Writing and Reading Across the Curriculum

Writing and Reading Across the Curriculum

Eighth Edition

Laurence Behrens
University of California
Santa Barbara

Leonard J. Rosen

Longman

New York • San Francisco • Boston
London • Toronto • Sydney • Tokyo • Singapore • Madrid
Mexico City • Munich • Paris • Cape Town • Hong Kong • Montreal

Senior Vice President and Publisher: Joseph Opiela
Acquisitions Editor: Susan Kunchandy
Development Editor: Michael Greer
Executive Marketing Manager: Ann Stypuloski
Supplements Editor: Donna Campion
Media Supplements Editor: Nancy Garcia
Production Manager: Douglas Bell
Project Coordination, Text Design, and Electronic Page Makeup: Elm Street Publishing Services, Inc.
Cover Designer/Manager: John Callahan
Manufacturing Buyer: Lucy Hebard
Printer and Binder: The Maple-Vail Book Manufacturing Group
Cover Printer: Coral Graphic Services, Inc.

For permission to use copyrighted material, grateful acknowledgment is made to the copyright holders on pp. 845–850, which are hereby made part of this copyright page.

Library of Congress Cataloging-in-Publication Data
Behrens, Laurence.
   Writing and reading across the curriculum / Laurence Behrens, Leonard J. Rosen—8th ed.
      p. cm.
   Includes bibliographical references and index.
   ISBN 0-321-09102-7
   1. College readers. 2. Interdisciplinary approach in education—Problems, exercises, etc.
      3. English language—Rhetoric—Problems, exercises, etc. 4. Academic writing—Problems, exercises, etc. I. Rosen, Leonard J. II. Title.

PE1417 .B396 2002
808'.0427—hr dc21

                                                                                2002066113

Please visit our website at http://www.ablongman.com/behrens

ISBN 0-321-09102-7

   4 5 6 7 8 9 10—PHX–05 04

To Bonnie and Michael—
and to L.C.R., Jonathan, and Matthew

Detailed Contents

Chapter 2
Critical Reading and Critique   50

Chapter 3
Introductions, Theses, and Conclusions   73

Chapter 5
Argument Synthesis   125

Chapter 6
Research   163

PART II
AN ANTHOLOGY OF READINGS   225

PSYCHOLOGY
Chapter 8
Obedience to Authority   304

"Cinderella": A Story of Sibling Rivalry and Oedipal Conflicts   567
Bruno Bettelheim

A psychoanalytic reading of "Cinderella": "Every child believes at some period in his life…that because of his secret wishes, if not also his clandestine actions, he deserves to be degraded, banned from the presence of others, relegated to a netherworld of smut."

"Cinderella" and the Loss of Father-Love   575
Jacqueline M. Schectman

A Jungian analyst finds in the wicked stepmother a sympathetic character—a woman who wanted a second chance at happiness but who found bitterness instead.

Cinderella's Stepsisters   590
Toni Morrison

In an address at Barnard College, the acclaimed novelist calls on women to treat one another more humanely than the stepsisters treated Cinderella.

LAW
Chapter 12
You, the Jury   598

The Maiden and the Pot of Gold: A Case of Emotional Distress   601
Several men play a cruel practical joke on a gullible woman. She suffers "mental suffering and humiliation." Then she sues.

The American Legal System   607
David Hricik
What is the purpose of law? Where does it come from? Why do we have "cases"? This attorney and teacher offers a primer for students of the law.

How to Present Your Case Systematically and Logically   617
Veda R. Charrow, Myra K. Erhardt, and Robert P. Charrow
How lawyers use the IRAC system to make persuasive arguments.

Venezia v. Miller Company: *A Defective Beer Bottle?*   629
Ruthi Erdman
Should a brewer be liable for injuries suffered by a child who smashed a beer bottle against a telephone pole? A model IRAC analysis.

Preface

When *Writing and Reading Across the Curriculum* (WRAC) was first published in 1982, it was—viewed from one angle—an experiment. We hoped to prove our hypothesis that both students and teachers would respond favorably to a composition reader organized by the kinds of specific topics that were typically studied in general education courses.

The response was both immediate and enthusiastic. Instructors found the topics in that first edition of *WRAC* both interesting and teachable, and students appreciated the links that such topics suggested to the courses they were taking concurrently in the humanities, the social sciences, and the sciences. Readers also told us how practical they found our "summary, synthesis, and critique" approach to writing college-level papers.

In developing each of the seven subsequent editions of *WRAC*, we have been guided by the same principle: to retain the essential multidisciplinary character of the text while providing ample new material to keep it fresh and timely. Some topics have proven particularly enduring—our "Cinderella" and "Obedience" chapters have been fixtures of *WRAC* since the first edition. But we take care to make sure that a third to one-half of the book is completely new every time, both by extensively revising existing chapters and by creating new ones. Over eight editions, our discussion of rhetoric has expanded to six chapters. While we have retained an emphasis on summary, critique, and synthesis, we continue to develop content on such issues as argumentation and online research and writing that addresses the issues and interests of today's classrooms.

STRUCTURE

Like its predecessors, the eighth edition of *Writing and Reading Across the Curriculum* is divided into two parts. The first part introduces the strategies of summary, critique, synthesis, and research. We take students step-by-step through the process of writing papers based on source material, explaining and demonstrating how summaries, critiques, and syntheses can be generated from the kinds of readings students will encounter later in the book—and throughout their academic careers. The second part of the text consists of a series of subject chapters drawn from both academic and professional disciplines. Each subject is not only interesting in its own right but is representative of the kinds of topics typically studied during the course of an undergraduate education. We also believe that students and teachers will discover connections among the thematic chapters of this edition that further enhance opportunities for writing, discussion, and inquiry.

CONTINUED FOCUS ON ARGUMENTATION

Part One of *Writing and Reading Across the Curriculum* is designed to prepare students for college-level assignments across the disciplines. The eighth edition continues the seventh edition's strengthened emphasis on the writing process and on argument, in particular. It provides coverage on the use of the World Wide Web for research and on citation of electronic sources. We now deal with argument synthesis in a separate chapter, emphasizing the following:

- **The Elements of Argument: Claim, Support, Assumption.** This section adapts the Toulmin approach to argument to the kinds of readings that students will encounter in Part Two of the text.
- **The Three Appeals of Argument:** *Logos, Ethos, Pathos.* This discussion may be used to analyze and develop arguments in the readings that students will encounter in Part Two of the book.
- **Developing and Organizing the Support for Your Arguments.** This section helps students to mine source materials for facts, expert opinions, and examples that will support their arguments.
- **Annotated Student Argument Paper.** A sample student paper highlights and discusses argumentative strategies that a student writer uses in drafting and developing a paper.

RESEARCHING ONLINE

Students who look for sources beyond this text will as likely do so on the Web as in the library. For that reason, in this edition we retain our focus on online research. Chapter 6 (Research) addresses the following topics:

- An updated section on **Citing Online Sources**, with current MLA and APA guidelines.
- **The Benefits and Pitfalls of Conducting Research on the World Wide Web.** In student papers, Web sources make up an increasingly large proportion of "Works Cited" and "References" lists. It's convenient to find and use Web sources, but how reliable are they? We explain how instructors and students should address this new reality—why the Web as a research aid should be welcomed, but why it should also be approached with caution.

PART ONE: NEW APPARATUS, TOPICS, READINGS, AND STUDENT PAPERS

New Apparatus, Chapters 1–6

New Boxes and Exercises

Throughout Part One, we have added boxed material that emphasizes the practical applications of writing summaries, syntheses, and critiques. We have also provided brief exercises so that students can practice reading and writing critically in a controlled environment, with specially chosen selections, as they work through the instructional materials.

Chapter 1: Summary, Paraphrase, and Quotation

A New Model for Marriage

Students are taken through the process of writing a summary of Barbara Graham's "The Future of Love: Kiss Romance Goodbye, It's Time for the Real Thing." We demonstrate how to annotate a source and divide it into sections, how to develop a thesis, and how to write and smoothly join section summaries. We also explain the following (for the most part with new readings related to the topic of dating):

- Summarizing narrative passages
- Summarizing figures and tables
- Paraphrasing sources
- Quoting sources

Chapter 4: Explanatory Synthesis

Computers, Communication, and Relationships

Like argument synthesis, explanatory synthesis is now treated in a separate chapter. Eight brief selections on the topic of relationships begun online precede discussion of the planning and writing of a student paper. The first draft is accompanied by detailed instructor comments. Exercises inviting students to prepare their own explanatory synthesis follow.

PART TWO: NEW THEMATIC CHAPTERS

As it has through seven editions, Part Two of *Writing and Reading Across the Curriculum* provides students with opportunities to practice the skills of summary, synthesis, and critique they have learned in Part One. We have prepared four new chapters for the eighth edition of *WRAC*. More than 50% of the reading selections in Part Two are new to this edition.

Chapter 7: Cyberspace and Identity: The E-Mail Revolution

E-mail has so thoroughly insinuated itself into the lives of Americans that one can hardly imagine life without it—an extraordinary development given that little more than a decade ago, the technology was not widely known beyond the scientific and engineering communities. That e-mail enhances—and distracts us from—our daily business is a given. Less clear, though, is the extent to which the technology has begun to alter our sense of self—an alteration that we explore in this chapter. Is the stockbroker who enters an online space to play one of the endless variants of *Dungeons and Dragons* the same starched professional she projects to her colleagues and clients at the office? When writing via e-mail to a prospective date in an online club, how does a young man represent himself, knowing that he cannot be seen?

Chapter 9: Business Ethics

This edition's chapter on Business Ethics is an updating, by popular demand, of a chapter that appeared originally in the third edition of *WRAC*. While we have replaced 80% of that chapter with new selections, we retain the original's guiding principle: to place student writers squarely in the middle of ethically complex issues of the sort they might encounter in the workplace. Fourteen years ago, when the third edition of *WRAC* was published, business ethics was a relatively young discipline. Today, discussions of ethics are infused throughout the business curriculum, and employers expect new hires to be attuned to issues of justice, individual rights, and the greater good. In this chapter, we explore these themes through the case method. The chapter opens with eleven brief cases that provide students with a chance to decide ethical courses of action informally, based on their personal values. These opening cases serve as a warm-up for the lengthier, more complex, cases to follow. In the "Principles" section of the chapter, we present three readings that outline ethical standards. Students can then apply these standards to the individual cases in the concluding section, "Cases for Analysis and Discussion." In every instance, whether students are making decisions about ethics based on their personal values or on a "system," they will need to argue for their decisions. To do so, they will draw on the skills learned in Part One of this text.

Chapter 10: Weight Debate

According to the Centers for Disease Control and Prevention and the *Journal of the American Medical Association* (*JAMA*), Americans are getting heavier—significantly so over the last decade—and are suffering the health-related consequences of their added pounds. In this chapter, we present readings on what the *JAMA* calls an "epidemic" of obesity that has seen the number of overweight and obese swell to more than 50% of the adult population in the United States. The chapter's opening selections from *JAMA*, the Centers for Disease Control, and *Scientific American* establish the nature of the problem in medical and biological terms. Readings that follow explore the ways in which cultural factors, including America's infatuation with slenderness, color the ways in which we perceive the overweight and the obese. We also include an inside look at the "flavor industry," which is responsible for making our foods so irresistible; and a surgeon's explanation of a curious and increasingly popular stomach-bypass operation. In all, "Weight Debate" offers students an opportunity to explore the place of food and weight, both in their own lives and in the broader cultural landscape.

Chapter 13: Good Take, Sweet Prince: *Hamlet* on Film

Much as the history of literary criticism is mirrored in the changing analyses of *Hamlet* over the centuries, so too can the history of film be seen in the more than 40 film adaptations of Shakespeare's play. No literary work, save for the Bible (or possibly, *Dracula*), has been filmed more often, and in this chapter we provide students with the tools to study four such adaptations: those by Laurence Olivier, Franco Zeffirelli, Kenneth Branagh, and Michael Almereyda, all of which are available on videotape and which the publisher is making available to adopters. Students will consider these, among other, questions: What constitutes an acceptable adaptation of a literary work? Can we say that one version is "more faithful" than another to the text? Can films based on a literary work be faithful without being literal? In what ways does a director's reading of the play inform such functional filmic elements as camera movement and lighting? How does the cinematography inform the drama's meaning? How does an adaptation reflect the era in which it was made? Why is *Hamlet* such fertile ground for filmmakers?

Following a set of three opening selections that introduce elements of Shakespeare's life, general themes in *Hamlet*, and "nonverbal expression" in Shakespearean films, the chapter readings are built around the four adaptations. Each film receives a cinematic outline—keyed to the appropriate act/scene number in *Hamlet* and to time elapsed in the film; a statement by the filmmaker explaining his approach to the play; and a review of the film. (The section devoted to Branagh's *Hamlet* also includes a diary that offers fascinating glimpses into the rehearsal and filming of this production.) Students will have ample opportunity to practice skills of comparison and contrast as they view multiple adaptations and (one hopes) read the play.

PART TWO: REVISED THEMATIC CHAPTERS

Chapter 8: Obedience to Authority

The Obedience chapter continues to build on the profoundly disturbing Milgram experiments. Other selections in this chapter, such as Philip Zimbardo's account of his Stanford prison experiment and Solomon Asch's "Opinions and Social Pressure," have provided additional perspectives on the significance of the obedience phenomenon. This edition adds two articles: one by Ian Parker, who researched how Milgram's experiments made him famous but may have ruined his career; and an article by David Brooks, "The Organization Kid," which observes how young people in elite colleges today tend to obey and conform in order to get ahead in a social and economic system that has largely benefited them.

Chapter 11: Fairy Tales: A Closer Look at "Cinderella"

This popular chapter includes variants of the Cinderella story along with the perspectives of a folklorist (Stith Thompson), a psychologist (Bruno Bettelheim), and a feminist (in this edition, novelist Toni Morrison). Restored to this edition is "Gudgekin the Thistle Girl," a variant of "Cinderella" written by novelist John Gardner. New to this edition is the fascinating "'Cinderella' and the Loss of Father-Love" by Jungian analyst Jacqueline Schectman, who sees in the stepmother a sympathetic figure who has sought a second chance at happiness but who has reaped only bitterness, instead. This chapter develops in students two basic skills: the ability to analyze by applying elements of a theoretical reading to one or more variants of "Cinderella"; and the ability to think and write comparatively by reading multiple versions of the story and by developing criteria by which to clarify similarities and differences.

Chapter 12: You, the Jury

As with the debut of "You, the Jury," in the seventh edition of *WRAC*, this chapter places students in the role of juror by asking that they apply points of law to facts of a case in order to arrive at a just verdict. Students must argue for their verdict (no prior legal education is necessary), principally by demonstrating the skill of analysis. More broadly, thinking and writing about legal issues is an ideal approach to the principles of effective argument: students must provide support (the facts of the case) for their claim (the verdict), based on relevant assumptions or warrants (the laws). New to this chapter are several child custody cases in which students are asked to make the difficult decision of which parent is to gain primary custody of a child (or children).

ANCILLARIES

Student Supplements

- *The Writing and Reading Across the Curriculum* Companion Website (www.ablongman.com/behrens) includes additional exercises, links, model papers, and many more student resources.

- Researching Online gives students detailed, step-by-step instructions for performing electronic searches; for researching with e-mail, listservs, newsgroups, IRC, MUDs, and MOOs; and for evaluating electronic sources. Includes excellent coverage of writing for the Web. Free when bundled with the text. ISBN 0-321-09277-5.

- *The New American Webster Handy College Dictionary,* Third Edition, is available as a free supplement for students, when bundled with the text. ISBN 0-451-18166-2.

- The Penguin Program—selected from a variety of Penguin Putnam titles, is available for a significant discount when packaged with the text (www.ablongman.com/penguin).

- *Take Note!* is a cross-platform CD-ROM that integrates note taking, outlining, and bibliography management into an easy-to-use package. ISBN 0-321-08232-X.

- *The Longman Writer's Journal* provides students with their own personal space for writing, complete with journal writing strategies, sample journal entries by other students, and many more writing prompts and topics to help get students writing. Free when bundled with the text. ISBN 0-321-08639-2.

Instructor Supplements

- The *Instructor's Manual* for the eighth edition of *Writing and Reading Across the Curriculum* provides sample syllabi and course calendars, chapter summaries, classroom ideas for writing assignments, introductions to each set of readings, case outcomes for the legal readings, and answers to review questions. Included as well are tips on how to incorporate the textbook's companion Web site into the course material. ISBN 0-321-10706-3.

- The Companion Website (www.ablongman.com/behrens) includes the full *Instructor's Manual* in a password-protected instructor section. The site includes additional exercises, links, model papers, and many more student resources. Instructors, please contact your Longman representative for further details.

ACKNOWLEDGMENTS

We have benefited over the years from the suggestions and insights of many teachers—and students—across the country. We would especially like to thank: Chris Anson, *North Carolina State University;* Anne Bailey, *Southeastern Louisiana University;* Joy Bashore, *Central Virginia Community College;* Nancy Blattner, *Southeast Missouri State University;* Mary Bly, *University of California, Davis;* Susan Callendar, *Sinclair Community College;* Jeff Carroll, *University of Hawaii;* Michael Colonnese, *Methodist College;* Cathy Dice, *University of Memphis;* Kathleen Dooley, *Tidewater Community College;* Judith Eastman, *Orange Coast College;* David Elias, *Eastern Kentucky University;* Deborah Gutschera, *College of DuPage;* Kip Harvigsen, *Ricks College;* Mark Jones, *University of Florida;* Jane Kaufman, *University of Akron;* Rodney Keller, *Ricks College;* Walt Klarner, *Johnson County Community College;* Dawn Leonard, *Charleston Southern University;* Krista May, *Texas A&M;* Stella Nesanovich, *McNeese State University;* Susie Paul, *Auburn University at Montgomery;* Nancy Redmond, *Long Beach City College;* Priscilla Riggle, *Bowling Green State University;* Joyce Smoot, *Virginia Tech;* Jackie Wheeler, *Arizona State University;* and Kristin Woolever, *Northeastern University.*

We would also like to thank the following reviewers for their help in the preparation of the seventh edition: James Allen, *College of DuPage;* Phillip Arrington, *Eastern Michigan University;* Carolyn Baker, *San Antonio College;* Bob Brannan, *Johnson County Community College;* Paige Byam, *Northern Kentucky University;* Anne Carr, *Southeast Community College;* Joseph Rocky Colavito, *Northwestern State University;* Timothy Corrigan, *Temple University;* Kathryn J. Dawson, *Ball State University;* Cathy Powers Dice, *University of Memphis;* Kathy Evertz, *University of Wyoming;* Bill Gholson, *Southern Oregon University;* Lila M. Harper, *Central Washington University;* M. Todd Harper, *University of Louisville;* Michael Hogan, *Southeast Missouri State University;* Sandra M. Jensen, *Lane Community College;* Alison Kuehner, *Ohlone College;*

William B. Lalicker, *West Chester University;* Krista L. May, *Texas A&M University;* Roark Mulligan, *Christopher Newport University;* Joan Mullin, *University of Toledo;* Aaron Race, *Southern Illinois University–Carbondale;* Deborah Reese, *University of Texas at Arlington;* Jeanette Riley, *University of New Mexico;* Sarah C. Ross, *Southeastern Louisiana University;* Raul Sanchez, *University of Utah;* Rebecca Shapiro, *Westminster College;* Philip Sipiora, *University of Southern Florida;* R. E. Stratton, *University of Alaska–Fairbanks;* Katherine M. Thomas, *Southeast Community College;* Victor Villanueva, *Washington State University;* and Pat Stephens Williams, *Southern Illinois University at Carbondale.*

We extend our gratitude to the following reviewers for their help in the preparation of this edition: Paul Buczkowski, *Eastern Michigan University;* Jennifer Bullis, *Whatcom Community College;* James A. Cornette, *Christopher Newport University;* Susan Boyd English, *Kirkwood Community College;* Karen Gordon, *Elgin Community College;* Anita Johnson, *Whatcom Community College;* Jeffery Klausman, *Whatcom Community College;* Clifford L. Lewis, *U Mass Lowell;* Signee Lynch, *Whatcom Community College;* Robert Rongner, *Whatcom Community College;* Mary Sheldon, *Washburn University;* Bonnie A. Spears, *Chaffey College;* and Bonnie Startt, *Tidewater Community College.*

We would like to especially acknowledge the invaluable assistance freely rendered to us by many people during and after the preparation of the law-oriented chapter, "You, the Jury." Amy Atchison, an attorney and law librarian at the Rand Corporation, provided numerous references, legal texts, and much-needed guidance through the legal research process. David Hricik, author of "The American Legal System" in You, the Jury, and an attorney at the Houston law firm Slusser and Frost, also provided useful feedback. Leonard Tourney, who teaches legal writing courses at the University of California at Santa Barbara, provided valuable advice before and during the composition of this chapter. Our gratitude also to Ruthi Erdman (whose model IRAC essay appears in this chapter) and her students at Central Washington University; Carolyn Baker and her students at San Antonio College; Gloria Dumler and her students at Bakersfield College; Lila Harper and her students at Central Washington University; Krista May and her students at Texas A&M University; Erik Peterson and his students at Central Washington University; and Sarah C. Ross and her students at Southeast Louisiana State University for helping us to field-test this chapter. The intelligent and perceptive comments of both instructors and students helped us make this chapter more focused and user friendly than it was when they received it.

A special thanks to Bonnie Beedles, who helped us gather and develop new materials for Part One and who also wrote the exercises and additional boxed material in that section. Thanks also to Susan Kunchandy, Rebecca Gilpin, and Douglas Bell of Longman, for helping shepherd the manuscript through the editorial and production process. Our special gratitude and appreciation to our development editor, Michael Greer, whose experience, resourcefulness, and humor helped make working on this edition a special pleasure. Michael wrote the "cinematic outline" of Almereyda's *Hamlet* and most of the questions accompanying that section. And he offered invaluable suggestions for selections in other chapters.

Laurence Behrens
Leonard J. Rosen

A Note to the Student

Your sociology professor asks you to write a paper on attitudes towards the homeless population of an urban area near your campus. You are expected to consult books, articles, Web sites and other online sources on the subject, and you are also encouraged to conduct surveys and interviews.

Your professor is making a number of assumptions about your capabilities. Among them:

- that you can research and assess the value of relevant sources;
- that you can comprehend college-level material, both print and electronic;
- that you can synthesize separate but related sources;
- that you can intelligently respond to such material.

In fact, these same assumptions underlie practically all college writing assignments. Your professors will expect you to demonstrate that you can read and understand not only textbooks but also critical articles and books, primary sources, Internet sources, online academic databases, CD-ROMs, and other material related to a particular subject of study. For example: for a paper on the progress of the Human Genome Project, you would probably look to articles and Internet sources for the most recent information. Using an online database, you would find articles on the subject in such print journals as *Nature, Journal of the American Medical Association,* and *Bioscience,* as well as leading newspapers and magazines. A Web search engine might lead you to a useful site called "A New Gene Map of the Human Genome" <http://www.ncbi.nlm.nih.gov/genemap99/> and the site of the "Human Genome Sequencing Department" at the Lawrence Berkeley National Laboratory <http://www-hgc.lbl.gov/>. You would be expected to assess the relevance of such sources to your topic and to draw from them the information and ideas you need. It's even possible that the final product of your research and reading may not be a conventional paper at all, but rather a Web site that you create which explains the science behind the Human Genome Project, explores a particular controversy about the project, or describes the future benefits geneticists hope to derive from the project.

You might, for a different class, be assigned a research paper on the films of director Martin Scorsese. To get started, you might consult your film studies textbook, biographical sources on Scorsese, and anthologies of criticism. Instructor and peer feedback on a first draft might lead you to articles in both popular magazines (such as *Time*) and scholarly journals (such as *Literature/Film Quarterly*), a CD-ROM database, *Film Index International,* and relevant Web sites (such as the "Internet Movie Database" <http://us.imdb.com>).

These two example assignments are very different, of course; but the skills you need to work with them are the same. You must be able to research relevant sources. You must be able to read and comprehend these sources. You must be able to perceive the relationships among several pieces of source material. And you must be able to apply your own critical judgments to these various materials.

Writing and Reading Across the Curriculum provides you with the opportunity to practice the three essential college-level skills we have just outlined and the forms of writing associated with them, namely:

- the *summary*
- the *critique*
- the *synthesis*

Each chapter of Part Two of this text represents a subject from a particular area of the academic curriculum: Technology/Communication, Psychology, Business, Health Sciences, Folklore, Law, and Film. These chapters, dealing with such topics as "Cyberspace and Identity," "Obedience to Authority," and "Business Ethics," illustrate the types of material you will study in your other courses.

Questions following the readings will allow you to practice typical college writing assignments. Review Questions help you recall key points of content. Discussion and Writing Suggestions ask you for personal, sometimes imaginative responses to the readings. Synthesis Activities at the end of each chapter allow you to practice assignments of the type that are covered in detail in Part One of this book. For instance, you may be asked to *describe* the Milgram experiment, and the reactions to it, or to *compare and contrast* a controlled experiment to a real-life (or fictional) situation. Finally, Research Activities ask you to go beyond the readings in this text in order to conduct your own independent research on these subjects.

In this book, you'll find articles and essays written by physicians, literary critics, sociologists, psychologists, lawyers, folklorists, political scientists, journalists, and specialists from other fields. Our aim is that you become familiar with the various subjects and styles of academic writing and that you come to appreciate the interrelatedness of knowledge. Biologists, sociologists, and historians have different ways of contributing to our understanding of weight gain. Fairy tales can be studied by literary critics, folklorists, psychologists, and feminists. Human activity and human behavior are classified into separate subjects only for convenience. The novel you read in your literature course may be able to shed some light upon an assigned article from your economics course—and vice versa.

We hope, therefore, that your writing course will serve as a kind of bridge to your other courses and that as a result of this work you can become more skillful at perceiving relationships among diverse topics. Because it involves such critical and widely applicable skills, your writing course may well turn out to be one of the most valuable—and one of the most interesting—of your academic career.

Laurence Behrens
Leonard J. Rosen

Writing and Reading Across the Curriculum

How to Write Summaries, Critiques, and Syntheses

Summary, Paraphrase, and Quotation

1

WHAT IS A SUMMARY?

The best way to demonstrate that you understand the information and the ideas in any piece of writing is to compose an accurate and clearly written summary of that piece. By a *summary* we mean a *brief restatement, in your own words, of the content of a passage* (a group of paragraphs, a chapter, an article, a book). This restatement should focus on the *central idea* of the passage. The briefest of all summaries (one or two sentences) will do no more than this. A longer, more complete summary will indicate, in condensed form, the main points in the passage that support or explain the central idea. It will reflect the order in which these points are presented and the emphasis given to them. It may even include some important examples from the passage. But it will not include minor details. It will not repeat points simply for the purpose of emphasis. And it will not contain any of your own opinions or conclusions. A good summary, therefore, has three central qualities: *brevity, completeness,* and *objectivity.*

CAN A SUMMARY BE OBJECTIVE?

Of course, this last quality of objectivity might be difficult to achieve in a summary. By definition, writing a summary requires you to select some aspects of the original and to leave out others. Since deciding what to select and what to leave out calls for your personal judgment, your summary really is a work of interpretation. And, certainly, your interpretation of a passage may differ from another person's. One factor affecting the nature and quality of your interpretation is your *prior knowledge* of the subject. For example, if you're attempting to summarize an anthropological article and you're a novice in the field, then your summary of the article might be quite different from that of your professor, who has spent 20 years studying this particular area and whose judgment about what is more significant and what is less significant is undoubtedly more reliable than your own. By the same token, your personal or professional *frame of reference* may also affect your interpretation. A union representative and a management representative attempting to summarize the latest management offer would probably come up with two very different accounts. Still, we believe that in most cases it's possible to produce a reasonably objective summary of a passage if you make a conscious, good-faith effort to be unbiased and not to allow your own feelings on the subject to distort your account of the text.

USING THE SUMMARY

In some quarters, the summary has a bad reputation—and with reason. Summaries often are provided by writers as substitutes for analyses. As students, many of us have summarized books that we were supposed to *review* critically. All the same, the summary does have a place in respectable college work. First, writing a summary is an excellent way to understand what you read. This in itself is an important goal of academic study. If you don't understand your source material, chances are you won't be able to refer to it usefully in an essay or research paper. Summaries help you to understand what you read because they force you to put the text into your own words. Practice with writing summaries also develops your general writing habits, since a good summary, like any other piece of good writing, is clear, coherent, and accurate.

Second, summaries are useful to your readers. Let's say you're writing a paper about the McCarthy era in America, and in part of that paper you want to discuss Arthur Miller's *Crucible* as a dramatic treatment of the subject. A summary of the plot would be helpful to a reader who hasn't seen or read—or who doesn't remember—the play. (Of course, if the reader is your American literature professor, you can safely omit the plot summary.) Or perhaps you're writing a paper about ballistic missile defenses. If your reader isn't familiar with the provisions of the 1972 Anti-Ballistic Missile Treaty, it would be a good idea to summarize these provisions at some early point in the paper. In many cases (a test, for instance), you can use a summary to demonstrate your knowledge of what your professor already knows; when writing a paper, you can use a summary to inform your professor about some relatively unfamiliar source.

Third, summaries are required frequently in college-level writing. For example, on a psychology midterm, you may be asked to explain Carl Jung's theory of the collective unconscious and to show how it differs from Freud's theory of the personal unconscious. The first part of this question requires you to *summarize* Jung's theory. You may have read about this theory in your textbook or in a supplementary article, or your instructor may have outlined it in his or her lecture. You can best demonstrate your understanding of Jung's theory by summarizing it. Then you'll proceed to contrast it with Freud's theory—which, of course, you must also summarize.

It may seem to you that being able to tell (or to retell) exactly what a passage says is a skill that ought to be taken for granted in anyone who can read at high school level. Unfortunately, this is not so: For all kinds of reasons, people don't always read carefully. In fact, it's probably safe to say that usually they don't. Either they read so inattentively that they skip over words, phrases, or even whole sentences, or, if they do see the words in front of them, they see them without registering their significance.

When a reader fails to pick up the meaning and the implications of a sentence or two, usually there's no real harm done. (An exception: You could lose credit on an exam or paper because you failed to read or to realize the

---

WHERE DO WE FIND WRITTEN SUMMARIES?

Here are just a few of the types of writing that involve summary:

Academic Writing

- **Critique papers.** Summarize material in order to critique it.
- **Synthesis papers.** Summarize to show relationships among sources.
- **Analysis papers.** Summarize theoretical perspectives before applying them.
- **Research papers.** Summarize to take notes and report on research.
- **Literature reviews.** Summarize multiple works on one topic.
- **Argument papers.** Summarize evidence and opposing arguments.
- **Essay exams.** Demonstrate understanding of course materials through summary.

Workplace Writing

- **Policy briefs.** Condense complex public policy.
- **Business plans.** Summarize costs, relevant environmental impacts, and other important matters.
- **Memos, letters, and reports.** Summarize procedures, product assessments, expenditures, and more.
- **Medical charts.** Record patient data in summary form.
- **Legal briefs.** Summarize relevant facts of cases.

significance of a crucial direction by your instructor.) But over longer stretches—the paragraph, the section, the article, or the chapter—inattentive or haphazard reading creates problems, for you must try to perceive the shape of the argument, to grasp the central idea, to determine the main points that compose it, to relate the parts of the whole, and to note key examples. This kind of reading takes a lot more energy and determination than casual reading. But, in the long run, it's an energy-saving method because it enables you to retain the content of the material and to use that content as a basis for your own responses. In other words, it allows you to develop an accurate and coherent written discussion that goes beyond summary.

HOW TO WRITE SUMMARIES

Every article you read will present a different challenge as you work to summarize it. As you'll discover, saying in a few words what has taken someone else a great many can be difficult. But like any other skill, the ability to summarize improves with practice. Here are a few pointers to get you started. They represent possible stages, or steps, in the process of writing a summary. These pointers are not meant to be ironclad rules; rather, they are designed to encourage habits of thinking that will allow you to vary your technique as the situation demands.

GUIDELINES FOR WRITING SUMMARIES

- *Read the passage carefully.* Determine its structure. Identify the author's purpose in writing. (This will help you distinguish between more important and less important information.) Make a note in the margin when you get confused, or when you think something is important; highlight or underline points sparingly, if at all.
- *Reread.* This time divide the passage into sections or stages of thought. The author's use of paragraphing will often be a useful guide. *Label,* on the passage itself, each section or stage of thought. *Highlight* key ideas and terms. Write notes in the margin.
- *Write one-sentence summaries,* on a separate sheet of paper, of each stage of thought.
- *Write a thesis: a one- or two-sentence summary of the entire passage.* The thesis should express the central idea of the passage, as you have determined it from the preceding steps. You may find it useful to keep in mind the information contained in the lead sentence or paragraph of most newspaper stories—the *what, who, why, where, when,* and *how* of the matter. For persuasive passages, summarize in a sentence the author's conclusion. For descriptive passages, indicate the subject of the description and its key feature(s). *Note: In some cases, a suitable thesis may already be in the original passage.* If so, you may want to quote it directly in your summary.
- *Write the first draft of your summary* by (1) combining the thesis with your list of one-sentence summaries or (2) combining the thesis with one-sentence summaries *plus* significant details from the passage. In either case, eliminate repetition and less important information. Disregard minor details or generalize them (e.g., George H. Bush and Bill Clinton might be generalized as "recent presidents"). Use as few words as possible to convey the main ideas.
- *Check your summary against the original passage* and make whatever adjustments are necessary for accuracy and completeness.
- *Revise your summary,* inserting transitional words and phrases where necessary to ensure coherence. Check for style. *Avoid a series of short, choppy sentences.* Combine sentences for a smooth, logical flow of ideas. Check for grammatical correctness, punctuation, and spelling.

DEMONSTRATION: SUMMARY

To demonstrate these points at work, let's go through the process of summarizing a passage of expository material. Read the following passage carefully. Try to identify its parts and to understand how these parts work together to create an overall point.

The Future of Love: Kiss Romance Goodbye, It's Time for the Real Thing
Barbara Graham

Author of the satire Women Who Run With Poodles: Myths and Tips for Honoring Your Mood Swings *(Avon, 1994), Barbara Graham has written articles for* Vogue, Self, Common Boundary *and other publications. She regularly contributes articles to the* Utne Reader, *from which this essay was taken.*

1 Freud and his psychoanalytic descendants are no doubt correct in their assessment that the search for ideal love—for that one perfect soulmate—is the futile wish of not fully developed selves. But it also seems true that the longing for a profound, all-consuming erotic connection (and the heightened state of awareness that goes with it) is in our very wiring. The yearning for fulfillment through love seems to be to our psychic structure what food and water are to our cells.

2 Just consider the stories and myths that have shaped our consciousness: Beauty and the Beast, Snow White and her handsome prince, Cinderella and Prince Charming, Fred and Ginger, Barbie and Ken. (Note that, with the exception of the last two couples, all of these lovers are said to have lived happily ever after—even though we never get details of their lives after the weddings, after children and gravity and loss have exacted their price.) Still, it's not just these lucky fairy tale characters who have captured our collective imagination. The tragic twosomes we cut our teeth on—Romeo and Juliet, Tristan and Iseult, Launcelot and Guinevere, Heathcliff and Cathy, Rhett and Scarlett—are even more compelling role models. Their love is simply too powerful and anarchic, too shattering and exquisite, to be bound by anything so conventional as marriage or a long-term domestic arrangement.

3 If recent divorce and remarriage statistics are any indication, we're not as astute as the doomed lovers. Instead of drinking poison and putting an end to our love affairs while the heat is still turned up full blast, we expect our marriages and relationships to be long-running fairy tales. When they're not, instead of examining our expectations, we switch partners and reinvent the fantasy, hoping that this

Barbara Graham, "The Future of Love: Kiss Romance Goodbye, It's Time for the Real Thing," *Utne Reader* Jan.–Feb. 1997: 20–23.

time we'll get it right. It's easy to see why: Despite all the talk of family values, we're constantly bombarded by visions of perfect romance. All you have to do is turn on the radio or TV or open any magazine and check out the perfume and lingerie ads. "Our culture is deeply regressed," says Florence Falk, a New York City psychotherapist. "Everywhere we turn, we're faced with glamorized, idealized versions of love. It's as if the culture wants us to stay trapped in the fantasy and does everything possible to encourage and expand that fantasy." Trying to forge an authentic relationship amidst all the romantic hype, she adds, makes what is already a tough proposition even harder.

4   What's most unusual about our culture is our feverish devotion to the belief that romantic love and marriage should be synonymous. Starting with George and Martha, continuing through Ozzie and Harriet right up to the present day, we have tirelessly tried to formalize, rationalize, legalize, legitimize, politicize, and sanitize rapture. This may have something to do with our puritanical roots, as well as our tendency toward oversimplification. In any event, this attempt to satisfy all of our contradictory desires under the marital umbrella must be put in historical context in order to be properly understood.

5   "Personal intimacy is actually quite a new idea in human history and was never part of the marriage ideal before the 20th century," says John Welwood, a Northern California-based psychologist and author, most recently, of *Love and Awakening.* "Most couples throughout history managed to live together their whole lives without ever having a conversation about what was going on within or between them. As long as family and society prescribed the rules of marriage, individuals never had to develop any consciousness in this area."

6   In short, marriage was designed to serve the economic and social needs of families, communities, and religious institutions, and had little or nothing to do with love. Nor was it expected to satisfy lust.

7   *In Myths To Live By,* Joseph Campbell explains how the sages of ancient India viewed the relationship between marriage and passion. They concluded that there are five degrees of love, he writes, "through which a worshiper is increased in the service and knowledge of his God." The first degree has to do with the relationship of the worshiper to the divine. The next three degrees of love, in order of importance, are friendship, the parent/child relationship, and marriage. The fifth and highest form is passionate, illicit love. "In marriage, it is declared, one is still possessed of reason," Campbell adds. "The seizure of passionate love can be, in such a context, only illicit, breaking in upon the order of one's dutiful life in virtue as a devastating storm."

8   No wonder we're having problems. The pressures we place on our tender unions are unprecedented. Even our biochemistry seems to militate against long-term sexual relationships. Dr. Helen Fisher, an anthropologist at Rutgers University and author of *Anatomy of Love,* believes that human pair-bonds originally evolved according to "the ancient blueprint of serial monogamy and clandestine adultery" and are originally meant to last around four years—at least long enough to raise a single dependent child through toddlerhood. The so-called seven-year-itch may be the remains of a four-year reproductive cycle, Fisher suggests.

9   Increasingly, Fisher and other researchers are coming to view what we call love as a series of complex biochemical events governed by hormones and enzymes. "People cling to the idea that romantic love is a mystery, but it's also a chemical experience," Fisher says, explaining that there are three distinct mating emotions and each is supported in the brain by the release of different chemicals. Lust, an emotion triggered by changing levels of testosterone in men and women, is associated with our basic sexual drive. Infatuation depends on the changing levels of dopamine, norepinephrine, and phenylethylamine (PEA), also called the "chemicals of love." They are natural—addictive—amphetaminelike chemicals that stimulate euphoria and make us want to stay up all night sharing our secrets. After infatuation and the dizzying highs associated with it have peaked—usually within a year or two—this brain chemistry reduces, and a new chemical system made up of oxytocin, vasopressin, and maybe the endorphins kicks in and supports a steadier, quieter, more nurturing intimacy. In the end, regardless of whether biochemistry accounts for cause or effect in love, it may help to explain why some people—those most responsive to the release of the attachment chemicals—are able to sustain a long-term partnership, while thrillseekers who feel depressed without regular hits of dopamine and PEA, are likely to jump from one liaison to the next in order to maintain a buzz.

10   But even if our biochemistry suggests that there should be term limits on love, the heart is a stubborn muscle and, for better or worse, most of us continue to yearn for a relationship that will endure. As a group, Generation Xers—many of whom are children of divorce—are more determined than any other demographic group to have a different kind of marriage than their parents and to avoid divorce, says Howard Markman, author of *Fighting For Your Marriage.* What's more, lesbians and gay men who once opposed marriage and all of its heterosexual, patriarchal implications, now seek to reframe marriage as a more flexible, less repressive arrangement. And, according to the U.S. National Center for Health Statistics, in one out of an estimated seven weddings, either the bride or the groom—or both—are tying the knot for at least the third time—nearly twice as many as in 1970. There are many reasons for this, from the surge in the divorce rate that began in the `70s, to our ever-increasing life span. Even so, the fact that we're still trying to get love right—knowing all we know about the ephemeral nature of passion, in a time when the stigmas once associated with being divorced or single have all but disappeared—says something about our powerful need to connect.

11   And, judging from the army of psychologists, therapists, clergy, and other experts who can be found dispensing guidance on the subject, the effort to save—or reinvent, depending on who's doing the talking—love and marriage has become a multimillion dollar industry. The advice spans the spectrum. There's everything from *Rules,* by Ellen Fein and Sherrie Schneider, a popular new book which gives 90's women 50's-style tips on how to catch and keep their man, to Harville Hendrix's *Getting The Love You Want,* and other guides to "conscious love." But regardless of perspective, this much is clear: Never before have our most intimate thoughts and actions been so thoroughly dissected, analyzed,

scrutinized, and medicalized. Now, people who fall madly in love over and over are called romance addicts. Their disease, modeled on alcoholism and other chemical dependencies, is considered "progressive and fatal."

12   Not everyone believes the attempt to deconstruct love is a good thing. The late philosopher Christopher Lasch wrote in his final (and newly released) book, *Women and the Common Life:* "The exposure of sexual life to scientific scrutiny contributed to the rationalization, not the liberation, of emotional life." His daughter, Elisabeth Lasch-Quinn, an historian at Syracuse University and the editor of the book, agrees. She contends that the progressive demystification of passionate life since Freud has promoted an asexual, dispassionate, and utilitarian form of love. Moreover, like her father, she believes that the national malaise about romance can be attributed to insidious therapeutic modes of social control—a series of mechanisms that have reduced the citizen to a consumer of expertise. "We have fragmented life in such a way," she says, "as to take passion out of our experience."

13   Admittedly, it's a stretch to picture a lovesick 12th century French troubadour in a 12-step program for romance addicts. Still, we can't overlook the fact that our society's past efforts to fuse together those historically odd bedfellows—passionate love and marriage—have failed miserably. And though it's impossible to know whether all the attention currently being showered on relationships is the last gasp of a dying social order—marriage—or the first glimmer of a new paradigm for relating to one another, it's obvious that something radically different is needed.

Read, Reread, Highlight

Let's consider our recommended pointers for writing a summary.

As you reread the passage, note important points, shifts in thought, and questions you may have in the margins of the essay. Consider the essay's significance as a whole and its stages of thought. What does it say? How is it organized? How does each part of the passage fit into the whole? What do all these points add up to?

Here is how the first few paragraphs of Graham's essay might look after you had marked the main ideas, by highlighting and by marginal notations.

psychic importance of love   Freud and his psychoanalytic descendants are no doubt correct in their assessment that the search for ideal love—for that one perfect soulmate—is the futile wish of not-fully-developed selves. But it also seems true that the longing for a profound, all-consuming erotic connection (and the heightened state of awareness that goes with it) is in our very wiring. The yearning for fulfillment through love seems to be to our psychic structure what food and water are to our cells.

Just consider the stories and myths that have shaped our consciousness: Beauty and the Beast, Snow White and her handsome prince,

fictional, sometimes tragic examples of ideal love

Cinderella and Prince Charming, Fred and Ginger, Barbie and Ken. (Note that, with the exception of the last two couples, all of these lovers are said to have lived happily ever after—even though we never get details of their lives after the weddings, after children and gravity and loss have exacted their price.) Still, it's not just these lucky fairy tale characters who have captured our collective imagination. The tragic twosomes we cut our teeth on—Romeo and Juliet, Tristan and Iseult, Launcelot and Guinevere, Heathcliff and Cathy, Rhett and Scarlett—are even more compelling role models. Their love is simply too powerful and anarchic, too shattering and exquisite, to be bound by anything so conventional as marriage or a long-term domestic arrangement.

difficulty of having a real relationship in a culture that glamorizes ideal love

If recent divorce and remarriage statistics are any indication, we're not as astute as the doomed lovers. Instead of drinking poison and putting an end to our love affairs while the heat is still turned up full blast, we expect our marriages and relationships to be long-running fairy tales. When they're not, instead of examining our expectations, we switch partners and reinvent the fantasy, hoping that this time we'll get it right. It's easy to see why: Despite all the talk of family values, we're constantly bombarded by visions of perfect romance. All you have to do is turn on the radio or TV or open any magazine and check out the perfume and lingerie ads. "Our culture is deeply regressed," says Florence Falk, a New York City psychotherapist. "Everywhere we turn, we're faced with glamorized, idealized versions of love. It's as if the culture wants us to stay trapped in the fantasy and does everything possible to encourage and expand that fantasy." Trying to forge an authentic relationship amidst all the romantic hype, she adds, makes what is already a tough proposition even harder.

contradictions of ideal love and marriage

What's most unusual about our culture is our feverish devotion to the belief that romantic love and marriage should be synonymous. Starting with George and Martha, continuing through Ozzie and Harriet right up to the present day, we have tirelessly tried to formalize, rationalize, legalize, legitimize, politicize, and sanitize rapture. This may have something to do with our puritanical roots, as well as our tendency toward oversimplification. In any event, this attempt to satisfy all of our contradictory desires under the marital umbrella must be put in historical context in order to be properly understood.

"personal intimacy" never considered part of marriage before 20th century

"Personal intimacy is actually quite a new idea in human history and was never part of the marriage ideal before the 20th century," says John Welwood, a Northern California-based psychologist and author, most recently, of *Love and Awakening.* "Most couples throughout history managed to live together their whole lives without ever having a conversation about what was going on within or between them. As long as family and society prescribed the rules of marriage, individuals never had to develop any consciousness in this area."

In short, marriage was designed to serve the economic and social needs of families, communities, and religious institutions, and had little or nothing to do with love. Nor was it expected to satisfy lust.

Divide into Stages of Thought

When a selection doesn't contain sections headed by thematic headings, as is the case with "The Future of Love," how do you determine where one stage of thought ends and the next one begins? Assuming that what you have read is coherent and unified, this should not be difficult. (When a selection is unified, all of its parts pertain to the main subject; when a selection is coherent, the parts follow one another in logical order.) Look, particularly, for transitional sentences at the beginning of paragraphs. Such sentences generally work in one or both of the following ways: (1) they summarize what has come before; (2) they set the stage for what is to follow.

For example, look at the sentence that opens paragraph 10: "But even if our biochemistry suggests that there should be term limits on love, the heart is a stubborn muscle, and for better or worse, most of us continue to yearn for a relationship that will endure." Notice how the first part of this sentence restates the main idea of the preceding section. The second part of the transitional sentence announces the topic of the upcoming section: three paragraphs devoted to the efforts people make to attain, save, or reinvent romantic relationships.

Each section of an article generally takes several paragraphs to develop. Between paragraphs, and almost certainly between sections of an article, you will usually find transitions that help you understand what you have just read and what you are about to read. For articles that have no subheadings, try writing your own section headings in the margins as you take notes. Then proceed with your summary.

The sections of Graham's article may be described as follows:

> **Section 1:** Introduction—a yearning for "fulfillment through love" pervades our culture, and that yearning is shaped by myths and romantic fantasies. (paragraphs 1–3).
>
> **Section 2:** Marriage and love—we expect passionate love to lead to happy, lifelong marriage. This is a relatively new and unique practice in human history (paragraphs 4–7).
>
> **Section 3:** Biochemistry and love—love has a biochemical component, which complicates our abilities to sustain long-term relationships (paragraphs 8–9).
>
> **Section 4:** Marriage and love revisited—many people are currently trying to preserve and/or reinvent marriage and love (paragraphs 10–12).
>
> **Section 5:** Conclusion—the fusion of passionate love with the institution of marriage hasn't worked very

well, and we need something "radically different"
to replace it (paragraph 13).

Write a One- or Two-Sentence Summary
of Each Stage of Thought

The purpose of this step is to wean you from the language of the original passage, so that you are not tied to it when writing the summary. Here are one-sentence summaries for each stage of thought in "The Future of Love" article's five sections:

Section 1: Introduction—a yearning for "fulfillment through love" pervades our culture, and that yearning is shaped by myths and romantic fantasies (paragraphs 1–3).

> Most members of American culture crave romantic
> love, but we have unreal expectations based upon
> idealized images of love that we learn from fan-
> tasies and fairy tales.

Section 2: Marriage and love—we expect passionate love to lead to happy, lifelong marriage. This is a relatively new and unique practice in human history (paragraphs 4–7).

> We expect the passionate love of fairy tales to
> lead to "happily ever after" in the institution of
> marriage, and when this fails, we move on and try
> it again. Ironically, the idea that marriage should
> be based on love—rather than upon social and eco-
> nomic concerns—is a relatively recent practice in
> Western history.

Section 3: Biochemistry and love—love has a biochemical component, which complicates our abilities to sustain long-term relationships (paragraphs 8–9).

> Biochemists are discovering that love and lust have
> hormonal causes, and their evidence suggests that
> our biological makeup predisposes us to seek the
> excitement of short-term relationships.

Section 4: Marriage and love revisited—many people are currently trying to preserve and/or reinvent marriage and love (paragraphs 10–12).

> Despite all the difficulties, we spend a lot of
> time analyzing the elements of relationships in

```
order to preserve or perhaps reinvent marriage. We
clearly want to make it work.
```

Section 5: Conclusion—the fusion of passionate love with the institution of marriage hasn't worked very well, and we need something "radically different" to replace it (paragraph 13).

```
Because confining passionate love to the institu-
tion of marriage hasn't worked very well, we need
to revise our model for human relationships.
```

Write a Thesis: A One- or Two-Sentence Summary of the Entire Passage

The thesis is the most general statement of a summary (or any other type of academic writing—see Chapter 3 for a more complete discussion of thesis statements). It is the statement that announces the paper's subject and the claim that you or—in the case of a summary—another author will be making about that subject. Every paragraph of a paper illuminates the thesis by providing supporting detail or explanation. The relationship of these paragraphs to the thesis is analogous to the relationship of the sentences within a paragraph to the topic sentence. Both the thesis and the topic sentences are general statements (the thesis being the more general) that are followed by systematically arranged details.

To ensure clarity for the reader, *the first sentence of your summary should begin with the author's thesis, regardless of where it appears in the article itself.* Authors may locate their thesis at the beginning of their work, in which case the thesis operates as a general principle from which details of the presentation follow. This is called a *deductive* organization: thesis first, supporting details second. Alternately, an author may locate his or her thesis at the end of the work, in which case the author begins with specific details and builds toward a more general conclusion, or thesis. This is called an *inductive* organization—an example of which you see in "The Future of Love."

A thesis consists of a subject and an assertion about that subject. How can we go about fashioning an adequate thesis for a summary of "The Future of Love"? Probably no two proposed thesis statements for this article would be worded identically, but it is fair to say that any reasonable thesis will indicate that the subject is the current state of love and marriage in American society. How does Graham view the topic? What *is* the current state of love and marriage, in her view? Looking back over our section summaries, we find that Graham's focus on the illusions of fairy tales and myths, on the difference between marriage in the present day and its earlier incarnations, and on the problems of divorce and "romance addiction" suggest she is not altogether positive in her assessment of the current state of marriage. Does she make a statement anywhere that pulls all this together somehow? Her conclusion, in paragraph 13, contains her main idea: "our society's past efforts to fuse together those historically odd bedfellows— passionate love and marriage—have failed miserably." Moreover, in the next sentence, she writes: "it's obvious that something radically different is needed." Further evidence that this is Graham's main point can be found in the complete title of the essay: "The Future of Love: Kiss Romance Goodbye, It's Time for the Real Thing." Mindful of Graham's subject and the assertion she makes about it, we can write a thesis statement *in our own words* and arrive at the following:

> The contemporary institution of marriage is in trouble, and this may be due to our unrealistic expectations that passionate love leads to lasting union. It may be time to develop a new model for love and relationships.

To clarify for our readers the fact that this idea is Graham's and not ours, we'll qualify the thesis as follows:

> In her article "The Future of Love: Kiss Romance Goodbye, It's Time for the Real Thing," Barbara Graham suggests that because unrealistic expectations for romantic love may undermine marriage, we should develop a new model for love and relationships.

The first sentence of a summary is crucially important, for it orients readers by letting them know what to expect in the coming paragraphs. The preceding example sentence provides the reader with a direct reference to an article, to its author, and to the thesis for the upcoming summary. The author and title reference could also be indicated in the summary's title (if this were a freestanding summary), in which case their mention could be dropped from the thesis. And lest you become frustrated too quickly, keep in mind that writing an acceptable thesis for a summary takes time—in this case, three drafts, or roughly seven minutes of effort spent on one sentence and another few minutes of fine-tuning after a draft of the entire summary was completed. That is, the first draft of the thesis was too vague and incomplete; the second draft was more specific and complete, but left out the author's point about correcting the problem; the third draft was more complete, but was cumbersome.

> **Draft 1:** Barbara Graham argues that our attempts to confine passionate love to the institution of marriage have failed.
> *(too vague—the problem isn't clear enough)*

Draft 2: Barbara Graham ~~argues that our attempts to confine passionate love to the institution of marriage have failed~~ describes how the contemporary institution of marriage is in trouble, and this may be due, she thinks, to our unrealistic expectations that passionate love will lead to lasting union. *(Incomplete—what about her call for a change?)*

Draft 3: In her article "The Future of Love: Kiss Romance Goodbye, It's Time for the Real Thing," Barbara Graham describes how ~~the contemporary institution of marriage is in trouble, and this may be due, she thinks, to~~ our unrealistic expectations that passionate love will lead to lasting union may be causing the troubles in the contemporary institution of marriage today, so she argues that perhaps it's time to develop a new model for love and relationships. *(Wordy)*

Final: In her article "The Future of Love: Kiss Romance Goodbye, It's Time for the Real Thing," Barbara Graham suggests that because unrealistic expectations for romantic love may undermine marriage, we should develop a new model for love and relationships.

Write the First Draft of the Summary

Let's consider two possible summaries of the example passage: (1) a short summary, combining a thesis with one-sentence section summaries, and (2) a longer summary, combining thesis, one-sentence section summaries, and some carefully chosen details. Again, realize that you are reading final versions; each of the following summaries is the result of at least two full drafts.

Summary 1: Combine Thesis Sentence with One-Sentence Section Summaries

In her article "The Future of Love: Kiss Romance Goodbye, It's Time for the Real Thing," Barbara Graham suggests that because unrealistic expectations for romantic love may undermine marriage, we should develop a new model for love and relationships. Most members of American culture crave romantic love, but we have unreal expectations based upon idealized images of love we learn from fantasies and fairy tales.

We expect the passionate love of fairy tales to lead to "happily ever after" in the institution of marriage, and when this fails, we move on and try it again. Ironically, the idea that marriage should be based on love—rather than upon social and economic concerns—is a relatively recent practice in Western history. While the romantic marriage ideal doesn't fit with tradition, biological evidence is mounting against it as well. Biochemists are discovering that love and lust have hormonal causes, and their evidence suggests that our biological makeup predisposes us to seek the excitement of short-term relationships.

Nonetheless, despite all the difficulties, we spend a lot of time analyzing the elements of relationships in order to preserve or perhaps reinvent marriage. We clearly want to make it work. Because confining passionate love to the institution of marriage hasn't worked very well, Graham ends by suggesting that we ought to revise our model for human relationships.

Discussion

This summary consists essentially of a restatement of Graham's thesis plus the section summaries, altered or expanded a little for stylistic purposes. The first sentence after the thesis encompasses the summary of Section 1 and is followed by the summaries of Sections 2, 3, 4, and 5. Notice the insertion of a transitional sentence between the summaries of Sections 2 and 3, helping to link the ideas more coherently.

Summary 2: Combine Thesis Sentence, Section Summaries, and Carefully Chosen Details

The thesis and one-sentence section summaries also can be used as the outline for a more detailed summary. Most of the details in the passage, however, won't be necessary in a summary. It isn't necessary even in a longer summary of this passage to discuss all of Graham's examples—specific romantic fairy tales, ancient Indian views of love and passion, the particular hormones involved with love and lust, or the examples of experts examining and writing about contemporary relationships. It would be appropriate, though, to mention one example of fairy-tale romance, to refer to the historical information on marriage as an economic institution, and to explain some of the biological findings about love's chemical basis.

None of these details appeared in the first summary, but in a longer summary, a few carefully selected details might be desirable for clarity. How do you decide which details to include? First, since the idea that love and marriage are not necessarily compatible is the main point of the essay, it makes sense to cite some of the most persuasive evidence supporting this idea. For example, you could mention that for most of Western history, marriage was meant "to serve the economic and social needs of families, communities, and religious institutions," not the emotional and sexual needs of individuals. Further, you might explain the biochemists' argument that "serial monogamy" based on mutual interests, and "clandestine adultery"—not lifelong, love-based marriage—are the forms of relationships best serving human evolution.

You won't always know which details to include and which to exclude. Developing good judgment in comprehending and summarizing texts is largely a matter of reading skill and prior knowledge (see page 3). Consider the analogy of the seasoned mechanic who can pinpoint an engine problem by simply listening to a characteristic sound that to a less experienced person is just noise. Or consider the chess player who can plot three separate winning strategies from a board position that to a novice looks like a hopeless jumble. In the same way, the more practiced a reader you are, the more knowledgeable you become about the subject, and the better able you will be to make critical distinctions between elements of greater and lesser importance. In the meantime, read as carefully as you can and use your own best judgment as to how to present your material.

Here's one version of a completed summary, with carefully chosen details. Note that we have highlighted phrases and sentences added to the original, briefer summary.

[margin note: Source, title, author are all named]

[margin note: (Thesis)]

> In her article "The Future of Love: Kiss Romance Goodbye, It's Time for the Real Thing," Barbara Graham suggests that because unrealistic expectations for romantic love may undermine marriage, we should develop a new model for love and relationships.

[margin note: examples →]

> Most members of American culture crave romantic love, but we have unreal expectations based upon idealized images of love we learn from fantasies and fairy tales such as Beauty and the Beast and Cinderella. Tragedies such as Romeo and Juliet teach us about the all-consuming nature of "true love," and these stories are tragic precisely because the lovers never get to fulfill what we've been taught is the ideal: living happily ever after, in wedded bliss. The idea that romantic love should be confined to marriage is perhaps the

(Section 1,
¶s 1–3)

biggest fantasy to which we subscribe. When we are unable to make this fantasy real—and it seems that often we are unable to do so—we end that marriage and move on to the next one. The twentieth century is actually the first century in Western history in which so much was asked of marriage. In earlier

(Section 2,
¶s 4–7)

eras, marriage was designed to meet social and economic purposes, rather than fulfill individual emotional and sexual desires.

Casting further doubt on the effectiveness of the current model of marriage, biochemists are discovering how hormones and enzymes influence feelings of love and lust. It turns out that the "chemistry" a person newly in love often feels for another has a basis in fact, as those early feelings of excitement and contentment are biochemical in nature. When people jump from one relationship to the next, they may be seeking that chemical "rush." Further, these biochemical discoveries fit with principles of evolutionary survival,

roughly 1/4 of the original is a good rule of thumb

(Section 3,
¶s 8–9)

because short-term relationships—and even adulterous affairs—help to more quickly propagate the species.

Nonetheless, despite such historical and biological imperatives, we don't seem interested in abandoning the pursuit of love and marriage. In order to preserve or perhaps reinvent marriage, we spend a lot of time scrutinizing and dissecting the dynamics of relationships. Self-help books on the

(Section 4,
¶s 10–12)

subject of love and relationships fill bookstore shelves and top best-seller lists.

fact

While some argue that such scrutiny ruins rather than reinvigorates love, perhaps our efforts to understand relationships can help us to invent some kind of revised model for human relationships—

(Section 5,
¶ 13)

since trying to confine passionate love to the institution of marriage clearly hasn't worked very well.

Discussion

The final two of our suggested steps for writing summaries are (1) to check your summary against the original passage, making sure that you have included all the important ideas, and (2) to revise so that the summary reads smoothly and coherently.

The structure of this summary generally reflects the structure of the original—with one notable departure. As we noted earlier, Graham uses an inductive approach, stating her thesis at the end of the essay. The summary, however, states the thesis right away, then proceeds deductively to develop that thesis.

Compared to the first, briefer summary, this effort mentions fairy tales and tragedy; develops the point about traditional versus contemporary versions of marriage; explains the biochemical/evolutionary point; and refers specifically to self-help books and their role in the issue.

How long should a summary be? This depends on the length of the original passage. A good rule of thumb is that a summary should be no longer than one-fourth of the original passage. Of course, if you were summarizing an entire chapter or even an entire book, it would have to be much shorter than that. The summary on pages 18–19 is about one-fourth the length of the original passage. Although it shouldn't be very much longer, you have seen (pages 16–17) that it could be shorter.

The length as well as the content of the summary also depends on its *purpose.* Let's suppose you decided to use Graham's piece in a paper that dealt with the biochemical processes of love and lust. In this case, you might summarize *only* Graham's discussion of Fisher's findings, and perhaps the point Graham makes about how biochemical discoveries complicate marriage. If, instead, you were writing a paper in which you argued against attempts to redefine marriage, you might summarize Graham's points in paragraph 10 about the persistent desire for lasting union found among members of Generation X and evidenced in the high numbers of marriages and remarriages. Thus, depending on your purpose, you would summarize either selected portions of a source or an entire source, as we will see more fully in the chapters on syntheses.

EXERCISE 1.1

Individual and Collaborative Summary Practice

Turn to Chapter 2 and read J. Morton Davis's essay "A Simple One-Step Plan to Solve the Education Crisis: A Message to the President and the Congress" (pages 54–55). Follow the steps for writing summaries outlined above—read, highlight, and divide into stages of thought. Write down a one- or two-sentence summary of each stage of thought in Davis's essay. Then, gather in groups of three or four classmates and compare your summary sentences. Discuss the differences in your sentences, and come to some consensus about the divisions in Davis's stages of thought—and the ways in which to best sum these up.

As a group, write a one- or two-sentence thesis statement summing up the entire passage. You could go even further. Using your individual summary sentences, or the versions of these your group revised, write a brief summary of Davis's essay, modeled upon the brief summary of Graham's essay on pages 16–17 (Summary 1: Combine Thesis Sentence with One-Sentence Section Summaries).

SUMMARIZING A NARRATIVE OR PERSONAL ESSAY

Narratives and personal essays differ from expository essays in that they focus upon personal experiences and/or views, aren't structured around an explicitly stated thesis, and are developed through the description of events or ideas rather than upon factual evidence or logical explanation. A narrative is a story, a retelling of a person's experiences. That person and those experiences may be imaginary, as is the case with fiction, or they may be real, as in biography. In first-person narratives, you can't assume that the narrator represents the author of the piece, unless you know the narrative is a memoir or biography. In a personal essay, on the other hand, the narrator is the author. And while the writer of a personal essay may tell stories about his or her experiences, usually writers of such essays discuss thoughts and ideas as much as or more than telling stories. Personal essays also tend to contain more obvious points than do narratives. Despite these differences, summarizing personal essays or narratives presents certain challenges—challenges that are different from those presented by summarizing expository writing.

You have seen that an author of an expository piece (such as Graham's "The Future of Love") follows assertions with examples and statements of support. Narratives, however, usually are less direct. The author relates a story—event follows event—the point of which may never be stated directly. The charm, the force, and the very point of the narrative lies in the telling; generally, narratives do not exhibit the same logical development of expository writing. They do not, therefore, lend themselves to summary in quite the same way. Narratives do have a logic, but that logic may be emotional, imaginative, or plot-bound. The writer who summarizes a narrative is obliged to give an overview—a synopsis—of the story's events and an account of how these events affect the central character(s). The summary must explain the significance or *meaning* of the events.

Similarly, while personal essays sometimes present points more explicitly than do narratives, their focus and structure link them to narratives. Personal essays often contain inexplicit main points, or multiple points; they tend to *explore* ideas and issues, rather than make explicit *assertions* about those ideas. This exploratory character often means that personal essays exhibit a loose structure, and they often contain stories or narratives within them. While summarizing a personal essay may not involve a synopsis of events, an account of the progression of thoughts and ideas is necessary and, as with a narrative, summaries of personal essays must explain the significance of what goes on in the piece being summarized.

In the following personal essay entitled "Why I Will Never Have a Girlfriend," Tristan Miller performs a statistical analysis that illustrates the low odds of his ever finding a girlfriend. While this piece portrays the frustration felt by many single people, at the same time it pokes fun at this focus on finding the one "right" person. If you were writing a paper on current attitudes toward relationships, you might reasonably want to include accounts from a single person's point of view. You could quote parts of such personal essays or narratives, and you could summarize them.

Why I Will Never Have A Girlfriend
Tristan Miller

This piece comes from Tristan Miller's personal Web site, at www.nothingisreal.com. Miller is currently a graduate student in computational linguistics at the University of Toronto.

Why don't I have a girlfriend? This is a question that practically every male has asked himself at one point or another in his life. Unfortunately, there is rarely a hard and fast answer to the query. Many guys try to reason their way through the dilemma nonetheless, often reaching a series of ridiculous explanations, each more self-deprecating than the last: "Is it because I'm too shy, and not aggressive enough? Is it my opening lines? Am I a boring person? Am I too fat or too thin? Or am I simply ugly and completely unattractive to women?" When all other plausible explanations have been discounted, most fall back on the time-honoured conclusion that "there must be Something Wrong™ with me" before resigning themselves to lives of perpetual chastity.[a]

Not me, though. I, for one, refuse to spend my life brooding over my lack of luck with women. While I'll be the first to admit that my chances of ever entering into a meaningful relationship with someone special are practically non-existent, I staunchly refuse to admit that it has anything to do with some inherent problem with me. Instead, I am convinced that the situation can be readily explained in purely scientific terms, using nothing more than demographics and some elementary statistical calculus.

Lest anyone suspect that my standards for women are too high, let me allay those fears by enumerating in advance my three criteria for the match. First, the potential girlfriend must be approximately my age—let's say 21 plus or minus three or four years. Second, the girl must be beautiful (and I use that term all-encompassingly to refer to both inner and outer beauty). Third, she must also be reasonably intelligent—she doesn't have to be Mensa material, but the ability to carry on a witty, insightful argument would be nice. So there you have it—

Tristan Miller, "Why I Will Never Have a Girlfriend," online essay, 1999, 7 Sept. 2000 <http://www.nothingisreal.com/girlfriend/>.

[a] After a short period of brooding, of course, these males will eventually come to the realization that the real reason they were never able to get a girlfriend is that they were too discriminating with their attentions. They will consequently return to the dating scene, entering a sequence of blasé relationships with mediocre girls for whom they don't really care, until they finally marry one out of fear of spending the rest of their lives alone. I am convinced that this behavior is the real reason for today's alarmingly high divorce rate.

three simple demands, which I'm sure you'll all agree are anything but unreasonable. That said, I now present my demonstration of why the probability of finding a suitable candidate fulfilling the three above-noted requirements is so small as to be practically impossible—in other words, why I will never have a girlfriend. I shall endeavor to make this proof as rigorous as the available data permits. And I should note, too, that there will be no statistical trickery involved here; I have cited all my sources and provided all relevant calculations[b] in case anyone wishes to conduct their own independent review. Let's now take a look at the figures, shall we?

Number of people on Earth (in 1998)   5, 592, 830, 000

We start with the largest demographic in which I am interested—namely, the population of this planet. That is not to say I'm against the idea of interstellar romance, of course; I just don't assess the prospect of finding myself a nice Altairian girl as statistically significant. Now anyway, the latest halfway-reliable figures we have for Earth's population come from the United States Census Bureau's 1999 World Population Profile. Due presumably to the time involved in compiling and processing census statistics, said report's data is valid only as of 1998, so later on we'll be making some impromptu adjustments to bring the numbers up to date.

...who are female   2 ,941, 118, 000[c]

I'd've thought that, given the title of this web page, this criterion goes without saying. In case anyone missed it, though, I am looking for exclusively female companionship. Accordingly, roughly half of the Earth's population must be discounted. Sorry, guys.

...in "developed" countries   605, 601, 000[d]

We now further restrict the geographical area of interest to so-called "first-world countries." My reasons for doing so are not motivated out of contempt for those who are economically disadvantaged, but rather by simple probability. My chances of meeting a babe from Bhutan or a goddess from Ghana, either in person or on the Internet, are understandably low. In fact, I will most likely spend nearly my entire life living and working in North America, Europe, and Australia, so it is to these types of regions that the numbers have been narrowed.

...currently (in 2000) aged 18 to 25   65, 399, 083[e]

Being neither a pedophile nor a geriatrophile, I would like to restrict my search for love to those whose age is approximately equal to my own. This is where things

---

[b] Due to rounding, figures cited may not add up exactly.

[c] U.S. Bureau of the Census, Report WP/98, Table A-3.

[d] U.S. Bureau of the Census, Report WP/98, Table A-7.

[e] U.S. Bureau of the Census, Report WP/98, Table A-7.

get a bit tricky, for two reasons: first, the census data is nearly two years old, and second, the "population by age" tables in WP/98 do not have a single listing for "16–23" but are instead quantified into "15–19" (of whom there are 39,560,000) and "20–44" (population 215,073,000). Women aged 15 to 19 in 1998 will be aged 17 to 21 in 2000[f]; in this group, I'm interested in dating those 18 or older, so, assuming the "15–19" girls' ages are uniformly distributed, we have

$$39,560,000 \times \frac{[21-18] + 1}{[19-15] + 1} = 31,648,000$$

Similarly, of 1998's "20–44" category, there are now

$$215,073,000 \times \frac{[25-22] + 1}{[44-20] + 1} = 34,411,680$$

females within my chosen age limit. The sum, 66,059,680, represents the total number of females aged 18 to 25 in developed countries in 2000. Unfortunately, roughly 1% of these girls will have died since the census was taken[g]; thus, the true number of so-far eligible bachelorettes is 65,399,083.

...who are beautiful   1, 487, 838[h]

Personal attraction, both physically and personality-wise, is an important instigator of any relationship. Of course, beauty is a purely subjective trait whose interpretation may vary from person to person. Luckily it is not necessary for me to define beauty in this essay except to state that for any given beholder, it will probably be normally distributed amongst the population.[i] Without going into the specifics of precisely which traits I admire, I will say that for a girl to be considered really beautiful to me, she should fall at least two standard deviations above the norm. From basic statistics theory, the area to the left of the normal curve at $z = 2$ is

$$\frac{1}{2} - \frac{1}{\sqrt{2\pi}} \int_0^2 e^{-\frac{1}{2}z^2} dz \approx 0.02275$$

and so it is this number with which we multiply our current population pool.

---

[f] Lest anyone think me out of touch with temporal reality, I am aware that it is still 1999 at the time of this writing; however, given that there remain less than two weeks until the new year, it would be more mathematically correct to make calculations based on the year 2000.

[g] WP/98 gives the annual death rate for developed countries as 10 per 1,000, but does not list death rates per age group. Presumably, the death rate graphs as a bathtub curve, but in absence of any numbers supporting this hypothesis, and for the sake of simplicity, I will conservatively estimate the death rate among this age group to be 1% biennially.

[h] U.S. Bureau of the Census, Report WP/98, Tables A-3 and A-7.

[i] Despite my efforts to research the matter, I could find no data on the distribution of beauty, either outer or inner, amongst the population. Perhaps attractiveness, being a largely subjective trait, does not lend itself to quantification. It is not unreasonable, however, to assume that like most other traits, it has a normal distribution. Indeed, this assumption seems to be backed up by informal observation and judgment—in any reasonably large group of people, most of them will be average-looking, and a tiny minority either exceedingly beautiful or exceedingly ugly.

...and intelligent   236, 053

Again, intelligence can mean different things to different people, yet I am once more relieved of making any explanation by noting that it, like most other characteristics, has a notionally normal distribution across the population. Let's assume that I will settle for someone a mere one standard deviation above the normal; in that case, a further

$$\frac{1}{2} - \frac{1}{\sqrt{2\pi}} \int_0^1 e^{-\frac{1}{2}z^2} dz \approx 84.1345\%$$

$= 84.1345\%$
of the population must be discounted.

...and not already committed   118, 027

I could find no hard statistics on the number of above-noted girls who are already married, engaged, or otherwise committed to a significant other, but informal observation and anecdotal evidence leads me to believe that the proportion is somewhere around 50%. (Fellow unattached males will no doubt have also noticed a preponderance of girls legitimately offering, "Sorry, I already have a boyfriend" as an excuse not to go on a date.) For reasons of morality (and perhaps too self-preservation), I'm not about to start hitting on girls who have husbands and boyfriends. Accordingly, that portion of the female population must also be considered off-limits.

...and also might like me   18, 726

Naturally, finding a suitable girl who I really like is no guarantee that she'll like me back. Assuming, as previously mentioned, that personal attractiveness is normally distributed, there is a mere 50% chance that any given female will consider me even marginally attractive. In practice, however, people are unlikely to consider pursuing a relationship with someone whose looks and personality just barely suffice. Let's make the rather conservative assumption, then, that a girl would go out with someone if and only if they were at least one standard deviation above her idea of average. In that case, referring to our previous calculation, only 15.8655% of females would consider someone with my physical characteristics and personality acceptable as a potential romantic partner.

Conclusion

It is here, at a pool of 18,726 acceptable females, that we end our statistical analysis. At first glance, a datable population of 18,726 may not seem like such a low number, but consider this: assuming I were to go on a blind date with a new girl about my age every week, I would have to date for 3,493 weeks before I found one of the 18,726. That's very nearly 67 years. As a North American male born in the late 1970s, my life expectancy is probably little more than 70 years, so we can safely say that I will be quite dead before I find the proverbial girl of my dreams. Come to think of it, she'll probably be dead too. So there you have it, my friends—finally, a cogent, scientific, non-self-deprecating argument for why I will never have a girlfriend. That said, if you happen to be a girl deluded enough to think that you and I have a chance together, feel free to drop me a line, but I warn you, you face odds of 157,060 to 1. I wouldn't bother if I were you.

Miller uses quantitative "data" to make light of his own search for a girlfriend—as well of the practice of statistical analysis itself. While he wants to find a girlfriend, his meticulous analysis of the numbers shows an ironic self-awareness about the ways in which that desire so easily slides into an obsessive preoccupation. This first-person account could be valuable in a paper otherwise dependent on newspaper and journal articles and on books explaining more factual elements of trends in modern romance. You might reasonably pause in your explanations to acknowledge the frustrations of those who want a relationship yet remain single (and the attempts these unfortunates make to understand their predicament), and Miller's piece could be useful for this.

How would you refer to Miller's essay? When you summarize a personal essay or a narrative, bear in mind the principles that follow, as well as those listed in the box.

HOW TO SUMMARIZE PERSONAL ESSAYS AND NARRATIVES

- Your summary will *not* be a narrative, but rather the synopsis of a narrative or personal account. Your summary will likely be a paragraph at most.
- You will want to name and describe the principal character(s) of the narrative and describe the narrative's main actions or events; or, in the case of the personal essay, identify the narrator and his or her relationship to the discussion.
- You should seek to connect the narrative's character(s) and events: describe the significance of events for (or the impact of events on) the character(s), and/or the narrator.

To summarize events, reread the narrative and make a marginal note each time you see that an action advances the story from one moment to the next. The key here is to recall that narratives take place *in time.* In your summary, be sure to re-create for your reader a sense of time flowing. Name and describe the character(s) as well. (For our purposes, *character* refers to the person, real or fictional, about whom the narrative is written.) The trickiest part of the summary will be describing the connection between events and characters. Earlier (page 3) we made the point that summarizing any selection involves a degree of interpretation, and this is especially true of summarizing narratives and personal essays. What, in the case of Miller, is the point of his statistical analysis? Is he really simply trying to prove why he'll never have a girlfriend? An answer belongs in a summary of this piece, yet developing an answer is tricky. Five readers would arrive at five different interpretations of his attitude toward the subject, would they not? Yes and no: yes, in the sense that these readers, given their separate experiences, will read from different points of view; no, in the sense that readers should be able to distinguish between Miller's attitude and their (the readers') attitude about the topic. A particular interpretation is only valid if textual details support it. For example, we should be able to agree that Miller's tone expresses an attitude not wholly serious, since he makes small jokes throughout his piece.

Noticing details such as the joking tone adopted by a writer is an example of the way you have to infer from clues in a personal essay or narrative the significance of events for a character; at other times, the writer will be more direct. In either case, remember that it is the piece's main character or narrator, real or imaginary, whose perspective should be represented in the summary. Here is a one-paragraph summary of Miller's essay. (The draft is the result of two prior drafts.)

> As the title of his essay "Why I Will Never Have a Girlfriend," suggests, Tristan Miller explores the reasons for his status as a single man. Providing a detailed, step-by-step breakdown of demographic data, Miller narrows down the number of eligible women available to him. He starts with the total population of the world and systematically reduces that number based on the actual number of women in the world, in his age group, and so on. Once arrived at his final number of eligible women, Miller offers an ironic argument that he's proven how statistical odds—rather than any deficiencies in him—are to blame for his lonely condition.

SUMMARIZING FIGURES AND TABLES

In your reading in the sciences and social sciences, you will often find data and concepts presented in nontext forms—as figures and tables. Such visual devices offer a snapshot, a pictorial overview of material that is more quickly and clearly communicated in graphic form than as a series of (often complicated) sentences. Note that in essence, figures and tables are themselves summaries. The writer uses a graph, which in an article or book is labeled as a numbered "figure," to present the quantitative results of research as points on a line or a bar, or as sections ("slices") of a pie. Pie charts show relative proportions, or percentages. Graphs, especially effective in showing patterns, relate one variable to another: for instance, income to years of education, or a college student's grade point average to hours of studying.

In the following sections, we present a number of figures and tables from two different sources, all dealing with topics related to romance and relationships. Figures 1.1, 1.2, 1.3, and Table 1.1 are based upon data generated by a study of the criteria used by participants on television dating shows in the United States and Israel to pick dating partners.* The categories are self-explanatory, although we should note that the category "physical appearance" denotes features of height, weight, facial features, and hair, while "sexual anatomy and bedroom behavior" refers to specifically sexual features of physical appearance, as well as to "kissing technique," "foreplay tactics," and the like. Figure 1.1 shows the percentage of American and Israeli men (out of a total of 266) who selected specific dating criteria as the most important ones used to screen potential dates among members of the opposite sex. Study this pie chart.

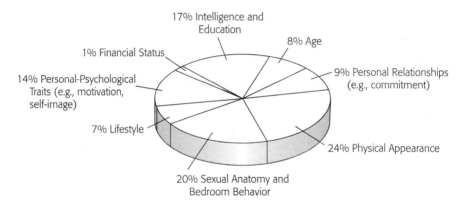

FIGURE 1.1   Categories Used by American and Israeli Males to Screen Dating Candidates

Here is a summary of the information presented:

> Males rated the categories of "physical appearance" and "sexual anatomy and bedroom behavior" as most important to them. Combined, at 44%, these two categories, which both center on external rather than internal characteristics, represent nearly half of males' chosen categories. Internal characteristics represented by the categories of "personal-psychological traits" and "intelligence and education" account for the next greatest amounts, for a com-

---

* Amir Hetsroni, "Choosing a Mate in Television Dating Games: The Influence of Setting, Culture, and Gender," *Sex Roles* 42.1–2 (2000): 90–97.

bined 31%. Males rated "relationship," "lifestyle," and "age" at nearly equal percentages, with an average rating of 8% for the three; interestingly, "financial status" was rated at the negligible 1%.

Figure 1.2 shows the percentages for women's ratings of dating criteria.

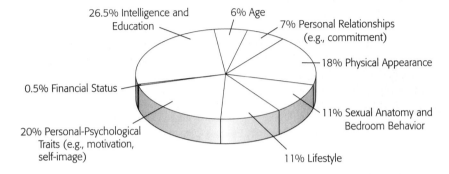

FIGURE 1.2   Categories Used by American and Israeli Females to Screen Dating Candidates

EXERCISE **1.2**

Summarizing Charts

Write a brief summary of the data in Figure 1.2. Use our summary of Figure 1.1 as a model, but structure and word your own summary differently.

Bar graphs are useful for comparing two sets of data. Figure 1.3 illustrates this with a comparison of the male and female choices.

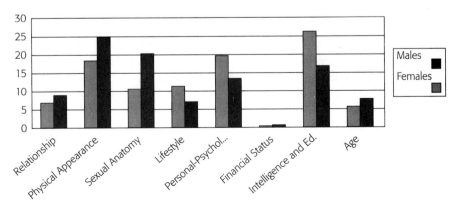

FIGURE 1.3   Comparison of Categories Used by American and Israeli Males and Females to Screen Dating Candidates

Here is a summary of the information in Figure 1.3:

> We find clear differences when comparing male and female choices of criteria for selecting a date. Males chose external characteristics such as "physical appearance" and especially "sexual anatomy and bedroom behavior" at significantly higher rates than did females. Conversely, females selected internal characteristics of "lifestyle," "personal-psychological traits," and "intelligence and education" at much higher rates than did males. There is virtually no significant difference between the male and female ratings of "relationship," "financial status," and "age"; all three of these criteria were rated at equally low levels of importance by both male and female participants.

A table presents numerical data in rows and columns for quick reference. Tabular information can be incorporated into graphs, if the writer chooses. Charts and graphs are preferable when the writer wants to emphasize a pattern or relationship; tables are used when the writer wants to emphasize numbers. While the previous charts and graphs combined all male and female data collected in the TV dating show study, Table 1.1 provides a breakdown of the categories chosen by males and females in the United States and in Israel. (Note: n refers to the total number of respondents in each category.)

TABLE 1.1   Categories Used by American and Israeli Males and Females to Screen Dating Candidates

Category	American Males (%) (n = 120)	Israeli Males (%) (n = 146)	American Females (%) (n = 156)	Israeli Females (%) (n = 244)
Relationship	9.5	8.0	9.5	5.0
Physical appearance	18.5	30.0	12.0	22.0
Sexual anatomy and bedroom behavior	11.5	27.5	4.5	15.0
Lifestyle	9.0	6.0	11.0	11.5
Personal-psychological traits	20.0	8.0	27.0	15.0
Financial status	1.5	—	—	1.0
Intelligence and education	22.5	12.5	29.0	24.5
Age	7.5	8.0	7.0	6.0
Total	100.0	100.0	100.0	100.0

Sometimes a single graph will present information on two or more populations, or data sets, all of which are tracked with the same measurements. Figure 1.4 comes from a study of 261 college students—93 males and 168 females.* The students were asked (among other things) to rate the acceptability of a hypothetical instance of sexual betrayal by both a male and a female heterosexual romantic partner who has agreed to be monogamous. The graph plots the ways in which gender of the transgressor played into the acceptability ratings given by male and female respondents. The researchers established mean values of 1 to 4 (indicating ratings of "totally unacceptable" to "totally acceptable"). A "mean" indicates the average of the ratings or scores given by a population or, in numerical terms, the sum of the scores divided by the number of scores. When respondents in the study were asked to assign a numerical rating of acceptability to instances of sexual betrayal, they chose numbers on a scale from 1 to 4, and these choices were averaged into mean acceptability ratings. None of the scores given by respondents in this study surpassed a mean acceptability rating of 2, but differences are evident between male and female ratings. The male respondents were more accepting of sexual betrayal than the females, with an overall mean acceptability score of 1.63, whereas the females' mean score was 1.31.

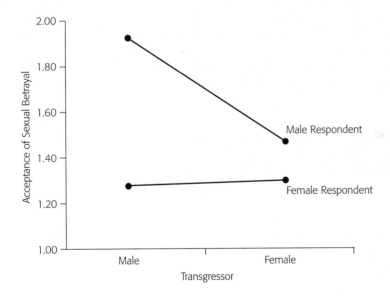

FIGURE 1.4   The Interaction of Sex of Respondent and Sex of Transgressor on the Acceptance of Sexual Betrayal

* S. Shirley Feldman, Elizabeth Cauffman, Lene Arnette Jensen, and Jeffrey J. Arnett, "The (Un)Acceptability of Betrayal: A Study of College Students' Evaluations of Sexual Betrayal by a Romantic Partner and Betrayal of a Friend's Confidence," *Journal of Youth and Adolescence* 29.4 (2000): 498–523.

A complete, scientific understanding of these findings would require more data, and statistical analysis of such data would yield precise information such as the exact amount of difference between male and female ratings. For example, in the original text of this study, the authors note that males were 11.6 times more accepting of sexual betrayal by male transgressors than were females. Even without such details, it is possible to arrive at a basic understanding of the data represented in the graph, and to summarize this information in simple terms. Here is a summary of the information reported in this graph:

> While males and females both rated sexual betrayal as unacceptable, males (with a mean rating of 1.63) were significantly more accepting overall than were females (with a mean rating of 1.31). Even more dramatic, however, is the difference between male and female ratings when the gender of the transgressor is factored in. Males rated male transgression as markedly more acceptable than female transgression, with approximate means of 1.90 for male transgressions and 1.43 for female transgressions. The males' ratings contrast sharply with those of females, who indicated a mean acceptability rating of approximately 1.25 for male transgressors, and 1.30 for female transgressors. Therefore, while both sexes found transgression by members of their own sex more acceptable than transgressions by the opposite sex, men were more accepting overall than women, and men believed male transgressors were significantly more acceptable than female transgressors. On the other hand, women found transgression overall less acceptable than males did, and women indicated far less difference in their ratings of male versus female transgressors than did the male respondents.

PARAPHRASE

In certain cases, you may want to *paraphrase* rather than summarize material. Writing a paraphrase is similar to writing a summary: It involves recasting a passage into your own words, so it requires your complete understanding of the material. The difference is that while a summary is a shortened version of the original, the paraphrase is approximately the same length as the original.

Why write a paraphrase when you can quote the original? You may decide to offer a paraphrase of material written in language that is dense, abstract, archaic, or possibly confusing. For example, suppose you were writing a paper on some aspect of human progress and you came across the following passage by the Marquis de Condorcet, a French economist and politician, written in the late eighteenth century:

> If man can, with almost complete assurance, predict phenomena when he knows their laws, and if, even when he does not, he can still, with great expectations of success, forecast the future on the basis of his experience of the past, why, then, should it be regarded as a fantastic undertaking to sketch, with some pretense to truth, the future destiny of man on the basis of his history? The sole foundation for belief in the natural science is this idea, that the general laws directing the phenomena of the universe, known or unknown, are necessary and constant. Why should this principle be any less true for the development of the intellectual and moral faculties of man than for the other operations of nature?

You would like to introduce Condorcet's idea on predicting the future course of human history, but you also don't want to slow down your narrative with this somewhat abstract quotation. You may decide to attempt a paraphrase, as follows:

> The Marquis de Condorcet believed that if we can predict such physical events as eclipses and tides, and if we can use past events as a guide to future ones, we should be able to forecast human destiny on the basis of history. Physical events, he maintained, are determined by natural laws that are knowable and predictable. Since humans are part of nature, why should their intellectual and moral development be any less predictable than other natural events?

Each sentence in the paraphrase corresponds to a sentence in the original. The paraphrase is somewhat shorter, owing to the differences of style between eighteenth- and twentieth-century prose (we tend to be more brisk and efficient, although not as eloquent). But the main difference is that we have replaced the language of the original with our own language. For example, we have paraphrased Condorcet's "the general laws directing the phenomena of the universe, known or unknown, are necessary and constant" with "Physical events, he maintained, are determined by natural laws that are knowable and predictable." To contemporary readers, "knowable and predictable" might be clearer than "necessary and constant" as a description of natural (i.e., physical) laws. Note that we added the specific examples of eclipses and tides to clarify what might have been a somewhat abstract idea. Note also that we included two attributions to Condorcet within the paraphrase to properly credit our source.

When you come across a passage that you don't understand, the temptation is strong to skip over it. Resist this temptation! Use a paraphrase as a tool for explaining to yourself the main ideas of a difficult passage. By translating another writer's language into your own, you can clarify what you understand and pinpoint what you don't. The paraphrase therefore becomes a tool for learning the subject.

The following pointers will help you write paraphrases.

HOW TO WRITE PARAPHRASES

- Make sure that you understand the source passage.
- Substitute your own words for those of the source passage; look for synonyms that carry the same meaning as the original words.
- Rearrange your own sentences so that they read smoothly. Sentence structure, even sentence order, in the paraphrase need not be based on that of the original. A good paraphrase, like a good summary, should stand by itself.

Let's consider some other examples. If you were investigating the ethical concerns relating to the practice of in vitro fertilization, you might conclude that you should read some medical literature. You might reasonably want to hear from the doctors themselves who are developing, performing, and questioning the procedures that you are researching. In professional journals and bulletins, physicians write to one another, not to the general public. They use specialized language. If you wanted to refer to a technically complex selection, you might need to write a paraphrase for the following selection:

In Vitro Fertilization: From Medical Reproduction to Genetic Diagnosis

Dietmar Mieth

[I]t is not only an improvement in the success-rate that participating research scientists hope for but rather, developments in new fields of research in in-vitro gene diagnosis and in certain circumstances gene therapy. In view of this, the French expert J. F. Mattei has asked the following question: "Are we forced to accept that in vitro fertilization will become one of the most compelling methods of genetic diagnosis?" Evidently, by the introduction of a new law in France and Sweden (1994), this acceptance (albeit with certain restrictions) has already occurred prior to the application of in vitro fertilization reaching a technically mature and clinically applicable phase. This may seem astonishing in view of the question placed by the above-quoted French expert: the idea of embryo production so as to withhold one or two embryos before implantation presupposes a definite "attitude towards eugenics." And to destroy an embryo merely because of its genetic characteristics could signify the reduction of a human life to the sum of its genes. Mattei asks: "In face of a molecular judgment on our lives, is there no possibility for appeal? Will the diagnosis of inherited monogenetic illnesses soon be extended to genetic predisposition for multi-factorial illnesses?"*

Like most literature intended for physicians, the language of this selection is somewhat forbidding to an audience of nonspecialists, who have trouble with phrases such as "predisposition for multi-factorial illnesses." As a courtesy to your readers and in an effort to maintain a consistent tone and level in your essay, you could paraphrase this paragraph of the medical newsletter. First, of course, you must understand the meaning of the passage, perhaps no small task. But, having read the material carefully (and perhaps consulting a dictionary), you might eventually prepare a paraphrase like this one:

> Writing in the *Newsletter of the European Network for Biomedical Ethics*, Dietmar Mieth reports that fertility specialists today want not only to improve the success rates of their procedures but also to diagnose and repair genetic problems before they implant fertilized eggs. Since the result of the in vitro process is often more fertilized eggs than can be used in a procedure, doctors may examine test-tube embryos for genetic defects and "withhold one or two" before implanting them. The practice of selectively implanting embryos raises concerns about eugenics and the rights of rejected embryos. On what genetic grounds will specialists distinguish flawed from healthy embryos and make a decision whether or not to implant? The appearance of single genes linked directly to specific, or "monogenetic," illnesses could be grounds for destroying an embryo. More complicated would be genes that predispose people to an illness but in no way guarantee the onset of that illness. Would these genes, which are only one factor in "multi-factorial illnesses," also be labeled undesirable and lead to embryo destruction? Advances in fertility science raise difficult questions. Already, even before techniques of genetic diagnosis are fully developed, legislatures are writing laws governing the practices of fertility clinics.

* Dietmar Mieth, "In Vitro Fertilization: From Medical Reproduction to Genetic Diagnosis," *Biomedical Ethics: Newsletter of the European Network for Biomedical Ethics* 1.1 (1996): 45.

We begin our paraphrase with the same "not only/but also" logic of the original's first sentence, introducing the concepts of genetic diagnosis and therapy. The next four sentences in the original introduce concerns of a "French expert." Rather than quoting Mieth, quoting the expert, and immediately mentioning new laws in France and Sweden, we decided (first) to explain that in vitro fertilization procedures can give rise to more embryos than needed. We reasoned that nonmedical readers would appreciate our making explicit the background knowledge that the author assumes other physicians possess. Then we quote Mieth briefly ("withhold one or two" embryos) to provide some flavor of the original. We maintain focus on the ethical questions and wait until the end of the paraphrase before mentioning the laws to which Mieth refers. Our paraphrase is roughly the same length as the original, and it conveys the author's concerns about eugenics. As you can see, the paraphrase requires a writer to make some decisions about the presentation of material. In many, if not most, cases, you will need to do more than simply "translate" from the original, sentence by sentence, to write your paraphrase.

Finally, let's consider a passage written by a fine writer that may, nonetheless, best be conveyed in paraphrase. In "Identify All Carriers," an article on AIDS, editor and columnist William F. Buckley makes the following statement:

> I have read and listened, and I think now that I can convincingly crystallize the thoughts chasing about in the minds of, first, those whose concern with AIDS victims is based primarily on a concern for them, and for the maintenance of the most rigid standards of civil liberties and personal privacy, and, second, those whose anxiety to protect the public impels them to give subordinate attention to the civil amenities of those who suffer from AIDS and primary attention to the safety of those who do not.

In style, Buckley's passage is more like Condorcet's than the medical newsletter: it is eloquent, balanced, and literate. Still, it is challenging, consisting of a lengthy sentence, perhaps a bit too eloquent for some readers to grasp. For your paper on AIDS, you decide to paraphrase Buckley. You might draft something like this:

```
Buckley finds two opposing sides in the AIDS
debate: those concerned primarily with the civil
liberties and the privacy of AIDS victims, and
those concerned primarily with the safety of the
public.
```

Our paraphrases have been somewhat shorter than the originals, but this is not always the case. For example, suppose you wanted to paraphrase this statement by Sigmund Freud:

> We have found out that the distortion in dreams which hinders our understanding of them is due to the activities of a censorship, directed against the unacceptable, unconscious wish-impulses.

If you were to paraphrase this statement (the first sentence in the Tenth Lecture of his *General Introduction to Psychoanalysis*), you might come up with something like this:

```
It is difficult to understand dreams because they
contain distortions. Freud believed that these dis-
tortions arise from our internal censor, which
attempts to suppress unconscious and forbidden
desires.
```

Essentially, this paraphrase does little more than break up one sentence into two and somewhat rearrange the sentence structure for clarity.

Like summaries, then, *paraphrases* are useful devices, both in helping you to understand source material and in enabling you to convey the essence of this source material to your readers. When would you choose to write a summary instead of a paraphrase (or vice versa)? The answer to this question depends on your purpose in presenting your source material. As we've said, summaries are generally based on articles (or sections of articles) or books. Paraphrases are generally based on particularly difficult (or important) paragraphs or sentences. You would seldom paraphrase a long passage, or summarize a short one, unless there were particularly good reasons for doing so. (For example, a lawyer might want to paraphrase several pages of legal language so that his or her client, who is not a lawyer, could understand it.) The purpose of a summary is generally to save your reader time by presenting him or her with a brief and quickly readable version of a lengthy source. The purpose of a paraphrase is generally to clarify a short passage that might otherwise be unclear. Whether you summarize or paraphrase may also depend on the importance of your source. A particularly important source—if it is not too long—may rate a paraphrase. If it is less important, or peripheral to your central argument, you may choose to write a summary instead. And, of course, you may choose to summarize only part of your source—the part that is most relevant to the point you are making.

EXERCISE 1.3

Summarizing and Paraphrasing

The following passage is excerpted from an article written in 1866 by Frederick Douglass, entitled "Reconstruction."* In this piece the famed advocate for African-American rights appeals to the Second Session of the Thirty-ninth United States Congress, as it considered issues of state and federal rights in the aftermath of the U.S. Civil War. Read this passage and write both a summary and a paraphrase.

Fortunately, the Constitution of the United States knows no distinction between citizens on account of color. Neither does it know any

---

* Frederick Douglass, "Reconstruction," *The Atlantic Monthly,* 18. 1866: 761–765.

difference between a citizen of a State and a citizen of the United States. Citizenship evidently includes all the rights of citizens, whether State or national. If the Constitution knows none, it is clearly no part of the duty of a Republican Congress now to institute one. The mistake of the last session was the attempt to do this very thing, by a renunciation of its power to secure political rights to any class of citizens, with the obvious purpose to allow the rebellious States to disfranchise, if they should see fit, their colored citizens. This unfortunate blunder must now be retrieved, and the emasculated citizenship given to the negro supplanted by that contemplated in the Constitution of the United States, which declares that the citizens of each State shall enjoy all the rights and immunities of citizens of the several States,—so that a legal voter in any State shall be a legal voter in all the States.

QUOTATIONS

A *quotation* records the exact language used by someone in speech or in writing. A *summary*, in contrast, is a brief restatement in your own words of what someone else has said or written. And a *paraphrase* also is a restatement, although one that is often as long as the original source. Any paper in which you draw upon sources will rely heavily on quotation, summary, and paraphrase. How do you choose among the three?

Remember that the papers you write should be your own—for the most part: your own language and certainly your own thesis, your own inferences, and your own conclusion. It follows that references to your source materials should be written primarily as summaries and paraphrases, both of which are built on restatement, not quotation. You will use summaries when you need a *brief* restatement, and paraphrases, which provide more explicit detail than summaries, when you need to follow the development of a source closely. When you quote too much, you risk losing ownership of your work: more easily than you might think, your voice can be drowned out by the voices of those you've quoted. So *use quotation sparingly,* as you would a pungent spice.

Nevertheless, *quoting just the right source at the right time can significantly improve your papers.* The trick is to know when and how to use quotations.

Choosing Quotations

You'll find that using quotations can be particularly helpful in several situations.

Quoting Memorable Language

Assume you're writing a paper on Napoleon Bonaparte's relationship with the celebrated Josephine. Through research you learn that two days after

---

WHEN TO QUOTE

- Use quotations when another writer's language is particularly memorable and will add interest and liveliness to your paper.
- Use quotations when another writer's language is so clear and economical that to make the same point in your own words would, by comparison, be ineffective.
- Use quotations when you want the solid reputation of a source to lend authority and credibility to your own writing.

---

their marriage, Napoleon, given command of an army, left his bride for what was to be a brilliant military campaign in Italy. How did the young general respond to leaving his wife so soon after their wedding? You come across the following, written by Napoleon from the field of battle on April 3, 1796:

> I have received all your letters, but none has such an impact on me as the last. Do you have any idea, darling, what you are doing, writing to me in those terms? Do you not think my situation cruel enough without intensifying my longing for you, overwhelming my soul? What a style! What emotions you evoke! Written in fire, they burn my poor heart!*

A summary of this passage might read as follows:

> On April 3, 1796, Napoleon wrote to Josephine, expressing how sorely he missed her and how passionately he responded to her letters.

You might write the following as a paraphrase of the passage:

> On April 3, 1796, Napoleon wrote to Josephine that he had received her letters and that one among all others had had a special impact, overwhelming his soul with fiery emotions and longing.

How feeble this summary and paraphrase are when compared with the original! Why not use the vivid language that your sources give you? Quote

---

* Francis Mossiker, *Napoleon and Josephine,* trans. (New York: Simon and Schuster, 1964): 437.

Napoleon in your paper to make your subject come alive with memorable detail:

> On April 3, 1796, a passionate, lovesick Napoleon responded to a letter from Josephine. She had written longingly to her husband, who, on a military campaign, acutely felt her absence. "Do you have any idea, darling, what you are doing, writing to me in those terms? [. . .] What emotions you evoke!" he said of her letters. "Written in fire, they burn my poor heart!"

Quotations can be direct or indirect. A *direct* quotation is one in which you record precisely the language of another, as we did with the sentences from Napoleon's letter. An *indirect* quotation is one in which you report what someone has said, although you are not obligated to repeat the words exactly as spoken (or written):

> **Direct quotation:** *Franklin D. Roosevelt said: "The only thing we have to fear is fear itself."*
>
> **Indirect quotation:** *Franklin D. Roosevelt said that we have nothing to fear but fear itself.*

The language in a direct quotation, which is indicated by a pair of quotation marks (" "), must be faithful to the language of the original passage. When using an indirect quotation, you have the liberty of changing words (although not changing meaning). For both direct and indirect quotations, *you must credit your sources,* naming them either in (or close to) the sentence that includes the quotation or in a parenthetical citation. (Note: We haven't included parenthetical citations in our examples here; see Chapter 6, pages 200–23 for specific rules on citing sources properly.)

Quoting Clear and Concise Language

You should quote a source when its language is particularly clear and economical—when your language, by contrast, would be wordy. Read this passage from a text on biology by Patricia Curtis:

> The honeybee colony, which usually has a population of 30,000 to 40,000 workers, differs from that of the bumblebee and many other social bees or wasps in that it survives the winter. This means that the bees must stay warm despite the cold. Like other bees, the isolated honeybee cannot fly if the temperature falls below 10°C (50°F) and cannot walk if the temperature is below 7°C (45°F). Within the wintering hive, bees maintain their temperature by clustering together in a dense ball; the lower the temperature, the denser the cluster. The clustered bees produce heat by constant muscular movements of their wings, legs, and abdomens. In very cold weather, the bees on the outside of the cluster keep moving toward the center, while those in the

core of the cluster move to the colder outside periphery. The entire cluster moves slowly about on the combs, eating the stored honey from the combs as it moves.*

A summary of this paragraph might read as follows:

> Honeybees, unlike many other varieties of bee, are able to live through the winter by "clustering together in a dense ball" for body warmth.

A paraphrase of the same passage would be considerably more detailed:

> Honeybees, unlike many other varieties of bee (such as bumblebees), are able to live through the winter. The 30,000 to 40,000 bees within a honeybee hive could not, individually, move about in cold winter temperatures. But when "clustering together in a dense ball," the bees generate heat by constantly moving their body parts. The cluster also moves within the hive, eating stored honey. This nutrition, in addition to the heat generated by the cluster, enables the honeybee to survive the cold winter months.

In both the summary and the paraphrase we've quoted Curtis's "clustering together in a dense ball," a phrase that lies at the heart of her description of wintering honeybees. For us to describe this clustering in any language other than Curtis's would be pointless since her description is admirably brief and precise.

Quoting Authoritative Language

You will also want to use quotations that lend authority to your work. When quoting an expert or some prominent political, artistic, or historical figure, you elevate your own work by placing it in esteemed company. Quote respected figures to establish background information in a paper, and your readers will tend to perceive that information as reliable. Quote the opinions of respected figures to endorse some statement that you've made, and your statement becomes more credible to your readers. For example, in an essay on the importance of reading well, you could make use of a passage from Thoreau's *Walden:*

> Reading well is hard work and requires great skill and training. It "is a noble exercise," writes Henry David Thoreau in *Walden*, "and one that will

---

* Patricia Curtis, "Winter Organization," *Biology*, 2nd ed. (New York: Worth, 1976): 822–823.

> task the reader more than any exercise which the
> customs of the day esteem. [. . .] Books must be
> read as deliberately and reservedly as they were
> written."

By quoting a famous philosopher and essayist on the subject of reading, you add legitimacy to your discussion. Not only do *you* regard reading to be a skill that is both difficult and important, so too does Henry David Thoreau, one of our most influential thinkers. The quotation has elevated the level of your work.

You can also quote to advantage well-respected figures who have written or spoken about the subject of your paper. Here is a discussion of space flight. Author David Chandler refers to a physicist and a physicist-astronaut:

> A few scientists—notably James Van Allen, discoverer of the Earth's radiation belts—have decried the expense of the manned space program and called for an almost exclusive concentration on unmanned scientific exploration instead, saying this would be far more cost-effective.
>
> Other space scientists dispute that idea. Joseph Allen, physicist and former shuttle astronaut, says, "It seems to be argued that one takes away from the other. But before there was a manned space program, the funding on space science was zero. Now it's about $500 million a year."

Note that in the first paragraph Chandler has either summarized or used an indirect quotation to incorporate remarks made by James Van Allen into the discussion on space flight. In the second paragraph, Chandler directly quotes his next source, Joseph Allen. Both quotations, indirect and direct, lend authority and legitimacy to the article, for both James Van Allen and Joseph Allen are experts on the subject of space flight. Note also that Chandler provides brief but effective biographies of his sources, identifying both so that their qualifications to speak on the subject are known to all:

> James Van Allen, *discoverer of the Earth's radiation belts* . . .
>
> Joseph Allen, *physicist and former shuttle astronaut* . . .

The phrases in italics are called *appositives.* Their function is to rename the nouns they follow by providing explicit, identifying detail. Any information about a person that can be expressed in the following sentence pattern can be made into an appositive phrase:

> James Van Allen is the *discoverer of the Earth's radiation belts.*
>
> He has decried the expense of the manned space program.

James Van Allen, *discoverer of the Earth's radiation belts,* has decried the expense of the manned space program.

Use appositives to identify authors whom you quote.

Incorporating Quotations into Your Sentences

Quoting Only the Part of a Sentence or Paragraph That You Need

We've said that a writer selects passages for quotation that are especially *vivid and memorable, concise,* or *authoritative.* Now put these principles into practice. Suppose that while conducting research on college sports, you've come across the following, written by Robert Hutchins, former president of the University of Chicago:

> If athleticism is bad for students, players, alumni, and the public, it is even worse for the colleges and universities themselves. They want to be educational institutions, but they can't. The story of the famous half-back whose only regret, when he bade his coach farewell, was that he hadn't learned to read and write is probably exaggerated. But we must admit that pressure from trustees, graduates, "friends," presidents, and even professors has tended to relax academic standards. These gentry often overlook the fact that a college should not be interested in a full-back who is a half-wit. Recruiting, subsidizing and the double educational standard cannot exist without the knowledge and the tacit approval, at least, of the colleges and universities themselves. Certain institutions encourage susceptible professors to be nice to athletes now admitted by paying them for serving as "faculty representatives" on the college athletic board.*

[handwritten annotation: Original Source]

Suppose that in this entire paragraph you find a gem, a sentence with quotable words that will enliven your discussion. You may want to quote part of the following sentence:

> These gentry often overlook the fact that a college should not be interested in a fullback who is a half-wit.

[handwritten annotation: key sentence]

Incorporating the Quotation into the Flow of Your Own Sentence

Once you've selected the passage you want to quote, work the material into your paper in as natural and fluid a manner as possible. Here's how we would quote Hutchins:

```
Robert Hutchins, former president of the University
of Chicago, asserts that "a college should not be
interested in a fullback who is a half-wit."
```

[handwritten annotation: correct use of quotation]

---

* Robert Hutchins, "Gate Receipts and Glory," *The Saturday Evening Post,* 3 Dec. 1983: 38.

Note that we've used an appositive to identify Hutchins. And we've used only the part of the paragraph—a single clause—that we thought memorable enough to quote directly.

Avoiding Freestanding Quotations

A quoted sentence should never stand by itself—as in the following example:

> Various people associated with the university admit that the pressures of athleticism have caused a relaxation of standards. "These gentry often over- look the fact that a college should not be inter- ested in a fullback who is a half-wit." But this kind of thinking is bad for the university and even worse for the athletes.

Even if it includes a parenthetical citation, a freestanding quotation would have the problem of being jarring to the reader. Introduce the quotation with a "signal phrase" that attributes the source not in a parenthetical citation, but in some other part of the sentence—beginning, middle, or end. Thus, you could write:

> As Robert Hutchins notes, "These gentry often over- look the fact that a college should not be inter- ested in a fullback who is a half-wit."

Here's a variation with the signal phrase in the middle:

> "These gentry," asserts Robert Hutchins, "often overlook the fact that a college should not be interested in a fullback who is a half-wit."

Another alternative is to introduce a sentence-long quotation with a colon:

> But Robert Hutchins disagrees: "These gentry often overlook the fact that a college should not be interested in a fullback who is a half-wit."

Use colons also to introduce indented quotations (as in the cases when we introduce long quotations in this chapter).

When attributing sources in signal phrases, try to vary the standard "states," "writes," "says," and so on. Other, stronger verbs you might con- sider: "asserts," "argues," "maintains," "insists," "asks," and even "wonders."

Incorporating Quotations

Go back to Tristan Miller's essay "Why I Will Never Have a Girlfriend," pages 22–26, and find some sentences that you think make interesting points. Imagine you want to use these points in an essay you're writing on contemporary attitudes toward dating. Write five different sentences that use a variety of the techniques discussed thus far to incorporate whole sentences as well as phrases from Miller's essay.

Using Ellipsis Marks

Using quotations becomes somewhat complicated when you want to quote the beginning and end of a passage but not its middle—as was the case when we quoted Henry David Thoreau. Here's part of the paragraph in *Walden* from which we quoted a few sentences:

> To read well, that is to read true books in a true spirit, is a noble exercise, and one that will task the reader more than any exercise which the customs of the day esteem. It requires a training such as the athletes underwent, the steady intention almost of the whole life to this object. Books must be read as deliberately and reservedly as they were written.*

And here was how we used this material:

```
Reading well is hard work and requires great skill
and training. It "is a noble exercise," writes
Henry David Thoreau in Walden, "and one that will
task the reader more than any exercise which the
customs of the day esteem. [. . .] Books must be
read as deliberately and reservedly as they were
written."
```

Whenever you quote a sentence but delete words from it, as we have done, indicate this deletion to the reader by bracketing three spaced periods—called an "ellipsis mark"—in the sentence at the point of deletion. The rationale for using an ellipsis mark is that a direct quotation must be reproduced *exactly* as it was written or spoken. When writers delete or change any part of the quoted material, readers must be alerted so they don't think the changes were part of the original. Brackets around the ellipsis mark indicate that the ellipsis was added by the person quoting, and was not contained in the original

---

* Henry David Thoreau, *Walden* (New York: Signet Classic, 1960): 72.

source. When deleting an entire sentence or sentences from a quoted paragraph, as in the example above, end the sentence you have quoted with a period, place the bracketed ellipsis, and continue the quotation.

If you are deleting the middle of a single sentence, use a bracketed ellipsis in place of the deleted words:

> ```
> "To read well [. . .] is a noble exercise, and one
> that will task the reader more than any exercise
> which the customs of the day esteem."
> ```

If you are deleting material from the end of a quoted sentence, add a period following the bracketed ellipsis:

> ```
> "It requires a training such as the athletes under-
> went [. . .]. Books must be read as deliberately and
> reservedly as they were written."
> ```

If you begin your quotation of an author in the middle of his or her sentence, you need not indicate deleted words with an ellipsis. Be sure, however, that the syntax of the quotation fits smoothly with the syntax of your sentence:

> ```
> Reading "is a noble exercise," writes Henry David
> Thoreau.
> ```

Using Brackets to Add or Substitute Words

In addition to using square brackets around ellipsis marks when you need to show that you've removed material, you also should use brackets whenever you need to add or substitute words in a quoted sentence. The brackets indicate to the reader a word or phrase that does not appear in the original passage but that you have inserted to avoid confusion. For example, when a pronoun's antecedent would be unclear to readers, delete the pronoun from the sentences and substitute an identifying word or phrase in brackets. When you make such a substitution, no ellipsis marks are needed. Assume that you wish to quote one or both of the underlined sentences in the following passage by Jane Yolen:

> Golden Press's *Walt Disney's Cinderella* set the new pattern for America's Cinderella. This book's text is coy and condescending. (Sample: "And her best friends of all were—guess who—the mice!") The illustrations are poor cartoons. And Cinderella herself is a disaster. She cowers as her sisters rip her homemade ball gown to shreds. (Not even homemade by Cinderella, but by the mice and birds.) <u>She answers her stepmother with whines and pleadings. She is a sorry excuse for a heroine, pitiable and useless.</u> She cannot perform even a simple action to save herself, though she is warned by her friends, the mice. She does not hear them because she is "off in a world of dreams."

Cinderella begs, she whimpers, and at last has to be rescued by—guess who—the mice!*

In quoting either of these sentences, you would need to identify to whom the pronoun *she* refers. You can do this inside the quotation by using brackets:

```
Jane Yolen believes that "[Cinderella] answers her
stepmother with whines and pleadings."
```

If the pronoun begins the sentence to be quoted, you can identify the pronoun outside of the quotation and simply begin quoting your source one word later:

```
Jane Yolen believes that Cinderella "is a sorry
excuse for a heroine, pitiable and useless."
```

Here's another example of a case where the pronoun needing identification occurs in the middle of the sentence to be quoted. Newspaper reporters must use brackets in these cases frequently when quoting sources, who in interviews might say something like the following:

After the fire they did not return to the station house for three hours.

If the reporter wants to use this sentence in an article, he or she needs to identify the pronoun:

An official from City Hall, speaking on the condition that he not be identified, said, "After the fire [the officers] did not return to the station house for three hours."

You also will need to add bracketed information to a quoted sentence when a reference essential to the sentence's meaning is implied but not stated directly. Read the following paragraphs from physicist Robert Jastrow's "Toward an Intelligence Beyond Man's":

These are amiable qualities for the computer; it imitates life like an electronic monkey. As computers get more complex, the imitation gets better. Finally, the line between the original and the copy becomes blurred. In another 15 years or so—two more generations of computer evolution, in the jargon of the technologists—we will see the computer as an emergent form of life.

The proposition seems ridiculous because, for one thing, computers lack the drives and emotions of living creatures. But when drives

---

* Jane Yolen, "America's 'Cinderella,'" *Children's Literature in Education* 8 (1977): 22.

are useful, they can be programmed into the computer's brain, just as nature programmed them into our ancestors' brains as a part of the equipment for survival. For example, computers, like people, work better and learn faster when they are motivated. Arthur Samuel made this discovery when he taught two IBM computers how to play checkers. They polished their game by playing each other, but they learned slowly. Finally, Dr. Samuel programmed in the will to win by forcing the computers to try harder—and to think out more moves in advance—when they were losing. Then the computers learned very quickly. One of them beat Samuel and went on to defeat a champion player who had not lost a game to a human opponent in eight years.*

If you wanted to quote only the underlined sentence, you would need to provide readers with a bracketed explanation; otherwise, the words "the proposition" would be unclear. Here is how you would manage the quotation:

> According to Robert Jastrow, a physicist and former official at NASA's Goddard Institute, "The proposition [that computers will emerge as a form of life] seems ridiculous because, for one thing, computers lack the drives and emotions of living creatures."

EXERCISE **1.5**

Using Brackets

Write your own sentences incorporating the following quotations. Use brackets to clarify references (such as pronouns, italicized below) that aren't clear outside of their original context. See the original sources to remind yourself of this context.

From the Robert Jastrow piece on computers and intelligence:
(a) Arthur Samuel made *this discovery* when he taught two IBM computers how to play checkers.
(b) *They* polished their game by playing each other, but *they* learned slowly.

From the Jane Yolen excerpt on Cinderella:
(c) *This book's* text is coy and condescending
(d) *She* cannot perform even a simple action to save herself, though she is warned by her friends, the mice.
(e) She does not hear *them* because she is "off in a world of dreams."

Remember that when you quote the work of another, you are obligated to credit—or cite—the author's work properly; otherwise, you may be guilty of plagiarism. See pages 200–223 for guidance on citing sources.

---

* Robert Jastrow, "Toward an Intelligence Beyond Man's," *Time* 20 Feb. 1978: 35.

WHEN TO SUMMARIZE, PARAPHRASE, AND QUOTE

Summarize:
- To present main points of a lengthy passage (article or book)
- To condense peripheral points necessary to a discussion

Paraphrase:
- To clarify a short passage
- To emphasize main points

Quote:
- To capture another writer's particularly memorable language
- To capture another writer's clearly and economically stated language
- To lend authority and credibility to your own writing

Practice Summary

Select one of the following articles in Part II of this book:

"We've Got Mail—Always," Andrew Leonard (pp. 229–34)

"Journey of an E-Mail," John Dyson (pp. 243–47)

"The Stanford Prison Experiment," Philip K. Zimbardo (pp. 347–59)

"The Tragedy of Hamlet, Prince of Denmark: A Critical Review," Edward Hubler (pp. 718–26)

Write a summary of the selected article, following the directions in this chapter for dividing the article into sections, for writing a one-sentence summary of each section, and then for joining section summaries with a thesis. Prepare for the summary by making notes in the margins. Your finished product should be the result of two or more drafts.

For a somewhat more challenging assignment, try summarizing one of the following articles:

"'Cinderella' and the Loss of Father Love," Jacqueline M. Schectman (pp. 575–89)

"Too 'Close to the Bone': The Historical Context for Women's Obsession with Slenderness," Roberta Seid (pp. 474–87)

2 Critical Reading and Critique

CRITICAL READING

When writing papers in college, you are often called on to respond critically to source materials. Critical reading requires the abilities to both summarize and evaluate a presentation. As you have seen in Chapter 1, a *summary* is a brief restatement in your own words of the content of a passage. An *evaluation,* however, is a more difficult matter.

In your college work, you read to gain and *use* new information; but as sources are not equally valid or equally useful, you must learn to distinguish critically among sources by evaluating them.

There is no ready-made formula for determining validity. Critical reading and its written analogue—the *critique*—require discernment, sensitivity, imagination, knowledge of the subject, and, above all, willingness to become involved in what you read. These skills cannot be taken for granted and are developed only through repeated practice. You must begin somewhere, though, and we recommend that you start by posing two broad categories of questions about passages, articles, and books that you read: (1) What is the author's purpose in writing? Does he or she succeed in this purpose? (2) To what extent do you agree with the author?

Question Category 1: What Is the Author's Purpose in Writing? Does He or She Succeed in This Purpose?

All critical reading *begins with an accurate summary.* Before attempting an evaluation, you must be able to locate an author's thesis and identify the selection's content and structure. You must understand the author's *purpose.* Authors write to inform, to persuade, and to entertain. A given piece may be primarily *informative* (a summary of the research on cloning), primarily *persuasive* (an argument on why the government must do something to alleviate homelessness), or primarily *entertaining* (a play about the frustrations of young lovers). Or it may be all three (as in John Steinbeck's novel *The Grapes of Wrath,* about migrant workers during the Great Depression). Sometimes, authors are not fully conscious of their purpose. Sometimes their purpose changes as they write. Also, more than one purpose can overlap—an article may need to inform the reader about an issue in order to make a persuasive point. But if the finished piece is coherent, it will have a primary reason for having been written,

---

WHERE DO WE FIND WRITTEN CRITIQUES?

Here are just a few of the different types of writing that involve critique:

Academic Writing

- **Synthesis, Analysis, and Research papers.** Critique sources in order to establish their usefulness.
- **Literature reviews.** Critique some of the sources being reviewed.
- **Book reviews.** Combine summary with critique.
- **Essay exams.** Demonstrate understanding of course material by critiquing it.

Workplace Writing

- **Legal briefs and legal arguments.** Critique previous rulings or arguments made by opposing counsel.
- **Business plans and proposals.** Critique other, less cost-effective approaches.
- **Policy briefs.** Communicate failings of policies and legislation through critique.

---

and it should be apparent that the author is attempting primarily to inform, persuade, or entertain a particular audience. To identify this primary reason, this purpose, is your first job as a critical reader. Your next job is to determine how successful the author has been. As a critical reader, you bring different criteria, or standards of judgment, to bear when you read pieces intended to inform, persuade, or entertain.

Writing to Inform

A piece intended to inform will provide definitions, describe or report on a process, recount a story, give historical background, and/or provide facts and figures. An informational piece responds to questions such as the following:

What (or who) is _____ ?

How does _____ work?

What is the controversy or problem about?

What happened?

How and why did it happen?

What were the results?

What are the arguments for and against _____ ?

To the extent that an author answers these and related questions and the answers are a matter of verifiable record (you could check for accuracy if you had the time and inclination), the selection is intended to inform. Having determined this, you can organize your response by considering three other criteria: accuracy, significance, and fair interpretation of information.

Evaluating Informative Writing

Accuracy of Information. If you are going to use any of the information presented, you must be satisfied that it is trustworthy. One of your responsibilities as a critical reader is to find out if it is accurate. This means you should check facts against other sources—sources you can locate by searching key terms in library databases, and by performing searches for related material on the Web. Since material on the Web is essentially "self-published," however, you must be especially vigilant in assessing the legitimacy of sources you find there. Government publications of data are often a good resource for verifying facts about political legislation, population data, crime statistics, and the like. In Chapter 6, on research, we provide a more detailed discussion of how you should approach Web sources. You will find a wealth of useful information on the Internet, but you will also find a tremendous amount of misinformation, distorted "facts," and unsupported opinion.

Significance of Information. One useful question that you can put to a reading is "So what?" In the case of selections that attempt to inform, you may reasonably wonder whether the information makes a difference. What can the person who is reading gain from this information? How is knowledge advanced by the publication of this material? Is the information of importance to you or to others in a particular audience? Why or why not?

Fair Interpretation of Information. At times you will read reports, the sole function of which is to relate raw data or information. In these cases, you will build your response on the two questions in category 1: What is the author's purpose in writing? Does she or he succeed in this purpose? More frequently, once an author has presented information, she or he will attempt to evaluate or interpret it—which is only reasonable, since information that has not been evaluated or interpreted is of little use. One of your tasks as a critical reader is to make a distinction between the author's presentation of facts and figures and his or her attempts to evaluate them. Watch for shifts from straightforward descriptions of factual information to assertions about what this information means, what its implications are, and so on. Pay attention to whether the logic with which the author connects interpretation with facts is sound. You may find that the information is valuable but the interpretation is not. Perhaps the author's conclusions are not justified. Could you offer a contrary explanation for the same facts? Does more information need to be gathered before firm conclusions can be drawn? Why?

Writing to Persuade

Writing is frequently intended to persuade—that is, to influence the reader's thinking. To make a persuasive case, the writer must begin with an assertion that is arguable, some statement about which reasonable people could disagree. Such an assertion, when it serves as the essential organizing principle of the article or book, is called a *thesis*. Here are two examples:

> Because they do not speak English, many children in this affluent land are being denied their fundamental right to equal educational opportunity.

> Bilingual education, which has been stridently promoted by a small group of activists with their own agenda, is detrimental to the very students it is supposed to serve.

Thesis statements such as these—and the subsequent assertions used to help support them—represent conclusions that authors have drawn as a result of researching and thinking about an issue. You go through the same process yourself when you write persuasive papers or critiques. And just as you are entitled to critically evaluate the assertions of authors you read, so your professors—and other students—are entitled to evaluate *your* assertions, whether they be encountered as written arguments or as comments made in class discussion.

EXERCISE **2.1**

Informative and Persuasive Thesis Statements

With a partner from your class, write one informative and one persuasive thesis statement for three of the following topics. For example, for the topic of prayer in schools, your informative thesis statement could read this way:

> Both advocates and opponents of school prayer frame their position as a matter of freedom.

Your persuasive thesis statement might be worded as follows:

> As long as schools don't dictate what kinds of prayers students should say, then school prayer should be allowed and even encouraged.

See what thesis statements you can come up with for the following issues (and don't worry about taking a position that you agree with or feel you could support—the exercise doesn't require that you write an essay at this point!).

Gun control; sex education in schools; grammar instruction in English class; violent lyrics in music; teaching computer skills in primary schools; curfews in college dormitories; course registration procedures.

Evaluating Persuasive Writing

Read the argument that follows: a proposal to exempt teachers from federal income tax. We will illustrate our discussion on defining terms, using information fairly, and arguing logically by referring to J. Morton Davis's argument. The example critique that follows these illustrations will be based on this same argument.

A Simple One-Step Plan to Solve the Education Crisis: A Message to the President and the Congress
J. Morton Davis

A Wall Street investment banker and entrepreneur, Davis is Chairman of the D.H. Blair Investment Banking Corporation. He is the author of Making America Work Again *(Crown Publishers 1983) and* From Hard Knocks to Hot Stocks *(William Morrow and Company 1998). This piece was originally published by the author as a full-page ad in the* New York Times, *January 18, 1998.*

1 Great teachers.

2 Thousands and thousands of great teachers.

3 We must attract our best and brightest to the one profession upon which truly rests our nation's freedom, security and future greatness—teaching. If we can enlist the best among us to train our children, we will surely have the best-prepared and best-educated students in the world, thereby assuring America's continued leadership.

4 **By enacting legislation to exempt teachers from all federal income taxes, Congress and the President can help assure that many of the best and brightest college students will choose to dedicate their careers and lives to teaching our children.**

5 Perhaps it could go without saying that the education crisis is the most important issue we as a nation face today, affecting daily our single most important natural resource—our children. Just as we as a nation could mount all of our resources and efforts for the Manhattan Project to win World War II, and, later, harness all of our best in industry and technology to win the race to put a man on the moon, today we must, with the same urgency, apply all our collective energies to improving the deplorable state of public education. And just as we use our tax system to advance many positive societal goals, our tax system here too offers a single, one-step opportunity to solve the current crisis in our education system. By exempting teachers from federal income taxes we will instantly put in place a mechanism sure to produce more and more great teachers.

6 First, this tax exemption would immediately and substantially increase teachers' salaries, thus incentivizing many of our top college graduates to pursue a

career in teaching. In the 30's and 40's, public education produced superior academic results because, during the Depression, many of our best were attracted to teaching as it was a relatively well paying and secure job in a time when few jobs were available. Teaching would again become an economically attractive career if it carried with it an exemption from federal income taxes. The cost to the Treasury would be small, and certainly any tax money invested in teaching will return many-fold as a generation of better-educated, more productive citizens enters the work force.

7   Second, and perhaps more importantly, an exemption from federal income taxes for teachers would distinctly and dramatically recognize the gifted dedication of those who devote their careers to inspiring the minds of our children and grandchildren. Freeing teachers from ever paying federal income tax would, in one grand gesture, symbolically designate teachers as the one professional group whom we respect, cherish and value above all others. This is not to devalue the life-and-death work of police officers and fire fighters, or the terribly important life-saving efforts of doctors, nurses and other medical professionals. But none is more important to our nation's future than teaching.

8   If we are going to produce the world's best-educated future generations, we must attract the best candidates to the job of teaching those generations. Professionally dedicated teachers will not only provide a basic education in the three R's and the sciences, but can also impart to our children values and visions, dreams and opportunities.

9   No profession is more important to society and the future of our country than teaching. Teaching should never be a fall-back position or a career compromise. It is the noblest of callings, and should be recognized as such—both in dollars and in respect. If our children and our nation are to succeed in an ever-more-competitive world, let us reward and upgrade the status of teachers so that the finest young minds will be drawn to the profession. This will undoubtedly produce the best-educated, most globally-competitive generation of Americans in our history.

10   Mr. President and members of the 105th Congress, a golden opportunity awaits you—a chance to cure the abysmal state of public education and go down in history as having made the nation and the world a better place. In a single, decisive, creative stroke you can solve the education crisis. By implementing a permanent income tax exemption for teachers you will raise their financial rewards and status to a level commensurate with their contributions, you will attract the best-and-brightest of our population to this noble profession, you will create a society in which "teacher" is the most exalted title in the land.

11   And you will leave a legacy that will endure forever.

Persuasive Strategies

Writers organize arguments by arranging evidence to support one conclusion and oppose (or dismiss) another. You can assess the validity of the argument and the conclusion by determining whether the author has (1) clearly defined key terms, (2) used information fairly, (3) argued logically and not fallaciously.

Clearly Defined Key Terms. The validity of an argument depends to some degree on how carefully key terms have been defined. Take the assertion, for example, that American society must be grounded in "family values." Just what do people who use this phrase mean by it? The validity of their argument depends on whether they and their readers agree on a definition of "family values"—as well as what it means to be "grounded in" family values. If an author writes that in the recent past, "America's elites accepted as a matter of course that a free society can sustain itself only through virtue and temperance in the people" (Charles Murray, "The Coming White Underclass," *Wall Street Journal,* 20 Oct. 1993), readers need to know what, exactly, the author means by "elites" and by "virtue and temperance" before they can assess the validity of the argument. In such cases, the success of the argument—its ability to persuade—hinges on the definition of a term. So, in responding to an argument, be sure you (and the author) are clear on what exactly is being argued. Only then can you respond to the logic of the argument, to the author's use of evidence, and to the author's conclusions.

Early in his argument, Davis refers to attracting "our best and brightest" to the teaching profession. He repeatedly uses the phrase, so it's fair to ask what, exactly, he means. "Best and brightest" was an expression associated with John F. Kennedy's administration, in which highly educated, exuberant people flocked to Washington with an explicit assumption that in committing themselves to public service they would do an exemplary job (because they were bright and committed). The closest Davis comes to defining "best and brightest" is "[p]rofessionally dedicated teachers," people "who devote their careers to inspiring the minds of our children and grandchildren." The phrase refers to academically talented, inspired, and inspiring college graduates. However, this same phrase took on an ironic twist when it was used by reporter David Halberstam as the title of a book about the tragic miscalculations made by these same talented and inspired people in getting the United States involved in the war in Vietnam.

Fair Use of Information. Information is used as evidence in support of arguments. When presented with such evidence, ask yourself two questions: First, "Is the information accurate and up-to-date?" At least a portion of an argument becomes invalid if the information used to support it is inaccurate or out-of-date. Second, "Has the author cited *representative* information?" The evidence used in an argument must be presented in a spirit of fair play. An author who presents only evidence favoring his views when he is well aware that contrary evidence exists is less than ethical. For instance, it would be dishonest to argue that an economic recession is imminent and to cite as evidence only those indicators of economic well-being that have taken a decided turn for the worse while ignoring and failing to cite contrary (positive) evidence. Davis seems to use information fairly and accurately in his essay; however, some of the cause-and-effect conclusions he draws based on that information are suspect, as we will see.

Logical Argumentation: Avoiding Logical Fallacies

At some point, you will need to respond to the logic of the argument itself. To be convincing, an argument should be governed by principles of logic— clear and orderly thinking. This does *not* mean that an argument should not be biased. A biased argument—that is, an argument weighted toward one point of view and against others—may be valid as long as it is logically sound.

Here are several examples of faulty thinking and logical fallacies to watch for:

Emotionally Loaded Terms. Writers sometimes will attempt to sway readers by using emotionally charged words: words with positive connotations to sway readers to their own point of view (e.g., "family values"); words with negative connotations (e.g., "liberal") to sway readers away from the opposing point of view. The fact that an author uses emotionally loaded terms does not necessarily invalidate the argument. Emotional appeals are perfectly legitimate and time-honored modes of persuasion. But in academic writing, which is grounded in logical argumentation, they should not be the *only* means of persuasion. You should be sensitive to *how* emotionally loaded terms are being used. In particular, are they being used deceptively or to hide the essential facts?

Davis uses the word "noble" throughout the argument—as in, teaching is a "noble" profession, "the noblest of callings" (paragraph 9). Our culture is quick to attach "nobility" to professions such as teaching that serve a necessary function but pay relatively low wages, as if the word itself could compensate teachers for lower salaries. Since American voters are unwilling to pay teachers more money but at the same time are eager to laud teachers as "noble," the word "nobility" has taken on a somewhat patronizing, disingenuous air among teachers. Some teachers may respond: "Sure we're flattered to be called noble. But raise our pay if you really care!" Davis does seem to be an outsider (that is, not a teacher) using the word "nobility" to heap familiar praise on teachers. He isn't being patronizing with his use of the term, however, since he's arguing for boosting teacher salaries and prestige. So teachers might well think him sincere.

Ad Hominem Argument. In an *ad hominem* argument, the writer rejects opposing views by attacking the person who holds them. By calling opponents names, an author avoids the issue. Consider this excerpt from a political speech:

> I could more easily accept my opponent's plan to increase revenues by collecting on delinquent tax bills if he had paid more than a hundred dollars in state taxes in each of the past three years. But the fact is, he's

TONE

Related to "emotionally loaded terms" is "tone." When we speak of the tone of a piece of writing, we refer to the overall emotional effect produced by the writer's choice of language.

- Were a film reviewer to repeatedly use such terms as "wonderful," "adorable," "magnificent performance," when discussing a film and its actors, we might call the tone "gushing."
- If a columnist, in referring to a politician's tax proposal, used such language as "obscene," "the lackeys of big business fat cats," and "sleazeball techniques," we would call the tone "angry."
- If another writer were to use language like "That's a great idea. Let's all give three cheers," when he meant just the opposite, we would call the tone "sarcastic."

These are examples of extreme kinds of tone; but tone can be more muted, particularly if the writer makes a special effort *not* to inject emotion into the writing. Almost any adjective describing human emotion can be attached to "tone" to convey the mood that is conveyed by the writer and the writing: playful, objective, brutal, dispassionate, sly, apologetic, rueful, cynical, hopeful, gleeful.

As we've indicated above in "Emotionally Loaded Terms," the fact that a writer's tone is highly emotional does not necessarily mean that the writer's argument is invalid. Conversely, a neutral tone does not ensure an argument's validity. One who argues passionately is not necessarily wrong, any more than one who comes across as objective and measured is necessarily right. In either case, we have to examine the validity of the argument on its own merits. We should recognize that we may have been manipulated into agreeing or disagreeing largely through an author's tone, rather than through her or his arguments.

Keep in mind, also, that many college instructors are likely to be put off by student writing that projects a highly emotional tone, a quality they will often consider more appropriate for the op-ed page of the student newspaper than for academic or pre-professional work. (One giveaway indicator of inappropriate emotion is the exclamation mark, which should be used very sparingly.)

a millionaire with a millionaire's tax shelters. This man hasn't paid a wooden nickel for the state services he and his family depend on. So I ask you: Is *he* the one to be talking about taxes to *us?*

It could well be that the opponent has paid virtually no state taxes for three years; but this fact has nothing to do with, and is a ploy to divert attention from, the merits of a specific proposal for increasing revenues. The proposal is lost in the attack against the man himself, an attack that violates the principles of logic. Writers (and speakers) must make their points by citing evidence in support of their views and by challenging contrary evidence.

Faulty Cause and Effect. The fact that one event precedes another in time does not mean that the first event has caused the second. An example: Fish begin dying by the thousands in a lake near your hometown. An environmental group immediately cites chemical dumping by several manufacturing plants as the cause. But other causes are possible: A disease might have affected the fish; the growth of algae might have contributed to the deaths; or acid rain might be a factor. The origins of an event are usually complex and are not always traceable to a single cause. So you must carefully examine cause-and-effect reasoning when you find a writer using it. In Latin, this fallacy is known as *post hoc, ergo propter hoc* ("after this, therefore because of this").

Davis makes two assertions that reveal questionable cause-and-effect thinking. First, he claims that enlisting our "best and brightest" into teaching will result in improved education: "If we can enlist the best among us to train our children, we will surely have the best-prepared and best-educated students in the world" (paragraph 3). The reader is entitled to ask: why *surely*? Where's the proof that teachers, alone, can effect so monumental a change? Davis also claims that a permanent exemption from federal taxes will result in more good teachers entering the classroom. Again, what assures this result? In both cases, Davis may be correct; but readers can legitimately expect support for such statements, and Davis offers none.

Either/Or Reasoning. Either/or reasoning also results from an unwillingness to recognize complexity. If an author analyzes a problem and offers only two courses of action, one of which he or she refutes, then you are entitled to object that the other is not thereby true. For usually, several other options (at the very least) are possible. For whatever reason, the author has chosen to overlook them. As an example, suppose you are reading a selection on genetic engineering and the author builds an argument on the basis of the following:

> Research in gene splicing is at a crossroads: Either scientists will be carefully monitored by civil authorities and their efforts limited to acceptable applications, such as disease control; or, lacking regulatory guidelines, scientists will set their own ethical standards and begin programs in embryonic manipulation that, however well intended, exceed the proper limits of human knowledge.

Certainly, other possibilities for genetic engineering exist beyond the two mentioned here. But the author limits debate by establishing an either/or choice. Such limitation is artificial and does not allow for complexity. As a critical reader, be on the alert for either/or reasoning.

Hasty Generalization. Writers are guilty of hasty generalization when they draw their conclusions from too little evidence or from unrepresentative evidence. To argue that scientists should not proceed with the human genome project because a recent editorial urged that the project be abandoned is to make a hasty generalization. This lone editorial may be unrepresentative of the views of most individuals—both scientists and laypeople—who have studied and written about the matter. To argue that one should never obey authority because Stanley Milgram's Yale University experiments in the 1960s show the dangers of obedience is to ignore the fact that Milgram's experiment was concerned primarily with obedience to *immoral* authority. Thus, the experimental situation was unrepresentative of most routine demands for obedience—for example, to obey a parental rule or to comply with a summons for jury duty—and a conclusion about the malevolence of all authority would be a hasty generalization.

False Analogy. Comparing one person, event, or issue to another may be illuminating, but it may also be confusing or misleading. The differences between the two may be more significant than the similarities, and conclusions drawn from one may not necessarily apply to the other. A writer who argues that it is reasonable to quarantine people with AIDS because quarantine has been effective in preventing the spread of smallpox is assuming an analogy between AIDS and smallpox that (because of the differences between the two diseases) is not valid.

Early in his argument, Davis exhorts the president and Congress to "mount all of our resources and efforts" (paragraph 5) to enlist great teachers in the same way we marshaled our resources to put humans on the moon and to win World War II by building an atomic bomb. Davis is making an analogy: we rallied and succeeded then; we can rally and succeed now. Readers can reasonably question the extent to which the challenges we face in education are similar to the challenges faced in building a bomb or rocket. To accept the parallel, we would have to believe that solving a problem in a mathematical science is equivalent to solving a problem in the social settings of the classroom and school. Are the problems and their solutions equivalent? Readers are entitled to question the parallel.

Begging the Question. To beg the question is to assume as a proven fact the very thesis being argued. To assert, for example, that America is not in decline because it is as strong and prosperous as ever is not to prove anything: it is merely to repeat the claim in different words. This fallacy is also known as circular reasoning.

Throughout his argument, Davis assumes a point he wants readers to accept—that enlisting our "best and brightest" will result in better-educated students. This is a cause-and-effect relationship that needs proof, but Davis assumes the correctness of the position and does not argue for it. This begging the question is especially evident when Davis writes: "Teaching would again become an economically attractive career if it carried with it an exemption from federal income taxes. The cost to the

Treasury would be small, and certainly any tax money invested in teaching will return many-fold as a generation of better-educated, more productive citizens enters the work force" (paragraph 6). To Davis, the end result of hiring bright teachers may be "certain," but readers are entitled to question his logic.

Non Sequitur. "Non sequitur" is Latin for "it does not follow"; the term is used to describe a conclusion that does not logically follow from a premise. "Since minorities have made such great strides in the last few decades," a writer may argue, "we no longer need affirmative action programs." Aside from the fact that the premise itself is arguable (*have* minorities made such great strides?), it does not follow that because minorities *may* have made great strides, there is no further need for affirmative action programs.

Oversimplification. Be alert for writers who offer easy solutions to complicated problems. "America's economy will be strong again if we all 'buy American,'" a politician may argue. But the problems of America's economy are complex and cannot be solved by a slogan or a simple change in buying habits. Likewise, a writer who argues that we should ban genetic engineering assumes that simple solutions ("just say 'no'") will be sufficient to deal with the complex moral dilemmas raised by this new technology.

Davis has likely never been a classroom teacher, which can be inferred both from his honorific use of the word "noble" (if teachers feel this way about themselves, they typically don't advertise it!) and from his failure to mention other possible sources of crisis in education aside from the lack of gifted teachers. Anyone with experience in public education knows, for instance, that school budgets are closely linked with successful student performance. Davis makes no mention of school budgets or of other factors such as economically depressed circumstances for students or political fights within school districts. Justifiably then, the later critique of Davis's letter objects that Davis oversimplifies the issue.

EXERCISE 2.2

Understanding Logical Fallacies

Make a list of the nine logical fallacies discussed in the last section. Briefly define each one in your own words. Then, in a group of three or four classmates, refer to your definitions and the examples we've provided for each logical fallacy, and collaborate with your group members to find or invent examples for each of the logical fallacies (or for some of them that your instructor assigns to each group). Compare these with the other groups in your class.

Writing to Entertain

Authors write not only to inform and persuade but also to entertain. One response to entertainment is a hearty laugh, but it is possible to entertain without laughter: A good book or play or poem may prompt you to ruminate, grow wistful, become elated, get angry. Laughter is only one of many possible reactions. You read a piece (or view a work) and react with sadness, surprise, exhilaration, disbelief, horror, boredom, whatever. As with a response to an informative piece or an argument, your response to an essay, poem, story, play, novel, or film should be precisely stated and carefully developed. Ask yourself some of the following questions (you won't have space to explore all of them, but try to consider some of the most important): Did I care for the portrayal of a certain character? Did that character (or a group of characters united by occupation, age, ethnicity, etc.) seem too sentimentalized, for example, or heroic? Did his adversaries seem too villainous or stupid? Were the situations believable? Was the action interesting or merely formulaic? Was the theme developed subtly or powerfully, or did the work come across as preachy or shrill? Did the action at the end of the work follow plausibly from what had come before? Was the language fresh and incisive or stale and predictable? Explain as specifically as possible what elements of the work seemed effective or ineffective and why. Offer an overall assessment, elaborating on your views.

Question Category 2: To What Extent Do You Agree or Disagree with the Author?

When formulating a critical response to a source, try to distinguish your evaluation of the author's purpose and success at achieving that purpose from your agreement or disagreement with the author's views. The distinction allows you to respond to a piece of writing on its merits. As an unbiased, even-handed critic, you evaluate an author's clarity of presentation, use of evidence, and adherence to principles of logic. To what extent has the author succeeded in achieving his or her purpose? Still withholding judgment, offer your assessment and give the author (in effect) a grade. Significantly, your assessment of the presentation may not coincide with your views of the author's conclusions: You may agree with an author entirely but feel that the presentation is superficial; you may find the author's logic and use of evidence to be rock solid but at the same time may resist certain conclusions. A critical evaluation works well when it is conducted in two parts. After evaluating the author's purpose and design for achieving that purpose, respond to the author's main assertions. In doing so, you'll want to identify points of agreement and disagreement and also evaluate assumptions.

Identify Points of Agreement and Disagreement

Be precise in identifying points of agreement and disagreement with an author. You should state as clearly as possible what *you* believe, and an effective way of doing this is to define your position in relation to that presented in the piece. Whether you agree enthusiastically, disagree, or agree with reservations, you can organize your reactions in two parts: first, summarize the author's position; second, state your own position and elaborate on your reasons for holding it. The elaboration, in effect, becomes an argument itself, and this is true regardless of the position you take. An opinion is effective when you support it by supplying evidence. Without such evidence, opinions cannot be authoritative. "I thought the article on cloning was lousy." Why? "I just thought so, that's all." This opinion is worthless because the criticism is imprecise: The critic has taken neither the time to read the article carefully nor the time to explore his own reactions carefully.

EXERCISE **2.3**

Exploring Your Viewpoints

Go to a Web site that presents short persuasive essays on current social issues, such as opinion-pages.org, drudgereport.com, or Speakout.com. Or go to an Internet search engine and type in a social issue together with the word "articles," "editorials," or "opinion," and see what you find. Once you've located an essay or Internet chat post that takes a position on the issue, write a paragraph or two articulating your agreement or disagreement with the position taken in this source. Be sure to explain why you feel the way you do and, wherever possible, cite relevant evidence—from your reading, experience, or observation. After stating your opinion, discuss what else you would need to know about the issue in order to make a convincing case for your viewpoint.

Explore the Reasons for Agreement and Disagreement: Evaluate Assumptions

One way of elaborating your reactions to a reading is to explore the underlying *reasons* for agreement and disagreement. Your reactions are based largely on assumptions that you hold and how these assumptions compare with the author's. An *assumption* is a fundamental statement about the world and its operations that you take to be true. A writer's assumptions may be explicitly stated; but just as often assumptions are implicit and you will have to "ferret them out," that is, to infer them. Consider an example:

> *In vitro* fertilization and embryo transfer are brought about outside the bodies of the couple through actions of third parties whose competence and technical activity determine the success of the procedure. Such fertilization entrusts the life and identity of the embryo into the power of doctors and biologists and establishes the domination of technology over the origin and destiny of the human person. Such a relationship of domination is in itself contrary to the dignity and equality that must be common to parents and children.*

---

* From the Vatican document *Instruction on Respect for Human Life in Its Origin and on the Dignity of Procreation,* given at Rome, from the Congregation for the Doctrine of the Faith, 22 Feb. 1987, as presented in *Origins: N.C. Documentary Service* 16.40. (19 Mar. 1987): 707.

This paragraph is quoted from the February 1987 Vatican document on artificial procreation. Cardinal Joseph Ratzinger, principal author of the document, makes an implicit assumption in this paragraph: that no good can come of the domination of technology over conception. The use of technology to bring about conception is morally wrong. Yet there are thousands of childless couples, Roman Catholics included, who reject this assumption in favor of its opposite: that conception technology is an aid to the barren couple; far from creating a relationship of unequals, the technology brings children into the world who will be welcomed with joy and love.

Assumptions provide the foundation on which entire presentations are built. If you find an author's assumptions invalid, i.e., not supported by factual evidence, or, if you disagree with value-based assumptions underlying an author's positions, you may well disagree with conclusions that follow from these assumptions. The author of a book on developing nations may include a section outlining the resources and time that will be required to industrialize a particular country and so upgrade its general welfare. Her assumption—that industrialization in that particular country will ensure or even affect the general welfare—may or may not be valid. If you do not share the assumption, in your eyes the rationale for the entire book may be undermined.

How do you determine the validity of assumptions once you have identified them? In the absence of more scientific criteria, validity may mean how well the author's assumptions stack up against your own experience, observations, reading, and values. A caution, however: The overall value of an article or book may depend only to a small degree on the validity of the author's assumptions. For instance, a sociologist may do a fine job of gathering statistical data about the incidence of crime in urban areas along the eastern seaboard. The sociologist also might be a Marxist, and you may disagree with the subsequent analysis of the data. Yet you may find the data extremely valuable for your own work.

In his open letter to the president and Congress, Davis makes several assumptions worth examining. The first is that we face a crisis in education. Davis assumes his readers agree and bases his entire proposal on this agreement. If we disagree with the assessment that America's schools are in crisis, then we're bound to reject the proposal. We may also believe America's schools face significant problems, but reject Davis's characterization of these problems as a "crisis." Davis's next assumption is implied: that the crisis in education is due, mainly, to the absence of good teachers. He never states this view directly; but we can reason that if the solution to the current crisis is to place our best and brightest into the classroom, then our current problems are due, mainly, to the absence of especially talented teachers. Davis does not offer support for this assumption, and the reader is entitled to suggest that there may be *other* reasons education is in crisis. (The critique that follows takes exactly this approach.) Davis assumes, as well, that a tax break will entice teachers—which it may. The underlying logic is that we are all motivated by personal gain. If we can boost pay to teachers, then we should be able to attract more candidates to the profession. Davis does not explain why an exemption will attract the best and brightest, as opposed to less inspired individuals looking for a stable career with decent pay. Finally, as discussed under "Begging the Question," Davis assumes the very point he wants to argue: that "If we can enlist the best among us to train our children, we will surely have the best-prepared and best-educated students in the world." Essentially, Davis asks readers to accept this conclusion on faith, for he offers no support. Readers are entitled to meet each of an author's assumptions with assumptions of their own; to evaluate the validity of those assumptions; and to begin formulating a critique, based on their agreement or disagreement.

CRITIQUE

In Chapter 1 we focused upon summary—the condensed presentation of ideas presented originally in another form. Summary is key to much of academic writing—even when we're not explicitly asked to summarize something, the reliance upon the works of others for support of claims made in the academic setting requires that we know how to summarize. It's not going too far to say that summarizing is the critical thinking skill from which a majority of academic writing builds. However, most academic thinking and writing does not stop at summary; usually we use summary to fully understand something, then we go on to do something else with it. The most direct activity following summary is critique. In critical thinking, we understand things, then we evaluate them. Critique is an essential element of critical thinking. Critique is also an important element of writing, and to address that fact, we now turn to writing critiques.

A *critique* is a *formalized, critical reading of a passage.* It also is a personal response; but writing a critique is considerably more rigorous than saying that a movie is "great," or a book is "fascinating," or "I didn't like it." These are all responses, and, as such, they're a valid, even essential, part of your understanding of what you see and read. But such responses don't help illuminate the subject for anyone—even you—if you haven't explained how you arrived at your conclusions.

Your task in writing a critique is to turn your critical reading of a passage into a systematic evaluation in order to deepen your reader's (and your own) understanding of that passage. Among other things, you're interested in determining what an author says, how well the points are made, what assumptions underlie the argument, what issues are overlooked, and what implications can be drawn from such an analysis. Critiques, positive or negative, should include a fair and accurate summary of the passage; they also should include a statement of your own assumptions. It is important to remember that you bring to bear an entire set of assumptions about the world. Stated or not, these assumptions underlie every evaluative comment you make; you therefore have an obligation, both to the reader and to yourself, to clarify your standards by making your assumptions explicit. Not only do your readers stand to gain by your forthrightness, but you do as well: In the process of writing a critical assessment, you are forced to examine your own knowledge, beliefs, and assumptions. Ultimately, the critique is a way of learning about yourself—yet another example of the ways in which writing is useful as a critical thinking tool!

How to Write Critiques

You may find it useful to organize your critiques in five sections: introduction, summary, analysis of the presentation, your response to the presentation, and conclusion.

The following box below contains some guidelines for writing critiques. Note that they are guidelines, not a rigid formula. Thousands of authors write

---

GUIDELINES FOR WRITING CRITIQUES

- *Introduction.* Introduce both the passage under analysis and the author. State the author's main argument and the point(s) you intend to make about it.

    Provide background material to help your readers understand the relevance or appeal of the passage. This background material might include one or more of the following: an explanation of why the subject is of current interest; a reference to a possible controversy surrounding the subject of the passage or the passage itself; biographical information about the author; an account of the circumstances under which the passage was written; or a reference to the intended audience of the passage.

- *Summary.* Summarize the author's main points, making sure to state the author's purpose for writing.

- *Analysis of the presentation.* Evaluate the validity of the author's presentation, as distinct from your points of agreement or disagreement. Comment on the author's success in achieving his or her purpose by reviewing three or four specific points. You might base your review on one (or more) of the following criteria:

    Is the information accurate?

    Is the information significant?

    Has the author defined terms clearly?

    Has the author used and interpreted information fairly?

    Has the author argued logically?

- *Your response to the presentation.* Now it is your turn to respond to the author's views. With which views do you agree? With which do you disagree? Discuss your reasons for agreement and disagreement, when possible, tying these reasons to assumptions—both the author's and your own.

- *Conclusion.* State your conclusions about the overall validity of the piece—your assessment of the author's success at achieving his or her aims and your reactions to the author's views. Remind the reader of the weaknesses and strengths of the passage.

critiques that do not follow the structure outlined here. Until you are more confident and practiced in writing critiques, however, we suggest you follow these guidelines. They are meant not to restrict you, but rather to provide you with a workable method of writing critical analyses that incorporates a logical sequence of development.

DEMONSTRATION: CRITIQUE

The critique that follows is based on J. Morton Davis's open letter to the president and the Congress (see pages 54–55). In this critique, you will see that it is possible to agree with an author's main point or proposal but disagree with his or her method of demonstration, or argument. Critiquing a different selection, you could just as easily accept the author's facts and figures but reject the conclusion he draws from them. As long as you carefully articulate the author's assumptions and your own, explaining in some detail your agreement and disagreement, the critique is yours to take in whatever direction you see fit.

The selections you will likely be inclined to critique are those, like Davis's, that argue a specific position. Indeed, every argument you read is an invitation to agreement or disagreement. It remains only for you to speak up and justify your position.

Model Essay:

A Critique of J. Morton Davis's Open Letter to the President and Congress

1 J. Morton Davis's open letter to the president and Congress, "A Simple One-Step Plan to Solve the Education Crisis," argues that teachers should be exempt from federal income taxes in order to entice our best and brightest into the profession. Few can deny what Davis, chairman of the D. H. Blair Investment Banking Corporation (and author of *Making America Work Again* and *From Hard Knocks to Hot Stocks*) calls the current "abysmal state of public education" (55). The problems in education are real, and Davis's proposal is both achievable and attractive—one that Congress could enact with relatively little political risk. So is a permanent federal income tax exemption for teachers a good idea? Davis's plan should be adopted; but it will not by itself solve our crisis in education.

2   In his open letter, Davis argues that we must solve America's education problems if we are to assert "continued leadership" in the world (54). The

[handwritten margin notes: "thesis", "thesis summary"]

---

best way to "cure" the problem is to "attract the best-and-brightest of our population to" teaching (55). Because teachers, like everyone else, are motivated by personal gain, we can entice prospective teachers into the profession with the incentive of a permanent exemption from federal income taxes. Aside from boosting take-home pay, an exemption also will confer on teachers special recognition and "would distinctly and dramatically recognize [their] gifted dedication" (55). With the inducements of a tax break and enhanced national respect, teachers would be more inclined to enter and remain in the profession. If we can attract and retain great teachers, writes Davis, we "can solve the education crisis" (55).

3   Teachers are paid less than are other professionals, and in our society a low salary translates into low stature. Davis's proposal to raise teachers' pay by enacting a permanent federal income tax exemption would, shrewdly, increase pay *and* prestige if teachers were the only tax-exempt professionals in the nation. Now that the country is enjoying budget surpluses, if we can afford the exemption we should enact it. Davis correctly notes that the federal government routinely uses the tax system to promote social objectives—as in the case of high taxes that discourage cigarette use. So why not use the system to promote a social end that everyone can endorse: a continuing supply of effective teachers?

4   While Davis does not say so openly, he mistakenly suggests that our current problems exist because the best and brightest are not presently in our classrooms. They are elsewhere. "Teaching should never be a fall-back position or a career compromise," he claims (55). Is it now? Is that how we got into the mess we're in, because our classrooms are led by people who could not succeed elsewhere? Without suggesting a single other cause for the current crisis in education, Davis apparently thinks so. We can't deny that poor teachers clog the system. But plenty of competent teachers exist who, while applauding Davis's proposed federal income tax exemption, would never agree that the poor teachers are the sole or even the main problem with education. Ask good teachers what ails the system and they will acknowledge deadwood colleagues, but also they will point to other problems: meager budgets, tensions within communities over how the schools should be run, and

severe social and economic conditions within local
school districts.

5   Bringing the best and brightest into America's
classrooms cannot solve the problem of under-financed
schools. State and local governments set expenditures
for schools; while Davis's suggestion will help the
cash flow of teachers already working, it will do
nothing to increase the *number* of teachers now available. The only way to increase the number of teachers
in the system is to raise local or state taxes or to
get federal support to hire them. But in the first
case, tax increases to local home owners are never
welcome; in the second, the federal government is not
likely to forego collecting taxes from teachers *and*
boost education dollars to states at the same time.
As long as annual budgets remain low, student-to-
teacher ratios will remain high and present barriers
to individualized instruction. Education suffers when
there are too few teachers, a problem that Davis's
tax exemption would not resolve.

6   Davis's open letter also avoids mention of structural problems within the educational community
itself: bloated administrations in which levels of
assistant principals and curriculum coordinators stay
out of the classroom, where they could do some direct
good, and instead over-manage the lives of teachers;
unions that militantly guard against increasing
teachers' hours and responsibilities, thereby causing
students to suffer; curricula that do not change with
the times or, conversely, change too easily, driven
by fads more than by careful review; and elected
school committees that clash with administrators over
policy. At the beginning of any given school year, at
least one major school system in America seems on the
verge of meltdown, with problems due mainly not to
lack of bright, dedicated teachers but to lack of
consensus among teachers, administrators, and towns.
Many of these problems are budgetary, and more money
could resolve them. But other problems are related to
the process of teaching itself, which is a social
activity based on philosophical principles.

7   Teaching is not an exact science. And while Davis
exhorts the president and Congress to mount a response
to the education crisis in the same way our nation
addressed the challenges of going to the moon or winning World War II (by building the atomic bomb), we
could not with respect to teaching agree on a single

course of action as we could (and did) with scientific and military challenges. Teaching is unlike physics and rocketry—sciences in which experts can isolate all factors that bear on a problem, predict how those factors will behave in any given circumstance, and then plan solutions accordingly. Teaching mixes contentious issues of politics, philosophy, and economics into a soup so complex that no one—not even well-meaning advocates in ideal circumstances—can agree on what, precisely, the problems are, let alone on how to solve them. Davis's hope for a national commitment to cure our schools is misinformed, because problems in education differ fundamentally from the problems to which he draws comparison.

8   Most seriously, Davis neglects the economic component of America's crisis in education. We have in this country a structural poverty that makes learning difficult for tens of thousands of students whose home environments foster neither the pride in education nor the basic economic security needed for success in school. When America's poorest children look around their communities and see disrepair, unemployment, crime, and the availability (mostly) of unskilled jobs, these students will see little reason to excel in the classroom. The truly motivated will rise above their conditions. But that takes hard work, and too few have the support structures of a steady home to make the transition out of poverty. The problem of structural poverty therefore persists, and its impact on the education system is immense. Davis's "simple" solution of exempting teachers from federal income taxes does not acknowledge what is perhaps the most profound and intractable cause of problems in American education.

9   Would prospective teachers approve of Davis's proposal? Forget for the moment the challenges to this proposal that other public servants such as firefighters and police would make. If Davis's proposed income tax exemption passed Congress, we could expect that those contemplating a career in teaching but who were wavering because of the low salaries would say yes and would join the profession. That would be good news. But until other problems that plague education—such as meager budgets, conflicting educational agendas, inefficient school bureaucracies, and structural poverty—are resolved, proposals such as Davis's, though they are welcome and *should*

be enacted, will not achieve their desired end.
Davis's proposal is a step in the right direction,
but it is only a step.

Informal Critique of Sample Essay

Before reading the Discussion of this student essay, write your own informal
response to the essay: what are its strengths and weaknesses? Does the essay
follow the general guidelines for writing critique that we outlined on page 66?
Jot down some ideas for a critique that take a different approach to Davis's
essay; what points might you bring up if you were going to argue that Davis's
proposal is an all around bad idea?

Discussion

- Paragraph 1 of this critique introduces the selection to be reviewed,
  along with the author, and sets a context for the reader. The paragraph
  ends with the writer's thesis: to adopt the proposed federal income tax
  exemption, even though that policy will not solve the educational crisis
  in America.
- Paragraph 2 summarizes Davis's letter. Note that the topic sentence
  clearly indicates that Davis has written a persuasive, rather than an
  informative, piece.
- Paragraph 3 explains the writer's basic agreement with Davis's federal
  income tax exemption proposal.
- Paragraph 4 begins the critical evaluation of Davis's letter, indicating
  that Davis assumes the problem with our current system is the absence
  of good teachers. Note how the paragraph's final sentence offers readers three arguments against Davis's assertion. These arguments are
  developed, in turn, in the next three paragraphs.
- Paragraph 5 raises the first problem Davis has failed to recognize—low
  budgets for school systems. Davis's proposal does not address this problem.
- Paragraph 6 raises a second problem Davis has failed to recognize:
  structural issues within the education community that lead to
  difficulties.
- Paragraph 7 continues this discussion and points out Davis's faulty logic
  in comparing the problems of education to problems faced by scientists
  during World War II and in the race to the moon.
- Paragraph 8 raises the third and most significant problem Davis has not
  acknowledged: the dire circumstances of many students and the effect
  of these circumstances on learning potential.

- Paragraph 9, the conclusion, summarizes the overall position of the critique—to accept the federal income tax exemption proposal, but to reject the expectation that the crisis in education will be solved with a single, "simple" solution.

Practice Critique

Select one of the following articles in Part II of this book:

"Too Much of a Good Thing," Greg Crister (pp. 461–64)

"Fat and Happy: In Defense of Fat Acceptance," Mary Ray Worley (pp. 469–74)

"Cinderella's Stepsisters," Toni Morrison (pp. 590–92)

Write a critique of the selected article, following the directions in this chapter for determining the author's purpose in writing the piece and for assessing the author's success in achieving that purpose.

   For a somewhat more challenging assignment, try writing a critique of one of the following articles:

"Disobedience as a Psychological and Moral Problem," Enrich Fromm (pp. 360–65)

"Ethics in Business," Gerald F. Cavanagh (pp. 394–408)

"'Cinderella': A Story of Sibling Rivalry and Oedipal Conflicts," Bruno Bettelheim (pp. 567–75)

Before writing your critique of the article, consider the earlier discussions of evaluating writing in this chapter. Examine the author's use of information and persuasive strategies. Review the logical fallacies and identify any of these in the selection you've chosen to critique. Work out your ideas on paper, perhaps producing a working outline. Then write a rough draft of your critique. Review the article, the subject of the critique—and revise your rough draft at least once before considering it finished.

Introductions, Theses, and Conclusions

3

WRITING INTRODUCTIONS

All writers, no matter how much they prepare, eventually have to face the question of writing their introduction. How to start? What's the best way to approach your subject? With high seriousness, a light touch, an anecdote? How best to engage your reader?

Many writers avoid such agonizing choices by putting them off—productively. Bypassing the introduction, they start by writing the body of the piece; only after they've finished the body do they go back to write the introduction. There's a lot to be said for this approach. Because you have presumably spent more time thinking and writing about the topic itself than about how you're going to introduce it, you are in a better position to begin directly with your presentation. And often, it's not until you've actually seen the piece on paper and read it over once or twice that a natural way of introducing it becomes apparent. Even if there is no natural way to begin, you are generally in better psychological shape to write the introduction after the major task of writing is behind you and you know exactly what you're leading up to.

Perhaps, however, you can't operate this way. After all, you have to start writing *somewhere,* and if you have evaded the problem by skipping the introduction, that blank page may loom just as large whenever you do choose to begin. If this is the case, then go ahead and write an introduction, knowing full well that it's probably going to be flat and awful. Write whatever comes to mind, as long as you have a working thesis. Assure yourself that whatever you put down at this point (except for the thesis) "won't count" and that when the time is right, you'll go back and replace it with something that's fit for eyes other than yours. But in the meantime, you'll have gotten started.

The *purpose* of an introduction is to prepare the reader to enter the world of your paper. The introduction makes the connection between the more familiar world inhabited by the reader and the less familiar world of the writer's particular subject; it places a discussion in a context that the reader can understand.

You have many ways to provide such a context. We'll consider just a few of the most common.

Quotation

Here is an introduction to a paper on democracy:

"Two cheers for democracy" was E. M. Forster's not-quite-whole-hearted judgment. Most Americans would not agree. To them, our democracy is one of the glories of civilization. To one American in particular, E. B. White, democracy is "the hole in the stuffed shirt through which the sawdust slowly trickles [. . .] the dent in the high hat [. . .] the recurrent suspicion that more than half of the people are right more than half of the time" (915). American democracy is based on the oldest continuously operating written constitution in the world—a most impressive fact and a testament to the farsightedness of the founding fathers. But just how farsighted can mere humans be? In *Future Shock,* Alvin Toffler quotes economist Kenneth Boulding on the incredible acceleration of social change in our time: "The world of today [. . .] is as different from the world in which I was born as that world was from Julius Caesar's" (13). As we move into the twenty-first century, it seems legitimate to question the continued effectiveness of a governmental system that was devised in the eighteenth century; and it seems equally legitimate to consider alternatives.

The quotations by Forster and White help set the stage for the discussion of democracy by presenting the reader with some provocative and well-phrased remarks. Later in the paragraph, the quotation by Boulding more specifically prepares us for the theme of change that will be central to the essay as a whole.

Historical Review

In many cases, the reader will be unprepared to follow the issue you discuss unless you provide some historical background. Consider the following introduction to an essay on the film-rating system:

Sex and violence on the screen are not new issues. In the Roaring Twenties there was increasing pressure from civic and religious groups to ban depictions of "immorality" from the screen. Faced with the threat of federal censorship, the film producers decided to clean their own house. In 1930, the Motion Picture Producers and Distributors of America established the Production Code. At first, adherence to the Code was voluntary; but in 1934 Joseph Breen, newly appointed head of the MPPDA, gave the Code teeth. Henceforth all newly produced films had to be submitted for approval to the Production Code Administration, which had the power to award or withhold the Code seal. Without a Code seal, it was virtually impossible for a film to be shown anywhere in the United States, since exhibitors would not accept it. At about the same time, the Catholic Legion of Decency was formed to advise the faithful which films were and were not objectionable. For several decades the Production Code Administration exercised powerful control over what was portrayed in American theatrical films. By the 1960s, however, changing standards of morality had considerably weakened the Code's grip. In 1968, the Production Code was replaced with a rating system designed to keep younger audiences away from films with high levels of sex or violence. Despite its imperfections, this rating system has proved more beneficial to American films than did the old censorship system.

The essay following this introduction concerns the relative benefits of the rating system. By providing some historical background on the rating system, the writer helps readers to understand his arguments. Notice the chronological development of details.

Review of a Controversy

A particular type of historical review is the review of a controversy or debate. Consider the following introduction:

> The *American Heritage Dictionary's* definition of civil disobedience is rather simple: "the refusal to obey civil laws that are regarded as unjust, usually by employing methods of passive resistance." However, despite such famous (and beloved) examples of civil disobedience as the movements of Mahatma Gandhi in India and the Reverend Martin Luther King, Jr., in the United States, the question of whether or not civil disobedience should be considered an asset to society is hardly clear cut. For instance, Hannah Arendt, in her article "Civil Disobedience," holds that "to think of disobedient minorities as rebels and truants is against the letter and spirit of a constitution whose framers were especially sensitive to the dangers of unbridled majority rule." On the other hand, a noted lawyer, Lewis Van Dusen, Jr., in his article "Civil Disobedience: Destroyer of Democracy," states that "civil disobedience, whatever the ethical rationalization, is still an assault on our democratic society, an affront to our legal order and an attack on our constitutional government." These two views are clearly incompatible. I believe, though, that Van Dusen's is the more convincing. On balance, civil disobedience is dangerous to society.*

The negative aspects of civil disobedience, rather than Van Dusen's essay, are the topic of this essay. But to introduce this topic, the writer has provided quotations that represent opposing sides of the controversy over civil disobedience, as well as brief references to two controversial practitioners. By focusing at the outset on the particular rather than the abstract aspects of the subject, the writer hoped to secure the attention of her readers and to involve them in the controversy that forms the subject of her essay.

From the General to the Specific

Another way of providing a transition from the reader's world to the less familiar world of the essay is to work from a general subject to a specific one.

---

* Michele Jacques, "Civil Disobedience: Van Dusen vs. Arendt," unpublished paper, 1993: 1. Used by permission.

The following introduction begins a paper on improving our air quality by inducing people to trade the use of their cars for public transportation.

> While generalizations are risky, it seems pretty safe to say that most human beings are selfish. Self-interest may be part of our nature, and probably aids the survival of our species, since self-interested pursuits increase the likelihood of individual survival and genetic reproduction. Ironically, however, our selfishness has caused us to abuse the natural environment upon which we depend. We have polluted, deforested, depleted, deformed, and endangered our earth, water, and air to such an extent that now our species' survival is gravely threatened. In America, air pollution is one of our most pressing environmental problems, and it is our selfish use of the automobile that poses the greatest threat to clean air, as well as the greatest challenge to efforts to stop air pollution. Very few of us seem willing to give up our cars, let alone use them less. We are spoiled by the individual freedom afforded us when we can hop into our gas-guzzling vehicles and go where we want, when we want. Somehow, we as a nation will have to wean ourselves from this addiction to the automobile, and we can do this by designing alternative forms of transportation that serve our selfish interests.*

From the Specific to the General: Anecdote, Illustration

The following paragraph quotes an anecdote in order to move from the specific to a general topic:

> In an article on the changing American family, Ron French tells the following story:
>
>> Six-year-old Sydney Papenheim has her future planned. "First I'm going to marry Jared," she told her mother. "Then I'm going to get divorced and marry Gabby." "No, honey," Lisa Boettcher says, "you don't plan it like that." That's news to Sydney. Her mother is divorced and remarried, as is her stepdad. Her grandparents are divorced and remarried, as are enough aunts and uncles to field a team for "Family Feud." She gets presents from her stepfather's ex-wife. Her stepfather's children sometimes play at the house of her father. "You never know what is going to happen from day to day," says Sydney's stepdad, Brian Boettcher. "It's an evolution." It's more like a revolution, from Norman Rockwell to Norman Lear.†

---

* Travis Knight, "Reducing Air Pollution with Alternative Transportation," unpublished paper, 1998: 1. Used by permission.

† Norman Lear: (b. 1922): American television writer and producer noted for developing groundbreaking depictions of the American family in the 1970s, such as "All in the Family," "Sanford and Son," and "Maude." Ron French, "Family: The D-Word Loses Its Sting as Households Blend," *Detroit News* 1 Jan. 2000, 17 Aug. 2000 <http://detnews.com/specialreports/2000/journey/family/family.htm>.

French continues on to report that by the year 2007, blended families such as the Boettcher's will outnumber traditional nuclear families. Yet most people continue to lament this change. We as a nation need to accept this new reality: the "till death do us part" version of marriage no longer works.[*]

The previous introduction went from the general (the statement that human beings are selfish) to the specific (how to decrease air pollution); this one goes from the specific (one little girl's understanding of marriage and divorce) to the general (the changing American family). The anecdote is one of the most effective means at your disposal for capturing and holding your reader's attention. Speakers have long begun their general remarks with a funny, touching, or otherwise appropriate story; in fact, there are plenty of books that are nothing but collections of such stories, arranged by subject.

Question

Frequently, you can provoke the reader's attention by posing a question or a series of questions:

Are gender roles learned or inherited? Scientific research has established the existence of biological differences between the sexes, but the effect of biology's influence on gender roles cannot be distinguished from society's influence. According to Michael Lewis of the Institute for the Study of Exceptional Children, "As early as you can show me a sex difference, I can show you the culture at work." Social processes, as well as biological differences, are responsible for the separate roles of men and women.[†]

Opening your essay with a question can be provocative, since it places the reader in an active role: He or she begins by considering answers. *Are* gender roles learned? *Are* they inherited? In this active role, the reader is likely to continue reading with interest.

Statement of Thesis

Perhaps the most direct method of introduction is to begin immediately with the thesis:

Every college generation is defined by the social events of its age. The momentous occurrences of an era—from war and economics to politics and inventions—give meaning to lives of the individuals who live

---

[*] Veronica Gonzalez, "New Family Formations," unpublished paper, 1999: 1. Used by permission.

[†] Tammy Smith, "Are Sex Roles Learned or Inherited?" unpublished paper, 1994: 1. Used by permission.

through them. They also serve to knit those individuals together by creating a collective memory and a common historic or generational identity. In 1979, I went to 26 college and university campuses, selected to represent the diversity of American higher education, and asked students what social or political events most influenced their generation. I told them that the children who came of age in the decade after World War I might have answered the Great Depression. The bombing of Pearl Harbor, World War II, or perhaps the death of Franklin Roosevelt might have stood out for those born a few years later. For my generation, born after World War II, the key event was the assassination of John F. Kennedy. We remember where we were when we heard the news. The whole world seemingly changed in its aftermath.*

This essay begins with a general assertion: that large-scale social events shape generations of college students. The advantage of beginning with a general thesis like this is that it immediately establishes the broader context and the point illustrated by the paper's subsequent focus on contemporary college students. Stating your thesis in the first sentence of an introduction also works when you make a controversial argument. Stating a provocative point right away, such as "Democracy is dead," for a paper examining the problems plaguing representative government in current society, forces the reader to sit up and take notice—perhaps even to begin protesting. This "hooks" a reader, who is likely to want to find out how your essay will support its strong thesis. In the example paragraph above, the general thesis is followed by specific examples of social events and their effects on college students, which prepares the reader to consider the experiences of current college students in comparison to those of earlier generations.

One final note about our model introductions: They may be longer than introductions you have been accustomed to writing. Many writers (and readers) prefer a shorter, snappier introduction. The length of an introduction can depend on the length of the paper it introduces, and it is also largely a matter of personal or corporate style: there is no rule concerning the correct length of an introduction. If you feel that a short introduction is appropriate, use one. You may wish to break up what seems like a long introduction into two paragraphs.

EXERCISE **3.1**

Drafting Introductions

Imagine that you are writing an essay using the topic, ideas, and thesis you developed in the earlier exercises in this book. Choose one of the seven types of introductions we've discussed—preferably one you have never used before—and draft an introduction that would work to open a paper on this topic. Use our examples as models to help you draft your practice introduction.

---

* Arthur Levine, "The Making of a Generation," *Change* Sept.–Oct. 1993: 8.

WRITING A THESIS

A thesis is a one-sentence summary of a paper's content. It is similar, actually, to a paper's conclusion (see pages 86–87) but lacks the conclusion's concern for broad implications and significance. The thesis is the product of your thinking; it therefore represents *your* conclusion about the topic on which you're writing, and therefore you have to have spent some time thinking (invention) in order to arrive at the thesis that begins your actual essay.

For a writer in the drafting stages, the thesis establishes a focus, a basis on which to include or exclude information. For the reader of a finished product, the thesis anticipates the author's discussion. *A thesis, therefore, is an essential tool for both writers and readers of academic material.*

This last sentence is our thesis for this section. Based on this thesis, we, as the authors, have limited the content of the section; and you, as the reader, will be able to form certain expectations about the discussion that follows. You can expect a definition of a thesis; an enumeration of the uses of a thesis; and a discussion focused on academic material. As writers, we will have met our obligations to you only if in subsequent paragraphs we satisfy these expectations.

The Components of a Thesis

Like any other sentence, a thesis includes a subject and a predicate, which consists of an assertion about the subject. In the sentence "Lee and Grant were different kinds of generals," "Lee and Grant" is the subject and "were different kinds of generals" is the predicate. What distinguishes a thesis from any other sentence with a subject and predicate is that *the thesis presents the controlling idea of the paper.* The subject of a thesis must present the right balance between the general and the specific to allow for thorough discussion within the allotted length of the paper. The discussion might include definitions, details, comparisons, contrasts—whatever is needed to illuminate a subject and carry on an intelligent conversation. (If the sentence about Lee and Grant were a thesis, the reader would assume that the rest of the paper contained comparisons and contrasts between the two generals.)

Bear in mind when writing theses that the more general your subject and the more complex your assertion, the longer your paper will be. For instance, you could not write an effective ten-page paper based on the following:

> Democracy is the best system of government.

Consider the subject of this sentence ("democracy") and the assertion of its predicate ("is the best system of government"). The subject is enormous in scope; it is a general category composed of hundreds of more specific subcategories, each of which would be appropriate for a paper ten pages in length. The predicate of our example is also a problem, for the claim that democracy is the best system of government would be simplistic unless accompanied by a thorough, systematic, critical evaluation of *every* form of government yet devised. A ten-page paper governed by such a thesis simply could not achieve the level of detail expected of college students.

Limiting the Scope of the Thesis

To write an effective thesis and thus a controlled, effective paper, you need to limit your subject and your claims about it. Two strategies for achieving a thesis of manageable proportions are (1) to begin with a working thesis (this strategy assumes that you are familiar with your topic) and (2) to begin with a broad area of interest and narrow it (this strategy assumes that you are unfamiliar with your topic).

Start with a Working Thesis

Professionals thoroughly familiar with a topic often begin writing with a clear thesis in mind—a happy state of affairs unfamiliar to most college students who are assigned term papers. But professionals usually have an important advantage over students: experience. Because professionals know their material, are familiar with the ways of approaching it, are aware of the questions important to practitioners, and have devoted considerable time to study of the topic, they are naturally in a strong position to begin writing a paper. In addition, many professionals are practiced at invention; the time they spend listing or outlining their ideas helps them work out their thesis statements. Not only do professionals have experience in their fields, but also they have a clear purpose in writing; they know their audience and are comfortable with the format of their papers.

Experience counts—there's no way around it. As a student, you are not yet an expert and therefore don't generally have the luxury of beginning your writing tasks with a definite thesis in mind. Once you choose and devote time to a major field of study, however, you will gain experience. In the meantime, you'll have to do more work than the professional to prepare yourself for writing a paper.

But let's assume that you *do* have an area of expertise, that you are in your own right a professional (albeit not in academic matters). We'll assume that you understand your nonacademic subject—say, backpacking—and have been given a clear purpose for writing: to discuss the relative merits of backpack designs. Your job is to write a recommendation for the owner of a sporting-goods chain, suggesting which line of backpacks the chain should carry. Because you already know a good deal about backpacks, you may already have some well-developed ideas on the topic before you start doing additional research.

Yet even as an expert in your field, you will find that beginning the writing task is a challenge, for at this point it is unlikely that you will be able to conceive a thesis perfectly suited to the contents of your paper. After all, a thesis is a summary, and it is difficult to summarize a presentation yet to be written—especially if you plan to discover what you want to say during the process of writing. Even if you know your material well, the best you can do at the early stages is to formulate a *working thesis*—a hypothesis of sorts, a well-informed hunch about your topic and the claim to be made about it. Once you have completed a draft, you can evaluate the degree to which your working thesis accurately summarizes the content of your paper. If the match is a good one, the working thesis becomes the thesis. If, however, sections of the paper drift from the focus set out in the working thesis, you'll need to revise the thesis and the paper itself to ensure that the presentation is unified. (You'll know that the match between the content and thesis is a good one when every paragraph directly refers to and develops some element of the thesis.)

This model works for approaching topics proper to your professor's territory, such as government or medieval poetry. The difference is that when approaching topics that are less familiar to you than something like backpacking, you will have to spend more time gathering data and brainstorming. Such labor prepares you to make assertions about your subject.

Choosing and Narrowing Your Subjects

Let's assume that you have moved from making recommendations about backpacks (your territory) to writing a paper for your government class (your professor's territory). Whereas you were once the professional who knew enough about your subject to begin writing with a working thesis, you are now the student, inexperienced and in need of a great deal of information before you can begin to think of thesis statements. It may be a comfort to know that your government professor would likely be in the same predicament if asked to recommend backpack designs. She would need to spend several weeks, at least, backpacking to become as experienced as you; and it is fair to say that you will need to spend several hours in the library before you are in a position to choose a topic suitable for an undergraduate paper.

Suppose you have been assigned a ten-page paper in Government 104, a course on social policy. Not only do you have to chose a subject, but also you have to narrow it sufficiently and decide upon your thesis. Where will you begin? First, you need to select a broad area of interest and make yourself knowledgeable about its general features. What if no broad area of interest occurs to you? Don't despair—usually there's a way to make use of material you've read in a text or heard in a lecture. The trick is to find a topic that can become personally important, for whatever reason. (For a paper in your biology class, you might write on the digestive system because a relative has stomach troubles. For an economics seminar, you might explore the factors that threaten banks with collapse because your great-grandparents lost their life savings during the Great Depression.) Whatever the academic discipline, try to discover a topic that you'll enjoy exploring; that way, you'll be writing for yourself as much as for your instructor. Some specific data gathering strategies to try if no topics occur to you: Review material covered during the semester, class by class if need be; review the semester's readings, actually skimming each assignment. Choose any subject that has held your interest, if even for a moment, and use that as your point of departure.

Imagine that you've reviewed each of your classes and recall that a lecture on AIDS aroused your curiosity. Your broad subject of interest, then, will be AIDS. At this point, the goal of your research is to limit this subject to a manageable scope. Although your initial, broad subject will often be more specific than our example, "AIDS," we'll assume for the purposes of discussion the most general case (the subject in greatest need of limiting).

A subject can be limited in at least two ways. First, a general article such as an encyclopedia entry may do the work for you by presenting the subject in the form of an outline, with each item in the outline representing a separate topic (which, for your purposes, may need further limiting). Second, you can limit a subject by asking several questions about it:

Who?

What aspects?

Where?

When?

How?

These questions will occur to you as you conduct your research and see the ways in which various authors have focused their discussions. Having read several sources and having decided that you'd like to use them, you might limit the subject "AIDS" by asking *who*—AIDS patients; and *which* aspect— civil rights of AIDS patients.

Certainly, "the civil rights of AIDS patients" offers a more specific focus than does "AIDS"; still, the revised focus is too broad for a ten-page paper in that a comprehensive discussion would obligate you to review numerous particular rights. So again you must try to limit your subject by posing a question. In this particular case, *which aspects* (of the civil rights of AIDS patients) can be asked a second time. Six aspects may come to mind:

- Rights in the workplace
- Rights to hospital care
- Rights to insurance benefits
- Rights to privacy
- Rights to fair housing
- Rights to education

Any *one* of these aspects could provide the focus of a ten-page paper, and you do yourself an important service by choosing one, perhaps two, of the aspects. To choose more would obligate you to too broad a discussion and you would frustrate yourself: Either the paper would have to be longer than ten pages or, assuming you kept to the page limit, the paper would be superficial in its treatment. In both instances, the paper would fail, given the constraints of the assignment. So it is far better to spend ample time gathering data, brainstorming, gathering data, and brainstorming, in order to limit your subject before you attempt to write about it. Let's assume that you settle on the following as an appropriately defined subject for a ten-page paper:

- The rights of AIDS patients in the workplace

The process of narrowing an initial subject (invention) depends heavily on the reading you do (data gathering). The more you read, the deeper your understanding of a topic. The deeper your understanding, the likelier it will be that you can divide a broad and complex topic into manageable—that is, researchable—categories. In the AIDS example, your reading in the literature suggested that the civil rights of AIDS patients was an issue at the center of recent national debate. So reading allowed you to narrow the subject "AIDS" by answering the initial questions—the *who* and *which* aspects. Once you narrowed your focus to "the civil rights of AIDS patients," you read further and quickly realized that civil rights in itself was a broad subject that also should be limited. In this way, reading provided an important stimulus as you worked to identify an appropriate subject for your paper. Your process here is recursive—you move back and forth between Stages 1 and 2 of the process, each movement bringing you closer to establishing a clear focus *before* you attempt to write your paper.

EXERCISE 3.2

Practice Narrowing Subjects

In groups of three or four classmates, choose one of the following subjects and respond to the questions listed above for narrowing subjects: Who? What aspects? Where? When? How? See if you can formulate a more narrow approach to the subject.

- Downloading music off the Internet
- College sports
- School violence
- Internet chat rooms
- America's public school system

Make an Assertion

Thesis statements arise out of essay subjects—they constitute an assertion or claim you wish to make *about* your essay's topic. If you have spent enough time reading and gathering information, and brainstorming ideas about the assignment, you will be knowledgeable enough to have something to say about the subject, based on a combination of your own thinking and the thinking of your sources.

If you have trouble making an assertion do some more invention: Try writing your topic at the top of a page and then listing everything you now know and feel about it. Often from such a list you will discover an assertion that you then can use to fashion a working thesis. A good way to gauge the reasonableness of your claim is to see what other authors have asserted about the same topic. In fact, keep good notes on the views of others; the notes will prove a useful counterpoint to your own views as you write and think about your claim, and you may want to use them in your paper. Next, make several assertions about your topic, in order of increasing complexity (as an example, we'll make three assertions). The earlier example of a subject, "the rights of AIDS patients in the workplace" (see page 83), might lead you to produce the following list of assertions:

1. During the past two decades, the rights of AIDS patients in the workplace have been debated by national columnists.
2. Several columnists have offered convincing reasons for protecting the rights of AIDS patients in the workplace.
3. The most sensible plan for protecting the rights of AIDS patients in the workplace has been offered by columnist Anthony Jones.

Keep in mind that these are *working theses*. Because you haven't written a paper based on any of them, they remain *hypotheses* to be tested. You might choose one of these and use it to focus your first essay draft. After completing a first draft, you would revise it by comparing the contents of the paper to the thesis and making adjustments as necessary for unity. The working thesis is an excellent tool for planning broad sections of the paper, but—again—don't let it prevent you from pursuing related discussions as they occur to you.

Using the Thesis to Plan Your Essay Structure

Establishing a working thesis helps you then move to the invention of your essay structure, because essay structure flows directly from the type of thesis contained in an essay.

Notice how the three statements about AIDS in the workplace differ from one another in the forcefulness of their assertions. The third thesis is *strongly argumentative*, or persuasive. "Most sensible" implies that the writer will explain several plans for protecting the rights of AIDS patients in the workplace. Following the explanation would come a comparison of plans and then a judgment in favor of Anthony Jones's plan. The thesis thus helps the writer plan the paper. Assuming that the paper follows the three-part structure we've proposed, the working thesis would become the final thesis, on the basis of which a reader could anticipate sections of the essay to come.

The first of the three thesis statements, by contrast, is *explanatory*, or informative:

> During the past two decades, the rights of AIDS patients in the workplace have been debated by national columnists.

In developing a paper based on this thesis, the writer would assert only the existence of a debate, obligating himself merely to a summary of the various positions taken. Readers, then, would use this thesis as a tool for anticipating the contours of the paper to follow. Based on this particular thesis, a reader would *not* expect to find the author strongly endorsing the views of one or another columnist. The thesis does not require the author to defend a personal opinion.

The second thesis *does* entail a personal, intellectually assertive commitment to the material, although the assertion is not as forceful as the one found in statement three:

> Several columnists have offered convincing reasons for protecting the rights of AIDS patients in the workplace.

Here we have an *explanatory, mildly argumentative* thesis that enables the writer to express an opinion. We infer from the use of the word *convincing* that the writer will judge the various reasons for protecting the rights of AIDS patients; and, we can reasonably assume, the writer believes in protecting these rights. Note the contrast between this second thesis and the first one, in which the writer was committed to no involvement in the debate whatsoever. Still, the second thesis is not as ambitious as the third one, whose writer implicitly accepted the general argument for safeguarding rights (an acceptance the writer would need to justify) and then took the additional step of evaluating the merits of those arguments in relation to each other.

As you can see, for any subject you might care to explore in a paper, you can make any number of assertions—some relatively simple, some complex. It is on the basis of these assertions that you set yourself an agenda in writing a paper—and readers set for themselves expectations for reading. The more ambitious the thesis, the more complex will be the paper and the greater will be the readers' expectations.

Using the Thesis

Different writing tasks require different theses. The *explanatory thesis* often is developed in response to short-answer exam questions that call for information, not analysis (e.g., "List and explain proposed modifications to contemporary American democracy"). The *explanatory but mildly argumentative thesis* is appropriate for organizing reports (even lengthy ones), as well as essay questions that call for some analysis (e.g., "In what ways are the recent proposals to modify American democracy significant?"). The *strongly argumentative thesis* is used to organize papers and exam questions that call for information, analysis, *and* the writer's forcefully stated point of view (e.g., "Evaluate proposed modifications to health maintenance organizations").

The strongly argumentative thesis, of course, is the riskiest of the three, since you must unequivocally state your position and make it appear reasonable—which requires that you offer evidence and defend against logical objections. But such intellectual risks pay dividends, and if you become involved enough in your work to make challenging assertions, you will provoke challenging responses that enliven classroom discussions. One of the important objectives of a college education is to extend learning by stretching, or challenging, conventional beliefs. You breathe new life into this broad objective, and you enliven your own learning as well, every time you adopt a thesis that sets a challenging agenda both for you (as writer) and for your readers. Of course, once you set the challenge, you must be equal to the task. As a writer, you will need to discuss all the elements implied by your thesis.

To review: A thesis (a one-sentence summary of your paper) helps you organize and your reader anticipate a discussion. Theses are distinguished by their carefully worded subjects and predicates, which should be just broad enough and complex enough to be developed within the length limitations of the assignment. Both novices and experts in a field typically begin the initial draft of a paper with a working thesis—a statement that provides writers with structure enough to get started but with latitude enough to discover what they want to say as they write. Once you have completed a first draft, you test the "fit" of your thesis with the paper that follows. Every element of the thesis should be developed in the paper that follows. Discussions that drift from your thesis should be deleted, or the thesis changed to accommodate the new discussions.

These concerns will be addressed more fully when we discuss the revision stage of the writing process. For now, let's move to a discussion of introduction and conclusions.

EXERCISE 3.3

Drafting Thesis Statements

After completing the group exercise where you narrowed a subject (Exercise 3.2, page 83), work individually or in small groups to draft three possible theses in relation to your earlier ideas. Draft one *explanatory thesis*, one *explanatory but mildly argumentative thesis*, and one *strongly argumentative thesis*.

WRITING CONCLUSIONS

One way to view the conclusion of your paper is as an introduction worked in reverse, a bridge from the world of your essay back to the world of your reader. A conclusion is the part of your paper in which you restate and (if necessary) expand on your thesis. Essential to many conclusions is the summary, which is not merely a repetition of the thesis but a restatement that takes advantage of the material you've presented. The *simplest conclusion is a summary of the paper,* but you may want more than this for the end of your paper. Depending on your needs, you might offer a summary and then build onto it a discussion of the paper's significance or its implications for future study, for choices that individuals might make, for policy, and so on. You might also want to urge the reader to change an attitude or to modify behavior. Certainly, you are under no obligation to discuss the broader significance of your work (and a summary, alone, will satisfy the formal requirement that your paper have an ending); but the conclusions of better papers often reveal authors who are "thinking large" and want to connect the particular concerns of their papers with the broader concerns of society.

Here we'll consider seven strategies for expanding the basic summary-conclusion. But two words of advice are in order. First, no matter how clever or beautifully executed, a conclusion cannot salvage a poorly written paper. Second, by virtue of its placement, the conclusion carries rhetorical weight. It is the last statement a reader will encounter before turning from your work. Realizing this, writers who expand on the basic summary-conclusion often wish to give their final words a dramatic flourish, a heightened level of diction. Soaring rhetoric and drama in a conclusion are fine as long as they do not unbalance the paper and call attention to themselves. Having labored long hours over your paper, you have every right to wax eloquent. But keep a sense of proportion and timing. Make your points quickly and end crisply.

Statement of the Subject's Significance

One of the more effective ways to conclude a paper is to discuss the larger significance of what you have written, providing readers with one more reason to regard your work as a serious effort. When using this strategy, you move from the specific concern of your paper to the broader concerns of the reader's world. Often, you will need to choose among a range of significances: A paper on the Wright brothers might end with a discussion of air travel as it affects economies, politics, or families; a paper on contraception might end with a discussion of its effect on sexual mores, population, or the church. But don't overwhelm your reader with the importance of your remarks. Keep your discussion well focused.

The following paragraphs conclude a paper on George H. Shull, a pioneer in the inbreeding and crossbreeding of corn:

> [...] Thus, the hybrids developed and described by Shull 75 years ago have finally dominated U.S. corn production.
>
> The adoption of hybrid corn was steady and dramatic in the Corn Belt. From 1930 through 1979 the average yields of corn in the U.S. increased from 21.9 to 95.1 bushels per acre, and the additional value to the farmer is now several billion dollars per year.
>
> The success of hybrid corn has also stimulated the breeding of other crops, such as sorghum hybrids, a major feed grain crop in arid parts of the world. Sorghum yields have increased 300 percent since 1930. Approximately 20 percent of the land devoted to rice production in China is planted with hybrid seed, which is reported to yield 20 percent more than the best varieties. And many superior varieties of tomatoes, cucumbers, spinach, and other vegetables are hybrids. Today virtually all corn produced in the developed countries is from hybrid

> seed. From those blue bloods of the plant kingdom has come a model
> for feeding the world.*

The first sentence of this conclusion is a summary, and from it the reader can infer that the paper included a discussion of Shull's techniques for the hybrid breeding of corn. The summary is followed by a two-paragraph discussion on the significance of Shull's research for feeding the world.

Call for Further Research

In the scientific and social scientific communities, papers often end with a review of what has been presented (as, for instance, in an experiment) and the ways in which the subject under consideration needs to be further explored. If you raise questions that you call on others to answer, however, make sure you know that the research you are calling for hasn't already been conducted.

This next conclusion comes from a sociological report on the placement of elderly men and women in nursing homes.

> Thus, our study shows a correlation between the placement of elder-ly citizens in nursing facilities and the significant decline of their motor and intellectual skills over the ten months following placement. What the research has not made clear is the extent to which this marked decline is due to physical as opposed to emotional causes. The elder-ly are referred to homes at that point in their lives when they grow less able to care for themselves—which suggests that the drop-off in skills may be due to physical causes. But the emotional stress of being placed in a home, away from family and in an environment that confirms the patient's view of himself as decrepit, may exacerbate—if not itself be a primary cause of—the patient's rapid loss of abilities. Further research is needed to clarify the relationship between depression and particular physical ailments as these affect the skills of the elderly in nursing facil-ities. There is little doubt that information yielded by such studies can enable health care professionals to deliver more effective services.

Notice how this call for further study locates the author in a large communi-ty of researchers on whom she depends for assistance in answering the ques-tions that have come out of her own work. The author summarizes her findings (in the first sentence of the paragraph), states what her work has not shown, and then extends her invitation.

Solution/Recommendation

The purpose of your paper might be to review a problem or controversy and to discuss contributing factors. In such a case, it would be appropriate, after

---

* William L. Brown, "Hybrid Vim and Vigor," *Science* Nov. 1984: 77–78.

summarizing your discussion, to offer a solution based on the knowledge you've gained while conducting research. If your solution is to be taken seriously, your knowledge must be amply demonstrated in the body of the paper.

> (1) [...] The major problem in college sports today is not commercialism—it is the exploitation of athletes and the proliferation of illicit practices which dilute educational standards.
>
> (2) Many universities are currently deriving substantial benefits from sports programs that depend on the labor of athletes drawn from the poorest sections of America's population. It is the responsibility of educators, civil rights leaders, and concerned citizens to see that these young people get a fair return for their labor both in terms of direct remuneration and in terms of career preparation for a life outside sports.
>
> (3) Minimally, scholarships in revenue-producing sports should be designed to extend until graduation, rather than covering only four years of athletic eligibility, and should include guarantees of tutoring, counseling, and proper medical care. At institutions where the profits are particularly large (such as Texas A & M, which can afford to pay its football coach $280,000 a year), scholarships should also provide salaries that extend beyond room, board, and tuition. The important thing is that the athlete be remunerated fairly and have the opportunity to gain skills from a university environment without undue competition from a physically and psychologically demanding full-time job. This may well require that scholarships be extended over five or six years, including summers.
>
> (4) Such a proposal, I suspect, will not be easy to implement. The current amateur system, despite its moral and educational flaws, enables universities to hire their athletic labor at minimal cost. But solving the fiscal crisis of the universities on the backs of America's poor and minorities is not, in the long run, a tenable solution. With the support of concerned educators, parents, and civil rights leaders, and with the help from organized labor, the college athlete, truly a sleeping giant, will someday speak out and demand what is rightly his—and hers—a fair share of the revenue created by their hard work.*

In this conclusion, the author summarizes his article in one sentence: "The major problem in college sports today is not commercialism—it is the exploitation of athletes and the proliferation of illicit practices which dilute educational standards." In paragraph 2, he continues with an analysis of the problem just stated and follows with a general recommendation—that "concerned educators, parents, and civil rights leaders" be responsible for the welfare of college athletes. In paragraph 3, he makes a specific proposal, and in the final paragraph, he anticipates resistance to the proposal. He concludes by discounting this resistance and returning to the general point, that college athletes should receive a fair deal.

---

* Mark Naison, "Scenario for Scandal," *Commonweal* 109.16 (1982).

Anecdote

An anecdote is a briefly told story or joke, the point of which in a conclusion is to shed light on your subject. The anecdote is more direct than an allusion. With an allusion, you merely refer to a story ("Too many people today live in Plato's cave..."); with the anecdote, you actually retell the story. The anecdote allows readers to discover for themselves the significance of a reference to another source—an effort most readers enjoy because they get to exercise their creativity.

The following anecdote concludes a political-philosophical essay. First, the author includes a paragraph summing up her argument, and she follows that with a brief story.

> Ironically, our economy is fueled by the very thing that degrades our value system. But when politicians call for a return to "traditional family values," they seldom criticize the business interests that promote and benefit from our coarsened values. Consumer capitalism values things over people; it thrives on discontent and unhappiness since discontented people make excellent consumers, buying vast numbers of things that may somehow "fix" their inadequacies. We buy more than we need, the economy chugs along, but such materialism is the real culprit behind our warped value systems. Anthony de Mello tells the following story:*
>
> > Socrates believed that the wise person would instinctively lead a frugal life, and he even went so far as to refuse to wear shoes. Yet he constantly fell under the spell of the marketplace and would go there often to look at the great variety and magnificence of the wares on display.
> > A friend once asked him why he was so intrigued with the allures of the market. "I love to go there," Socrates replied, "to discover how many things I am perfectly happy without." (27)

The writer chose to conclude the article with this anecdote. She could have developed an interpretation, but this would have spoiled the dramatic value for the reader. The purpose of using an anecdote is to make your point with subtlety, so resist the temptation to interpret. Keep in mind three guidelines when selecting an anecdote: It should be prepared for (readers should have all the information they need to understand it), it should provoke the reader's interest, and it should not be so obscure as to be unintelligible.

Quotation

A favorite concluding device is the quotation—the words of a famous person or an authority in the field on which you are writing. The purpose of quoting another is to link your work to theirs, thereby gaining for your work authori-

---

* Frances Wageneck, *Family Values in the Marketplace,* unpublished paper, 2000: 6. Used by permission.

ty and credibility. The first criterion for selecting a quotation is its suitability to your thesis. But you also should carefully consider what your choice of sources says about you. Suppose you are writing a paper on the American work ethic. If you could use a line by comedian David Letterman or one by the current secretary of labor to make the final point of your conclusion, which would you choose and why? One source may not be inherently more effective than the other, but the choice certainly sets a tone for the paper. The following two paragraphs conclude an essay examining the popularity of vulgar and insulting humor in television shows, movies, and other popular culture:

> But studies on the influence of popular culture suggest that cruel humor serves as more than a release in modern society. The ubiquitous media pick up on our baser nature, exaggerate it to entertain, and, by spitting it back at us, encourage us to push the boundaries even further. As a result, says Johns Hopkins' Miller, "We're gradually eroding the kinds of social forms and inhibitions that kept [aggressive] compulsions contained."
>
> Before the cycle escalates further, we might do well to consider the advice of Roman statesman and orator Cicero, who wrote at the peak of the Roman empire: "If we are forced, at ever hour, to watch or listen to horrible events, this constant stream of ghastly impressions will deprive even the most delicate among us of all respect for humanity."*

The two quotations used here serve different but equally effective ends. The first idea provides one last expert's viewpoint, then leads nicely into the cautionary note the writer introduces by quoting Cicero. The Roman's words, and the implied parallel being drawn between Rome and contemporary culture, are strong enough that the author ends there, without stepping in and making any statements of her own. In other cases, quotations can be used to set up one last statement by the author of an essay.

There is a potential problem with using quotations: If you end with the words of another, you may leave the impression that someone else can make your case more eloquently than you can. The language of the quotation will put your own prose into relief. If your own prose suffers by comparison—if the quotations are the best part of your paper—you'd be wise to spend some time revising. The way to avoid this kind of problem is to make your own presentation strong.

Question

Questions are useful for opening essays, and they are just as useful for closing them. Opening and closing questions function in different ways, however. The introductory question promises to be addressed in the paper that follows. But the concluding question leaves issues unresolved, calling on the readers to assume an active role by offering their own answers. Take a look at

---

* Nina J. Easton, "The Meaning of America," *Los Angeles Times Magazine* 7 Feb. 1993: 21.

the following two paragraphs, written to conclude an essay on genetically modified (GM) food:

> Are GM foods any more of a risk than other agricultural innovations that have taken place over the years, like selective breeding? Do the existing and potential future benefits of GM foods outweigh any risks that do exist? And what standard should governments use when assessing the safety of transgenic crops? The "frankenfood" frenzy has given life to a policy-making standard known as the "precautionary principle," which has been long advocated by environmental groups. That principle essentially calls for governments to prohibit any activity that raises concerns about human health or the environment, even if some cause-and-effect relationships are not fully established scientifically. As Liberal Democrat MP [Member of Parliament] Norman Baker told the BBC: "We must always apply the precautionary principle. That says that unless you're sure of adequate control, unless you're sure the risk is minimal, unless you're sure nothing horrible can go wrong, you don't do it."
>
> But can any innovation ever meet such a standard of certainty—especially given the proliferation of "experts" that are motivated as much by politics as they are by science? And what about those millions of malnourished people whose lives could be saved by transgenic foods? [Is] the "precautionary principle" [really] so precautionary after all [?]*

Perhaps you will choose to raise a question in your conclusion and then answer it, based on the material you've provided in the paper. The answered question challenges a reader to agree or disagree with your response and thus also places the reader in an active role. The following brief conclusion ends a student paper entitled "Is Feminism Dead?"

> So the answer to the question "Is the feminist movement dead?" is no, it's not. Even if most young women today don't consciously identify themselves as "feminists"—due to the ways in which the term has become loaded with negative associations—the principles of gender equality that lie at feminism's core are enthusiastically embraced by the vast number of young women, and even a large percentage of young men.

Speculation

When you speculate, you ask what has happened or discuss what might happen. This kind of question stimulates the reader because its subject is the unknown.

---

* "Frankenfoods Frenzy," *Reason* 13 Jan. 2000, 17 Aug. 2000 <http://reason.com/bi/bi-gmf.html>.

The following paragraph concludes "The New Generation Gap" by Neil Howe and William Strauss. In this essay, Howe and Strauss discuss the differences among Americans of various ages, including the "GI Generation" (born between 1901 and 1924), the "Boomers" (born 1943–1961), the "Thirteeners" (born 1961–1981), and the "Millennials" (born 1981–2000):

> If, slowly but surely, Millennials receive the kind of family protection and public generosity that GIs enjoyed as children, then they could come of age early in the next century as a group much like the GIs of the 1920s and 1930s—as a stellar (if bland) generation of rationalists, team players, and can-do civic builders. Two decades from now Boomers entering old age may well see in their grown Millennial children an effective instrument for saving the world, while Thirteeners entering midlife will shower kindness on a younger generation that is getting a better deal out of life (though maybe a bit less fun) than they ever got at a like age. Study after story after column will laud these "best damn kids in the world" as heralding a resurgent American greatness. And, for a while at least, no one will talk about a generation gap.*

Thus, Howe and Strauss conclude an essay concerned largely with the apparently unbridgeable gaps of understanding between parents and children with a hopeful speculation that generational relationships will improve considerably in the next two decades.

EXERCISE 3.4

Drafting Conclusions

Imagine that you have written a paper using the topic, ideas, and thesis you developed in the earlier exercises in this chapter. Choose one of the seven types of conclusions we've discussed—preferably one you have never used before—and draft a conclusion that would work to end your paper. Use our examples as models to help you draft your practice conclusion.

---

* Neil Howe and William Strauss, "The New Generation Gap," *Atlantic Monthly* Dec. 1992: 65.

4 Explanatory Synthesis

WHAT IS A SYNTHESIS?

A *synthesis* is a written discussion that draws on two or more sources. It follows that your ability to write syntheses depends on your ability to infer relationships among sources—essays, articles, fiction, and also nonwritten sources, such as lectures, interviews, and observations. This process is nothing new for you, since you infer relationships all the time—say, between something you've read in the newspaper and something you've seen for yourself, or between the teaching styles of your favorite and least favorite instructors. In fact, if you've written research papers, you've already written syntheses. In an *academic synthesis,* you make explicit the relationships that you have inferred among separate sources.

The skills you've already learned and practiced from the previous three chapters will be vital in writing syntheses. Clearly, before you're in a position to draw relationships between two or more sources, you must understand what those sources say; in other words, you must be able to *summarize* these sources. It will frequently be helpful for your readers if you provide at least partial summaries of sources in your synthesis essays. At the same time, you must go beyond summary to make judgments—judgments based, of course, on your *critical reading* of your sources. You should already have drawn some conclusions about the quality and validity of these sources; and you should know how much you agree or disagree with the points made in your sources and the reasons for your agreement or disagreement.

Further, you must go beyond the critique of individual sources to determine the relationship among them. Is the information in source B, for example, an extended illustration of the generalizations in source A? Would it be useful to compare and contrast source C with source B? Having read and considered sources A, B, and C, can you infer something else—D (not a source, but your own idea)?

Because a synthesis is based on two or more sources, you will need to be selective when choosing information from each. It would be neither possible nor desirable, for instance, to discuss in a ten-page paper on the American Civil War every point that the authors of two books make about their subject. What you as a writer must do is select from each source the ideas and information that best allow you to achieve your purpose.

| **WHERE DO WE FIND WRITTEN SYNTHESES?** |

Here are just a few of the types of writing that involve synthesis:

Academic Writing

- **Analysis papers.** Apply one or more theoretical approaches to an object or event under study.
- **Research papers.** Synthesize multiple sources in order to answer a well defined question.
- **Essay exams.** Demonstrate understanding by comparing and contrasting theories, viewpoints, or approaches.

Work-Place Writing

- **Newspaper and magazine articles.** Synthesize primary and secondary sources.
- **Position papers and policy briefs.** Compare and contrast different solutions for solving problems.
- **Business plans.** Synthesize ideas and proposals into one coherent plan.
- **Memos and letters.** Synthesize multiple ideas, events, and proposals into concise form.
- **Web sites.** Synthesize information presented in Web pages and related links.

PURPOSE

Your purpose in reading source materials and then in drawing on them to write your own material is often reflected in the wording of an assignment. For instance, consider the following assignments on the Civil War:

American History: Evaluate the author's treatment of the origins of the Civil War.

Economics: Argue the following proposition, in light of your readings: "The Civil War was fought not for reasons of moral principle but for reasons of economic necessity."

Government: Prepare a report on the effects of the Civil War on Southern politics at the state level between 1870 and 1917.

Mass Communications: Discuss how the use of photography during the Civil War may have affected the perceptions of the war by Northerners living in industrial cities.

Literature: Select two twentieth-century Southern writers whose work you believe was influenced by the divisive effects of the Civil War. Discuss the ways this influence is apparent in a novel or a group of short stories written by each author. The works should not be *about* the Civil War.

Applied Technology: Compare and contrast the technology of warfare available in the 1860s with the technology available a century earlier.

Each of these assignments creates for you a particular purpose for writing. Having located sources relevant to your topic, you would select, for possible use in a paper, only those parts that helped you in fulfilling this purpose. And how you used those parts, how you related them to other material from other sources, would also depend on your purpose. For instance, if you were working on the government assignment, you might possibly draw on the same source as another student working on the literature assignment by referring to Robert Penn Warren's novel *All the King's Men*, about Louisiana politics in the early part of the twentieth century. But because the purposes of these assignments are different, you and the other student would make different uses of this source. Those same parts or aspects of the novel that you find worthy of detailed analysis might be mentioned only in passing by the other student.

USING YOUR SOURCES

Your purpose determines not only what parts of your sources you will use but also how you will relate them to one another. Since the very essence of synthesis is the combining of information and ideas, you must have some basis on which to combine them. *Some relationships among the material in your sources must make them worth synthesizing.* It follows that the better able you are to discover such relationships, the better able you will be to use your sources in writing syntheses. Notice that the mass communications assignment requires you to draw a *cause-and-effect* relationship between photographs of the war and Northerners' perceptions of the war. The applied technology assignment requires you to *compare and contrast* state-of-the-art weapons technology in the eighteenth and nineteenth centuries. The economics assignment requires you to *argue* a proposition. In each case, *your purpose will determine how you relate your source materials to one another.*

Consider some other examples. You may be asked on an exam question or in instructions for a paper to *describe* two or three approaches to prison reform during the past decade. You may be asked to *compare and contrast* one country's approach to imprisonment with another's. You may be asked to develop an *argument* of your own on this subject, based on your reading. Sometimes (when you are not given a specific assignment) you determine your own purpose: You are interested in exploring a particular subject; you are interested in making a case for one approach or another. In any event, your purpose shapes your essay. Your purpose determines which sources you research, which ones you use, which parts of them you use, at which points in your essay you use them, and in what manner you relate them to one another.

TYPES OF SYNTHESES: EXPLANATORY AND ARGUMENT

In this and the next chapter we categorize syntheses into two main types: *explanatory* and *argument.* The easiest way to recognize the difference between these two types may be to consider the difference between a newspaper article and an editorial on the same subject. Most likely, we'd say that the main purpose of the newspaper article is to convey *information,* and the main purpose of the editorial is to convey *opinion* or *interpretation.* Of course, this distinction is much too simplified: newspaper articles often convey opinion or bias, sometimes subtly, sometimes openly; and editorials often convey unbiased information, along with opinion. But as a practical matter, we can generally agree on the distinction between a newspaper article that *primarily* conveys information and an editorial that *primarily* conveys opinion.

We'll say, for the sake of convenience, that the newspaper article provides an *explanation* and that the editorial provides an *argument.* This is essentially the distinction we make between explanatory and argument syntheses.

As an example, consider the following paragraph:

> Researchers now use recombinant DNA technology to analyze genetic changes. With this technology, they cut and splice DNA from different species, then insert the modified molecules into bacteria or other types of cells that engage in rapid replication and cell division. The cells copy the foreign DNA right along with their own. In short order, huge populations produce useful quantities of recombinant DNA molecules. The new technology also is the basis of genetic engineering, by which genes are isolated, modified, and inserted back into the same organism or into a different one.*

Now consider this paragraph:

> Many in the life sciences field would have us believe that the new gene splicing technologies are irrepressible and irreversible and that any attempt to oppose their introduction is both futile and retrogressive. They never stop to even consider the possibility that the new genetic science might be used in a wholly different manner than is currently being proposed. The fact is, the corporate agenda is only one of two potential paths into the Biotech Century. It is possible that the growing

---

* Cecie Starr and Ralph Taggart, "Recombinant DNA and Genetic Engineering," *Biology: The Unity and Diversity of Life* (New York: Wadsworth: 1998).

number of anti-eugenic activists around the world might be able to ignite a global debate around alternative uses of the new science—approaches that are less invasive, more sustainable and humane and that conserve and protect the genetic rights of future generations.*

Both of these passages deal with the topic of biotechnology, but the two take quite different approaches. The first passage came from a biology textbook, while the second appeared in a magazine article. As we might expect from a textbook on the broad subject of biology, the first passage is explanatory and informative; it defines and explains some of the key concepts of biotechnology without taking a position or providing commentary about the implications of the technology. Magazine articles often present information in the same ways; however, many magazine articles take specific positions, as we see in the second passage. This passage is argumentative or persuasive. Its primary purpose is to convey a point of view regarding the topic of biotechnology.

While each of these excerpts presents a clear instance of writing that is either explanatory or argumentative, it is important to note that the sources for these excerpts—the textbook chapter and the magazine article—both contain elements of explanation and argument. The textbook writers, while they refrain from taking a particular position, do go on to note the controversies surrounding biotechnology and genetic engineering. They might even subtly reveal a certain bias in favor of one side of the issue, through their word choice, tone, and perhaps through devoting more space and attention to one point of view. Explanatory and argumentative writing are not entirely mutually exclusive. The overlap in the categories of explanation and argument is also found in the magazine article: In order to make his case against genetic engineering, the writer has to explain certain elements of the issue. Yet, even while these categories overlap to a certain extent, the second passage clearly has argument as its primary purpose, while the first passage is primarily explanatory.

In Chapter 2 we noted that the primary purpose in a piece of writing is either informative, persuasive, or entertaining (or some combination of the three). Some scholars of writing argue that all writing is essentially persuasive, and even without entering into that complex argument, we've just seen how the varying purposes in writing do overlap. In order to persuade someone of a particular position we typically must also inform them about it; conversely, a primarily informative piece of writing also must work to persuade the reader that its claims are truthful. Both informative and persuasive writing often include entertaining elements, and writing intended primarily to entertain also typically contains information and persuasion. For practical purposes, however, it is possible—and useful—to identify the *primary* purpose in a piece of writing as informative/explanatory, persuasive/argumentative, or entertaining. Entertainment as a primary purpose is the one least often

---

* Jeremy Rifkin, "The Ultimate Therapy: Commercial Eugenics on the Eve of the Biotech Century," *Tikkun* May–June 1998: 35.

practiced in purely academic writing—perhaps to your disappointment!—but information and persuasion are ubiquitous. Thus, while recognizing the overlap between these categories, we distinguish in this and the following chapter between two types of synthesis writing: explanatory (or informative), and argument (or persuasive). Just as distinguishing the primary purpose in a piece of writing helps you to critically read and evaluate it, distinguishing the primary purpose in your own writing helps you to make the appropriate choices regarding your approach.

In this chapter we'll first present some guidelines for writing syntheses in general, then we'll proceed to focus on explanatory syntheses. In the following chapter, we'll discuss the argument synthesis.

HOW TO WRITE SYNTHESES

Although writing syntheses can't be reduced to a lockstep method, it should help you to follow the guidelines listed in the following box.

GUIDELINES FOR WRITING SYNTHESES

- **Consider your purpose in writing.** What are you trying to accomplish in your essay? How will this purpose shape the way you approach your sources?
- **Select and carefully read your sources**, according to your purpose. Then reread the passages, mentally summarizing each. Identify those aspects or parts of your sources that will help you in fulfilling your purpose. When rereading, *label* or *highlight* the sources for main ideas, key terms, and any details you want to use in the synthesis.
- **Take notes on your reading.** In addition to labeling or underlining key points in the readings, you might write brief one- or two-sentence summaries of each source. This will help you in formulating your thesis statement, and in choosing and organizing your sources later.
- **Formulate a thesis.** Your thesis is the main idea that you want to present in your synthesis. It should be expressed as a complete sentence. You might do some predrafting about the ideas discussed in the readings in order to help you work out a thesis. If you've written one-sentence summaries of the readings, looking these over will help you to brainstorm connections between readings and devise a thesis.

  When you write your paper drafts, you will need to consider where your thesis fits in your paper. Sometimes the thesis is the first sentence, but more often it is *the final sentence of the first paragraph.* If you are writing an *inductively arranged* synthesis (see page 148), the thesis sentence may not appear until the final paragraphs. (See Chapter 3 for more information on writing an effective thesis.)

- **Decide how you will use your source material.** How will the information and the ideas in the passages help you fulfill your purpose?
- **Develop an organizational plan,** according to your thesis. How will you arrange your material? It is not necessary to prepare a formal outline. But you should have some plan that will indicate the order in which you will present your material and that will indicate the relationships among your sources.
- **Draft the topic sentences for the main sections.** This is an optional step, but you may find it a helpful transition from organizational plan to first draft.
- **Write the first draft** of your synthesis, following your organizational plan. Be flexible with your plan, however. Frequently, you will use an outline to get started. As you write, you may discover new ideas and make room for them by adjusting the outline. When this happens, reread your work frequently, making sure that your thesis still accounts for what follows and that what follows still logically supports your thesis.
- **Document your sources.** You must do this by crediting them within the body of the synthesis—citing the author's last name and page number from which the point was taken and by providing full citation information in a list of "Works Cited" at the end. (See Chapter 6 for more information on documenting sources.)
- **Revise your synthesis,** inserting transitional words and phrases where necessary. Make sure that the synthesis reads smoothly, logically, and clearly from beginning to end. Check for grammatical correctness, punctuation, spelling.

Note: The writing of syntheses is a recursive process, and you should accept a certain amount of backtracking and reformulating as inevitable. For instance, in developing an organizational plan (Step 6 of the procedure), you may discover a gap in your presentation that will send you scrambling for another source—back to Step 2. You may find that formulating a thesis and making inferences among sources occur simultaneously; indeed, inferences often are made before a thesis is formulated. Our recommendations for writing syntheses will give you a structure; they will get you started. But be flexible in your approach; expect discontinuity and, if possible, be assured that through backtracking and reformulating you will eventually produce a coherent, well-crafted essay.

THE EXPLANATORY SYNTHESIS

Many of the papers you write in college will be more or less explanatory in nature. An explanation helps readers understand a topic. Writers explain when they divide a subject into its component parts and present them to the reader in a clear and orderly fashion. Explanations may entail descriptions that recreate in words some object, place, emotion, event, sequence of events, or state of affairs. As a student reporter, you may need to explain an event—to relate when, where, and how it took place. In a science lab, you would observe the conditions and results of an experiment and record them for review by others. In a political science course, you might review research on a particular subject—say, the complexities underlying the debate over school vouchers—and then present the results of your research to your professor and the members of your class.

Your job in writing an explanatory paper—or in writing the explanatory portion of an argumentative paper—is not to argue a particular point, but rather *to present the facts in a reasonably objective manner*. Of course, explanatory papers, like other academic papers, should be based on a thesis. But the purpose of a thesis in an explanatory paper is less to advance a particular opinion than to focus the various facts contained in the paper.

DEMONSTRATION: EXPLANATORY SYNTHESIS—COMPUTERS, COMMUNICATION, AND RELATIONSHIPS

To illustrate how the process of synthesis works, we'll begin with a number of short extracts from several articles on the same subject.

Suppose you were writing a paper on a matter that many computer users are discussing these days: the ways in which communication via computers (that is, computer mediated communication, or CMC) is changing human patterns of interaction, communication, and relationships. In this Information Age when people all over the world can use various forums on the Internet to communicate with one another, many questions arise about this relatively new form of communication. Some writers and thinkers are excited about the world of possibilities opened up by this technological medium; others are skeptical about whether the Internet will lead to more interaction and connection between people, or will harm the quality of such connections. Still others argue that this new mode of communication is likely to further isolate us from each other, and "real" human contact will become a rare and precious thing.

EXERCISE 4.1

Exploring the Topic

Before reading what others have written on the subject of computers, communication, and relationships, write several paragraphs exploring what you know and what you think about this topic. You might focus your first paragraph on discussing your own experience with computer communication and relationships. How much have you used e-mail, instant messaging, and other Internet-related activity? How have these technologies affected your ability to communicate with others? What are some of the positive and negative impacts of such communication on relationships? In your second paragraph try broadening the focus by discussing what you know about these issues in the world at large. What are some of the concerns people have about computers and their effects on communication? What do you think most interests journalists, professors, politicians, and businesspeople about computer communication and relationships?

Because this is a topic that bears upon a broader subject—the ways that computers and the Internet affect our lives—you decide to investigate what has been written on the subject, both in print and electronic texts. In the following pages we present excerpts from the kinds of articles your research might locate.

Note: To save space and for the purpose of demonstration, the following passages are brief excerpts only. In preparing your paper, naturally you would draw upon the entire articles from which these extracts were made.

Cyberspace: A New Frontier for Fighting Words
Sanjiv N. Singh

Sanjiv N. Singh holds a J.D. from the UCLA School of Law. The article from which this piece is excerpted appeared in the Rutgers Computer and Technology Law Journal *in 1999.*

[T]he Internet has begun to transform the way in which people interact. Various mediums now exist that allow for cheap and almost instantaneous communication via computer. For example, e-mail is now an increasingly common way to communicate with family, friends, and acquaintances. In fact, more than fifteen percent of the U.S. adult population use e-mail [...]. Technology research firms estimate that by the year 2001, fifty percent of the U.S. population will communicate via e-mail [...].

Many colleges and graduate schools routinely provide students with, and in some cases require, use of e-mail accounts. As a result, significant segments of our population are being socialized in an environment where cyberspace communication is an encouraged form of establishing and confirming social engagements or simply corresponding with friends.

Social Relationships in Electronic Forums: Hangouts, Salons, Workplaces and Communities
Rob Kling

Rob Kling is a professor of Information Systems and Information Science in the School for Library and Information Science at the University of Indiana at Bloomington. He has

published numerous articles examining the impact of information technologies on organi-
zations, the workplace, publishing and education, as well as social life. His books include
Computerization and Controversy: Value Conflicts and Social Choices *(1996), and* Computers
and Politics: High Technology in American Local Governments *(1982). The following reading*
is excerpted from an essay that appeared in CMC Magazine.*

Enthusiasts for [Internet] forums argue that they are building new forms of community life (Rheingold, 1993). But other analysts observe that not every collection
of people who happen to talk (or write) to each other form the sense of trust,
mutual interest, and sustained commitments that automatically deserve to be
labeled as communities (Jones, 1995). [...]

In the United States, communities seem to be deteriorating from a complex
combination of causes. In the inner cities of big urban centers, many people fear
street crime and stay off the streets at night. In the larger suburban and post-sub-
urban areas, many people hardly know their neighbors and "latch key" children
often have little adult contact after school. An African proverb which says that "it
takes a whole village to raise a child" refers to a rich community life with a sense
of mutual responsibility that is difficult to find in many new neighborhoods. Some
advocates believe that computer technology in concert with other efforts could
play a role in rebuilding community life by improving communication, economic
opportunity, civic participation, and education (Schuler, 1994; Civille, Fidelman, and
Altobello, 1993).

Signs of Life in the USA
Sonia Maasik and Jack Solomon

Sonia Maasik is a member of the Writing Program faculty at UCLA, and Jack Solomon is an
English professor at California State College, Northridge. In addition to their popular textbook
(from which this excerpt comes) Signs of Life in the USA: Readings on Popular Culture for
Writers *(3rd edition, 2000), the two have also collaborated on* California Dreams and
Realities: Readings for Critical Thinkers and Writers *(1999).†*

The emerging outlines of the Web's global village have some people very excited
and others worried. The worried contingent are concerned that the relationships
people are building on the Net lack an essential core of humanity. The unreal world
of virtual culture, they believe, the world in which you can pretend to be just about
anything, is being substituted for a social reality made up of real human beings.
And such a world, based entirely on the transmission of electronic signals, is potentially a world in which human beings will be unable to conceive of others as

---

* Rob Kling, "Social Relationships in Electronic Forums: Hangouts, Salons, Workplaces and Communities,"
CMC Magazine 22 July 1996, 4 Feb. 2000 <http://www.december.com/cmc/mag/1996/jul/kling.html>.

† Sonia Maasik and Jack Solomon, eds., *Signs of Life in the USA* (Boston: Bedford Books, 1997) 701.

human beings. When all interaction is electronic, they ask, where is the ground for true human empathy and relatedness?

Life at High-Tech U
Deborah Branscum

A contributing editor to Newsweek, *a columnist for* Fortune.com's *"Valley Talk," and a free-lance technology writer, Deborah Branscum has written articles for a number of publications, including* Wired, The New York Times, Infoworld, *and* Yahoo Internet Life. *She operates a web site called* MonsterBuzz.com, *and founded its affiliated* BUZZ *executive conference.**

Some academics dismiss [e-mail] as an unhealthy substitute for human contact. But Stanford's Richard Holeton, who tracked e-mail discussions of first-year students in one dorm, found that 87 percent of their messages involved important social or critical dialogue. Those issues included "pornography, free speech, a potential grape boycott on campus and a sexual-harassment allegation," says Holeton. And the people who dominated dorm life in face-to-face encounters were not the same folks who ruled the e-mail debates. Electronic discourse, it seems, offered a voice to some students who might not otherwise be heard.

Developing Personal and Emotional Relationships Via Computer-Mediated Communication
Brittney G. Chenault

Brittney G. Chenault holds a degree from the Graduate School of Library and Information Science at the University of Illinois, Urbana-Champaign. This article appeared in the online journal, CMC Magazine, *and has been widely read and quoted since its publication in 1998.*†

The idea of a community accessible only via my computer screen sounded cold to me at first, but I learned quickly that people can feel passionately about e-mail and computer conferences. I've become one of them. I care about these people I met through my computer [...] (Rheingold, 1993, p. 1). [...]

---

* Deborah Branscum, "Life at High-Tech U," *Newsweek* 27 Oct. 1997: 78–80.

† Brittney G. Chenault, "Developing Personal and Emotional Relationships Via Computer-Mediated Communication," *CMC Magazine* May 1998, 20 March 2000. <http://www.december.com/cmc/mag/1998/may/chenault.html>.

People meet via CMC every day, exchange information, debate, argue, woo, commiserate, and support. They may meet via a mailing list or newsgroup, and continue the interaction via e-mail. Their relationships can range from the cold, professional encounter, to the hot, intimate rendezvous. Rheingold describes people in virtual communities as using the words they type on screens to exchange pleasantries and argue, engage in intellectual discourse, conduct commerce, exchange knowledge, share emotional support, make plans, brainstorm, gossip, feud, fall in love, find friends and lose them, play games, flirt, create a little high art and a lot of idle talk.

Cyberspace Romances: Interview with Jean-François Perreault of *Branchez-vous*
John Suler

John Suler is a Professor of Psychology at Rider University in New Jersey, and a practicing psychologist. His publications include Contemporary Psychoanalysis *and* Eastern Thought *(1993) as well as the online hypertext book (Web site)* The Psychology of Cyberspace. *This excerpt comes from that Web site and represents a comment by the interviewee, Jean-François Perreault, of the Quebec, Canada based online magazine* Branchez-Vous.

Perreault: My guess is that in a "true" romance on the Internet, the couple eventually will want to meet each other face-to-face. They may HAVE to meet each other for the relationship to fully develop and to be fully satisfying. For these people, the Internet simply was a way to meet each other. I say "simply" but this feature of the Internet shouldn't be underestimated. It is a POWERFUL way for people with compatible interests and personalities to find each other.

There are some people who may NOT want to meet the lover face-to-face. My guess is that these people prefer living with the fantasy that they have created (consciously or unconsciously) about the cyber-lover [...]. They may not want to meet each other face-to-face because the fantasy might be destroyed by the hard facts of reality. Who can say whether this is "wrong" or "dangerous?" Many people allow themselves the luxury of fantasy—either through books, or TV, or movies. And most people don't confuse this fantasy with reality. A cyber-lover is just another type of "escape fantasy"—only it's much more interactive, and therefore much more exciting, than the more usual methods.

John Suler, "Cyberspace Romances: Interview with Jean-François Perreault of *Branchez-vous*," *The Psychology of Cyberspace*, 11 Dec. 1996, 7 April 2000 <http://www.rider.edu/users/suler/psycyber/psycyber.html>.

Click Here for Romance
Jennifer Wolcott

A staff writer for The Christian Science Monitor, *Jennifer Wolcott writes on a wide range of topics, including social issues, the arts, and popular culture.**

Online chat can sprout real-life romances that begin with surprisingly honest communication and realistic expectations, traits that many traditional relationships lack at first, according to an Ohio University sociologist who is studying relationships that begin in cyberspace. "I really feel the basis of these relationships is better and deeper than many real-life meetings because the couples are honest with each other in their writings," says Andrea Baker, assistant professor of sociology at Ohio University's Lancaster campus [...]. Baker's study suggests the written word tends to promote frank conversation in cyberspace, especially between couples who eventually want to meet face-to-face. Study participants said this immediate sincerity when meeting online was a pleasant switch from the typical blind date scenario. "Couples say this kind of honesty is absolutely necessary to forming a good relationship," Baker says. "In most cases, they are extremely honest and really cover the downsides as well as the upsides so there won't be any surprises when they meet." [...]

Honesty is what most appealed to California resident John Dwyer about the online approach. Disillusioned with the bar scene, he decided to give it a whirl. He posted a personal ad and photograph, got hundreds of responses, and eventually connected with Debbie. They married this past New Year's Eve—a year and a half after she answered his online ad. "If you are honest when talking online, you can strip away all the superficial stuff and really get to know someone," says Debbie. How did she know John was being honest? "I got a sense from the conversation whether it was real or contrived," she says. "I could tell after a while that he wasn't just someone trying to land a fish."

You've Got Romance! Seeking Love Online: Net-Based Services Change the Landscape, If Not the Odds, of Finding the Perfect Mate
Bonnie Rothman Morris

Bonnie Rothman Morris is a journalist and screenwriter who writes frequently for The New York Times, *which is the source for this excerpt. Morris's screenplays include the comedies "Guy and Doll," and "Taking the Leap."*†

---

* Jennifer Wolcott, "Click Here for Romance," *The Christian Science Monitor* 13 Jan. 1999, 23 Feb. 2000 <http://www.csmonitor.com/durable/1991/01/13/fp11s1-csm.shtml>.

† Bonnie R. Morris, "You've Got Romance! Seeking Love Online: Net-Based Services Change the Landscape, If Not the Odds, of Finding the Perfect Mate," *New York Times on the Web* 26 Aug. 1999, 23 Feb. 2000 <http://www.nytimes.com/library/tech/yr/mo/circuits/index.html>.

Tom Buckley didn't have much use for a dating service, or so he thought. "I didn't need to pay a company to help set me up to get a date, a girlfriend, a fiancée, a wife," said Buckley, 30, a steel broker in Portland, Ore., who plays rugby in his spare time. But after a lonely Thanksgiving dinner where he was the only single adult at the family dinner table, Buckley signed up for a free week on Match.com. What ensued on the matchmaking service was an e-mail romance with Terri Muir, a schoolteacher on Vancouver Island in British Columbia. "Anybody who knew us would never have thought we would have gone down that road," Buckley said in a telephone interview. Reflecting on the couple's instant attraction, he said, "e-mail made it easier to communicate because neither one of us was the type to walk up to someone in the gym or a bar and say, 'You're the fuel to my fire.'"

Thirteen months after their first feverish exchanges, Buckley and Ms. Muir lied to their family and friends and sneaked away to Vancouver to meet for the first time. At their wedding one year later, they finally told the tale of how they had met to their 100 guests. More and more single people, used to finding everything else on the Internet, are using it to search for love. More than 2,500 Web sites for adults are now devoted to matchmaking, said Daniel Bender, founder of Cupid's Network, an Internet portal for personals sites. [...]

[Robert Spradling] struck up an online romance with a Ukrainian woman whom he had met on American Singles. The woman immediately asked him for money to pay the agency she was using to translate and send her romantic e-mails back to him. There are many such agencies in the former Soviet Union, Spradling said. Next she told Spradling she wanted to start her own matchmaking agency. Spradling, 42, an employee in the development office at Morehead State University in Kentucky, footed the bill for that, too. After sending her about $8,000, Spradling asked her to marry him, via e-mail. She said yes and invited him to Kiev. "When you meet some-body and you think you're in love, you never see any faults," said Spradling, who said the couple had made wedding plans when he was visiting. After his return to the United States, Spradling never heard from her again. He's sworn off finding love through the Internet for now [...]. "I caution a lot of guys to be careful and keep their head and learn a lot about who they're dating online," Spradling said.

Consider Your Purpose

Here, then, are brief selections from eight sources on computer mediated communication. How do you go about synthesizing these sources?

First, remember that before considering the *how,* you must consider the *why.* In other words, what is your *purpose* in synthesizing these sources? You might use them for a paper dealing with a broader issue: the effects of computer technology on our daily lives, or on daily human interactions and relationships. If this were your purpose, these sources would be used for only one section of your discussion, and the paper as a whole would advance an *argument* for a particular viewpoint about technology in modern society. Or, for a communications course you might consider the impact technology is having on communication, comparing this kind of communication with other forms of written communication and/or with face-to-face, verbal communication. The various positions and uses of computer mediated conversation (CMC) would be important examples of how communication is changing. Or, moving out of the academic world and into the commercial one, you might be a computer consultant preparing a brochure for a new Internet application or matchmaking Web site. In this brochure, you might want to address the personal uses to which people put these kinds of applications, or for the Web site, you would focus on the positive aspects of forming relationships on the Internet.

But for now let's keep it simple: you want to write a paper, or a section of a paper, that simply explains the impact the Internet is having on relationships between people so that people who may be interested, but who know little or nothing about these issues, will understand some aspects of the CMC phenomenon. Your job, then, is to write an *explanatory* synthesis—one that presents a focused overview of computer mediated communication but does not advance your own opinion on the subject.

EXERCISE 4.2

Critical Reading for Synthesis

Look over the preceding readings and make a list of the different ways they address the broad topics of computers, communication, and relationships. Make your list as specific and detailed as you can. Then write several lists grouping together the readings that deal with similar aspects of the overall topics. Imagine that you are planning to write a very short synthesis on one small aspect of the broad topic. For different aspects of the topic, which readings would you use?

We asked one of our students, Alyssa Mellott, to read these passages and to use them as sources in a short paper on some of the issues surrounding CMC. We also asked her to write some additional comments describing the process of developing her ideas into a draft. We'll draw upon some of these comments in the following discussion.

Formulate a Thesis

The difference between a purpose and a thesis is a difference primarily of focus. Your purpose provides direction to your research and focus to your paper. Your thesis sharpens this focus by narrowing it and formulating it in the words of a single declarative statement. (Refer to Chapter 3 for additional discussion on formulating thesis statements.)

Since Alyssa's purpose in this case was simply to summarize source material with little or no comment, her thesis would be the most obvious statement she could make about the relationship among these passages. By "obvious" we mean a statement that characterizes all of these readings' main points. Taken as a whole, what do they *mean*? Here Alyssa describes the process she followed in coming up with a preliminary thesis for her explanatory synthesis:

I began my writing process by looking over all the readings and noting the main point of each reading in a sentence on a piece of paper.

Then I reviewed all of these points and identified the patterns in the readings. These I listed as follows: (1) All the readings focus on Internet communication, or CMC. (2) The readings address several different kinds of relationships the authors believe are affected by CMC: communal relationships, relationships between long-distance friends, those between students and instructors, and love relationships. (3) Some authors discuss positive views, others negative views, of CMC and relationships.

Looking over these points, I drafted a preliminary thesis. This thesis summed up the different issues in the sources and stated how these interrelated.

> The Internet is changing the ways people interact and form relationships.

This was a true statement, but it was also too vague and too obvious. I didn't feel it adequately represented the readings' points, since the readings explored a number of specific kinds of interactions and relationships impacted by CMC. I wanted my thesis to more fully reflect the complexity of people's concern regarding technology and relationships. My next version followed:

> Computers and the Internet add new ways for people to interact, but we have yet to see whether or not these new modes of communication will improve human interaction.

This thesis was more comprehensive, but it still didn't quite work. It was still vague, and the last part seemed bland; it didn't reflect the strong feelings the writers expressed about the possible effects of CMC on different kinds of relationships. In my next attempt, I tried to be more specific and a little more dramatic:

> With so many computer users forming a variety of online relationships, no one can deny that this new technology is affecting our modes of communication; however, reactions to these changes range widely from excitement over our abilities to forge global connections, to fear that such connections will

```
prove much less satisfying than old-fashioned human
interactions.
```

```
     This sentence was quite long, but I felt the
first part of the sentence introduced the real
point of my essay: that people have certain mixed
reactions to how CMC will affect relationships. I
thought this would be a good working thesis because
it would help me structure my essay around specif-
ic views on CMC. Now I proceeded to the next step
in writing—organizing my material.
```

Decide How You Will Use Your Source Material

The easiest way to deal with sources is to summarize them. But because you are synthesizing *ideas* rather than sources, you will have to be more selective than if you were writing a simple summary. You don't have to treat *all* the ideas in your sources, only the ones related to your thesis. Some sources might be summarized in their entirety; others, only in part. Look over your earlier notes or sentences summarizing each reading, and refer back to the readings themselves. Focusing on some of the more subtle elements of the issues addressed by the authors, expand your earlier summary sentences. Write brief phrases in the margin, highlight key phrases or sentences, or take notes on a separate sheet of paper or in a word processing file or electronic data filing program. Decide how your sources can help you achieve your purpose and support your thesis. For example, how, if at all, will you use the quotations by Rheingold contained in the passage by Chenault? How could you incorporate the personal experiences reported by some of the people who formed romantic attachments online?

Develop an Organizational Plan

An organizational plan is your map for presenting material to the reader. What material will you present? To find out, examine your thesis. Do the content and structure of the thesis (that is, the number and order of assertions) suggest an organizational plan for the paper? Expect to devote at least one paragraph of your paper to developing each section of this plan. Having identified likely sections, think through the possibilities of arrangement. Ask yourself: What information does the reader need to understand first? How do I build on this first section—what block of information will follow? Think of each section in relation to others until you have placed them all and have worked your way through to a plan for the whole paper.

Study your thesis, and let it help suggest an organization. Bear in mind that any one paper can be written—successfully—according to a variety of plans. Your job before beginning your first draft is to explore possibilities. Sketch a series of rough outlines: Arrange and rearrange your paper's likely sections until you develop a plan that both fosters the reader's understanding and achieves your objectives as a writer. Think carefully about the logical order of your points: Does one idea or point lead to the next? If not, can you find a more logical place for the point, or are you just not clearly articulating the connections between the ideas?

Your final paper may well deviate from your final sketch, since in the act of writing you may discover the need to explore new material, to omit planned material, to refocus or to reorder your entire presentation. Just the same, a well-conceived organizational plan will encourage you to begin writing a draft.

Alyssa describes the process of organizing the material as follows:

> In reviewing my sources and writing summary statements, I noted the most important aspects of the computer interaction issue, according to the authors:
>
> - An increasing number of people use the Internet to interact in new ways (Singh 102).
> - In this era when community life is threatened by social and economic hardships, advocates of Internet communication believe this technology could help improve community life by "improving communication, economic opportunity, civic participation, and education" (Kling 103).
> - Some fear the ways in which real human interaction is being taken over by "virtual culture" (Maasik and Solomon 103).
> - The Internet offers college students additional opportunities for meaningful "social or critical" discussions. It may be a useful outlet for otherwise quiet people (Branscum 104).
> - Although the idea of interacting through the computer may sound impersonal, people who are involved in the many varieties of virtual communication come to form meaningful attachments to each other. (Chenault 104–105).
> - Whether or not romances that begin over the Internet end up moving out into the real world, this form of communication has enormous potential for bringing together people with similar interests (Suler 105).
> - A sociologist studying Internet romances found that participants were generally quite honest and open with one another at

the start of their relationships—perhaps even more honest than people beginning relationships in more traditional ways. (Wolcott 106).

· A large number of Web sites offer matchmaking services, and people using such services report both positive and negative outcomes. People should be cautious, however, as some experiences show that it's easy to be duped by a potential partner via computer (Morris 107).

I tried to group some of these topics into categories that would have a logical order. The first thing that I wanted to communicate was the growing prevalence of the Internet in our everyday lives and the variety of relationships that can develop online, which has sparked a debate over the quality of these.

Next, I thought I should explain what Internet enthusiasts are so excited about. I wanted to discuss the idea of using the Internet to rebuild community life.

I also wanted to explain the position of those who feel that Internet relationships will prove to be less satisfying than old-fashioned human interactions. On the other hand, I wanted to explain that some people feel that the Internet can add additional qualities to communication that traditional human interaction lacks.

Next, I intended to counter this optimistic view with words of caution from Internet skeptics about romantic relationships that begin online.

Finally, I planned to conclude with a short summary of the debate.

I returned to my thesis:

With so many computer users forming a variety of online relationships, no one can deny that this new technology is affecting our modes of communication; however, reactions to these changes range widely from excitement over our abilities to forge global connections, to fear that such connections will prove much less satisfying than old-fashioned human interactions.

Based on her thesis, Alyssa developed an outline for a seven-paragraph paper, including introduction and conclusion:

A. Introduction: explanation of the debate surrounding CMC.

B. Enthusiasm over the possibilities that the Internet provides for communication.

C. Skepticism about the quality of Internet relationships.

D. Advantages of Internet relationships over old-fashioned relationships.

E. Specific example of a relationship formed online.

F. Words of caution and a negative example.

G. Conclusion: summing up.

Write the Topic Sentences

This is an optional step, but writing draft versions of topic sentences will get you started on each main idea of your synthesis and will help give you the sense of direction you need to proceed. Here are Alyssa's draft topic sentences for sections based on the thesis and organizational plan she developed. Note that when read in sequence following the thesis, these sentences give an idea of the logical progression of the essay as a whole.

- An increasing number of people are becoming Internet users every day.

- Using the Internet to strengthen community life may sound like a good idea; however, skeptics warn that the quality of relationships formed through the Internet is not up to par with those formed through face-to-face human interactions.

- The argument has been taken a step further by those who contend that the Internet offers certain advantages for communication that face-to-face human interactions cannot.

- Research indicates that at the start of a relationship, participants in Internet romances are often more honest and open with one another than their counterparts in traditional dating situations.

- With increasing numbers of people using Internet matchmaking services, skeptics remind us that people should exercise caution in getting to know people via CMC.

Write Your Synthesis

Here is the first draft of Alyssa's explanatory synthesis. Thesis and topic sentences are highlighted. Modern Language Association (MLA) documentation style, explained in Chapter 6, is used throughout. Note that for the sake of clarity, parenthetical references are to pages in *Writing and Reading Across the Curriculum*.

Opposite each page of this first draft, we have included Alyssa's instructor's comments and suggestions for revision.

Model Synthesis

Advantages and Disadvantages of Computer Mediated Communication
Alyssa Mellott

1 From the home, to the workplace, to the classroom, the Internet has clicked its way into our everyday lives. On any given day, research papers may be e-mailed to professors, ads are posted to sell just about anything, and arrangements to meet significant others for dinner and a movie can be made—all with the help of the Internet. In addition to providing us with such conveniences, computer mediated communication (CMC) provides a medium for fostering new relationships. Whether you are looking for a business partner, fellow political enthusiasts, or a future spouse, the Internet can be a powerful tool for uniting people with similar interests. With so many computer users forming a variety of online relationships, no one can deny that this new technology is affecting our modes of communication; however, reactions to these changes range widely from excitement over our abilities to forge global connections, to fear that such connections will prove much less satisfying than old-fashioned human interactions.

2 An increasing number of people are becoming Internet users every day. It is estimated that by the year 2001, "fifty percent of the U.S. population will communicate via e-mail" (Singh 102). Is the growing popularity of the Internet as a form of communication and its effect on our modes of communication a positive trend? Champions of the Internet point out that in transforming the way people interact, the Internet has made communication faster, more efficient, and less expensive. Internet enthusiasts also feel that Internet

Discussion and Suggestions for Revision

The following section summarizes the key points and suggestions for revision made during Alyssa's conference with her instructor.

Title and Paragraph 1

Your title could be more interesting and less mechanical. Your first paragraph introduces the subject with some good, specific examples, but you sound a bit too much like a proponent of the new technology, rather than a writer who is objectively presenting various positions on CMC's potential.

Your thesis statement could be shortened and tightened up. While it's good that you aim to specifically characterize the two overall positions regarding CMC, you end up over-simplifying things a bit.

Suggestions for Revision: Make the current title more interesting and less focused on a clear-cut set of oppositions.

In order to maintain an objective stance—since this essay is meant to be explanatory rather than argumentative—you might cut some of your examples here and get to the point sooner. You could then follow your introduction with a paragraph in which you develop some of the background points you raise in your current introduction—that the Internet has enormous potential for "uniting people with similar interests," as you say. You could refer to points from the readings to make your discussion more objectively explanatory.

Shorten your thesis statement by separating the two ideas you've currently joined with a semicolon: the first clause introduces the thesis you state in the second clause, so separating these ideas will help emphasize your essay's main point. More important, rephrase your thesis so that it more accurately characterizes the positions offered in the readings. For example, none of the readings emphasizes the "global" dimension to the connections forged on the Internet, nor does the notion of "fear" that Internet relations will be "less satisfying than old-fashioned...interactions" adequately account for the negative views regarding CMC. Back up a bit and formulate a slightly less specific—and more comprehensive—statement.

Edit your use of passive voice—*who* e-mails papers to professors? Avoid clichéd phrases such as "on any given day...."

Paragraph 2

This paragraph starts with a good background point about the prevalence of the Internet in our lives, then you shift to one of the key reasons some people are excited about CMC. The first idea does lead to the second, but could bear more development, as could your second point about CMC's community-building potential.

Suggestions for Revision: Consider splitting this paragraph in two. As suggested in the comments on paragraph 1, some of the points raised in your introduction could be moved to a background paragraph—and the first two sentences in this current paragraph 2 would fit there. Look back over the

forums "are building new forms of community life" (Kling 103). It has been suggested that CMC could play a role in "rebuilding [deteriorating] community life" in inner cities, suburban, and postsuburban areas of the United States. Kling quotes an African proverb "it takes a whole village to raise a child" to express the need for a "rich community life" based on "mutual responsibility" that seems to be lacking in our modern neighborhoods (103). Some observers feel CMC can improve "communication, economic opportunity, civic participation, and education" (Kling 103).

3   Using the Internet to strengthen community life may sound like a good idea; however, skeptics warn that the quality of relationships formed through the Internet is not up to par with those formed through face-to-face human interactions. Analysts have observed that not everyone who communicates via the Internet forms "the sense of trust, mutual interest, and sustained commitments" that characterize communities (Kling 103). Others are concerned that the relationships people are building through the Internet "lack an essential core of humanity" (Maasik and Solomon 103). They feel that our social reality made up of real people is being taken over by a virtual culture. It is within this virtual culture that a danger exists for people to become "unable to conceive of others as human beings," resulting in an environment lacking in "human empathy and relatedness" (Maasik and Solomon 103–104). Similarly, some teachers consider e-mail to be "an unhealthy substitute for human contact" (Branscum 104).

4   The argument has been taken a step further by some who contend that the Internet can provide certain advantages to communication that face-to-face human interactions cannot. In a study of first-year college students, Stanford's Richard Holeton found that students who were ordinarily reserved were often the most active participants in Internet discussions (Branscum 104). Similarly, the Internet can serve as a way for people who are having trouble dating to find romantic partners. For instance, Tom Buckley met his wife after signing up with Match.com. Buckley noted that the Internet helped him to meet his wife because "neither one of us was the type to walk up to someone in the gym or a bar and say, 'You're the fuel to my fire'" (qtd. in Morris 107). Holeton's research and Tom Buckley's experience suggest that the Internet may

readings for more ideas that would help you develop points about CMC's prevalence and its general, positive potential. After discussing that, you could begin a third paragraph focused on the point about the Internet's potential for building communities. Spend more time defining "community" and explaining how, according to its advocates, CMC could replace lost community.

Edit your sentences—you have some repetitive and choppy sentence structures and passive constructions that could be rephrased in the active voice.

Paragraph 3

Paragraph 3 follows logically from paragraph 2, and you make a clear transition in your topic sentence. However, this paragraph's points would be stronger if you had explained the arguments about the Internet's community-building potential in the last paragraph.

In your effort to paraphrase points from the Maasik and Solomon reading, and to intersperse their quoted words with your own, you end up producing wordy and awkward sentences. Furthermore, when you paraphrase the authors in the sentence "They feel that our social reality…," you haven't changed the wording enough to qualify as a legitimate paraphrase.

In the last sentence of this paragraph you throw in another reference that doesn't really add anything to your points. Why do you need this point?

Suggestions for Revision: Once you've added development of your points in paragraph 2, rework the points expressed by the "skeptics" in this paragraph to more clearly relate back to the ideas of community you've just discussed.

Consider dealing with the ideas from Maasik and Solomon in a block quote, or else rework your sentences to more smoothly incorporate their ideas without using their sentence structures and wording.

If you feel the added point in your last sentence is important, then make that importance more clear; if it's really not necessary, then leave it out.

Paragraph 4

The topic sentence is confusing. You write, "The argument has been taken a step further…," and this wording suggests that you're referring to the argument *against* CMC since this is the last argument about which you've written. In actuality, however, you seem to be referring to the entire argument over CMC, not just one side of it. Other than that, this paragraph contains interesting points and good examples.

Suggestions for Revision: Change your opening sentence to more accurately reflect the paragraph's focus.

provide an avenue of expression and opportunity for otherwise quiet or timid individuals.

5   Research indicates that at the start of a relationship, participants in Internet romances are often more honest and open with one another than their counterparts in traditional dating situations. Andrea Baker, assistant professor of sociology at Ohio University's Lancaster campus who is studying romances that start over the Internet, reports that relationships that start online are "better and deeper" than traditional relationships because the couples are honest in the words they write (qtd. in Wolcott 106). Like the participants in Baker's study, California resident John Dwyer found the sincerity present in online communication to be a pleasant change from more traditional dating scenes (Wolcott 106). After posting a personal ad on the Internet, Dwyer met his future wife, Debbie, who commented, "'If you are honest when talking online, you can strip away all the superficial stuff and really get to know someone'" (qtd. in Wolcott 106).

6   With increasing numbers of people using Internet matchmaking services, skeptics remind us that people should exercise caution in getting to know people via CMC. After having his heart broken and his wallet drained by a romantic partner that he met online, Robert Spradling has sworn off using the Internet to find love and warns others to "be careful and keep their head and learn a lot about who they're dating online" (qtd. in Morris 107).

7   Wouldn't it be nice if the saying was "What you read is what you get"? Anyone who has spent even five minutes playing with e-mail cannot deny that the enthusiasm surrounding the possibilities posed for communication by the Internet is warranted. Nevertheless, we must constantly be reminded that the computer screen poses as an effective poker face for those with insincere intentions.

Works Cited

Branscum, Deborah. "Life at High-Tech U." <u>Newsweek</u> 27 Oct. 1997: 78–80.

Kling, Rob. "Social Relationships in Electronic Forums: Hangouts, Salons, Workplaces and Communities." <u>CMC Magazine</u> 22 July 1996. 4 Feb. 2000. <http://www.december.com/cmc/mag/1996/jul/kling.html>.

Maasik, Sonia, and Jack Solomon, eds. <u>Signs of Life in the USA</u>. Boston: Bedford Books, 1997. 701.

Paragraph 5

In paragraph 5 you do a nice job of extending the points in your last paragraph; however, your first sentence here doesn't make that relationship clear. By starting with "Research indicates..." you imply that you're moving on to a new element of CMC, rather than adding to the last point.

Suggestions for Revision: Write a topic sentence that spells out how your new points relate to the last ones. You also might add a sentence that sums up your overall point at the end of the paragraph to help improve the logical "flow" between this paragraph and paragraph 6.

Paragraph 6

Again, you're lacking an effective transition here, one that makes clear the way these new points qualify or limit the positive assessments offered in paragraph 5. The Spradling story provides a nice counterpoint to the happy couple's experience in the last paragraph, but as a reader I don't get a complete picture of the actual events in Spradling's experience.

Suggestions for Revision: Write a better transitional sentence to open the paragraph. Slow down a little and tell Spradling's story more clearly. Review the reading by Suler: is there a way in which a cyberlove relationship might apply to Spradling's difficulties in moving his romance from the online to the off line realm?

Paragraph 7

Your conclusion focuses too much on the last issue raised in your essay, while failing to bring a sense of closure to the essay by pulling together all the points of the essay.

Suggestions for Revision: Think about what all these points add up to. Yes, as your current conclusion states, the Internet can help people hide malignant intentions—but is this the whole story? Are people able to lie and conceal things in real life as well as in the virtual world? And what about your earlier points about community-building and human connection? Try to wrap things up more comprehensively, rather than focusing narrowly on the one issue of deceit.

Morris, Bonnie R. "You've Got Romance! Seeking Love Online: Net-Based Services Change the Landscape, If Not the Odds, of Finding the Perfect Mate." <u>New York Times on the Web</u> 26 Aug. 1996. 23 Feb. 2000 <http://www.nytimes.com/library/tech/yr/mo/circuits/index.html>.

Singh, Sanjiv N. "Cyberspace: A New Frontier for Fighting Words." <u>Rutgers Computer and Technology Law Journal</u> 25.2 (1999): 283.

Wolcott, Jennifer. "Click Here for Romance." <u>The Christian Science Monitor</u> 13 Jan. 1999. 23 Feb. 2000 <http://www.csmonitor.com/durable/1991/01/13/fp11s1-csm.shtml>.

EXERCISE **4.3**

Revising the Sample Synthesis

Try your hand at creating a final draft of this essay by following the suggestions above, together with using your own best judgment about how to improve the first draft. After trying your own version of the essay, compare it to the revised version (below) Alyssa produced after the discussion on revision.

Revised Model Synthesis

Computer Mediated Communication: New and Improved Human Relations Or The End of Real Interaction?
Alyssa Mellott

From the home, to the workplace, to the classroom, the Internet has clicked its way into our everyday lives. Today's students can e-mail as file attachments their end-of-term papers to their professors and can then turn around and use e-mail to gather a group of friends for a party or to celebrate the term's completion. These online exchanges, called CMC (or computer mediated communication) sound fairly commonplace at the turn of the millennium. But what we have yet to discover is how CMC might change both the ways we communicate and the quality of our relationships. While many praise CMC's potential to bridge barriers and promote meaningful dialogue, others caution that CMC is fraught with dangers.

Very soon, half of America will communicate via e-mail, according to analysts (Singh 102). We can only assume that figure will grow—rapidly—as children who have matured in the Internet era move on to college and into careers. With e-mail becoming an increasingly

common form of communication, people are discovering
and conversing with one another in a variety of ways
that bring a new twist to old, familiar patterns.
Using e-mail, people meet "to exchange pleasantries
and argue, engage in intellectual discourse, conduct
commerce, exchange knowledge, share emotional support,
make plans, brainstorm, gossip, feud, [and] fall in
love" (Chenault 105). That is, through e-mail people
do what they have always done: communicate. But the
medium of that communication has changed, which
excites some people and concerns others.

Advocates argue that the Internet has not only made
existing types of communication faster, more convenient, more efficient, and less expensive; it has also
made possible "new forms of community life," such as
chat rooms and discussion lists, in which people from
all over the country and the world gather to share
information and exchange points of view (Kling 103).
CMC is potentially so powerful a medium of exchange
that some believe it can promote dialogue within communities that are declining. A community, after all,
is built on people acting in the interests of their
neighbors for the common good. Via e-mail, online
newsgroups, and e-forums, neighbors will have new ways
of looking out for one another (Kling 103).

Still, skeptics aren't convinced that electronic
communication can provide the basis of lasting personal
relationships, primarily because relationships initiated on a cathode ray tube lack immediacy and physical
presence. What may be missing in the electronic village, say the critics, is "an essential core of humanity" (Maasik and Solomon 103):

> The unreal world of virtual culture [. . .] is being sub-
> stituted for a social reality made up of real human
> beings. And such a world, based entirely on the trans-
> mission of electronic signals, is potentially a world in
> which human beings will be unable to conceive of others
> as human beings. When all interaction is electronic,
> [the critics] ask, where is the ground for true human
> empathy and relatedness? (Maasik and Solomon 103–104)

The fact that people communicate—via e-mail, snail
(written) mail, or in person—does not guarantee that
their exchanges lead to community. Members of a community trust and care for one another; they extend themselves and offer help (Kling 103). Critics of CMC
argue that the supporters gloss over this important

distinction when they assume that electronic forums are "building new forms of community life" (Kling 103). Talking, electronically or otherwise, marks only the *beginning* of a process. Community building is hard work and takes time.

Notwithstanding these concerns, proponents of CMC confidently point to examples in which the new technologies of communication bring people together in meaningful, healthy ways. In a study of first-year college students, researcher Richard Holeton of Stanford University found that students who were ordinarily reserved were often the most active participants in Internet discussions (Branscum 104). Similarly, the Internet can serve as a way for people who are having trouble dating to find partners. For instance, Tom Buckley of Portland, Oregon, met his wife after signing up with Match.com. Buckley noted that the Internet helped him to meet his wife because "neither one of us was the type to walk up to someone in the gym or a bar and say, 'You're the fuel to my fire'" (qtd. in Morris 107). Holeton's research and Buckley's experience suggest that the Internet may provide a way for otherwise quiet or timid individuals to express themselves.

Beyond simply providing a safe and lower-stress place to meet, the Internet may actually promote honest communication. An Ohio University sociologist, Andrea Baker, concluded from her research that individuals who begin their romance online can be at an advantage: writing via e-mail can promote a "better and deeper" relationship than one begun in person because writing itself promotes a frank, honest exchange (qtd. in Wolcott 106). Certainly this was the experience of John Dwyer, a Californian who tired of meeting women in bars and decided instead to post an advertisement online. He eventually met the woman who would become his wife—Debbie, who said: "'If you are honest when talking online, you can strip away all the superficial stuff and really get to know someone'" (qtd. in Wolcott 106). When it works, CMC can promote a sincere exchange among those looking for lasting relationships.

Skeptics are not so easily convinced, however. Show them an example of a relationship that blossomed online and they will point to another in which one party was betrayed emotionally or financially. Take, for instance, the experience of Robert Spradling. He met and formed a romantic attachment to a Ukrainian woman online. She encouraged the romance via e-mail and eventually asked for money to set up a business. He sent $8,000 and later, again online, asked her to marry him. She agreed, they met in Kiev, and after Spradling returned home she disappeared—his money gone and his heart broken (Morris 107). Perhaps Spradling was one of the Internet romantics for whom it is wiser to avoid face-to-face meetings. That way, he could have enjoyed the interactive fantasy of a "cyber-lover" without ever having to ruin the fun with the uncomfortable truths of real life (Suler 105).

It is far from certain, then, that all or even most relationships begun online develop positively. Closer to the truth is that both online and offline, some relationships begin—and end—in deceit while others blossom. Experts do not yet know whether computer mediated communication, because of its electronic format, alters relationships as they are forming or, rather, is simply a new territory in which to find others. Time will tell. In the meantime, the advice that loved ones give us when we set off to find new friends—Be careful!—makes sense whether we are looking in the virtual world or down the street.

Works Cited

Branscum, Deborah. "Life at High-Tech U." <u>Newsweek</u> 27 Oct. 1997: 78–80.

Chenault, Brittney G. "Developing Personal and Emotional Relationships Via Computer-Mediated Communication." <u>CMC Magazine</u> May 1998. 20 March 2000. <http://www.december.com/cmc/mag/1998/may/chenault.html>.

Kling, Rob. "Social Relationships in Electronic Forums: Hangouts, Salons, Workplaces and Communities." <u>CMC Magazine</u> 22 July 1996. 4 Feb. 2000. <http://www.december.com/cmc/mag/1996/jul/kling.html>.

Maasik, Sonia, and Jack Solomon, eds. <u>Signs of Life in the USA</u>. Boston: Bedford Books, 1997. 701.

Morris, Bonnie R. "You've Got Romance! Seeking Love Online: Net-Based Services Change the Landscape, If Not the Odds, of Finding the Perfect Mate." <u>New York Times on the Web</u> 26 Aug. 1999. 23 Feb. 2000 <http://www.nytimes.com/library/tech/yr/mo/circuits/index.html>.

Singh, Sanjiv N. "Cyberspace: A New Frontier for Fighting Words." <u>Rutgers Computer and Technology Law Journal</u> 25.2 (1999): 283.

Suler, John. "Cyberspace Romances: Interview with Jean-Francois Perreault of *Branchez-vous*." <u>The Psychology of Cyberspace</u> 11 Dec. 1996. 7 April 2000 <http://www.rider.edu/users/suler/psycyber/psycyber.html>.

Wolcott, Jennifer. "Click Here for Romance." <u>The Christian Science Monitor</u> 13 Jan. 1999. 23 Feb. 2000 <http://www.csmonitor.com/durable/1991/01/13/fp11s1-csm.shtml>.

Practice Explanatory Synthesis

Now we'll give you an opportunity to practice your skills in planning and writing an explanatory synthesis. In Chapter 7, "Cyberspace and Identity: The E-Mail Revolution," you'll find additional readings on computer mediated communication (CMC). Review the table of contents for that chapter, selecting a group of at least five articles of interest to you, based on the descriptive annotations. Read these additional sources; then plan and write an explanatory synthesis dealing with some aspect of their subject matter. We encourage you to incorporate what you have learned about CMC from the brief selections included in the previous pages and worked into the model student paper. Don't feel compelled to bring in every last source, however.

Argument Synthesis

5

THE ARGUMENT SYNTHESIS

The explanatory synthesis, as we have seen, is fairly modest in purpose. It emphasizes the materials in the sources themselves, not the writer's interpretation. Because your reader is not always in a position to read your sources, this kind of synthesis, if done well, can be very informative. But the main characteristic of the explanatory synthesis is that it is designed more to *inform* than to *persuade*. As we have said, the thesis in the explanatory synthesis is less a device for arguing a particular point than a device for providing focus and direction to an objective presentation of facts or opinions. As the writer of an explanatory synthesis, you remain, for the most part, a detached observer.

Recall the thesis our student devised for her final draft of the explanatory synthesis on computer mediated communication in Chapter 4:

> While many praise CMC's potential to bridge barriers and promote meaningful dialogue, others caution that CMC is fraught with dangers.

This thesis provides a summation of the viewpoints people espouse in regard to CMC, neither arguing for or against any one viewpoint.

In contrast to an explanatory thesis, an argumentative thesis is *persuasive* in purpose. Writers working with the same source material might conceive of and support other, opposite theses. So the thesis for an argument synthesis is a claim about which reasonable people could disagree. It is a claim with which—given the right arguments—your audience might be persuaded to agree. The strategy of your argument synthesis is therefore to find and use convincing *support* for your *claim*.

The Elements of Argument: Claim, Support, Assumption

Let's consider the terminology we've just used. One way of looking at an argument is to see it as an interplay of three essential elements: claim, support, and assumption. A *claim* is a proposition or conclusion that you are trying to prove. You prove this claim by using *support* in the form of fact or expert opinion. Linking your supporting evidence to your claim is your *assumption* about the subject. This assumption, also called a *warrant,* is—as we've discussed in Chapter 2—an underlying belief or principle about some aspect of the world and how it operates. By nature, assumptions (which are often unstated) tend to be more general than either claims or supporting evidence. What we do when we *analyze* is to apply the principles that underlie our assumptions to the specific evidence that we will use as support for our claims.

For example, here are the essential elements of an argument advocating parental restriction of television viewing for their high school children:

> `Claim`
> High school students should be restricted to no more than two hours of TV viewing per day.
>
> `Support`
> An important new study, as well as the testimony of educational specialists, reveals that students who watch more than two hours of TV a night have, on average, lower grades than those who watch less TV.
>
> `Assumption`
> Excessive TV viewing adversely affects academic performance.

As another example, if we converted the thesis for our explanatory synthesis into a *claim* suitable for an argument synthesis, it might read as follows:

> CMC threatens to undermine human intimacy, connection, and ultimately, community.

Here are the other elements of this argument:

> `Support`
> While the Internet presents us with increased opportunities to meet people, these meetings are limited by geographical distance.
>
> People are spending increasing amounts of time in cyberspace: In 1998, the average Internet user spent over four hours per week online, and by 2000, this figure had nearly doubled.
>
> College health officials report that excessive Internet usage threatens many college students' academic and psychological well-being.
>
> New kinds of relationships fostered on the Internet often pose challenges to pre-existing relationships.

```
Assumptions
There is a fundamental difference between the com-
munication skills used and the connections formed
via the Internet and face-to-face contact.

"Real" connection and a sense of community are sus-
tained by face-to-face contact, not by Internet
interactions.
```

For the most part, arguments should be constructed logically, or rationally, so that claims are supported by evidence in the form of facts or expert opinions. As we'll see, however, logic is only one component of effective arguments.

EXERCISE 5.1

Practicing Claim, Support, and Assumption

Devise a one-sentence claim addressing the positive impact (or potential impact) of CMC on relationships—whether or not you personally agree with such a claim. Then, drawing on materials read in the last chapter (102–107), list supporting statements and assumptions that might underlie this claim.

The Three Appeals of Argument: *Logos, Ethos, Pathos*

Speakers and writers have never relied upon logic alone in advancing and supporting their claims. More than 2,000 years ago, the Athenian philosopher and rhetorician Aristotle explained how speakers attempting to persuade others to their point of view could achieve their purpose primarily by relying on one or more *appeals*, which he called *logos, ethos,* and *pathos.*

Since we frequently find these three appeals employed in political argument, we'll use political examples in the following discussion. But keep in mind that these appeals are also used extensively in advertising, in legal cases, in business documents, and in many other types of argument.

Logos

Logos is the rational appeal, the appeal to reason. If they expect to persuade their audiences, speakers must argue logically and must supply appropriate evidence to support their case. Logical arguments are commonly of two types (often combined). The *deductive* argument begins with a generalization, then cites a specific case related to that generalization, from which follows a conclusion. A familiar example of deductive reasoning, used by Aristotle himself, is the following:

All men are mortal. (*generalization*)

Socrates is a man. (*specific case*)

Socrates is mortal. (*conclusion about the specific case*)

In the terms we've just been discussing, this deduction may be restated as follows:

> Socrates is mortal. (*claim*)
>
> Socrates is a man. (*support*)
>
> All men are mortal. (*assumption*)

An example of a more contemporary deductive argument may be seen in President John F. Kennedy's address to the nation in June 1963 on the need for sweeping civil rights legislation. Kennedy begins with the generalizations that it "ought to be possible [...] for American students of any color to attend any public institution they select without having to be backed up by troops" and that "it ought to be possible for American citizens of any color to register and vote in a free election without interference or fear of reprisal." Kennedy then provides several specific examples (primarily recent events in Birmingham, Alabama) and statistics to show that this was not the case. He concludes:

> We face, therefore, a moral crisis as a country and a people. It cannot be met by repressive police action. It cannot be left to increased demonstrations in the streets. It cannot be quieted by token moves or talk. It is time to act in the Congress, in your state and local legislative body, and, above all, in all of our daily lives.

Underlying Kennedy's argument is the following reasoning:

> All Americans should enjoy certain rights.
>
> Some Americans do not enjoy these rights.
>
> We must take action to ensure that all Americans enjoy these rights.

Another form of logical argumentation is *inductive* reasoning. A speaker or writer who argues inductively begins not with a generalization, but with several pieces of specific evidence. The speaker then draws a conclusion from this evidence. For example, in a 1990 debate on gun control, Senator Robert C. Byrd (Democrat, Virginia) cites specific examples of rampant crime: "I read of young men being viciously murdered for a pair of sneakers, a leather jacket, or $20." He also offers statistical evidence of the increasing crime rate: "in 1951, there were 3.2 policemen for every felony committed in the United States; this year [1990] nearly 3.2 felonies will be committed per every police officer [...]." He concludes, "Something has to change. We have to stop the crimes that are distorting and disrupting the way of life for so many innocent, law-respecting Americans. The bill that we are debating today attempts to do just that."

Statistical evidence also was used by Senator Edward M. Kennedy (Democrat, Massachusetts) in arguing for passage of the Racial Justice Act of 1990, designed to ensure that minorities were not disproportionately singled out for the death penalty. Kennedy points out that 17 defendants in Fulton County, Georgia, between 1973 and 1980, were charged with killing police officers but the only defendant who received the death sentence was a black man. Kennedy also cites statistics to show that "those who killed whites were 4.3 times more likely to receive the death penalty than were killers of blacks," and that "in Georgia, blacks who killed whites received the death penalty 16.7 percent of the time, while whites who killed received the death penalty only 4.2 percent of the time."

Of course, the mere piling up of evidence does not in itself make the speaker's case. As Donna Cross explains in "Politics: The Art of Bamboozling,"* politicians are very adept at "card-stacking." And statistics can be selected and manipulated to prove anything, as demonstrated in Darrell Huff's landmark book *How to Lie with Statistics* (1954). Moreover, what appears to be a logical argument may, in fact, be fundamentally flawed. (See Chapter 2 for a discussion of logical fallacies and faulty reasoning strategies.) On the other hand, the fact that evidence can be distorted, statistics misused, and logic fractured does not mean that these tools of reason can be dispensed with or should be dismissed. It means only that audiences have to listen and read critically—perceptively, knowledgeably, and skeptically (though not necessarily cynically).

Sometimes, politicians can turn their opponents' false logic against them. Major R. Owens, a Democratic Representative from New York, attempted to counter what he took to be the reasoning on welfare adopted by his opponents:

> Welfare programs create dependency and so should be reformed or abolished.
>
> Aid to Families with Dependent Children (AFDC) is a welfare program.
>
> AFDC should be reformed or abolished.

In his speech opposing the Republican welfare reform measure of 1995, Owens simply changes the specific (middle) term, pointing out that federal subsidies for electric power in the West and Midwest and farmers' low-rate home loan mortgages are, in effect, welfare programs ("We are spoiling America's farmers by smothering them with socialism [...]"). The logical conclusion—that we should reform or eliminate farmers' home loan mortgages—would clearly be unacceptable to many of those pushing for reform of AFDC. Owens thus suggests that opposition to AFDC is based less on reason than on lack of sympathy for its recipients.

EXERCISE 5.2

Using Deductive and Inductive Logic

Choose an issue currently being debated at your school, or a college-related issue about which you are concerned. Write down a claim about this issue. Then write two paragraphs addressing your claim—one in which you organize your points deductively, and one in which you organize them inductively. Some sample issues might include college admissions policies, classroom crowding, or grade inflation.

---

* Donna Cross, *Word Abuse: How the Words We Use Use Us* (New York: Coward, 1979).

Ethos

Ethos, or the ethical appeal, is an appeal based not on the ethical rationale for the subject under discussion, but rather on the ethical nature of the person making the appeal. A person making an argument must have a certain degree of credibility: That person must be of good character, be of sound sense, and be qualified to hold the office or recommend policy.

For example, Elizabeth Cervantes Barrón, running for senator as the peace and freedom candidate, begins her statement, "I was born and raised in central Los Angeles. I grew up in a multiethnic, multicultural environment where I learned to respect those who were different from me [...]. I am a teacher and am aware of how cutbacks in education have affected our children and our communities."

On the other end of the political spectrum, American Independent gubernatorial candidate Jerry McCready also begins with an ethical appeal: "As a self-employed businessman, I have learned firsthand what it is like to try to make ends meet in an unstable economy being manipulated by out-of-touch politicians." Both candidates are making an appeal to *ethos,* based on the strength of their personal qualities for the office they seek.

L. A. Kauffman is not running for office but rather writing an article arguing against socialism as a viable ideology for the future ("Socialism: No." *Progressive,* April 1, 1993). To defuse objections that he is simply a tool of capitalism, Kauffman begins with an appeal to *ethos:* "Until recently, I was executive editor of the journal *Socialist Review.* Before that I worked for the Marxist magazine, *Monthly Review.* My bookshelves are filled with books of Marxist theory, and I even have a picture of Karl Marx up on my wall." Thus, Kauffman establishes his credentials to argue knowledgeably about Marxist ideology.

Conservative commentator Rush Limbaugh frequently makes use of the ethical appeal by linking himself with the kind of Americans he assumes his audiences to be (what author Donna Cross calls "glory by association"):

> In their attacks [on me], my critics misjudge and insult the American people. If I were really what liberals claim—racist, hatemonger, blowhard—I would years ago have deservedly gone into oblivion. The truth is, I provide information and analysis the media refuses to disseminate, information and analysis the public craves. People listen to me for one reason: I am effective. And my credibility is judged in the marketplace every day [...]. I represent America's rejection of liberal elites [...]. I validate the convictions of ordinary people.*

EXERCISE 5.3

Using Ethos

Return to the claim you used for Exercise 5.2, and write a paragraph in which you use an appeal to *ethos* to make a case for that claim.

---

* Rush Limbaugh, "Why I Am a Threat to the Left," *Los Angeles Times,* 9 Oct. 1994.

Pathos

Finally, speakers and writers appeal to their audiences by use of *pathos*, the appeal to the emotions. There is nothing inherently wrong with using an emotional appeal. Indeed, since emotions often move people far more powerfully than reason alone, speakers and writers would be foolish not to use emotion. And it would be a drab, humorless world if human beings were not subject to the sway of feeling, as well as reason. The emotional appeal becomes problematic only if it is the *sole* or *primary* basis of the argument. This is the kind of situation that led, for example, to the internment of Japanese Americans during World War II or that leads to periodic political spasms to enact anti-flag-burning legislation.

President Reagan was a master of emotional appeal. He closed his first inaugural address with a reference to the view from the Capitol to the Arlington National Cemetery, where lie thousands of markers of "heroes":

> Under one such marker lies a young man, Martin Treptow, who left his job in a small-town barbershop in 1917 to go to France with the famed Rainbow Division. There, on the western front, he was killed trying to carry a message between battalions under heavy artillery fire. We're told that on his body was found a diary. On the flyleaf under the heading, "My Pledge," he had written these words: "America must win this war. Therefore, I will work, I will save, I will sacrifice, I will endure, I will fight cheerfully and do my utmost, as if the issue of the whole struggle depended on me alone." The crisis we are facing today does not require of us the kind of sacrifice that Martin Treptow and so many thousands of others were called upon to make. It does require, however, our best effort and our willingness to believe in ourselves and to believe in our capacity to perform great deeds, to believe that together with God's help we can and will resolve the problems which now confront us.

Surely, Reagan implies, if Martin Treptow can act so courageously and so selflessly, we can do the same. The logic is somewhat unclear, since the connection between Martin Treptow and ordinary Americans of 1981 is rather tenuous (as Reagan concedes); but the emotional power of Martin Treptow, whom reporters were sent scurrying to research, carries the argument.

A more recent president, Bill Clinton, also uses *pathos.* Addressing an audience of the nation's governors about his welfare plan, Clinton closed his remarks by referring to a conversation he had held with a welfare mother who had gone through the kind of training program Clinton was advocating. Asked by Clinton whether she thought that such training programs should be mandatory, the mother said, "I sure do." When Clinton asked her why, she said:

> "Well, because if it wasn't, there would be a lot of people like me home watching the soaps because we don't believe we can make anything of ourselves anymore. So you've got to make it mandatory." And I said, "What's the best thing about having a job?" She said, "When my boy goes to school, and they say, 'What does your mama do for a living?' he can give an answer."

Clinton uses the emotional power he counts on in that anecdote to set up his conclusion: "We must end poverty for Americans who want to work. And we must do it on terms that dignify all of the rest of us, as well as help our country to work better. I need your help, and I think we can do it."

EXERCISE 5.4

Using Pathos

Return to the claim you used for Exercises 5.2 and 5.3, and write a paragraph in which you use an appeal to *pathos* to make a case for that claim.

DEMONSTRATION: DEVELOPING AN ARGUMENT SYNTHESIS—THE WAL-MART CONTROVERSY

To demonstrate how to plan and draft an argument synthesis, let's consider another subject. If you were taking an economics or business economics course, you would probably at some point consider the functioning of the market economy. For consumers, one of the most striking trends in this economy in recent times has been the rise of superstores such as Wal-Mart, Home Depot, Costco, Staples, and Best Buy. Most consumers find these vast shopping outlets convenient and economical. Others find them an abomination, contending that these ugly and predatory outlets drive out of business the Mom-and-Pop stores that were the staple of small-town America.

Suppose, in preparing to write a short paper on Wal-Mart, you came up with the following sources. Read them carefully, noting as you do the kinds of information and ideas you could draw upon to develop an *argument synthesis*.

Note: To save space and for the purpose of demonstration, the following passages are excerpts only. In preparing your paper, naturally you would draw upon entire articles from which these extracts were made.

Ban the Bargains
Bob Ortega

Bob Ortega, reporter for the Wall Street Journal, *introduces the Wal-Mart debate with a particular slant: the involvement of aging activists from the 1960s and 1970s.*

"Ultimate Predator"

To denizens of the counterculture, Wal-Mart stands for everything they dislike about American society—mindless consumerism, paved landscapes and homogenization of community identity.

Bob Ortega, "Ban the Bargains," *Wall Street Journal* 11 Oct. 1994: B6.

"We've lost a sense of taste, of refinement—we're destroying our culture and replacing it with…Wal-Mart," says Allan B. Wolf, a Kent State University alumnus now trying to keep Wal-Mart out of Cleveland Heights, Ohio, where he is a high-school teacher.

"We'd never have fought another business as hard as we've fought Wal-Mart," says Alice Doyle, of Cottage Grove, Ore., who calls the giant discounter "the ulti-mate predator."

At Wal-Mart headquarters in Bentonville, Ark., company officials characterize all opponents, ex-hippie and otherwise, as "a vocal minority." They deny that their store has become, for some activists, a kind of successor to Vietnam.

Don Shinkle, a Wal-Mart vice president, says "there are maybe eight to 10 sites where there is opposition." However, there are at least 40 organized groups active-ly opposing proposed or anticipated Wal-Mart stores in communities such as Oceanside, Calif.; Gaithersburg, Md.; Quincy, Mass.; East Lampeter, Penn.; Lake Placid, N.Y.; and Gallatin, Tenn.

Local opposition has delayed some stores and led the company to drop its plans in Greenfield, Mass., and two other towns in that state, as well as in Bath, Maine; Simi Valley, Calif.; and Ross and West Hempfield, Pa.

Protest March

The residents of Cleveland Heights hope to join that list. On a recent Monday there, a large crowd, including some people who had been tear-gassed at Kent State 24 years ago for protesting the war, led a march on city hall and chanted, "One, two, three, four—we don't want your Wal-Mart store." Says Jordan Yin, a leader of the anti–Wal-Mart coalition, "Old hippies describes the whole town."

In Fort Collins, Colo., Shelby Robinson, a former Vietnam War protester and member of the George McGovern campaign, has little success these days per-suading her old companions to join her lobbying for solar power, animal rights or vegetarianism. But when Wal-Mart proposed coming to town, the activist impuls-es of her old friends came alive, and many joined her in fighting the store.

"I really hate Wal-Mart," says Ms. Robinson, a self-employed clothing designer. "Everything's starting to look the same, everybody buys all the same things—a lot of small-town character is being lost. They disrupt local communities, they hurt small businesses, they add to our sprawl and pollution because everybody drives farther, they don't pay a living wage—and visually, they're atrocious."

In Boulder, Colo., Wal-Mart real-estate manager Steven P. Lane tried appeasing the city's ex-hippies by proposing a "green store" that he said would be environ-mentally friendly, right up to the solar-powered sign out front. But when city coun-cil member Spencer Havlick, who helped organize the first Earth Day in 1970, suggested that the whole store be solar-powered, Mr. Lane fell silent. Dr. Havlick, professor of environmental design at the University of Colorado, says, "Their pro-posal wasn't as green as they thought it was."

These activists have hardly slowed Wal-Mart's overall expansion—it expects to add 125 stores next year to its existing 2,504. But even so, some Wal-Mart sym-pathizers find them irritating. William W. Whyte, who bid good riddance to hippies when he graduated from Kent State in 1970, now finds himself annoyed by them again, as an analyst following Wal-Mart for Stephens Inc.

"The same types of people demonstrating then are demonstrating now," grumbles Mr. Whyte. "If they had to worry about putting food on the table, they'd probably be working for Wal-Mart instead of protesting them."

Some Wal-Mart supporters call the protesters elitists for opposing a purveyor of low-priced goods. But Tim Allen, who at age 26 has been active in the development of a "green" housing co-op and an organizer of the Wal-Mart protest movement in Ithaca, replies that "people aren't poor because they're paying 15 cents more for a pair of underwear."

Eight Ways to Stop the Store
Albert Norman

Albert Norman is a well-known opponent of Wal-Mart and a former anti-Vietnam activist. In this article, Norman outlines his strategies for blocking Wal-Mart. Norman's bias is clear—and will be balanced by some of the other selections that follow.

Last week I received another red-white-and-blue invitation to a Wal-Mart grand opening in Rindge, New Hampshire. I say "another" because Wal-Mart has already invited me to its new store in Hinsdale, New Hampshire, just twenty miles away. With over $67 billion in annual sales, and more than 2,000 stores, Wal-Mart holds a grand opening somewhere in America almost every other day. But it will never invite me to its new store in Greenfield, Massachusetts, my home town, because Greenfield voters recently rejected Wal-Mart at the ballot box.

The Arkansas mega-retailer has emerged as the main threat to Main Street, U.S.A. Economic impact studies in Iowa, Massachusetts, and elsewhere suggest that Wal-Mart's gains are largely captured from other merchants. Within two years of a grand opening, Wal-Mart stores in an average-size Iowa town generated $10 million in annual sales—by "stealing" $8.3 million from other businesses.

Since our victory in Greenfield, we have received dozens of letters from "Stop the WAL" activists in towns like East Aurora, New York; Palatine, Illinois; Mountville, Pennsylvania; Williston, Vermont; Branford, Connecticut—small communities fighting the battle of Jericho. If these towns follow a few simple rules of engagement, they will find that the WAL *will* come tumbling down:

Quote scripture: Wal-Mart founder Sam Walton said it best in his autobiography: "If some community, for whatever reason, doesn't want us in there, we aren't interested in going in and creating a fuss." Or, as one company V.P. stated, "We have so many opportunities for building in communities that want Wal-Marts, it would be foolish of us to pursue construction in communities that don't want us." The greater the fuss raised by local citizens, the more foolish Wal-Mart becomes.

Learn Wal-Math: Wal-Mathematicians only know how to add. They never talk about the jobs they destroy, the vacant retail space they create or their impact on

---

Albert Norman, "Eight Ways to Stop the Store," *Nation* 28 Mar. 1994: 10.

commercial property values. In our town, the company agreed to pay for an impact study that gave enough data to kill three Wal-Marts. Dollars merely shifted from cash registers on one side of town to Wal-Mart registers on the other side of town. Except for one high school scholarship per year, Wal-Mart gives very little back to the community.

Exploit their errors: Wal-Mart always makes plenty of mistakes. In our community, the company tried to push its way onto industrially zoned land. It needed a variance not only to rezone land to commercial use but also to permit buildings larger than 40,000 square feet. This was the "hook" we needed to trip the company up. Rezoning required a Town Council vote (which it won), but our town charter allowed voters to seek reconsideration of the vote, and ultimately, a referendum. All we needed was the opportunity to bring this to the general public—and we won. Wal-Mart also violated state law by mailing an anonymous flier to voters.

Fight capital with capital: In our town (pop. 20,000) Wal-Mart spent more than $30,000 trying to influence the outcome of a general referendum. It even created a citizen group as a front. But Greenfield residents raised $17,000 to stop the store—roughly half of which came from local businesses. A media campaign and grass-roots organizing costs money. If Wal-Mart is willing to spend liberally to get into your town, its competitors should be willing to come forward with cash also.

Beat them at the grass roots: Wal-Mart can buy public relations firms and telemarketers but it can't find bodies willing to leaflet at supermarkets, write dozens of letters to the editor, organize a press conference or make calls in the precincts. Local coalitions can draw opinion-makers from the business community (department, hardware and grocery stores, pharmacies, sporting goods stores), environmentalists, political activists and homeowners. Treat this effort like a political campaign: The Citizens versus the WAL.

Get out your vote: Our largest expenditure was on a local telemarketing company that polled 4,000 voters to identify their leanings on Wal-Mart. Our volunteers then called those voters leaning against the WAL two days before the election. On election day, we had poll-watchers at all nine precincts. If our voters weren't at the polls by 5 P.M., we reminded them to get up from the dinner table and stop the mega-store.

Appeal to the heart as well as the head: One theme the Wal-Mart culture has a hard time responding to is the loss of small-town quality of life. You can't buy rural life style on any Wal-Mart shelf—once you lose it, Wal-Mart can't sell it back to you. Wal-Mart's impact on small-town ethos is enormous. We had graphs and bar charts on job loss and retail growth—but we also communicated with people on an emotional level. Wal-Mart became the WAL—an unwanted shove into urbanization, with all the negatives that threaten small-town folks.

Hire a professional: The greatest mistake most citizen groups make is trying to fight the world's largest retailer with a mimeo-machine mentality. Most communities have a political consultant nearby, someone who can develop a media campaign and understand how to get a floppy disk of town voters with phone numbers. Wal-Mart uses hired guns; so should anti–Wal-Mart forces.

"Your real mission," a Wal-Mart executive recently wrote to a community activist, "is to be blindly obstructionist." On the contrary, we found it was Wal-Mart that would blindly say anything and do anything to bulldoze its way toward another grand opening in America. But if community coalitions organize early, bring their case directly to the public and trumpet the downside of mega-store development, the WALs will fall in Jericho.

Wal-Mart's War on Main Street
Sarah Anderson

Sarah Anderson is an economic analyst for a think tank in Washington, D.C.

Across the country, thousands of rural people are battling to save their local downtowns. Many of these fights have taken the form of anti–Wal-Mart campaigns. In Vermont, citizens' groups allowed Wal-Mart to enter the state only after the company agreed to a long list of demands regarding the size and operation of the stores. Three Massachusetts towns and another in Maine have defeated bids by Wal-Mart to build in their communities. In Arkansas, three independent drugstore owners won a suit charging that Wal-Mart had used "predatory pricing," or selling below cost, to drive out competitors. Canadian citizens are asking Wal-Mart to sign a "Pledge of Corporate Responsibility" before opening in their towns. In at least a dozen other U.S. communities, groups have fought to keep Wal-Mart out or to restrict the firm's activities.

By attacking Wal-Mart, these campaigns have helped raise awareness of the value of locally owned independent stores on Main Street. Their concerns generally fall in five areas:

- *Sprawl Mart*—Wal-Mart nearly always builds along a highway outside town to take advantage of cheap, often unzoned land. This usually attracts additional commercial development, forcing the community to extend services (telephone and power lines, water and sewage services, and so forth) to that area, despite sufficient existing infrastructure downtown.
- *Wal-Mart channels resources out of a community*—studies have shown that a dollar spent on a local business has four or five times the economic spin-off of a dollar spent at a Wal-Mart, since a large share of Wal-Mart's profit returns to its Arkansas headquarters or is pumped into national advertising campaigns.
- *Wal-Mart destroys jobs in locally owned stores*—a Wal-Mart-funded community impact study debunked the retailer's claim that it would create a lot of jobs in Greenfield, Massachusetts. Although Wal-Mart planned to hire 274 people at its Greenfield store, the community could expect to gain only eight net jobs, because of projected losses at other businesses that would have to compete with Wal-Mart.

Sarah Anderson, "Wal-Mart's War on Main Street," *The Progressive* Nov. 1994.

- *Citizen Wal-Mart?*—in at least one town—Hearne, Texas—Wal-Mart destroyed its Main Street competitors and then deserted the town in search of higher returns elsewhere. Unable to attract new businesses to the devastated Main Street, local residents have no choice but to drive long distances to buy basic goods.
- *One-stop shopping culture*—in Greenfield, where citizens voted to keep Wal-Mart out, anti–Wal-Mart campaign manager Al Norman said he saw a resurgence of appreciation for Main Street. "People realized there's one thing you can't buy at Wal-Mart, and that's small-town quality of life," Norman explains. "This community decided it was not ready to die for a cheap pair of underwear."

Small towns cannot return to the past, when families did all their shopping and socializing in their hometown. Rural life is changing and there's no use denying it. The most important question is, who will define the future? Will it be Wal-Mart, whose narrow corporate interests have little to do with building healthy communities? Will it be the department of transportation, whose purpose is to move cars faster? Will it be the banks and suppliers primarily interested in doing business with the big guys? Or will it be the people who live in small towns, whose hard work and support are essential to any effort to revitalize Main Street?

Who's Really the Villain?
Jo-Ann Johnston

A freelance writer based in Greenfield, Massachusetts—a town that successfully fought off the construction of a Wal-Mart superstore—Jo-Ann Johnston challenges the logic of anti–Wal-Mart forces and argues that the store would have helped to address fundamental problems with the local economy.

Cheap underwear. That's all Wal-Mart Corp. contributes as it squeezes the life out of a community's downtown, according to Albert Norman, an outspoken Wal-Mart critic. His sentiment—and talent for rousing support—led folks in rural Greenfield, Massachusetts, to block the company's plans to build a store there. It also established the political consultant as one of the best known opponents to "Sprawl-mart" in the country. But fighting off Wal-Mart hasn't done much for the 18,845 residents of Greenfield.

As in numerous other communities during the past ten years, Wal-Mart simply found a site just a short distance away from its original target. In this case, it's in Orange, a smaller town located up the road about twenty-five minutes from downtown Greenfield. Meanwhile, this area ranks as the state's second poorest in per capita income. And in January, it posted an unemployment rate of 6.1 percent—attributable partly to the recent closings of a paper plant, a container factory, and

Jo-Ann Johnston, "Who's Really the Villain?" *Business Ethics* May–June 1995.

a large store that sold liquidated merchandise. Wal-Mart would have brought to Greenfield 240 tax-paying jobs and increased retail traffic.

Set to open later this year, the store in Orange will be yet another example of how saying "go away" to the likes of Wal-Mart overlooks a much deeper problem facing small-town America: the need to change a way of doing business while maintaining, or improving, a deeply valued way of life. An increasing number of people are beginning to realize that small-town merchants need to adapt to changes in their communities, the economy, and their industries instead of chastising an outside company. That means accepting the fact that a Wal-Mart, or a similar retailer, may become a neighbor.

Such thinking is hogwash as far as anti–Wal-Marters are concerned. Consumerism has run amok if a town figures it needs a Wal-Mart, says Norman [see "Eight Ways to Stop the Store"], who today works with people in Illinois, Ohio, New England, and other regions to stop Wal-Marts and other large discount retailers from setting up shop. His list of reasons to fight such chain stores is lengthy, with perhaps one of the most popular being the potential loss of small-town quality of life. People move to small towns from urban or suburban America in part to escape from mall and shopping strip development, he says, not to see it duplicated.

That emotional argument carries weight, especially in New England, where twelve cities and one state, Vermont, have fought Wal-Mart. A current battle is taking place in Sturbridge, a historic town in eastern Massachusetts where community activists are fighting to keep Wal-Mart out. The town draws 60 percent of its general business from tourism-related trade, says local Wal-Mart opponent Carol Goodwin. "We market history," she says. The town and its re-creation of an early American village are the state's second largest tourist attraction. A big cookie-cutter mart off the freeway could obscure this town of eight thousand's special appeal, she says.

Sturbridge may want to take a lesson from its neighbor to the northwest, however. Merchants in Greenfield face the possible loss of business due to the fact that Wal-Mart found a location "just over the hill" from where it was first looking to build. Kenneth Stone, an economist at Iowa State University and the country's leading researcher on the economic impacts of Wal-Marts, found that towns in the Midwest and East suffered a "retail leakage" of shoppers who instead drove to the closest regional shopping center with a discount store.

Does that mean Greenfield shoppers will now drive to Orange? Well, several of the town's shoppers complained during the Wal-Mart battle that area merchants could use competition because of their poor selection, high prices, limited hours, and lackluster service. Meanwhile, Wal-Mart has a good reputation for service. A *Consumer Reports* reader poll in late 1994 found that fifty thousand people rated Wal-Mart the highest in customer satisfaction of "value-oriented chains."

In many ways, what is happening to small-town retail corridors is similar to how mom-and-pop corporations were caught off guard during the takeover frenzy of the 1980s. Survivors became more efficient to avoid being picked off by raiders looking to maximize shareholder profits. With Wal-Mart, it's a matter of maximizing retailing opportunities for consumers.

By the time a community knows the demographically astute Wal-Mart has its eye on an area, it's virtually too late to stop *somebody* from coming into town, says

Bill Sakelarios, president of the Concord-based Retail Merchants Association of New Hampshire. In Greenfield, for instance, the threat of competition to that town's small retailers didn't disappear with the Wal-Mart vote. BJ's Wholesale club is considering the town for a store.

Wal-Mart is viewed as a threat, though, because it uses bulk buying, discount pricing, and tight inventory and distribution management that smaller retailers can't keep up with. It also has the competitive advantage of size: The company's sales surged 22 percent to more than $82 billion, while net income climbed 15 percent to more than $2.6 billion in the year ended January 31, 1995, compared with year-earlier results.

Because it's so huge, the best defense against Wal-Mart for small-town retailers is to adapt, evolve, and create some stronghold that will make them viable and worth keeping, even in the face of new competition, says Robert Kahn, a Lafayette, California, management consultant who has worked with the chain and publishes a newsletter called *Retailing Today*. All kinds of stores have found ways to survive in the shadow of Wal-Mart, he says. Grocery stores have maintained check cashing, hardware stores and nurseries have offered classes, women's clothing retailers have filled in the gaps in the Wal-Mart line. Others point to pharmacies that have been able to compete with Wal-Marts. Stone met one druggist who kept a loyal clientele of shut-ins who spent $200 to $300 a month individually on prescriptions by offering home delivery, something Wal-Mart didn't do in his market.

The argument that self-improvement and change for small retailers may be the answer is definitely scorned in some circles. But stores that balk at such notions may not get much sympathy from customers who have had to change jobs or learn new skills—all because of shifts in the structure of the economies in the fields in which they work.

"You read stories about how towns don't want Wal-Mart, but in many cases that's a very few people getting a lot of publicity. And I may have on my desk a petition signed by fifteen thousand people saying, 'Please come, ignore the one hundred people who are trying to block the store,'" Wal-Mart President and CEO David Glass told a press gathering in December. "In retailing, you have a very simple answer to all that. Any community that didn't want a Wal-Mart store—all they've got to do is not shop there. And I guarantee a store, even if it's [just] built, won't be there long."

Another thing to consider is what happens if Wal-Mart, or a store like it, comes into town, stays for ten years, and then leaves. Where that's happened, retailers who found ways to adapt to Wal-Mart's presence still believe they're much better as a result. In Nowata, Oklahoma, Wal-Mart pulled up stakes last year and deserted a town of 3,900 people who had come to depend on it as their second largest taxpayer, as well as their major retailing center. But several local merchants survived Wal-Mart's stay of fourteen years because they learned to adjust their business practices. Wayne Clark, whose father opened Clark's Sentry Hardware in 1938, says he survived Wal-Mart's presence by providing better service and a more specialized inventory.

Nowata also brings up another interesting question on the Wal-Mart controversy: Could it be that old-time downtowns simply are obsolete and an impediment to efficient retailing? Many retailers have probably been in a precarious position for a long time, for a number of reasons, and then place the blame for problems or eventual demise on the highly visible Wal-Mart, says Sakelarios. "Wal-Mart is being singled out. Small-town business districts brought a lot of this on themselves," agrees Iowa State's Stone.

As cars have drawn shopping to other locales, downtown districts haven't worked hard enough to remain competitive and efficient, data suggest. "Small retailers often believe that the community *owes them* rather than *they owe* the community," Kahn wrote in his December newsletter.

He cites as evidence a recent survey of more than 1,500 Illinois retailers conducted by the state's merchant association. Kahn found it stunning that 54 percent reorder inventory for their stores only when they're already out of stock. That translates into poor selection and service, Kahn says, because small retailers often can't get priority shipments from vendors and most often wait for five to fifteen days to get fresh stock in, leaving customers without that selection in the interim. "That's not providing any service. If it's not in stock, eventually the customer is going to go somewhere else," Kahn points out.

Kahn also criticized the 63 percent of the retailers surveyed who claimed to know what their customers want, even though they didn't track customer purchases.

Apart from self-inflicted injuries, retailers are also pressured on other fronts, says John Donnellan, a member of the Consumer Studies faculty at the University of Massachusetts in Ames. The growth of the mail-order catalogs, cable TV shopping networks, specialized category stores such as Toys 'R' Us, and now, possibly, shopping via on-line computer services, all present more competition for small merchants that draw from local markets.

The only difference with Wal-Mart is that it's the biggest, most identifiable source of that new and increasing competition. As a result, it has become a lightning rod for all the angst and anxiety of struggling shop keepers—deserved or not.

Wal-Mart Stores, Inc.
Hoover's Handbook of American Business 2002

Founded by Gary Hoover, this handbook provides detailed proprietary information on American companies

Overview

Different cultures call a divine power by various names; retailers call it Wal-Mart. Bentonville, Arkansas-based Wal-Mart Stores is the world's largest retailer, operating more than 4,150 stores. Store types include discount stores (Wal-Mart), members-

Hoover's Handbook of American Business 2002 (Austin: Hoover's, 2001).

only warehouse stores (Sam's Club, serving small-business and individual customers), and combination discount and grocery stores (Wal-Mart Supercenters; ASDA in the UK). Wal-Mart also sells products online.

Wal-Mart is best known for its breadth of merchandise and low prices. Another part of the retailing leviathan's appeal is its efforts to promote a small-town flavor, with friendly greeters and simple trappings. The chain doesn't just compete in discount staples such as clothing—it is a force in several other categories including electronics, health and beauty products, sporting goods, and toys. Its prescription drug sales make it North America's #3 pharmacy operator (behind Walgreen and CVS). Wal-Mart plans to start offering unlimited Internet access, and it is testing the sale of household appliances and bedding in some stores. Already a leading food retailer through its Supercenters, Wal-Mart is expanding its Neighborhood Market format (smaller stores focusing on groceries, prescription drugs, and health and beauty products).

Wal-Mart has stores in all 50 states and is the #1 retailer in Canada and Mexico. (It holds a majority stake in Wal-Mart de México.) The company also has stores in Asia, Europe, and South America. In addition, Wal-Mart owns the largest US convenience store distributor, McLane Company.

The heirs of the late Sam Walton (Wal-Mart's founder) own about 38% of the company.

History

Sam Walton began his retail career as a J. C. Penney management trainee and later leased a Ben Franklin-franchised dime store in Newport, Arkansas, in 1945. In 1950 he relocated to Bentonville, Arkansas, and opened a Walton 5 & 10. By 1962 Walton owned 15 Ben Franklin stores under the Walton 5 & 10 name.

After Ben Franklin management rejected his suggestion to open discount stores in small towns, Walton, with his brother James "Bud" Walton, opened the first Wal-Mart Discount City in Rogers, Arkansas, in 1962. Wal-Mart Stores went public in 1970 with 18 stores.

Avoiding regional retailers, Walton opened stores in small and midsized towns in the 1970s. The company sold its Ben Franklin stores in 1976. By 1980 Wal-Mart's 276 stores had sales of $1.2 billion.

In 1983 Wal-Mart opened Sam's Wholesale Club, a concept based on the successful cash-and-carry, membership-only warehouse format pioneered by the Price Company of California.

The company started Hypermart*USA in 1987 as a joint venture with Dallas-based supermarket chain Cullum Companies (now Randall's Food Markets). The 200,000-sq.-ft. discount store/supermarket hybrid was later retooled as Wal-Mart Supercenters. Sam stepped down as CEO in 1988 and president David Glass was appointed CEO. Wal-Mart bought out Cullum the next year.

Wal-Mart acquired wholesale distributor McLane Company in 1990. In 1992, the year Sam died, the company expanded into Mexico through a joint venture to open Sam's Clubs with Mexico's largest retailer Cifra (renamed Wal-Mart de México in 2000). Wal-Mart acquired 122 former Woolco stores in Canada in 1994. Co-founder Bud died a year later.

More international expansion included the acquisition of German hypermarket chain Wertkauf in 1997; the purchase of Brazilian retailer Lojas Americanas' 40%

interest in a joint venture (1998); and the addition of four stores and other sites in South Korea. Also in 1998 the company began testing the Neighborhood Market format, a 40,000-sq.-ft. grocery-and-drug combination store. In 1999 Wal-Mart bought 74 German-based Interspar hypermarkets and acquired ASDA Group, the UK's third-largest supermarket chain. COO Lee Scott succeeded Glass as CEO in 2000; Glass stayed on as chairman of the executive committee.

Wal-Mart formed an alliance with America Online to offer Internet access in 2001. Later that same year a group of six current and former female Wal-Mart employees filed a sex-discrimination lawsuit (seeking to represent up to 500,000 current and former Wal-Mart workers) against the company.

Also in 2001 Wal-Mart said it would acquire all the minority interest in Walmart.com and integrate its online operations with its store operations. It also laid off 100 employees at its corporate headquarters and eliminated 300 unfilled positions. It began offering college textbooks discounted up to 30% at its online College Bookstore.

Officers

Chairman: S. Robson Walton, age 56
Chairman of the Executive Committee: David D. Glass, age 65, $2,900,308 pay
President and CEO: H. Lee Scott Jr., age 52, $2,742,308 pay
EVP and CFO: Thomas M. Schoewe, age 48
EVP; President and CEO, Sam's Club Division: Thomas R. Grimm, age 56, $1,198,785 pay
EVP; President and CEO, Wal-Mart International Division: John B. Menzer, age 50, $1,277, 385 pay
EVP and Director; President and CEO, Wal-Mart Stores Division: Thomas M. Coughlin, age 52, $1,916,923 pay
EVP; President, Wal-Mart Realty: Paul R. Carter
EVP and COO, Wal-Mart Stores Division; Jim H. Haworth, age 39
EVP and Senior General Counsel: Thomas D. Hyde, age 52
EVP, Administration: Michael Duke
EVP, Food Merchandise: Doug Degn, age 44
EVP, General Merchandise: Don S. Harris, age 43
EVP, Marketing and Consumer Communications: Robert Connolly, age 57
EVP, People Division: Coleman Peterson
EVP, Specialty Division: David Dible
SVP and Chief Information Officer: Kevin Turner
SVP, Finance and Treasurer: Joseph J. Fitzsimmons, age 53
SVP, General Counsel and Secretary: Robert K. Rhoads, age 46
Auditors: Ernst & Young LLP

Locations

HQ: 702 SW 8th St., Bentonville, AR 72716
Phone: 501-273-4000   **Fax:** 501-273-1917
Web: www.walmartstores.com

Products/Operations		
2001 Sales	$ mil.	% of total
Wal-Mart Stores	121,889	64
SAM's Clubs	26,798	14
International	32,100	17
Other	10,542	5
Total	**191,329**	**100**

Selected Operations

ASDA (large stores offering a combination of general merchandise of food)
McLane Distribution Centers (distribution centers supplying convenience stores and Sam's Clubs, Supercenters, and Wal-Marts)
Sam's Club (members-only warehouse clubs)
Supercenters (large stores offering a combination of general merchandise and food)
Wal-Mart International Division (foreign operations)
Wal-Mart Stores (general merchandise)

Competitors

Ace Hardware
Albertsons'
Army and Air Force
    Exchange
AutoZone
Best Buy
Big Lots
BJs Wholesale Club
Carrefour
Circuit City
CompUSA
Core-Mark
Costco Wholesale
CVS

Dollar General
Eby-Brown
Family Dollar Stores
Home Depot
Hudson's Bay
J.C. Penney
Kmart
Kroger
Loblaw
Lowe's
Meijer
METRO AG
Office Depot
OfficeMax

Pep Boys
RadioShack
Rite Aid
Royal Ahold
Safeway
Sears
Service Merchandise
Staples
Target
TJX
Toys "R" Us
TruServ
Walgreen

Historical Financials & Employees

NYSE symbol: WMT FYE: January 31	Annual Growth	1/92	1/93	1/94	1/95	1/96	1/97	1/98	1/99	1/00	1/01
Sales ($ mil.)	17.8%	43,887	55,484	67,345	82,494	93,627	104,859	117,958	137,634	165,013	191,329
Net income ($ mil.)	16.4%	1,609	1,995	2,333	2,681	2,740	3,056	3,526	4,430	5,377	6,295
Income as % of sales	—	3.7%	3.6%	3.5%	3.2%	2.9%	2.9%	3.0%	3.2%	3.3%	3.3%
Earnings per share ($)	16.7%	0.35	0.44	0.51	0.59	0.60	0.67	0.78	0.99	1.21	1.40
Stock price—FY high ($)	—	14.97	16.47	17.06	14.63	13.81	14.13	20.97	43.22	70.25	64.94
Stock price—FY low ($)	—	8.19	12.53	11.50	10.31	9.55	10.06	11.50	20.09	38.88	41.44
Stock price—FY close ($)	17.3%	13.47	16.28	13.25	11.44	10.19	11.88	19.91	43.00	54.75	56.80
P/E—high	—	43	37	33	25	23	21	27	44	56	46
P/E—low	—	23	28	23	17	16	15	15	20	31	29
Dividends per share ($)	19.0%	0.05	0.06	0.07	0.09	0.10	0.11	0.14	0.16	0.20	0.24
Book value per share ($)	18.5%	1.52	1.90	2.34	2.77	3.22	3.75	4.13	4.75	5.80	7.01
Employees	14.4%	371,000	434,000	528,000	622,000	675,000	728,000	825,000	910,000	1,140,000	1,244,000

Stock Price History

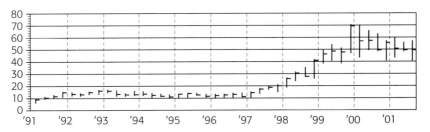

2001 Fiscal Year-End

Debt ratio: 33.3%
Return on equity: 22.0%
Cash ($ mil.): 2,054
Current ratio: 0.92
Long-term debt ($ mil.): 15,655
No. of shares (mil.): 4,470
Dividends
    Yield: 0.4%
    Payout: 17.1%
Market value ($ mil.): 253,896

Victorious Secret
Albert Norman

The following communities have either voted to reject a big box retail development at least once, or pressured the developer to withdraw. Developers don't want you to know that towns can beat sprawl, so this list is a victorious secret. Updated to August, 2001

Chandler, AZ	North Auburn, CA	Plainville, CT
Gilbert, AZ	San Juan Capistrano, CA	Orange, CT
Glendale, AZ	Santa Rosa, CA	New Milford, CT
Mesa, AZ	Santa Maria, CA	Old Saybrook, CT
Phoenix, AZ	Simi Valley, CA	Tolland, CT
Tucson, AZ	S. San Francisco, CA	Fort Collins, CO
Eureka, CA	Yucaipa, CA	Jefferson County CO
Grass Valley, CA	Colchester, CT	Silverthorne, CO

Albert Norman, "Victorious Secret," *Sprawl-Busters,* Sept. 2001, 3 Sept. 2001
<http://www.sprawl-busters.com/victoryz.html>.

Woodland Park, CO	Bangor, ME	Strongsville, OH
Rehobeth, DE	Belfast, ME	Yellow Springs, OH
Bonita Springs, FL	Wells, ME	Westlake, OH
Clermont, FL	Fenton, MI	Warren, OR
Hallandale, FL	Buffalo, MN	Lower Gwynned, PA
Lake Forest, FL	Burnsville, MN	Milford, PA
Naples, FL	Olivette, MO	Mount Joy, PA
St. Petersburg, FL	Springfield, MO	Warwick, PA
Temple Terrace, FL	St. Louis, MO	West Hempfield, PA
Atlanta, GA	Warsaw, MO	Barranquitas, PR
Athens, GA	Lincoln, NB	Utuado, PR
Hawaii Kai, HI	Asheville, NC	Middletown, RI
Mason City, IA	Durham, NC	Clemson, SC
Hailey, ID	Hickory, NC	Arlington, TX
Evergreen Park, IL	Claremont, NH	Cooleyville, TX
Lake in the Hills, IL	Peterboro, NH	Fort Worth, TX
Wheaton, IL	Stratham, NH	Kennedale, TX
Lawrence, KS	Walpole, NH	Murphy, TX
New Albany, IN	Deptford, NJ	Richardson, TX
Manhattan, KS	Englewood, NJ	Layton, UT
Overland Park, KS	Hamilton, NJ	Taylorsville, UT
Wichita, KS	Manalapan, NJ	Accomac, VA
Fort Wright, KY	Albuquerque, NM	Ashland, VA
Henderson, KY	Tijeras, NM	Charlottesville, VA
Barnstable, MA	Reno, NV	Fredericksburg, VA
Billerica, MA	Aurora, NY	Roanoke, VA
Boxboro, MA	Buffalo, NY	Warrenton, VA
Braintree, MA	East Aurora, NY	Williamsburg, VA
Easthampton, MA	Cazenovia, NY	Gig Harbor, WA
Greenfield, MA	Hornell, NY	Port Townsend, WA
Lee, MA	Hyde Park, NY	Brookfield, WI
Northboro, MA	Ithaca, NY	Menomonee Falls, WI
Plymouth, MA	Lake Placid, NY	Racine, WI
Reading, MA	Leeds, NY	Waukesha, WI
Saugus, MA	New Platz, NY	Morgantown, WV
Somerset, MA	North Greenbush, NY	St. Albans, VT
Westford, MA	New Rochelle, NY	St. Johnsbury, VT
Yarmouth, MA	Saranac Lake, NY	Willison, VT
Accokeek, MD	Beavercreek, OH	Brampton, ONT
Chestertown, MD	Broadview Hts., OH	Guelph, ONT
Gaithersburg, MD	Highland Hts., OH	Oakville, ONT
Paradise, MD	Lorain, OH	Waterloo, ONT
Kent Island, MD	North Olmstead, OH	Surrey, BC
Rockland, ME	Ottawa, OH	Park Royal, BC

Critical Reading for Synthesis

Look over the preceding readings and develop a list of the different points they make regarding Wal-Mart. Make your list as specific and detailed as you can. Then make several more lists in which you group readings that take similar positions, noting the variations among them.

Next go back over the readings, examining the kinds of arguments made by the writers. Do you see examples of faulty logic? (You might review the logical fallacies we discussed in Chapter 2 to help you here.) Do any of the writers use appeals to *ethos* or *pathos*? If so, are these effective or not, and why?

Once you've critically examined the writer's arguments, look over the factual information presented in the charts and lists. How does this information fit into the claims made in the argumentative pieces?

Finally, identify which arguments you find most persuasive. How does your agreement with these arguments relate to your own experiences with—or lack of experience with—Wal-Mart and other "megastores"?

Consider Your Purpose

As with the explanatory synthesis, your specific purpose in writing an argument synthesis is crucial. What, exactly, you want to do will affect your claim, the evidence you select to support your claim, and the way you organize the evidence. Your purpose may be clear to you before you begin research, may emerge during the course of research, or may not emerge until after you have completed your research. (Of course, the sooner your purpose is clear to you, the fewer wasted motions you will make. On the other hand, the more you approach research as an exploratory process, the likelier that your conclusions will emerge from the sources themselves, rather than from preconceived ideas. For a discussion of the research process, see Chapter 6.)

Let's say that while reading these sources, your own encounters with Wal-Mart influence your thinking on the subject and you find yourself agreeing more with the supporters than with the detractors of Wal-Mart. Perhaps you didn't grow up in a small town, so you don't have much experience with or knowledge of the kind of retail stores that the megastores have been displacing.

On the one hand, you can understand and even sympathize with the viewpoints of critics such as Norman and Anderson. (You may have shopped in the smaller stores in towns you have visited, or seen them portrayed in movies, or perhaps even visited reconstructed small-town stores in museums such as the Smithsonian or in the "Main Street" area in Disneyland.) On the other hand, it seems to you unrealistic in this day and age to expect that stores like Wal-Mart can be stopped or should be. For you, the prices and the convenience are a big plus. Your purpose, then, is formed from this kind of response to the source material.

Making a Claim: Formulate a Thesis

As we indicated in the introduction to argument synthesis, one useful way of approaching an argument is to see it as making a *claim*. A claim is a proposition, a conclusion that you are trying to prove or demonstrate. If your purpose is to demonstrate that it is neither possible nor desirable to stop the spread of Wal-Mart, then that is the claim at the heart of your argument. The claim is generally expressed in one-sentence form as a *thesis*. You use the information—and sometimes appeals to *ethos* and *pathos* (see pages 130–32)—in sources to *support* your claim.

Of course, not every piece of information in a source is useful for supporting a claim. By the same token, you may draw support for your own claim from sources that make entirely different claims. You may use as support for your own claim—for example, that Wal-Mart is growing at an alarming rate—data from *Hoover's Handbook,* which indicates the exact opposite: that Wal-Mart's growth is good for both customers and stockholders.

Similarly, you might use one source as part of a *counterargument*—an argument opposite to your own—so that you can demonstrate its weaknesses and, in the process, strengthen your own claim. On the other hand, the author of one of your sources may be so convincing in supporting a claim that you adopt it yourself, either partially or entirely. The point is that *the argument is in your hands*: you must devise it yourself and must use your sources in ways that will support the claim expressed in your thesis.

You may not want to divulge your thesis until the end of the paper, to draw the reader along toward your conclusion, allowing the thesis to flow naturally out of the argument and the evidence on which it is based. If you do this, you are working *inductively.* Or you may wish to be more direct and *begin* with your thesis, following the thesis statement with evidence to support it. If you do this, you are working *deductively.* In academic papers, deductive arguments are far more common than inductive arguments.

Based on your reactions to reading the sources, you decide to concede that the case against Wal-Mart has some merit and certainly some homespun appeal, but that opponents of such megastores are being unrealistic in expecting most people to sacrifice convenience and economy for the sake of retaining a vanishing way of life. After a few tries, you arrive at the following provisional thesis:

> Opponents of the giant discount chains have made powerful arguments against them, and it's too bad that these megastores are helping to make a way of life extinct; but opponents should realize that stores such as Wal-Mart are so successful because most people prefer bargains and convenience to tradition and small-town charm.

Decide How You Will Use Your Source Material

Your claim commits you to (1) recognize the arguments made by opponents of Wal-Mart, and (2) argue that Wal-Marts will prevail because they offer people advantages that the traditional retail shops can't match. The sources provide plenty of information and ideas—that is, evidence—that will allow you to support your claim. Norman and Anderson sum up the anti–Wal-Mart case, one that is also described more objectively by Ortega. Johnston offers the primary argument for Wal-Mart, and other data showing the growth of the chain are provided by the chart from *Hoover's Handbook.*

Develop an Organizational Plan

Having established your overall purpose and your claim, having developed a provisional thesis, and having decided how to use your source materials, how do you logically organize your essay? In many cases, including this one, a well-written thesis will suggest an overall organization. Thus, the first part of your synthesis will address the powerful arguments made by opponents of Wal-Mart. The second part will cover the even more powerful case (in your judgment) to be made on the other side. Sorting through your material and categorizing it by topic and subtopic, you might arrive at the following outline:

A. Introduction. The emotional anti—Wal-Mart case; conflict of values: consumerism vs. small-town America. *Thesis*.

B. Spectacular growth of Wal-Mart.

C. The case against Wal-Mart.

   1. Arguments against Wal-Mart.

   2. Al Norman's crusade.

D. Transition: the case for Wal-Mart.

E. Concession: charm of small-town stores. But—problems with small-town stores.

F. Changes in American economy and lifestyle and their effect on Main Street.

G. How traditionalists and store owners can deal with Wal-Mart.

   1. Fight it.

   2. Adjust by competing in ways that Wal-Mart can't.

H. Conclusion. Wal-Mart is not a "villain" because it offers what people want.

Argument Strategy

The argument represented by this outline deals with a claim of *value,* rather than a claim of *fact.* In other words, this is not an argument over whether Wal-Marts *are* better, according to some objective standard, than Main Street variety stores, since there is no such standard about which most people would agree. (Of course, if "better" were defined as more profitable, then this argument *would* become one of fact and would be easily disposed of, since numbers would provide sufficient support for the claim.) Rather, it is an argument that turns on those values which for some people take priority—convenience and economy versus charm and traditional small-town life. This *claim,* therefore, is based not only upon the *supporting evidence,* but also upon *assumptions* about the relative value of convenience and economy, on the one hand, and charm and traditional small-town life, on the other. Accordingly, while some of the arguments are based upon an appeal to *logos,* most are based upon the appeal to *pathos.* Some are even based upon *ethos,* since the writer will occasionally imply that her view is representative of that of most people.

To *support* her *claim,* the writer will rely upon a combination of summary, paraphrase, and quotation—much of it *testimony* from either "average" customers or from proponents of one side or the other of the debate. Note that despite her own essentially pro–Wal-Mart position, the writer provides *counterarguments* and *concessions,* indicating that she is not afraid to fairly represent the views of the other side, and even to give them some credit (the concession) before she responds and reinforces her own argument.

Draft and Revise Your Synthesis

The final draft of a completed synthesis,* based upon the above outline, follows. Thesis, transitions, and topic sentences are underlined; Modern Language Association (MLA) documentation style, explained in Chapter 6, is used throughout. Note that for the sake of clarity, references in the following essay are to pages in *Writing and Reading Across the Curriculum.*

Model Synthesis

A Vote for Wal-Mart

1   According to one critic, Wal-Mart is waging a "War on Main Street." Anti—Wal-Mart activists such as Bob Ortega think that we should "Ban the Bargains." A pro—Wal-Mart writer asks "Who's Really the Villain?" (Johnston 137). Obviously, the ever-expanding Wal-Mart

---

*This synthesis draws upon one additional article not reprinted here: "Shopping with the Enemy," *The Economist,* 14 Oct. 1995: 33.

brings some people's emotions to the boiling point. This seems strange. After all, Wal-Mart doesn't seem one of those hot-button issues like abortion or capital punishment. But for many, this is not just about discount department stores; it's about conflicting values: the values of small-town America versus the values of "mindless consumerism" (Ortega 132). I don't consider myself a mindless consumerist, but I happen to like Wal-Marts. Opponents of the giant discount chains have made powerful arguments against them, and it's too bad that these megastores are helping to make a way of life extinct; but opponents should realize that stores like Wal-Mart are so successful because most people prefer bargains and convenience to tradition and small-town charm.

2   Wal-Mart's growth has been spectacular. Launched in 1962, by 2000 Wal-Mart had over 4,150 stores, including 1,100 "Supercenters" (Hoover's 140). Al Norman, one of Wal-Mart's most vocal critics, reported that in 1994 Wal-Mart had over $67 billion in sales (134). Six years later, Wal-Mart's annual sales climbed to $165 billion (Hoover's 144). Wal-Mart also owns Sam's Club, another discount chain, which opened in 1983 and in 2001 had sales of more than $26 billion (Hoover's 143).

3   To its critics, Wal-Mart seems to represent everything that's wrong with modern American society. Sarah Anderson, an economist and the daughter of a small-town retailer, argues that Wal- Mart encourages urban sprawl, drains money from local economies, kills downtowns and local jobs, and destroys the quality of small-town life (136–37). Others blame Wal-Mart for the "homogenization of community identity" (Ortega 132). One local resident complains, "Everything's starting to look the same, everybody buys all the same things—a lot of small-town character is being lost." She adds, "Visually, [Wal-Marts are] atrocious" (qtd. in Ortega 133). Wal-Marts' ugliness is a common theme: the stores have been described as "huge, charmless boxes" ("Shopping" 33).

4   Activist Al Norman has helped organize local communities to fight the spread of Wal-Mart. His Web site, "Sprawl-Busters," proudly lists 156 communities that have succeeded in beating back Wal-Mart's advance on their town. (He also lists communities that have rejected other large discounters like Home Depot, Costco, and K-Mart.) Norman argues that "Wal-Mart's

gains are largely captured from other merchants"
("Eight Ways" 134). His rallying cry is that communities are "not ready to die for a cheap pair of underwear" (qtd. in Anderson 137).

5   But rhetoric like this is overkill. Norman might
as well blame computer makers for the death of typewriters or automakers for the death of horse-and-
buggy rigs. Horses and buggies may be more
picturesque and romantic than cars, but most
Americans drive cars these days because they're a lot
faster and more convenient. If customers choose to
buy underwear at Wal-Mart instead of the mom-and-pop
store downtown, that's because it's easier to get to
Wal-Mart—and to park there—and because cheapness is a
quality that matters to them.

6   I agree that Wal-Marts are unattractive and
"charmless." They just don't have the warmth or individuality of some of the small shops you find in
downtown areas, especially the ones that have been in
business for generations. But like most people, I'm
willing to sacrifice warmth and individuality if I
can get just what I want at a price I can afford.
As Jo-Ann Johnston points out, mom-and-pop stores
have brought on a lot of their own problems by not
being sufficiently responsive to what their customers
need. She notes, "several of the town's shoppers complained during the Wal-Mart battle that area merchants could use competition because of their poor
selection, high prices, limited hours, and lackluster
service" (138). Johnston points out that if customers
can't find what they want at the price they want at
local stores, it's not surprising that they go to
Wal-Mart. Even residents of Vermont, one of the areas
most likely to resist the intrusion of Wal-Mart, come
flocking to Wal-Mart for the bargains and the selection ("Shopping" 33). Russ Walker, store manager of
the Bennington Wal-Mart, dismisses opposition to the
discount chain as "'a handful of non-natives' who
care more about prettiness than economic development"
("Shopping" 33).

7   As even opponents of Wal-Mart admit, American
downtowns were in trouble long before Wal- Mart
arrived on the scene. Changes in the economy and in
the American lifestyle have contributed to the end of
a traditional way of life. In other words, stores such

as Wal-Mart are a symptom rather than a cause of the changes in Main Street. Blaming Wal-Mart "overlooks a much deeper problem facing small-town America," writes Jo-Ann Johnston: "the need to change a way of doing business while maintaining, or improving, a deeply valued way of life" (138). As Sarah Anderson admits, "Small towns cannot return to the past, when families did all their shopping and socializing in their hometown. Rural life is changing and there's no use denying it" (137).

8   In "Eight Ways to Stop the Store," Norman provides tips for community activists on how to fight Wal-Mart. I agree that if most people don't want Wal-Mart in their community, they should campaign against it and keep it out. I even think that the community might be a more pleasant place to live without the huge discount chains. But I also believe that residents of these communities should be aware of the price they will pay, both financially and in convenience, for maintaining their traditional way of doing business. Even without Wal-Mart, local downtowns will have trouble holding on to their customers. A better plan than keeping the big discounters out would be for local retailers to adapt to the changing times and to the competition. Some store owners have found ways of offering their customers what Wal-Mart can't provide: personalized services, such as home delivery or special orders, along with merchandise not available in the chain stores (Johnston 139).

9   Wal-Mart did not become the huge success it is by forcing its products on an unwilling public. People shop there because they want to. They want to save money and they want to find what they're looking for. Who can blame them? Wal-Mart may not be pretty, but it's also not "the villain."

Works Cited

Anderson, Sarah. "Wal-Mart's War on Main Street." <u>Progressive</u> Nov. 1994: 19–21.

<u>Hoover's Handbook of American Business 2002</u>. Austin, TX: Hoover's Business Press, 2001.

Johnston, Jo-Ann. "Who's Really the Villain?" <u>Business Ethics</u> May–June 1995: 16–18.

Norman, Albert. "Eight Ways to Stop the Store." <u>The Nation</u> 28 Mar. 1994: 418.

---."Victorious Secret." <u>Sprawl-Busters</u> Sept. 2001. 3 Sept. 2001 <http://www.sprawl-busters.com/victoryz.html>.

Ortega, Bob. "Ban the Bargains." <u>The Wall Street Journal</u> 11 Oct. 1994: 1.

"Shopping with the Enemy." <u>Economist</u> 14 Oct. 1995: 33.

Discussion

The writer of this argument synthesis on Wal-Mart attempts to support a *claim*—one that essentially favors Wal-Mart—by offering *support* in the form of facts (examples and statistics) and opinions (testimony of experts and "average" customers). However, since the writer's claim is one of *value*, as opposed to fact, its effectiveness depends partially upon the extent to which we, as readers, agree with the *assumptions* underlying the argument. (See our discussion of assumptions in Chapter 2, pages 63–65). An assumption (sometimes called a *warrant*) is a generalization or principle about how the world works or should work—a fundamental statement of belief about facts or values. In this particular case, the underlying assumption is that the values of cheapness and convenience are preferable, as a rule, to the values of charm and small-town tradition. Assumptions often are deeply rooted in people's psyches, sometimes deriving from lifelong experiences and observations, and are not easily changed, even by the most logical arguments. People who grew up in small-town America and remember it fondly are therefore far less likely to be persuaded by the support offered for this writer's claim than those who have lived in urban and suburban areas.

- **Paragraph 1:** The writer summarizes some of the most heated arguments against Wal-Mart by citing titles of recent articles about the store. The writer goes on to explain the intensity of emotion generated by stores such as Wal-Mart by linking it to a larger conflict of values: the values of small-town America vs. the values of consumerism. The writer then states her own preference for Wal-Mart, which leads to her *claim* (represented in the *thesis* at the end of the first paragraph).

  Argument strategy: The writer sets up the argument as one of conflicting *values*, relying here upon summary and quotations that support an appeal to *pathos* (emotions of the reader). The writer also provides the beginning of an appeal to *ethos* (establishing herself as credible) by stating her own views as a consumer in the sentence before the thesis.

- **Paragraph 2:** Here the writer discusses the spectacular growth of Wal-Mart. This growth is indirectly, rather than directly, relevant to the debate itself, since it is this apparently unstoppable growth that has caused Wal-Mart to be perceived as such a threat by opponents.

Argument strategy: This paragraph relies primarily upon the appeal to *logos* (logic) since its main purpose is to establish Wal-Mart's spectacular success. The argument here is supported primarily with statistics.

- **Paragraphs 3 and 4:** In these paragraphs, the writer discusses the case against Wal-Mart. The third paragraph covers the objections most commonly advanced by Wal-Mart critics. Three articles (Anderson, Ortega, and "Shopping with the Enemy") provide the source material for this paragraph. In the next paragraph, the writer focuses on Al Norman, one of the most prominent anti–Wal-Mart activists, who has helped localities organize campaigns against new Wal-Marts, some of them successful.
  Argument strategy: The third paragraph, part of the *counterargument*, attempts to support emotional arguments (that is, *pathos*) with a combination of summary (topic sentence), paraphrase (second sentence), and quotation (following sentences). The fourth paragraph, a continuation of the counterargument, relies on a combination of appeals to *logos* (the numbers of communities that, according to Norman, have rejected Wal-Mart) and *pathos* (the quotation in the final sentence of the paragraph).

- **Paragraph 5:** This paragraph begins the transition to the opposite side. The writer begins advancing her own claim—that people aren't willing to sacrifice convenience and price to charm and tradition. She also suggests that the small-town American Main Street that Wal-Mart is replacing was dying anyway.
  Argument strategy: This paragraph makes a transition from the counterargument to the writer's own argument. Initially, the appeal is to *logos*: she draws an analogy between the passing of traditional Main Street stores and the passing of typewriters and horses and buggies. This is followed by another appeal to *pathos*—the importance of efficiency, convenience, and cheapness.

- **Paragraph 6:** The writer admits that Wal-Marts are not pretty, charming, or unique, but argues that the mom-and-pop stores have their own problems: small selection, nonresponsiveness to customer needs, indifferent service, and relatively high prices.
  Argument strategy: In this paragraph, the writer makes an important *concession* (part of the counterargument) that charm is important; but she continues to use the appeal to *pathos* to support the primary claim. Note that in the middle of the paragraph, the writer makes an appeal to *ethos* ("like most people, I'm willing to sacrifice warmth and individuality if I can get just what I want at a price I can afford"). This statement aligns the writer with what most people want from their shopping experiences. After all, the writer implies, this is a matter of good sense—a quality the reader is likely to think valuable, a quality that she or he appears to share with the writer.

- **Paragraph 7:** This paragraph deals more explicitly than the fifth paragraph with the passing away of traditional small-town America, owing to changes in the economy and in lifestyle.

    Argument strategy: In this paragraph the writer follows through with her strategy of relying upon a combination of *logos* and *pathos* to support her claim. Beginning by summarizing the reasons for the decline of Main Street, she concludes the paragraph with quotations focusing on the sad but inevitable passing of a way of life.

- **Paragraph 8:** Here the writer concedes that people are free to fight Wal-Mart coming to their town if they don't want the giant store; but a better course of action might be for local merchants to adjust to Wal-Mart by offering goods and services that the giant store is unwilling or unable to, such as home delivery and specialty merchandise.

    Argument strategy: At this point, the writer focuses almost all her attention on the appeal to logic: she summarizes both the essential nature of the conflict and suggestions offered by one source for counteracting the Wal-Mart threat.

- **Paragraph 9:** The writer concludes by reemphasizing her claim: Wal-Mart is successful because it gives customers what they want.

    Argument strategy: The writer wraps up her argument by reemphasizing the reasons offered for Wal-Mart's success. She rounds off her discussion by repeating, in quotation marks, the "villain" epithet with which the paper begins. The final sentence again combines the appeal to *pathos* (we admittedly cannot call Wal-Mart "pretty") and *logos* (in view of the evidence offered as support, it makes no sense to label Wal-Mart a "villain").

Of course, many other approaches to an argument synthesis would be possible based on the sources provided here. One, obviously, would be the opposite argument: that in embracing Wal-Marts and other giant chains, America is losing part of its soul—or, at a less profound level, small towns are losing part of their charm and distinctive character. Another might be to assess the quality of the various positions according, for example, to the nature of the evidence provided or the type of logic employed. Another might be to de-emphasize the more concrete issue of stores such as Wal-Mart and to focus on the broader issue of changes in small-town life. Whatever your approach to the subject, in first *critically examining* the various sources and then *synthesizing* them to support your argument, you are engaging in the kind of critical thinking that is essential to success in a good deal of academic and professional work.

DEVELOPING AND ORGANIZING THE SUPPORT FOR YOUR ARGUMENTS

Experienced writers seem to have an intuitive sense of how to develop and present the supporting evidence for their claims; this sense is developed through much hard work and practice. Less experienced writers wonder what to say first, and having decided on that, wonder what to say next. There is no single method of presentation. But the techniques of even the most experienced writers often boil down to a few tried and tested arrangements.

As we've seen in the model synthesis in this chapter, the key to devising effective arguments is to find and use those kinds of support that most persuasively strengthen your claim. Some writers categorize support into two broad types: *evidence* and *motivational appeals.* Evidence, in the form of facts, statistics, and expert testimony, helps make the appeal to *logos* or reason. Motivational appeals—appeals to *pathos* and to *ethos*—are employed to get people to change their minds, to agree with the writer or speaker, or to decide upon a plan of activity.

Following are some of the most common principles for using and organizing support for your claims.

Summarize, Paraphrase, and Quote Supporting Evidence

In most of the papers and reports you will write in college and the professional world, evidence and motivational appeals derive from summarizing, paraphrasing, and quoting material in the sources that either have been provided to you or that you have independently researched. (See Chapter 1 on when to summarize, paraphrase, and quote material from sources.) As we noted above, the third paragraph of the Wal-Mart synthesis offers all three treatments of evidence: in the first sentence, the writer *summarizes* anti–Wal-Mart sentiment in the sources; in the second sentence, she *paraphrases* Sarah Anderson; in the third sentence, she *quotes* Bob Ortega.

Provide Various Types of Evidence and Motivational Appeals

Keep in mind the appeals to both *logos* and *pathos.* As we've discussed, the appeal to *logos* is based on evidence that consists of a combination of *facts, statistics,* and *expert testimony.* In the Wal-Mart synthesis, the writer uses all of these varieties of evidence: facts (the economic decline of small-town America, as discussed in paragraph 7), statistics (the growth of Wal-Mart, as documented in paragraph 2), and testimony (the quotations in paragraph 3). The appeal to *pathos* is based on the appeal to the needs and values of the audience. In the Wal-Mart synthesis, this appeal is exemplified in the use of support (for example, the quotations in paragraph 6 about the limitations of mom-and-pop stores) that are likely to make readers upset or dissatisfied because they feel that they need greater selection, efficiency, and economy than the smaller stores can offer them.

Use Climactic Order

Organize by climactic order when you plan to offer a number of different categories or elements of support for your claim. Recognize, however, that some are more important—that is, are likely to be more persuasive—than others. The basic principle here is that you should *save the most important evidence for the end,* since whatever you have said last is what readers are likely to most remember. A secondary principle is that whatever you say first is what they are *next* most likely to remember. Therefore, when you have several reasons to support your claim, an effective argument strategy is to present the second most important, then one or more additional reasons, and finally, the most important reason.

Use Logical or Conventional Order

Using logical or conventional order means that you use as a template a preestablished pattern or plan for arguing your case.

- One common pattern is describing or arguing a *problem/solution.* Using this pattern, you begin with an introduction in which you typically define the problem, then perhaps explain its origins, then offer one or more solutions, then conclude.

- Another common pattern is presenting *two sides of a controversy.* Using this pattern, you introduce the controversy and (if an argument synthesis) your own point of view or claim, then explain each side's arguments, providing reasons that your point of view should prevail. This was the pattern of our argument synthesis: After an introduction to the controversy, the writer defined the problem by establishing the spectacular growth of Wal-Mart, then presented both sides of the controversy—taking care, because of the principle of climactic order, to present the pro–Wal-Mart side last.

- Another common pattern is *comparison-contrast.* In fact, this pattern is so important that we will discuss it separately in the next section.

- The order in which you present elements of an argument is sometimes dictated by the conventions of the discipline in which you are writing. For example, lab reports and experiments in the sciences and social sciences often follow this pattern: *Opening* or *Introduction, Methods and Materials* [of the experiment or study], *Results, Discussion.*

Present and Respond to Counterarguments

As we have seen in the Wal-Mart synthesis, people who develop arguments on a controversial topic can effectively use *counterargument* to help support their claims. When you use counterargument, you present an argument *against* your claim, but then show that this argument is weak or flawed. The advantage of this technique is that you demonstrate that you are aware of the other side of the argument and that you are prepared to answer it.

Here is how a counterargument typically is developed:

A. Introduction and claim
B. Main opposing argument
C. Refutation of opposing argument
D. Main positive argument

In the Wal-Mart synthesis, the writer gives a fair representation—using summary, paraphrase, and quotation—of the anti–Wal-Mart case for the purpose of showing that it is weaker than the pro–Wal-Mart case.

Use Concession

Concession is a variation of counterargument. As in counterargument, you present the opposing viewpoint, but instead of demolishing that argument, you concede that it does have some validity and even some appeal, although your own argument is the stronger one. This bolsters your own standing—your own ethos—as a fair-minded person who is not blind to the virtues of the other side.

Here is an outline for a concession argument:

A. Introduction and claim
B. Important opposing argument
C. Concession that this argument has some validity
D. Positive argument(s)

Sometimes, when you are developing a *counterargument* or *concession argument*, you may become convinced of the validity of the opposing point of view and change your own views. Don't be afraid of this happening. Writing is a tool for learning. To change your mind because of new evidence is a sign of flexibility and maturity, and your writing can only be the better for it.

Use Comparison-Contrast

A particularly important type of argument synthesis uses a comparison and contrast pattern. Comparison-and-contrast techniques enable you to examine two subjects (or sources) in terms of one another. When you compare, you consider *similarities*. When you contrast, you consider *differences*. By comparing and contrasting, you perform a multifaceted analysis that often suggests subtleties that otherwise might not have come to your (or the reader's) attention.

To organize a comparison-and-contrast argument, you must carefully read sources in order to discover *significant criteria for analysis*. A *criterion* is a specific point to which both of your authors refer and about which they may agree or disagree. (For example, in a comparative report on compact cars, criteria for *comparison and contrast* might be road handling, fuel economy, and comfort of ride.) The best criteria are those that allow you not only to account for obvious similarities and differences between sources but also to plumb deeper, to more subtle and significant similarities and differences.

Organizing Comparison-and-Contrast Syntheses

There are two basic approaches to organizing a comparison-and-contrast synthesis: organization by *source* and organization by *criteria*.

1. *Organizing by source.* You can organize a comparative synthesis as a sequence of summaries of your sources, followed by a discussion in which you point out significant similarities and differences between passages. Having read the summaries and become familiar with the distinguishing features of each passage, your readers will likely be able to appreciate the more obvious similarities and differences. Follow up on these summaries by discussing both the obvious and subtle comparisons and contrasts, focusing on the most significant.

   Organization by source is best saved for passages that are briefly summarized. If the summary of your source becomes too long, your readers might forget the remarks you made in the first summary as they are reading the second. A comparison-and-contrast synthesis organized by source might proceed like this:

   I. Introduce the essay; lead to thesis.

   II. Summarize passage A by discussing its significant features.

   III. Summarize passage B by discussing its significant features.

   IV. Write a paragraph (or two) in which you discuss the significant points of comparison and contrast between passages A and B. Alternatively, you could begin the process of comparison-contrast in section III.

   End with a conclusion in which you summarize your points and, perhaps, raise and respond to pertinent questions.

2. *Organizing by criteria.* Instead of summarizing entire passages one at a time with the intention of comparing them later, you could discuss two passages simultaneously, examining the views of each author point by point (criterion by criterion), comparing and contrasting these views in the process. The criterion approach is best used when you have a number of points to discuss or when passages are long and/or complex. A comparison-and-contrast synthesis organized by criteria might look like this:

   I. Introduce the essay; lead to thesis.

   II. Criterion 1
      A. Discuss what author A says about this point.
      B. Discuss what author B says about this point, comparing and contrasting B's treatment of the point with A's.

III. Criterion 2
    A. Discuss what author A says about this point.
    B. Discuss what author B says about this point, comparing and contrasting B's treatment of the point with A's.

And so on. Proceed criterion by criterion until you have completed your discussion. Be sure to arrange criteria with a clear method; knowing how the discussion of one criterion leads to the next will ensure smooth transitions throughout your paper. End with a conclusion in which you summarize your points and, perhaps, raise and respond to pertinent questions.

EXERCISE 5.6

Comparing and Contrasting

Refer back to two of the readings on the Wal-Mart controversy that take opposing sides, such as Sarah Anderson's "Wal-Mart's War on Main Street" on pages 136–37 and Jo-Ann Johnston's "Who's Really the Villain?" on pages 137–40. Identify at least three significant criteria for comparative analysis—three specific points to which both authors refer, and about which they agree or disagree. Then imagine you are preparing to write a short comparison-and-contrast paper and devise two detailed outlines: the first organized by source, and the second organized by criteria.

Avoid Common Fallacies in Developing and Using Support

In Chapter 2, in the section on "Critical Reading," we considered some of the criteria that, as a reader, you may use for evaluating informative and persuasive writing (see pages 50–61). We discussed how you can assess the accuracy, the significance, and the author's interpretation of the information presented. We also considered the importance in good argument of clearly defined key terms and the pitfalls of emotionally loaded language. Finally, we saw how to recognize such logical fallacies as either/or reasoning, faulty cause-and-effect reasoning, hasty generalization, and false analogy. As a writer, no less than as a critical reader, be aware of these common problems and try to avoid them.

EXERCISE 5.7

Practicing Arguments

Devise a one-sentence claim about the Wal-Mart controversy that differs from that made in the model synthesis. Then write several paragraphs discussing the argument strategies that you could use to develop this claim. What types of evidence—facts, statistics, and expert opinions—from the readings would you use? What motivational appeals (*ethos* and *pathos*) would be appropriate? Which counterarguments would you address, and how would you address them? What concessions would you make?

SUMMARY

In this chapter and Chapter 4 preceding it, we've considered two main types of synthesis: the *explanatory synthesis* and the *argument synthesis.* Although for ease of comprehension we've placed them into separate categories, these types are not, of course, mutually exclusive. Both explanatory syntheses and argument syntheses often involve elements of one another. Which format you choose will depend upon your *purpose* and the method that you decide is best suited to achieve this purpose.

If your main purpose is to help your audience understand a particular subject, and in particular to help them understand the essential elements or significance of this subject, then you will be composing an explanatory synthesis. If your main purpose, on the other hand, is to persuade your audience to agree with your viewpoint on a subject, or to change their minds, or to decide upon a particular course of action, then you will be composing an argument synthesis. If one effective technique of making your case is to establish similarities or differences between your subject and another one, then you will compose a comparison-contrast synthesis—which may well be just *part* of a larger synthesis.

In planning and drafting these syntheses, you can draw upon a variety of strategies: supporting your claims by summarizing, paraphrasing, and quoting from your sources; using appeal to *logos, pathos,* and *ethos;* and choosing from among formats such as climactic or conventional order, counterargument, and concession, that will best help you to achieve your purpose.

The strategies of synthesis you've practiced in these last two chapters will be dealt with again in Chapter 6, on Research, where we'll consider a category of synthesis commonly known as the research paper. The research paper involves all of the skills in summary, critique, and synthesis that we've discussed so far, the main difference being, of course, that you won't find the sources you need in this particular text. We'll discuss approaches to locating and critically evaluating sources, selecting material from among them to provide support for your claims, and finally, documenting your sources in standard professional formats.

Research

6

GOING BEYOND THIS TEXT

In this chapter we'll discuss how you can use the skills you've learned in writing summaries, critiques, syntheses, and analyses to conduct research and to compose research papers and reports. Research is a wide-ranging process that can result in a number of types of written documents (see the box on page 164). When we need to find answers or to make discoveries, we engage in research. In your work as an undergraduate college student, you are usually asked to conduct research in order to produce a particular type of written document: the research paper. A research paper is generally considered a major academic endeavor, and frequently it is. But even a paper based on only one or two sources outside the scope of assigned reading has been researched. Research requires you to (1) locate and take notes on relevant sources and organize your findings; (2) summarize or paraphrase these sources; (3) critically evaluate them for their value and relevance to your subject; (4) synthesize information and ideas from several sources that best support your own critical viewpoint; and (5) analyze concepts and phenomena, often by applying theoretical concepts to them.

RESEARCH PAPERS IN THE ACADEMIC DISCIPLINES

Though most of your previous experience with research papers may have been in English classes, you should be prepared for instructors in other academic disciplines to assign papers with significant research components. Here, for example, is a sampling of research topics that have been assigned recently in a broad range of undergraduate courses:

Anthropology: Identify, observe, and gather data pertaining to a particular subculture within the campus community; describe the internal dynamics of this group, and account for these dynamics in terms of theories of relevant anthropologists and sociologists.

Art History: Discuss the main differences between Romanesque and Gothic sculpture, using the sculptures of Jeremiah (St. Pierre Cathedral) and St. Theodore (Chartres Cathedral) as major examples.

163

Asian-American Studies:	Address an important socio-psychological issue for Asian-American communities and/or individuals—for example, the effects of stereotypes, mental health problems, gender relations, academic achievement, assertiveness, or interracial marriage. Review both the theoretical and research literature on the issue, conduct personal interviews, and draw conclusions from your data.
Environmental Studies:	Choose a problem or issue of the physical environment at any level from local to global. Use both field and library work to explore the situation. Include coverage of the following: (1) the history of the issue or problem; (2) the various interest groups involved, taking note of conflicts among them; (3) critical facts and theories from environmental science necessary to understand and evaluate the issue or problem; (4) impact and significance of management measures already taken or proposed; (5) your recommendations for management of the solution.
Film Studies:	Choose a particular period of Italian film and discuss major film trends or production problems within that period.

WHERE DO WE FIND WRITTEN RESEARCH?

Here are just a few types of writing that involve research:

Academic Writing

- **Research papers.** Research an issue and write a paper incorporating the results of that research.
- **Literature reviews.** Research and review relevant studies and approaches to a particular science or social-science topic.
- **Experimental reports.** Research previous studies in order to refine—or show need for—your current approach; conduct primary research.
- **Case studies.** Conduct both primary and secondary research.
- **Position papers.** Research approaches to an issue in order to formulate your own approach.

Workplace Writing

- **Reports in business, science, engineering, social services, medicine**
- **Market analysis**
- **Business Plans**
- **Environmental Impact Reports**
- **Legal Research: Memorandum of Points and Authorities**

History: Write a paper analyzing the history of a public policy (for example, the U.S. Supreme Court's role in undermining the civil rights of African-Americans between 1870 and 1896), drawing your sources from the best, most current scholarly histories available.

Physics: Research and write a paper on solar cell technology, covering the following areas: basic physical theory, history and development, structure and materials, types and characteristics, practical uses, state of the art, and future prospects.

Political Science: Explain the contours of California's water policy in the last few decades and then, by focusing on one specific controversy, explain and analyze the way in which policy was adapted and why. Consider such questions as these: Where does the water comes from? How much is there? Who uses it? Who pays for it? How much does it cost? Should more water resources be developed?

Psychology: Explore some issue related to the testing of mental ability; for example, the effects of time limits upon test reliability.

Religious Studies: Select a particular religious group or movement present in the nation for at least twenty years and show how its belief or practice has changed since members of the group have been in America or, if the group began in America, since its first generation.

Sociology: Write on one of the following topics: (1) a critical comparison of two (or more) theories of deviance; (2) a field or library research study of those in a specific deviant career: thieves, drug addicts, prostitutes, corrupt politicians, university administrators; (3) portrayals of deviance in popular culture—e.g., television accounts of terrorism, incest, domestic violence; (4) old age as a form of deviance in the context of youth culture; (5) the relationship between homelessness and mental illness.

Some of these research papers allow students a considerable range of choice (within the general subject); others are highly specific in requiring students to address a particular issue. Most of these papers call for some library research; a few call for a combination of library and field research; others may be based entirely on field research. As with all academic writing, your first task is to make sure you understand the assignment. Remember to critically read and analyze the specific task(s) required of you in a research paper assignment.

FINDING A SUBJECT

When you are not assigned a specific subject to research, you're faced with finding your own subject (usually within the parameters of the course you're

---

WRITING THE RESEARCH PAPER

Here is an overview of the main steps involved in writing research papers. Keep in mind that, as with other writing projects, writing research papers is a recursive process. For instance, you will gather data at various stages of your writing, as the list below illustrates.

Data Gathering and Invention 1

- **Find a subject.** Decide what subject you are going to research and write about.
- **Develop a research question.** Formulate an important question that you would like to answer through your research.
- **Conduct preliminary research.** Consult knowledgeable people, general and specialized encyclopedias, overviews and bibliographies in recent books, the *Bibliographic Index*, and subject heading guides.
- **Refine your research question.** Based on your preliminary research, brainstorm about your topic and ways to answer your research question. Sharpen your focus, refining your question and planning the sources you'll need to consult.
- **Conduct focused research.** Consult books, electronic databases, general and specialized periodicals, biographical indexes, general and specialized dictionaries, government publications, and other appropriate sources. Conduct interviews and surveys, as necessary.

Data Gathering and Invention 2

- **Develop a working thesis.** Based on your initial research, formulate a working thesis that attempts to respond to your research question.
- **Develop a working bibliography.** Keep a working bibliography (either paper or electronic) of your sources. Make this bibliography easy to sort and rearrange.

---

writing for). Within a course's broad subject area, you must narrow your focus. Review course readings and notes, and think back to issues of interest to you or questions you may have had. If you have trouble choosing a topic, do some writing to help free up your thoughts. Review the discussion of narrowing a subject in Chapter 3, pages 81–83.

THE RESEARCH QUESTION

Research handbooks generally advise students to narrow their subjects as much as possible. A ten-page paper on the modern feminist movement would be unmanageable. You would have to do an enormous quantity of

- **Evaluate sources.** Attempt to determine the veracity and reliability of your sources; use your critical reading skills; check *Book Review Digest;* look up biographies of authors.
- **Take notes from sources.** Paraphrase and summarize important information and ideas from your sources. Copy down important quotations. Note page numbers from sources of this quoted and summarized material.
- **Arrange your notes according to your outline.** Develop a working outline of topics to be covered in your paper. Arrange your notes according to this outline.

Drafting

- **Write your draft.** Write the preliminary draft of your paper, working from your notes, according to your outline.
- **Avoid plagiarism.** Take care to cite all quoted, paraphrased, and summarized source material, making sure that your own wording and sentence structure differ from those of your sources.
- **Cite sources.** Use in-text citations and a Works Cited or References list, according to the conventions of the discipline (e.g., MLA, APA, CBE).

Revision

- **Revise your draft.** Check that your thesis still fits with your paper's focus. Use transitional words and phrases to ensure coherence. Make sure that the research paper reads smoothly, logically, and clearly from beginning to end. Check for development.

Editing

- **Edit your draft.** Check for style, combining short, choppy sentences and ensuring variety in your sentence structures. Check for grammatical correctness, punctuation, and spelling.

research (a preliminary computer search of this subject would yield several thousand items), and you couldn't hope to produce anything other than a superficial treatment of such a broad subject. You could, however, write a paper on the contemporary feminist response to a particular social issue, or the relative power of current feminist political organizations. It's difficult to say, however, how narrow is narrow enough. (A literary critic once produced a twenty-page article analyzing the first paragraph of Henry James's *The Ambassadors.*)

Perhaps more helpful as a guideline on focusing your research is to seek to answer a particular question, a *research question.* For example, how did the Clinton administration respond to criticisms of bilingual education? To what extent is America perceived by European critics to be in decline? Did Exxon behave responsibly in handling the *Valdez* oil spill? How has the debate over genetic engineering evolved during the past decade? To what extent do contemporary cigarette ads perpetuate sexist attitudes? Or how do contemporary cigarette ads differ in message and tone from cigarette ads in the 1950s? Focusing on questions such as these and approaching your research as a way of answering such questions is probably the best way to narrow your subject and ensure focus in your paper. The essential answer to this research question eventually becomes your *thesis;* in the paper, you present evidence that systematically supports your thesis.

EXERCISE 6.1

Constructing Research Questions

Moving from a broad topic or idea to a well-focused research question can be challenging. Practice this skill by working with small groups of your classmates to construct research questions about the following topics (or come up with some topics of your own). Write at least one research question for each topic listed; then discuss these topics and questions with the other groups in class.

Racial or gender stereotypes in television shows

Drug addiction in the U.S. adult population

Global environmental policies

Employment trends in high-technology industries

United States energy policy

PRELIMINARY RESEARCH

Once you have a research question, you want to see what references are available. You want to familiarize yourself quickly with the basic issues and generate a preliminary list of sources. This will help you refine your research question and conduct efficient research once you've attained more focus. There are many ways to go about finding preliminary sources; some of the more effective ones are listed in the box on page 169. We'll consider a few of these suggestions in more detail.

Consulting Knowledgeable People

When you think of research, you may immediately think of libraries and print material. But don't neglect a key reference—other people. Your *instructor* probably can suggest fruitful areas of research and some useful sources. Try to see your instructor during office hours, however, rather than immediately before or after class, so that you'll have enough time for a productive discussion.

Once you get to the library, ask a *reference librarian* which reference sources (e.g., bibliographies, specialized encyclopedias, periodical indexes, statistical

---

**HOW TO FIND PRELIMINARY SOURCES
AND NARROW THE SUBJECT**

- Ask your instructor to recommend sources on the subject.
- Ask your college librarian for useful reference tools in your subject area.
- Read an encyclopedia article on the subject and use the bibliography following the article to identify other sources.
- Read the introduction to a recent book on the subject and review that book's bibliography to identify more sources.
- Consult the annual *Bibliographic Index* (see pages 171–72 for details).
- Use an Internet search engine to explore your topic. Type in different key-word or search term combinations and browse the sites you find for ideas and references to sources you can look up later (see the box on pages 174–75 for details).
- If you need help in narrowing a broad subject, try one or more of the following:
  —search by subject in an electronic database to see how the subject breaks down into components;
  —search the subject heading in an electronic periodical catalog, such as *InfoTrac*, or in a print catalog such as the *Readers' Guide to Periodical Literature;*
  —search the *Library of Congress Subject Headings* catalog (see Subject-Heading Guides, page 172 for details).

---

almanacs) you need for your particular area of research. Librarians won't do your research for you, but they'll be glad to show you how to research efficiently and systematically.

You can also obtain vital primary information from people when you interview them, ask them to fill out questionnaires or surveys, or have them participate in experiments. We'll cover this aspect of research in more detail below.

Encyclopedias

Reading an encyclopedia entry about your subject will give you a basic understanding of the most significant facts and issues. Whether the subject is American politics or the mechanics of genetic engineering, the encyclopedia article—written by a specialist in the field—offers a broad overview that may serve as a launching point to more specialized research in a particular area. The article may illuminate areas or raise questions that you feel motivated to pursue further. Equally important, the encyclopedia article frequently concludes with an *annotated bibliography* describing important books and articles on the subject.

Encyclopedias have certain limitations. First, most professors don't accept encyclopedia articles as legitimate sources for academic papers. You should use encyclopedias primarily to familiarize yourself with (and to select a particular aspect of) the subject area and as a springboard for further research. Also, because new editions appear only once every five or ten years, the information they contain—including bibliographies—may not be current. Current editions of the *Encyclopaedia Britannica* and the *Encyclopedia Americana,* for instance, may not include information about the most recent developments in biotechnology.

Some of the most useful general encyclopedias include the following:

American Academic Encyclopedia

Encyclopedia Americana

New Encyclopaedia Britannica

Keep in mind that the library also contains a variety of more *specialized encyclopedias.* These encyclopedias restrict themselves to a particular disciplinary area, such as chemistry, law, or film, and are considerably more detailed in their treatment of a subject than are general encyclopedias. Here are examples of specialized encyclopedias:

Social Sciences

Encyclopedia of Education

Encyclopedia of Psychology

Guide to American Law

International Encyclopedia of the Social Sciences

Humanities

Encyclopedia of American History

Encyclopedia of Art

Encyclopedia of Religion and Ethics

International Encyclopedia of Film

The New College Encyclopedia of Music

Science and Technology

Encyclopedia of Biological Sciences

Encyclopedia of Computer Science and Engineering

Encyclopedia of Physics

McGraw-Hill Encyclopedia of Environmental Science

Van Nostrand's Scientific Encyclopedia

Business

Encyclopedia of Banking and Finance

Encyclopedia of Economics

Exploring Specialized Encyclopedias

Go to the Reference section of your campus library and locate several specialized encyclopedias within your major or area of interest. Look through the encyclopedias, noting their organization, and read entries on topics that interest you. Jot down some notes describing the kinds of information you find. You might also use this opportunity to look around at the other materials available in the Reference section of the library, including the *Bibliographic Index*, *Biographical Indexes*, the *Book Review Digest*, and *Periodical Indexes* (see below).

Overviews and Bibliographies in Recent Books

If your professor or a bibliographic source directs you to an important recent book on your subject, skim the introductory (and possibly the concluding) material to the book, along with the table of contents, for an overview of key issues. Look also for a bibliography, works cited, and/or references list. These lists are extremely valuable resources for locating material for research. For example, Zvi Dor-Ner's book *Columbus and the Age of Discovery* includes a four-page annotated bibliography of important reference sources on Columbus and the age of exploration.

Keep in mind that authors are not necessarily objective about their subjects, and some have particularly biased viewpoints that you may unwittingly carry over to your paper, treating them as objective truth.* However, you may still be able to get some useful information out of such sources. Alert yourself to authorial biases by looking up the reviews of your book in the *Book Review Digest* (described on page 173). Additionally, look up biographical information on the author (see Biographical Indexes, page 184), whose previous writings or professional associations may suggest a predictable set of attitudes on the subject of your book.

Bibliographic Index

The *Bibliographic Index* is a series of annual volumes that enables you to locate bibliographies on a particular subject. The bibliographies it refers to generally appear at the end of book chapters or periodical articles, or they may themselves be book or pamphlet length. Browsing through the

---

*Bias is not necessarily bad. Authors, like all other people, have certain preferences and predilections that influence the way they view the world and the kinds of arguments they make. As long as they inform you of their biases, or as long as you are aware of them and take them into account, you can still use these sources judiciously. (You might gather valuable information from a book about the Watergate scandal, even if it were written by former President Richard Nixon or one of his top aides, as long as you make proper allowance for their understandable biases.) Bias becomes a potential problem only when it masquerades as objective truth or is accepted as such by the reader. For suggestions on identifying and assessing authorial bias, see the material on persuasive writing (pages 53–61) and evaluating assumptions (pages 63–65) in Chapter 2.

Bibliographic Index in a general subject area may give you ideas for further research in particular aspects of the subject, along with particular references.

Subject-Heading Guides

Seeing how a general subject (e.g., education) is broken down in other sources also could stimulate research in a particular area (e.g., bilingual primary education in California). As in the table of contents of a book, the general subject (the book title) is analyzed into its secondary subject headings (the chapter titles). To locate such sets of secondary subject headings, consult:

- an electronic database or a subject directory as found at yahoo.com
- an electronic or print periodical catalog (e.g., *InfoTrac, Readers' Guide, Social Science Index*)
- *The Library of Congress Subject Headings* catalog
- The *Propaedia* volume of the *New Encyclopaedia Britannica* (1998)

FOCUSED RESEARCH

Once you've narrowed your scope to a particular subject and a particular research question (or set of research questions), you're ready to undertake more focused research. Your objective now is to learn as much as you can about your particular subject. Only in this way will you be qualified to make an informed response to your research question. This means you'll have to become something of an expert on the subject—or, if that's not possible, given time constraints, you can at least become someone whose critical viewpoint is based solidly on the available evidence. In the following pages we'll suggest how to find sources for this kind of focused research. In most cases, your research will be *secondary* in nature, based on (1) *books;* (2) *electronic databases;* (3) *articles;* and (4) *specialized reference sources.* In certain cases, you may gather your own *primary* research, using (5) *interviews, surveys,* structured observation, or content/textual analysis.

Books

Books are useful in providing both breadth and depth of coverage of a subject. Because they generally are published at least a year or two after the events treated, they also tend to provide the critical distance that is sometimes missing from articles. Conversely, this delay in coverage also means that the information you find in books will not be as current as information you find in journals. And of course, books also may be shallow, inaccurate, outdated, or hopelessly biased. (For help in making such determinations, see *Book Review Digest,* next.) You can locate relevant books through the electronic or card catalog. When using this catalog, you may search in three ways: (1) by *author,* (2) by *title,* and (3) by *subject.* Entries include the call number, publication information, and, frequently, a summary of the book's contents. Larger libraries use the Library of Congress cataloging system for call numbers (e.g., E111/C6); smaller ones use the Dewey Decimal System (e.g., 970.015/C726).

Book Review Digest

Perhaps the best way to determine the reliability and credibility of a book you may want to use is to look it up in the annual *Book Review Digest.* These volumes list (alphabetically by author) the most significant books published during the year, supply a brief description of each, and, most importantly, provide excerpts from (and references to) reviews. If a book receives bad reviews, you don't necessarily have to avoid it (the book still may have something useful to offer, and the review itself may be unreliable). But you should take any negative reaction into account (particularly ones concerning the reliability and accuracy of the author's information) when using that book as a source.

Electronic Databases

Much of the information that is available in print—and a good deal that is not—is available in electronic form. Almost certainly, your library card catalog has been computerized, allowing you to conduct searches much faster and more easily than in the past. Increasingly, researchers are accessing magazine, newspaper, and journal articles and reports, abstracts, and other forms of information through *online* databases (many of them on the Internet) and through databases on *CD-ROMs.* One great advantage of using databases (as opposed to print indexes) is that you can search several years' worth of different periodicals at the same time.

Online databases—that is, those that originate outside your computer—are available through international, national, or local (e.g., campus) networks. The largest such database is DIALOG, which provides access to more than 300 million records in more than 400 databases, ranging from sociology to business to chemical engineering. Another large database is LEXIS-NEXIS (like DIALOG, available only through online subscription). LEXIS-NEXIS, and its "Academic Universe" version, provides access to numerous legal, medical, business, and news sources. In addition to being efficient and comprehensive, online databases are generally far more up-to-date than print sources. If you have an Internet connection from your own computer, you can access many of these databases—including those available through commercial online services such as CompuServe and America Online—without leaving your room.

Access to online databases often requires an account and a password, which you may be able to obtain by virtue of your student status. In some cases, you will have to pay a fee to the local provider of the database, based on how long you are online. But many databases will be available to you free of charge. For

USING KEYWORDS AND BOOLEAN LOGIC TO REFINE ONLINE SEARCHES

You will find more—and more relevant—sources on Internet search engines and library databases if you carefully plan your search strategies. *Note: Some search engines and online databases have their own systems for searching—review the "Help" section of different search engines, and use "Advanced Search" options where available. The following tips are general guidelines and their applicability in different search engines may vary somewhat.*

1. **Identify multiple keywords:**
    Write down your topic and/or your research question, then brainstorm synonyms and related terms for the words in that topic/question.

Sample topic: Political activism on college campuses.

Sample research question: What kinds of political activism are college students involved in today?

Keywords: Political activism; college students

Synonyms and related terms: politics; voting; political organizations; protests; political issues; universities; colleges; campus politics.

2. **Conduct searches using different combinations of synonyms and related terms.**

3. **Find new terms in the sources you locate and search with these.**

4. **Use quotation marks around terms you want linked.**
    "political activism"

example, your library may offer access through its computer terminals to magazine and newspaper databases, as well as to the Internet itself.

Various sites and files on the Internet may be accessed through their *gopher* or *ftp* (file transfer protocol) addresses. (Once you locate a file, you may have to download it to your disk or to your e-mail address.) More user-friendly is the *World Wide Web,* which offers graphics, multimedia, and "hyperlinks" to related material in numerous sources. To access these sources, you can either browse (i.e., follow your choice of paths or links wherever they lead) or type in a site's address.

To search for Web information on a particular topic, try using one of the more popular search engines:

5. Use "Boolean operators" to link keywords:
The words AND, OR, and NOT are used in "Boolean logic" to combine search terms and get more precise results than using keywords alone.

AND: Connecting keywords with AND narrows a search by retrieving only sources that contain *both* keywords:

> *Political activism AND college students*

OR: Connecting keywords with OR broadens a search by retrieving all sources that contain at least one of the search terms. This operator is useful when you have a topic/keyword for which there are a number of synonyms. Linking synonyms with OR will lead you to the widest array of sources:

> *Political activism OR protests OR political organizing OR voting OR campus politics*

> *College OR university OR campus OR students*

AND and OR: You can use these terms in combination, by putting the OR phrase in parentheses:

> *(political activism OR protests) AND (college OR university)*

NOT: Connecting keywords with NOT (or, in some cases, AND NOT) narrows a search by excluding certain terms. If you want to focus upon a very specific topic, NOT can be used to limit what the search engine retrieves; however, this operator should be used carefully as it can cause you to miss sources that may actually be relevant:

> *College students NOT high school*

> *Political activism NOT voting*

Google: http://www.google.com

Yahoo: http://www.yahoo.com

AltaVista: http://altavista.com

WebCrawler: http://webcrawler.com

SearchCom: http://www.search.com

Lycos: http://www.lycos.com

Review the "Help" and "Advanced Search" sections of search engines to achieve the best results. See the box on pages 174–75 for some general tips on searching online.

CD-ROMs (compact disk-read only memory) are useful sources for research. Many newspapers, magazines, and journals are available on CD-ROM: for example, the *Readers' Guide to Periodical Literature, The New York Times, Film Index International, PAIS International,* and *America: History and Life,* as are other standard reference sources, such as *Statistical Abstract of the U.S., The Encyclopaedia Britannica, Bibliography of Native North Americans, Environment Reporter,* and *National Criminal Justice Reference Service.* Of particular interest is *InfoTrac,* which provides access to more then 1,000 general interest, business, government, and technological periodicals.

Keep in mind, however, that while electronic sources make it far easier to access information than do their print counterparts, they often do not go back more than twenty years. For earlier information, therefore (e.g., contemporary reactions to the Milgram experiments of the 1960s), you would have to rely on print indexes.

EXERCISE **6.3**

Exploring Electronic Sources

Go to the library and ask a Reference librarian how to access the available CD-ROMs (different libraries have different systems for finding these materials). Check out one or two CD-ROMs with information of interest to you, and spend some time familiarizing yourself with this method of finding information. Next, use the library's Internet connection (or use your home computer if you have Internet access) to access a search engine. Pick a topic/research question of interest to you, review the box on "Using Keywords and Boolean Logic to Refine Online Searches" (pages 174–75), and try different combinations of keywords and Boolean operators to see what sources you can find for your topic. Jot down notes describing the kinds of sources you find, which terms seem to yield the best results, etc. Effective searching on the Internet takes practice; you'll save time when conducting research if you have a good sense of how to use these search strategies.

The Benefits and Pitfalls of the World Wide Web

In the past few years, the Web has become not just a research tool, but a cultural phenomenon. The pop artist Andy Warhol once said that in the future everyone would be famous for fifteen minutes. He might have added that everyone would also have a personal Web site. People use the Web not just to look up information, but also to shop, to make contact with long-lost friends and relatives, to grind their personal or corporate axes, to advertise themselves and their accomplishments.

The Web makes it possible for people sitting at home, work, or school to gain access to the resources of large libraries and to explore corporate and government databases. In her informative book *The Research Paper and the World Wide Web,* Dawn Rodrigues quotes Bruce Dobler and Harry Bloomberg on the essential role of the Web in modern research:

> It isn't a matter anymore of using computer searches to locate existing documents buried in some far-off library or archive. The Web is

providing documents and resources that simply would be too expensive to publish on paper or CD-ROM.

Right now—and not in some distant future—doing research without looking for resources on the Internet is, in most cases, not really looking hard enough. [...] A thorough researcher cannot totally avoid the Internet and the Web.*

And indeed, Web sites are increasingly showing up as sources in both student and professional papers. But like any other rapidly growing and highly visible cultural phenomenon, the Web has created its own backlash. First, as anyone who has tried it knows, for many subjects, systematic research on the Web is not possible. For all the information that is on the Internet, there's a great deal more that is not and never will be converted to digital format. One library director has estimated that only about 4,000 of 150,000 published scholarly journals are available online, and many of these provide only partial texts of relatively recent articles in the paper editions. *The New York Times* is available on the Web, but the online edition includes only a fraction of the content of the print edition, and online versions of the articles generally are abridged and often must be paid for. If you are researching the rise of McCarthyism in America during the early 1950s or trying to determine who else, since Stanley Milgram, has conducted psychological experiments on obedience, you are unlikely to find much useful information for your purpose on the Web.

Moreover, locating what *is* available is not always easy, since there's no standardized method—like the Library of Congress subheading and call number system—of cataloging and cross-referencing online information. The tens of thousands of Web sites and millions of Web pages, together with the relative crudity of search engines such as Yahoo, Google, AltaVista, and WebCrawler, have made navigating an ever-expanding cyberspace an often daunting and frustrating procedure.

Second, it is not a given that people who do research on the Web will produce better papers as a result. David Rothenberg, a professor of philosophy at New Jersey Institute of Technology, believes that "his students' papers had declined in quality since they began using the Web for research."[†] Neil Gabler, a cultural critic, writes:

The Internet is such a huge receptacle of rumor, half-truth, misinformation and disinformation that the very idea of objective truth perishes in the avalanche. All you need to create a "fact" in the web world is a bulletin board or chat room. Gullible cybernauts do the rest.[‡]

---

*Dawn Rodrigues, *The Research Paper and the World Wide Web* (Upper Saddle River, NJ: Prentice Hall, 1997).

[†]Steven R. Knowlton, "Students Lost in Cyberspace," *Chronicle of Higher Education* 2 Nov. 1997: 21

[‡]Neil Gabler, "Why Let Truth Get in the Way of a Good Story?" *Los Angeles Times* "Opinion," 26 Oct. 1997: 1.

Another critic is even blunter: "Much of what purports to be serious information is simply junk—neither current, objective, nor trustworthy. It may be impressive to the uninitiated, but it is clearly not of great use to scholars."*

Of course, print sources are not necessarily objective or reliable either, and in Chapter 2, Critical Reading and Critique, we discussed some criteria by which readers may evaluate the quality of information and ideas in *any* source (pages 51–65). Web sources, however, present a special problem. In most cases, material destined for print has to go through one or more editors and fact checkers before being published, since most authors don't have the resources to publish and distribute their own writing. But anyone with a computer and a modem can "publish" on the Web; furthermore, those with a good Web authoring program and graphics software can create sites that, outwardly at least, look just as professional and authoritative as those of the top academic, government, and business sites. These personal sites will appear in search-engine listings—generated through keyword matches rather than through independent assessments of quality or relevance—and uncritical researchers, using their information as a factual basis for the claims they make in their papers, do so at their peril.

The Internet has also led to increased problems with plagiarism. Many college professors complain these days about receiving work copied directly off of Web sites. Such copying runs the gamut from inadvertent plagiarism of passages copied and pasted off the Web into notes and then transferred verbatim to papers, to intentional theft of others' work, pasted together into a document and claimed as the student's own. In one recent case, an instructor reports that she received a student paper characterized by a more professional writing style than usual for that student. The instructor typed a few keywords from the paper into an Internet search engine, and one of the first sources retrieved turned out to be a professional journal article from which the student had copied whole passages and pasted them together to create a "report." This student received an "F" in the course and was referred to a university disciplinary committee for further action.

The Internet sometimes proves a very tempting source from which to lift materials. But not only is such activity ethically wrong, it is also likely to result in serious punishment, such as permanent notations on your academic transcript or expulsion from school. One of the things all students should know is that while cheating is now made easier by the Internet, the converse is also true: Instructors can often track down the sources for material plagiarized from the Internet just as easily as the student found them in the first place. (Easier, in fact, because now instructors can scan papers into software or Internet programs that will search the Web for matching text.) For more on plagiarism, see the section devoted to this subject later in the chapter, on pages 198–99.

We certainly don't mean to discourage Web research. There are thousands of excellent sites in cyberspace. The reference department of most college and

---

*William Miller, "Troubling Myths About On-Line Information," *Chronicle of Higher Education* 1 Aug. 1997: A44.

university libraries will provide lists of such sites, arranged by discipline, and the most useful sites also are listed in the research sections of many handbooks. Most people locate Web sites, however, by using search engines and by "surfing" the hyperlinks. And for Web sources, more than print sources, the warning *caveat emptor*—let the buyer beware—applies.

Evaluating Web Sources

In their extremely useful site "Evaluating Web Resources" (http://www2.widener.edu/Wolfgram-Memorial-Library/webevaluation/webeval.htm), reference librarians Jan Alexander and Marsha Tate offer some important guidelines for assessing Web sources. First, they point out, it's important to determine what *type* of Web page you are dealing with. Web pages generally fall into one of six types, each with a different purpose: (1) entertainment, (2) business/marketing, (3) reference/information, (4) news, (5) advocacy of a particular point of view or program, (6) personal page. The purpose of the page—informing, selling, persuading, entertaining—has a direct bearing upon the objectivity and reliability of the information presented.

Second, when evaluating a Web page, one should apply the same general criteria as are applied to print sources: (1) accuracy, (2) authority, (3) objectivity, (4) currency, (5) coverage. As we've noted, when assessing the *accuracy* of a Web page, it's important to consider the likelihood that its information has been checked by anyone other than the author. When assessing the *authority* of the page, one considers the author's qualifications to write on the subject and the reputability of the publisher. In many cases, it's difficult to determine not just the qualifications, but the very identity of the author. When assessing the *objectivity* of a Web page, one considers the bias on the part of the author or authors and the extent to which they are trying to sway their reader's opinion. Many Web pages passing themselves off as informational are in fact little more than "infomercials." When assessing the *currency* of a Web page, one asks whether the content is up-to-date and whether the publication date is clearly labeled. Dates on Web pages often are missing or are not indicated clearly. If a date is provided, does it refer to the date the page was written, the date it was placed on the Web, or the date it was last revised? Finally, when assessing the *coverage* of a Web page, one considers which topics are included (and not included) in the work and whether the topics are covered in depth. Depth of coverage has generally not been a hallmark of Web information.

Other pitfalls of Web sites: Reliable sites may include links to other sites that are inaccurate or outdated. Web pages also are notoriously unstable, frequently changing or even disappearing without notice.

Finally, the ease with which it's possible to surf the net can encourage intellectual laziness and make researchers too dependent upon Web resources. Professors are increasingly seeing papers largely or even entirely based upon information in Web sites. While Web sources are indeed an important new source of otherwise unavailable information, there's usually no substitute for library or primary research, such as interviews or field study. The vast majority of printed material in even a small college library—much of it essential to informed research—does not appear on the Web, nor is it likely to in the immediate future. Much of the material you will research in the next few years remains bound within covers. You may well learn of its existence in electronic databases, but at some point you'll have to walk over to a library shelf, pull out a book, and turn printed pages.

Above all, remember that you must apply the critical reading skills you've been practicing throughout this textbook to all your sources—no matter their form or type or where you found them.

EXERCISE 6.4

Practice Evaluating Web Sources

To practice applying the criteria for evaluating Web sources discussed in the section above, go to an Internet search engine and look for sources addressing a topic of interest to you (perhaps following completion of Exercise 6.3, page 176). Try to locate one source representing each of the six types listed above (i. e., entertainment, business/marketing, reference/information, etc.). Print out the main page of each of these sources and bring the copies to class. In small groups of your classmates look over the different sites each student found and make notes on each example's (1) accuracy; (2) authority; (3) objectivity; (4) currency; (5) coverage.

Periodicals: General

Magazines

Because many more periodical articles than books are published every year, you are likely (depending on the subject) to find more information in periodicals than in books. By their nature, periodical articles tend to be more current than books. The best way, for example, to find out about the federal government's current policy on cloning is to look for articles in periodicals and newspapers. However, periodical articles may have less critical distance than books, and they also may date more rapidly—to be superseded by more recent articles.

General periodicals (such as *Time, The New Republic,* and *The Nation*) are intended for nonspecialists. Their articles, which tend to be highly readable, may be written by staff writers, freelancers, or specialists. But usually they do not provide citations or other indications of sources, and so are of limited usefulness for scholarly research.

The most well-known general index is the *Readers' Guide to Periodical Literature,* an index of articles in several hundred general-interest magazines and a few more specialized magazines such as *Business Week* and *Science Digest.* Articles in the *Readers' Guide* are indexed by author, title, and subject.

Another general reference for articles is the *Essay and General Literature Index,* which indexes articles contained in anthologies.

Increasingly, texts and abstracts of articles are available on online databases. These texts may be downloaded to your floppy disk or hard drive or e-mailed to your e-mail address.

Newspapers

News stories, feature stories, and editorials (even letters to the editor) may be important sources of information. Your library certainly will have the *New York Times* index, and it may have indexes to other important newspapers, such as the *Washington Post*, the *Los Angeles Times*, the *Chicago Tribune*, the *Wall Street Journal*, and the *Christian Science Monitor*. Newspaper holdings will be on microfilm (your library may have the *New York Times* on CD-ROM), and you will need a microprinter/viewer to get hard copies.

Note: Because of its method of cross-referencing, the *New York Times* index may at first be confusing. Suppose that you want to find stories on bilingual education during a given year. When you locate the "Bilingual education" entry, you won't find citations but rather a *"See also* Education" reference that directs you to seven dates (August 14, 15, and 17; September 11; October 20, 29, and 30) under the heading of "Education." Under this major heading, references to stories on education are arranged in chronological order from January to December. When you look up the dates to which you were directed, you'll see brief descriptions of these stories on bilingual education.

Periodicals: Specialized

Journal Articles

Many professors will expect at least some of your research to be based on articles in specialized periodicals or "scholarly journals." So instead of (or in addition to) relying on an article from *Psychology Today* for an account of the effects of crack cocaine on mental functioning, you might (also) rely on an article from the *Journal of Abnormal Psychology*. If you are writing a paper on the satirist Jonathan Swift, you may need to locate a relevant article in *Eighteenth-Century Studies*. Articles in such journals normally are written by specialists and professionals in the field, rather than by staff writers or freelancers, and the authors will assume that their readers already understand the basic facts and issues concerning the subject.

To find articles in specialized periodicals, you'll use specialized indexes—that is, indexes for particular disciplines. You also may find it helpful to refer to *abstracts*. Like specialized indexes, abstracts list articles published in a particular discipline over a given period, but they also provide summaries of the articles listed. Abstracts tend to be more selective than indexes, since they consume more space (and involve considerably more work to compile); but, because they also describe the contents of the articles covered, they can save you a lot of time in determining which articles you should read and which ones you can safely skip. Don't treat abstracts alone as sources for research; if you find useful material in an abstract, you need to locate the article to which it applies and use that as your source of information.

Here are some of the more commonly used specialized periodical indexes and abstracts in the various disciplines.

Note: Lists of electronic databases follow the print indexes, but some listed print indexes (e.g., PAIS) also are available in electronic form, such as CD-ROM.

Social Science Indexes
Abstracts in Anthropology
Education Index
Index to Legal Periodicals
Psychological Abstracts
Public Affairs Information Service (PAIS)
Social Science Index
Sociological Abstracts
Women's Studies Abstracts

Social Science Databases
ERIC (Educational Resources Information Center)
PAIS (Public Affairs Information Service)
PSYCHINFO (psychology)
Psychological Abstracts
Social SciSearch
Sociological Abstracts

Humanities Indexes
Abstracts of English Studies
America: History and Life
Art Index
Cambridge Bibliography of English Literature
Essay and General Literature Index
Film/Literature Index
Historical Abstracts
Humanities Index
International Index of Film Periodicals
MLA International Bibliography of Books and Articles on Modern Languages and Literature
Music Index
Religion Index
Year's Work in English Studies

Humanities Databases
Arts and Humanities Citation Index

MLA Bibliography
Philosophers' Index
Historical Abstracts

Science and Technology Indexes
Applied Science and Technology Index
Biological Abstracts
Engineering Index
General Science Index
Index to Scientific and Technical Proceedings

Science and Technology Databases
Aerospace Database
Agricola (agriculture)
Biosis Previews (biology, botany)
Chemical Abstracts search (chemistry)
Compendex (engineering)
Environment Abstracts
MathSci
MEDLINE (medical)
ScienceCitation Index
SciSearch
WSPEC (physics, electronics, computer science)

Business Indexes
Business Index
Business Periodicals Index
Economic Titles/Abstracts
Wall Street Journal *Index*

Business Databases
ABI/INFORM
Econ Abstracts International
Labor Statistics
Standard & Poor's News

Law Databases
LEXIS-NEXIS
Westlaw

Exploring Specialized Periodicals

Visit your campus library and locate the specialized periodical indexes for your major or area of interest (ask a reference librarian to help you). Note the call numbers for specialized periodicals (also called academic journals) in your field, and visit the periodical room or section of the library where recent editions of academic journals are usually housed. Locate the call numbers you've noted, and spend some time looking through the different specialized periodicals in your field. The articles you find in these journals represent some of the most recent scholarship in your field—the kind of scholarship many of your professors are busy conducting. Write half a page or so describing some of the articles you find interesting, and why.

Biographical Indexes

To look up information on particular people, you can use not only encyclopedias but an array of biographical sources. (You can also use biographical sources to alert yourself to potential biases on the part of your source authors.) A brief selection follows:

Living Persons

Contemporary Authors: A Biographical Guide to Current Authors and Their Works

Current Biography

International Who's Who

Who's Who in America

Persons No Longer Living

Dictionary of American Biography

Dictionary of National Biography (Great Britain)

Dictionary of Scientific Biography

Who Was Who

Persons Living or Dead

Biography Almanac

McGraw-Hill Encyclopedia of World Biography

Webster's Biographical Dictionary

Dictionaries

Use dictionaries to look up the meaning of general or specialized terms. Here are some of the most useful dictionaries:

General

Oxford English Dictionary
Webster's New Collegiate Dictionary
Webster's Third New International Dictionary of the English Language

Social Sciences

Black's Law Dictionary
Dictionary of the Social Sciences
McGraw-Hill Dictionary of Modern Economics

Humanities

Dictionary of American History
Dictionary of Films
Dictionary of Philosophy
Harvard Dictionary of Music
McGraw-Hill Dictionary of Art

Science and Technology

Computer Dictionary and Handbook
Condensed Chemical Dictionary
Dictionary of Biology
Dorland's Medical Dictionary

Business

Dictionary of Advertising Terms
Dictionary of Business and Economics
Mathematical Dictionary for Economics and Business Administration
McGraw-Hill Dictionary of Modern Economics: A Handbook of Terms and Organizations

Other Sources/Government Publications

You also may find useful information in other sources. For statistical and other basic reference information on a subject, consult a *handbook* (example: *Statistical Abstracts of the United States*). For current information on a subject as of a given year, consult an *almanac* (example: *World Almanac*). For annual updates of information, consult a *yearbook* (example: *The Statesman's Yearbook*). For maps and other geographic information, consult an *atlas* (example: *New York Times Atlas of the World*). (Often, simply browsing through the reference shelves for data on your general subject—such as

---

CRITICAL READING FOR RESEARCH

- **Read for relationships to your research question.** How does the source help you to formulate and clarify your research question?
- **Read for relationships between sources.** How does each source illustrate, support, expand upon, contradict, or offer an alternative perspective to those of your other sources?
- **Consider the relationship between your source's form and content.** How does the form of the source—specialized encyclopedia, book, article in a popular magazine, article in a professional journal, etc.— affect its content, the manner in which that content is presented, and its relationship to other sources?
- **Pay special attention to the legitimacy of Internet sources.** Consider how the content and validity of the information on the Web page may be affected by the purpose of the site. Assess Web-based information for its (1) accuracy; (2) authority; (3) objectivity; (4) currency; and (5) coverage (Alexander and Tate).

---

biography, public affairs, psychology—will reveal valuable sources of information.) And of course, much reference information is available on government sites on the Web.

Many libraries keep pamphlets in a *vertical file* (i.e., a file cabinet). For example, a pamphlet on AIDS might be found in the vertical file rather than in the library stacks. Such material is accessible through the *Vertical File Index* (a monthly subject-and-title index to pamphlet material).

Finally, note that the U.S. government regularly publishes large quantities of useful information. Some indexes to government publications include the following:

American Statistics Index

Congressional Information Service

The Congressional Record

Information U.S.A.

Interviews and Surveys

Depending on the subject of your paper, some or all of your research may be conducted outside the library. In conducting such primary research, you may perform experiments in science labs, make observations or gather data in courthouses, in city government files, in shopping malls (if you are observing, say, patterns of consumer behavior), in the quad in front of the humanities building, or in front of TV screens (if you are analyzing, say, situation comedies or commercials, or if you are drawing on documentaries or interviews—in which cases you should try to obtain transcripts or tape the programs).

You may want to *interview* you professors, your fellow students, or other individuals who know about your subject. Before interviewing your subject(s), become knowledgeable enough about the topic that you can ask intelligent questions. You also should prepare most of your questions beforehand. Ask "open-ended" questions designed to elicit meaningful responses, rather than "forced choice" questions that can be answered with a word or two, or "leading questions" that presume a particular answer. (Example: Instead of asking "Do you think that men should be more sensitive to women's concerns for equality in the workplace?" ask, "To what extent do you see evidence that men are insufficiently sensitive to women's concerns for equality in the workplace?") Ask follow-up questions to elicit additional insights or details. If you record the interview (in addition to or instead of taking notes), get your subject's permission, preferably in writing.

Surveys or *questionnaires,* when well prepared, can produce valuable information about the ideas or preferences of a group of people. Before preparing your questions, determine your purpose in conducting the survey, exactly what kind of information you want to obtain, and whom you are going to ask for the information. Decide also whether you want to collect the questionnaires as soon as people have filled them out or whether you want the responses mailed back to you. (Obviously, in the latter case, you have to provide stamped, self-addressed envelopes and specify a deadline for return.) Keep in mind that the larger and more representative your sample of people, the more reliable the survey. As with interviews, it's important to devise and word questions carefully so that they (1) are understandable and (2) don't reflect your own biases. If you're surveying attitudes on capital punishment, for example, and you ask, "Do you believe that the state should endorse legalized murder?" you've loaded the questions to influence people to answer in the negative, and thus you've destroyed the reliability of your survey.

Unlike interview questions, survey questions should be short answer or multiple choice; open-ended questions encourage responses that are difficult to quantify. (You may want to leave space, however, for "additional comments.") Conversely, "yes" or "no" responses or rankings on a 5-point scale are easy to quantify. For example, you might ask a random sample of students in your residence hall the extent to which they are concerned that genetic information about themselves might be made available to their insurance companies—on a scale of 1 (unconcerned) to 5 (extremely concerned). For surveys on certain subjects (and depending on the number of respondents), it may be useful to break out the responses by as many meaningful categories as possible—for example, gender, age, ethnicity, religion, education, geographic locality, profession, and income. Obtaining these kinds of statistical breakdowns, of course, means more work on the part of your respondents in filling out the surveys and more work for you in compiling the responses. If the survey is too long and involved, some subjects won't participate or won't return the questionnaires.

FROM RESEARCH TO WORKING THESIS

The search strategy we've just described isn't necessarily a straight-line process. In other words, you won't always proceed from the kinds of things you do in "preliminary research" to the kinds of things you do in "focused research." You may not formulate a research question until you've done a good deal of focused research. And the fact that we've treated, say, specialized periodical articles before biographical sources does not mean that you should read articles before you read biographical materials. We've described the process as we have for convenience; and, *in general*, it is a good idea to proceed from more general sources to more particular ones. In practice, however, the research procedure often is considerably less systematic. You might begin, for example, by reading a few articles on the subject, and continue by looking up an encyclopedia article or two. Along the way, you might consult specialized dictionaries, book review indexes, and a guide to reference books in the area. Or, instead of proceeding in a straight line through the process, you might find yourself moving in circular patterns—backtracking to previous steps and following up leads you missed or ignored earlier. There's nothing wrong with such variations of the basic search strategy, as long as you keep in mind the kinds of resources that are available to you, and as long as you plan to look up as many of these resources as you can—given the constraints on your time.

One other thing you'll discover as you proceed: research is to some extent a self-generating process. That is, one source will lead you—through references in the text, citations, and bibliographic entries—to others. Your authors will refer to other studies on the subject; and frequently they'll indicate which ones they believe are the most important and why. At some point, if your research has been systematic, you'll realize that you've already looked at most of the key work on the subject. At that point you can be reasonably assured that the research stage of your paper is nearing its end.

As you progress in this, the "data-gathering" stage of your research and writing process, you will typically find yourself moving in and out of the next stage of the process, "invention." Thus, as you locate and read your sources, you may find that your preliminary research question undergoes a change. Suppose you are researching bilingual education. At first you may have been primarily interested in the question of whether bilingual education is a good idea. During your research, you come across S. I. Hayakawa's controversial proposal that English be made the official language of the United States, and you decide to shift the direction of your research toward this particular debate. Or, having made an initial assessment that bilingual education is a good idea, you conclude that Hayakawa is wrong. Be prepared for such shifts: They're a natural—and desirable—part of the research (and learning) process. They indicate that you haven't made up your mind in advance, that you're open to new evidence and ideas.

You're now ready to respond to your modified research questions with a *working thesis*—a statement that controls and focuses your entire paper, points toward your conclusion, and is supported by your evidence. See our earlier discussion in Chapter 3 (pages 79–85) on the process of devising and narrowing a thesis.

THE WORKING BIBLIOGRAPHY

As you conduct your research, keep a working bibliography—that is, a set of bibliographic information on all the sources you're likely to use in preparing the paper. Compile full bibliographic information as you consider each source. It's better to spend time during the research process noting information on a source you don't eventually use than to go back to retrieve information—such as the publisher or the date—just as you're writing your final draft.

Now that library catalogs and databases are available online, it's easy to copy and paste your sources' (or potential sources') bibliographic information into a document, or to e-mail citations to yourself for cutting and pasting later. A more traditional but still very efficient way to compile bibliographic information is on 3" x 5" cards. (Note, however, that certain software programs allow you to create sortable electronic cards.) You can easily add, delete, and rearrange cards as your research progresses. Whether you keep bibliographic information on 3" x 5" cards or in a document, be sure to record the following:

a. the author or editor (last name first)

b. the title (and subtitle) of the book or article

c. the publisher and place of publication (if a book) or the title of the periodical

d. the date of publication; if periodical, volume and issue number

e. the inclusive page numbers (if article)

You also may want to include:

f. a brief description of the source (to help you recall it later in the research process)

g. the library call number (to help you relocate the source if you haven't checked it out)

h. a code number, which you can use as a shorthand reference to the source in your notes

Your final bibliography, known as "Works Cited" in Modern Language Association (MLA) format and "References" in American Psychological Association (APA) format, consists of the sources you have actually summarized, paraphrased, or quoted in your paper. When you compile the bibliography, arrange your sources alphabetically by authors' last names.

Here is an example of a working bibliography notation or card for a book:

> *Sale, Kirkpatrick. The Conquest of Paradise: Christopher Columbus and the Columbian Legacy. New York: Knopf, 1990.*
>
> *Attacks Columbian legacy for genocide and ecocide. Good treatment of Columbus's voyages (Chaps. 6–8).*

Here is an example of a working bibliography record for an article:

> *Axtell, James. "Europeans, Indians, and the Age of Discovery in American History Textbooks." American Historical Review. 92.3 (1987): 621–32.*
>
> *Finds treatments of subjects in title of article inadequate in most college-level American history texts. Specifies "errors," "half-truths" and "misleading assertions." Recommends changes in nine areas.*

Some instructors may ask you to prepare—either in addition to or instead of a research paper—an *annotated bibliography*. This is a list of relevant works on a subject, with the contents of each briefly described or assessed. The bibliography cards shown provide examples of two entries in an annotated bibliography on the Columbian legacy. Annotations are different from *abstracts* in that they do not claim to be comprehensive summaries; they indicate, rather, how the items may be useful to the researcher.

EVALUATING SOURCES

As you sift through what seems a formidable mountain of material, you'll need to work quickly and efficiently; you'll also need to do some selecting. This means, primarily, distinguishing the more important from the less important (and the unimportant) material. The hints in the box on page 191 can simplify the task.

NOTE-TAKING

People have their favorite ways of note-taking. Some use cards; others use legal pads or spiral notebooks; yet others type notes into a laptop computer, perhaps using a database program. We prefer 4" x 6" cards for note-taking. Such cards have some of the same advantages as 3" x 5" cards for working bibliographies: They can easily be added to, subtracted from, and rearranged to accommodate changing organizational plans. Also, discrete pieces of information from the same source can easily be arranged (and

---

> ## GUIDELINES FOR EVALUATING SOURCES
>
> - **Skim** the source. With a book, look over the table of contents, the introduction and conclusion, and the index; zero in on passages that your initial survey suggests are important. With an article, skim the introduction and the headings.
> - Be on the alert for **references** in your sources to other important sources, particularly to sources that several authors treat as important.
> - Other things being equal, the more **recent** the source, the better. Recent work usually incorporates or refers to important earlier work.
> - If you're considering making multiple references to a book, look up the **reviews** in the *Book Review Digest* or the *Book Review Index*. Also, check the author's credentials in a source such as *Contemporary Authors* or *Current Biography*.
> - Draw on your **critical reading** skills to help you determine the reliability and value of a source. (Review Chapter 2 on Critical Reading and Critique.)

rearranged) into subtopics—a difficult task if you have three pages of notes on an entire article.

Whatever your preferred approach, we recommend including, along with the note itself,

a. a topic or subtopic label, corresponding to your outline (see below)

b. a code number, corresponding to the number assigned the source in the working bibliography

c. a page reference at end of note

Here is a sample notecard for an article by Charles Krauthammer entitled "Hail Columbus, Dead White Male" (*Time*, May 27, 1991):

> *Defenses of Columbus (III B)*
>
> *Defends Columbus against revisionist attacks. Our civilization "turned out better" than that of the Incas. "And mankind is the better for it. Infinitely better. Reason enough to honor Columbus and 1492" (74).*

Here is a notecard for the specialized periodical article by Axtell (see bibliography card on page 190):

Problems with Textbooks (II A)   ⑫

American history textbooks do not give adequate coverage to the Age of
Discovery. An average of only 4% of the textbook pages covering first-
semester topics is devoted to the century that accounts for 30% of the
time between Columbus and Reconstruction. "The challenge of
explaining some of the most complex, important, and interesting events
in human history—the discovery of a new continent, the religious
upheavals of the sixteenth century, the forging of the Spanish empire,
the Columbian biological exchange, the African diaspora—all in
twenty or twenty-five pages—is one that few, if any, textbook authors
have met or are likely to meet" (623).

The notecard is headed by a topic label followed by the tentative location
in the paper outline where the information will be used. The number in the
upper right corner is coded to the corresponding bibliography card. The note
itself in the first card uses *summary* ("Defends Columbus against revisionist
attacks") and *quotation.* The note in the second card uses *summary* (sentence
1), *paraphrase* (sentence 2), and *quotation* (sentence 3). Summary is used to condense important ideas treated in several paragraphs in the sources; paraphrase, for the important detail on textbook coverage; quotation, for
particularly incisive language by the source authors. For general hints on
when to use each of these three forms, see Chapter 1, page 49.

At this point we must stress the importance of using quotation marks
around quoted language *in your notes.* Making sure to note the difference
between your own and quoted language will help you avoid unintentionally
using someone else's words or ideas without crediting them properly. Such
use constitutes plagiarism—a serious academic offense—something that professors don't take lightly; you don't want to invite suspicion of your work,
even unintentionally. See the discussion of plagiarism on pages 198–99 for
more details.

INVENTION STRATEGIES

Brainstorming without Your Notes

As we've mentioned, while you're in the first, data-gathering stage of your
research and writing process—as you're locating, reading, and taking notes on
your sources—you usually move in and out of the next stage, invention. As you
see what work has been conducted on your topic, as you read what others think
and write about the topic, you are naturally led to revise and refine your own
thinking on your topic and research question. So while these two stages in the
process of conducting research and writing about it overlap, at some point you
will have gathered enough materials (although you may not be finished gathering data yet) to be ready to make a more definite move from data-gathering to

invention (but this doesn't mean you won't move back to data-gathering again!)

A useful strategy for making this transition is to put aside your notes and, based on the reading and note-taking you have done, sit down and write about your ideas. What have you learned about your topic? What answers to your research question have you generated? Begin by developing ideas and sorting out your thoughts about your topic. Spending time formulating and clarifying your thoughts *away* from your notes can help you retain authorship of the paper you ultimately write. That is, research papers are meant to represent *your synthesis* of your sources. Too often, students produce research papers that read like patchwork quilts of sources "sewn" together without a clear guiding point. It's up to you have a point that is your own (the thesis, or answer to your research question), and to use your sources to make that point, rather than letting your sources take over and turn your paper into an "information dump."

Brainstorming with Your Notes

Once you have spent time clarifying your thoughts and your understanding of your sources, go back to your notes and check your understanding for accuracy. Revise your thoughts if necessary.

Now it's time to carefully and critically review your notes. Recall that your research originally was stimulated by one or more *research questions,* to which you may have made a tentative response in your *working thesis* (see page 79). As you review your notes, patterns should begin to emerge that either substantiate, refute, or otherwise affect your working thesis. These patterns represent the relationships you discern among the various ideas and pieces of evidence that you investigate. They may be patterns of cause and effect, of chronology, of logical relationships, of comparison and contrast, of pro and con, of correspondence (or lack of correspondence) between theory and reality. Once these patterns begin to emerge, you are ready to begin outlining the structure of your paper.

ARRANGING YOUR NOTES: THE OUTLINE

Working from your original working thesis—or a new thesis that you have developed during the course of data-gathering and invention, you can begin constructing a preliminary outline. This outline indicates the order in which you plan to support your thesis.

For example, on deciding to investigate new genetic technologies, you devise a working thesis focused on the intensity of the debate over the applications of such technologies. Much of the debate, you discover, focuses on arguments about the morality of (1) testing for genetic abnormalities in the fetus, (2) using genetic information to screen prospective employees, and (3) disrupting the ecosystem by creating new organisms. Based on this discovery, you might create a brief outline, numbering each of these three main categories (as examples of the pro-con debates) and using these numbers on your notecards to indicate how you have (at least provisionally) categorized each note. As you continue your research, you'll be able to expand or reduce the scope of your paper, modifying your outline as necessary. Your developing outline becomes a guide to continuing research.

Some people prefer not to develop an outline until they have more or less completed their research. At that point they will look over their notecards or notes, consider the relationships among the various pieces of evidence, possibly arrange their cards into separate piles, and then develop an outline based on their perceptions and insights about the material. They will then rearrange and code the notecards to conform to their newly created outline.

In the past, instructors commonly required students to develop multileveled formal outlines (complete with Roman and Arabic numerals) before writing their first drafts. But many writers find it difficult to generate papers from such elaborate outlines, which sometimes restrict, rather than stimulate, thought. Now, instructors often recommend only that students prepare an *informal outline,* indicating just the main sections of the paper and possibly one level below that. Thus, a paper on how the significance of Columbus's legacy has changed over the years may be informally outlined as follows:

```
Intro: Different views of Columbus, past and
       present;

       -thesis: view of Columbus varies with
       temper of times

Pre-20th century assessments of Columbus and
legacy

The debate over the quincentennial (1992)

       -positive views

       -negative views

Conclusion: How to assess Columbian heritage
```

Such an outline will help you organize your research and should not be unduly restrictive as a guide to writing.

The *formal outline* (a multileveled plan with Roman and Arabic numerals, capital and small lettered subheadings) may still be useful, not so much as an exact blueprint for composition—although some writers do find it useful for this purpose—but rather as a guide to revision. That is, after you have written your draft, outlining it may help you discern structural problems: illogical sequences of material; confusing relationships between ideas; poor unity or coherence; sections that are too abstract or underdeveloped. Many instructors also require that formal outlines accompany the finished research paper.

The formal outline should indicate the logical relationships in the evidence relating to your particular subject (see example below). But it also may reflect the general conventions of presenting academic ideas. Thus, after an *introduction,* papers in the social sciences often proceed with a description of the *methods* of collecting information, continue with a description of the *results* of the investigation, and end with a *conclusion*. Papers in the sciences often follow a similar pattern. Papers in the humanities are generally less standardized in form. In devising a logical organization for your paper, ask yourself how your reader might best be introduced to the subject, be guided through a discussion of the main issues, and be persuaded that your viewpoint is a sound one.

Formal outlines are generally of two types: *topic* and *sentence outlines.* In the topic outline, headings and subheadings are indicated by words or phrases—as in the informal outline above. In the sentence outline, each heading and subheading is indicated in a complete sentence. Both topic and sentence outlines generally are preceded by the *thesis.*

Here is an example of a sentence outline:

> *Thesis:* Assessment of Columbus, his voyages, and his legacy varies, depending on the values of the times.
>
> I. Early—19th century and late—20th century assessments of Columbus are 180 degrees apart.
>
>   A. 19th-century commentators idolize him.
>
>   B. 20th-century commentators often demonize him.
>
>   C. Shifting assessments are based less on hard facts about Columbus than on the values of the culture that assesses him.
>
> II. In the 16th and 17th centuries, Columbus was not yet being used for political purposes.
>
>   A. In the early 16th century, his fame was eclipsed by that of others.
>
>   1. Amerigo Vespucci and Vasco da Gama were considered more successful mariners.
>
>   2. Cortés and Pizarro were more successful in bringing back wealth from the New World.
>
>   B. In the next century, historians and artists began writing of the achievements of Columbus, but without an overt political purpose.
>
>   1. The first biography of Columbus was written by his son Fernando.
>
>   2. Plays about Columbus were written by Lope de Vega and others.
>
>   C. An important exception was that in 1542 the monk Bartolomé de las Casas attacked the Spanish legacy in the Americas—although he did not attack Columbus personally.
>
> III. In the 18th and 19th centuries, Columbus and his legacy began to be used for political purposes.

A. During the late 18th century, Columbus' stature in America increased as part of the attempt to stir up anti-British sentiment.

 1. Columbus was opposed by kings, since he "discovered" a land free of royal authority.

 2. Columbus, the bold visionary who charted unknown territories, became symbolic of the American spirit.

B. During the 19th century, Columbus's reputation reached its peak.

 1. For some, Columbus represented geographical and industrial expansion, optimism, and faith in progress.

 2. For others, Columbus' success was the archetypal rags-to-riches story at the heart of the American Dream.

 3. After the Civil War, Catholics celebrated Columbus as an ethnic hero.

 4. The 400th anniversary of Columbus's landfall both celebrated the past and expressed confidence in the future. Columbus became the symbol of American industrial success.

IV. By the quincentennial of Columbus's landfall, the negative assessments of Columbus were far more evident than were positive assessments.

A. Historians and commentators charged that the consequences of Columbus's "discoveries" were imperialism, slavery, genocide, and ecocide.

B. The National Council of Churches published a resolution blasting the Columbian legacy.

C. Kirkpatrick Sale's *The Conquest of Paradise* also attacked Columbus.

D. Native Americans and others protested the quincentennial and planned counterdemonstrations.

V. Conclusion: How should we judge Columbus?

A. In many ways, Columbus was a man of his time and did not rise above his time.

B. In his imagination and boldness and in the impact of his discoveries, Columbus stands above others of his time.

    C. When we assess Columbus and his legacy, we
       also assess our own self-confidence, our
       optimism, and our faith in progress.

WRITING THE DRAFT

Your goal in drafting your paper is to support your thesis by clearly and logically presenting your evidence—evidence that you summarize, critique, synthesize, and analyze. In effect, you are creating and moderating a conversation among your sources that supports the conclusions you have drawn from your exploration and analysis of the material. The finished paper, however, should not merely represent an amalgam of your sources; it should present your own particular critical perspective on the subject. Your job is to select and arrange your material in such a way that your conclusions seem inevitable (or at least reasonable). You also must select and arrange your material in a way that is fair and logical; remember that your paper will be evaluated to some degree on whether it meets the standards of logical argumentation discussed on pages 57–61. Try not to be guilty of such logical fallacies as hasty generalization, false analogy, and either/or reasoning.

As we suggested in the section on introductions (pages 73–78), when writing the first draft it's sometimes best to skip the introduction (you'll come back to it later when you have a better idea of just what's being introduced) and to start with the main body of your discussion. What do you have to tell your audience about your subject? It may help to imagine yourself sitting opposite your audience in an informal setting like the student center, telling them what you've discovered in the course of your research and why you think it's interesting and significant. The fact that you've accumulated a considerable body of evidence (in your notes) to support your thesis should give you confidence in presenting your argument. Keep in mind, too, that there's no one right way to organize this argument; any number of ways will work, provided each makes logical sense. And if you're working on a computer, it is particularly easy to move whole paragraphs and sections from one place to another, as logic dictates.

Begin the drafting process by looking at your notecards. Arrange the cards to correspond to your outline (or number entries in your notes, if you haven't used notecards). Summarize, paraphrase, and quote from your notecards as you draft. (If you write your first draft by hand, one timesaving technique is to tape photocopied quotations in the appropriate places in your draft.) If necessary, review the material on explanatory and argument syntheses (Chapters 4 and 5). In particular, note the box "Guidelines for Writing Syntheses" (pages 99–100) and the section "Developing and Organizing the Support for Your Arguments" (pages 156–61). When presenting your argument, consider such rhetorical strategies as counterargument, concession, and comparison and contrast. The model student papers in Chapters 4 and 5 on synthesis may serve as models for your own research paper.

As you work through your notes, be selective. Don't provide more evidence or discussion than you need to prove your point. Resist the urge to use *all* of your material just to show how much research you've done. (One author and experienced teacher Susan M. Hubbuch, scornfully refers to papers with too much information as "memory dumps"—consisting of nothing but "mindless regurgitation of everything you have read about a subject.") Also avoid going into extended discussions of what are essentially tangential issues. Keep focused on your research questions and on providing support for your thesis.

At the same time, remember that you *are* working on a rough draft—one that will probably have all kinds of problems, from illogical organization to awkward sentence structure to a banal conclusion. Don't worry about it; you can deal with all such problems in subsequent drafts. The important thing now is get the words on paper or on your disk.

AVOIDING PLAGIARISM

Plagiarism is generally defined as the attempt to pass off the work of another as one's own. Whether born out of calculation or desperation, plagiarism is the least tolerated offense in the academic world. The fact that most plagiarism is unintentional—arising from ignorance of conventions rather than deceitfulness—makes no difference to many professors.

You can avoid plagiarism and charges of plagiarism by following the basic rules below:

RULES FOR AVOIDING PLAGIARISM

- Cite *all* quoted material and *all* summarized and paraphrased material, unless the information is common knowledge (e.g., the Civil War was fought from 1861 to 1865).
- Make sure that both the *wording* and the *sentence structure* of your summaries and paraphrases are substantially your own.

Following is a passage of text, along with several student versions of the ideas represented. (The passage is from Richard Rovere's article on Senator Joseph P. McCarthy, titled "The Most Gifted and Successful Demagogue This Country Has Ever Known."*)

> McCarthy never seemed to believe in himself or in anything he had said. He knew that Communists were not in charge of American foreign policy. He knew that they weren't running the United States

---

*Richard Rovere, "The Most Gifted and Successful Demagogue This Country Has Ever Known," *New York Times Magazine* 30 Apr. 1967.

Army. He knew that he had spent five years looking for Communists in the government and that—although some must certainly have been there, since Communists had turned up in practically every other major government in the world—he hadn't come up with even one.

One student version of this passage reads as follows:

> McCarthy never believed in himself or in anything he had said. He knew that Communists were not in charge of American foreign policy and weren't running the United States Army. He knew that he had spent five years looking for Communists in the government, and although there must certainly have been some there, since Communists were in practically every other major government in the world, he hadn't come up with even one.

Clearly, this is intentional plagiarism. The student has copied the original passage almost word for word.

Here is another version of the same passage:

> McCarthy knew that Communists were not running foreign policy or the Army. He also knew that although there must have been some Communists in the government, he hadn't found a single one, even though he had spent five years looking.

This student has attempted to put the ideas into her own words, but both the wording and the sentence structure still are so heavily dependent on the original passage that even if it *were* cited, most professors would consider it plagiarism.

In the following version, the student has sufficiently changed the wording and sentence structure, and she uses a *signal phrase* (a phrase used to introduce a quotation or paraphrase, signaling to the reader that the words to follow come from someone else) to properly credit the information to Rovere, so that there is no question of plagiarism:

> According to Richard Rovere, McCarthy was cynical enough to know that Communists were running neither the government nor the Army. He also knew that he hadn't found a single Communist in government, even after a lengthy search (192).

Apart from questions of plagiarism, it's essential to quote accurately. You are not permitted to change any part of a quotation or to omit any part of it without using brackets or ellipses (see Chapter 1, pages 45–49).

CITING SOURCES

When you refer to or quote the work of another, you are obligated to credit or cite your source properly. There are two types of citations—in-text citations and full citations at the end of a paper—and they work in tandem.

If you are writing a paper in the humanities, you probably will be expected to use the Modern Language Association (MLA) format for citation. This format is fully described in the *MLA Handbook for Writers of Research Papers*, 5th ed. (New York: Modern Language Association of America, 1999). A paper in the social sciences will probably use the American Psychological Association (APA) format. This format is fully described in the *Publication Manual of the American Psychological Association*, 5th ed. (Washington, D.C.: American Psychological Association, 2001).

In the following section, we will focus on MLA and APA styles, the ones you are most likely to use in your academic work. Keep in mind, however, that instructors often have their own preferences. Some require the documentation style specified in the *Chicago Manual of Style*, 14th ed. (Chicago: University of Chicago Press, 1993). This style is similar to the American Psychological Association style, except that publication dates are not placed within parentheses. Instructors in the sciences often follow the Council of Biology Editors (CBE) format. Or they may prefer a number format: Each source listed on the bibliography page is assigned a number, and all text references to the source are followed by the appropriate number within parentheses. Some instructors like the old MLA style, which calls for footnotes and endnotes. Check with your instructor for the preferred documentation format if this is not specified in the assignment itself.

In-Text Citation

The general rule for in-text citation is to include only enough information to alert the reader to the source of the reference and to the location within that source. Normally, this information includes the author's last name and the page number (plus the year of publication, if using APA guidelines). But if you have already named the author in the preceding text, just the page number is sufficient.

TYPES OF CITATIONS

- Citations that indicate the source of quotations, paraphrases, and summarized information and ideas—these citations appear *in text*, within parentheses.
- Citations that appear in an alphabetical list of "Works Cited" or "References" following the paper.

Content Notes

Occasionally, you may want to provide a footnote or an endnote as a *content note*—one that provides additional information bearing on or illuminating, but not directly related to, the discussion at hand. For example

> ¹ Equally well-known is Forster's distinc-
> tion between story and plot: In the former, the
> emphasis is on sequence ("the king died and
> then the queen died"); in the latter, the
> emphasis is on causality ("the king died and
> then the queen died of grief").

Notice the format: The first line is indented five spaces or one-half inch and the note number is raised one-half line. A single space from there, the note begins. Subsequent lines of the note are flush with the left margin. If the note is at the bottom of the page (a footnote), it is placed four spaces below the text of the page, and the note itself is single-spaced. Content notes are numbered consecutively throughout the paper; do not begin renumbering on each page. Most word-processing programs have functions for inserting consecutive footnotes, formatting them, and placing them in the appropriate position on your pages.

Full Citations

In MLA format, your complete list of sources, with all information necessary for a reader to locate a source, is called "Works Cited." Entries in this listing should be double-spaced, with second and subsequent lines of each entry indented (a "hanging indent")—five spaces or one-half inch. In both styles, a single space follows the period. Here are two samples for comparison:

Sample MLA Full Citation (for a journal article)

> Haan, Sarah C. "The 'Persuasion Route' of the Law:
>
> Advertising and Legal Persuasion." <u>Columbia Law</u>
>
> <u>Review</u> 100.5 (June 2000): 1281–1326.

Sample APA Full Citation (for a journal article)

> Haan, S. C. (2000). The "persuasion route" of the law:
>
> Advertising and legal persuasion. *Columbia Law*
>
> *Review 100* (5). 1281–1326.

The main difference between MLA and APA styles is that in MLA style, the date of the publication follows the name of the publisher; in APA style, the date is placed within parentheses following the author's name. Other differences: In APA style, only the initial of the author's first name is indicated, and only the first word (and any proper noun) of the book or article title and subtitle is capitalized. The first letter of any word after a colon in a title is also capitalized. In MLA style, all words following the first word (except articles and prepositions) are capitalized. For APA style, do *not* place quotation marks around journal/magazine article titles. However, do use "p." and "pp." to indicate page numbers of newspaper articles. In APA format, italicize titles of books and journals, extending italics to include punctuation and volume (but not issue) numbers. When citing books, both MLA and APA rules dictate that publishers' names should be abbreviated; thus, "Random House" becomes "Random"; "William Morrow" becomes "Morrow."

Note: While the hanging indent (second and subsequent lines indented) is the recommended format for APA style references in student papers, manuscripts intended for publication follow paragraph indent format, in which only the first line of each reference is indented.

Provided below are some of the most commonly used citations in MLA and APA formats. For a more complete listing, consult the MLA *Handbook,* the APA *Manual,* or whichever style guide your instructor has specified.

MLA STYLE

In-Text Citation

Here are sample in-text citations using the MLA system:

```
From the beginning, the AIDS antibody test has been
"mired in controversy" (Bayer 101).
```

Notice that in the MLA system there is no punctuation between the author's name and the page number within the parentheses. Notice also that the parenthetical reference is placed *before* the final punctuation of the sentence, because it is considered part of the sentence.

If you have already mentioned the author's name in the text—in a *signal phrase*—it is not necessary to repeat it in the citation:

```
According to Bayer, from the beginning, the AIDS
antibody test has been "mired in controversy" (101).
```

In MLA format, you must supply page numbers for summaries and paraphrases, as well as for quotations:

```
According to Bayer, the AIDS antibody test has been
controversial from the outset (101).
```

Use a block, or indented form, for quotations of five lines or more. In block quotations, place the parenthetical citation *after* the period:

Robert Flaherty's refusal to portray primitive people's contact with civilization arose from an inner conflict:

> He had originally plunged with all his heart into the role of explorer and prospector; before Nanook, his own father was his hero. Yet as he entered the Eskimo world, he knew he did so as the advance guard of industrial civilization, the world of United States Steel and Sir William Mackenzie and railroad and mining empires. The mixed feeling this gave him left his mark on all his films. (Barnouw 45)

Again, were Barnouw's name mentioned in the sentence leading into the quotation, the parenthetical reference would be simply (45).

Usually parenthetical citations appear at the end of your sentences; however, if the reference applies only to the first part of the sentence, the parenthetical information is inserted at the appropriate points *within* the sentence:

While Baumrind argues that "the laboratory is not the place to study degree of obedience" (421), Milgram asserts that such arguments are groundless.

There are times when you must modify the basic author/page number reference. Depending on the nature of your source(s), you may need to use one of the following citation formats:

Quoted Material Appearing in Another Source

(qtd. in Garber 211)

An Anonymous Work

("Obedience" 32)

Two Authors

(Bernstein and Politi 208)

A Particular Work by an Author, When You List Two or More Works by That Author in the List of Works Cited

(Toffler, <u>Wave</u> 96—97)

Two or More Sources as the Basis of Your Statement

```
(Butler 109; Carey 57)
```

The Location of a Passage in a Literary Text

```
for example, Hardy's The Return of the Native (224;

ch. 7)
```

[Page 224 in the edition used by the writer; the chapter number, 7, is provided for the convenience of those referring to another edition.]

A Multivolume Work

```
(3: 7–12) [volume number: page number]
```

The Location of a Passage in a Play

```
(1.2.308–22) [act.scene.line number(s)]
```

The Bible

```
(John 3.16) [book.chapter.verse]
```
```
(Col. 3.14)
```

In-Text Citation of Electronic Sources (MLA)

Web sites, CD-ROM data, and e-mail generally do not have numbered pages. Different browsers may display and printers may produce differing numbers of pages for any particular site. You should therefore omit both page numbers and paragraph numbers from in-text citations to electronic sources, unless these page or paragraph numbers are provided within the source itself. For parenthetical citations of electronic sources, MLA style dictates that you cite the author's name. In APA style, cite the author's name and the year of publication.

Examples of MLA Citations in Works Cited List

Books (MLA)

One Author

```
Kolodny, Annette. The Land Before Her: Fantasy and

    Experience of the American Frontiers, 1630–1860.

    Chapel Hill: U of North Carolina P, 1984.
```

Note: MLA convention dictates abbreviating the names of university presses (e.g., Oxford UP for Oxford University Press or the above for University of North Carolina Press). Commercial publishing companies are also shortened by dropping such endings as "Co.," or "Inc."

Two or More Books by the Same Author

Gubar, Susan. <u>Critical Condition: Feminism at the Turn of</u>

    <u>the Century</u>. New York: Columbia UP, 2000.

---. <u>Racechanges: White Skin, Black Face in American</u>

    <u>Culture</u>. New York: Oxford UP, 1997.

Note: For MLA style, references to works by the same author are listed in alphabetical order of title. UP is an abbreviation of University Press.

Two Authors

Chambliss, William J., and Thomas F. Courtless. <u>Criminal</u>

    <u>Law, Criminology, and Criminal Justice: A Casebook</u>.

    Pacific Grove: Brooks/Cole, 1992.

Three Authors

Young, Richard E., Alton L. Becker, and Kenneth L. Pike.

    <u>Rhetoric: Discovery and Change</u>. New York: Harcourt,

    1970.

More Than Three Authors

Maimon, Elaine, et al. <u>Writing in the Arts and Sciences</u>.

    Boston: Little, 1982.

Book with an Editor

Grant, Michael, ed. <u>T. S. Eliot: The Critical Heritage</u>.

    Boston: Routledge, 1982.

Later Edition

Houp, Kenneth W., and Thomas E. Pearsall. <u>Reporting</u>

    <u>Technical Information</u>. 8th ed. Boston: Allyn, 1995.

Republished Book

Dreiser, Theodore. <u>An American Tragedy.</u> 1925. Cambridge:

    Bentley, 1978.

One Volume of a Multivolume Work

Bailey, Thomas A. <u>The American Spirit: United States</u>

    <u>History as Seen by Contemporaries</u>. 6th ed. 2 vols.

    Lexington: Heath, 1987.

Translation

Kundera, Milan. <u>The Book of Laughter and Forgetting</u>.

    Trans. Michael Henry Heim. New York: Penguin, 1987.

Selection from an Anthology

Rueckert, William. "An Experiment in Ecocriticism." <u>The</u>

    <u>Ecocriticism Reader: Landmarks in Literary Ecology</u>.

    Ed. Cheryll Glotfelty and Harold Fromm. Athens: U of

    Georgia P, 1996. 105—21.

Reprinted Material in an Edited Collection

McGinnis, Wayne D. "The Arbitrary Cycle of

    <u>Slaughterhouse-Five</u>: A Relation of Form to Theme."

    <u>Critique: Studies in Modern Fiction</u> 17. 1 (1975):

    55—68. Rpt. in <u>Contemporary Literary Criticism</u>. Ed.

    Dedria Bryfonski and Phyllis Carmel Mendelson. Vol.

    8. Detroit: Gale, 1978. 530—31.

Government Publication

United States Commission on Child and Family Welfare.

    <u>Parenting our Children: In the Best Interest of the</u>

    <u>Nation: A Report of the U. S. Commission on Child and</u>

    <u>Family Welfare</u>. Washington: GPO, 1996.

United States. Congress. House. Committee on Energy and

    Commerce. Subcommittee on Health and the

    Environment. <u>Health Consequences of Smoking:</u>

    <u>Nicotine Addiction: Hearing Before the Subcommittee</u>

    <u>on Health and the Environment of the Committee on</u>

    <u>Energy and Commerce</u>. 100th Cong., 2nd sess.

    Washington: GPO, 1988.

The Bible

    <u>The New English Bible</u>. New York: Oxford UP, 1972.

Signed Encyclopedia Article

    Lack, David L. "Population." <u>Encyclopaedia Britannica:</u>

    <u>Macropaedia</u>. 15th ed. 1998.

Unsigned Encyclopedia Article

    "Tidal Wave." <u>Encyclopedia Americana</u>. 1982 ed.

Periodicals (MLA)

Continuous Pagination throughout Annual Cycle

    Binder, Sarah. "The Dynamics of Legislative Gridlock,

    1947–1996." <u>American Political Science Review</u> 93

    (1999): 519–31.

Separate Pagination Each Issue

    O'Mealy, Joseph H. "Royal Family Values: The

    Americanization of Alan Bennett's <u>The Madness of King</u>

    <u>George III</u>." <u>Literature/Film Quarterly</u> 27.2 (1999):

    90–97.

Monthly Periodical

    Davison, Peter. "Girl, Seeming to Disappear." <u>Atlantic</u>

    <u>Monthly</u> May 2000: 108–11.

Signed Article in Weekly Periodical

Gladwell, Malcolm. "The New-Boy Network." <u>New Yorker</u> 29

May 2000: 68—86.

Unsigned Article in Weekly Periodical

"GOP Speaker Admits 'Exaggerations.'" <u>New Republic</u> 14

Aug. 2000: 10—11.

Signed Article in Daily Newspaper

Vise, David A. "FBI Report Gauges School Violence

Indicators." <u>Washington Post</u> 6 Sept. 2000: B1+.

Unsigned Article in Daily Newspaper

"The World's Meeting Place." <u>New York Times</u> 6 Sept. 2000:

A11.

Review

Barber, Benjamin R. "The Crack in the Picture Window."

Rev. of <u>Bowling Alone: The Collapse and Revival of</u>

<u>American Community</u>, by Robert D. Putnam. <u>Nation</u> 7

Aug. 2000: 29-34.

Other Sources (MLA)

Interview

Emerson, Robert. Personal interview. 10 Oct. 1998.

Dissertation (Abstracted in Dissertation Abstracts International)

Sheahan, Mary Theresa. "Living on the Edge: Ecology and

Economy in Willa Cather's 'Wild Land': Webster County

Nebraska, 1870-1900." Diss. Northern Illinois U,

1999. <u>DAI</u> 60/04 (1999): 1298.

Note: If the dissertation is available on microfilm, give the University Microfilms order number at the conclusion of the reference. Example, in MLA format: UMI, 1999. 9316566.

Lecture

Osborne, Michael. "The Great Man Theory: Caesar."

Lecture. History 41. University of California, Santa

Barbara, 5 Nov. 1999.

Paper Delivered at a Professional Conference

Worley, Joan. "Texture: The Feel of Writing." Conference

on College Composition and Communication. Cincinnati,

21 Mar. 1992.

Film

Howard's End. Dir. James Ivory. Perf. Emma Thompson and

Anthony Hopkins. Merchant/Ivory and Film Four

International, 1992.

Recording of a TV Program or Film

Legacy of the Hollywood Blacklist. Dir. Judy Chaikin. One

Step Productions and Public Affairs TV.

Videocassette. 1987.

Audio Recording

Hersh, Kristen. "Rock Candy Brains." Strange Angels.

Rykodisc, 1998.

Schumann, Robert. Symphonies Nos. 1 & 4. Cond. George

Szell. Cleveland Orchestra. Columbia, 1978

[Or, to emphasize the conductor rather than the composer:]

```
Szell, George, cond. Symphonies 1 & 4. By Robert

    Schumann. Cleveland Orchestra. Columbia, 1978.
```

Electronic Sources (MLA)

According to guidelines in the 1999 *MLA Handbook for Writers of Research Papers,* writers of research papers should credit the electronic sources they use by following these general conventions: 1. Name of the author (if given); 2. Title of the work, underlined; 3. Name of editor, compiler, or translator (if relevant); 4. Electronic publication information, including edition, volume number, release, or version (if relevant); 5. Date of electronic publication or latest update; 6. Name of any sponsoring organization or institution; 7. Date of access; 8. Pathway or method of access. Include a full and accurate URL for any source taken from the Internet (with access-mode identifier—*http, ftp, gopher,* or *telnet*). Enclose URLs in angle brackets(< >). When a URL continues from one line to the next, break it only after a slash. Do not add a hyphen; 9. *For portable sources:* City of publication and name of publisher (e.g., Redmond: Microsoft), or name of the vendor (e.g., Silverplatter), and electronic publication date.

If you cannot find some of this information within your sources, cite what is available. Note that the order of this information may vary depending upon the type of source cited. Follow the formatting conventions illustrated by the following models:

An Online Scholarly Project or Database

```
The Walt Whitman Hypertext Archive. Eds. Kenneth M.

    Price and Ed Folsom. 16 Mar. 1998. College of

    William and Mary. 3 Apr. 1998

    <http://jefferson.village.Virginia.EDU/whitman/>.
```

1. Title of project or database; 2. name of the editor of project; 3. electronic publication information; 4. date of access and URL

A Short Work within a Scholarly Project

```
Whitman, Walt. "Crossing Brooklyn Ferry." The Walt

    Whitman Hypertext Archive. Ed. Kenneth M. Price and

    Ed Folsom. 16 Mar. 1998. College of William and Mary.

    3 Apr. 2001 <http://jefferson.village.virginia.edu/

    whitman/works/leaves/1891/text/index.html>.
```

A Personal or Professional Site

Winter, Mick. <u>How to Talk New Age.</u> 6 Apr. 2000

<http://www.well.com/user/mick/newagept.html>.

An Online Book Published Independently

Smith, Adam. <u>The Wealth of Nations</u>. New York: Methuen,

1904. 3 Mar. 2001 <http://www.mk.net/~dt/Bibliomania/

NonFiction/Smith/Wealth/index.html>.

An Online Book within a Scholarly Project

Whitman, Walt. <u>Leaves of Grass</u>. Philadelphia: McKay,

1891–2. <u>The Walt Whitman Hypertext Archive</u>. Ed.

Kenneth M. Price and Ed Folsom. 16 Mar. 1998.

College of William and Mary. 3 Apr. 1998

<http://jefferson.village.virginia.edu/whitman/works/

leaves/1891/text/title.html>.

An Article in a Scholarly Journal

Jackson, Francis L. "Mexican Freedom: The Idea of the

Indigenous State." <u>Animus</u> 2.3 (1997): 15 pars. 4 Apr.

1998 <http://www.mun.ca/animus/1997vol2/jackson2.htm>.

An Unsigned Article in a Newspaper or on a Newswire

"Drug Czar Wants to Sharpen Drug War." <u>TopNews</u> 6 Apr.

1998. 6 Apr. 1998 <http://news.lycos.com/stories/

TopNews?19980406_NEWS-DRUGS.asp>.

A Signed Article in a Newspaper or on a Newswire

Davis, Robert. "Drug May Prevent Breast Cancer." <u>USA Today</u>

6 Apr. 1998. 8 Apr. 1998 <http://www.usatoday.com/

news/nds14.htm>.

An Article in a Magazine

Pitta, Julie. "Un-Wired?" <u>Forbes</u> 20 Apr. 1998. 12 May 1998

    <http://www.forbes.com/Forbes/98/0420/6108045a.htm>.

A Review

Beer, Francis A. Rev. of <u>Evolutionary Paradigms in the</u>

    <u>Social Sciences. Special Issue, International Studies</u>

    <u>Quarterly</u> 40.3 (1996). <u>Journal of Mimetics</u> 1 (1997).

    4 Jan. 1998 <http://www.cpm.mmu.ac.uk/jomemit/1997/vol1/

    beer_fa.html>.

An Editorial or Letter to the Editor

"The Net Escape Censorship? Ha!" Editorial. <u>Wired</u> 3.09. 1

    Apr. 1998. 22 Aug. 2000 <http://www.wired.com/wired/

    3.09/departments/baker.if.html>.

An Abstract

Maia, Ana Couto. "Prospects for United Nations

    Peacekeeping: Lessons from the Congo Experience."

    <u>MAI</u> 36.2 (1998): 400. Abstract. 6 Apr. 1998

    <http://www.lib.umi.com/dissertations/fullcit?289845>.

A Periodical Source on CD-ROM, Diskette, or Magnetic Tape

Ellis, Richard. "Whale Killing Begins Anew." <u>Audubon</u>

    [GAUD] 94.6 (1992): 20–22. <u>General Periodicals</u>

    <u>Ondisc-Magazine Express</u>. CD-ROM. UMI-Proquest. 1992.

A Non-Periodical Source on CD-ROM, Diskette, or Magnetic Tape

Clements, John. "War of 1812." <u>Chronology of the United</u>

    <u>States</u>. CD-ROM. Dallas: Political Research, Inc. 1997.

Electronic Mail

Mendez, Michael R. "Re: Solar power." E-mail to Edgar V.

   Atamian. 11 Sept. 1996.

Armstrong, David J. E-mail to the author. 30 Aug. 1996.

An Online Posting

For online postings or synchronous communications, try to cite a version stored as a Web file, if one exists, as a courtesy to the reader. Label sources as needed (e.g., Online posting, Online defense of dissertation, etc., with neither underlining nor quotation marks). Follow the following models as appropriate.

Message from an Electronic Mailing List

Kosten, A. "Major update of the WWWVL Migration and

   Ethnic Relations." Online posting. 7 Apr. 1998.

   ERCOMER News. 7 May 1998 <http://www.ercomer.org/

   archive/ercomer-news/0002.html>.

Message from an Online Forum or Discussion Group

Dorsey, Michael. "Environmentalism or Racism." Online

   posting. 25 Mar. 1998. 1 Apr. 1998

   <news:alt.org.sierra-club>.

Synchronous Communication

Mendez, Michael R. "Solar Power Versus Fossil Fuel

   Power." Online debate. 3 Apr. 1998. CollegeTownMOO.

   3 Apr. 1998 <telnet://next.cs.bvc.edu.7777>.

Computer Software on CD-ROM

Gamma UniType for Windows 1.5. Vers. 1.1. San Diego:

   Gamma Productions, Inc., 1997.

Note: If software is downloaded, include the date of download in the citation.

APA STYLE

In-Text Citation

Here are the sample in-text citations using the APA system:

> From the beginning, the AIDS antibody test has been
>
> "mired in controversy" (Bayer, 1989, p. 101).

Notice that in the APA system, there is a comma between the author's name, the date, and the page number, and the number itself is preceded by "p." or "pp." Notice also that the parenthetical reference is placed *before* the final punctuation of the sentence.

If you have already mentioned the author's name in the text, it is not necessary to repeat it in the citation:

> According to Bayer (1989), from the beginning, the
>
> AIDS antibody test has been "mired in controversy"
>
> (p. 101).

or:

> According to Bayer, from the beginning, the AIDS
>
> antibody test has been "mired in controversy"
>
> (1989, p. 101).

When using the APA system, provide page numbers only for direct quotations, not for summaries or paraphrases. If you do not refer to a specific page, simply indicate the date:

> Bayer (1989) reported that there are many precedents
>
> for the reporting of AIDS cases that do not unduly
>
> violate privacy.

For quotations of 40 words or more, use block (indented) quotations. In these cases, place the parenthetical citation *after* the period:

> Robert Flaherty's refusal to portray primitive
>
> people's contact with civilization arose from an
>
> inner conflict:
>
> > He had originally plunged with all his heart into
> >
> > the role of explorer and prospector; before

```
Nanook, his own father was his hero. Yet as he en-
tered the Eskimo world, he knew he did so as the
advance guard of industrial civilization, the
world of United States Steel and Sir William
Mackenzie and railroad and mining empires. The
mixed feeling this gave him left his mark on all
his films. (Barnouw, 1974, p. 45)
```

Again, were Barnouw's name mentioned in the sentence leading into the quotation, the parenthetical reference would be simply (1974, p. 45) for APA style.

If the reference applies only to the first part of the sentence, the parenthetical reference is inserted at the appropriate points *within* the sentence:

```
While Baumrind (1963) argued that "the laboratory
is not the place to study degree of obedience" (p.
421), Milgram asserts that such arguments are
groundless.
```

On occasion, you must modify the basic author/page number reference. Depending on the nature of your source(s), you may need to use one of the following citation formats:

Quoted Material Appearing in Another Source

```
(cited in Garber, 2000, p. 211)
```

An Anonymous Work

```
("Obedience," 1993, p. 32)
```

Two Authors

```
(Bernstein & Politi, 1996, p. 208)
```

A Particular Work by an Author, When You List Two or More Works by That Author in the List of References

```
(Toffler, 1973, pp. 96–97)
```

Two or More Sources as the Basis of Your Statement (Arrange Entries in Alphabetic Order of Surname)

```
(Butler, 1990, p. 109; Carey, 1987, p. 57)
```

A Multivolume Work

> (Vol. 2, p. 88)

In-Text Citation of Electronic Sources (APA)

Web sites, CD-ROM data, and e-mail generally do not have numbered pages, and different printers may produce different numbers of pages for any particular site. You should therefore omit both page numbers and paragraph numbers from in-text citations to electronic sources, unless these page or paragraph numbers are provided within the source itself.

Examples of APA Citations in References List

Books (APA)

One Author

> Kolodny, A. (1984). *The land before her: Fantasy and experience of the American frontiers, 1630–1860.* Chapel Hill, NC: University of North Carolina Press.

Two or More Books by the Same Author

> Gubar, S. (1997). *Racechanges: White skin, black face in American culture.* New York: Oxford University Press.

> Gubar, S. (2000). *Critical condition: Feminism at the turn of the century.* New York: Columbia University Press.

Note: For APA style, references to works by the same author are listed in chronological order of publication, earliest first.

Two Authors

> Chambliss, W. J., & Courtless, T. F. (1992). *Criminal law, criminology, and criminal justice: A casebook.* Pacific Grove, CA: Brooks/Cole.

Three Authors

> Young, R. E., Becker, A. L., & Pike, K. L. (1970). *Rhetoric: Discovery and change.* New York: Harcourt.

More Than Three Authors

Maimon, E., Belcher, G. L., Hearn, G. W., Nodine, B. N.,

     & O'Connor, F. W. (1982). *Writing in the arts and*

     sciences. Boston: Little.

Book with an Editor

Grant, M. (Ed.). (1982). *T. S. Eliot: The critical*

     heritage. Boston: Routledge.

Later Edition

Houp, K. W., & Pearsall, T. E. (1995). *Reporting*

     technical information (8th ed.). Boston: Allyn and

     Bacon.

Republished Book

Dreiser, T. (1978). *An American tragedy.* Cambridge, MA:

     R. Bentley. (Original work published 1925).

One Volume of a Multivolume Work

Bailey, T. A. (1987). *The American spirit: United States*

     history as seen by contemporaries (6th ed., Vol. 2).

     Lexington, MA: Heath.

Translation

Kundera, M. (1987). *The book of laughter and forgetting.*

     (M. H. Heim, Trans.). New York: Penguin.

Selection from an Anthology

Rueckert, W. (1996). An experiment in ecocriticism. In C.

     Glotfelty & H. Fromm (Eds.), *The ecocriticism reader:*

     Landmarks in literary ecology. (pp. 105–121). Athens,

     GA: University of Georgia Press.

Reprinted Material in an Edited Collection

McGinnis, W. D. (1975). The arbitrary cycle of

Slaughterhouse-five: A relation of form to theme. In

D. Bryfonski and P. C. Mendelson (Eds.), *Contemporary*

literary criticism (Vol. 8, pp. 530–531). Detroit:

Gale. (Reprinted from *Critique: Studies in modern*

fiction 17, (1) 1975, pp. 55–68.)

Government Publication

U. S. Commission on Child and Family Welfare. (1996).

Parenting our children: In the best interest of the

nation: A report of the U. S. commission on child and

family welfare. Washington, DC: U. S. Government

Printing Office.

U. S. Congress. House. Committee on Energy and Commerce.

Subcommittee on Health and the Environment. (1988).

Health consequences of smoking: Nicotine addiction:

Hearing before the subcommittee on health and the

environment of the committee on energy and commerce.

100th Congress, 2nd session. HR. Washington, DC:

Government Printing Office.

Signed Encyclopedia Article

Lack, D. L. (1998). In *The New Encyclopaedia Britannica.*

(Vol. 20, pp. 368–372). Chicago: Encyclopaedia

Britannica.

Unsigned Encyclopedia Article

Tidal wave. (1982). In *The Encyclopedia Americana.* (Vol.

28, pp. 213–216). New York: Americana.

Periodicals (APA)

Continuous Pagination throughout Annual Cycle

Binder, S. (1999). The dynamics of legislative gridlock,

1947–1996. *American Political Science Review, 93,*

519–531.

Separate Pagination Each Issue

O'Mealy, J. H. (1999). Royal family values: The

Americanization of Alan Bennett's *The Madness of King*

George III. Literature/Film Quarterly, 27 (2), 90–97.

Monthly Periodical

Davison, P. (2000, May). Girl, seeming to disappear.

Atlantic Monthly, 108–111.

Signed Article in Weekly Periodical

Gladwell, M. (2000, May 29). The new-boy network. *The New*

Yorker, 68–86.

Unsigned Article in Weekly Periodical

GOP speaker admits 'exaggerations.' (2000, August 14).

New Republic, 10–11.

Signed Article in Daily Newspaper

Vise, D. A. (2000, September 6). FBI report gauges school

violence indicators. *The Washington Post,* pp. B1, B6.

Unsigned Article in Daily Newspaper

The world's meeting place. (2000, September 6). *The New*

York Times, p. A11.

Review

Barber, B. R. (2000, August 7). The crack in the picture

window. [Review of the book *Bowling alone: The collapse and revival of American community*]. *The Nation*, 29–34.

Other Sources (APA)

Dissertation (Abstracted in Dissertation Abstracts International)

Pendar, J. E. (1982). Undergraduate psychology majors: Factors influencing decisions about college, curriculum and career. *Dissertation Abstracts International, 42,* 4370A.

Note: If the dissertation is available on microfilm, give the University Microfilms order number in parentheses at the conclusion of the reference: (UMI No.AAD9315947)

Lecture

Baldwin, J. (1999, January 11). *The self in social interactions.* Sociology 2 lecture, University of California, Santa Barbara.

Paper Delivered at a Professional Conference

Worley, J. (1992, March). *Texture: The feel of writing.* Paper presented at the Conference on College Composition and Communication, Cincinnati, OH.

Film

Thomas, J. (Producer), & Cronenberg, D. (Director). (1991). *Naked lunch* [Motion Picture]. United States: 20th Century Fox.

TV Series

Chase, D. (Producer). (2001). *The Sopranos* [Television series] New York: HBO.

Music Recording

```
Hersh, K. (1998). Rock candy brains. On Strange Angels

     [CD]. Salem, MA: Rykodisc.
```

Electronic Sources (APA)

The general APA order of items for electronic sources is as follows: 1. Name of the author (if given); 2. Date of publication; 3. Title of electronic source, in italics; 4. Edition, volume number, release, or version (if relevant); 5. Date source was retrieved; 6. Pathway or method of access. 7. *For portable sources:* City of publication and name of publisher (e.g., Redmond: Microsoft), or name of the vender (e.g., SilverPlatter).

The general APA format for online periodical sources is as follows:

> Author, I. (date). Title of article. *Name of Periodical. Volume number.*
> Retrieved month, day, year, from source

Remember: For online sources do not add periods or other punctuation immediately following path statements; such extra marks may prevent you from accessing the source.

An Article in an Internet-Only Scholarly Journal

```
Sheehan, K. B., & Hoy, M. G. (1999). Using e-mail to survey

     internet users in the United States: Methodology and

     assessment. Journal of Computer-Mediated

     Communication. Retrieved August 14, 2001, from

     http://www.ascusc.org/jcmc/vol4/issue3/sheehan.html
```

Note: The APA guidelines distinguish between Internet articles that are based on a print source, and those that appear in Internet-only journals. When an Internet article is reproduced from a print source, simply follow the usual journal article reference format, and include the phrase "Electronic version" in brackets following the title of the article. In such a case, you don't need to include the URL or date retrieved from the Internet.

A Personal or Professional Site

```
Winter, M. (n.d.) How to talk new age. Retrieved April 6,

     2000, from http://www.well.com/user/mick/

     newagept.html
```

Note: When no date of publication is given, indicate this with n.d. for "no date" in parentheses where the date usually would appear.

An Unsigned Article in a Newspaper or on a Newswire

```
Drug czar wants to sharpen drug war. (1998, April 6)

    Retrieved April 6, 1998, from http://news.lycos.com/

    stories/TopNews?19980406_NEWS-DRUGS.asp
```

A Signed Article in a Newspaper or on a Newswire

```
Davis, R. (1998, April 6). Drug may prevent breast

    cancer. USA Today. Retrieved April 8, 1998, from

    http://www.usatoday.com/news/nds14.htm
```

An Article in a Magazine

```
Pitta, J. (1998, April 20). Un-wired? Forbes. Retrieved

    May 12, 1998, from http://www.forbes.com/Forbes/

    98/0420/6108045a.htm
```

An Abstract

```
Maia, A. C. (1998). Prospects for United Nations

    peacekeeping: Lessons from the Congo experience. MAI

    36 (2). Abstract retrieved April 6, 1998, from

    http:/www.lib.umi.com/dissertations/fullcit?289845
```

A Periodical Source on CD-ROM, Diskette, or Magnetic Tape

```
Ellis, R. (1992). Whale killing begins anew. Audubon 94

    (6) 20—22. Retrieved from General Periodicals Ondisc-

    Magazine Express [CD-ROM] UMI-Proquest.
```

A Non-Periodical Source on CD-ROM, Diskette, or Magnetic Tape

```
Clements, J. (1997). War of 1812. Retrieved from

    Chronology of the United States [CD-ROM]. Dallas:

    Political Research, Inc.
```

An Online Posting

For online postings or synchronous communications, the APA recommends referencing only those sources which are maintained in archived form, since non-archived postings are not retrievable by your readers. If you must include sources that are not archived—and this includes e-mail communications between individuals—the APA suggests citing them as personal communications in the text of your work, but leaving them out of the References list. For archived sources, follow these models as appropriate.

Message from an Electronic Mailing List

Kosten, A. (1998, April 7). Major update of the WWWVL

migration and ethnic relations. Message posted to

ERCOMER News, archived at http://www.ercomer.org/

archive/ercomer-news/0002.html

Message from an Online Forum or Discussion Group

Pagdin, F. (2001, July 3). New medium for therapy [Msg

498]. Message posted to http://www.groups.yahoo.com/

group/cybersociology/message/498

Computer Software on CD-ROM

Gamma UniType for Windows 1.5 (Version 1.1) [Computer

software]. (1997). San Diego: Gamma Productions, Inc.

Writing Assignment: Short Research Paper

Using the methods we have outlined in this chapter—and incorporating the skills covered in this textbook as a whole—conduct your own research on a topic and research question that falls within your major or your area of interest. Your research process should then culminate in a 1,500–1,700 word research paper in which you use your sources to present an answer to your research question.

An Anthology
of Readings

Cyberspace and Identity: The E-Mail Revolution

7

A cartoon in *The New Yorker* a few years ago showed two dogs sitting near a computer. One dog says to the other, "On the Internet, nobody knows you're a dog." That's as succinct a statement as one can make about the benefits and the drawbacks of electronic communication. On the one hand, the Internet is a great democratizer: everyone is equal because anyone can publish anything. On the other hand, if anyone can publish anything, then for all we know, some of the material we read online might be written by "dogs."

The speed with which e-mail has become an essential medium of personal, business, and professional communication is truly breathtaking. Virtually unknown to the general public little more than a decade ago, e-mail is now so ubiquitous that it's hard to imagine how we ever got along without it. (Quite well, thank you, skeptics will respond.) Many people obsessively check their e-mail ten or more times a day. We appear to measure our worth and status according to how many people (and canines) are sending us messages. We are daily bombarded with megabytes of spam and other useless communications. On the other hand, e-mail provides many with lifelines to family and friends. In Times Square, New York, an all-night Internet café provides immigrants with inexpensive means of staying in touch with loved ones in their home countries. On the AskMe.com Web site, people who need answers to questions in any of hundreds of categories can get free advice from "experts." (Let the buyer beware, however: as an article later in this chapter shows, one top-rated legal expert on AskMe.com turned out to be a 15-year-old high schooler with no legal training.)

Is e-mail a truly new mode of communication, or is it just an electronic hybrid of the conventional letter and the telephone conversation? The 1999 movie *You've Got Mail* delighted audiences with the very contemporary situation of a couple enjoying an e-mail relationship that was more intense than the relationships they were simultaneously experiencing with their live-in lovers. The comic mileage was generated by the fact that in real life they actually knew and detested each other. Is this kind of situation only possible because of the distinctive nature of e-mail? Significantly, *You've Got Mail* was a remake of a 1940 Ernst Lubitsch film called *The Shop Around the Corner*. The latter film was also remade in 1949 as an MGM musical, *In the Good Old Summertime*, and in the 1960s as a Broadway show, *She Loves Me*. In the first three versions, the lovers are pen pals who work side by side in the same shop but don't know the identities of their correspondents. More recently, of course, when few people write personal letters, the same situation calls for a new mode of communication—though one sharing certain essential features of the old mode of communication.

As some of the writers in this chapter point out, e-mail is a mixed blessing—if not an actual curse. Increasingly, employers monitor their employees' e-mail and sometimes impose penalties (even to the point of firing people) for inappropriate use of company e-mail facilities. A spouse going through a divorce or custody proceeding may obtain a warrant to search the e-mail of the other spouse, in an attempt to find incriminating evidence. The veil of anonymity provided by the Internet can expose people to vicious "flaming" attacks—abusive, sometimes threatening messages. And because "nobody knows you're a dog," people can pretend to be what they are not. For some, assuming alternate identities can be a healthy form of play and self-development; for others, it can be a mode of perpetrating deception or even criminal fraud.

A fascinating recent case of such e-deception involved the online magazine *Slate*. In February 2002 an individual named Robert Klingler, who claimed to be the North American head of BMW, sent an e-mail to one of the magazine's editors, proposing to write a series of five diary entries for *Slate* about his activities as a top-level executive of a major automobile manufacturer. *Slate* took Klingler up on his offer and the first two entries appeared in the magazine. Deputy editor Jack Shafer recounts what happened next:

> When *Slate* readers pointed out to the editors that neither Google.com nor Nexis searchers produced any hits for a "Robert Klingler and the automobile industry," we assumed the worst and took the entries down from the site. A phone call to the European auto company in question confirmed that no "Robert Klingler" worked for them.*

Subsequent efforts to track down and contact "Robert Klingler" proved unsuccessful. Meanwhile, *Slate,* with egg on its face, ruefully admitted that it had been duped, apologized to its readers, candidly posted all of the evidence on its site, and promised "greater vigilance in the future."[†]

In this chapter, we will explore some of the many facets of the e-mail revolution, focusing particularly on the interrelationship between e-mail (both in its private and its public forums) and identity. Our identity is generally thought of as our essential self—that unique core of personhood and personality that makes us different from anyone else. But what is our "true" identity? Is it the self that we create for ourselves over the years and project to the world at large—our families, our friends, our coworkers, the general public? Is it the self to which we retreat when we are alone, perhaps fantasizing about operating in some alternate universe? Is it some combination of these? And

---

* Jack Shafer, "*Slate* Gets Duped," *Slate* 5 March 2002. <http://slate.msn.com/?id=2062867>.

[†] See the above selection by Shafer for additional links to the "Klingler" affair, including Shafer's subsequent (12 March 2002) investigative article, "Who is 'Robert Klingler'?: On the Trail of the Man who Duped *Slate*," as well as Klingler's diary entries and readers' responses to the imbroglio.

under what circumstances is our "true" identity (assuming there is such a thing) most likely to emerge?

Some writers think that the Internet offers fertile fields of play for experimenting with our identities. Even so simple an act as choosing a screen name for ourselves places a label on a particular aspect of our identity (or one that may not previously have existed); and when we create alternate screen names, we create alternate identities, each of which may have a distinctive personality, each of which we may explore and develop in e-mail messages, electronic bulletin boards, chat rooms, online gaming, and other arenas of the Internet.

In "We've Got Mail—Always," Andrew Leonard surveys the revolution wrought by e-mail and considers some of its benefits and drawbacks. In "Going Postal," Tony Schwartz focuses primarily on the drawbacks, and in particular, the way that checking and responding to e-mail can become addictive, crowding out other, possibly more useful and necessary activities. In "The A-List E-List," David Brooks offers a humorous perspective on how we can use e-mail for one-upmanship over our correspondents. The technical aspects of e-mail—just how does a message get from sender to recipient?—are engagingly outlined by John Dyson in "Journey of an E-Mail." In "Not Exactly the Most Reliable Way to Win a War, IMHO," Roy Rivenburg wonders what would happen if an army fighting a war had to depend on the kind of e-mail servers and software available to the general public.

"A Shared Sadness," by Russ Parsons, shows the coming together of a small online community when one of their members faces major surgery. The next piece explores the phenomenon of online romances: In "Virtual Love," Meghan Daum writes of her own experience with a passionate e-mail affair. In "The Anonymous Voice," business consultant Esther Dyson considers the benefits and drawbacks of anonymous communication. Sociologist Sherry Turkle then explains how creating and experimenting with multiple identities on the Internet can be psychologically healthy. Two examples of this kind of identity-creation follow. In "Boy, You Fight Like a Girl," Alex Pham discusses why gender-switching is so popular among online gamers. And in "Faking It: The Virtual Lawyer," Michael Lewis recounts how a 15-year-old youth with no legal training became the top legal expert on a widely used information Web site.

We've Got Mail—Always
Andrew Leonard

We begin this chapter with a broad survey of the e-mail revolution. Andrew Leonard's first sentence introduces his basic approach: "Is e-mail a blessing or a curse?" He goes on to illustrate areas in which it is one or the other—or both at once. Leonard begins and ends with his own experiences, but in the course of the article, he covers many areas of contemporary life in which e-mail has changed the way that we communicate with one another. This article first appeared as part of a "Special Report" issue of Newsweek *(devoted to computers), dated September 20, 1999. Leonard is a contributing editor for* Newsweek *and a senior technology correspondent of the online magazine* Salon.com .

1   Is e-mail a blessing or a curse? Last month, after a week's vacation, I discovered 1,218 unread e-mail messages waiting in my IN box. I pretended to be dismayed, but secretly I was pleased. This is how we measure our wired worth in the late 1990s—if you aren't overwhelmed by e-mail, you must be doing something wrong.

2   Never mind that after subtracting the stale office chitchat, spam, flame wars, dumb jokes forwarded by friends who should have known better and other e-mail detritus, there were perhaps seven messages actually worth reading. I was doomed to spend half my workday just deleting junk. E-mail sucks.

3   But wait—what about those seven? A close friend in Taipei I haven't seen in five years tells me he's planning to start a family. A complete stranger in Belgium sends me a hot story tip. Another stranger offers me a job. I'd rather lose an eye than lose my e-mail account. E-mail rocks!

4   E-mail. Can't live with it, can't live without it. Con artists and real artists, advertisers and freedom fighters, lovers and sworn enemies—they've all flocked to e-mail as they would to any new medium of expression. E-mail is convenient, saves time, brings us closer to one another, helps us manage our ever-more-complex lives. Books are written, campaigns conducted, crimes committed—all via e-mail. But it is also inconvenient, wastes our time, isolates us in front of our computers and introduces more complexity into our already too-harried lives. To skeptics, e-mail is just the latest chapter in the evolving history of human communication. A snooping husband now discovers his wife's affair by reading her private e-mail—but he could have uncovered the same sin by finding letters a generation ago.

5   Yet e-mail—and all online communication—is in fact something truly different; it captures the essence of life at the close of the 20th century with an authority that few other products of digital technology can claim. Does the pace of life seem ever faster? E-mail simultaneously allows us to cope with that acceleration and contributes to it. Are our attention spans shriveling under barrages of new, improved forms of stimulation? The quick and dirty e-mail is made to order for those whose ability to concentrate is measured in nanoseconds. If we accept that the creation of the globe-spanning Internet is one of the most important technological innovations of the last half of this century, then we must give e-mail—the living embodiment of human connection across the Net—pride of place. The way we interact with each other is changing; e-mail is both the catalyst and the instrument of that change.

6   The scope of the phenomenon is mind-boggling. Worldwide, 225 million people can send and receive e-mail. Forget about the Web or e-commerce or even online pornography: e-mail is the Internet's true killer app—the software application that we simply must have, even if it means buying a $2,000 computer and plunking down $20 a month to America Online. According to Donna Hoffman, a professor of marketing at Vanderbilt University, one survey after another finds that when online users are asked what they do on the Net, "e-mail is always No. 1."

7   Oddly enough, no one planned it, and no one predicted it. When research scientists first began cooking up the Internet's predecessor, the Arpanet, in 1968, their primary goal was to enable disparate computing centers to share resources. "But it didn't take very long before they discovered that the most important thing was the ability to send mail around, which they had not anticipated at all," says Eric Allman, chief technical officer of Sendmail, Inc., and the primary author of a 20-year-old program—Sendmail—that still transports the vast majority of the world's e-mail across the Internet. It seems that what all those top computer scientists really wanted to use the Internet for was as a place to debate, via e-mail, such crucially important topics as the best science-fiction novel of all time. Even though Allman is now quite proud that his software helps hundreds of millions of people communicate, he says he didn't set out originally to change the world. As a systems administrator at UC Berkeley in the late '70s, he was constantly hassled by computer-science researchers in one building who wanted to get their e-mail from machines in another location. "I just wanted to make my life easier," says Allman.

8   Don't we all? When my first child was born in 1994, e-mail seemed to me some kind of Promethean gift perfectly designed to help me cope with the irreconcilable pressures of new-fatherhood and full-time freelance writing. It saved me time and money without ever requiring me to leave the house; it salvaged my social life, allowed me to conduct interviews as a reporter and kept a lifeline open to my far-flung extended family. Indeed, I finally knew for sure that the digital world was viscerally potent when I found myself in the middle of a bitter fight with my mother—on e-mail. Again, new medium, old story.

9   My mother had given me an e-mail head start. In 1988, she bought me a modem so I could create a CompuServe account. The reason? Her younger brother had contracted a rapidly worsening case of Parkinson's disease. He wasn't able to talk clearly, and could hardly scrawl his name with a pen or pencil. But he had a computer, and could peck out words on a keyboard. My mom figured that if the family all had CompuServe accounts, we could send him e-mail. She grasped, long before the Internet became a household word, how online communication offered new possibilities for transcending physical limitations, how as simple a thing as e-mail could bring us closer to those whom we love.

10   It may even help us find those whom we want to love in the first place. Jenn Shreve is a freelance writer in the San Francisco Bay Area who keeps a close eye on the emerging culture of the new online generation. For the last couple of years, she's seen what she considers to be a positive change in online dating habits. E-mail, she argues, encourages the shy. "It offers a semi-risk-free environment to initiate romance," says Shreve. "Because it lacks the immediate threat of physical rejection, people who are perhaps shy or had painful romantic failures in the past can use the Internet as a way to build a relationship in the early romantic stages."

11   But it's not just about lust. E-mail also flattens hierarchies within the bounds of an office. It is far easier, Shreve notes, to make a suggestion to your superiors and colleagues via e-mail than it is to do so in a pressure-filled meeting room. "Any time when you have something that is difficult to say, e-mail can make it easier," she says. "It serves as a buffer zone."

12   Of course, e-mail's uses as a social lubricant can be taken to extremes. There is little point in denying the obvious dark side to the lack of self-constraint encouraged by e-mail. Purveyors of pornography rarely call us on the phone and suggest out loud that we check out some "hot teen action." But they don't think twice about jamming our e-mail boxes full of outrageously prurient advertisements. People who would never insult us face to face will spew the vilest, most objectionable, most appalling rhetoric imaginable via e-mail or an instant message, or in the no-holds-barred confines of a chat room.

13   Cyberspace's lapses in gentility underscores a central contradiction inherent in online communication. If it is true that hours spent on the Net are often hours subtracted from watching television, one could argue that the digital era has raised the curtains on a new age of literacy—more people are writing more words than ever before! But what kind of words are we writing? Are we really more literate, or are we sliding ever faster into a quicksand of meaningless irrelevance, of pop-cultural triviality—expressed, usually, in lowercase letters—run amok? E-mail is actually too easy, too casual. Gone are the days when one would worry over a letter to a lover or a relative or a colleague. Now there's just time for that quick e-mail, a few hastily cobbled together thoughts written in a colloquial style that usually borders on unedited stream of consciousness. The danger is obvious: snippy comments to a friend, overly sharp retorts to one's boss, insults mistakenly sent to the target, not the intended audience. E-mail allows us to act before we can think—the perfect tool for a culture of hyperstimulation.

14   So instead of creating something new, we forward something old. Instead of crafting the perfect phrase, we use a brain-dead abbreviation: IMHO for In My Humble Opinion, or ROTFLMAO, for Rolling On The Floor Laughing My A— Off. Got a rumor? E-mail it to 50 people! Instant messaging and chat rooms just accentuate the casual negative. If e-mail requires little thought, then instant messaging—flashing a message directly onto a recipient's computer monitor—is so insubstantial as to be practically nonexistent.

15   E-mail, ultimately, is a fragile thing, easy to forge, easy to corrupt, easy to destroy. A few weeks ago a coworker of mine accidentally and irretrievably wiped out 1,500 of his own saved messages. For a person who conducts the bulk of his life online, such a digital tragedy is akin to erasing part of your own memory. Suddenly, nothing's left. It is comforting to think that, if preserved in a retrievable way, all the notes the world is passing back and forth today constitute a vast historical archive, but the opposite may also be true. Earlier this summer, I visited some curators at the Stanford University Library who are hard at work compiling a digital archive of Silicon Valley history. They bemoaned a new, fast-spreading corporate policy that requires the deletion of all corporate e-mails after every 60 or 90 days. As Microsoft and Netscape have learned to their dismay, old e-mails, however trivial they seem when they are written, can and will come back to haunt you. It is best, say the lawyers, to just wipe them all out.

16   Still, e-mail is enabling radically new forms of worldwide human collaboration. Those 225 million people who can send and receive it represent a network of potentially cooperating individuals dwarfing anything that even the mightiest corporation or government can muster. Mailing-list discussion groups and online conferencing allow us to gather together to work on a multitude of

projects that are interesting or helpful to us—to pool our collective efforts in a fashion never before possible. The most obvious place to see this collaboration right now is in the world of software. For decades, programmers have used e-mail to collaborate on projects. With increasing frequency, this collaboration is occurring across company lines, and often without even the spur of commercial incentives. It's happening largely because it can—it's relatively easy for a thousand programmers to collectively contribute to a project using e-mail and the Internet. Perhaps each individual contribution is small, but the scale of the Internet multiplies all efforts dramatically.

17   Meanwhile, now that we are all connected, day and night, across time zones and oceans and corporate firewalls, we are beginning to lose sight of the distinction between what is work and what is play.

18   Six years after I logged onto CompuServe for the first time, I went to Australia for three weeks. Midway through my visit, I ended up in Alice Springs, a fraying-at-the-edges frontier town about a thousand miles away from anywhere in the middle of the great Australian outback. An exotic place, nestled among the oldest mountain remnants of the world, where flocks of parrots swoop and flutter through the downtown shopping district. But instead of wandering through the desert seeking out wallabies and feral camels, I found myself dialing long distance to a friend's University of Melbourne Internet account, and transferring from there via a telnet program to my own account at the Well in San Francisco. Once on the Well, I checked my mail to see if a fact checker for *Wired* magazine had any fresh queries for me concerning a story I had recently submitted.

19   I was on the job—in large part because I had an e-mail address and had made the Devil's bargain with the wired world. As I listened for the sound of the modem connecting in Alice Springs, I felt in the pit of my stomach that I had lost control over some valuable part of my life. Your employer will refrain from calling you at 11:30 at night, but not from sending an inquiring, hectoring, must-be-promptly-answered-as-soon-as-you-log-on e-mail. E-mail doesn't just collapse distance, it demolishes all boundaries. And that can be, depending on the moment, either a blessing or a curse.

Review Questions

1. Summarize some of the ways that e-mail can be, as Leonard puts it, either a "blessing or a curse."

2. What was the original purpose of the people who invented e-mail?

3. How does Leonard inject himself into his discussion of e-mail?

Discussion and Writing Suggestions

1. What part does e-mail play in your own life? Explain how you have experienced some of the e-mail "blessings" and "curses" to which Leonard refers, illustrating your account with relevant anecdotes.

2. Many people bemoan the e-mail revolution, complaining that it has replaced letter-writing, which they see as a superior form of communication. Consider the advantages and disadvantages of e-mail communication versus those of communication by letter and communication by telephone. Begin by creating a table, with rows for e-mail, letter-writing, and telephone calls, and with columns for advantages and disadvantages. Develop this table into a short paper. In your discussion consider particular situations that illustrate the benefits and drawbacks of each form of communication.

3. According to freelance writer Jenn Shreve, e-mail "offers a semi-risk-free environment to initiate romance." To what extent have you found this to be true, either in your own experience or the experience of others you know? Why "semi-risk-free," as opposed to "risk-free"?

4. Leonard notes that "E-mail allows us to act before we can think." Recount an occasion when you have written an e-mail message in the heat of anger (or passion), pushed the "Send" button "in haste" and then "at leisure" regretted sending your words. What was the aftermath? Did the incident change how you wrote and sent e-mail in the future?

5. One of the ways that e-mail changes its users, according to Leonard, is to reduce their "gentility" when communicating with others, particularly others they don't know personally. To what extent has e-mail changed the way you think about yourself, changed your concept of your own identity? For example, when you send e-mail messages to particular individuals, do you, in effect, redefine yourself or reconstruct yourself according to the type of person you would like to be, to those individuals? By the same token, do the e-mail messages you receive from certain people imply a certain "you"—one who may be somewhat different from the "you" that exists apart from e-mail? Why do you think e-mail is a good tool for bringing about these redefinitions and reconstructions of your self?

Going Postal
Tony Schwartz

The previous selection by Andrew Leonard focused on the world of e-mail, covering both its "blessings" and its "curses." The following article by Tony Schwartz deals primarily with the "curses," and one in particular: the addictive nature of e-mail. See if you can recognize yourself or others you know in some of the people Schwartz writes about. This article first appeared in New York *magazine on July 19, 1999.*

1 I am sitting at my desk, looking for ways to avoid writing this piece.

2 That's nothing new, and I know I am in good company. Writers have long looked for excuses not to write. It used to be that I spent the early part of each day lingering over the newspaper, or walking down two flights of stairs in my house to get a cup of tea or toast up a bagel. But eventually—after 20 or 30 minutes, sometimes an hour—I would settle down and put in two, three, or sometimes even four hours of solid work before lunch and then repeat the ritual in the afternoon.

3 E-mail has changed all that. Suddenly, it seems to have invaded my life, an intermittent but relentless demand on my attention from early in the morning until shortly before sleep. What began as the mildest of diversions—a couple of notes a day from friends in distant cities with whom I was happy to be more connected—has grown into as many as two or three dozen exchanges, most of them focused on work. I now find myself logging on as many as ten times each day to see what new e-mail has arrived. In the evenings, after dinner, I walk up to my office yet again, knowing that my wife won't object because she, too, regularly checks her e-mail.

4 E-mail's intoxicating qualities are now well-known: It's convenient, efficient, simple, and informal, a way to stay connected to more people, a democratizing force in the workplace and less intrusive than the telephone. But as e-mail proliferates, its more pernicious effects are increasingly evident. Much as it facilitates the conduct of business, e-mail is threatening to overrun people's lives. It's no longer uncommon for executives—even those at middle levels—to receive 100 to 150 e-mails a day—a veritable torrent that floods "24–7," to use the macho shorthand of e-business. At a subtler level, e-mail celebrates transaction more than engagement, bite-size information rather than considered reflection, connection without commitment. In the name of better and speedier communication, e-mail can be rude, clipped, superficial, and depressingly desiccated. A boon when it comes to making lunch dates and answering yes-or-no questions, it is also an insistent source of distraction from more demanding work. E-mail has proved fiercely addictive—cocaine for compulsive achievers.

5 Robert Iger, the chairman of ABC, is nothing if not disciplined. He awakens in the dark each day at 4:30 A.M. in order to read four newspapers. After that, he works out at the gym near his office on the Upper West Side, eats a small breakfast, and arrives at his desk by seven. For years, nothing interfered with this regimen. Then along came e-mail.

6 "It's just completely changed the rhythms of my workday." Iger admitted recently, sounding sheepish. "I try to avoid turning on the computer when I wake up now, because I know if I do, I won't read my newspapers. By the time I do log on, around 6 A.M., 25 messages have accumulated from Europe and California since I last checked before going to sleep. When I get to work and sit down at my desk, there's often some document in my in-box that I need to read. But meanwhile, the e-mails keep arriving. It really affects your attention span. All of a sudden, you find yourself turning around in your chair just to see what's there. Without thinking about it, you start answering them, and before long, 40 minutes has gone by. I now find myself purposely avoiding meetings just to handle the increasing volume of e-mail. I haven't been able to discipline myself yet to put off looking at them—and I'm not sure if I ever will."

7   At least two factors feed e-mail's seductive power. One is the middle ground that it offers between the desire to be productive (or at least to *feel* productive) and the utterly human inclination to avoid challenging work. "We typically choose to do the thing that demands the least of us first," says Sherry Turkle, a sociologist affiliated with MIT's Science, Technology and Society program and author of *Life on the Screen.* "E-mail has been constructed so that you can do the business at hand easily and efficiently. You have the sense, sitting at your keyboard, of orchestrating a life. It feels satisfying and productive without much effort."

8   The other irresistible lure of e-mail is more primal. "It's the power of intermittent reinforcement," argues Lee Sproull, a professor of business at New York University who has spent the past fifteen years studying e-mail. "The computer is now the ultimate Skinner box. You keep coming back for the reward."

9   There is considerable gratification that comes from forever being needed, wanted—popular, even. "It's sort of the way you used to feel about mail arriving from the postman," explains Sarah Crichton, the publisher of Little, Brown. "Possibly, just possibly, there would be something wonderful in one of those envelopes that would delight you, make your heart race a little faster. The difference with e-mail is that it keeps arriving all day long."

10   All this compulsive checking and replying necessarily carves up days into smaller and smaller bits. What gets sacrificed is the depth and richness that grows out of sustained, absorbed attention to a single task. Instead, multitasking—the capacity to do more than one thing at a time—has become a desirable skill for overburdened executives. "I can do my e-mail while I'm talking on the phone," says Lauren Zalaznick, head of original programming for VH1. "I know it's rude, but I can also take a meeting and do e-mail at the same time. Basically, e-mail goes with almost everything."

11   Zalaznick is sitting across the desk from me as we talk. She never strikes me as harried, but there are several odd moments when I sense that she isn't completely there. Only later does she acknowledge that during our time together, she received fourteen e-mails and managed to quietly respond to most of them, tapping away at a silent keyboard hidden below desk height. As far as she's concerned, there's no choice. If Zalaznick doesn't multitask, there's no way to get all of her work done—much less leave the office in time to hang out with her two young children and put them to bed.

12   "There's no question that e-mail increases efficiency," explains Esther Dyson, who heads the high-tech consulting company EDventure Holdings. "The problem is that it increases the efficiency of the next guy, too, so no one really feels more efficient."

13   The next time I experience what I have come to call The Pause is during a telephone conversation with Sarah Crichton. This time, I can't resist a small dig. "You don't happen to be answering your e-mail, do you?" I ask.

14   "How did you know?" Crichton replies, slightly abashed. Then she makes a confession: "During meetings in my office, when I have to dig in deep and really think about something that makes me antsy, I'll often swivel in my chair and start answering e-mails. I don't even notice I'm doing it, but the people I work with have learned to call me on it."

15   Andrew Heyward, the president of CBS News, has recognized another way that e-mail costs him. "It's a refuge when you don't want to grapple with something else, but it also works the other way," he says. "Whenever I have a free moment now, I turn to e-mail. It's probably taken away the last few minutes in my life that were available for pure reflection."

16   For many, leaving the office scarcely means logging off. "The umbilical cord is longer than it's ever been," explains ABC's Iger. On the weekends, like many of his fellow executives, he still manages to check his e-mail at least three times a day—and does so just as frequently when he's in Tokyo or Shanghai on business. America Online recently commissioned a study of Internet use and found that 47 percent of users now take their laptops on vacation, and 26 percent check their e-mail. "I've played the game of not taking my laptop on vacation," explains Barry Schuler, president of AOL Interactive Services. "What happens is that you sit there on the beach, gazing out into the ocean, but you can't relax because you're thinking about how many e-mails are accumulating in your in-box. I finally decided that I'm willing to take a couple of hours each day on vacation discreetly off in a corner doing my e-mail. It's worth feeling like a jerk in order to know that I'm on top of everything and I'm not going to return to 1,000 unanswered e-mails."

17   Not long ago, Schuler and his boss, Robert Pittman, got to talking about feeling enslaved by e-mail. They decided that one antidote might be to institute companywide e-mail-free weekends: If you don't have a piece of pressing business, you are encouraged not to log on at all. Of course, Schuler sees most of his business as pressing, so he rarely abstains. When VH1's Zalaznick had her second child two years ago, she found that nights afforded an unexpected opportunity. "I'd get up at 3 or 4 A.M. each night to nurse my baby," she explains. "In the peacefulness and bondingness of it all, I'd find myself holding her in one arm while reading and typing e-mails with the other."

18   In the emerging e-mail etiquette, a great deal is sacrificed in the name of efficiency. "E-mail may be the rudest form of communication yet invented," says Nathan Myhrvold, until recently the chief technology officer at Microsoft.

19   E-mail eliminates tone of voice, body language, and the sort of social cues and contexts that make it possible to distinguish between different messages intended by the same words. In technological terms, e-mail has a limited emotional bandwidth. Because messages are typically written quickly and in compressed form, it's scarily easy for misunderstandings to occur. An abbreviated response that would fly smoothly in conversation can be read as brusque or dismissive in e-mail, partly because no greeting or sign-off is expected. And even highly literate people feel free to send e-mails filled with typos, spelling errors, incomplete sentences, bad grammar, and no capital letters or punctuation at all.

20   Of course, it plays both ways. The same breezy informality that frees people to be curt, sloppy, and rude in e-mail also promotes a certain openness and intimacy not encouraged by other forms of communication. NYU's Sproull refers to it as a "disinhibiting" effect. "It's not unlike what happens when people put on masks and Halloween costumes," she explains.

21   "I am much more intimate and personal in e-mail than I am anywhere else," says Barry Diller, chairman and CEO of USA Networks. "That may be just because

everyone, including me, is all closed off and constipated, but whatever the reasons, there's a real value to it. In talking, my cognitive process is instinctive and reactive. With e-mail, the process is primarily written. I have to focus on what I'm going to say, compose sentences, make myself understood, reflect before I react. I might be just as tough in writing as I would be verbally—but then I read what I've written and edit myself."

22   Nathan Myhrvold has had just the opposite experience. With this loosening of inhibitions, he says, comes a certain rashness—a tendency to act out. "Just because you have a little more time to reflect with e-mail doesn't mean you do," Myhrvold argues. "E-mail emboldens people. It makes them more extreme. There's something cathartic about pushing the SEND button, even when you're sending something you may later regret."

23   The instant intimacy fostered by e-mail is not unlike the exchange you might have with someone in a bar late at night after a couple of drinks, when even the most revelatory exchanges somehow don't fully count. "E-mail relationships are a way to bond very quickly," says Zalaznick. "You don't have to spend much time on them. They're safe. And you can bail out at any point without significant consequences." That's also precisely their limitation: Real engagement is messy, time-consuming, and exacting in a way that e-mail is not. "E-mail is sort of deadening—a little bit like turning Technicolor into black and white," says Arlie Hochschild, a professor of sociology at the University of California at Berkeley and author of *Time Bind: When Work Becomes Home and Home Becomes Work.*

24   One of the ironies of e-mail is that it can be so isolating. "When you log on, you feel like you're in touch with everything that's going on in the world," says Judith Regan, publisher of Regan Books. "But what you really are is out of touch—literally. There is no touching anymore. We started this century with small communities and large families and neighbors visiting each other. We're ending it alone in a room with a joystick." As it happens, Regan herself is so busy that I've only been able to catch up with her by calling on a Sunday morning. "This is a perfect example," she says. "Here I am, sitting at home in front of my computer answering e-mail at ten in the morning when I should be in bed with a handsome guy making love."

25   Instead, the handsome guy has been replaced by hundreds of semi-strangers forever wanting to do virtual business. "The convenience of e-mail is far outweighed by the fact that more people have my attention," says Hochschild. "What happens is that because people can reach me more easily by e-mail, I end up in communication with more people who are peripheral to my life while not making enough time for the people who are primary."

26   One solution for overburdened e-mail users is to use multiple addresses, including one that is made available only to a small number of key people. Of course, that means checking for e-mail at more than one address, itself time-consuming. Some people are turning to filters, now built into most e-mail programs, to sort and prioritize their incoming mail.

27   Brian Reid is a research manager at Lucent who has been using e-mail since the late sixties: he helped develop the technology as a Carnegie Mellon grad student. Reid, who receives as many as 2,000 messages a day, has perhaps the most sophisticated sorting system yet devised. One filter displays any block of

messages from the same address or on the same subject as a cluster so that he can decide in a quick glance whether any of them merit his attention. Another tells him when he has received multiple messages from the same sender in a certain period of time—on the grounds that it might suggest an emergency. (It's never happened, but you can't be too careful.) Incoming mail from close family members beeps in different tones that Reid can recognize.

28   But in the end, even the most elaborate systems can do only so much. Like many others, Reid now spends much of his day checking, reading, and sending e-mail, including at least a couple of hours at home each night. In virtuality, the attempt to log off is the equivalent of trying to eat just one potato chip. "My wife will often say to me. 'Dear, will you turn that thing off and come to bed?'" Reid acknowledges. "But for me, being plugged in is just part of who I am."

29   Sarah Crichton manages to take a few hours off from work between the time she gets home and when her 9-year-old daughter goes to bed. Then she's back in front of her laptop around 10:30 or 11 answering e-mail. The difference is that she does so while sitting in bed, alongside her husband, who has his own laptop. "This wasn't the sort of romantic image we had of ourselves when we fell in love twenty years ago," Crichton acknowledges. "But the truth is, we're both pretty content doing it."

30   As for the telephone conversation we've been having. Crichton insists she's resisted answering a single e-mail during our 45-minute chat. But that doesn't mean she hasn't stolen an occasional glance at the incoming flow. "I've got twelve new messages," she suddenly volunteers. "This is very exciting. It's been good talking with you, but I have to hang up now."

Review Questions

1. How has e-mail changed Schwartz's life—and the lives of many others?

2. What is multi-tasking? How does e-mail communication facilitate multi-tasking?

3. Aside from refusing to read or send e-mail, how have some people managed to cope with the onslaught of e-mail messages sent to them every day?

Discussion and Writing Suggestions

1. Schwartz writes (paragraph 4): "E-mail has proved fiercely addictive—cocaine for compulsive achievers." Assuming a measure of truth to this observation, why do you think that e-mail has proved addictive for *achievers* ? Which characteristics of achievement-oriented people make them particularly likely to rely heavily upon e-mail?

2. Schwartz quotes former Microsoft technology executive Nathan Myhrvold as saying, "E-mail may be the rudest form of communication yet invented." What do you think he means? To what extent

do you agree? For example, why is e-mail any "ruder" than letter-writing?

3. Schwartz indicates that at least two of the people he interviewed by phone proceeded to either read or respond to their e-mail messages while they talked to him. Other kinds of routine "multi-tasking" include conversing on our cell phones while walking down the street or driving. Such routine phenomena of contemporary life suggest that people are much more productive now than they were before we had cell phones or e-mail. After all, when people had to do such tasks consecutively, rather than simultaneously, their days must have been much longer. Or were they? To what extent do you think that the daily tasks and workload of life have been eased—or increased—by such high-tech developments as e-mail?

4. Barry Diller and Nathan Myhrvold have differing opinions about the desirability of what Schwartz calls the "openness and intimacy" of e-mail. Have you ever been offended by an e-mail message? If so, why? To what extent might you have had a different reaction if the person composing the message had used another medium (letter, telephone, or face-to-face conversation) or had not been so quick to take advantages of the unique qualities of e-mail?

5. "One of the ironies of e-mail is that it can be so isolating," writes Schwartz. To what extent do you agree? Cite examples from your own experience or the experiences of others you have talked to.

The A-List E-List
David Brooks

We are endlessly resourceful in finding ways to gain status over our fellow creatures. Some do it through possessions—a bigger and fancier house; a state-of-the-art home theater system; the fastest, sleekest computer; the most monstrous sport utility vehicle. Others employ what British humorist Steven Potter called "one-upmanship": the art of gaining psychological advantage over your rival by implying—often without any basis in fact—that you have better social or professional connections, that you are more skillful and talented, that you are more desirable or in demand.

In this light-hearted piece, David Brooks ponders the latest ploy in the status wars: casually using your e-mail address list to impress recipients with how well-connected you are. Brooks's piece first appeared in the "Shouts and Murmurs" section of The New Yorker, *on September 13, 1999.*

1   I spend my days trying to contribute to a more just, caring, and environmentally sensitive society, but, like most Americans, I'm always on the lookout for

subtle ways to make myself seem socially superior. So I was thrilled recently to learn about E-name dropping, a new and extremely petty form of one-upmanship made possible by recent strides in information technology.

2   I first became aware of this new status ploy when a colleague sent out a mass message. "Dear friends," his E-mail began. But before I could go on to the text my eye was drawn up to the list of other people it had been sent to. My friend had apparently sent this message—it was a request for help on an article—to his entire E-mail address book. There were three hundred and four names, listed alphabetically, along with their E-mail addresses. It was like a roster of young media meritocrats. There were newsweek.coms, wsj.coms, nytimes.coms, as well as your assorted berkeley.edus, stanford.edus, microsoft.coms, and even a UN.org.

3   I realized that I had stumbled across the *Social Register* of the information age. We all carry our own select social clubs on our hard drives, and when we send out a mass mailing we can flaunt our splendiferous connections to arouse the envy of friend and foe alike. It's as if you were walking down the street with your Rolodex taped to your lapel—only better, since having an E-mail friendship with someone suggests that you are trading chatty badinage, not just exchanging stiff missives under a formal letterhead.

4   So in theory a strategic striver could structure his E-mail address list to reveal the entire trajectory of his career ascent. He could include a few of his early thesis advisers—groton.org, yale.edu, oxford.ac.uk—then a few internship-era mentors—imf.org, whitehouse.gov—and, finally, a few social/professional contacts—say, davosconference.com or trilat.org. When he inflicts this list on his friends' in-boxes, they will be compelled, like unwilling list archeologists, to retrace his perfect life, triumph by triumph.

5   My friend with the three-hundred-and-four-name list hadn't exploited the full potentialities of the genre, so I cast about for other lists and began to analyze them. I learned a lot from these lists. For example, my view of *The Nation's* columnist Eric Alterman has been transformed by the knowledge that he has just stopped using "Tom-seaver" as part of his E-mail address. But, frankly, reading through the address lists of my friends, I found that there were longueurs. Entire passages were filled with names of insignificant people, such as family members I'd never heard of. I came to realize, as Capability Brown must have, that in the making of any beautiful vista pruning is key.

6   If Aristotle were alive, he would note that there are four types of E-mail lists. There are lists that remind you that the sender went to a better college than you did. There are lists that remind you that he has a better job than you do. There are those that remind you that he has more sex than you do. And, finally, there are those that remind you that he is better than you in every respect: spiritually, professionally, and socially.

7   I have begun fantasizing about assembling the mother of all E-mail lists, the sort that would be accumulated by a modern Renaissance man. Such a list would be studded with jewels (HisHoliness@vatican.com, QEII@windsor.org). But, more than that, it would suggest a series of high achievements across the full range of human endeavor. It would include whopping hints about mysterious other lives (coupboy@theagency.gov, Ahmed@mujahedin.com). It would reveal intimate connections with the great but socially selective (JDSal@aol.com, Solzhenits@archi.org). Of

course, I wouldn't want only celebrities on my list; that would be vulgar. I would leave room for talk-show bookers, upper-bracket realtors, Sherpas, airline presidents, night-club publicists, rain-forest tour guides, underprivileged kids, members of the Gotti family, and a rotating contingent of the people I actually know, for whose edification the whole list has been constructed in the first place.

8   To take advantage of this list, I would need excuses to send out mass mailings as frequently as possible. I would have to change my address a lot ("From now on you can reach me at genius24@MacArthurgrant.com…"). I would send out a lot of general queries ("Does anybody know who is handling Ike Berlin's estate? I'm trying to find a first edition of the complete works of Hérzen…"). And I'd send out a few accidental mass mailings by hitting the Reply All button by "mistake" ("Your Holiness, it turns out I can't make it to Rome Tuesday. Maybe somebody else can bring the beer and soda…").

9   No longer would I be the ninety-eight-pound cyberweakling that I am now. Alec Baldwin would start sending me dirty jokes in hopes of making it onto my E-mail list. People would actually begin replying to my messages. The fact is, in the new information age, we can now be snobs on a scale never dreamed of by our ancestors. Is this a great time to be alive, or what?

Discussion and Writing Suggestions

1. To what extent is status important to you? In what areas of endeavor is status particularly necessary, perhaps even crucial? What kinds of things have you done to enhance your status, relative to your peers or others you know? How do you think the universal search for status affects the way we deal with one another, affects our success in achieving our goals?

2. To what extent do Brooks's observations about gaining social status through e-mail communications resonate with you? Have you ever studied the names and addresses of others who have been copied on an e-mail sent to you in a way that changes your opinion of the sender? Have you ever purposely used the "copy to" function as a way of impressing—or intimidating—your intended recipient with whom else you know and communicate with?

3. Of course, e-mail is only one of the latest means by which people attempt to raise their status in the eyes of others. Among the people you are most familiar with, what other status-seeking practices are most common, most striking? Do people generally attempt, by the acquisition and display of various kinds of objects, to impress others with their importance? Do they adopt certain modes of behavior calculated to impress, or inspire envy? To what extent are such practices successful with their target audience?

4. Compose one or two e-mail messages, in the manner of Brooks's "fantasizing" toward the end of his piece.

Journey of an E-Mail
John Dyson

Every day, we operate and depend upon a multitude of technical devices without having the foggiest idea how they work. Forget high-tech computers: how many of us could explain the operation of a radio, a telephone, a light bulb, the electric motor that powers our fan? How many of us could give an accurate and coherent account of the internal workings of a low-tech device like a flush toilet?

The main job of a science writer is to explain to nontechnically inclined people how the technology that we take for granted works. In the following selection, freelance writer John Dyson explains just what happens when we click "Send" on our e-mail screen.

1　Doug and Julie Young raise Dandie Dinmont terriers. They also publish a newsletter for fellow lovers of the breed. Not too long ago they wanted a picture of Mr. D, our family pet.

2　I could have sent the photo by ordinary mail, but that would have taken at least four days. Instead, sitting down at the computer in my den overlooking London's River Thames, I sent an e-mail. I typed in an address, young@montizard.com, composed a short message, then attached a photograph I'd scanned into my PC. Finally I clicked Send. Mr. D instantly vanished from my screen—headed to a farmhouse in rural Ohio.

3　Along with more than 150 million others around the world, I use e-mail all the time and can't imagine living without it. How it actually works, of course, was a mystery. So one day I decided to find out. Mounting my bicycle, I pedaled off to follow my dog through cyberspace.

4　The first stop was a brick office plaza between a canal and an elevated highway in Brentford, west London. This was one of the homes of Cable & Wireless, the company that connects my computer to the Internet by telephone lines.

5　Escorted through security checks and card-swipe doors, I entered a brightly lit, windowless room with rows of fridge-size metal cabinets called racks, containing computers the size of TV sets, each costing as much as a car. In an adjoining control room, engineers, some of whom were wearing earrings, were monitoring rows of complicated numbers on video screens. As the racks tend to look the same, engineers give them names. "This is Marvin," said Jason Semple, pointing to one. "He's your postbox."

6　A burly 27-year-old, Semple hooked a finger over the spine of what looked like one of scores of videocassettes on a shelf. He slid out a circuit board glittering with tiny gold wires and silver connectors.

7　"When your PC dials our number, it's answered by one of these modems," Semple explained. "It checks your name and password with another computer, then asks what you want."

8   My computer had replied, "I've got mail."

9   Next, Mr. D was fed into a "mail server"—a bunch of computers filling five racks. One read my e-mail's destination and checked another, which stored Internet addresses like a gigantic phone directory.

10   The Cable & Wireless directory could do ten look-ups a second. It didn't find montizard.com, so it asked a bigger directory, storing ten million addresses in Europe and Africa. That didn't work either, so it asked one of 13 core directories (ten in the United States, two in Europe, one in Japan) holding every Internet address in the world.

11   Back came the answer: "Send mail to BuckeyeNet." This is the company connecting the Youngs to the Internet. BuckeyeNet's Internet address—209.41.2.152—was clipped like a dog tag to Mr. D's collar.

12   Next, something bizarre happened. Imagine a postal clerk who chops your letter into little bits and puts them in separate envelopes. This is done to every e-mail. All the bits and bytes representing Mr. D were instantly divided among about 120 packets. Every one was stamped with BuckeyeNet's address, plus my own address, so the jigsaw puzzle could be reassembled at the other end.

13   But they didn't go all at once. Instead, a single packet was sent off like a scout car, to knock on the door of BuckeyeNet, say hello and make a connection. The first stop was a gateway router, which would help the scout car find the way.

14   Picture the Internet as 65,000 interstate highways crisscrossing the globe and connected to smaller roads and streets. Like a cop with a walkie-talkie on every crossroad, the router learns the fastest way to get an e-mail to its destination. It knows all the routes and, by talking with other "cops" down the road every half-minute, it discovers where the delays are—say, heavy telephone traffic or a cut cable.

15   A Cable & Wireless router sent Mr. D's hello packet across London to the company's transmission center in Docklands, where another router fed it into the stream of e-mail packets heading for the westerly tip of Cornwall, the nearest part of England to America.

16   All this happened in four milliseconds—like a lightning flash.

17   I took a decidedly slower train to Cornwall and went to Porthcurno, a cliff-top village. There, in a barn-size room, is the base station of the transatlantic Gemini cable.

18   Take a hair-thin fiber of glass, wrap it in a protective jacket, then incorporate it with others in a rubbery protective tube. This is fiber-optic cable, known in the trade as pipe.

19   A flashing laser at one end fires digital on/off signals along the fiber. At about 120,000 miles a second—more than half the speed of light—they zip to the other end.

20   "It's the high-tech equivalent of two kids signaling each other with flashlights," explained Dave Shirt, operations director. With pretty quick fingers, I'd say: the lasers flash ten billion times a second.

21   Mr. D's packet next jostled for elbowroom with a torrent of transatlantic electronic traffic—equivalent to 100,000 closely typed pages every second, or 400,000 simultaneous phone calls. Think that's a lot? At present six parallel

lanes of traffic hurtle along every glass fiber. Newly laid cables will soon have 128 lanes, preparing for the explosion of Internet traffic when every movie ever made could be available online.

22   I returned to London, hopped a plane to New York and rented a car, then picked up Mr. D's trail again on a long, flat beach in Manasquan, N.J., where the Gemini cable comes ashore. Next the e-mail zipped along poles and beside railroad tracks before flashing into 60 Hudson Street, in downtown Manhattan. Time taken from London: approximately 40 milliseconds, or one-tenth of a blink of the eye.

23   This 22-floor art-deco building is a "telco hotel" where telephone companies own or rent space for equipment so they can connect to one another more easily. The scout packet was switched into high-capacity "fat pipes" crossing the continent. It also hit what engineers call ATM—asynchronous transfer mode.

24   Now Mr. D was diced yet again into dozens of identically sized cells which flashed through the back of a telephone exchange in West Orange, N.J., just west of New York.

25   But from there the cells had a really wild ride, zipping through pipe beside railroad tracks, into and out of Philadelphia, up the Ohio Valley, through Cleveland and into another telephone exchange at Willow Springs, outside Chicago. Here the bits came together, and the original packet was restored. It all took a fraction of a second.

26   Barely pausing for a breath, so to speak, the scout packet next raced through Chicago and Detroit, before landing in a building in Columbus, Ohio—headquarters of Fiber Network Solutions. There I met the company's co-founder, Kyle Bacon, a laid-back 27-year-old wearing two gold earrings.

27   Bacon, who used to duck classes to work on his university's computer system, helped set up a network that controls Internet pipes so businesses and industry have to pay the company to open the tap. That was three years ago. Now the company employs 45 people, and Bacon drives a silver BMW whose license plate reads FAT PIPE.

28   A router in the company switched Mr. D into a skinny pipe running direct to the home of BuckeyeNet—then a two-room office with a dirt parking lot, some five miles from rural Lancaster. BuckeyeNet has over a thousand clients and 13 computers. By way of comparison, the biggest Internet-access provider in the world, America Online, has some 19 million subscribers and servers covering football fields of floor space.

29   Dressed in shorts and, naturally, sporting a gold earring, Jonathan Sheline, 27, told me he'd set up the company after leaving the Army, where he'd served hitches in the infantry and counterintelligence. In just 18 months his net was one of the largest in the town. Our friends the Youngs are among its $17.95-a-month clients.

30   BuckeyeNet's mail server unwrapped Mr. D's scout packet, which carried a message. "Helo," it said. "I am j.dyson at cwcom.net." "Helo" means *hello* in a computer language called Simple Mail Transfer Protocol (SMTP).

31   BuckeyeNet's mail server sent an acknowledgment to London, which took one-tenth of a second to arrive. Next the two computers negotiated the connection. Their conversation, using codes as well as plain text, went like this:

32   Ohio: Okay, I'm listening. SMTP is spoken here.

33   London: I have mail from j.dyson at cwcom.net.

34   Ohio: Pleased to meet you.

35   London: I've got mail for montizard.com.

36   Ohio (checking list of clients): Okay, I can handle that.

37   London: I'm ready to send data.

38   Ohio: Start mail input.

39   From London, five packets hit the road. If any crashed or failed to arrive, the Ohio dispatcher would let London know and they'd be sent again. When this bunch arrived, Ohio said: "I got the first five, give me five more."

40   Despite all the messages Ping-Ponging across the Atlantic, the last bit of Mr. D straggled into BuckeyeNet's server less than half a minute after I had origi-nally clicked Send. For me it had been nine hours in the air, four hours waiting for a connection and an hour and a half in cars. And my luggage was left behind. But Mr. D still had to go the last five miles.

41   When I arrived in their old farmhouse on nearly five acres outside Rushville, Doug and Julie Young were making breakfast for 35 dogs, 30 ferrets, two llamas and a parrot. Julie had an armful of cans, bowls and milk cartons, difficult to carry because they were all different sizes.

42   Meanwhile, from a big paper bag, Doug filled a container with pellets of dog food—the perfect metaphor for understanding why e-mails are minced and shredded into packets and cells. Like pellets, they pour more easily and there-fore travel much faster.

43   A big, jovial man of 51, Doug uses e-mail to talk with breeders all over the world. When he clicked Get Mail, the BuckeyeNet server checked his mailbox and forwarded its contents down the phone line. The stream of bits material-ized into Mr. D gazing imperially out of the screen from his kitchen chair, not a bit ruffled after his 4000-mile dash.

Review Questions

1. How did Dyson's own server computer in West London know where to send his message?

2. Why are e-mail messages chopped into numerous electronic pieces (or "packets") before they are transmitted?

3. What is SMTP?

Discussion and Writing Suggestions

1. Write a summary (one or two paragraphs) of the process Dyson describes without using any of the specifics: personal or place names. Your summary should represent a general description of how a piece of e-mail makes its way from sender to recipient.

2. Discuss the ways in which Dyson attempts to make what is essen-tially a complex process intelligible and interesting to his readers. To what extent do you think he succeeds?

3. To what extent were you surprised by the mechanics of e-mail routing, as explained by Dyson? Before you read this article, what did you imagine happened when you hit the "send" button to transmit your e-mail message to its intended recipient(s)?

4. Think of a technical or scientific process that you understand reasonably well, but that many other people don't. Using Dyson's article as a model, describe what happens in a way that removes some of the mystery from the process, without unduly simplifying it. Examples: what happens when you turn the ignition key in your car; explain how rain or snow starts falling; how insects pollinate plants; how beer or wine is made; what happens when you push down the flush lever of a toilet.

Not Exactly the Most Reliable Way to Run a War, IMHO[1]
Roy Rivenburg

System crashes and program freeze-ups are two of the less endearing aspects of life in the computer age. In this humorous sketch, Los Angeles Times *staff writer Roy Rivenburg speculates, through a series of imaginary e-mail messages, about how the Army might have to fight a war if it were dependent upon the same kind of Internet connections and software as the rest of us. This piece originally appeared in the* Times *on May 1, 2001.*

1   News item: The U.S. Army is considering a program to give every soldier a handheld computer equipped with wireless Internet access. "This has the potential to greatly enhance the Army's ability to fight," said one defense analyst.

2   Then again…

3   **E-mail from:** Sgt. Bill Koe

4   **To:** B Company troops

5   **Subject:** Attack enemy position NOW!

6   Operation Desert Drizzle is now officially underway, men. This is a tightly coordinated land, sea and air attack. Our specific mission is detailed in the attached map file. I'm also sending a jpg file containing a blessing from our chaplain.

7   **From:** Pvt. G. Pyle

8   **To:** Sgt. Bill Koe

9   Sarge, we need to postpone. Henderson's server crashed; Ballard and Smith are in the middle of downloading songs off Napster; and I just got to Level Eight on Donkey Kong, which I've never done before. I can't stop now.

10   **From:** Cpl. Agarn

11   **To:** Sgt. Bill Koe

---

[1]IMHO: in my humble opinion.

12 Sir, there's a virus in the chaplain attachment. It won't open.

13 **From:** B Company
14 **To:** 38th Artillery Brigade
15 Dudes, we're pinned down by sniper fire. :-(
16 Need you to shell the coordinates marked on attached file.

17 **From:** 38th Artillery Brigade
18 **To:** B Company
19 Roger. Fed your data into Microsoft Blitzkrieg 5.0. Should take care of sniper problem. ;-)

20 **From:** B Company
21 **To:** 38th Artillery Brigade
22 Oops, you just blew up the Belgian Embassy. LOL.[2]

23 **From:** 38th Artillery Brigade
24 **To:** B Company
25 Ha. I knew we should've upgraded to Blitzkrieg 5.2. Hang on, will try again. In meantime, check out the babes at www.hotmilitarymamas.com.

26 **From:** Col. Robert Hogan
27 **To:** 29th Regiment—All Officers and Soldiers
28 Preliminary reconnaissance indicates that 38% of Air Force's "smart bombs" failed to detonate or veered off course. Recommend logging onto E-Trade ASAP and selling your defense stocks before news breaks back home.

29 **From:** Pfc. Ryan
30 **To:** killkillkill@aol.com, bmurray@doowahdiddy.org, binghampton@make-warnotlove.net, harrison@UNpeacekeeper.com, duvall22@lovethesmellofna-palminmorning.com
31 This is not a joke! I am forwarding this e-mail because the person who sent it to me studied law in ROTC and says it's for real. The U.S. Army and Microsoft are considering a merger to form a corporate military power capable of ruling the world. As a prelude to assuming total control over every aspect of our lives, Microsoft is running an e-mail beta test. When you forward this e-mail to other soldiers, the CIA will track it and the Army will increase your veterans' benefits by $5 a year per forward. If you send it to 100 people, you will also be given a Silver Star. If you forward it to 1,000 people, you will be named commander of an entire city under the new Microsoft regime. Maybe this is bogus, but what have we got to lose??!!? Send this e-mail to every soldier you know!

32 **From:** B Company
33 **To:** Allied Command HQ
34 May Day! We've just captured the enemy's secret antiaircraft headquarters but need IMMEDIATE REINFORCEMENTS or we could be driven out.

35 **From:** Mail Delivery Subsystem
36 **To:** B Company

---

[2]LOL: laughing out loud.

37 DELIVERY FAILURE. Error code 255: Message did not reach intended recipient due to system delays. Try again later.

Discussion and Writing Suggestions

1. What particular aspects of computer and e-mail activity are the subjects of Rivenburg's satire? To what extent does this piece remind you of your own frustrations with the Internet? Detail two or three incidents, based on personal experience.

2. Did you find Rivenburg's piece funny? If so, what is the source of the humor? Why does it work? (If not, why *didn't* it work?)

3. Think of an area of contemporary life (not necessarily computer-related) that annoys or frustrates you. Compose a series of e-mail messages—like Rivenburg's—humorously dramatizing, in a particular situation, this irritating aspect of life (e.g., college administrators planning how to "ease" the student registration process; advertisers brainstorming about how to make cigarettes more appealing to prospective customers).

A Shared Sadness
Russ Parsons

Most e-mail messages are private communications between a sender and one or more specifically designated recipients. Increasingly popular, however, are public electronic forums, such as chat groups, bulletin boards, newsgroups, the Usenet, and "Multi-User Domains" (MUDs). These groups, or electronic communities, are generally organized around particular personal or professional interests—e.g., Shakespeare studies, cancer survival, environmental issues, online romance. In these forums, to which users generally register or subscribe, senders post messages that can be read by all members of the group, and to which any member can respond. New and old members can also read discussion "threads" that transpired among members of the group days or even months ago.

In the following article, Los Angeles Times *staff writer Russ Parsons recounts one such discussion thread concerning a person he had never met, but whose fate touched him, and many others, deeply. Parsons' article offers another perspective on how electronic communication has helped foster new ways of relating to one another. "A Shared Sadness" first appeared in* The Los Angeles Times *on August 7, 1998.*

1 People who haven't spent much time there seem to imagine cyberspace as their own private nightmare brought to life. To some people it is a scary place, full of predators of one stripe or another. To some it is a virtual Gomorrah, a RAM-charged peep show catering to unimaginable perversions.

2   Others fear it as a cold place, a place of separation peopled only by the lonely, locked in their own little worlds. Though they may talk to one another, do they communicate?

3   "What about a sense of community?" asked a friend of mine the other day. "What about things like communication on shared subjects other than the narrow topics at hand, those things that provide the glue that transforms a group of people into a community?" (He is a professor, and he does talk that way.)

4   So I told him about Gary Holleman. Gary helped start one of the Internet discussion groups, or chat lists, I belong to. A chat list, for the uninitiated, is kind of like an ongoing letter dedicated to a specific topic. If you have something to say about that topic, you e-mail your comment to a central computer, which then forwards it to everyone else on the list. If they have something to add, they can either respond to you privately or send another message back to the central computer.

5   You can find a chat list for just about any special interest imaginable. I belong to five: one devoted to mysteries, one for wine, one for the organization Slow Food, one for cookbooks and another—the one Holleman started—for chefs and cooks.

6   There are a couple of hundred people who are on the list: not all of them are chefs and cooks. Some are culinary students or work in related fields. Some are merely curious eavesdroppers (called lurkers).

7   Conversations—that is the only way to describe them—cover everything from practical matters like Alto-Sham slow cookers (from context, I gather that this is a kind of steam oven used in production kitchens) to a rather heated philosophical argument about whether cooking is an art or a craft. At any one time, several of these topics (called threads) are happening at the same time.

8   One day early last October, in the midst of these workaday discussions, there was a note titled "Gary Holleman's Broken Heart." In it, with surprising wit and panache (we're talking chefs, remember?), Gary, a corporate chef who did product research and development, informed us that he had suddenly learned he needed some heart surgery.

9   *As you may or may not know, I recently found out that I need some spare parts for my heart—an operation that my doctors perform every day and is analogous to a medical "slam-dunk." However, for my friends, family and especially me, the prospects are somewhat more intimidating.*

10   The problem, he wrote, began at lunch at a food conference in Portland, Ore.:

11   *"The mean age of the population is gradually moving upward, and with it a new concern for fat-free, heart-healthy foods," the luncheon speaker from Noble Assn. said as he discussed food trends for the late 1990s. The woman next to me was full of questions for me about the Internet. I heard neither the speaker nor my lunch partner. My heart felt as if it were jumping through my chest. I was sure I had taken on a cartoonish figure [and that] everyone in the room could see my heart beating two feet in front of my body. In fact, I was worried my heart had invaded the personal space of the gentleman across the table.*

12   The problem recurred the next morning. He called his doctor back home in Minnesota and was told to go immediately to a cardiologist. There he learned that he had a leaky heart valve and would need to have open-heart surgery within a couple of weeks. Since the nearest major medical center was in Fargo, N.D., that's where he headed.

13   *I was stunned. The doctor says I have a four-plus aortic insufficiency (on a scale of one to four, four being the worst). While over the past year I had been unable to keep up my 15–20-miles-a-week jogging schedule, I had no idea*

that the problem was a lack of oxygen due to a broken heart. I thought I was just getting old.

14   After a couple of days of tests, he was told there was a complication: He also had an enlarged aortic artery that might have to be replaced as well.

15   *"While not technically difficult, this would be a much more complex operation," Dr. Damle said with his beautiful East Indian accent. Complex means longer. And slightly more risk, I assume.*

16   To keep everyone updated on his progress, Gary created a small mailing list that he would post to regularly. If we sent him a note, he'd add our names.

17   I didn't know Gary and, to be perfectly honest, his name hadn't registered from his postings in the past. His was a face in the crowd of postings that comes through my computer every day—someone I saw everyday but never thought much about.

18   But I was touched by the hopeful, funny tone of the note. It was a nice piece of writing. I sent him a note, telling him so and suggested that when it was all over, he should collect these essays for a book. That got me on the list.

19   The next day another missive arrived.

20   *Can a heartbroken man in Minnesota find happiness in a Fargo operating room? Read on.*

21   *"Allergic to any foods?" the intake nurse asked as she diligently filled out the proper forms.*

22   *"No, but I am a vegetarian. Ovolacto," I replied.*

23   *"A chef AND a vegetarian?"*

24   *An hour later the food arrived. A splendid vegetarian feast—sort of. One cup of hot, canned, diced beets. Another cup of hot, canned, diced beets. One scoop of instant mashed potatoes (I recognize the flavor: NIFDA Red Label). Another scoop of instant mashed potatoes.*

25   There was worse news than lunch, though.

26   *The CT scan is in, and the results are clear. I have an aortic aneurysm. "The walls of the aortic artery are weak and enlarged. I am sure that is what is causing the failure of the valve," said Dr. Damle.*

27   *The word "aneurysm" was not what I wanted to hear. It means, in Damle's words, that "we have increased the magnitude of the operation significantly." This means more risk, and, as I think it, he says it.*

28   Gary sounded more upbeat after the weekend.

29   *The "rose-colored glasses" in pill form prescribed by my surgeon, also known as antianxiety medicine, are working well. I know this for several reasons:*

30   *1) I just traveled 500 miles round-trip over 24 hours with three of my teens and my wife, and I still think I have had an absolutely marvelous weekend. We went to visit my four grandkids. Yes, at 42 years old I am too young for either heart surgery or grandkids, but I am blessed with both. However, I don't think there is a correlation.*

31   *2) I also know the antianxiety medicine is working because I have forgotten what I had anxiety about in the first place.*

32   Well, not entirely. He told of talking with one of his kids over lunch.

33   *"So, did your mother tell you there has been a change in plans for the operation? I need more extensive surgery."*

34   *"Yeah, I guess I heard. But it's still routine surgery, right?"*

35   *It's always a hard thing to know, much less tell someone else, just how risky an operation is. There is always balance—honesty and plain talk countered by hope, comfort and matter-of-factness.*

36   *"Well, yes, routine…I guess." How routine can open-heart surgery get, I wonder?*

37   *"Oh, that's good."*

38   *"But you know when we talked before, I said it was a slam-dunk medical procedure? Well, now it's more like a three-point shot."*

39   *I see the panic in his eyes. He is remembering how well I play basketball. In fact, I am remembering how well I play basketball. Thinking quickly, I add, "But, uh, Michael Jordan is taking the three-point shot!" The concern fades from his face, and we eat our salads in silence.*

40   The next post was full of news of the next day's surgery. It turns out that because of the location of the aneurysm, the surgery was going to be even more complex to avoid starving the brain of blood.

41   *The risk here is substantial. It's starting to feel more like a half-court shot by a random spectator trying to win a million dollars. I exaggerate. The doctor I have chosen is the finest doctor in North Dakota for this type of operation. (OK, I admit it. There aren't that many doctors in N.D., but Damle is excellent.)*

42   Getting ready for the surgery, he and his wife, Lois, rented a suite in a hotel across the street from the hospital. Since there was a kitchen, why not fix dinner? It had to be better than hospital food.

43   *My only disappointment making dinner was a result of the apparent dearth of fresh basil in Fargo, N.D. We went to Hornbacher's grocery store—the biggest in town—only to find REALLY shabby looking herbs, none of which resembled basil. I inquired at the checkout counter.*

44   *"Where is the best produce section in town?" I asked the checkout person. She thought for a moment, as if it were a trick question. "Uh, here?"*

45   *"Excuse me, I don't THINK so. Not in a MILLION YEARS! Your herbs look like they are left over from the floods of '97! They look like they went THROUGH the floods!" I could feel my blood pressure rising. And then I remember that I forgot to take my midday antianxiety pill.*

46   *And that brings me to the night before the dawn that has consumed my thoughts for the last two weeks. The blood tests are in. The doctor is ready. My family is by my side. I have my Ambien sleeping pills. And from reading the flood of e-mail I have received, I know my friends are thinking of me and praying for me. It is not generally my nature to try and attract attention (in the grocery store, from my friends or God for that matter), but I am indeed comforted and joyful over the love and affection that has been uploaded to my little port on the Net. Thank you, God bless you all. I'll key you soon.*

47   The next day, in order to keep calls to the family at a minimum, a member of the chat list was designated to act as go-between. I checked in every hour to see how Gary was doing.

48   There were constant updates. First:

49   *The surgery is taking longer than expected, but that's not necessarily a bad sign.*

50   Then:

51   *I have just spoken with the nurse's station, and Gary has been returned to surgery. I am hoping things are going well, but this may be the time to start praying.*

52   It got worse.

53   *Gary is in very, very critical condition. Please stop what you are doing for just a moment and pray however and to whomever you do it.*

54   By 4, it seemed a corner had been turned.

55   *Gary is out of surgery. His heart is being supported by a left ventricular assist device. He is much improved. He is currently in intensive care and will be in the recovery room soon.*

56   But at 5:

57   *I just spoke with Lois. Gary has been taken back into surgery for the third time. She does not know for what. We all continue to hope and pray.*

58   A couple of minutes later:

59   *I just spoke to Gary's brother Michael, and Gary's condition has taken an unforeseen turn toward critical.*

60   After that, a maddening silence. I found things to straighten up around my desk, staying late and doing busy work in between logging on to check for news. Finally, just after 7:

61   *Gary Holleman left us half an hour ago. We all loved him.*

62   Messages flew back and forth as the news spread. It seemed everyone had been doing just what I had been doing—staying close to the computer to check in. The next day—Oct. 22, 1997—was declared a day of silence in Gary's honor. We took up a collection for his children and—this being cyberspace, again—someone added a tribute section to his home page where anyone who wanted could write a note about Gary. (If you want to visit, it's still up: *http://www.churchstreet.com/co/gary.htm*)

63   Just like anyplace else, we grieved for a friend we'd lost and knew that our little community had been changed forever.

Review Questions

1. What is a chat list?

2. Summarize "A Shared Sadness." Avoid direct quotations, but try to convey the sense of the changing circumstances of Holleman's condition, particularly once he undergoes surgery.

Discussion and Writing Suggestions

1. Discuss the significance of the title "A Shared Sadness." In your discussion consider how Parsons uses the word "community." What kind of community developed in the wake of Holleman's illness and surgery? How was this virtual community different from what we generally think of as a "community?"

2. Many people who have read this article have found it unusually touching. Given that thousands of people die of heart disease every year, which aspects of "A Shared Sadness" make the story of this particular death so moving?

3. Visit the Web site devoted to Gary Holleman <http://www.churchstreet.com/co/gary.htm> mentioned by Parsons. Read some of the postings by those who knew Holleman, either in person, or through the chat list, and write a short account of what you find.

4. Have you ever been in the waiting room or been waiting at home while someone you know underwent major surgery? Describe your reactions and the reactions of others around you, or others you were in contact with, as the surgery approached, and as news of its progress filtered out. To what extent were your reactions similar to those of Parsons and his virtual community?

Virtual Love
Meghan Daum

Star-vehicles like You've Got Mail *aside, the popular media abounds with stories—some inspirational, some cautionary—about online romances. In a typical pattern, couples first meet one another in public chat rooms, then retire to private spaces for one-on-one e-mail conversations, then at some point, perhaps, "progress" to cyber-sex. (In no small number of cases, one or both parties are already married, and the discovery of the online romance by the outraged spouse leads to divorce. Question: does engaging in an online, entirely text-based romance constitute infidelity to one's spouse or significant other?) Many of these relationships remain at a virtual level; in other cases, couples begin communicating by telephone, and then, perhaps, decide to meet one other in person. Some of these stories have happy endings; most don't. Disappointment seems almost a given: even in those cases not involving outright fraud or misrepresentation (a male representing himself as female, a 50-year-old married woman representing herself as a 30-year-old single, a request by one party to the other for "travel expenses"), the reality is seldom able to match the expectation raised by the intoxication of an idealized cyber-romance.*

Online dating originates not only in special-interest chat rooms, but also in numerous matchmaking sites on the Web, like Matchmaker.com, AmericanSingles.com, Altmatch.com, CatholicSingles.com, and ThirdAge.com. One site, Match.com, takes credit for about 1,000 weddings that have resulted from couples meeting at its site. In the following article, the author describes how she met her partner in yet another way: when he unexpectedly e-mailed her after reading some of her published work. The progress of this relationship is detailed in "Virtual Love." Meghan Daum is a freelance writer whose articles have appeared in such magazines as Harper's, Vogue, *and* The New Yorker. *This article first appeared in the August 25–September 1, 1997, issue of* The New Yorker.

1 It was last November; fall was drifting away into an intolerable chill. I was at the end of my twenty-sixth year, and was living in New York City, trying to sup-

port myself as a writer, and taking part in the kind of urban life that might be construed as glamorous were it to appear in a memoir in the distant future. At the time, however, my days felt more like a grind than like an adventure: hours of work strung between the motions of waking up, getting the mail, watching TV with my roommates, and going to bed. One morning, I logged on to my America Online account to find a message under the heading "is this the real meghan daum?" It came from someone with the screen name PFSlider. The body of the message consisted of five sentences, written entirely in lowercase letters, of perfectly turned flattery: something about PFSlider's admiration of some newspaper and magazine articles I had published over the last year and a half, something about his resulting infatuation with me, and something about his being a sportswriter in California.

2   I was engaged for the thirty seconds that it took me to read the message and fashion a reply. Though it felt strange to be in the position of confirming that I was indeed "the real meghan daum," I managed to say, "Yes, it's me. Thank you for writing." I clicked the "Send Now" icon, shot my words into the void, and forgot about PFSlider until the next day, when I received another message, this one headed "eureka."

3   "wow, it is you," he wrote, still in lowercase. He chronicled the various conditions under which he'd read my few-and-far-between articles—a boardwalk in Laguna Beach, the spring-training pressroom for a baseball team that he covered for a Los Angeles newspaper. He confessed to having a crush on me. He referred to me as "princess daum." He said he wanted to have lunch with me during one of his two annual trips to New York.

4   The letter was outrageous and endearingly pathetic, possibly the practical joke of a friend trying to rouse me out of a temporary writer's block. But the kindness pouring forth from my computer screen was bizarrely exhilarating, and I logged off and thought about it for a few hours before writing back to express how flattered and "touched"—this was probably the first time I had ever used that word in earnest—I was by his message.

5   I am not what most people would call a computer person. I have no interest in chat rooms, newsgroups, or most Web sites. I derive a palpable thrill from sticking a letter in the United States mail. But I have a constant low-grade fear of the telephone, and I often call people with the intention of getting their answering machines. There is something about the live voice that I have come to find unnervingly organic, as volatile as live television. E-mail provides a useful antidote for my particular communication anxieties. Though I generally send and receive only a few messages a week, I take comfort in their silence and their boundaries.

6   PFSlider and I tossed a few innocuous, smart-assed notes back and forth over the week following his first message. Let's say his name was Pete. He was twenty-nine, and single. I revealed very little about myself, relying instead on the ironic commentary and forced witticisms that are the conceit of so many E-mail messages. But I quickly developed an oblique affection for PFSlider. I was excited when there was a message from him, mildly depressed when there wasn't. After a few weeks, he gave me his phone number. I did not give him mine, but he looked it up and called me one Friday night. I was home. I picked up the phone. His voice was jarring, yet not unpleasant. He held up more than his end

of the conversation for an hour, and when he asked permission to call me again I granted it, as though we were of an earlier era.

7   Pete—I could never wrap my mind around his name, privately thinking of him as PFSlider, "E-mail guy," or even "baseball boy"—began phoning me two or three times a week. He asked if he could meet me, and I said that that would be O.K. Christmas was a few weeks away, and he told me that he would be coming back East to see his family. From there, he would take a short flight to New York and have lunch with me.

8   "It is my off-season mission to meet you," he said.

9   "There will probably be a snowstorm," I said.

10   "I'll take a team of sled dogs," he answered.

11   We talked about our work and our families, about baseball and Bill Clinton and Howard Stern and sex, about his hatred for Los Angeles and how much he wanted a new job. Sometimes we'd find each other logged on simultaneously and type back and forth for hours.

12   I had previously considered cyber-communication an oxymoron, a fast road to the breakdown of humanity. But, curiously, the Internet—at least in the limited form in which I was using it—felt anything but dehumanizing. My interaction with PFSlider seemed more authentic than much of what I experienced in the daylight realm of living beings. I was certainly putting more energy into the relationship than I had put into many others. I also was giving Pete attention that was by definition undivided, and relishing the safety of the distance between us by opting to be truthful instead of doling out the white lies that have become the staple of real life. The outside world—the place where I walked around avoiding people I didn't want to deal with, peppering my casual conversations with half-truths, and applying my motto "Let the machine take it" to almost any scenario—was sliding into the periphery of my mind.

13   For me, the time on-line with Pete was far superior to the phone. There were no background noises, no interruptions from "call waiting," no long-distance charges. Through typos and misspellings, he flirted maniacally. "I have an absurd crush on you," he said. "If I like you in person, you must promise to marry me." I was coy and conceited, telling him to get a life, baiting him into complimenting me further, teasing him in a way I would never have dared to do in person, or even on the phone. I would stay up until 3 A.M. typing with him, smiling at the screen, getting so giddy that when I quit I couldn't fall asleep. I was having difficulty recalling what I used to do at night. It was as if he and I lived together in our own quiet space—a space made all the more intimate because of our conscious decision to block everyone else out. My phone was tied up for hours at a time. No one in the real world could reach me, and I didn't really care.

14   Since my last serious relationship, I'd had the requisite number of false starts and five-night stands, dates that I wasn't sure were dates, and emphatically casual affairs that buckled under their own inertia. With PFSlider, on the other hand, I may not have known my suitor, but, for the first time in my life, I knew the deal: I was a desired person, the object of a blind man's gaze. He called not only when he said he would call but unexpectedly, just to say hello. He was protected by the shield of the Internet; his guard was not merely down but nonexistent. He let his phone bill grow to towering proportions. He told me that he

thought about me all the time, though we both knew that the "me" in his mind consisted largely of himself. He talked about me to his friends, and admitted it. He arranged his holiday schedule around our impending date. He managed to charm me with sports analogies. He didn't hesitate. He was unblinking and unapologetic, all nerviness and balls to the wall.

15   And so PFSlider became my everyday life. All the tangible stuff fell away. My body did not exist. I had no skin, no hair, no bones. All desire had converted itself into a cerebral current that reached nothing but my frontal lobe. There was no outdoors, no social life, no weather. There was only the computer screen and the phone, my chair, and maybe a glass of water. Most mornings, I would wake up to find a message from PFSlider, composed in Pacific time while I slept in the wee hours. "I had a date last night," he wrote. "And I am not ashamed to say it was doomed from the start because I couldn't stop thinking about you."

16   I fired back a message slapping his hand. "We must be careful where we tread," I said. This was true but not sincere. I wanted it, all of it. I wanted unfettered affection, soul-mating, true romance. In the weeks that had elapsed since I picked up "is this the real meghan daum?" the real me had undergone some kind of meltdown—a systemic rejection of all the savvy and independence I had worn for years, like a grownup Girl Scout badge.

17   Pete knew nothing of my scattered, juvenile self, and I did my best to keep it that way. Even though I was heading into my late twenties, I was still a child, ignorant of dance steps and health insurance, a prisoner of credit-card debt and student loans and the nagging feeling that I didn't want anyone to find me until I had pulled myself into some semblance of an adult. The fact that Pete had literally seemed to discover me, as if by turning over a rock, lent us an aura of fate which I actually took half-seriously. Though skepticism seemed like the obvious choice in this strange situation, I discarded it precisely because it was the obvious choice, because I wanted a more interesting narrative than cynicism would ever allow. I was a true believer in the urban dream: the dream of years of struggle, of getting a break, of making it. Like most of my friends, I wanted someone to love me, but I wasn't supposed to need it. To admit to loneliness was to smack the face of progress, to betray the times in which we lived. But PFSlider derailed me. He gave me all of what I'd never even realized I wanted.

18   My addiction to PFSlider's messages indicated a monstrous narcissism, but it also revealed a subtler desire, which I didn't fully understand at the time. My need to experience an old-fashioned kind of courtship was stronger than I had ever imagined. And the fact that technology was providing an avenue for such archaic discourse was a paradox that both fascinated and repelled me. Our relationship had an epistolary quality that put our communication closer to the eighteenth century than to the impending millennium. Thanks to the computer, I was involved in a well-defined courtship, a neat little space in which he and I were both safe to express the panic and the fascination of our mutual affection. Our interaction was refreshingly orderly, noble in its vigor, dignified despite its shamelessness. It was far removed from the randomness of real-life relationships. We had an intimacy that seemed custom-made for our strange, lonely times. It seemed custom-made for me.

19   The day of our date, a week before Christmas, was frigid and sunny. Pete was sitting at the bar of the restaurant when I arrived. We shook hands. For a split second, he leaned toward me with his chin, as if to kiss me. He was shorter than I had pictured, though he was not short. He struck me as clean-cut. He had very nice hands. He wore a very nice shirt. We were seated at a very nice table. I scanned the restaurant for people I knew, saw none, and couldn't decide how I felt about that.

20   He talked, and I heard nothing he said. I stared at his profile and tried to figure out whether I liked him. He seemed to be saying nothing in particular, but he went on forever. Later, we went to the Museum of Natural History and watched a science film about storm chasers. We walked around looking for the dinosaurs, and he talked so much that I wanted to cry. Outside, walking along Central Park West at dusk, through the leaves, past the yellow cabs and the splendid lights of Manhattan at Christmas, he grabbed my hand to kiss me and I didn't let him. I felt as if my brain had been stuffed with cotton. Then, for some reason, I invited him back to my apartment. I gave him a few beers and finally let him kiss me on the lumpy futon in my bedroom. The radiator clanked. The phone rang and the machine picked up. A car alarm blared outside. A key turned in the door as one of my roommates came home. I had no sensation at all—only a clear conviction that I wanted Pete out of my apartment. I wanted to hand him his coat, close the door behind him, and fight the ensuing emptiness by turning on the computer and taking comfort in PFSlider.

21   When Pete finally did leave, I berated myself from every angle: for not kissing him on Central Park West, for letting him kiss me at all, for not liking him, for wanting to like him more than I had wanted anything in such a long time. I was horrified by the realization that I had invested so heavily in a made-up character—a character in whose creation I'd had a greater hand than even Pete himself. How could I, a person so self-congratulatingly reasonable, have been sucked into a scenario that was more akin to a television talk show than to the relatively full and sophisticated life I was so convinced I led? How could I have received a fan letter and allowed it to go this far?

22   The next day, a huge bouquet of FTD flowers arrived from him. No one had ever sent me flowers before. I forgave him. As human beings with actual flesh and hand gestures and Gap clothing, Pete and I were utterly incompatible, but I decided to pretend otherwise. He returned home and we fell back into the computer and the phone, and I continued to keep the real world safely away from the desk that held them. Instead of blaming him for my disappointment, I blamed the earth itself, the invasion of roommates and ringing phones into the immaculate communication that PFSlider and I had created.

23   When I pictured him in the weeks that followed, I saw the image of a plane lifting off over an overcast city. PFSlider was otherworldly, more a concept than a person. His romance lay in the notion of flight, the physics of gravity defiance. So when he offered to send me a plane ticket to spend the weekend with him in Los Angeles I took it as an extension of our blissful remoteness, a three-dimensional E-mail message lasting an entire weekend.

24   The temperature on the runway at J.F.K. was seven degrees Fahrenheit. Our DC-10 sat for three hours waiting for deicing. Finally, it took off over the frozen

city, and the ground below shrank into a drawing of itself. Phone calls were made, laptop computers were plopped onto tray tables. The recirculating air dried out my contact lenses. I watched movies without the sound and told myself that they were probably better that way. Something about the plastic interior of the fuselage and the plastic forks and the din of the air and the engines was soothing and strangely sexy.

25   Then we descended into LAX. We hit the tarmac, and the seat-belt signs blinked off. I hadn't moved my body in eight hours, and now I was walking through the tunnel to the gate, my clothes wrinkled, my hair matted, my hands shaking. When I saw Pete in the terminal, his face seemed to me just as blank and easy to miss as it had the first time I'd met him. He kissed me chastely. On the way out to the parking lot, he told me that he was being seriously considered for a job in New York. He was flying back there next week. If he got the job, he'd be moving within the month. I looked at him in astonishment. Something silent and invisible seemed to fall on us. Outside, the wind was warm, and the Avis and Hertz buses ambled alongside the curb of Terminal 5. The palm trees shook, and the air seemed as heavy and palpable as Pete's hand, which held mine for a few seconds before dropping it to get his car keys out of his pocket. He stood before me, all flesh and preoccupation, and for this I could not forgive him.

26   Gone were the computer, the erotic darkness of the telephone, the clean, single dimension of Pete's voice at 1 A.M. It was nighttime, yet the combination of sight and sound was blinding. It scared me. It turned me off. We went to a restaurant and ate outside on the sidewalk. We strained for conversation, and I tried not to care that we had to. We drove to his apartment and stood under the ceiling light not really looking at each other. Something was happening that we needed to snap out of. Any moment now, I thought. Any moment and we'll be all right. These moments were crowded with elements, with carpet fibers and automobiles and the smells of everything that had a smell. It was all wrong. The physical world had invaded our space.

27   For three days, we crawled along the ground and tried to pull ourselves up. We talked about things that I can no longer remember. We read the Los Angeles *Times* over breakfast. We drove north past Santa Barbara to tour the wine country. I felt like an object that could not be lifted, something that secretly weighed more than the world itself. Everything and everyone around us seemed imbued with a California lightness. I stomped around the countryside, an idiot New Yorker in my clunky shoes and black leather jacket. Not until I studied myself in the bathroom mirror of a highway rest stop did I fully realize the preposterousness of my uniform. I was dressed for war. I was dressed for my regular life.

28   That night, in a tiny town called Solvang, we ate an expensive dinner. We checked into a Marriott and watched television. Pete talked at me and through me and past me. I tried to listen. I tried to talk. But I bored myself and irritated him. Our conversation was a needle that could not be threaded. Still, we played nice. We tried to care, and pretended to keep trying long after we had given up. In the car on the way home, he told me that I was cynical, and I didn't have the presence of mind to ask him just how many cynics he had met who would travel three thousand miles to see someone they barely knew.

29   Pete drove me to the airport at 7 A.M. so I could make my eight-o'clock flight home. He kissed me goodbye—another chaste peck that I recognized from countless dinner parties and dud dates. He said that he'd call me in a few days when he got to New York for his job interview, which we had discussed only in passing and with no reference to the fact that New York was where I happened to live. I returned home to frozen January. A few days later, he came to New York, and we didn't see each other. He called me from the plane taking him back to Los Angeles to tell me, through the static, that he had got the job. He was moving to my city.

30   PFSlider was dead. There would be no meeting him in distant hotel lobbies during the baseball season. There would be no more phone calls or E-mail messages. In a single moment, Pete had completed his journey out of our mating dance and officially stepped into the regular world—the world that gnawed at me daily, the world that fostered those five-night stands, the world where romance could not be sustained, because so many of us simply did not know how to do it. Instead, we were all chitchat and leather jackets, bold proclaimers of all that we did not need. But what struck me most about this affair was the unpredictable nature of our demise. Unlike most cyber-romances, which seem to come fully equipped with the inevitable set of misrepresentations and false expectations, PFSlider and I had played it fairly straight. Neither of us had lied. We'd done the best we could. Our affair had died from natural causes rather than virtual ones.

31   Within a two-week period after I returned from Los Angeles, at least seven people confessed to me the vagaries of their own E-mail affairs. This topic arose, unprompted, in the course of normal conversation. I heard most of these stories in the close confines of smoky bars and crowded restaurants, and we all shook our heads in bewilderment as we told our tales, our eyes focused on some point in the distance. Four of these people had met their correspondents, by traveling from New Haven to Baltimore, from New York to Montana, from Texas to Virginia, and from New York to Johannesburg. These were normal people, writers and lawyers and scientists. They were all smart, attractive, and more than a little sheepish about admitting just how deeply they had been sucked in. Mostly, it was the courtship ritual that had seduced us. E-mail had become an electronic epistle, a yearned-for rule book. It allowed us to do what was necessary to experience love. The Internet was not responsible for our remote, fragmented lives. The problem was life itself.

32   The story of PFSlider still makes me sad, not so much because we no longer have anything to do with each other but because it forces me to see the limits and the perils of daily life with more clarity than I used to. After I realized that our relationship would never transcend the screen and the phone—that, in fact, our face-to-face knowledge of each other had permanently contaminated the screen and the phone—I hit the pavement again, went through the motions of everyday life, said hello and goodbye to people in the regular way. If Pete and I had met at a party, we probably wouldn't have spoken to each other for more than ten minutes, and that would have made life easier but also less interesting. At the same time, it terrifies me to admit to a firsthand understanding of the way the heart and the ego are snarled and entwined like diseased trees that

have folded in on each other. Our need to worship somehow fuses with our need to be worshipped. It upsets me still further to see how inaccessibility can make this entanglement so much more intoxicating. But I'm also thankful that I was forced to unpack the raw truth of my need and stare at it for a while. It was a dare I wouldn't have taken in three dimensions.

33   The last time I saw Pete, he was in New York, three thousand miles away from what had been his home, and a million miles away from PFSlider. In a final gesture of decency, in what I later realized was the most ordinary kind of closure, he took me out to dinner. As the few remaining traces of affection turned into embarrassed regret, we talked about nothing. He paid the bill. He drove me home in a rental car that felt as arbitrary and impersonal as what we now were to each other.

34   Pete had known how to get me where I lived until he came to where I lived: then he became as unmysterious as anyone next door. The world had proved to be too cluttered and too fast for us, too polluted to allow the thing we'd attempted through technology ever to grow in the earth. PFSlider and I had joined the angry and exhausted living. Even if we met on the street, we wouldn't recognize each other, our particular version of intimacy now obscured by the branches and bodies and falling debris that make up the physical world.

Discussion and Writing Suggestions

1. Daum remarks that, contrary to what she had previously assumed about cyber-communication, her e-mail correspondence with Pete was "anything but dehumanizing. My interaction with PFSlider seemed more authentic than much of what I experienced in the daylight realm of living beings. I was certainly putting more energy into the relationship than I had put into many others." To what extent have you experienced this same reaction to virtual correspondence (if not virtual romance)? How do you account for this phenomenon?

2. Daum writes that PFSlider told her that "he thought about me all the time, though we both knew that the 'me' in his mind consisted largely of himself." What do you think she means? In what sense did they "both" know this? Do you think that this statement would have been less true had Pete and she first encountered one another face-to-face? Or if they had first made contact by letter and telephone, rather than by e-mail?

3. Daum notes that as her virtual relationship developed, "the real me had undergone some kind of meltdown—a systematic rejection of all the savvy and independence I had worn for years, like a grownup Girl Scout badge." Why do you think this happened? To what extent do your own experiences or those of others you know bear out this phenomenon? To what extent is the Internet (as opposed to the power of new romance, virtual or old-fashioned) the key factor in causing such a "meltdown"?

4. How do you account for the particular way in which Daum's and Pete's relationship developed, both before they physically met and after? Consider, in particular, Daum's reflections to herself (paragraph 21) immediately after their first date. Was the relationship doomed from the start, because of the unrealistic expectations that each had developed, or might people different from these particular two have been able to sustain their relationship over the long term? To what extent does Daum's case provide a general lesson about online romances?

5. Daum remarks (paragraph 30) that her affair with Pete "died from natural causes rather than virtual ones." And she concludes (paragraph 34) that her and Pete's "particular version of intimacy [was] now obscured by the branches and bodies and falling debris that make up the physical world." What do you think she means by these statements? What were the "natural causes"? What are the "branches and bodies and falling debris"?

The Anonymous Voice
Esther Dyson

Sometimes people are never so powerful as when they assume a mask of anonymity. They can say whatever they want to whomever they want, confident that they can escape accountability for their words and the effects of those words. Of course, anonymous communications did not begin with the Internet: people have been sending unsigned letters and messages for centuries, and anonymous telephone calls have been a fact of life for decades. Anonymous e-mail and chat-room messages are only the latest variant of this age-old phenomenon. As Esther Dyson points out in the following piece, there are sometimes legitimate reasons for Internet anonymity; but there are also opportunities for abuse and serious harm to people's reputations.

After earning a degree in economics from Harvard, Esther Dyson began her career as a fact checker and then a reporter for Forbes, *a business magazine. In 1974 she authored* Help Wanted: Minorities and Women in the Retail Industry, *a pamphlet published by the New York Council on Economic Priorities. Subsequently, Dyson became a researcher for Rosen Research, a company devoted to emerging information technology. In 1983, she bought the company from her employer and re-named it EDventure Holdings. EDventure publishes* Release 1.0, *a monthly computer-industry newsletter, and sponsors the annual PC Forum for important players in the high-tech industry. A frequent public speaker and a highly influential voice in the field of information technology, as it relates to venture capital and emerging markets, Dyson has published articles in* The New York Times, The Washington Post, Wired, Forbes, *and* Harvard Business Review. *The following passage is from her book* Release 2.0: A Design for Living in the Digital Age *(1997). (* Release 2.1 *was published in 1998.)*

1 We were standing around the barbecue at a spruced-up country inn outside Lisbon, after a long day of discussions about anonymity, censorship, regulation,

and the like. I took off my badge and quipped, "I'm anonymous now!"

2   "Well, I can think of many reasons to be anonymous," leered a bystander, "but I can't discuss them in polite company!"

3   That's the general attitude to anonymity: You've probably got something to hide, and it's probably disgusting. Good people don't need anonymity.

4   Well, good people wouldn't need anonymity if everyone around them were good, too, but there are too many people everywhere willing to take advantage of others' weaknesses, betray their confidences, or otherwise misuse a totally open world. (Of course, in a truly open world blackmail would be impossible.)

5   Socially, anonymity is a useful mechanism for people to let off steam, explore ideas or fantasies, and hide from social disapproval with a minimum of consequences. Whatever you think of this, it's probably better than the alternative, which is to explore those fantasies or face oppression in real life. It's not that you can't get hurt by emotions engendered online, but you're less likely to. A lot of the anonymous chatter is harmless because no one believes it anyway.

6   Anonymity may not be desirable in itself, but it is often a rational, best-of-a-bad-situation response to a less than perfect world. Or it may just be an outlet for a kid going through a phase.

My Other Self

7 Growing up in the fifties, I didn't know how to be a teenager around my parents, who had immigrated from Europe after I was born. They were reasonable and flexible, but they would have been nonplussed if I had talked about dating, asked to take driving lessons, started wearing makeup. There was just no concept of teenager in my family—only grown-ups and children. I left at the age of fifteen, although for the "respectable" reason of going to college, where I changed identity to become a teenager with a vengeance. It took about ten years for me to feel comfortable at home again.

8   Had the online world existed, I might have tried out being a teenager online and had less need to leave home—or perhaps the support from outside to stay home and change. I might not even have needed to be anonymous, since my parents probably wouldn't have been in the same circles online, but someone might have forwarded them something I wrote. I might have written something untrue, just because I didn't want to be burdened with my real identity of a slightly dumpy fifteen-year-old with braces and horn-rimmed glasses. I might have wanted to pretend my parents were wicked tyrants—or I simply might have wanted to discuss them in ways I wouldn't have wanted them to see.

9   That is one powerful reason for anonymity on the Net: You may be perfectly happy to be open in a specific community—a circle of your teenaged friends, for example—but you might not want to see your words copied out of context, or even read in full by someone outside that community. Think of all the banal or silly or indiscreet conversations you have had over the years at cocktail parties, in movie lines, at kids' soccer games, in locker rooms, among strangers on holiday…Imagine if all that were online and could be searched and retrieved. Haven't you ever told a stranger on a bus or airplane something you might not tell your best friend? Or your mother?

10   Why else would someone choose to be anonymous? Reasons range broadly:

- discussing personal problems (especially those involving a third party) with others. You could be an abused spouse, a parent with a rebellious teenager, or simply a government lawyer trying to decide if she really wants to stay in that career.
- testing ideas you may not want to be associated with. Are you a politician trying to float a trial balloon? Or perhaps a teenager wondering if there's a case for virginity?
- playing a harmless joke on a friend. This could backfire.
- complaining about anything from messy washrooms to a sexually abusive boss, a corrupt politician, or a tyrannical teacher. Or you could anonymously warn a friend that his job is in trouble, her loud music is annoying the neighborhood, or his kid is skipping school.
- asking dumb questions. One example offered by anonymity service provider Johan Helsingius was that of a C-language programmer who needed answers to some elementary questions and didn't want to reveal his ignorance to his boss.
- trying out a different identity—real or imagined. Many of these cases have to do with sexual orientation, but they could have to do with age or other aspects of identity. In less innocent cases, people pretend to be experts when they're not, and can cause considerable damage. (But this list is about *good* reasons.)
- rallying support and arousing political consciousness in an oppressive political regime. Often political dissent is crushed because dissidents don't know that others feel the same way. Repressive governments, of course, also *benefit* from anonymity: It hides the extent of dissatisfaction and makes people afraid to trust one another—which is a downside of anonymity.
- voting—perhaps the most widely recognized and approved form of anonymous behavior. The answer to "Who voted for the opposition?" is properly: No one knows. But their voices will be counted.

Anonymity in Practice

11 Many anonymous communities work perfectly well by their own standards. Those include a large variety of newsgroups where people discuss troubling subjects such as addictions, diseases, fantasies, fears, and other potentially uncomfortable topics. Others simply revel in anonymity as part of their culture. For example, there's a strange thing called the Internet Oracle (formerly the Usenet Oracle), where anonymity is accepted and encouraged. People e-mail questions to the Oracle and other players supply the answers for their own and others' pleasure. That is, you e-mail in a question, and that question is forwarded to another person on the list, who answers it. The organizers cull the best of the questions and answers and post them for all to see. The underlying conceit is that the Oracle embodies the collective wisdom of all the players; he has his own crotchety whims, human frailties, and of course an ever-changing personality. The convention for contributors is anonymity, although it is not

required. The system automatically removes people's return e-mail addresses, but the instructions say, "If you do not wish to remain anonymous, you may include a phrase in your answer like 'incarnated as <insert your name and/or address here>.'" Fewer than 1 percent of the contributors identified themselves.

12   Consider it a giant party game played over the Net. Although it went through a rough spot for a couple of years as a large number of newcomers entered the fray without respect for the Oracle culture, they eventually dropped out and the Oracle retains its spirit of intellectual playfulness. The questions and answers are a mix of pseudomythology, programmer jargon, sophomoric jokes, and truly elegant irony. Entertainment on the Net isn't all virtual reality, video clips, and twitch games.

13   One of the organizers, veteran online user, editor, online columnist, and former English professor David Sewell, surveyed some of the participants about their perceptions of anonymity. He says, "Anonymity provides two crucial advantages: freedom of self-expression, and the shared aesthetic illusion of an Oracle persona. Like college professors who publish murder mysteries or romance novels under pseudonyms for fear of being thought unprofessional, Oracle writers sometimes feel safer when unidentified." In an article published by *First Monday,* an online Internet journal, he quotes some participants and then goes on to explain further one lure of anonymity:

> "I think [anonymity is] essential. I wouldn't have the guts to use the Oracle if I knew my name was going with everything I wrote."

> "It helps me to give answers which are much more uninhibited. If I knew my identity would be made public I might be a little reluctant to write, since I would not want co-workers to know how much I am involved."

14   But the second reason for accepting anonymity more resembles that of the medieval author, who, in Hans Robert Jauss's words, wrote "in order to praise and to extend his object, not to express himself or to enhance his personal reputation." The "object" in this case is the collection of a corpus of work by a personality, the Oracle, whose characteristics derive from the collective efforts of contributors…. And in fact the Oracle has accreted an identifiable personality. Like a Greek god, he is polymorphous: now a crochety old man, now a super-intelligent computer program, now a deity. A jealous, omniscient and omnipotent being, he is apt to strike with lightning supplicants who insult him or fail to grovel sufficiently. Nevertheless he is vulnerable to having his plug pulled by his creator Kinzler, his computer's system administrator, or an irate "god@heaven.com." Like Zeus, he has a consort: Lisa evolved from the cliche-geek's fantasy-fulfilling "net.sex.goddess" to the Oracle's companion. It may be that one reason for leaving Oracle submissions unsigned is generic constraint: like Scripture, Oracularities should seem to participants to proceed directly from the voice of God. As E. M. Forster once observed of unsigned newspaper editorials, "anonymous statements have…a universal air about them. Absolute truth, the collected wisdom of the universe, seems to be speaking, not the feeble voice of a man." A number of Oracle authors who responded to the questionnaire identified similar reasons for leaving their contributions unsigned:

"I'd put less effort into writing for the Oracle if [my identity] were public. I prefer the idea of an all-powerful Oracle rather than the various incarnations scenario.… Sometimes it would be nice to say, 'I wrote that!' but I prefer to just smile knowingly…"

"I don't care who wrote it, but it sort of loses something when I see a signature line. Destroys the myth, so to speak."

"When I read Oracularities…I prefer to think of a faceless deity in a cave somewhere, not joe@lharc.netcom.edu. I prefer anonymity."

[…]

Why Anonymity Is Sometimes Not Such a Great Idea After All

15 Johan Helsingius, the Oracle and my teenage self all make a good case *for* anonymity. But why is it not something we want to promote in general?

16   First, because it can be done to excess and is not healthy for individuals, though this is a free country and a free Net. Second, because even good people tend to be "less good" when they're not recognized and building (or keeping) a reputation. And finally, because bad people can use anonymity to get away with truly harmful behavior.

17   Like alcohol, anonymity can be useful in moderation. For some people it's a harmless release and an outlet; others can overuse it and abuse it to avoid everyday responsibilities and challenges. No, you should not just go and live the rest of your life anonymously online, flitting from identity to identity. Nor should you drown yourself in alcohol, lose yourself in gambling, or escape into drugs. The Net can be an addiction like any other, although it is probably easier on your body than most of them.

18   It may not be nice to say it, but people are not all always nice, and therefore a little social pressure can be a good thing. For example, I consider myself basically "good," but I'm a lot less nice in airport lines (for instance) than in places where I know someone. Haven't you ever lost your patience with a clerk or a waiter and then been embarrassed when you found out someone you know was watching? Unfortunately, I have! (This is why people usually behave better in tight communities than in big cities, and tourists abroad behave in ways they wouldn't at home. Consider the well-known reprimand: "Would you do this in your mother's home?")

19   If you want to be scientific rather than moralistic about it, consider a variety of experiments in game and market theory. The basic finding of all of them is that people work together best by telling the truth, on any task from avoiding jail to setting prices for goods. Sometimes people can gain a short-term advantage by lying, but they usually can't benefit in the long run. Over time markets work better and produce better average outcomes, when people (1) tell the truth and (2) can earn a reputation for doing so.

20   When people operate anonymously, there's no incentive to tell the truth; dishonest people easily betray others for their own gain. Overall, anonymous

markets don't work well. The wrong people get put into jail; the market prices are volatile and misallocate goods or investment; investment doesn't take place because no one can count on long-term gains. Overall, everyone is worse off on average, and the crooks do better than the honest people. However, they must always live in fear of encountering even bigger crooks. (This all sounds very much like the current situation in much of Russia to me. It has markets, yes, but it lacks the rules of disclosure and accountability that make them work.)

21   But the issue isn't just markets: Visibility leads to healthier communities in general. There should be occasions and places where anonymity is practiced but they should be clearly marked. The worst difficulties arise when you get something in-between—especially when people pretend to be other, known people rather than anonymous characters, as happened not long ago in one of the first online communities.

The Experience at the WELL

22 The WELL (perhaps too cutely, it stands for Whole Earth 'Lectronic Link) was started in San Francisco by Stewart Brand, also founder of the Whole Earth Catalogue. It attracted an elite crowd of early adopters. Brand had earlier been part of one of the first online services, called EIES (for Electronic Information Exchange System). On it was one small group of scientists and corporate people who were using it for an ongoing conference in the early '80s. That group had a brief but devastating encounter with anonymity. Recalls Stewart (by e-mail, of course): "They were all respected men and women with responsible positions in the world. Suddenly one was behaving like a 'you can't catch me' prankster. The whole discussion swerved to dealing with that. Amusement turned to resentment and then turned to distrust and distaste. The group fell apart online. The bad odor from that experience lasted for a long time."

23   That experience led Stewart to make personal identities required on the WELL. Besides, many of them already knew each other offline; others joined the community online and then met face-to-face. Over a couple of years, the few hundred members formed a tight little community, full of friendship and gossip, petty rivalries and deep affection, a few romances, some shared secrets…a normal community. Then a group of members decided to start a subgroup that allowed anonymity, over Brand's skepticism—but he figured the results might be different the second time around. They were not.

24   Strange things began to happen. First people posted unpleasant truths, attacking one another. In such a tight little community, it was pretty easy to figure out who was saying what—and trying to guess was fun. Then people started pretending to be one another, and it became harder to tell what was going on. Says Stewart in retrospect: "Because the people actually knew each other, they could pretend to be one another more convincingly. They could reveal secrets. It was far worse than a group of strangers could have been."

25   He continues: "Now, there were several conferences on the WELL where it was permitted, almost encouraged, for people to say absolutely vicious things about each other, and the strong WELL opinion against censorship made those conferences as sacrosanct as any other.

26   "But anonymous parody was apparently unacceptable where accountable viciousness was okay. Several people asked Cliff Figallo, who ran the WELL at the time [and who used to work at EFF] to shut down the Anonymous conference, and he promptly did. Nobody mourned. [The experiment] lasted at most two weeks with the world's most permissive online community.

27   "The two experiences add up to a proof for me. They were wholly separate— different systems, different people, different times. Both had fairly high-minded expectations of anonymity online. Both failed horribly. Different pathologies emerged and became decisive in the two occasions. On EIES, one of a close, trusted group turned into an unaccountable demon and never recanted. On the WELL, people pretended to be other people destructively. In both cases, trust was the casualty. It was easy to destroy; hard to rebuild."

Problems with Anonymity

28 Relatively speaking, the WELL was a mild case. Far worse than its tendency to foster bad behavior (and perhaps allowing people to work out their hostilities online rather than in real life), the fundamental argument against anonymity is the third one cited on page 266: lack of accountability for serious wrongdoing by seriously bad people. You might not want your neighbors to know you occasionally exercise your right to read pornography—or that you're the one who keeps correcting the school principal's grammar. But what if you're abusing children and posting the pictures online, then what?

29   Indeed, the possibility of anonymity is one of the scariest features of the Net—for parents, for law enforcement, for employers hiring new workers, for victims of nasty rumors, scams, and other misdeeds. It's troubling for merchants who want to know who their customers are, for debt collectors, and for others to whom obligations are owed.

30   On the other hand, anonymity is also a problem for repressive governments who want to know who is criticizing them, for maniacs who want to track and pester people they're obsessed with, for con artists trolling for new victims, and in general for people who want to know others' secrets. For anyone, anonymity can make it hard to assess the reliability and value of information.

Accountability

31 If society suspects someone (for whatever reason) of a crime, what right does it have to find out who it is and catch that person? Presumably, the same right online as offline. If it can find the person, following due process with appropriate search warrants and the like, society should be able to prosecute him. There is no ISP-client privilege similar to attorney-client privilege. But at the same time, people should not be forced to make it easy—just as the law doesn't force us to live without window shades or to use postcards instead of letters in envelopes.

32   In this sense, anonymity online is akin to conditions we take for granted in the terrestrial world. If we required each shopper to show an ID each time she entered a store, that would certainly both reduce crime and make it easier to catch criminals, but it is not likely (thank goodness!) that we will do so in the United States. Law-abiding citizens in the United States are not required to carry

their documents with them, although they must do so when driving a car, buying a gun, passing a border, or getting on an airplane. All these are infringements on our liberty, but we accept them (or most of us do) because they reduce real risks. But I don't think the risk someone will do something bad is large enough or grave enough to require forcible identification of everyone online.

33   That means that anonymity in itself should not be illegal. There are enough good reasons for people to be anonymous that it should be considered part of the normal range of social behavior—at least in some places on the Net (again as in real life).

[...]

True-Life Experience

34 As I sit here writing this chapter on anonymity, I have just received a strange missive from a stranger, someone calling himself ******. I have no idea who he (?) is, but he knows a fair amount about me. Nothing he couldn't have read somewhere; it's probably not someone I know. But it's familiar enough: He knows the shape of my family, some of my background (Russia), and he's clever enough to make some inside jokes that only I could appreciate. How much do I want to say here? If he's obsessed with me, surely he'll be reading these words, too. As Carly Simon sings: "You're so vain, bet you think this song is about you." But it isn't, it's about the other one; take that! But he hasn't harmed me, asks nothing of me other than to read his quite clever ramblings.

35   What should I do? His e-mail comes from a commercial service; I could probably track him down if I wanted to. But why should I? To ask him to stop? Time enough to do that if he starts bothering me. First, I could filter and automatically delete everything he sends. If I got seriously unpleasant or threatening mail, I could go to his Internet service provider and ask it to ask him to stop. But the best approach is probably simply to ignore it.

36   Yet it feels creepy. And I have to compare it with several other anonymous messages, from a single different source, that I got after attending a conference last fall. They referred to two other people, one of whom was at the conference and one of whom wasn't. Could the messages have been from one of the people I had met there? Certainly, they spoiled my memory of the previous three days. These particular messages were quite obscene and offensive, but in some sense they were less troubling than the one I just received. This writer didn't seem to know much about me other than my gender; his comments were graphic and disgusting, but they had nothing to do with me personally. And besides, I was one of three well known (in the Internet community) people he was attacking; the messages seemed to come *from him* rather than *to me*. It's invasion of privacy coupled with anonymity that's so creepy in this most recent message.

37   All these messages are the result of a trade-off I have made. I have become well known, and now strangers can write to me anonymously and disturb me. I could filter them out, taking mail only from people I know, but that would be ridiculous. As time passes, presumably I will become even more visible and get more e-mail, some of it helpful and enlightening, some of it wasteful of time,

and some of it no doubt hurtful. That's the trade-off I'm making, and one I'm increasingly aware of. But I *do* have the choice.

38   Choice is what I want to preserve. Other people may choose differently. I would like the choice to have a secret e-mail account for my special friends. Perhaps I'd like to join some communities under a false name, if only to avoid the assumptions people will make when they hear my real one. While anonymity gives other people the opportunity to annoy me and others, it also gives me the opportunity to avoid those annoyers.

39   What will I do when they start posting lies, not just to me but to the world at large? That's when it gets more troubling.

40   I hope I'll have the fortitude to live by what I say here. At the same time, I hope people in general start to get wiser. It's one thing to read a lie about yourself in the *New York Times,* another to read it in the *National Enquirer.* It's one thing when it's said by a friend you know, another when it's said by someone who doesn't even dare to publish his name. Why honor him with attention?

Review Questions

1. What are some of the benefits of anonymity, according to Dyson?

2. What are some of the drawbacks of anonymity?

3. What is the Internet Oracle? What is the basis of its appeal and particular power?

4. What was the significance of the experience at the WELL?

Discussion and Writing Suggestions

1. Recount a situation in which you have taken advantage of your anonymity—or one in which someone else has rendered themselves anonymous to you. (The situation may have involved a conversation by computer, or by telephone, or even a face-to-face encounter in which one person did not know the identity of the other.) In either case, what were the reasons for anonymity? (What was one party trying to hide?) What were the effects? What were the advantages and disadvantages of anonymity to either party?

2. Dyson writes, "Anonymity may not be desirable in itself, but it is often a rational, best-of-a-bad situation response to a less than perfect world." To what extent do you agree with this statement? Explain, using specific examples.

3. According to Dyson, "people are not all always nice, and therefore a little social pressure can be a good thing." Recall a situation in which you were restrained by "social pressure" from acting out your impulses, particularly a situation in which you concluded that the hoped-for veil of anonymity might at some point fall away.

4. In her section on "Accountability" (paragraphs 31–33) Dyson concludes that Internet anonymity should not be illegal. To what extent do you agree with her reasoning on this question?

5. In the final section Dyson discusses a "creepy" message from an anonymous stranger. She concludes that the best course of action is to ignore the message. Do you think you would make the same choice as she did?

Cyberspace and Identity
Sherry Turkle

What we think of as our identity is generally our unique inner self—that core personality that makes us different from our friends, our brothers or sisters, even our identical twin. Not only do we like to think of our identity as unique, but we also see it as unified and whole. People who have multiple personalities, like those we read about in the cases of The Three Faces of Eve *or* Sybil *are clinical aberrations. Increasingly, however, this view of the unitary self is being challenged. We have long known that personalities can fragment; but it is only recently that the concept of fragmented or "decentered" selves has been seen not only as normal, but actually as psychologically healthy. Certainly, in some extreme cases, the personality can fragment to the point where the individual cannot function normally (particularly if one personality is not aware of the existence of the others). But if Superman and his alternate identity Clark Kent can healthfully coexist in the same body, then why not DrJane and Hellraiser as two different screen names of a single Internet subscriber?*

It is not that one side of the self excludes the other; it is rather that both (or in fact several) sides are aspects of the same individual, and there is no reason why one cannot "cycle through" the various sides of oneself while remaining a balanced, functioning member of society. In the following article, sociologist Sherry Turkle explores this concept of multiple identity, as it has been fostered by the development of cyberspace communication.

Sherry Turkle did her undergraduate work at Radcliff and earned a joint doctorate in sociology and personality psychology from Harvard in 1976. A licensed clinical psychologist, Turkle is Professor of the Sociology of Science in the Program in Science, Technology, and Society at the Massachusetts Institute of Technology. One of the most highly regarded authorities in the field, Turkle has written numerous articles on computer technologies and virtual communities in such periodicals as The Utne Reader, Sociological Inquiry, Social Research, Sciences, American Prospect, Signs, *and* Daedalus. *Her books include* Psychoanalytic Politics: Jacques Lacan and Freud's French Revolution *(1981),* The Second Self: Computers and the Human Spirit *(1984), and* Life on the Screen: Identity in the Age of the Internet *(1995). In 1995 she was selected by* Newsweek *as one of the "50 For the Future: the Most Influential People to Watch in Cyberspace." Turkle has been featured on the cover of* Wired *(April 1996) and* Technology Review *(February/March 1996). She has also been profiled in* Scientific

---

For a fuller discussion of the themes in this essay, see Turkle (1995).

American *(April 1998) and* The New York Times *(18 June 1998). This article, originally enti-tled "Looking Toward Cyberspace: Beyond Grounded Sociology: Cyberspace and Identity," first appeared in* Contemporary Sociology *in November 1999.*

1   We come to see ourselves differently as we catch sight of our images in the mirror of the machine. Over a decade ago, when I first called the computer a "second self" (1984), these identity-transforming relationships were most usu-ally one-on-one, a person alone with a machine. This is no longer the case. A rapidly expanding system of networks, collectively known as the Internet, links millions of people together in new spaces that are changing the way we think, the nature of our sexuality, the form of our communities, our very identities. In cyberspace, we are learning to live in virtual worlds. We may find ourselves alone as we navigate virtual oceans, unravel virtual mysteries, and engineer virtual skyscrapers. But increasingly, when we step through the looking glass, other people are there as well.

2   Over the past decade, I have been engaged in the ethnographic and clinical study of how people negotiate the virtual and the "real" as they represent them-selves on computer screens linked through the Internet. For many people, such experiences challenge what they have traditionally called "identity," which they are moved to recast in terms of multiple windows and parallel lives. Online life is not the only factor that is pushing them in this direction; there is no simple sense in which computers are causing a shift in notions of identity. It is, rather, that today's life on the screen dramatizes and concretizes a range of cultural trends that encourage us to think of identity in terms of multiplicity and flexibility.

Virtual Personae

3   In this essay, I focus on one key element of online life and its impact on iden-tity: the creation and projection of constructed personae into virtual space. In cyberspace, it is well known, one's body can be represented by one's own tex-tual description: The obese can be slender, the beautiful plain. The fact that self-presentation is written in text means that there is time to reflect upon and edit one's "composition," which makes it easier for the shy to be outgoing, the "nerdy" sophisticated. The relative anonymity of life on the screen—one has the choice of being known only by one's chosen "handle" or online name—gives people the chance to express often unexplored aspects of the self. Additionally, multiple aspects of self can be explored in parallel. Online services offer their users the opportunity to be known by several different names. For example, it is not unusual for someone to be BroncoBill in one online community, ArmaniBoy in another, and MrSensitive in a third.

4   The online exercise of playing with identity and trying out new identities is perhaps most explicit in "role playing" virtual communities (such as Multi-User Domains, or MUDs) where participation literally begins with the creation of a persona (or several); but it is by no means confined to these somewhat exotic locations. In bulletin boards, newsgroups, and chat rooms, the creation of per-sonae may be less explicit than on MUDs, but it is no less psychologically real. One IRC (Internet Relay Chat) participant describes her experience of online talk: "I go from channel to channel depending on my mood.... I actually feel a

part of several of the channels, several conversations…I'm different in the different chats. They bring out different things in me." Identity play can happen by changing names and by changing places.

5   For many people, joining online communities means crossing a boundary into highly charged territory. Some feel an uncomfortable sense of fragmentation, some a sense of relief. Some sense the possibilities for self-discovery. A 26-year-old graduate student in history says, "When I log on to a new community and I create a character and know I have to start typing my description, I always feel a sense of panic. Like I could find out something I don't want to know." A woman in her late thirties who just got an account with America Online used the fact that she could create five "names" for herself on her account as a chance to "lay out all the moods I'm in—all the ways I want to be in different places on the system."

6   The creation of site-specific online personae depends not only on adopting a new name. Shifting of personae happens with a change of virtual place. Cycling through virtual environments is made possible by the existence of what have come to be called "windows" in modern computing environments. Windows are a way to work with a computer that makes it possible for the machine to place you in several contexts at the same time. As a user, you are attentive to just one of windows on your screen at any given moment, but in a certain sense, you are a presence in all of them at all times. You might be writing a paper in bacteriology and using your computer in several ways to help you: You are "present" to a word processing program on which you are taking notes and collecting thoughts, you are "present" to communications software that is in touch with a distant computer for collecting reference materials, you are "present" to a simulation program that is charting the growth of bacterial colonies when a new organism enters their ecology, and you are "present" to an online chat session where participants are discussing recent research in the field. Each of these activities takes place in a "window," and your identity on the computer is the sum of your distributed presence.

7   The development of the windows metaphor for computer interfaces was a technical innovation motivated by the desire to get people working more efficiently by "cycling through" different applications, much as time-sharing computers cycle through the computing needs of different people. But in practice, windows have become a potent metaphor for thinking about the self as a multiple, distributed, "time-sharing" system.

8   The self no longer simply plays different roles in different settings—something that people experience when, for example, one wakes up as a lover; makes breakfast as a mother; and drives to work as a lawyer. The windows metaphor suggests a distributed self that exists in many worlds and plays many roles at the same time. The "windows" enabled by a computer operating system support the metaphor, and cyberspace raises the experience to a higher power by translating the metaphor into a life experience of "cycling through."

Identity, Moratoria, and Play

9 Cyberspace, like all complex phenomena, has a range of psychological effects. For some people, it is a place to "act out" unresolved conflicts, to play and

replay characterological difficulties on a new and exotic stage. For others, it pro-vides an opportunity to "work through" significant personal issues, to use the new materials of cybersociality to reach for new resolutions. These more posi-tive identity effects follow from the fact that for some, cyberspace provides what Erik Erikson ([1950]1963) would have called a "psychosocial moratorium," a central element in how he thought about identity development in adolescence. Although the term moratorium implies a "time out," what Erikson had in mind was not withdrawal. On the contrary, the adolescent moratorium is a time of intense interaction with people and ideas. It is a time of passionate friendships and experimentation. The adolescent falls in and out of love with people and ideas. Erikson's notion of the moratorium was not a "hold" on significant expe-riences but on their consequences. It is a time during which one's actions are, in a certain sense, not counted as they will be later in life. They are not given as much weight, not given the force of full judgment. In this context, experimen-tation can become the norm rather than a brave departure. Relatively conse-quence-free experimentation facilitates the development of a "core self," a personal sense of what gives life meaning that Erikson called "identity."

10   Erikson developed these ideas about the importance of a moratorium during the late 1950s and early 1960s. At that time, the notion corresponded to a common understanding of what "the college years" were about. Today, 30 years later, the idea of the college years as a consequence-free "time out" seems of another era. College is pre-professional, and AIDS has made consequence-free sexual experimentation an impossibility. The years associated with adolescence no longer seem a "time out." But if our culture no longer offers an adolescent moratorium, virtual communities often do. It is part of what makes them seem so attractive.

11   Erikson's ideas about stages did not suggest rigid sequences. His stages describe what people need to achieve before they can move ahead easily to another developmental task. For example, Erikson pointed out that successful intimacy in young adulthood is difficult if one does not come to it with a sense of who one is, the challenge of adolescent identity building. In real life, how-ever, people frequently move on with serious deficits. With incompletely resolved "stages," they simply do the best they can. They use whatever mate-rials they have at hand to get as much as they can of what they have missed. Now virtual social life can play a role in these dramas of self-reparation. Time in cyberspace reworks the notion of the moratorium because it may now exist on an always-available "window."

Expanding One's Range in the Real

12 Case, a 34-year-old industrial designer happily married to a female co-worker, describes his real-life (RL) persona as a "nice guy," a "Jimmy Stewart type like my father." He describes his outgoing, assertive mother as a "Katharine Hepburn type." For Case, who views assertiveness through the prism of this Jimmy Stewart/Katharine Hepburn dichotomy, an assertive man is quickly perceived as "being a bastard." An assertive woman, in contrast, is perceived as being "modern and together." Case says that although he is comfortable with his tem-perament and loves and respects his father, he feels he pays a high price for his

own low-key ways. In particular, he feels at a loss when it comes to confrontation, both at home and at work. Online, in a wide range of virtual communities, Case presents himself as females whom he calls his "Katharine Hepburn types." These are strong, dynamic, "out there" women who remind Case of his mother, who "says exactly what's on her mind." He tells me that presenting himself as a woman online has brought him to a point where he is more comfortable with confrontation in his RL as a man.

13   Case describes his Katharine Hepburn personae as "externalizations of a part of myself." In one interview with him, I used the expression "aspects of the self," and he picked it up eagerly, for his online life reminds him of how Hindu gods could have different aspects or subpersonalities, all the while being a whole self. In response to my question "Do you feel that you call upon your personae in real life?" Case responded:

> Yes, an aspect sort of clears its throat and says, "I can do this. You are being so amazingly conflicted over this and I know exactly what to do. Why don't you just let me do it?"… In real life, I tend to be extremely diplomatic, non-confrontational. I don't like to ram my ideas down anyone's throat. [Online] I can be, "Take it or leave it." All of my Hepburn characters are that way. That's probably why I play them. Because they are smart-mouthed, they will not sugarcoat their words.

In some ways, Case's description of his inner world of actors who address him and are able to take over negotiations is reminiscent of the language of people with multiple-personality disorder. But the contrast is significant: Case's inner actors are not split off from each other or from his sense of "himself." He experiences himself very much as a collective self, not feeling that he must goad or repress this or that aspect of himself into conformity. He is at ease, cycling through from Katharine Hepburn to Jimmy Stewart. To use analyst Philip Bromberg's language (1994), online life has helped Case learn how to "stand in the spaces between selves and still feel one, to see the multiplicity and still feel a unity." To use computer scientist Marvin Minsky's (1987) phrase, Case feels at ease cycling through his "society of mind," a notion of identity as distributed and heterogeneous. Identity, from the Latin *idem*, has been used habitually to refer to the sameness between two qualities. On the Internet, however, one can be many, and one usually is.

An Object to Think with for Thinking About Identity

14 In the late 1960s and early 1970s, I was first exposed to notions of identity and multiplicity. These ideas—most notably that there is no such thing as "the ego," that each of us is a multiplicity of parts, fragments, and desiring connections—surfaced in the intellectual hothouse of Paris; they presented the world according to such authors as Jacques Lacan, Gilles Deleuze, and Felix Guattari. But despite such ideal conditions for absorbing theory, my "French lessons" remained abstract exercises. These theorists of poststructuralism spoke words that addressed the relationship between mind and body, but from my point of view had little to do with my own.

15   In my lack of personal connection with these ideas, I was not alone. To take one example, for many people it is hard to accept any challenge to the idea of an autonomous ego. While in recent years, many psychologists, social theorists, psychoanalysts, and philosophers have argued that the self should be thought of as essentially decentered, the normal requirements of everyday life exert strong pressure on people to take responsibility for their actions and to see themselves as unitary actors. This disjuncture between theory (the unitary self is an illusion) and lived experience (the unitary self is the most basic reality) is one of the main reasons why multiple and decentered theories have been slow to catch on—or when they do, why we tend to settle back quickly into older, centralized ways of looking at things.

16   When, 20 years later, I used my personal computer and modem to join online communities, I had an experience of this theoretical perspective which brought it shockingly down to earth. I used language to create several characters. My textual actions are my actions—my words make things happen. I created selves that were made and transformed by language. And different personae were exploring different aspects of the self. The notion of a decentered identity was concretized by experiences on a computer screen. In this way, cyberspace becomes an object to think with for thinking about identity—an element of cultural bricolage.

17   Appropriable theories—ideas that capture the imagination of the culture at large—tend to be those with which people can become actively involved. They tend to be theories that can be "played" with. So one way to think about the social appropriability of a given theory is to ask whether it is accompanied by its own objects-to-think-with that can help it move out beyond intellectual circles.

18   For example, the popular appropriation of Freudian ideas had little to do with scientific demonstrations of their validity. Freudian ideas passed into the popular culture because they offered robust and down-to-earth objects to think with. The objects were not physical but almost-tangible ideas, such as dreams and slips of the tongue. People were able to play with such Freudian "objects." They became used to looking for them and manipulating them, both seriously and not so seriously. And as they did so, the idea that slips and dreams betray an unconscious began to feel natural.

19   In Freud's work, dreams and slips of the tongue carried the theory. Today, life on the computer screen carries theory. People decide that they want to interact with others on a computer network. They get an account on a commercial service. They think that this will provide them with new access to people and information, and of course it does. But it does more. When they log on, they may find themselves playing multiple roles; they may find themselves playing characters of the opposite sex. In this way, they are swept up by experiences that enable them to explore previously unexamined aspects of their sexuality or that challenge their ideas about a unitary self. The instrumental computer, the computer that does things for us, has revealed another side: a subjective computer that does things *to* us as people, to our view of ourselves and our relationships, to our ways of looking at our minds. In simulation, identity can be fluid and multiple, a signifier no longer clearly points to a thing that is signified, and understanding is less likely to proceed through analysis than by navigation through virtual space.

20   Within the psychoanalytic tradition, many "schools" have departed from a unitary view of identity, among these the Jungian, object-relations, and Lacanian. In different ways, each of these groups of analysts was banished from the ranks of orthodox Freudians for such suggestions, or somehow relegated to the margins. As the United States became the center of psychoanalytic politics in the mid-twentieth century, ideas about a robust executive ego began to constitute the psychoanalytic mainstream.

21   But today, the pendulum has swung away from that complacent view of a unitary self. Through the fragmented selves presented by patients and through theories that stress the decentered subject, contemporary social and psychological thinkers are confronting what has been left out of theories of the unitary self. It is asking such questions as, What is the self when it functions as a society? What is the self when it divides its labors among its constituent "alters"? Those burdened by posttraumatic dissociative disorders suffer these questions; I am suggesting that inhabitants of virtual communities play with them. In our lives on the screen, people are developing ideas about identity as multiplicity through new social *practices* of identity as multiplicity.

22   With these remarks, I am not implying that chat rooms or MUDs or the option to declare multiple user names on America Online are causally implicated in the dramatic increase of people who exhibit symptoms of multiple-personality disorder (MPD), or that people on MUDs have MPD, or that MUDding (or online chatting) is like having MPD. I am saying that the many manifestations of multiplicity in our culture, including the adoption of online personae, are contributing to a general reconsideration of traditional, unitary notions of identity. Online experiences with "parallel lives" are part of the significant cultural context that supports new theorizing about nonpathological, indeed healthy, multiple selves.

23   In thinking about the self, *multiplicity* is a term that carries with it several centuries of negative associations, but such authors as Kenneth Gergen (1991), Emily Martin (1994), and Robert Jay Lifton (1993) speak in positive terms of an adaptive, "flexible" self. The flexible self is not unitary, nor are its parts stable entities. A person cycles through its aspects, and these are themselves ever-changing and in constant communication with each other. Daniel Dennett (1991) speaks of the flexible self by using the metaphor of consciousness as multiple drafts, analogous to the experience of several versions of a document open on a computer screen, where the user is able to move between them at will. For Dennett, knowledge of these drafts encourages a respect for the many different versions, while it imposes a certain distance from them. Donna Haraway (1991), picking up on this theme of how a distance between self states may be salutory, equates a "split and contradictory self" with a "knowing self." She is optimistic about its possibilities: "The knowing self is partial in all its guises, never finished, whole, simply there and original; it is always constricted and stitched together imperfectly; and therefore able to join with another, to see together without claiming to be another." What most characterizes Haraway's and Dennett's models of a knowing self is that the lines of communication between its various aspects are open. The open communication encourages an attitude of respect for the many within us and the many within others.

24   Increasingly, social theorists and philosophers are being joined by psycho-analytic theorists in efforts to think about healthy selves whose resilience and capacity for joy comes from having access to their many aspects. For example, Philip Bromberg (1994) insists that our ways of describing "good parenting" must now shift away from an emphasis on confirming a child in a "core self" and onto helping a child develop the capacity to negotiate fluid transitions between self states. The healthy individual knows how to be many but to smooth out the moments of transition between states of self. Bromberg says: "Health is when you are multiple but feel a unity. Health is when different aspects of self can get to know each other and reflect upon each other." Here, within the psychoanalytic tradition, is a model of multiplicity as a state of easy traffic across selves, a conscious, highly articulated "cycling through."

From a Psychoanalytic to a Computer Culture?

25 Having literally written our online personae into existence, they can be a kind of Rorschach test. We can use them to become more aware of what we project into everyday life. We can use the virtual to reflect constructively on the real. Cyberspace opens the possibility for identity play, but it is very serious play. People who cultivate an awareness of what stands behind their screen personae are the ones most likely to succeed in using virtual experience for personal and social transformation. And the people who make the most of their lives on the screen are those who are able to approach it in a spirit of self-reflection. What does my behavior in cyberspace tell me about what I want, who I am, what I may not be getting in the rest of my life?

26   As a culture, we are at the end of the Freudian century. Freud, after all, was a child of the nineteenth century; of course, he was carrying the baggage of a very different scientific sensibility than our own. But faced with the challenges of cyberspace, our need for a practical philosophy of self-knowledge, one that does not shy away from issues of multiplicity, complexity, and ambivalence, that does not shy away from the power of symbolism, from the power of the word, from the power of identity play, has never been greater as we struggle to make meaning from our lives on the screen. It is fashionable to think that we have passed from a psychoanalytic culture to a computer culture—that we no longer need to think in terms of Freudian slips but rather of information processing errors. But the reality is more complex. It is time to rethink our relationship to the computer culture and psychoanalytic culture as a proudly held joint citizenship.

References

Bromberg, Philip. 1994. "Speak that I May See You: Some Reflections on Dissociation, Reality, and Psychoanalytic Listening." *Psychoanalytic Dialogues* 4 (4): 517–47.

Dennett, Daniel. 1991. *Consciousness Explained.* Boston: Little, Brown.

Erikson, Erik. [1950] 1963. *Childhood and Society,* 2nd Ed. New York: Norton.

Haraway, Donna. 1991. "The Actors are Cyborg, Nature is Coyote, and the Geography is Elsewhere: Postscript to 'Cyborgs at Large.'" In *Technoculture,* edited by Constance Penley and Andrew Ross. Minneapolis: University of Minnesota Press.

Gergen, Kenneth. 1991. *The Saturated Self-Dilemmas of Identity in Contemporary Life.* New York: Basic Books.

Lifton, Robert Jay. 1993. *The Protean Self: Human Resilience in an Age of Fragmentation.* New York: Basic Books.

Martin, Emily. 1994. *Flexible Bodies: Tracking Immunity in American Culture from the Days of Polio to the Days of AIDS.* Boston: Beacon Press.

Minsky, Martin. 1987. *The Society of Mind.* New York: Simon & Schuster.

Turkle, Sherry. [1978] 1990. *Psychoanalytic Politics: Jacques Lacan and Freud's French Revolution.* 2nd Ed. New York: Guilford Press.

———1984. *The Second Self: Computers and the Human Spirit.* New York: Simon & Schuster.

———1995. *Life on the Screen: Identity in the Age of the Internet.* New York: Simon & Schuster.

Review Questions

1. As she draws upon the ideas of psychologist Erik Erikson, how does Turkle examine the implications of creating multiple cyber-personalities on the Internet?

2. For Turkle, how did the Internet help support the theory that the "unitary self" is an illusion?

3. What is the basis of the analogy between Freud's theories about dreams and slips of the tongue and people assuming multiple identities on the Internet?

Discussion and Writing Suggestions

1. For Turkle, one of the most exciting—and healthy—aspects of the Internet is that it allows us to create—and explore—multiple personae and personalities for ourselves. To what extent have you experienced this sense of creation and re-creation of yourself as you communicate with individuals and groups in various cyber-contexts?

2. Turkle discusses Case, the man who cycles between his "Katherine Hepburn" and "Jimmy Stewart" personas. What is the significance of this phenomenon? Turkle argues that this "collective self" phenomenon is different from multiple personality disorder, in that there is unity in multiplicity. To what extent do you agree?

3. Turkle writes (paragraph 21), "In our lives on the screen, people are developing ideas about identity as multiplicity through new social *practices* of identity as multiplicity." Write a paper using this sentence as a thesis. Develop specific examples from your own experience or the experiences of people you know.

4. Turkle argues that there is a difference between people who have Multiple Personality Disorder (MPD) and people who assume multiple personalities or who explore multiple aspects of themselves on the Internet. What is the difference? To what extent do you agree with Turkle's ideas on this point?

5. Turkle contends that we need "a practical philosophy of self-knowledge, one that does not shy away from issues of multiplicity, complexity, and ambivalence, that does not shy away from the power of symbolism, from the power of the word, from the power of identity play." Assuming that you agree, how should a philosophy of such self-knowledge be fostered? Do schools have a role here? Or do adolescents need to develop such awareness on their own?

Boy, You Fight Like a Girl
Alex Pham

In a previous article in this chapter Esther Dyson considers some implications of online anonymity. Following Dyson, Sherry Turkle discusses how people on the Net are able to "cycle" through multiple personae. Both of these phenomena are exemplified in a particular Internet subculture: online gaming. In "Boy, You Fight Like a Girl," Los Angeles Times *staff writer Alex Pham discusses the penchant of many online gamers for gender-switching—and the reactions they encounter. This article first appeared in the* Los Angeles Times *on May 17, 2001.*

1   In her flowing crimson cape, thigh-high leather boots and metal-studded red leather bustier, Cardinal is a bow-and-arrow-toting *femme fatale.*

2   But not only is Cardinal not real—she's a character in the popular computer game "Ultima Online"—she's not really female. Cardinal is the alter-ego of Kenn Gold, a 33-year-old former Army sergeant with thorny green-and-black tattoos covering both of his muscular arms.

3   As one of the thousands of online gamers who play characters of the opposite gender, Gold created Cardinal as a tactical move: Female characters generally get treated better in the male-dominated world of virtual adventuring. Yet he was unprepared for the shock of seeing the world through a woman's eyes.

4   "I can't even begin to tell you how funny it is to watch guys trip all over themselves and be dumb," Gold said. "It's very amusing to see them try to be really sophisticated and cool, when they're turning out to be just the opposite."

5   Changing genders has long been a piece of online role-playing games—part juvenile mischievousness, part theatrical posing and part psychological release. But as the genre explodes—online games now attract hundreds of thousands of players—it's prompted a blossoming of cross-gender experimentation and created sexually amorphous virtual worlds that some revel in and others curse.

6   Men find they must constantly brush off unwanted advances, and their female characters are not taken as seriously. But they also find it easier to chat with other players and escape the relentless competition among male characters.

7   The story is the same for women who play men to avoid cheesy pick-up lines. They discover that moving among predominantly male groups involves participating in constant one-upmanship. And as their male characters move up the ranks, they fear losing the respect of other players if their true gender is discovered.

8   Online adventures are one of the fastest-growing segments of the computer game market, with titles such as "EverQuest," "Asheron's Call" and "Ultima Online." And it's not just kids with nothing better to do. Teachers, nurses, construction workers and accountants create alter-egos and join with others to explore virtual realms and slay imaginary beasts.

9   In "EverQuest," the most popular of the games with more than 360,000 subscribers, players spend an average of 20 hours a week online. Players call it "EverCrack" because it's so addictive. Much of the allure is the ability to put mundane daily life aside and pretend to be something they're not—an elf, a woodsman, a knight.

10   The ultimate challenge: to be another gender. Although some gamers swap genders to explore their own sexuality—a tiny fraction are cross-dressers in real life—the vast majority do it as a test of skill.

11   "There's a long history of this as a performance genre," said Henry Jenkins, director of comparative media studies at the Massachusetts Institute of Technology. "There is Glenda Jackson who plays Hamlet. Dustin Hoffman played Tootsie. It's a great challenge, a way to show virtuosity."

Virtual Experience Can Have Real Ramifications

12 Encouraging the make-believe are online avatars—the graphic representation of a player's character. Scantily clad females are impossibly thin and full-bosomed. Males are muscular and rendered in heroic proportions. As a result, the contrast between avatar and player can be striking, even when gamers are playing their own gender.

13   In "EverQuest," only 20% of subscribers are female, but 40% of avatars are. Even accounting for the number of women who play male characters, that amounts to roughly half the female characters in "EverQuest" being played by men such as Gold.

14   This might be fun and games, but as any serious player of such adventures will attest, online experiences—with their power to make people laugh, cry or become angry—can have real-life consequences.

15   "It certainly makes you more aware of how men treat women," said Raph Koster, 29, who has played a female character for years in an early online text-based game, "LegendMUD." "You're more aware that there are a lot of gendered interactions that we don't recognize as such. It makes you think more about what you're saying and how you're sending subtle messages without being aware of it."

16   For instance, "if you're a female character, just something as innocent as smiling might get read wrong." And if a male character tries to help a female character, it's assumed he wants something. Often, he does.

17   Mark Wight, a 28-year-old heavy-equipment operator from Ramona, Calif., said he wanted to hook his female character, Cytarack, into a hunting group so she could gain experience and advance in the game.

18   "There was this one guy who traveled halfway across the game's virtual continent to hunt with her, but it seemed he was more interested in other things," Wight said, explaining that some players engage in online "cybersex" with each other—basically a modern twist on phone sex in which acts are described in real-time chat. "I don't play her anymore because people get other ideas. Many adults play because they're looking for somebody on the other side."

19   In his Mission Viejo apartment, Gold jockeys two computers as he maneuvers Cardinal around "Ultima Online's" virtual realm. He chain smokes Camels, surrounded by stacks of "X-Men" comic books and an exhaustive collection of "Star Trek" video tapes.

20   In the Army, Gold commanded a Black Hawk helicopter maintenance crew. These days, he's a graduate student in English at Cal State Fullerton, where he teaches freshman composition.

21   At this moment, however, he is Cardinal, a spell-casting huntress on horseback with a mane of pink hair, leather gloves and black tights.

22   Gold confesses that he has another female character—this one in "EverQuest"—whom he declines to name because no one knows she is played by a man. His character is a longtime member of a "guild," a band of players who agree to play together.

23   Many of his band would be upset, explained Gold, who spends about 35 hours each week playing "EverQuest" and "Ultima Online." "They'd feel they couldn't trust me anymore. I'd be ostracized. These are guys who think they're worldly, and it scares them to think that there are women they're interested in who may actually be guys."

24   The deception cuts both ways. Louise, a 44-year-old Sacramento house painter who declined to give her last name, plays a male character and is the leader of her "EverQuest" guild. She said she fears that if the members of her guild were to discover not only her gender but her age, she would lose their respect.

25   "Some of them are teenage boys," Louise said. "I don't think they'd take it too well. There's a belief that women can't be aggressive. But that's not true at all. I love to be aggressive. It gives me a real adrenaline rush."

26   In daily life, though, she is shy. It is only when she slips into a role-playing mode that Louise says she can fully express her aggressive nature without fear of being belittled.

27   But because online relationships can be as intense as their real-world counterparts, there is the potential to wreak psychological havoc.

Emboldened Under Veil of Online Anonymity

28 Gold five years ago attended an online wedding involving two characters in a game called "Meridian 59." Once the vows were exchanged, the bride declared that she was actually a man and that the two had had cybersex, humiliating the groom in front of their virtual guests. It was all a revenge plot the "bride" had devised because the groom had killed another of the player's characters months earlier in the game.

29   What makes such behavior possible, of course, is the anonymous nature of the Web. Online players are less accountable for their words and, therefore, less inhibited with their expressions.

30   "The Internet makes you bolder," said Rick Hall, a game producer at Origin Systems, the company that created "Ultima Online." "If you're the type of guy who wouldn't approach a girl in real life, you can do it online. And if you get shot down, who cares."

31   Similarly, anonymity gives people the freedom to emphasize a particular personality trait or mood they would stifle in real life. Many players maintain a stable of characters they can pull out to match their mood.

32   Geoffrey Zatkin, a senior game designer for the company that wrote "EverQuest," rotates between three characters—a male fencer, a male rogue and a female druid. Each represents a facet of his identity. The fencer is witty, the rogue aloof and the druid outgoing. Zatkin plays the female character when feeling chatty.

33   For Ramin Shokrizade, playing female characters allows him to escape the competitiveness that pervades the male culture.

34   "Among power gamers, it gets to be very competitive," said Shokrizade, 35, an exercise trainer and math and science tutor in Palm Desert who says he plays online role-playing games an average of 80 hours a week. "If you're female, they don't do that with you. I enjoy chatting with other players and helping people out. I've been a track coach for 15 years, so I'm used to helping people. This is just a way of practicing what I know."

35   Still, Shokrizade was surprised at how differently he was treated as a female character.

36   "It was strange," he said. "If you don't mind being in a supportive role, life is a lot easier for you. You're not expected to be in a leadership role."

37   Players who wish to escape gender constraints online ironically find themselves in a medium that, if anything, reinforces sexual stereotypes.

38   "Females tend to get in groups faster, but we get harassed," said Aaron Harvey, a 26-year-old freelance Web designer from Ventura who plays a female gnome in "EverQuest." "People are constantly trying to pick us up. I've been offered [more powerful weaponry] for cybersex, which I turn down rather quickly."

39   Often, players who gender-swap online are reluctant to talk about their reasons.

40   "It's not something you would talk about or be proud of," said Pavel Curtis, who developed a well-known text-based online community called LambdaMOO when he was a researcher at Xerox's Palo Alto Research Center. "Society doesn't see it as a healthy form of experimentation. At best, it's seen as duplicitous. At worst, it's sick and perverted."

41   Such strongly held views underscore how important gender identity is to people—even online, where physical appearances are not supposed to matter.

42   "We tailor our actions based on who we think we're talking to," said Amy Bruckman, assistant professor in the College of Computing at Georgia Tech in Atlanta. "Because these factors shape our interactions, we're often uncomfortable when we don't know these cues on age, race and gender."

43   As a result, much effort goes into spotting fakes. The clues cited by players are telling indications of how people perceive gender. Bruckman recalled a time when she tried to pass as a male character but was instantly pegged as an

impostor. How? "It was just my style of speaking. I used long sentences with lots of adjectives, which is seen as stereotypic of females," Bruckman said.

44   "Everybody, it seems, needs to know," Koster said. "It's like a void that needs to be filled, and it's deeply ingrained in our culture. There's this notion that the Internet will give us this utopia where gender, age and race don't matter. The idea that we'll all be disembodied floating lights just ain't gonna happen."

Discussion and Writing Suggestions

1. Do you or anyone you know engage in online gaming? To what extent can you confirm the kinds of behavior Pham discusses in "Boy, You Fight Like a Girl"—particularly, gender switching and the reaction to gender switching? What is your take on this phenomenon?

2. What kind of gender stereotypes are revealed in the experiences of people who engage in gender-switching while participating in online games? To what extent do you think such gender stereotyping is aggravated by the very experience of participating in such games? That is, to what extent might the anonymity of the Internet make sexists of people who, in their "real world" interpersonal relations, generally behave with more tolerance and sensitivity? To what extent (on the other hand) might online gaming attract people with sexist mindsets?

3. How does the type of online behavior discussed in Pham's article tie into Dyson's observations on Internet anonymity and Turkle's discussion of multiple personae? To what extent are Dyson, on the one hand, and Turkle, on the other, likely to regard gender-switching during online gaming as psychologically healthy?

4. Amy Bruckman recalls that she tried to pass as a male while playing online games, but was immediately spotted because of her "style of speaking." In general, do you believe that males and females have different styles of speaking (or writing)? If so, what characterizes these different styles? Do you think you are likely to be successful in passing yourself off as a member of the opposite sex?

   You might try an experiment along these lines: divide a group of people into an equal number of males and females. Have some in each group adopt personas in which they switch genders. Have people write an anonymous series of notes to one another, asking and answering questions, devising a system by which the notes are transmitted from one person to another. (E-mailing would work only if anonymity can be maintained; otherwise, notes would have to be written on paper.) Have writers attempt to determine the actual genders of their anonymous correspondents. Ask people who successfully determined the gender of their correspondents (as opposed to just guessed correctly) what were the "giveaways"?

Faking It: The Virtual Lawyer
Michael Lewis

The last few selections have focused on how people create new identities for themselves on the Internet—or perhaps more accurately, how they create new aspects of their selves as they communicate online. Esther Dyson indicated the possibilities for fraud and misrepresentation afforded by Internet anonymity; Sherry Turkle focused on the creation of new selves as an exploration of different personae. And in the introduction to this chapter, we described the "Robert Klingler" affair, in which an individual, claiming to be the North American head of a major European automobile manufacturer, succeeded in getting a couple of his "Diary" entries published in the online magazine Slate *before the editors realized that they had been taken in by a skillful con-artist.*

In the following article, Michael Lewis, a contributing editor for The New York Times Magazine, *details the fascinating account of how a 15-year-old with no legal training posed as an expert attorney on the Web—and not only got away with it but was confirmed in his expert status, both by his "clients" and by actual, practicing attorneys! That this is possible raises questions not only about the special status of the law as an elite profession, but also about how the Internet tends to make anyone with a little knowledge into an authority. This article first appeared in* The New York Times Magazine *on July 15, 2001 and appears in a different form in Lewis's book* Next *(2001).*

1   When Internet stocks began their free fall in March 2000, the Internet was finally put in its proper place. It was nothing more than a fast delivery service for information—that was what serious people who had either lost a lot of money in the late stages of the Internet boom or, more likely, failed to make money began to say now. The profit-making potential of the Internet had been overrated, and so the social effects of the Internet were presumed to be overrated. But they weren't. Speeding up information was not the only thing the Internet had done. The Internet had made it possible for people to thwart all sorts of rules and conventions. It wasn't just the commercial order that was in flux. Many forms of authority were secured by locks waiting to be picked. The technology and money-making potential of the Internet were far less interesting than the effects people were allowing it to have on their lives and what these, in turn, said about those lives.

2   What was happening on the Internet buttressed a school of thought in sociology known as role theory. The role theorists argue that we have no "self" as such. Our selves are merely the masks we wear in response to the social situations in which we find ourselves. The Internet had offered up a new set of social situations, to which people had responded by grabbing for a new set of masks. People take on the new tools they are ready for and make use of only what they need, how they need it. If they were using the Internet to experiment with their identities, it was probably because they found their old identities inadequate. If the Internet was giving the world a shove in a certain direction, it was probably because the world already felt inclined to move in that direction. The Internet was telling us what we wanted to become.

3   I have already written here about Jonathan Lebed, the 15-year-old boy in the New Jersey suburbs who used the Internet to transform himself into a stock market manipulator. Jonathan's story suggested that you couldn't really understand what was happening on the Internet unless you understood the conditions in the real world that led to what was happening on the Internet—and you couldn't understand those unless you went there in person and looked around. Once you did that, you came to appreciate all sorts of new truths. For instance, the Internet was rock 'n' roll all over again. Not rock 'n' roll now, but rock 'n' roll in the 1950's and 1960's, when it actually terrified grown-ups. The Internet was enabling a great status upheaval and a subversion of all manner of social norms. And the people quickest to seize on its powers were the young.

4   A Finnish company, Nokia, figured this out before I did. Nokia has come to dominate the mobile-phone business to the point where pretty much everyone now agrees that the Finns will be the first to connect mobile phones to the Internet in a way that the rest of us will find necessary. The Finns were successful because they were especially good at guessing what others would want from their mobile phones. One big reason for this—or so the people at Nokia believe—was that they spent a lot of time studying children. The kids came to each new technology fresh, without preconceptions, and they picked it up more quickly. They dreamed up uses for their phones that, for reasons no one fully understood, never occurred to grown-ups. The instant text message, for instance.

5   To create an instant message, you punched it by hand into your telephone, using the keypad as a typewriter. On the face of it, this is not an obvious use of a telephone keypad. The difference between the number of letters in the alphabet and the number of keys on the pad meant you wound up having to type a kind of Morse code. The technique had been popularized by Finnish schoolboys who were nervous about asking girls out on dates to their faces and Finnish schoolgirls who wanted to tell one another what had happened on those dates as soon as it happened. They had proved that if the need to communicate indirectly is sufficiently urgent, words can be typed into a telephone keypad with amazing speed. Five and a half million Finns sent one another more than a billion instant messages in the year 2000.

6   The instant message has fast become a staple of European corporate communication. The technique spread from Finnish children to businessmen because the kids taught their parents. Nokia employed anthropologists to tell them this. Finland has become the first nation on earth to acknowledge formally the childcentric model of economic development: if you wanted a fast-growing economy, you needed to promote rapid technical change, and if you intended to promote rapid technical change, you needed to cede to children a strange measure of authority.

7   When capitalism encourages ever more rapid change, children enjoy one big advantage over adults: they haven't decided who they are. They haven't sunk a lot of psychological capital into a particular self. When a technology comes along that rewards people who are willing to chuck overboard their old selves for new ones, the people who aren't much invested in their old selves have an edge. The things that get tossed overboard with a 12-year-old self don't seem like much to give up at the time.

8   I spent my childhood in New Orleans. I would like now to consider this otherwise uninteresting fact, as it is bound up with my interest in identity and change. New Orleans has always been an excellent place to observe progress. To know progress, you need to know what it has rolled over or left behind, and when progress is moving as fast as it is now, recalling its victims is difficult. New Orleans keeps its anachronisms alive long enough for them to throw the outside world into sharp relief. For instance, until the mid–1990's you could find actual gentlemen lawyers in New Orleans, who thought of themselves mainly as members of an honorable and dignified profession. One of these dinosaurs was my father.

9   Right up until it collapsed, the old family law firm that my father managed clung to its charming habits. The gentlemen lawyers wrote notes to one another arguing over the correct pronunciation of certain phrases in ancient Greek. They collected strange artifacts from dead cultures. They treated education as a branch of religion. They wore bow ties. They were terrifyingly at ease with themselves but did not know the meaning of casual Friday. Their lives had been premised on a frankly elitist idea: an attorney was above the fray. He possessed special knowledge. He observed a strict code of conduct without ever having to say what it was. He viewed all entreaties to change with suspicion. The most important thing in the world to him was his stature in the community, and yet so far as anyone else could determine, he never devoted an ounce of his mental energy to worrying about it. Status wasn't a cause; it was an effect of the way he led his life.

10   The first hint I had that this was no longer a tenable pose—and would not be a tenable pose for me—came from a man I had never met called Morris Bart. I was some kind of teenager at the time. My father and I were driving along the Interstate highway that ran through town when we came upon a giant billboard. It said something like: "Are you a victim? Have you been injured? No one represents your interests? Call Morris Bart, attorney-at-law." And there was a big picture of Morris Bart. He had the easy smile of a used-car dealer.

11   "Do you do the same thing as Morris Bart?" I asked my father.

12   "Not exactly."

13   "But his billboard says he's a lawyer."

14   "We have a different kind of law firm."

15   "How?"

16   "We don't have billboards."

17   "Why not?"

18   "It's just not something a lawyer does."

19   That was true. It was true right up to the moment Morris Bart stuck up his picture beside the Interstate. My father and his colleagues remained unmoved, but the practice of law was succumbing to a general force, the twin American instincts to democratize and to commercialize. (Often they amount to the same thing.) These are the two forces that power the Internet and in turn are powered by it.

20   Morris Bart was a tiny widget inside the same magnificent American instrument of destruction that the Internet has so eloquently upgraded. A few years after Bart put up his billboard, the lawyers in my father's firm began to receive

calls from "consultants" who wanted to help teach them how to steal clients and lawyers from other firms—a notion that would have been unthinkable a few years earlier and remained unthinkable to some. A few years after that, the clients insisted that lawyers bill by the hour—and then questioned the bills! The old game was over. The minute the market intruded too explicitly, the old prestige began to seep out of the law. For the gentlemen lawyers, it ended about as well as it could. But still it ended. And for people whose identity was wrapped up in the idea, the end gave their story the shape of tragedy.

21   I recall the feeling when it first dawned on me that the ground beneath my teenage feet was moving. I did not enjoy the premonition of doom in my father's world. But what troubled me even more was that some part of me wanted my father to have his own billboard beside the highway—which of course he would never do. My response was to leave home and invent another self for myself. Had the Internet been available, I might have simply gone online.

22   That's what Jonathan Lebed did. And that's what another teenager with an AOL account named Marcus Arnold began doing last summer—putting on a mask that would cause even Morris Bart to shudder and delivering another insult to the social order and its reigning notions of status and expertise.

23   The AskMe Corporation was created in 1999 by former Microsoft employees. The software it sold enabled the big companies that bought it—3M, Procter & Gamble—to create a private Web for their workers. This private Web was known as "knowledge sharing." The knowledge exchange was a screen on a computer where employees could put questions to the entire company. The appeal of this was obvious. Once an AskMe-style knowledge exchange was up and running, it didn't matter where inside the company any particular expertise resided. So long as expertise didn't leave the company, it was always on tap for whoever needed it.

24   AskMe soon found that it was able to tell a lot about a company from its approach to the new software. In pyramid-shaped hierarchical organizations, the bosses tended to appoint themselves or a few select subordinates as the "experts." Questions rose from the bottom of the organization, the answers flowed down from the top and the original hierarchy was preserved, even reinforced. In less-hierarchical pancake-shaped companies, the bosses used the software to create a network of all the company's employees and to tap intelligence wherever in that network it happened to be. That way, anyone in the company could answer anyone else's questions. Anyone could be the expert. Of course, it didn't exactly inspire awe in the ranks to see the intern answering a question posed by the vice president for strategic planning. But many companies decided that a bit of flattening was a small price to pay to tap into the collective knowledge bank.

25   The people who created the AskMe software believed that it gave companies whose bosses were willing to risk their own prestige and authority an advantage over the hierarchical companies whose bosses were not. They didn't say this publicly, because they wanted to sell their software to the pyramid-shaped organizations too. But they knew that once the software was deployed, companies that flattened their organization charts to encourage knowledge to

flow freely in every direction would beat companies that didn't. Knowledge came from the strangest places; employees knew a lot more than they thought they did; and the gains in the collective wisdom outweighed any losses to the boss's authority.

26   In short, the software subtly changed the economic environment. It bestowed new rewards on the egalitarian spirit. It made life harder for pyramids and easier for pancakes.

27   Out in the field, AskMe's salespeople, like salespeople everywhere, found themselves running into the same five or six objections from potential buyers— even when the buyers were pancake-shaped. One was "How do you know that your software won't break down when all of our 200,000 employees are using it heavily?" To prove that it wouldn't, AskMe created a Web site and offered a version of its software to the wider public. The site, called AskMe.com, went up on the Web in February 2000 and quickly became the most heavily used of a dozen or so knowledge exchanges on the Internet. In its first year, the site had more than 10 million visitors.

28   This was striking in view of how peripheral the site was to the ambitions of the AskMe Corporation. The company made no money from the site and did not bother to monitor what went on there or even to advertise its existence. The millions of people using the site were drawn by word of mouth. The advice on the site was freely offered. The experts were self-appointed and ranked by the people who sought the advice. Experts with high rankings received small cash prizes from AskMe.com. The prizes—and the free publicity—attracted a lot of people who don't normally work for nothing. Accountants, lawyers and financial consultants mingled their licensed knowledge with experts in sports trivia, fortune telling and body piercing.

29   AskMe Corporation didn't think of it this way, but its public Web site suggested a number of questions. What is the wider society's instinctive attitude toward knowledge? Are we willing to look for it wherever it might be found or only from the people who are supposed to possess it? Does the world want to be a pyramid or a pancake?

30   In the summer of 2000, in a desert town called Perris, halfway between Los Angeles and Palm Springs, 15-year-old Marcus Arnold offered his reply to those questions, and a thousand or so more besides. Marcus's parents had immigrated to Perris from Belize by way of South Central Los Angeles. Why anyone would move to Perris from anywhere was not immediately clear. Perris was one of those nonplaces that America specializes in creating. One day, it was a flat, hazy stretch of sand and white rock beneath an endless blue sky into which recreational skydivers routinely plunged; the next, some developer had laid out a tract of 10,000 identical homes; and the day after that, it was teeming with people who were there mainly because it was not someplace else. The decision of human beings to make a home of it had little effect on the identity of Perris. Even after the tract houses had been deposited in the desert, Perris was known chiefly as a place to leap onto from an airplane.

31   Marcus lived with his parents and his twin brother in a small brick house a mile or so from the big drop zone. Over the family's two-car garage, from morning until night, people stepped out of planes and plummeted to earth, and the

blue sky above Marcus was permanently scarred by parachutes. Marcus himself was firmly earthbound, a great big bear of a boy. He was six feet tall and weighed maybe 200 pounds. He did not walk but lumbered from the computer to the front door, then back again. The computer squatted on a faux-antique desk in the alcove between the dining room and the living room, which were as immaculately kept as showrooms in a model home. It was the only computer in the house. In theory, the family shared it; in practice, it belonged to him. He now needed as much time on it as he could get, as he was a leading expert on AskMe.com. His field was the law.

32   When I first visited Marcus, the blue screen displayed the beginning of an answer to a question on AskMe.com that he had bashed out before I arrived:

33   "Your son should not be in jail or on trial. According to Miranda versus Arizona the person to be arrested must be read his rights before he was asked any questions. If your son was asked any questions before the reading of his rights he should not be in prison. If you want me to help you further write me back on this board privately."

34   The keyboard vanished beneath Marcus's jumbo hands, and another page on AskMe.com popped up on the screen. Marcus wanted to show me the appallingly weak answer to a question that had been offered by one of the real lawyers on the site. "I can always spot a crummy attorney," he said. "There are people on the Web site who have no clue what they're talking about—they are just there to get rankings and to sell their services and to get paid." Down went his paws, out of sight went the keyboard and up popped one of Marcus's favorite Web sites. This one listed the menus on death row in Texas. Photographs of men put to death by the state appeared next to hideous lists of the junk food they had ordered for their last meals. Marcus browsed these for a minute or two, searching for news, then moved on, without comment.

35   One privilege of adolescence is that you can treat everything around you as normal, because you have nothing to compare it with, and Marcus appeared to be taking full advantage of it. To Marcus, it was normal that you could punch a few buttons into a machine and read what a man who was executed by the state this morning had eaten last night. It was normal that the only signs of life outside his house were the people floating down from the sky and into the field out back. It was normal that his parents had named his identical twin brother Marc. Marc and Marcus. And it was normal that he now spent most of the time he was not in school on the Internet, giving legal advice to grown-ups.

36   Marcus had stumbled upon AskMe.com late in the spring of 2000. He was studying for his biology exam and looking for an answer to a question. He noticed that someone had asked a question about the law to which he knew the answer. Then another. A thought occurred: why not answer them himself? To become an official expert, he only needed to fill in a form. He did this on June 5, 2000—a day already enshrined in Marcus's mind. "I always wanted to be an attorney since I was, like, 12," he said, "but I couldn't do it because everyone is going to be: 'Like, what? Some 12-year-old kid is going to give me legal advice?'"

37   "They'd feel happier with a 15-year-old?"

38   He drew a deep breath and made a face that indicated that he took this to be a complicated question. "So when I first went on AskMe," he said, "I told

everybody I was 20, roughly about 20, and everyone believed me." Actually, he claimed to be 25, which to a boy of 15 is, I suppose, roughly 20. To further that impression, he adopted the handle LawGuy 1975. People who clicked onto his page found him described as "LawGuy1975 aka Billy Sheridan." Billy Sheridan was Marcus's handle on America Online.

39   A few days after he appointed himself a legal expert, Marcus recounted, he was logging onto the Internet solely to go to AskMe.com and deal with grownups' legal problems.

40   What sort of legal problems? I asked him.

41   "Simple ones," he said. "Some of them are like, 'My husband is in jail for murder, and he didn't do it, and I need to file a motion for dismissal, how do I do it?' I have received questions from people who are just, like, you know, 'I am going to be put in jail all of a sudden, can somebody help me plead before they come cart me off?' And it's just, like, well, come on, that's a cry for help. You're not just going to sit there. But most of them are simple questions. 'What's a felony?' Or 'How many years will I get if I commit this crime?' Or 'What happens if I get sued?' Simple questions." He said all this in the self-conscious rapid-fire patter of a television lawyer.

42   Once he became an expert, Marcus's career took on a life of its own. The AskMe rankings were driven by the number of questions the expert answered, the speed of his replies and the quality of those replies, as judged by the recipients, who bestowed on them a rating of one to five stars. By July 1, Marcus was ranked No. 10 out of 150 or so experts in AskMe.com's criminal-law division, many of whom were actual lawyers. As he tells it, that's when he decided to go for the gold. "When I hit the Top 10, I got some people who were like, 'Congratulations, blah blah blah.' So my adrenaline was pumping to answer more questions. I was just, like: You know what? Let me show these people I know what I'm doing." He needed to inspire even more people to ask him questions, and to reply to them quickly, and in a way that prompted them to reward him with lots of stars. To that end, he updated the page that advertised his services. When he was done it said:

43   "I am a law expert with two years of formal training in the law. I will help anyone I can! I have been involved in trials, legal studies and certain forms of jurisprudence. i am not accredited by the state bar association yet to practice law.… sincerely, Justin Anthony Wyrick Jr."

44   "Justin was the name I always wanted—besides mine," Marcus said. Justin Anthony Wyrick Jr.—a pseudonym on top of a pseudonym on top of a pseudonym. Justin Anthony Wyrick Jr. had a more authoritative ring to it, in Marcus's opinion, and in a lot of other people's too. On one day, Marcus received and answered 110 questions. Maybe a third of them came from the idly curious, a third from people who were already in some kind of legal trouble and the final third from people who appeared to be engaged in some sort of odd cost-benefit analysis.

45   **Q:** What amount of money must a person steal or gain through fraud before it is considered a felony in Illinois?

46   **A:** In Illinois you must have gained $5,001+ in an illegal fashion in order to constitute fraud. If you need anything else please write back! Sincerely, Justin Anthony Wyrick Jr.

47 **Q:** Can a parole officer prevent a parolee from marrying?

48 **A:** Hey! Unless the parolee has "no marriage" under the special conditions in which he is released, he can marry. If you have any questions, please write back. Sincerely, Justin Anthony Wyrick Jr.

49 The more questions Marcus answered, the more people who logged onto the boards looking for legal advice wanted to speak only to him. In one two-week stretch he received 943 legal questions and answered 939. When I asked him why he hadn't answered the other four, a look of profound exasperation crossed his broad face. "Traffic law," he said. "I'm sorry. I don't know traffic law." By mid-July, he was the No. 3 rated expert in criminal law on AskMe.com. Beneath him in the rankings were 125 licensed attorneys and a wild assortment of ex-cops and ex-cons. The next-youngest person on the board was 31.

50 In a few weeks, Marcus had created a new identity for himself: legal wizard. He now viewed school not so much as preparation for a future legal career as material for an active one. He investigated a boondoggle taken by the local school board and discovered that it had passed off on the taxpayer what to him appeared to be the expenses for a private party. He brought that, and a lot more, up at a public hearing. Why grown-up people with grown-up legal problems took him seriously was the great mystery Marcus didn't much dwell on—except to admit that it had nothing to do with his legal training. He had had no legal training, formal or informal.

51 On the top of the Arnold family desk was a thin dictionary, plus stacks and stacks of court cases that people from AskMe who had come to rely on Marcus's advice had mimeographed and sent to him for his review. (The clients sent him the paperwork, and he wrote motions, which the clients then passed on to licensed attorneys for submission to a court.) But there was nothing on the desk or in the house even faintly resembling a book about the law. The only potential sources of legal information were the family computer and the big-screen TV.

52 "Where do you find books about the law?" I asked.

53 "I don't," he said, tap-tap-tapping away on his keyboard. "Books are boring. I don't like reading."

54 "So you go on legal Web sites?"

55 "No."

56 "Well, when you got one of these questions did you research your answer?"

57 "No, never. I just know it."

58 "You just know it."

59 "Exactly."

60 The distinct whiff of an alternate reality lingered in the air. It was just then that Marcus's mother, Priscilla, came through the front door. She was a big lady, teetering and grunting beneath jumbo-size sacks of groceries. A long box of doughnuts jutted out of the top of one.

61 "Hi, Marcus, what you doing?" she said, gasping for breath.

62 "Just answering some questions," he said.

63 "What were you answering?" she asked with pleasure. She radiated pride.

64 "I got one about an appellate bond—how to get one," he said. "Another one about the Supreme Court. A petition to dismiss something."

65 "We got some chili-cheese dogs here."

66   "That's cool."

67   Priscilla nipped into the kitchen, where she heaped the doughnuts onto a plate and tossed the dogs into boiling water. Strange new smells wafted out over the computer.

68   "Where did you acquire your expertise?" I asked.

69   "Marcus was born with it!" Priscilla shouted. Having no idea how to respond, I ignored her.

70   "What do you mean?" Marcus asked me. He was genuinely puzzled by my question.

71   "Where does your information come from?"

72   "I don't know," he said. "Like, I really just don't know."

73   "How can you not know where knowledge comes from?" I asked.

74   "After, like, watching so many TV shows about the law," he said, "it's just like you know everything you need to know." He gave a little mock shiver. "It's scary. I just know these things."

75   Again Priscilla shouted from the kitchen, "Marcus has got a gift!"

76   Marcus leaned back in his chair—every inch the young prodigy—pleased that his mother was saving him the trouble of explaining the obvious to a fool. It was possible to discern certain lines in Marcus's character, but the general picture was still out of focus. He had various personas: legal genius, humble Internet helpmate, honest broker, ordinary kid who liked the Web. Now he cut a figure familiar to anyone who has sat near a front row in school—the fidgety, sweet-natured know-it-all.

77   What he knew, exactly, was unclear. On the Web, he had come across to many as a font of legal expertise. In the flesh, he gave a more eclectic perfor-mance—which was no doubt one reason he found the Internet as appealing as he did. Like Jonathan Lebed, he was the kind of person high school is designed to suppress, and like Jonathan Lebed, he had refused to accept his assigned status. When the real world failed to diagnose his talents, he went looking for a second opinion. The Internet offered him as many opinions as he needed to find one he liked. It created the opportunity for new sorts of self-perceptions, which then took on a reality all their own.

78   There was something else familiar about the game Marcus was playing, but it took me a while to put my finger on it. He was using the Internet the way adults often use their pasts. The passage of time allows older people to remem-ber who they were as they would like to have been. Young people do not enjoy access to that particular escape route from their selves—their pasts are still unpleasantly present—and so they tend to turn the other way and imagine themselves into some future adult world. The sentiment that powers their fan-tasies goes by different names—hope, ambition, idealism—but at bottom it is nostalgia. Nostalgia for the future. These days nostalgia for the future is a lot more fashionable than the traditional kind. And the Internet has made it possi-ble to act on the fantasy in whole new ways.

79   Priscilla shouted from the kitchen: "Marcus had his gift in the womb. I could feel it."

80   Now Marcus had his big grin on. "Welcome to my brain," he said.

81   "What?"

82   "Welcome to my brain."

83   He had said it so much like a genial host offering his guest the comfortable chair that I had to stop myself from saying "Thanks." Behind him was a long picture window overlooking the California desert—the view was the reason Priscilla loved her house. Beyond that, brown mountains. In the middle distance between white desert and brown mountain, a parachute ripped open and a body jerked skyward.

84   "Let's try this again," I said.

85   "O.K.," he said, cheerfully.

86   "Basically, you picked up what you know from watching 'Court TV' shows," I said.

87   "Basically," he said.

88   "And from these Web sites that you browse."

89   "Basically."

90   Priscilla shouted out from the kitchen, "How many dogs you want, Marcus?"

91   "Two, and some doughnuts," Marcus hollered.

92   "What do you think these people would have done if you weren't there to answer their questions?" I asked.

93   "They would have paid an attorney," he said. But as he said it, his big grin vanished and a cloud shadowed his broad, open face. All of a sudden he was the soul of prudence.

94   He may well have been recalling the P.R. fiasco that followed the discovery by a hundred or so licensed attorneys on AskMe.com of the true identity of the new expert moving up their ranks. In any case, he lifted his giant palms toward me in the manner of the Virgin Mary resisting the entreaties of the Holy Spirit and said: "Look, I'm not out there to take business away from other people. That's not my job."

95   "But you think that legal expertise is overrated?"

96   "Completely."

97   Once Marcus attained his high AskMe.com rankings, a lot of people he didn't really know began to ask for his phone number and his fee structure. For the first time, for some reason he was unable to explain fully, his conscience began to trouble him. He decided it was time to come clean with his age. To do this, he changed his expert profile. Where it had read "legal expert," it now read "15-year-old intern attorney expert."

98   A few hours after he posted his confession, hostile messages came hurtling toward him. A few of them came from his "clients," but most came from the lawyers and others who competed with him for rankings and publicity. A small war broke out on the message boards, with Marcus accusing the lawyers of ganging up on him to undermine his No. 3 ranking and the lawyers accusing Marcus of not knowing what he was talking about. The lawyers began to pull up Marcus's old answers and bestow on them lowly one-star ratings—thus dragging down his average. Then they did something even worse: they asked him detailed questions about the finer points of the law. When he couldn't supply similarly detailed answers, they laid into him.

99   Marcus's replies to the e-mail lashings read less like the work of a defense lawyer than like those of a man trying to talk his torturers into untying him:

100   "I am reporting your abusive response, for it hurts my reputation, and my dignity as an expert on this board."

101   "Please don't e-mail me threats."

102   "Leave me alone! I am not even practicing law!"

103   "Please, I beg of you, stop sending me letters saying that you'll be watching me, because you are scaring my parents."

104   "I really just want to be friends."

105   "Let's try to be friends, or something?"

106   To which Marcus's wittiest assailant replied: "In your last two posts you've ended by asking that I be your friend. That's like the mortally wounded gladiator wanting to be friends with the lion."

107   On the one hand, the whole episode was absurd—Marcus Arnold was a threat to no one but himself and, perhaps, the people who sought his advice. To practice law, you still needed a license, and no 15-year-old boy was going to be granted one. At the same time, Marcus had wandered into an arena alive with combustible particles. The Internet had arrived at an embarrassing moment for the law.

108   The knowledge gap between lawyers and nonlawyers had been shrinking for some time, and the Internet was closing it further. Legal advice was being supplied over the Internet, often free—and it wasn't just lawyers doing the supplying. Students, cops, dicks, even ex-cons went onto message boards to help people with their questions and cases. At the bottom of this phenomenon was a corrosively democratic attitude toward legal knowledge, which the legal profession now simply took for granted. "If you think about the law," the co-chairman of the American Bar Association task force on "e-lawyering," Richard S. Granat, said in an interview in *The New York Times,* in an attempt to explain the boom in do-it-yourself Internet legal services, "a large component is just information. Information by itself can go a long way to help solve legal problems."

109   In that simple sentence you could hear whatever was left of the old professional mystique evaporating. The status of lawyering was in flux, had been for some time. An anthology that will cause elitists to weep will one day be culled from the long shelf of diatribes about the descent into mass culture of the American lawyer at the end of the 20th century. Separate chapters will detail the advent of the billable hour, the 1977 Supreme Court decision permitting lawyers to advertise their services and a magazine called *The American Lawyer,* which in 1985 began to publish estimates of lawyers' incomes. Once the law became a business, it was on its way to becoming a commodity. Reduce the law to the sum of its information, and, by implication, anyone can supply it.

110   That idea had already traveled a long way, and the Internet was helping it to travel faster. After all, what did it say about the law that even a 15-year-old boy who had never read a law book could pass as an expert in it to a huge audience? It said that a lot of people felt that legal knowledge was accessible to the amateur. Who knows? Maybe they were right. Perhaps legal expertise was overrated. Completely.

111   By its nature, the Internet undermined anyone whose status depended on a privileged access to information. But you couldn't fairly blame the Internet for Marcus Arnold, any more than you could blame the Internet for Jonathan

Lebed. The Internet was merely using Marcus to tell us something about ourselves: we doubted the value of formal training. A little knowledge had always been a dangerous thing. Now it was becoming a respectable thing. A general collapse in the importance of formal training was a symptom of post-Internet life; knowledge, like the clothing that went with it, was being informalized. Casual thought went well with casual dress.

112   And so the situation in which Marcus Arnold found himself in the late summer of 2000, while bizarre, was revealing. Marcus had been publicly humiliated by the real lawyers, but it didn't stop him from offering more advice. He clung by his big mitts to a lower ranking. Then the clients began to speak. With pretty much one voice they said, "Leave the kid alone!" A lot of people seemed to believe that any 15-year-old who had risen so high in the ranks of AskMe.com legal experts must be some kind of wizard. They began to seek him out more than ever before; they wanted his, and only his, advice.

113   Marcus wiped himself off and gave it to them. In days his confidence was fully restored. "You always have your critics," he said. "I mean, with the real lawyers, it's a pride issue. They can't let someone who could be their son beat them. Plus they have a lot more time than I do. I'm always stretched for time. Six hours a day of school, four hours of homework, sometimes I can't get online to answer the questions until after dinner."

114   Despite this and other handicaps, Marcus's ranking rebounded. Two weeks after he disclosed his age, he was on the rise; two weeks later he hit No. 1. The legal advice he gave to a thousand or so people along the way might not have withstood the scrutiny of the finest legal minds. Some of it was the sort of stuff you could glean directly from Judge Judy; more of it was a simple restating of the obvious in a friendly tone. Marcus didn't have much truck with the details; he didn't handle complexity terribly well. But that was the whole point of him—he didn't need to. A lot of what a real lawyer did was hand out simple information in a way that made the client feel served, and this Marcus did well. He may have had only the vaguest idea of what he was talking about and a bizarre way of putting what he did know. But out there in the void, they loved him.

115   Marcus's father, Melvin, worked at a furniture retail outlet two hours' drive from home and so wasn't usually around when his son was handing out advice on the Internet. Not that it mattered; he wouldn't have known what Marcus was up to in any case. "I'm not the sort of person who gets on the computer," Melvin said when he arrived home and saw Marcus bashing away for my benefit. "I never get on the computer, as a matter of fact." And he said this matter-of-factly, in a spirit in no way defiant or angry, just gently resigned to the Way Things Are. "When I need something from the computer," he also said, "I ask Marcus."

116   "It just gives me more computer time," Marcus said and resumed his furious typing.

117   What with the computer smack in the center of the place, the Arnolds' house didn't allow me to talk to Melvin without disrupting Marcus. When Marcus realized that he was about to be forced to listen to whatever his father might have to say about his Internet self, he lost interest. He called for Marc, and the twin bear-boys lumbered out the front door. On the way out, he turned and asked me if I knew anyone in Hollywood he might talk to. "I think what I really want

to do," he said, "is be an actor." With that final non sequitur, he left me to cross-examine his parents.

118   The first thing that was instantly clear was that, unlike their son, they were aware that their lives were no longer what anyone would call normal. The Lebeds had proved that if your adolescent child was online, you didn't need to leave your house to feel uprooted. The Arnolds were already uprooted, so they didn't prove anything. They had moved from Belize to South Central Los Angeles. They had moved from there to Perris for a reason, which Melvin now calmly explained to me. At the family's Los Angeles home, Marcus's older brother had been murdered. He had been shot dead in cold blood by an acquaintance in the middle of a family barbecue. The man who shot him was up for parole in 2013. "Marcus didn't tell you about that, did he?" Melvin asked rhetorically. "In my opinion, that's how Marcus got interested in the law. He saw that it wasn't fair."

119   The Arnolds moved to Perris shortly after their son's murder. Not long after they arrived, Marcus asked for a computer. He had waited until he crashed the Top 10 on AskMe.com before he let his parents know why, suddenly, he was up at all hours bashing away on the family keyboard. His parents had had radically different reactions to the news. His mother nearly burst with pride—she always knew that Marcus was special, and the Internet was giving him a chance to prove it. His father was mildly skeptical. He couldn't understand how a 15-year-old boy could be functioning as a lawyer. The truth is, Melvin hadn't taken Marcus all that seriously, at least not at first. He assumed that he was reacting to the grief of his older brother's murder. Then the phone started to ring...and ring. "These were grown-up people," Melvin said, still incredulous at the events taking place under his roof. "They call this house and ask for Marcus. These people are like 40, 45 years old, and they're talking to Marcus about their legal problems, but they're not including the parents. That's where I get scared, because it's not supposed to work like that."

120   "Well...," Priscilla said. She scrunched up her big friendly face in what was clearly intended to be disapproval. "They're not acknowledging the fact that he's 15. They're acknowledging the fact that he can give them some legal advice."

121   "But the phone," Melvin said. "It is always ringing. These people want Marcus to give them legal advice. I mean, really, it's like what he does people do as a job. And he's doing it right here. I get so frustrated. I always say, 'Marcus, you're talking too much, you're talking too much.'"

122   "But that's what attorneys do," Priscilla said. "They talk a lot."

123   Melvin gave up on his wife and turned to me. "I tell him to stay off the phone, stay off the computer. This is the thing I keep on saying to him. Nobody else in this house can ever use the phone. There's no way I can stop him, but still—."

124   "But attorneys talk—that's what they do," Priscilla said.

125   "I don't use the phone anyway, really," Melvin said. "The calls come, they're never mine, you know. It's always Marcus, Marcus, Marcus—people calling him from everywhere."

126   They were off and running on what was clearly a familiar conversational steeplechase. "I don't understand," I said. "How do all these people have your phone number?" But neither of them was listening. Priscilla, having seized on

her main point, was now intent on spearing Melvin on the end of it. "But that's what he's got to do," she said. "That's what attorneys do! Talk!"

127   "Yeah, but he's not an attorney," Melvin said. He turned to me again in a bid for arbitration. "He drives you nuts with his talk. Nuts!"

128   "How do they get your phone number?" I asked again.

129   "But he will be one day," Priscilla said. "He has that gift."

130   "He's a kid," Melvin said.

131   "How did they get your phone number?" I asked for the third time.

132   Priscilla looked up. "Marcus puts it on the Internet," she said. To her, it was the most normal of things.

133   Melvin took a different view. Maybe it was the distinct feeling he had that a lot of Marcus's "clients" had had to stand in line at a pay phone to make their calls. Or that they always seemed to prefer to wait on hold rather than call back later. Or their frantic tones of voice. Whatever the reason, he didn't like it. "I told Marcus," he said wearily, "that we don't even know who these people are—they might be criminals out there—that you're not supposed to give them our phone number, our address."

134   Priscilla furrowed her brow and tried to conjure concern. "What really scared me one time," she said, less with fear than in the spirit of cooperation, "was this lady that he was assisting with her criminal case. The lady sent him the whole book of her court case. I said: 'Marcus, why would you want to take this upon yourself? You've got to tell this lady you're just 15 years old!' But he didn't listen to me. The point came that the lady actually wanted him to go to court with her, and I said, 'No, we've got to stop it here, because you don't have a license for that, you don't study law.' He said: 'Mom, you've got to drive me to the court. I know what I'm doing.' I said: 'No way. You don't have a license to dictate the law.'"

135   I could see that her heart wasn't in this soliloquy. She stopped and brightened, as if to say she had done her best to meet her husband halfway, then said, "But I think all of this Internet is good for Marcus."

136   "Do you think Marcus knows what he's doing?" I asked.

137   "Oh, yes, very much," she said. "Because there's a lot of times that we would watch these court shows, and he would come up with the same suggestions and the same answers like the attorneys would do."

138   That appeared to settle the matter; even Melvin could not disagree. Marcus knew his "Court TV."

139   "Can you see him charging for this advice?" I asked.

140   "At what age?" Melvin said. A new alarm entered his voice.

141   "Thirty."

142   "I hope," Melvin said with extreme caution, "I hope he will do well."

143   "He's supposed to have his own law firm by then," Priscilla said.

Review Questions

1. What is the significance of Nokia's success in mobile telephones, according to Lewis?

2. What, for Lewis, was the significance of Morris Bart? How was this new kind of lawyer emblematic of what was happening on the Internet?

3. What are "pyramids" and "pancakes," according to Lewis? How did the AskMe software favor pancakes and undermine pyramids?

4. From what sources did Marcus get the answers he was providing to people who asked him questions about the law?

Discussion and Writing Suggestions

1. Lewis writes that role theorists claim that "we have no 'self' as such. Our selves are merely the masks we wear in response to the social situations in which we find ourselves. The Internet had offered up a new set of social situations, to which people had responded by grabbing for a new set of masks." To what extent do you agree with this assertion? Support your response with illustrations from your own experience or the experiences of people you know. Relate your comments at some point to Lewis' discussion of Marcus Arnold.

2. To what extent do you approve of what Marcus Arnold did? Do you think that he is a healthy or an unhealthy symptom of what is happening on the Internet? To what extent would you be prepared to seek legal advice from Arnold?

3. Lewis argues that Marcus "was using the Internet the way adults often use their pasts." But since young people like Marcus do not have much of a past, they turn to the future and "imagine themselves into some future adult world." To what extent do you think that this theory accounts for the fascination of many young people for the Internet—i.e., that it provides a means of fantasizing about their lives in the future?

4. Go to the AskMe site <*www.AskMe.com*>, find a category and subcategory with which you are reasonably familiar, and browse through the answers to questions that some of the experts have provided. How good are their answers? Could you have provided better ones? (Try a few.) Do the more reliable and complete answers appear to come from experts who—according to their own description of their qualifications and credentials—have had the most training and experience?

SYNTHESIS ACTIVITIES

1. Write an article for a newsmagazine exploring the various facets of the e-mail revolution. Use Leonard as a model for survey articles of

this type, but avoid using more than one or two of Leonard's own examples. Focus in particular on how e-mail provides a means of exploring and defining aspects of our identity. Keep the article relatively objective—that is, it should essentially take the form of an *explanatory* synthesis—but don't be afraid of venturing mildly argumentative assessments of the e-mail phenomenon or the directions in which our Internet culture is headed.

2. Argue that the net effects of the e-mail revolution are positive—*or* that they are negative. In formulating your argument, acknowledge and explain that e-mail has both positive and negative aspects, but assert that on-balance, the positive outweighs the negative (or vice versa) in terms of how e-mail has affected both private and public discourse. Draw upon as many articles and selections in this chapter as will be helpful in supporting your case.

3. How has e-mail changed the way we think about identity? Draw upon the selections in the latter part of the chapter—Daum, Dyson, Turkle, Pham, and Lewis, to explore this topic. Consider such matters as (1) the identity or identities we create when we send messages; (2) the implied identities of those who send us messages; (3) the relationship or conflict between our actual identity and our implied identity or identities; (4) the relationship between our physical selves and our implied selves.

4. The Internet allows us to pretend to be what we are not. From different perspectives, David Brooks ("The A-List E-List'), Alex Pham ("Boy, You Fight Like a Girl") and Michael Lewis ("Faking It: The Virtual Lawyer") focus on this phenomenon. (Dyson and Turkle consider this matter in a more general way.) Compare and contrast Brooks's, Pham's, and Lewis's articles as they explore this matter. Consider not only the individuals discussed in their articles and the different ways in which they offer false fronts to the world, but also the tone and the style in which each author presents his article. To what extent can we draw general conclusions about what we read in these three selections?

5. Daum's experience with online romance is common, if not universal. While some lucky souls do indeed find their future mates over the Internet, most who attempt online romance find that the relationships burn brightly for awhile and then smolder and die—particularly, once the parties actually meet.

   Why should this be so? What accounts for the eventual failure of so many online romances? Aren't we expressing our "true" selves in e-mail messages? Or are the selves we project simply idealized versions of our selves that cannot survive in the "real world"? To what extent is there an inherent conflict, a tension, between our physical selves and our cyber-selves? In your response, draw not only upon Daum and other selections in this chapter, but also upon some of the short readings on online romance (e.g., Suler, Wolcott, Morris, Eggett) in Chapter Four.

6. The e-mail revolution appears to have changed some of the rules of communication, often for the worse. One of the more unpleasant developments of the new medium is "flaming": the sending of abusive, insulting, sometimes vicious messages, or even threats, to another with whom one may have a minor disagreement. Considerably less serious, but still annoying to many e-mail recipients, is the tendency of some writers not to use punctuation or capital letters, indeed not to bother proofreading (or even signing) their messages at all. While some believe that e-mail messages do not require strict adherence to stylistic conventions, others take issue. In *The Elements of E-Mail Style*, authors David Angell and Brent Heslop assert, "Using all lower-case letters is annoying for the recipient and can result in your message being misunderstood or not read at all."*

Do you regard such casual disregard of conventions as breaches of communication etiquette or are they simply part of the distinctive nature of e-mail culture? Attempt to explain these and perhaps other negative features of e-mail communication, drawing upon some of the selections that you have read in this chapter, particularly Leonard, Schwartz, and Dyson.

7. Compare and contrast Pham's article on gender-switching among online gamers with Lewis's article about the make-believe lawyer. What kinds of phenomena are common to both situations? In what ways do they fundamentally differ? What is the role, for example, of deception in the two situations? How do the role players differ in their purpose? What are the consequences of exposure of the deception?

8. In a piece called "The Return of the Word" Adam Gopnik writes, "E-mail has succeeded brilliantly for the same reason that the videophone failed miserably: what we actually want from our exchanges is the minimum human contact commensurate with the need to connect with other people. 'Only connect.' Yes, but *only* connect."[†] What do you think Gopnik means. Why "*only* connect"? Just what kind of contact do we crave, do we need from our e-mail correspondents? In your response, draw upon some of the following selections: Leonard, Schwartz, Parsons, Daum, Turkle.

The Elements of E-Mail Style: Communicate Effectively via Electronic Mail. Reading: Addison-Wesley, 1994.

[†]*The New Yorker*, 6 Dec. 1999: The quotation "Only connect" is from *Howard's End* (1910) by E.M. Forster.

9. In the manner of Roy Rivenburg, devise a situation involving characters of your own creation; and compose a series of e-mail exchanges dramatizing this situation. Or instead of creating a new situation, you may want to dramatize one based on events in real life, your own, or someone else's.

RESEARCH ACTIVITIES

1. Explore some aspect of online romance. What services are available for people who want to find love on the Internet? What are the benefits and drawbacks of using such services? What are the special thrills and the hazards of seeking love online? How is online romance similar to and different from the old-fashioned kind? What happens when two people who have met and fallen in love (or lust) online meet in person? Begin your research by reviewing some of the selections in this chapter that focus on these matters, and then pursue the matter further by seeking additional sources.

2. One of the most popular offshoots of e-mailing is "instant messaging," a process that allows people to have e-mail exchanges in real time, one that represents a kind of hybrid between the letter (in that messages are written) and the telephone (in that an exchange takes place over a relatively brief, unbroken period of time). Write an article for a newsmagazine exploring the phenomenon of instant messaging— how it got started, why it has become so popular, how it became a legal issue (when America Online initially refused to license its Instant Messaging software), where it seems headed.

3. As Andrew Leonard explains in "We've Got Mail—Always," e-mail was invented in the late 1960s when scientists in different locations who used the Arpanet, the predecessor of the Internet, sought to develop a way of sharing resources and information with one another. Write a report on the early history of e-mail, focusing on the period before 1990 when it became a mass phenomenon. Who were the main players? What were the key moments? What were the technical challenges? At what point did it become apparent that e-mail was going to have far broader applications than was originally conceived?

4. Like anything else, e-mail has a significant legal dimension. Of increasing concern to employees is the privacy of their e-mail and the extent to which employers can monitor their e-mail and use it against them. Employers have been known to send fake e-mails to employees pretending to be other employers offering more lucrative or prestigious jobs. Employees who responded favorably were deemed disloyal and subsequently denied promotion. In 2000, civil libertarians became alarmed when the FBI revealed that it was using a software program called Carnivore to monitor all e-mail

passing through a particular Internet Service Provider (ISP), ostensibly in an attempt to catch terrorists, drug dealers, and child pornographers. During a divorce proceeding, one spouse may obtain a court order to search the e-mail records of the other spouse for incriminating information about extramarital affairs. Explore some of the ways that e-mail monitoring and searching has been used against people, along with some of the ways that civil libertarians and others have been resisting activities in court.

5. "Lurk" for a while in some chat rooms or electronic bulletin boards. (To "lurk" over electronic communications is to read what others are writing without announcing your own presence.) Visit forums on a variety of subjects. For example, if you are a member of America Online, you'll find chat rooms available on numerous subjects. If you read electronic publications like Slate.com or Salon.com, you can trace discussion threads in which readers react to articles that have been published. Report on what you find. What tentative conclusions can you draw about the types of communication that occur in such places? Categorize the types of comments made. What appear to be the effects of anonymity? To what extent do you detect that writers are creating personas for themselves, ones that may be different from what they are like in person?

6. Conduct a survey about e-mail use. Try to keep the group you survey relatively homogenous (e.g., undergraduates) and organize that group by subcategories (e.g., class standing, major, gender, whether an individual has her or his own computer or must use college equipment). Develop a questionnaire, as well as a set of interview questions, exploring such issues as the main purposes of sending e-mail messages, the average length of messages, how often e-mail is checked, and the use of chat rooms and electronic bulletin boards. Write a report based on your findings. Use tables and graphs or charts to summarize your data. Use standard social science format for developing your report: an *introduction*, a section on *methods* of gathering data, a section on *results*, a *discussion* of the results, and a *conclusion*.

7. Visit AskMe.com and browse through the questions and answers by various "experts" in one of the numerous categories listed. It's best to select a category—whether movies, computer software, or refinishing cabinets—with which you have some "expert" knowledge, yourself. Notice how many of the responses have been rated (on a scale of one to five stars) by the questioner and by other experts. Assess the quality of the responses, based on your own knowledge of the subject, and compare them with the ratings posted. Write a report, possibly for a magazine like *Consumer Reports*, assessing the quality of information provided by particular experts in this area on AskMe.com.

8 Obedience to Authority

Would you obey an order to inflict pain on another person? Most of us, if confronted with this question, would probably be quick to answer: "Never!" Yet if the conclusions of researchers are to be trusted, it is not psychopaths who kill noncombatant civilians in wartime and torture victims in prisons around the world but rather ordinary people following orders. People obey. This is a basic, necessary fact of human society. As psychologist Stanley Milgram has written, "Obedience is as basic an element in the structure of social life as one can point to. Some system of authority is a requirement of all communal living."

The question, then, is not, "Should we obey the orders of an authority figure?" but rather, "To what *extent* should we obey?" Each generation seems to give new meaning to these questions. During the Vietnam War, a number of American soldiers followed a commander's orders and murdered civilians in the hamlet of My Lai. In 1987 former White House military aide Oliver North was prosecuted for illegally diverting money raised by selling arms to Iran—considered by the U.S. government to be a terrorist state—to fund the anti-communist Contra (resistance) fighters in Nicaragua. North's attorneys claimed that he was following the orders of his superiors. And, although North was found guilty,* the judge who sentenced him to perform community service (there was no prison sentence) largely agreed with this defense when he called North a pawn in a larger game played by senior officials in the Reagan administration. In the 1990s the world was horrified by genocidal violence in Rwanda and in the former nation of Yugoslavia. These were civil wars, in which people who had been living for generations as neighbors suddenly, upon the instigation and orders of their leaders, turned upon and slaughtered one another.

In less dramatic ways, conflicts over the extent to which we obey orders surface in everyday life. At one point or another, you may face a moral dilemma at work. Perhaps it will take this form: The boss tells you to overlook File X in preparing a report for a certain client. But you're sure that File X pertains directly to the report and contains information that will alarm the client. What should you do? The dilemmas of obedience also emerge on some campuses with the rite of fraternity or sports-related hazing. Psychologists Janice Gibson and Mika Haritos-Fatouros have made the startling observation that whether the obedience in question involves a pledge's joining a fraternity or a torturer's joining an elite military corps, the *process*

---

*In July 1990, North's conviction was overturned on appeal.

by which one acquiesces to a superior's order (and thereby becomes a member of the group) is remarkably the same:

> There are several ways to teach people to do the unthinkable, and we have developed a model to explain how they are used. We have also found that college fraternities, although they are far removed from the grim world of torture and violent combat, use similar methods for initiating new members, to ensure their faithfulness to the fraternity's rules and values. However, this unthinking loyalty can sometimes lead to dangerous actions: Over the past 10 years, there have been countless injuries during fraternity initiations and 39 deaths. These training techniques are designed to instill obedience in people, but they can easily be a guide for an intensive course in torture.
>
> 1. *Screening to find the best prospects:* Normal, well-adjusted people with the physical, intellectual, and, in some cases, political attributes necessary for the task.
>
> 2. *Techniques to increase binding among these prospects:* Initiation rites to isolate people from society and introduce them to a new social order, with different rules and values.
>
>   Elitist attitudes and "in-group" language, which highlight the differences between the group and the rest of society.
>
> 3. *Techniques to reduce the strain of obedience:* Blaming and dehumanizing the victims, so it is less disturbing to harm them.
>
>   Harassment, the constant physical and psychological intimidation that prevents logical thinking and promotes the instinctive responses needed for acts of inhuman cruelty.
>
>   Rewards for obedience and punishments for not cooperating.
>
>   Social modeling by watching other group members commit violent acts and then receive rewards.
>
>   Systematic desensitization to repugnant acts by gradual exposure to them, so they appear routine and normal despite conflicts with previous moral standards.*

In this chapter, you will explore the dilemmas inherent in obeying the orders of an authority. First, in a brief essay adapted from a lecture, British novelist Doris Lessing helps set a context for the discussion by questioning the manner in which we call ourselves individualists yet fail to understand how groups define and exert influence over us. Next, psychologist Solomon Asch describes an experiment he devised to demonstrate the powerful influence of group pressure upon individual judgment. Psychologist Stanley Milgram then reports on his own landmark study in which he set out to determine the extent

---

*"The Education of a Torturer" by Janice T. Gibson and Mika Haritos-Fatouros from *Psychology Today*, November 1986. Reprinted with permission from *Psychology Today Magazine*. Copyright 1986 Sussex Publishers, Inc.

to which ordinary individuals would obey the clearly immoral orders of an authority figure. The results were shocking, not only to the psychiatrists who predicted that few people would follow such orders but also to many other social scientists and people—some of whom applauded Milgram for his fiendishly ingenious design, some of whom bitterly attacked him for unethical procedures. We include one of these attacks, a scathing review by psychologist Diana Baumrind. Another, and later, perspective on the reaction to Milgram's experiment is provided by British writer Ian Parker in his essay "Obedience."

Next Philip Zimbardo reports on his famous (and controversial) Stanford Prison Experiment, in which volunteers exhibited astonishingly convincing authoritarian and obedient attitudes as they play-acted at being prisoners and guards. Two essays conclude the chapter. In "Disobedience as a Psychological and Moral Problem," psychoanalyst and philosopher Erich Fromm discusses the comforts of obedient behavior. Finally, in "The Organization Kid," David Brooks wonders if the new generation of "elite" students is being systematically trained almost from birth to find happiness in conforming and doing what their elders tell them to do.

Group Minds
Doris Lessing

Doris Lessing sets a context for the discussion on obedience by illuminating a fundamental conflict: We in the Western world celebrate our individualism, but we're naïve in understanding the ways that groups largely undercut our individuality. "We are group animals still," says Lessing, "and there is nothing wrong with that. But what is dangerous is ... not understanding the social laws that govern groups and govern us." This chapter is largely devoted to an exploration of these tendencies. As you read selections by Milgram and the other authors here, bear in mind Lessing's troubling question: If we know that individuals will violate their own good common sense and moral codes in order to become accepted members of a group, why then can't we put this knowledge to use and teach people to be wary of group pressures?

Doris Lessing, the daughter of farmers, was born in Persia, now Iran, in 1919. She attended a Roman Catholic convent and a girls' high school in southern Rhodesia (now Zimbabwe). From 1959 through to the present, Lessing has written more than twenty works of fiction and has been called "the best woman novelist" of the postwar era. Her work has received a great deal of scholarly attention. She is, perhaps, best known for her Five Short Novels *(1954),* The Golden Notebook *(1962), and* Briefing for a Descent into Hell *(1971).*

1 People living in the West, in societies that we describe as Western, or as the free world, may be educated in many different ways, but they will all emerge with an idea about themselves that goes something like this: I am a citizen of a free society, and that means I am an individual, making individual choices. My mind is my

own, my opinions are chosen by me, I am free to do as I will, and at the worst the pressures on me are economic, that is, I may be too poor to do as I want.

2   This set of ideas may sound something like a caricature, but it is not so far off how we see ourselves. It is a portrait that may not have been acquired consciously, but is part of a general atmosphere or set of assumptions that influence our ideas about ourselves.

3   People in the West therefore may go through their entire lives never thinking to analyze this very flattering picture, and as a result are helpless against all kinds of pressures on them to conform in many kinds of ways.

4   The fact is that we all live our lives in groups—the family, work groups, social, religious, and political groups. Very few people indeed are happy as solitaries, and they tend to be seen by their neighbors as peculiar or selfish or worse. Most people cannot stand being alone for long. They are always seeking groups to belong to, and if one group dissolves, they look for another. We are group animals still, and there is nothing wrong with that. But what is dangerous is not the belonging to a group, or groups, but not understanding the social laws that govern groups and govern us.

5   When we're in a group, we tend to think as that group does: we may even have joined the group to find "like-minded" people. But we also find our thinking changing because we belong to a group. It is the hardest thing in the world to maintain an individual dissident opinion, as a member of a group.

6   It seems to me that this is something we have all experienced—something we take for granted, may never have thought about it. But a great deal of experiment has gone on among psychologists and sociologists on this very theme. If I describe an experiment or two, then anyone listening who may be a sociologist or psychologist will groan, oh God not *again*—for they will have heard of these classic experiments far too often. My guess is that the rest of the people will never have heard of these experiments, never have had these ideas presented to them. If my guess is true, then it aptly illustrates my general thesis, and the general idea behind these talks, that we (the human race) are now in possession of a great deal of hard information about ourselves, but we do not use it to improve our institutions and therefore our lives.

7   A typical test, or experiment, on this theme goes like this. A group of people are taken into the researcher's confidence. A minority of one or two are left in the dark. Some situation demanding measurement or assessment is chosen. For instance, comparing lengths of wood that differ only a little from each other, but enough to be perceptible, or shapes that are almost the same size. The majority in the group—according to instruction—will assert stubbornly that these two shapes or lengths are the same length, or size, while the solitary individual, or the couple, who have not been so instructed will assert that the pieces of wood or whatever are different. But the majority will continue to insist—speaking metaphorically—that black is white, and after a period of exasperation, irritation, even anger, certainly incomprehension, the minority will fall into line. Not always, but nearly always. There are indeed glorious individuals who stubbornly insist on telling the truth as they see it, but most give in to the majority opinion, obey the atmosphere.

8   When put as badly, as unflatteringly, as this, reactions tend to be incredulous: "I certainly wouldn't give in, I speak my mind...." But would you?

9   People who have experienced a lot of groups, who perhaps have observed their own behavior, may agree that the hardest thing in the world is to stand out against one's group, a group of one's peers. Many agree that among our most shameful memories is this, how often we said black was white because other people were saying it.

10   In other words, we know that this is true of human behavior, but how do we know it? It is one thing to admit it, in a vague uncomfortable sort of way (which probably includes the hope that one will never again be in such a testing situation) but quite another to make that cool step into a kind of objectivity, where one may say, "Right, if that's what human beings are like, myself included, then let's admit it, examine and organize our attitudes accordingly."

11   This mechanism, of obedience to the group, does not only mean obedience or submission to a small group, or one that is sharply determined, like a religion or political party. It means, too, conforming to those large, vague, ill-defined collections of people who may never think of themselves as having a collective mind because they are aware of differences of opinion—but which, to people from outside, from another culture, seem very minor. The underlying assumptions and assertions that govern the group are never discussed, never challenged, probably never noticed, the main one being precisely this: that it *is* a group mind, intensely resistant to change, equipped with sacred assumptions about which there can be no discussion.

12   But suppose this kind of thing were taught in schools?

13   Let us just suppose it, for a moment....But at once the nub of the problem is laid bare.

14   Imagine us saying to children, "In the last fifty or so years, the human race has become aware of a great deal of information about its mechanisms; how it behaves, how it must behave under certain circumstances. If this is to be useful, you must learn to contemplate these rules calmly, dispassionately, disinterestedly, without emotion. It is information that will set people free from blind loyalties, obedience to slogans, rhetoric, leaders, group emotions." Well, there it is.

Review Questions

1. What is the flattering portrait Lessing paints of people living in the West?

2. Lessing believes that individuals in the West are "helpless against all kinds of pressures on them to conform in many kinds of ways." Why?

3. Lessing refers to a class of experiments on obedience. Summarize the "typical" experiment.

Discussion and Writing Suggestions

1. Lessing writes that "what is dangerous is not the belonging to a group, or groups, but not understanding the social laws that govern groups and govern us." What is the danger Lessing is speaking of here?

2. Lessing states that "we (the human race) are now in possession of a great deal of hard information about ourselves, but we do not use it to improve our institutions and therefore our lives." First, do you agree with Lessing? Can you cite other examples (aside from information on obedience to authority) in which we do not use our knowledge to better humankind?

3. Explore some of the difficulties in applying this "hard information" about humankind that Lessing speaks of. Assume she's correct in claiming that we don't incorporate our knowledge of human nature into the running of our institutions. Why don't we? What are the difficulties of *acting* on information?

4. Lessing speaks of "people who remember how they acted in school" and of their guilt in recalling how they succumbed to group pressures. Can you recall such an event? What feelings do you have about it now?

Opinions and Social Pressure
Solomon E. Asch

In the early 1950s, Solomon Asch (b. 1907), a social psychologist at Rutgers University in New Brunswick, New Jersey, conducted a series of simple but ingenious experiments on the influence of group pressure upon the individual. Essentially, he discovered, individuals can be influenced by groups to deny the evidence of their own senses. Together with the Milgram experiments of the following decade (see the following selections), these studies provide powerful evidence of the degree to which individuals can surrender their own judgment to others, even when those others are clearly in the wrong. The results of these experiments have implications far beyond the laboratory: they can explain a good deal of the normal human behavior we see every day—at school, at work, at home.

1 That social influences shape every person's practices, judgments, and beliefs is a truism to which anyone will readily assent. A child masters his "native" dialect down to the finest nuances; a member of a tribe of cannibals accepts cannibalism as altogether fitting and proper. All the social sciences take their departure from the observation of the profound effects that groups exert on their members. For psychologists, group pressure upon the minds of individual raises a host of questions they would like to investigate in detail.

2   How, and to what extent, do social forces constrain people's opinions and attitudes? This question is especially pertinent in our day. The same epoch that has witnessed the unprecedented technical extension of communication has also brought into existence the deliberate manipulation of opinion and the "engineering of consent." There are many good reasons why, as citizens and as scientists, we should be concerned with studying the ways in which human beings form their opinions and the role that social conditions play.

3   Studies of these questions began with the interest in hypnosis aroused by the French physician Jean Martin Charcot (a teacher of Sigmund Freud) toward the end of the 19th century. Charcot believed that only hysterical patients could be fully hypnotized, but this view was soon challenged by two other physicians, Hyppolyte Bernheim and A. A. Liébault, who demonstrated that they could put most people under hypnotic spell. Bernheim proposed that hypnosis was but an extreme form of a normal psychological process which became known as "suggestibility." It was shown that monotonous reiteration of instructions could induce in normal persons in the waking state involuntary bodily changes such as swaying or rigidity of the arms, and sensations such as warmth and odor.

4   It was not long before social thinkers seized upon these discoveries as a basis for explaining numerous social phenomena, from the spread of opinion to the formation of crowds and the following of leaders. The sociologist Gabriel Tarde summed it all up in the aphorism: "Social man is a somnambulist."

5   When the new discipline of social psychology was born at the beginning of this century, its first experiments were essentially adaptations of the suggestion demonstration. The technique generally followed a simple plan. The subjects, usually college students, were asked to give their opinions or preferences concerning various matters; some time later they were again asked to state their choices, but now they were also informed of the opinions held by authorities or large groups of their peers on the same matters. (Often the alleged consensus was fictitious.) Most of these studies had substantially the same result: confronted with opinions contrary to their own, many subjects apparently shifted their judgments in the direction of the views of the majorities or the experts. The late psychologist Edward L. Thorndike reported that he had succeeded in modifying the esthetic preferences of adults by this procedure. Other psychologists reported that people's evaluations of the merit of a literary passage could be raised or lowered by ascribing the passage to different authors. Apparently the sheer weight of numbers or authority sufficed to change opinions, even when no arguments for the opinions themselves were provided.

6   Now the very ease of success in these experiments arouses suspicion. Did the subjects actually change their opinions, or were the experimental victories scored only on paper? On grounds of common sense, one must question whether opinions are generally as watery as these studies indicate. There is some reason to wonder whether it was not the investigators who, in their enthusiasm for a theory, were suggestible, and whether the ostensibly gullible subjects were not providing answers which they thought good subjects were expected to give.

7   The investigations were guided by certain underlying assumptions, which today are common currency and account for much that is thought and said

about the operations of propaganda and public opinion. The assumptions are that people submit uncritically and painlessly to external manipulation by suggestion or prestige, and that any given idea or value can be "sold" or "unsold" without reference to its merits. We should be skeptical, however, of the supposition that the power of social pressure necessarily implies uncritical submission to it: independence and the capacity to rise above group passion are also open to human beings. Further, one may question on psychological grounds whether it is possible as a rule to change a person's judgment of a situation or an object without first changing his knowledge or assumptions about it.

8   In what follows I shall describe some experiments in an investigation of the effects of group pressure which was carried out recently with the help of a number of my associates. The tests not only demonstrate the operations of group pressure upon individuals but also illustrate a new kind of attack on the problem and some of the more subtle questions that it raises.

9   A group of seven to nine young men, all college students, are assembled in a classroom for a "psychological experiment" in visual judgment. The experimenter informs them that they will be comparing the lengths of lines. He shows two large white cards [see Figure 1]. On one is a single vertical black line—the standard whose length is to be matched. On the other card are three vertical lines of various lengths. The subjects are to choose the one that is of the same length as the line on the other card. One of the three actually is of the same length; the other two are substantially different, the difference ranging from three quarters of an inch to an inch and three quarters.

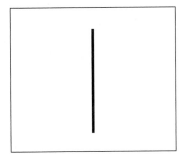 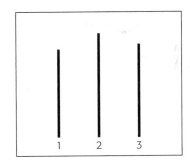

FIGURE 1   Subjects were shown two cards. One bore a standard line. The other bore three lines, one of which was the same length as the standard. The subjects were asked to choose this line.

10   The experiment opens uneventfully. The subjects announce their answers in the order in which they have been seated in the room, and on the first round every person chooses the same matching line. Then a second set of cards is exposed; again the group is unanimous. The members appear ready to endure politely another boring experiment. On the third trial there is an unexpected disturbance. One person near the end of the group disagrees with all the others in his selection of the matching line. He looks surprised, indeed incredulous,

about the disagreement. On the following trial he disagrees again, while the others remain unanimous in their choice. The dissenter becomes more and more worried and hesitant as the disagreement continues in succeeding trials; he may pause before announcing his answer and speak in a low voice, or he may smile in an embarrassed way.

11   What the dissenter does not know is that all the other members of the group were instructed by the experimenter beforehand to give incorrect answers in unanimity at certain points. The single individual who is not a party to this pre-arrangement is the focal subject of our experiment. He is placed in a position in which, while he is actually giving the correct answers, he finds himself unexpectedly in a minority of one, opposed by a unanimous and arbitrary majority with respect to a clear and simple fact. Upon him we have brought to bear two opposed forces: the evidence of his senses and the unanimous opinion of a group of his peers. Also, he must declare his judgments in public, before a majority which has also stated its position publicly.

12   The instructed majority occasionally reports correctly in order to reduce the possibility that the naive subject will suspect collusion against him. (In only a few cases did the subject actually show suspicion; when this happened, the experiment was stopped and the results were not counted.) There are 18 trials in each series, and on 12 of these the majority responds erroneously.

13   How do people respond to group pressure in this situation? I shall report first the statistical results of a series in which a total of 123 subjects from three institutions of higher learning (not including my own Swarthmore College) were placed in the minority situation described above.

14   Two alternatives were open to the subject: he could act independently, repudiating the majority, or he could go along with the majority, repudiating the evidence of his senses. Of the 123 put to the test, a considerable percentage yielded to the majority. Whereas in ordinary circumstances individuals matching the lines will make mistakes less than 1 per cent of the time, under group pressure the minority subjects swung to acceptance of the misleading majority's wrong judgments in 36.8 per cent of the selections.

15   Of course individuals differed in response. At one extreme, about one quarter of the subjects were completely independent and never agreed with the erroneous judgments of the majority. At the other extreme, some individuals went with the majority nearly all the time. The performances of individuals in this experiment tend to be highly consistent. Those who strike out on the path of independence do not, as a rule, succumb to the majority even over an extended series of trials, while those who choose the path of compliance are unable to free themselves as the ordeal is prolonged.

16   The reasons for the startling individual differences have not yet been investigated in detail. At this point we can only report some tentative generalizations from talks with the subjects, each of whom was interviewed at the end of the experiment. Among the independent individuals were many who held fast because of staunch confidence in their own judgment. The most significant fact about them was not absence of responsiveness to the majority but a capacity to recover from doubt and to reestablish their equilibrium. Others who acted independently came to believe that the majority was correct in its answers, but

they continued their dissent on the simple ground that it was their obligation to call the play as they saw it.

17   Among the extremely yielding persons we found a group who quickly reached the conclusion: "I am wrong, they are right." Others yielded in order "not to spoil your results." Many of the individuals who went along suspected that the majority were "sheep" following the first responder, or that the majority were victims of an optical illusion; nevertheless, these suspicions failed to free them at the moment of decision. More disquieting were the reactions of subjects who construed their difference from the majority as a sign of some general deficiency in themselves, which at all costs they must hide. On this basis they desperately tried to merge with the majority, not realizing the longer-range consequences to themselves. All the yielding subjects underestimated the frequency with which they conformed.

18   Which aspect of the influence of a majority is more important—the size of the majority or its unanimity? The experiment was modified to examine this question. In one series the size of the opposition was varied from one to 15 persons. The results showed a clear trend. When a subject was confronted with only a single individual who contradicted his answers, he was swayed little: he continued to answer independently and correctly in nearly all trials. When the opposition was increased to two, the pressure became substantial: minority subjects now accepted the wrong answer 13.6 per cent of the time. Under the pressure of a majority of three, the subjects' errors jumped to 31.8 per cent. But further increases in the size of the majority apparently did not increase the weight of the pressure substantially. Clearly the size of the opposition is important only up to a point.

19   Disturbance of the majority's unanimity had a striking effect. In this experiment the subject was given the support of a truthful partner—either another individual who did not know of the prearranged agreement among the rest of the group, or a person who was instructed to give correct answers throughout.

20   The presence of a supporting partner depleted the majority of much of its power. Its pressure on the dissenting individual was reduced to one fourth: that is, subjects answered incorrectly only one fourth as often as under the pressure of a unanimous majority. The weakest persons did not yield as readily. Most interesting were the reactions to the partner. Generally the feeling toward him was one of warmth and closeness; he was credited with inspiring confidence. However, the subjects repudiated the suggestion that the partner decided them to be independent.

21   Was the partner's effect a consequence of his dissent, or was it related to his accuracy? We now introduced into the experimental group a person who was instructed to dissent from the majority but also to disagree with the subject. In some experiments the majority was always to choose the worst of the comparison lines and the instructed dissenter to pick the line that was closer to the length of the standard one; in others the majority was consistently intermediate and the dissenter most in error. In this manner we were able to study the relative influence of "compromising" and "extremist" dissenters.

22   Again the results are clear. When a moderate dissenter is present the effect of the majority on the subject decreases by approximately one third, and

extremes of yielding disappear. Moreover, most of the errors the subjects do make are moderate, rather than flagrant. In short, the dissenter largely controls the choice of errors. To this extent the subjects broke away from the majority even while bending to it.

23   On the other hand, when the dissenter always chose the line that was more flagrantly different from the standard, the results were of quite a different kind. The extremist dissenter produced a remarkable freeing of the subjects; their errors dropped to only 9 percent. Furthermore, all the errors were of the moderate variety. We were able to conclude that dissents *per se* increased independence and moderated the errors that occurred, and that the direction of dissent exerted consistent effects.

24   In all the foregoing experiments each subject was observed only in a single setting. We now turned to studying the effects upon a given individual of a change in the situation to which he was exposed. The first experiment examined the consequences of losing or gaining a partner. The instructed partner began by answering correctly on the first six trials. With his support the subject usually resisted pressure from the majority: 18 of 27 subjects were completely independent. But after six trials the partner joined the majority. As soon as he did so, there was an abrupt rise in the subjects' errors. Their submission to the majority was just about as frequent as when the minority subject was opposed by a unanimous majority throughout.

25   It was surprising to find that the experience of having had a partner and of having braved the majority opposition with him had failed to strengthen the individuals' independence. Questioning at the conclusion of the experiment suggested that we had overlooked an important circumstance; namely, the strong specific effect of "desertion" by the partner to the other side. We therefore changed the conditions so that the partner would simply leave the group at the proper point. (To allay suspicion it was announced in advance that he had an appointment with the dean.) In this form of the experiment, the partner's effect outlasted his presence. The errors increased after his departure, but less markedly than after a partner switched to the majority.

26   In a variant of this procedure the trials began with the majority unanimously giving correct answers. Then they gradually broke away until on the sixth trial the naive subject was alone and the group unanimously against him. As long as the subject had anyone on his side, he was almost invariably independent, but as soon as he found himself alone, the tendency to conform to the majority rose abruptly.

27   As might be expected, an individual's resistance to group pressure in these experiments depends to a considerable degree on how wrong the majority was. We varied the discrepancy between the standard line and the other lines systematically, with the hope of reaching a point where the error of the majority would be so glaring that every subject would repudiate it and choose independently. In this we regretfully did not succeed. Even when the difference between the lines was seven inches, there were still some who yielded to the error of the majority.

28   The study provides clear answers to a few relatively simple questions, and it raises many others that await investigation. We would like to know the degree of consistency of persons in situations which differ in content and structure. If

consistency of independence or conformity in behavior is shown to be a fact, how is it functionally related to qualities of character and personality? In what ways is independence related to sociological or cultural conditions? Are leaders more independent than other people, or are they adept at following their followers? These and many other questions may perhaps be answerable by investigations of the type described here.

29   Life in society requires consensus as an indispensable condition. But consensus, to be productive, requires that each individual contribute independently out of his experience and insight. When consensus comes under the dominance of conformity, the social process is polluted and the individual at the same time surrenders the powers on which his functioning as a feeling and thinking being depends. That we have found the tendency to conformity in our society so strong that reasonably intelligent and well-meaning young people are willing to call white black is a matter of concern. It raises questions about our ways of education and about the values that guide our conduct.

30   Yet anyone inclined to draw too pessimistic conclusions from this report would do well to remind himself that the capacities for independence are not to be underestimated. He may also draw some consolation from a further observation: those who participated in this challenging experiment agreed nearly without exception that independence was preferable to conformity.

Review Questions

1. What is "suggestibility"? How is this phenomenon related to social pressure?

2. Summarize the procedure and results of the Asch experiment. What conclusions does Asch draw from these results?

3. To what extent did varying the size of the majority and its unanimity affect the experimental results?

4. What distinction does Asch draw between consensus and conformity?

Discussion and Writing Suggestions

1. Before discussing the experiment, Asch considers how easily people's opinions or attitudes may be shaped by social pressure. To what extent do you agree with this conclusion? Write a short paper on this subject, drawing upon examples from your own experience or observation or from your reading.

2. Do the results of this experiment surprise you? Or do they confirm facts about human behavior that you had already suspected, observed, or experienced? Explain, in two or three paragraphs. Provide examples, relating these examples to features of the Asch experiment.

3. Frequently, the conclusions drawn from a researcher's experimental results are challenged on the basis that laboratory conditions do not accurately reflect the complexity of human behavior. Asch draws certain conclusions about the degree to which individuals are affected by group pressures based on an experiment involving subjects choosing matching line lengths. To what extent, if any, do you believe that these conclusions lack validity because the behavior at the heart of the experiment is too dissimilar to real-life situations of group pressure on the individual? Support your opinions with examples.

4. We are all familiar with the phenomenon of "peer pressure." To what extent do Asch's experiments demonstrate the power of peer pressure? To what extent do you think that other factors may be at work? Explain, providing examples.

5. Asch's experiments, conducted in the early 1950s, involved groups of "seven to nine young men, all college students." To what extent do you believe that the results of a similar experiment would be different today? To what extent might they be different if the subjects had included women, as well, and subjects of various ages, from children, to middle-aged people, to older people? To what extent do you believe that the social class or culture of the subjects might have an impact upon the experimental results? Support your opinions with examples and logical reasoning. (Beware, however, of overgeneralizing, based upon insufficient evidence.)

The Perils of Obedience
Stanley Milgram

In 1963, a Yale psychologist conducted one of the classic studies on obedience that Doris Lessing refers to in "Group Minds." Stanley Milgram designed an experiment that forced participants either to violate their conscience by obeying the immoral demands of an authority figure or to refuse those demands. Surprisingly, Milgram found that few participants could resist the authority's orders, even when the participants knew that following these orders would result in another person's pain. Were the participants in these experiments incipient mass murderers? No, said Milgram. They were "ordinary people, simply doing their jobs." The implications of Milgram's conclusions are immense.

Consider: Where does evil reside? What sort of people were responsible for the Holocaust, and for the long list of other atrocities that seem to blight the human record in every generation? Is it a lunatic fringe, a few sick but powerful people who are responsible for atrocities? If so, then we decent folk needn't ever look inside ourselves to understand evil since (by our definition) evil lurks out there, in "those sick ones." Milgram's study suggested otherwise: that under a special set of circumstances the obedience we naturally show authority figures can transform us into agents of terror.

The article that follows is one of the longest in this text, and it may help you to know in advance the author's organization. In paragraphs 1–11, Milgram discusses the larger significance and the history of dilemmas involving obedience to authority; he then summarizes his basic experimental design and follows with a report of one experiment. Milgram organizes the remainder of his article into sections, which he has subtitled "An Unexpected Outcome," "Peculiar Reactions," "The Etiquette of Submission," and "Duty without Conflict." He begins his conclusion in paragraph 108. If you find the article too long to complete in a single sitting, then plan to read sections at a time, taking notes on each until you're done. Anticipate the article immediately following Milgram's: it reviews his work and largely concerns the ethics of his experimental design. Consider these ethics as you read so that you, in turn, can respond to Milgram's critics.

Stanley Milgram (1933–1984) taught and conducted research at Yale and Harvard universities and at the Graduate Center, City University of New York. He was named Guggenheim Fellow in 1972–1973 and a year later was nominated for the National Book Award for Obedience to Authority. *His other books include* Television and Antisocial Behavior *(1973),* The City and the Self *(1974),* Human Aggression *(1976), and* The Individual in the Social World *(1977).*

1   Obedience is as basic an element in the structure of social life as one can point to. Some system of authority is a requirement of all communal living, and it is only the person dwelling in isolation who is not forced to respond, with defiance or submission, to the commands of others. For many people, obedience is a deeply ingrained behavior tendency, indeed a potent impulse overriding training in ethics, sympathy, and moral conduct.

2   The dilemma inherent in submission to authority is ancient, as old as the story of Abraham, and the question of whether one should obey when commands conflict with conscience has been argued by Plato, dramatized in *Antigone,* and treated to philosophic analysis in almost every historical epoch. Conservative philosophers argue that the very fabric of society is threatened by disobedience, while humanists stress the primacy of the individual conscience.

3   The legal and philosophic aspects of obedience are of enormous import, but they say very little about how most people behave in concrete situations. I set up a simple experiment at Yale University to test how much pain an ordinary citizen would inflict on another person simply because he was ordered to by an experimental scientist. Stark authority was pitted against the subjects' strongest moral imperatives against hurting others, and with the subjects' ears ringing with the screams of the victims, authority won more often than not. The extreme willingness of adults to go to almost any lengths on the command of an authority constitutes the chief finding of the study and the fact most urgently demanding explanation.

4   In the basic experimental design, two people come to a psychology laboratory to take part in a study of memory and learning. One of them is designated as a "teacher" and the other a "learner." The experimenter explains that the study is concerned with the effects of punishment on learning. The learner is conducted into a room, seated in a kind of miniature electric chair; his arms are strapped to prevent excessive movement, and an electrode is attached to his

wrist. He is told that he will be read lists of simple word pairs, and that he will then be tested on his ability to remember the second word of a pair when he hears the first one again. Whenever he makes an error, he will receive electric shocks of increasing intensity.

5   The real focus of the experiment is the teacher. After watching the learner being strapped into place, he is seated before an impressive shock generator. The instrument panel consists of thirty level switches set in a horizontal line. Each switch is clearly labeled with a voltage designation ranging from 15 to 450 volts. The following designations are clearly indicated for groups of four switches, going from left to right: Slight Shock, Moderate Shock, Strong Shock, Very Strong Shock, Intense Shock, Extreme Intensity Shock, Danger: Severe Shock. (Two switches after this last designation are simply marked XXX.)

6   When a switch is depressed, a pilot light corresponding to each switch is illuminated in bright red; an electric buzzing is heard; a blue light, labeled "voltage energizer," flashes; the dial on the voltage meter swings to the right; and various relay clicks sound off.

7   The upper left-hand corner of the generator is labeled SHOCK GENERATOR, TYPE ZLB, DYSON INSTRUMENT COMPANY, WALTHAM, MASS. OUTPUT 15 VOLTS–450 VOLTS.

8   Each subject is given a sample 45-volt shock from the generator before his run as teacher, and the jolt strengthens his belief in the authenticity of the machine.

9   The teacher is a genuinely naive subject who has come to the laboratory for the experiment. The learner, or victim, is actually an actor who receives no shock at all. The point of the experiment is to see how far a person will proceed in a concrete and measurable situation in which he is ordered to inflict increasing pain on a protesting victim.

10   Conflict arises when the man receiving the shock begins to show that he is experiencing discomfort. At 75 volts, he grunts; at 120 volts, he complains loudly; at 150, he demands to be released from the experiment. As the voltage increases, his protests become more vehement and emotional. At 285 volts, his response can be described only as an agonized scream. Soon thereafter, he makes no sound at all.

11   For the teacher, the situation quickly becomes one of gripping tension. It is not a game for him; conflict is intense and obvious. The manifest suffering of the learner presses him to quit; but each time he hesitates to administer a shock, the experimenter orders him to continue. To extricate himself from this plight, the subject must make a clear break with authority.[1]

12   The subject, Gretchen Brandt,[2] is an attractive thirty-one-year-old medical technician who works at the Yale Medical School. She had emigrated from Germany five years before.

13   On several occasions when the learner complains, she turns to the experimenter coolly and inquires, "Shall I continue?" She promptly returns to her task when the experimenter asks her to do so. At the administration of 210 volts,

---

[1]The ethical problems of carrying out an experiment of this sort are too complex to be dealt with here, but they receive extended treatment in the book from which this article is adapted.

[2]Names of subjects described in this piece have been changed.

she turns to the experimenter, remarking firmly, "Well, I'm sorry, I don't think we should continue."

14 EXPERIMENTER: The experiment requires that you go on until he has learned all the word pairs correctly.

15 BRANDT: He has a heart condition. I'm sorry. He told you that before.

16 EXPERIMENTER: The shocks may be painful but they are not dangerous.

17 BRANDT: Well, I'm sorry, I think when shocks continue like this, they *are* dangerous. You ask him if he wants to get out. It's his free will.

18 EXPERIMENTER: It is absolutely essential that we continue....

19 BRANDT: I'd like you to ask him. We came here of our free will. If he wants to continue I'll go ahead. He told you he had a heart condition. I'm sorry. I don't want to be responsible for anything happening to him. I wouldn't like it for me either.

20 EXPERIMENTER: You have no other choice.

21 BRANDT: I think we are here on our own free will. I don't want to be responsible if anything happens to him. Please understand that.

22   She refuses to go further and the experiment is terminated.

23   The woman is firm and resolute throughout. She indicates in the interview that she was in no way tense or nervous, and this corresponds to her controlled appearance during the experiment. She feels that the last shock she administered to the learner was extremely painful and reiterates that she "did not want to be responsible for any harm to him."

24   The woman's straightforward, courteous behavior in the experiment, lack of tension, and total control of her own action seem to make disobedience a simple and rational deed. Her behavior is the very embodiment of what I envisioned would be true for almost all subjects.

An Unexpected Outcome

25 Before the experiments, I sought predictions about the outcome from various kinds of people—psychiatrists, college sophomores, middle-class adults, graduate students, and faculty in the behavioral sciences. With remarkable similarity, they predicted that virtually all subject would refuse to obey the experimenter. The psychiatrists, specifically, predicted that most subjects would not go beyond 150 volts, when the victim makes his first explicit demand to be freed. They expected that only 4 percent would reach 300 volts, and that only a pathological fringe of about one in a thousand would administer the highest shock on the board.

26   These predictions were unequivocally wrong. Of the forty subjects in the first experiment, twenty-five obeyed the orders of the experimenter to the end, punishing the victim until they reached the most potent shock available on the generator. After 450 volts were administered three times, the experimenter called a halt to the session. Many obedient subjects then heaved sights of relief, mopped their brows, rubbed their fingers over their eyes, or nervously fumbled cigarettes. Others displayed only minimal signs of tension from beginning to end.

27   When the very first experiments were carried out, Yale undergraduates were used as subjects, and about 60 percent of them were fully obedient. A colleague of mine immediately dismissed these findings as having no relevance to "ordinary" people, asserting that Yale undergraduates are a highly aggressive, competitive bunch who step on each other's necks on the slightest provocation. He assured me that when "ordinary" people were tested, the results would be quite different. As we moved from the pilot studies to the regular experimental series, people drawn from every stratum of New Haven life came to be employed in the experiment: professionals, white-collar workers, unemployed persons, and industrial workers. *The experiment's total outcome was the same as we had observed among the students.*

28   Moreover, when the experiments were repeated in Princeton, Munich, Rome, South Africa, and Australia, the level of obedience was invariably somewhat *higher* than found in the investigation reported in this article. Thus one scientist in Munich found 85 percent of his subjects to be obedient.

29   Fred Prozi's reactions, if more dramatic than most, illuminate the conflicts experienced by others in less visible form. About fifty years old and unemployed at the time of the experiment, he has a good-natured, if slightly dissolute, appearance, and he strikes people as a rather ordinary fellow. He begins the session calmly but becomes tense as it proceeds. After delivering the 180-volt shock, he pivots around in his chair and, shaking his head, addresses the experimenter in agitated tones:

30 PROZI: I can't stand it. I'm not going to kill that man in there. You hear him hollering?

31 EXPERIMENTER: As I told you before, the shocks may be painful, but …

32 PROZI: But he's hollering. He can't stand it. What's going to happen to him?

33 EXPERIMENTER: (*his voice patient, matter-of-fact*): The experiment requires that you continue, Teacher.

34 PROZI: Aaah, but unh, I'm not going to get that man sick in there—know what I mean?

35 EXPERIMENTER: Whether the learner likes it or not, we must go on, through all the word pairs.

36 PROZI: I refuse to take the responsibility. He's in there hollering!

37 EXPERIMENTER: It's absolutely essential that you continue, Prozi.

38 PROZI: (*indicating the unused questions*): There's too many left here. I mean, Jeez, if he gets them wrong, there's too many of them left. I mean, who's going to take the responsibility if anything happens to that gentleman?

39 EXPERIMENTER: I'm responsible for anything that happens to him. Continue, please.

40 PROZI: All right. (*Consults list of words.*) The next one's "Slow—walk, truck, dance, music." Answer, please (*A buzzing sound indicates the learner has signaled his answer.*) Wrong. A hundred and ninety-five volts. "Dance." (*Zzumph!*)

41 LEARNER: (*yelling*): Let me out of here! My heart's bothering me! (*Teacher looks at experimenter.*)

42 EXPERIMENTER: Continue, please.

43 LEARNER (*screaming*): Let me out of here! You have no right to keep me here! Let me out of here, my heart's bothering me, let me out!

44 PROZI: (*shakes head, pats the table nervously*): You see, he's hollering. Hear that? Gee, I don't know.

45 EXPERIMENTER: The experiment requires …

46 PROZI (*interrupting*): I know it does, sir, but I mean—hunh! He don't know what he's getting in for. He's up to 195 volts! (*Experiment continues, through 210 volts, 225 volts, 240 volts, 255 volts, 270 volts, at which point Prozi, with evident relief, runs out of word-pair questions.*)

47 EXPERIMENTER: You'll have to go back to the beginning of that page and go through them again until he's learned them all correctly.

48 PROZI: Aw, no. I'm not going to kill that man. You mean I've got to keep going up with the scale? No sir. He's hollering in there. I'm not going to give him 450 volts.

49 EXPERIMENTER: The experiment requires that you go on.

50 LEARNER: Ohhh. I absolutely refuse to answer anymore. (*Shouting urgently now.*) Let me out of here! You can't hold me here! Get me out. Get-me-out-of-here!

51 EXPERIMENTER: Continue. The next word is "Green," please.

52 PROZI: "Green—grass, hat, ink, apple." (*Nothing happens. No answering buzz. Just gloomy silence.*)

53 PROZI: I don't think he is going to answer.

54 EXPERIMENTER: If the learner doesn't answer in a reasonable time, about four or five seconds, consider the answer wrong. And follow the same procedures you have been doing for wrong answers. Say, "Wrong," tell him the number of volts, give him the punishment, read him the correct answer. Continue, please.

55 PROZI: "Green—grass, hat, ink, apple." Answer, please. (*More silence. Subject just sits there.*)

56 EXPERIMENTER: Go on with the procedure, please.

57 PROZI: Three hundred and fifteen volts. The answer is "ink." (*Zzumph!*)

58 LEARNER: Ohh. Ooohh.

59 PROZI: (*relieved to hear response*): Next one …

60 LEARNER: I absolutely refuse to answer.

61 PROZI: You got to. You get a shock if you don't answer. (*Experiment continues with learner refusing to answer, and finally, failing even to grunt or groan. At 375 volts, the subject stands up.*)

62 PROZI: I think something's happened to that fellow in there. I don't get no answer. He was hollering at less voltage. Can't you check in and see if he's all right, please?

63 EXPERIMENTER: (*with same detached calm*): Not once we've started. Please continue, Teacher.

64 PROZI (*sits down, sighs deeply*): "Cool—day, shade, water, paint." Answer, please. Are you all right in there? Are you all right?

65 EXPERIMENTER: Please continue, Teacher. Continue, please. (*Subject pushes lever. Zzumph!*)

66 PROZI (*swiveling around in his chair*): Something's happened to that man in there. (*Swiveling back.*) Next one. "Low—dollar, necklace, moon, paint."

(*Turning around again.*) Something's happened to that man in there. You better check on him, sir. He won't answer or nothing.

67 EXPERIMENTER: Continue. Go on, please.

68 PROZI: You accept all responsibility?

69 EXPERIMENTER: The responsibility is mine. Correct. Please go on. (*Subject returns to his list, starts running through words as rapidly as he can read them, works through to 450 volts.*)

70 PROZI: That's that.

71 EXPERIMENTER: Continue using the 450 switch for each wrong answer. Continue, please.

72 PROZI: But I don't get anything!

73 EXPERIMENTER: Please continue. The next word is "white."

74 PROZI: Don't you think you should look in on him, please?

75 EXPERIMENTER: Not once we've started the experiment.

76 PROZI: What if he's dead in there? (*Gestures toward the room with the electric chair.*) I mean, he told me he can't stand the shock, sir. I don't mean to be rude, but I think you should look in on him. All you have to do is look in on him. All you have to do is look in the door. I don't get no answer, no noise. Something might have happened to the gentleman in there, sir.

77 EXPERIMENTER: We must continue. Go on, please.

78 PROZI: You mean keep giving him what? Four-hundred-fifty volts, what he's got now?

79 EXPERIMENTER: That's correct. Continue. The next word is "white."

80 PROZI: (*now at a furious pace*): "White—cloud, horse, rock, house." Answer, please. The answer is "horse." Four hundred and fifty volts. (*Zzumph!*) Next word, "Bag—paint, music, clown, girl." The answer is "paint." Four hundred and fifty volts. (*Zzumph!*) Next word is "Short—sentence, movie …"

81 EXPERIMENTER: Excuse me, Teacher. We'll have to discontinue the experiment.

Peculiar Reactions

82 Morris Braverman, another subject, is a thirty-nine-year-old social worker. He looks older than his years because of his bald head and serious demeanor. His brow is furrowed, as if all the world's burdens were carried on his face. He appears intelligent and concerned.

83   When the learner refuses to answer and the experimenter instructs Braverman to treat the absence of an answer as equivalent to a wrong answer, he takes his instruction to heart. Before administering 300 volts he asserts officiously to the victim, "Mr. Wallace, your silence has to be considered as a wrong answer." Then he administers the shock. He offers half-heartedly to change places with the learner, then asks the experimenter, "Do I have to follow these instructions literally?" He is satisfied with the experimenter's answer that he does. His very refined and authoritative manner of speaking is increasingly broken up by wheezing laughter.

84   The experimenter's notes on Mr. Braverman at the last few shocks are:

> Almost breaking up now each time gives shock. Rubbing face to hide laughter. Squinting, trying to hide face with hand, still laughing. Cannot control his laughter at this point no matter what he does. Clenching fist, pushing it onto table.

85   In an interview after the session, Mr. Braverman summarizes the experiment with impressive fluency and intelligence. He feels the experiment may have been designed also to "test the effects on the teacher of being in an essentially sadistic role, as well as the reactions of a student to a learning situation that was authoritative and punitive." When asked how painful the last few shocks administered to the learner were, he indicates that the most extreme category on the scale is not adequate (it read EXTREMELY PAINFUL) and places his mark at the edge of the scale with an arrow carrying it beyond the scale.

86   It is almost impossible to convey the greatly relaxed, sedate quality of his conversation in the interview. In the most relaxed terms, he speaks about his severe inner tension.

87 EXPERIMENTER: At what point were you most tense or nervous?

88 MR. BRAVERMAN: Well, when he first began to cry out in pain, and I realized this was hurting him. This got worse when he just blocked and refused to answer. There was I. I'm a nice person, I think, hurting somebody, and caught up in what seemed a mad situation... and in the interest of science, one goes through with it.

89   When the interviewer pursues the general question of tension, Mr. Braverman spontaneously mentions his laughter.

90   "My reactions were awfully peculiar. I don't know if you were watching me, but my reactions were giggly, and trying to stifle laughter. This isn't the way I usually am. This was a sheer reaction to a totally impossible situation. And my reaction was to the situation of having to hurt somebody. And being totally helpless and caught up in a set of circumstances where I just couldn't deviate and I couldn't try to help. This is what got me."

91   Mr. Braverman, like all subjects, was told the actual nature and purpose of the experiment, and a year later he affirmed in a questionnaire that he had learned something of personal importance: "What appalled me was that I could possess this capacity for obedience and compliance to a central idea, i.e., the value of a memory experiment, even after it became clear that continued adherence to this value was at the expense of violation of another value, i.e., don't hurt someone who is helpless and not hurting you. As my wife said, 'You can call yourself Eichmann.'[3] I hope I deal more effectively with any future conflicts of values I encounter."

The Etiquette of Submission

92 One theoretical interpretation of this behavior holds that all people harbor deeply aggressive instincts continually pressing for expression, and that the experiment provides institutional justification for the release of these impulses. According to this view, if a person is placed in a situation in which he has complete power

---

[3]*Adolf Eichmann* (1906–1962), the Nazi official responsible for implementing Hitler's "Final Solution" to exterminate the Jews, escaped to Argentina after World War II. In 1960, Israeli agents captured him and brought him to Israel, where he was tried as a war criminal and sentenced to death. At his trial, Eichmann maintained that he was merely following orders in arranging murders of his victims.

over another individual, whom he may punish as much as he likes, all that is sadistic and bestial in man comes to the fore. The impulse to shock the victim is seen to flow from the potent aggressive tendencies, which are part of the motivational life of the individual, and the experiment, because it provides social legitimacy, simply opens the door to their expression.

93   It becomes vital, therefore, to compare the subject's performance when he is under orders and when he is allowed to choose the shock level.

94   The procedure was identical to our standard experiment, except that the teacher was told that he was free to select any shock level on any of the trials. (The experimenter took pains to point out that the teacher could use the highest levels on the generator, the lowest, any in between, or any combination of levels.) Each subject proceeded for thirty critical trials. The learner's protests were coordinated to standard shock levels, his first grunt coming at 75 volts, his first vehement protest at 150 volts.

95   The average shock used during the thirty critical trials was less than 60 volts— lower than the point at which the victim showed the first signs of discomfort. Three of the forty subjects did not go beyond the very lowest level on the board, twenty-eight went no higher than 75 volts, and thirty-eight did not go beyond the first loud protest at 150 volts. Two subjects provided the exception, administering up to 325 and 450 volts, but the overall result was that the great majority of people delivered very low, usually painless, shocks when the choice was explicitly up to them.

96   This condition of the experiment undermines another commonly offered explanation of the subjects' behavior—that those who shocked the victim at the most severe levels came only from the sadistic fringe of society. If one considers that almost two-thirds of the participants fall into the category of "obedient" subjects, and that they represented ordinary people drawn from working, managerial, and professional classes, the argument becomes very shaky. Indeed, it is highly reminiscent of the issue that arose in connection with Hannah Arendt's 1963 book, *Eichmann in Jerusalem.* Arendt contended that the prosecution's efforts to depict Eichmann as a sadistic monster was fundamentally wrong, that he came closer to being an uninspired bureaucrat who simply sat at his desk and did his job. For asserting her views, Arendt became the object of considerable scorn, even calumny. Somehow, it was felt that the monstrous deeds carried out by Eichmann required a brutal, twisted personality, evil incarnate. After witnessing hundreds of ordinary persons submit to the authority in our own experiments, I must conclude that Arendt's conception of the banality of evil comes closer to the truth than one might dare imagine. The ordinary person who shocked the victim did so out of a sense of obligation—an impression of his duties as a subject—and not from any peculiarly aggressive tendencies.

97   This is, perhaps, the most fundamental lesson of our study: ordinary people, simply doing their jobs, and without any particular hostility on their part, can become agents in a terrible destructive process. Moreover, even when the destructive effects of their work become patently clear, and they are asked to carry out actions incompatible with fundamental standards of morality, relatively few people have the resources needed to resist authority.

98   Many of the people were in some sense against what they did to the learner, and many protested even while they obeyed. Some were totally convinced of the wrongness of their actions but could not bring themselves to make an open break with authority. They often derived satisfaction from their thoughts and felt that—within themselves, at least—they had been on the side of the angels. They tried to reduce strain by obeying the experimenter but "only slightly," encouraging the learner, touching the generator switches gingerly. When interviewed, such a subject would stress that he had "asserted my humanity" by administering the briefest shock possible. Handling the conflict in this manner was easier than defiance.

99   The situation is constructed so that there is no way the subject can stop shocking the learner without violating the experimenter's definitions of his own competence. The subject fears that he will appear arrogant, untoward, and rude if he breaks off. Although these inhibiting emotions appear small in scope alongside the violence being done to the learner, they suffuse the mind and feelings of the subject, who is miserable at the prospect of having to repudiate the authority to his face. (When the experiment was altered so that the experimenter gave his instructions by telephone instead of in person, only a third as many people were fully obedient through 450 volts.) It is a curious thing that a measure of compassion on the part of the subject—an unwillingness to "hurt" the experimenter's feelings—is part of those binding forces inhibiting his disobedience. The withdrawal of such deference may be as painful to the subject as to the authority he defies.

Duty without Conflict

100 The subjects do not derive satisfaction from inflicting pain, but they often like the feeling they get from pleasing the experimenter. They are proud of doing a good job, obeying the experimenter under difficult circumstances. While the subjects administered only mild shocks on their own initiative, one experimental variation showed that, under orders, 30 percent of them were willing to deliver 450 volts even when they had to forcibly push the learner's hand down on the electrode.

101   Bruno Batta is a thirty-seven-year-old welder who took part in the variation requiring the use of force. He was born in New Haven, his parents in Italy. He has a rough-hewn face that conveys a conspicuous lack of alertness. He has some difficulty in mastering the experimental procedure and needs to be corrected by the experimenter several times. He shows appreciation for the help and willingness to do what is required. After the 150-volt level, Batta has to force the learner's hand down on the shock plate, since the learner himself refuses to touch it.

102   When the learner first complains, Mr. Batta pays no attention to him. His face remains impassive, as if to dissociate himself from the learner's disruptive behavior. When the experimenter instructs him to force the learner's hand down, he adopts a rigid, mechanical procedure. He tests the generator switch. When it fails to function, he immediately forces the learner's hand onto the shock plate. All the while he maintains the same rigid mask. The learner, seated alongside him, begs him to stop, but with robotic impassivity he continues the procedure.

103   What is extraordinary is his apparent total indifference to the learner; he hardly takes cognizance of him as a human being. Meanwhile, he relates to the experimenter in a submissive and courteous fashion.

104   At the 330-volt level, the learner refuses not only to touch the shock plate but also to provide any answers. Annoyed, Batta turns to him, and chastises him: "You better answer and get it over with. We can't stay here all night." These are the only words he directs to the learner in the course of an hour. Never again does he speak to him. The scene is brutal and depressing, his hard, impassive face showing total indifference as he subdues the screaming learner and gives him shocks. He seems to derive no pleasure from the act itself, only quiet satisfaction at doing his job properly.

105   When he administers 450 volts, he turns to the experimenter and asks, "Where do we go from here, Professor?" His tone is deferential and express-es his willingness to be a cooperative subject, in contrast to the learner's obstinacy.

106   At the end of the session he tells the experimenter how honored he has been to help him, and in a moment of contrition, remarks, "Sir, sorry it could-n't have been a full experiment."

107   He has done his honest best. It is only the deficient behavior of the learner that has denied the experimenter full satisfaction.

108   The essence of obedience is that a person comes to view himself as the instrument for carrying out another person's wishes, and he therefore no longer regards himself as responsible for his actions. Once this critical shift of viewpoint has occurred, all of the essential features of obedience follow. The most far-reaching consequence is that the person feels responsible *to* the authority directing him but feels no responsibility *for* the content of the actions that the authority prescribes. Morality does not disappear—it acquires a radically differ-ent focus: the subordinate person feels shame or pride depending on how ade-quately he has performed the actions called for by authority.

109   Language provides numerous terms to pinpoint this type of morality: *loyal-ty, duty, discipline* all are terms heavily saturated with moral meaning and refer to the degree to which a person fulfills his obligations to authority. They refer not to the "goodness" of the person per se but to the adequacy with which a subordinate fulfills his socially defined role. The most frequent defense of the individual who has performed a heinous act under command of authority is that he has simply done his duty. In asserting this defense, the individual is not intro-ducing an alibi concocted for the moment but is reporting honestly on the psy-chological attitude induced by submission to authority.

110   For a person to feel responsible for his actions, he must sense that the behavior has flowed from "the self." In the situation we have studied, subjects have precisely the opposite view of their actions—namely, they see them as originating in the motives of some other person. Subjects in the experiment fre-quently said, "If it were up to me, I would not have administered shocks to the learner."

111   Once authority has been isolated as the cause of the subject's behavior, it is legitimate to inquire into the necessary elements of authority and how it must be perceived in order to gain compliance. We conducted some investigations

into the kinds of changes that would cause the experimenter to lose his power and to be disobeyed by the subject. Some of the variations revealed that:

- *The experimenter's physical presence has a marked impact on his authority.* As cited earlier, obedience dropped off sharply when orders were given by telephone. The experimenter could often induce a disobedient subject to go on by returning to the laboratory.
- *Conflicting authority severely paralyzes action.* When two experimenters of equal status, both seated at the command desk, gave incompatible orders, no shocks were delivered past the point of their disagreement.
- *The rebellious action of others severely undermines authority.* In one variation, three teachers (two actors and a real subject) administered a test and shocks. When the two actors disobeyed the experimenter and refused to go beyond a certain shock level, thirty-six of the forty subjects joined their disobedient peers and refused as well.

112   Although the experimenter's authority was fragile in some respects, it is also true that he had almost none of the tools used in ordinary command structures. For example, the experimenter did not threaten the subjects with punishment—such as loss of income, community ostracism, or jail—for failure to obey. Neither could he offer incentives. Indeed, we should expect the experimenter's authority to be much less than that of someone like a general, since the experimenter has no power to enforce his imperatives, and since participation in a psychological experiment scarcely evokes the sense of urgency and dedication found in warfare. Despite these limitations, he still managed to command a dismaying degree of obedience.

113   I will cite one final variation of the experiment that depicts a dilemma that is more common in everyday life. The subject was not ordered to pull the lever that shocked the victim, but merely to perform a subsidiary task (administering the word-pair test) while another person administered the shock. In this situation, thirty-seven of forty adults continued to the highest level on the shock generator. Predictably, they excused their behavior by saying that the responsibility belonged to the man who actually pulled the switch. This may illustrate a dangerously typical arrangement in a complex society: it is easy to ignore responsibility when one is only an intermediate link in a chain of action.

114   The problem of obedience is not wholly psychological. The form and shape of society and the way it is developing have much to do with it. There was a time, perhaps, when people were able to give a fully human response to any situation because they were fully absorbed in it as human beings. But as soon as there was a division of labor things changed. Beyond a certain point, the breaking up of society into people carrying out narrow and very special jobs takes away from the human quality of work and life. A person does not get to see the whole situation but only a small part of it, and is thus unable to act without some kind of overall direction. He yields to authority but in doing so is alienated from his own actions.

115   Even Eichmann was sickened when he toured the concentration camps, but he had only to sit at a desk and shuffle papers. At the same time the man in

the camp who actually dropped Cyclon-b into the gas chambers was able to justify *his* behavior on the ground that he was only following orders from above. Thus there is a fragmentation of the total human act; no one is confronted with the consequences of his decision to carry out the evil act. The person who assumes responsibility has evaporated. Perhaps this is the most common characteristic of socially organized evil in modern society.

Review Questions

1. Milgram states that obedience is a basic element in the structure of social life. How so?

2. What is the dilemma inherent in obedience to authority?

3. Summarize the obedience experiments.

4. What predictions did experts and laypeople make about the experiments before they were conducted? How did these predictions compare with the experimental results?

5. What are Milgram's views regarding the two assumptions bearing on his experiment that (1) people are naturally aggressive and (2) a lunatic, sadistic fringe is responsible for shocking learners to the maximum limit?

6. How do Milgram's findings corroborate Hannah Arendt's thesis about the "banality of evil"?

7. What, according to Milgram, is the "essence of obedience"?

8. How did being an intermediate link in a chain of action affect a subject's willingness to continue with the experiment?

9. In the article's final two paragraphs, Milgram speaks of a "fragmentation of the total human act." To what is he referring?

Discussion and Writing Suggestions

1. "Conservative philosophers argue that the very fabric of society is threatened by disobedience, while humanists stress the primacy of the individual conscience." Develop the arguments of both the conservative and the humanist regarding obedience to authority. Be prepared to debate the ethics of obedience by defending one position or the other.

2. Would you have been glad to have participated in the Milgram experiments? Why or why not?

3. The ethics of Milgram's experimental design came under sharp attack. Diana Baumrind's review of the experiment typifies the crit-

icism; but before you read her work, try to anticipate the objections she raises.

4. Given the general outcome of the experiments, why do you suppose Milgram gives as his first example of a subject's response the German émigré's refusal to continue the electrical shocks?

5. Does the outcome of the experiment upset you in any way? Do you feel the experiment teaches us anything new about human nature?

6. Comment on Milgram's skill as a writer of description. How effectively does he portray his subjects when introducing them? When recreating their tension in the experiment?

7. Mrs. Braverman said to her husband: "You can call yourself Eichmann." Do you agree with Mrs. Braverman? Explain.

8. Reread paragraphs 29 through 81, the transcript of the experiment in which Mr. Prozi participated. Appreciating that Prozi was debriefed, that is, was assured that no harm came to the learner, imagine what Prozi might have been thinking as he drove home after the experiment. Develop your thoughts into a monologue, written in the first person, with Prozi at the wheel of his car.

Review of Stanley Milgram's Experiments on Obedience
Diana Baumrind

Many of Milgram's colleagues saluted him for providing that "hard information" about human nature that Doris Lessing speaks of. Others attacked him for violating the rights of his subjects. Still others faulted his experimental design and claimed he could not, with any validity, speculate on life outside the laboratory based on the behavior of his subjects within.

In the following review, psychologist Diana Baumrind excoriates Milgram for "entrapping" his subjects and potentially harming their "self-image or ability to trust adult authorities in the future." In a footnote (p. 334), we summarize Milgram's response to Baumrind's critique.

Diana Baumrind is a psychologist who, when writing this review, worked at the Institute of Human Development, University of California, Berkeley. The review appeared in American Psychologist *shortly after Milgram published the results of his first experiments in 1963.*

1   …The dependent, obedient attitude assumed by most subjects in the experimental setting is appropriate to that situation. The "game" is defined by the experimenter and he makes the rules. By volunteering, the subject agrees implicitly to assume a posture of trust and obedience. While the experimental conditions leave him exposed, the subject has the right to assume that his security and self-esteem will be protected.

2   There are other professional situations in which one member—the patient or client—expects help and protection from the other—the physician or psychologist. But the interpersonal relationship between experimenter and subject additionally has unique features which are likely to provoke initial anxiety in the subject. The laboratory is unfamiliar as a setting and the rules of behavior ambiguous compared to a clinician's office. Because of the anxiety and passivity generated by the setting, the subject is more prone to behave in an obedient, suggestible manner in the laboratory than elsewhere. Therefore, the laboratory is not the place to study degree of obedience or suggestibility, as a function of a particular experimental condition, since the base line for these phenomena as found in the laboratory is probably much higher than in most other settings. Thus experiments in which the relationship to the experimenter as an authority is used as an independent condition are imperfectly designed for the same reason that they are prone to injure the subjects involved. They disregard the special quality of trust and obedience with which the subject appropriately regards the experimenter.

3   Other phenomena which present ethical decisions, unlike those mentioned above, *can* be reproduced successfully in the laboratory. Failure experience, conformity to peer judgment, and isolation are among such phenomena. In these cases we can expect the experimenter to take whatever measures are necessary to prevent the subject from leaving the laboratory more humiliated, insecure, alienated, or hostile than when he arrived. To guarantee that an especially sensitive subject leaves a stressful experimental experience in the proper state sometimes requires special clinical training. But usually an attitude of compassion, respect, gratitude, and common sense will suffice, and no amount of clinical training will substitute. The subject has the right to expect that the psychologist with whom he is interacting has some concern for his welfare, and the personal attributes and professional skill to express his good will effectively.

4   Unfortunately, the subject is not always treated with the respect he deserves. It has become more commonplace in sociopsychological laboratory studies to manipulate, embarrass, and discomfort subjects. At times the insult to the subject's sensibilities extends to the journal reader when the results are reported. Milgram's (1963) study is a case in point. The following is Milgram's abstract of his experiment:

This article describes a procedure for the study of destructive obedience in the laboratory. It consists of ordering a naive S to administer increasingly more severe punishment to a victim in the context of a learning experiment.[1] Punishment is administered by means of a shock generator with 30 graded switches ranging from Slight Shock to Danger: Severe Shock. The victim is a confederate of E. The primary dependent variable is the maximum shock the S is willing to administer before he refuses to continue further.[2] 26 Ss obeyed the experimental commands fully,

---

[1]In psychological experiments, *S* is an abbreviation for *subject; E* is an abbreviation for *experimenter.*

[2]In the context of a psychological experiment, a *dependent variable* is a behavior that is expected to change as a result of changes in the experimental procedure.

and administered the highest shock on the generator. 14 Ss broke off the experiment at some point after the victim protested and refused to provide further answers. The procedure created extreme levels of nervous tension in some Ss. Profuse sweating, trembling, and stuttering were typical expressions of this emotional disturbance. One unexpected sign of tension—yet to be explained—was the regular occurrence of nervous laughter, which in some Ss developed into uncontrollable seizures. The variety of interesting behavioral dynamics observed in the experiment, the reality of the situation for the S, and the possibility of parametric variations[3] within the framework of the procedure point to the fruitfulness of further study [p. 371].

5   The detached, objective manner in which Milgram reports the emotional disturbance suffered by his subjects contrasts sharply with his graphic account of that disturbance. Following are two other quotes describing the effects on his subjects of the experimental conditions:

> I observed a mature and initially poised businessman enter the laboratory smiling and confident. Within 20 minutes he was reduced to a twitching, stuttering wreck, who was rapidly approaching a point of nervous collapse. He constantly pulled on his earlobe, and twisted his hands. At one point he pushed his fist into his forehead and muttered: "Oh God, let's stop it." And yet he continued to respond to every word of the experimenter, and obeyed to the end [p. 377].
>
> In a large number of cases the degree of tension reached extremes that are rarely seen in sociopsychological laboratory studies. Subjects were observed to sweat, tremble, stutter, bite their lips, groan, and dig their fingernails into their flesh. These were characteristic rather than exceptional responses to the experiment.
>
> One sign of tension was the regular occurrence of nervous laughing fits. Fourteen of the 40 subjects showed definite signs of nervous laughter and smiling. The laughter seemed entirely out of place, even bizarre. Full-blown, uncontrollable seizures were observed for 3 subjects. On one occasion we observed a seizure so violently convulsive that it was necessary to call a halt to the experiment...[p. 375].

Milgram does state that,

> After the interview, procedures were undertaken to assure that the subject would leave the laboratory in a state of well being. A friendly reconciliation was arranged between the subject and the victim, and an effort was made to reduce any tensions that arose as a result of the experiment [p. 374].

It would be interesting to know what sort of procedures could dissipate the type of emotional disturbance just described. In view of the effects on subjects, traumatic to a degree which Milgram himself considers nearly unprecedented in sociopsychological experiments, his casual assurance that these tensions were dissipated before the subject left the laboratory is unconvincing.

---

[3]*Parametric variation* is a statistical term that describes the degree to which information based on data for one experiment can be applied to data for a slightly different experiment.

6   What could be the rational basis for such a posture of indifference? Perhaps Milgram supplies the answer himself when he partially explains the subject's destructive obedience as follows, "Thus they assume that the discomfort caused the victim is momentary, while the scientific gains resulting from the experiment are enduring" [p. 378]. Indeed such a rationale might suffice to justify the means used to achieve his end if that end were of inestimable value to humanity or were not itself transformed by the means by which it was attained.

7   The behavioral psychologist is not in as good a position to objectify his faith in the significance of his work as medical colleagues at points of breakthrough. His experimental situations are not sufficiently accurate models of real-life experience; his sampling techniques are seldom of a scope which would justify the meaning with which he would like to endow his results; and these results are hard to reproduce by colleagues with opposing theoretical views. Unlike the Sabin vaccine,[4] for example, the concrete benefit to humanity of his particular piece of work, no matter how competently handled, cannot justify the risk that real harm will be done to the subject. I am not speaking of physical discomfort, inconvenience, or experimental deception per se, but of permanent harm, however slight. I do regard the emotional disturbance described by Milgram as potentially harmful because it could easily effect an alteration in the subject's self-image or ability to trust adult authorities in the future. It is potentially harmful to a subject to commit, in the course of an experiment, acts which he himself considers unworthy, particularly when he has been entrapped into committing such acts by an individual he has reason to trust. The subject's personal responsibility for his actions is not erased because the experimenter reveals to him the means which he used to stimulate these actions. The subject realizes that he would have hurt the victim if the current were on. The realization that he also made a fool of himself by accepting the experimental set results in additional loss of self-esteem. Moreover, the subject finds it difficult to express his anger outwardly after the experimenter in a self-acceptant but friendly manner reveals the hoax.

8   A fairly intense corrective interpersonal experience is indicated wherein the subject admits and accepts his responsibility for his own actions, and at the same time gives vent to his hurt and anger at being fooled. Perhaps an experience as distressing as the one described by Milgram can be integrated by the subject, provided that careful thought is given to the matter. The propriety of such experimentation is still in question even if such a reparational experience were forthcoming. Without it I would expect a naive, sensitive subject to remain deeply hurt and anxious for some time, and a sophisticated, cynical subject to become even more alienated and distrustful.

9   In addition the experimental procedure used by Milgram does not appear suited to the objectives of the study because it does not take into account the special quality of the set which the subject has in the experimental situation.

---

[4]The Sabin vaccine provides immunization against polio.

Milgram is concerned with a very important problem, namely, the social consequences of destructive obedience. He says,

> Gas chambers were built, death camps were guarded, daily quotas of corpses were produced with the same efficiency as the manufacture of appliances. These inhumane policies may have originated in the mind of a single person, but they could only be carried out on a massive scale if a very large number of persons obeyed orders [p. 371].

But the parallel between authority-subordinate relationships in Hitler's Germany and in Milgram's laboratory is unclear. In the former situation the SS man or member of the German Officer Corps, when obeying orders to slaughter, had no reason to think of his superior officer as benignly disposed towards himself or their victims. The victims were perceived as subhuman and not worthy of consideration. The subordinate officer was an agent in a great cause. He did not need to feel guilt or conflict because within his frame of reference he was acting rightly.

10   It is obvious from Milgram's own description that most of his subjects were concerned about their victims and did trust the experimenter, and that their distressful conflict was generated in part by the consequences of these two disparate but appropriate attitudes. Their distress may have resulted from shock at what the experimenter was doing to them as well as from what they thought they were doing to their victims. In any case there is not a convincing parallel between the phenomena studied by Milgram and destructive obedience as the concept would apply to the subordinate-authority relationship demonstrated in Hitler's Germany. If the experiments were conducted "outside of New Haven and without any visible ties to the university," I would still question their validity on similar although not identical grounds. In addition, I would question the representativeness of a sample of subjects who would voluntarily participate within a noninstitutional setting.

11   In summary, the experimental objectives of the psychologist are seldom incompatible with the subject's ongoing state of well being, provided that the experimenter is willing to take the subject's motives and interests into consideration when planning his methods and correctives. Section 4b in *Ethical Standards of Psychologists* (APA, undated) reads in part:

> Only when a problem is significant and can be investigated in no other way is the psychologist justified in exposing human subjects to emotional stress or other possible harm. In conducting such research, the psychologist must seriously consider the possibility of harmful aftereffects, and should be prepared to remove them as soon as permitted by the design of the experiment. Where the danger of serious aftereffects exists, research should be conducted only when the subjects or their responsible agents are fully informed of this possibility and volunteer nevertheless [p. 12].

From the subject's point of view procedures which involve loss of dignity, self-esteem and trust in rational authority are probably most harmful in the long run and require the most thoughtfully planned reparations, if engaged in at all. The public image of psychology as a profession is highly related to our own actions, and some of these actions are changeworthy. It is important that as research psychologists we protect our ethical sensibilities rather than adapt our personal standards to include as appropriate the kind of indignities to which Milgram's subjects were exposed. I would not like to see experiments such as Milgrams' proceed unless the subjects were fully informed of the dangers of serious after-effects and his correctives were clearly shown to be effective in restoring their state of well being.[5]

---

[5]Stanley Milgram replied to Baumrind's critique in a lengthy critique of his own [From Stanley Milgram, "Issues in the Study of Obedience: A Reply to Baumrind," *American Psychologist* 19, 1964, pp. 848-851]. Following are his principal points:

• Milgram believed that the experimental findings were in large part responsible for Baumrind's criticism. He writes:

Is not Baumrind's criticism based as much on the unanticipated findings as on the method? The findings were that some subjects performed in what appeared to be a shockingly immoral way. If, instead, every one of the subjects had broken off at "slight shock," or at the first sign of the learner's discomfort, the results would have been pleasant, and reassuring, and who would protest?

• Milgram objected to Baumrind's assertion that those who participated in the experiment would have trouble justifying their behavior. Milgram conducted follow-up questionnaires. The results, summarized in Table 1, indicate that 84 percent of the subjects claimed they were pleased to have been a part of the experiment.

TABLE 1 Excerpt from Questionnaire Used in a Follow-up Study of the Obedience Research			
Now That I Have Read the Report, and All Things Considered...	Defiant	Obedient	All
1. I am very glad to have been in the experiment	40.0%	47.8%	43.5%
2. I am glad to have been in the experiment	43.8%	35.7%	40.2%
3. I am neither sorry nor glad to have been in the experiment	15.3%	14.8%	15.1%
4. I am sorry to have been in the experiment	0.8%	0.7%	0.8%
5. I am very sorry to have been in the experiment	0.0%	1.0%	0.5%

Note—Ninety-two percent of the subjects returned the questionnaire. The characteristics of the nonrespondents were checked against the respondents. They differed from the respondents only with regard to age; younger people were overrepresented in the nonresponding group.

• Baumrind objected that studies of obedience cannot meaningfully be carried out in a laboratory setting, since the obedience occurred in a context where it was appropriate. Milgram's response: "I reject Baumrind's argument that the observed obedience does not count because it occurred where it is appropriate. That is precisely why it *does* count. A soldier's obedience is no less meaningful because it occurs in a pertinent military context."
• Milgram concludes his critique in this way: "If there is a moral to be learned from the obedience study, it is that every man must be responsible for his own actions. This author accepts full responsibility for the design and execution of the study. Some people may feel it should not have been done. I disagree and accept the burden of their judgment."

References

American Psychological Association. *Ethical standards of psychologists: A summary of ethical principles.* Washington, D.C.: APA, undated.

Milgram, S. Behavioral study of obedience. *J. Abnorm. Soc. Psychol.* 67, 1963, pp. 371–378.

Review Questions

1. Why might a subject volunteer for an experiment? Why do subjects typically assume a dependent, obedient attitude?

2. Why is a laboratory not a suitable setting for a study of obedience?

3. For what reasons does Baumrind feel that the Milgram experiment was potentially harmful?

4. For what reasons does Baumrind question the relationship between Milgram's findings and the obedient behavior of subordinates in Nazi Germany?

Discussion and Writing Suggestions

1. Baumrind contends that the Milgram experiment is imperfectly designed for two reasons: (1) The laboratory is not the place to test obedience; (2) Milgram disregarded the trust that subjects usually show an experimenter. To what extent do you agree with Baumrind's objections? Do you find them all equally valid?

2. Baumrind states that the ethical procedures of the experiment keep it from having significant value. Do you agree?

3. Do you agree with Baumrind that the subjects were "entrapped" into committing unworthy acts?

4. Assume the identity of a participant in Milgram's experiment who obeyed the experimenter by shocking the learner with the maximum voltage. You have just returned from the lab, and your spouse asks you about your day. Compose the conversation that follows.

Obedience
Ian Parker

As Ian Parker points out, Milgram's experiment became "the most cited, celebrated—and reviled—experiment in the history of social psychology." Parker also explains, however, that for Milgram himself the experiment was a mixed blessing: it would both "make his name and destroy his reputation."

Milgram was fascinated by the Asch experiment, but when all was said and done, this experiment was only about lines. He wondered if it were possible "to make Asch's conformity experiment more humanely significant." Milgram's breakthrough, his "incandescent moment," came when he asked himself "Just how far would a person go under the experimenter's orders?" We have seen the results in the experiment he describes and discusses in an earlier selection.

In the following passage, Ian Parker, a British writer who lives in New York, focuses on both the immediate and the long-term reaction to Milgram's experiments among both the general public and Milgram's professional colleagues and also of the effect of the experiment upon the experimenter himself. This selection is excerpted from an article that Parker wrote for the Autumn 2000 issue of Granta. *Parker writes regularly for* The New Yorker *and has also written for* Human Sciences, History of the Human Sciences, Political Studies, *and* Human Relations.

1   Milgram had a world exclusive. He had caught evil on film. He had invented a kind of torture machine. But it was not immediately clear what he should do with his discovery. When he began the study, he had no theory, nor was he planning to test another man's theory. His idea had sprung from contemplation of Solomon Asch, but the 'incandescent' moment at Princeton was a shift away from theory into experimental practice. He had had an idea for an experiment. Now, he was in an odd situation: he had caused something extraordinary to happen, but, technically, his central observation counted for nothing. With no provocation, a New Haven man had hit a fellow citizen with 450 volts. To the general observer, this will come as a surprise, but it is not a social scientific discovery, as Edward E. Jones, the distinguished editor of the *Journal of Personality*, made clear to Milgram when he declined the invitation to publish Milgram's first paper. 'The major problem,' Jones wrote to Milgram, 'is that this is really the report of some pilot research on a method for inducing stress or conflict…your data indicate a kind of triumph of social engineering…we are led to no conclusions about obedience, really, but rather are exhorted to be impressed with the power of your situation as an influence context.' The *Journal of Abnormal and Social Psychology* also rejected the paper on its first submission, calling it a 'demonstration' rather than an experiment.

2   Milgram had described only one experimental situation. When he resubmitted the paper to the same journal, he now included experimental variables, and it was publishable. In the rewrite, Milgram put the emphasis on the way in which differences in situation had caused differences in degrees of obedience: the closer the learner to the teacher, the greater the disobedience, and so on. These details were later lost as the experiment moved out of social psychology into the larger world. But it could hardly have happened otherwise. The thought that people were zapping each other in a Yale laboratory is bound to be more striking than the thought that zapping occurs a little less often when one is looking one's victim in the eye. The unscientific truth, perhaps, is that the

central comparison in Milgram's study is not between any two experimental variables: it is between what happened in the laboratory, and what we thought would happen. The experimental control in Milgram's model is our hopelessly flawed intuition.

3   "Somehow," Milgram told a friend in 1962, "I don't write as fast or as easily as I run experiments. I have done about all the experiments I plan to do on Obedience, am duly impressed with the results, and now find myself acutely constipated." Milgram found it hard to knock the experiment into social scientific shape. It would be another decade before he incorporated his findings into a serious theory of the sources of human obedience. When he did so, in the otherwise absorbing and beautifully written book *Obedience to Authority* (1974), his thoughts about an 'agentic state'—a psychological zone of abandoned autonomy—were not widely admired or developed by his peers, not least because they were so evidently retrospective. Most readers of *Obedience to Authority* are more likely to take interest in the nods of acknowledgment made to Arthur Koestler's *The Ghost in the Machine,* and to Alex Comfort, the English anarchist poet, novelist, and author of *The Joy of Sex.* Most readers will take more pleasure—and feel Milgram took more pleasure—in the novelistic and strikingly unscientific descriptions of his experimental subjects. ("Mrs Dontz," he wrote, "has an unusually casual, slow-paced way of speaking, and her tone expresses constant humility; it is as if every assertion carries the emotional message: 'I'm just a very ordinary person, don't expect a lot from me.' Physically, she resembles Shirley Booth in the film *Come Back, Little Sheba.*")

4   But while Milgram was struggling to place his findings in a proper scientific context, they seemed to have found a natural home elsewhere. Stanley Milgram—a young social psychology professor at the start of his career—appeared to be in a position to contribute to one of the late twentieth century's most pressing intellectual activities: making sense of the Holocaust. Milgram always placed the experiments in this context, and the figure of Adolf Eichmann, who was seized in Buenos Aires in the spring of 1960, and whose trial in Jerusalem began a year later, loomed over his proceedings. (In a letter that urged Alan Elms to keep up the supply of experimental volunteers, Milgram noted that this role bore "some resemblance to Mr Eichmann's position.") The trial, as Peter Novick has recently written in *The Holocaust in American Life,* marked "the first time that what we now call the Holocaust was presented to the American public as an entity in its own right, distinct from Nazi barbarism in general." When Milgram published his first paper on the obedience studies in 1963, Hannah Arendt's articles about the trial had just appeared in the *New Yorker,* and in her book, *Eichmann in Jerusalem,* and they had given widespread currency to her perception about "the banality of evil." Milgram put Eichmann's name in the first paragraph of his first obedience paper, and so claimed a place in a pivotal contemporary debate. His argument was this: his study showed how ordinary people are surprisingly prone to destructive obedience; the crimes of the Holocaust had been committed by people obeying orders; those people, therefore, could now be thought ordinary. The argument

had its terrifying element and its consoling element: according to Milgram, Americans had to see themselves as potential murderers; at the same time we could understand Nazis to be no more unusual than any New Haven guy in a check shirt.

5   It may seem bizarre now: Milgram returned to ordinary Nazis their Nuremberg defense, nicely polished in an American laboratory. But the idea struck a chord, and news quickly spread of Milgram's well-meaning, all-American torturers. "Once the [Holocaust] connection was in place," said Arthur G. Miller, a leading Milgram scholar, "then the experiments took on a kind of a larger-than-life quality." Milgram's work was reported in the *New York Times* (65% IN TEST BLINDLY OBEY ORDER TO INFLICT PAIN), and the story was quickly picked up by *Life, Esquire,* ABC television, UPI, and the British press. The fame of the experiments spread, and as the Sixties acquired their defining spirit, Holocaust references were joined by thoughts of My Lai; this was a good moment in history to have things to say about taking orders. By the time Milgram had published his book and released a short film of the experiment, his findings had spread into pop-ular culture, and into theological, medical, and legal discussions. Thomas Blass, a social psychologist at the University of Maryland, Baltimore County, who is preparing a Milgram biography, has a large collection of academic references, including a paper in the context of accountancy ethics. (Is it unthinking obedi-ence that causes accountants to act unlawfully on behalf of clients?) Outside the academy, Dannie Abse published an anti-Milgram play, *The Dogs of Pavlov,* in 1973, and two years later, in America, CBS broadcast a television movie, *The Tenth Level,* that made awkward melodrama out of the obedience experiments, and starred William Shatner as a spookily obsessed and romantically disengaged version of Professor Milgram. ("You may know your social psychology, Professor, but you have a lot to learn about the varieties of massage.") Peter Gabriel sang "We Do What We're Told (Milgram's 37)" in 1986. And there would be more than a whiff of Milgram in the 1990 episode of *The Simpsons,* "There's No Disgrace Like Home," in which the family members repeatedly electrocute one another until the lights across Springfield flicker and dim. Last year, "The Stanley Milgram Experiment"—a comedy sketch duo—made its off-off-Broadway debut in New York. Robbie Chafitz, one of the pair, had been startled and amused by the Milgram film as a teenager, and had always vowed to use the name one way or another. Besides, as he told me, "anything with electricity and people is funny."

6   But however celebrated the experiments became, there was a question they could never shake off. It was an ethical issue: had Stanley Milgram mis-treated his subjects? Milgram must have seen the storm coming, at least from the moment when Herbert Winer marched into his office, talking of heart attacks. In the summer of 1962, other subjects recorded their feelings about the experiment in response to a questionnaire sent out by Milgram along with a report explaining the true purpose of the experiment. Replies were transferred on to index cards and are now held—unpublished and anonymous—at Yale. "Since taking part in the experiment," reads one card, "I have suffered a mild heart attack. The one thing my doctor tells me that I

must avoid is any form of tension." Another card: "Right now I'm in group therapy. Would it be OK if I showed this report to [the] group and the doctors at the clinic?"

7   Since then, the experiment has been widely attacked from within the profession and from outside. To many, Milgram became a social psychological demon; Alan Elms has met people at parties who have recoiled at the news that he was a Milgram lieutenant. The psychologist Bruno Bettelheim described Milgram's work as "vile" and "in line with the human experiments of the Nazis." In his defense, Milgram would always highlight the results of post-experimental psychological studies—which had reported "no evidence of any traumatic reactions"—and the fact of the debriefings in Linsly-Chittenden Hall, in which care had been taken to give obedient subjects reasons not to feel bad about themselves. They were told to remember, for example, that doctors routinely hurt people in a thoroughly good cause. (Alan Elms wonders if this debriefing was *too* effective, and that subjects should have been obliged to confront their actions more fully.)

8   But Milgram never quite won the ethical argument. And the controversy was immediately damaging to his career. Someone—perhaps a Yale colleague, according to Thomas Blass—quickly brought the experiment to the attention of the American Psychological Association, and Milgram's application for APA membership was delayed while the case against him was considered. Today, although the APA is happy to include Milgram's shock generator in a traveling psychology exhibition, it is careful to describe the experiments as "controversial" in its accompanying literature. As the APA points out, modern ethical guidelines (in part inspired by Milgram) would prevent the obedience studies from being repeated today.

9   The controversy followed him. In 1963 Milgram left Yale for Harvard. He was happy there. This is where his two children were born. And when a tenured job came up, he applied. But he needed the unanimous support of his colleagues, and could not secure it. He was blackballed by enemies of the obedience work. (According to Alexandra Milgram, her husband once devised a board game based on the tenure of university professors.) The late Roger Brown, a prominent Harvard psychologist, told Thomas Blass that there had been those in the department who thought of Milgram as "sort of manipulative, or the mad doctor. They felt uneasy about him."

10   So in 1967 Stanley Milgram left Harvard to become head of the social psychology programme in the psychology department in the Graduate Center of the City University of New York (CUNY). In one sense, it was a promotion; he was a full professor at thirty-three. "But after Yale and Harvard, it was the pits," said Milgram's friend and fellow social psychologist, Philip Zimbardo. "Most people I know who didn't get tenure, it had a permanent effect on their lives. You don't get to Yale or Harvard unless you've been number one from kindergarten on, you've been top—so there's this discontinuity. It's the first time in your life you've failed. You're Stanley Milgram, and people all over the world are talking about your research, and you've failed." Milgram was the most cited man in social psychology—Roger Brown, for example, considered his research to be

of "profound importance and originality"—yet in later life, he was able to tell Zimbardo that he felt under-appreciated.

11   The ethical furor preyed on Milgram's mind—in the opinion of Arthur G. Miller, it may have contributed to his premature death—but one of its curious side effects was to reinforce the authenticity of his studies in the world outside psychology departments. Among those with a glancing knowledge of Milgram, mistreatment of experimental subjects became the only Milgram controversy. The studies remained intellectually sound, a minor building block of Western thought, a smart conversational gambit at cocktail parties. "People identified the problem with Milgram as just a question of ethics," says Henderikus Stam, of the University of Calgary in Canada, who trained as a social psychologist, but who lost faith and is now a psychological theoretician and historian. "So in a way people never got beyond that. Whereas there's a deeper epistemological question, which is: what can we actually know when we've done an experiment like that, what are we left with? What have we learned about obedience?"

12   Within the academy, there was another, quieter, line of criticism against Milgram: this was methodological. In a paper in 1968 the social psychologists Martin Orne and Charles Holland raised the issue of incongruity, pointing out that Milgram's subjects had been given two key pieces of information: a man in apparent danger, and another man—a man in a lab coat—whose lack of evident concern suggested there was no danger. It seemed possible that obedient subjects had believed in the more plausible piece of information (no danger), and thus concluded, at some conscious or semi-conscious level, that the experiment was a fake, and—in a "pact of ignorance"—been generous enough to role-play for the sake of science. In other words, they were only obeying the demands of amateur dramatics.

13   Perhaps forgetting that people weep in the theatre, Milgram's response was to argue that the subjects' signs of distress or tension—the twitching and stuttering and racing heartbeats—could be taken as evidence that they had accepted the experiment's reality. He also drew upon the questionnaire he had sent out in 1962, in which his volunteers—now entirely in the know—had been asked to agree with one of five propositions, running from, "I fully believed the learner was getting painful shocks" to "I was certain the learner was not getting the shocks." Milgram was pleased to note that three-quarters of the subjects said they believed the learner was definitely or probably getting the shocks. (He added, reasonably, "It would have been an easy out at this point to deny that the hoax had been accepted.")

14   Herbert Winer reports that he was fully duped, and Alan Elms told me that, watching through the mirror during the summer of 1961, he saw very little evidence of widespread disbelief. But it is worth pointing out that Milgram could have reported his questionnaire statistics rather differently. He could have said that only fifty-six per cent accepted his first proposition: "I fully believed the learner was getting painful shocks." Forty-four per cent of Milgram's subjects claimed to be at least partially unpersuaded. (Indeed, on his own questionnaire, Winer said he had some doubts.) These people do not have much of a presence in Milgram's writings, but you catch a glimpse of them in the Yale Library

index cards. One reads: "I was quite sure 'grunts and screams' were electrical-
ly reproduced from a speaker mounted in [the] students' room." (They were.)
"If [the learner] was making the sounds I should have heard the screams from
under the door—which was a poorly fit [*sic*] thin door. I'm sorry that I didn't have
enough something to get up and open this door. Which was not locked. To see
if student was still there." On another card: "I think that one of the main reasons
I continued to the end was that…I just couldn't believe that Yale would concoct
anything that would be [as] dangerous as the shocks were supposed to be."
Another subject had noticed how the experimenter was watching him rather
than the learner. Another hadn't understood why he was not allowed to volunteer to be the learner. And another wrote, "I had difficulty describing the
experiment to my wife as I was so overcome with laughter—haven't had such a
good laugh since the first time I saw the 4 Marx Bros—some 25 years ago."

15   For an experiment supposed to involve the undeserved torture of an innocent Irish-American man, there was a lot of laughter in Yale's Interaction
Laboratory. Frequently, Milgram's subjects could barely contain themselves as
they moved up the shock board ("On one occasion," Milgram later wrote, "we
observed a seizure so violently convulsive that it was necessary to call a halt to
the experiment.") Behind their one-way mirror, Milgram and Elms were at times
highly amused. And when students are shown the Milgram film today, there
tends to be loud laughter in the room. People laugh, and—despite the alleged
revelation of a universal heart of darkness—they go home having lost little faith
in their friends and their families.

16   According to Henderikus Stam, the laughter of the students, and perhaps
that of the subjects, is a reasonable response to an absurd situation. It's a
reaction to the notion that serious and complex moral issues, and the subtleties of human behaviour, can reasonably be illuminated through play-acting
in a university laboratory. The experiment does nothing but illuminate itself.
"What it does is it says, 'Aren't we clever?' If you wanted to demonstrate obedience to authority wouldn't you be better showing a film about the
Holocaust, or news clips about Kosovo? Why do you need an experiment,
that's the question? What does the experiment do? The experiment says that
if we really want to know about obedience to authority we need an abstract
representation of that obedience, removed from all real forms of the abuse
of authority. But what we then do is to use that representation to refer back
to the real historical examples."

17   What happens when we refer back to historical examples? Readers of *Hitler's
Willing Executioners,* Daniel Jonah Goldhagen's study of the complicity of ordinary German citizens in the Holocaust, will learn within one paragraph of a
German policeman, Captain Wolfgang Hoffmann, a "zealous executioner of
Jews," who "once stridently disobeyed a superior order that he deemed morally objectionable." The order was that he and members of his company should
sign a declaration agreeing not to steal from Poles. Hoffmann was affronted that
anyone would think the declaration necessary, that anyone would imagine his
men capable of stealing. "I feel injured," he wrote to his superiors, "in my sense
of honour." The genocidal killing of thousands of Jews was one thing, but

plundering from Poles was another. Here was an order to which he was opposed, and which he felt able to disobey.

18   Goldhagen is impatient with what he calls "the paradigm of external compulsion," which sets the actions of the Holocaust's perpetrators in the context of social-psychological or totalitarian state forces. His book aims to show how the crimes of the Holocaust were carried out by people obeying their own consciences, not blindly or fearfully obeying orders. "If you think that certain people are evil," he told me, "and that it's necessary to do away with them—if you hate them—and then someone orders you to kill them, you're not carrying out the deed only because of the order. You're carrying it out because you think it's right. So in all those instances where people are killing people they hate—their enemies or their perceived enemies—then Milgram is just completely inapplicable."

19   Goldhagen wonders if the Milgram take on the Holocaust met a particular need, during the Cold War, for America's new German allies "to be thought well of." He also wonders if, by robbing people of their agency, "of the fact that they're moral beings," the experiment tapped into the kind of reductive universalism by which, he says, Americans are easily seduced—the belief that all men are created equal, and in this case equally obedient. Goldhagen has no confidence in the idea that Milgram was measuring obedience at all. The experimental conditions did not properly control for other variables, such as trust, nor did they allow for the way decisions are made in the real world—over time, after consultation. Besides, said Goldhagen, in a tone close to exasperation, "people disobey all the time! Look around the world. Do people always pay all their taxes? Do what their bosses tell them? Or quietly accept what any government decides? Even with all kinds of sanctions available, one of the greatest problems that institutions face is to get their members to comply with rules and orders." Milgram's findings, he says, "are roundly, repeatedly and glaringly falsified by life."

20   In the opinion of Professor Stam, this comes close to defining the problems of social psychology itself. It is a discipline, he says, that makes the peculiar claim that "if you want to ask questions about the social world, you have to turn them into abstract technical questions." The Milgram experiment, he says, "has the air of scientificity about it. But it's not scientific, it's…*scientistic.*"

21   And there is Milgram's problem: he devised an intensely powerful piece of tragicomic laboratory theatre, and then had to smuggle it into the faculty of social science. His most famous work—which had something to say about trust, embarrassment, low-level sadism, willingness to please, exaggerated post-war respect for scientific research, the sleepy, heavy-lidded pleasure of being asked to *take part*, and, perhaps, too, the desire of a rather awkward young academic to secure attention and respect—had to pass itself off as an event with a single, steady meaning. And that disguise has not always been convincing. It's odd to hear Arthur G. Miller—one of the world's leading Milgram scholars—acknowledge that there have been times when he has wondered, just for a moment, if the experiments perhaps mean nothing at all.

22   But the faculty of social psychology is not ready to let Milgram go. And there may be a new way to rescue the experiments from their ungainly ambiguity. This is the route taken by Professors Lee Ross and Richard E. Nisbett (at

Stanford and the University of Michigan respectively), whose recent synthesis of social psychological thinking aims to give the subject new power. According to Professor Ross, the experiments may be "performance," but they still have social psychological news to deliver. If that is true, then we can do something that the late professor was not always able to do himself: we can make a kind of reconciliation between the artist and the scientist in Stanley Milgram.

23   Ross and Nisbett find a seat for Stanley Milgram at social psychology's high table. They do this slyly, by taking the idea of obedience—Milgram's big idea— and putting it quietly to one side. When Ross teaches Milgram at Stanford, he makes a point of giving his students detailed instructions on how to prepare for the classes—instructions that he knows will be thoroughly ignored. He is then able to stand in front of his students and examine their disobedience. "I asked you to do something that's good for you rather than bad for you," he tells them. "And I'm a legitimate authority rather than an illegitimate one, and I actually have power that the Milgram experimenter doesn't have. And yet you didn't obey. So the study can't just be about obedience." What it is primarily about, Ross tells his students—and it may be about other things too—is the extreme power of a situation that has been built without obvious escape routes. (As Herbert Winer said: "At no time was there a pause or a break when anything could be raised...") "There was really no exit," Ross told me, "there was no channel for disobedience. People who were discomforted, who wanted to disobey, didn't quite know how to do it. They made some timid attempts, and it got them nowhere. In order to disobey they have to step out of the whole situation, and say to the experimenter, 'Go to hell! You can't tell me what to do!' As long as they continue to function within that relationship, they're asking the experimenter for permission not to give shocks, and as long as the experimenter denies them that permission, they're stuck. They don't know how to get out of it." Ross suspects that things would have turned out very differently given one change to the situation. It's a fairly big change: the addition of a prominent red button in the middle of the table, combined with a clearly displayed notice signed by the "Human Subjects' Committee" explaining that the button could be pressed "by any subject in any experiment at any time if he or she absolutely refuses to continue."

24   According to Ross and Nisbett (who are saying something that Milgram surely knew, but something he allowed to become obscured), the Obedience Experiments point us towards a great social psychological truth, perhaps *the* great truth, which is this: people tend to do things because of where they are, not who they are, and we are slow to see it. We look for character traits to explain a person's actions—he is clever, shy, generous, arrogant—and we stubbornly underestimate the influence of the situation, the way things *happened to be* at that moment. So, if circumstances had been even only subtly different (if she hadn't been running late; if he'd been *told* the film was a comedy), the behaviour might have been radically different. Under certain controlled circumstances, then, people can be induced to behave unkindly: to that extent, Milgram may have something to say about a kind of destructive obedience. But under other circumstances, Professor Ross promised me, the same people would be nice. Given the correct situation, he said, we could be led to do

"terrifically altruistic and self-sacrificing things that we would never have agreed to before we started."

25   So the experiment that has troubled us for nearly forty years (that buzzing and howling), and which caused Milgram to have dark thoughts about America's vulnerability to fascism, suddenly has a new complexion. Now, it is about the influence of *any* situation on behaviour, good or bad: "You stop on the highway to help someone," Professor Ross said, "and then the help you try to give doesn't prove to be enough, so you give the person a ride, and then you end up lending them money or letting them stay in your house. It wasn't because that was the person in the world you cared about the most, it was just one thing led to another. Step by step."

26   That's the Milgram situation. "We can take ordinary people," Ross said, "and make them show a degree of obedience or conformity—or for that matter altruism or bravery, whatever—to a degree that we would normally assume you would only see in the rare few. And that's relevant to telling us what we're capable of making people do, but it also tells us that when we observe the world, we are often going to be making an attribution error, because lots of times, the situational factors have been opaque to us, and therefore we are making erroneous inferences about people. The South African government says, 'Can we deal with this fellow Mandela?' and the answer is, 'No, he's a terrorist.' But a social psychologist would say, 'Mandela, in *one* context, given *one* set of situations, was a terrorist.'" According to Ross, that's the key lesson of social psychology; that's how the discipline can be useful in education, the work place, and law. "Our emphasis," he says, "should be on creating situations that promote what we want to promote, rather than searching endlessly for the right person. Don't assume that people who commit atrocities are atrocious people, or people who do heroic things are heroic. Don't get overly carried away; don't think, because you observed someone under one set of discrete situational factors, that you know *what they're like,* and therefore can predict what they would do in a very different set of circumstances."

27   It's hard not to think of Stanley Milgram in another set of circumstances—to imagine the careers he did not have in films or in the theatre, and to wonder how things would have turned out if his work had appeared at another time, or had been read a little differently. It may now be possible to place the Obedience Experiments somewhere near the center of the social psychological project, but that's not how it felt in the last years of Milgram's life. He had failed to secure tenure at Harvard. Disappointed, he moved to New York, assuming he would soon be leaving again, to take up a post at a more glamorous institution. But he was still at CUNY seventeen years later, at the time of his premature death. "He had hoped it would be just for five years," Alexandra Milgram told me, "But things got much more difficult to move on to other places. You were glad to have what you had. And he was happy to do the work that he did. I don't think he was as happy at the university as he was at, say, Harvard, but he was a very independent person: he had his ideas, he had his research."

28   The research pushed Milgram into a kind of internal exile. Confirming his reputation as social psychology's renegade, he pursued work that, although often brilliantly conceived and elegantly reported, could look eccentric and old-fash-

ioned to colleagues, and that ran the risk of appearing to place method ahead of meaning. "It would flash and then burn out," says Professor Miller, "and then he'd go on to something else." He sent his (young, able-bodied) students on to the New York subway to ask people to give up their seats. He co-wrote a paper about *Candid Camera's* virtues as an archive for students of human behaviour. Pre-empting the play *Six Degrees of Separation,* he studied the "small world" phenomenon, investigating the chains of acquaintance that link two strangers. He took photographs of rail commuters and showed them to those who travelled on the same route, to explore the notion of the "familiar stranger." In an expensive, elaborate, and ultimately inconclusive experiment in 1971, he explored the links between antisocial acts seen on television and similar acts in real life by getting CBS to produce and air two versions of a hit hospital drama, *Medical Center.* He asked students to try to give away money on the street. He tested how easy it was for people to walk between a pavement photographer and his subject. And when he was recuperating from one of a series of heart attacks, he made an informal study of the social psychology of being a hospital patient. He was only fifty-one when he died.

29   Once, shortly before the Obedience Experiments had begun, Milgram had written from Yale about his fear of having made the wrong career move. "Of course," he told a friend, "I am glad that the present job sometimes engages my genuine interests, or at least, a part of my interests, but there is another part that remains submerged and somehow, perhaps because it is not expressed, seems most important." He described his routine: pulling himself out of bed, dragging himself to the lecture room "where I misrepresent myself for two hours as an efficient and persevering man of science…I should not be here, but in Greece shooting films under a Mediterranean sun, hopping about in a small boat from one Aegean isle to the next." He added, in a spirit of comic self-laceration, "Fool!"

Review Questions

1. Why was Milgram's article rejected when it was first submitted for publication? What did Milgram do to assure its professional acceptability?

2. What does Parker mean when he says (paragraph 5) that "Milgram returned to ordinary Nazis their Nuremberg defense, nicely polished in an American laboratory"?

3. In what sense did his obedience experiments ruin Milgram's career?

4. Based on what you have read about Daniel Jonah Goldhagen, explain the meaning of the title of his book, *Hitler's Willing Executioners.*

5. What does Henderikus Stam mean when he charges that Milgram's experiment is "not scientific, it's… *scientistic"*?

Discussion and Writing Suggestions

1. Parker charts the course of the Milgram experiments working their way into popular consciousness—from magazine articles to TV dramas, to episodes of *The Simpsons.* Why do you think that the obedience experiments, more than thousands of other social science experiments, performed during the 1960s, made such an indelible impact, even outside the profession of social psychology?

2. Parker focuses in part upon the ethical problems with Milgram's experiments. To what extent do you believe that these experiments were unethical? To what extent does Milgram's chief rejoinder— that his surveys taken after the fact show that the vast majority of his subjects suffered no permanent ill effects—effectively rebut the ethical objections?

3. One theory about why many of Milgram's subjects behaved as they did—going all the way to the top of the shock register—is that they did not really believe that the subjects were being shocked; they simply went along with the experimenter because they did not think it possible that a prestigious institution like Yale would be a party to inflicting harm on people. To what extent do you find this theory plausible?

4. Parker notes that not only did many of Milgram's subjects laugh during the experiments and later, in recounting it to others, but many students also laugh when they watch Milgram's film in class. Did you laugh when you saw the film? Did others? Attempt to account for this apparently incongruous reaction.

5. How necessary was Milgram's experiment? Parker notes that many have argued that if we want to learn about the power of authority to compel obedience, all we need do is study the numerous historical examples (the Holocaust being the one most often cited) of obedience to malign authority. To what extent do the results of Milgram's experiments add anything to what we already know about obedience from actual historical events?

6. Parker quotes Daniel Jonah Goldhagen, author of *Hitler's Willing Executioners,* to the effect that "If you think that certain people are evil and that it's necessary to do away with them—if you hate them—and then someone orders you to kill them, you're not carrying out the deed only because of the order. You're carrying it out because you think it's right." In other words, people who commit evil acts do so less because they feel compelled to obey external authority figures than because they are following their own consciences, their own sense of who is the enemy. To what extent do you find that this theory accounts for many of the evil acts in the world?

7. Parker cites Ross' theory that an important reason that so many of Milgram's subjects were fully obedient is that they had no "escape route"—the experimenter never gave them time or opportunity to call a halt to the experimental procedure. To what extent do you find this theory plausible? Would a "red button" to stop the experiment likely have led to a different set of results?

8. Lee Ross and Richard E. Nisbet believe that the main factor determining the obedience of Milgram's subjects was not the *character* of the subjects, but rather the *situation*—that given a different situation (i.e., a situation not involving a carefully controlled laboratory experiment), the same subjects who were so obedient might have behaved very differently. To what extent do you find this theory plausible? Can you think of examples in which people will behave in different ways in different situations?

The Stanford Prison Experiment
Philip K. Zimbardo

As well known—and as controversial—as the Milgram obedience experiments, the Stanford Prison Experiment (1973) raises troubling questions about the ability of individuals to resist authoritarian or obedient roles, if the social setting requires these roles. Philip K. Zimbardo, professor of psychology at Stanford University, set out to study the process by which prisoners and guards "learn" to become compliant and authoritarian, respectively. To find subjects for the experiment, Zimbardo placed an advertisement in a local newspaper:

> Male college students needed for psychological study of prison life. $15 per day for 1–2 weeks beginning Aug. 14. For further information & applications, come to Room 248, Jordan Hall, Stanford U.

The ad drew 75 responses. From these Zimbardo and his colleagues selected 21 college-age men, half of whom would become "prisoners" in the experiment, the other half "guards." The elaborate role-playing scenario, planned for two weeks, had to be cut short due to the intensity of subjects' responses. This article first appeared in the New York Times Magazine *(April 8, 1973).*

> *In prison, those things withheld from and denied to the prisoner become precisely what he wants most of all.*
>
> —Eldridge Cleaver, "Soul on Ice"

Our sense of power is more vivid when we break a man's spirit than when we win his heart.

—Eric Hoffer, "The Passionate State of Mind"

Every prison that men build is built with bricks of shame,
and bound with bars lest Christ should see how men their brothers maim.
—Oscar Wilde, "The Ballad of Reading Gaol"

Wherever anyone is against his will that is to him a prison.
—Epictetus, "Discourses"

1   The quiet of a summer morning in Palo Alto, Calif., was shattered by a screech-ing squad car siren as police swept through the city picking up college students in a surprise mass arrest. Each suspect was charged with a felony, warned of his constitutional rights, spread-eagled against the car, searched, handcuffed, and carted off in the back seat of the squad car to the police station for booking.

2   After fingerprinting and the preparation of identification forms for his "jacket" (central information file), each prisoner was left isolated in a detention cell to wonder what he had done to get himself into this mess. After a while, he was blindfolded and transported to the "Stanford County Prison." Here he began the process of becoming a prisoner—stripped naked, skin-searched, deloused, and issued a uniform, bedding, soup, and towel.

3   The warden offered an impromptu welcome:

4   "As you probably know, I'm your warden. All of you have shown that you are unable to function outside in the real world for one reason or another—that somehow you lack the responsibility of good citizens of this great country. We of this prison, your correctional staff, are going to help you learn what your responsibilities as citizens of this country are. Here are the rules. Sometime in the near future there will be a copy of the rules posted in each of the cells. We expect you to know them and to be able to recite them by number. If you follow all of these rules and keep your hands clean, repent for your misdeeds, and show a proper attitude of penitence, you and I will get along just fine."

5   There followed a reading of the 16 basic rules of prisoner conduct, "Rule Number One: Prisoners must remain silent during rest periods, after lights are out, during meals, and whenever they are outside the prison yard. Two: Prisoners must eat at mealtimes and only at mealtimes. Three: Prisoners must not move, tamper, deface, or damage walls, ceilings, windows, doors, or other prison prop-erty.... Seven: Prisoners must address each other by their ID number only. Eight: Prisoners must address the guards as 'Mr. Correctional Officer.'... Sixteen: Failure to obey any of the above rules may result in punishment."

6   By late afternoon these youthful "first offenders" sat in dazed silence on the cots in their barren cells trying to make sense of the events that had trans-formed their lives so dramatically.

7   If the police arrests and processing were executed with customary detach-ment, however, there were some things that didn't fit. For these men were now part of a very unusual kind of prison, an experimental mock prison, created by social psychologists to study the effects of imprisonment upon volunteer research subjects. When we planned our two-week-long simulation of prison

life, we sought to understand more about the process by which people called "prisoners" lose their liberty, civil rights, independence, and privacy, while those called "guards" gain social power by accepting the responsibility for controlling and managing the lives of their dependent charges.

8   Why didn't we pursue this research in a real prison? First, prison systems are fortresses of secrecy, closed to impartial observation, and thereby immune to critical analysis from anyone not already part of the correctional authority. Second, in any real prison, it is impossible to separate what each individual brings into the prison from what the prison brings out in each person.

9   We populated our mock prison with a homogeneous group of people who could be considered "normal-average" on the basis of clinical interviews and personality tests. Our participants (10 prisoners and 11 guards) were selected from more than 75 volunteers recruited through ads in the city and campus newspapers. The applicants were mostly college students from all over the United States and Canada who happened to be in the Stanford area during the summer and were attracted by the lure of earning $15 a day for participating in a study of prison life. We selected only those judged to be emotionally stable, physically healthy, mature, law-abiding citizens.

10   The sample of average, middle-class, Caucasian, college-age males (plus one Oriental student) was arbitrarily divided by the flop of a coin. Half were randomly assigned to play the role of guards, the others of prisoners. There were no measurable differences between the guards and the prisoners at the start of the experiment. Although initially warned that as prisoners their privacy and other civil rights would be violated and that they might be subjected to harassment, every subject was completely confident of his ability to endure whatever the prison had to offer for the full two-week experimental period. Each subject unhesitatingly agreed to give his "informed consent" to participate.

11   The prison was constructed in the basement of Stanford University's psychology building, which was deserted after the end of the summer-school session. A long corridor was converted into the prison "yard" by partitioning off both ends. Three small laboratory rooms opening onto this corridor were made into cells by installing metal barred doors and replacing existing furniture with cots, three to a cell. Adjacent offices were refurnished as guards' quarters, interview-testing rooms, and bedrooms for the "warden" (Jaffe) and the "superintendent" (Zimbardo). A concealed video camera and hidden microphones recorded much of the activity and conversation of guards and prisoners. The physical environment was one in which prisoners could always be observed by the staff, the only exception being when they were secluded in solitary confinement (a small, dark storage closet, labeled "The Hole").

12   Our mock prison represented an attempt to simulate the psychological state of imprisonment in certain ways. We based our experiment on an in-depth analysis of the prison situation, developed after hundreds of hours of discussion with Carlo Prescott (our ex-con consultant), parole officers, and correctional personnel, and after reviewing much of the existing literature on prisons and concentration camps.

13   "Real" prisoners typically report feeling powerless, arbitrarily controlled, dependent, frustrated, hopeless, anonymous, dehumanized, and emasculated.

It was not possible, pragmatically or ethically, to create such chronic states in volunteer subjects who realize that they are in an experiment for only a short time. Racism, physical brutality, indefinite confinement, and enforced homosexuality were not features of our mock prison. But we did try to reproduce those elements of the prison experience that seemed most fundamental.

14   We promoted anonymity by seeking to minimize each prisoner's sense of uniqueness and prior identity. The prisoners wore smocks and nylon stocking caps; they had to use their ID numbers; their personal effects were removed and they were housed in barren cells. All of this made them appear similar to each other and indistinguishable to observers. Their smocks, which were like dresses, were worn without undergarments, causing the prisoners to be restrained in their physical actions and to move in ways that were more feminine than masculine. The prisoners were forced to obtain permission from the guard for routine and simple activities such as writing letters, smoking a cigarette, or even going to the toilet; this elicited from them a childlike dependency.

15   Their quarters, though clean and neat, were small, stark, and without esthetic appeal. The lack of windows resulted in poor air circulation, and persistent odors arose from the unwashed bodies of the prisoners. After 10 P.M. lockup, toilet privileges were denied, so prisoners who had to relieve themselves would have to urinate and defecate in buckets provided by the guards. Sometimes the guards refused permission to have them cleaned out, and this made the prison smell.

16   Above all, "real" prisons are machines for playing tricks with the human conception of time. In our windowless prison, the prisoners often did not even know whether it was day or night. A few hours after falling asleep, they were roused by shrill whistles for their "count." The ostensible purpose of the count was to provide a public test of the prisoners' knowledge of the rules and of their ID numbers. But more important, the count, which occurred at least once on each of the three different guard shifts, provided a regular occasion for the guards to relate to the prisoners. Over the course of the study, the duration of the counts was spontaneously increased by the guards from their initial perfunctory 10 minutes to a seemingly interminable several hours. During these confrontations, guards who were bored could find ways to amuse themselves, ridiculing recalcitrant prisoners, enforcing arbitrary rules, and openly exaggerating any dissension among the prisoners.

17   The guards were also "deindividualized": They wore identical khaki uniforms and silver reflector sunglasses that made eye contact with them impossible. Their symbols of power were billy clubs, whistles, handcuffs, and the keys to the cells and the "main gate." Although our guards received no formal training from us in how to be guards, for the most part they moved with apparent ease into their roles. The media had already provided them with ample models of prison guards to emulate.

18   Because we were as interested in the guards' behavior as in the prisoners', they were given considerable latitude to improvise and to develop strategies and tactics of prisoner management. Our guards were told that they must maintain "law and order" in this prison, that they were responsible for handling any trouble that might break out, and they were cautioned about the seriousness and potential dangers of the situation they were about to enter. Surprisingly, in

most prison systems, "real" guards are not given much more psychological preparation or adequate training than this for what is one of the most complex, demanding, and dangerous jobs our society has to offer. They are expected to learn how to adjust to their new employment mostly from on-the-job experience, and from contacts with the "old bulls" during a survival-of-the-fittest orientation period. According to an orientation manual for correctional officers at San Quentin, "the only way you really get to know San Quentin is through experience and time. Some of us take more time and must go through more experiences than others to accomplish this; some really never do get there."

19   You cannot be a prisoner if no one will be your guard, and you cannot be a prison guard if no one takes you or your prison seriously. Therefore, over time a perverted symbiotic relationship developed. As the guards became more aggressive, prisoners became more passive; assertion by the guards led to dependency in the prisoners; self-aggrandizement was met with self-deprecation, authority with helplessness, and the counterpart of the guards' sense of mastery and control was the depression and hopelessness witnessed in the prisoners. As these differences in behavior, mood, and perception became more evident to all, the need for the now "righteously" powerful guards to rule the obviously inferior and powerless inmates became a sufficient reason to support almost any further indignity of man against man:

20   Guard K: "During the inspection, I went to cell 2 to mess up a bed which the prisoner had made and he grabbed me, screaming that he had just made it, and he wasn't going to let me mess it up. He grabbed my throat, and although he was laughing I was pretty scared....I lashed out with my stick and hit him in the chin (although not very hard), and when I freed myself I became angry. I wanted to get back in the cell and have a go with him, since he attacked me when I was not ready."

21   Guard M: "I was surprised at myself...I made them call each other names and clean the toilets out with their bare hands. I practically considered the prisoners cattle, and I kept thinking: 'I have to watch out for them in case they try something.'"

22   Guard A: "I was tired of seeing the prisoners in their rags and smelling the strong odors of their bodies that filled the cells. I watched them tear at each other on orders given by us. They didn't see it as an experiment. It was real and they were fighting to keep their identity. But we were always there to show them who was boss."

23   Because the first day passed without incident, we were surprised and totally unprepared for the rebellion that broke out on the morning of the second day. The prisoners removed their stocking caps, ripped off their numbers, and barricaded themselves inside the cells by putting their beds against the doors. What should we do? The guards were very much upset because the prisoners also began to taunt and curse them to their faces. When the morning shift of guards came on, they were upset at the night shift who, they felt, must have been too permissive and too lenient. The guards had to handle the rebellion themselves, and what they did was startling to behold.

24   At first they insisted that reinforcements be called in. The two guards who were waiting on stand-by call at home came in, and the night shift of guards

voluntarily remained on duty (without extra pay) to bolster the morning shift. The guards met and decided to treat force with force. They got a fire extinguisher that shot a stream of skin-chilling carbon dioxide and forced the prisoners away from the doors; they broke into each cell, stripped the prisoners naked, took the beds out, forced the prisoners who were the ringleaders into solitary confinement, and generally began to harass and intimidate the prisoners.

25   After crushing the riot, the guards decided to head off further unrest by creating a privileged cell for those who were "good prisoners" and then, without explanation, switching some of the troublemakers into it and some of the good prisoners out into the other cells. The prisoner ringleaders could not trust these new cellmates because they had not joined in the riot and might even be "snitches." The prisoners never again acted in unity against the system. One of the leaders of the prisoner revolt later confided:

26   "If we had gotten together then, I think we could have taken over the place. But when I saw the revolt wasn't working, I decided to toe the line. Everyone settled into the same pattern. From then on, we were really controlled by the guards."

27   It was after this episode that the guards really began to demonstrate their inventiveness in the application of arbitrary power. They made the prisoners obey petty, meaningless, and often inconsistent rules, forced them to engage in tedious, useless work, such as moving cartons back and forth between closets and picking thorns out of their blankets for hours on end. (The guards had previously dragged the blankets through thorny bushes to create this disagreeable task.) Not only did the prisoners have to sing songs or laugh or refrain from smiling on command; they were also encouraged to curse and vilify each other publicly during some of the counts. They sounded off their numbers endlessly and were repeatedly made to do pushups, on occasion with a guard stepping on them or a prisoner sitting on them.

28   Slowly the prisoners became resigned to their fate and even behaved in ways that actually helped to justify their dehumanizing treatment at the hands of the guards. Analysis of the tape-recorded private conversations between prisoners and of remarks made by them to interviewers revealed that fully half could be classified as nonsupportive of other prisoners. More dramatic, 85 percent of the evaluative statements by prisoners about their fellow prisoners were uncomplimentary and deprecating.

29   This should be taken in the context of an even more surprising result. What do you imagine the prisoners talked about when they were alone in their cells with each other, given a temporary respite from the continual harassment and surveillance by the guards? Girl friends, career plans, hobbies or politics?

30   No, their concerns were almost exclusively riveted to prison topics. Their monitored conversations revealed that only 10 percent of the time was devoted to "outside" topics, while 90 percent of the time they discussed escape plans, the awful food, grievances or ingratiating tactics to use with specific guards in order to get a cigarette, permission to go to the toilet, or some other favor. Their obsession with these immediate survival concerns made talk about the past and future an idle luxury.

31   And this was not a minor point. So long as the prisoners did not get to know each other as people, they only extended the oppressiveness and reality of their

life as prisoners. For the most part, each prisoner observed his fellow prisoners allowing the guards to humiliate them, acting like compliant sheep, carrying out mindless orders with total obedience, and even being cursed by fellow prisoners (at a guard's command). Under such circumstances, how could a prisoner have respect for his fellows, or any self-respect for what *he* obviously was becoming in the eyes of all those evaluating him?

32   The combination of realism and symbolism in this experiment had fused to create a vivid illusion of imprisonment. The illusion merged inextricably with reality for at least some of the time for every individual in the situation. It was remarkable how readily we all slipped into our roles, temporarily gave up our identities, and allowed these assigned roles and the social forces in the situation to guide, shape, and eventually to control our freedom of thought and action.

33   But precisely where does one's "identity" end and the one's "role" begin? When the private self and the public role behavior clash, what direction will attempts to impose consistency take? Consider the reactions of the parents, relatives, and friends of the prisoners who visited their forlorn sons, brothers, and lovers during two scheduled visitors' hours. They were taught in short order that they were our guests, allowed the privilege of visiting only by complying with the regulations of the institution. They had to register, were made to wait half an hour, were told that only two visitors could see any one prisoner; the total visiting time was cut from an hour to only 10 minutes, they had to be under the surveillance of a guard, and before any parents could enter the visiting area, they had to discuss their son's case with the warden. Of course they complained about these arbitrary rules, but their conditioned, middle-class reaction was to work within the system to appeal privately to the superintendent to make conditions better for their prisoners.

34   In less than 36 hours, we were forced to release prisoner 8612 because of extreme depression, disorganized thinking, uncontrollable crying, and fits of rage. We did so reluctantly because we believed he was trying to "con" us—it was unimaginable that a volunteer prisoner in a mock prison could legitimately be suffering and disturbed to that extent. But then on each of the next three days another prisoner reacted with similar anxiety symptoms, and we were forced to terminate them, too. In a fifth case, a prisoner was released after developing a psychosomatic rash over his entire body (triggered by rejection of his parole appeal by the mock parole board). These men were simply unable to make an adequate adjustment to prison life. Those who endured the prison experience to the end could be distinguished from those who broke down and were released early in only one dimension—authoritarianism. On a psychological test designed to reveal a person's authoritarianism, those prisoners who had the highest scores were best able to function in this authoritarian prison environment.

35   If the authoritarian situation became a serious matter for the prisoners, it became even more serious—and sinister—for the guards. Typically, the guards insulted the prisoners, threatened them, were physically aggressive, used instruments (night sticks, fire extinguishers, etc.) to keep the prisoners in line, and referred to them in impersonal, anonymous, deprecating ways: "Hey, you," or "You [obscenity], 5401, come here." From the first to the last day, there was a significant increase in the guards' use of most of these domineering, abusive tactics.

36   Everyone and everything in the prison was defined by power. To be a guard who did not take advantage of this institutionally sanctioned use of power was to appear "weak," "out of it," "wired up by the prisoners," or simply a deviant from the established norms of appropriate guard behavior. Using Erich Fromm's definition of sadism, as "the wish for absolute control over another living being," all of the mock guards at one time or another during this study behaved sadistically toward the prisoners. Many of them reported—in their diaries, on critical-incident report forms, and during post-experimental interviews—being delighted in the new-found power and control they exercised and sorry to see it relinquished at the end of the study.

37   Some of the guards reacted to the situation in the extreme and behaved with great hostility and cruelty in the forms of degradation they invented for the prisoners. But others were kinder; they occasionally did little favors for the prisoners, were reluctant to punish them, and avoided situations where prisoners were being harassed. The torment experienced by one of these good guards is obvious in his perceptive analysis of what if felt like to be responded to as a "guard":

38   "What made the experience most depressing for me was the fact that we were continually called upon to act in a way that just was contrary to what I really feel inside. I don't feel like I'm the type of person that would be a guard, just constantly giving out [orders]…and forcing people to do things, and pushing and lying—it just didn't seem like me, and to continually keep up and put on a face like that is just really one of the most oppressive things you can do. It's almost like a prison that you create yourself—you get into it, and it becomes almost the definition you make of yourself, it almost becomes like walls, and you want to break out and you want just to be able to tell everyone that 'this isn't really me at all, and I'm not the person that's confined in there—I'm a person who wants to get out and show you that I am free, and I do have my own will, and I'm not the sadistic type of person that enjoys this kind of thing.'"

39   Still, the behavior of these good guards seemed more motivated by a desire to be liked by everyone in the system than by a concern for the inmates' welfare. No guard ever intervened in any direct way on behalf of the prisoners, ever interfered with the orders of the cruelest guards, or ever openly complained about the subhuman quality of life that characterized this prison.

40   Perhaps the most devastating impact of the more hostile guards was their creation of a capricious, arbitrary environment. Over time the prisoners began to react passively. When our mock prisoners asked questions, they got answers about half the time, but the rest of the time they were insulted and punished—and it was not possible for them to predict which would be the outcome. As they began to "toe the line," they stopped resisting, questioning and, indeed, almost ceased responding altogether. There was a general decrease in all categories of response as they learned the safest strategy to use in an unpredictable, threatening environment from which there is no physical escape—do nothing, except what is required. Act not, want not, feel not, and you will not get into trouble in prisonlike situations.

41   Can it really be, you wonder, that intelligent, educated volunteers could have lost sight of the reality that they were merely acting a part in an elaborate game that would eventually end? There are many indications not only that they did,

but that, in addition, so did we and so did other apparently sensible, responsible adults.

42   Prisoner 819, who had gone into an uncontrollable crying fit, was about to be prematurely released from the prison when a guard lined up the prisoners and had them chant in unison, "819 is a bad prisoner. Because of what 819 did to prison property we all must suffer. 819 is a bad prisoner." Over and over again. When we realized 819 might be overhearing this, we rushed into the room where 819 was supposed to be resting, only to find him in tears, prepared to go back into the prison because he could not leave as long as the others thought he was a "bad prisoner." Sick as he felt, he had to prove to them he was not a "bad" prisoner. He had to be persuaded that he was not a prisoner at all, that the others were also just students, that this was just an experiment and not a prison and the prison staff were only research psychologists. A report from the warden notes, "While I believe that it was necessary for *staff* [me] to enact the warden role, at least some of the time, I am startled by the ease with which I could turn off my sensitivity and concern for others for 'a good cause.'"

43   Consider our overreaction to the rumor of a mass escape plot that one of the guards claimed to have overheard. It went as follows: Prisoner 8612, previously released for emotional disturbance, was only faking. He was going to round up a bunch of his friends, and they would storm the prison right after visiting hours. Instead of collecting data on the pattern of rumor transmission, we made plans to maintain the security of our institution. After putting a confederate informer into the cell 8612 had occupied to get specific information about the escape plans, the superintendent went back to the Palo Alto Police Department to request transfer of our prisoners to the old city jail. His impassioned plea was only turned down at the last minute when the problem of insurance and city liability for our prisoners was raised by a city official. Angered at this lack of cooperation, the staff formulated another plan. Our jail was dismantled, the prisoners, chained and blindfolded, were carted off to a remote storage room. When the conspirators arrived, they would be told the study was over, their friends had been sent home, there was nothing left to liberate. After they left, we would redouble the security features of our prison making any future escape attempts futile. We even planned to lure ex-prisoner 8612 back on some pretext and imprison him again, because he had been released on false pretenses! The rumor turned out to be just that—a full day had passed in which we collected little or no data, worked incredibly hard to tear down and then rebuilt our prison. Our reaction, however, was as much one of relief and joy as of exhaustion and frustration.

44   When a former prison chaplain was invited to talk with the prisoners (the grievance committee had requested church services), he puzzled everyone by disparaging each inmate for not having taken any constructive action in order to get released. "Don't you know you must have a lawyer in order to get bail, or to appeal the charges against you?" Several of them accepted his invitation to contact their parents in order to secure the services of an attorney. The next night one of the parents stopped at the superintendent's office before visiting time and handed him the name and phone number of her cousin who was a public defender. She said that a priest had called her and suggested the need for a

lawyer's services! We called the lawyer. He came, interviewed the prisoners, discussed sources of bail money, and promised to return again after the weekend.

45   But perhaps the most telling account of the insidious development of this new reality, of the gradual Kafkaesque metamorphosis of good into evil, appears in excerpts from the diary of one of the guards, Guard A:

46   *Prior to start of experiment:* "As I am a pacifist and nonaggressive individual. I cannot see a time when I might guard and/or maltreat other living things."

47   *After an orientation meeting:* "Buying uniforms at the end of the meeting confirms the gamelike atmosphere of this thing. I doubt whether many of us share the expectations of 'seriousness' that the experimenters seem to have."

48   *First Day:* "Feel sure that the prisoners will make fun of my appearance and I evolve my first basic strategy—mainly not to smile at anything they say or do which would be admitting it's all only a game.... At cell 3 I stop and setting my voice hard and low say to 5486, 'What are you smiling at?' 'Nothing, Mr. Correctional Officer.' 'Well, see that you don't.' (As I walk off I feel stupid.)"

49   *Second Day:* "5704 asked for a cigarette and I ignored him—because I am a non-smoker and could not empathize.... Meanwhile since I was feeling empathetic towards 1037, I determined not to talk with him.... after we had count and lights out [Guard D] and I held a loud conversation about going home to our girl friends and what we were going to do to them."

50   *Third Day (preparing for the first visitors' night):* "After warning the prisoners not to make any complaints unless they wanted the visit terminated fast, we finally brought in the first parents. I made sure I was one of the guards on the yard, because this was my first chance for the type of manipulative power that I really like—being a very noticed figure with almost complete control over what is said or not. While the parents and prisoners sat in chairs, I sat on the end of the table dangling my feet and contradicting anything I felt like. This was the first part of the experiment I was really enjoying.... 817 is being obnoxious and bears watching."

51   *Fourth Day:* "...The psychologist rebukes me for handcuffing and blindfolding a prisoner before leaving the [counseling] office, and I resentfully reply that it is both necessary security and my business anyway."

52   *Fifth Day:* "I harass 'Sarge' who continues to stubbornly overrespond to all commands. I have singled him out for the special abuse both because he begs for it and because I simply don't like him. The real trouble starts at dinner. The new prisoner (416) refuses to eat his sausage...we throw him into the Hole ordering him to hold sausages in each hand. We have a crisis of authority; this rebellious conduct potentially undermines the complete control we have over the others. We decide to play upon prisoner solidarity and tell the new one that all the others will be deprived of visitors if he does not eat his dinner.... I walk by and slam my stick into the Hole door.... I am very angry at this prisoner for causing discomfort and trouble for the others. I decided to force-feed him, but he wouldn't eat. I let the food slide down his face. I didn't believe it was me doing it. I hated myself for making him eat but I hated him more for not eating."

53   *Sixth Day:* "The experiment is over. I feel elated but am shocked to find some other guards disappointed somewhat because of the loss of money and some because they are enjoying themselves."

54   We were no longer dealing with an intellectual exercise in which a hypothesis was being evaluated in the dispassionate manner dictated by the canons of the scientific method. We were caught up in the passion of the present, the suffering, the need to control people, not variables, the escalation of power, and all the unexpected things that were erupting around and within us. We had to end this experiment: So our planned two-week simulation was aborted after only six (was it only six?) days and nights.

55   Was it worth all the suffering just to prove what everybody knows—that some people are sadistic, others weak, and prisons are not beds of roses? If that is all we demonstrated in this research, then it was certainly not worth the anguish. We believe there are many significant implications to be derived from this experience, only a few of which can be suggested here.

56   The potential social value of this study derives precisely from the fact that normal, healthy, educated young men could be so radically transformed under the institutional pressures of a "prison environment." If this could happen in so short a time, without the excesses that are possible in real prisons, and if it could happen to the "cream-of-the-crop of American youth," then one can only shudder to imagine what society is doing both to the actual guards and prisoners who are at this very moment participating in that unnatural "social experiment."

57   The pathology observed in this study cannot be reasonably attributed in pre-existing personality differences of the subjects, that option being eliminated by our selection procedures and random assignment. Rather, the subjects' abnormal social and personal reactions are best seen as a product of their transaction with an environment that supported the behavior that would be pathological in other settings, but was "appropriate" in this prison. Had we observed comparable reactions in a real prison, the psychiatrist undoubtedly would have been able to attribute any prisoner's behavior to character defects or personality maladjustment, while critics of the prison system would have been quick to label the guards as "psychopathic." This tendency to locate the source of behavior disorders inside a particular person or group underestimates the power of situational forces.

58   Our colleague, David Rosenhan, has very convincingly shown that once a sane person (pretending to be insane) gets labeled as insane and committed to a mental hospital, it is the label that is the reality which is treated and not the person. This dehumanizing tendency to respond to other people according to socially determined labels and often arbitrarily assigned roles is also apparent in a recent "mock hospital" study designed by Norma Jean Orlando to extend the ideas in our research.

59   Personnel from the staff of Elgin State Hospital in Illinois role-played either mental patients or staff in a weekend simulation on a ward in the hospital. The mock mental patients soon displayed behavior indistinguishable from that we usually associate with the chronic pathological syndromes of acute mental patients: Incessant pacing, uncontrollable weeping, depression, hostility, fights, stealing from each other, complaining. Many of the "mock staff" took advantage of their power to act in ways comparable to our mock guards by dehumanizing their powerless victims.

60 During a series of encounter debriefing sessions immediately after our experiment, we all had an opportunity to vent our strong feelings and to reflect upon the moral and ethical issues each of us faced, and we considered how we might react more morally in future "real-life" analogues to this situation. Year-long follow-ups with our subjects via questionnaires, personal interviews, and group reunions indicate that their mental anguish was transient and situationally specific, but the self-knowledge gained has persisted.

61 By far the most disturbing implication of our research comes from the parallels between what occurred in that basement mock prison and daily experiences in our own lives—and we presume yours. The physical institution of prison is but a concrete and steel metaphor for the existence of more pervasive, albeit less obvious, prisons of the mind that all of us daily create, populate, and perpetuate. We speak here of the prisons of racism, sexism, despair, shyness, "neurotic hang-ups," and the like. The social convention of marriage, as one example, becomes for many couples a state of imprisonment in which one partner agrees to be prisoner or guard, forcing or allowing the other to play the reciprocal role—invariably without making the contract explicit.

62 To what extent do we allow ourselves to become imprisoned by docilely accepting the roles others assign us or, indeed, choose to remain prisoners because being passive and dependent frees us from the need to act and be responsible for our actions? The prison of fear constructed in the delusions of the paranoid is no less confining or less real than the cell that every shy person erects to limit his own freedom in anxious anticipation of being ridiculed and rejected by his guards—often guards of his own making.

Review Questions

1. What was Zimbardo's primary goal in undertaking the prison experiment?

2. What was the profile of the subjects in the experiments? Why is this profile significant?

3. Zimbardo claims that there is a "process" (paragraphs 2, 7) of becoming a prisoner. What is this process?

4. What inverse psychological relationships developed between prisoners and guards?

5. What was the result of the prison "riot"?

6. Why did prisoners have no respect for each other or for themselves?

7. How does the journal of Guard A illustrate what Zimbardo calls the "gradual Kafkaesque metamorphosis of good into evil"? See paragraphs 45–54.

8. What are the reasons people would voluntarily become prisoners?

9. How can the mind keep people in jail?

Discussion and Writing Suggestions

1. Reread the four epigraphs to this article. Write a paragraph of response to any one of them, in light of Zimbardo's discussion of the prison experiment.

2. You may have thought, before reading this article, that being a prisoner is a physical fact, not a psychological state. What are the differences between these two views?

3. In paragraph 8, Zimbardo explains his reasons for not pursuing his research in a real prison. He writes that "it is impossible to separate what each individual brings into the prison from what the prison brings out in each person." What does he mean? And how does this distinction prove important later in the article (see paragraph 58)?

4. Zimbardo reports that at the beginning of the experiment each of the "prisoner" subjects "was completely confident of his ability to endure whatever the prison had to offer for the full two-week experimental period" (paragraph 10). Had you been a subject, would you have been so confident, prior to the experiment? Given what you've learned of the experiment, do you think you would have psychologically "become" a prisoner or guard if you had been selected for these roles? (And if not, what makes you so sure?)

5. Identify two passages in this article: one that surprised you relating to the prisoners; and one that surprised you relating to the guards. Write a paragraph explaining your response to each. Now read the two passages in light of each other. Do you see any patterns underlying your responses?

6. Zimbardo claims that the implications of his research matter deeply—that the mock prison he created is a metaphor for prisons of the mind "that all of us daily create, populate, and perpetuate" (paragraph 61). Zimbardo mentions the prisons of "racism, sexism, despair, [and] shyness." Choose any one of these and discuss how it might be viewed as a mental prison.

7. Reread paragraphs 61 and 62. Zimbardo makes a metaphorical jump from his experiment to the psychological realities of your daily life. Prisons—the artificial one he created and actual prisons—stand for something: social systems in which there are those who give orders and those who obey. All metaphors break down at some point. Where does this one break down?

8. Zimbardo suggests that we might "choose to remain prisoners because being passive and dependent frees us from the need to act and be responsible for our actions" (paragraph 62). Do you agree? What are the burdens of being disobedient?

Disobedience as a Psychological and Moral Problem
Erich Fromm

Erich Fromm (1900–1980) was one of the twentieth century's distinguished writers and thinkers. Psychoanalyst and philosopher, historian and sociologist, he ranged widely in his interests and defied easy characterization. Fromm studied the works of Freud and Marx closely, and published on them both, but he was not aligned strictly with either. In much of his voluminous writing, he struggled to articulate a view that could help bridge ideological and personal conflicts and bring dignity to those who struggled with isolation in the industrial world. Author of more than thirty books and contributor to numerous edited collections and journals, Fromm is best known for Escape from Freedom *(1941),* The Art of Loving *(1956), and* To Have or To Be? *(1976).*

In the essay that follows, first published in 1963, Fromm discusses the seductive comforts of obedience, and he makes distinctions among varieties of obedience, some of which he believes are destructive, and others, life affirming. His thoughts on nuclear annihilation may seem dated in these days of post–cold war cooperation, but it is worth remembering that Fromm wrote his essay just after the Cuban missile crisis, when fears of a third world war ran high. (We might note that despite the welcome reductions of nuclear stockpiles, the United States and Russia still possess, and retain battle plans for, thousands of warheads.) On the major points of his essay, concerning the psychological and moral problems of obedience, Fromm remains as pertinent today as when he wrote some forty years ago.

1   For centuries kings, priests, feudal lords, industrial bosses, and parents have insisted that *obedience is a virtue* and that *disobedience is a vice.* In order to introduce another point of view, let us set against this position the following statement: *human history began with an act of disobedience, and it is not unlikely that it will be terminated by an act of obedience.*

2   Human history was ushered in by an act of disobedience according to the Hebrew and Greek myths. Adam and Eve, living in the Garden of Eden, were part of nature; they were in harmony with it, yet did not transcend it. They were in nature as the fetus is in the womb of the mother. They were human, and at the same time not yet human. All this changed when they disobeyed an order. By breaking the ties with earth and mother, by cutting the umbilical cord, man emerged from a prehuman harmony and was able to take the first step into independence and freedom. The act of disobedience set Adam and Eve free and opened their eyes. They recognized each other as strangers and the world outside them as strange and even hostile. Their act of disobedience broke the primary bond with nature and made them individuals. "Original sin," far from corrupting man, set him free; it was the beginning of history. Man had to leave the Garden of Eden in order to learn to rely on his own powers and to become fully human.

3   The prophets, in their messianic concept, confirmed the idea that man had been right in disobeying; that he had not been corrupted by his "sin," but freed from the fetters of pre-human harmony. For the prophets, *history* is the place where man becomes human; during its unfolding he develops his powers of

reason and of love until he creates a new harmony between himself, his fellow man, and nature. This new harmony is described as "the end of days," that period of history in which there is peace between man and man, between man and nature. It is a "new" paradise created by man himself, and one which he alone could create because he was forced to leave the "old" paradise as a result of his disobedience.

4   Just as the Hebrew myth of Adam and Eve, so the Greek myth of Prometheus sees all human civilization based on an act of disobedience. Prometheus, in stealing the fire from the gods, lays the foundation for the evolution of man. There would be no human history were it not for Prometheus' "crime." He, like Adam and Eve, is punished for his disobedience. But he does not repent and ask for forgiveness. On the contrary, he proudly says: "I would rather be chained to this rock than be the obedient servant of the gods."

5   Man has continued to evolve by acts of disobedience. Not only was his spiritual development possible only because there were men who dared to say no to the powers that be in the name of their conscience or their faith, but also his intellectual development was dependent on the capacity for being disobedient—disobedient to authorities who tried to muzzle new thoughts and to the authority of long-established opinions which declared a change to be nonsense.

6   If the capacity for disobedience constituted the beginning of human history, obedience might very well, as I have said, cause the end of human history. I am not speaking symbolically or poetically. There is the possibility, or even the probability, that the human race will destroy civilization and even all life upon earth within the next five to ten years. There is no rationality or sense in it. But the fact is that, while we are living technically in the Atomic Age, the majority of men—including most of those who are in power—still live emotionally in the Stone Age; that while our mathematics, astronomy, and the natural sciences are of the twentieth century, most of our ideas about politics, the state, and society lag far behind the age of science. If mankind commits suicide it will be because people will obey those who command them to push the deadly buttons; because they will obey the archaic passions of fear, hate, and greed; because they will obey obsolete clichés of State sovereignty and national honor. The Soviet leaders talk much about revolutions, and we in the "free world" talk much about freedom. Yet they and we discourage disobedience—in the Soviet Union explicitly and by force, in the free world implicitly and by the more subtle methods of persuasion.

7   But I do not mean to say that all disobedience is a virtue and all obedience is a vice. Such a view would ignore the dialectical relationship between obedience and disobedience. Whenever the principles which are obeyed and those which are disobeyed are irreconcilable, an act of obedience to one principle is necessarily an act of disobedience to its counterpart and vice versa. Antigone is the classic example of this dichotomy. By obeying the inhuman laws of the State, Antigone necessarily would disobey the laws of humanity. By obeying the latter, she must disobey the former. All martyrs of religious faiths, of freedom, and of science have had to disobey those who wanted to muzzle them in order to obey their own consciences, the laws of humanity, and of reason. If a man can only obey and not disobey, he is a slave; if he can only disobey and not

obey, he is a rebel (not a revolutionary); he acts out of anger, disappointment, resentment, yet not in the name of a conviction or a principle.

8   However, in order to prevent a confusion of terms an important qualification must be made. Obedience to a person, institution, or power (heteronomous obedience) is submission; it implies the abdication of my autonomy and the acceptance of a foreign will or judgment in place of my own. Obedience to my own reason or conviction (autonomous obedience) is not an act of submission but one of affirmation. My conviction and my judgment, if authentically mine, are part of me. If I follow them rather than the judgment of others, I am being myself; hence the word *obey* can be applied only in a metaphorical sense and with a meaning which is fundamentally different from the one in the case of "heteronomous obedience."

9   But this distinction still needs two further qualifications, one with regard to the concept of conscience and the other with regard to the concept of authority.

10   The word *conscience* is used to express two phenomena which are quite distinct from each other. One is the "authoritarian conscience" which is the internalized voice of an authority whom we are eager to please and afraid of displeasing. This authoritarian conscience is what most people experience when they obey their conscience. It is also the conscience which Freud speaks of, and which he called "Super-Ego." This Super-Ego represents the internalized commands and prohibitions of father, accepted by the son out of fear. Different from the authoritarian conscience is the "humanistic conscience"; this is the voice present in every human being and independent from external sanctions and rewards. Humanistic conscience is based on the fact that as human beings we have an intuitive knowledge of what is human and inhuman, what is conducive of life and what is destructive of life. This conscience serves our functioning as human beings. It is the voice which calls us back to ourselves, to our humanity.

11   Authoritarian conscience (Super-Ego) is still obedience to a power outside of myself, even though this power has been internalized. Consciously I believe that I am following *my* conscience; in effect, however, I have swallowed the principles of *power;* just because of the illusion that humanistic conscience and Super-Ego are identical, internalized authority is so much more effective than the authority which is clearly experienced as not being part of me. Obedience to the "authoritarian conscience," like all obedience to outside thoughts and power, tends to debilitate "humanistic conscience," the ability to be and to judge oneself.

12   The statement, on the other hand, that obedience to another person is *ipso facto* submission needs also to be qualified by distinguishing "irrational" from "rational" authority. An example of rational authority is to be found in the relationship between student and teacher; one of irrational authority in the relationship between slave and master. Both relationships are based on the fact that the authority of the person in command is accepted. Dynamically, however, they are of a different nature. The interests of the teacher and the student, in the ideal case, lie in the same direction. The teacher is satisfied if he succeeds in furthering the student; if he has failed to do so, the failure is his and the student's. The slave owner, on the other hand, wants to exploit the slave as much as possible. The more he gets out of him the more satisfied he is. At the same time, the slave tries to defend as best he can his claims for a minimum of hap-

piness. The interests of slave and master are antagonistic, because what is advantageous to the one is detrimental to the other. The superiority of the one over the other has a different function in each case; in the first it is the condition for the furtherance of the person subjected to the authority, and in the second it is the condition for his exploitation. Another distinction runs parallel to this: rational authority is rational because the authority, whether it is held by a teacher or a captain of a ship giving orders in an emergency, acts in the name of reason which, being universal, I can accept without submitting. Irrational authority has to use force or suggestion, because no one would let himself be exploited if he were free to prevent it.

13   Why is man so prone to obey and why is it so difficult for him to disobey? As long as I am obedient to the power of the State, the Church, or public opinion, I feel safe and protected. In fact it makes little difference what power it is that I am obedient to. It is always an institution, or men, who use force in one form or another and who fraudulently claim omniscience and omnipotence. My obedience makes me part of the power I worship, and hence I feel strong. I can make no error, since it decides for me; I cannot be alone, because it watches over me; I cannot commit a sin, because it does not let me do so, and even if I do sin, the punishment is only the way of returning to the almighty power.

14   In order to disobey, one must have the courage to be alone, to err, and to sin. But courage is not enough. The capacity for courage depends on a person's state of development. Only if a person has emerged from mother's lap and father's commands, only if he has emerged as a fully developed individual and thus has acquired the capacity to think and feel for himself, only then can he have the courage to say "no" to power, to disobey.

15   A person can become free through acts of disobedience by learning to say no to power. But not only is the capacity for disobedience the condition for freedom; freedom is also the condition for disobedience. If I am afraid of freedom, I cannot dare to say "no," I cannot have the courage to be disobedient. Indeed, freedom and the capacity for disobedience are inseparable; hence any social, political, and religious system which proclaims freedom, yet stamps out disobedience, cannot speak the truth.

16   There is another reason why it is so difficult to dare to disobey, to say "no" to power. During most of human history obedience has been identified with virtue and disobedience with sin. The reason is simple: thus far throughout most of history a minority has ruled over the majority. This rule was made necessary by the fact that there was only enough of the good things of life for the few, and only the crumbs remained for the many. If the few wanted to enjoy the good things and, beyond that, to have the many serve them and work for them, one condition was necessary: the many had to learn obedience. To be sure, obedience can be established by sheer force. But this method has many disadvantages. It constitutes a constant threat that one day the many might have the means to overthrow the few by force; furthermore there are many kinds of work which cannot be done properly if nothing but fear is behind the obedience. Hence the obedience which is only rooted in the fear of force must be transformed into one rooted in man's heart. Man must want and even need to obey, instead of only fearing to disobey. If this is to be achieved, power must

assume the qualities of the All Good, of the All Wise; it must become All Knowing. If this happens, power can proclaim that disobedience is sin and obedience virtue; and once this has been proclaimed, the many can accept obedience because it is good and detest disobedience because it is bad, rather than to detest themselves for being cowards. From Luther to the nineteenth century one was concerned with overt and explicit authorities. Luther, the pope, the princes, wanted to uphold it; the middle class, the workers, the philosophers, tried to uproot it. The fight against authority in the State as well as in the family was often the very basis for the development of an independent and daring person. The fight against authority was inseparable from the intellectual mood which characterized the philosophers of the enlightenment and the scientists. This "critical mood" was one of faith in reason, and at the same time of doubt in everything which is said or thought, inasmuch as it is based on tradition, superstition, custom, power. The principles *sapere aude* and *de omnibus est dubitandum*—"dare to be wise" and "of all one must doubt"—were characteristic of the attitude which permitted and furthered the capacity to say "no."

17   The case of Adolf Eichmann [see note, page 323] is symbolic of our situation and has a significance far beyond the one in which his accusers in the courtroom in Jerusalem were concerned with. Eichmann is a symbol of the organization man, of the alienated bureaucrat for whom men, women and children have become numbers. He is a symbol of all of us. We can see ourselves in Eichmann. But the most frightening thing about him is that after the entire story was told in terms of his own admissions, he was able in perfect good faith to plead his innocence. It is clear that if he were once more in the same situation he would do it again. And so would we—and so do we.

18   The organization man has lost the capacity to disobey, he is not even aware of the fact that he obeys. At this point in history the capacity to doubt, to criticize, and to disobey may be all that stands between a future for mankind and the end of civilization.

Review Questions

1. What does Fromm mean when he writes that disobedience is "the first step into independence and freedom"?

2. Fromm writes that history began with an act of disobedience and will likely end with an act of obedience. What does he mean?

3. What is the difference between "heteronomous obedience" and "autonomous obedience"?

4. How does Fromm distinguish between "authoritarian conscience" and "humanistic conscience"?

5. When is obedience to another person *not* submission?

6. What are the psychological comforts of obedience, and why would authorities rather have people obey out of love than out of fear?

Discussion and Writing Suggestions

1. Fromm suggests that scientifically we live in the twentieth century but that politically and emotionally we live in the Stone Age. As you observe events in the world, both near and far, would you agree? Why?

2. Fromm writes: "If a man can only obey and not disobey, he is a slave; if he can only disobey and not obey, he is a rebel (not a revolutionary)." Explain Fromm's meaning here. Explain, as well, the implication that to be fully human one must have the freedom to both obey and disobey.

3. Fromm writes that "obedience makes me part of the power I worship, and hence I feel strong." Does this statement ring true for you? Discuss, in writing, an occasion in which you felt powerful because you obeyed a group norm.

4. In paragraphs 15 and 16, Fromm equates obedience with cowardice. Can you identify a situation in which you were obedient but, now that you reflect on it, also were cowardly? That is, can you recall a time when you caved in to a group but now wish you hadn't? Explain.

5. Fromm says that we can see ourselves in Adolf Eichmann—that as an organization man he "has lost the capacity to disobey, he is not even aware of the fact that he obeys." To what extent do you recognize yourself in this portrait?

The Organization Kid
David Brooks

In the following article David Brooks focuses less on the sometimes startling, sometimes horrifying effects of obedience to authority than on the making of the kind of conformist mind that is a prerequisite for such obedience. Ian Parker, in his article on Stanley Milgram, reviewed some of the reasons that people are likely to become overly obedient—not only that they willingly put themselves into Milgram's "agentic state," but also that they find themselves in a particular set of circumstances that foments obedience. They may also be predisposed (through cultural or educational influences) to aggression toward their victims and, thus, to carry out orders to hurt or even kill their perceived enemies. Recent history, not only in Nazi Germany, but also in places like Rwanda, the Middle East, and the former Yugoslavia offers ample evidence of this phenomenon.

In this article David Brooks focuses on the roots of obedience in education and socialization—and particularly the type of education and socialization undergone by upper-middle-class young people at elite institutions. Brooks doesn't suggest that students who go to schools like Princeton are Nazis in training. He does assert that in the past decade or so—after a period in the 1960s and 1970s during which young people prized freedom, experimentation, and rebellion against authority—today's generation is experiencing the results of a social backlash, one in which productivity, conformity, and compliance with authority have become some of the main goals of social conditioning among parents and school administrators.

The title of Brooks' article, "The Organization Kid," is a variation on the title of a pioneering 1956 sociological study by William H. Whyte called The Organization Man. *In this highly influential book the author considered the origins, the mentality, and the behavior of a particular social type that developed in the post–World War II period: the man (Whyte did not focus on women) who was the ideal employee because he was a well-fitting cog in the wheel of the business (or military) organization where he worked, as much as possible like his fellow workers, inclined not to make waves, inclined to think the company always knew best. The organization man was also a model member of his community, where he lived in a house and drove a car that looked just like everyone else's in the neighborhood, had the standard-issue wife and 2.4 kids, and believed that the government always had his best interests at heart. (The organization man was also known as "the man in the gray flannel suit," after Sloan Wilson's 1955 novel about postwar suburbia. For a comic look at the 1950s-type organization man—and his office setting—see Billy Wilder's 1960 Academy Award-winning film* The Apartment.*)*

David Brooks is a senior editor at The Weekly Standard. *His book* Bobos in Paradise *was published in 2000. This selection is excerpted from an article that originally appeared in the April 2001 issue of* The Atlantic Monthly. *As he explains in the first part of his article (not included here), Brooks' conclusions apply primarily to middle and upper-middle-class young people attending "elite" schools: he formulated his ideas after talking to faculty and students at Princeton University. (Results at your institution may vary.)*

1 [Y]oung people today are […] likely to defer to and admire authority figures. Responding to a 1997 Gallup survey, 96 percent of teenagers said they got along with their parents, and 82 percent described their home life as "wonderful" or "good." Roughly three out of four said they shared their parents' general values. When asked by Roper Starch Worldwide in 1998 to rank the major problems facing America today, students aged twelve to nineteen most frequently named as their top five concerns selfishness, people who don't respect law and the authorities, wrongdoing by politicians, lack of parental discipline, and courts that care too much about criminals' rights. It is impossible to imagine teenagers a few decades ago calling for stricter parental discipline and more respect for authority. In 1974 a majority of teenagers reported that they could not "comfortably approach their parents with personal matters of concern." Forty percent believed they would be "better off not living with their parents."

2 Walk through any mall in America. Browse through the racks at Old Navy and Abercrombie & Fitch and the Gap. The colors are bright and chipper. The sales staff is peppy. The look is vaguely retro—upbeat 1962 pre-assassination innocence. The Gap's television ads don't show edgy individualists; they show perky conformists, a bunch of happy kids all wearing the same clothes and all swing-dancing the same moves.

3 In short, at the top of the meritocratic ladder we have in America a generation of students who are extraordinarily bright, morally earnest, and incredibly industrious. They like to study and socialize in groups. They create and join organizations with great enthusiasm. They are responsible, safety-conscious, and

mature. They feel no compelling need to rebel—not even a hint of one. They not only defer to authority; they admire it. "Alienation" is a word one almost never hears from them. They regard the universe as beneficent, orderly, and meaningful. At the schools and colleges where the next leadership class is being bred, one finds not angry revolutionaries, despondent slackers, or dark cynics but the Organization Kid.

4   To understand any generation, or even the elite segment of any generation, we have to keep reminding ourselves when it was born and what it has experienced. Most of today's college students were born from 1979 to 1982. That means they were under ten years old when the Berlin Wall fell, and so have no real firsthand knowledge of global conflict or Cold War anxieties about nuclear war. The only major American armed conflict they remember is Desert Storm, a high-tech cakewalk. Moreover, they have never known anything but incredible prosperity: low unemployment and low inflation are the normal condition; crime rates are always falling; the stock market rises. If your experience consisted entirely of being privileged, pampered, and recurringly rewarded in the greatest period of wealth creation in human history, you'd be upbeat too. You'd defer to authority. You'd think that the universe is benign and human nature is fundamentally wonderful.*

5   But the outlook of these young people can't be explained by economics and global events alone. It must also have something to do with the way they were raised. As the University of Michigan time-analysis data show, this is a group whose members have spent the bulk of their lives in structured, adult-organized activities. They are the most honed and supervised generation in human history. If they are group-oriented, deferential to authority, and achievement-obsessed, it is because we achievement-besotted adults have trained them to be. We have devoted our prodigious energies to imposing a sort of order and responsibility on our kids' lives that we never experienced ourselves. The kids have looked upon this order and have decided that it's good.

6   Childhood is indeed a journey, a series of stations on the way to adulthood. Snapshots of a few of the stations of contemporary childhood will show how the Organization Kid came to be. [...]

Elementary School

7   No one has done a meticulous scientific study of the subject, but my impression is that the big-backpack era began in the mid-1980s. Kids began carrying larger and larger backpacks to school every year; by the early 1990s I saw elementary school students lugging storage containers that were bigger than they were. I'd watch them trooping into the school yard and wonder what would happen to a kid who lost his balance and tipped backward onto his pack. He'd lie there like a stranded beetle, face skyward, arms and legs flailing in the air, unable to flip over again. Would he simply be stuck, pinned to the pavement by the weight of his mathematics texts, until someone came to the rescue?

---

*This article was written before the terrorist attacks on the World Trade Center and the Pentagon on September 11, 2001. [eds.]

8   Perhaps the most important event in ushering in the big-backpack era was the release of the report *A Nation at Risk,* on April 26, 1983. Commissioned by Terrel Bell, Ronald Reagan's Secretary of Education, the report decried the "rising tide of mediocrity" plaguing American schools and it caused an immediate sensation. The problem, it said, was that schools had become too loose and free-flowing. Students faced a "cafeteria style curriculum" that gave them too many choices. They were graduating from high school having spent much of their time in elective gut classes. They didn't do enough homework. They weren't given enough "rigorous examinations" and standardized tests, nor were they forced to meet stringent college-admissions requirements.

9   The report represented a rejection of an era that celebrated "natural" education, student-centered diversity, and spontaneity, and that cultivated creativity over discipline and nonconformity over conformity. *A Nation at Risk* bid farewell to all that, and said it was time to reassert authority and re-establish order. Schools needed to get back to basics.

10   The message took, and the effect has been dramatic. During the 1960s and 1970s schools assigned less and less homework, so that by 1981 the average six-to-eight-year-old was doing only fifty-two minutes of homework a week. By 1997 the amount of homework assigned to the average child of the same age had doubled, to more than two hours a week. Meanwhile, the school day, which had shortened during the sixties and seventies, has steadily lengthened since, as has the school year. Requirements have stiffened. Before 1983 the average school district required one year of math and one year of science for high school graduation. Now the average high school calls for two years of each. The culture of schools has tightened. In the 1970s, rebelling against the rigid desks-in-a-row pedagogy of the 1950s, schools experimented with open campuses and classes without walls. Now the language of education reform has changed, and the emphasis is on testing, accountability, and order.

11   Especially order: increasingly, and in surprising numbers, kids whose behavior subverts efficient learning are medicated so that they and their classmates can keep pace. The United States produces and uses about 90 percent of the world's Ritalin and its generic equivalents. In 1980 it was estimated that somewhere between 270,000 and 541,000 elementary school students were taking Ritalin. By 1987 around 750,000 were. And the use of the drug didn't really take off until the 1990s. In 1997 around 30,000 pounds were produced—an increase of more than 700 percent over the 1990 production level.

12   Far from all of that Ritalin goes to elementary school kids, but the Ritalin that does is prescribed most frequently in upper-middle-class suburban districts—where, one suspects, the achievement ethos is strongest. Some physicians believe that 10 percent of all children have the sort of conduct disorder—attention-deficit disorder, oppositional defiant disorder—that could be eased with Ritalin or some other drug. It is stunning how quickly we have moved from the idea that children should be given freedom to chart their own learning to a belief that adults have a responsibility to reshape the minds of kids whose behavior deviates from the standard. As Ken Livingston wrote in *The Public Interest* in 1997, "In late twentieth-century America, when it is difficult or inconvenient to change the environment, we don't think twice about changing the

brain of the person who has to live in it." And as Howe and Strauss wrote in *Millennials Rising,* "Ironically, where young Boomers once turned to drugs to prompt impulses and think outside the box, today they turn to drugs to suppress their kids' impulses and keep their behavior inside the box…Nowadays, Dennis the Menace would be on Ritalin, Charlie Brown on Prozac."

13   The end result of these shifts in pedagogy and in pharmacology is that schools are much more efficient and productive places, geared more than ever toward projecting children into the stratosphere of success. Authority and accountability have replaced experimentation and flexibility. […]

Adolescence

14 Adolescence is a complicated time, and maybe no single snapshot can sum it up. But reading through some of the best recent literature on the subject— Patricia Hersch's *A Tribe Apart,* Kay Hymowitz's *Ready or Not,* Thomas Hine's *The Rise and Fall of the American Teenager*—one is struck by how many people are grappling in different ways with a common quandary: too much space. At some point in the past sophisticated parents cottoned on to the idea that rebellion and experimentation are part of the natural order of growing up, and that parents of teenagers should therefore give their kids enough freedom and space to explore and define themselves. But these new books and a shelf's worth of foundation reports now assert that kids today do not seem to want as much freedom and space as they have been granted. So the task for parents is to define boundaries for their adolescents, to offer continual guidance and discipline. Two decades ago parents were advised to withdraw from their teens' lives as those teens flew off to adulthood. Now they are advised to serve as chaperones at all-night graduation parties.

15   The U-turn is dramatic. In 1967 the U.S. Supreme Court heralded the liberationist age with its decision in the *Gault case.* The Court held that students have the same due-process rights as adults. That decision restricted the ways in which schools could assert paternalistic authority, but it was also a sign of the times. Children and teens should be left free to be themselves. As the legal scholar Martha Minow summarized it in an essay in *From Children to Citizens* (1987), the decision was part of a cultural and "legal march away from the conception of the child as a dependent person." Many high schools in the seventies and eighties adopted open-campus policies. Students had to show up for class, but beyond that they were free to come and go as they pleased; the high school was essentially turned into a college campus. The Emancipation of Minors Act, passed by the California legislature in 1982, enabled teenagers to sign contracts, own property, and keep their earnings. It transformed them into quasi adults.

16   The prevailing view today couldn't be more different. The 1997 *National Longitudinal Study of Adolescent Health* emphasized that the most powerful factor in determining the well-being of young people is the presence of parents and adults who are actively engaged in supervising and setting goals for teenagers' lives. A 1993 study, *Talented Teenagers,* found that teens need security and support if they are going to explore. Hersch's highly acclaimed *A Tribe*

Apart is an angry rebuke to parents who have given their teens too much space. Hersch writes,

> The lives of the kids in this book illustrate in subtle and not so subtle ways the need for adult presence to help them learn the new lessons of growing up. Kids need adults who bear witness to the details of their lives and count them as something. They require the watchful eyes and the community standards that provide greater stability…The kids in the book who do best are those who have a strong interactive family and a web of relationships and activities that surround them consistently.

17   So when we survey American childhood today, we see that a quiet revolution has taken place. The Romantics—and the neo-Romantics of the 1960s and 1970s—thought that children were born with an innate wisdom and purity. They were natural beings, as yet uncontaminated by the soul-crushing conventions of adult society. Hence they should be left free to explore, to develop their own creative tendencies, to learn at their own pace. Now, in contrast, children are to be stimulated and honed. Parents shouldn't hesitate to impose their authority. On the contrary, it is now pretty widely believed that the killings at Columbine and similar tragedies teach us that parents have a duty to be highly involved in the lives of their kids.

18   Today's ramped-up parental authority rests on three pillars: science, safety, and achievement. What we ambitious parents know about the human brain tells us that children need to be placed in stimulating and productive environments if they are going to reach their full potential. What we know about the world tells us that it is a dangerous place: there are pesticides on our fruit, cigarettes in the school yards, rocks near the bike paths, kidnappers in the woods. Children need to be protected. And finally, what we know about life is that sorting by merit begins at birth and never ends. Books about what to expect in the first year lay out achievement markers starting in the first month, and from then on childhood is one long progression of measurements, from nursery school admissions to SATs. Parents need to be coaching at their child's side.

19   Imagine being a product of this regimen—one of the kids who thrived in it, the sort who winds up at elite schools. All your life you have been pleasing your elders, performing and enjoying the hundreds of enrichment tasks that dominated your early years. You are a mentor magnet. You spent your formative years excelling in school, sports, and extracurricular activities. And you have been rewarded with a place at a wonderful university filled with smart, successful, and cheerful people like yourself. Wouldn't you be just like the students I found walking around Princeton?

The Moral Life of the Organization Kid

20 When students enter college today, they are on familiar ground. After throwing off curfews, dress codes, and dormitory supervision in the 1970s, most colleges are reimposing their authority and reasserting order, just as high schools and families are. Some universities are trying to restrict or eliminate drinking. Many are cracking down on fraternity hazing rites. Others have banned Dionysian rituals such as lascivious costume balls and Princeton's Nude Olympics. University

regulations intrude far more into the personal lives of students, and the students seem to approve.

21   As part of an effort to cajole students into behaving responsibly, many colleges have tried to provide places where they can go to amuse themselves without alcohol or drugs. Princeton has just completed a new student facility in the Frist Campus Center, formerly Palmer Hall, an old science building. On a walk from the library to Frist one may pass Prospect House, formerly the president's residence and now the faculty club, with a sparkling, glass-walled restaurant overlooking beautifully maintained gardens. On the lawns nearby, if the weather is tolerable, a drama group might be rehearsing, and other students might be bent over heavy books or laptops. The students are casual, but they look every bit as clean-cut as students in the early 1960s did, as if the intervening forty years of collegiate scruffiness had never happened. Almost all the men shave every day. Their hair is trim and freshly shampooed. Very few students wear tattoos or have had their bodies pierced—so far as one can see—in unapproved places. Many of the women wear skirts, or sundresses when the weather is warm. "I lived an incredibly ragged life," Kathryn Taylor, class of 1974, now an administrator in alumni affairs, told me of her college days. "It never would have dawned on me to try to look nice. They seem to be much more conscious of apparel."

22   It was only relatively recently that Princeton went coed, but one wouldn't know it. The male students are modern, enlightened men, sensitized since the first grade to apologize for their testosterone. The women are assertive and make a show of self-confidence, especially the athletes. Members of the women's soccer team have T-shirts that read YOUNG, WILD AND READY TO SCORE. Posters advertising a weekend's races say CROSS COUNTRY! IT'S EXCITING TO WATCH SEXY WOMEN RUN!—brashness that would be socially unacceptable if the boys tried it.

23   The Frist Campus Center is a Neo-Gothic structure, built in 1907, that once housed nuclear experiments. Coats of arms are etched in stone on the façade, from which an imposing statue of Benjamin Franklin looks down at visitors. But that is the old Princeton; the building's ground level has been turned into the up-to-date student center, where rows of computer stations allow students to check their e-mail and where modern banalities have been painted on the walls: "Only by deliberating together about moral questions will we find mutual respect and common ground.—Amy Guttman." "The locusts sang and they were singing for me.—Bob Dylan." "Race matters.—Cornel West." "If I'm not out there training, someone else is.—Lynn Jennings."

24   Beyond are a billiards room, a set of low chairs where students can read while watching ESPN on a big-screen TV, a kiosk selling Princeton memorabilia, and a convenience store in which you can buy Nantucket Nectars, Arizona green tea with ginseng, raspberry Snapple, and the full array of Gatorade and Powerade, in flavors such as Fierce Melon and Arctic Shatter.

25   Bulletin boards throughout are festooned with recruiting posters from investment firms. One, from Goldman Sachs, shows a photo of a group of wholesome-looking young people relaxing after a game of lunchtime basketball. The text reads "Wanted: Strategists, Quick Thinkers, Team Players, Achievers." Another, from the business-consulting firm KPMG, shows a picture of a pair of

incredibly hip-looking middle-aged people staring warmly into the camera. The text reads "Now that you've made your parents proud, join KPMG and give them something to smile about." It's hard to imagine a recruiting poster of a few decades ago appealing to students' desire to make their parents happy.

26   Downstairs is a cafeteria with a variety of food stations—pasta, a grill, salads, daily specials. Except that the drinks are not free, it reminded me of the dining hall at Microsoft, in Redmond, Washington. A wall of glass looks out over a lawn. Small groups of happy-looking people—Asian-American kids here, African-American kids there—sit at the tables. They are talking mostly about their work-loads, and even their conversational style is polite and slightly formal. "Hello, ladies …" one young woman calls out to a group of her friends. "How are you?" a young man asks a young woman in greeting. "I'm fine, thanks," she replies. "How are you?"

27   They're so clean, inside and out. They seem like exactly the sort of young people we older folks want them to be. Baby Boomers may be tempted to utter a little prayer of gratitude: Thank God our kids aren't the royal pains in the ass that we were to our parents.

28   But the more I talked to them and observed them, the more I realized that the difference between this and preceding generations is not just a matter of dress and comportment. It's not just that these students work harder, are more neatly groomed, and defer to their teachers more readily. There are more-fun-damental differences: they have different mental categories.

29   It takes a while to realize this, because unlike their predecessors, they don't shout out their differences or declare them in political or social movements. In fact, part of what makes them novel is that they don't think they are new. They don't see themselves as a lost generation or a radical generation or a beatnik generation or even a Reaganite generation. They have relatively little genera-tional consciousness. That's because this generation is for the most part not fighting to emancipate itself from the past. The most sophisticated people in preceding generations were formed by their struggle to break free from some-thing. The most sophisticated people in this one aren't.

30   "On or about December 1910 human character changed," Virginia Woolf famously declared. Gone, she wrote, were the old certainties, the old manners, the deference to nineteenth-century authority. Instead human beings—at least the ones in Woolf's circle—were starting to see the world as full of chaos and discontinuity. Einstein smashed the notion of absolute time and space. Artists from Seurat to Picasso deconstructed visual perceptions. James Joyce's *Ulysses* scrambled the narrative order of the traditional novel. Rebels upended Victorian sexual mores. And later in the century, when the modernists were exhausted, the postmodernists came along to tell us that life is even more disordered and contingent than even Virginia Woolf could have imagined. Words are detach-able from their meanings. History has no grand narratives. Everything is just shifting modes of perception, a maelstrom of change and diversity.

31   For those growing into adulthood during most of the twentieth century, there-fore, the backdrop to life was the loss of faith in coherent systems of thought and morality. Sophisticated people knew they were supposed to rebel against authority, reject old certainties, and liberate themselves from hidebound cus-

toms and prejudices. Artists rebelled against the stodgy mores of the bourgeoisie. Radicals rebelled against the commercial and capitalist order. Feminists rebelled against the patriarchal family. And in the latter half of the twentieth century a youth culture emerged, which distilled these themes. Every rock anthem, every fashion statement, every protest gesture, every novel about rebellious youth—from *The Catcher in the Rye* to *On the Road*—carried the same cultural message: It's better to be a nonconformist than a conformist, a creative individualist than a member of a group, a rebel than a traditionalist, a daring adventurer than a safe and responsible striver. "We hope for nonconformists among you," the theologian Paul Tillich preached to college audiences in 1957, "for your sake, for the sake of the nation, and for the sake of humanity."

32   Today's elite college students don't live in that age of rebellion and alienation. They grew up in a world in which the counterculture and the mainstream culture have merged with, and co-opted, each other. For them, it's natural that one of the top administrators at Princeton has a poster of the Beatles album *Revolver* framed on her office wall. It's natural that hippies work at ad agencies and found organic-ice-cream companies, and that hi-tech entrepreneurs quote Dylan and wear black jeans to work. For them, it's natural that parents should listen to Led Zeppelin, Jimi Hendrix, and the Doors—just like kids. They don't have the mental barriers that exist between, say, the establishment and rebels, between respectable society and the subversive underground. For them, all those categories are mushed together. "They work for Save the Children and Merrill Lynch and they don't see a contradiction," says Jeffrey Herbst, the politics professor. Moreover, nothing in their environment suggests that the world is ill constructed or that life is made meaningful only by revolt. There have been no senseless bloodbaths like World War I and Vietnam, no crushing economic depressions, no cycles of assassination and rioting to foment disillusionment. They've mostly known parental protection, prosperity, and peace.

33   During most of the twentieth century the basic ways of living were called into question, but now those fundamental debates are over, at least among the young elite. Democracy and dictatorship are no longer engaged in an epic struggle; victorious democracy is the beneficent and seemingly natural order. No more fundamental arguments pit capitalism against socialism; capitalism is so triumphant that we barely even contemplate an alternative. Radicals no longer assault the American family and the American home; we accept diverse family patterns but celebrate family and community togetherness. The militant feminists of the 1960s are mostly of a grandmotherly age now. Even theological conflicts have settled down; it's fashionable to be religious so long as one is not aggressively so.

34   Unlike their elders, in other words, these young people are not part of an insurrection against inherited order. They are not even part of the conservative reaction against the insurrection. The debates of the Reagan years are as distant as the trial of the Chicago Seven, which is as distant as the Sacco and Vanzetti case. It's not that they reject one side of that culture war, or embrace the other. They've just moved on. As people in northern California would say, they're living in a different place.

35   The world they live in seems fundamentally just. If you work hard, behave pleasantly, explore your interests, volunteer your time, obey the codes of political correctness, and take the right pills to balance your brain chemistry, you will be rewarded with a wonderful ascent in the social hierarchy. You will get into Princeton and have all sorts of genuinely interesting experiences open to you. You will make a lot of money—but more important, you will be able to improve yourself. You will be a good friend and parent. You will be caring and conscientious. You will learn to value the really important things in life. There is a fundamental order to the universe, and it works. If you play by its rules and defer to its requirements, you will lead a pretty fantastic life.

Review Questions

1. What are some of the indications of the emergent "organization kid" at elementary schools, according to Brooks?

2. How does Brooks contend that high schools prepare "elite" students to be obedient to authority?

3. What do the decorations inside the Frist Campus Center at Princeton indicate to Brooks about today's elite college generation?

4. What kind of historical forces account for the different mentality of today's elite younger generation, from that of their parents, according to Brooks?

Discussion and Writing Suggestions

1. To what extent do you recognize yourself and your generation in the description provided by Brooks in the first two paragraphs of this selection? If you disagree, explain why.

2. Brooks writes that as a result of educational reforms during the 1980s and 1990s, "the emphasis [in top schools] is on testing, accountability, and order." Later, he says that "schools are much more efficient and productive places [than they were a decade or so earlier], geared more than ever toward projecting children into the stratosphere of success. Authority and accountability have replaced experimentation and flexibility." To what extent does your own experience bear out this contention?

3. To what degree do you find in the wider culture any indications of a move toward re-imposition of authority, and the regimentation of young minds, as discussed by Brooks? Consider, for example, the growing demand for school uniforms or the movement to control offensive lyrics from popular music. Do these and other moves toward greater social control of young people indicate that we are living in the age of "the organization kid"?

4. Why do you think Brooks labels such slogans and aphorisms as "The locusts sang and they were singing for me" and "Race matters" (paragraph 23) as "modern banalities"?

5. Brooks repeatedly draws comparisons and contrasts between today's generation of students and those who came of age in the 1960s and 1970s. To what extent does what your own parents or older relatives have told you about their lives as students confirm Brooks' conclusions about the difference between the older and younger generations?

6. Brooks suggests that because the younger generation has never experienced social upheavals of the magnitude of the Civil Rights movement or the anti-war movement of the 1960s, or the struggle against communism from the 1950s to the 1980s, but on the contrary, has only experienced economic prosperity, they have, in effect, nothing to rebel against. They are therefore far more inclined to be conformist than were their parents at the same age. To what extent do you accept this analysis?

7. In addition to the kind of economic and social sailing that Brooks claims today's younger generation has enjoyed, he asserts that to this generation "[t]here is a fundamental order to the universe, and it works." To what extent do you think that the terrorist attacks on the World Trade Center and the Pentagon on September 11, 2001 have rendered this optimistic viewpoint obsolete?

8. Brooks' analysis is concerned only with students "at the top of the meritocratic ladder," the kinds of students who go to Princeton, Yale, Harvard, and other elite schools. To what extent do you think that his comments about "the organization kid" apply to students at less elite institutions? Is nonconformity and disobedience to authority more likely to be tolerated (or encouraged) in such places?

9. Assuming that what Brooks says has a degree of truth, to what extent do you believe that the kind of conformity and obedience he notes of the younger generation makes this generation more likely to be similar to the kind of obedient subjects that Stanley Milgram encountered during his experiments?

SYNTHESIS ACTIVITIES

1. Compare and contrast the Asch and the Milgram experiments, considering their separate (1) objectives, (2) experimental designs and procedures, (3) results, and (4) conclusions. To what extent do the findings of these two experiments reinforce one another? To what extent do they highlight different, if related, social phenomena? To

what extent do their results reinforce those of Zimbardo's prison experiment?

2. Assume for the moment you agree with Doris Lessing: Children need to be taught how to disobey so they can recognize and avoid situations that give rise to harmful obedience. If you were the curriculum coordinator for your local school system, how would you teach children to disobey responsibly? What would be your curriculum? What homework would you assign? What class projects? What field trips? One complicated part of your job would be to train children to understand the difference between *responsible* disobedience and anarchy. What is the difference?

   Take up these questions in an essay that draws on both your experiences as a student and your understanding of the selections in this chapter. Points that you might want to consider in developing the essay: defining overly obedient children; appropriate classroom behavior for responsibly disobedient children (as opposed to inappropriate behavior); reading lists; homework assignments; field trips; class projects.

3. A certain amount of obedience is a given in society. Stanley Milgram and others observe that social order, civilization itself, would not be possible unless individuals were willing to surrender a portion of their autonomy to the state. Allowing that we all are obedient (we must be), define the point at which obedience to a figure of authority becomes dangerous.

   As you develop your definition, consider the ways you might use the work of authors in this chapter and their definitions of acceptable and unacceptable levels of obedience. Do you agree with the ways in which others have drawn the line between reasonable and dangerous obedience? What examples from current stories in the news or from your own experience can you draw on to test various definitions?

4. Describe a situation in which you were faced with a moral dilemma of whether or not to obey a figure of authority. After describing the situation and the action you took (or didn't take), discuss your behavior in light of any two readings in this chapter. You might consider a straightforward, four-part structure for your essay: (1) your description; (2) your discussion, in light of source A; (3) your discussion, in light of source B; and (4) your conclusion—an overall appraisal of your behavior.

5. At one point in his essay (paragraphs 15 and 16), Erich Fromm equates obedience with cowardice. Earlier in the chapter, Doris Lessing (paragraph 9) observes that "among our most shameful memories is this, how often we said black was white because other people were saying it." Using the work of these authors as a point of departure, reconsider an act of obedience or disobedience in

your own life. Describe pertinent circumstances for your reader. Based on what you have learned in this chapter, reassess your behavior. Would you behave similarly if given a second chance in the same situation?

6. Discuss the critical reaction to the Milgram experiments. Draw upon Baumrind and Parker, as well as Milgram himself, in summarizing both the ethical and procedural objections to the experiments. Following these summaries, develop your own critique, positive or negative, bringing in Milgram himself, where appropriate.

7. In his response to Diana Baumrind, Stanley Milgram makes a point of insisting that follow-up interviews with subjects in his experiments show that a large majority were pleased, in the long run, to have participated. (See Table 1 in the footnote to Baumrind, page 334.) Writing on his own post-experiment surveys and interviews, Philip Zimbardo writes that his subjects believed their "mental anguish was transient and situationally specific, but the self-knowledge gained has persisted" (paragraph 60). Why might they *and* the experimenters nonetheless have been eager to accept a positive, final judgment of the experiments? Develop an essay in response to this question, drawing on the selections by Milgram, Zimbardo, and Baumrind.

8. Develop a synthesis in which you extend Baumrind's critique of Milgram (and possibly, the critiques of others, as discussed by Parker) to the Stanford Prison Experiment. This assignment requires that you understand the core elements of Baumrind's critique; that you have a clear understanding of Zimbardo's experiment; and that you systematically apply elements of the critiques, as you see fit, to Zimbardo's work. In your conclusion, offer your overall assessment of the Stanford Prison Experiment. To do this, you might answer Zimbardo's own question in paragraph 55: "Was [the experiment] worth all the suffering?" Or you might respond to another question: Do you agree that Zimbardo is warranted in extending the conclusions of his experiment to the general population?

9. In response to the question "Why is man so prone to obey and why is it so difficult for him to disobey?" Erich Fromm suggests that obedience lets people identify with the powerful and invites feelings of safety. Disobedience is psychologically more difficult and requires an act of courage. (See paragraphs 13 and 14.) Solomon Asch notes that the tendency to conformity is generally stronger than the tendency to independence. And in his final paragraph, Philip Zimbardo writes that a "prison of fear" keeps people compliant and frees them of the need to take responsibility for their own actions. In a synthesis that draws on these three sources, explore the interplay of *fear* and its opposite, *courage*, in relation to obedience. To prevent the essay from becoming too abstract, direct your attention repeatedly to a single case, the details of which will help to

keep your focus. This case may be based upon a particular event from your own life or the life of someone you know.

10. To what extent are students particularly prone to obedience? Draw upon Zimbardo and Brooks, as well as your own outside reading, observations, and experience, in developing your response. If the Zimbardo experiment were conducted today, do you think that the results would be about the same as they were in the early 1970s? Why or why not?

RESEARCH ACTIVITIES

1. When Milgram's results were first published in book form in 1974, they generated heated controversy. The reactions reprinted here (by Baumrind and Parker) represent only a very small portion of that controversy. Research other reactions to the Milgram experiments and discuss your findings. Begin with the reviews listed and excerpted in the *Book Review Digest;* also use the *Social Science Index,* the *Readers' Guide to Periodical Literature,* and newspaper indexes to locate articles, editorials, and letters to the editor on the experiments. (Note that editorials and letters are not always indexed. Letters appear within two to four weeks of the weekly magazine articles to which they refer, and within one to two weeks of newspaper articles.) What were the chief types of reactions? To what extent were the reactions favorable?

2. Milgram begins his article "Obedience to Authority" with a reference to Nazi Germany. The purpose of his experiment, in fact, was to help throw light on how the Nazi atrocities could have happened. Research the Nuremberg war crimes tribunals following World War II. Drawing specifically on the statements of those who testified at Nuremberg, as well as those who have written about it, show how Milgram's experiments do help explain the Holocaust and other Nazi crimes. In addition to relevant articles, see Telford Taylor, *Nuremberg and Vietnam: An American Tragedy* (1970); Hannah Arendt, *Eichmann in Jerusalem: A Report on the Banality of Evil* (1963); Richard A. Falk, Gabriel Kolko, and Robert J. Lifton (eds.), *Crimes of War* (1971).

3. Obtain a copy of the transcript of the trial of Adolf Eichmann—the Nazi official who carried out Hitler's "final solution" for the extermination of the Jews. Read also Hannah Arendt's *Eichmann in Jerusalem: A Report on the Banality of Evil,* along with the reviews of this book. Write a critique both of Arendt's book and of the reviews it received.

4. The My Lai massacre in Vietnam in 1969 was a particularly egregious case of overobedience to military authority in wartime. Show the connections between this event and Milgram's experiments.

Note that Milgram himself treated the My Lai massacre in the epilogue to his *Obedience to Authority: An Experimental View* (1974).

5. Investigate the court-martial of Lt. William Calley, convicted for his role in the My Lai massacre. Discuss the question of whether President Nixon was justified in commuting his sentence. Examine in detail the dilemmas the jury must have faced when presented with Calley's defense that he was only following orders.

6. Research the Watergate break-in of 1972 and the subsequent cover-up by Richard Nixon and members of his administration, as an example of overobedience to authority. Focus on one particular aspect of Watergate (e.g., the role of the counsel to the president, John Dean, or why the crisis was allowed to proceed to the point where it actually toppled a presidency). In addition to relevant articles, see Robert Woodward and Carl Bernstein, *All the President's Men* (1974); Leon Jaworski, *The Right and the Power: The Prosecution of Watergate* (1976); *RN: The Memoirs of Richard Nixon* (1978); John Dean, *Blind Ambition* (1976); John Sirica, *To Set the Record Straight: The Break-in, the Tapes, the Conspirators, the Pardon* (1979); Sam Ervin, *The Whole Truth: The Watergate Conspiracy* (1980); John Ehrlichman, *Witness to Power: The Nixon Years* (1982).

7. Examine conformity as a social phenomenon (and a particular manifestation of obedience to group authority) in some particular area. For example, you may choose to study conformity as it exists among school children, adolescent peer groups, social clubs or associations, or businesspeople. You may want to draw upon such classic studies as William H. Whyte's *The Organization Man* (1956) or David Riesman's *The Lonely Crowd* (1950), or focus upon more recent books and articles, such as Rosabeth Moss Kantor's *A Tale of "O": On Being Different in an Organization* (1980) and John Goldhammer's 1996 book *Under the Influence: The Destructive Effects of Group Dynamics* (1996), including your sociology or social psychology textbooks. You may also find enlightening some fictional treatments of conformity, such as Sinclair Lewis' *Babbitt* (1922), Sloan Wilson's *The Man in the Gray Flannel Suit* (1950), and Herman Wouk's *The Caine Mutiny: A Novel of World War II* (1951). What are the main factors creating the urge to conform among the particular group you are examining? What kind of forces may be able to counteract conformity?

8. At the outset of his article, Stanley Milgram refers to imaginative works revolving around the issue of obedience to authority: the story of Abraham and Isaac; three of Plato's dialogues, "Apology," "Crito," and "Phaedo;" and the story of Antigone (dramatized by both the fifth-century B.C. Athenian Sophocles and the twentieth-century Frenchman Jean Anouilh). Many other fictional works deal with obedience to authority—for example, George Orwell's *1984* (1949), Herman Wouk's novel *The Caine Mutiny* (and his subsequent

play *The Caine Mutiny Court Martial*), and Shirley Jackson's "The Lottery." Check with your instructor, with a librarian, and with such sources as the *Short Story Index* to locate other imaginative works on this theme. Write a paper discussing the various ways in which the subject has been treated in fiction and drama. To ensure coherence, draw comparisons and contrasts among works showing the connections and the variations on the theme of obedience to authority.

Business Ethics

9

Business ethics—both as an academic discipline and as an evolving set of principles used to guide decision making in large and small companies—is a relatively new concept in American life. Before the 1960s and 1970s, the proper role of business was understood as providing goods and services to a consuming public, for profit. Most Americans might have agreed with the sentiment that "what's good for General Motors is good for the country" and trusted General Motors to define "good" on its own terms. No longer. Scandals in business saw corporations dumping toxic chemicals and withholding information about product defects from the public; and with the increasing tendency of large companies to gobble up smaller ones came a general wariness of corporations. In response to this wariness, businesses began to consider their social responsibilities. Increasingly confronted with the reality of government regulation, managers and executives felt compelled to provide the public with an account of hazards in the workplace or in the environment, of questionable labor or management practices, or of economic decisions that might disrupt entire communities. Business also began to take into consideration public concern over corporate policy *before* decisions were made.

By the 1970s, corporations around the country began accepting the view that they had responsibilities to stakeholders as well as to shareholders—to all who were affected by the conduct of business, be that effect monetary, physical, psychological, or environmental. Money was no longer the only concern. Writing in 1971, the Committee for Economic Development noted:

> Today it is clear that the terms of the contract between society and business are, in fact, changing in substantial and important ways. Business is being asked to assume broader responsibilities to society than ever before and to serve a wider range of human values. Business enterprises, in effect, are being asked to contribute more to the quality of American life than just supplying quantities of goods and services.*

The acknowledgment of corporate America's social responsibilities came just in time, apparently, as Americans began showing their impatience with "business as usual." In a survey conducted in 1968, 70 percent of respondents felt that businesses

---

Social Responsibilities of Business Corporations by the Committee for Economic Development (New York: CED, 1971), pp. 29–30.

were managing to earn profits while at the same time showing decent concern for the public's welfare. In 1978, only 15 percent of respondents felt the same way. By 1985, more than half of the respondents to selected surveys claimed that corporate executives are dishonest, that businesses show little regard for the society in which they operate, and that executives violate the public trust whenever money is to be made. For example, in 1992, a leading ethicist who consults with some of America's largest companies reported that, based on in-house surveys, "between 20 percent and 30 percent of middle managers have written deceptive internal reports." That is to say, one-fifth to one-third of the managers surveyed admit to lying.

The news is rife with examples of ethical misconduct. Recall the space shuttle *Challenger* disaster, in which the decision to launch was made over the protest of engineers who warned of potentially disastrous defects in the very parts that failed. Recall the Exxon *Valdez* fiasco that saw hundreds of miles of pristine Alaskan coastal waters despoiled by crude oil: The oil leaked from the ruptured hold of a tanker whose captain had left the bridge command to a subordinate unqualified to navigate the vessel in Prince William Sound; setting the causes of the accident aside, Exxon representatives argued with Alaskan and federal officials over the limits of corporate liability in cleaning up the mess. The corporate impulse was to limit corporate cost, whatever the larger environmental cost to the people of Alaska. And in 2000, recall the more than 200 deaths and 700 injuries linked to the Ford Explorer. Ford accused its long-time tire supplier, Firestone, of knowingly providing substandard tires that failed at high speeds and caused Explorers to roll. Firestone returned the charge, arguing that Ford knowingly built a dangerously unstable car. The manufacturers recalled nearly 20 million tires and have faced numerous lawsuits. More pervasive than these high-profile stories, and perhaps more damaging, are the "little" violations of ethical standards forced on managers or other employees who are asked, or forced, everyday to sacrifice personal values for company gain.

The study of ethics, of course, is not new. From the time of Aristotle (384–322 B.C.), philosophers have debated the standards by which we judge right or good behavior. The systematic study of ethics as applied to business, however, *is* new, and we see in it (according to a past president of the Society for Business Ethics) "an attempt…to revive the importance and legitimacy of making moral claims in the world of practical affairs.* Two associated developments have accompanied the rise of business ethics. First, corporations have begun drafting codes of ethics for their employees. Second, courses in business ethics are being taught at the graduate and undergraduate levels in schools around the country. The thrust of these courses has been both to justify the need for ethics in business and to provide a model by which students, future business leaders, can make ethical judgments in the world of work.

It is likely that in your life as a person who conducts business of one sort or another you will face an ethical dilemma: You could act one way and

---

*W. Michael Hoffman. "Business Ethics in the United States: Its Past Decade and Its Future," *Business Insights* 5, No. 1 (Spring/Summer, 1989): 8.

maintain your principles—but, perhaps, lose a job or an important account; you could act another way and help to secure your fortune—but, perhaps, at the expense of your integrity. The pressures on people in business to make money, on the one hand, but to do the "right" thing, on the other, are real and often painfully difficult. It is these pressures—clearly defining them and responding to them—that form the subject matter of this chapter. We begin with eleven brief scenarios that pose ethical dilemmas and will get you thinking about fair and just courses of action. To encourage your thinking we provide a short primer on business ethics in the form of eight "rules" for ethical conduct, from Robert Solomon's *New World of Business: Ethics and Free Enterprise in the Global 1990s.* Next, writing on "The Case of the Collapsed Mine," Richard T. De George poses a series of questions that effectively surveys the field of business ethics. Gerald F. Cavanagh then presents a detailed system for "Ethics in Business" that, along with Solomon's eight rules, you can use to analyze the six cases concluding the chapter: "Peter Green's First Day," "Romance on the Job," "Is Family-Friendly Always Fair?," "The Serpent Was There," "Is This the Right Time to Come Out?" and "Why Should My Conscience Bother Me?" Like the brief cases that begin the chapter, these will challenge you to recommend reasonable courses of action.

OPENING CASES

The eleven brief cases that follow will whet your appetite for the ethically more complex cases appearing later in the chapter. Here, you will have a chance to familiarize yourself with the types of puzzling questions you may encounter in the world of business. For instance, what should you do when you observe questionable manufacturing processes that may endanger public safety? How loyal should you be to a current employer if a competitor offers you a better salary? As you read, try to identify what is ethically troubling or problematic in these scenarios and begin a process of considering appropriate responses. For the moment, keep your analysis informal: recommend responsible courses of action based on your own value system, not on any formal ethical guidelines (which you will find later in the chapter).

These cases were prepared for textbooks written by Business School faculty at three institutions: John R. Boatright of Loyola University Chicago, for the third edition of his *Ethics and the Conduct of Business* (Prentice Hall, 2000); Robert C. Solomon of the University of Texas at Austin, for *The New World of Business: Ethics and Free Enterprise in the Global 1990s* (Littlefield Adams, 1994); and Gerald F. Cavanagh, University of Detroit, for the third edition of *American Business Values* (Prentice Hall, 1990). If you need guidance on discussing these cases, see Robert Solomon's "Thinking Ethics: The Rules of the Game," which immediately follows this opening section with a set of eight rules for thinking ethically. You might use any of Solomon's rules to analyze one or more of these initial cases.

John R. Boatright

The Sales Rep

A sales representative for a struggling computer supply firm has a chance to close a multimillion-dollar deal for an office system to be installed over a two-year period. The machines for the first delivery are in the company's warehouse, but the remainder would have to be ordered from the manufacturer. Because the manufacturer is having difficulty meeting the heavy demand for the popular model, the sales representative is not sure that subsequent deliveries can be made on time. Any delay in converting to the new system would be costly to the customer; however, the blame could be placed on the manufacturer. Should the sales representative close the deal without advising the customer of the problem?

The Research Director

The director of research in a large aerospace firm recently promoted a woman to head an engineering team charged with designing a critical component for a new plane. She was tapped for the job because of her superior knowledge of the engineering aspects of the project, but the men under her direction have been expressing resentment at working for a woman by subtly sabotaging the work of the team. The director believes that it is unfair to deprive the woman of advancement merely because of the prejudice of her male colleagues, but quick completion of the designs and the building of a prototype are vital to the success of the company. Should he remove the woman as head of the engineering team?

The Marketing VP

The vice president of marketing for a major brewing company is aware that college students account for a large proportion of beer sales and that people in this age group form lifelong loyalties to particular brands of beer. The executive is personally uncomfortable with the tasteless gimmicks used by her competitors in the industry to encourage drinking on campuses, including beach parties and beer-drinking contests. She worries about the company's contribution to underage drinking and alcohol abuse among college students. Should she go along with the competition?

The CEO

The CEO of a midsize producer of a popular line of kitchen appliances is approached about merging with a larger company. The terms offered by the suitor are very advantageous to the CEO, who would receive a large severance package. The shareholders of the firm would also benefit, because the offer for their stock is substantially above the current market price. The CEO learns, however, that plans call for closing a plant that is the major employer in a small town. The firm has always taken its social responsibility seriously, but the CEO is now unsure of how to balance the welfare of the employees who would be thrown out of work and the community where the plant is located against the interests of the shareholders. He is also not sure how much to take his own interests into account. Should he bail out in order to enrich himself?

Robert C. Solomon

The Better Offer

You are in charge of new-product development at Company A in the midst of a fierce competition for the development of a new and more efficient gizmo. The research department has come up with a workable model, and the engineering department is just now in the midst of "getting the bugs out." One of your main competitors, Company B, has obviously fallen behind and offers you a lucrative position, more than commensurate with your present duties and at almost double the salary. Your current employer insists that he cannot possibly match the offer but does give you a 20 percent raise, "to show our appreciation."

Should you feel free to accept the competing offer from Company B?

If you do accept it, should you feel free to develop for Company B the gizmo designed by Company A?

The Faulty Hood Latch

You are a worker in an automobile factory and you become convinced that the hood latch on the new-model Crocodiliac is insufficiently secure and may well pop open at high speeds in a small number of cars, probably causing an accident or, at the least, considerable damage to the car itself. You go to your supervisor and insist that the latch be redesigned, but you are told that production is too far under way; the cost would be formidable and the delay intolerable. You go to the president of the firm and get the same response. What should you do?

Third-World Pharmaceuticals

Your company sells pharmaceutical products in a developing country, in which one of your products, Wellness Plus, promises to provide an effective cure for a common infantile illness. But you find, much to your horror, that the product is being systematically misused, with sometimes serious medical consequences, by people who are mostly illiterate and have no medical supervision. At the same time, the product is selling like hotcakes. What should you do?

Fashion Jeans

Your Fashion Jean Co. could save almost 30 percent on labor costs by moving your main manufacturing plant from El Paso, Texas, across the river to Juarez, Mexico. Should you do so?

Hello—You're Fired

Your bank has a standing policy of firing almost half of its new employees at the end of their first six months. "It makes them more competitive." "It weeds out the slow learners." What effect do you think this has on their efficiency? What effect on their morale and their attitudes toward the bank? Is such a policy ethical?

The Sick Day

A young man in your employ took two weeks off "for illness," but a picture in the local paper happens to show him at the shopping mall during one of his supposed "sick" days. He is a good employee, a hard worker, and he has been under a lot of pressure lately. How do you handle the situation? What considerations are most impressive, as far as you are concerned, in deciding whether or not to fire him?

Gerald F. Cavanagh

Double Expense Account

Frank Waldron is a second-year MBA student at Eastern State University. Although he has had many job offers, he continues to have the university placement office arrange interviews. He reasons that the interview experience will be valuable and a better offer may even come along. Frank has also discovered a way to make money from job interviews.

On one occasion, two firms invited him to New York City for visits to their home offices. He managed to schedule both visits on the same day and then billed each of them for his full travel expenses. In this way he was able to pocket $700. When a friend objected that this was dishonest, Frank replied that each firm had told him to submit an expense account and that therefore he was not taking something to which he had no right. One firm had not asked for receipts, which he interpreted to mean that it intended to make him a gift of the money.

What advice would you give Frank? Is what he is doing unethical? Which norms are most helpful in deciding the question?

PRINCIPLES OF BUSINESS ETHICS

Thinking Ethics: The Rules of the Game
Robert C. Solomon

For thousands of years philosophers have been discussing principles to guide ethical behavior. Much more recently, prompted by questionable practices taken in the name of advancing the bottom line, faculty in business schools and business professionals themselves have discussed the particular ways in which ethics applies to business. Of the many guides now available, Robert C. Solomon's is among the more succinct and easily applied. Solomon, Quincy Lee Centennial Professor of Philosophy and Business at the University of Texas at Austin, is the author of three books on business ethics. The selection that follows appears in his New World of Business: Ethics and Free Enterprise in the Global 1990s *(Littlefield Adams, 1994).*

...by thinking, nobody can ever get worse but will only get better.
—Anne Frank, Diary of a Young Girl

1   Ethics is, first of all, a way of thinking.

2   Being ethical is also—of course—*doing* the right thing, but what one does is hardly separable from how one thinks. Most people in business who do wrong do so not because they are wicked but because they think they are trapped and do not even consider the ethical significance or implications of their actions.

3   What is thinking ethically? It is thinking in terms of *compliance* with the rules, implicit as well as explicit, thinking in terms of the *contributions* one can make as well as one's own possible gains, thinking in terms of avoiding harmful *consequences* to others as well as to oneself. Accordingly, here are eight crucial rules for ethical thinking in business.

Rule No. 1: Consider other people's well-being, including the well-being of nonparticipants.

4   In virtually every major religion this is the golden rule: "Do unto others as you would have them do unto you"; or, negatively, "Do not do unto others as you would not have them do unto you." Ideally, this might mean that one should try to maximize everyone's interests, but this is unreasonable. First of all, no one really expects that a businessman (or anyone else) would or should sacrifice his own interests for everyone else's. Second, it is impossible to take everyone into account; indeed, for any major transaction, the number of people who will be affected—some unpredictably—may run into the tens or hundreds of thousands. But we can readily accept a minimum version of this rule, which is to make a *contribution* where it is reasonable to do so and to avoid *consequences* that are harmful to others. There is nothing in the golden rule that demands that one deny one's own interests or make sacrifices to the public good. It says only that one must take into account human effects beyond one's own bottom line and weigh one's own gain against the losses of others.

Rule No. 2: Think as a member of the business community and not as an isolated individual.

5   Business has its own rules of propriety and fairness. These are not just matters of courtesy and protocol; they are the conditions that make business possible. Respect for contracts, paying one's debts, and selling decent products at a reasonable price are not only to one's own advantage; they are necessary for the very existence of the business community.

Rule No. 3: Obey, but do not depend solely on, the law.

6   It goes without saying, as a matter of prudence if not of morality, that businesses and business people ought to obey the law—the most obvious meaning of *compliance*. But what needs to be added is that ethical thinking is not limited to legal obedience. There is much unethical behavior that is not illegal, and the question of what is right is not always defined by the law. The fact is that many things that are not immoral or illegal are repulsive, disgusting, unfair, and unethical—belching aloud in elevators, throwing a disappointing dish at one's host at dinner, paying debts only after the "final notice," fleecing the feebleminded, taking advantage of trust and good faith, selling

faulty if not dangerous merchandise under the rubric "Buyer beware." Check the law—but don't stop there.

Rule No. 4: Think of yourself—and your company—as part of society, not just "the market."

7 Businesspeople and businesses are citizens in society. They share the fabric of feelings that make up society and, in fact, contribute much of that feeling themselves. Business is not a closed community. It exists and thrives because it serves and does not harm society. It is sometimes suggested that business has its own ethical rules and that they are decidedly different from those of the larger society. Several years ago business writer Alfred Carr raised a major storm in the *Harvard Business Review* by arguing that business, like poker, had its own rules and that these were not to be confused with the moral rules of the larger society. The comparison with poker has its own problems, but, leaving those aside for now, we can see how such a view not only invites but *demands* the most rigorous regulation of business. Business is subject to the same ethical rules as everyone else because businessmen do *not* think of themselves as separate from society. A few years ago, the then chairman of the Ford Foundation put it bluntly: "Either we have a social fabric that embraces us all, or we're in real trouble." So too with ethics.

Rule No. 5: Obey moral rules.

8 [This is the] most obvious and unavoidable rule of ethical thinking. [...] There may be room for debate about whether a moral rule applies. There may be questions of interpretation. But there can be no excuse of ignorance ("Oh, I didn't know that one isn't supposed to lie and cheat") and there can be no unexcused exceptions ("Well, it would be all right to steal in *this* case"). The German philosopher Immanuel Kant called moral rules "categorical imperatives," meaning that they are absolute and unqualified commands for everyone, in every walk of life, without exception, even for harried executives. This is, perhaps, too extreme to be practical, but moral rules are the heart of ethics, and there can be no ethics—and no business—without them.

Rule No. 6: Think "objectively."

9 Ethics is not a science, but it does have one feature in common with science: The rules apply equally to everyone, and being able to be "disinterested"—that is, to think for a moment from other people's perspectives and from a larger viewpoint—is essential. Whether an action is *right* is a matter quite distinct from whether or not it is in *your* interest. For that matter, it is quite independent of your personal opinions as well.

Rule No. 7: Ask the question, "What sort of person would do such a thing?"

10 Our word "ethics" comes from the Greek word *ethos,* meaning "character." Accordingly, ethics is not just obedience to rules so much as it is the concern

for your personal (and company) character—your reputation and "good name"—and, more important, how you feel about yourself. Peter Drucker summarizes the whole of business ethics as "being able to look at your face in the mirror in the morning."

Rule No. 8: Respect the customs and beliefs of others, but not at the expense of your own ethics.

11 The most difficult kind of ethical thinking that people in business have to do concerns not a conflict between ethics and profits but rather the conflict between two ethical systems. In general, it is an apt rule of thumb that one should follow the customs and ethics of the community. But suppose there is a conflict not only of mores but of morals, as in the apartheid policies of South Africa. Then the rule to obey (and support) one's own moral principles takes priority. What is even more difficult is what one should do when the moral issue is not clear and moral categories vary from culture to culture. A much-debated example is the question of giving money to expedite a transaction in many third-world countries. It is "bribery" in our system, "supporting public servants" in theirs. Bribery is illegal and unethical here because it contradicts our notion of a free and open market. But does the same apply in the third world, where business (and social life) have very different presuppositions?

12   Ethical thinking is ultimately no more than considering oneself and one's company as citizens of the business community and of the larger society, with some concern for the well-being of others and—the mirror image of this—respect for oneself and one's character. Nothing in ethics excludes financially sound thinking, and there is nothing about ethics that requires sacrificing the bottom line. In both the long and the short run, ethical thinking is essential to strategic planning. There is nothing unethical about making money, but money is not the currency of ethical thinking in business.

Review Questions

1. What distinction does Solomon make between behaving ethically and thinking ethically?

2. Explain the "minimum" version of the golden rule.

3. What does Solomon say are the essential requirements of the golden rule?

4. Is there a difference between ethical behavior and legal behavior, according to Solomon?

5. What are categorical imperatives?

Discussion and Writing Suggestions

1. Select one of the eleven brief cases for analysis that open the chapter and analyze that case by applying any *one* or *two* of Solomon's rules. Use the rule(s) to guide you in recommending an ethical course of action in the case. Prepare a one- or two-paragraph written analysis explaining your recommendation(s).

2. How comprehensive are Solomon's eight rules for thinking ethically? Can you think of other rules that he should have mentioned? Any that should be omitted?

3. Which of Solomon's rules seems most difficult to apply in the actual practice of business?

4. Solomon writes that "[t]here is nothing in the golden rule that demands that one deny one's own interests or make sacrifices to the public good." Is this your reading of the golden rule?

5. Describe an example of a business action that you believe is legal but unethical.

6. Solomon quotes Peter Drucker as summarizing "the whole of business ethics as 'being able to look at your face in the mirror in the morning.'" Does this strike you as a useful summary? Discuss.

The Case of the Collapsed Mine
Richard T. De George

Studying business ethics can make one sensitive to issues and questions that might otherwise have escaped notice, had no formal training been available. A business situation fraught with dilemmas for one person might for another simply be business as usual, and this is the problem: one person sees conflict; another person sees none. So we offer a selection that demonstrates how someone who is sensitive to ethical dilemmas would approach a particular incident. In "The Case of the Collapsed Mine," Richard T. De George presents a case study and then raises a series of questions that, in effect, provides an overview of business ethics. For instance, De George takes up questions of the value of human life as measured against the cost of designing very safe, or relatively safe, products; and the need to restructure systems that reward loyalty at the expense of morality. These are questions you will read more about in the selections to follow. You may be surprised (as we were) by the number of questions De George can draw from the case.

Richard T. De George is University Distinguished Professor of Philosophy and Courtesy Professor of Management at the University of Kansas. He is the author or editor of over fifteen books and more than one hundred scholarly articles concerning business ethics. De George has traveled worldwide in discussing issues of applied ethics; he has served as president of the American Philosophical Association (Central Division) and at the University of Kansas has won awards for his teaching and scholarship. De George was educated at Fordham University (B.A.), University of Louvain, Belgium (Ph.B.), and Yale (M.A. and Ph.D.).

1   The following case illustrates the sorts of questions that might arise in business ethics and various ways to approach them. Consider the case of the collapsed mine shaft. In a coal mining town of West Virginia, some miners were digging coal in a tunnel thousands of feet below the surface. Some gas buildup had been detected during the two preceding days. This had been reported by the director of safety to the mine manager. The buildup was sufficiently serious to have closed down operations until it was cleared. The owner of the mine decided that the buildup was only marginally dangerous, that he had coal orders to fill, that he could not afford to close down the mine, and that he would take the chance that the gas would dissipate before it exploded. He told the director of safety not to say anything about the danger. On May 2nd, the gas exploded. One section of the tunnel collapsed, killing three miners and trapping eight others in a pocket. The rest managed to escape.

2   The explosion was one of great force and the extent of the tunnel's collapse was considerable. The cost of reaching the men in time to save their lives would amount to several million dollars. The problem facing the manager was whether the expenditure of such a large sum of money was worth it. What, after all, was a human life worth? Whose decision was it and how should it be made? Did the manager owe more to the stockholders of the corporation or to the trapped workers? Should he use the slower, safer, and cheaper way of reaching them and save a large sum of money or the faster, more dangerous, and more expensive way and possibly save their lives?

3   He decided on the latter and asked for volunteers. Two dozen men volunteered. After three days, the operation proved to be more difficult than anyone had anticipated. There had been two more explosions and three of those involved in the rescue operation had already been killed. In the meantime, telephone contact had been made with the trapped men who had been fortunate enough to find a telephone line that was still functioning. They were starving. Having previously read about a similar case, they decided that the only way for any of them to survive long enough was to draw lots, and then kill and eat the one who drew the shortest straw. They felt that it was their duty that at least some of them should be found alive; otherwise, the three volunteers who had died rescuing them would have died in vain.

4   After twenty days the seven men were finally rescued alive; they had cannibalized their fellow miner. The director of safety who had detected the gas before the explosion informed the newspapers of his report. The manager was charged with criminal negligence; but before giving up his position, he fired the director of safety. The mine eventually resumed operation.

5   There are a large number of issues in the above account....

6   The director of safety is in some sense the hero of the story. But did he fulfill his moral obligation before the accident in obeying the manager and in not making known either to the miners, the manager's superior, or to the public the fact that the mine was unsafe? Did he have a moral obligation after the explosion

and rescue to make known the fact that the manager knew the mine was unsafe? Should he have gone to the board of directors of the company with the story or to someone else within the company rather than to the newspapers? All these questions are part of the phenomenon of worker responsibility. To whom is a worker responsible and for what? Does his moral obligation end when he does what he is told? Going public with inside information such as the director of safety had is commonly known as "blowing the whistle" on the company. Frequently those who blow the whistle are fired, just as the director of safety was. The whole phenomenon of whistle blowing raises serious questions about the structure of companies in which employees find it necessary to take such drastic action and possibly suffer the loss of their jobs. Was the manager justified in firing the director of safety?

7   The manager is, of course, the villain of the story. He sent the miners into a situation which he knew was dangerous. But, he might argue, he did it for the good of the company. He had contracts to fulfill and obligations to the owners of the company to show a profit. He had made a bad decision. Every manager has to take risks. It just turned out that he was unlucky. Does such a defense sound plausible? Does a manager have an obligation to his workers as well as to the owners of a company? Who should take precedence and under what conditions does one group or the other become more important? Who is to decide and how?

8   The manager decided to try to save the trapped miners even though it would cost the company more than taking the slower route. Did he have the right to spend more of the company's money in this way? How does one evaluate human life in comparison with expenditure of money? It sounds moral to say that human life is beyond all monetary value. In a sense it is. However, there are limits which society and people in it can place on the amount they will, can, and should spend to save lives. The way to decide, however, does not seem to be to equate the value of a person's life with the amount of income he would produce in his remaining years, if he lives to a statistically average age, minus the resources he would use up in that period. How does one decide? How do and should people weigh human lives against monetary expenditure? In designing automobiles, in building roads, in making many products, there is a trade-off between the maximum safety that one can build into the product and the cost of the product. Extremely safe cars cost more to build than relatively safe cars. We can express the difference in terms of the number of people likely to die driving the relatively safe ones as opposed to the extremely safe ones. Should such decisions be made by manufacturers, consumers, government, or in some other way?

9   The manager asked for volunteers for the rescue work. Three of these volunteers died. Was the manager responsible for their deaths in the same way that he was responsible for the deaths of the three miners who had died in the first mine explosion? Was the company responsible for the deaths in either case? Do companies have obligations to their employees and the employees' families in circumstances such as these, or are the obligations only those of the managers? If the manager had warned the miners that the level of gas was dangerous, and they had decided that they wanted their pay for that day and would

work anyway, would the manager have been responsible for their deaths? Is it moral for people to take dangerous jobs simply to earn money? Is a system that impels people to take such jobs for money a moral system? To what extent is a company morally obliged to protect its workers and to prevent them from taking chances?

10   The manager was charged with criminal negligence under the law. Was the company responsible for anything? Should the company have been sued by the family of the dead workers? If the company were sued and paid damages to the families, the money would come from company profits and hence from the profits of the shareholders. Is it fair that the shareholders be penalized for an incident they had nothing to do with? How is responsibility shared and/or distributed in a company, and can companies be morally responsible for what is done in their name? Are only human beings moral agents and is it a mistake to use moral language with respect to companies, corporations, and businesses?

11   The decision of the trapped miners to cast lots to determine who would be killed and eaten also raises a number of moral issues. Our moral intuitions can provide in this case no ready answer as to whether their decision was morally justifiable, since the case is not an ordinary one. How to think about such an issue raises the question of how moral problems are to be resolved and underscores the need for some moral theory as guidelines by which we can decide unusual cases. A number of principles seem to conflict—the obligation not to kill, the consideration that it is better for one person to die rather than eight, the fact noted by the miners that three persons had already died trying to rescue them, and so on. The issue here is not one peculiar to business ethics, but it is rather a moral dilemma that requires some technique of moral argument to solve.

12   The case does not tell us what happened to either the manager or the director of safety. Frequently the sequel to such cases is surprising. The managers come off free and ultimately rewarded for their concern for the company's interest, while the whistle blower is black-balled throughout the industry. The morality of such an outcome seems obvious—justice does not always triumph. What can be done to see that it triumphs more often is a question that involves restructuring the system.

13   Business ethics is sometimes seen as conservative and is also used as a defense of the status quo. Sometimes it is seen as an attack on the status quo and hence viewed as radical. Ideally it should be neither. It should strive for objectivity. When there are immoral practices, structures, and actions occurring, business ethics should be able to show that these actions are immoral and why. But it should also be able to supply the techniques with which the practices and structures that are moral can be defended as such. The aim of business ethics is neither defense of the status quo nor its radical change. Rather it should serve to remedy those aspects or structures that need change and protect those that are moral. It is not a panacea. It can secure change only if those in power take the appropriate action. But unless some attention is paid to business ethics, the moral debate about practices and principles central to our society will be more poorly and probably more immorally handled than otherwise.

Discussion and Writing Suggestions

1. Of the many questions that De George poses regarding "The Case of the Collapsed Mine," which question or set of questions seems most likely to get at the heart of the case? Explain your choice.

2. De George writes: "When there are immoral practices, structures, and actions occurring, business ethics should be able to show that these actions are immoral and why. But it should also be able to supply the techniques with which the practices and structures that are moral can be defended as such." Based on what you've read and seen on news reports, and based on your own experience, perhaps, to what extent are people in business amenable to discussing reasons that an action may or may not be ethical?

3. In paragraph 6, De George poses several questions and then writes: "All these questions are part of the phenomenon of worker responsibility." *Worker responsibility*, then, becomes a category of questions. Reread the selection and create categories for the other questions that De George asks. For instance, some questions concern corporate responsibility, some concern the prohibition against killing, and so on. Compare your categories with a classmate's. (These categories will provide something of an index to the issues addressed in this chapter and, more generally, an index to the concerns of business ethicists.)

4. Summarize the significant details of an event in your own work experience and draw out those elements that raised ethical dilemmas for you or someone you know. In the fashion of De George, write a brief essay in which you pose a series of questions about the event and the behaviors of the people involved.

Ethics in Business
Gerald F. Cavanagh

The case method is used as an instructional strategy in schools of business and departments of business ethics in colleges and universities around the country. Students read varied accounts (real or hypothetical) of life in the world of business and then are asked to analyze a case and advise the principals what to do. For instance, students of business might read about specific business transactions (or the preliminaries leading up to such transactions); accounts of interpersonal behaviors within organizations that call for management to take action; or accounts of organizational structures and how these impede or promote productivity. One class of cases that students are increasingly being asked to read involves ethical dilemmas faced by corporate executives, managers, and individual contributors. In all these cases, students are expected to conduct a systematic analysis and make specific, defensible recommendations.

In cases concerning financial analysis, you would perhaps be asked to use spreadsheets in arriving at your recommendations. In cases concerning ethical analysis, you would be expect-

ed to use one or another model—a set of well-defined criteria—in arriving at your recommendations. Gerald Cavanagh offers such a model in his "Ethics in Business," which appeared originally in his American Business Values *(1990)*, a text written for college course work. You'll find Cavanagh's discussion clearly written and organized (divided into sections and subsections), but you may also find the discussion somewhat difficult, for Cavanagh must define three ethical theories in order to establish his model for decision making. Read slowly, take notes, and respond to all the review questions on page 408 as you read, and you will find the discussion in your grasp—which is important, because you'll be asked to apply Cavanagh's model to several cases.

Gerald Cavanagh is professor of management, associate dean, and director of Graduate Programs in the University of Detroit's College of Business and Administration. Cavanagh holds a B.S. in engineering, has graduate degrees in philosophy, theology, and management (Ph.D., Michigan State University), and was ordained a Jesuit priest in 1964. He has served on boards of trustees of several universities, and he referees papers for several scholarly journals and for national meetings of the Academy of Management. He has also given ethics workshops at universities throughout the country.

1   The basic method of making ethical judgments involves just three steps: (1) gathering relevant factual information, (2) determining the moral norm that is most applicable, and (3) making the ethical judgment on the rightness or wrongness of the act or policy (see Figure 1).

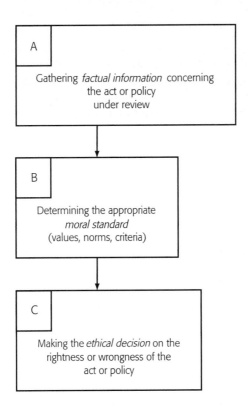

FIGURE 1   Steps in Ethical Decision Making

2   Nevertheless, ethical judgments are not always easy to make. The facts of the case are often not clear-cut, and the ethical criteria or principles to be used are not always agreed on, even by the experts themselves. Hence, ethics seems to most businesspeople, indeed to most Americans, to be subjective, amorphous, ill-defined, and thus not very useful. Just as with politics and religion, there is often more heat than light generated by ethical discussions. This lack of confidence in ethics is unfortunate, since without agreed ethical principles, it is everyone for him- or herself. In such a situation, trust, which is basic to all business and commerce, is undermined.

Dilemmas to Decisions

3   Let us begin our examination of ethical decision making by assessing a case that was first judged by 1,700 business executive readers of the *Harvard Business Review.* This case was part of a classical large-scale study of business ethics by Raymond C. Baumhart, S.J.[1]

> An executive earning $120,000 a year has been padding his or her expense account by about $6,000 a year.

4   First some background: An expense account is available for expenses that are incurred in the course of one's work. It is not fair to ask an employee to use personal funds, without reimbursement, for legitimate business expenses.

5   To return to the case, how ethical is it to pad one's expense account? On numerous occasions over the years hundreds of other managers have been asked to judge the case, and the results have been substantially the same. Replying to an anonymous questionnaire and speaking for themselves, 85 percent of executives think that this sort of behavior is simply unacceptable. Perhaps more important, almost two-thirds of them think their business colleagues would also see such behavior as unacceptable under any circumstances.

6   Why would padding an expense account be considered wrong by these executives? An expense account is not a simple addition to someone's salary. It is designed to cover the actual expenses that are incurred by employees in the course of doing their work.

7   Pocketing a company pencil or making a personal long-distance phone call from the office may seem relatively trivial. Perhaps, but fabricating expenses up to 5 percent of one's salary is not trivial; it is a substantial violation of justice. The executive in the case is taking more compensation than he or she is entitled to. Presumably the executive's salary is ample compensation for the work, and the extra $6,000 is not intended as direct compensation, nor is it recognized by law as such.

8   Circumstances are often cited that might seem to mitigate the injustice. Some might say, "Many others are also doing it" or "My superior knows about

---

[1]Raymond C. Baumhart, S.J., *Ethics in Business* (New York: Holt, Rinehart & Winston, 1968), p. 21. The dollar figures in the case have been adjusted for inflation. For an updating of Baumhart's findings, see Steven Brenner and Earl Molander, "Is the Ethics of Business Changing?" *Harvard Business Review* 55 (January–February 1977): 57–71.

it and says nothing." In the cited study, only about a quarter of the executives thought that their peers would justify such actions on these counts. A mere handful (about 10 percent) said that they themselves thought that it would be acceptable in such circumstances. An examination of these circumstances follows.

The Actions of Other People

9   The fact that many people are doing actions of a certain kind can never in itself justify those actions. For example, the fact that superiors ordered actions and others did them was no legal defense for concentration camp officers at the post–World War II Nuremberg war crime trials. Even though these Nazi officers were under orders, and even though many of their peers felt that killing "undesirables" was alright, it was not accepted as a defense. Even less so is it an ethical defense. Although ethics is influenced by conditions, a moral principle is not established by voting.

10   Let us assume in the case of the expense account that the executive is a woman. We must acknowledge that it would be to her benefit if she could increase her salary by 5 percent. To have that extra $6,000 would be in her self-interest. Focusing primarily on her self-interest could easily lead her to be less objective in her search for the right action and would make her more prone to look for excuses to do that which would benefit her.

11   Justice calls for a fair distribution of the benefits and burdens of society. In this case, we are concerned with benefits. When is it ethical to take funds from an expense account? Assuming that the executive's family is not starving because she has an abnormally low salary, justice tells us that the expense account should be used for expenses, not as a salary supplement. Ignorance and coercion can lessen responsibility. However, in this case, the executive could hardly claim that she did not know what an expense account was or that she was coerced into taking the money.

12   But if she can get away with it, why shouldn't she pad her expense account? Is there any real difference between an executive who is ethical and one who isn't? A basic assumption that almost all businesspeople support is that a businessperson should be ethical. That is, individuals should try to do good and avoid evil, not only on the job but in all aspects of life. The foundation for business transactions is confidence that most businesspeople are trustworthy, truthful, and ethical. If most businesspeople were not ethical, it would be almost impossible to purchase supplies, sell goods or securities, or do most of the buying and selling that we are accustomed to doing in modern society.

13   Admittedly there can be a short-term financial advantage for an embezzler or a supplier who takes ten million dollars and delivers defective goods. It is because of individuals like this that we have laws, courts, and jails. Yet we also know that not all activities can be regulated, nor can all unethical acts be fully punished (in this life, anyway). If a large percentage of businesspeople did not pay their bills and took advantage of their business partners, the business system would collapse.

Ethical Norms for Business Decisions

14 Ethical criteria and ethical models have been the subject of much reflection over the centuries. Of all ethical theories, utilitarianism is the one businesspeople feel most at home with. This is not surprising, as the theory traces its origins to Adam Smith, the father of modern economics. The main proponents of utilitarianism, however, were Jeremy Bentham[2] and John Stuart Mill,[3] both of whom helped to formulate the theory more precisely. Utilitarianism evaluates actions in terms of their consequences. In any given situation, the one action which would result in the greatest net gain for all concerned parties is considered to be the right, or morally obligatory, action. The theory of rights focuses on the entitlements of individual persons. Immanuel Kant[4] (personal rights) and John Locke[5] (property rights) were the first to fully develop the theory of rights. The theory of justice has a longer tradition, going back to Plato and Aristotle in the fourth century B.C.[6] Theoretical work in each of these traditional theories has continued to the present.[7] For an overview of these three theories—their history, strengths, weaknesses, and areas of application—see Table 1.

The Norm of Utilitarianism

15 Utilitarianism judges that an action is right if it produces the greatest utility, "the greatest good for the greatest number." The decision process is very much like a cost-benefit analysis applied to all parties who would be touched by the decision. That action is right which produces the greatest net benefit when all the costs and benefits to all the affected parties are taken into account. Although it would be convenient if these costs and benefits could be measured in some comparable unit, this is rarely possible. Many important values (e.g., human life and liberty) cannot be quantified. Thus, the best that can be done is to enumerate the effects and the magnitude of their costs and benefits as clearly and accurately as possible.

16   The utilitarian principle says that the right action is that which produces the greatest net benefit over any other possible action. This does not mean that the right action produces the greatest good for the person performing the action. Rather, it is the action that produces the greatest net good for all those who are affected by the action. Utilitarianism can handle some ethical cases quite well,

---

[2]Jeremy Bentham, *An Introduction to the Principles of Morals and Legislation* (New York: Hafner, 1948).

[3]John Stuart Mill, *Utilitarianism* (Indianapolis: Bobbs-Merrill, 1957).

[4]Immanuel Kant, *The Metaphysical Elements of Justice,* trans. J. Ladd (New York: Library of Liberal Arts, 1965).

[5]John Locke, *The Second Treatise of Government* (New York: Liberal Arts Press, 1952).

[6]Aristotle, *Ethics,* trans. J. A. K. Thomson (London: Penguin, 1953).

[7]For example, John Rawls, *A Theory of Justice* (Cambridge, Mass.: Harvard University Press, 1971). See two books of readings: Thomas Donaldson and Patricia Werhane, *Ethical Issues in Business* (Englewood Cliffs, N.J.: Prentice-Hall, 1979); Tom Beauchamp and Norman Bowie, *Ethical Theory and Business,* 2d ed. (Englewood Cliffs, N.J.: Prentice-Hall, 1983).

TABLE 1   Ethical Models for Business Decisions

Definition and Origin	Strengths	Weaknesses	When Used	
			Example	Summary
UTILITARIANISM				
"The greatest good for the greatest number": Bentham (1748–1832), Adam Smith (1723–1790), David Ricardo (1772–1823).	1. Concepts, terminology, methods are easiest for businesspersons to work with; justifies a profit maximization system. 2. Promotes view of entire system of exchange beyond "this firm." 3. Encourages entrepreneurship, innovation, productivity.	1. Impossible to measure or quantify all important elements. 2. "Greatest good" can degenerate into self-interest. 3. Can result in abridging person's rights. 4. Can result in neglecting less powerful segments of society.	1. Plant closing. 2. Pollution. 3. Condemnation of land or buildings for "development."	1. Use in all business decisions, and will be dominant criteria in 90%. 2. Version of model is implicitly used already, although scope is generally limited to "this firm."
THEORY OF RIGHTS				
Individual's freedom is not to be violated: Locke (1635–1701)—property; Kant (1724–1804)—personal rights.	1. Ensures respect for individual's property and personal freedom. 2. Parallels political "Bill of Rights."	1. Can encourage individualistic, selfish behavior.	1. Unsafe workplace. 2. Flammable children's toys. 3. Lying to superior or subordinate.	1. Where individual's property or personal rights are in question. 2. Use with, for example, employee privacy, job tenure, work dangerous to person's health.
THEORY OF JUSTICE				
Equitable distribution of society's benefits and burdens: Aristotle (384–322 B.C.), Rawls (1921–).	1. The "democratic" principle. 2. Does not allow a society to become status- or class-dominated. 3. Ensures that minorities, poor, handicapped receive opportunities and a fair share of output.	1. Can result in less risk, incentive, and innovation. 2. Encourages sense of "entitlement."	1. Delivery of shoddy goods. 2. Low wages to Hispanic or black workers. 3. Bribes, kickbacks, fraud.	1. In product decisions usefulness to *all* in society. 2. In setting salaries for unskilled workers, executives. 3. In public policy decisions: to maintain a floor of living standards for all. 4. Use with, for example, performance appraisal, due process, distribution of rewards and punishments.

especially those that are complex and affect many parties. Although the model and the methodology are clear in theory, carrying out the calculations is often difficult. Taking into account so many affected parties, along with the extent to which the action touches them, can be a tallying nightmare.

17   Hence several shortcuts have been proposed that can reduce the complexity of utilitarian calculations. Each shortcut involves a sacrifice of accuracy for ease of calculation. Among these shortcuts are (1) adherence to a simplified rule (e.g., the Golden Rule, "Do unto others as you would have them do unto you"); (2) calculation of costs and benefits in dollar terms for ease of comparison; (3) restriction of consideration to those directly affected by the action, putting aside indirect effects. In using these shortcuts, an individual should be aware that they result in simplification and that some interests may not be sufficiently taken into consideration.

18   In the popular mind, the term *utilitarianism* sometimes suggests selfishness and exploitation. For our purposes, the term should be considered not to have these connotations. However, a noteworthy weakness of utilitarianism as an ethical norm is that it can advocate, for example, abridging an individual's right to a job or even life for the sake of the greater good of a larger number of people. This and other difficulties are discussed elsewhere.[8] One additional caution in using utilitarian rules is in order: It is considered unethical to opt for narrower benefits (e.g., personal goals, career, or money) at the expense of the good of a larger number, such as a nation or a society. Utilitarian norms emphasize the good of the group; it is a large-scale ethical model. As a result, an individual and what is due that individual may be overlooked. The theory of rights has been developed to emphasize the individual and the standing of that individual with peers and within society.

The Norm of Individual Rights

19 A right is a person's entitlement to something.[9] Rights may flow from the legal system, such as our constitutional rights of freedom of conscience or freedom of speech. The U.S. Bill of Rights and the United Nations Universal Declaration of Human Rights are examples of documents that spell out individual rights in detail. Legal rights, as well as others which may not be written into law, stem from the human dignity of persons. Moral rights have these characteristics: (1) They enable individuals to pursue their own interests, and (2) they impose correlative prohibitions or requirements on others.

20   Hence, every right has a corresponding duty. My right to freedom of conscience is supported by the prohibition of other individuals from unnecessarily limiting that freedom of conscience. From another perspective, my right to be paid for my work corresponds to a duty of mine to perform "a fair day's work for a fair day's pay." In the latter case, both the right and duty stem from the right

---

[8]Gerald F. Cavanagh, Dennis J. Moberg, and Manuel Velasquez, "The Ethics of Organizational Politics," *Academy of Management Review,* 6 (July 1981): 363–74. For a more complete treatment, see Manuel Velasquez, *Business Ethics: Concepts and Cases* (Englewood Cliffs, N.J.: Prentice-Hall, 1982), pp. 46–58.

[9]Velasquez, *Business Ethics,* p. 29; see also Thomas Donaldson, *Corporations and Morality* (Englewood Cliffs, N.J.: Prentice-Hall, 1982).

to private property, which is a traditional pillar of American life and law. However, the right to private property is not absolute. A factory owner may be forced by law, as well as by morality, to spend money on pollution control or safety equipment. For a listing of selected rights and other ethical norms, see Table 2.

TABLE 2   Some Selected Ethical Norms

UTILITARIAN

1. *Organizational goals* should aim at *maximizing the satisfactions* of the organization's constituencies.
2. The members of an organization should attempt to attain its goals as *efficiently* as possible by consuming as few inputs as possible and by minimizing the external costs which organizational activities impose on others.
3. The employee should use *every effective means* to achieve the goals of the organization and should neither jeopardize those goals nor enter situations in which personal interests conflict significantly with the goals.

RIGHTS

1. *Life and safety:* The individual has the right not to have her or his life or safety unknowingly and unnecessarily endangered.
2. *Truthfulness:* The individual has a right not to be intentionally deceived by another, especially on matters about which the individual has the right to know.
3. *Privacy:* The individual has the right to do whatever he or she chooses to do outside working hours and to control information about his or her private life.
4. *Freedom of conscience:* The individual has the right to refrain from carrying out any order that violates those commonly accepted moral or religious norms to which the person adheres.
5. *Free speech:* The individual has the right to criticize conscientiously and truthfully the ethics or legality of corporate actions so long as the criticism does not violate the rights of other individuals within the organization.
6. *Private property:* The individual has a right to hold private property, especially insofar as this right enables the individual and his or her family to be sheltered and to have the basic necessities of life.

JUSTICE

1. *Fair treatment:* Persons who are similar to each other in the relevant respects should be treated similarly; persons who differ in some respect relevant to the job they perform should be treated differently in proportion to the difference between them.
2. *Fair administration of rules:* Rules should be administered consistently, fairly, and impartially.
3. *Fair compensation:* Individuals should be compensated for the cost of their injuries by the party that is responsible for those injuries.
4. *Fair blame:* Individuals should not be held responsible for matters over which they have no control.
5. *Due process:* The individual has a right to a fair and impartial hearing when he or she believes that personal rights are being violated.

Source: Quoted and adapted from Manuel Velasquez, Gerald Cavanagh, and Dennis Moberg, "Organizational Statesmanship and Dirty Politics: Ethical Guidelines for the Organizational Politician," *Organizational Dynamics,* (Fall, 1983).

21   People also have the right not to be lied to or deceived, especially on matters which they have a right to know about. A supervisor has the duty to be truthful in giving feedback on work performance even if it is difficult for the supervisor to do so. Each of us has the right not to be lied to by salespeople or advertisements. Perjury under oath is a serious crime; lying on matters where another has a right to accurate information is also seriously unethical. Truthfulness and honesty are basic ethical norms.

22   Judging morality by reference to individual rights is quite different from using utilitarian standards. Rights express the requirements of morality from the standpoint of the individual; rights protect the individual from the encroachment and demands of society or the state. Utilitarian standards promote society's interests and are relatively insensitive regarding a single individual except insofar as the individual's welfare affects the overall good of society.

23   A business contract establishes rights and duties that did not exist before: The right of the purchaser to receive what was agreed and the right of the seller to be paid what was agreed. Formal written contracts and informal verbal agreements are essential to business transactions.

24   Immanuel Kant recognized that an emphasis on rights can lead people to focus largely on what is due them. So he formulated what he called "categorical imperatives." The first is that "I ought never to act except in such a way that I can also will that my maxim should become a universal law." Another formulation is this: An action is morally right for a person in a certain situation if and only if the person's reason for carrying out the action is a reason that he or she would be willing to have every person act on, in any similar situation.[10]

25   Kant's second categorical imperative cautions us against using other people as a means to our own ends: Never treat humanity simply as a means, but always also as an end. One interpretation of the second imperative is this: An action is morally right for a person if and only if in performing the action the person does not use others merely as a means for advancing his or her own interests, but also both respects and develops their capacity to choose for themselves.[11] Capital, plants, and machines are all to be used to serve the purposes of individuals. On the other hand, individuals themselves are not to be used merely as instruments for achieving the goals of others. This rules out deception, manipulation, and exploitation in dealing with people.

The Norm of Justice

26 Justice requires all persons, and thus managers too, to be guided by fairness, equity, and impartiality. Justice calls for evenhanded treatment of groups and individuals (1) in the distribution of the benefits and burdens of society, (2) in the administration of laws and regulations, and (3) in the imposition of sanctions and the rewarding of compensation for wrongs suffered. An action or policy is just if it is comparable to the treatment accorded to others.

---

[10]Immanuel Kant, *Groundwork of the Metaphysics of Morals,* trans. H. J. Paton (New York: Harper & Row, 1964), pp. 62–90.

[11]Ibid; see also Velasquez, *Business Ethics,* p. 68.

27   Standards of justice are generally considered to be more important than the utilitarian consideration of consequences. If a society is unjust to a minority group (e.g., apartheid treatment of blacks in South Africa), we generally consider that society to be unjust and we condemn it, even if the results of the injustices bring about greater economic productivity. On the other hand, we seem willing to trade off some equity if the results will bring about greater benefits for all. For example, income and wealth differences are justified only if they bring greater benefits for all.

28   Standards of justice are not as often in conflict with individual rights as are utilitarian norms.[12] This is not surprising, since justice is largely based on the moral rights of individuals. The moral right to be treated as a free and equal person, for example, undergirds the notion that benefits and burdens should be distributed equitably. Personal moral rights (e.g., freedom of conscience, the right to due process, the right to free consent, the right to privacy) are so basic that they generally may not be taken away to bring about a better distribution of benefits within a society. On the other hand, property rights may be abridged for the sake of a fairer distribution of benefits and burdens (e.g., graduated income tax, limits on pollution).

29   Distributive justice becomes important when a society has sufficient goods but not everyone's basic needs are satisfied. The question then becomes, What is a just distribution? The fundamental principle is that equals should be treated equally and that unequals should be treated in accord with their inequality. For example, few would argue that a new person hired for a job should receive the same pay as a senior worker with twenty years experience. People who perform work of greater responsibility or who work longer hours should be eligible for greater pay. However, it is clear that pay differentials should be based on the work itself, not on some arbitrary bias of the employer.

30   Even knowing all of the above, we still wouldn't be able to determine what is a fair distribution of society's benefits and burdens. In fact, quite different notions of equity are generally proposed. For example, the capitalist model (benefits based on contribution) is radically different from the socialist (from each according to abilities, to each according to needs). An important contribution to the theory of justice has been made by John Rawls.[13] Rawls would have us construct a system of rules and laws for society as if we did not know what roles we were to play in that society. We do not know if we would be rich or poor, male or female, African or European, manager or slave, handicapped or physically and mentally fit. Rawls calls this the "veil of ignorance." Constructing a system of rules under the veil of ignorance is intended to allow us to rid ourselves of the biases we have as a result of our status. In such circumstances, each of us would try to construct a system that would be of the greatest benefit to all and that would not undermine the position of any group. Rawls proposes that people under the veil of ignorance would agree to two principles:

---

[12]Jerald Greenberg, "A Taxonomy of Organizational Justice Theories," *Academy of Management Review* 12 (January 1987): 9–22.

[13]Rawls, *Theory of Justice.*

1. Each person is to have an equal right to the most extensive liberty compatible with similar liberty for others.
2. Social and economic inequalities are to be arranged so that they are both reasonably expected to be to everyone's advantage and attached to positions and offices open to all.

The first principle is consonant with the American sense of liberty and thus is not controversial in the United States. The second principle is more egalitarian and also more controversial. However, Rawls maintains that if people honestly choose as if they were under the veil of ignorance, they would opt for a system of justice that is most fair to all members of society. Let us now use these ethical norms in making ethical decisions.

Solving Ethical Problems

31 Any human judgment is preceded by two steps: gathering the facts and determining the appropriate criteria (see Figure 1). Before any ethically sensitive situation can be assessed, it is essential that all the relevant data be on hand. As an aid to determining the appropriate criteria, we have presented the classical norms of utility, rights, and justice. Figure 2 is a schematic diagram of how ethical decision making should proceed. Although it contains greater detail than Figure 1, the same three steps (A, B, and C) are underscored. Even Figure 2 is simplified, but nevertheless it can aid in handling ethical problems.

32   Let us apply our scheme to the case of the executive who padded her expense account. We will accept the limited data provided in the case. Using the utility criterion, we judge that although padding her expense account is in the interest of the executive, it does not optimize benefits for others. Her actions hurt shareholders, customers, more honest executives, and people in other firms in similar situations. Padding one's expense account also adds to the expense of doing business and to this extent violates utility. The rights norm is not so useful here: The executive has no right to the extra money, although we might make the case that the shareholders' and customers' right to private property is being violated. With regard to justice, salary and commissions constitute ordinary compensation for individuals. Expense accounts have a quite different purpose. In this instance, most managers responding to the case held that it was unethical for the executive to pad her expense account. John Rawls would maintain that all of us would set the rules in this fashion if we did not know what roles we ourselves would have in society. Hence, we conclude that padding one's expense account is judged unethical on all three ethical norms, and is therefore clearly wrong. Note that 73 percent of the executives who were asked came to the same judgment.

[...]

Decision Making Using the Model

33 Let us examine another case:

> Brian Curry, financial vice president of Digital Robotics Corporation, is about to retire and has been asked to recommend one of his two assistants for promotion to vice

president. Curry knows that his recommendations will be acted on. He also knows that since both assistants are about the same age, the one not chosen will have difficulty getting future promotions. Debra Butler is the most qualified for the position. She is bright and outgoing and has better leadership ability. Moreover, her father is president of the largest customer of Digital, and Curry correctly reasons that Digital will more likely keep this business if the daughter is made an officer. On the other hand, John McNichols has been with the company longer, has worked seventy-hour weeks, and has pulled the company through some very difficult situations. He has continued putting in extra effort because he was told

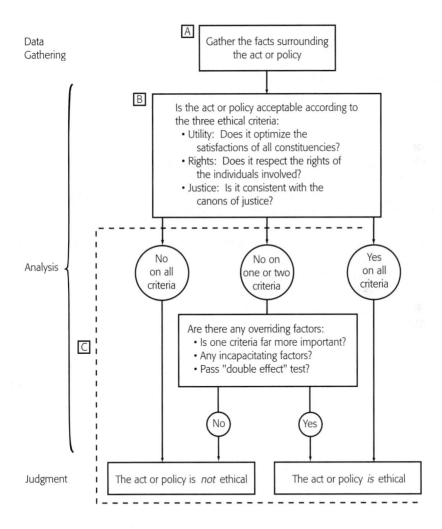

FIGURE 2   Flow Diagram of Ethical Decision Making

Source: Adapted from Manuel Velasquez, Gerald F. Cavanagh, and Dennis J. Moberg, "Organizational Statesmanship and Dirty Politics: Ethical Guidelines for the Organizational Politician." *Organizational Dynamics* (Fall, 1983).

some time ago that he was in line for the vice presidency. Nevertheless, Curry recommends Butler for the job.

34   Let us again use our norms and Figure 2 to decide this case. Utility tells us that the selection of Debra Butler optimally benefits top management, shareholders, customers, and most of the workers, because she is a better leader. The principal cost is to John McNichols. As for justice, we conclude that because the promotional decision was made on the basis of relevant abilities, it did constitute fair treatment. On the other hand, McNichols worked extra hours because of the promised promotion. Much of his work effort was based on a false promise. McNichols had a right to know the truth and to be treated fairly.[14]

35   Thus, according to the criterion of utility, the appointment of Butler is morally acceptable, since there will be a net gain for most parties. However, because of the promise made earlier to McNichols, which resulted in extended workweeks, he is being treated unjustly. We can then ask if there are any "overriding factors" that ought to be taken into consideration.

Overriding Factors

36 Overriding factors are factors which may, in a given case, justify overriding one of the three ethical criteria: utility, rights, or justice (see Figure 2). Overriding factors can be examined when there is a conflict in the conclusions drawn from the ethical norms. For example, there might be incapacitating factors. If there are any elements that coerce an individual into doing a certain action, then that individual is not held to be fully responsible. Managers at a H. J. Heinz plant were under great pressure from top management to show a profit. They were not able to do as well as was expected, so they began to juggle the books. This resulted in a cumulative overstatement of profits of $8.5 million. Nevertheless, the managers who falsified the books would probably be judged less unethical than the top managers who exerted the unrelenting pressure. Even though making false entries in the books is objectively unethical, the plant managers did not bear full responsibility because they were pressured by superiors.[15]

37   Also, someone might not be able to utilize the criteria owing to lack of information. A manager might think that another employee is embezzling from the firm. However, to report that employee to superiors might ruin his or her reputation. Therefore, even though stealing is a violation of justice, in this instance there is not yet sufficient information to utilize the criteria. In addition, the manager may be sincerely uncertain of the criteria or their applicability in this particular case.

38   Consider again the case of appointing a financial vice president. Utility calls for recommending Debra Butler for the position. The right to full information and perhaps justice support McNichols' claim. McNichols has worked more

---

[14]Marshall Sashkin has developed a set of questions whereby a manager can score him- or herself as being predominantly a user of the utility, justice, or rights norm. See Sashkin, *Managerial Values Profile* (Bryn Mawr, Pa.: Organizational Design and Development, 1986).

[15]"Some Middle Managers Cut Corners to Achieve High Corporate Goals," *Wall Street Journal*, November 8, 1979, pp. 1, 19.

hours and harder because of a promised reward. Since the position was promised to him, fair treatment requires giving him special consideration. On the basis of the importance of a verbal promise and of justice, we might conclude that McNichols should get the position.

39   Because there is now a conflict between these two norms, any overriding factors should be taken into account. Is one criteria more important? The effective operation of the firm is an important ethical goal. How much better a manager is Butler and how would her selection affect the firm's performance and the jobs of others at Digital?

40   With regard to incapaciting factors, there seems to be little coercion involved, certainly no physical coercion. That Debra Butler's father is president of Digital's largest customer might constitute psychological coercion. However, Curry seems to have made his decision freely.

41   Another important factor to consider is exactly what sort of promise was made to McNichols? Was it clear and unequivocal? If the "promise" was in fact a mere statement that McNichols had a good chance at the promotion or if Butler's performance is expected to be significantly better than McNichols', then Curry could ethically recommend Butler. However, some sort of compensation should then be made to McNichols.

42   Another kind of overriding factor occurs when people using different criteria come to varying conclusions on the same case. The so-called principle of double effect can be useful. Let us take an example of firing a worker who is not a very good performer but who is the sole provider of a family. Using the utility norm, we would probably say the firing was ethical. But using the justice norm, we might call it unethical, because an entire family would be deprived of income. There is a conflict between the conclusions reached using the different norms, so the principal of the double effect is appropriate. The principle is applicable when an act has both a good effect (e.g., bringing greater efficiency to the firm and providing honest feedback to the worker) and a bad effect (e.g., elimination of the principal support for the family). One may ethically perform such an act under three conditions: (1) One does not directly intend the bad effect (e.g., depriving the family of income); (2) the bad effect is not a means to the good end but is simply a side effect (e.g., depriving the family of income is not a means of making the firm more efficient); and (3) the good effect sufficiently outweighs the bad (e.g., the benefits of greater firm efficiency are sufficiently greater than the difficulties the family will face). Going back to the preceding case, would the appointment of Butler pass the double effect test?

43   The above ethical model, which has been used in many books on management,[16] enables the manager to integrate ethical analysis into business decisions. It is intended to stand alongside economic analysis—to complement and correct it.

---

[16]See, for example, Harold Koontz and Helnz Weihrich, *Management,* 9th ed. (New York: McGraw-Hill, 1988), pp. 611–13; John Schermerhorn, James Hunt, and Richard Osborn, *Managing Organization Behavior,* 2d ed. (New York: Wiley, 1985); Richy Griffin and Gregory Moorhead, *Organization Behavior,* 2d ed. (Boston: Houghton Mifflin, 1989).

Review Questions

1. Summarize the basic steps in making an ethical judgment.

2. Name and briefly define the three ethical norms that Cavanagh presents as criteria for making ethical decisions in business.

3. What are the main differences between Utilitarianism and Individual Rights, according to Cavanagh?

4. What is the "veil of ignorance"?

5. What is an "overriding factor"?

Discussion and Writing Suggestions

1. Study Figure 2, Cavanagh's "Flow Diagram of Ethical Decision Making." Do you agree with the ways Cavanagh uses this system to analyze the "Expense Padding" case (see paragraphs 3 and 32) and the "Digital Robotics" case (see paragraphs 33–42)? Note that you will be asked to use the diagram when analyzing the cases immediately following this selection.

2. Regardless of your response to Cavanagh's system for making ethical decisions, why is it important for businesspeople to make such decisions systematically? What would be the consequences if each person decided ethically complicated matters based on his or her own personal values?

3. Cavanagh provides a succinct summary of Utilitarianism, Justice, and Individual Rights—three philosophical approaches to ethical behavior. Follow Cavanagh's footnotes and research one of these approaches. Report to your class on its history and the philosophers most closely associated with it.

4. Think of a decision you've made recently that involved a question of ethics—if possible, business ethics. In a few sentences, describe the situation. Then apply Cavanagh's system to the situation. Is the decision that follows from using Cavanagh's system consistent with the decision you made?

CASES FOR ANALYSIS AND DISCUSSION

Following, you'll find a number of cases for analysis and discussion. In business schools around the country, the "case method" is an instructional technique of long standing. For all courses in the business curriculum, the rationale for presenting cases is the same. The "case," usually a narrative account, re-creates a problem or a particular challenge in a business context. The case amounts to raw data that the student reviews in light of principles learned in class or through reading. The student is then asked to gather facts, to define a problem, to select an appropriate principle by which to study those facts, and to recommend or evaluate courses of action, based on a clear method of analysis.

All the cases that follow present ethical dilemmas that arise from business dealings, some hypothetical and some based on actual events. Your job in reading these cases is to analyze them in light of Cavanagh's (or Solomon's) principles for making ethical decisions. What would you do in similar circumstances or if you were asked to advise those involved? What business decisions would follow from your recommendations? Who would be affected by those decisions? These, among other questions, are fundamental to case-method instruction.

Case 1: Peter Green's First Day
Laura L. Nash

1   Peter Green came home to his wife and new baby a dejected man. What a contrast to the morning, when he had left the apartment full of enthusiasm to tackle his first customer in his new job at Scott Carpets. And what a customer! Peabody Rug was the largest carpet retailer in the area and accounted for 15% of the entire volume of Peter's territory. When Peabody introduced a Scott product, other retailers were quick to follow with orders. So when Bob Franklin, the owner of Peabody Rug, had called District Manager John Murphy expressing interest in "Carpet Supreme," Scott's newest commercial-duty home carpet, Peter knew that a $15,000–$20,000 order was a real profitability, and no small show for his first sale. And it was important to do well at the start, for John Murphy had made no bones about his scorn for the new breed of salespeople at Scott Carpet.

2   Murphy was of the old school: in the business since his graduation from a local high school, he had fought his way through the stiffest retail competition in the nation to be District Manager of the area at age fifty-eight. Murphy knew his textiles, and he knew his competitors' textiles. He knew his customers, and he knew how well his competitors knew his customers. Formerly, when Scott Carpet had needed to fill sales positions, it had generally raided the competition for experienced personnel, put them on a straight commission, and thereby managed to increase sales and maintain its good reputation for service at the same time. When Murphy had been promoted eight years ago to the position of District Manager, he had passed on his sales territory to Harvey Katchorian, a sixty-year-old mill rep and son of an immigrant who had also spent his life in the carpet trade. Harvey had had no trouble keeping up his sales and had retired from the company the previous spring after forty-five years of successful service in the industry. Peter, in turn, was to take over Harvey's accounts, and Peter knew that John Murphy was not sure that his original legacy to Harvey was being passed on to the best salesperson.

3   Peter was one of the new force of salespeople from Scott's Sales Management Program. In 1996 top management had created a training program to compensate for the industry's dearth of younger salespeople with long-term management potential. Peter, a college graduate, had entered Scott's five-month training program immediately after college and was the first graduate of the program to be assigned to John Murphy's district. Murphy had made it known to top management from the start that he did not think the training program could compensate for on-the-job experience, and he was clearly withholding optimism about Peter's prospects as a salesperson despite Peter's fine performance during the training program.

4   Peter had been surprised, therefore, when Murphy volunteered to accompany him on his first week of sales "to ease your transition into the territory." As they entered the office at Peabody Rug, Murphy had even seemed friendly and said reassuringly, "I think you'll get along with Bob. He's a great guy—knows the business and has been a good friend of mine for years."

5   Everything went smoothly. Bob liked the new line and appeared ready to place a large order with Peter the following week, but he indicated that he would require some "help on the freight costs" before committing himself definitely. Peter was puzzled and unfamiliar with the procedure, but Murphy quickly stepped in and assured Bob that Peter would be able to work something out.

6   After the meeting, on their way back to Scott Carpets' district office, Peter asked Murphy about freight costs. Murphy sarcastically explained the procedure: Because of its large volume, Peabody regularly "asked for a little help to cover shipping costs," and got it from all or most suppliers. Bob Franklin was simply issued a credit for defective merchandise. By claiming he had received second-quality goods, Bob was entitled to a 10%–25% discount. The discount on defective merchandise had been calculated by the company to equal roughly the cost of shipping the 500-lb. rolls back to the mill, and so it just about covered Bob's own freight costs. The practice had been going on so long that Bob demanded "freight assistance" as a matter of course before placing a large order. Obviously, the merchandise was not defective, but by making an official claim, the sales representative could set in gear the defective-merchandise compensation system. Murphy reiterated, as if to a two-year-old, the importance of a Peabody account to any sales rep, and shrugged off the freight assistance as part of doing business with such an influential firm.

7   Peter stared at Murphy. "Basically, what you're asking me to do, Mr. Murphy, is to lie to the front office."

8   Murphy angrily replied, "Look, do you want to make it here or not? If you do, you ought to know you need Peabody's business. I don't know what kind of fancy think they taught you at college, but where I come from you don't call your boss a liar."

9   From the time he was a child, Peter Green had been taught not to lie or steal. He believed these principles were absolute and that one should support one's beliefs at whatever personal cost. But during college the only even remote test of his principles was his strict adherence to the honor system in taking exams.

10   As he reviewed the conversation with Murphy, it seemed to Peter that there was no way to avoid losing the Peabody account, which would look bad on

his own record as well as Murphy's—not to mention the loss in commissions for them both. He felt badly about getting into a tiff with Murphy on his first day out in the territory, and knew Murphy would feel betrayed if one of his salespeople purposely lost a major account.

11   The only out he could see, aside from quitting, was to play down the whole episode. Murphy had not actually *ordered* Peter to submit a claim for damaged goods (was he covering himself legally?), so Peter could technically ignore the conversation and simply not authorize a discount. He knew very well, however, that such a course was only superficially passive, and that in Murphy's opinion he would have lost the account on purpose. As Peter sipped halfheartedly at a martini, he thought bitterly to himself, "Boy, they sure didn't prepare me for this in Management Training. And I don't even know if this kind of thing goes on in the rest of Murphy's district, let alone in Scott's eleven other districts."

Review Questions

1. Why was John Murphy skeptical about Peter Green's abilities as a salesperson?

2. What are "freight costs," and how do they tie in to the general question of business ethics?

Discussion and Writing Suggestions

1. What would you do if you were Peter Green? Apply the criteria set out by Cavanagh or Solomon.

2. If Green decides to "lie to the front office," who will be hurt? Is it in the best interest of Scott Carpets (as well as of Bob Franklin, John Murphy, and Peter himself) to go along with the lie that Peabody Rug had received defective merchandise and so was entitled to a credit?

3. Murphy is an experienced, successful salesman, and Scott Carpets is a successful company. Yet the way they do business is being questioned by a young man fresh out of college, with little or no practical experience—a young man who relies primarily on the "absolute" principles of honor and integrity that he had been taught as a child. To what extent do you think that there is an inherent conflict or incompatibility between basic ethical principles and business success?

4. Assume for the moment that a sales representative from a competing carpeting manufacturer was willing and eager to issue a defective merchandise credit to Peabody Rug. If you were Peter Green, would this knowledge make it easier for you to issue the credit?

Case 2: Romance on the Job:
(a) Dating at Wal-Mart
John R. Boatright

1 The company's position is crystal-clear: "Wal-Mart strongly believes and supports the 'family unit.'" For this reason, the handbook that all newly hired employees must read and sign stipulates, "A dating relation between a married associate with another associate, other than his or her own spouse, is not consistent with this belief and is prohibited." This policy was designed in part to maintain businesslike relations among employees and to avoid the turmoil that extramarital affairs can cause in the workplace. An added, and perhaps not unintended, benefit of the policy is to reinforce the wholesome, down-home image that Wal-Mart carefully fosters. The policy was challenged, however, when the manager of a Wal-Mart store in Johnstown, New York, discovered that two sales associates—one a twenty-year-old single man and the other a twenty-three-year-old woman who was married but separated from her husband—were dating. The romantic tie between the two came to the manager's attention when the woman was served with custody papers at the store. The manager immediately fired them both. The woman could not remember reading the no-dating rule in the handbook but expressed her disagreement nonetheless. "I felt it was my personal life," she said.

(b) Love and Business
Thomas I. White

1 Most of the public controversy about invasions of employees' privacy has centered on a company's attempt to find out if its workers are doing something illegal, such as using drugs. More pressing, however, is the practice by many companies of regulating its employees' lives in an area that is not simply legal, but also normal, healthy, and the source of great joy—personal relationships. Numerous corporations limit the kinds of relationships its employees may enter. In some cases, they are barred from dating coworkers; in other cases, competitors.

2 A major U.S. food corporation, for example, does not let its employees date one another. Nonetheless, two executives met and fell in love. Despite the fact that the man and woman worked in different parts of the company and had no formal business relationship with each other, their actions now jeopardized both of their jobs. For a year they lived together secretly. Before they publicly announced their plans to marry, however, the man left the company.

3 In 1982, the Coca-Cola Company fired Amanda Blake, a manager of data processing at the Coca-Cola bottler in Northampton, Massachusetts, when she refused to break her engagement with an accountant at a rival Pepsi bottler. An

attorney representing the company said that she might have accidentally leaked confidential information to her husband. In a similar case in 1979, Virginia Rulon-Miller lost her job as a marketing manager at IBM because she continued to date a former IBM account manager who now worked for a competitor. Former IBM Chairman Thomas J. Watson, Jr., however, at one time had said that "we have concern with an employee's off-the-job behavior only when it reduces his ability to perform regular job assignments." Rulon-Miller sued and received a judgment of $300,000.

4   Critics of these restrictions claim that they are unwarranted intrusions into employees' private lives. Moreover, they argue that finding a suitable companion is not only critical to one's well-being but also can be so difficult that such restrictions are an unreasonable price to pay for a job. Proponents, however, argue that the matter is not so simple. Personal relationships between coworkers can lead to favoritism and even to an unfair competitive advantage over other workers. One member of the relationship may be in a position to pass along useful information that his or her partner's peers lack. And even if there are no problems when the relationship is going well, there may be significant problems if it sours. Particularly if the former lovers work together, their professional relationship may be affected. There may be tension, hostility, and difficulty communicating with each other in a way that affects their own performance and that of their colleagues. Relationships with competitors are seen as even more dangerous because of the risk of the spread of confidential information that could cost a company sales and, ultimately, jobs.

Review Questions

1. What risks do companies feel they run when employees date?

2. What objections can be raised to company prohibitions against dating?

3. When a company prohibits employees from dating, what assumption does the company make about the employees' ability to keep their private and professional lives separate?

Discussion and Writing Suggestions

1. Use the criteria set out by Cavanagh or Solomon to decide whether or not the manager should have fired the employees in the "Dating at Wal-Mart" case. Be prepared to defend your conclusions.

2. Use the criteria set out by Cavanagh or Solomon to decide ethical courses of action in the Coca-Cola and IBM cases in "Love and Business." Be prepared to defend your conclusions.

3. In "Dating at Wal-Mart," we learn that the company makes a distinction between married employees dating (someone other than

their spouse) and unmarried ones dating. Do you understand and approve of the distinction? Discuss.

4. For a moment adopt the position that fellow employees should not have a romantic relationship. How would you respond to the objection that because on-the-job friendships as well as romantic relationships can lead to problems at work, employees should not be friends? Should friendships on the job be disallowed? Why or why not?

5. Do you believe a company has the right to regulate an employee's romantic life on the job?

Case 3: Is Family-Friendly Always Fair?
John R. Boatright

1 Martha Franklin had never seen Bill so angry. It was past seven-thirty on a Friday evening, and both were tired from a long day. The November sales report had been due at four o'clock, but Martha's assistant, Janet, had taken the last two days off to be with her ten-year-old daughter, who had undergone emergency surgery to remove an abdominal obstruction. Martha had attempted to pull the figures together herself but was slowed by her unfamiliarity with the new computerized sales-reporting system. As the regional sales director, the report was her responsibility, but she generally relied on others to generate the numbers. Just before lunch, she asked Bill Stevens, one of three district sales managers, to help out until the job was finished. As he dropped the completed report on her desk, he slumped down in a chair and began to complain, calmly at first and then with increasing agitation.

2 "Don't get me wrong," he said. "I'm willing to do my part, and it's great that Janet was able to spend this time with her daughter. Many employers are not as caring as we are here. But every time someone in this office gets time off to care for a family member, one of us single people takes up the slack. I feel that I'm doing my own job and a bit of everyone else's. If you recall, I spent half the day on Thanksgiving straightening out a billing problem for Frank, so that he wouldn't have to disrupt his family's plans. Many people in the office jealously guard their time, leaving at five sharp in order to attend a son's Little League game or get their children to a birthday party.

3 "This is a very family-friendly place. But what about those of us without families? It's as if we're expected to be married to the company. No one considers that we have a life to lead too. Also, no one wanted to be transferred to the office in Omaha, but Susan was selected to go because she had no family to relocate. She's been transferred three times while most people with families have managed to stay put. And most of the fringe benefits are for families, so we lose out yet again. We've got a great child-care center but no workout room.

It's unfair. This company is discriminating against single people and childless couples, and a lot of us are beginning to resent the unequal treatment."

4   As Martha heard Bill out, she sympathized with his complaints and wondered what could be done. She supported the family-friendly programs for which the company had received national recognition. Was Bill describing the inevitable trade-off, or could the company treat everyone fairly and yet differently?

Review Questions

1. Summarize Bill's complaint.

2. What is the manager's response to Bill's complaint?

Discussion and Writing Suggestions

1. Use the criteria set out by Cavanagh or Solomon to decide an ethical and fair course of action in this case. In developing a response, answer the question that concludes the case: "[C]ould the company treat everyone fairly and yet differently?" Be prepared to defend your conclusions.

2. Consider your own experience as an employee, or the experiences of someone you know well—perhaps a friend or family member. To what extent have you or your friend (or family member) either benefited or suffered from pro-family practices like the ones described in the case? Have you seen single people bear the brunt of pro-family policies? Discuss.

3. Is there an "inevitable trade-off" between the benefits available to working mothers or fathers and an increased dedication to work expected of single employees? That is, if benefits are given to one part of the work force, must benefits be taken from another part?

4. What might treating "everyone fairly and yet differently" look like? Design a singles-friendly employee program that would be as enlightened as this company's family-friendly program.

Case 4: The Serpent Was There
Margot Adam Langstaff and Joseph Badaracco, Jr.

In 1979, a young woman who later graduated from the Harvard Business School was an unwitting participant in a medical tragedy in Trinidad and Tobago. This case first describes the accident and then explains how the woman and her coworkers reacted to it. It is told in her own words.

1 In 1981, I faced a serious ethical dilemma that arose from a failed surgical procedure. It was an incident I will remember for the rest of my life. To this day I reflect on the outcome and hope that the correct decision was made.

2 I was a nurse supervisor in charge of training an operating room hospital staff of locals in Trinidad and Tobago for World Health, Inc. This is a nonprofit American organization whose chief purpose is to provide modern treatment for surgical disorders suffered by residents of developing countries.

3 It was late on a Friday afternoon. The intense heat of the August day was finally dissipating when an elderly woman was wheeled into the operating room for a cataract removal, our last surgical procedure in an exhausting week.

4 The patient lay before us in the center of the sterile, green operating room. The tiles may have been what made the room appear deceivingly cool. Perhaps it was the empty quality of the room itself; only an instrument table and stark aluminum lamp, jutting out from the center ceiling, were visible. No back-up generator existed; it was a very primitive operating room. There was a damp quality to the air, like that of a closed basement on a humid summer day.

5 Dark and deeply furrowed like the soil she tilled, the patient's face reflected years of hardship. She had obviously never seen such a clean and modern medical facility before. Beneath the uncertainty and fear, her expression revealed years of oppression and severe poverty. Yet she radiated a sense of dignity that I could only appreciate but never fully comprehend.

6 Speaking Spanish, the highly trained young American surgeon gently assured the woman that this was a routine, simple, and painless operation; it would be over shortly. The student nurse reached for the woman's hand as the doctor promised that the sight in her left eye would soon be restored.

7 The surgeon, straddling a small black stool at the head of the surgical table, glanced at the instrument tray to his left. Hand outstretched, he paused for a moment, looked up, and asked where the local anesthetic was. The student nurse turned toward me; I nodded. She walked out of the operating room into a small stock room next door. Seconds later she returned with a small bottle. Resuming her position alongside me, she handed me a bottle whose label read "Lidocaine." I passed it to the surgeon for a third verification. I held the bottle up so the surgeon could withdraw the Lidocaine into a sterile syringe. He then injected the clear liquid through the long, needled syringe deeply into the patient's left tear duct.

8 Only the sound of a whirring fan broke the silence in that room. I felt a stream of tropical air brush my face momentarily as it rotated in its arc. I closed my eyes for an eternal moment.

9 The fan whirled by me again. Suddenly the woman began groaning and writhing in pain while lifting herself off the table. Purely out of reflex, I grabbed her upper arms—thinking how ironic it was that her arms were as slender as the stalks of sugar cane she spent her days harvesting. My thumb and forefinger touched while strongly encircling these arms. I forced her to resume a reclining position. She turned her head from side to side mumbling in Spanish. We tried to restrain her as she continued to shake her head frantically. Something was seriously wrong.

10   The fan continued in the wave of its arc, but now it was spreading a distinctive smell throughout the musty room. In an instant the young surgeon's eyes met mine, and mirrored the panic and fear there.

11   The surgeon froze. "Do you smell something?" I remember his question vividly.

12   "Formaldehyde." I replied without thinking.

13   The syringe slipped from the surgeon's grasp to the floor. "Irrigate her eye," he said in a quiet yet controlling way. I ripped the seal from the sterile solution bottle and poured it into her eye. As he held her head firmly, I kept the colorless fluid gushing into her eye. It was no use; the intervening seconds were too long to save the eye from the sightless glaze that had now hardened over it.

14   The surgeon grasped the small bottle of Lidocaine, now lying empty on the tray. Pulling off his mask he held the bottle under his nose and then let it drop back alongside the unused instruments. We looked at each other, unable to move. This woman would never see again out of that eye. Her other eye remained shuttered by its cataract. We had injected formaldehyde directly into her eye. How could formaldehyde have gotten into the Lidocaine bottle?

15   I watched the surgeon pick up the phone and dial the familiar number of the chief surgeon's home residence. We stood in the now-empty operating room. Even the instrument tray was gone; no evidence pertaining to the recent events existed. I studied the surgeon's expression as the conversation ensued with our boss, aware of the cool tiles pressed against the bare skin on the back of my neck and legs as I leaned against the wall.

16   The circle of orange settled on top of the peaked mountains; sunlight was dimming and, hence, the heat diminished. The surgeon and I were silent as we drove up the winding, bumpy roads to the outskirts of the city. As we climbed higher our separation from the true existence of the people our work was designed to help grew. The surroundings were now beautiful; only the scent of flamingo trees in full bloom could be detected. We passed high forbidding iron gates, barely able to detect the exquisite colored tiles on the Victorian-styled rooftops nestled behind. We paused at the most impressive gate and honked. An armed guard ran toward us, paused, then unlocked the gate; we were allowed to enter the residence of the chief surgeon.

17   The sunset was magnificent from the veranda. The peaked mountains were blackened by the shadows. The sun had slipped behind them and left an orange disappearing rainbow. How deceiving the beauty was. The sunset had blackened the poverty; one could not focus on what really lay below us in the city.

18   Following dinner, we became silent while the servant refilled our coffee cups. The chief surgeon nodded, and his wife quickly left through the ceiling-high French doors. He did not speak until her footsteps on the marble floor could no longer be heard. I watched and listened closely. Here was a man, highly trained in the States, board certified, and still teaching part-time at a medical school in Milwaukee. He knew of poverty; he understood poverty, but would not accept it as being inevitable. He had grown up in the city that we could no longer see

clearly from this view. He understood this oppressive country, its culture, heritage, and the complexity of its leaders and people; his people. I could not imagine what those deep-set brown eyes had seen in their 60 years of existence; 60 years of unselfish dedication.

19   His words were quiet and firm. We all knew that someone on the clinic staff had made a gross mistake and mislabeled a bottle. He said that we could not undo the tragic mishap of that afternoon, but that we would have to think how best to handle the situation. He felt that no matter what course of action we took, in no way should we put ourselves or the continued practice of providing safe and clean surgery to locals at risk. We had restored the sight of hundreds of people and would help perhaps thousands more. The young surgeon and I did not say a word, knowing that, if this had occurred in the United States, our careers could well be over before they ever started. The three of us were dedicated to helping people, yet we had taken the eye of a woman.

20   We discussed the complexity of the day's tragedy late into the night. If the error were made public, there was a chance that the people who most desperately needed our care would stay away. The trust that had taken so long to establish would be broken. We also recognized that acknowledging the tragic incident could put our training program in jeopardy, thus denying local citizens the opportunity to learn medical skills. We considered the successes of our education program and the direct impact that we had made in improving both the health care system and the economy of Trinidad and Tobago. If made public, the reputation of the chief surgeon as well as that of World Health, Inc., could be irreversibly damaged, through a mistake that we still did not have a full understanding of. The government had been trying to obstruct our teachings; they would now have reason to end the training program that was fully under way.

21   The toughest issue for each of us was that of honesty. By not admitting the tragic mistake to the woman or the community, in essence we were lying. This violated values that we all held dear. Yet we knew what might happen if we told the truth. Honesty seemed inconsistent with our dedication to providing outstanding medical care to all. Somehow, we had already made a grave error; would we make it worse or better by lying about it?

22   Together that night we made the difficult decision, one that we would live with for the rest of our lives, that we would let the incident pass without further comment. We agreed that halting our work would be a far greater tragedy than what occurred in that operating room.

23   As the formaldehyde was destroying her eye, in her agony the woman had cried out in Spanish, "Why is the serpent causing me so much pain?"

24   In voodoo, the serpent is the devil. Maybe in a sense the woman was right; the serpent was there that Friday afternoon. The woman will always believe this, as will the others in her village. Perhaps she was right. It could be that the serpent dwells in human errors and carelessness. It may be that the devil feeds on the lofty expectation placed on the most careful, highly trained, and ethical medical professionals. The serpent reminds us that they are human, too, and make errors from time to time. Should their careers be therefore ruined? Should their

capacity for good vanish because the serpent appears from time to time? That seems to me to be a far greater evil than what happened in the operating room in Trinidad and Tobago that day. If fear of failure ends human attempts to do good, the devil will have won.

Review Questions

1. Recount the events in the clinic.

2. What ethical questions emerged as a result of the surgical mistake?

3. To what does the "serpent" refer in the case's title?

Discussion and Writing Suggestions

1. Applying the ethical norms of Utilitarianism and Individual Rights to this case leads to a question: to what extent does the greater good of future people who might be helped at this clinic override the individual rights of the woman who has permanently lost her sight in one eye? Discuss this question in a multi-paragraph essay. [Hint: See Cavanagh for definitions of the ethical norms. Also, see his paragraph 42 for a definition of "double effect," a principle that comes into play when one action—in this case, not reporting the mistake in the clinic—can have both a positive and a negative effect.]

2. Use the criteria set out by Cavanagh or Solomon to determine an ethical course of action in this case. Did the nurse supervisor, the attending surgeon, and the chief surgeon make the right decision? In developing your answer, consider the Discussion and Writing Suggestion immediately above.

3. The narrator concludes with a question: "Should [the]capacity for good [among people who have made an error] vanish because the serpent appears from time to time?" Your answer? Consider the extent to which this question is validly drawn from the facts of the case. That is, who would seriously dispute that the answer should be *Of course the capacity for good should not vanish?*

4. The nurse supervisor, the surgeon performing the procedure, and the chief surgeon make the decision not to report the mistake. The narrator seems to have been genuinely shaken by the events described and continues to "hope that the correct decision was made." Are you convinced they made their decision for the greater good—and that their noble-seeming vision of helping others, used to justify their decision, was not in fact a justification to save themselves?

5. In the United States, the reporting of this incident might have abruptly ended the careers of those involved (see paragraph 19). In not reporting the incident, the nurse supervisor, the surgeon performing the procedure, and the chief surgeon believed that standards of medical oversight and accountability should differ in the United States and in Third World countries. Do you agree?

Case 5: Is This the Right Time to Come Out?
Alistair D. Williamson

1 George Campbell, assistant vice president in mergers and acquisitions at Kirkham McDowell Securities, a St. Louis underwriting and financial advisory firm, looked up as Adam Lawson, one of his most promising associates, entered his office. Adam, 29 years old, had been with the firm for only two years but had already distinguished himself as having great potential. Recently, he had helped to bring in an extremely lucrative deal, and in six weeks, he and several other associates would be honored for their efforts at the firm's silver anniversary dinner.

2 As Adam closed the door and sat down, he said, "George, I'd like to talk to you about the banquet. I've thought about this very carefully, and I want you to know that I plan to bring my partner, Robert Collins, as my escort."

3 George was taken aback. "Well, Adam," he said, "I don't quite know what to say. I have to be honest with you; I'm a little surprised. I had no idea that you were gay. I would never have guessed." He looked at Adam for clues on how to proceed: his subordinate did seem nervous but not defiant or hostile.

4 Though only a 50-person operation, Kirkham McDowell had long since secured its status as one of the region's leading corporate financial advisers. The firm's client roster included established and successful regional companies as well as one of the country's largest defense contractors, a very conservative company for which the firm managed part of an impressive pension portfolio. Representatives of Kirkham McDowell's major clients and many of the area's most influential political and business leaders were expected to attend the banquet. All this raced through George's mind as he asked Adam, "Why do you want to do this? Why do you want to mix your personal and professional lives?"

5 "For the same reason that you bring your wife to company social events," Adam replied.

6 A look of confusion flickered across George's face while Adam continued. "Think about it for a moment, George. Success in this business depends in great part on the relationships you develop with your clients and the people you work with. An important part of those relationships is letting people know about your life away from the office, and that includes the people who are important to you. Some of the other associates already know Robert. Whenever his schedule permits, he accompanies me when I'm invited by one of my colleagues to

have dinner with his or her spouse. Granted, that isn't very often—Robert is a corporate attorney, and his work is very demanding—but he joins me whenever he can."

7   "But, Adam, a wife isn't the same thing as a—"

8   "It *is* the same thing, George. Robert and I have made a commitment to each other. We have been together for almost five years now, and I would feel very uncomfortable telling him that I was going to a major social event alone— on a weekend, no less."

9   "Well, I'm sure you'd agree that it wouldn't be appropriate for an associate to bring a date—someone he barely knows—to such an event."

10   "Come on, George. I think you know me well enough to realize that I have better judgment than that. If Robert and I had known each other for only six months, I wouldn't be having this conversation with you right now. But, as I said, we've been together for over five years!"

11   George thought for a moment. "Adam," he said slowly, "I'm just not sure you should try to make an issue of this at such an important time for the company. Why bring it up now? Think of our clients. We work with some very conservative companies. They could very well decide to give their business to a firm whose views seem to agree more with their own. You're not just making a personal statement here. You're saying something about the culture at Kirkham McDowell, something that some of our clients might fundamentally oppose. How are they going to react?"

12   Adam leaned forward. "This is only an issue if people make it an issue," he said, "I have resolved never to lie about myself or about anything that is important to me—and that includes my sexuality. Since I joined the firm, as I've become comfortable sharing details of my personal life with certain colleagues, I've come out to them and often introduced them to Robert. If people ask me if I'm gay, I'm honest with them. Likewise, if people ask me if I have a girlfriend, I tell them about my relationship with Robert. With the silver anniversary celebration coming up, I thought the time was right to speak with you. This is the first large social event the company has held since I started working here. And after a lot of discussion with Robert and some of the associates here, I've decided that I need to be as open at the banquet as I have tried to be in other areas within the organization.

13   "It's not a decision that I've taken lightly. I've seen what has happened to some of my gay friends who have come out at work. Even at much less conservative companies, some are never invited to important social events with colleagues and customers, no matter how much business they bring in. They'll never know whether or not their bonuses have been affected by prejudice related to their sexuality. I know my career could be adversely influenced by this decision, but I believe that my work should stand on its own merits. George, I've been a top contributor at this firm since I walked in the door. I hope I can rely on you to back me up on this."

14   Adam stood up but waited for George to reply. "You've given me a lot to think about," George said. "And I don't want to say anything until I've had a chance to consider all the implications. I appreciate the confidence you've shown in me by being so open. I wish I had something conclusive to say at this

point, but the fact of the matter is that I have never had to face this issue before. I am one of your biggest supporters here at the firm. Your work has been exemplary. And, until today, I would have said that you could look forward to a very successful career here. But I'm concerned about how this will play with our clients and, as a result, about how senior management will react. I personally don't have any problems with your being gay, but I'd hate to see you torpedo your career over this. It's possible that this could jeopardize some of our relationships with significant clients. Let me think about it for a few days. We can have lunch next week and map out a strategy."

15   After Adam left his office, George sat in silence for a few minutes, trying to make sense of the conversation. He was unsure of his next move. Adam clearly had *not* come into his office looking for permission to bring his lover to the banquet. George realized that he could do nothing and let events simply unfold. After all, Adam had not asked that Robert be included in his benefits coverage nor had he requested a specific managerial decision. There was no company policy on paper to guide him through his dilemma. But Adam wouldn't have come to him if he hadn't wanted a response of some kind. And shouldn't he at least tell his superior in order to head off any awkward moments at the banquet?

16   Just how negative an effect could Robert have on Adam's career with the firm and on the firm's relationship with its clients? Wasn't it possible, even likely, that the party would come off without incident? That the issue would blow over? That even the firm's most conservative clients wouldn't realize the significance of Adam's guest or would simply decide that it was a personal issue, not a business one? Or would George's worst fears be realized? Adam had to recognize that the potential risks were great. It was one thing for him to come out of the closet at the office. But wasn't he pushing things too far?

Review Questions

1. Summarize the facts of this case.

2. What are George Campell's conflicts?

3. What are the ethical issues?

4. What evidence do you find in the case that Adam is a highly qualified, valuable professional?

Discussion and Writing Suggestions

1. Use the criteria set out by Cavanagh or Solomon to decide an ethical, fair course of action in this case. How should the manager, George, handle Adam's announcement that he intends to bring his partner to the company's social event?

2. George asks Adam: "Why do you want to mix your personal and professional lives?" Adam responds: "For the same reason that you

bring your wife to company social events." To what extent is it appropriate for people at work to mix their personal and professional lives? (Note that in the "Romance on the Job" cases, the companies in question assume that it is impossible for employees *not* to mix their personal and professional lives. The companies therefore discourage on-the-job dating and dating employees of rival companies.)

3. George claims that by coming out, Adam is "saying something about the culture at Kirkham McDowell." If Adam is making a statement, what is it, and why does George see this as problematic?

4. What assumptions about sexual preference and business is George making? Are these valid assumptions? Who, in your view, is in greater need of instruction: George or Adam?

5. Adam says: "I believe that my work should stand on its own merits." In your experience as an employee, on what can an appraisal of someone's work depend *aside* from its merits?

Case 6: Why Should My Conscience Bother Me?
*Kermit Vandivier**

1 The B. F. Goodrich Co. is what business magazines like to speak of as "a major American corporation." It has operations in a dozen states and as many foreign countries, and of these far-flung facilities, the Goodrich plant at Troy, Ohio, is not the most imposing. It is a small, one-story building, once used to manufacture airplanes. Set in the grassy flatlands of west-central Ohio, it employs only about six hundred people. Nevertheless, it is one of the three largest manufacturers of aircraft wheels and brakes, a leader in a most profitable industry. Goodrich wheels and brakes support such well-known planes as the F111, the C5A, the Boeing 727, the XB70, and many others. Its customers include almost every aircraft manufacturer in the world.

2 Contracts for aircraft wheels and brakes often run into millions of dollars, and ordinarily a contract with a total value of less than $70,000, though welcome, would not create any special stir of joy in the hearts of Goodrich sales personnel. But purchase order P-23718, issued on June 18, 1967, by the LTV Aerospace Corporation, and ordering 202 brake assemblies for a new Air Force plane at a total price of $69,417, was received by Goodrich with considerable glee. And there was good reason. Some ten years previously, Goodrich had built a brake for LTV that was, to say the least, considerably less than a rousing success. The brake had not lived up to Goodrich's promises, and after experiencing considerable

---

* Reporter, *Daily News,* in Troy, Ohio.

difficulty, LTV had written off Goodrich as a source of brakes. Since that time, Goodrich salesmen had been unable to sell so much as a shot of brake fluid to LTV. So in 1967, when LTV requested bids on wheels and brakes for the new A7D light attack aircraft it proposed to build for the Air Force, Goodrich submitted a bid that was absurdly low, so low that LTV could not, in all prudence, turn it down.

3   Goodrich had, in industry parlance, "bought into the business." Not only did the company not expect to make a profit on the deal; it was prepared, if necessary, to lose money. For aircraft brakes are not something that can be ordered off the shelf. They are designed for a particular aircraft, and once an aircraft manufacturer buys a brake, he is forced to purchase all replacement parts from the brake manufacturer. The $70,000 that Goodrich would get for making the brake would be a drop in the bucket when compared with the cost of the linings and other parts the Air Force would have to buy from Goodrich during the lifetime of the aircraft. Furthermore, the company which manufactures brakes for one particular model of an aircraft quite naturally has the inside track to supply other brakes when the planes are updated and improved.

4   Thus, that first contract, regardless of the money involved, is very important, and Goodrich, when it learned that it had been awarded the A7D contract, was determined that while it may have slammed the door on its own foot ten years before, this time, the second time around, things would be different. The word was soon circulated throughout the plant: "We can't bungle it this time. We've got to give them a good brake, regardless of the cost."

5   There was another factor which had undoubtedly influenced LTV. All aircraft brakes made today are of the disk type, and the bid submitted by Goodrich called for a relatively small brake, one containing four disks and weighing only 106 pounds. The weight of any aircraft part is extremely important. The lighter a part is, the heavier the plane's payload can be. The four-rotor, 106-pound brake promised by Goodrich was about as light as could be expected, and this undoubtedly had helped move LTV to award the contract to Goodrich.

6   The brake was designed by one of Goodrich's most capable engineers, John Warren. A tall, lanky blond and a graduate of Purdue, Warren had come from the Chrysler Corporation seven years before and had become adept at aircraft brake design. The happy-go-lucky manner he usually maintained belied a temper which exploded whenever anyone ventured to offer any criticism of his work, no matter how small. On these occasions, Warren would turn red in the face, often throwing or slamming something and then stalking from the scene. As his coworkers learned the consequences of criticizing him, they did so less and less readily, and when he submitted his preliminary design for the A7D brake, it was accepted without question.

7   Warren was named project engineer for the A7D, and he, in turn, assigned the task of producing the final production design to a newcomer to the Goodrich engineering stable, Searle Lawson. Just turned twenty-six, Lawson had been out of the Northrup Institute of Technology only one year when he came to Goodrich in January 1967. Like Warren, he had worked for a while in the automotive industry, but his engineering degree was in aeronautical and astronautical sciences, and when the opportunity came to enter his special field, via Goodrich, he took it. At the Troy plant, Lawson had been assigned to various

"paper projects" to break him in, and after several months spent reviewing statistics and old brake designs, he was beginning to fret at the lack of challenge. When told he was being assigned to his first "real" project, he was elated and immediately plunged into his work.

8   The major portion of the design had already been completed by Warren, and major assemblies for the brake had already been ordered from Goodrich suppliers. Naturally, however, before Goodrich could start making the brakes on a production basis, much testing would have to be done. Lawson would have to determine the best materials to use for the linings and discover what minor adjustments in the design would have to be made.

9   Then, after the preliminary testing and after the brake was judged ready for production, one whole brake assembly would undergo a series of grueling, simulated braking stops and other severe trials called qualification tests. These tests are required by the military, which gives very detailed specifications on how they are to be conducted, the criteria for failure, and so on. They are performed in the Goodrich plant's test laboratory, where huge machines called dynamometers can simulate the weight and speed of almost any aircraft. After the brakes pass the laboratory tests, they are approved for production, but before the brakes are accepted for use in military service, they must undergo further extensive flight tests.

10   Searle Lawson was well aware that much work had to be done before the A7D brake could go into production, and he knew that LTV had set the last two weeks in June 1968 as the starting dates for flight tests. So he decided to begin testing immediately. Goodrich's suppliers had not yet delivered the brake housing and other parts, but the brake disks had arrived, and using the housing from a brake similar in size and weight to the A7D brake, Lawson built a prototype. The prototype was installed in a test wheel and placed on one of the big dynamometers in the plant's test laboratory. The dynamometer was adjusted to simulate the weight of the A7D and Lawson began a series of tests, "landing" the wheel and brake at the A7D's landing speed, and braking it to a stop. The main purpose of these preliminary tests was to learn what temperatures would develop within the brake during the simulated stops and to evaluate the lining materials tentatively selected for use.

11   During a normal aircraft landing the temperatures inside the brake may reach 1000 degrees, and occasionally a bit higher. During Lawson's first simulated landings, the temperature of his prototype brake reached 1500 degrees. The brake glowed a bright cherry-red and threw off incandescent particles of metal and lining material as the temperature reached its peak. After a few such stops, the brake was dismantled and the linings were found to be almost completely disintegrated. Lawson chalked this first failure up to chance and, ordering new lining materials, tried again.

12   The second attempt was a repeat of the first. The brake became extremely hot, causing the lining materials to crumble into dust.

13   After the third such failure, Lawson, inexperienced though he was, knew that the fault lay not in defective parts or unsuitable lining material but in the basic design of the brake itself. Ignoring Warren's original computations, Lawson made his own, and it didn't take him long to discover where the trouble lay—the brake

was too small. There simply was not enough surface area on the disks to stop the aircraft without generating the excessive heat that caused the linings to fail.

14   The answer to the problem was obvious but far from simple—the four-disk brake would have to be scrapped, and a new design, using five disks, would have to be developed. The implications were not lost on Lawson. Such a step would require the junking of all the four-disk-brake subassemblies, many of which had now begun to arrive from the various suppliers. It would also mean several weeks of preliminary design and testing and many more weeks of waiting while the suppliers made and delivered the new subassemblies.

15   Yet, several weeks had already gone by since LTV's order had arrived, and the date for delivery of the first production brakes for flight testing was only a few months away.

16   Although project engineer John Warren had more or less turned the A7D over to Lawson, he knew of the difficulties Lawson had been experiencing. He had assured the young engineer that the problem revolved around getting the right kind of lining material. Once that was found, he said, the difficulties would end.

17   Despite the evidence of the abortive tests and Lawson's careful computations, Warren rejected the suggestion that the four-disk brake was too light for the job. Warren knew that his superior had already told LTV, in rather glowing terms, that the preliminary tests on the A7D brake were very successful. Indeed, Warren's superiors weren't aware at this time of the troubles on the brake. It would have been difficult for Warren to admit not only that he had made a serious error in his calculations and original design but that his mistakes had been caught by a green kid, barely out of college.

18   Warren's reaction to a five-disk brake was not unexpected by Lawson, and, seeing that the four-disk brake was not to be abandoned so easily, he took his calculations and dismal test results one step up the corporate ladder.

19   At Goodrich, the man who supervises the engineers working on projects slated for production is called, predictably, the projects manager. The job was held by a short, chubby and bald man named Robert Sink. A man truly devoted to his work, Sink was as likely to be found at his desk at ten o'clock on Sunday night as ten o'clock on Monday morning. His outside interests consisted mainly of tinkering on a Model-A Ford and an occasional game of golf. Some fifteen years before, Sink had begun working at Goodrich as a lowly draftsman. Slowly, he worked his way up. Despite his geniality, Sink was neither respected nor liked by the majority of the engineers, and his appointment as their supervisor did not improve their feelings about him. They thought he had only gone to high school. It quite naturally rankled those who had gone through years of college and acquired impressive specialties such as thermodynamics and astronautics to be commanded by a man whom they considered their intellectual inferior. But, though Sink had no college training, he had something even more useful: a fine working knowledge of company politics.

20   Puffing upon a Meerschaum pipe, Sink listened gravely as young Lawson confided his fears about the four-disk brake. Then he examined Lawson's calculations and the results of the abortive tests. Despite the fact that he was not a qualified engineer, in the strictest sense of the word, it must certainly have

been obvious to Sink that Lawson's calculations were correct and that a four-disk brake would never have worked on the A7D.

21   But other things of equal importance were also obvious. First, to concede that Lawson's calculations were correct would also mean conceding that Warren's calculations were incorrect. As projects manager, he not only was responsible for Warren's activities, but, in admitting that Warren had erred, he would have to admit that he had erred in trusting Warren's judgment. It also meant that, as projects manager, it would be he who would have to explain the whole messy situation to the Goodrich hierarchy, not only at Troy but possibly on the corporate level at Goodrich's Akron offices. And, having taken Warren's judgment of the four-disk brake at face value (he was forced to do this since, not being an engineer, he was unable to exercise any engineering judgment of his own), he had assured LTV, not once but several times, that about all there was left to do on the brake was pack it in a crate and ship it out the back door.

22   There's really no problem at all, he told Lawson. After all, Warren was an experienced engineer, and if he said the brake would work, it would work. Just keep on testing and probably, maybe even on the very next try, it'll work out just fine.

23   Lawson was far from convinced, but without the support of his superiors there was little he could do except keep on testing. By now, housings for the four-disk brake had begun to arrive at the plant, and Lawson was able to build up a production model of the brake and begin the formal qualification tests demanded by the military.

24   The first qualification attempts went exactly as the tests on the prototype had. Terrific heat developed within the brakes and, after a few, short, simulated stops, the linings crumbled. A new type of lining material was ordered and once again an attempt to qualify the brake was made. Again, failure.

25   On April 11, the day the thirteenth test was completed, I became personally involved in the A7D situation.

26   I had worked in the Goodrich test laboratory for five years, starting first as an instrumentation engineer, then later becoming a data analyst and technical writer. As part of my duties, I analyzed the reams and reams of instrumentation data that came from the many testing machines in the laboratory, then transcribed it to a more usable form for the engineering department. And when a new-type brake had successfully completed the required qualification tests, I would issue a formal qualification report.

27   Qualification reports were an accumulation of all the data and test logs compiled by the test technicians during the qualification tests, and were documentary proof that a brake had met all the requirements established by the military specifications and was therefore presumed safe for flight testing. Before actual flight tests were conducted on a brake, qualification reports had to be delivered to the customer and to various government officials.

28   On April 11, I was looking over the data from the latest A7D test, and I noticed that many irregularities in testing methods had been noted on the test logs.

29   Technically, of course, there was nothing wrong with conducting tests in any manner desired, so long as the test was for research purposes only. But qualification test methods are clearly delineated by the military, and I knew that this

test had been a formal qualification attempt. One particular notation on the test logs caught my eye. For some of the stops, the instrument which recorded the brake pressure had been deliberately miscalibrated so that, while the brake pressure used during the stops was recorded as 1000 psi (the maximum pressure that would be available on the A7D aircraft), the pressure had actually been 1100 psi!

30   I showed the test logs to the test lab supervisor, Ralph Gretzinger, who said he had learned from the technician who had miscalibrated the instrument that he had been asked to do so by Lawson. Lawson, said Gretzinger, readily admitted asking for the miscalibration, saying he had been told to do so by Sink.

31   I asked Gretzinger why anyone would want to miscalibrate the data-recording instruments.

32   "Why? I'll tell you why," he snorted. "That brake is a failure. It's way too small for the job, and they're not ever going to get it to work. They're getting desperate, and instead of scrapping the damned thing and starting over, they figure they can horse around down here in the lab and qualify it that way."

33   An expert engineer, Gretzinger had been responsible for several innovations in brake design. It was he who had invented the unique brake system used on the famous XB70. A graduate of Georgia Tech, he was a stickler for detail and he had some very firm ideas about honesty and ethics. "If you want to find out what's going on," said Gretzinger, "ask Lawson, he'll tell you."

34   Curious, I did ask Lawson the next time he came into the lab. He seemed eager to discuss the A7D and gave me the history of his months of frustrating efforts to get Warren and Sink to change the brake design. "I just can't believe this is really happening," said Lawson, shaking his head slowly. "This isn't engineering, at least not what I thought it would be. Back in school, I thought that when you were an engineer, you tried to do your best, no matter what it cost. But this is something else."

35   He sat across the desk from me, his chin propped in his hand. "Just wait," he warned. "You'll get a chance to see what I'm talking about. You're going to get in the act, too, because I've already had the word that we're going to make one more attempt to qualify the brake, and that's it. Win or lose, we're going to issue a qualification report!"

36   I reminded him that a qualification report could only be issued after a brake had successfully met all military requirements, and therefore, unless the next qualification attempt was a success, no report would be issued.

37   "You'll find out," retorted Lawson. "I was already told that regardless of what the brake does on test, it's going to be qualified." He said he had been told in those exact words at a conference with Sink and Russell Van Horn.

38   This was the first indication that Sink had brought his boss, Van Horn, into the mess. Although Van Horn, as manager of the design engineering section, was responsible for the entire department, he was not necessarily familiar with all phases of every project, and it was not uncommon for those under him to exercise the what-he-doesn't-know-won't-hurt-him philosophy. If he was aware of the full extent of the A7D situation, it meant that matters had truly reached a desperate stage—that Sink had decided not only to call for help but was looking toward that moment when blame must be borne and, if possible, shared.

39   Also, if Van Horn had said, "Regardless what the brake does on test, it's going to be qualified," then it could only mean that, if necessary, a false qualification report would be issued! I discussed this possibility with Gretzinger, and he assured me that under no circumstances would such a report ever be issued.

40   "If they want a qualification report, we'll write them one, but we'll tell it just like it is," he declared emphatically. "No false data or false reports are going to come out of this lab."

41   On May 2, 1968, the fourteenth and final attempt to qualify the brake was begun. Although the same improper methods used to nurse the brake through the previous tests were employed, it soon became obvious that this too would end in failure.

42   When the tests were about half completed, Lawson asked if I would start preparing the various engineering curves and graphic displays which were normally incorporated in a qualification report. "It looks as though you'll be writing a qualification report shortly," he said.

43   I flatly refused to have anything to do with the matter and immediately told Gretzinger what I had been asked to do. He was furious and repeated his previous declaration that under no circumstances would any false data or other matter be issued from the lab.

44   "I'm going to get this settled right now, once and for all," he declared. "I'm going to see Line [Russell Line, manager of the Goodrich Technical Services Section, of which the test lab was a part] and find out just how far this thing is going to go!" He stormed out of the room.

45   In about an hour, he returned and called me to his desk. He sat silently for a few moments, then muttered, half to himself, "I wonder what the hell they'd do if I just quit?" I didn't answer and I didn't ask him what he meant. I knew. He had been beaten down. He had reached the point when the decision had to be made. Defy them now while there was still time—or knuckle under, sell out.

46   "You know," he went on uncertainly, looking down at his desk, "I've been an engineer for a long time, and I've always believed that ethics and integrity were every bit as important as theorems and formulas, and never once has anything happened to change my beliefs. Now this…. Hell, I've got two sons I've got to put through school and I just…." His voice trailed off.

47   He sat for a few more minutes, then, looking over the top of his glasses, said hoarsely, "Well, it looks like we're licked. The way it stands now, we're to go ahead and prepare the data and other things for the graphic presentation in the report, and when we're finished, someone upstairs will actually write the report.

48   "After all," he continued, "we're just drawing some curves, and what happens to them after they leave here, well, we're not responsible for that."

49   He was trying to persuade himself that as long as we were concerned with only one part of the puzzle and didn't see the completed picture, we really weren't doing anything wrong. He didn't believe what he was saying, and he knew I didn't believe it either. It was an embarrassing and shameful moment for both of us.

50   I wasn't at all satisfied with the situation and decided that I too would discuss the matter with Russell Line, the senior executive in our section.

51 Tall, powerfully built, his teeth flashing white, his face tanned to a coffee-brown by a daily stint with a sun lamp, Line looked and acted every inch the executive. He was a crossword-puzzle enthusiast and an ardent golfer, and though he had lived in Troy only a short time, he had been accepted into the Troy Country Club and made an official of the golf committee. He commanded great respect and had come to be well liked by those of us who worked under him.

52 He listened sympathetically while I explained how I felt about the A7D situation, and when I had finished, he asked me what I wanted him to do about it. I said that as employees of the Goodrich Company we had a responsibility to protect the company and its reputation if at all possible. I said I was certain that officers on the corporate level would never knowingly allow such tactics as had been employed on the A7D.

53 "I agree with you," he remarked, "but I still want to know what you want me to do about it."

54 I suggested that in all probability the chief engineer at the Troy plant, H. C. "Bud" Sunderman, was unaware of the A7D problem and that he, Line, should tell him what was going on.

55 Line laughed, good-humoredly. "Sure, I could, but I'm not going to. Bud probably already knows about this thing anyway, and if he doesn't, I'm sure not going to be the one to tell him."

56 "But why?"

57 "Because it's none of my business, and it's none of yours. I learned a long time ago not to worry about things over which I had no control. I have no control over this."

58 I wasn't satisfied with this answer, and I asked him if his conscience wouldn't bother him if, say, during flight tests on the brake, something should happen resulting in death or injury to the test pilot.

59 "Look," he said, becoming somewhat exasperated, "I just told you I have no control over this thing. Why should my conscience bother me?"

60 His voice took on a quiet, soothing tone as he continued. "You're just getting all upset over this thing for nothing. I just do as I'm told, and I'd advise you to do the same."

61 He had made his decision, and now I had to make mine.

62 I made no attempt to rationalize what I had been asked to do. It made no difference who would falsify which part of the report or whether the actual falsification would be by misleading numbers or misleading words. Whether by acts of commission or omission, all of us who contributed to the fraud would be guilty. The only question left for me to decide was whether or not I would become a party to the fraud.

63 Before coming to Goodrich in 1963, I had held a variety of jobs, each a little more pleasant, a little more rewarding than the last. At forty-two, with seven children, I had decided that the Goodrich Company would probably be my "home" for the rest of my working life. The job paid well, it was pleasant and challenging, and the future looked reasonably bright. My wife and I had bought a home and we were ready to settle down into a comfortable, middle-age, middle-class

rut. If I refused to take part in the A7D fraud, I would have to either resign or be fired. The report would be written by someone anyway, but I would have the satisfaction of knowing I had had no part in the matter. But bills aren't paid with personal satisfaction, nor house payments with ethical principles. I made my decision.*

Review Questions

1. Why did Lawson conclude that Warren's design was flawed?

2. Why did Warren not consider redesigning the brakes? Why did Sink choose to support Warren, instead of Lawson, when he must have realized that Lawson was right about the brakes?

3. Both Ralph Gretzinger and Vandivier at first refused to go along with the demand that they falsify test data. Why did both men eventually cave in to their superiors?

4. At what point did Vandivier consult a lawyer? Why then—and not earlier?

Discussion and Writing Suggestions

1. If you were Vandivier, would you have acted as he did? (Consider especially the personal dilemma he describes in paragraphs 62–63.) Do you believe that he acted responsibly at all stages of this case? Explain.

2. In paragraph 71 on page 432, Vandivier says that he and Lawson "discussed such things as the Nuremberg trials [the post World War II tribunals at which Nazi officials were found guilty of war crimes] and how they related to our guilt and complicity in the A7D situation." To what extent do you see parallels between these two situations?

3. Apply Cavanagh's ethical decision-making model to this case. To what extent do the principles of utilitarianism, rights, and justice apply? Are there any "overwhelming factors" that could help determine which principles are more important in this case?

4. Assume that you are a member of a commission charged with investigating the Goodrich case. Assume also that you found Vandivier's account of the matter to be credible. Consider all of the

---

* Turn to page 432 for the author's concluding discussion on what happened in this case. Before reading that discussion, however, try to anticipate Vandivier's decision.

things that went wrong, and try to devise safeguards—in the form of a series of recommendations—to prevent such mishaps in the future.

5. Ethically, what similarities do you find between this case and the Peter Green case? (Consider, for example, the similarities between Peter Green and Searle Lawson.) What differences do you find?

Following are the concluding paragraphs to the Vandivier case, presented earlier.

Conclusion to "Why Should My Conscience Bother Me?"

64 …The next morning, I telephoned Lawson and told him I was ready to begin on the qualification report.

65 In a few minutes, he was at my desk, ready to begin. Before we started, I asked him, "Do you realize what we are going to do?"

66 "Yeah," he replied bitterly, "we're going to screw LTV. And speaking of screwing," he continued, "I know now how a whore feels, because that's exactly what I've become, an engineering whore. I've sold myself. It's all I can do to look at myself in the mirror when I shave. I make me sick."

67 I was surprised at his vehemence. It was obvious that he too had done his share of soul-searching and didn't like what he had found. Somehow, though, the air seemed clearer after his outburst, and we began working on the report.

68 I had written dozens of qualification reports, and I knew what a "good" one looked like. Resorting to the actual test data only on occasion, Lawson and I proceeded to prepare page after page of elaborate, detailed engineering curves, charts, and test logs, which purported to show what had happened during the formal qualification tests. Where temperatures were too high, we deliberately chopped them down a few hundred degrees, and where they were too low, we raised them to a value that would appear reasonable to the LTV and military engineers. Brake pressure, torque values, distances, times—everything of consequence was tailored to fit the occasion.

69 Occasionally, we would find that some test either hadn't been performed at all or had been conducted improperly. On those occasions, we "conducted" the test—successfully, of course—on paper.

70 For nearly a month we worked on the graphic presentation that would be a part of the report. Meanwhile, the fourteenth and final qualification attempt had been completed, and the brake, not unexpectedly, had failed again.

71 During that month, Lawson and I talked of little else except the enormity of what we were doing. The more involved we became in our work, the more apparent became our own culpability. We discussed such things as the Nuremberg trials and how they related to our guilt and complicity in the A7D situation. Lawson often expressed his opinion that the brake was downright dangerous and that, once on flight tests, "anything is liable to happen."

72 I saw his boss, John Warren, at least twice during that month and needled him about what we were doing. He didn't take the jibes too kindly but managed to laugh the situation off as "one of those things." One day I remarked that what

we were doing amounted to fraud, and he pulled out an engineering handbook and turned to a section on laws as they related to the engineering profession.

73   He read the definition of fraud aloud, then said, "Well, technically I don't think what we're doing can be called fraud. I'll admit it's not right, but it's just one of those things. We're just kinda caught in the middle. About all I can tell you is, do like I'm doing. Make copies of everything and put them in your SYA file."

74   "What's an 'SYA' file?" I asked.

75   "That a 'save your ass' file." He laughed.

76   On June 5, 1968, the report was officially published and copies were delivered in person to the Air Force and LTV. Within a week, flight tests were begun at Edwards Air Force Base in California. Searle Lawson was sent to California as Goodrich's representative. Within approximately two weeks, he returned because some rather unusual incidents during the tests had caused them to be canceled.

77   His face was grim as he related stories of several near crashes during landings—caused by brake troubles. He told me about one incident in which, upon landing, one brake was literally welded together by the intense heat developed during the test stop. The wheel locked, and the plane skidded for nearly 1500 feet before coming to a halt. The plane was jacked up and the wheel removed. The fused parts, within the brake had to be pried apart.

78   Lawson had returned to Troy from California that same day, and that evening, he and others of the Goodrich engineering department left for Dallas for a high-level conference with LTV.

79   That evening I left work early and went to see my attorney. After I told him the story, he advised that, while I was probably not actually guilty of fraud, I was certainly part of a conspiracy to defraud. He advised me to go to the Federal Bureau of Investigation and offered to arrange an appointment. The following week he took me to the Dayton office of the FBI, and after I had been warned that I would not be immune from prosecution, I disclosed the A7D matter to one of the agents. The agent told me to say nothing about the episode to anyone and to report any further incident to him. He said he would forward the story to his superiors in Washington.

80   A few days later, Lawson returned from the conference in Dallas and said that the Air Force, which had previously approved the qualification report, had suddenly rescinded that approval and was demanding to see some of the raw test data taken during the tests. I gathered that the FBI had passed the word.

81   Finally, early in October 1968, Lawson submitted his resignation, to take effect on October 25. On October 18, I submitted my own resignation, to take effect on November 1. In my resignation, addressed to Russell Line, I cited the A7D report and stated: "As you are aware, this report contained numerous deliberate and willful misrepresentations which, according to legal counsel, constitute fraud and expose both myself and others to criminal charges of conspiracy to defraud.... The events of the past seven months have created an atmosphere of deceit and distrust in which it is impossible to work...."

82   On October 25, I received a sharp summons to the office of Bud Sunderman. As chief engineer at the Troy plant, Sunderman was responsible for the entire engineering division. Tall and graying, impeccably dressed at all times,

he was capable of producing a dazzling smile or a hearty chuckle or immobilizing his face into marble hardness, as the occasion required.

83   I faced the marble hardness when I reached his office. He motioned me to a chair. "I have your resignation here," he snapped, "and I must say you have made some rather shocking, I might even say irresponsible, charges. This is very serious."

84   Before I could reply, he was demanding an explanation. "I want to know exactly what the fraud is in connection with the A7D and how you can dare accuse this company of such a thing!"

85   I started to tell some of the things that had happened during the testing, but he shut me off saying, "There's nothing wrong with anything we've done here. You aren't aware of all the things that have been going on behind the scenes. If you had known the true situation, you would never have made these charges." He said that in view of my apparent "disloyalty" he had decided to accept my resignation "right now," and said it would be better for all concerned if I left the plant immediately. As I got up to leave he asked me if I intended to "carry this thing further."

86   I answered simply, "Yes," to which he replied, "Suit yourself." Within twenty minutes, I had cleaned out my desk and left. Forty-eight hours later, the B. F. Goodrich Company recalled the qualification report and the four-disk brake, announcing that it would replace the brake with a new, improved, five-disk brake at no cost to LTV.

87   Ten months later, on August 13, 1969, I was the chief government witness at a hearing conducted before Senator William Proxmire's Economy in Government Subcommittee of the Congress's Joint Economic Committee. I related the A7D story to the committee, and my testimony was supported by Searle Lawson, who followed me to the witness stand. Air Force officers also testified, as well as a four-man team from the General Accounting Office, which had conducted an investigation of the A7D brake at the request of Senator Proxmire. Both Air Force and GAO investigators declared that the brake was dangerous and had not been tested properly.

88   Testifying for Goodrich was R. G. Jeter, vice-president and general counsel of the company, from the Akron headquarters. Representing the Troy plant was Robert Sink. These two denied any wrongdoing on the part of the Goodrich Company, despite expert testimony to the contrary by Air Force and GAO officials. Sink was quick to deny any connection with the writing of the report or of directing any falsifications, claiming to be on the West Coast at the time. John Warren was the man who supervised its writing, said Sink.

89   As for me, I was dismissed as a high-school graduate with no technical training, while Sink testified that Lawson was a young, inexperienced engineer. "We tried to give him guidance," Sink testified, "but he preferred to have his own convictions."

90   About changing the data and figures in the report, Sink said: "When you take data from several different sources, you have to rationalize among those data what is the true story. This is part of your engineering know-how." He admitted that changes had been made in the data, "but only to make them more consistent with the overall picture of the data that is available."

91   Jeter pooh-poohed the suggestion that anything improper occurred, saying: "We have thirty-odd engineers at this plant…and I say to you that it is incredible that these men would stand idly by and see reports changed or falsified.… I mean you just do not have to do that working for anybody.… Just nobody does that."

92   The four-hour hearing adjourned with no real conclusion reached by the committee. But, the following day the Department of Defense made sweeping changes in its inspection, testing, and reporting procedures. A spokesman for the DOD said the changes were a result of the Goodrich episode.

93   The A7D is now in service, sporting a Goodrich-made five-disk brake, a brake that works very well, I'm told. Business at the Goodrich plant is good. Lawson is now an engineer for LTV and has been assigned to the A7D project. And I am now a newspaper reporter.

94   At this writing, those remaining at Goodrich are still secure in the same positions, all except Russell Line and Robert Sink. Line has been rewarded with a promotion to production superintendent, a large step upward on the corporate ladder. As for Sink, he moved up into Line's old job.

SYNTHESIS ACTIVITIES

1. Analyze the ethical dilemma in any of the cases you've read in this chapter. Consider the case in two ways:

    -   Analyze the dilemma based on Gerald Cavanagh's strategy for making ethical business decisions.
    -   Analyze the case following the questions set out in Solomon.

    Having conducted your two analyses, choose one as the basis for writing a memo in which you review the dilemma and suggest a course of action. Assume you are a business consultant, writing to a company owner faced with the dilemma presented in the case. Your memo should review the pertinent facts, identify the dilemma, analyze the dilemma (according to materials provided by Cavanagh or Solomon), and present a course of action—which you justify based on your analysis.

2. Devise your own criteria for making ethical business decisions. As you devise these criteria, bear in mind that a decision maker in business must seek to balance financial needs with the rights of employees, consumers, owners (shareholders), and the community. Then, using your criteria, analyze one of the cases presented in this chapter. Write a memo, as described in the first Synthesis Activity.

3. Present one of the cases in this chapter to five or more college-age people. Present the same case to several older people you know who are in business. Try for an equal representation of women and men. Ask respondents in each group, "What would you do?" Study

your notes or your tape-recorded transcripts. Do any gender or generational patterns emerge? Present your findings in a comparison-contrast synthesis.

4. How effective is studying and discussing hypothetical dilemmas (that is, studying cases) in preparing you for the pressures of actual dilemmas in the workplace? Develop an answer into an argument synthesis that draws on three or more cases in this chapter. If possible, refer to actual ethical dilemmas with which you've struggled in your own work.

5. Compare and contrast Solomon's and Cavanagh's approaches to making ethical decisions in business. To what extent do the approaches overlap in their underlying philosophies? In the method and ease of their application? In their comprehensiveness? Having made notes on these points, apply each approach to a single case presented in this chapter. Do the two approaches lead you to making different recommendations? Develop your analysis into a comparison-contrast synthesis.

6. To what extent do you feel that dilemmas of business ethics originate in a confusion of two codes of ethics: what we might call "church" ethics and business ethics? That is, do you feel that people in business operate according to one code of conduct and that the same people, after business hours, operate according to a different code? In your view, should one code predominate both in and out of business? Develop an argument synthesis in which you take a stand on the question. In an effort to keep the discussion from becoming too abstract, try to ground your discussion in a particular case—either from this chapter or from your own experience.

Research Activities

1. Research the practice of intelligence gathering in business. A business professional must pay close attention to competitors, but how close? Is espionage permissible? In looking for sources, consult the cumulative indexes of two journals: *Business Ethics* and *Business Horizons*. The following books should be of use:

   Jerry Miller, ed. *Millennium Intelligence: Understanding and Conducting Competitive Intelligence in the Digital Age* (2000); Larry Kahaner, *Competitive Intelligence: How to Gather, Analyze, and Use Information to Move Your Business to the Top* (1998); Leonard M. Fuld, *New Competitor Intelligence: The Complete Resource for Finding, Analyzing, and Using Information about Your Competitors* (1994); Ian Gordon, *Beat the Competition: How to Use Competitive Intelligence to Develop Winning Business Strategies* (1989); Howard Sutton, *Competitive Intelligence* (1988).

2. Research the history of business ethics in America, and address this question: To what extent have Americans, over their history, been careful to observe standards of ethical behavior in their business dealings? The following study will be especially helpful: Peter Baida, *Poor Richard's Legacy: American Business Values from Benjamin Franklin to Donald Trump* (1990).

3. Locate as many books as you can on the topic of "climbing-the-ladder-to-corporate-success." Make a study of the advice in these books and report on the ethical values implicit in them. Can you classify varieties of advice? Do you find yourself agreeing with any particular strategies? What does your agreement reveal about *you?*

4. Investigate the topic of whistleblowing, the action a lone employee takes when he or she feels that a company's unethical behavior may harm the public. Under what conditions should an employee blow the whistle? What are the personal ramifications of blowing the whistle? How do companies and fellow employees respond to whistleblowers? What are the laws that protect whistleblowers? Three possible sources: David Lewis, *Whistleblowing at Work* (2001); Terance D. Miethe, *Whistleblowing at Work: Tough Choices in Exposing Fraud, Waste, and Abuse on the Job* (1999); Sissela Bok, *On the Ethics of Concealment and Revelation* (1989). Many books on the general topic of business ethics have chapters devoted to whistleblowing.

5. Choose some company that interests you, and to which you have at least limited access. Investigate the extent to which the topic of business ethics is on people's minds and on the company's agenda. Does the company have a formal code of ethics? Does the company have in place a procedure for employees who wish to raise questions about the ethics of particular practices? Has the company asked any of its employees to attend workshops on business ethics? Does the company feel the need to address any of these questions?

6. Investigate and report on any of the insider trading scandals of the 1980s. You might begin by doing a literature search on two names: Ivan Boesky and Michael Milken. In your paper, explain how insider trading works and why it is both ethically problematic and illegal.

7. Research the Ford Explorer scandal of 2000–01. What are the basic facts of the case? (On the Internet you should be able to locate Congressional testimony, since Ford's and Firestone's chairmen were called before a Congressional committee investigating the matter.) What claims did drivers and their families make against the company? What claims did Ford make against Firestone Tires? What counter claims did Firestone make? What resolutions, if any, were reached? Based on what you have read in this chapter, in what ways does the Explorer case involve issues of business ethics?

10 Weight Debate

You've probably heard of the "Freshman 15"—the extra weight that first-year students gain when they settle down to unlimited helpings of high-calorie dorm food. More calories in than out (no time for exercise with all that studying—right?) is the basic equation for weight gain. And in record numbers, Americans—college students included—are packing on the pounds. At the same time, an alarmingly high number of girls and young women are voluntarily starving themselves (sometimes to death) in an effort to achieve an idealized image of slenderness promoted by the media. Not only is this ideal unrealistic, it is wholly arbitrary. As recently as 100 years ago, the culturally approved ideal weight was significantly heavier than it is today. Indeed, undergarment manufacturers used to provide padding so that those who were too thin could avoid the stigma of being labeled sickly or impoverished.

Open most newspapers or magazines, and the chances are excellent that you will find advertisements featuring images of slender models. Television shows and movies bombard us with an endless stream of fit, toned actors. Everywhere we turn, our culture reminds us none too subtly that slenderness is America's ideal. Whole industries have emerged to help us achieve this lean and hungry look, but recent statistics show that fewer and fewer of us are succeeding. According to the Centers for Disease Control and the *Journal of the American Medical Association,* the number of Americans who are overweight or obese has reached epidemic proportions.* One in two American adults is overweight; one in five is obese—statistics that result in $70 billion (annually) in lost productivity and direct health care expenses. Add to that an additional $30 billion Americans spend trying to *lose* weight each year, and the magnitude of the problem begins to take shape.

But monetary losses represent only the measurable portion of the problem. In a culture infatuated with youthful athleticism, the obese too often suffer from profound lack of self-esteem as friends, family, coworkers, and strangers unfairly equate being fat with flaws of character. And it is not as if the overweight and obese don't try to lose weight. Dieting, it seems, is America's favorite occupation. But diets—95% of them—do *not* work, according to recent studies; and so those who have every intention of thinning down find themselves doomed to a cycle of losing weight and,

---

*In 2001, the United States Surgeon General published a "Call to Action to Prevent and Decrease Overweight and Obesity." You can find the full report along with comprehensive statistics on the state of America's weight at <http://www.surgeongeneral.gov/topics/obesity/default.htm>.

within months or a few years, gaining all or most of it back. At the other end of the scale, literally and figuratively, the psychological costs of monitoring one's weight are equally overwhelming to the nation's 7 to 10 million anorexics and bulimics. For well over a decade, physicians and therapists have sought to help their patients get the nutrition they need to thrive, but their conditions remain stubbornly resistant to change.

On the one hand, then, our culture screams at us to remain thin and exacts a heavy price in self-esteem for not doing so. On the other, competitive forces have led the food industry to invest millions in manipulating the flavors and textures of their goods so that we will buy and eat more. Couple this effort with clever advertising campaigns and bright packaging, and one wonders why every American isn't either overweight or terrified to eat anything at all. One author whose work appears in this chapter, Roberta Seid, actually argues that "anorexia nervosa could be called the paradigm of our age, for our creed encourages us all to adopt the behavior and attitudes of the anorexic. The difference is one of degree, not of kind." As consumers of food, we are caught in a strange tug-of-war in which we are urged to consume—even to excess, while at the same time admonished not to show any visible signs of excess consumption. Some are pulled tragically in one direction, choosing self-starvation; record numbers are pulled in the other direction, eating all that good food even as we look miserably each morning at the bathroom scale. At the end of every day, well over half of this nation thinks constantly, even obsessively, about weight.

This chapter gathers some provocative articles and essays on being overweight and obese: that is, on being *fat*. We use this politically incorrect word neutrally, not pejoratively, following the usage of several authors whose work appears in the pages that follow.* The readings open with a statement by physicians Jeffrey Koplan and William Dietz writing the lead editorial in the 27 October 1999 issue of the *Journal of the American Medical Association.* The authors begin with the provocative claim that "Obesity is epidemic in the United States." Next we offer two tables summarizing data from a recent study by the Centers for Disease Control on the "Prevalence of Obesity Among U.S. Adults, by Characteristics and by Region and State." W. Wayt Gibbs, staff writer for *Scientific American,* then reports on the biological causes of being overweight and obese and on various pharmacological responses. Next, in an op-ed piece for the *Los Angeles Times,* Greg Crister argues that we should stigmatize the behavior of unhealthy overeating, teaching children (especially) that "[e]ating too much food is a bad thing."

The second part of the chapter consists of readings that critique our culture's preoccupation with thinness. This section begins with a policy statement

---

* The literature on anorexia nervosa and bulimia is so extensive that we could not represent it with any reasonably comprehensive coverage here. If you have an interest in these subjects, you will find many books and articles readily available in community as well as academic libraries, and also on the Web.

by NAAFA, the National Association to Advance Fat Acceptance, on the subject of "Dieting and the Diet Industry." Mary Ray Worley, a NAAFA member, writes of the debilitating self-hatred among fat people and of her life-changing decision to join "a growing number of people [who] believe it's possible to be happy with your body even if it happens to be fat."

Roberta Seid follows with "Too 'Close to the Bone': The Historical Context for Women's Obsession with Slenderness." In a startlingly original critique, Seid examines the spiritual dimensions of our obsession with thinness as well as the historical changes that led to a new—and thinner—body ideal. Next, Hillel Schwartz argues that our culture is caught in the grip of a "despotism of slenderness." He imagines a fat "utopia" in which fat people accept themselves and are accepted by the culture at large. In "Why the Fries Taste Good," from Eric Schlosser's *Fast Food Nation*, the author provides a fascinating, inside look at the flavor industry and the biochemical tricks that food manufacturers use to seduce our tastebuds. Finally, writing for the *New Yorker,* Atul Gawande, a surgeon who assisted on a gastric-bypass, tells the story of Vincent Caselli, a Boston-area contractor whose efforts to lose weight proved so futile that he submitted to an increasingly popular surgical procedure that reduced his stomach to a one-ounce sized pouch.

Caloric Imbalance and Public Health Policy
Jeffrey P. Koplan, MD, MPH
William H. Dietz, MD, PhD

On October 27, 1999, the Journal of the American Medical Association (JAMA), *one of the country's most prestigious medical journals, devoted an entire issue to obesity—a publication decision that got the attention of the American public. Articles in this issue reported on the increased mortality and disease risk associated with obesity. Working with data that had been recently gathered by the Centers for Disease Control and Prevention (CDC) in Atlanta, Koplan and Dietz open their editorial with a brief, dramatic statement. As public health professionals, they define a problem and make a call to action. Dr. Koplan is director of the CDC.*

1   Obesity is epidemic in the United States. More than 50% of US adults are now overweight, based on a body mass index (BMI)* of 25 kg/m² or more.[1] Furthermore, 22% of the U.S. adult population is obese, based on a BMI of 30 kg/m² or more, equivalent to approximately 13.5 kg (30 lb) overweight. Three percent of U.S. adults have a BMI of 40 kg/m² or more, which represents

---

* Your Body Mass Index is your weight in kilograms divided by the square of your height in meters. See the BMI chart immediately following this editorial. [editors]

[1] Flegal KM, Carroll MD, Kuczmarski RJ, Johnson CL. Overweight and obesity in the United States: prevalence and trends, 1960–1994. *Int J Obesity,* 1998;22:39–47.

a weight excess of approximately 45 kg (100 lb). Blacks and Hispanics are disproportionately affected. As the study by Mokdad and colleagues in this issue of *The Journal*[2] clearly demonstrates, the increase in the prevalence of obesity has been rapid. No area of the country has been spared.

2   Obesity is not simply a cosmetic disorder. Approximately 60% of overweight 5- to 10-year-old children already have 1 associated biochemical or clinical cardiovascular risk factor, such as hyperlipidemia, elevated blood pressure, or increased insulin levels, and 25% have 2 or more.[3] As Must and colleagues[4] demonstrate in their article, the risk factors observed in children will become chronic diseases in adults. Almost 80% of obese adults have diabetes, high blood cholesterol levels, high blood pressure, coronary artery disease, gallbladder disease, or osteoarthritis, and almost 40% have 2 or more of these comorbidities. Based on the study by Allison and colleagues,[5] only smoking exceeds obesity in its contribution to total mortality rates in the United States. A recent estimate suggesting that the direct and indirect costs of obesity in the United States approximated 10% of the national health care budget[6] underscores why the nation can no longer afford to ignore obesity as a major medical problem.

3   Genes related to obesity are clearly not responsible for the epidemic of obesity because the gene pool in the United States did not change significantly between 1980 and 1994. However, comparison of the differences in BMI in children and adolescents on a percentile by percentile basis indicates that the changes in BMI were limited to the upper half of the BMI distribution; the mean BMI increased by substantially more than the median.[7] These observations suggest either that 50% of children and adolescents had obesity susceptibility genes that were acted on by environmental changes, or that environmental changes only affected 50% of the population.

4   The human body, like any system, obeys the laws of thermodynamics. An excess of energy intake over expenditure leads to storage of energy in the form of fat. What may have developed as an evolutionary response to periods of famine and sparse foodstuffs has become a burden with negative health consequences in contemporary society. Only during the last several decades has

[2]Mokdad AH, Serdula MK, Djetz WH, Bowman BA, Marks JS, Koplan JP. The spread of the obesity epidemic in the United States, 1991–1998. *JAMA*. 1999;282:1519–1522.

[3]Freedman DS, Dietz WH, Srinivasan SR, Berenson GS. The relation of overweight to cardiovascular risk factors among children and adolescents: the Bogalusa Heart Study. *Pediatrics*. 1999;103:1175–1182.

[4]Must A, Spadano J, Coakley EH, Field AE, Colditz G, Dietz WH. The disease burden associated with overweight and obesity. *JAMA*. 1999;282:1523–1529.

[5]Allison DB, Fontaine KR, Manson JE, Stevens J, VanItallie TB. Annual deaths attributable to obesity in the United States. *JAMA*. 1999;282:1530–1538.

[6]Wolf AM, Colditz GA. Current estimates of the economic costs of obesity in the United States. *Obesity Res*. 1998;6:97–106.

[7]Troiano RP, Flegal KM. Overweight children and adolescents: description, epidemiology, and demographics. *Pediatrics*. 1998;101(suppl):497–504.

an imbalance of energy intake and output occurred for a large proportion of the American population.

5   Between surveys conducted from 1977 through 1978 and 1994 through 1996, reported daily energy intakes increased from 9404 (2239) to 10 311 kJ (2455 kcal) in men and from 6443 (1534) to 6913 kJ (1646 kcal) in women.[8,9] Innumerable environmental changes that foster eating more frequently have occurred: the availability of more food and foods with higher energy content, the growth of the fast food industry, the increased numbers and marketing of snack foods, and an increased time for socializing along with a custom of socializing with food and drink. In a parallel development, opportunities in daily life to burn energy have diminished: children watch more television daily, physical education has been markedly reduced in our schools, many neighborhoods lack sidewalks for safe walking, the workplace has become increasingly automated, household chores are assisted by labor saving machinery, and walking or bicycling has been replaced by automobile travel for all but the shortest distances.

6   Public health and clinical strategies to address the obesity epidemic must begin with weight maintenance for the adult population, weight loss for the obese, and increased physical activity for all. Weight maintenance for the obese as well as the nonobese will prevent further increases in the prevalence and the severity of obesity and also will prevent new cases of obesity in those who currently have weights within the healthy range. Modest weight losses of 5% to 10% of body weight improve glucose tolerance, hyperlipidemia, and blood pressure in obese adults.[10] Because physical activity may prevent obesity, improve obesity-associated comorbidities,[11] reduce mortality,[12,13] and have beneficial effects on a variety of other chronic diseases,[14] strategies to increase physical activity must be implemented for the entire population. Implementation of these strategies will require a shift in emphasis from a cosmetic ideal weight for height to an acceptable weight for health.

---

[8]Federation of American Societies for Experimental Biology, Life Sciences Research Office. *Third Report on Nutrition Monitoring in the United States.* Vol 2. Washington DC: US Government Printing Office; 1995.

[9]Frazao E. *America's Eating Habits: Changes and Consequences.* Washington, DC: US Dept of Agriculture; 1999. Information Bulletin AIB–750.

[10]National Institutes of Health. *Clinical Guidelines on the Identification, Evaluation, and Treatment of Overweight and Obesity in Adults.* Bethesda, Md: National Institutes of Health; 1998. Publication 98–4083.

[11]US Department of Health and Human Services. *Physical Activity and Health: A Report of the Surgeon General.* Atlanta, Ga: Centers for Disease Control and Prevention; 1996.

[12]Lee CD, Blair SN, Jackson AS. Cardiorespiratory fitness, body composition, and all-cause and cardiovascular disease mortality in men. *Am J Clin Nutr.* 1999;69:373–380.

[13]Wei M, Kampert JB, Barlow CE, et al. Relationship between low cardiorespiratory fitness and mortality in normal-weight, overweight, and obese men. *JAMA.* 1999;282:1547–1553.

[14]Powell KE, Carperson CJ, Koplan JP, Ford ES. Physical activity and chronic disease. *Am J Clin Nutr.* 1989;49:999–1006.

7   The time has come to develop a national comprehensive obesity prevention strategy that incorporates educational, behavioral, and environmental components analogous to those already in place for tobacco use. For example, the decline in tobacco use not only reflects an increased awareness of the health consequences of its use but also reflects a broad social strategy to reduce exposure. Prevention of tobacco use includes health warnings on cigarette packages, creation of tobacco-free spaces in restaurants and public buildings, enforcement of laws that prohibit tobacco sales to minors, and taxes that make cigarettes expensive.

8   Solutions to the obesity epidemic will differ from those that have reduced tobacco use. In contrast to tobacco use, energy intake derives from multiple foods rather than a single product. Furthermore, people can choose not to smoke, whereas they cannot easily choose not to eat without adverse health consequences. As in the case of tobacco users, obese individuals must not become the target of discrimination but should be seen as persons with a chronic health condition in need of support and treatment. Nonetheless, without comprehensive population-based efforts to prevent and treat obesity, the prevalence of obesity and its expensive associated diseases and mortality are likely to continue to increase. Like rickets, pellagra, goiter, and dental caries, the most effective solutions to the obesity epidemic are likely environmental. However, in contrast to single-nutrient deficiency diseases, which can be addressed by nutrient fortification, environmental solutions to obesity will be more complex.

9   Because obesity has not been the focus of major preventive efforts, a desperate need exists for research to identify effective interventions and programs to prevent obesity. Several promising directions are already apparent. As Robinson[15] demonstrates in this issue of *The Journal*, reduced television viewing by children slows rates of weight gain. A recent school-based intervention that focused on increased physical activity, increased fruit and vegetable consumption, reduced consumption of high-fat foods, and reduced inactivity significantly reduced obesity prevalence in preadolescent girls.[16] One successful experimental approach to make fruits and vegetables or other nutritious foods more competitive is to offer more diverse, attractive, and less-expensive alternatives to high energy value foods in vending machines and cafeteria lines.[17] Schools also provide one of the few supervised locations where children can be physically active. The significant health benefits associated with physical activity and the reduced opportunities for children to be active make restoration of daily physical education in schools a priority. Nonetheless, some communities lack the facilities or have chosen not to support physical education programs.

---

[15]Robinson TN. Reducing children's television viewing to prevent obesity: a randomized controlled trial. *JAMA*. 1999;282:1561–1567.

[16]Gortmaker SL, Peterson K, Wiecha J, et al. Reducing obesity via a school-based interdisciplinary intervention among youth: Planet Health. *Arch Pediatr Adolesc Med*. 1999;153:409–418.

[17]French SA, Story M, Jeffery RW, et al. Pricing strategy to promote fruit and vegetable purchase in high school cafeterias: *J Am Diet Assoc*. 1997;97:1008–1010.

10   In response to the high costs of health care associated with obesity and inactivity, a number of major corporations have initiated effective programs that include weight loss and increased physical activity.[18] However, given the economics and dynamics of the small- to medium-sized workplaces in which 50% of the U.S. workforce is employed, broader dissemination of such programs may be limited. With relatively high turnover of members in managed care plans and uncertain cost recovery of investments in diet and exercise programs whose benefits may not be apparent for a year or two, managed care plans may be less motivated to institute such health promotion programs. The health and financial benefits, such as reduced workdays lost to illness or reduced health care costs, are increasingly supported by data but will require wide acceptance by employers and health plans before workers become the focus of activities promoting healthful diets and levels of physical activity.

11   Because work-site physical activity programs will not be an option for many adults, changes in the community environment to promote physical activity may offer the most practical approach to prevent obesity or reduce its comorbidities. Restoration of physical activity as part of the daily routine represents a critical goal. As recent studies have shown, physical activity need not be vigorous or continuous to produce health benefits.[19-21] Changes that promote physical activity may be as mundane as improving the location and appearance of stairwells or as complex as the redesign of communities. In many parts of the United States, community infrastructure to support physical activity already exists, such as sidewalks and bicycle trails, and work-sites, schools, and shopping areas in close proximity to residential areas. Such infrastructure makes walking or bicycling to school, to work, or to shop part of daily physical activity. In these areas, strategies to promote physical activity may be easier to implement than in communities that lack such infrastructure.

12   Automobile trips that can be safely replaced by walking or bicycling offer the first target for increased physical activity in communities. Recent data indicate that approximately 25% of all trips are less than 1 mile, and 75% of these are by car[22] (Paul Schimek, oral communication, September 14, 1999). Reliance on physical activity as an alternative to car use is less likely to occur in many cities and towns unless they are designed or retro-fitted to permit walking or

[18]Tully S. America's healthiest companies. *Fortune.* 1995;131:98–106.

[19]Dunn AL, Marcus BH, Kampert JB, Garcla ME, Kohl HW III, Blair SN. Comparisons of lifestyle and structured interventions to increase physical activity and cardiorespiratory fitness. *JAMA.* 1999;281:327–334.

[20]Andersen RE, Wadden TA, Bartlett SJ, Zemel B, Verde TJ, Franckowiak SC. Effects of lifestyle activity vs structured aerobic exercise in obese women. *JAMA.* 1999;281:335–340.

[21]Manson JE, Hu FB, Rich-Edwards JW, et al. A prospective study of walking as compared with vigorous exercise in the prevention of coronary heart disease in women. *N Engl J Med.* 1999;341:650–658.

[22]Schimek P. Unpublished calculations from 1995 Nationwide Personal Transportation Survey. US Department of Transportation, Federal Highway Administration, Research and Technical Support Center. Lanham, Md: Federal Highway Administration; 1997.

bicycling. The location of schools, work sites, and shopping areas near residential areas will require substantial changes in community or regional design. Several incentives may promote such changes. Alternatives to automobiles will reduce air pollution as well as increase physical activity. Community recreation areas or facilities may promote physical activity during leisure time. Such facilities clearly improve the desirability of communities. For example, a recent survey of new home buyers indicated that almost all of the amenities that made communities desirable places to live were features that promoted physical activity, such as walking and jogging trails, outdoor swimming pools, playgrounds, and parks.[23]

13   People in the United States are proud of the nation's magnificent geography and enjoy exploration of and adventures in it. U.S. mythology is filled with images of vigorous physicality and glorified hard work—cowboys, farmers, longshoremen, miners, and athletes. Most U.S. citizens value the image of physically active presidents—from the boxing and hunting of Teddy Roosevelt to the swimming of Franklin Delano Roosevelt, the touch football of John Kennedy, the jogging of Jimmy Carter and Bill Clinton, the wood-splitting and horseback riding of Ronald Reagan, and the golf and horseshoe tossing of George Bush. Similar role models are needed for women and minorities.

14   However, despite the pervasive conceptual preference for being lean and active, the environments and behaviors that have been developed make both characteristics difficult to achieve. Far too many people appear to have accepted the determinants of the problems of overweight and inactivity, and rely on "treatments" in the forms of myriad ineffective diet remedies and nostrums. As with many health issues, it is essential to emphasize prevention as the only effective and cost-effective approach. There is a particular need to focus on children and adolescents whose excess weight and sedentary lifestyle will form the basis for a lifetime of preventable morbidity and increased premature mortality.

15   Obesity, overweight, and a sedentary lifestyle are serious health issues now and will only worsen without thoughtful and scientifically based interventions that address societal and individual attitudes and behaviors and their environmental context. Physicians and other health care professionals, elected officials, educators, employers, and parents need to recognize the magnitude and impact of this major health problem and provide the will and energy to correct it through preventive approaches. In the past 25 years, several newer areas have been incorporated as targets for clinical and public health concern, such as tobacco control and injury prevention. It is now time to promote weight control and physical activity.

Acknowledgments: We thank Martha Katz, MA, Steve Gortmaker, PhD, and Tom Robinson, MD, for their comments and suggestions.

[23]Fletcher J. Is this Disneyland? no, the new suburbs. *Wall Street Journal.* June 4, 1999:W12.

Body Mass Index Chart

	19	20	21	22	23	24	25	26	27	28	29	30	31	32	33	34	35	36
Height (inches)							Body Weight (pounds)											
58	91	96	100	105	110	115	119	124	129	134	138	143	148	153	158	162	167	172
59	94	99	104	109	114	119	124	128	133	138	143	148	153	158	163	168	173	178
60	97	102	107	112	118	123	128	133	138	143	148	153	158	163	168	174	179	184
61	100	106	111	116	122	127	132	137	143	148	153	158	164	169	174	180	185	190
62	104	109	115	120	126	131	136	142	147	153	158	164	169	175	180	186	191	196
63	107	113	118	124	130	135	141	146	152	158	163	169	175	180	186	191	197	203
64	110	116	122	128	134	140	145	151	157	163	169	174	180	186	192	197	204	209
65	114	120	126	132	138	144	150	156	162	168	174	180	186	192	198	204	210	216
66	118	124	130	136	142	148	155	161	167	173	179	186	192	198	204	210	216	223
67	121	127	134	140	146	153	159	166	172	178	185	191	198	204	211	217	223	230
68	125	131	138	144	151	158	164	171	177	184	190	197	203	210	216	223	230	236
69	128	135	142	149	155	162	169	176	182	189	196	203	209	216	223	230	236	243
70	132	139	146	153	160	167	174	181	188	195	202	209	216	222	229	236	243	250
71	136	143	150	157	165	172	179	186	193	200	208	215	222	229	236	243	250	257
72	140	147	154	162	169	177	184	191	199	206	213	221	228	235	242	250	258	265
73	144	151	159	166	174	182	189	197	204	212	219	227	235	242	250	257	265	272
74	148	155	163	171	179	186	194	202	210	218	225	233	241	249	256	264	272	280
75	152	160	168	176	184	192	200	208	216	224	232	240	248	256	264	272	279	287
76	156	164	172	180	189	197	205	213	221	230	238	246	254	263	271	279	287	295

Body Mass Index Chart

	37	38	39	40	41	42	43	44	45	46	47	48	49	50	51	52	53	54
Height (inches)							Body Weight (pounds)											
58	177	181	186	191	196	201	205	210	215	220	224	229	234	239	244	248	253	258
59	183	188	193	198	203	208	212	217	222	227	232	237	242	247	252	257	262	267
60	189	194	199	204	209	215	220	225	230	235	240	245	250	255	261	266	271	276
61	195	201	206	211	217	222	227	232	238	243	248	254	259	264	269	275	280	285
62	202	207	213	218	224	229	235	240	246	251	256	262	267	273	278	284	289	295
63	208	214	220	225	231	237	242	248	254	259	265	270	278	282	287	293	299	304
64	215	221	227	232	238	244	250	256	262	267	273	279	285	291	296	302	308	314
65	222	228	234	240	246	252	258	264	270	276	282	288	294	300	306	312	318	324
66	229	235	241	247	253	260	266	272	278	284	291	297	303	309	315	322	328	334
67	236	242	249	255	261	268	274	280	287	293	299	306	312	319	325	331	338	344
68	243	249	256	262	269	276	282	289	295	302	308	315	322	328	335	341	348	354
69	250	257	263	270	277	284	291	297	304	311	318	324	331	338	345	351	358	365
70	257	264	271	278	285	292	299	306	313	320	327	334	341	348	355	362	369	376
71	265	272	279	286	293	301	308	315	322	329	338	343	351	358	365	372	379	386
72	272	279	287	294	302	309	316	324	331	338	346	353	361	368	375	383	390	397
73	280	288	295	302	310	318	325	333	340	348	355	363	371	378	386	393	401	408
74	287	295	303	311	319	326	334	342	350	358	365	373	381	389	396	404	412	420
75	295	303	311	319	327	335	343	351	359	367	375	383	391	399	407	415	423	431
76	304	312	320	328	336	344	353	361	369	377	385	394	402	410	418	426	435	443

BMI Tables. To use these tables, find your height in the left-hand column. Move across to a given weight. The number at the top of the column is your BMI.

Review Questions

1. What percentage of Americans is overweight, and what percentage is obese? What is the source of this data?

2. What is the relationship between obesity and general health, according to the authors?

3. Why, according to the authors, can the United States "no longer afford to ignore obesity as a major medical problem"?

4. What causes obesity?

5. What are the authors' recommendations for combating the epidemic of obesity?

6. Why will environmental strategies play an especially important role in the fight against obesity, and in what ways will these strategies prove complex?

7. The authors urge readers to accept prevention as an approach to obesity, as opposed to treatment. Why?

Discussion and Writing Suggestions

1. Scan the footnotes of this article from *Journal of the American Medical Association*. For what sorts of statements do the authors cite sources? Generally, how dependable do you find the information in this editorial?

2. What elements of the editorial identify it *as* an editorial? (You might reflect on the editorials you read in newspapers.) To what extent does the piece by Koplan and Dietz fit the same genre of writing?

3. The authors review a good deal of information in their discussion of "caloric imbalance." Do you find that the authors are *not* discussing any elements of being overweight or obese that you consider to be important?

4. Koplan and Dietz use the highly charged word "epidemic" in their article. Physicians use this word to denote a specific set of circumstances. Look up "epidemic" in a dictionary and discuss the ways in which the rising incidence of obesity compels the authors to use this word.

5. The authors state that their recommendations for reducing obesity "will require a shift in emphasis from a cosmetic ideal weight for height to an acceptable weight for health." What forces are at work in the culture that help to define and promote a cosmetically ideal weight? What success do you envision for moving Americans away from such an ideal?

6. The *JAMA* is calling for a major national mobilization against obesity that is reminiscent of the mobilization against tobacco use. To what extent do you feel that the authors have made the case in this editorial for such a broad-scale, expensive, and extended campaign? Have they convinced you that obesity poses a major health risk to the well-being of the nation?

Prevalence of Obesity Among U.S. Adults, by Characteristics and by Region and State
Centers for Disease Control and Prevention

In 1999, the Centers for Disease Control and Prevention (CDC) published a report entitled "U.S. Obesity Trends in Adults from 1991–1998." Two broad conclusions emerged from this study:

- *The prevalence of obesity [...] increased from 12% in the U.S. population in 1991 to 17.9% in 1998.*

- *Obesity increased in every state, for both men and women, across all age categories, all races, all educational levels, and regardless of an individual's smoking status.*

On its Web site, the CDC describes itself as "the lead federal agency for protecting the health and safety of people—at home and abroad, providing credible information to enhance health decisions, and promoting health through strong partnerships." As such, CDC is charged with devising and implementing strategies for preventing disease. The first stage in developing a strategy, of course, is to understand the extent of a problem, which the CDC attempted to do with its study. Note that Dr. Jeffrey Koplan, lead author of the JAMA editorial immediately preceding these tables, is the Director of CDC. Following are two tables from the 1999 study. To see complete data, go to this Web site: http://www.cdc.gov/nccdphp/dnpa/obesity/.

Prevalence of Obesity Among U.S. Adults, by Characteristics

Characteristics	1991	1995	1998	1999
Total	12.0	15.3	17.9	18.9
Sex				
Men	11.7	15.6	17.7	19.1
Women	12.2	15.0	18.1	18.6
Age groups				
18–29	7.1	10.1	12.1	12.1
30–39	11.3	14.4	16.9	18.6

Characteristics	1991	1995	1998	1999
40–49	15.8	17.9	21.2	22.4
50–59	16.1	21.6	23.8	24.2
60–69	14.7	19.4	21.3	22.3
>70	11.4	12.1	14.6	16.1
Race, ethnicity				
White	11.3	14.5	16.6	17.7
Black	19.3	22.6	26.9	27.3
Hispanic	11.6	16.8	20.8	21.5
Other	7.3	9.6	11.9	12.4
Educational level				
Less than high school	16.5	20.1	24.1	25.3
High school	13.3	16.7	19.4	20.6
Some college	10.7	15.1	17.8	18.1
College or above	8.0	11.0	13.1	14.3
Smoking status				
Never smoked	12.0	15.2	17.9	19.0
Ex-smoker	14.0	17.9	20.9	21.5
Current smoker	9.9	12.3	14.8	15.7

Prevalence of Obesity Among U.S. Adults, Region and State

	1991	1995	1998	1999
New England	9.9	12.1	14.4	14.9
Maine	12.1	13.7	17.0	18.9
New Hampshire	10.4	14.7	14.7	13.8
Vermont	10.0	14.2	14.4	17.2
Massachusetts	8.8	11.1	13.8	14.3
Rhode Island	9.1	12.9	16.2	16.1
Connecticut	10.9	11.9	14.7	14.5
Mid Atlantic	12.7	14.4	16.7	17.8
New York	12.8	13.3	15.9	16.9
New Jersey	9.7	14.2	15.2	16.8
Pennsylvania	14.4	16.1	19.0	19.9
East north central	14.1	17.2	19.1	20.3
Ohio	14.9	17.2	19.5	19.8
Indiana	14.8	19.6	19.5	19.4
Illinois	12.7	16.4	17.9	20.2
Michigan	15.2	17.7	20.7	22.1
Wisconsin	12.7	15.3	17.9	19.3
West north central	12.2	16.5	18.0	19.0
Kansas	n/a	15.8	17.3	18.5
Minnesota	10.6	15.0	15.7	15.0
Iowa	14.4	17.2	19.3	20.9
Missouri	12.0	18.0	19.8	20.8
North Dakota	12.9	15.6	18.7	21.2
South Dakota	12.8	13.6	15.4	19.0
Nebraska	12.5	15.7	17.5	20.2
South Atlantic	11.1	15.6	18.6	19.3
District of Columbia	15.2	n/a	19.9	17.9

	1991	1995	1998	1999
South Atlantic (continued)				
Delaware	14.9	16.2	16.6	17.1
Maryland	11.2	15.8	19.8	17.6
Virginia	10.1	15.2	18.2	18.6
West Virginia	15.2	17.8	22.9	23.9
North Carolina	13.0	16.5	19.0	21.0
South Carolina	13.8	16.1	20.2	20.2
Georgia	9.2	12.6	18.7	20.7
Florida	10.1	16.5	17.4	17.9
East south central	13.1	17.8	20.0	21.2
Kentucky	12.7	16.6	19.9	21.1
Tennessee	12.1	18.0	18.5	20.1
Alabama	13.2	18.3	20.7	21.8
Mississippi	15.7	18.6	22.0	22.8
West south central	13.1	15.2	19.9	21.0
Arkansas	12.8	17.3	19.2	21.9
Louisiana	15.7	17.4	21.3	21.5
Oklahoma	11.9	13.0	18.7	20.2
Texas	12.7	15.0	19.9	21.1
Mountain	9.6	12.0	14.1	14.5
Montana	9.5	12.6	14.7	14.7
Idaho	11.7	13.8	16.0	19.5
Colorado	8.4	10.0	14.0	14.3
New Mexico	7.8	12.7	14.7	17.3
Arizona	11.0	12.8	12.7	11.6
Wyoming	n/a	13.9	14.5	16.4
Utah	9.7	12.6	15.3	16.3
Pacific	10.2	14.2	17.0	18.1
Washington	9.9	13.5	17.6	17.7
Nevada	n/a	13.3	13.4	15.3
Oregon	11.2	14.7	17.8	19.6
California	10.0	14.4	16.8	18.1
Alaska	13.1	19.2	20.7	19.2
Hawaii	10.4	10.4	15.3	15.3
U.S. Total	12.0	15.3	17.9	18.9

Review Questions

1. As you study the Characteristics table, what correlation do you find between race/ethnicity and obesity?

2. In the Characteristics table, what correlation do you find between level of education and incidence of obesity?

3. Review both CDC tables and summarize the general trend in incidence of obesity.

4. According to the Region/State table, which are the least and most obese areas of the country?

Discussion and Writing Suggestions

1. Select your age group, race/ethnicity, educational level, and smoking status in the Characteristics table. To what extent do the percentages reported reflect what you have observed about the prevalence of obesity?

2. Select your region and state in the Region/State table. Do the percentages reported reflect what you have observed about the prevalence of obesity?

3. Focus on the 1991 through 1999 percentages of obesity among people who have smoked and quit, never smoked, or presently smoke. What inferences can you draw between smoking status and obesity?

4. Speculate on possible explanations for the relationship between obesity and level of education.

5. To what extent are you surprised to find state and regional differences in levels of obesity? Identify one such difference and speculate on the causes of the difference.

6. Why might those older than 70 tend to be less obese than those aged 30–69?

7. Do you find any surprises in the CDC's data? Discuss.

8. Write a paragraph summarizing what for you are the key findings in one of the two tables.

Gaining on Fat
W. Wayt Gibbs

The following article appeared in the August 1996 issue of Scientific American. *Staff writer W. Wayt Gibbs reports on the causes and potential treatments of what he and others refer to as the "disease" of obesity. Gibbs examines genetic factors that may contribute to obesity and reviews the "set point" and "settling point" hypotheses for weight maintenance and weight gain. You can find this article online, with related links, at http://www.sciam.com/0896issue/0896gibbs.html.*

1 Throughout most of human history, a wide girth has been viewed as a sign of health and prosperity. It seems both ironic and fitting, then, that corpulence now poses a growing threat to the health of many inhabitants of the richest nations. The measure of the hazard in the U.S. is well known: 59 percent of the adult population meets the current definition of clinical obesity, according to a 1995 report by the Institute of Medicine, easily qualifying the disease for epidemic status. Epidemiologists at Harvard University conservatively estimate that treating

obesity and the diabetes, heart disease, high blood pressure and gall stones caused by it rang up $45.8 billion in health care costs in 1990, the latest year studied. Indirect costs because of missed work pitched another $23 billion onto the pile. That year, a congressional committee calculated, Americans spent about $33 billion on weight-loss products and services. Yet roughly 300,000 men and women were sent early to their graves by the damaging effects of eating too much and moving too little.

2   The problem is as frustrating as it is serious. Quick and easy solutions—liquid diets, support groups, acupressure, appetite-suppressing "aroma sticks," and even the best-intentioned attempts to eat less and exercise more—have all failed in well-controlled trials to reduce the weight of more than a small fraction of their obese adherents by at least 10 percent for five years—an achievement shown to increase life expectancy sharply.

3   The discovery last summer of leptin, a natural hormone that cures gross obesity when injected into mutant mice that lack it, raised hopes of a better quick fix. Those hopes have faded as subsequent studies have found no fat people who share the leptin-related mutations seen in mice. But the identification of leptin is only one of many important advances over the past several years that have opened a new chapter in the understanding of obesity.

4   Armed with powerful new tools in molecular biology and genetic engineering, scientists are seeking physiological explanations for some of the most puzzling aspects of the fattening of industrial society. Why is obesity on the rise, not just in the U.S. but in nearly all affluent countries? How is it that some individuals remain fat despite constant diets, whereas others eat what they want without gaining a pound? Why is it so hard to lose a significant amount of weight and nearly impossible to keep it off? Perhaps most important, what can be done to slow and eventually reverse this snowballing trend? The traditional notion that obesity is simply the well-deserved consequence of sloth and gluttony has led to unhelpful and sometimes incorrect answers to these questions. Science may at last offer better.

What Makes the World Go Round

5   Contrary to conventional wisdom, the U.S. is not the fattest nation on earth. Obesity is far more common on Western Samoa and several other Pacific islands. On Nauru, a mere dot of eight square miles once covered to overflowing with seabird guano, the 7,500 islanders have traded that valuable source of phosphate to fertilizer companies in exchange for one of the highest per capita incomes in the world. Many also traded their plows for lounge chairs and their traditional diet of fish and vegetables for Western staples such as canned meats, potato chips and beer. Within the course of a generation, the change has taken its toll on their bodies. By 1987 well over 65 percent of men and 70 percent of women on Nauru were obese, and one third suffered from diabetes.

6   Many countries, developed and developing, are heading in the same direction at an alarming pace. Changes in diet alone do not explain the trend. Surveys—some of which admittedly are of dubious accuracy—show that the proportion of calories Americans get from fat has dropped about eight points since the 1980s, to 34 percent. Yet the prevalence of obesity has risen by a similar

amount in nearly the same period. Britons ate 10 percent fewer calories overall in 1991 than in 1980, according to government estimates, while the number
of heavyweights doubled. Polls that show gasoline consumption and hours
spent watching television rising about as quickly as the rate of obesity in some
countries seem to explain part of the disparity.

7   Evolutionary biology may provide a deeper explanation, however. In 1962
James V. Neel of the University of Michigan proposed that natural selection pressured our distant ancestors to acquire "thrifty genes," which boosted the ability to store fat from each feast in order to sustain people through the next
famine. In today's relative surfeit, Neel reasoned, this adaptation has become a
liability. The theory is supported by the Nauruans' plight and also by studies of
the Pima Indians, a tribe whose progenitors split into two groups sometime
during the Middle Ages. One group settled in southern Arizona; the other
moved into the Sierra Madre Mountains in Mexico. By the 1970s most of the
Indians in Arizona had been forced out of farming and had switched to an
American diet with 40 percent of its calories from fat. They now endure the
highest incidence of obesity reported anywhere in the world—far higher than
among their white neighbors. About half develop diabetes by age 35.

8   Eric Ravussin, a researcher with the National Institute of Diabetes and
Digestive and Kidney Diseases (NIDDK), has compared Pimas in Arizona with
their distant relatives in Maycoba, Mexico, who still live on subsistence farming
and ranching. Although the groups share most of the same genes, Pimas in
Maycoba are on average 57 pounds (26 kilograms) lighter and about one inch
(2.5 centimeters) shorter. Few have diabetes. Maycobans also eat about half as
much fat as their counterparts to the north, and they spend more than 40 hours
a week engaged in physical work. The fact that Mexican Pimas remain lean provides strong evidence that the high rate of obesity among American Pimas is
the result not of a genetic defect alone but of a genetic susceptibility—excep-
tionally thrifty genes—turned loose in an environment that offers easy access to
high-energy food while requiring little hard labor.

9   Because all human populations seem to share this genetic susceptibility to
varying degrees, "we are going to see a continuing increase in obesity over the
next 25 years" as standards of living continue to rise, predicts F. Xavier Pi-Sunyer,
director of the obesity research center at St. Luke's-Roosevelt Hospital in New
York City. He warns that "some less developed countries are particularly at risk.
It is projected that by 2025, more than 20 percent of the population of Mexico
will have diabetes."

10   Studies of Pimas, islanders and migrants "all seem to indicate that among
different populations, the prevalence of obesity is largely determined by environmental conditions," Ravussin concludes. A few doctors have proposed
changing those conditions by levying a "fat tax" on high-calorie foods or raising
insurance rates for those who fail to show up at a gym regularly.

11   But economic and legal punishments are unlikely to garner much popular
support, and no one knows whether they would effectively combat obesity. So
most researchers are turning back to factors they think they can control: the
genetic and biological variables that make one person gain weight while others
in the same circumstances stay lean.

Finding Genes That Fit

12 Doctors have long known that the tendency to gain weight runs in families—how strongly is still under debate. Numerous analyses of identical twins reared apart have shown that genetic factors alone control a large part of one's body mass index, an estimate of body fat commonly used to define obesity. A few have found weight to be as dependent on genes as height: about 80 percent. But the majority have concluded that genetic influences are only about half that potent.

13   Investigators at the National Institutes of Health who examined more than 400 twins over a period of 43 years concluded that "cumulative genetic effects explain most of the tracking in obesity over time," including potbellies sprouting in middle age. Interestingly, the researchers also determined that "shared environmental effects were not significant" in influencing the twins' weight gain. That result is bolstered by five studies that compared the body mass indexes of adopted children with their biological and adoptive parents. All found that the family environment—the food in the refrigerator, the frequency of meals, the type of activities the family shares—plays little or no role in determining which children will grow fat. Apparently, only dramatic environmental differences, such as those between the mountains of Mexico and the plains of Arizona, have much effect on the mass of a people.

14   Just which genes influence our eating, metabolism and physical activity, and how they exert their power, remains a mystery. But geneticists do have some encouraging leads. Five genes that can cause rodents to balloon have now been pinpointed.

15   *Obese,* cloned by Jeffrey M. Friedman and others at the Rockefeller University, encodes a blueprint for leptin, a hormone produced by fat cells. Mice with a mutation in this gene produce either no leptin or a malformed version and quickly grow to three times normal weight. *Diabetes,* cloned last December by a team at Millennium Pharmaceuticals in Cambridge, Mass., codes for a receptor protein that responds to leptin by reducing appetite and turning up metabolism. Mice with a bad copy of this gene do not receive the leptin signal, and they, too, get very fat from infancy.

16   Within the past year scientists at the Jackson Laboratory in Bar Harbor, Maine, have cloned two other fat genes, named *fat* and *tubby.* Mice with a mutation in either of these genes put on weight gradually—more like humans do. The *fat* gene gets translated into an enzyme that processes insulin, the hormone that signals the body that it has been fed. But the protein produced by the *tubby* gene is unlike any ever seen. Researchers do not yet know why mice with errors in *fat, tubby* or *agouti yellow,* a fifth obesity gene discovered several years ago, put on extra ounces.

17   Although geneticists have located versions of all five genes within human DNA, "so far, when we have looked for human mutations on these genes, we haven't found them," reports L. Arthur Campfield, a research leader at Hoffmann-La Roche, the drug company that has bought the rights to Millennium's work on the leptin receptor. In fact, clinical studies by Friedman and others have shown that unlike *obese* and *diabetes* mice, heavy humans generally produce a normal amount of leptin given the amount of fat they are

carrying. At least at first glance, there seems to be nothing wrong with their leptin systems.

18   All of which is no surprise to most obesity researchers, who have long maintained that there must be multiple genes that interact with one another and with economic and psychological pressures to set an individual's susceptibility to weight gain. Although identifying clusters of interrelated genes is considerably trickier than finding single mutations, some labs have made headway in mice. David West of the Pennington Biomedical Research Center in Baton Rouge, La., has been crossing one strain that fattens dramatically on a high-fat diet with a closely related strain that remains relatively lean on the same menu. By tracking the way the trait is passed from one generation to the next, West has proved that the fat sensitivity is carried by one to four dominant genes, and he has narrowed down the chromosome segments on which they could lie. Interestingly, the *tubby* gene happens to rest within one of these segments.

19   Eventually the genes involved in human weight regulation should be found. But that is the simple part. To make a dent in obesity, physiologists will then have to figure out how all these genes work in real bodies outside the lab. The first step will be to resolve once and for all an old dieters' debate: Do we or do we not have set points—predetermined weights at which our bodies are happiest—and can they be changed?

Set Up for Failure

20 A typical American adult gains about 20 pounds between the ages of 25 and 55. "If you figure that an adult ingests 900,000 to one million calories a year and you calculate the energy cost of those additional 20 pounds," observes Rudolph L. Leibel, co-director of the human metabolism laboratory at Rockefeller, you find that "just a few tenths of 1 percent of the calories ingested are in fact being stored. That degree of control or balance is extraordinary."

21   Multiple feedback loops maintain the body at a stable weight by shunting messages through the bloodstream and the autonomic nervous system between the brain, the digestive tract, muscle—and, it turns out, fat. Until recently, fat was generally considered just a passive storage tissue. In fact, says Ronald M. Evans of the Salk Institute in La Jolla, Calif., "it is a type of endocrine tissue. Fat secretes signals—hormones such as leptin—and also monitors and responds to signals from other cells."

22   Last December, Evans reported his discovery of a new hormone, with the catchy name of 15d-PGJ$_2$, that is produced inside fat cells and seems to trigger the formation of new ones, at least in children. Any drug that tried to interfere with the hormone to prevent new fat from forming would probably work only in children, Evans says, because fat cells in adults usually inflate in size rather than increase in number. But a synthetic molecule that mimics 15d-PGJ$_2$, called troglitazone, does appear to be an effective drug for the type II diabetes associated with obesity, because it also signals muscle cells to respond normally to insulin.

23   In mapping the maze of intertwined pathways that control short-term appetite as well as factors (such as fat and carbohydrate levels) that change over days or weeks, researchers are slowly working out how all these signals

combine to hold weight steady. Two major theories vie for acceptance: set point and settling point.

24   The set-point hypothesis is the older and more deterministic. It asserts that the brain continuously adjusts our metabolism and subconsciously manipulates our behavior to maintain a target weight. Although the set point may change with age, it does so according to a fixed genetic program; diet or exercise can move you away from your set point, at least for a time, but the target itself cannot change—or so the theory goes. Last year Leibel and his colleagues Michael Rosenbaum and Jules Hirsch, who are three of the strongest proponents of the set-point theory, completed a study that seems to support their hypothesis.

25   The physicians admitted 66 people to the Rockefeller hospital. Some of the patients were obese, and some had never been overweight, but all had been at the same weight for at least six months. Over the next three months the subjects ate only precisely measured liquid meals. The doctors ran an extensive battery of tests on the volunteers and then increased the calories that some were fed and put the others on restricted diets. When the subjects had gained 10 percent or lost either 10 or 20 percent of their original weight, the tests were run again to see what had changed.

26   The investigation disproved some tidbits of weight-gain folklore, such as that thin people do not digest as much of their food as heavyweights. The study also found that "the idea that you will be fatter—or will require fewer calories to maintain your starting body weight—as a result of having yo-yoed down and back up again is wrong," Rosenbaum adds. Moreover, the research showed that obese people, when their weight is stable, do not eat significantly more than lean people with the same amount of muscle but less fat.

27   But the trial's real purpose was to determine how much of a fight the body puts up when people attempt to change the weight they have maintained for a long time—why, in other words, dieters tend to bounce back to where they started. When both lean and obese subjects dropped weight, "it seemed to set off a bunch of metabolic alarms," Leibel recalls. The subjects' bodies quickly started burning fewer calories—15 percent fewer, on average, than one would expect given their new weight. Surprisingly, the converse also seems to be true for weight gain. Even rotund people have to eat about 15 percent more than one would expect to stay very far above their set point.

28   That fact raises a major problem for set-point theory: How does it explain the rapid increase in the prevalence of obesity? "Clearly, set points have to be rising, just as we are getting taller in every generation," Rosenbaum says. "But set points are not changeable in adulthood, as far as we can tell. So there must be a window of opportunity sometime in childhood where the environment influences the set point," he speculates. "If you could figure out when and how that occurs, maybe you could modify the environment then, and you wouldn't have to worry about your kids getting fat 20 years down the line."

29   That will remain wishful thinking until set-point advocates demonstrate how weight is centrally controlled. Their best guess now, explains Louis A. Tartaglia, a scientist at Millennium, is that "the body's set point is something like a thermostat"—a lipostat, some have called it—and leptin acts like the thermometer.

30   As you gain weight, Friedman elaborates, "you make more leptin. That shuts off appetite, increases energy expenditure and undoubtedly does other things to restore body weight to the set point. Conversely, if you get too thin, levels of leptin fall, and now you eat more, burn less, and again your weight returns to where it started. Now that we know what the gene and its product are, we can test that simpleminded theory."

31   Amgen, a biotechnology firm in Thousand Oaks, Calif., that has reportedly promised Rockefeller up to $100 million for the right to produce leptin, has begun injecting the hormone into obese people in clinical trials. "The goal," Rosenbaum says, "is to co-opt your body into working with you rather than against you to maintain an altered body weight" by tricking it into believing it is fatter than it is.

32   But the body may not be easily fooled. In May, scientists at the University of Washington reported that they had engineered mice that lack the gene for neuropeptide Y (NPY), the most powerful appetite stimulant known. Leptin curtails NPY production; this, it was thought, is how it quells hunger. But mice lacking NPY do not lose weight—something else compensates.

33   Critics of the set-point hypothesis also protest that it fails to explain the high rates of obesity seen in Nauruans and American Pimas. Moreover, if body fat is centrally controlled, they argue, the amount of fat in your diet should have little impact on your weight. Numerous studies have found the contrary. One recent survey of some 11,600 Scotsmen observed that obesity was up to three times more common among groups that ate the most fat than among those who relied on sugars for most of their energy.

Fat in the Balance

34 At a conference last year, researchers reviewed the evidence and judged that although the set-point hypothesis has not been disproved, there is more "biological merit" to the idea of a "settling point." This newer theory posits that we maintain weight when our various metabolic feedback loops, tuned by whatever susceptibility genes we carry, settle into a happy equilibrium with our environment. Economic and cultural changes are upsetting this equilibrium and propelling more people—those with more genetic risk factors—into obesity.

35   The prime culprit suspected in this trend is hardly surprising: it is the fat dripping off hamburgers, smoothing out ice cream and frying every meat imaginable. But biochemists are at last working out precisely why fat is bad. For years, they have known that people fed a high-fat meal will consume about the same amount as those given a high-carbohydrate meal. Because fat has more calories per bite, however, the subjects with greasy grins tend to ingest more energy than they can burn, a phenomenon known as passive overconsumption.

36   One reason for this, according to biopsychologist John E. Blundell of the University of Leeds, seems to be that the systems controlling hunger and satiety respond quickly to protein and carbohydrates but slowly to fat—too slowly to stop a high-fat meal before the body has had too much. Metabolic systems seem to favor carbohydrates (which include sugars and starches) as well. Knock down a soda or a plate of pasta, and your body will soon speed up its carbohydrate combustion. Polish off a bag of pork rinds, however, and your fat

oxidation rate hardly budges, points out Jean-Pierre Flatt, a biochemist at the University of Massachusetts Medical School. Most incoming fat is shipped directly to storage, then burned later only if carbohydrate reserves dip below some threshold, which varies from person to person.

37　　There is another way to increase the rate at which fat is burned for energy: pack on the pounds. More fat on the body yields more fatty acids circulating in the bloodstream. That in turn boosts fat oxidation, so that eventually a "fat balance" is reached where all the fat that is eaten is combusted, and weight stabilizes. Many genetic and biological factors can influence the fat oxidation rate and thus affect your settling point in a particular environment.

38　　Olestra, an artificial fat approved earlier this year by the Food and Drug Administration, may change that rate as well. Olestra tastes more or less like an ordinary fat, but it flows undigested through the body. A preliminary study by George A. Bray, Pennington's executive director, suggests that the ingredient may short-circuit passive overconsumption. For two weeks, Bray replaced the natural fat in his subjects' meals with olestra. "They did not compensate at all by eating more food," he reports, adding that "it remains to be seen whether that holds up in longer-term studies."

39　　The fat balance explains in part why settling points vary among people who overeat fat: some oxidize fat efficiently at normal weights; others burn too little until excess pounds force the oxidation rate up. But the model does not by itself explain why some do not overeat at all. To answer that, Flatt has proposed a "glycogen hypothesis."

40　　The human body can store about a day's supply of carbohydrates in the form of glycogen, a simple starch. Glycogen reserves function somewhat like fuel tanks; we partially refill the stores with each meal but rarely top them off. In fact, the range between "empty" and "full" appears to be a matter of individual preference, influenced by such factors as the diversity and palatability of food at hand, social pressures and meal habits. People who are content with lower glycogen levels or who frequently deplete them through exercise burn fat more readily than those who like to keep their tanks full, Flatt suggests. But he concedes that the "crucial link from glycogen stores to appetite remains to be proven."

41　　Researchers need more evidence before they can pronounce either set point or settling point—or neither—correct. James O. Hill of the University of Colorado Health Sciences Center has begun collecting some of those critical data. He is assembling a registry of the most precious resource in obesity research: the people who have lost a large amount of weight and kept it off for several years without relapse. Hill has already identified about 1,000 such individuals and has begun examining a handful for biochemical clues to their success.

42　　Unfortunately, no current explanation of weight regulation leaves much room for voluntary control; all the metabolic cycles involved are governed subconsciously. Settling-point theory does at least suggest that sufficiently drastic changes in lifestyle might prod the body to resettle at a new weight. But without assistance, changes radical enough to make a difference are evidently uncomfortable enough to be infeasible—for millions of dieters have tried this strategy and failed.

Getting over the Hump

43 Increasingly, obesity researchers argue that the most effective assistance they can provide their patients will probably be pharmacological. "The treatment philosophy of the past 40 years, which has been to train patients to eat differently, is simply not going to cure the epidemic of obesity that we see worldwide," asserts Barbara C. Hansen, director of the obesity research center at the University of Maryland School of Medicine.

44 Untangling the biology beneath body fat has created a plethora of new drug targets that has drawn dozens of pharmaceutical firms off the sidelines. The potential market is enormous, not only because obesity is common and growing but also because even an ideal drug will have to be taken indefinitely, according to Hansen and others. "Obesity isn't curable," Bray says. "It's like high blood pressure. If you don't take the medication, your blood pressure won't stay down. And if you don't take drugs—or do something—to treat obesity, your weight won't stay down."

45 Part of the reason for the resurgence of commercial interest is a shift in policy at the FDA, which decided in April to allow the appetite suppressant dexfenfluramine to be prescribed for obesity in the U.S., as it already is in 65 other countries. It is the first weight-loss drug approved in the U.S. in 23 years, and nearly all obesity researchers agree it has been too long coming. The FDA also recently relaxed its guidelines for obesity-drug applications. "As our compromise right now, we're suggesting that a company can present us with two years of data—in some cases, one year if the data look good enough and the company gives us a firm commitment to do follow-up studies under tight controls," says Leo Lutwak, a medical officer with the FDA's Center for Drug Evaluation & Research.

46 Lutwak admits that with only two years of information, the FDA may approve drugs that turn out to have serious long-term side effects.* "The best we can hope for is something like insulin for the treatment of diabetes," Leibel says. Insulin rescues a type I diabetic by replacing a hormone that is missing. "But after 15 years, you begin to have complications of our inability to perfectly mimic the biology," Leibel continues. "If we're lucky, that's the kind of problem we'll face in the treatment of obesity." Lutwak responds that "when that happens, the public will be informed, and they will have to make a decision about whether it is worth it."

47 If the long-term cost of treatment is unknown, the benefits are becoming clearer, thanks to studies on people who have an operation, called gastroplasty, that reduces the size of the stomach. Although infrequently used in the U.S., the procedure has proved remarkably effective in Sweden. A long-term study there of 1,150 obese patients who underwent gastric surgery found that they typically dropped 66 pounds over two years—88 pounds if a more severe procedure was used—whereas control subjects given standard dietary treatment lost nothing. The surgery cured more than two thirds of those with diabetes, compared with 16 percent cured in the control group. Likewise, twice as many (43 percent) of the hypertension cases were cured by the operation.

---

* In September 1997 (a year after this article was published), the FDA ordered dexfenfluramine (marketed as Redux, half of the popular "fen-phen" diet cocktail combination) pulled from the market after the drug was linked to life-threatening heart-valve leaks. Numerous lawsuits were instituted against the manufacturer, Interneuron Pharmaceuticals, and the marketer, Wyeth–Ayerst Laboratories.

48   Gastroplasty has drawbacks in addition to the risks that always accompany major surgery—principally a high rate of digestive complications. Drug treatments might be better, but Hansen's work with rhesus monkeys suggests that prevention would be best. A decade ago her team began a trial on young adult monkeys, equivalent in maturity to 20-year-old men. The researchers adjusted the animals' food supply so that they neither gained nor lost weight. "In the past 10 years we have had 100 percent success preventing both obesity and type II diabetes," Hansen asserts. "In the control group, which was simply allowed to feed freely on the same diet, half are diabetic. Because everything we know about human obesity is also true of nonhuman primate obesity, that shows you the power of weight control."

49   It does not, unfortunately, demonstrate a feasible way to achieve it. The NIDDK has launched a program to educate Americans about ways to avoid weight gain, but Susan Z. Yanovski, the program's director, admits that so far it has had little perceptible impact. There is no major lobbying organization for the disease, notes Pi-Sunyer, and the NIH directs less than 1 percent of its research funding at obesity. "Many people seem to be unaware of how big a health problem this is now and how big it is going to grow, particularly when you look at the increasing obesity of children," Yanovski says. Because obese adolescents usually become fat adults, "we're really heading for trouble in another 20 to 30 years," she adds.

50   At least one grade school intervention has had modest success, knocking a few percentage points off the number of children who turn into overweight adolescents by taking fat out of the children's lunches, giving them more strenuous recreation and educating their parents about weight control. "We have to be very careful about putting children on restrictive diets," Yanovski warns. "That is inappropriate. But we can be more proactive in getting our kids away from the television set, more physically active, riding their bikes instead of being driven everywhere. If people recognize that this is a serious public health problem affecting their children, then maybe they will start taking some action." If not, economists should start adjusting their models now to account for the tremendous health care cost increases that lie ahead.

Review Questions

1. What is the problem regarding obesity, as Gibbs sees it, and what questions need to be addressed?

2. What is the "thrifty genes" explanation of the rising incidence of obesity, and what evidence exists to support this explanation?

3. What do studies about identical twins reveal about the importance of genetics in causing obesity?

4. What is the role of laboratory mice in helping to understand the mechanisms of obesity in humans?

5. What is a "set point"? What evidence is there for the set point as an explanation of how weight is maintained? What is the main problem with the set point hypothesis?

6. What is the "settling point" hypothesis, and what is the evidence for it as an explanation of obesity?

7. According to Gibbs, from what area of research will the most effective assistance to obesity come?

Discussion and Writing Suggestions

1. What is your view of the proposed "fat tax" that would add expense to high calorie food (presumably so that people will not buy and eat as much) or an insurance rate hike for those who don't exercise regularly?

2. If a person can be predisposed genetically to obesity in the way, say, a person can be predisposed to contracting cancer, what explains the social stigma attached to being overweight and obese? Why are obese people blamed for their condition while cancer sufferers are not?

3. Gibbs reports that "no current explanation of weight regulation leaves much room for voluntary control; all the metabolic cycles involved are governed subconsciously" (paragraph 42). How do you regard this news? Given these findings, do you believe that dieters should continue to diet?

4. Gibbs and others have remarked on the importance of preventing obesity by working with children and adolescents. Think of various kids you know—siblings, cousins, neighbors, and friends. How agreeable would they be (or have they been) to anti-obesity messages? Do you see them easily cutting back on, let alone giving up, fast food? Could you, personally, make that kind of sacrifice in the name of slenderness?

Too Much of a Good Thing
Greg Crister

In an op-ed essay for the Los Angeles Times *(July 22, 2001), Greg Crister argues that, faced with a rising obesity epidemic, we should stigmatize overeating. Crister is careful to distinguish between stigmatizing the person and the act, but he makes no apologies for urging that we teach children that "[e]ating too much food is a bad thing." Crister has written a book on the obesity epidemic:* Supersize *(Houghton Mifflin, 2002).*

1   Sometime over the next month or so, United Nations health and nutrition experts will convene in New York to begin discussing what many consider to be the pivotal medical issue of our day: obesity and its impact on children. For the

UN, traditionally concerned with starvation and malnutrition, it is a historic first, following up on an alarm it sounded about obese adults in 1999. "Obesity," the U.N. proclaimed, "is the dominant unmet global health issue, with Westernized countries topping the list."

2   Solid epidemiological data drives the effort. In Canada, Great Britain, Japan, Australia—even coastal China and Southeast Asia—the rate of childhood obesity has been soaring for more than a decade. Closer to home, at least 25% of all Americans under age nineteen are overweight or obese, a figure that has doubled over the last 30 years and a figure that moved the surgeon general to declare childhood obesity an epidemic. The cost in health care dollars to treat obesity's medical consequences—from diabetes to coronary heart disease to a variety of crippling bone conditions—will eventually make the battle against HIV/AIDS seem inexpensive. Yet in the U.S., the most important foot soldiers against obesity are increasingly paralyzed by years of media-induced food hysteria, over-generalized and outdated nutritional wisdom, and, truth be told, an unwillingness to set firm and sometimes unpopular food parameters. That infantry is the much-strained American family and its increasingly harried commandant, *Parentis americanus.* What it needs to promulgate is dietary restraint, something our ancestors knew simply as avoiding gluttony.

3   This is not to say that parents should be blamed for the nation's growing dietary permissiveness. They are wary of confronting their children's eating habits for a reason: For years, conventional wisdom held that food should never become a dinner table battleground. "Pressure causes tension," write Harvey and Marilyn Diamond, authors of the classic *Fit for Life,* which has sold more than 3 million copies. "Where food is concerned, tension is always to be avoided." The operative notion is that a child restrained from overeating will either rebel by secretly gorging when away from the table or, worse, will suffer such a loss of self-esteem that a lifetime of disastrous eating behavior will follow.

4   Of course, no one should be stigmatized for being overweight. But stigmatizing the unhealthful behaviors that cause obesity would conform with what we know about effective health messages. In both the campaign against unsafe sex and the campaign against smoking, stigmatizing such behaviors proved highly effective in reducing risk and harm. It's true, smokers—and homosexuals—may have experienced a modicum of stereotyping in the short run, but such is the price of every public health advance: short term pain for long term gain.

5   Another inhibition to imposing dietary restraint is the belief, promoted in handbook after handbook of parental advice, that 'kids know when they are full.' But perhaps not. In fact, new research suggests just the opposite: Kids don't know when they are full.

6   In a recent study, Pennsylvania State University nutritional scholar Barbara Rolls and her associates examined the eating habits of two groups of kids, one of three-year-olds, another of five-year-olds. The children were presented with a series of plates of macaroni and cheese. The first plate was a normal serving built around baseline nutritional needs; the second was slightly larger; the third was what might be called "supersized."

7   What the researchers found is that the younger children consistently ate the same baseline amount, leaving more food on the plates with larger servings.

The 5-year-olds, though, altered their eating behavior dramatically depending on the amount they were served, devouring whatever was on the plate. Something had happened. The mere presence of an oversized portion had induced exaggerated eating. The authors concluded that "these early years may provide a unique opportunity for interventions that reduce the risk of developing overweight." Those interventions "should include clear information on appropriate portion sizes for children."

8   Theorizing aside, our disinclination to restrain eating flies in the face of overwhelming evidence that, of all age groups, children seem to be the ones who respond most positively to dietary advice. In four randomized studies of obese 6- to 12-year-olds, those who were offered frequent, simple behavioral advice were substantially less overweight 10 years later than kids who did not get the advice. In fact, 30% of those studied were no longer obese at all.

9   The case for early intervention has been further buttressed by new studies on another age-old medical injunction: never put a kid on a diet. (The concern was that under-nutrition could lead to stunted growth.) But as the authors of a study of 1,062 kids under age three concluded in the journal *Pediatrics,* "a supervised, low-saturated-fat and low-cholesterol diet has no influence on growth during the first three years of life." Overweight kids who were put on such a diet ended up with better, more moderate eating habits.

10   Changing the eating habits of children, though, is antithetical to some notions many parents hold dear. And to some it seems a relic of an earlier, more religious era of moral certainties when gluttony was vilified as one of the seven deadly sins. Many boomer parents believe, as one parent and nutritionist said at a recent summit on childhood obesity, that "kids have the right to make bad nutrition decisions." That may be true. But ours is a world where at least a billion dollars a year is spent by just one fast-food chain to convince families to visit a crazy-looking clown with his own playground and purchase a thousand supersize calories for a mere $2.50. McDonald's official line today is that three meals a week at its restaurants are perfectly acceptable for an average kid. That's three meals a week of grease, refined flour, and a jumbo shot of sugar.

11   Given today's bounty of cheap and unhealthful food alternatives, and given the inconvenience that goes with making good nutritional choices, one might wonder if a campaign against over-consumption, a campaign advocating restraint, could work. On this point, we might take a cue from the French. In the early 20th century France, in response to its first experiences with widespread child obesity, launched the puericulture movement, which focused on excessive weight gain in early childhood and adolescence. Its prescription: All meals should be adult-supervised; all portions should be moderate, with 'seconds' a rare treat. All but an occasional small snack were forbidden. As its historian Peter N. Stearns writes in *Fat History,* puericulture's message was simple: Eating too much food is a bad thing.

12   Therein lies at least part of the explanation for the legendary leanness of the French: They were taught in childhood not to overeat. And it didn't seem to do much harm to their self-esteem.

Review Questions

1. With what particular problem is Crister concerned in this essay?

2. According to conventional wisdom, how should parents set limits with respect to their children's intake of food?

3. Notwithstanding conventional wisdom, what are the three arguments (two supported by research studies) that Crister makes for curtailing the food intake of children?

4. What objections does Crister anticipate to his proposals, and how does he rebut these objections?

Discussion and Writing Suggestions

1. Crister advocates that we teach children that "[e]ating too much food is a bad thing." Do you agree? In your view, what are a parent's responsibilities in teaching children about eating and over-eating?

2. What do you make of the following objection to Crister's proposed instruction of children—that children "have the right to make bad nutrition decisions"? Who is more persuasive on this point (discussed in paragraph 10), Crister or those who argue for a child's nutritional autonomy?

3. Reread paragraph 4, which Crister begins: "Of course, no one should be stigmatized for being overweight." In fact, is Crister advocating stigmatization? What is the difference between stigmatizing an act (that is, overeating) and stigmatizing an actor (the person who overeats)?

4. Notwithstanding Crister's assertion that "no one should be stigmatized for being overweight," to what extent do you find him to be morally intolerant in this essay? Of whom does he disapprove—children who overeat, their parents, the broader culture that fosters overeating? Or do you find that his objection is to overeating itself?

5. What assumptions does Crister make about the origins of overeating? In considering this question, you might think about the roles of individual will power, genes, parental and institutional authority, and a child's autonomy.

NAAFA Policy on Dieting and the Diet Industry
National Association to Advance Fat Acceptance

The National Association to Advance Fat Acceptance (NAAFA) was founded in 1969 as a "non-profit human rights organization dedicated to improving the quality of life for fat people." NAAFA is both an advocacy group, publishing and advocating for positions on issues that affect fat people, like the following policy statement on dieting, and a support group that offers members "tools for self empowerment." You can visit the NAAFA Web site at http://www.NAAFA.org for a closer look at the organization's official documents, informational brochures, book service, and more. What you will find consistently is a content and a tone that promotes fat acceptance.

History/Existing Condition

1   The term "diet" within this policy refers exclusively to weight reduction diets. "Dieting" is defined as any attempt to achieve or maintain lower body weight by intentionally limiting or manipulating the amount or type of food intake. Weight reduction diets include medically supervised diets; self-administered diets; commercial diet organizations and centers; weight-loss support groups or behavior modification programs; "fad" diets; "sensible, well-balanced" diets; in-hospital fasts; very-low-calorie diets (VLCDs); prepackaged food plans; and diets supplemented by drugs or artificial food products or supplements.

2   "Dieting" does not refer to attempts to lower fat sugar, salt, or cholesterol intake, increase fiber intake, exercise or pursue a medically mandated nutritional regimen prescribed for specific medical conditions. Weight-loss diets have long been promoted as a permanent cure for "obesity," although they rarely produce long-lasting or permanent results. According to existing medical research, fewer than five percent of all dieters succeed in losing a significant amount of weight and maintaining that weight loss over a five-year period. Ninety percent of all dieters regain some or all of the weight originally lost and at least one-third gain more. In recent years, an increasing body of research has substantiated this diet failure rate and acknowledged genetic and physiological factors in the determination of body size.

3   Although these statistics apply to all types of diets, even those considered "sensible," physicians continue to prescribe weight-loss diets as a viable treatment for fat patients; and researchers, the media, and the diet industry continue to urge fat people to resist their body's natural predisposition and struggle harder to lose weight. As diet failure rates become widely publicized, some "experts" pretend to abandon "dieting" and encourage their clients to "just eat less and exercise more."

4   Promoting diets and diet products is a major industry in the United States. According to Marketdata Enterprises, the annual revenue for the diet industry was over $30 billion dollars in 1990. This figure includes money spent on diet centers and programs, group and individual weight-loss, diet camps, prepackaged foods; over-the-counter and prescription diet drugs; weight-loss books and magazines; and physicians, nurses, nutritionists, and other health professionals specializing in weight-loss (total 1990 revenue—$8 billion); commercial and residential exercise clubs with weight-loss programs (total 1990 revenue—$8 billion); and sugar-free, fat-free, and reduced calorie ("lite") food products, imitation fats and sugar substitutes (total 1990 revenue—$14 billion).

5   The diet industry's advertising and marketing strategy is based on the creation and perpetuation of fear, biases, and stereotypes. Fat people are portrayed as unhealthy, unattractive, asexual, weak-willed, lazy, and gluttonous. Weight loss or a thin figure are equated with virtue, health, and success. Failure to participate in

dieting or lack of success in losing weight are blamed on a lack of willpower or determination and a lack of moral values. Fat people are taught to feel guilty and blame themselves for the failures of weight-loss programs, and to expect and accept rejection, mistreatment, and discrimination regarding their weight. This negative media campaign has a devastating impact on millions of fat people. These messages lower fat people's self-esteem and foster discontent, self-doubt, and self-hatred, especially during the weight regain state of the dieting "yo-yo" cycle.

6   Diet promoters also emphasize dieting's supposed health benefits and minimize risks related to dieting. People of all sizes are misled about the extent and severity of the health risks associated with being fat and are told that being thin is the only way to good health, and that dieting makes people thin. Many health problems traditionally attributed to "obesity," such as high blood pressure, heart problems, high cholesterol, and gallbladder problems, are often caused by the dieting process itself. Recent studies indicate that repeated "yo-yo" dieting may actually reduce one's life span rather than increase longevity.

7   Currently there are very few controls or regulations to inform and protect the dieting consumer. Weight loss "success" is only vaguely defined using short-term results, and weight loss "failure is always blamed on the consumer, and health risks are not disclosed. The few regulations that do exist are rarely, or at most, loosely enforced.

NAAFA's Official Position

8   Since reducing diets rarely achieve permanent weight loss and can result in negative health consequences, since laws and regulations protecting the consumer are nonexistent or remain unenforced, and since people undertaking diets are rarely given sufficient information to allow them to give true informed consent, the National Association to Advance Fat Acceptance strongly discourages participation in weight-reduction dieting. Further, NAAFA strongly condemns any diet marketing strategy based on guilt and fear. Such approaches cause untold suffering to fat people by ruining their self-esteem and by perpetuating negative stereotypes. NAAFA demands that local, state, and federal governments regulate the diet industry to protect the consumer from misleading claims regarding safety and long-term effectiveness.

NAAFA Advocates:

- That local, state, and federal legislatures introduce, pass, enact, and enforce legislation which protects consumers against dangerous or ineffective diets and misleading diet advertising.
- That state and federal regulatory agencies, such as the Food and Drug Administration (FDA) and the Federal Trade Commission (FTC), adopt regulations based on NAAFA's "Guidelines for the Diet Industry" and closely monitor and control all aspects of the multi-billion-dollar diet industry.
- That all commercials for weight-loss diets and diet products be banned from radio and television because of lack of product success, negative health consequences, and the extreme negative impact of anti-fat propaganda on the self-esteem and quality of life of fat people.

- That federal regulations require all diets and weight-loss products to clearly display a health warning (similar to those found on cigarettes) regarding possible hazards and side effects.
- That regulations be adopted that require the diet industry to publish five-year (minimum) follow-up studies and "success" rates. All such statistics must be verifiable by objective outside researchers and clearly displayed on all diet products and advertising.
- That the Centers for Disease Control track morbidity and mortality caused by dieting and make the findings available to the public.
- That the National Institutes of Health (NIH) include input from consumer advocacy groups in establishing public health policy about dieting and obesity.
- That consumer protection agencies, such as Consumers Union, conduct biannual studies on the efficacy of diet products and programs.
- That institutions such as the military, hospitals, schools, mental institutions, or prisons provide adequate food and not force anyone to diet against their will.
- That employers, schools, and judges never use weight loss or dieting as a condition for employment, promotion, admission, or avoiding incarceration.
- That health care professionals and medical institutions never deny other medical treatment to patients who choose not to diet.
- That the diet industry refrain from creating or perpetuating negative stereotypes about fat people in its marketing strategies.
- That diet companies and diet industry trade organizations voluntarily comply with NAAFA's "Guidelines for the Diet Industry."
- That individuals considering dieting study available literature on long-term results and side effects and carefully weigh dieting's possible benefits and risks.
- That dieters refuse to feel guilty or blame themselves for presumed lack of willpower if a diet fails.
- That no one allow themselves to be coerced into dieting against their will.
- That no one make assumptions or judge another person on the basis of body size or dietary preferences.

NAAFA Resolves to:
- Educate the public, the media, and potential dieters as to the low long-term success rates and possible negative health consequences of weight reduction dieting.
- Discourage the diet industry from basing their product advertising on fear and guilt and from using and perpetuating negative stereotypes of fat people.
- Promote alternatives to weight-loss diets in a manner which is sensitive to the emotional and financial investment which many fat people have made in repeated weight-loss attempts.
- Provide advice and emotional support to individuals who have dieted unsuccessfully and blame themselves, rather than the product, for the diet's failure.

- Alert consumers to diets or weight-loss schemes which have been determined to be dangerous or fraudulent, have lawsuits pending against them, or are being investigated by government agencies.
- Assist plaintiffs and/or their attorneys engaged in litigation involving diet fraud and ill effects of dieting, by providing them with referrals to expert witnesses who might testify on their behalf.
- Advocate for the safety and emotional and physical well-being of consumers by attempting to influence public policy about dieting, obesity, and diet industry regulation.

Review Questions

1. How does NAAFA define "dieting"?

2. What percentage of dieters lose weight and keep it off five years after beginning their diet?

3. How much money was spent on the diet industry in 1990? (In 2001 the amount was $50 billion.)

4. What are the risks of dieting, according to NAAFA?

5. What is NAAFA's official position on dieting, and what action does it want taken regarding the dieting industry?

Discussion and Writing Suggestions

1. NAAFA states that "[t]he diet industry's advertising and marketing strategy is based on the creation and perpetuation of fear, biases, and stereotypes." Locate a print, television, or radio ad for a diet program and analyze its content for "fear, biases, and stereotypes." Discuss the ways in which NAAFA's assertion is or is not validated by your research.

2. How does NAAFA summarize the stereotypes of fat people? What stereotypes about fat people have you encountered in your experience? List these and compare your list with those of others in your class.

3. Do you believe that the regulation of weight-loss diets is feasible? How do you imagine this regulation would be accomplished?

4. Explore the NAAFA Web site <http://www.naafa.org>. What are your reactions to the content on the Web site? How would you describe its tone? To what extent does NAAFA present itself as a well-run organization?

5. Review the positions that NAAFA advocates. Which strike you as most workable? least workable? Why?

Fat and Happy: In Defense of Fat Acceptance
Mary Ray Worley

Mary Ray Worley is a member of NAAFA, the National Association to Advance Fat Acceptance. Hers is the only first-person account you will read in this chapter of the social and psychological pressures that fat people can experience. She does much to elucidate anti-fat stereotypes and, through her spirited writing, does much to dispel them. As you read, you might bear in mind the contrasts between Worley's position on obesity and that of Greg Crister, who argues that we should stigmatize the act of overeating.

1   If you've grown up in twentieth-century American society, you probably believe that being fat is a serious personal, social, and medical liability. Many Americans would rather die or cut off a limb than be fat, many believe that fatness is a serious health risk, and many are convinced that it is a simple matter to reduce one's body size and are so offended by body fat that they believe it is acceptable to shun fat people and make them the butt of cruel jokes. Those who are fat quickly learn to be deeply ashamed of their bodies and spend their lives trying to become what they are not and hide what cannot be hidden. Our society believes that thinness signals self-discipline and self-respect, whereas fatness signals self-contempt and lack of resolve. We're so accustomed to this way of thinking that many of us have never considered that there might be an alternative.

2   Nevertheless, a growing number of people believe it's possible to be happy with your body even if it happens to be fat. In August 2000 I attended the annual convention of the National Association to Advance Fat Acceptance (NAAFA) in San Diego, and it was like visiting another planet altogether. I hadn't realized how deeply my body shame affected my life until I spent a glorious week without it. I'll never be the same again.

3   The first time I had that "different planet" feeling was at the pool party on the first night of the convention. Here were all these fat people in stylish swimsuits and cover-ups, and whereas on my home planet a fat person was expected to feel apologetic and embarrassed about her body—especially in a swimsuit—here were a hundred or so fat people who were enjoying being in their bodies without a shred of self-consciousness. They were having so much fun it was infectious. I felt light-headed and giddy. I kept noticing how great everyone looked. They were confident and radiant and happy—and all sizes of fat. Definitely not my planet.

4   One of the features of NAAFA's conventions is that they invite vendors who sell stylish large-size clothing. So whereas on my home planet, you're lucky if you can find a swimsuit that fits at all, on this planet you have choices and can find a swimsuit that's made from beautiful fabric and looks absolutely smashing on you. Where I come from, you're grateful if you can find clothes that you can actually get on, and forget finding clothes that really fit you. But on this planet there were play clothes, dress-up clothes, you name it. Choices galore. Beautiful fabrics with an elegant drape and a certain panache. I'd never before

had so many choices. The clothes I tried on (and bought) not only fit me but looked terrific. As the week wore on and everyone had visited the vendors' booths, we all looked snazzier and snazzier, and the ones who had been to past conventions looked snazzy from the get-go.

5   The next night at the talent show those of us who didn't get a part in the high school musical because we were too fat had a chance to play the lead for five minutes. (I sang a snappy little number by Stephen Sondheim called "The Ladies Who Lunch," from *Company,* and hammed it up big time. I had a blast!) Top billing was given to a troupe of belly dancers called the Fatimas. Now, I had read about this attraction in the literature I received about the convention, and I have to admit that I thought it would be some kind of a spoof or a joke. I just couldn't conceive of a group of fat women doing serious belly dancing, but it was no joke. These women were indeed serious—and excellent—belly dancers. They wore the full belly-dancing regalia—that is, gauze and bangles and beads and not much else. When they first looped and bobbed their way out into the middle of the room, I think my chin must have dropped through the floor. They were exquisitely beautiful and voluptuous and graceful and serene. I thought that anyone, no matter how acculturated to my home planet, would have to be just about dead not to recognize how beautiful they were. And they were all so different from each other. We are accustomed to seeing mostly thin bodies that look more or less the same, but these bodies showed an amazing degree of delightful diversity. Body fat does not distribute itself on every fat person in the same way, so there's lots of variety. Plus they weren't all young. A couple of them had to have been past fifty, and they were so beautiful. And exotic, and mesmerizing. I had always assumed that as a fat woman I could never do that, and especially not as a fat woman past fifty. Wrong, wrong, wrong. I felt a jolt as my old assumptions were jettisoned out into space. Bag that old paradigm. This one is definitely a lot more fun.

6   One of the featured speakers at the convention was Dr. Diane Budd, who spoke about the medical and scientific communities' take on fatness. Although the data gathered for most current studies indicate that body size is primarily determined by one's genetic makeup, most researchers conclude—in spite of their own findings—that fat individuals should try to lose weight anyway. There are no data that indicate (a) that such efforts are likely to be effective (in fact, more than 90 percent of those who lose weight gain it back), (b) that a person's overall health would be improved by losing weight, or (c) that the effort to lose weight won't in fact turn out to have lasting harmful effects on one's appetite, metabolism, and self-esteem. Our assumptions about the desirability of thinness are so deeply ingrained that scientists find it next to impossible to align their recommendations with their findings; apparently they cannot bring themselves to say that since body size is largely a result of one's genetic makeup it's best to get on with the business of learning to live in the body you have, whatever its size.

7   Moreover, none of the studies take into account the physical implications of the social ostracism and body hate that are a regular part of most fat people's lives. Fat people are often taunted in public and are pressured by family members to lose weight. Complete strangers feel they are not out of line to criticize

the contents of a fat person's grocery cart, and family members may evaluate everything a fat person puts on her plate. Fat people need to be active and strong enough to carry their body weight comfortably, but they may feel ill at ease exercising in public because of unkind stares and comments. They may feel that they can't wear shorts or sleeveless t-shirts or swimsuits for fear of offending the delicate sensibilities of others and inviting rude comments, and so they will be too hot and too embarrassed and will give up on regular exercise because they don't have the support they need to continue. Now *that* is a health risk.

8   Moreover, fat people are often reluctant to seek medical attention because health professionals are among the most prejudiced people around. Regardless of the ailment you are seeking treatment for, if you are fat, your doctor may put you on a diet before she treats your cough, and attribute whatever complaint you have to your weight. Pressures like these must certainly contribute to the shortening of many fat people's lives, quite apart from any physical risk resulting from a preponderance of body fat.

9   The upshot is that it's very likely that the health risks of being fat have been highly overestimated. In combination with other risk factors, being fat may occasionally contribute to compromised health, but not nearly to the degree that many people think. When a fat person goes to a weight-loss clinic, the goal is usually to lose weight as quickly as possible, as though to snatch the poor fat soul out of the jaws of imminent death. And often the harsh methods used to effect that weight loss are in and of themselves much more harmful than being fat is. In fact, it is my understanding that statistically a person is much less likely to regain weight that is lost very slowly. So what's the big rush? The big rush is that we hate fat and want to put as much distance between ourselves and it as quickly as possible. Quick and dramatic weight loss sells; slow and gradual weight loss does not. There's nothing compassionate, rational, or scientific about it. We just hate fat.

10   Many fat people have made numerous efforts and spent thousands of dollars throughout their lives to lose weight and each time regained the lost pounds plus a few more. Have this happen to you enough times and you will be apprehensive at the prospect of losing weight for fear of gaining back more than you lose. On my own account, there's no way I want to diet again, because it will just make me fatter in the long run. Help like that I don't need, and I sure as spitfire don't need to pay through the nose for it.

11   After years and years of dieting it slowly dawned on me that my body rebelled when I tried to restrict my food intake. All those years I figured that it was me who was failing, and then I began to realize that it was the method that was failing. I began to wonder whether the problem itself was being incorrectly defined. I began raising new questions just about the time that researchers were discovering that, rather than being a simple intake-outtake equation, body weight resulted from a complex interplay of set point (the body's tendency to stay within a certain narrow weight range), appetite and satiety cues, metabolism, and genes. Moreover, our bodies are designed to protect us from starvation and have some powerful defenses against it. They react to dieting just as they do to starving. They don't know there is a McDonald's around every corner.

For all they know, we're still living in the Ice Age, when the next meal may be hours or days or miles away. So when we decrease the amount of food we eat, our bodies slow the metabolic rate to fend off possible starvation. It's a great system, really. In my case I'm convinced that as determined as I have been to become thin, my body has always been more determined to save me from starvation. My body is more stubborn than I am. Amazing.

12   So I stopped dieting and began to make peace with food and with my body. I slowly stopped being afraid of food. In 1999 I became a vegetarian, and somehow that change—and the culture that seems to go with it—put food in a new light for me. Food was no longer the enemy; it was a gift and a source of joy. I began to slow down and relish my meals, to enjoy food and be grateful for all the ways that it nourishes me.

13   Over the last fifteen years or so I've made many attempts to become more active on a regular basis with varying degrees of success. I often would go swimming three or four times a week for two, three, or four months followed by a hiatus of several weeks or months. About two years ago, I realized that I always felt better when I was being active. So why the long hiatuses? Because I was exercising in hopes of losing weight. After months of dogged discipline with what I considered to be meager results at best, I would naturally become discouraged and stop. Within a few weeks I would stop feeling the surge of energy and well-being that comes with regular exercise.

14   So what would happen if I just exercised because I felt better when I did? How about moving just for the fun of it? So I gave up the notion of losing weight and consequently gave up feeling hopeless, and as a result the hiatuses have become fewer and shorter in duration. I began to vary my workouts more, so that I got less bored and enjoyed myself more. Who knew that moving, even in a large body, could be this much fun? I'd never allowed myself to have this kind of fun in my body before.

15   I discovered to my delight that the more physically competent I became, the better I felt about my body. My husband, Tom, and I go for long hikes in the woods, and some of those hikes have been challenging for me—not too challenging, but just enough. Two years ago we visited Yosemite National Park, and we hiked partway up to the top of Vernal Fall. It was a demanding hike, and pretty much everybody was huffing and puffing. We made it up to the bridge that's just shy of halfway to the top. It was good to know when to stop, but it rankled me that I didn't have the energy or stamina to make it all the way. So I decided that next time I will. Next spring we're planning another trip to Yosemite, and I'm going to make it to the top of Vernal Fall. I don't care how long it takes me or how much I have to huff and puff. My only stipulation is that I have to be strong enough to have fun doing it. I don't want it to be a torture session.

16   I've been training with that goal in mind for months now. Instead of avoiding stairs, I look for them. I'm no longer ashamed of huffing and puffing—I'm proud. I'm pushing myself just enough so that I'm becoming stronger and have more endurance all the time. This summer I discovered that I can hike all day long. What a thrill! In July, Tom and I hiked in Copper Falls State Park from 12 noon until 8 P.M. (we stopped to rest three times). And in August I traipsed around

the San Diego Wild Animal Park from 9 A.M. until 8 P.M. (again with three rests). How wonderful to have a body that will carry me through an entire day of fun! I never realized before what a miracle my body is, its glorious ability to build muscle and save me from starvation. I'm only beginning to discover what a marvelous gift it is.

17   After years of fighting our set points, our metabolism, our genes, and our hunger, after decades of being ashamed, hating our bodies, and trying to manipulate them into being something they're not, after spending mountains of money and energy trying to conform to someone else's ideal, it isn't surprising that some of us question whether this is the best way to for us to live. A few of us brave adventurers have found another way, and it involves much less agony, costs much less money, and is much more fun.

18   We're not giving up, and we're not letting ourselves go. Rather we're forging a new relationship with our bodies, one that doesn't involve self-loathing, one that appreciates the miraculous bodies we have, one that brings joy. There's plenty of room on this new planet, and here you needn't apologize for your size. You're entitled to the space you take up. You can find clothes that show off the gorgeous person you are, you can play and dance without self-consciousness, you can be proud of yourself and never dread unwanted attention, you can be a brave pioneer and a friend to those who have suffered on planets less kind and less joyous than this one.

Discussion and Writing Suggestions

1. How would you characterize Worley's point of view in this essay? Distilled to a single statement, what is she arguing? To what extent do you find yourself sympathetic to her point of view?

2. Worley writes: "Our society believes that thinness signals self-discipline and self-respect, whereas fatness signals self-contempt and lack of resolve." To what extent do you find this statement a fair and accurate representation of how our society views fat people? How do you define "society" in this case? Who (or what) are its agents?

3. What role has NAAFA played in helping Worley think and feel differently about herself?

4. Is Worley's self-acceptance the same thing as complacency about her obesity? Explain your answer.

5. Writing an editorial in the *Journal of the American Medical Association*, Koplan and Dietz claim that "[g]enes related to obesity are clearly not responsible for the epidemic of obesity" (page 441). To what extent does their claim negate the force of Worley's argument (paragraph 6) that "it's best to get on with the business of learning to live in the body you have, whatever its size"?

6. Reread paragraphs 7 and 8 on "the social ostracism and body hate that are a regular part of most fat people's lives." Even if one allows that, in light of new research, Worley is wrong about the causes and medical impact of being fat, to what extent do the points she makes about the social, psychological, and emotional costs of obesity still have force?

7. What are the differences between exercising to lose weight and exercising to feel better? (See paragraphs 13–16.) What lessons are embedded in this distinction?

8. Comment on the "old planet" / "new planet" distinction that Worley develops in paragraphs 2, 3, and 18.

Too "Close to the Bone": The Historical Context for Women's Obsession with Slenderness
Roberta Seid

In "Too 'Close to the Bone,'" Roberta Seid critiques our culture's "religion" of thinness and explains how Americans have come to be adherents of this religion, as well of the psychological and even spiritual costs of adherence. You will find in Seid's essay an excellent example of how scholarship—historical and cultural scholarship, in this case—can shine a light on complex problems, helping us to view them in entirely new ways. When she wrote this piece in 1994, Seid was a lecturer in the Program for the Study of Women and Men in Society at the University of Southern California, Los Angeles.

1   Why have Americans, particularly American women, become fatphobic? Why and how have they come to behave as though the shape of their lives depends on the shape of their bodies? Why have they clung to these beliefs despite the toll they take on private lives, and especially despite their most extreme and dangerous manifestation, eating disorders? This chapter addresses these questions by placing the phenomenon in a broad historical context, with particular focus on fashion and the unique and dangerous twist it has taken in our era.

2   Although current explanations for our thinness mania are valuable, they often leave many questions unanswered. Feminists have often blamed fashion for oppressing and subordinating women, but fashion has rarely had the destructive effects we see today. Moreover, the fashion for thinness, which has prevailed only for the past 40 years or so, requires explanation itself. The eating disorders literature, often focused on individual psychopathology, has found neither a consistent etiological profile nor a universally accepted explanation for why eating disorders have swelled into a social disease. Nor does it explain why millions of women without clinical cating disorders mimic the behavior and mind set of affected women. Finally, a much weaker body of literature attributes the phenomenon to the mass media's influence. Although the media's power to shape our perceptions cannot be underestimated, this explanation

also begs the question. Why would the media necessarily promote slenderness?

3   A more comprehensive explanation emerges when we stand back and, employing a broad historical perspective, look at the underlying cultural beliefs that affect both genders. Our culture is swept up in a web of peculiar and distorted beliefs about beauty, health, virtue, eating, and appetite. We have elevated the pursuit of a lean, fat-free body into a new religion. It has a creed: "I eat right, watch my weight, and exercise." Indeed, anorexia nervosa could be called the paradigm of our age, for our creed encourages us all to adopt the behavior and attitudes of the anorexic. The difference is one of degree, not of kind. Like any religion worthy of the name, ours also has its damnation. Failure to follow the creed—and the corporeal stigmata of that failure, fatness and flabbiness—produce a hell on earth. The fat and flabby are damned to failure, regardless of professional and personal successes. Our religion also has its rewards, its salvation. In following the creed, one is guaranteed beauty, energy, health, and a long successful life. Followers are even promised self-transformation: The "thin person within," waiting to burst through the fat, is somehow a more exciting, sexy, competent, successful self. Virtue can be quantified by the numbers on the scale, the lean-to-fat ratio, clothing size, and body measurements. And, in a curious inversion of capitalist values, less is always better.

Body Ideals Before the 20th Century

4   The creed of thinness is composed of prejudices, and they have a history. A cursory review of Western civilization's aesthetic and health ideals indicates the novelty and arbitrariness of current beliefs. The female body has not altered for thousands of years; the range of body types in the past does not differ from the range we know today. What has changed is the body type (or types) regarded as ideal, as well as the effort put into meeting this ideal and the methods used to do so. Although styles of dress have tended to change at an ever-quickening tempo since the 12th century, body ideals have changed slowly. By looking at the visual evidence provided by paintings of dressed people and of the nude, we can see that never before have men or women desired a body so "close to the bone."

5   There have been, of course, other periods when slenderness was admired. During the 15th century, paintings of long-limbed ladies reverberated with the vaulting reaches of Gothic cathedrals. Sixteenth-century Mannerists in northern Europe painted elongated nudes, such as the nymphs in Cranach the Elder's *The Judgment of Paris*. More recently, the Romantic vogue for slenderness in the 1830s–1850s encouraged young ladies to strive for the tiny waist favored by fashion—an effort later immortalized in *Gone with the Wind* when Scarlett O'Hara's stays are tightened to achieve a 17-inch waist.[1]

---

[1]For a fuller discussion of past body ideals, see Roberta P. Seid, *Never Too Thin: Why Women Are at War with Their Bodies* (New York: Prentice-Hall Press, 1989), 37–81. The best sources for a general overview are Francois Boucher, *20,000 Years of Fashion: The History of Costume and Personal Adornment,* expanded edition (New York: Harry N. Abrams, 1987) and Kenneth Clark, *The Nude: A Study in Ideal Form* (Princeton, NJ: Princeton University Press, 1956).

6   Nonetheless, it would be misleading to assume that these eras resembled our own. Gothic and Mannerist nudes had not a bone or muscle showing; they were sweetly and fully fleshed. Women of the Romantic period may have wanted tiny waists, but they also wanted their shoulders, arms, calves, and bosoms ample, indicating an "amorous plenitude."[2] Indeed, thinness was considered ugly, a woman's misfortune. The French epicure J. A. Brillat-Savarin defined thinness as those of his epoch typically did—as "the condition of the individual whose muscular flesh, not being filled with fat, reveals the forms and angles of the bony structure." Thinness in women was, he observed, "a terrible misfortune.... The most painstaking toilette, the sublimest costume, cannot hide certain absences, or disguise certain angles."[3] Nor did the Romantic lady equate slenderness with health and energy as we do today; health was not part of her aesthetic ideal. Rather, slenderness signified delicacy and fragility, the qualities she sought.

7   Just a century ago, body ideals and ideas were the reverse of our own, underscoring the fact that there was no folk wisdom about the value of slenderness that science has recently confirmed. Indeed, the female ideal was Junoesque: tall, full-busted, full-figured, mature. Dimpled flesh—what we today shudderingly call "cellulite"—was considered desirable. Sinewy, "close to the bone" women "no bigger than a whipping post" suffered disdain, not those with amply fleshed curves properly distributed and disciplined only by the corset.[4] The undergarment industry even came to the aid of the slighted thin woman with inflatable rubber garments (replete with dimples) for her back, calves, shoulders, and hips. They may have provided meager comfort, for they could deflate at unexpected moments.[5]

8   Fat was seen as a "silken layer" that graced the frames of elegant ladies. It was regarded as "stored-up force," equated with reserves of energy and strength. Plumpness was deemed a sign of emotional well-being; it was identified with a good temperament, with a clean conscience, with temperate and disciplined habits, and above all with good health. Today, of course, we have totally inverted these associations.[6]

9   In the mid-19th century, the prolific writer Catherine Beecher described healthy weight. If you felt heavy and got on the scale (a rare experience in the 19th century), and weighed either heavy or light, you were in bad health. But

---

[2]See the excellent discussion of this ideal in Valerie Steele, *Fashion and Eroticism: Ideals of Feminine Beauty from the Victorian Era to the Jazz Age* (New York: Oxford University Press, 1985), 108–110.

[3]Jean Anthelme Brillat-Savarin, *The Physiology of Taste or Meditations on Transcendental Gastronomy* (New York: Doubleday, 1926 [orig. 1826]), 172, 187.

[4]Steele, 1985, 218–223; Hillel Schwartz, *Never Satisfied: A Cultural History of Diets, Fantasies, and Fat* (New York: Free Press, 1986), Illustration 5 (1857 cartoon from *Harper's Weekly*).

[5]David Kunzle, "The Corset as Erotic Alchemy: From Rococo Galanterie to Montaut's Physiologies," in Thomas Hess and Linda Nochlin, eds., *Art News Annual*, vol. 38, *Woman as Sex Object: Erotic Art, 1730–1970* (1972); Steele, 1985, 128, 221.

[6]Seid, 1989, 70–80.

if you felt light and weighed heavy, then you were in excellent health; weighing heavy was good. More importantly, Beecher distinguished between feelings and actual weight—a distinction lost to many today, who determine how they feel by the numbers on the scale.[7]

Development of the Obsession with Thinness

10 The transformation of these values began at about the turn of the present century, when slenderness came into fashion. This occurred for a variety of reasons, among them the modernist aesthetic with its idealization of speed and motion, and its penchant for stripping things down to their essential forms. (Some called it the revenge of the thin who for so long had been slighted.) But "slim" is a relative term, and the women who boasted the new form would by contemporary standards be called overweight. In addition, in the first half of this century, the belief that plumpness signaled robust health remained strong.

11 The culture of slimming as we know it is really a post–World War II phenomenon.[8] Fashion continued to value a slender (if curving) form, and the health industry, finally convinced by insurance companies, launched massive campaigns to persuade Americans to lose weight. Key ideas that would take full force in subsequent decades began to emerge. Chief among these was "fatphobia," the conviction that animal fat of any kind—on the body, in the blood, on the plate—was dangerous. The perception developed that Americans were too fat and getting fatter; that they ate too much, ate the wrong foods, and were sedentary and therefore flabby. Americans' self-perception shifted to that of a diseased, unhealthy group, even though they enjoyed the best health and greatest longevity ever known in American society. These pronouncements did not abate, even though average life expectancy continued to improve. Most important was the growing fear that Americans were getting physically and *morally* soft. For at the heart of all the campaign literature was a moral concern about how Americans would react to postwar plenty and leisure—how they would handle modernization.

12 In subsequent decades, these ideas intensified. Weight loss techniques began to be seen as life-prolonging in and of themselves. The fitness ethic emerged from these beliefs and fueled obsession with exercise. But the new emphasis on fitness was just a variation on the theme of slenderness. The ideal remained a fat-free body. The "health food" craze played on the same dynamic, growing out of and then later helping to fuel and dignify diet obsessions. In addition, the standards of slenderness grew more extreme, both in charts of ideal weight and in fashion. The famous 1960s model Twiggy, at 5 feet 7 inches and 98 pounds, represented the boundary beyond which no ambulatory person could go; however, her image became one that women thereafter aspired to meet. Female beauty had come to be represented by a gawky, bare-boned adolescent. Simultaneously, definitions of "overweight" and "obesity" began to include normal-sized Americans.

---

[7]Beecher's standards are quoted by Harvey Green, *Fit for America: Health–Fitness–Sport and American Society* (New York: Pantheon Books, 1986), 64.

[8]For a fuller discussion with citations of sources, see Seid, 1989, Chapters 12 and 13.

13   More compelling, however, were the principles underlying fatphobia, which turned it into a national obsession. The health industry embraced the questionable concept of "ideal weight"—the idea that the weight associated with optimum health and longevity could be determined by height. It was then decreed that everyone of the same height and bone structure should meet this ideal. But this injunction assumed that body weight and the ratios of fat to lean tissue were direct functions of exercise and eating habits. The obvious corollary was that everybody should reduce to ideal weight and that everybody could easily do so—if they exerted enough willpower. In short, these decrees blamed the victim: if you were fat, it was your fault. This is the most powerful and pernicious aspect of fatphobia; indeed, in modern America, being fat is as shameful as being dirty. We seem to believe that slenderness is as attainable as cleanliness, and as crucial to respectable grooming. We can easily embrace these ideas because they fit so well with America's self-help-oriented, democratic ideology. We can all be body aristocrats, we believe, if we just try hard enough. This set of beliefs fuels prejudices against fat and has allowed the thinness mania to spiral into a religion.

14   More and more evidence is emerging that discredits this whole ideology and shows that its premises are empirically flawed. The thinner are not necessarily healthier, nor are they more fit. Our fundamental beliefs—that people of the same height should have the same weight, and that people can exercise absolute control over their body weights—are also flawed. Numerous studies demonstrate that the majority of the "fat" cannot slim down permanently. The problem is not their lack of willpower, but the unreasonable expectation placed on them to weigh a certain amount. Animal breeders have long known that nature did not intend everyone to be the same size, but modern science seems to have temporarily forgotten.

15   Sadly, efforts to squeeze into the ideal size are often useless and destructive—not only because they can exacerbate the problem they are designed to cure, but because they trigger psychological, physiological, and behavioral consequences, including binge eating, food obsessions, and, in susceptible individuals, eating disorders. Even worse, dieters pay a price in sense of well-being, in health, and in the ability to lead rich and productive lives. The contemporary and historical literature on famine describes ennui, tension, irritability, preoccupation with food, loss of libido, and lassitude created by diets equivalent to those advised for weight loss. The United Nations World Health Organization has established a daily intake of 1000 calories as the border of semistarvation; modern diets often recommend less. The famine literature attributes these symptoms to hunger and undernourishment; the literature on overweight attributes them to lack of willpower or to psychopathology.

16   Laboring under perverse notions about food and appetite, we believe that permanent dieting and chronic hunger are healthy and energy-giving; we are convinced that food does not nourish, but rather kills. If we find ourselves eating with unbridled appetite, we believe that there is either something wrong with us or with the food itself, which must be "addictive." In truth, the well-nourished, not the undernourished, grow strong, healthy, and productive. Poor appetite is a sign of the depressed and the ill; indeed, women are often grateful for an illness—it makes dieting easier.

17   It is hard to resist the parallel between Victorian attributes toward sex and modern attitudes toward food. In the 19th century, the control of sexual instincts was the acme of virtue; sexual behavior was the yardstick of goodness. Today, eating habits and body weights have become the yardsticks of virtue, and food rules have become as dour and inhibitory as the sex rules of the 19th century. Perhaps cultures require some kind of instinctual control to feel that they qualify as "civilized."

Why Women More Than Men?

18 Given that this belief system pervades our culture, why does it affect women so much more than men? Why do more women than men suffer from eating disorders, obesity, and distorted body image? Why are women, not men, at war with their bodies? There are many reasons, some more obvious than others.

19   One reason is biological. Standards for males simply are not as extreme or as inimical to normal masculine body builds as are women's standards. Indeed, our female ideal violates the anthropomorphic reality of the average female body. The ideal female weight, represented by actresses, models, and Miss Americas, has progressively decreased to that of the thinnest 5–10% of American women. Consequently, 90–95% of American women feel that they don't "measure up."[9] Societies have never been kind to deviants, but in America a statistical deviation has been normalized, leading millions of women to believe that they are abnormal.

20   In addition, the taut, lean, muscled body—the "fit" form so many strive to achieve—is more like the body of a male than of a female. The goal is to suppress female secondary sexual characteristics, from dimpled flesh to plumpness in thighs, behinds, hips, and bosom. Women consequently are pitted in a war against their own biologies to meet the standard.

21   It is not just biology that confounds women. They strive to meet this unreasonable standard because it has become a moral imperative in our society, and because, despite a quarter-century of feminism, the quest for physical beauty

---

[9]Although exact figures on this subject remain elusive, many sources confirm this general trend. This percentage was suggested by Rita Freedman, *Beauty Bound* (Lexington, Mass.: Lexington Books, 1986), 149, but it is corroborated by other sources. I studied statistics of Miss America contenders with data for the earlier periods from Frank Deford, *There She Is: The Life and Times of Miss America* (New York: Viking Press, 1971) 313–316, and from Miss America Pageant Yearbooks, 1972–1983, and found a dramatic slenderizing trend. For more details, see Seid, 1989, Chapter 10. For a study of a similar development in the *Playboy* centerfolds, whose average weights dropped from 11% below the national average in 1970 to 17% below it in 1978, see Paul E. Garfinkel and David M. Garner, *Anorexia Nervosa: A Multidimensional Perspective* (New York: Brunner/Mazel, 1982), 108–109, and D. M. Garner, P. E. Garfinkel, D. Schwartz, and M. Thompson, "Cultural Expectations of Thinness in Women," *Psychological Reports* 47 (1980): 483–491. On the rise of an emaciated ideal in the ballet subculture, see L. M. Vincent, *Competing with the Sylph* (New York: Andrews & McNeel, 1979). Jennifer Brenner, professor of psychology at Brandeis University, and Dr. Joseph Cunningham recently reported the results of their study comparing the weights of New York fashion models and Brandeis students. "Female models are 9 percent taller and 16 percent thinner than average women," Brenner reported in an article by Lena Williams, "Girl's Self-Image Is Mother of the Woman," *New York Times* (National Edition), February 6, 1992, A1, A12.

remains deeply powerful. On even a practical level, women's self-image, their social and economic success, and even their survival can still be determined largely by their beauty and by the men it allows them to attract, while for men these are based largely on how they act and what they accomplish. Looks simply are of secondary importance for male success.

22   But the impulse toward beauty runs much deeper than the desire for social acceptance and success. Beauty and fashion are intertwined, and women try to meet unreasonable weight standards also because fashion—our system of dress—requires them to do so. Though many have castigated fashion as a shallow and frivolous vanity, it is propelled by profound impulses, which it shares with all dress systems. Dress and adornment are basic to all human cultures. Even the most primitive tribes find ways to decorate the body. The overwhelming importance of dress is underscored by the fact that from the moment we slip out of the womb to the moment of our deaths, we alter our natural appearance. How we choose to dress is a complex cultural phenomenon. Clothing and adornment are simultaneously a material object, a social signal, a ritual, and a form of art. Every facet of a society—from its economic base to its social structure, from its values about human beings and their bodies to its loftiest spiritual and aesthetic ideals—influences the forms and rules of dress. Each culture sets up its own rules, and in following them, people defer to and perpetuate fundamental social values and norms.

23   In obeying fashion's dictates, we are bowing to powerful constraints about self-presentation and about how others should interpret our attitudes, behavior, and identity. The enormous time and energy women (and men) devote to it is simply another of civilization's many demands and, possibly, pleasures. For in dressing, in following fashion, we are engaged in a game, a plastic art, a process whereby we partially create ourselves. We are involved in social and private play of the profoundest type—trying to transcend our uncivilized, animal state, to make ourselves human. Friedrich Nietzsche, in *The Birth of Tragedy,* argued that "We derive such dignity as we possess from our status as art works." Fun, fantasy, humor, artistic creativity, and our deepest aspirations exist in the dress constraints of everyday life.[10]

24   Fashion, the dress system of the West, has, however, taken a rather peculiar twist in recent decades—one that helps explain our body obsessions. Fashionable beauty is no longer about the clothes covering the body, but about the naked body itself. This has not been true before in the history of fashion. Fashion is, as we have seen, a plastic art. Although it would be foolhardy to describe the past as Edenic, it nonetheless is true that fashion has traditionally been a handmaiden to beauty. It allowed people to approach the reigning ideal by manipulating cosmetics and clothing—that is, by manipulating what they put *on* themselves, not what they *were* underneath those clothes, stays, girdles, and so forth.

---

[10]Nietzsche's statement is quoted in Steele, 1985, 245. For a fuller theoretical discussion and bibliography on the role of dress and adornment in human culture, see Roberta P. Seid, *The Dissolution of Traditional Rural Culture in Nineteenth-Century France: A Study of the Bethmale Costume* (New York: Garland Press, 1987), 1–45.

25   By the late 20th century, however, women's bodies, which heretofore had never been exposed to the public eye, virtually became wholly exposed. With the introduction of the miniskirt and teeny tops, women's legs, thighs, and upper bodies were suddenly revealed, bereft of the aid of body-shaping undergarments. The fitness craze and the growing liberalization in censorship and in acceptable norms of nudity intensified the trend.

26   By the 1980s, even fashion magazines showed naked or leotarded bodies more than they showed clothing. The undressed body—the bare bones of being, celebrated as liberating and "natural"—had become the focus of fashion. No longer did a woman have the luxury of manipulating only what was outside her body, the "not me"; now she had to manipulate her self, the once private stretches of the body.

27   This new, "natural" look could not really be liberating, because fashion is antithetical (almost by definition) to nature, so stringent standards began being set for the now-exposed form. Suddenly, the average American woman became aware of flaws she never knew existed; pronouncements were made about how every private crevice of her anatomy was to look. Women consequently ran smack into a dilemma between the naked and the nude.

28   The art historian Sir Kenneth Clark argued that the nude is a form of art; the naked is merely the human body undressed, replete with all its flaws and blemishes. The naked becomes the nude through art, with the artist transforming that humble and flawed form into an ideal of beauty.[11] Yet today, bombarded by verbal and visual commercial images of the nude, women have been seduced into believing that they should—and could, with enough effort—have one of those perfect bodies. They expect the image reflected in their mirrors to look like the nude. It almost never does. And so they renew their battle against their recalcitrant bodies.

29   Changes in the structure of fashion contributed further to the battle: No authorities put brakes on the urge to meet the slender ideal. This, too, was new in fashion's history. Although there has always been considerable harmony among standards of feminine beauty, health, and the gestalt of an era, excesses of fashion were heretofore severely criticized by social authorities, including doctors, teachers, and clergy, parents, and, since the 19th century, feminists. The clergy and moralists, in particular, stressed that there were values more important than outward appearance; that the soul and one's deeds mattered, not fashion standards; that, in the words of the old adage, "Pretty is as pretty does." In the late 20th century—at least until alarm about eating disorders spread—all these authorities, especially physicians, seemed to agree that one could never be too thin. This unholy alliance between societal and fashion authorities allowed the vogue for thinness to go to extremes.

30   Even contemporary feminists have been slow to resist the slenderness fashion. They were initially seduced, perhaps, by its underlying message that biology is not destiny. Even more, the rhetoric of the slenderness ideal—that health is beauty and beauty health, and both are fit and thin—may have persuaded

---

[11]Clark, 1956, 3–9.

them. They applauded the fact that physical strength and health were now feminine ideals. It took a while for them to realize that what was sought, what had become ideal, was merely the *appearance* of health and vigor—and that dangerous means were being used to achieve it.

31   Despite the historical uniqueness of these developments, some rather cruel historical consistencies remain. More stringent bodily controls are still required of the female than of the male. Animal-like functions, such as belching, nose wiping, urinating, sweating, scratching, spitting, masturbating, farting, and even body odor, remain less permissible for women than for men. In the male subculture, unlike female subcultures, there is an acceptance of and a certain humor about these behaviors, which sometimes become the subject of good-natured contests. Men simply are permitted to be more comfortable about natural functions and to exhibit them to a greater extent in public. They do not compromise masculinity; rather, they often confirm it. Women, on the other hand, compromise their femininity if they do not control these behaviors. The same discrepancy applies to diet and body size: Women are expected to manage these even more stringently than men. Similarly, as long as control of appetite and body weight is regarded as virtuous, women must exercise this control more than men. Once again, women are expected to be the custodians and embodiments of virtue for the culture.

Thinness and Our Cultural and Spiritual Values

32 What remains puzzling about this unique fashion for bare-boned skinniness is what it suggests about our aesthetic ideals—and, even more importantly, about our values, our gestalt. If we step back a moment and look at our ideal of beauty from a more distant perspective (perhaps that of a future historian or anthropologist), we can perhaps see how peculiar it is that we celebrate the living version of Giacometti sculptures, anorexics with barbells.

33   Future historians might conjecture that Americans had fallen in love with death, or at least with mortification of the flesh. They might speculate that terror of nuclear destruction had made fashion play with cadavers and turn them into images of beauty. Or they might argue that we had been so influenced by modern art, Bauhaus aesthetics, and contemporary steel architecture that our ideal human body also had come to consist only of the scaffolding that held it up and of the machinery that made it move. Or they might suggest that we had come to see technology, not human beings, as the prime force in history, and so had chosen to resemble our conquerors.

34   Alternatively, they might argue that our fascination with the unconscious, and our new awareness that scientific reality was concealed from us—that the universe was made up of particles we could not see and governed by laws that defied the logic of our senses—led us to strip the outer body of any meaning or significance and of any possible beauty. Or, more simply, they might conjecture that in an era of population density, it was more practical and economical to have skinny people. Thin people would need less room, so more of them could be squeezed into the spaces on mass transit and into workplaces, and they could live in smaller houses. It certainly also might be interpreted as democratic. No one had the right to take up more space than another or to command

respect through the imposing grandeur of body size.

35   They might also conjecture that late 20th-century America had so confused its image of women that what looked female could no longer be considered beautiful. Even more, they might contend that we had dehumanized, not just masculinized, the human form. We had reduced it to its smallest, least imposing form. They might argue that we had come to idealize technology, and also (befitting our secular age) to distinguish humans from other animals and the civilized from the uncivilized not by the presence of consciousness, a soul, and a conscience, but by the suppression of animal fat. They might even suggest that we had become so terrified of what made us human—especially our passions and our vulnerability—that we didn't want our bodies to betray any softness, curves, or idiosyncracies. Or they might think that we had suppressed tender flesh because we no longer saw human beings as sources of comfort and nurture.

36   From a purely aesthetic perspective, our fat-free beauties might come out no better. Indeed, even unprejudiced present-day observers may be taken aback. Faces are gaunt and angular; necks are steeples of bones. Unfleshed arms and legs, full of sharp angles, look gangly and disproportionately long. Indeed, dieted women look as though the life and color have been sucked out of them. Nor, for all the paeans to strength, do these scrawny, narrow women look strong or stable, or as if they have a stature to be reckoned with. Indeed, the lean body looks as repressed and controlled as the spirit that must have gotten it that way.

37   It is odd, too, that we have developed an erotic ideal that suppresses flesh and minimizes sexual characteristics. There is little to linger over, to explore, to discover. When the body has been efficiently reduced to a flat surface, it offers no softness, no warmth, no tenderness, no mysteries—qualities once integral to images of sexuality. Our erotic ideal has become as hard and unyielding, perhaps, as the love relationships that dominate social life.

38   In criticizing our new religion, I am not suggesting that we gorge wantonly or that we ignore our health and our physical appearance. This would be a surrender to the treacherous polarities that dominate our thinking: Our choices seem to be thinness or fatness, gluttony or starvation, vigorous exercise or lethargy, ascetic rituals or self-indulgence, youthfulness or old age, beauty or ugliness. I am suggesting that we recultivate our tastes and find a saner middle ground where our bodies can round out with more life, flesh, and health; where we can relish the fruits of our prosperity without self-punishment; and where we understand that the nourishment that is one of life's greatest pleasures is also one of its most basic necessities.

39   It would be a tragedy, after 25 years of the women's movement, if women did not rebel against this "religion" that threatens to sabotage their hard-won victories. Is the "liberated woman," supposedly at ease in the boardroom, really consumed with self-loathing and obsessed with tallying calories, exercise, and the vital statistics of the body (weight, muscle-to-fat ratio, inches of breast, hip, and thigh)? Never measuring quite right, she may be as victimized by biology as her predecessors.

40   I am not suggesting, as many past and present feminists have, that we do away with beauty and fashion standards altogether. It would be a bleak world

if we did not celebrate beauty and if we did not encourage the imagination and play involved in bedecking ourselves and molding our own images. The impulses toward adornment and self-beautification run deep in human culture and are connected to its noblest aspirations. Nor am I suggesting that fashion standards of the past were always benign. Each era has exacted its own price for beauty, though our era is unique in producing a standard based exclusively on the bare bones of being, which can be disastrous for human health, happiness, and productivity.

41   But I am urging that we dismantle this new religion, because it is misguided and destructive. It does not provide reasonable guidelines by which to live. Our bodies, our fitness, and our food should not be our paramount concerns. They have nothing to do with ethics, or relationships, or community responsibilities, or with the soul. They have nothing to say about the purpose of life, except that we should survive as well and as long and as beautifully as we can. They give us no purpose beyond ourselves. This is a religion appropriate only for a people whose ideals do not extend beyond their physical existence, and whose vision of the future and of the past is strangely empty. Surely Americans can produce a worthier creed.

42   In making the denial of hunger and its physical manifestations, thinness, into a primary virtue, our "religion" is unique among the major world religions. Although there is a long history of fasting for spiritual cleansing or purity, no religion has set it up as a virtue; indeed, most have condemned it. Buddha rejected fasting because he did not find it a way to enlightenment. Judaism prescribes only a few fast days a year. Otherwise, it proscribes such deprivation: According to the Talmud, people must be well nourished so they can do what is important in life—follow God's commandments and perform *mitzvot* (good deeds). The early fathers of the Christian Church, too, condemned fasting, and the Church exacted higher penances for the sin of not eating than it did for the sin of gluttony. The Muslims, even during their great fast of Ramadan, do not abstain from food. They are merely proscribed from eating during certain hours, and the other hours are given to feasting. In these religions, food has not been seen as a temptation put in humanity's path, but as vital for people to carry out their larger spiritual tasks.

43   It is one thing to follow a rigid dietary code and rituals of behavior in accordance with the laws of a God or gods we worship. The faithful are trying to fulfill God's or the gods' commandments, not only for their own salvation, but also to hasten the arrival of a more perfect world. It is quite another thing to follow rigid dietary and behavior codes only to improve our physical selves. Such actions are not part of a larger system of morals. They have no vision of a higher good or of a better future that their rituals might help create. This is a solipsistic religion in the narrowest and strictest sense, in that it is only about the bare bones of being. If avoiding fatness and possible disease is the main preoccupation of our lives, then what are we living for?

44   Our new religion bankrupts us. Historically unprecedented numbers of us are healthy—able to enjoy sex without fear of unwanted pregnancy, to go through childbirth without the once omnipresent threat of death, to treat once-fatal

infectious diseases easily, and to alleviate the minor aches and pains that caused discomfort to our forebears (from toothaches to earaches to headaches to skin eruptions to upset stomachs). Advances in technology, medicine, and food production, wrought by painstaking human efforts, have given us a well-being virtually unknown in previous centuries. We should be grateful, but instead we hate our bodies because they bulge here or are flabby there or fail to respond to our most rigorous diets. Surely this is the worst form of hubris—to despise our bodies because they are not perfect. Our new religion neither puts checks on this kind of vanity nor underscores how trivial is the accomplishment of weight loss and of physical perfection. Instead, it seduces us into believing that this quest is the worthiest of human goals.

45   We must abandon our new religion because it trivializes human life itself. We must restore a humanistic vision in which self-improvement means cultivating the mind and enlarging the soul; developing generosity, humor, dignity, and humility; living more graciously with biology, aging, and death; living with our limitations. We need a concept of self-improvement that reminds us to learn from the past, to build on it, and to bequeath wisdom to future generations. We stand poised between a past for which we have lost respect and a future we must now struggle to envision.

Review Questions

1. According to Seid, what is our "new religion," and what is its creed?

2. In what ways is the 20th- and 21st-century ideal of beauty arbitrary?

3. To what does "close to the bone" of Seid's title refer?

4. In what ways has the ideal of female beauty changed in the last 100 years?

5. Why did the current "fatphobia" take hold?

6. What, according to Seid, is the "most [...] pernicious aspect of fatphobia"?

7. In what ways is the blame-the-victim logic directed against fat people flawed, according to Seid?

8. In paragraph 18, Seid asks: "Why do more women than men suffer from eating disorders, obesity, and distorted body image?" What is her answer?

9. After launching her extended critique against the "religion" of dieting and the "close to the bone" ideal of beauty, what recommendation does Seid make?

Discussion and Writing Suggestions

1. In paragraph 3, Seid challenges the reader with a daring assertion: "[A]norexia nervosa could be called the paradigm of our age, for our creed encourages us all to adopt the behavior and attitudes of the anorexic. The difference is one of degree, not of kind." Two questions: First, if you have followed the logic of Seid's argument, does this assertion follow? Second, to what extent do you agree?

2. In paragraphs 13–14, Seid explains the logic by which Americans come to blame fat people for being fat. Summarize that logic—and then comment on it. For instance, have you ever encountered this type of blame-the-victim thinking? Is it reasonable, in your view, to regard fat people as victims?

3. In your experience, or in the experience of people you know, to what extent is it true that "dieters pay a price in sense of well-being, in health, and in the ability to lead rich and productive lives"?

4. In paragraph 15, Seid juxtaposes the "contemporary and historical literature on famine" to the messages implied in and stated directly by our dieting culture. What is your response?

5. How do you respond to Seid's assertion in paragraph 17 comparing our culture's preoccupation with weight to Victorian culture's preoccupation with sex?

6. Seid argues that in the 20th century the world of fashion has focused not only on clothes but on the body, the result being that a woman who wants to dress fashionably must attend to the body beneath the clothes as well as to the clothes themselves (see paragraphs 24–27). How consciously aware are you of having to "manipulate" yourself—that is your body—in order to be fashionably correct? After you have answered this question, meet in a group of four or more classmates, with equal numbers of men and women. Compare answers.

7. In paragraph 29, Seid speaks of an "unholy alliance between societal and fashion authorities." What, in her view, is so unholy? Do you agree?

8. Seid writes in paragraph 41: "Our bodies, our fitness, and our food [...] have nothing to do with ethics, or relationships, or community responsibilities, or with the soul." In paragraph 43 she writes that severe dieting for the sake of thinness, alone, is a "solipsistic religion" and contributes nothing to the greater good of society. Seid makes a strong and cogent argument in this essay against the "religion" of thinness and the ways in which it "trivializes human life itself." Discuss her conclusions and recommendations. Do you agree? Could you imagine yourself or others agreeing and *still* wanting to diet?

9. Notwithstanding Seid's arguments, statistical trends are clear (see the selections in this chapter from the *Journal of the American Medical Association* and the *Centers for Disease Control*) that the number of overweight and obese people is rising, which in turn is leading to increased levels of illness and death. In what ways do these scientific reports affect your reading of Seid?

Fat and Happy?
Hillel Schwartz

"Fat and Happy" forms the final chapter of historian Hillel Schwartz's book-length study of dieting, Never Satisfied *(Free Press, 1986). Like Seid, who critiques what she terms a "religion" of thinness, Schwartz critiques what he calls a "despotism of slenderness." The selection has a satiric feel to it, but underlying all satire—this included—are points seriously made. Indeed, much of the logic presented here you will find shared by other writers, such as Seid and Worley. In the two sections of the chapter reproduced here, Schwartz presents a "Vindication of Fat" and an image of "The Fat Society: A Utopia."*

Recently there has been a growing protest against the despotism of slenderness, and a scientific debate over the dangers of a moderate fatness. Underlying the protest and the debate is a utopian vision of a Fat Society where neither overweight nor obesity stands in the way of social freedom or personal happiness.

The Vindication of Fat

1 Fatness is fine.

2 If fat people are unhappy people, blame not their fat but their fellow citizens who bill them as clowns, clodhoppers, cannibals, or criminals; who spread such commercial rumors as "To be fat is the end of life"; who sport bumper stickers on their vans, "No fat chicks"; who print posters which read, "It's in to be thin. It's out to be stout."[1] Blame the kindergarten teachers, the coaches, the friends and physicians who goad fat people into a maze of diets from which they may never return. Dieting makes everything worse, for the chances are high that fat people will fail. They will be saddened and frustrated by their failures, and they will come to agree with everyone else that they are failures in all of life. Because they have failed they are fat, and because they are fat they fail.

[1]Marvin Grosswirth, *Fat Pride* (NY, 1971) 161, D-Zerta ad, and American Physical Fitness Research Institute poster, "Fit to Quote" (Santa Monica, Calif., 1969).

3   It is the taking off and the putting on of weight that endangers the body. Not the fat or the pounds but the dieting itself, the frustration, and the constant hunger. No one has been able to prove that fatness *per se* cuts life short. If left alone, 99 percent of human beings will reach a plateau weight, a set point at which their metabolisms will be satisfied and their bodies healthy. It is the dieting, the anxiety, and the perpetual scrimmaging with food that lead to illness. "What causes the most damage is not the actual weight itself, but the fear of weight." People who drive their weights down and up through a series of diets are those most likely to become fatter and unhappier than before, for they upset the natural equilibrium of their bodies. In self-defense, their bodies stockpile fat whenever and wherever possible, hedging as they may against the next (self-imposed) privation. Meanwhile hearts suffer through cycles of feast and famine, strained at each new feast, shocked at each new famine. "To fat, to starve—/Perchance to die of it! Ah, there's the rub." Pokeberry, dinitrophenol, rainbow pills, liquid protein—there is no end to death by dieting.[2]

4   And still the dieting goes on, as fat people are compromised and persecuted. Like other minorities, fat people are treated like children, given silly nicknames, considered socially and sexually immature. The "Diet Conscience," an electronic guardian, sneers when the refrigerator door is opened, "Are you eating again? Shame on you! No wonder you look the way you do! Ha! Ha! Ha! You'll be sorry, fatty. Do yourself a favor; *shut the door!*"[3]

---

[2]Louis I. Dublin believed that he had demonstrated that weight-reducing decreased mortality: "Overweight shortens life," *MLIC* 32 (Oct 1951) 1–4, and idem, "Relation of obesity to longevity," *NEJM* 248 (1953) 971–74. But see Public Health Service, *Obesity and Health* (Washington, D.C., 1966) 59; George V. Mann, "Obesity, the national spook," *AJPH* 61 (1971) 1491–98; idem, "Influence of obesity on health," *NEJM* 291 (1974) 178–85, 226–32; and William Bennett and Joel Gurin, *The Dieter's Dilemma* (NY, 1982) 134–35.

On the absence of a causal relationship between fatness or overweight and increased mortality, see Ancel Keys et al., "Coronary heart disease: overweight and obesity as risk factors," *AIM* 77 (1972) 15–27; Tavia Gordon and William B. Kannel, "Obesity and cardiovascular disease: the Framingham study," *Clinics in Endocrinology and Metabolism* 5 (1976) 367–75; Susan C. Wooley et al., "Obesity and women—I. A closer look at the facts," *Women's Studies Int Q* 2 (1979) 74; Reubin Andres, "Effect of obesity on total mortality," *IJO* 4 (1980) 381–86; Kelly D. Brownell, "Obesity," *J of Consulting and Clinical Psych* 50 (1982) 820; and Carol Sternhill, "We'll always be fat, but fat can be fit," *Ms.* (May 1985) 142.

On the dangers of a weight-loss/weight-gain cycle, see Vinne Young, *It's Fun to Be Fat* (NY, 1953) 10, 26 and quote on 23; Nick Lyons, *Locked Jaws* (NY, 1979) 13 quote; and Sharon G. Patton, "Why dieting can make you fat," *New Woman* (Aug 1984) 34.

On deaths from dieting, see Roland C. Curtin, "The heart and its danger in the treatment of obesity," *J of Balneology and Climatology* 12 (1908) 223 on pokeberry; Chapter Seven on dinitrophenol and amphetamines; House of Representatives Subcommittee on Health and the Environment, *Hearing…on the Most Popular Diet in America Today, Liquid Protein, Dec 28, 1977* (Washington, D.C., 1978) 3–7; Center for Disease Control, "Follow-up on deaths associated with liquid protein diets," *Morbidity and Mortality Weekly Report* 27 (1978) 223–24; Harold E. Sours et al., "Sudden death associated with very low calorie weight reduction regimens," *AJCN* 34 (1981) 453–61, and see also 1639–40, 2855–57.

[3]Ann M. Lingg, "A plump girl talks back," *Amer Mercury* 78 (March 1954) 30, an early reference to minority status; Lew Louderback, "More people should be fat," *SEP* 240 (Nov 4, 1967) 10; Grosswirth, *Fat Pride,* 40; and Mildred Klingman, *Secret Lives of Fat People* (Boston, 1981) 72 on Diet Conscience. See also Lisa Schoenfielder and Barb Wieser, eds., *Shadow on a Tightrope: Writings by Women on Fat Oppression* (Iowa City, Ia., 1983).

5   Like other minorities, fat people are seen as throwbacks to a more primitive time. Neanderthals in museum dioramas are squat and fat; cannibals
stirring pots are fat; Oriental despots are fat; harems are full of slothful fat
women and supervised by fat eunuchs. The modern world is passing them
by. Fat people are stuck in the past, so much so that modern businessmen
and scientists prefer an employee who has been in jail or in a mental ward
to one who is fat. Criminality and insanity seem less intransigent, less rooted,
than obesity.[4]

6   If fat people are not such atavisms, why do they do so poorly in school
and in business? The same vicious circle surrounding other minorities surrounds fat people, who have more difficulty getting into the best colleges and
who are not promoted as quickly as their leaner rivals. How they look is more
important than how well they do their jobs. The New York City Traffic
Department in 1965 dismissed six meter maids for being overweight;
National Airlines fired a stewardess for being 4 lbs overweight. As of 1982
only Michigan had a law specifically banning discrimination on account of
weight. In 1980 a *New Yorker* cartoon depicted a judge sentencing a defendant: "It is the Court's opinion that, although innocent, you are dangerously
overweight." This comedy had already been played out in Miami, where a
woman being sentenced for a misdemeanor assault explained that at 315
lbs she was too heavy to work. The judge gave her three years' probation on
the condition that she lose 65 lbs at 3 lbs per week; if she went off her diet,
she would go to prison.[5]

7   Physicians are equally unsympathetic. They find fat patients distasteful. Fat
people seem more difficult to examine, less likely to cooperate. Fat people
are waddling reminders of the failure of medicine to come up with a safe,
workable program for long-term weight reduction, just as poor people and
homeless people are stark reminders of the failure of the economic system.
Like politicians, physicians blame the victims. It is not the doctor's fault if fat
people are weak, dishonest, lazy, and childish. All one can do with such
people is to threaten them with disease and death, play on their fears. "If,
knowing these dangers—as you now do—you continue to overeat, it must be
obvious that you are acting in a childish fashion. You are immature. This

---

[4]Robert J. Homant and Daniel B. Kennedy, "Attitudes toward ex-offenders: a comparison of social stig-
mas," *J of Criminal Justice* 10 (1982) 383–91.

[5]Peter L. Benson et al., "Social costs of obesity," *Social Behavior and Personality* 8 (1980) 91–96 on
colleges; Llewellyn Louderback, *Fat Power* (NY, 1970) 47, 52, 53, 55; Chris Chase, *The Great American
Waistline* (NY, 1981) 196 on stewardesses; *New Yorker* (Sept 29, 1980) 49; and "Better than prison,"
Time 97 (June 7, 1971) 39. Concerning weight discrimination at law, see David H. Tucker for the
Maryland Commission on Human Relations, *Report on the Study of Weight and Size Discrimination,*
typescript (Baltimore, 1980); Jane O. Baker, "The Rehabilitation Act of 1973: protection for victims of
weight discrimination?" *UCLA Law R* 29 (April 1982) 947–71; David Berreby, "Is being fat a handicap?
Courts differ," *National Law J* 4 (Aug 30, 1982) 3:1; Lynne Reaves, "Fat folks' rights: weight bias issues
emerging," *Amer Bar Assoc J* 69 (1983) 878; and Lauren R. Reskin, "Employers must give obese job
applicants a fat chance," *Amer Bar Assoc J* 71 (Sept 1985) 104.

alone will prove to you that you are acting *like a child* if you continue to be fat. Now it is up to you.... Be childish and die, or grow up and live!"[6]

8   Yet nearly half of all dieters get their dieting information from such patronizing doctors, doctors who until recently have had no specific training in nutrition. In 1970, three-quarters of doctors surveyed found obesity and overweight to be very frequent among their patients, yet few have pursued the study of obesity (bariatrics) in order to improve their courses of treatment. Nor have they been in particularly good shape themselves; the Scarsdale diet doctor Herman Tarnower was 15 lbs overweight according to his own charts. Physicians are no better than gamblers playing "statistical roulette with the lives of fat people," prescribing diet pills that affect blood pressure and kidneys, dictating diets that are subtle forms of sadism, calling for a "grim, dour self-punishment. If we submit we become miserable, if not actually neurotic."[7]

9   And then? "Then you are told that your frustrations, your worries, your inhibitions, and your insecurities turn into fat." Tranquilizers will not work; they make you fatter. You need psychological help. A woman in the 1950s was given the name of a psychiatrist because she was fat. She wrote to Dear Abby, "Now Abby, I am not *crazy*, I am just a little overweight. Have you ever heard of anything so insulting?" Abby thought a psychiatrist might do her a world of good, but Abby had no statistics to support such a claim, and there are none now. Psychiatrists are as inept with fat people as they are, still, with the schizophrenics whom they often use as a model for the obese. Perhaps because they are so inept, they demand much more of their fat patients. "Goddammit!" cried one fat woman at her psychiatrist, "You call *me* insatiable; you're the one who's never satisfied."[8]

10   Society itself will not be satisfied until all fat people are gone. Aldebaran, a member of the Los Angeles Fat Underground, wrote an open letter to a doctor in 1977: "You see fat as suicide, I see weight-loss as murder—genocide, to be precise—the systematic murder of a biological minority by organized medicine." But not just by organized medicine. By society as a whole. In the United States, a fat person's prior identification is with fatness; as a status, fatness comes

---

[6]George L. Maddox et al., "Overweight as a problem of medical management in a public outpatient clinic," *AJMS* 252 (Oct 1966) 394–402; Hilde Bruch, *The Importance of Overweight* (NY, 1957) 318–24; Howard D. Kurland, "Obesity: an unfashionable problem," *Psychiatric Opinion* 7,6 (1970) 20–24; and Alfred J. Cantor, *How to Lose Weight the Doctor's Way* (NY, 1959) quote on 40.

[7]Ruth Adams, *Did You Ever See a Fat Squirrel?* (Emmaus, Pa., 1972) 197; Tillie Lewis Tasti Diet ad in *Supermarket News* (March 29, 1976) on "Where Do Diet Food Customers Get Their Information?"; Louis Harris and Associates, *Harris Survey Yearbook* (NY, 1971) 203, 213; Diana Trilling, *Mrs. Harris: The Death of the Scarsdale Diet Doctor* (NY, 1981) 85 and cf. Peter Wyden and Barbara Wyden, *How the Doctors Diet* (NY, 1968); interview with Dr. Frederick J. Stare, Sept 27, 1984, concerning physician education in nutrition; and Martin Lederman, *The Slim Gourmet* (NY, 1955) quote on 8.

[8]Vinne Young, "Don't get ill getting thin," *Science Digest* 36 (Aug 1954) 1 (quote); Abigail van Buren (= Pauline Phillips), *Dear Abby* (Englewood Cliffs, N.J., 1958) 121; Walter W. Hamburger, "Psychology of dietary change," *AJPH* 48 (1958) 1342–48; Robert M. Lindner, *The Fifty-Minute Hour* (NY, 1955) 133 (quote); Albert J. Stunkard and A. J. Rush, "Dieting and depression reexamined," *AIM* 81 (1974) 526–33; and Colleen S. W. Rand, "Treatment of obese patients in psychoanalysis," *Psychiatric Clinics of North Amer* 1 (1978) 661–72.

before religion, race, sexual preference, income, gender. Only in a society intent on doing away with fat people could fatness become so distinct and so negative a stigma. George Nathan Blomberg, fat hero of the 1978 novel by Mark Dintenfass, *The Case Against Org,* becomes defiant in the face of such genocide: "Listen, one must choose to be obese: it is an act of courage." Near the end he knows, "There is no skinny guy inside me struggling to get out. I am Org forever." And on the last page he imagines "I and the world and a chocolate cherry all melting together, becoming one and everything."[9]

The Fat Society: A Utopia

11 If the tables could be turned, if this were a fat society, a society that admired and rewarded fatness—a society that has never existed in this country for both sexes at the same time—things would be very much different and very much better. It would be like Servia, Indiana, in 1899, "A Town of Fat People," population 206, temperate, quiet, and affluent. Or like Roseto, Pennsylvania, in the 1960s, population 1,700, nearly all of the residents obese and hardly a heart murmur among them.[10]

12 In a fat society, dinners would be scrumptious, sociable, and warm. No Mixed Gelatinoids as hors d'oeuvres, no Strained Nitrogen Gumbo for the soup, no Grilled Proteids with Globulin Patties for the entrée, no Compôte of Assorted Vitamins for dessert. There would be 101 Things To Do With Cottage Cheese—use it as a facial, take it out on a leash for a walk, build a snowman—but no one would have to eat it.[11]

13 In a fat society, children would be fed and fed well when hungry. When they were fed, they would be satisfied, because there would be no snares laid around food. Feeding would be calm and loving, always sufficient, never forced. Children as they grew into adolescence would acquire no eating disorders, since fat people and thin people would be on equal terms and there would be none of that anxious dieting which so often starts off the career of an anorectic or bulimic. No one would be obsessed with food because all people would have the opportunity to be powerful and expressive beyond the dining table.[12]

14 In a fat society, fat people would dress expressively. Their fashions would no longer be called "oversize" or "halfsize," and they would have the same choice

---

[9]Aldebaran, "Fat liberation—a luxury?" *State and Mind* 5 (June–July 1977) 34; Stuart Byron, "The unmaking of a fattie," *Village Voice* (Dec 17, 1970) 10; and Mark Dintenfass, *The Case Against Org* (Boston, 1978) 5, 189, 246, quoted with permission from Little, Brown & Co.

[10]*NYDT* (Sept 3, 1899) illus, supp. 20:3; Louderback, *Fat Power,* 167.

[11]Irvin S. Cobb, *At His Best* (Garden City, N.Y., 1929) 244 on gelatinoids, and Totie Fields, *I Think I'll Start on Monday: The Official 81/2 Oz Mashed Potato Diet* (NY, 1972) 32 on cottage cheese. On conviviality and its suppression by dieters, see James A. Pike and Howard A. Johnson, *Man in the Middle* (Greenwich, Conn., 1956) 53; Robert Waithman, "Plea to the joyless eaters," *NYT Mag* (Feb 12, 1956) 19, 62; and Jean Kerr, *Please Don't Eat the Daisies* (NY, 1957) 172.

[12]Cf. Margaret Atwood, *Lady Oracle* (NY, 1976) esp. 74, 321; Susan C. Wooley and Orland W. Wooley, "Should obesity be treated at all?" in *Eating and Its Disorders,* eds. A. J. Stunkard and E. Stellar (NY, 1984) 185–92.

of fabrics and designs as everyone else. Not just pantyhose but all clothes would be "Just my Size." Full-size models would be featured in the salons of *haute couture;* full-size fiberglass mannequins would pose with others in the most elite shop-windows. Fat people would no longer need to buy their clothes at specialty shops like The Forgotten Woman and Catherine Stout, or discreetly through the mails from Lane Bryant, Roaman's, and King-Size. A fat woman could wear dramatic colors and horizontal stripes when the fancy struck; a fat man could indulge a secret desire to wear a large-checked light gray suit.[13]

15   A fat society would be forthright about the body beneath the clothes. It would be relaxed about bodily functions, assured about sensuality, confident with sexuality. Compulsive weighing would disappear; no longer would the scale (always described as a male) lord it over anyone's body. The prudery of weight-watching, the overzealous guardianship of the body, would vanish. Beauty and sexuality would be independent of pounds and of calipers. The fat person would be a "strikingly *unavoidable* creature," and neither the fat man nor the fat woman would be typed as nonsexual or sexually corrupt. "I am touchable," fat people would say to themselves, and they would think of their pounds as "voluptuous planes." Like Sarah Fay Cohen Campbell in the novel *Fat People* (1982), they would accept their bodies as loving instruments and learn to play them in an open tuning.[14]

16   Women in particular would wear their weight with new conviction. They would affirm their physiological gifts, their genetic and cultural tendencies to put on flesh, their extra layering of body fat. Fat women would not live in the future conditional, suspended between what they are and who they will be when they are finally thin. Fat women would not have to invent fantasy selves a quarter their bulk and four times as lovely. "I've earned my wrinkles and padding," women would say with Ruthanne Olds. "They represent a lot of rewarding life experience." So everyone would at last welcome back the Earth Mother, the Venus of Willendorf, the female colossus, the grand diva, "La Stupenda," and divinity would once more be nurturant rather than vindictive.[15]

---

[13]Margaret Dana, *Behind the Label* (Boston, 1938) 117–20; Marya Mannes, "Juno in limbo: the trauma of size 16," *Harper's Mag* (July 1964) 37–40; Grosswirth, *Fat Pride,* 69; Susie Orbach, *Fat Is a Feminist Issue* (NY, 1979) 90–91; Jean DuCoffe and Sherry Suib Cohen, *Making It Big* (NY, 1980) 12, 22, 25–31; Evelyn Roaman and Dee Ratterree, *The Evelyn Roaman Book: An Expert Shows You How Heavy Can Be Happy* (NY, 1980); Dale Godey, *Your Guide to Dressing Thin* (NY, 1981) 12–27; Ann Harper and Glenn Lewis, *The Big Beauty Book* (NY, 1982) 104; and William Johnston, "The fun of being a fat man," *Amer Mag* 94 (July 1922) 54–55.

[14]Lila Austin, "I'm fat, and I like it!" *GH* III (Sept 1940) 48; Nora S. Kinzer, *Put Down and Ripped Off* (NY, 1977) 34, 49–50; Marcia Millman, *Such a Pretty Face: Being Fat in America* (NY, 1980) 106, 162–63; Harper and Lewis, *Big Beauty Book,* quote on 3; DuCoffe and Cohen, *Making It Big,* 258 (quote), 260–63; David Newman and Robert Benton, "Fat power," *Esquire* 66 (Dec 1966) 212–15 on visual grandeur of fat men; Carol S. Smith, *Fat People* (NY, 1978); and see "Fatso" film (20th-Century Fox, 1980).

[15]Charlotte C. Rowett, "Success, avoirdupois, and clothes," *Woman Beautiful* 4 (June 1910) 40–41; DuCoffe and Cohen, *Making It Big,* 334; Anne Scott Beller, *Fat and Thin* (NY, 1977) esp. ch. 7; Kim Chernin, *The Obsession: Reflections on the Tyranny of Slenderness* (NY, 1981) esp. 133, 139; Jean Stafford, "The echo and the nemesis," *Children Are Bored on Sunday* (NY, 1953) 10–39, a fantasy self; Ruthanne Olds, *Big and Beautiful: Overcoming Fat Phobia* (Washington, D.C., 1982) 13; Stella J. Reichman, *Great Big Beautiful Doll* (NY, 1977) 26–28; and Marion Woodman, *The Owl Was a Baker's Daughter* (Toronto, 1980) 10, 18.

17   A fat society would be a comforting society, less harried, more caring. It would favor the gourmet over the glutton, slow food over fast food, matriarchy and communal affection over patriarchy and self-hate, eroticism over pornography, philanthropy and art over greed and blind technology. It would mean therefore an end to narcotics and narcissism. In a fat society, there would be no "flight from feelings," no need to resort to a form of privacy that kills as it protects. No one would have such stingy personal boundaries that the self would seem always under siege. Mirrors would neither frighten nor enchant. There would be more to the person than a mercurial reflection from shopwindows. "Sizing up" a person would be a wonderfully complex experience; tape measures and scales would have nothing to do with it.[16]

18   A fat society would be less harshly competitive, less devouring. People could be assertive without seeming aggressive or threatening. There would be no cannibalism, no fear of swallowing or being swallowed up. Accepting one's own bulk, one need not consume others or gnaw at one's self. Dieting is cannibalism. Dieters eat off their own bodies: "You start to get thin when you begin to *live on your own fat.* " Dieters are encouraged to be cannibals: "If your body-republic doesn't get enough food to support all the citizens, some will die and be cannibalized to feed the others.... In this body-politic of cell-citizens, you can fool all of the people all of the time, and if you want to *get* thin and *stay* thin, that's what you must do." Dieters have no recourse but to be cannibals: "To reduce weight, an obese person must burn his own body fat. It's as simple as that. He must eat himself up! A bit cannibalistic? I'm afraid so. But it's the only way to lose weight." That legendary diet drug which was nothing but a live tapeworm was the folkloric representation of such cannibalism. In a fat society, no one would be eaten up from within and no one would be eaten alive. Fat people, weighted, solid, would not fear the desires of others or their own desires. If fat people now lie or steal or hide, that is because they are always trying to save face ("such a pretty face") and disguise their needs. They must act surreptitiously, with the night and the bathroom as their refuge. In a fat society, no one would be forced to such humiliating secrecy. All hunger would be honest hunger.[17]

Review Questions

1. What is the "vicious circle" that affects fat people and "other minorities," according to Schwartz?

2. Schwartz asserts that physicians play an important, and largely negative, role in the lives of fat people. What is this role?

---

[16]See Donald B. Meyer, *The Positive Thinkers* (Garden City, N.Y., 1965) 120 on the "flight from feelings"; Véronique Nahoum, "La belle femme ou le stade du miroir en histoire," *Communications* 31 (1979) 22–32 on mirrors; and Susan Griffin, *Pornography and Silence* (NY, 1981) esp. 60–62.

[17]Nina W. Putnam, *Tomorrow We Diet* (NY, 1922) 89; Phillip W. Haberman, Jr., "How to diet if you have no character at all," *Vogue* 135 (June 1960) 148; and Thyra S. Winslow, *Think Yourself Thin* (NY, 1951) 113. On tapeworms, Ronald L. Baker, *Hoosier Folk Legends* (Bloomington, Ind., 1982) 226, and Jane Fonda, *Workout Book* (NY, 1981) 10.

3. In the section titled "The Fat Society: A Utopia" (paragraphs 11–18), what attributes of our current culture does Schwartz link to slenderness?

4. List any three of Schwartz's especially strong assertions, what you would consider to be his "zingers"—his most highly charged, argumentative statements. Quote carefully, cite paragraph numbers, and explain in a sentence or two what makes each statement argumentative.

Discussion and Writing Suggestions

1. In his prelude to "Fat and Happy?"—the final chapter in his book *Never Satisfied*—Hillel Schwartz observes that "[r]ecently there has been a growing protest against the despotism of slenderness." In what sense can the culture of slenderness be said to be despotic?

2. To what extent does modern medical evidence contradict Schwartz's assertion that "[no] one has been able to prove that fatness *per se* cuts life short"? [See Gawande, the editorial in the *Journal of the American Medical Association,* and the Surgeon General's "Call to Action" (at <http://www.surgeongeneral.gov/topics/obesity/default.htm>.)] If medical evidence invalidates Schwartz's assertion about fatness and duration of life, does this same evidence also invalidate Schwartz's other points about being fat and happy?

3. In paragraph 10, Schwartz makes an extreme assertion, quoting a fat activist to suggest that weight-loss regimes are a species of "murder" by organized medicine and the larger society. Your response?

4. Schwartz observes that in "the United States, […] fatness comes before religion, race, sexual preference, income, [and] gender." Is Schwartz's observation accurate? Do you find yourself ordering your initial impressions of people by weight first? How might you argue against Schwartz on this point?

5. To what extent does Schwartz's "fat utopia" appeal to you? Would it, in fact, be a more enjoyable world than our currently "despotic" world of slenderness? What problems can you anticipate in Schwartz's utopia?

6. Schwartz has carefully cited evidence for many of his claims, even the seemingly extreme ones. Locate one such footnoted claim (perhaps—"a fat man could indulge a secret desire to wear a large-checked light gray suit") and then locate and read some of the cited sources. Report to your class on what you find.

7. Schwartz wrote the book *Never Satisfied,* in which this selection appears, in 1986. In the nearly two decades that have elapsed, how well does his critique of slim culture and his imagined utopia of fat culture hold up for you?

Why the Fries Taste Good
Eric Schlosser

An award-winning correspondent for the Atlantic Monthly, *Eric Schlosser offers a fascinating behind-the-scenes look at the flavoring industry—the $1.4 billion per year enterprise that prepares recipes for the "artificial" and "natural" flavors you find in the ingredients list of virtually all processed foods. By revealing how dedicated the food industry is to making its products taste so good, Schlosser provides a useful context for this chapter's readings on obesity. The producers of processed foods want us to eat; our physicians want us to lose weight. And we're caught in the middle, tugged this way by all those delicious flavors and that way by unpleasant readouts on the bathroom scale. The selection is excerpted from Schlosser's best-seller,* Fast Food Nation: The Dark Side of the All-American Meal *(Houghton Mifflin, 2001). A* New York Times *reviewer, Michiko Kakutani, writes that Schlosser's book will "make you think about the fallout that the fast food industry has had on America's social and cultural landscape: how it has affected everything from ranching and farming to diets and health, from marketing and labor practices to larger economic trends."*

1   The taste of McDonald's french fries has long been praised by customers, competitors, and even food critics. James Beard loved McDonald's fries. Their distinctive taste does not stem from the type of potatoes that McDonald's buys, the technology that processes them, or the restaurant equipment that fries them. Other chains buy their french fries from the same large processing companies, use Russet Burbanks, and have similar fryers in their restaurant kitchens. The taste of a fast food fry is largely determined by the cooking oil. For decades, McDonald's cooked its french fries in a mixture of about 7 percent cottonseed oil and 93 percent beef tallow. The mix gave the fries their unique flavor—and more saturated beef fat per ounce than a McDonald's hamburger.

2   Amid a barrage of criticism over the amount of cholesterol in their fries, McDonald's switched to pure vegetable oil in 1990. The switch presented the company with an enormous challenge: how to make fries that subtly taste like beef without cooking them in tallow. A look at the ingredients now used in the preparation of McDonald's french fries suggests how the problem was solved. At the end of the list is a seemingly innocuous, yet oddly mysterious phrase: "natural flavor." That ingredient helps to explain not only why the fries taste so good, but also why most fast food—indeed, most of the food Americans eat today—tastes the way it does.

3   Open your refrigerator, your freezer, your kitchen cupboards, and look at the labels on your food. You'll find "natural flavor" or "artificial flavor" in just about

every list of ingredients. The similarities between these two broad categories of flavor are far more significant than their differences. Both are man-made additives that give most processed food its taste. The initial purchase of a food item may be driven by its packaging or appearance, but subsequent purchases are determined mainly by its taste. About 90 percent of the money that Americans spend on food is used to buy processed food. But the canning, freezing, and dehydrating techniques used to process food destroy most of its flavor. Since the end of World War II, a vast industry has arisen in the United States to make processed food palatable. Without this flavor industry, today's fast food industry could not exist. The names of the leading American fast food chains and their best-selling menu items have become famous worldwide, embedded in our popular culture. Few people, however, can name the companies that manufacture fast food's taste.

4   The flavor industry is highly secretive. Its leading companies will not divulge the precise formulas of flavor compounds or the identities of clients. The secrecy is deemed essential for protecting the reputation of beloved brands. The fast food chains, understandably, would like the public to believe that the flavors of their food somehow originate in their restaurant kitchens, not in distant factories run by other firms.

5   The New Jersey Turnpike runs through the heart of the flavor industry, an industrial corridor dotted with refineries and chemical plants. International Flavors & Fragrances (IFF), the world's largest flavor company, has a manufacturing facility off Exit 8A in Dayton, New Jersey; Givaudan, the world's second-largest flavor company, has a plant in East Hanover. Haarmann & Reimer, the largest German flavor company, has a plant in Teterboro, as does Takasago, the largest Japanese flavor company. Flavor Dynamics has a plant in South Plainfield; Frutarom is in North Bergen; Elan Chemical is in Newark. Dozens of companies manufacture flavors in New Jersey industrial parks between Teaneck and South Brunswick. Indeed, the area produces about two-thirds of the flavor additives sold in the United States.

6   The IFF plant in Dayton is a huge pale blue building with a modern office complex attached to the front. It sits in an industrial park, not far from a BASF plastics factory, a Jolly French Toast factory, and a plant that manufactures Liz Claiborne cosmetics. Dozens of tractor-trailers were parked at the IFF loading dock the afternoon I visited, and a thin cloud of steam floated from the chimney. Before entering the plant, I signed a nondisclosure form, promising not to reveal the brand names of products that contain IFF flavors. The place reminded me of Willy Wonka's chocolate factory. Wonderful smells drifted through the hallways, men and women in neat white lab coats cheerfully went about their work, and hundreds of little glass bottles sat on laboratory tables and shelves. The bottles contained powerful but fragile flavor chemicals, shielded from light by the brown glass and the round plastic caps shut tight. The long chemical names on the little white labels were as mystifying to me as medieval Latin. They were the odd-sounding names of things that would be mixed and poured and turned into new substances, like magic potions.

7   I was not invited to see the manufacturing areas of the IFF plant, where it was thought I might discover trade secrets. Instead, I toured various laboratories

and pilot kitchens, where the flavors of well-established brands are tested or adjusted, and where whole new flavors are created. IFF's snack and savory lab is responsible for the flavor of potato chips, corn chips, breads, crackers, breakfast cereals, and pet food. The confectionery lab devises the flavor for ice cream, cookies, candies, toothpastes, mouthwashes, and antacids. Everywhere I looked, I saw famous, widely advertised products sitting on laboratory desks and tables. The beverage lab is full of brightly colored liquids in clear bottles. It comes up with the flavor for popular soft drinks, sport drinks, bottled teas, and wine coolers, for all-natural juice drinks, organic soy drinks, beers, and malt liquors. In one pilot kitchen I saw a dapper chemist, a middle-aged man with an elegant tie beneath his lab coat, carefully preparing a batch of cookies with white frosting and pink-and-white sprinkles. In another pilot kitchen I saw a pizza oven, a grill, a milk-shake machine, and a french fryer identical to those I'd seen behind the counter at countless fast food restaurants.

8   In addition to being the world's largest flavor company, IFF manufactures the smell of six of the ten best-selling fine perfumes in the United States. It makes the smell of Estée Lauder's Beautiful, Clinique's Happy, Ralph Lauren's Polo, and Calvin Klein's Eternity. It also makes the smell of household products such as deodorant, dishwashing detergent, bath soap, shampoo, furniture polish, and floor wax. All of these aromas are made through the same basic process: the manipulation of volatile chemicals to create a particular smell. The basic science behind the scent of your shaving cream is the same as that governing the flavor of your TV dinner.

9   The aroma of a food can be responsible for as much as 90 percent of its flavor. Scientists now believe that human beings acquired the sense of taste as a way to avoid being poisoned. Edible plants generally taste sweet; deadly ones, bitter. Taste is supposed to help us differentiate food that's good for us from food that's not. The taste buds on our tongues can detect the presence of half a dozen or so basic tastes, including: sweet, sour, bitter, salty, astringent, and umami (a taste discovered by Japanese researchers, a rich and full sense of deliciousness triggered by amino acids in foods such as shellfish, mushrooms, potatoes, and seaweed). Taste buds offer a relatively limited means of detection, however, compared to the human olfactory system, which can perceive thousands of different chemical aromas. Indeed "flavor" is primarily the smell of gases being released by the chemicals you've just put in your mouth.

10   The act of drinking, sucking, or chewing a substance releases its volatile gases. They flow out of the mouth and up the nostrils, or up the passageway in the back of the mouth, to a thin layer of nerve cells called the olfactory epithelium, located at the base of the nose, right between the eyes. The brain combines the complex smell signals from the epithelium with the simple taste signals from the tongue, assigns a flavor to what's in your mouth, and decides if it's something you want to eat.

11   Babies like sweet tastes and reject bitter ones; we know this because scientists have rubbed various flavors inside the mouths of infants and then recorded their facial reactions. A person's food preferences, like his or her personality, are formed during the first few years of life, through a process of socialization. Toddlers can learn to enjoy hot and spicy food, bland health food, or fast

food, depending upon what the people around them eat. The human sense of smell is still not fully understood and can be greatly affected by psychological factors and expectations. The color of a food can determine the perception of its taste. The mind filters out the overwhelming majority of chemical aromas that surround us, focusing intently on some, ignoring others. People can grow accustomed to bad smells or good smells; they stop noticing what once seemed overpowering. Aroma and memory are somehow inextricably linked. A smell can suddenly evoke a long-forgotten moment. The flavors of childhood foods seem to leave an indelible mark, and adults often return to them, without always knowing why. These "comfort foods" become a source of pleasure and reassurance, a fact that fast food chains work hard to promote. Childhood memories of Happy Meals can translate into frequent adult visits to McDonald's, like those of the chain's "heavy users," the customers who eat there four or five times a week.

12   The human craving for flavor has been a largely unacknowledged and unexamined force in history. Royal empires have been built, unexplored lands have been traversed, great religions and philosophies have been forever changed by the spice trade. In 1492 Christopher Columbus set sail to find seasoning. Today the influence of flavor in the world marketplace is no less decisive. The rise and fall of corporate empires—of soft drink companies, snack food companies, and fast food chains—is frequently determined by how their products taste.

13   The flavor industry emerged in the mid-nineteenth century, as processed foods began to be manufactured on a large scale. Recognizing the need for flavor additives, the early food processors turned to perfume companies that had years of experience working with essential oils and volatile aromas. The great perfume houses of England, France, and the Netherlands produced many of the first flavor compounds. In the early part of the twentieth century, Germany's powerful chemical industry assumed the technological lead in flavor production. Legend has it that a German scientist discovered methyl anthranilate, one of the first artificial flavors, by accident while mixing chemicals in his laboratory. Suddenly the lab was filled with the sweet smell of grapes. Methyl anthranilate later became the chief flavoring compound of grape Kool-Aid. After World War II, much of the perfume industry shifted from Europe to the United States, settling in New York City near the garment district and the fashion houses. The flavor industry came with it, subsequently moving to New Jersey to gain more plant capacity. Man-made flavor additives were used mainly in baked goods, candies, and sodas until the 1950s, when sales of processed food began to soar. The invention of gas chromatographs and mass spectrometers—machines capable of detecting volatile gases at low levels—vastly increased the number of flavors that could be synthesized. By the mid-1960s the American flavor industry was churning out compounds to supply the taste of Pop Tarts, Bac-Os, Tab, Tang, Filet-O-Fish sandwiches, and literally thousands of other new foods.

14   The American flavor industry now has annual revenues of about $1.4 billion. Approximately ten thousand new processed food products are introduced every year in the United States. Almost all of them require flavor additives. And about nine out of every ten of these new food products fail. The latest flavor innovations and corporate realignments are heralded in publications such as *Food*

Chemical News, Food Engineering, Chemical Market Reporter, and *Food Product Design.* The growth of IFF has mirrored that of the flavor industry as a whole. IFF was formed in 1958, through the merger of two small companies. Its annual revenues have grown almost fifteenfold since the early 1970s, and it now has manufacturing facilities in twenty countries.

15   The quality that people seek most of all in a food, its flavor, is usually present in a quantity too infinitesimal to be measured by any traditional culinary terms such as ounces or teaspoons. Today's sophisticated spectrometers, gas chromatographs, and headspace vapor analyzers provide a detailed map of a food's flavor components, detecting chemical aromas in amounts as low as one part per billion. The human nose, however, is still more sensitive than any machine yet invented. A nose can detect aromas present in quantities of a few parts per trillion—an amount equivalent to 0.000000000003 percent. Complex aromas, like those of coffee or roasted meat, may be composed of volatile gases from nearly a thousand different chemicals. The smell of a strawberry arises from the interaction of at least 350 different chemicals that are present in minute amounts. The chemical that provides the dominant flavor of bell pepper can be tasted in amounts as low as .02 parts per billion; one drop is sufficient to add flavor to five average size swimming pools. The flavor additive usually comes last, or second to last, in a processed food's list of ingredients (chemicals that add color are frequently used in even smaller amounts). As a result, the flavor of a processed food often costs less than its packaging. Soft drinks contain a larger proportion of flavor additives than most products. The flavor in a twelve-ounce can of Coke costs about half a cent.

16   The Food and Drug Administration does not require flavor companies to disclose the ingredients of their additives, so long as all the chemicals are considered by the agency to be GRAS (Generally Regarded As Safe). This lack of public disclosure enables the companies to maintain the secrecy of their formulas. It also hides the fact that flavor compounds sometimes contain more ingredients than the foods being given their taste. The ubiquitous phrase "artificial strawberry flavor" gives little hint of the chemical wizardry and manufacturing skill that can make a highly processed food taste like a strawberry.

17   A typical artificial strawberry flavor, like the kind found in a Burger King strawberry milk shake, contains the following ingredients: amyl acetate, amyl butyrate, amyl valerate, anethol, anisyl formate, benzyl acetate, benzyl isobutyrate, butyric acid, cinnamyl isobutyrate, cinnamyl valerate, cognac essential oil, diacetyl, dipropyl ketone, ethyl acetate, ethyl amylketone, ethyl butyrate, ethyl cinnamate, ethyl heptanoate, ethyl heptylate, ethyl lactate, ethyl methylphenylglycidate, ethyl nitrate, ethyl propionate, ethyl valerate, heliotropin, hydroxyphenyl-2-butanone (10 percent solution in alcohol), α-ionone, isobutyl anthranilate, isobutyl butyrate, lemon essential oil, maltol, 4-methylacetophenone, methyl anthranilate, methyl benzoate, methyl cinnamate, methyl heptine carbonate, methyl naphthyl ketone, methyl salicylate, mint essential oil, neroli essential oil, nerolin, neryl isobutyrate, orris butter, phenethyl alcohol, rose, rum ether, γ-undecalactone, vanillin, and solvent.

18   Although flavors usually arise from a mixture of many different volatile chemicals, a single compound often supplies the dominant aroma. Smelled alone,

that chemical provides an unmistakable sense of the food. Ethyl-2-methyl butyrate, for example, smells just like an apple. Today's highly processed foods offer a blank palette: whatever chemicals you add to them will give them specific tastes. Adding methyl-2-peridylketone makes something taste like popcorn. Adding ethyl-3-hydroxybutanoate makes it taste like marshmallow. The possibilities are now almost limitless. Without affecting the appearance or nutritional value, processed foods could even be made with aroma chemicals such as hexanal (the smell of freshly cut grass) or 3-methyl butanoic acid (the smell of body odor).

19   The 1960s were the heyday of artificial flavors. The synthetic versions of flavor compounds were not subtle, but they did not need to be, given the nature of most processed food. For the past twenty years food processors have tried hard to use only "natural flavors" in their products. According to the FDA, these must be derived entirely from natural sources—from herbs, spices, fruits, vegetables, beef, chicken, yeast, bark, roots, etc. Consumers prefer to see natural flavors on a label, out of a belief that they are healthier. The distinction between artificial and natural flavors can be somewhat arbitrary and absurd, based more on how the flavor has been made than on what it actually contains. "A natural flavor," says Terry Acree, a professor of food science technology at Cornell University, "is a flavor that's been derived with an out-of-date technology." Natural flavors and artificial flavors sometimes contain exactly the same chemicals, produced through different methods. Amyl acetate, for example, provides the dominant note of banana flavor. When you distill it from bananas with a solvent, amyl acetate is a natural flavor. When you produce it by mixing vinegar with amyl alcohol, adding sulfuric acid as a catalyst, amyl acetate is an artificial flavor. Either way it smells and tastes the same. The phrase "natural flavor" is now listed among the ingredients of everything from Stonyfield Farm Organic Strawberry Yogurt to Taco Bell Hot Taco Sauce.

20   A natural flavor is not necessarily healthier or purer than an artificial one. When almond flavor (benzaldehyde) is derived from natural sources, such as peach and apricot pits, it contains traces of hydrogen cyanide, a deadly poison. Benzaldehyde derived through a different process—by mixing oil of clove and the banana flavor, amyl acetate—does not contain any cyanide. Nevertheless, it is legally considered an artificial flavor and sells at a much lower price. Natural and artificial flavors are now manufactured at the same chemical plants, places that few people would associate with Mother Nature. Calling any of these flavors "natural" requires a flexible attitude toward the English language and a fair amount of irony.

21   The small and elite group of scientists who create most of the flavor in most of the food now consumed in the United States are called "flavorists." They draw upon a number of disciplines in their work: biology, psychology, physiology, and organic chemistry. A flavorist is a chemist with a trained nose and a poetic sensibility. Flavors are created by blending scores of different chemicals in tiny amounts, a process governed by scientific principles but demanding a fair amount of art. In an age when delicate aromas, subtle flavors, and microwave ovens do not easily coexist, the job of the flavorist is to conjure illusions about

processed food and, in the words of one flavor company's literature, to ensure "consumer likeability." The flavorists with whom I spoke were charming, cosmopolitan, and ironic. They were also discreet, in keeping with the dictates of their trade. They were the sort of scientist who not only enjoyed fine wine, but could also tell you the chemicals that gave each vintage its unique aroma. One flavorist compared his work to composing music. A well-made flavor compound will have a "top note," followed by a "dry-down," and a "leveling-off," with different chemicals responsible for each stage. The taste of a food can be radically altered by minute changes in the flavoring mix. "A little odor goes a long way," one flavorist said.

22   In order to give a processed food the proper taste, a flavorist must always consider the food's "mouthfeel"—the unique combination of textures and chemical interactions that affects how the flavor is perceived. The mouthfeel can be adjusted through the use of various fats, gums, starches, emulsifiers, and stabilizers. The aroma chemicals of a food can be precisely analyzed, but mouthfeel is much harder to measure. How does one quantify a french fry's crispness? Food technologists are now conducting basic research in rheology, a branch of physics that examines the flow and deformation of materials. A number of companies sell sophisticated devices that attempt to measure mouthfeel. The Universal TA-XT2 Texture Analyzer, produced by the Texture Technologies Corporation, performs calculations based on data derived from twenty-five separate probes. It is essentially a mechanical mouth. It gauges the most important rheological properties of a food—the bounce, creep, breaking point, density, crunchiness, chewiness, gumminess, lumpiness, rubberiness, springiness, slipperiness, smoothness, softness, wetness, juiciness, spreadability, spring-back, and tackiness.

23   Some of the most important advances in flavor manufacturing are now occurring in the field of biotechnology. Complex flavors are being made through fermentation, enzyme reactions, fungal cultures, and tissue cultures. All of the flavors being created through these methods—including the ones being synthesized by funguses—are considered natural flavors by the FDA. The new enzyme-based processes are responsible for extremely lifelike dairy flavors. One company now offers not just butter flavor, but also fresh creamy butter, cheesy butter, milky butter, savory melted butter, and super-concentrated butter flavor, in liquid or powder form. The development of new fermentation techniques, as well as new techniques for heating mixtures of sugar and amino acids, have led to the creation of much more realistic meat flavors. The McDonald's Corporation will not reveal the exact origin of the natural flavor added to its french fries. In response to inquiries from *Vegetarian Journal*, however, McDonald's did acknowledge that its fries derive some of their characteristic flavor from "animal products."

24   Other popular fast foods derive their flavor from unexpected sources. Wendy's Grilled Chicken Sandwich, for example, contains beef extracts. Burger King's BK Broiler Chicken Breast Patty contains "natural smoke flavor." A firm called Red Arrow Products Company specializes in smoke flavor, which is added to barbecue sauces and processed meats. Red Arrow manufactures natural smoke flavor by charring sawdust and capturing the aroma chemicals released into the air. The

smoke is captured in water and then bottled, so that other companies can sell food which seems to have been cooked over a fire.

25   In a meeting room at IFF, Brian Grainger let me sample some of the company's flavors. It was an unusual taste test; there wasn't any food to taste. Grainger is a senior flavorist at IFF, a soft-spoken chemist with graying hair, an English accent, and a fondness for understatement. He could easily be mistaken for a British diplomat or the owner of a West End brasserie with two Michelin stars. Like many in the flavor industry, he has an Old World, old-fashioned sensibility which seems out of step with our brand-conscious, egocentric age. When I suggested that IFF should put its own logo on the products that contain its flavors—instead of allowing other brands to enjoy the consumer loyalty and affection inspired by those flavors—Grainger politely disagreed, assuring me such a thing would never be done. In the absence of public credit or acclaim, the small and secretive fraternity of flavor chemists praises one another's work. Grainger can often tell, by analyzing the flavor formula of a product, which of his counterparts at a rival firm devised it. And he enjoys walking down supermarket aisles, looking at the many products that contain his flavors, even if no one else knows it.

26   Grainger had brought a dozen small glass bottles from the lab. After he opened each bottle, I dipped a fragrance testing filter into it. The filters were long white strips of paper designed to absorb aroma chemicals without producing off-notes. Before placing the strips of paper before my nose, I closed my eyes. Then I inhaled deeply, and one food after another was conjured from the glass bottles. I smelled fresh cherries, black olives, sautéed onions, and shrimp. Grainger's most remarkable creation took me by surprise. After closing my eyes, I suddenly smelled a grilled hamburger. The aroma was uncanny, almost miraculous. It smelled like someone in the room was flipping burgers on a hot grill. But when I opened my eyes, there was just a narrow strip of white paper and a smiling flavorist.

Review Questions

1. To what does the flavor industry owe its origins?

2. What basic tastes can the human taste buds distinguish? How does the ability to taste compare with the ability to smell?

3. Primarily, what constitutes the flavor of a food? How does our brain process the flavor of a food?

4. Where and when did the flavor industry begin? To where did it move—and why?

5. How much artificial flavor is typically required to flavor a food?

6. What are the differences between "natural" and "artificial" flavors? In what important respect are natural and artificial flavorings alike?

Discussion and Writing Suggestions

1. Schlosser writes: "The fast food chains, understandably, would like the public to believe that the flavors of their food somehow originate in their restaurant kitchens, not in distant factories run by other firms." What evidence do you find, both direct and indirect, that fast food restaurants want you to believe this? Why would they want to foster this belief?

2. In paragraph 7, Schlosser writes that one flavor manufacturer's "snack and savory lab is responsible for the flavor of potato chips, corn chips, breads, crackers, breakfast cereals, and pet food." Why would pet food be flavored?

3. In paragraph 17, Schlosser lists the chemical ingredients responsible for the taste of artificial strawberry. What was your response to reading this list?

4. Reread the description of "flavorists" and their abilities in paragraph 21. Your reactions? Does the job of flavorist appeal to you?

5. Prior to reading this article, were you at all aware of the science put to work in the service of appealing to your taste buds and sense of smell? With such sophisticated resources backing the fast food industry—creating the complex taste and "mouthfeel" of a french fry, for instance, is there any sense in which you think the flavorists and rheologists are making the individual eater's attempt to maintain a healthy weight more difficult?

6. Are you at all disappointed—amused? pleased?—to learn how the products you eat get their "natural smoke flavor?" (See paragraph 24.) More broadly, on completing this selection, do you have any sense that the processed food you eat is inauthentic? Explain.

The Man Who Couldn't Stop Eating
Atul Gawande

Atul Gawande tells the story of Vincent Caselli, who underwent a gastric bypass to lose weight by making him physically incapable of eating and absorbing the nutrients from more than an ounce of food at a sitting. Gawande, who assisted on the surgery, calls this "among the strangest operations surgeons perform" in that it "is intended to control a person's will—to manipulate his innards so that he does not overeat." Those who, like Caselli, are morbidly obese and whose weight profoundly reduces their quality of life are turning to the gastric bypass more frequently. Gawande, a surgical resident and also a staff writer for the New Yorker, *uses the story of Caselli to "contemplate the human appetite." As such, he provides a fitting and compelling end to the selections in this chapter on obesity. The essay appeared originally in the July 9, 2001 issue of the* The New Yorker. *Gawande is the author of the recently published* Complications: A Surgeon's Notes on an Imperfect Science.

1 At 7:30 A.M. on September 13, 1999, an anesthesiologist and two orderlies rolled our patient, whom I will call Vincent Caselli, into the operating room, where his attending surgeon and I awaited him. Caselli was a short man of middle age—five feet seven, fifty-four years old. The son of Italian immigrants, he had worked as a heavy-machine operator and road-construction contractor. (He and his men had paved a rotary in my own neighborhood.) He had been married for thirty-five years; he and his wife had three girls, all grown now. And he weighed four hundred and twenty-eight pounds. Housebound, his health failing, he no longer had anything resembling a normal life. And so, although he was afraid of surgery, he had come for a Roux-en-Y gastric-bypass operation. It is the most drastic treatment we have for obesity. It is also among the strangest operations surgeons perform. It removes no disease, repairs no defect or injury. It is an operation that is intended to control a person's will—to manipulate his innards so that he does not overeat—and it is soaring in popularity. Some forty-five thousand patients underwent obesity surgery in 1999, and the number is expected to double by 2003.

2 For the very obese, general anesthesia alone is a dangerous undertaking; major abdominal surgery can easily become a disaster. Obesity substantially increases the risk of respiratory failure, heart attacks, wound infections, hernias—almost every complication possible, including death. Nevertheless, Dr. Sheldon Randall, the attending surgeon, was relaxed, having done more than a thousand of these operations. I, the assisting resident, remained anxious. Watching Caselli struggle to shift himself from the stretcher onto the operating table and then stop halfway to catch his breath, I was afraid that he would fall in between. Once he was on the table, his haunches rolled off the sides, and I double-checked the padding that protected him from the table's sharp edges. He was naked except for his "universal"–size johnny, which covered him like a napkin, and a nurse put a blanket over his lower body for the sake of modesty. When we tried to lay him down, he lost his breath and started to turn blue, and the anesthesiologist had to put him to sleep sitting up. Only with the breathing tube and a mechanical ventilator in place were we able to lay him flat.

3 He was a mountain on the table. I am six feet two, but even with the table as low as it goes I had to stand on a step stool; Dr. Randall stood on two stools stacked together. He nodded to me, and I cut down the middle of our patient's belly, through skin and then dense inches of glistening yellow fat, and we opened the abdomen. Inside, his liver was streaked with fat, too, and his bowel was covered by a thick apron of it, but his stomach looked ordinary—a smooth, grayish-pink bag the size of two fists. We put metal retractors in place to hold the wound open and keep the liver and the slithering loops of bowel out of the way. Working elbow deep, we stapled his stomach down to the size of an ounce. Before the operation, it could accommodate a quart of food and drink; now it would hold no more than a shot glass. We then sewed the opening of this little pouch to a portion of bowel two feet past his duodenum—past the initial portion of the small bowel, where bile and pancreatic juices break food down. This was the bypass part of the operation, and it meant that what food the stomach could accommodate would be less readily absorbed.

4   The operation took us a little over two hours. Caselli was stable throughout, but his recovery was difficult. Patients are usually ready to go home three days after surgery; it was two days before Caselli even knew where he was. His kidneys failed for twenty-four hours, and fluid built up in his lungs. He became delirious, seeing things on the walls, pulling off his oxygen mask, his chest leads for the monitors, even yanking out the I.V. We were worried, and his wife and daughters were terrified, but gradually he pulled through.

5   By the third day after surgery, he was well enough to take sips of clear liquids (water, apple juice, ginger ale), up to one ounce every four hours. On my afternoon rounds, I asked him how he'd done. "O.K.," he said. We began giving him four-ounce servings of Carnation Instant Breakfast for protein and modest calories. He could finish only half, and that took him an hour. It filled him up and, when it did, he felt a sharp, unpleasant pain. This was to be expected, Dr. Randall told him. It would be a few days before he was ready for solid food. But he was doing well. He no longer needed I. V. fluids. And, after he'd had a short stay in a rehabilitation facility, we sent him home.

6   A couple of weeks later, I asked Dr. Randall how Caselli was getting on. "Just fine," the surgeon said. Although I had done a few of these cases with him, I had not seen how the patients progressed afterward. Would he really lose all that weight? I asked. And how much could he eat? Randall suggested that I see Caselli for myself. So one day that October, I gave him a call, and he invited me to stop by.

7   Vincent Caselli and his wife live in an unassuming saltbox house not far outside Boston. To get there, I took Route 1, past four Dunkin' Donuts, four pizzerias, three steak houses, two McDonald's, two Ground Rounds, a Taco Bell, a Friendly's, and an International House of Pancakes. (A familiar roadside vista, but that day it seemed a sad tour of our self-destructiveness.) I rang the doorbell, and a long minute passed. I heard a slow footfall coming toward the door, and Caselli, visibly winded, opened it. But he smiled broadly when he saw me and gave my hand a warm squeeze. He led me—his hand on table, wall, doorjamb for support—to a seat at a breakfast table in his flowered-wallpaper kitchen.

8   I asked him how things were going. "Real good," he said. He had no more pain from the operation, the incision had healed, and, though it had been only three weeks, he'd already lost forty pounds. But, at three hundred and ninety, and still stretching his size-64 slacks and size-XXXXXXL T-shirts (the largest he could find at the local big-and-tall store), he did not yet feel different. Sitting, he had to keep his legs apart to let his abdomen sag between them, and the weight of his body on the wooden chair forced him to shift every minute or two because his buttocks would fall asleep. Sweat rimmed the folds of his forehead and made his thin salt-and-pepper hair stick to his pate. His brown eyes were rheumy, above dark bags. He breathed with a disconcerting wheeze.

9   We talked about his arrival home from the hospital. The first solid food he had tried was a spoonful of scrambled eggs. Just that much, he said, made him so full it hurt, "like something was ripping," and he threw it up. He was afraid that nothing solid would ever go down. But he gradually found that he could tolerate small amounts of soft foods—mashed potatoes, macaroni, even chicken if it was

finely chopped and moist. Breads and dry meats, he found, got "stuck," and he'd have to put a finger down his throat and make himself vomit.

10   Caselli's battle with obesity, he explained, began in his late twenties. "I always had some weight on me," he said—he was two hundred pounds at nineteen, when he married Teresa (as I'll call her), and a decade later he reached three hundred. He would diet and lose seventy-five pounds, then put a hundred back on. By 1985, he weighed four hundred pounds. On one diet, he got down to a hundred and ninety, but he gained it all back. "I must have gained and lost a thousand pounds," he told me. He developed high blood pressure, high cholesterol, and diabetes. His knees and his back ached all the time, and he had limited mobility. He used to get season tickets to Boston Bruins games, and go out regularly to the track at Seekonk every summer to see the auto racing. Years ago, he drove in races himself. Now he could barely walk to his pickup truck. He hadn't been on an airplane since 1983, and it had been two years since he had been to the second floor of his own house, because he couldn't negotiate the stairs. "Teresa bought a computer a year ago for her office upstairs, and I've never seen it," he told me. He had to move out of their bedroom, upstairs, to a small room off the kitchen. Unable to lie down, he had slept in a recliner ever since. Even so, he could doze only in snatches, because of sleep apnea, which is a common syndrome among the obese and is thought to be related to excessive fat in the tongue and in the soft tissues of the upper airway. Every thirty minutes, his breathing would stop, and he'd wake up asphyxiating. He was perpetually exhausted.

11   There were other troubles, too, the kind that few people speak about. Good hygiene, he said, was nearly impossible. He could no longer stand up to urinate, and after moving his bowels he often had to shower in order to get clean. Skin folds would become chafed and red, and sometimes develop boils and infections. And, he reported, "Sex life is nonexistent. I have real hopes for it." For him, though, the worst part was his diminishing ability to earn a livelihood.

12   Vincent Caselli's father had come to Boston from Italy in 1914 to work in construction, and he soon established his own firm. In 1979, Vincent went into business for himself. He was skilled at operating heavy equipment—his specialty was running a Gradall, a thirty-ton, three-hundred-thousand-dollar hydraulic excavator—and he employed a team of men year-round to build roads and sidewalks. Eventually, he owned his own Gradall, a ten-wheel Mack dump truck, a backhoe, and a fleet of pickup trucks. But in the past three years he had become too big to operate the Gradall or keep up with the daily maintenance of the equipment. He had to run the business from his house, and pay others to do the heavy work; he enlisted a nephew to help manage the men and the contracts. Expenses rose, and since he could no longer go around to city halls himself, he found contracts harder to get. If Teresa hadn't had a job—she is the business manager for an assisted-living facility in Boston—they would have gone bankrupt.

13   Teresa, a freckled redhead, had been pushing him for a long time to diet and exercise. He, too, wanted desperately to lose weight, but the task of controlling himself, day to day, meal to meal, seemed beyond him. "I'm a man of habits," he told me. "I'm very prone to habits." And eating, he said, was his worst

habit. But, then, eating is everyone's habit. What was different about *his* habit? I asked. Well, the portions he took were too big, and he could never leave a crumb on his plate. If there was pasta left in the pot, he'd eat that, too. But why, I wanted to know. Was it that he just loved food? He pondered this question for a moment. It wasn't love, he decided. "Eating felt good instantaneously," he said, "but it only felt good instantaneously." Was it excessive hunger that drove him? "I was never hungry," he said.

14   As far as I could tell, Caselli ate for the same reasons that everyone eats: because food tasted good, because it was seven o'clock and time for dinner, because a nice meal had been set out on the table. And he stopped eating for the same reason everyone stops: because he was full and eating was no longer pleasurable. The main difference seemed to be that it took an unusual quantity of food to make him full. (He could eat a large pizza as if it were a canapé.) To lose weight, he faced the same difficult task that every dieter faces—to stop eating before he felt full, while the food still tasted good, and to exercise. These were things that he could do for a little while, and, with some reminding and coaching, for perhaps a bit longer, but they were not, he had found, things that he could do for long. "I am not strong," he said.

15   In the spring of 1999, Caselli developed serious infections in both legs: as his weight increased, and varicosities appeared, the skin thinned and broke down, producing open, purulent ulcers. Despite fevers and searing pain, it was only after persistent coaxing from his wife that he finally agreed to see his doctor. The doctor diagnosed a serious case of cellulitis, and he spent a week in the hospital receiving intravenous antibiotics.

16   At the hospital, he was given an ultrasound scan to check whether blood clots had formed in the deep veins of his legs. A radiologist came to give him the results. Caselli recounted the conversation to me. "He says, 'You don't have blood clots, and I'm really surprised. A guy like you, in the situation you're in, the odds are you're gonna have blood clots. That tells me you're a pretty healthy guy'"—but only, he went on, if Caselli did something about his weight. A little later, the infectious-disease specialist came by to inspect his wounds. "I'm going to tell you something," Caselli recalls the man saying. "I've been reading your whole file—where you were, what you were, how you were. You take that weight off— and I'm not telling you this to bust your ass—you take that weight off and you're a very healthy guy. Your heart is good. Your lungs are good. You're strong."

17   "I took that seriously," Caselli said. "You know, there are two different doctors telling me this. They don't know me other than what they're reading from their records. They had no reason to tell me this. But they knew the weight was a problem. And if I could get it down somewhere near reality…"

18   When he got home, he remained sick in bed for another two weeks. Meanwhile, his business collapsed. Contracts stopped coming in entirely, and he knew that when his men finished the existing jobs he would have to let them go. Months before, his internist had suggested that he consider surgery and he had dismissed the notion. But he didn't now. He went to see Dr. Randall, who spoke with him frankly about the risks involved. There was a one-in-two-hundred chance of death and a one-in-ten chance of a significant complication, such as bleeding, infection, gastric ulceration, blood clots, or leakage

into the abdomen. The doctor also told him that it would change how he ate forever. Unable to work, humiliated, ill, and in pain, Vincent Caselli decided that surgery was his only hope.

19   It is hard to contemplate the human appetite without wondering if we have any say over our lives at all. We believe in will—in the notion that we have a choice over such simple matters as whether to sit still or stand up, to talk or not talk, to have a slice of pie or not. Yet very few people, whether heavy or slim, can voluntarily reduce their weight for long. The history of weight-loss treatment is one of nearly unremitting failure. Whatever the regimen—liquid diets, high-protein diets, or grapefruit diets, the Zone, Atkins, or Dean Ornish diet—people lose weight quite readily, but they do not keep it off. A 1993 National Institutes of Health expert panel reviewed decades of diet studies and found that between ninety and ninety-five per cent of people regained one-third to two-thirds of any weight lost within a year—and all of it within five years. Doctors have wired patients' jaws closed, inflated plastic balloons inside their stomachs, performed massive excisions of body fat, prescribed amphetamines and large amounts of thyroid hormone, even performed neurosurgery to destroy the hunger centers in the brain's hypothalamus—and still people do not keep the weight off. Jaw wiring, for example, can produce substantial weight loss, and patients who ask for the procedure are highly motivated; yet some still take in enough liquid calories through their closed jaws to gain weight, and the others regain it once the wires are removed. We are a species that has evolved to survive starvation, not to resist abundance.

20   Children are the surprising exception to this history of failure. Nobody would argue that children have more self-control than adults; yet in four randomized studies of obese children between the ages of six and twelve, those who received simple behavioral teaching (weekly lessons for eight to twelve weeks, followed by monthly meetings for up to a year) ended up markedly less over-weight ten years later than those who didn't; thirty percent were no longer obese. Apparently, children's appetites are malleable. Those of adults are not.

21   There are at least two ways that humans can eat more than they ought to at a sitting. One is by eating slowly but steadily for far too long. This is what people with Prader-Willi syndrome do. Afflicted with a rare inherited dysfunction of the hypothalamus, they are incapable of experiencing satiety. And though they eat only half as quickly as most people, they do not stop. Unless their access to food is strictly controlled (some will eat garbage or pet food if they find nothing else), they become mortally obese.

22   The more common pattern, however, relies on rapid intake. Human beings are subject to what scientists call a "fat paradox." When food enters your stomach and duodenum (the upper portion of the small intestine), it triggers stretch receptors, protein receptors, and fat receptors that signal the hypothalamus to induce satiety. Nothing stimulates the reaction more quickly than fat. Even a small amount, once it reaches the duodenum, will cause a person to stop eating. Still we eat too much fat. How can this be? It turns out that foods can trigger receptors in the mouth which get the hypothalamus to *accelerate* our intake—and, again, the most potent stimulant is fat. A little bit on the tongue, and the receptors push us to eat fast, before the gut signals

shut us down. The tastier the food, the faster we eat—a phenomenon called "the appetizer effect." (This is accomplished, in case you were wondering, not by chewing faster but by chewing less. French researchers have discovered that, in order to eat more and eat it faster, people shorten their "chewing time"—they take fewer "chews per standard food unit" before swallowing. In other words, we gulp.)

23   Apparently, how heavy one becomes is determined, in part, by how the hypothalamus and the brain stem adjudicate the conflicting signals from the mouth and the gut. Some people feel full quite early in a meal; others, like Vincent Caselli, experience the appetizer effect for much longer. In the past several years, much has been discovered about the mechanisms of this control. We now know, for instance, that hormones, like leptin and neuropepide Y, rise and fall with fat levels and adjust the appetite accordingly. But our knowledge of these mechanisms is still crude at best.

24   Consider a 1998 report concerning two men, "BR" and "RH," who suffered from profound amnesia. Like the protagonist in the movie *Memento,* they could carry on a coherent conversation with you, but, once they had been distracted, they recalled nothing from as recently as a minute before, not even that they were talking to you. (BR had had a bout of viral encephalitis; RH had had a severe seizure disorder for twenty years.) Paul Rozin, a professor of psychology at the University of Pennsylvania, thought of using them in an experiment that would explore the relationship between memory and eating. On three consecutive days, he and his team brought each subject his typical lunch (BR got meat loaf, barley soup, tomatoes, potatoes, beans, bread, butter, peaches, and tea; RH got veal parmigiana with pasta, string beans, juice, and apple crumb cake). Each day, BR at all his lunch, and RH could not quite finish. Their plates were then taken away. Ten to thirty minutes later, the researchers would reappear with the same meal. "Here's lunch," they would announce. The men ate just as much as before. Another ten to thirty minutes later, the researchers again appeared with the same meal. "Here's lunch," they would say, and again the men would eat. On a couple of occasions, the researchers even offered RH a fourth lunch. Only then did he decline, saying that his "stomach was a little tight." Stomach stretch receptors weren't completely ineffectual. Yet, in the absence of a memory of having eaten, social context alone—someone walking in with lunch—was enough to re-create appetite.

25   You can imagine forces in the brain vying to make you feel hungry or full. You have mouth receptors, smell receptors, visions of tiramisu pushing one way and gut receptors another. You have leptins and neuropeptides saying you have either too much fat stored or too little. And you have your own social and personal sense of whether eating more is a good idea. If one mechanism is thrown out of whack, there's trouble.

26   Given the complexity of appetite and our imperfect understanding of it, we shouldn't be surprised that appetite-altering drugs have had only meagre success in making people eat less. (The drug combination of fenfluramine and phentermine, or "fen-phen," had the most success, but it was linked to heart-valve abnormalities and was withdrawn from the market.) University researchers and pharmaceutical companies are searching intensively for a drug that will

effectively treat serious obesity. So far, no such drug exists. Nonetheless, one treatment has been found to be effective, and, oddly enough, it turns out to be an operation.

27   At my hospital, there is a recovery-room nurse who is forty-eight years old and just over five feet tall, with boyish sandy hair and an almost athletic physique. Over coffee one day at the hospital café, not long after my visit with Vincent Caselli, she revealed that she once weighed more than two hundred and fifty pounds. Carla (as I'll call her) explained that she had had gastric-bypass surgery some fifteen years ago.

28   She had been obese since she was five years old. She started going on diets and taking diet pills—laxatives, diuretics, amphetamines—in junior high school. "It was never a problem losing weight," she said. "It was a problem keeping it off." She remembers how upset she was when, on a trip with friends to Disneyland, she found that she couldn't fit through the entrance turnstile. At the age of thirty-three, she reached two hundred and sixty-five pounds. One day, accompanying her partner, a physician, to a New Orleans medical convention, she found that she was too short of breath to walk down Bourbon Street. For the first time, she said, "I became fearful for my life—not just the quality of it but the longevity of it."

29   This was 1985. Doctors were experimenting with radical obesity surgery, but there was dwindling enthusiasm for it. Two operations had held considerable promise. One, known as jejunoileal bypass—in which nearly all the small intestine was bypassed, so that only a minimum amount of food could be absorbed—was killing people. The other, stomach stapling, was proving not to be very effective over time; people tended to adapt to the tiny stomach, eating densely caloric foods more and more frequently.

30   Working in the hospital, however, Carla heard encouraging reports about the gastric-bypass operation—stomach stapling plus a rerouting of the intestine so that food bypassed only the duodenum. She knew that the data about its success was still sketchy, that other operations had failed, but in May of 1986, after a year of thinking about it, she had the surgery.

31   "For the first time in my life, I experienced fullness," she told me. Six months after the operation, she was down to a hundred and eighty-five pounds. Six months after that, she weighed a hundred and thirty pounds. She lost so much weight that she had to have surgery to remove the aprons of skin that hung from her belly and thighs down to her knees. She was unrecognizable to anyone who had known her before, and even to herself. "I went to bars to see if I could get picked up—and I did," she said. "I always said no," she quickly added, laughing. "But I did it anyway."

32   The changes weren't just physical, though. She said she felt a profound and unfamiliar sense of will power. She no longer *had* to eat anything: "Whenever I eat, somewhere in the course of that time I end up asking myself, 'Is this good for you? Are you going to put on weight if you eat too much of this?' And I can just stop." She knew, intellectually, that the surgery was why she no longer ate as much as she used to. Yet she felt as if she were choosing not to do it.

33   Studies report this to be a typical experience of a successful gastric-bypass patient. "I do get hungry, but I tend to think about it more," another woman who

had had the operation told me, and she described an internal dialogue very much like Carla's: "I ask myself, 'Do I really need this?' I watch myself." For many, this feeling of control extends beyond eating. They become more confident, even assertive—sometimes to the point of conflict. Divorce rates, for example, have been found to increase significantly after the surgery. Indeed, a few months after her operation, Carla and her partner broke up.

34   Carla's dramatic weight loss has proved to be no aberration. Published case series now show that most patients undergoing gastric bypass lose at least two-thirds of their excess weight (generally more than a hundred pounds) within a year. They keep it off, too: ten-year follow-up studies find an average regain of only ten to twenty pounds. And the health benefits are striking: patients are less likely to have heart failure, asthma, or arthritis; eighty percent of those with diabetes are completely cured of it.

35   I stopped in to see Vincent Caselli one morning in January of 2000, about four months after his operation. He didn't quite spring to the door, but he wasn't winded this time. The bags under his eyes had shrunk. His face was more defined. Although his midriff was vast, it seemed smaller, less of a sack.

36   He told me that he weighed three hundred and forty-eight pounds—still far too much for a man who was only five feet seven inches tall, but ninety pounds less than he weighed on the operating table. And it had already made a difference in his life. Back in October, he told me, he missed his youngest daughter's wedding because he couldn't manage the walking required to get to the church. But by December he had lost enough weight to resume going to his East Dedham garage every morning. "Yesterday, I unloaded three tires off the truck," he said. "For me to do that three months ago? There's no way." He had climbed the stairs of his house for the first time since 1997. "One day around Christmastime, I say to myself, 'Let me try this. I gotta try this.' I went very slow, one foot at a time." The second floor was nearly unrecognizable to him. The bathroom had been renovated since he last saw it, and Teresa had, naturally, taken over the bedroom, including the closets. He would move back up eventually, he said, though it might be a while. He still had to sleep sitting up in a recliner, but he was sleeping in four-hour stretches now—"Thank God," he said. His diabetes was gone. And although he was still unable to stand up longer than twenty minutes, his leg ulcers were gone, too. He lifted his pants legs to show me. I noticed that he was wearing regular Red Wing work boots—in the past, he had to cut slits along the sides of his shoes in order to fit into them.

37   "I've got to lose at least another hundred pounds," he said. He wanted to be able to work, pick up his grandchildren, buy clothes off the rack at Filenes, go places without having to ask himself, "Are there stairs? Will I fit in the seats? Will I run out of breath?" He was still eating like a bird. The previous day, he'd had nothing all morning, a morsel of chicken with some cooked carrots and a small roast potato for lunch, and for dinner one fried shrimp, one teriyaki chicken strip, and two forkfuls of chicken-and-vegetable lo mein from a Chinese restaurant. He was starting up the business again, and, he told me, he'd gone out for a business lunch one day recently. It was at a new restaurant in Hyde Park—"beautiful"—and he couldn't help ordering a giant burger and a plate of fries. Just two bites into the burger, though, he had to stop. "One of the fellas says to me,

'Is that all you're going to eat?' And I say, 'I can't eat any more.' 'Really?' I say, 'Yeah, I can't eat any more. That's the truth.'"

38   I noticed, however, that the way he spoke about eating was not the way Carla had spoken. He did not speak of stopping because he wanted to. He spoke of stopping because he had to. You want to eat more, he explained, but "you start to get that feeling in your insides that one more bite is going to push you over the top." Still, he often took that bite. Overcome by waves of nausea, pain, and bloating—the so-called dumping syndrome—he'd have to vomit. If there were a way to eat more, he would. This scared him, he admitted. "It's not right," he said.

39   Three months later, in April, Caselli invited me and my son to stop by his garage in East Dedham. My son was four years old and, as Vince remembered my once saying, fascinated with all things mechanical. The garage was huge, cavernous, with a two-story rollup door and metal walls painted yellow. There, in the shadows, was Vince's beloved Gradall, a handsome tank of a machine, as wide as a county road, painted yield-sign yellow, with shiny black tires that came up to my chest and his company name emblazoned in curlicue script along its flanks. On the chassis, six feet off the ground, was a glass-enclosed control cab and a thirty-foot telescoping boom, mounted on a three-hundred-and-sixty-degree swivel. Vince and a friend of his, a fellow heavy-equipment contractor I'll call Danny, were sitting on metal folding chairs in a sliver of sunlight, puffing fat Honduran cigars, silently enjoying the day. They both rose to greet us. Vince introduced me as "one of the doctors who did my stomach operation."

40   I let my son go off to explore the equipment and asked Vince how his business was going. Not well, he said. Except for a few jobs in late winter plowing snow for the city in his pickup truck, he had brought in no income since the previous August. He'd had to sell two of his three pickup trucks, his Mack dump truck, and most of the small equipment for road building. Danny came to his defense. "Well, he's been out of action," he said. "And you see we're just coming into the summer season. It's a seasonal business." But we all knew that wasn't the issue.

41   Vince told me that he weighed about three hundred and twenty pounds. This was about thirty pounds less than when I had last seen him, and he was proud of that. "He don't eat," Danny said. "He eats half of what I eat." But Vince was still unable to climb up into the Gradall and operate it. And he was beginning to wonder whether that would ever change. The rate of weight loss was slowing down, and he noticed that he was able to eat more. Before, he could eat only a couple of bites of a burger, but now he could sometimes eat half of one. And he still found himself eating more than he could handle. "Last week, Danny and this other fellow, we had to do some business," he said. "We had Chinese food. Lots of days, I don't eat the right stuff—I try to do what I can do, but I ate a little bit too much. I had to bring Danny back to Boston College, and before I left the parking lot there I just couldn't take it anymore. I had to vomit.

42   "I'm finding that I'm getting back into that pattern where I've always got to eat," he went on. His gut still stopped him, but he was worried. What if one day it didn't? He had heard about people whose staples gave way, returning their stomach to its original size, or who managed to put the weight back on in some other way.

43   I tried to reassure him. I told him what I knew Dr. Randall had already told him during a recent appointment: that a small increase in the capacity of his stomach pouch was to be expected, and that what he was experiencing seemed normal. But could something worse happen? I didn't want to say.

44   Among the gastric-bypass patients I had talked with was a man whose story remains a warning and a mystery to me. He was forty-two years old, married, and had two daughters, both of whom were single mothers with babies and still lived at home, and he had been the senior computer-systems manager for a large local company. At the age of thirty-eight, he had had to retire and go on disability because his weight—which had been above three hundred pounds since high school—had increased to more than four hundred and fifty pounds and was causing unmanageable back pain. He was soon confined to his home. He could not walk half a block. He could stand for only brief periods. He went out, on average, once a week, usually for medical appointments. In December, 1998, he had a gastric bypass. By June of the following year, he had lost a hundred pounds.

45   Then, as he put it, "I started eating again." Pizzas. Boxes of sugar cookies. Packages of doughnuts. He found it hard to say how, exactly. His stomach was still tiny and admitted only a small amount of food at a time, and he experienced the severe nausea and pain that gastric-bypass patients get whenever they eat sweet or rich things. Yet his drive was stronger than ever. "I'd eat right through pain—even to the point of throwing up," he told me. "If I threw up, it was just room for more. I would eat straight through the day." He did not pass a waking hour without eating something. "I'd just shut the bedroom door. The kids would be screaming. The babes would be crying. My wife would be at work. And I would be eating." His weight returned to four hundred and fifty pounds, and then more. The surgery had failed. And his life had been shrunk to the needs of pure appetite.

46   He is among the five to twenty percent of patients—the published reports conflict on the exact number—who regain weight despite gastric-bypass surgery. (When we spoke, he had recently submitted to another, more radical gastric bypass, in the desperate hope that something would work.) In these failures, one begins to grasp the power that one is up against. An operation that makes overeating both extremely difficult and extremely unpleasant—which, for more than eighty percent of patients, is finally sufficient to cause appetite to surrender and be transformed—can sometimes be defeated after all. Studies have yet to uncover a single consistent risk factor for this outcome. It could, apparently, happen to anyone.

47   It was a long time before I saw Vince Caselli again. Earlier this year, I called him to ask about getting together, and he suggested that we go out to see a Boston Bruins game. A few days later, he picked me up at the hospital in his rumbling Dodge Ram. For the first time, he looked almost small in the out-sized truck. He was down to about two hundred and fifty pounds. "I'm still no Gregory Peck," he said, but he was now one of the crowd—chubby, in an ordinary way. The rolls beneath his chin were gone. His face had a shape. His middle no longer rested between his legs. And, almost a year and a half after the surgery, he was still losing weight. At the FleetCenter, where the Bruins play, he walked

up the escalator without getting winded. Our tickets were taken at the gate—the Bruins were playing the Pittsburgh Penguins—and we walked through the turnstiles. Suddenly, he stopped and said, "Look at that. I went right through, no problem. I never would have made it through there before." It was the first time he'd gone to an event like this in years.

48   We took our seats about two dozen rows up from the ice, and he laughed a little about how easily he fit. The seats were as tight as coach class, but he was quite comfortable. (I, with my long legs, was the one who had trouble finding room.) Vince was right at home here. He had been a hockey fan his whole life, and could supply me with all the details: the Penguins' goalie Garth Snow was a local boy from Wrentham and a friend of one of Vince's cousins; Joe Thornton and Jason Allison were the Bruins' best forwards, but neither could hold a candle to the Penguins' Mario Lemieux. There were nearly twenty thousand people at the game, but within ten minutes Vince had found a friend from his barbershop sitting just a few rows away.

49   The Bruins won, and we left cheered and buzzing. Afterward, we went out to dinner at a grill near the hospital. Vince told me that his business was finally up and running. He could operate the Gradall without difficulty, and he'd had full-time Gradall work for the past three months. He was even thinking of buying a new model. At home, he had moved back upstairs. He and Teresa had taken a vacation in the Adirondacks; they were going out evenings, and visiting their grandchildren.

50   I asked him what had changed since I saw him the previous spring. He could not say precisely, but he gave me an example. "I used to love Italian cookies, and I still do," he said. A year ago, he would have eaten to the point of nausea. "But now they're, I don't know, they're too sweet. I eat one now, and after one or two bites I just don't want it." It was the same with pasta, which had always been a problem for him. "Now I can have a bite and I'm satisfied."

51   Partly, it appeared that his taste in food had changed. He pointed to the nachos and buffalo wings and hamburgers on the menu, and said that, to his surprise, he no longer felt like eating any of them. "It seems like I lean toward protein and vegetables nowadays," he said, and he ordered a chicken Caesar salad. But he also no longer felt the need to stuff himself. "I used to be real reluctant to push food away," he told me. "Now it's just—it's different." But when did this happen? And how? He shook his head. "I wish I could pinpoint it for you," he said. He paused to consider. "As a human, you adjust to conditions. You don't think you are. But you are."

52   These days, it isn't the failure of obesity surgery that is prompting concerns but its success. Physicians have gone from scorning it to encouraging, sometimes imploring, their most severely overweight patients to undergo a gastric-bypass operation. That's not a small group. More than five million adult Americans meet the strict definition of morbid obesity. (Their "body mass index"—that is, their weight in kilograms divided by the square of their height in metres—is forty or more, which for an average man is roughly a hundred pounds or more overweight.) Ten million more weigh just under the mark but may nevertheless have obesity-related health problems that are serious enough to warrant the surgery. There are ten times as many candidates for obesity

surgery right now as there are for heart-bypass surgery in a year. So many patients are seeking the procedure that established surgeons cannot keep up. The American Society of Bariatric Surgery has only five hundred members nationwide who perform gastric-bypass operations, and their waiting lists are typically months long. Hence the too familiar troubles associated with new and lucrative surgical techniques (the fee can be as much as twenty thousand dollars): newcomers are stampeding to the field, including many who have proper training but have not yet mastered the procedure, and others who have no training at all. Complicating matters further, individual surgeons are promoting a slew of variations on the standard operation which haven't been fully researched—the "duodenal switch," the "long limb" bypass, the laparoscopic bypass. And a few surgeons are pursuing new populations, such as adolescents and people who are only moderately obese.

53   Perhaps what's most unsettling about the soaring popularity of gastric-bypass surgery, however, is simply the world that surrounds it. Ours is a culture in which fatness is seen as tantamount to failure, and get-thin-quick promises—whatever the risks—can have an irresistible allure. Doctors may recommend the operation out of concern for their patients' health, but the stigma of obesity is clearly what drives many patients to the operating room. "How can you let yourself look like that?" is society's sneering, unspoken question, and often its spoken one as well. Women suffer even more than men from the social sanction, and it's no accident that seven times as many women as men have had the operation. (Women are only an eighth more likely to be obese.)

54   Indeed, deciding *not* to undergo the surgery, if you qualify, is at risk of being considered the unreasonable thing to do. A three-hundred-and-fifty-pound woman who did not want the operation told me of doctors browbeating her for her choice. And I have learned of at least one patient with heart disease being refused treatment by a doctor unless she had a gastric bypass. If you don't have the surgery, you will die, some doctors tell their patients. But we actually do not know this. Despite the striking improvements in weight and health, studies have not yet proved a corresponding reduction in mortality.

55   There are legitimate grounds for being wary of the procedure. As Paul Ernsberger, an obesity researcher at Case Western Reserve University, pointed out to me, many patients undergoing gastric bypass are in their twenties and thirties. "But is this really going to be effective and worthwhile over a forty-year span?" he asked. "No one can say." He was concerned about the possible long-term effects of nutritional deficiencies (for which patients are instructed to take a daily multivitamin). And he was concerned about evidence from rats that raises the possibility of an increased risk of bowel cancer.

56   We want progress in medicine to be clear and unequivocal, but of course it rarely is. Every new treatment has gaping unknowns—for both patients and society—and it can be hard to decide what to do about them. Perhaps a simpler, less radical operation will prove effective for obesity. Perhaps the long-sought satiety pill will be found. Nevertheless, the gastric bypass is the one thing we have now that works. Not all the questions have been answered, but there are more than a decade of studies behind it. And so we forge ahead. Hospitals everywhere are constructing obesity-surgery centers, ordering reinforced

operating tables, training surgeons and staff. At the same time, everyone expects that, one day, something new and better will be discovered that will make what we're now doing obsolete.

57   Across from me, in our booth at the grill, Vince Caselli pushed his chicken Caesar salad aside only half eaten. "No taste for it," he said, and he told me he was grateful for that. The operation, he said, had given him his life back. But, after one more round of drinks, it was clear that he still felt uneasy.

58   "I had a serious problem and I had to take serious measures," he said. "I think I had the best technology that is available at this point. But I do get concerned: Is this going to last my whole life? Someday, am I going to be right back to square one—or worse?" He fell silent for a moment, gazing into his glass. "Well, that's the cards that God gave me. I can't worry about stuff I can't control."

Review Questions

1. "The Man Who Couldn't Stop Eating" is a long article, which the author has broken into unlabeled sections. Identify these sections—and label them.

2. What made Vince Caselli a candidate for stomach bypass surgery?

3. What does the research show on the success of weight loss among adults? among children?

4. Identify some of the ways that people can overeat.

5. What are some of the conflicting body signals regarding appetite that make the scientific understanding of obesity so complex and difficult to understand?

6. What are the positive and negative effects of the surgery?

7. Why is the stomach-bypass surgery beginning to concern physicians?

Discussion and Writing Suggestions

1. How would you describe Gawande's attitude toward gastric-bypass surgery? toward obesity itself?

2. What evidence can you find—for instance, in the tone of his writing, in the questions that he poses, or in his choice of subject matter—that Gawande is a physician?

3. In paragraph 7, Gawande writes that on his way to Vince Caselli's house he passes several fast food restaurants. What effect does this paragraph have on you? Why do you think he includes it in the essay?

4. Discuss Gawande's use of Vincent Caselli's story as a structural backbone to this essay. Citing examples, show how Gawande builds the essay by retelling, and playing off, Vince's story. (Note that the essay is not about Vince Caselli, per se, but about obesity, obesity surgery, and the place of obesity in the larger culture.)

5. In paragraph 19, Gawande writes: "It is hard to contemplate the human appetite without wondering if we have any say over our lives at all." What does Gawande mean by this? What is your reaction to the statement?

6. Given the increasing incidence of obesity in America, how reasonable a solution do you think gastric-bypass surgery is? As a society, how much emphasis should we be placing on treating obesity, as opposed to preventing it?

SYNTHESIS ACTIVITIES

1. In the opening of "Fat and Happy?" Hillel Schwartz remarks that fat people are unhappy largely due to the pressures that the larger culture places on them to go on diets that inevitably fail. Worley makes a similar point about the futility of dieting. And medical specialists (see Gawande and also Koplan and Dietz, the authors of the editorial in the *Journal of the American Medical Association*) observe that most dieters are doomed to regain the weight they lose. Given such overwhelming agreement on the prospects for successful dieting, what, then, is an overweight or obese person to do? Drawing on the selections in this chapter, write an argument synthesis structured in a problem-solution format. Use your sources to define the problem: the apparent fact that diets don't work, and that we're facing a marked increase in overweight and obese people who need to lose weight. Use the remainder of your essay to formulate a sensible response to this problem.

2. For cultural reasons (see Seid, Schwartz, and Worley), women and men may feel the need to lose weight. But the scientific reality is that many should lose weight to maintain good health (see the CDC tables, Gawande, Gibbs, and the *JAMA*). Compare and contrast the argument that being overweight or obese is a socially constructed problem with the argument that excess weight is a medical condition. Recall that your comparison and contrast should lead to a central claim. That claim, your thesis, will help you to organize the synthesis.

3. Drawing primarily on the selections by Seid, Schwartz, and Worley, write an explanatory synthesis that presents the ways in which fat people are made to feel inadequate by the culture at large.

4. If, as several of the authors in this chapter report, diets are ineffective for the great majority of dieters, then one could conclude that dieters themselves are not to blame for their failure to lose weight. If there is no one to blame, if we can't point an accusing finger to a dieter's lack of willpower, how should we think about the problems of being overweight and obese? What evidence do you see, if any, that we as a culture are prepared to approach problems *without* laying blame? In preparing an argument synthesis that responds to this question, reread the selections by Gibbs, Worley, Crister, Seid (especially paragraph 13), Schwartz, and Schlosser. Focus your reading on discussions of blame-making—of who takes or should take responsibility for the problems of being overweight or obese. What patterns emerge that you can discuss in your synthesis?

5. Hillel Schwartz writes that our culture promotes a "despotism of slenderness." First, do you agree that the ideal body type in our culture is slender? Second, do you agree that this slender ideal is despotic? Despotism requires a despot, does it not? Who—or what—in this case is the despot? Drawing on the selections by Schwartz and others in this chapter, write a synthesis that argues for or against a cultural "despotism of slenderness." In making your case, you might refer to sources outside this chapter—for instance, to the worlds of advertising, fashion, weight-loss products, and fast food.

6. In a synthesis that draws upon your own experiences or those of someone you know, explain the challenges of trying to maintain your weight in a culture that does not readily forgive being overweight or obese. In your synthesis, refer to the selections in this chapter that discuss the cultural pressures of being fat—including Seid, Schwartz, Crister, and Worley.

7. Prior to reading Eric Schlosser's, "Why the Fries Taste Good," were you at all aware of the science put to work in the service of appealing to your taste buds and sense of smell? With such sophisticated resources backing the fast food industry—creating the complex taste and "mouthfeel" of a french fry, for instance, is there any sense in which you think the fast food industry is making the individual eater's attempt to maintain a healthy weight especially difficult? More broadly, observe the tug-of-war taking place over the American consumer of food: on the one hand, the food industry is helping scientists to create delectable products that scream "Eat Me!" while on the other fashion houses, magazines, and various (powerful) forces that Seid and others identify scream "Be Skinny!" In an explanatory synthesis that draws on the selections in this chapter, discuss this tug-of-war. Who is being fought over? What are the forces arrayed on each side of the fight? Who is winning? (To answer this last question, you can draw on the tables from the

Centers for Disease Control, the editorial by Koplan and Dietz, and the article by Gibbs.)

8. Compare and contrast Greg Crister's belief that bad eating behaviors should be stigmatized with Worley's realization that she should accept being fat and forge "a new relationship" with her body.

9. How extreme do you find the gastric-bypass surgery described by Gawande? Do you understand why morbidly obese people would elect to undergo the operation? Do you understand why "moderately obese" people would do so? Write a synthesis in which you discuss the various cultural pressures to be thin (see Seid and Schwartz) and the various remedies available to achieve this goal—including dieting, exercise, and surgery (see Gibbs, Koplan and Dietz, and Gawande). You will write an explanatory synthesis if you have no strongly held views on the topic. You will write an argument synthesis if you do. Either way, your synthesis should be governed by a carefully constructed thesis.

10. The medical community is now calling for a War on Fat, reminiscent of the War on Tobacco. Adopting strategies for anti-smoking campaigns, activists have considered suing food companies for creating unhealthy, "addictive" products. They have also discussed taxing junk food both to make it less affordable and to create funds for combating obesity. Compare and contrast these two "wars." Draw on readings in this chapter to develop your essay. At some point in your writing, you may want to consider the roles of individual choice and willpower in eating and in smoking.

RESEARCH ACTIVITIES

1. Research the debate surrounding the creation of the U.S. government's "Food Pyramid." You will readily be able to locate official government publications online that describe the pyramid. Locate articles in the library and online describing the disagreements and compromises involved in designing the pyramid. You may want to consult Walter C. Willett's *Eat, Drink, and Be Healthy* (Simon & Schuster, 2001) for a critique of the pyramid on nutritional grounds.

2. In the *Scientific American* article appearing in this chapter, W. Wayt Gibbs concludes that pharmaceutical research may hold out the best hope for addressing the problems of obesity. Conduct research into the history of and present state-of-the-art regarding diet pills. When were they introduced? To date, how effective have they been? You may want to reserve special attention for the recent "fen-phen" diet pill scare, in which a potent combination of appetite suppressants was found to cause heart-valve problems.

3. Conduct research into the "BMI," or Body Mass Index, which you can find on p. 446, and which is mentioned prominently in the *Journal of the American Medical Association* editorial by Koplan and Dietz. In your report, answer these basic questions: Why and when was the index developed? By whom? What did it replace? What medical assumptions underlie the index? How has it been used, and how is it being used today?

4. Hillel Schwartz' article contains extensive footnotes. Review the entries in his list and select several to track down and read, according to your interests. Based on your findings, devise a research question and conduct additional research. Write a paper in which you present your results.

5. Roberta Seid observes that the modern conception of being overweight and obese came into being at an identifiable historical moment—her point being that ideal body types have changed over time and that we live in a time in which the ideal is "close to the bone." Write a research paper that presents an explanatory overview of the changing conceptions of the ideal body type, from ancient times through to the present. You can take Seid's article as your starting point. As a next step, you might move outward from her footnotes. You may want to consult Peter Stearns's *Fat History* (New York University Press, 1997).

6. Select one of the commercially successful dieting programs. Collect the company's literature and then conduct an inquiry, over the Internet and in the library, on the effectiveness of that program. Locate, if you can, any complaints—you can try the local Better Business Bureau, and prepare a final report in which you assess the program's credibility.

7. Research the prevalence of obesity in other countries or cultures. For instance, you might research obesity among the French, whom Greg Crister says are known for their "legendary leanness." Or you might investigate the Pima Indians or inhabitants of Nauru (see the selection by W. Wayt Gibbs). Consider beginning your research with an article that appeared in the Boston *Globe* on February 26, 2002: "Developing Nations Taking on West's Flabby Look," by Stephen Smith. (You can access the *Globe*'s archives at <http://www.globe.com>.)

8. Research the various elective surgical techniques for managing weight, including liposuction and the gastric-bypass described by Gawande. Where were these procedures developed? By whom? What is their rate of success? The dangers associated with them? What new weight reduction surgeries are being developed?

Fairy Tales: A Closer Look at "Cinderella"

11

In August 2001, when the crown prince of Norway married a single mother and former waitress, hundreds of thousands of Norwegians cheered, along with an estimated 300 million television viewers worldwide. Observers called it a "Cinderella" tale—and everyone everywhere understood the reference. Mette-Marit Tjessem Hoiby had become a Cinderella figure. But why had the bride's humble beginnings so endeared her to a nation? We can begin to offer answers by examining an ancient and universally known tale in which a young girl—heartsick at the death of her mother, deprived of her father's love, and scorned by her new family—is nonetheless recognized for her inner worth.

"Once upon a time...."Millions of children around the world have listened to these (or similar) words. And, once upon a time, such words were magic archways into a world of entertainment and fantasy for children and their parents. But in our own century, fairy tales have come under the scrutiny of anthropologists, linguists, educators, psychologists, and psychiatrists, as well as literary critics, who have come to see them as a kind of social genetic code—a means by which cultural values are transmitted from one generation to the next. Some people, of course, may scoff at the idea that charming tales like "Cinderella" or "Snow White" are anything other than charming tales, at the idea that fairy tales may really be ways of inculcating young and impressionable children with culturally approved values. But even if they are not aware of it, adults and children use fairy tales in complex and subtle ways. We can, perhaps, best illustrate this by examining variants of a single tale—"Cinderella."

"Cinderella" appears to be the best-known fairy tale in the world. In 1892, Marian Roalfe Cox published 345 variants of the story, the first systematic study of a single folktale. In her collection, Cox gathered stories from throughout Europe in which elements or motifs of "Cinderella" appeared, often mixed with motifs of other tales. All told, more than 700 variants exist throughout the world—in Europe, Africa, Asia, and North and South America. Scholars debate the extent to which such a wide distribution is explained by population migrations or by some universal quality of imagination that would allow people at different times and places to create essentially the same story. But for whatever reason, folklorists agree that "Cinderella" has appealed to storytellers and listeners everywhere.

The great body of folk literature, including fairy tales, comes to us from an oral tradition. Written literature, produced by a particular author, is preserved through the generations just as the author recorded it. By contrast, oral literature changes with every telling: The childhood game comes to mind in which one child whispers a sentence into the ear of another; by the time the second child repeats the sentence to a third, and the third to a fourth (and so on), the sentence has changed considerably. And so it is with oral literature, with the qualification that these stories are also changed quite consciously when a teller wishes to add or delete material.

The modern student of folk literature finds her- or himself in the position of *reading* as opposed to hearing a tale. The texts we read tend to be of two types, which are at times difficult to distinguish. We might read a faithful transcription of an oral tale or a tale of *literary* origin—a tale that was originally written (as a short story would be), not spoken, but that nonetheless may contain elements of an oral account. In this chapter, we include tales of both oral and literary origin. Jakob and Wilhelm Grimm published their transcription of "Cinderella" in 1812. The version by Charles Perrault (1697) is difficult to classify as the transcription of an oral source, since he may have heard the story originally but appears (according to Bruno Bettelheim) to have "freed it of all content he considered vulgar, and refined its other features to make the product suitable to be told at court." Of unquestionable literary origin are the Walt Disney version of the story, based on Perrault's text; Anne Sexton's poem; Tanith Lee's "When the Clock Strikes," a version in which the Cinderella figure is a witch bent on avenging the murder of her royal family; and John Gardner's "Gudgekin the Thistle Girl."

Preceding these nine variants of "Cinderella," we present a general reading on fairy-tale literature by Stith Thompson. Following the variants are three selections that respond directly to the tale. We hear from Bruno Bettelheim, who, following psychoanalytic theory, finds in "'Cinderella': A Story of Sibling Rivalry and Oedipal Conflicts." A Jungian analyst, Jacqueline Schectman, then examines the tale to find a sympathetic Stepmother in "'Cinderella' and the Loss of Father-Love." The chapter concludes with a feminist perspective offered by Nobel laureate Toni Morrison, who in an address at Barnard College calls on her women listeners to treat one another more humanely than the stepsisters treated Cinderella.

A note on terminology: "Cinderella," "Jack and the Beanstalk," "Little Red Riding Hood," and the like are commonly referred to as fairy tales, although, strictly speaking, they are not. True fairy tales concern a "class of supernatural beings of diminutive size, who in popular belief are said to possess magical powers and to have great influence for good or evil over the affairs of humans" (*Oxford English Dictionary*). "Cinderella" and the others just mentioned concern no beings of diminutive size, although extraordinary, magical events do occur in the stories. Folklorists would be more apt to call these stories "wonder tales." We retain the traditional "fairy tale," with the proviso that in popular usage the term is misapplied. You may notice that the authors in this chapter use the terms "folktale" and "fairy tale" interchangeably. The expression "folktale" refers to *any* story conceived orally and passed on in an oral tradition. Thus, "folktale" is a generic term that incorporates both fairy tales and wonder tales.

Universality of the Folktale
Stith Thompson

*Folklorists travel around the world, to cities and rural areas alike, recording the facts, tradi-
tions, and beliefs that characterize ethnic groups. Some folklorists record and compile jokes;
others do the same with insults or songs. Still others, like Stith Thompson, devote their professional careers to studying tales. And, as it turns out, many aspects of stories and storytelling are worth examining. Among them: the art of narrative—how tellers captivate their
audiences; the social and religious significance of tale telling; the many types of tales that
are told; the many variants, worldwide, of single tales (such as "Cinderella"). In a preface
to one of his own books, Thompson raises the broad questions and the underlying assumptions that govern the folklorist's study of tales. We begin this chapter with Thompson's
overview to set a context for the variants of "Cinderella" that you will read.*

*Note the ways that Thompson's approach to fairy tales differs from yours. Whether or not
you're conscious of having an approach, you do have one: Perhaps you regard stories such
as "Cinderella" as entertainment. Fine—this is a legitimate point of view, but it's only one of
several ways of regarding folktales. Stith Thompson claims that there's much to learn in
studying tales. He assumes, as you might not, that tales should be objects of study as well
as entertainment.*

*Stith Thompson (1885–1976) led a distinguished life as an American educator, folklorist,
editor, and author. Between 1921 and 1955, he was a professor of folklore and English, and
later dean of the Graduate School and Distinguished Service Professor at Indiana University,
Bloomington. Five institutions have awarded Thompson honorary doctorates for his work
in folklore studies. He published numerous books on the subject, including* European Tales
Among North American Indians *(1919),* The Types of the Folktales *(1928), and* Tales of the
North American Indian *(1929). He is best known for his six-volume* Motif Index of Folk
Literature *(1932–1937; 1955–1958, 2nd ed.).*

1   The teller of stories has everywhere and always found eager listeners. Whether
his tale is the mere report of a recent happening, a legend of long ago, or an
elaborately contrived fiction, men and women have hung upon his words and
satisfied their yearnings for information or amusement, for incitement to heroic
deeds, for religious edification, or for release from the overpowering monotony
of their lives. In villages of central Africa, in outrigger boats on the Pacific, in the
Australian bush, and within the shadow of Hawaiian volcanoes, tales of the present and of the mysterious past, of animals and gods and heroes, and of men
and women like themselves, hold listeners in their spell or enrich the conversation of daily life. So it is also in Eskimo igloos under the light of seal-oil lamps,
in the tropical jungles of Brazil, and by the totem poles of the British Columbian
coast. In Japan too, and China and India, the priest and the scholar, the peasant and the artisan all join in their love of a good story and their honor for the
man who tells it well.

2   When we confine our view to our own occidental world, we see that for at
least three or four thousand years, and doubtless for ages before, the art of the

story-teller has been cultivated in every rank of society. Odysseus entertains the court of Alcinous with the marvels of his adventures. Centuries later we find the long-haired page reading nightly from interminable chivalric romances to entertain his lady while her lord is absent on his crusade. Medieval priests illustrate sermons by anecdotes old and new, and only sometimes edifying. The old peasant, now as always, whiles away the winter evening with tales of wonder and adventure and the marvelous workings of fate. Nurses tell children of Goldilocks or the House that Jack Built. Poets write epics and novelists novels. Even now the cinemas and theaters bring their stories directly to the ear and eye through the voices and gestures of actors. And in the smoking-rooms of sleeping cars and steamships and at the banquet table the oral anecdote flourishes in a new age.

3   In the present work we are confining our interest to a relatively narrow scope, the traditional prose tale—the story which has been handed down from generation to generation either in writing or by word of mouth. Such tales are, of course, only one of the many kinds of story material, for, in addition to them, narrative comes to us in verse as ballads and epics, and in prose as histories, novels, dramas, and short stories. We shall have little to do with the songs of bards, with the ballads of the people, or with poetic narrative in general, though stories themselves refuse to be confined exclusively to either prose or verse forms. But even with verse and all other forms of prose narrative put aside, we shall find that in treating the traditional prose tale—the folktale—our quest will be ambitious enough and will take us to all parts of the earth and to the very beginnings of history.

4   Although the term "folktale" is often used in English to refer to the "household tale" or "fairy tale" (the German *Märchen*), such as "Cinderella" or "Snow White," it is also legitimately employed in a much broader sense to include all forms of prose narrative, written or oral, which have come to be handed down through the years. In this usage the important fact is the traditional nature of the material. In contrast to the modern story writer's striving after originality of plot and treatment, the teller of a folktale is proud of his ability to hand on that which he has received. He usually desires to impress his readers or hearers with the fact that he is bringing them something that has the stamp of good authority, that the tale was heard from some great story-teller or from some aged person who remembered it from old days.

5   So it was until at least the end of the Middle Ages with writers like Chaucer, who carefully quoted authorities for their plots—and sometimes even invented originals so as to dispel the suspicion that some new and unwarranted story was being foisted on the public. Though the individual genius of such writers appears clearly enough, they always depended on authority, not only for their basic theological opinions but also for the plots of their stories. A study of the sources of Chaucer or Boccaccio takes one directly into the stream of traditional narrative.

6   The great written collections of stories characteristic of India, the Near East, the classical world, and Medieval Europe are almost entirely traditional. They copy and recopy. A tale which gains favor in one collection is taken over into others, sometimes intact and sometimes with changes of plot or characteriza-

tion. The history of such a story, passing it may be from India to Persia and Arabia and Italy and France and finally to England, copied and changed from manuscript to manuscript, is often exceedingly complex. For it goes through the hands of both skilled and bungling narrators and improves or deteriorates at nearly every retelling. However well or poorly such a story may be written down, it always attempts to preserve a tradition, an old tale with the authority of antiquity to give it interest and importance.

7   If use of the term "folktale" to include such literary narratives seems somewhat broad, it can be justified on practical grounds if on no other, for it is impossible to make a complete separation of the written and the oral traditions. Often, indeed, their interrelation is so close and so inextricable as to present one of the most baffling problems the folklore scholar encounters. They differ somewhat in their behavior, it is true, but they are alike in their disregard of originality of plot and of pride of authorship.

8   Nor is complete separation of these two kinds of narrative tradition by any means necessary for their understanding. The study of the oral tale [...] will be valid so long as we realize that stories have frequently been taken down from the lips of unlettered taletellers and have entered the great literary collections. In contrary fashion, fables of Aesop, anecdotes from Homer, and saints' legends, not to speak of fairy tales read from Perrault or Grimm, have entered the oral stream and all their association with the written or printed page has been forgotten. Frequently a story is taken from the people, recorded in a literary document, carried across continents or preserved through centuries, and then retold to a humble entertainer who adds it to his repertory.

9   It is clear then that the oral story need not always have been oral. But when it once habituates itself to being passed on by word of mouth it undergoes the same treatment as all other tales at the command of the raconteur. It becomes something to tell to an audience, or at least to a listener, not something to read. Its effects are no longer produced indirectly by association with words written or printed on a page, but directly through facial expression and gesture and repetition and recurrent patterns that generations have tested and found effective.

10   This oral art of taletelling is far older than history, and it is not bounded by one continent or one civilization. Stories may differ in subject from place to place, the conditions and purposes of taletelling may change as we move from land to land or from century to century, and yet everywhere it ministers to the same basic social and individual needs. The call for entertainment to fill in the hours of leisure has found most peoples very limited in their resources, and except where modern urban civilization has penetrated deeply they have found the telling of stories one of the most satisfying of pastimes. Curiosity about the past has always brought eager listeners to tales of the long ago which supply the simple man with all he knows of the history of his folk. Legends grow with the telling, and often a great heroic past evolves to gratify vanity and tribal pride. Religion also has played a mighty role everywhere in the encouragement of the narrative art, for the religious mind has tried to understand beginnings and for ages has told stories of ancient days and sacred beings. Often whole cosmologies have unfolded themselves in these legends, and hierarchies of gods and heroes.

11   Worldwide also are many of the structural forms which oral narrative has assumed. The hero tale, the explanatory legend, the animal anecdote—certainly these at least are present everywhere. Other fictional patterns are limited to particular areas of culture and act by their presence or absence as an effective index of the limits of the area concerned. The study of such limitations has not proceeded far, but it constitutes an interesting problem for the student of these oral narrative forms.

12   Even more tangible evidence of the ubiquity and antiquity of the folktale is the great similarity in the content of stories of the most varied peoples. The same tale types and narrative motifs are found scattered over the world in most puzzling fashion. A recognition of these resemblances and an attempt to account for them brings the scholar closer to an understanding of the nature of human culture. He must continually ask himself, "Why do some peoples borrow tales and some lend? How does the tale serve the needs of the social group?" When he adds to his task an appreciation of the aesthetic and practical urge toward storytelling, and some knowledge of the forms and devices, stylistic and histrionic, that belong to this ancient and widely practiced art, he finds that he must bring to his work more talents than one man can easily possess. Literary critics, anthropologists, historians, psychologists, and aestheticians are all needed if we are to hope to know why folktales are made, how they are invented, what art is used in their telling, how they grow and change and occasionally die.

Review Questions

1. According to Thompson, why do people venerate a good storyteller?

2. For Thompson, what features distinguish a "folktale" from modern types of fiction?

3. How does religion help encourage the existence of folktale art?

4. What is a strong piece of evidence for the great antiquity and universality of folktales?

Discussion and Writing Suggestions

1. Based on Thompson's explanation of the qualities of oral folktales, what do you feel is gained by the increasing replacement of this form of art and entertainment by TV?

2. What do you suppose underlies the apparent human need to tell stories, given that storytelling is practiced in every culture known?

3. Interview older members of your family, asking them about stories they were told as children. As best you can, record a story. Then examine your work. How does it differ from the version you heard?

Write an account of your impressions on the differences between an oral and written rendering of a story. Alternately, you might record a story and then speculate on what the story might mean in the experiences of the family member who told it to you.

Nine Variants of "Cinderella"

The existence of Chinese, French, German, African, and Native American versions of the popular "Cinderella," along with 700 other versions worldwide, comes as a surprise to many. Which is the real "Cinderella"? The question is misleading in that each version is "real" for a particular group of people in a particular place and time. Certainly, you can judge among versions and select the most appealing. You can also draw comparisons and contrasts. Indeed, the grouping of the stories that we present here invites comparisons. A few of the categories you might wish to consider as you read:

- *Cinderella's innocence or guilt, concerning the treatment she receives at the hands of her stepsisters*

- *Cinderella's passive (or active) nature*

- *Sibling rivalry—the relationship of Cinderella to her sisters*

- *The father's role*

- *The rule that Cinderella must return from the ball by midnight*

- *Levels of violence*

- *Presence or absence of the fairy godmother*

- *Cinderella's relationship with the prince*

- *Characterization of the prince*

- *The presence of Cinderella's dead mother*

- *The function of magic*

- *The ending*

Cinderella
Charles Perrault

Charles Perrault (1628–1703) was born in Paris of a prosperous family. He practiced law for a short time and then devoted his attentions to a job in government, in which capacity he was instrumental in promoting the advancement of the arts and sciences and in securing pensions for writers, both French and foreign. Perrault is best known as a writer for his Contes de ma mère l'oie (Mother Goose Tales), *a collection of fairy tales taken from popular folklore. He is widely suspected of having changed these stories in an effort to make them more acceptable to his audience—members of the French court.*

1 Once there was a nobleman who took as his second wife the proudest and haughtiest woman imaginable. She had two daughters of the same character, who took after their mother in everything. On his side, the husband had a daughter who was sweetness itself; she inherited this from her mother, who had been the most kindly of women.

2 No sooner was the wedding over than the stepmother showed her ill-nature. She could not bear the good qualities of the young girl, for they made her own daughters seem even less likable. She gave her the roughest work of the house to do. It was she who washed the dishes and the stairs, who cleaned out Madam's room and the rooms of the two Misses. She slept right at the top of the house, in an attic, on a lumpy mattress, while her sisters slept in panelled rooms where they had the most modern beds and mirrors in which they could see themselves from top to toe. The poor girl bore everything in patience and did not dare to complain to her father. He would only have scolded her, for he was entirely under his wife's thumb.

3 When she had finished her work, she used to go into the chimney-corner and sit down among the cinders, for which reason she was usually known in the house as Cinderbottom. Her younger stepsister, who was not so rude as the other, called her Cinderella. However, Cinderella, in spite of her ragged clothes, was still fifty times as beautiful as her sisters, superbly dressed though they were.

4 One day the King's son gave a ball, to which everyone of good family was invited. Our two young ladies received invitations, for they cut quite a figure in the country. So there they were, both feeling very pleased and very busy choosing the clothes and the hair-styles which would suit them best. More work for Cinderella, for it was she who ironed her sisters' underwear and goffered their linen cuffs. Their only talk was of what they would wear.

5 "I," said the elder, "shall wear my red velvet dress and my collar of English lace."

6 "I," said the younger, "shall wear just my ordinary skirt; but, to make up, I shall put on my gold-embroidered cape and my diamond clasp, which is quite out of the common."

7 The right hairdresser was sent for to supply double-frilled coifs, and patches were bought from the right patch-maker. They called Cinderella to ask her opinion, for she had excellent taste. She made useful suggestions and even offered to do their hair for them. They accepted willingly.

8 While she was doing it, they said to her:

9 "Cinderella, how would you like to go to the ball?"

10 "Oh dear, you are making fun of me. It wouldn't do for me."

11 "You are quite right. It would be a joke. People would laugh if they saw a Cinderbottom at the ball."

12 Anyone else would have done their hair in knots for them, but she had a sweet nature, and she finished it perfectly. For two days they were so excited that they ate almost nothing. They broke a good dozen laces trying to tighten their stays to make their waists slimmer, and they were never away from their mirrors.

13 At last the great day arrived. They set off, and Cinderella watched them until they were out of sight. When she could no longer see them, she began to cry. Her godmother, seeing her all in tears, asked what was the matter.

14   "If only I could…If only I could…" She was weeping so much that she could not go on.

15   Her godmother, who was a fairy, said to her: "If only you could go to the ball, is that it?"

16   "Alas, yes," Said Cinderella with a sigh.

17   "Well," said the godmother, "be a good girl and I'll get you there."

18   She took her into her room and said: "Go into the garden and get me a pumpkin."

19   Cinderella hurried out and cut the best she could find and took it to her god-mother, but she could not understand how this pumpkin would get her to the ball. Her godmother hollowed it out, leaving only the rind, and then tapped it with her wand and immediately it turned into a magnificent gilded coach.

20   Then she went to look in her mouse-trap and found six mice all alive in it. She told Cinderella to raise the door of the trap a little, and as each mouse came out she gave it a tap with her wand and immediately it turned into a fine horse. That made a team of six horses, each of fine mouse-coloured grey.

21   While she was wondering how she would make a coachman, Cinderella said to her:

22   "I will go and see whether there is a rat in the rat-trap, we could make a coachman of him."

23   "You are right," said the godmother. "Run and see."

24   Cinderella brought her the rat-trap, in which there were three big rats. The fairy picked out one of them because of his splendid whiskers and, when she had touched him, he turned into a fat coachman, with the finest moustaches in the district.

25   Then she said: "Go into the garden and you will find six lizards behind the watering-can. Bring them to me."

26   As soon as Cinderella had brought them, her godmother changed them into six footmen, who got up behind the coach with their striped liveries, and stood in position there as though they had been doing it all their lives.

27   Then the fairy said to Cinderella:

28   "Well, that's to go to the ball in. Aren't you pleased?"

29   "Yes. But am I to go like this, with my ugly clothes?"

30   Her godmother simply touched her with her wand and her clothes were changed in an instant into a dress of gold and silver cloth, all sparkling with precious stones. Then she gave her a pair of glass slippers, most beautifully made.

31   So equipped, Cinderella got into the coach: but her godmother warned her above all not to be out after midnight, telling her that, if she stayed at the ball a moment later, her coach would turn back into a pumpkin, her horses into mice, her footmen into lizards, and her fine clothes would become rags again.

32   She promised her godmother that she would leave the ball before midnight without fail, and she set out, beside herself with joy.

33   The King's son, on being told that a great princess whom no one knew had arrived, ran out to welcome her. He handed her down from the coach and led her into the hall where his guests were. A sudden silence fell; the dancing stopped, the violins ceased to play, the whole company stood fascinated by the beauty of the unknown princess. Only a low murmur was heard: "Ah, how lovely

she is!" The King himself, old as he was, could not take his eyes off her and kept whispering to the Queen that it was a long time since he had seen such a beautiful and charming person. All the ladies were absorbed in noting her clothes and the way her hair was dressed, so as to order the same things for themselves the next morning, provided that fine enough materials could be found, and skillful enough craftsmen.

34   The King's son placed her in the seat of honour, and later led her out to dance. She danced with such grace that she won still more admiration. An excellent supper was served, but the young Prince was too much occupied in gazing at her to eat anything. She went and sat next to her sisters and treated them with great courtesy, offering them oranges and lemons which the Prince had given her. They were astonished, for they did not recognize her.

35   While they were chatting together, Cinderella heard the clock strike a quarter to twelve. She curtsied low to the company and left as quickly as she could.

36   As soon as she reached home, she went to her godmother and, having thanked her, said that she would very much like to go again to the ball on the next night—for the Prince had begged her to come back. She was in the middle of telling her godmother about all the things that had happened, when the two sisters came knocking at the door. Cinderella went to open it.

37   "How late you are!" she said, rubbing her eyes and yawning and stretching as though she had just woken up (though since they had last seen each other she had felt very far from sleepy).

38   "If you had been at the ball," said one of the sisters, "you would not have felt like yawning. There was a beautiful princess there, really ravishingly beautiful. She was most attentive to us. She gave us oranges and lemons."

39   Cinderella could have hugged herself. She asked them the name of the princess, but they replied that no one knew her, that the King's son was much troubled about it, and that he would give anything in the world to know who she was. Cinderella smiled and said to them:

40   "So she was very beautiful? Well, well, how lucky you are! Couldn't I see her? Please, Miss Javotte, do lend me that yellow dress which you wear about the house."

41   "Really," said Miss Javotte, "what an idea! Lend one's dress like that to a filthy Cinderbottom! I should have to be out of my mind."

42   Cinderella was expecting this refusal and she was very glad when it came, for she would have been in an awkward position if her sister really had lent her her frock.

43   On the next day the two sisters went to the ball, and Cinderella too, but even more splendidly dressed than the first time. The King's son was constantly at her side and wooed her the whole evening. The young girl was enjoying herself so much that she forgot her godmother's warning. She heard the clock striking the first stroke of midnight when she thought that it was still hardly eleven. She rose and slipped away as lightly as a roe-deer. The Prince followed her, but he could not catch her up. One of her glass slippers fell off, and the Prince picked it up with great care.

44   Cinderella reached home quite out of breath, with no coach, no footmen, and wearing her old clothes. Nothing remained of all her finery, except one of

her little slippers, the fellow to the one which she had dropped. The guards at the palace gate were asked if they had not seen a princess go out. They answered that they had seen no one go out except a very poorly dressed girl, who looked more like a peasant than a young lady.

45   When the two sisters returned from the ball, Cinderella asked them if they had enjoyed themselves again, and if the beautiful lady had been there. They said that she had, but that she had run away when it struck midnight, and so swiftly that she had lost one of her glass slippers, a lovely little thing. The Prince had picked it up and had done nothing but gaze at it for the rest of the ball, and undoubtedly he was very much in love with the beautiful person to whom it belonged.

46   They were right, for a few days later the King's son had it proclaimed to the sound of trumpets that he would marry the girl whose foot exactly fitted the slipper. They began by trying it on the various princesses, then on the duchesses and on all the ladies of the Court, but with no success. It was brought to the two sisters, who did everything possible to force their feet into the slipper, but they could not manage it. Cinderella, who was looking on, recognized her own slipper, and said laughing:

47   "Let me see if it would fit me!"

48   Her sisters began to laugh and mock at her. But the gentleman who was trying on the slipper looked closely at Cinderella and, seeing that she was very beautiful, said that her request was perfectly reasonable and that he had instructions to try it on every girl. He made Cinderella sit down and, raising the slipper to her foot, he found that it slid on without difficulty and fitted like a glove.

49   Great was the amazement of the two sisters, but it became greater still when Cinderella drew from her pocket the second little slipper and put it on her other foot. Thereupon the fairy godmother came in and, touching Cinderella's clothes with her wand, made them even more magnificent than on the previous days.

50   Then the two sisters recognized her as the lovely princess whom they had met at the ball. They flung themselves at her feet and begged her forgiveness for all the unkind things which they had done to her. Cinderella raised them up and kissed them, saying that she forgave them with all her heart and asking them to love her always. She was taken to the young Prince in the fine clothes which she was wearing. He thought her more beautiful than ever and a few days later he married her. Cinderella, who was as kind as she was beautiful, invited her two sisters to live in the palace and married them, on the same day, to two great noblemen of the Court.

Ashputtle
Jakob and Wilhelm Grimm

Jakob Grimm (1785–1863) and Wilhelm Grimm (1786–1859) are best known today for the 200 folktales they collected from oral sources and reworked in Kinder- und Hausmärchen *(popularly known as* Grimm's Fairy Tales*), which has been translated into seventy languages.*

The techniques Jakob and Wilhelm Grimm used to collect and comment on these tales became a model for other collectors, providing a basis for the science of folklore. Although the Grimm brothers argued for preserving the tales exactly as heard from oral sources, scholars have determined that they sought to "improve" the tales by making them more readable. The result, highly pleasing to lay audiences the world over, nonetheless represents a literary reworking of the original oral sources.

1   A rich man's wife fell sick and, feeling that her end was near, she called her only daughter to her bedside and said: "Dear child, be good and say your prayers; God will help you, and I shall look down on you from heaven and always be with you." With that she closed her eyes and died. Every day the little girl went out to her mother's grave and wept, and she went on being good and saying her prayers. When winter came, the snow spread a white cloth over the grave, and when spring took it off, the man remarried.

2   His new wife brought two daughters into the house. Their faces were beautiful and lily-white, but their hearts were ugly and black. That was the beginning of a bad time for the poor stepchild. "Why should this silly goose sit in the parlor with us?" they said. "People who want to eat bread must earn it. Get into the kitchen where you belong!" They took away her fine clothes and gave her an old gray dress and wooden shoes to wear. "Look at the haughty princess in her finery!" they cried and, laughing, led her to the kitchen. From then on she had to do all the work, getting up before daybreak, carrying water, lighting fires, cooking and washing. In addition the sisters did everything they could to plague her. They jeered at her and poured peas and lentils into the ashes, so that she had to sit there picking them out. At night, when she was tired out with work, she had no bed to sleep in but had to lie in the ashes by the hearth. And they took to calling her Ashputtle because she always looked dusty and dirty.

3   One day when her father was going to the fair, he asked his two stepdaughters what he should bring them. "Beautiful dresses," said one. "Diamonds and pearls," said the other. "And you, Ashputtle. What would you like?" "Father," she said, "break off the first branch that brushes against your hat on your way home, and bring it to me." So he brought beautiful dresses, diamonds, and pearls for his two stepdaughters, and on the way home, as he was riding through a copse, a hazel branch brushed against him and knocked off his hat. So he broke off the branch and took it home with him. When he got home, he gave the stepdaughters what they had asked for, and gave Ashputtle the branch. After thanking him, she went to her mother's grave and planted the hazel sprig over it and cried so hard that her tears fell on the sprig and watered it. It grew and became a beautiful tree. Three times a day Ashputtle went and sat under it and wept and prayed. Each time a little white bird came and perched on the tree, and when Ashputtle made a wish the little bird threw down what she had wished for.

4   Now it so happened that the king arranged for a celebration. It was to go on for three days and all the beautiful girls in the kingdom were invited, in order that his son might choose a bride. When the two stepsisters heard they had been asked, they were delighted. They called Ashputtle and said: "Comb our hair, brush our shoes, and fasten our buckles. We're going to the wedding at the king's palace." Ashputtle obeyed, but she wept, for she too would have liked

to go dancing, and she begged her stepmother to let her go. "You little sloven!" said the stepmother. "How can you go to a wedding when you're all dusty and dirty? How can you go dancing when you have neither dress nor shoes?" But when Ashputtle begged and begged, the stepmother finally said: "Here, I've dumped a bowlful of lentils in the ashes. If you can pick them out in two hours, you may go." The girl went out the back door to the garden and cried out: "O tame little doves, O turtledoves, and all the birds under heaven, come and help me put

the good ones in the pot,
the bad ones in your crop."

Two little white doves came flying through the kitchen window, and then came the turtledoves, and finally all the birds under heaven came flapping and fluttering and settled down by the ashes. The doves nodded their little heads and started in, peck peck peck peck, and all the others started in, peck peck peck peck, and they sorted out all the good lentils and put them in the bowl. Hardly an hour had passed before they finished and flew away. Then the girl brought the bowl to her stepmother, and she was happy, for she thought she'd be allowed to go to the wedding. But the stepmother said: "No, Ashputtle. You have nothing to wear and you don't know how to dance; the people would only laugh at you." When Ashputtle began to cry, the stepmother said: "If you can pick two bowlfuls of lentils out of the ashes in an hour, you may come." And she thought: "She'll never be able to do it." When she had dumped the two bowlfuls of lentils in the ashes, Ashputtle went out the back door to the garden and cried out: "O tame little doves, O turtledoves, and all the birds under heaven, come and help me put

the good ones in the pot,
the bad ones in your crop."

Two little white doves came flying through the kitchen window, and then came the turtledoves, and finally all the birds under heaven came flapping and fluttering and settled down by the ashes. The doves nodded their little heads and started in, peck peck peck peck, and all the others started in, peck peck peck peck, and they sorted out all the good lentils and put them in the bowls. Before half an hour had passed, they had finished and they all flew away. Then the girl brought the bowls to her stepmother, and she was happy, for she thought she'd be allowed to go to the wedding. But her stepmother said: "It's no use. You can't come, because you have nothing to wear and you don't know how to dance. We'd only be ashamed of you." Then she turned her back and hurried away with her two proud daughters.

5   When they had all gone out, Ashputtle went to her mother's grave. She stood under the hazel tree and cried:

"Shake your branches, little tree,
Throw gold and silver down on me."

Whereupon the bird tossed down a gold and silver dress and slippers embroidered with silk and silver. Ashputtle slipped into the dress as fast as she could and went to the wedding. Her sisters and stepmother didn't recognize her. She was so beautiful in her golden dress that they thought she must be the daughter of some foreign king. They never dreamed it could be Ashputtle, for they thought she was sitting at home in her filthy rags, picking lentils out of the ashes. The king's son came up to her, took her by the hand and danced with her. He wouldn't dance with anyone else and he never let go her hand. When someone else asked for a dance, he said: "She is my partner."

6   She danced until evening, and then she wanted to go home. The king's son said: "I'll go with you, I'll see you home," for he wanted to find out whom the beautiful girl belonged to. But she got away from him and slipped into the dovecote. The king's son waited until her father arrived, and told him the strange girl had slipped into the dovecote. The old man thought: "Could it be Ashputtle?" and he sent for an ax and a pick and broke into the dovecote, but there was no one inside. When they went indoors, Ashputtle was lying in the ashes in her filthy clothes and a dim oil lamp was burning on the chimney piece, for Ashputtle had slipped out the back end of the dovecote and run to the hazel tree. There she had taken off her fine clothes and put them on the grave, and the bird had taken them away. Then she had put her gray dress on again, crept into the kitchen and lain down in the ashes.

7   Next day when the festivities started in again and her parents and stepsisters had gone, Ashputtle went to the hazel tree and said:

"Shake your branches, little tree,
Throw gold and silver down on me."

Whereupon the bird threw down a dress that was even more dazzling than the first one. And when she appeared at the wedding, everyone marveled at her beauty. The king's son was waiting for her. He took her by the hand and danced with no one but her. When others came and asked her for a dance, he said: "She is my partner." When evening came, she said she was going home. The king's son followed her, wishing to see which house she went into, but she ran away and disappeared into the garden behind the house, where there was a big beautiful tree with the most wonderful pears growing on it. She climbed among the branches as nimbly as a squirrel and the king's son didn't know what had become of her. He waited until her father arrived and said to him: "The strange girl has got away from me and I think she has climbed up in the pear tree." Her father thought: "Could it be Ashputtle?" He sent for an ax and chopped the tree down, but there was no one in it. When they went into the kitchen, Ashputtle was lying there in the ashes as usual, for she had jumped down on the other side of the tree, brought her fine clothes back to the bird in the hazel tree, and put on her filthy gray dress.

8   On the third day, after her parents and sisters had gone, Ashputtle went back to her mother's grave and said to the tree:

"Shake your branches, little tree,
Throw gold and silver down on me."

Whereupon the bird threw down a dress that was more radiant than either of the others, and the slippers were all gold. When she appeared at the wedding, the people were too amazed to speak. The king's son danced with no one but her, and when someone else asked her for a dance, he said: "She is my partner."

9   When the evening came, Ashputtle wanted to go home, and the king's son said he'd go with her, but she slipped away so quickly that he couldn't follow. But he had thought up a trick. He had arranged to have the whole staircase brushed with pitch, and as she was running down it the pitch pulled her left slipper off. The king's son picked it up, and it was tiny and delicate and all gold. Next morning he went to the father and said: "No girl shall be my wife but the one this golden shoe fits." The sisters were overjoyed, for they had beautiful feet. The eldest took the shoe to her room to try it on and her mother went with her. But the shoe was too small and she couldn't get her big toe in. So her mother handed her a knife and said: "Cut your toe off. Once you're queen you won't have to walk any more." The girl cut her toe off, forced her foot into the shoe, gritted her teeth against the pain, and went out to the king's son. He accepted her as his bride-to-be, lifted her up on his horse, and rode away with her. But they had to pass the grave. The two doves were sitting in the hazel tree and they cried out:

> *"Roocoo, roocoo,*
> *There's blood in the shoe.*
> *The foot's too long, the foot's too wide,*
> *That's not the proper bride."*

He looked down at her foot and saw the blood spurting. At that he turned his horse around and took the false bride home again. "No," he said, "this isn't the right girl; let her sister try the shoe on." The sister went to her room and managed to get her toes into the shoe, but her heel was too big. So her mother handed her a knife and said: "Cut off a chunk of your heel. Once you're queen you won't have to walk any more." The girl cut off a chunk of her heel, forced her foot into the shoe, gritted her teeth against the pain, and went out to the king's son. He accepted her as his bride-to-be, lifted her up on his horse, and rode away with her. As they passed the hazel tree, the two doves were sitting there, and they cried out:

> *"Roocoo, roocoo,*
> *There's blood in the shoe.*
> *The foot's too long, the foot's too wide,*
> *That's not the proper bride."*

He looked down at her foot and saw that blood was spurting from her shoe and staining her white stocking all red. He turned his horse around and took the false bride home again. "This isn't the right girl, either," he said. "Haven't you got another daughter?" "No," said the man, "there's only a puny little kitchen drudge that my dead wife left me. She couldn't possibly be the bride." "Send her up," said the king's son, but the mother said: "Oh, no, she's much too dirty to be seen." But he insisted and they had to call her. First she washed her face and hands, and when they were clean, she went upstairs and curtseyed to the king's son. He handed her the golden slipper and sat down on a footstool, took her foot out of her heavy wooden shoe, and put it into the slipper. It fitted perfectly. And when she stood up and the king's son looked into her face, he recognized the beautiful girl he had danced with and cried out: "This is my true bride!" The stepmother and the two sisters went pale with fear and rage. But he lifted Ashputtle up on his horse and rode away with her. As they passed the hazel tree, the two white doves called out:

"Roocoo, roocoo,
No blood in the shoe.
Her foot is neither long nor wide,
This one is the proper bride."

Then they flew down and alighted on Ashputtle's shoulders, one on the right and one on the left, and there they sat.

10   On the day of Ashputtle's wedding, the two stepsisters came and tried to ingratiate themselves and share in her happiness. On the way to church the elder was on the right side of the bridal couple and the younger on the left. The doves came along and pecked out one of the elder sister's eyes and one of the younger sister's eyes. Afterward, on the way out, the elder was on the left side and younger on the right, and the doves pecked out both the remaining eyes. So both sisters were punished with blindness to the end of their days for being so wicked and false.

When the Clock Strikes
Tanith Lee

Tanith Lee has written what might be called an inversion of "Cinderella" wherein the heroine is a witch. You will find all elements of the traditional tale here, and Lee's rendering is unmistakably "Cinderella." But with devious consistency, Lee turns both the magic and the unrighted wrong that lie at the heart of the tale to a dark purpose: revenge. Tanith Lee is a prolific writer of stories for young adults and of adult fantasy and science fiction. Born in 1947 in London, Lee had her first story published when she was twenty-four and has written more than two dozen stories and plays since.

1   Yes, the great ballroom is filled only with dust now. The slender columns of white marble and the slender columns of rose-red marble are woven together by cobwebs. The vivid frescoes, on which the Duke's treasury spent so much, are dimmed by the dust; the faces of the painted goddesses look grey. And the velvet curtains—touch them they will crumble. Two hundred years now, since

anyone danced in this place on the sea-green floor in the candle-gleam. Two hundred years since the wonderful clock struck for the very first time.

2   I thought you might care to examine the clock. It was considered exceptional in its day. The pedestal is ebony and the face fine porcelain. And these figures, which are of silver, would pass slowly about the circlet of the face. Each figure represents, you understand, an hour. And as the appropriate hours came level with this golden bell, they would strike it the correct number of times. All the figures are unique, as you see. Beginning at the first hour, they are, in this order, a girl-child, a dwarf, a maiden, a youth, a lady, and a knight. And here, notice, the figures grow older as the day declines: a queen and king for the seventh and eighth hours, and after these, an abbess and a magician and next to last, a hag. But the very last is strangest of all. The twelfth figure; do you recognize him? It is Death. Yes, a most curious clock. It was reckoned a marvelous thing then. But it has not struck for two hundred years. Possibly you have been told the story? No? Oh, but I am certain that you have heard it, in another form, perhaps.

3   However, as you have some while to wait for your carriage, I will recount the tale, if you wish.

4   I will start with what was said of the clock. In those years, this city was prosperous, a stronghold—not as you see it today. Much was made in the city that was ornamental and unusual. But the clock, on which the twelfth hour was Death, caused something of a stir. It was thought unlucky, foolhardy, to have such a clock. It began to be murmured, jokingly by some, by others in earnest, that one night when the clock struck the twelfth hour, Death would truly strike with it.

5   Now life has always been a chancy business, and it was more so then. The Great Plague had come but twenty years before and was not yet forgotten. Besides, in the Duke's court there was much intrigue, while enemies might be supposed to plot beyond the city walls, as happens even in our present age. But there was another thing.

6   It was rumored that the Duke had obtained both his title and the city treacherously. Rumor declared that he had systematically destroyed those who had stood in line before him, the members of the princely house that formerly ruled here. He had accomplished the task slyly, hiring assassins talented with poisons and daggers. But rumor also declared that the Duke had not been sufficiently thorough. For though he had meant to rid himself of all that rival house, a single descendant remained, so obscure he had not traced her—for it was a woman.

7   Of course, such matters were not spoken of openly. Like the prophecy of the clock, it was a subject for the dark.

8   Nevertheless, I will tell you at once, there was such a descendant he had missed in his bloody work. And she was a woman. Royal and proud she was, and seething with bitter spite and a hunger for vengeance, and as bloody as the Duke, had he known it, in her own way.

9   For her safety and disguise, she had long ago wed a wealthy merchant in the city, and presently bore the man a daughter. The merchant, a dealer in silks, was respected, a good fellow but not wise. He rejoiced in his handsome and aristocratic wife. He never dreamed what she might be about when he was not

with her. In fact, she had sworn allegiance to Satanas. In the dead of night she would go up into an old tower adjoining the merchant's house, and there she would say portions of the Black Mass, offer sacrifice, and thereafter practise witchcraft against the Duke. This witchery took a common form, the creation of a wax image and the maiming of the image that, by sympathy, the injuries inflicted on the wax be passed on to the living body of the victim. The woman was capable in what she did. The Duke fell sick. He lost the use of his limbs and was racked by excruciating pains from which he could get no relief. Thinking himself on the brink of death, the Duke named his sixteen-year-old son his heir. This son was dear to the Duke, as everyone knew, and be sure the woman knew it too. She intended sorcerously to murder the young man in his turn, preferably in his father's sight. Thus, she let the Duke linger in his agony, and commenced planning the fate of the prince.

10   Now all this while she had not been toiling alone. She had one helper. It was her own daughter, a maid of fourteen, that she had recruited to her service nearly as soon as the infant could walk. At six or seven, the child had been lisping the satanic rite along with her mother. At fourteen, you may imagine, the girl was well versed in the Black Arts, though she did not have her mother's natural genius for them.

11   Perhaps you would like me to describe the daughter at this point. It has a bearing on the story, for the girl was astonishingly beautiful. Her hair was the rich dark red of antique burnished copper, her eyes were the hue of the reddish-golden amber that traders bring from the East. When she walked, you would say she was dancing. But when she danced, a gate seemed to open in the world, and bright fire spangled inside it, but she was the fire.

12   The girl and her mother were close as gloves in a box. Their games in the old tower bound them closer. No doubt the woman believed herself clever to have got such a helpmate, but it proved her undoing.

13   It was in this manner. The silk merchant, who had never suspected his wife for an instant of anything, began to mistrust the daughter. She was not like other girls. Despite her great beauty, she professed no interest in marriage, and none in clothes or jewels. She preferred to read in the garden at the foot of the tower. Her mother had taught the girl her letters, though the merchant himself could read but poorly. And often the father peered at the books his daughter read, unable to make head or tail of them, yet somehow not liking them. One night very late, the silk merchant came home from a guild dinner in the city, and he saw a slim pale shadow gliding up the steps of the old tower, and he knew it for his child. On impulse, he followed her, but quietly. He had not considered any evil so far, and did not want to alarm her. At an angle of the stair, the lighted room above, he paused to spy and listen. He had something of a shock when he heard his wife's voice rise up in glad welcome. But what came next drained the blood from his heart. He crept away and went to his cellar for wine to stay himself. After the third glass he ran for neighbours and for the watch.

14   The woman and her daughter heard the shouts below and saw the torches in the garden. It was no use dissembling. The tower was littered with evidence of vile deeds, besides what the woman kept in a chest beneath her unknowing

husband's bed. She understood it was all up with her, and she understood too how witchcraft was punished hereabouts. She snatched a knife from the altar.

15   The girl shrieked when she realized what her mother was at. The woman caught the girl by her red hair and shook her.

16   "Listen to me, my daughter," she cried, "and listen carefully, for the minutes are short. If you do as I tell you, you can escape their wrath and only I need die. And if you live I am satisfied, for you can carry on my labor after me. My vengeance I shall leave you, and my witchcraft to exact it by. Indeed, I promise you stronger powers than mine. I will beg my lord Satanas for it and he will not deny me, for he is just, in his fashion, and I have served him well. Now, will you attend?"

17   "I will," said the girl.

18   So the woman advised her, and swore her to the fellowship of Hell. And then the woman forced the knife into her own heart and dropped dead on the floor of the tower.

19   When the men burst in with their swords and staves and their torches and their madness, the girl was ready for them.

20   She stood blank-faced, blank-eyed, with her arms hanging at her sides. When one touched her, she dropped down at his feet.

21   "Surely she is innocent," this man said. She was lovely enough that it was hard to accuse her. Then her father went to her and took her hand and lifted her. At that the girl opened her eyes and she said, as if terrified: "How did I come here? I was in my chamber and sleeping—"

22   "The woman has bewitched her," her father said.

23   He desired very much that this be so. And when the girl clung to his hand and wept, he was certain of it. They showed her the body with the knife in it. The girl screamed and seemed to lose her senses totally.

24   She was put to bed. In the morning, a priest came and questioned her. She answered steadfastly. She remembered nothing, not even of the great books she had been observed reading. When they told her what was in them, she screamed again and apparently would have thrown herself from the narrow window, only the priest stopped her.

25   Finally, they brought her the holy cross in order that she might kiss it and prove herself blameless.

26   Then she knelt, and whispered softly, that nobody should hear but one— "Lord Satanas, protect thy handmaid." And either that gentleman has more power than he is credited with or else the symbols of God are only as holy as the men who deal in them, for she embraced the cross and it left her unscathed.

27   At that, the whole household thanked God. The whole household saving, of course, the woman's daughter. She had another to thank.

28   The woman's body was burnt, and the ashes put into unconsecrated ground beyond the city gates. Though they had discovered her to be a witch, they had not discovered the direction her witchcraft had selected. Nor did they find the wax image with its limbs all twisted and stuck through with needles. The girl had taken that up and concealed it. The Duke continued in his distress, but he did not die. Sometimes, in the dead of night, the girl would unearth the image from

under a loose brick by the hearth, and gloat over it, but she did nothing else. Not yet. She was fourteen and the cloud of her mother's acts still hovered over her. She knew what she must do next.

29   The period of mourning ended.

30   "Daughter," said the silk merchant to her, "why do you not remove your black? The woman was malign and led you into wickedness. How long will you mourn her, who deserves no mourning?"

31   "Oh my father," she said, "never think I regret my wretched mother. It is my own unwitting sin I mourn." And she grasped his hand and spilled her tears on it. "I would rather live in a convent," said she, "than mingle with proper folk. And I would seek a convent too, if it were not that I cannot bear to be parted from you."

32   Do you suppose she smiled secretly as she said this? One might suppose it. Presently she donned a robe of sackcloth and poured ashes over her red-copper hair. "It is my penance," she said, "I am glad to atone for my sins."

33   People forgot her beauty. She was at pains to obscure it. She slunk about like an aged woman, a rag pulled over her head, dirt smeared on her cheeks and brow. She elected to sleep in a cold cramped attic and sat all day by a smoky hearth in the kitchens. When someone came to her and begged her to wash her face and put on suitable clothes and sit in the rooms of the house, she smiled modestly, drawing the rag or a piece of hair over her face. "I swear," she said, "I am glad to be humble before God and men."

34   They reckoned her pious and they reckoned her simple. Two years passed. They mislaid her beauty altogether, and reckoned her ugly. They found it hard to call to mind who she was exactly, as she sat in the ashes, or shuffled unattended about the streets like a crone.

35   At the end of the second year, the silk merchant married again. It was inevitable, for he was not a man who liked to live alone.

36   On this occasion, his choice was a harmless widow. She already had two daughters, pretty in an unremarkable style. Perhaps the merchant hoped they would comfort him for what had gone before, this normal cheery wife and the two sweet, rather silly daughters, whose chief interests were clothes and weddings. Perhaps he hoped also that his deranged daughter might be drawn out by company. But that hope foundered. Not that the new mother did not try to be pleasant to the girl. And the new sisters, their hearts grieved by her condition, went to great lengths to enlist her friendship. They begged her to come from the kitchens or the attic. Failing in that, they sometimes ventured to join her, their fine silk dresses trailing on the greasy floor. They combed her hair, exclaiming, when some of the ash and dirt were removed, on its color. But no sooner had they turned away, than the girl gathered up handfuls of soot and ash and rubbed them into her hair again. Now and then, the sisters attempted to interest their bizarre relative in a bracelet or a gown or a current song. They spoke to her of the young men they had seen at the suppers or the balls which were then given regularly by the rich families of the city. The girl ignored it all. If she ever said anything it was to do with penance and humility. At last, as must happen, the sisters wearied of her, and left her alone. They had no cares and did not want to share in hers. They came to resent her moping greyness, as indeed the merchant's second wife had already done.

37   "Can you do nothing with the girl?" she demanded of her husband. "People will say that I and my daughters are responsible for her condition and that I ill-treat the maid from jealousy of her dead mother."

38   "Now how could anyone say that?" protested the merchant, "when you are famous as the epitome of generosity and kindness."

39   Another year passed, and saw no huge difference in the household.

40   A difference there was, but not visible.

41   The girl who slouched in the corner of the hearth was seventeen. Under the filth and grime she was, impossibly, more beautiful, although no one could see it.

42   And there was one other invisible item—her power (which all this time she had nurtured, saying her prayers to Satanas in the black of midnight), her power was rising like a dark moon in her soul.

43   Three days after her seventeenth birthday, the girl straggled about the streets as she frequently did. A few noted her and muttered it was the merchant's ugly simple daughter and paid no more attention. Most did not know her at all. She had made herself appear one with the scores of impoverished flotsam which constantly roamed the city, beggars and starvelings. Just outside the city gates, these persons congregated in large numbers, slumped around fires of burning refuse or else wandering to and fro in search of edible seeds, scraps, the miracle of a dropped coin. Here the girl now came, and began to wander about as they did. Dusk gathered and the shadows thickened. The girl sank to her knees in a patch of earth as if she had found something. Two or three of the beggars sneaked over to see if it were worth snatching from her—but the girl was only scrabbling in the empty soil. The beggars, making signs to each other that she was touched by God—mad—left her alone. But, very far from mad, the girl presently dug up a stoppered clay urn. In this urn were the ashes and charred bones of her mother. She had got a clue as to the location of the urn by devious questioning here and there. Her occult power had helped her to be sure of it.

44   In the twilight, padding along through the narrow streets and alleys of the city, the girl brought the urn homewards. In the garden at the foot of the old tower, gloom-wrapped, unwitnessed, she unstoppered the urn and buried the ashes freshly. She muttered certain unholy magics over the grave. Then she snapped off the sprig of a young hazel tree, and planted it in the newly turned ground.

45   I hazard you have begun to recognize the story by now. I see you suppose I tell it wrongly. Believe me, this is the truth of the matter. But if you would rather I left off the tale…No doubt your carriage will soon be here—No? Very well. I shall continue.

46   I think I should speak of the Duke's son at this juncture. The prince was nineteen, able, intelligent, and of noble bearing. He was of that rather swarthy type of looks one finds here in the north, but tall and slim and clear-eyed. There is an ancient square where you may see a statue of him, but much eroded by two centuries, and the elements. After the city was sacked, no care was lavished on it.

47   The Duke treasured his son. He had constant delight in the sight of the young man and what he said and did. It was the only happiness the invalid had.

48   Then, one night, the Duke screamed out in his bed. Servants came running with candles. The Duke moaned that a sword was transfixing his heart, an inch at a time. The prince hurried into the chamber, but in that instant the Duke

spasmed horribly and died. No mark was on his body. There had never been a mark to show what ailed him.

49   The prince wept. They were genuine tears. He had nothing to reproach his father with, everything to thank him for. Nevertheless, they brought the young man the seal ring of the city, and he put it on.

50   It was winter, a cold blue-white weather with snow in the streets and countryside and a hard wizened sun that drove thin sharp blades of light through the sky, but gave no warmth. The Duke's funeral cortege passed slowly across the snow, the broad open chariots draped with black and silver, the black-plumed horses, the chanting priests with their glittering robes, their jeweled crucifixes and golden censers. Crowds lined the roadways to watch the spectacle. Among the beggar women stood a girl. No one noticed her. They did not glimpse the expression she veiled in her ragged scarf. She gazed at the bier pitilessly. As the young prince rode by in his sables, the seal ring on his hand, the eyes of the girl burned through her ashy hair, like a red fox through grasses.

51   The Duke was buried in the mausoleum you can visit to this day, on the east side of the city. Several months elapsed. The prince put his grief from him, and took up the business of the city competently. Wise and courteous he was, but he rarely smiled. At nineteen his spirit seemed worn. You might think he guessed the destiny that hung over him.

52   The winter was a hard one, too. The snow had come, and having come was loath to withdraw. When at last the spring returned, flushing the hills with color, it was no longer sensible to be sad.

53   The prince's name day fell about this time. A great banquet was planned, a ball. There had been neither in the palace for nigh on three years, not since the Duke's fatal illness first claimed him. Now the royal doors were to be thrown open to all men of influence and their families. The prince was liberal, charming, and clever even in this. Aristocrat and rich trader were to mingle in the beautiful dining room, and in this very chamber, among the frescoes, the marbles and the candelabra. Even a merchant's daughter, if the merchant were notable in the city, would get to dance on the sea-green floor, under the white eye of the fearful clock.

54   The clock. There was some renewed controversy about the clock. They did not dare speak to the young prince. He was a skeptic, as his father had been. But had not a death already occurred? Was the clock not a flying in the jaws of fate? For those disturbed by it, there was a dim writing in their minds, in the dust of the street or the pattern of blossoms. *When the clock strikes*—But people do not positively heed these warnings. Man is afraid of his fears. He ignores the shadow of the wolf thrown on the paving before him, saying: It is only a shadow.

55   The silk merchant received his invitation to the palace, and to be sure, thought nothing of the clock. His house had been thrown into uproar. The most luscious silks of his workshop were carried into the house and laid before the wife and her two daughters, who chirruped and squealed with excitement. The merchant stood smugly by, above it all yet pleased at being appreciated. "Oh, father!" cried the two sisters, "may I have this one with the gold piping?" "Oh, father, this one with the design of pineapples?" Later, a jeweler arrived and set

out his trays. The merchant was generous. He wanted his women to look their best. It might be the night of their lives. Yet all the while, at the back of his mind, a little dark spot, itching, aching. He tried to ignore the spot, not scratch at it. His true daughter, the mad one. Nobody bothered to tell her about the invitation to the palace. They knew how she would react, mumbling in her hair about her sin and her penance, paddling her hands in the greasy ash to smear her face. Even the servants avoided her, as if she were just the cat seated by the fire. Less than the cat, for the cat saw to the mice—Just a block of stone. And yet, how fair she might have looked, decked in the pick of the merchant's wares, jewels at her throat. The prince himself could not have been unaware of her. And though marriage was impossible, other less holy, though equally honorable contracts, might have been arranged to the benefit of all concerned. The merchant sighed. He had scratched the darkness after all. He attempted to comfort himself by watching the two sisters exult over their apparel. He refused to admit that the finery would somehow make them seem but more ordinary than they were by contrast.

56   The evening of the banquet arrived. The family set off. Most of the servants sidled after. The prince had distributed largesse in the city; oxen roasted in the squares and the wine was free by royal order.

57   The house grew somber. In the deserted kitchen the fire went out.

58   By the hearth, a segment of gloom rose up.

59   The girl glanced around her, and she laughed softly and shook out her filthy hair. Of course, she knew as much as anyone, and more than most. This was to be her night, too.

60   A few minutes later she was in the garden beneath the old tower, standing over the young hazel tree which thrust up from the earth. It had become strong, the tree, despite the harsh winter. Now the girl nodded to it. She chanted under her breath. At length a pale light began to glow, far down near where the roots of the tree held to the ground. Out of the pale glow flew a thin black bird, which perched on the girl's shoulder. Together, the girl and the bird passed into the old tower. High up, a fire blazed that no one had lit. A tub steamed with scented water that no one had drawn. Shapes that were not real and barely seen flitted about. Rare perfumes, the rustle of garments, the glint of gems as yet invisible filled and did not fill the restless air.

61   Need I describe further? No. You will have seen paintings which depict the attendance upon a witch of her familiar demons. Now one bathes her, another anoints her, another brings clothes and ornaments. Perhaps you do not credit such things in any case. Never mind that. I will tell you what happened in the courtyard before the palace.

62   Many carriages and chariots had driven through the square, avoiding the roasting oxen, the barrels of wine, the cheering drunken citizens, and so through the gates into the courtyard. Just before ten o'clock (the hour, if you recall the clock, of the magician) a solitary carriage drove through the square and into the court. The people in the square gawked at the carriage and pressed forward to see who would step out of it, this latecomer. It was a remarkable vehicle that looked to be fashioned of solid gold, all but the domed roof that was transparent flashing crystal. Six black horses drew it. The coachman and postillions were clad in crimson,

and strangely masked as curious beasts and reptiles. One of these beast-men now hopped down and opened the door of the carriage. Out came a woman's figure in a cloak of white fur, and glided up the palace stair and in at the doors.

63   There was dancing in the ballroom. The whole chamber was bright and clamorous with music and the voices of men and women. There, between those two pillars, the prince sat in his chair, dark, courteous, seldom smiling. Here the musicians played, the deep-throated viol, the lively mandolin. And there the dancers moved up and down on the sea-green floor. But the music and the dancers had just paused. The figures on the clock were themselves in motion. The hour of the magician was about to strike.

64   As it struck, through the doorway came the figure in the fur cloak. And, as if they must, every eye turned to her.

65   For an instant she stood there, all white, as though she had brought the winter snow back with her. And then she loosed the cloak from her shoulders, it slipped away, and she was all fire.

66   She wore a gown of apricot brocade embroidered thickly with gold. Her sleeves and the bodice of her gown were slashed over ivory satin sewn with large rosy pearls. Pearls, too, were wound in her hair that was the shade of antique burnished copper. She was so beautiful that when the clock was still, nobody spoke. She was so beautiful it was hard to look at her for very long.

67   The prince got up from his chair. He did not know he had. Now he started out across the floor, between the dancers, who parted silently to let him through. He went toward the girl in the doorway as if she drew him by a chain.

68   The prince had hardly ever acted without considering first what he did. Now he did not consider. He bowed to the girl.

69   "Madam," he said. "You are welcome. Madam," he said. "Tell me who you are."

70   She smiled.

71   "My rank," she said. "Would you know that, my lord? It is similar to yours, or would be were I now mistress in my dead mother's palace. But, unfortunately, an unscrupulous man caused the downfall of our house."

72   "Misfortune indeed," said the prince. "Tell me your name. Let me right the wrong done you."

73   "You shall," said the girl. "Trust me, you shall. For my name, I would rather keep it secret for the present. But you may call me, if you will, a pet name I have given myself—Ashella."

74   "Ashella…. But I see no ash about you," said the prince, dazzled by her gleam, laughing a little, stiffly, for laughter was not his habit.

75   "Ash and cinders from a cold and bitter hearth," said she. But she smiled again. "Now everyone is staring at us, my lord, and the musicians are impatient to begin again. Out of all these ladies, can it be you will lead me in the dance?"

76   "As long as you will dance," he said. "You shall dance with me."

77   And that is how it was.

78   There were many dances, slow and fast, whirling measures and gentle ones. And here and there, the prince and the maiden were parted. Always then he looked eagerly after her, sparing no regard for the other girls whose hands lay in his. It was not like him, he was usually so careful. But the other young men

who danced on that floor, who clasped her fingers or her narrow waist in the dance, also gazed after her when she was gone. She danced, as she appeared, like fire. Though if you had asked those young men whether they would rather tie her to themselves, as the prince did, they would have been at a loss. For it is not easy to keep pace with fire.

79 The hour of the hag struck on the clock.

80 The prince grew weary of dancing with the girl and losing her in the dance to others and refinding her and losing her again.

81 Behind the curtains there is a tall window in the east wall that opens on the terrace above the garden. He drew her out there, into the spring night. He gave an order, and small tables were brought with delicacies and sweets and wine. He sat by her, watching every gesture she made, as if he would paint her portrait afterward.

82 In the ballroom, here, under the clock, the people murmured. But it was not quite the murmur you would expect, the scandalous murmur about a woman come from nowhere that the prince had made so much of. At the periphery of the ballroom, the silk merchant sat, pale as a ghost, thinking of a ghost, the living ghost of his true daughter. No one else recognized her. Only he. Some trick of the heart had enabled him to know her. He said nothing of it. As the step-sisters and wife gossiped with other wives and sisters, an awful foreboding weighed him down, sent him cold and dumb.

83 And now it is almost midnight, the moment when the page of the night turns over into day. Almost midnight, the hour when the figure of Death strikes the golden bell of the clock. And what will happen when the clock strikes? Your face announces that you know. Be patient; let us see if you do.

84 "I am being foolish," said the prince to Ashella on the terrace. "But perhaps I am entitled to foolish, just once in my life. What are you saying?" For the girl was speaking low beside him, and he could not catch her words.

85 "I am saying a spell to bind you to me," she said.

86 "But I am already bound."

87 "Be bound then. Never go free."

88 "I do not wish it," he said. He kissed her hands and he said, "I do not know you, but I will wed you. Is that proof your spell has worked? I will wed you, and get back for you the rights you have lost."

89 "If it were only so simple," said Ashella, smiling, smiling. "But the debt is too cruel. Justice requires a harsher payment."

90 And then, in the ballroom, Death struck the first note on the golden bell.

91 The girl smiled and she said,

92 "I curse you in my mother's name."

93 The second stroke.

94 "I curse you in my own name."

95 The third stroke.

96 "And in the name of those that your father slew."

97 The fourth stroke.

98 "And in the name of my Master, who rules the world."

99 As the fifth, the sixth, the seventh strokes pealed out, the prince stood non-plussed. At the eighth and ninth strokes, the strength of the malediction

seemed to curdle his blood. He shivered and his brain writhed. At the tenth stroke, he saw a change in the loveliness before him. She grew thinner, taller. At the eleventh stroke, he beheld a thing in a ragged black cowl and robe. It grinned at him. It was all grin below a triangle of sockets of nose and eyes. At the twelfth stroke, the prince saw Death and knew him.

100   In the ballroom, a hideous grinding noise, as the gears of the clock failed. Followed by a hollow booming, as the mechanism stopped entirely.

101   The conjuration of Death vanished from the terrace.

102   Only one thing was left behind. A woman's shoe. A shoe no woman could ever have danced in. It was made of glass.

103   Did you intend to protest about the shoe? Shall I finish the story, or would you rather I did not? It is not the ending you are familiar with. Yes, I perceive you understand that, now.

104   I will go quickly, then, for your carriage must soon be here. And there is not a great deal more to relate.

105   The prince lost his mind. Partly from what he had seen, partly from the spells the young witch had netted him in. He could think of nothing but the girl who had named herself Ashella. He raved that Death had borne her away but he would recover her from Death. She had left the glass shoe as token of her love. He must discover her with the aid of the shoe. Whomsoever the shoe fitted would be Ashella. For there was this added complication, that Death might hide her actual appearance. None had seen the girl before. She had disappeared like smoke. The one infallible test was the shoe. That was why she had left it for him.

106   His ministers would have reasoned with the prince, but he was past reason. His intellect had collapsed as totally as only a profound intellect can. A lunatic, he rode about the city. He struck out at those who argued with him. On a particular occasion, drawing a dagger, he killed, not apparently noticing what he did. His demand was explicit. Every woman, young or old, maid or married, must come forth from her home, must put her foot into the shoe of glass. They came. They had no choice. Some approached in terror, some weeping. Even the aged beggar women obliged, and they cackled, enjoying the sight of royalty gone mad. One alone did not come.

107 Now it is not illogical that out of the hundreds of women whose feet were put into the shoe, a single woman might have been found that the shoe fitted. But this did not happen. Nor did the situation alter, despite a lurid fable that some, tickled by the idea of wedding the prince, cut off their toes that the shoe might fit them. And if they did, it was to no avail, for still the shoe did not.

108   Is it really surprising? The shoe was sorcerous. It constantly changed itself, its shape, its size, in order that no foot, save one, could ever be got into it.

109   Summer spread across the land. The city took on its golden summer glaze, its fetid summer smell.

110   What had been a whisper of intrigue, swelled into a steady distant thunder. Plots were being hatched.

111   One day, the silk merchant was brought, trembling and grey of face, to the prince. The merchant's dumbness had broken. He had unburdened himself of

his fear at confession, but the priest had not proved honest. In the dawn, men had knocked on the door of the merchant's house. Now he stumbled to the chair of the prince.

112   Both looked twice their years, but, if anything, the prince looked the elder. He did not lift his eyes. Over and over in his hands he turned the glass shoe.

113   The merchant, stumbling too in his speech, told the tale of his first wife and his daughter. He told everything, leaving out no detail. He did not even omit the end: that since the night of the banquet the girl had been absent from his house, taking nothing with her—save a young hazel from the garden beneath the tower.

114   The prince leapt from his chair.

115   His clothes were filthy and unkempt. His face was smeared with sweat and dust…it resembled, momentarily, another face.

116   Without guard or attendant, the prince ran through the city toward the merchant's house, and on the road, the intriguers waylaid and slew him. As he fell, the glass shoe dropped from his hands, and shattered in a thousand fragments.

117   There is little else worth mentioning.

118   Those who usurped the city were villains and not merely that, but fools. Within a year, external enemies were at the gates. A year more, and the city had been sacked, half burnt out, ruined. The manner in which you find it now, is somewhat better than it was then. And it is not now anything for a man to be proud of. As you were quick to note, many here earn a miserable existence by conducting visitors about the streets, the palace, showing them the dregs of the city's past.

119   Which was not a request, in fact, for you to give me money. Throw some from your carriage window if your conscience bothers you. My own wants are few.

120   No, I have no further news of the girl, Ashella, the witch. A devotee of Satanas, she has doubtless worked plentiful woe in the world. And a witch is long-lived. Even so, she will die eventually. None escapes Death. Then you may pity her, if you like. Those who serve the gentleman below—who can guess what their final lot will be? But I am very sorry the story did not please you. It is not, maybe, a happy choice before a journey.

121   And there is your carriage at last.

122   What? Ah, no, I shall stay here in the ballroom where you came on me. I have often paused here through the years. It is the clock. It has a certain—what shall I call it—power, to draw me back.

123   I am not trying to unnerve you. Why should you suppose that? Because of my knowledge of the city, of the story? You think that I am implying that I myself am Death? Now you laugh. Yes, it is absurd. Observe the twelfth figure on the clock. Is he not as you have always heard Death described? And am I in the least like that twelfth figure?

124   Although, of course, the story was not as you have heard it, either.

A Chinese "Cinderella"
Tuan Ch'êng-shih

"The earliest datable version of the Cinderella story anywhere in the world occurs in a Chinese book written about 850–860 A.D." Thus begins Arthur Waley's essay on the Chinese "Cinderella" in the March 1947 edition of Folk-Lore. *The recorder of the tale is a man named Tuan Ch'êng-shih, whose father was an important official in Szechwan and who himself held a high post in the office arranging the ceremonies associated with imperial ancestor worship.*

1 Among the people of the south there is a tradition that before the Ch'in and Han dynasties there was a cave-master called Wu. The aborigines called the place the Wu cave. He married two wives. One wife died. She had a daughter called Yeh-hsien, who from childhood was intelligent and good at making pottery on the wheel. Her father loved her. After some years the father died, and she was ill-treated by her step-mother, who always made her collect firewood in dangerous places and draw water from deep pools. She once got a fish about two inches long, with red fins and golden eyes. She put it into a bowl of water. It grew bigger every day, and after she had changed the bowl several times she could find no bowl big enough for it, so she threw it into the back pond. Whatever food was left over from meals she put into the water to feed it. When she came to the pond, the fish always exposed its head and pillowed it on the bank; but when anyone else came, it did not come out. The step-mother knew about this, but when she watched for it, it did not once appear. So she tricked the girl, saying, "Haven't you worked hard! I am going to give you a new dress." She then made the girl change out of her tattered clothing. Afterwards she sent her to get water from another spring and reckoning that it was several hundred leagues, the step-mother at her leisure put on her daughter's clothes, hid a sharp blade up her sleeve, and went to the pond. She called to the fish. The fish at once put its head out, and she chopped it off and killed it. The fish was now more than ten feet long. She served it up and it tasted twice as good as an ordinary fish. She hid the bones under the dunghill. Next day, when the girl came to the pond, no fish appeared. She howled with grief in the open countryside, and suddenly there appeared a man with his hair loose over his shoulders and coarse clothes. He came down from the sky. He consoled her, saying, "Don't howl! Your step-mother has killed the fish and its bones are under the dung. You go back, take the fish's bones and hide them in your room. Whatever you want, you have only to pray to them for it. It is bound to be granted." The girl followed his advice, and was able to provide herself with gold, pearls, dresses, and food whenever she wanted them.

2 When the time came for the cave-festival, the step-mother went, leaving the girl to keep watch over the fruit-trees in the garden. She waited till the step-mother was some way off, and then went herself, wearing a cloak of stuff spun from kingfisher feathers and shoes of gold. Her step-sister recognized her and said to the step-mother, "That's very like my sister." The step-mother suspected the same thing. The girl was aware of this and went away in such a hurry that she lost one shoe. It was picked up by one of the people of the cave. When

the step-mother got home, she found the girl asleep, with her arms around one of the trees in the garden, and thought no more about it.

3   This cave was near to an island in the sea. On this island was a kingdom called T'o-han. Its soldiers had subdued twenty or thirty other islands and it had a coast-line of several thousand leagues. The cave-man sold the shoe in T'o-han, and the ruler of T'o-han got it. He told those about him to put it on; but it was an inch too small even for the one among them that had the smallest foot. He ordered all the women in his kingdom to try it on, but there was not one that it fitted. It was light as down and made no noise even when treading on stone. The king of T'o-han thought the cave-man had got it unlawfully. He put him in prison and tortured him, but did not end by finding out where it had come from. So he threw it down at the wayside. Then they went everywhere[1] through all the people's houses and arrested them. If there was a woman's shoe, they arrested them and told the king of T'o-han. He thought it strange, searched the inner-rooms and found Yeh-hsien. He made her put on the shoe, and it was true.

4   Yeh-hsien then came forward, wearing her cloak spun from halcyon feathers and her shoes. She was as beautiful as a heavenly being. She now began to render service to the king, and he took the fish-bones and Yeh-hsien, and brought them back to his country.

5   The step-mother and step-sister were shortly afterwards struck by flying stones, and died. The cave people were sorry for them and buried them in a stone-pit, which was called the Tomb of the Distressed Women. The men of the cave made mating-offerings there; any girl they prayed for there, they got. The king of T'o-han, when he got back to his kingdom, made Yeh-hsien his chief wife. The first year the king was very greedy and by his prayers to the fish-bones got treasures and jade without limit. Next year, there was no response, so the king buried the fish-bones on the seashore. He covered them with a hundred bushels of pearls and bordered them with gold. Later there was a mutiny of some soldiers who had been conscripted and their general opened (the hiding-place) in order to make better provision for his army. One night they (the bones) were washed away by the tide.

6   This story was told me by Li Shih-yuan, who has been in the service of my family a long while. He was himself originally a man from the caves of Yung-chou and remembers many strange things of the South.

The Maiden, the Frog, and the Chief's Son
(An African "Cinderella")

The version of the tale that follows was recorded in the (West African) Hausa language and published, originally, in 1911 by Frank Edgar. The tale remained unavailable to nonspeakers of Hausa until 1965, when Neil Skinner (of UCLA) completed an English translation.

---

[1]Something here seems to have gone slightly wrong with the text. [Waley]

1   There was once a man had two wives, and they each had a daughter. And the one wife, together with her daughter, he couldn't abide; but the other, with her daughter, he dearly loved.

2   Well, the day came when the wife that he disliked fell ill, and it so happened that her illness proved fatal, and she died. And her daughter was taken over by the other wife, the one he loved; and she moved into that wife's hut. And there she dwelt, having no mother of her own, just her father. And every day the woman would push her out, to go off to the bush to gather wood. When she returned, she had to pound up the *fura.* Then she had the *tuwo* to pound, and, after that, to stir. And then they wouldn't even let her eat the *tuwo.* All they gave her to eat were the burnt bits at the bottom of the pot. And day after day she continued thus.

3   Now she had an elder brother, and he invited her to come and eat regularly at his home—to which she agreed. But still when she had been to the bush, and returned home, and wanted a drink of water, they wouldn't let her have one. Nor would they give her proper food—only the coarsest of the grindings and the scrapings from the pot. These she would take, and going with them to a borrow-pit, throw them in. And the frogs would come out and start eating the scrapings. Then, having eaten them up, they would go back into the water; and she too would return home.

4   And so things went on day after day, until the day of the Festival arrived. And on this day, when she went along with the scrapings and coarse grindings, she found a frog squatting here; and realized that he was waiting for her! She got there and threw in the bits of food. Whereupon the frog said, "Maiden, you've always been very kind to us, and now we—but just you come along tomorrow morning. That's the morning of the Festival. Come along then, and we'll be kind to you, in our turn." "Fine," she said, and went off home.

5   Next morning was the Festival, and she was going off to the borrow-pit, just as the frog had told her. But as she was going, her half-sister's mother said to her, "Hey—come here, you good-for-nothing girl! You haven't stirred the *tuwo,* or pounded the *fura,* or fetched the wood or the water." So the girl returned. And the frog spent the whole day waiting for her. But she, having returned to the compound, set off to fetch wood. Then she fetched water, and set about pounding the *tuwo,* and stirred it till it was done and then took it off the fire. And presently she was told to take the scrapings. She did so and went off to the borrow-pit, where she found the frog. "Tut tut, girl!" said he, "I've been waiting for you here since morning, and you never came." "Old fellow," she said, "You see, I'm a slave." "How come?" he asked. "Simple" she said, "My mother died— died leaving me her only daughter. I have an elder brother, but he is married and has a compound of his own. And my father put me in the care of his other wife. And indeed he had never loved my mother. So I was moved into the hut of his other wife. And, as I told you, slavery is my lot. Every morning I have to go off to the bush to get wood. When I get back from that I have to pound the *fura,* and then I pound the *tuwo,* and then start stirring it. And even when I have finished stirring the *tuwo,* I'm not given it to eat—just the scrapings." Says the frog, "Girl, give us your hand." And she held it out to him, and they both leaped into the water.

6   Then he went and picked her up and swallowed her. (And he vomited her up.) "Good people," said he, "Look and tell me, is she straight or crooked?" And they looked and answered, "She is bent to the left." So he picked her up and swallowed her again and then brought her up, and again asked them the same question. "She's quite straight now," they said. "Good," said he.

7   Next he vomited up cloths for her, and bangles, and rings, and a pair of shoes, one of silver, one of gold. "And now," said he, "Off you go to the dancing." So all these things were given to her, and he said to her, "When you get there, and when the dancing is nearly over and the dancers dispersing, you're to leave your golden shoe, the right one, there." And the girl replied to the frog, "Very well, old fellow, I understand," and off she went.

8   Meanwhile the chief's son had caused the young men and girls to dance for his pleasure, and when she reached the space where they were dancing he saw her. "Well!" said the chief's son, *"There's* a maiden for you, if you like. Don't you let her go and join in the dancing—I don't care whose home she comes from. Bring her here!" So the servants of the chief's son went over and came back with her to where he was. He told her to sit down on the couch, and she took her seat there accordingly.

9   They chatted together for some time, till the dancers began to disperse. Then she said to the chief's son, "I must be going home." "Oh, are you off?" said he. "Yes," said she and rose to her feet. "I'll accompany you on your way for a little" said the chief's son, and he did so. But she had left her right shoe behind. Presently she said, "Chief's son, you must go back now," and he did so. And afterwards she too turned and made her way back.

10   And there she found the frog by the edge of the water waiting for her. He took her hand and the two of them jumped into the water. Then he picked her up and swallowed her, and again vomited her up; and there she was just as she had been before, a sorry sight. And taking her ragged things she went off home.

11   When she got there, she said, "Fellow-wife of my mother, I'm not feeling very well." And the other said, "Rascally slut! You have been up to no good—refusing to come home, refusing to fetch water or wood, refusing to pound the *fura* or make the *tuwo.* Very well then! No food for you today!" And so the girl set off to her elder brother's compound, and there ate her food, and so returned home again.

12   But meanwhile, the chief's son had picked up the shoe and said to his father, "Dad, I have seen a girl who wears a pair of shoes, one of gold, one of silver. Look, here's the golden one—she forgot it and left it behind. She's the girl I want to marry. So let all the girls of this town, young and old, be gathered together, and let this shoe be given to them to put on." "Very well," said the chief.

13   And so it was proclaimed, and all the girls, young and old, were collected and gathered together. And the chief's son went and sat there beside the shoe. Each girl came, and each tried on the shoe, but it fitted none of them, none of the girls of the town; until only the girl who had left it was left. Then someone said "Just a minute! There's that girl in so-and-so's compound, whose mother died." "Yes, that's right," said another, "Someone go and fetch her." And someone went and fetched her.

14   But the minute she arrived to try it on, the shoe itself of its own accord, ran across and made her foot get into it. Then said the chief's son, "Right, here's my wife."

15   At this, the other woman—the girl's father's other wife—said, "But the shoe belongs to my daughter; it was she who forgot it at the place of the dancing, not this good-for-nothing slut." But the chief's son insisted that, since he had seen the shoe fit the other girl, as far as he was concerned, she was the one to be taken to his compound in marriage. And so they took her there, and there she spent one night.

16   Next morning she went out of her hut and round behind it, and there saw the frog. She knelt respectfully and said, "Welcome, old fellow, welcome," and greeted him. Says he, "Tonight we shall be along to bring some things for you." "Thank you" said she, and he departed.

17   Well, that night, the frog rallied all the other frogs, and all his friends, both great and small came along. And he, their leader, said to them, "See here—my daughter is being married. So I want every one of you to make a contribution." And each of them went and fetched what he could afford, whereupon their leader thanked them all, and then vomited up a silver bed, a brass bed, a copper bed, and an iron bed, and went on vomiting up things for her—such as woollen blankets, and rugs, and satins, and velvets.

18   "Now" said he to the girl, "If your heart is ever troubled, just lie down on this brass bed," and he went on, "And when the chief's son's other wives come to greet you, give them two calabashes of cola-nuts and ten thousand cowrie shells; then, when his concubines come to greet you, give them one calabash of cola-nuts and five thousand cowries." "Very well," said she. Then he said, "And when the concubines come to receive corn for making *tuwo*, say to them, 'There's a hide-bag full, help yourselves.'" "Very well," she said. "And," he went on, "If your father's wife comes along with her daughter and asks you what it is like living in the chief's compound, say 'Living in the chief's compound is a wearisome business—for they measure out corn there with the shell of a Bambara groundnut.'"

19   So there she dwelt, until one day her father's favorite wife brought her daughter along at night, took her into the chief's compound, and brought the other girl out and took her to her own compound. There she said, "Oh! I forgot to get you to tell her all about married life in the chief's compound." "Oh, it's a wearisome business," answered our girl. "How so?" asked the older woman, surprised. "Well, they use the shell of a Bambara groundnut for measuring out corn. Then, if the chief's other wives come to greet you, you answer them with the 'Pf' of contempt. If the concubines come to greet you, you clear your throat, hawk, and spit. And if your husband comes into your hut, you yell at him." "I see," said the other—and her daughter stayed behind the chief's son's compound.

20   Next morning when it was light, the wives came to greet her—and she said "Pf" to them. The concubines came to greet her, and she spat at them. Then when night fell, the chief's son made his way to her hut, and she yelled at him. And he was amazed and went aside, and for two days pondered the matter.

21   Then he had his wives and concubines collected and said to them, "Look,

now—I've called you to ask you. They haven't brought me the same girl. How did that one treat all of you?" "Hm—how indeed!" they all exclaimed. "Each morning, when we wives went to greet her, she would give us cola-nuts, two calabashes full, and cowries, ten thousand of them to buy tobacco flowers. And when the concubines went to greet her, she would give them a calabash of cola-nuts, and five thousand cowries to buy tobacco flowers with; and in the evening, for corn for *tuwo,* it would be a whole hide-bag full." "You see?" said he, "As for me, whenever I came to enter her hut, I found her respectfully kneeling. And she wouldn't get up from there, until I had entered and sat down on the bed."

22 "Hey," he called out, "Boys, come over here!" And when they came, he went into her hut and took a sword, and chopped her up into little pieces, and had them collect them and wrap them up in clothing; and then taken back to her home.

23 And when they got there, they found his true wife lying in the fireplace, and picking her up they took her back to her husband.

24 And next morning when it was light, she picked up a little gourd water-bottle and going around behind her hut, there saw the frog. "Welcome, welcome, old fellow," said she, and went on. "Old fellow, what I should like is to have a well built; and then you, all of you, can come and live in it and be close to me." "All right" said the frog, "You tell your husband." And she did so.

25 And he had a well dug for her, close to her hut. And the frogs came and entered the well and there they lived. That's all. *Kungurus kan kusu.*

Oochigeaskw—The Rough-Faced Girl (A Native American "Cinderella")

The following version of the tale was told, originally, in the Algonquin language. Native Americans who spoke Algonquian lived in the Eastern Woodlands of what is now the United States and in the northern, semiarctic areas of present-day Canada.

1 There was once a large village of the MicMac Indians of the Eastern Algonquins, built beside a lake. At the far end of the settlement stood a lodge, and in it lived a being who was always invisible. He had a sister who looked after him, and everyone knew that any girl who could see him might marry him. For that reason there were very few girls who did not try, but it was very long before anyone succeeded.

2 This is the way in which the test of sight was carried out: at evening-time, when the Invisible One was due to be returning home, his sister would walk with any girl who might come down to the lakeshore. She, of course, could see her brother, since he was always visible to her. As soon as she saw him, she would say to the girls:

3   "Do you see my brother?"

4   "Yes," they would generally reply—though some of them did say "No."

5   To those who said that they could indeed see him, the sister would say:

6   "Of what is his shoulder strap made?" Some people say that she would enquire:

7   "What is his moose-runner's haul?" or "With what does he draw his sled?"

8   And they would answer:

9   "A strip of rawhide" or "a green flexible branch," or something of that kind.

10   Then she, knowing that they had not told the truth, would say:

11   "Very well, let us return to the wigwam!"

12   When they had gone in, she would tell them not to sit in a certain place, because it belonged to the Invisible One. Then, after they had helped to cook the supper, they would wait with great curiosity, to see him eat. They could be sure he was a real person, for when he took off his moccasins they became visible, and his sister hung them up. But beyond this they saw nothing of him, not even when they stayed in the place all the night, as many of them did.

13   Now there lived in the village an old man who was a widower, and his three daughters. The youngest girl was very small, weak, and often ill: and yet her sisters, especially the elder, treated her cruelly. The second daughter was kinder, and sometimes took her side: but the wicked sister would burn her hands and feet with hot cinders, and she was covered with scars from this treatment. She was so marked that people called her *Oochigeaskw,* the Rough-Faced Girl.

14   When her father came home and asked why she had such burns, the bad sister would at once say that it was her own fault, for she had disobeyed orders and gone near the fire and fallen into it.

15   These two elder sisters decided one day to try their luck at seeing the Invisible One. So they dressed themselves in their finest clothes, and tried to look their prettiest. They found the Invisible One's sister and took the usual walk by the water.

16   When he came, and when they were asked if they could see him, they answered: "Of course." And when asked about the shoulder strap or sled cord, they answered: "A piece of rawhide."

17   But of course they were lying like the others, and they got nothing for their pains.

18   The next afternoon, when the father returned home, he brought with him many of the pretty little shells from which wampum was made, and they set to work to string them.

19   That day, poor Little Oochigeaskw, who had always gone barefoot, got a pair of her father's moccasins, old ones, and put them into water to soften them so that she could wear them. Then she begged her sisters for a few wampum shells. The elder called her a "little pest," but the younger one gave her some. Now, with no other clothes than her usual rags, the poor little thing went into the woods and got herself some sheets of birch bark, from which she made a dress, and put marks on it for decoration, in the style of long ago. She made a petticoat and a loose gown, a cap, leggings, and a handkerchief. She put on her father's large old moccasins, which were far too big for her, and went forth to

try her luck. She would try, she thought, to discover whether she could see the Invisible One.

20   She did not begin very well. As she set off, her sisters shouted and hooted, hissed and yelled, and tried to make her stay. And the loafers around the village, seeing the strange little creature, called out "Shame!"

21   The poor little girl in her strange clothes, with her face all scarred, was an awful sight, but she was kindly received by the sister of the Invisible One. And this was, of course, because this noble lady understood far more about things than simply the mere outside which all the rest of the world knows. As the brown of the evening sky turned to black, the lady took her down to the lake.

22   "Do you see him?" the Invisible One's sister asked.

23   "I do indeed—and he is wonderful!" said Oochigeaskw.

24   The sister asked:

25   "And what is his sled-string?"

26   The little girl said:

27   "It is the Rainbow."

28   "And, my sister, what is his bow-string?"

29   "It is The Spirit's Road—the Milky Way."

30   "So you *have* seen him," said his sister. She took the girl home with her and bathed her. As she did so, all the scars disappeared from her body. Her hair grew again, as it was combed, long, like a blackbird's wing. Her eyes were now like stars: in all the world there was no other such beauty. Then, from her treasures, the lady gave her a wedding garment, and adorned her.

31   Then she told Oochigeaskw to take the *wife's* seat in the wigwam: the one next to where the Invisible One sat, beside the entrance. And when he came in, terrible and beautiful, he smiled and said:

32   "So we are found out!"

33   "Yes," said his sister. And so Oochigeaskw became his wife.

Walt Disney's "Cinderella"
Adapted by Campbell Grant

Walter Elias Disney (1901–1966), winner of thirty-two Academy Awards, is world famous for his cartoon animations. After achieving recognition with cartoon shorts populated by such immortals as Mickey Mouse and Donald Duck, he produced the full-length animated film version of Snow White and the Seven Dwarfs *in 1937. He followed with other animations, including "Cinderella" (1950), which he adapted from Perrault's version of the tale. A Little* Golden Book, *the text of which appears here, was then adapted from the film by Campbell Grant.*

1   Once upon a time in a far-away land lived a sweet and pretty girl named Cinderella. She made her home with her mean old stepmother and her two stepsisters, and they made her do all the work in the house.

2   Cinderella cooked and baked. She cleaned and scrubbed. She had no time left for parties and fun.

3   But one day an invitation came from the palace of the king.

4   A great ball was to be given for the prince of the land. And every young girl in the kingdom was invited.

5   "How nice!" thought Cinderella. "I am invited, too."

6   But her mean stepsisters never thought of her. They thought only of themselves, of course. They had all sorts of jobs for Cinderella to do.

7   "Wash this slip. Press this dress. Curl my hair. Find my fan."

8   They both kept shouting, as fast as they could speak.

9   "But I must get ready myself. I'm going, too," said Cinderella.

10   "You!" they hooted. "The Prince's ball for you?"

11   And they kept her busy all day long. She worked in the morning, while her stepsisters slept. She worked all afternoon, while they bathed and dressed. And in the evening she had to help them put on the finishing touches for the ball. She had not one minute to think of herself.

12   Soon the coach was ready at the door. The ugly stepsisters were powdered, pressed, and curled. But there stood Cinderella in her workaday rags.

13   "Why, Cinderella!" said the stepsisters. "You're not dressed for the ball."

14   "No," said Cinderella. "I guess I cannot go."

15   Poor Cinderella sat weeping in the garden.

16   Suddenly a little old woman with a sweet, kind face stood before her. It was her fairy godmother.

17   "Hurry, child!" she said. "You are going to the ball!"

18   Cinderella could hardly believe her eyes! The fairy godmother turned a fat pumpkin into a splendid coach.

19   Next her pet mice became horses, and her dog a fine footman. The barn horse was turned into a coachman.

20   "There, my dear," said the fairy godmother. "Now into the coach with you, and off to the ball you go."

21   "But my dress—" said Cinderella.

22   "Lovely, my dear," the fairy godmother began. Then she really looked at Cinderella's rags.

23   "Oh, good heavens," she said. "You can never go in that." She waved her magic wand.

"Salaga doola,
Menchicka boola,
Bibbidi bobbidi boo!" she said.

24   There stood Cinderella in the loveliest ball dress that ever was. And on her feet were tiny glass slippers!

25   "Oh," cried Cinderella. "How can I ever thank you?"

26   "Just have a wonderful time at the ball, my dear," said her fairy godmother. "But remember, this magic lasts only until midnight. At the stroke of midnight, the spell will be broken. And everything will be as it was before."

27   "I will remember," said Cinderella. "It is more than I ever dreamed of."

28   Then into the magic coach she stepped, and was whirled away to the ball.

29   And such a ball! The king's palace was ablaze with lights. There was music and laughter. And every lady in the land was dressed in her beautiful best.

30   But Cinderella was the loveliest of them all. The prince never left her side, all evening long. They danced every dance. They had supper side by side. And they happily smiled into each other's eyes.

31   But all at once the clock began to strike midnight, Bong Bong Bong—

32   "Oh!" cried Cinderella. "I almost forgot!"

33   And without a word, away she ran, out of the ballroom and down the palace stairs. She lost one glass slipper. But she could not stop.

34   Into her magic coach she stepped, and away it rolled. But as the clock stopped striking, the coach disappeared. And no one knew where she had gone.

35   Next morning all the kingdom was filled with the news. The Grand Duke was going from house to house, with a small glass slipper in his hand. For the prince had said he would marry no one but the girl who could wear that tiny shoe.

36   Every girl in the land tried hard to put it on. The ugly stepsisters tried hardest of all. But not a one could wear the glass shoe.

37   And where was Cinderella? Locked in her room. For the mean old stepmother was taking no chances of letting her try on the slipper. Poor Cinderella! It looked as if the Grand Duke would surely pass her by.

38   But her little friends the mice got the stepmother's key. And they pushed it under Cinderella's door. So down the long stairs she came, as the Duke was just about to leave.

39   "Please!" cried Cinderella. "Please let me try."

40   And of course the slipper fitted, since it was her very own.

41   That was all the Duke needed. Now his long search was done. And so Cinderella became the prince's bride, and lived happily ever after—and the little pet mice lived in the palace and were happy ever after, too.

Cinderella
Anne Sexton

Anne Sexton (1928–1974) has been acclaimed as one of America's outstanding contemporary poets. In 1967, she won the Pulitzer Prize for poetry for Live or Die. *She published four other collections of her work, including* Transformations, *in which she recast, with a modern twist, popular European fairy tales such as "Cinderella." Sexton's poetry has appeared in* The New Yorker, Harper's, *the* Atlantic, *and* Saturday Review. *She received a Robert Frost Fellowship (1959), a scholarship from Radcliffe College's New Institute for Independent Study (1961–1963), a grant from the Ford Foundation (1964), and a Guggenheim Award (1969). In her book* All My Pretty Ones, *Sexton quoted Franz Kafka: "The books we need are the kind that act upon us like a misfortune, that make us suffer like the death of someone*

we love more than ourselves. A book should serve as the axe for the frozen sea within us."
Asked in an interview (by Patricia Marz) about this quotation, Sexton responded: "I think
[poetry] should be a shock to the senses. It should almost hurt."

You always read about it;
the plumber with twelve children
who wins the Irish Sweepstakes.
From toilets to riches.
5   That story.

Or the nursemaid,
some luscious sweet from Denmark
who captures the oldest son's heart.
From diapers to Dior.
10   That story.

Or a milkman who serves the wealthy,
eggs, cream, butter, yogurt, milk,
the white truck like an ambulance
who goes into real estate
15   and makes a pile.
From homogenized to martinis at lunch.

Or the charwoman
who is on the bus when it cracks up
and collects enough from the insurance.
20   From mops to Bonwit Teller.
That story.

Once
the wife of a rich man was on her deathbed
and she said to her daughter Cinderella:
25   Be devout. Be good, Then I will smile
down from heaven in the seam of a cloud.
The man took another wife who had
two daughters, pretty enough
but with hearts like blackjacks.
30   Cinderella was their maid.
She slept on the sooty hearth each night
and walked around looking like Al Jolson.
Her father brought presents home from town,
jewels and gowns for the other women
35   but the twig of a tree for Cinderella.
She planted that twig on her mother's grave
and it grew to a tree where a white dove sat.
Whenever she wished for anything the dove
would drop it like an egg upon the ground.
40   The bird is important, my dears, so heed him.

Next came the ball, as you all know.
It was a marriage market.
The prince was looking for a wife.
All but Cinderella were preparing
45   and gussying up for the big event.
Cinderella begged to go too.
Her stepmother threw a dish of lentils
into the cinders and said: Pick them
up in an hour and you shall go.
50   The white dove brought all his friends;
all the warm wings of the fatherland came,
and picked up the lentils in a jiffy.
No, Cinderella, said the stepmother,
you have no clothes and cannot dance.
55   That's the way with stepmothers.

Cinderella went to the tree at the grave
and cried forth like a gospel singer:
Mama! Mama! My turtledove,
send me to the prince's ball!
60   The bird dropped down a golden dress
and delicate little gold slippers.
Rather a large package for a simple bird.
So she went. Which is no surprise.

Her stepmother and sisters didn't
65   recognize her without her cinder face
and the prince took her hand on the spot
and danced with no other the whole day.

As nightfall came she thought she'd better
get home. The prince walked her home
70   and she disappeared into the pigeon house
and although the prince took an axe and broke
it open she was gone. Back to her cinders.
These events repeated themselves for three days.
However on the third day the prince
75   covered the palace steps with cobbler's wax
and Cinderella's gold shoe stuck upon it.
Now he would find whom the shoe fit
and find his strange dancing girl for keeps.
He went to their house and the two sisters
80   were delighted because they had lovely feet.
The eldest went into a room to try the slipper on
but her big toe got in the way so she simply
sliced it off and put on the slipper.
The prince rode away with her until the white dove
85   told him to look at the blood pouring forth.
That is the way with amputations.

They don't just heal up like a wish.
The other sister cut off her heel
but the blood told as blood will.
90   The prince was getting tired.
He began to feel like a shoe salesman.
But he gave it one last try.
This time Cinderella fit into the shoe
like a love letter into its envelope.

95   At the wedding ceremony
the two sisters came to curry favor
and the white dove pecked their eyes out.
Two hollow spots were left
like soup spoons.

100   Cinderella and the prince
lived, they say, happily ever after,
like two dolls in a museum case
never bothered by diapers or dust,
never arguing over the timing of an egg,
105   never telling the same story twice,
never getting a middle-aged spread,
their darling smiles pasted on for eternity.

Regular Bobbsey Twins.
That story.

Gudgekin the Thistle Girl
John Gardner

John Gardner (1933–1982), accomplished novelist, critic, and much-loved teacher of writing at the State University of New York, Binghamton, received the National Book Critics Award for his novel October Light *in 1976. His other works include* Grendel *(1971),* The Sunlight Dialogues *(1972),* Nickel Mountain *(1973), and numerous short stories and critical pieces for magazines such as* Esquire *and the* Hudson Review. *Folktale literature fascinated Gardner, and he wrote three collections of tales himself:* The King's Indian and Other Fireside Tales *(1974),* Dragon, Dragon and Other Tales *(1975), and* Gudgekin the Thistle Girl and Other Tales *(1976). Gardner died at the age of 49 in a motorcycle accident.*

1   In a certain kingdom there lived a poor little thistle girl. What thistle girls did for a living—that is, what people did with thistles—is no longer known, but whatever the reason that people gathered thistles, she was one of those who did it. All day long, from well before sunrise until long after sunset, she wandered the countryside gathering thistles, pricking her fingers to the bone, piling the thistles into her enormous thistle sack and carrying them back to her stepmother. It was a bitter life, but she always made the best of it and never felt the least bit sorry for herself, only for the miseries of others. The girl's name was Gudgekin.

2   Alas! The stepmother was never satisfied. She was arrogant and fiercely competitive, and when she laid out her thistles in her market stall, she would rather be dead than suffer the humiliation of seeing that some other stall had more thistles than she had. No one ever did, but the fear preyed on her, and no matter how many sacks of thistles poor Gudgekin gathered, there were never enough to give the stepmother comfort. "You don't earn your keep," the stepmother would say, crossing her arms and closing them together like scissors. "If you don't bring more thistles tomorrow, it's away you must go to the Children's Home and good riddance!"

3   Poor Gudgekin. Every day she brought more than yesterday, but every night the same. "If you don't bring more thistles tomorrow, it's away to the Home with you." She worked feverishly, frantically, smiling through her tears, seizing the thistles by whichever end came first, but never to her stepmother's satisfaction. Thus she lived out her miserable childhood, blinded by burning tears and pink with thistle pricks, but viewing her existence in the best light possible. As she grew older she grew more and more beautiful, partly because she was always smiling and refused to pout, whatever the provocation; and soon she was as lovely as any princess.

4   One day her bad luck changed to good. As she was jerking a thistle from between two rocks, a small voice cried, "Stop! You're murdering my children!"

5   "I beg your pardon?" said the thistle girl. When she bent down she saw a beautiful little fairy in a long white and silver dress, hastily removing her children from their cradle, which was resting in the very thistle that Gudgekin had been pulling.

6   "Oh," said Gudgekin in great distress.

7   The fairy said nothing at first, hurrying back and forth, carrying her children to the safety of the nearest rock. But then at last the fairy looked up and saw that Gudgekin was crying. "Well," she said. "What's this?"

8   "I'm sorry," said Gudgekin. "I always cry. It's because of the misery of others, primarily. I'm used to it."

9   "Primarily?" said the fairy and put her hands on her hips.

10   "Well," sniffled Gudgekin, "to tell the truth, I do sometimes imagine I'm not as happy as I might be. It's shameful, I know. Everyone's miserable, and it's wrong of me to whimper."

11   "Everyone?" said the fairy, "—miserable? Sooner or later an opinion like that will make a fool of you!"

12   "Well, I really don't know," said Gudgekin, somewhat confused. "I've seen very little of the world, I'm afraid."

13   "I see," said the fairy thoughtfully, lips pursed. "Well, that's a pity, but it's easily fixed. Since you've spared my children and taken pity on my lot, I think I should do you a good turn."

14   She struck the rock three times with a tiny golden straw, and instantly all the thistles for miles around began moving as if by their own volition toward the thistle girl's sack. It was the kingdom of fairies, and the beautiful fairy with whom Gudgekin had made friends was none other than the fairies' queen. Soon the fairies had gathered all the thistles for a mile around, and had filled the sack that Gudgekin had brought, and had also filled forty-three more, which they'd fashioned on the spot out of gossamer.

15   "Now," said the queen, "it's time that you saw the world."

16   Immediately the fairies set to work all together and built a beautiful chariot as light as the wind, all transparent gossamer woven like fine thread. The chariot was so light that it needed no horses but flew along over the ground by itself, except when it was anchored with a stone. Next they made the thistle girl a gown of woven gossamer so lovely that not even the queen of the kingdom had anything to rival it; indeed, no one anywhere in the world had such a gown or has ever had, even to this day. For Gudgekin's head the fairies fashioned a flowing veil as light and silvery as the lightest, most silvery of clouds, and they sprinkled both the veil and the gown with dew so they glittered as if with costly jewels.

17   Then, to a tinny little trumpeting noise, the queen of the fairies stepped into the chariot and graciously held out her tiny hand to the thistle girl.

18   No sooner was Gudgekin seated beside the queen than the chariot lifted into the air lightly, like a swift little boat, and skimmed the tops of the fields and flew away to the capital.

19   When they came to the city, little Gudgekin could scarcely believe her eyes. But there was no time to look at the curious shops or watch the happy promenading of the wealthy. They were going to the palace, the fairy queen said, and soon the chariot had arrived there.

20   It was the day of the kingdom's royal ball, and the chariot was just in time. "I'll wait here," said the kindly queen of the fairies. "You run along and enjoy yourself, my dear."

21   Happy Gudgekin! Everyone was awed by her lovely gown and veil; and even the fact that the fairies had neglected to make shoes for her feet, since they themselves wore none, turned out to be to Gudgekin's advantage. Barefoot dancing immediately became all the rage at court, and people who'd been wearing fine shoes for years slipped over to the window and slyly tossed them out, not to be outdone by a stranger. The thistle girl danced with the prince himself, and he was charmed more than words can tell. His smile seemed all openness and innocence, yet Gudgekin had a feeling he was watching her like a hawk. He had a reputation throughout the nine kingdoms for subtlety and shrewdness.

22   When it was time to take the thistle sacks back to her cruel stepmother, Gudgekin slipped out, unnoticed by anyone, and away she rode in the chariot.

23   "Well, how was it?" asked the queen of the fairies happily.

24   "Wonderful! Wonderful!" Gudgekin replied. "Except I couldn't help but notice how gloomy people were, despite their merry chatter. How sadly they frown

when they look into their mirrors, fixing their make-up. Some of them frown because their feet hurt, I suppose; some of them perhaps because they're jealous of someone; and some of them perhaps because they've lost their youthful beauty. I could have wept for them!"

25   The queen of the fairies frowned pensively. "You're a good-hearted child, that's clear," she said, and fell silent.

26   They reached the field, and the thistle girl, assisted by a thousand fairies, carried her forty-four sacks to her wicked stepmother. The stepmother was amazed to see so many thistle sacks, especially since some of them seemed to be coming to the door all by themselves. Nevertheless, she said—for her fear of humiliation so drove her that she was never satisfied—"A paltry forty-four, Gudgekin! If you don't bring more thistles tomorrow, it's away to the Home with you!"

27   Little Gudgekin bowed humbly, sighed with resignation, forced to her lips a happy smile, ate her bread crusts, and climbed up the ladder to her bed of straw.

28   The next morning when she got to the field, she found eighty-eight thistle sacks stuffed full and waiting. The gossamer chariot was standing at anchor, and the gossamer gown and veil were laid out on a rock, gleaming in the sun.

29   "Today," said the queen of the fairies, "we're going on a hunt."

30   They stepped into the chariot and flew off light as moonbeams to the royal park, and there, sure enough, were huntsmen waiting, and huntswomen beside them, all dressed in black riding-pants and riding-skirts and bright red jackets. The fairies made the thistle girl a gossamer horse that would sail wherever the wind might blow, and the people all said she was the most beautiful maiden in the kingdom, possibly an elf queen. Then the French horns and bugles blew, and the huntsmen were off. Light as a feather went the thistle girl, and the prince was so entranced he was beside himself, though he watched her, for all that, with what seemed to her a crafty smile. All too soon came the time to carry the thistle sacks home, and the thistle girl slipped from the crowd, unnoticed, and rode her light horse beside the chariot where the queen of the fairies sat beaming like a mother.

31   "Well," called the queen of the fairies, "how was it?"

32   "Wonderful!" cried Gudgekin, "it was truly wonderful! I noticed one thing, though. It's terrible for the fox!"

33   The queen of the fairies thought about it. "Blood sports," she said thoughtfully, and nodded. After that, all the rest of the way home, she spoke not a word.

34   When the thistle girl arrived at her stepmother's house, her stepmother threw up her arms in amazement at sight of those eighty-eight thistle-filled sacks. Nonetheless, she said as sternly as possible, "Eighty-eight! Why not a hundred? If you don't bring in more sacks tomorrow, it's the Home for you for sure!"

35   Gudgekin sighed, ate her dry crusts, forced a smile to her lips, and climbed the ladder.

36   The next day was a Sunday, but Gudgekin the thistle girl had to work just the same, for her stepmother's evil disposition knew no bounds. When she got to the field, there stood two times eighty-eight thistle sacks, stuffed to the tops and waiting. "*That* ought to fix her," said the queen of the fairies merrily. "Jump into your dress."

37   "Where are we going?" asked Gudgekin, as happy as could be.

38   "Why, to church, of course!" said the queen of the fairies. "After church we go to the royal picnic, and then we dance on the bank of the river until twilight."

39   "Wonderful!" said the thistle girl, and away they flew.

40   The singing in church was thrilling, and the sermon filled her heart with such kindly feelings toward her friends and neighbors that she felt close to dissolving in tears. The picnic was the sunniest in the history of the kingdom, and the dancing beside the river was delightful beyond words. Throughout it all the prince was beside himself with pleasure, never removing his eyes from Gudgekin, for he thought her the loveliest maiden he'd met in his life. For all his shrewdness, for all his aloofness and princely self-respect, when he danced with Gudgekin in her bejeweled gown of gossamer, it was all he could do to keep himself from asking her to marry him on the spot. He asked instead, "Beautiful stranger, permit me to ask you your name."

41   "It's Gudgekin," she said, smiling shyly and glancing at his eyes.

42   He didn't believe her.

43   "Really," she said, "it's Gudgekin." Only now did it strike her that the name was rather odd.

44   "Listen," said the prince with a laugh, "I'm *serious*. What is it really?"

45   "I'm serious too," said Gudgekin bridling. "It's Gudgekin the Thistle Girl. With the help of the fairies I've been known to collect two times eighty-eight sacks of thistles in a single day."

46   The prince laughed more merrily than ever at that. "Please," he said, "don't tease me, dear friend! A beautiful maiden like you must have a name like bells on Easter morning, or like songbirds in the meadow, or children's laughing voices on the playground! Tell me now. Tell me the truth. What's your name?"

47   "Puddin Tane," she said angrily, and ran away weeping to the chariot.

48   "Well," said the queen of the fairies, "how was it?"

49   "Horrible," snapped Gudgekin.

50   "Ah!" said the queen. "Now we're getting there!"

51   She was gone before the prince was aware that she was leaving, and even if he'd tried to follow her, the gossamer chariot was too fast, for it skimmed along like wind. Nevertheless, he was resolved to find and marry Gudgekin— he'd realized by now that Gudgekin must indeed be her name. He could easily understand the thistle girl's anger. He'd have felt the same himself, for he was a prince and knew better than anyone what pride was, and the shame of being made to seem a fool. He advertised far and wide for information on Gudgekin the Thistle Girl, and soon the news of the prince's search reached Gudgekin's cruel stepmother in her cottage. She was at once so furious she could hardly see, for she always wished evil for others and happiness for herself.

52   "I'll never in this world let him find her," thought the wicked stepmother, and she called in Gudgekin and put a spell on her, for the stepmother was a witch. She made Gudgekin believe that her name was Rosemarie and sent the poor baffled child off to the Children's Home. Then the cruel stepmother changed herself, by salves and charms, into a beautiful young maiden who looked exactly like Gudgekin, and she set off for the palace to meet the prince.

53   "Gudgekin!" cried the prince and leaped forward and embraced her. "I've been looking for you everywhere to implore you to forgive me and be my bride!"

54   "Dearest prince," said the stepmother disguised as Gudgekin, "I'll do so gladly!"

55   "Then you've forgiven me already, my love?" said the prince. He was surprised, in fact, for it had seemed to him that Gudgekin was a touch more sensitive than that and had more personal pride. He'd thought, in fact, he'd have a devil of a time, considering how he'd hurt her and made a joke of her name. "Then you really forgive me?" asked the prince.

56   The stepmother looked slightly confused for an instant but quickly smiled as Gudgekin might have smiled and said, "Prince, I forgive you everything!" And so, though the prince felt queer about it, the day of the wedding was set.

57   A week before the wedding, the prince asked thoughtfully, "Is it true that you can gather, with the help of the fairies, two times eighty-eight thistle sacks all in one day?"

58   "Haven't I told you so?" asked the stepmother disguised as Gudgekin and gave a little laugh. She had a feeling she was in for it.

59   "You did say that, yes," the prince said, pulling with two fingers at his beard. "I'd surely like to see it!"

60   "Well," said the stepmother, and curtsied, "I'll come to you tomorrow and you shall see what you shall see."

61   The next morning she dragged out two times eighty-eight thistle sacks, thinking she could gather in the thistles by black magic. But the magic of the fairies was stronger than any witch's, and since they lived in the thistles, they resisted all her fiercest efforts. When it was late afternoon the stepmother realized she had only one hope: she must get the real Gudgekin from the Children's Home and make her help.

62   Alas for the wicked stepmother, Gudgekin was no longer an innocent simpleton! As soon as she was changed back from simple Rosemarie, she remembered everything and wouldn't touch a thistle with an iron glove. Neither would she help her stepmother now, on account of all the woman's cruelty before, nor would she do anything under heaven that might be pleasing to the prince, for she considered him cold-hearted and inconsiderate. The stepmother went back to the palace empty-handed, weeping and moaning and making a hundred excuses, but the scales had now fallen from the prince's eyes—his reputation for shrewdness was in fact well founded—and after talking with his friends and advisers, he threw her in the dungeon. In less than a week her life in the dungeon was so miserable it made her repent and become a good woman, and the prince released her. "Hold your head high," he said, brushing a tear from his eye, for she made him think of Gudgekin. "People may speak of you as someone who's been in prison, but you're a better person now than before." She blessed him and thanked him and went her way.

63   Then once more he advertised far and wide through the kingdom, begging the real Gudgekin to forgive him and come to the palace.

64   "Never!" thought Gudgekin bitterly, for the fairy queen had taught her the importance of self-respect, and the prince's offense still rankled.

65   The prince mused and waited, and he began to feel a little hurt himself. He was a prince, after all, handsome and famous for his subtlety and shrewdness, and she was a mere thistle girl. Yet for all his beloved Gudgekin cared, he might as well have been born in some filthy cattle shed! At last he understood how things were, and the truth amazed him.

66   Now word went far and wide through the kingdom that the handsome prince had fallen ill for sorrow and was lying in his bed, near death's door. When the queen of the fairies heard the dreadful news, she was dismayed and wept tears of remorse, for it was all, she imagined, her fault. She threw herself down on the ground and began wailing, and all the fairies everywhere began at once to wail with her, rolling on the ground, for it seemed that she would die. And one of them, it happened, was living among the flowerpots in the bedroom of cruel little Gudgekin.

67   When Gudgekin heard the tiny forlorn voice wailing, she hunted through the flowers and found the fairy and said, "What in heaven's name is the matter, little friend?"

68   "Ah, dear Gudgekin," wailed the fairy, "our queen is dying, and if she dies we will all die of sympathy, and that will be that."

69   "Oh, you mustn't!" cried Gudgekin, and tears filled her eyes. "Take me to the queen at once, little friend, for she did a favor for me and I see I must return it if I possibly can!"

70   When they came to the queen of the fairies, the queen said, "Nothing will save me except possibly this, my dear: ride with me one last time in the gossamer chariot for a visit to the prince."

71   "Never!" said Gudgekin, but seeing the heartbroken looks of the fairies, she instantly relented.

72   The chariot was brought out from its secret place, and the gossamer horse was hitched to it to give it more dignity, and along they went skimming like wind until they had arrived at the dim and gloomy sickroom. The prince lay on his bed so pale of cheek and so horribly disheveled that Gudgekin didn't know him. If he seemed to her a stranger it was hardly surprising; he'd lost all signs of his princeliness and lay there with his nightcap on sideways and he even had his shoes on.

73   "What's this?" whispered Gudgekin. "What's happened to the music and dancing and the smiling courtiers? And where is the prince?"

74   "Woe is me," said the ghastly white figure on the bed. "I was once that proud, shrewd prince you know, and this is what's become of me. For I hurt the feelings of the beautiful Gudgekin, whom I've given my heart and who refuses to forgive me for my insult, such is her pride and uncommon self-respect."

75   "My poor beloved prince!" cried Gudgekin when she heard this, and burst into a shower of tears. "You have given your heart to a fool, I see now, for I am your Gudgekin, simple-minded as a bird! First I had pity for everyone but myself, and then I had pity for no one but myself, and now I pity all of us in this miserable world, but I see by the whiteness of your cheeks that I've learned too late!" And she fell upon his bosom and wept.

76   "You give me your love and forgiveness forever and will never take them back?" asked the poor prince feebly, and coughed.

77   "I do," sobbed Gudgekin, pressing his frail, limp hand in both of hers.

78   "Cross your heart?" he said.

79   "Oh, I do, I *do!*"

80   The prince jumped out of bed with all his wrinkled clothes on and wiped the thick layer of white powder off his face and seized his dearest Gudgekin by the waist and danced around the room with her. The queen of the fairies laughed like silver bells and immediately felt improved. "Why you fox!" she told the prince. All the happy fairies began dancing with the prince and Gudgekin, who waltzed with her mouth open. When she closed it at last it was to pout, profoundly offended.

81   "Tr-tr-*tricked!*" she spluttered.

82   "Silly goose," said the prince, and kissed away the pout. "It's true, I've tricked you, I'm not miserable at all. But you've promised to love me and never take it back. My advice to you is, make the best of it!" He snatched a glass of wine from the dresser as he merrily waltzed her past, and cried out gaily, "As for myself, though, I make no bones about it: I intend to watch out for witches and live happily ever after. You must too, my Gudgekin! Cross your heart!"

83   "Oh, very well," she said finally, and let a little smile out. "It's no worse than the thistles."

84   And so they did.

"Cinderella": A Story of Sibling Rivalry and Oedipal Conflicts
Bruno Bettelheim

Having read several variants of "Cinderella," you may have wondered what it is about this story that's prompted people in different parts of the world, at different times, to show interest in a child who's been debased but then rises above her misfortune. Why are people so fascinated with "Cinderella"?

Depending on the people you ask and their perspectives, you'll find this question answered in various ways. As a Freudian psychologist, Bruno Bettelheim believes that the mind is a repository of both conscious and unconscious elements. By definition, we aren't aware of what goes on in our unconscious; nonetheless, what happens there exerts a powerful influence on what we believe and on how we act. This division of the mind into conscious and unconscious parts is true for children no less than for adults. Based on these beliefs about the mind, Bettelheim analyzes "Cinderella" first by pointing to what he calls the story's essential theme: sibling rivalry, or Cinderella's mistreatment at the hands of her stepsisters. Competition among brothers and sisters presents a profound and largely unconscious problem to children, says Bettelheim. By hearing "Cinderella," a story that speaks directly to their unconscious, children are given tools that can help them resolve conflicts. Cinderella resolves her difficulties; children hearing the story can resolve theirs as well: This is the unconscious message of the tale.

Do you accept this argument? To do so, you'd have to agree with the author's reading of "Cinderella's" hidden meanings; and you'd have to agree with his assumptions concerning the conscious and unconscious mind and the ways in which the unconscious will seize upon the content of a story in order to resolve conflicts. Even if you don't accept Bettelheim's analysis, his essay makes fascinating reading. First, it is internally consistent—that is, he begins with a set of principles and then builds logically upon them, as any good writer will. Second, his analysis demonstrates how a scholarly point of view—a coherent set of assumptions about the way the world (in this case, the mind) works—creates boundaries for a discussion. Change the assumptions and you'll change the analyses that follow from them.

Bettelheim's essay is long and somewhat difficult. While he uses no subheadings, he has divided his work into four sections: paragraphs 2–10 are devoted to sibling rivalry; paragraphs 11–19, to an analysis of "Cinderella's" hidden meanings; paragraphs 20–24, to the psychological makeup of children at the end of their Oedipal period; and paragraphs 25–27, to the reasons "Cinderella," in particular, appeals to children in the Oedipal period.

Bruno Bettelheim, a distinguished psychologist and educator, was born in 1903 in Vienna. He was naturalized as an American citizen in 1939 and served as a professor of psychology at Rockford College and the University of Chicago. Awarded the honor of fellow by several prestigious professional associations, Bettelheim was a prolific writer and contributed articles to numerous popular and professional publications. His list of books includes Love Is Not Enough: The Treatment of Emotionally Disturbed Children *(1950),* The Informed Heart *(1960), and* The Uses of Enchantment *(1975), from which this selection has been excerpted. Bettelheim died in 1990.*

1   By all accounts, "Cinderella" is the best-known fairy tale, and probably also the best-liked. It is quite an old story; when first written down in China during the ninth century A.D., it already had a history. The unrivaled tiny foot size as a mark of extraordinary virtue, distinction, and beauty, and the slipper made of precious material are facets which point to an Eastern, if not necessarily Chinese, origin.[1] The modern hearer does not connect sexual attractiveness and beauty in general with extreme smallness of the foot, as the ancient Chinese did, in accordance with their practice of binding women's feet.

2   "Cinderella," as we know it, is experienced as a story about the agonies and hopes which form the essential content of sibling rivalry; and about the degraded heroine winning out over her siblings who abused her. Long before Perrault gave "Cinderella" the form in which it is now widely known, "having to live among the ashes" was a symbol of being debased in comparison to one's siblings, irrespective of sex. In Germany, for example, there were stories in which such an ash-boy later becomes king, which parallels Cinderella's fate. "Aschenputtel" is the title of the Brothers Grimm's version of the tale. The term originally designated a lowly, dirty kitchenmaid who must tend to the fireplace ashes.

3   There are many examples in the German language of how being forced to dwell among the ashes was a symbol not just of degradation, but also of sibling rivalry, and of the sibling who finally surpasses the brother or brothers who

---

[1]Artistically made slippers of precious material were reported in Egypt from the third century on. The Roman emperor Diocletian in a decree of A.D. 301 set maximum prices for different kinds of footwear, including slippers made of fine Babylonian leather, dyed purple or scarlet, and gilded slippers for women. [Bettelheim]

have debased him. Martin Luther in his *Table Talks* speaks about Cain as the God-forsaken evildoer who is powerful, while pious Abel is forced to be his ash-brother (*Asche-brüdel*), a mere nothing, subject to Cain; in one of Luther's sermons he says that Esau was forced into the role of Jacob's ash-brother. Cain and Able, Jacob and Esau are Biblical examples of one brother being suppressed or destroyed by the other.

4   The fairy tale replaces sibling relations with relations between step-siblings—perhaps a device to explain and make acceptable an animosity which one wishes would not exist among true siblings. Although sibling rivalry is universal and "natural" in the sense that it is the negative consequence of being a sibling, this same relation also generates equally as much positive feeling between siblings, highlighted in fairy tales such as "Brother and Sister."

5   No other fairy tale renders so well as the "Cinderella" stories the inner experiences of the young child in the throes of sibling rivalry, when he feels hopelessly outclassed by his brothers and sisters. Cinderella is pushed down and degraded by her stepsisters; her interests are sacrificed to theirs by her (step)mother; she is expected to do the dirtiest work and although she performs it well, she receives no credit for it; only more is demanded of her. This is how the child feels when devastated by the miseries of sibling rivalry. Exaggerated though Cinderella's tribulations and degradations may seem to the adult, the child carried away by sibling rivalry feels, "That's me; that's how they mistreat me, or would want to; that's how little they think of me." And there are moments—often long time periods—when for inner reasons a child feels this way even when his position among his siblings may seem to give him no cause for it.

6   When a story corresponds to how the child feels deep down—as no realistic narrative is likely to do—it attains an emotional quality of "truth" for the child. The events of "Cinderella" offer him vivid images that give body to his overwhelming but nevertheless often vague and nondescript emotions; so these episodes seem more convincing to him than his life experiences.

7   The term "sibling rivalry" refers to a most complex constellation of feelings and their causes. With extremely rare exceptions, the emotions aroused in the person subject to sibling rivalry are far out of proportion to what his real situation with his sisters and brothers would justify, seen objectively. While all children at times suffer greatly from sibling rivalry, parents seldom sacrifice one of their children to the others, nor do they condone the other children's persecuting one of them. Difficult as objective judgments are for the young child—nearly impossible when his emotions are aroused—even he in his more rational moments "knows" that he is not treated as badly as Cinderella. But the child often feels mistreated, despite all his "knowledge" to the contrary. That is why he believes in the inherent truth of "Cinderella," and then he also comes to believe in her eventual deliverance and victory. From her triumph he gains the exaggerated hopes for his future which he needs to counteract the extreme misery he experiences when ravaged by sibling rivalry.

8   Despite the name "sibling rivalry," this miserable passion has only incidentally to do with a child's actual brothers and sisters. The real source of it is the child's feelings about his parents. When a child's older brother or sister is more

competent than he, this arouses only temporary feelings of jealousy. Another child being given special attention becomes an insult only if the child fears that, in contrast, he is thought little of by his parents, or feels rejected by them. It is because of such an anxiety that one or all of a child's sisters or brothers may become a thorn in his flesh. Fearing that in comparison to them he cannot win his parents' love and esteem is what inflames sibling rivalry. This is indicated in stories by the fact that it matters little whether the siblings actually possess greater competence. The Biblical story of Joseph tells that it is jealousy of parental affection lavished on him which accounts for the destructive behavior of his brothers. Unlike Cinderella's, Joseph's parent does not participate in degrading him, and, on the contrary, refers him to his other children. But Joseph, like Cinderella, is turned into a slave, and, like her, he miraculously escapes and ends by surpassing his siblings.

9   Telling a child who is devastated by sibling rivalry that he will grow up to do as well as his brothers and sisters offers little relief from his present feelings of dejection. Much as he would like to trust our assurances, most of the time he cannot. A child can see things only with subjective eyes, and comparing himself on this basis to his siblings, he has no confidence that he, on his own, will someday be able to fare as well as they. If he could believe more in himself, he would not feel destroyed by his siblings no matter what they might do to him, since then he could trust that time would bring about a desired reversal of fortune. But since the child cannot, on his own, look forward with confidence to some future day when things will turn out all right for him, he can gain relief only through fantasies of glory—a domination over his siblings—which he hopes will become reality through some fortunate event.

10   Whatever our position within the family, at certain times in our lives we are beset by sibling rivalry in some form or other. Even an only child feels that other children have some great advantages over him, and this makes him intensely jealous. Further, he may suffer from the anxious thought that if he did have a sibling, his parents would prefer this other child to him. "Cinderella" is a fairy tale which makes nearly as strong an appeal to boys as to girls, since children of both sexes suffer equally from sibling rivalry, and have the same desire to be rescued from their lowly position and surpass those who seem superior to them.

11   On the surface, "Cinderella" is as deceptively simple as the story of Little Red Riding Hood, with which it shares greatest popularity. "Cinderella" tells about the agonies of sibling rivalry, of wishes coming true, of the humble being elevated, of true merit being recognized even when hidden under rags, of virtue rewarded and evil punished—a straightforward story. But under this overt content is concealed a welter of complex and largely unconscious material, which details of the story allude to just enough to set our unconscious associations going. This makes a contrast between surface simplicity and underlying complexity which arouses deep interest in the story and explains its appeal to the millions over centuries. To begin gaining an understanding of these hidden meanings, we have to penetrate behind the obvious sources of sibling rivalry discussed so far.

12   As mentioned before, if the child could only believe that it is the infirmities of his age which account for his lowly position, he would not have to suffer so wretchedly from sibling rivalry, because he could trust the future to right mat-

ters. When he thinks that his degradation is deserved, he feels his plight is utterly hopeless. Djuna Barnes's perceptive statement about fairy tales—that the child knows something about them which he cannot tell (such as that he likes the idea of Little Red Riding Hood and the wolf being in bed together)—could be extended by dividing fairy tales into two groups: one group where the child responds only unconsciously to the inherent truth of the story and thus cannot tell about it; and another large number of tales where the child preconsciously or even consciously knows what the "truth" of the story consists of and thus could tell about it, but does not want to let on that he knows. Some aspects of "Cinderella" fall into the latter category. Many children believe that Cinderella probably deserves her fate at the beginning of the story, as they feel they would, too; but they don't want anyone to know it. Despite this, she is worthy at the end to be exalted, as the child hopes he will be too, irrespective of his earlier shortcomings.

13   Every child believes at some period of his life—and this is not only at rare moments—that because of his secret wishes, if not also his clandestine actions, he deserves to be degraded, banned from the presence of others, relegated to a netherworld of smut. He fears this may be so, irrespective of how fortunate his situation may be in reality. He hates and fears those others—such as his siblings—whom he believes to be entirely free of similar evilness, and he fears that they or his parents will discover what he is really like, and then demean him as Cinderella was by her family. Because he wants others—most of all, his parents—to believe in his innocence, he is delighted that "everybody" believes in Cinderella's. This is one of the great attractions of this fairy tale. Since people give credence to Cinderella's goodness, they will also believe in his, so the child hopes. And "Cinderella" nourishes this hope, which is one reason it is such a delightful story.

14   Another aspect which holds large appeal for the child is the vileness of the stepmother and stepsisters. Whatever the shortcomings of a child may be in his own eyes, these pale into insignificance when compared to the stepsisters' and stepmother's falsehood and nastiness. Further, what these stepsisters do to Cinderella justifies whatever nasty thoughts one may have about one's siblings: they are so vile that anything one may wish would happen to them is more than justified. Compared to their behavior, Cinderella is indeed innocent. So the child, on hearing her story, feels he need not feel guilty about his angry thoughts.

15   On a very different level—and reality considerations coexist easily with fantastic exaggerations in the child's mind—as badly as one's parents or siblings seem to treat one, and much as one thinks one suffers because of it, all this is nothing compared to Cinderella's fate. Her story reminds the child at the same time how lucky he is, and how much worse things could be. (Any anxiety about the latter possibility is relieved, as always in fairy tales, by the happy ending.)

16   The behavior of a five-and-a-half-year-old girl, as reported by her father, may illustrate how easily a child may feel that she is a "Cinderella." This little girl had a younger sister of whom she was very jealous. The girl was very fond of "Cinderella," since the story offered her material with which to act out her feelings, and because without the story's imagery she would have been hard

pressed to comprehend and express them. This little girl had used to dress very neatly and liked pretty clothes, but she became unkempt and dirty. One day when she was asked to fetch some salt, she said as she was doing so, "Why do you treat me like Cinderella?"

17   Almost speechless, her mother asked her, "Why do you think I treat you like Cinderella?"

18   "Because you make me do all the hardest work in the house!" was the little girl's answer. Having thus drawn her parents into her fantasies, she acted them out more openly, pretending to sweep up all the dirt, etc. She went even further, playing that she prepared her little sister for the ball. But she went the "Cinderella" story one better, based on her unconscious understanding of the contradictory emotions fused into the "Cinderella" role, because at another moment she told her mother and sister, "You shouldn't be jealous of me just because I am the most beautiful in the family."

19   This shows that behind the surface humility of Cinderella lies the conviction of her superiority to mother and sisters, as if she would think: "You can make me do all the dirty work, and I pretend that I am dirty, but within me I know that you treat me this way because you are jealous of me because I am so much better than you." This conviction is supported by the story's ending, which assures every "Cinderella" that eventually she will be discovered by her prince.

20   Why does the child believe deep within himself that Cinderella deserves her dejected state? This question takes us back to the child's state of mind at the end of the oedipal period.[2] Before he is caught in oedipal entanglements, the child is convinced that he is lovable, and loved, if all is well within his family relationships. Psychoanalysis describes this stage of complete satisfaction with oneself as "primary narcissism." During this period the child feels certain that he is the center of the universe, so there is no reason to be jealous of anybody.

21   The oedipal disappointments which come at the end of this developmental stage cast deep shadows of doubt on the child's sense of his worthiness. He feels that if he were really as deserving of love as he had thought, then his parents would never be critical of him or disappoint him. The only explanation for parental criticism the child can think of is that there must be some serious flaw in him which accounts for what he experiences as rejection. If his desires remain unsatisfied and his parents disappoint him, there must be something wrong with him or his desires, or both. He cannot yet accept that reasons other than those residing within him could have an impact on his fate. In this oedipal jealousy, wanting to get rid of the parent of the same sex had seemed the most natural thing in the world, but now the child realizes that he cannot have his own way, and that maybe this is so because the desire was wrong. He is no longer so sure that he is preferred to his siblings, and he begins to suspect that this may be due to the fact that *they* are free of any bad thoughts or wrongdoing such as his.

---

[2]*Oedipal:* Freud's theory of the Oedipus complex held that at an early stage of development a child wishes to replace the parent of the same sex in order to achieve the exclusive love of the parent of the opposite sex.

22   All this happens as the child is gradually subjected to ever more critical attitudes as he is being socialized. He is asked to behave in ways which run counter to his natural desires, and he resents this. Still he must obey, which makes him very angry. This anger is directed against those who make demands, most likely his parents; and this is another reason to wish to get rid of them, and still another reason to feel guilty about such wishes. This is why the child also feels that he deserves to be chastised for his feelings, a punishment he believes he can escape only if nobody learns what he is thinking when he is angry. The feeling of being unworthy to be loved by his parents at a time when his desire for their love is very strong leads to the fear of rejection, even when in reality there is none. This rejection fear compounds the anxiety that others are preferred and also maybe preferable—the root of sibling rivalry.

23   Some of the child's pervasive feelings of worthlessness have their origin in his experiences during and around toilet training and all other aspects of his education to become clean, neat, and orderly. Much has been said about how children are made to feel dirty and bad because they are not as clean as their parents want or require them to be. As clean as a child may learn to be, he knows that he would much prefer to give free rein to his tendency to be messy, disorderly, and dirty.

24   At the end of the oedipal period, guilt about desires to be dirty and disorderly becomes compounded by oedipal guilt, because of the child's desire to replace the parent of the same sex in the love of the other parent. The wish to be the love, if not also the sexual partner, of the parent of the other sex, which at the beginning of the oedipal development seemed natural and "innocent," at the end of the period is repressed as bad. But while this wish as such is repressed, guilt about it and about sexual feelings in general is not, and this makes the child feel dirty and worthless.

25   Here again, lack of objective knowledge leads the child to think that he is the only bad one in all these respects—the only child who has such desires. It makes every child identify with Cinderella, who is relegated to sit among the cinders. Since the child has such "dirty" wishes, that is where he also belongs, and where he would end up if his parents knew of his desires. This is why every child needs to believe that even if he were thus degraded, eventually he would be rescued from such degradation and experience the most wonderful exaltation—as Cinderella does.

26   For the child to deal with his feelings of dejection and worthlessness aroused during this time, he desperately needs to gain some grasp on what these feelings of guilt and anxiety are all about. Further, he needs assurance on a conscious and an unconscious level that he will be able to extricate himself from these predicaments. One of the greatest merits of "Cinderella" is that, irrespective of the magic help Cinderella receives, the child understands that essentially it is through her own efforts, and because of the person she is, that Cinderella is able to transcend magnificently her degraded state, despite what appear as insurmountable obstacles. It gives the child confidence that the same will be true for him, because the story relates so well to what has caused both his conscious and his unconscious guilt.

27   Overtly "Cinderella" tells about sibling rivalry in its most extreme form: the jealousy and enmity of the stepsisters, and Cinderella's sufferings because of it. The many other psychological issues touched upon in the story are so covertly alluded to that the child does not become consciously aware of them. In his unconscious, however, the child responds to these significant details which refer to matters and experiences from which he consciously has separated himself, but which nevertheless continue to create vast problems for him.

Review Questions

1. What does living among ashes symbolize, according to Bettelheim?

2. What explanation does Bettelheim give for Cinderella's having stepsisters, not sisters?

3. In what ways are a child's emotions aroused by sibling rivalry?

4. To a child, what is the meaning of Cinderella's triumph?

5. Why is the fantasy solution to sibling rivalry offered by "Cinderella" appropriate for children?

6. Why is Cinderella's goodness important?

7. Why are the stepsisters and stepmother so vile, according to Bettelheim?

8. In paragraphs 20–26, Bettelheim offers a complex explanation of oedipal conflicts and their relation to sibling rivalry and the child's need to be debased, even while feeling superior. Summarize these seven paragraphs, and compare your summary with those of your classmates. Have you agreed on the essential information in this passage?

Discussion and Writing Suggestions

1. One identifying feature of psychoanalysis is the assumption of complex unconscious and subconscious mechanisms in human personality that explain behavior. In this essay, Bettelheim discusses the interior world of a child in ways that the child could never articulate. The features of this world include the following:

   All children experience sibling rivalry.

   The real source of sibling rivalry is the child's parents.

   Sibling rivalry is a miserable passion and a devastating experience.

   Children have a desire to be rescued from sibling rivalry (as opposed to rescuing themselves, perhaps).

Children experience an Oedipal stage, in which they wish to do away with the parent of the same sex and be intimate with the parent of the opposite sex.

"Every child believes at some point in his life…that because of his secret wishes, if not also his clandestine actions, he deserves to be degraded, banned from the presence of others, relegated to a netherworld of smut."

To what extent do you agree with these statements? Take one of the statements and respond to it in a four- or five-paragraph essay.

2. A critic of Bettelheim's position, Jack Zipes, argues that Bettelheim distorts fairy-tale literature by insisting that the tales have therapeutic value and speak to children almost as a psychoanalyst might. Ultimately, claims Zipes, Bettelheim's analysis corrupts the story of "Cinderella" and closes down possibilities for interpretation. What is your view of Bettelheim's psychoanalytic approach to fairy tales?

"Cinderella" and the Loss of Father-Love
Jacqueline M. Schectman

Jacqueline Schectman, director of training for the Jung Institute of Boston, is a therapist who draws on the theories of Carl Jung to help clients understand and address the root causes of their unhappiness. Jung (1875–1961) was the founder of Analytical Psychology. A one-time associate of Sigmund Freud, he developed the theory of the collective unconscious: a set of unconscious patterns in the psyche by which we order our world. These patters emerge from the unconscious as "archetypes" in stories, myths, and religions—as elements we seem to recognize instantly (perhaps without knowing why) and find deeply resonant, whichever culture we call our own. In "Cinderella," at least four archetypes—Father, Mother, wicked Stepmother, and the Shadow—figure prominently.

In her preface to the book in which "'Cinderella' and the Loss of Father-Love" appears, The Stepmother in Fairy Tales: Bereavement and the Feminine Shadow (1993), Schectman writes: "My approach to fairy tales is a reflection of my work with families and young children in that I tend to read the tales as bridges between inner and outer life, as stories of the struggle to find and define one's place in the world." For Schectman, the archetypal Stepmother is an important—and sympathetic—force both in the tale and in our lives, for "[s]he is a force against which the child can test his growing strength and maturity."

Throughout her essay, Schectman interweaves her analyst's notes on various clients with her analysis of "Cinderella." It is fascinating to watch how her understanding of her clients' inner lives informs her understanding of "Cinderella," and vice versa.

1   In my work with young children I have always been moved by the child's miraculous ability to find and use just those materials—games, stories, images,

even pieces of furniture—best suited for the healing of his or her wounds. So it was with Ginny, the quick and independent sister of a chronically ill child. Given her sister's special needs, Ginny was always second in her parents' hearts and minds; her frequent misbehavior was her only means of briefly holding center stage. In therapy she learned to use her hours in most expressive ways, directing me to play the role of rescuer/protector/friend, Godmother, Good Fairy or the Prince. At not quite four years of age, "Cinderella" was her chosen tale.

> Ginny's favorite made-up game was to run into the waiting room and hide in a space behind her mother's chair. In my part as Prince, I was to enter with an object, meant to be a shoe, in hand. I'd make a show of searching for the proper foot to fit the shoe, then discover Ginny in her niche. Thus found, she'd emerge in triumph from behind the chair, try on the "shoe", and prance around the room, a tiny Cinderella ready to be seen and loved.

2   "Cinderella" is a story for the Stepchild in us all, for the lonely one waiting for her Prince, for the one who feels unseen by those she loves. We weep with Cinderella when we feel harried and abused, when a Stepmother within warns against our dreams. Joy, she seems to say, is gold that will surely turn to lead at the stroke of twelve. Cinderella's triumph at the ball is a victory for all who'd prove Stepmother wrong, who would naysay her mocking, deprecating voice. When Cinderella dances with The Prince she dances for all who dare to wish for love, for recognition, for better days to come.[1]

3   When we recall the Cinderellas of our youth we probably remember Disney's lovely, laughing film, or the genteel stories of Perrault, in which a graciously forgiving Cinderella brings her sisters to her royal court.[2] The Grimms' Germanic version that we'll look at here is a darker tale, bloody and vengeful and full of mutilating loss.[3] Like most Stepmother tales, this "Cinderella" is a tale of grief. It begins, fittingly, with Mother's death-bed scene:

> The wife of a wealthy man fell ill, and was close to death. As her end drew near, she called her beloved daughter to her side, and said: "My dear and only child, remember to be pious and be good. God, then, will protect you, and I shall watch from heaven and be ever near." With that she died. The young girl visited her mother's grave each day and wept...

---

[1]A recent version of this tale, the movie *Pretty Woman,* takes great pleasure in proving the disapproving wrong. The heroine, dressed in her newly purchased clothes, returns to the store where she'd been insulted and ignored the day before. The look of shocked recognition on the saleswomen's faces sends a cheer up in the audience every time the film is shown.

[2]C. F. Neil Philip, *The Cinderella Story: The Origins and Variations of the Story Known as "Cinderella,"* for the history and evolution of this tale. In 1892, M.R. Cox compiled 345 variants of "Cinderella" in a collection reissued by Kraus Reprinted Limited in 1967.

[3]Children take great pleasure in the gory details of this tale, in which they find their fantasies of vengeance played out to the full. Adults, on the other hand, are shocked and prefer the prettied versions they recall.

4   In this bereavement tale, every member of the family responds to loss. Cinderella weeps and pines in her attachment to her grief; Stepmother and her daughters carry coldness and envy in their hearts, while father meets their cruel, unconscious power with an equally unconscious weakness and withdrawal. Cinderella is not the only orphan in this tale; her stepsisters have suffered loss and will suffer more throughout this tale, as cruelty turns upon itself in a mockery of Mother Love. The story begins with the Good Mother's death, ends with her punishing revenge and is taken up throughout with a desperate search for masculine security and love. When Mother dies, Father's love is lost as well, buried in the coldness of his grief.

> Winter came and went, and with the Spring the man had found another wife. The woman had two daughters of her own, beautiful like she, but vile in temperament and black of heart.

5   Cinderella's father takes a wife to ease his family's pain. Instead, he brings home grief equal to his own; each family amplifies the others' need. This "proud and haughty" Stepmother[4] has no softness for her husband's child; her widowhood has left her hard and dry. Her husband and the father of her family has gone, and she's raised two daughters as lonely and unhappy as herself. "Beautiful and fair of face" they may well be, but they seem to lack a lens through which to view the beauty that is theirs. It brings them little joy.

6   The bereavement that binds all the women in this tale—Stepmother, her daughters, surely the heroine herself—is that of father-loss. Each plays out an aspect of this loss, Cinderella in her flights from love, her sisters in their wish to win the Prince, Stepmother in her desperate need to see her daughters wed. She has had to raise her family alone, and her pride and haughtiness may well be her defense against the helplessness she has felt along the way. She's determined that her daughters have a better life than she, a life safely in a husband's care. Her stepchild is a mere distraction from her overall campaign, another burden in her overburdened life.

7   Fathers have played minor, seemingly unimportant, roles in the other tales we've looked at here. In "The Laidly Worm…," and in "Snow White," the widowed fathers seek and find their second wives, and then all but disappear, seemingly enchanted by the witches in their homes. "Hansel and Gretel"'s Woodsman-Father can do little more throughout the tale than wring his hands. In each of these tales, a son or brother or some passing foreign prince has appeared to defeat the Witch, rescue the princess and bring balance and completion to the tale. These young heroes are stepping into Father's shoes, for once-upon-a-time the Old King was a hero too, with a vitally important role in family life.

8   Neumann (1973:198) sees Father as the bearer of "tradition, culture and the development of consciousness," without whom the child might be lost in a

---

[4]So she is described in Perrault's French version of the tale, in which Stepmother is also called "the most disagreeable lady in the whole country." (Philip, 1989), and (Howell, 1985).

maternal uroboric state. In familial terms, one might understand Father as a necessary third to the perfect twoness of the mother-child bond. His presence moves the child from the paradise of mother's arms into an awareness of others in the world, and thus into awareness of himself as separate being. This archetypal Father carries conflict, therefore consciousness, into the child's life.

9   In Freudian terms, the Oedipal father stands between a mother and her son, challenging the child to take him on or to forego instinctual desire. A daughter, too, must give up her desire for her father, but not before experiencing, at a feeling level, the mutuality of that desire. Father's love, returned, is an acknowledgement of her as a sexual being. Samuels (1986) speaks to the importance of this relationship in feminine development:

> [The] erotic element guarantees the significance of the relationship.... The father could not be more different from his daughter; he is male and from another generation. This is what gives him his potential to stimulate an expansion and deepening of her personality. But he is also part of the same family as his daughter; that should make him "safe" as regards physical expression of this necessary sexuality and also provides a reason for his own emotional investment.

10   Aside from his role in his children's development, father's greatest contribution to a family's life may be in his support of mother in her nurturing and containing role. Ideally, he provides her with a place of rest, with a means of regathering her strength and her stores of loving care. A year ago I joined family and friends in the huge public picnic that marks Boston's celebration of the Fourth of July. A young woman sat among us and nursed her infant child, while her husband knelt beside her, feeding her while she fed their son. The small circle they created for themselves was so protective and complete that neither the surrounding crowd nor the fireworks could disturb their peace. In the absence of Father, this loving and protective third to the mother-child pair, the demands of mothering may make Stepmothers of us all. A depleted, isolated mother has less and less to give her child, and raising one's family alone may well evoke the Witch:

> Janet's husband, a submariner in the nuclear fleet, spent half his year at sea, three months on shore, three months on the sub. The first month of his seatime went relatively well; Janet, warmed by the last weeks of his time with her, felt cared-for and relaxed, and while she missed him she could feel his presence in their home. Her children felt this too, and joined her in her efforts toward a structured family life. By the second month they'd begin to test her limits and her will, and her unsupported weariness would begin to show: the grass would go unmowed, dishes go unwashed, and she'd lose her patience earlier each day. By the time the petty officer returned he'd find his children wild, his home a mess and his wife a screaming hag. They'd repair the damage over several weeks, but by then it was nearly time for him to leave again.

11   Father's absence need not be so stark to bring Stepmother to the scene. His partial withdrawal, born of helplessness and fear, and played out in rigidity of roles, can be just as keenly felt and not so easily addressed:

Anne was five, her brother seven, when her parents were divorced. Her father, at a loss for how to spend his weekend visit time with her, left her with his new young bride while he and brother washed the car, mowed the lawn and made household repairs. The four would meet only around meals. No one openly complained; father, after all, was a conscientious man trying hard to do his best. As one might guess, his wife and daughter blamed one another for their loneliness and loss, and their shared resentment grew into week-end dread. The stepmother acted out her archetypal role and Anne responded as a weepy, angry stepchild in her father's home.

12   "Cinderella" brings the theme of father-loss into sharp relief. In no other tale is his distance quite so darkly felt, his grief-borne blindness to the women's needs so stark. He takes no protective role in any version of the tale, and in some he is altogether gone. A Spanish "Cinderella"[5] has it thus:

> All were very happy for some months, until the father had to take a long trip, from which he never returned. With the absence of [Cinderella's] father, things began to change…

13   We can imagine the rage and disappointment in Cinderella's home. A widow remarries, seeking that second chance at life: comfort, warmth, an end to loneliness; a partner in parenting her difficult, demanding girls. Instead, she finds herself in sole charge of a grieving child, a child so attached to mourning that ashes seem her natural milieu. The widow, having been betrayed into a caretaker's role, is clearly having none of it; she has no comfort left to give. The child becomes the target of her wrath and her daughters join her in her outraged sense of loss. They've made do with very little loving parent-care, and scarcity has fed their greed. They are not about to share the little that they have.

> …the sisters plagued her with their insults and their ugly ways. They took her pretty clothes and bade her dress in rags and wooden shoes. "Where is the proud princess now?" they laughed, and had her work from dawn to dusk…

14   What deprivation lies behind the sisters' mocking cries, their need to taunt the grieving girl? Do they sense in her her mother's parting gift, the ever present nearness of the love they have never known? Like Psyche's sisters, they must destroy this stranger Eros in their midst, that which never has been, never can be, theirs. Love, beginning with a love of self, is an alien invader in their home, always longed for, always pushed away.

15   How does one empathize with ugliness, with the heartless lack of empathy played out by the sisters in this tale? Sitting with such darkness in an analytic hour is the most difficult of therapeutic tasks, for it constellates one's hateful sister when an understanding soulmate is the patient's desperate need:

---

[5]Tardy, William T., *Treasury of Children's Classics in Spanish and English,* Lincolnwood, National Textbook Company, 1987.

Beth, the fourth of seven girls, spent her childhood vying for her mother's ear, her father's eye. She feels today that she was never truly seen or heard. At thirty-five she is talented, quite beautiful, and by her own sad doing, utterly alone. At family gatherings she provokes her sisters and their mates until they turn their backs on her and leave. She undermines her colleagues, challenges her boss, and throws away her lovers whenever they want loving in return. I am often flooded with revulsion as she tells her tales; she seems so totally devoid of the capacity for empathy and love. Finally, at the nadir of my own disgust, I find that I am with her after all. The rage, and the separateness from her I feel are what she suffers through every hour of her life. I have a glimpse into the depth of her misery and pain.

16   The suffering of the "vile and black of heart" can be profound—a hopeless, lonely journey that would seem to have no end. In a gathering following one of my "Stepmother" talks, a young woman handed me this poem, then slipped away:

The Ugly Stepsister

I am an ugly stepsister.
Never have I lovingly done work.
Only cried and wanted to be rescued
By the Prince divinely dancing.
But my feet
They're too big.
Size nine.
Some seem to think
I could have been
  Cinderella if I'd only tried.
She who was born from love
And knew her true worth.
What did I have to sing about?
                    —D.M., Vancouver

17   What to sing about, indeed? A young woman growing up needs a mother, well-grounded in her own femininity, with whom she can identify if she's to value the woman in herself. Cinderella's mother, close to her child even in the moment of her death, provides the girl with that sense of self that shines through all her ashes and her tattered clothes. This centeredness provokes the envy that her sisters feel. The sisters, it would seem, lack that model in their lives; they've only known their mother in her darkness, in the incompleteness of her widow's grief. Worse, they've missed the sparkle in their father's eye, the admiring glance that can take a daughter's beauty in and return it to her with delight and love. Without that loving and reflective eye, what can these sisters know of their true worth? Samuels continues:

Many fathers and daughters fail to achieve this [erotic] link. This is because men tend to be extremely cautious about becoming erotically involved with their daughters (even in fantasy).... The father's failure to participate in a mutual attraction and mutual, painful renunciation of erotic fulfillment with his daughter deprives her of psychological enhancement. This can take many forms: mockery of her sexuality, over-strictness, indifference—and, if the symbolic dimension is savagely repressed, actual incest. In the absence of eros or its excess the daughter loses sight of herself as a sexually viable adult, with disastrous consequences. (Samuels, 1986)

18   All that the sisters in this tale know about father is his absence in their lives. Their loss is so profoundly felt it can only be expressed in surface greed, in a need for all the glitter that the world provides:

> One day, when [Cinderella's] father was about to travel to the nearest town, he asked his step-daughters what he might bring them from the fair. "Pretty dresses," said the one, while her sister asked for emeralds and pearls.

19   Their wish, in its essence, is to be remembered while father journeys to and from the fair. The child (of any age) who assaults the returning traveler with cries of "What did you bring for me?" wants to know that he was missed along the way. Cinderella has what seems, at first, to be a different sort of wish, but she, too, needs to be carried in her father's mind; good mothering is never quite enough:

> "Father, bring me the first branch to touch your hat as you ride toward home."

Nature herself seems to tap father on the head. He returns with a hazel twig, a symbol of hidden wisdom, divine inspiration and the Earth Goddess's chthonic powers (Cooper, 80). A grateful Cinderella plants the twig on her mother's grave:

> The Hazel twig, watered by Cinderella's many tears, grew to be a handsome tree, and a small white bird nestled in the tree and granted Cinderella's every wish.

20   This bird—the departed mother's spirit, always near—brings Cinderella everything but her father's loving eye. He seems to be oblivious to the abuse she suffers at her sisters' hands, nor does he see the envy eating at his stepdaughters' hearts. Could this father be determined not to see the younger women in his home, in an effort to deny the erotic energy he feels? In "Thousandfurs" (Grimm, #65), a variant on the Cinderella theme, a King is enjoined to incest by his dying wife; he promises to marry no one not as beautiful as she. As his daughter grows to be the beauty that her mother was, she becomes the object of the King's desire, and must protect herself by running off, hidden in a cloak of many furs. In family life, fathers may protect their daughters and themselves from their desires by turning a blind eye, by not seeing the young beauties growing up before their eyes. While father-daughter incest, acted out, may be the worst sort of sexual abuse, this denial of incestuous desire abuses sexuality in its most delicate and nascent state (cf. Samuels, above). When father turns away in fear, the admiring glances of a passing Prince may take on great importance for a Princess coming into bloom:

> Kate remembers the party for her "Sweet Sixteen," one of her first dates with
> the boy she'd eloped with at eighteen: "I'd had my hair cut short that day in
> a becoming style and I wore a dance dress I'd picked out for myself. When my
> father saw me he was furious, and told me I looked ugly, like some sort of
> tramp. Even I could see that wasn't so, but he had me close to tears. J. arrived
> just then and he was so impressed he could barely speak; I was a different girl
> than the one he'd seen that afternoon in school! The look on his face meant
> everything to me."

21   The longed for Prince may arrive in more pernicious forms. In Chapter One
we looked at brother-sister incest as a saving grace. When kept at the level of
desire, this intensity of sibling love serves as container for familial eros, for love
that has no other place to go. Sadly, separating action from desire is at times
too great a task for a child prince to bear. Brother-sister incest, acted out and
then repressed, becomes a hidden source of shame in adult life, a shadow on
one's erotic life.

> Gwen and her brother Josh grew up with a father who'd learned to keep his
> feelings under wraps. He viewed his wife and children from an icy distance that
> left all in a state of aching need. At some time early in their lives Gwen and
> Josh discovered comfort in one another's sexual touch. Gwen cannot yet say
> when this activity began, nor when it ceased to be. She only knows that plea-
> sure, now, is inextricably bound with shame; her body's needs evoke her great-
> est fears.

22   In our tale, as in the memory above, father's distance keeps everyone in a
state of need. As we might expect, the announcement of the Prince's Ball stirs
a flurry of excitement in Cinderella's home:

> The king in those days had a son, and the son was looking for a bride.
> Accordingly, the King ordered that a feast be held to last three days, to which
> all the beautiful young maidens in the country were to come. When the sisters
> learned that they would go they began ordering their stepsister about... "We
> will soon be dancing with the King!" Cinderella did as she was told, but longed
> to go herself...

23   Here, indeed, is the answer to all the women's prayers: A young man with eyes
for the beauties in his realm, with a heart ready to be won, with a throne to give
his bride. The sisters primp and preen and prepare to meet their Prince; Cinderella
weeps, and begs her Stepmother for leave to go along. The woman is aghast:

> "You go to the Feast? How can it be? You have no clothes and shoes, but you
> would dance? Nonsense!"

24   Three times Cinderella cries and pleads, and twice Stepmother sends her off
to pick the lentils from the ashes in the hearth. Like Psyche, enjoined by
Aphrodite to separate a pile of grain, Cinderella too—with the help of all the
creatures of the air—must sort things out before she can hope to meet her Eros
in the Prince. This sifting through the ashes of one's life, "The good for the pot,

the bad for the crop," is the torturous inner task that must precede true marriages of heart and mind. Note that nothing here is thrown away; the "bad" is recognized, and taken in. This is the work on Shadow, a task so painful only a Stepmother would demand that it be done.

> Paul spent his hour in recital of his lover's faults. They'd had one of their frequent fights and he wanted sympathy from me, support for his anger and his sense of being wronged. Instead, I asked him to examine his part in what transpired. How had he provoked her wrath, what might he have done to bring things to a different end? Such reflections were the last things on his mind and he snarled his disgust with me. What good was I if I couldn't take his side?

25   Cinderella never questions the rightness of her task. Always the good and pious child, she does as she is told, only to be turned away again:

> Cinderella thought: "Now I can go to the feast!" But her stepmother said again: "No Cinderella, you may not go. You have no gown and you cannot dance. The King would only laugh!"

26   Stepmother, in all her harshness, tells Cinderella one more necessary truth: the sackcloth and ashes of her grief are hardly proper dress for a royal ball, nor has she learned to dance while weeping on her mother's grave. If she's to meet The Prince she must put her mournful piety away.

> In the years in which I led discussion groups for single and divorced adults, I watched participants arrive in every stage of need, some still in mourning for the lover (husband, wife) they'd lost, or indeed had never had. Others were more ready to explore their newly "liberated" lives. The former frequently found sympathy and kindly nods of understanding in the group. Just as frequently they left the social hour alone. Something in their bearing said, "Not Yet," in words that all could understand.

27   Cinderella, having served her mourning time, is more ready than anyone can know. She calls upon her source of strength, and wastes no time in dressing for the ball:

> When all had gone, Cinderella repaired to her mother's grave, where she wept and wished beneath the tree:

> > *"Tremble, tremble little tree,*
> > *Gold and silver rain on me."*

> And the bird let fall a ballgown made of silver and of gold, and dancing shoes embroidered with the finest silk. Quickly Cinderella dressed, and just as quickly made her way to the palace of the King. There no one knew her in her golden gown…

28   We can imagine the fury and dismay of the sisters here, as they watch this lovely stranger dancing with the Prince. Why can't they catch his eye? They too

have done just as mother said, but her motherly advice to them has been very different than she offered to the stepchild in their home. All of their energies and hopes have gone into selection of their clothes and jewels; into polishing their courtly manners and their nails. Their every hair is perfectly in place, but they've not been asked to do the inner work demanded of this "foreign princess" clothed in gold. How are they to understand the apparent ease with which she's captured the young man's heart? Neither Stepmother nor her daughters can recognize the hard-working maiden within the golden dress; they see only that she has what they have not.

> After years of agonizing work, Gloria is in reunion with her gifted inner Prince. She plays piano with a local band, sings through her days and steals the time to write the poetry she loves. Her husband, however, feels great envy when he sees her living out her gifts; he is tied to work that brings him little joy. While he rationally connects her blossoming with her therapeutic work he is nonetheless enraged; how dare she find the inner fire that still eludes his life?

29   Cinderella's sisters need not have envied her so much; for all her work, she is unprepared for the suddenness of her success, and flies away in fear:

> Cinderella danced until evening fell. But then she begged her leave. The Prince wished to see her home but Cinderella fled from him…

30   How can Cinderella trust the love and admiration of the Prince when her own father seems to see her not at all? Like his wife and stepdaughters, he's failed to recognized the beautiful young woman dancing at the ball.

> Bridget's father died when she was just thirteen, too soon to see his "little nurse" become the sprightly beauty she would grow to be. Today she is indeed a nurse, and she has married well, to a man who loves her more than she can quite believe. When they meet with friends she compares herself to all the other women in the room, and imagines that her husband finds her wanting in some way; they must be more desirable than she. She cannot find that father-voice within herself to say: You are the fairest in *this* land!

31   How is Cinderella's Prince to capture the mysterious, elusive girl? He asks the man who ought to know her best:

> The Prince waited until Cinderella's father came, and told him of the unknown princess hidden in the pigeon-house. Her father thought: "Could it be Cinderella?" At that the old man took an axe and chopped the pigeon-house to bits, but no one was inside.

32   "Can it be Cinderella?" We can hear the shock and wonder in the old man's voice. As the veil of his denial slowly lifts, he must contemplate his daughter in all of her nubility and charm. Can this lovely woman be his little girl? When he attacks the pigeon-house, and then the pear tree into which the Prince has seen the maiden flee, it's as if the very nature of her feminine allure must be

destroyed before she leaves him for a younger man! When we ask, "Who gives this bride to wed?" we are asking father no small thing. His sense of loss at such a time may well evoke an angry, vengeful "Stepfather," not unlike the "Stepmother" who is forced to see her sons off into the world.

33   The father Kate recalls could not bear to see her sexuality emerge. When she eloped with the man who'd caught her eye, father's pain and grief made for an encounter he'd regret throughout his life.

> When Kate eloped, her father, furious, summoned her, her husband and his parents to a meeting at his home. He told her husband that he'd made a terrible mistake: his bride was lazy, disobedient, dishonest and a tramp. "She will be a rope around your neck for life!" The bridegroom was not inclined to "give her back," but the father-daughter rift took many years to heal.

34   Three times Cinderella ventures out to dance, and three times runs away, to hide once more among the ashes by the hearth. This retreat until the time is right, until the world feels safe enough for love, is part of the connection to the earth Cinderella demonstrates throughout this tale. There is safety in her dirty rags, and she'll hide in them until her doubts and fears release her into life.

> Anne's first forays into sexuality were frightening and harsh; she needed time then to withdraw into herself, to feel into her fear and rage, to learn to be more conscious of the woman she'd become. Accordingly, she made herself as unattractive as her natural beauty would allow: cropped her hair, gained thirty pounds, dressed in shapeless, faded clothes. She remained thus, to her family's dismay, for several years. When a gentle Prince appeared, with the capacity to see the woman hidden in the rags, she allowed herself to venture forth, to see and to be seen. The Prince has come and gone, but Anne has thrown her rags away.

35   Cinderella's Prince has made his choice, and as the festival comes to an end he determines not to let his disappearing partner go again:

> [The Prince]...had seen that the palace steps were smeared with tar and pitch, and when she fled one of her golden slippers remained, caught in the sticky tar. The Prince held the slipper in his hand, and felt he would surely find the maiden now.
>   When morning came, he took the golden slipper to Cinderella's house, and showed it to her father, saying: "I will only wed the maid who fits this shoe." Then the sisters had some hope, for they had dainty feet.

36   Now begins the darkest portion of this tale, for while Cinderella hides herself and waits, her sisters try to fit themselves into her tiny shoe. As they try the slipper on their soft, uncalloused feet we hear that most dangerous of sounds, the well-intentioned voice of an ambitious mother-who-knows-best:

> The elder of the two took the shoe into another room to try it on, her mother at her side. Alas, the slipper would not fit. But her mother handed

her a knife and said: "Cut off your toe; you'll have no need to walk when you are Queen." This the maiden did, and despite her pain, forced her foot into the tiny shoe. The King's son, seeing her thus shod, carried her away to be his bride.

37   With the advent of an eligible Prince, mothers may see a life of ease ahead for their daughters—better lives, indeed, than they have had! They beseech their daughters to conform, to fit themselves into some pre-formed, perfect mold. There is freedom in security, they say, and time enough ahead for all your little quirks and dreams, for all the imperfections that make you who you are. There will be a time to take a stand, to run that race or write that book, time enough for wholeness when you are safely married to The Prince.

38   Perhaps modern women should know better, should know that a woman must accept herself—stand on her own two feet—if she hopes to find a Prince. But for all of that, one can't quite shut out the loud, collective voice that joins the desperate-mother voice within. "Reshape your nose," one hears. "File down your teeth and suck the fat out of your thighs; don't you know the competition's terrible out there?" When one's sense of self depends upon a Prince out in the world, no sacrifice of flesh, no loss of spirit feels too great.

39   What is tragic for the sisters in this tale is that their sacrifices are in vain. The Prince carries each of the pain-wracked maidens off in turn, only to be cautioned by the pigeons perched in Cinderella's magic tree: his bloodied bride is false. Now the younger of the sisters has her turn:

> Then the second sister took the shoe into another room, where her mother waited with a knife. Again, the shoe was just too small, and the mother said, "Cut a bit off your heel..."[6]

and once more, the Prince is warned as he carries the false sister by the hazel tree. Both young women offer up their mutilated feet, but the Prince has no desire for a bloodied, martyred bride.

> Linda recalls her mother when her family was young: "She had a joyful, playful side to her that she completely put away whenever my father was at home. None of us ever saw him laugh, and she assumed, I think, that laughter was not permitted in our house. I know she loved to swim and run and play out in the woods—other people told me this—but she simply let this go in an effort to 'grow up.' Eventually my father found his pleasure far from home; he told my mother that she'd ceased to move him long ago."

---

[6]"Cinderella" has its source in seventh-century China, and this version of the tale may be a commentary on the practice of binding female feet. In China, highborn female children had their feet bound into tiny, lotus shapes. "The four smaller toes were folded under the sole, the whole foot was folded so the underside of the heel and toes were brought together." Women with bound feet were the essence of beauty and nobility. "Chinese men were conditioned to intense fetishistic passion for deformed female feet. Chinese poets sang ecstatic praises of the lotus feet that aroused their desire to fever pitch. The crippled woman was considered immeasurably charming by reason of her vulnerability, her suffering and her helplessness—she couldn't even escape an attacker by running away (Walker 319).

40   We must admire the determination of the Prince. He returns each of the injured sisters to her home, and asks Cinderella's father, one more time, for assistance in finding his true bride. Father must finally release his only child, his last reminder of the wife and happy home he'd once enjoyed. His answer is so cruel and final in its disavowal that it serves to free Cinderella from his grasp. If she'd ever hoped to catch her father's eye, to win his love, that hope is surely gone with his reply:

> "These maids have proved themselves untrue. Have you none other here beneath your roof?" "No," said the man; "only a scrawny servant-girl, here before my late wife died. She could not be your bride, I know." But when the Prince persisted, they called Cinderella in.

41   For Cinderella and her Prince, what follows is the moment of surrender, recognition, and a sense that all is as it's meant to be. Cinderella, her face washed clean of ashes and of grief, tries on the golden shoe that fits her perfectly:

> When Cinderella stood to face her dancing partner once again, the King's son knew her then, and cried out in great joy, "That is my true bride!"

42   Such moments are the stuff of which romantic literature and art are made.[7] Our beloved—the one we've dreamed of all our lives and have always known within ourselves—suddenly appears, fantasy made flesh. All of our ambivalence is gone, there is nothing left to do but bow to love, and pray that it will last.

43   As the Prince carries Cinderella off, we're told that Stepmother and her daughters become "pale with rage"—and pale, perhaps, with the sisters' loss of blood. One would think the tale could end right there: justice has been done, Cinderella has her man, her vain and selfish sisters have their mutilated feet and empty beds. But the worst is yet to come for the unhappy sisters in this tale:

> On the wedding day, the false sisters came to join the royal train, hoping to find favor in their sister's eyes. On the way to the church they walked at Cinderella's side, the elder on the left, the younger on the right. The birds pecked out one eye of each. On their return from church, each walked on Cinderella's other side, and the doves pecked out their remaining eyes. Thus the sisters were struck blind, and were punished for their falseness all their days.

44   Blindness has been a theme throughout this tale: Father, blind with hope, seeks a second wife, then shuts his eyes to the redoubled family grief within his home, to his daughters' needs and the abuse being perpetrated out of unmet needs. His blindness in the dark further darkens every facet of his family's life. The stepsisters, blinded by their envy of Cinderella's glowing inner light, attempt to douse it with their cruel and mocking taunts. And Stepmother, who can see very well what *Cinderella* needs to bring her into life, cannot provide her daughters with the guidance they require. She is too close to them to see them as they are, too attached to their "well being" to offer them an honestly reflective

---

[7] Cf. Haule, John, *Divine Madness: Archetypes of Romantic Love,* Boston, Shambhala Press, 1990.

eye. As a "good" mother she has indeed been blind, closed against the wisdom that the harsh, truth-telling Stepmother can, and does, provide.

45   The pigeons in this tale, embodiments of mother-nurturance throughout, provide the sisters with the sort of cursed gift a Stepmother might give. What might blindness to the outer world mean to the "vile, black-hearted" daughters we have come to know? Their focus has always been "out there," on all the pretty things that shine and glow in the material world, on all the treasures others might possess. They've had no insight, for to peer inside themselves would have revealed an emptiness too terrible to bear. Their sunlight gone, perhaps their helpless groping in the dark will provide the inward shift of vision that their souls require, the clear reflective eye always absent from their lives.

46   Cinderella's tale begins with her loving mother's death; her time in rags and ashes prepares her for her life ahead. Her sisters face another sort of death. They can never be the prancing, carefree careless girls they were; their hopes of dancing at another ball are gone. What their lives will be we cannot know, but the necessary darkness that precedes all inner work has come. It is in this darkness that the sisters' tale begins.

Bibliography

Cooper, J.C., *An Illustrated Encyclopedia of Traditional Symbols.* London: Thames and Hudson, Ltd., 1979.

Neumann, Erich, *The Child.* Ralph Manheim, Translator; New York: Harper & Row, 1973.

———. *The Great Mother,* Ralph Manheim, Translator; Princeton: Princeton University Press, 1963.

Walker, Barbara G., *The Woman's Encyclopedia of Myths and Secrets.* San Francisco: Harper & Row, 1983.

Review Questions

1. Schectman explains that "Cinderella" is a "bereavement tale [in which] every member of the family responds to loss." What does she mean? More particularly, what role does "father-loss" play in this bereavement? Why is father-loss so significant in this story?

2. In which ways, according to Schectman, can the Stepmother and the Stepsisters be seen in a sympathetic light?

3. In paragraph 10, Schectman writes that "the demands of mothering may make Stepmothers of us all." How so? What is the father's role in a mother's becoming a "wicked" Stepmother?

4. In the tale, the Stepmother orders Cinderella to separate lentils from ashes in the hearth. What is the Jungian explanation of this cruel task, and why is it the Stepmother's job to inflict this cruelty?

5. What is the significance of Cinderella's three visits to the ball?

6. What is the significance of the sisters' cutting off parts of their feet to fit the slipper, according to Schectman? Psychologically, why does Cinderella not need to cut off parts of her feet?

7. According to Schectman, what is the significance of the birds pecking out the eyes of the Stepsisters?

Discussion and Writing Suggestions

1. Schectman has presented the Stepmother and Stepsisters of "Cinderella" sympathetically, making it possible for us to empathize with them. Given your reading of this essay, are you convinced? Do you now see the Stepmother and Stepsisters in a new light?

2. Comment on Schectman's use of notes made about her clients to inform her reading of "Cinderella"—and, conversely, of her use of the fairy tale to better understand issues in the lives of her clients. Make a few general observations about this use of an analyst's notes, and then discuss one particular example in depth.

3. In paragraph 8, Schectman writes that the father's "presence moves the child from the paradise of mother's arms into an awareness of others in the world, and thus into awareness of himself as separate being. This archetypal Father carries conflict, therefore consciousness, into the child's life." Schectman is claiming a necessary relationship between conflict and consciousness. How can conflict lead to consciousness?

4. What is the process by which a good mother can turn into a wicked Stepmother? (See paragraph 10—especially Schectman's analyst's notes—for a starting point.) How can good mother and wicked Stepmother co-exist in one person?

5. Identify one of Schectman's insights into "Cinderella" that seems especially new and powerful. How has Schectman used principles of Jungian analysis to arrive at this insight?

6. Are there any instances in which Schectman's use of Jungian analysis leads to a strained or unconvincing insight into "Cinderella," in your view? Discuss.

7. Reread the poem that Schectman quotes, "The Ugly Stepsister" (paragraph 16). Your comments? (If you're temporarily stumped for reactions, consider: What assumption does the author of the poem make about the relationship between readers of "Cinderella" and the tale itself? Do you share this assumption? Have you ever identified with a character in a fairy tale?)

Cinderella's Stepsisters
Toni Morrison

Toni Morrison (b. 1931), an African American novelist of such acclaimed works as The Bluest Eye *(1970),* Song of Solomon *(1977),* Tar Baby *(1981), Pulitzer-prize winning* Beloved *(1987),* Jazz *(1992), and* Paradise *(1998), received the Nobel Prize for literature in 1993. Critics have hailed her work as being at once both mythic, in its themes and characters, and intensely realistic in its depictions of the sorrows, struggles, and hopes of black people. The selection that follows is excerpted from an address Morrison delivered at Barnard College. In it, she exhorts her women listeners to treat their "stepsisters" more humanely than Cinderella's stepsisters treated her.*

1 Let me begin by taking you back a little. Back before the days at college. To nursery school, probably, to a once-upon-a-time time when you first heard, or read, or, I suspect, even saw "Cinderella." Because it is Cinderella that I want to talk about; because it is Cinderella who causes me a feeling of urgency. What is unsettling about that fairy tale is that it is essentially the story of a household—a world, if you please—of women gathered together and held together in order to abuse another woman. There is, of course, a rather vague absent father and a nick-of-time prince with a foot fetish. But neither has much personality. And there are the surrogate "mothers," of course (god- and step-), who contribute both to Cinderella's grief and to her release and happiness. But it is her stepsisters who interest me. How crippling it must have been for those young girls to grow up with a mother, to watch and imitate that mother, enslaving another girl.

2 I am curious about their fortunes after the story ends. For contrary to recent adaptations, the stepsisters were not ugly, clumsy, stupid girls with outsize feet. The Grimm collection describes them as "beautiful and fair in appearance." When we are introduced to them they are beautiful, elegant, women of status, and clearly women of power. Having watched and participated in the violent dominion of another woman, will they be any less cruel when it comes their turn to enslave other children, or even when they are required to take care of their own mother?

3 It is not a wholly medieval problem. It is quite a contemporary one: feminine power when directed at other women has historically been wielded in what has been described as a "masculine" manner. Soon you will be in a position to do the very same thing. Whatever your background—rich or poor—whatever the history of education in your family—five generations or one—you have taken advantage of what has been available to you at Barnard and you will therefore have both the economic and social status of the stepsisters *and* you will have their power.

4 I want not to *ask* you but to *tell* you not to participate in the oppression of your sisters. Mothers who abuse their children are women, and another woman, not an agency, has to be willing to stay their hands. Mothers who set fire to school buses are women, and another woman, not an agency, has to tell them to stay their hands. Women who stop the promotion of other women in careers are women, and another woman must come to the victim's aid. Social and wel-

fare workers who humiliate their clients may be women, and other women colleagues have to deflect their anger.

5   I am alarmed by the violence that women do to each other: professional violence, competitive violence, emotional violence. I am alarmed by the willingness of women to enslave other women. I am alarmed by a growing absence of decency on the killing floor of professional women's worlds. You are the women who will take your place in the world where *you* can decide who shall flourish and who shall wither; you will make distinctions between the deserving poor and the undeserving poor; where you can yourself determine which life is expendable and which is indispensable. Since you will have the power to do it, you may also be persuaded that you have the right to do it. As educated women the distinction between the two is first-order business.

6   I am suggesting that we pay as much attention to our nurturing sensibilities as to our ambition. You are moving in the direction of freedom and the function of freedom is to free somebody else. You are moving toward self-fulfillment, and the consequences of that fulfillment should be to discover that there is something just as important as you are and that just-as-important thing may be Cinderella—or your stepsister.

7   In your rainbow journey toward the realization of personal goals, don't make choices based only on your security and your safety. Nothing is safe. That is not to say that anything ever was, or that anything worth achieving ever should be. Things of value seldom are. It is not safe to have a child. It is not safe to challenge the status quo. It is not safe to choose work that has not been done before. Or to do old work in a new way. There will always be someone there to stop you. But in pursuing your highest ambitions, don't let your personal safety diminish the safety of your stepsister. In wielding the power that is deservedly yours, don't permit it to enslave your stepsisters. Let your might and your power emanate from that place in you that is nurturing and caring.

8   Women's rights is not only an abstraction, a cause; it is also a personal affair. It is not only about "us"; it is also about me and you. Just the two of us.

Discussion and Writing Suggestions

1. Cinderella "is essentially the story of a household—a world, if you please—of women gathered together and held together in order to abuse another woman." Do you agree with Morrison's characterization of the story?

2. Morrison finds *Cinderella* to be a story that teaches girls unhealthy ways of treating other girls—their "stepsisters." The assumption is that fairy tales, heard while young, can have a lasting influence on attitudes later in life. Do you accept the assumption?

3. In paragraph 5, Morrison writes: "Since you will have the power to [wield influence over others], you may also be persuaded that you have the right to do it." What is the difference between having the

power to take an action and assuming that you have the right to take that action? Specifically, in the terms of this essay, what does Morrison mean?

4. Morrison writes that she is "alarmed by the violence that women do to each other: professional violence, competitive violence, emotional violence." Is it your sense that the "violence" women do to one another is different in degree or kind than the violence they do to men—or that men do to men?

5. Morrison suggests an opposition between women's ambition and their "nurturing sensibilities." First, what are "nurturing sensibilities?" Are they learned (from fairy tales, for instance)? Are they inborn? What is the difference between ambition and nurturing sensibilities? How might this difference manifest itself in the workplace? In the Perrault version of Cinderella? In the Grimm version?

6. In Morrison's view, female power differs from male power. How so?

7. Why should women be any less likely "to participate in the oppression" of other women than they are in the oppression of men? Do women owe it to other women to show special consideration? Why?

8. What is your response to this address, delivered at Barnard College? If you're a woman, what do you take from this selection? If you're a man, what do you take? Do you suppose that responses to the address will differ along gender lines? Explain.

SYNTHESIS ACTIVITIES

1. In 1910, Antti Aarne published one of the early classifications of folktale types as an aid to scholars who were collecting tales and needed an efficient means for telling where, and with what changes, similar tales had appeared. In 1927, folklorist Stith Thompson, translating and enlarging Aarne's study, produced a work that is now a standard reference for folklorists the world over. We present the authors' description of type 510 and its two forms, 510A ("Cinderella") and 510B. Use this description as a basis on which to compare and contrast any three versions of "Cinderella."

510. *Cinderella and Cap o' Rushes.*

   I. *The Persecuted Heroine.* (a) The heroine is abused by her stepmother and stepsisters, or (b) flees in disguise from her father who wants to marry her, or (c) is cast out by him because she has said that she loved him like salt, or (d) is to be killed by a servant.

II. *Magic Help.* While she is acting as servant (at home or among strangers) she is advised, provided for, and fed (a) by her dead mother, (b) by a tree on the mother's grave, or (c) by a supernatural being, or (d) by birds, or (e) by a goat, a sheep, or a cow. When the goat is killed, there springs up from her remains a magic tree.

III. *Meeting with Prince.* (a) She dances in beautiful clothing several times with a prince who seeks in vain to keep her, or she is seen by him in church. (b) She gives hints of the abuse she has endured, as servant girl, or (c) she is seen in her beautiful clothing in her room or in the church.

IV. *Proof of Identity.* (a) She is discovered through the slipper-test, or (b) through a ring which she throws into the prince's drink or bakes in his bread. (c) She alone is able to pluck the gold apple desired by the knight.

V. *Marriage with the Prince.*

VI. *Value of Salt.* Her father is served unsalted food and thus learns the meaning of her earlier answer.

Two forms of the type follow.

A. *Cinderella.* The two stepsisters. The stepdaughter at the grave of her own mother, who helps her (milks the cow, shakes the apple tree, helps the old man). Threefold visit to church (dance). Slipper-test.

B. *The Dress of Gold, of Silver, and of Stars. (Cap o' Rushes).* Present of the father who wants to marry his own daughter. The maiden as servant of the prince, who throws various objects at her. The threefold visit to the church and the forgotten shoe. Marriage.

2. Speculate on the reasons folktales are made and told. As you develop a theory, rely first on your own hunches regarding the origins and functions of folktale literature. You might want to recall your experiences as a child listening to tales so that you can discuss their effects on you. Rely as well on the variants of "Cinderella," which you should regard as primary sources (just as scholars do). And make use of the critical pieces you've read—Thompson, Bettelheim, Schectman, and Morrison—selecting pertinent points from each that will help clarify your points. *Remember:* Your own speculation should dominate the paper. Use sources to help you make *your* points.

3. At the conclusion of his article, Stith Thompson writes:

> Literary critics, anthropologists, historians, psychologists, and aestheticians are all needed if we are to hope to know why folktales are made, how they are invented, what art is used in their telling, how they grow and change and occasionally die.

What is your opinion of the critical work you've read on "Cinderella"? Writing from various perspectives, authors in this chapter have analyzed the tale. To what extent have the analyses illuminated "Cinderella" for you? (Have the analyses in any way "ruined" your ability to enjoy "Cinderella"?) To what extent do you find the analyses off the mark? Are the attempts at analysis inappropriate for a children's story? In your view, what place do literary critics, anthropologists, historians, and psychologists have in discussing folktales?

In developing a response to these questions, you might begin with Thompson's quotation and then follow directly with a statement of your thesis. In one part of your paper, critique the work of Bettelheim, Schectman, and/or Morrison as a way of demonstrating which analyses of folktales (if any) seem worthwhile to you. In another section of the paper (or, perhaps, woven into the critiques), you'll refer directly to the variants of "Cinderella." For the sake of convenience, you might refer to a single variant. If so, state as much to the reader and explain your choice of variant.

4. Review the variants of "Cinderella" and select two you would read to your child. In an essay, justify your decision. Which of the older European variants do you prefer: Grimm? Perrault? How do the recent versions by Sexton, Lee, Disney, and Gardner affect you? And what of the Chinese, African, and Algonquin versions—are they recognizably "Cinderella"?

You might justify the variants you've selected by defining your criteria for selection and then analyzing the stories separately. (Perhaps you will use Aarne and Thompson's classification—see Synthesis Activity 1.) You might justify your choices negatively— that is, by defining your criteria and then *eliminating* certain variants because they don't meet the criteria. In concluding the paper, you might explain how the variants you've selected work as a pair. How do they complement each other? (Or, perhaps, they *don't* complement each other and this is why you've selected them.)

5. Try writing a version of "Cinderella" and setting it on a college campus. For your version of the story to be an authentic variant, you'll need to retain certain defining features, or motifs. See Aarne and Thompson—Synthesis Activity 1. As you consider the possibilities for your story, recall Thompson's point that the teller of a folktale borrows heavily on earlier versions; the virtue of telling is not in rendering a new story but in retelling an old one and *adapting* it to local conditions and needs. Unless you plan to write a commentary "Cinderella," as Sexton's poem is, you should retain the basic motifs of the old story and add details that will appeal to your particular audience: your classmates.

6. In her 1981 book *The Cinderella Complex,* Colette Dowling wrote:

> It is the thesis of this book that personal, psychological dependency—
> the deep wish to be taken care of by others—is the chief force holding
> women down today. I call this "The Cinderella Complex"—a network
> of largely repressed attitudes and fears that keep women in a kind of
> half-light, retreating from the full use of their minds and creativity.
> Like Cinderella, women today are still waiting for something external
> to transform their lives.

In an essay, respond to Dowling's thesis. First, apply her
thesis to a few of the variants of "Cinderella." Does the thesis
hold in each case? Next, respond to her view that "the chief force
holding women down today" is psychological dependency, or the
need for "something external" (i.e., a Prince) to transform their
lives. In your experience, have you observed a Cinderella complex at work?

7. Discuss the process by which Cinderella falls in love in these tales.
The paper that you write will be an extended comparison and contrast in which you observe this process at work in the variants and
then discuss similarities and differences. (In structuring your paper,
you'll need to make some choices: Which variants will you discuss
and in what order?) At the conclusion of your extended comparison
and contrast, try to answer the "so what" question. That is, pull
your observations together and make a statement about
Cinderella's falling in love. What is the significance of what you've
learned? Share this significance with your readers.

8. Write an explanatory synthesis in which you attempt to define a
feminist perspective on "Cinderella" as this is expressed by Sexton
and Morrison. If you are feeling ambitious, you can write a second
part to this essay by *applying* that definition to one variant.
Essentially, you would be writing a critique of that variant, based
on the principles defined in the opening section of your essay.
Conclude by giving your assessment of the variant, based on the
feminist principles you have defined.

9. Compare and contrast Bettelheim's Freudian analysis of
"Cinderella" with Schectman's Jungian analysis. Which seems the
more illuminating? Realize that you are not comparing the work of
Freud and Jung (a daunting task!). Rather (and more modestly),
concentrate on the limited material at hand. Two analysts, working
in different traditions, apply the principles of their traditions in
order to better understand a fairy tale—and ourselves. What are the
relative strengths and weaknesses of these two efforts?

RESEARCH ACTIVITIES

1. Research the fairy-tale literature of your ancestors, both the tales and any critical commentary that you can find on them. Once you have read the material, talk with older members of your family to hear any tales they have to tell. (Seek, especially, oral versions of stories you have already read.) In a paper, discuss the role that fairy-tale literature has played, and continues to play, in your family.

2. Locate the book *Morphology of the Folktale* (1958), by Russian folklorist Vladimir Propp. Use the information you find there to analyze the elements of any three fairy tales of your choosing. In a paper, report on your analysis and evaluate the usefulness of Propp's system of classifying the key elements of fairy-tale literature.

3. Bruno Bettelheim's *Uses of Enchantment* (1975) generated a great deal of reaction on its publication. Read Bettelheim and locate as many reviews of his work as possible. Based on your own reactions and on your reading of the reviews, write an evaluation in which you address Bettelheim's key assumption that fairy-tale literature provides important insights into the psychological life of children.

4. Locate and study multiple versions of any fairy tale other than "Cinderella." Having read the versions, identify—and write your paper on—what you feel are the defining elements that make the tales variants of a single story. See if you can find the tale listed as a "type" in Aarne and Thompson, *The Types of Folk-Tales.* If you wish, argue that one version of the tale is preferable to others.

5. Jack Zipes, author of *Breaking the Magic Spell* (1979), takes the approach that fairy tales are far from innocuous children's stories; rather, they inculcate the unsuspecting with the value systems of the dominant culture. Write a paper in which you evaluate an interpretation of fairy-tale literature. In your paper, explicitly address the assumption that fairy tales are not morally or politically neutral but, rather, imply a distinct set of values.

6. Write a children's story. Decide on the age group that you will address, and then go to a local public library and find several books directed to the same audience. (1) Analyze these books and write a brief paper in which you identify the story elements that seem especially important for your intended audience. (2) Then attempt your own story. (3) When you have finished, answer this question: What values are implicit in your story? What will children who read or hear the story learn about themselves and their world? Plan to submit your brief analytical paper, your story, and your final comment.

7. Videotape, and then study, several hours of Saturday morning cartoons. Then locate and read a collection of Grimm's fairy tales. In a comparative analysis, examine the cartoons and the fairy tales along any four or five dimensions that you think are important. The point of your comparisons and contrasts will be to determine how well the two types of presentations stack up against each other. Which do you find more entertaining? Illuminating? Ambitious? Useful? (These criteria are suggestions only. You should generate your own criteria as part of your research.)

8. Arrange to read to your favorite young person a series of fairy tales. Based on your understanding of the selections in this chapter, develop a list of questions concerning the importance or usefulness of fairy-tale literature to children. Read to your young friend on several occasions and, if possible, talk about the stories after you read them (or while you are reading). Then write a paper on your experience, answering as many of your initial questions as possible. (Be sure in your paper to provide a profile of the child with whom you worked; to review your selection of stories; and to list the questions you wanted to explore.)

You, the Jury

WILLIAM ROPER: So now you'd give the Devil benefit of law!

MORE: Yes. What would you do? Cut a great road through the law to get after the Devil?

ROPER: I'd cut down every law in England to do that!

MORE: Oh? And when the last law was down, and the Devil turned round on you—where would you hide, Roper, the laws all being flat? This country's planted thick with laws from coast to coast—man's laws, not God's—and if you cut them down—and you're just the man to do it—d'you really think you could stand upright in the winds that would blow then? [*Quietly.*] Yes, I'd give the Devil benefit of law, for my own safety's sake.

—Robert Bolt, *A Man for All Seasons*

The above lines indicate one way of looking at the law, but clearly, many people take a different view of the legal profession. One of Shakespeare's characters declares, "The first thing we do, let's kill all the lawyers" (*Henry VI*, Pt II). Never mind that while playing off the public's perennial resentment of lawyers, Shakespeare intended this line as a sardonic commentary on mob mentality. Still, everyone loves a good lawyer joke. ("Why didn't the shark eat the lawyer who fell out of his boat? Professional courtesy.") Of course, in these litigious times, the same people who tell lawyer jokes hurry to get their own after they slip on the ice in their neighbor's driveway or when they're arrested on a drunk driving charge.

In Robert Bolt's play, Thomas More views the law as civilized society's first line of defense against chaos and anarchy. Without the law, he argues, we would have no protection against "the winds that would blow" in a lawless society. But even if we don't accept this exalted view of the law, it's certainly true that all of us, at some points in our lives, will have dealings with the law (not necessarily as a defendant, we hasten to add), and that as citizens of society, most of us rely upon the law to protect us against those who would violate our rights and to impose damages upon those who have injured us. (Those who don't rely on the law often rely instead on their own private arsenals to repel invaders and predators.)

If the average citizen is not the plaintiff or the defendant in a court case, then her or his most common direct experience with the law may be as a juror. Chosen at random from a cross-section of the population, jurors may be called upon to render a verdict in a civil case (a case of product liability, for example, or negligence, or libel) or in a criminal case (such as robbery or murder). After the lawyers on both sides have presented their witnesses and their evidence, after they have made their arguments and rebutted their opponents, and after the judge has explained the law to the jury in language they can understand, it falls to the jury to apply the law to the facts of the particular case. They must decide whether or not a rule has been violated, and if it has, the price the defendant must pay—perhaps a fine, perhaps a jail term, perhaps even the forfeiture of his or her life.

Underlying this chapter is the assumption that you are a jury member (or perhaps a judge) in a particular case. You will be presented with the facts of the case. You will also be presented with the relevant law. It will be your task to study the issues, to render a verdict either for the plaintiff or for the defendant, and—most importantly, for our purposes—to explain your reasoning. Don't worry about becoming tangled in the thickets of the law (and some of these thickets are very dense indeed). We will assume no previous legal knowledge, and for each case we will present enough facts and enough statements about the law to enable you to make an educated judgment, just as if you were a member of a jury.

Don't worry, either, about making the "right" choice. The most important thing is not that you come out on the correct side or even the side that actually prevailed in the end. (Keep in mind that through the appeals process, a higher court can reverse the ruling of a lower court—saying, in effect, that the lower court was wrong.) What is important is that you carefully analyze the case, that you go through the reasoning process systematically and logically, in a manner consistent with the facts.

In one sense, this chapter previews a particular situation in which you might one day find yourself—fulfilling your civic duty as a juror in an actual case. More generally, it will provide you with some interesting cases through which you can practice a very fundamental intellectual task in the academic and professional worlds: the task of applying a general rule or principle to a particular case or circumstance. Obviously, this is a process that doesn't happen only in law. As a student in a sociology course, for example, you might show how some principles relating to the ways that individuals obey authority apply in particular cases (for example, the suicides in the Heaven's Gate cult) and even allow you to make certain broad predictions about behavior. As a film student, you might show how the general features of the typical *film noir* operate in particular films, such as *The Big Sleep* or *A Touch of Evil.*

Besides exercising your intellectual faculties, you'll see that it's often fascinating to plunge into legal battles. After all, legal cases are, at heart, conflicts, and conflicts are inherently interesting. That's why we like to read books or watch TV shows or movies that are set in the courtroom.

We begin our chapter with a number of civil cases (that is, cases of private wrongs), starting with "The Maiden and the Pot of Gold: A Case of Emotional

Distress," in which a woman sues some men who tricked her into believing that she had recovered a pot of gold from a field. Following are three selections that will help orient you to the legal system and legal reasoning. In "The American Legal System," attorney David Hricik explains where the law comes from and describes the process of the typical lawsuit. In "How to Present Your Case Systematically and Logically," Veda R. Charrow, Myra K. Erhardt, and Robert P. Charrow describe legal thinking and legal writing, focusing particularly on the important IRAC (issue, rule, application, conclusion) technique. In *"Venezia v. Miller Brewing Company:* A Defective Beer Bottle?" writing instructor Ruthi Erdman offers a model analysis, in IRAC format, of a case in which parents sued a brewer when their young son was injured after shattering a beer bottle against a telephone pole.

"The Ridiculed Employee" deals with an additional case of emotional distress upon which you, as a jury member, can deliberate. (Can a man collect damages from a supervisor who repeatedly makes fun of his stuttering?) This selection is followed by "Assault and Battery on the Gridiron: A Case of Reckless Disregard of Safety," an unusual case in which one football player sues another for injuries sustained on the playing field. In "Who Gets the Kids? Some Cases of Child Custody," you will get a chance to consider some of the bitterest lawsuits that pass through the civil courts. In "'Urban War Zone': A Case of Public Nuisance" you will consider opposing viewpoints on whether a city has a constitutional right to restrict gang activities—both criminal and noncriminal—in its neighborhoods.

The next part of the chapter deals with criminal cases. In "The Felled Stop Signs," you will decide the legal responsibility of some teenagers who pulled down highway signs, including a stop sign—a piece of "fun" that resulted in a fatal accident. In "Drag Racing and Death: Some Cases of Manslaughter," you will consider the question of how seriously the law should deal with someone who participates in a fatal drag race, even though he may not have driven the car actually involved in the accident. Next, as a guide to the entire chapter, we offer a "Legal Glossary" to help you understand the unfamiliar legal language you will encounter while working with these cases. Finally, an expanded section on "Research Activities" shows how to conduct respectable legal research without actually being enrolled in law school.

Each selection dealing with a particular case consists of two elements. The first element presents the "Facts of the Case," as written by the panel of appeals court judges who ruled upon the case. All of the cases you will read in this chapter are cases that have been appealed by either the plaintiff or the defendant to an appeals court after the original jury verdict. The second element presents the "Statements of the Law," statements that you will apply to the facts of the case, just as if you were following the judge's instructions. In some selections, these statements do consist of the kind of instructions that a judge would give to a jury in such cases. In others, they will be the actual statutes that may or may not have been violated. You may also read excerpts from case law—judicial opinions from previous cases dealing with similar issues that may have bearing upon the case you are currently considering.

What you will not find, however, as you consider these cases, is the ultimate outcome. If you know the outcome in advance, you are likely to be unduly swayed in your reasoning, attempting to bring it in line with the arguments of the side that prevailed. As we suggested earlier, which side won is less important for our purposes than the process of logically applying general principles to specific cases. Nevertheless, if you have to know which side won, ask your instructor; she or he will be able to consult the *Instructor's Manual.*

Occasionally, however, it will be difficult or even impossible to find out which side ultimately won. That's because some cases are sent back by the appeals court to the trial court, and most trial court cases are not published—though photocopied transcripts are available (for a hefty fee) from the clerk of the court—and the more newsworthy cases are covered by reporters. Also, a good many civil cases, after going up and down through the appeals process, are ultimately settled out of court—and frequently, the terms of the settlement are not publicly available.

This chapter offers considerable opportunities for group work. After all, work on a jury is a collective enterprise, and before a jury arrives at a verdict, unanimous or otherwise, its individual members must engage in a good deal of discussion, perhaps even argument. In some cases, your papers may be written collectively by the group; but even when individually written, they could reflect the views of more than one viewpoint. In fact, as you will see in the Charrow/Erhardt selection, the IRAC format, used widely in legal writing, should include a consideration and a rebuttal of opposing arguments.

A NOTE ON SYNTHESIS ACTIVITIES

Because of the special nature of legal reasoning, we include synthesis activities, where appropriate, as part of the Discussion and Writing Suggestions following some of the grouped case selections, rather than at the end of the chapter.

Lawyers synthesize cases as a matter of course, but only when they are closely related, in order to point out legal precedents. We do include a few closely related cases in this chapter (for example, *Nickerson v. Hodges* and *Harris v. Jones,* both in the "emotional distress" section, as well as in the "drag racing" and "stop sign" cases); but for the most part, the cases we have selected are too different in facts and legal issues to be usefully synthesized.

The Maiden and the Pot of Gold: A Case of Emotional Distress
(Nickerson v. Hodges)

You may have heard the phrase "emotional distress" in connection with a lawsuit and wondered how such a vague term could possibly have legal meaning. After all, people are always doing things that distress other people. Bosses inflict distress on their employees, teachers distress students, lovers distress each other. Undoubtedly, your parents drive you to emotional distress (and vice versa) yet few children sue their parents—though that has *happened.*

Still, there's emotional distress and there's emotional distress; some people seem to go out of their way to maliciously and outrageously distress others, and the distress they occasion sometimes is particularly severe. In these cases, we feel that the perpetrators should be legally liable—meaning that they should be forced to pay financial damages to their victims. But plaintiffs must do more than claim *that they have suffered emotional distress at the hands of the defendants. They must* prove *such a claim, by showing how the legal definition of emotional distress applies to their particular case, or by showing how their particular case is similar, if not identical, to one or more previous cases of proven emotional distress.*

The following passage presents one such case: it is part of an opinion by the Supreme Court of Louisiana in 1920. First, we present the "Facts of the Case" as summarized by the panel of judges who wrote the opinion. (Their ruling itself and the reasoning behind it are not presented here; these are for you to decide. Your instructor, however, will be able to consult the Instructor's Manual *and tell you how the case turned out.) Following the facts of the case, we offer a set of instructions that the judge might give to the jury before they begin deliberating in a case involving emotional distress. Strictly speaking, these instructions are anachronistic, since they were written in the latter part of the century (and are intended for California juries.) Nonetheless, they embody the same essential assumptions about liability for emotional distress that were considered by the judges who decided the case of* Nickerson v. Hodges.

Note: In civil (as opposed to criminal) cases, such as this one, a jury will render a verdict of either "liable" or "not liable" (as opposed to "guilty" or "not guilty").

Carrie E. NICKERSON et al.

v.

A. J. HODGES et al.
Supreme Court of Louisiana
Feb. 2, 1920

The Facts of the Case*

1   Miss Carrie E. Nickerson brought this suit against H.R. Hayes, William or "Bud" Baker, John W. Smith, Mrs. Fannie Smith, Miss Minnie Smith, A.J. Hodges, G.G. Gatling, R.M. Coyle, Sam P.D. Coyle, and Dr. Charles Coyle, claiming $15,000 as damages, alleged to have been caused in the form of financial outlay, loss in business, mental and physical suffering, humiliation, and injury to reputation and social standing, all growing out of an alleged malicious deception and conspiracy with respect to the finding of a supposed pot of gold. Subsequent to the filing of the petition, and before the trial, the said Miss Nickerson died, and her legal heirs, some 10 in number, were made parties plaintiff, and now prosecute this suit.

2   Miss Nickerson was a kinswoman of Burton and Lawson Deck, the exact degree of relationship not being fully shown by the record, and there had been, in the family, a tradition that these two gentlemen, who died many years ago, had, prior to their deaths, buried a large amount of gold coin on the place now owned by the defendant John W. Smith, or on another near by. She was employed by the California Perfume Company to solicit orders for their wares

---

Nickerson v. Hodges. 84 So. 37 (1920).

in the towns, villages, etc., in Webster and other parishes, and on the occasion of a visit to the city of Shreveport seems to have interviewed a fortune teller, who told her that her said relatives had buried the gold, and gave her what purported to be a map or plat showing its location on the property of Smith.

3   Thereafter, with the help of some three or four other persons, principally relatives, and one Bushong, she spent several months digging, at intervals, around the house and on the premises of Smith, who seems to have extended them a cordial welcome, and to have permitted them to dig almost without limit as to time and place, and in addition boarded the fortune hunters, while so engaged, without charge. We assume that this was due, perhaps, to the fact that he, too, had a slight hope that they might find something, and he was to receive a part thereof for his concessions. At any rate, the diggers pursued their course with such persistence and at such lengths, digging around the roots of shade tees, the pillars of his house, etc., until finally, his daughter, the said Minnie Smith, William or "Bud" Baker, and H.R. Hayes conceived the idea of themselves providing a "pot of gold" for the explorers to find.

4   Accordingly they obtained an old copper kettle or bucket, filled it with rocks and wet dirt, and buried it in an old chimney seat on the adjoining place, where the searchers had been or were intending to also prospect for the supposed treasure. Two lids or tops were placed on the pot, the first being fastened down with hay wire; then a note was written by Hayes, dated, according to some July 1, 1884, and, as to others, 1784, directing whoever should find the pot not to open it for three days, and to notify all the heirs. This note was wrapped in tin, placed between the first and second lids, and the latter was also securely fastened down with hay wire. This took place some time toward the latter part of March, and, according to these three defendants, was to have been an April fool; but plans miscarried somewhat, and the proper opportunity for the "find" did not present itself until April 14th.

5   On that day Miss Nickerson and her associates were searching and digging near the point where the pot had been buried, when Grady Hayes, a brother of H.R. Hayes, following directions from the latter, and apparently helping the explorers to hunt for the gold, dug up the pot and gave the alarm. All of those in the vicinity, of course, rushed to the spot, those who were "in" on the secret being apparently as much excited as the rest, and, after some discussion, it was decided to remove the lid. When this was done, the note was discovered, and H.R. Hayes advised Miss Nickerson that he thought it proper that its directions should be carried out, and that the bank at Cotton Valley, a few miles distant, was the best place to deposit the "gold" for safe-keeping, until the delays could run and the heirs be notified, as requested. Following this suggestion, the pot was placed in a gunny sack, tied up, and taken to the bank for deposit. Defendant Gatling was the cashier of the bank, but refused to give a receipt for the deposit as a "pot of gold," because, as he insisted, he did not know what it contained.

6   As might have been supposed, it did not take long for the news to spread that Miss Nickerson and her associates in the search for fortune, had found a pot of gold, and the discussion and interest in the matter became so general that defendant A.J. Hodges, vice president of the bank, went over from his place of business in Cotton Valley to the bank, and he and Gatling, after talking the matter over,

decided to examine the pot, so that, in event it did contain gold, proper precautions to guard the bank might be taken, pending the return of Miss Nickerson and the appearance of those who might claim the fortune. These two undid the wire sufficiently to peep into the pot, and discovered that it apparently contained only dirt. They then replaced the lid and held their tongues until the reappearance of Miss Nickerson. However, the secret leaked out from other sources, that the whole matter was a joke, and this information too, became pretty well distributed.

7   After depositing the pot in the bank, Miss Nickerson went to Minden, La., and induced Judge R.C. Drew to agree to accompany her to Cotton Valley on the following Monday (the deposit at the bank having been made on Saturday) for the purpose of seeing that the ceremonies surrounding the opening of the treasure were properly conducted. Judge Drew swears that he had heard in some way that the matter was a joke, and so informed Miss Nickerson, warning her not to place too much faith in the idea that she was about to come into a fortune, but that finally, because of his friendly relations with and kindly feeling toward her, he consented and did go, mainly to gratify her wishes in the premises. Some half a dozen other relatives of Burton and Lawson Deck were notified, and either accompanied or preceded Miss Nickerson to Cotton Valley.

8   With the stage thus set, the parties all appeared at the bank on Monday morning at about 11 o'clock, and among the number were H.R. Hayes, one of the defendants, who seems to have been one of the guiding spirits in the scheme, and one Bushong, the latter, we infer, from intimations thrown out by witnesses in the record, being at the time either an avowed or supposed suitor of Miss Nickerson's. Judge Drew, as the spokesman for the party, approached Gatling and informed him that it was desired that the pot be produced for the purpose of opening and examining the contents for the benefit of those thus assembled. The testimony of the witnesses varies a little as to just when the storm began; some say, as soon as the sack was brought out. Miss Nickerson discovered that the string was tied near the top, instead of down low around the pot, and immediately commenced to shout that she had been robbed; others insist that she was calm until the package was opened and the mocking earth and stones met her view. Be that as it may, she flew into a rage, threw the lid of the pot at Gatling, and for some reason, not clearly explained, turned the force of her wrath upon Hayes to such an extent that he appealed for protection, and Bushong, with another, held her arms to prevent further violence.

9   Miss Nickerson was a maiden, nearing the age of 45 years, and some 20 years before had been an inmate of an insane asylum, to the knowledge of those who had thus deceived her. She was energetic and self-supporting in her chosen line of employment, as a soap drummer, until she met the fortune teller who gave her the "information" which she evidently firmly believed would ultimately enable her to find the fortune which the family tradition told her had been left hidden by her deceased relatives. The conspirators, no doubt, merely intended what they did as a practical joke, and had no willful intention of doing the lady any injury. However, the results were quite serious indeed, and the mental suffering and humiliation must have been quite unbearable, to say nothing of the disappointment and conviction, which she carried to her grave some two years later, that she had been robbed.

Judge's Instructions to the Jury*

1 Ladies and Gentlemen of the Jury:

2   It is now my duty to instruct you on the law that applies to this case. It is your duty to follow the law.

3   As jurors it is your duty to determine the effect and value of the evidence and to decide all questions of fact.

4   You must not be influenced by sympathy, prejudice, or passion.

5   The plaintiff *Carrie E. Nickerson* seeks to recover damages based upon on a claim of intentional infliction of emotional distress.

6   The essential elements of such a claim are:

1. The defendant engaged in outrageous, [unprivileged] conduct;
2. [a. The] defendant intended to cause plaintiff to suffer emotional distress; [or [b.] [(1) The defendant engaged in the conduct with reckless disregard of the probability of causing plaintiff to suffer emotional distress;
   (2) The plaintiff was present at the time the outrageous conduct occurred; and
   (3) The defendant knew that the plaintiff was present;]
3. The plaintiff suffered severe emotional distress; and
4. Such outrageous conduct of the defendant was a cause of the emotional distress suffered by the plaintiff.

7   The term "emotional distress" means mental distress, mental suffering, or mental anguish. It includes all highly unpleasant mental reactions, such as fright, nervousness, grief, anxiety, worry, mortification, shock, humiliation, and indignity, as well as physical pain.

8   The word "severe," in the phrase "severe emotional distress," means substantial or enduring as distinguished from trivial or transitory. Severe emotional distress is emotional distress of such substantial quantity or enduring quality that no reasonable person in a civilized society should be expected to endure it.

9   In determining the severity of emotional distress you should consider its intensity and duration.

10   Extreme and outrageous conduct is conduct which goes beyond all possible bounds of decency so as to be regarded as atrocious and utterly intolerable in a civilized community.

11   Extreme and outrageous conduct is not mere insults, indignities, threats, annoyances, petty oppressions or other trivialities. All persons must necessarily be expected and required to be hardened to a certain amount of rough language and to occasional acts that are definitely inconsiderate and unkind.

12   Extreme and outrageous conduct, however, is conduct which would cause an average member of the community to immediately react in outrage.

California Jury Instructions, Civil: Book of Approved Jury Instructions (BAJI). 8th ed. Prepared by The Committee on Standard Jury Instruction Civil, of the Superior Court of Los Angeles County, California. Hon. Stephen M. Lachs, Judge of the Superior Court, Chairman. Compiled and Edited by Paul G. Breckenridge, Jr. St. Paul, MN: West Publishing Co., 1994.

13   The extreme and outrageous character of a defendant's conduct may arise from defendant's knowledge that a plaintiff is peculiarly susceptible to emotional distress by reason of some physical or mental condition or peculiarity. Conduct may become extreme and outrageous when a defendant proceeds in the face of such knowledge, where it would not be so if defendant did not know.

14   If you find that plaintiff is entitled to a verdict against defendant, you must then award plaintiff damages in an amount that will reasonably compensate plaintiff for all loss or harm, provided that you find it was [or will be] suffered by plaintiff and was caused by the defendant's conduct. The amount of such award shall include:

15   Reasonable compensation for any fears, anxiety and other emotional distress suffered by the plaintiff.

16   No definite standard [or method of calculation] is prescribed by law by which to fix reasonable compensation for emotional distress. Nor is the opinion of any witness required as to the amount of such reasonable compensation. [Furthermore, the argument of counsel as to the amount of damages is not evidence of reasonable compensation.] In making an award for emotional distress you shall exercise your authority with calm and reasonable judgment and the damages you fix shall be just and reasonable in the light of the evidence.

Discussion and Writing Suggestions

1. If you were a member of the jury in the case of *Nickerson v. Hodges,* would you vote for a verdict of "liable for intentional infliction of emotional distress" against the defendants? Explain your vote, applying the "Judge's Instructions to the Jury"—and in particular, the definitions concerning "emotional distress"—to the particular facts of this case.

2. If you vote "liable," what damages would you award the plaintiffs? Keep in mind that Miss Nickerson herself has died and the plaintiffs are now her heirs.

3. Notice that the instructions to the jury include the admonition that "All persons must necessarily be expected and required to be hardened [...] to occasional acts that are definitely inconsiderate and unkind." This is distinguished from conduct that is "[e]xtreme and outrageous." Define the conduct at issue according to one set of terms or the other, explaining your reasoning.

4. How do the particular circumstances of the plaintiff, Miss Nickerson, affect your vote on the verdict? For example, if Miss Nickerson were a different kind of person, or if the "practical joke" had been differently handled, how (if at all) would this have changed your view of the case and your view of whether the plaintiff had suffered emotional distress and was due financial damages?

5. Of the ten defendants charges, only three (Minnie Smith, William or "Bud" Baker, and H.R. Hayes) admitted to being in on the phony

pot of gold scheme, but they denied "any malicious or unlawful intent." As a juror, how would you respond to this defense? How do you assess the moral and legal responsibility of some of the other figures in the case—such as the bank cashier G.G. Gatling and bank vice president A.H. Hodges?

The American Legal System
David Hricik

Where does the law come from? What is a plaintiff? Why does this country need so many different kinds of law courts? How does a case get to the Supreme Court? These basic questions about American law are addressed by David Hricik in the following selection from his book Law School Basics: A Preview of Law School and Legal Reasoning *(1996). Hricik's explanations—intended for prospective law students as an introduction to law school—will provide an important foundation for your understanding of the cases you read and write about in this chapter.*

A graduate of Northwestern University School of Law, Hricik practices at the Houston law firm of Slusser and Frost. He teaches legal writing at the University of Houston Law School Center, helped create the Law School Basics computer course at America Online, and has published articles and given lectures on topics ranging from legal ethics, to patent litigation, to judicial reform.

1   Here are some basic questions: What is the "law"? Where does "law" come from? What is the purpose of law?

2   The last question first: What is the purpose of law?

A. What Is the Purpose of Law?

3   For our purposes, it is easier to begin by saying what the purpose of law is not, rather than what it is. Laws are not the same as personal or individual morality. This is easy to prove: some things are legal, yet are considered immoral by some people. *See, e.g., Roe v. Wade,* 410 U.S. 113, 119 (1973) (abortion is protected by the United States Constitution)...[1]

---

[1]You have just seen a case cited…as a lawyer would do in a brief or memorandum. A few words about case *citations* is in order here. Look at the cite for *Roe.* The words *"See, e.g .,"* mean "See, for example." *"Roe v. Wade"* means that someone named Roe is involved in a suit with someone named Wade. (You can't tell who sued whom, though, not just from the *style* of the case.) "410 U.S. 113, 119" means that the Roe versus Wade case is "reported" (*i.e.* printed) at volume 410 of the United States Reporters, beginning at page 113, and that the specific words from the case to which I'm referring are on page 119 of that Reporter. The fact that it is in the United States Reporters means it was decided by the United States Supreme Court, as that particular reporter publishes only its decisions. The date in the parentheses is when the case was decided. The parenthetical explanation of "abortion is protected by the United States Constitution" is what *I* say that the court said. It is one way to let the reader know what a case says.

4   Some things which are moral to some people are nonetheless always illegal. *See, e.g., Reynolds v. United States,* 98 U.S. 145, 167 (1878) (polygamy is illegal). Some laws even require people to do things which they find utterly immoral. For example, Christian Scientists may be forced to accept blood transfusions, even though they believe it damns them to eternal hell. Laws are not morals—at least not an individual's or a particular group's morals. That much is clear.

5   There are many theories about why we have laws, about what purpose is served by our explicit, institutionalized and complex legal system. Some view law as merely a tool to oppress people; others argue that laws express reason and order. Many view law as a system of rules which, when applied to facts by judges and juries, should result in rational and reasonable results to particular cases—to particular facts. We will not decide who is right. As with most things, the truth no doubt lies somewhere in between.

6   For our purpose, we do not care too much about what the purpose of law is, at least not on this fundamental level. For lawyers and law students, the law is a set of "rules" which create "duties," the breaking of which may result in "liability," usually in the form of money damages. Put at its simplest, "the law" is an expression of the social policy that people have a duty to follow the rules, and those who don't will incur liability for any harm they cause.

7   The "rule" is very often something so vague as having a duty to "act reasonably under the circumstances." Or, the rule can be very specific: having to stop at a stop sign, having to drive no more than 30 miles per hour, having to do what you have agreed in a contract to do.

8   "Liability" for breaking a rule often comes in the form of a "judgment" for money damages, which is a court's order for one person to pay money to another person. It can also take the form of an "injunction," which is a court order prohibiting someone from doing something. For example, a court could enjoin a party from selling dangerous products. (In criminal cases, "liability" can take the form of a jail or prison sentence or a fine—which is a court's order that a person pay money to the government.)

9   So the "purpose" of law is to have rules which create duties which, when broken, result in some sort of liability to the injured party. Obviously that is an oversimplification: for example, some of the law comprises those rules that define *how much* someone who breaks a "rule" must pay the injured party. But, as a general concept, law is meant to define the duties which people owe one another.

B. Where Does "Law" Come From?

10 As to where this "law" comes from, it is again probably easiest to first say what the law is *not.* The western world's legal systems are of two primary kinds: common law and civil law. For our purposes, the "common law" system which we have in the United States can be described by contrasting it to civil law systems. By illuminating the differences, we can better see the common law methods. Understanding how the common law system works will help you understand why you spend so much of law school reading cases.

11   Civil law jurisdictions[2] place their primary emphasis on legislation—statutes or codes enacted by a parliament or similar legislative body. The governing legislatures of civil law countries try to enact comprehensive codes on every subject. These statutes or codes provide the main source of the legal rules. In theory, everything necessary for the legal operation of society is covered in a code or statute. Consequently, in civil law countries, decisions by courts are not as important as those codes. The courts play a role, to be sure, but it is comparatively less than in common law countries.

12   In contrast, under the common law system, like we have in the United States, the society places less overall emphasis on statutes and codes. The "common" law plays a much greater role because there are *no* statutes or codes governing *most* legal issues. Instead, most of the "rules" are in the form of previously-decided judicial opinions, not statutes or codes. Unlike civil law systems, in common law countries, *judicially*-developed "rules"—that have never been approved by any voters or elected legislative body, such as a Congress, a state legislature, or even a city council—provide much of the governing legal framework.

13   The common law method means building up the law by court opinions, case-by-case, as opposed to creating the law by legislative enactment. The facts surrounding origins of the English system are illuminating:

> England had laws just as Continental countries did, even though these laws were not "written" in the Romanist sense of being declared in authoritative texts. The rules established by general custom were declared not by a single judge alone but by the whole court of the king, which represented the magnates of the kingdom; *but there was no authorized version of these rules.*[3]

14   Under our common law system, most law comes in the form of these judicial opinions: there is no big encyclopedia of "rules" setting out what can, must, or should be done under any set of facts or circumstances. You will seldom go to a "rule book" to find an "outline" of legal rules on the issue you are researching. As will become more clear later, the common law is really a series of *cases*—not rules—which can be applied to later fact patterns.

15   The point is so important that it bears repeating: most "law" in common law systems is case law, decided by judges and memorialized only in written "opinions"—not statutes, codes, or other "rule books." For instance, the "elements" which must be alleged to effectively claim that a party was negligent in injuring another person were essentially created by the courts of England in the sixteenth century, and were adopted by America's state courts throughout the nineteenth century. Likewise, most contract law is primarily found only in cases decided over hundreds of years by judges. Similarly, the rules governing real property come from cases which were written by judges in England long, long

---

[2]An example of a civil law jurisdiction is France.

[3]*Dictionary of the History of Ideas* 694 (emphasis added).

ago involving fee tails, fee simples, and other legal concepts whose importance has left us, but whose labels have not.

16   Of course, there are specialized statutes in common law jurisdictions such as the United States. Statutes provide a very comprehensive set of legal rules for some issues. For instance, significant federal legislation, called ERISA, governs employee benefit plans. ERISA is a complex statute, and the government has promulgated hundreds of pages of rules and regulations which further clarify and add to the statute. The patent statutes are comprehensive, as are some of the federal environmental statutes. Similarly, many state legislatures have enacted very detailed state statutes on various subjects. For example, the Texas Deceptive Trade Practices Act (often called the "DTPA"), provides a fairly complex codification of law designed to protect consumers. There are also a *lot* of federal and state regulations which are relatively comprehensive.

17   Nonetheless, with certain exceptions, statutes play a comparatively insignificant role in the common law system. For example, even though the DTPA is probably one of the longer Texas statutes, the legislature left many issues for the courts to decide by applying the statute to various facts. Those judicial interpretations are as important—if not more so—than the words of the DTPA statute itself.

18   The main supposed benefit of the common law system is its flexibility: a judge can decide that the facts before him or her are different enough under the rules so that a different *result* from an earlier case should be reached. Courts can also create a different, new rule when needed to apply to new problems or social changes. The common law has an additional benefit: judges decide cases based on actual, concrete disputes, not hypotheticals. A statute cannot be written which will govern every possible fact pattern, but a court can decide what rule should apply to specific facts, and a jury can decide what result is just under all kinds of different and unforeseeable fact patterns. The common law system allows for a lot of discretion in order to achieve justice in each dispute.

19   Most people are surprised to learn that many, if not most, of the laws that lawyers rely on in their day-to-day practice were never passed by a legislature or by Congress, but instead evolved over hundreds of years as courts developed and applied judge-made rules to the facts presented in each new dispute brought before them. That arguably makes judges very powerful. That power, in turn, means that *your* ability to effectively argue the law can shape the outcome of your client's cases. Knowing how to find the law and how to write about it will make you a more effective, and therefore a more powerful, lawyer.

20   To sum up, the "purpose" of law is to create duties which, if broken, mean that the wrong-doer must compensate the injured party. This "set of rules," however, exists only in the form of case law; there is no "rule book," as there is in civil law countries.

C. Why Do We Have "Cases" Anyway?

21 Lawyers use the word "case" to refer to many very different things. "Case" means a dispute: your client has been sued by IBM. That is a case. "Case" also refers to the published opinions which judges have written when they decided earlier dis-

putes. Thus, if IBM's case against your client went to trial and the judge wrote an opinion explaining the case, that opinion is also a "case." I will refer to the latter kinds of "cases" as "opinions" whenever I think the context is confusing.

22   How are opinions created? As next shown a court may, when it decides a case, write an opinion that will be published in a reporter. Those published opinions then become *precedent*—the law—for other courts to use when deciding later cases. To understand why opinions get written, you need to understand how lawsuits are resolved. To illustrate, I will give you something you will not get in law school: a brief and over-simplified synopsis of a lawsuit.

23   The *plaintiff* is the party which sues. The plaintiff files a "complaint." The complaint lays out the allegations which, plaintiff claims to show, why the defendant (the party being sued) owes the plaintiff money. Put in terms of the "purpose" of law: the plaintiff alleges facts which show that the defendant owed a duty to the plaintiff, breached that duty, and injured the plaintiff. For example, in a case you will read as a 1-L,[4] the plaintiff claims that the defendant had agreed to deliver a load of coal to the plaintiff's lumber mill; because the defendant failed to deliver the coal on time and as promised, the mill had to shut down, causing the plaintiff to lose business; because he had no coal, he could not run the mill, and so could not cut wood to sell to his customers.

24   After being served with the plaintiff's complaint, a defendant must file an "answer." The defendant will "deny" those allegations in the plaintiff's complaint which, the defendant contends, are not true, and will assert any "affirmative defenses" he might have. Again, for example, the defendant will deny that there was a contract to deliver coal; if there was a contract, it is legally unenforceable because it was not in writing; even if there were an enforceable contract, the damages were caused or at least exacerbated by plaintiff's failure to order coal from some other supplier.

25   The judge will then issue a "scheduling order." Scheduling orders typically set the case for trial in a year or so, and establish certain deadlines along the way, the most important of which is a "discovery cut-off" deadline. The parties will have up to that date to take "discovery" of each other. Discovery consists of asking each other written questions (called "interrogatories"); asking each other to produce documents which are relevant to the suit (called "requests for production"); and taking each other's sworn answers to oral questions (called "depositions"). [...]

26   Typically, at some point near the end of the discovery period, one side or the other will file a "motion for summary judgment." This motion says that the moving party is entitled to "win as a matter of law": the *movant* will argue that given the undisputed facts and under the controlling case law, it is entitled to have the court enter judgment in its favor. For example, the defendant coal supplier could file a motion for summary judgment contending that there had been no enforceable written contract, and so a judgment should be entered in the defendant's favor ordering that the plaintiff "take nothing" for the lawsuit. The other side will oppose this motion by filing a response in which it argues either

---

[4] 1-L—a first-year law student.

that a jury must be allowed to decide the case because there are disputed facts, or, for various legal reasons, that the controlling opinions do not mean that the movant should win as a matter of law. So, the plaintiff in our coal case might contend that there really was a written contract and that a jury needs to decide whether to believe the plaintiff's story that his dog had eaten it.

27   When the trial court judge grants or denies the motion for summary judgment, he may write an opinion which explains the facts of the case and the controlling legal principles, and then *applies* those legal principles to the facts of that particular lawsuit to explain why the court reached the result it did. Judges write opinions so that the parties understand why he ruled as he did; so that the appellate court can review whether his decision was correct (if there is a later appeal); and, in a larger sense, so that in the future other parties can conduct themselves in accordance with the law. This is one way the published opinions are created: district court judges sometimes write and publish opinions when deciding cases.

28   If the trial judge determines that the movant is entitled to win the case as a matter of law, the losing side can appeal after he writes the opinion. If the judge denies the motion, then there must be a jury trial, after which the losing side can still appeal. Judges sometimes write an opinion even after a jury trial, when denying the losing party's motion for new trial or motion for judgment as a matter of law. This is another way published opinions are created: by district judges when explaining why the result reached after a trial by jury was correct and fair.

29   Any appeal will be decided by an intermediate appellate court (the exact name of which depends on whether the suit is in state or federal court). The party that *lost* in the lower court will appeal, and will be called the "appellant." The party that won will be called the "appellee." The parties will file their *briefs* in the appellate court. After reading the briefs and perhaps allowing a short oral argument, the appellate court will write an opinion that either *affirms* the trial court's judgment as correct, or *reverses* the trial court because it committed some reversible error. Any appellate court opinion which is published becomes part of the common law that can be applied by later courts. This is another way the published opinions are created.

30   The loser in the court of appeals can then try to appeal to the highest appellate court (usually called a supreme court). As with appellate court decisions, the published opinions of the supreme court join the common law decision.

31   Thus, we have opinions because of the way by which we resolve lawsuits in the common law system. The parties need to know *why* one side won. The reviewing appellate court needs to be able to check whether the lower court got it right. Society needs to know what the legal rules are so that in the future, people can avoid breaking the rules. That's why we have all these opinions.

D. The State and Federal Court Systems

32 The next piece of the puzzle which no one will ever *explain* to you in law school is how the courts are structured. You are just supposed to already know it, or you are supposed to figure it out from reading opinions for class.

33   There are at least two reasons why you need to understand the court systems. (Systems, not system.) First, it will help you understand cases better when
you are preparing for class. When you read the case, and it says that the plaintiff lost in the trial court, but won a reversal in the appellate court, you will know
that the plaintiff will be the appellee in the decision in the supreme court.
Second, the fundamental principle of legal reasoning is the doctrine of precedent. You have to know which earlier cases are *controlling* precedent over the
particular court your case is in. In order to know which cases are *binding* on your
court, you have to understand how the state and federal judicial systems in the
United States are structured. (You'll see why in a moment.) The doctrine of
precedent is crucial in the practice of law and in the United States legal systems.

34   The fact that the United States has the federal judiciary, along with fifty independent state court systems, as well as countless administrative and quasi-judi-
cial bodies, makes it probably the most complex judicial system in the world.
Welcome to it!

1. The Structure of the Federal Court System

35 The federal court system has a pyramid structure. The federal district courts, of
which there are about ninety, are at the base. Twelve federal appellate (or "circuit") courts make up the middle. At the top of the judicial pyramid sits the
United States Supreme Court.

36   We'll study the federal judicial pyramid from the bottom up.

37   *A. United States District Courts*   As mentioned, there are about ninety federal district courts. Each state has at least one, and most states are divided into
several districts.

38   Lawsuits must originally be filed in district courts. All federal trials take place
in the district courts. Witnesses testify, evidence is received, and juries reach
their decisions *only* in these district courts. District courts are the only courts
which *find facts;* appellate courts cannot do so, but instead merely apply the
law to the facts as found by the district court, or determine whether there is evidence to support the district court's fact-findings. Appellate courts merely review
the written "record" of testimony and exhibits taken in by the trial court and
apply the law to double-check whether the trial court was correct.… .

39   *B. United States Courts of Appeal—The Circuit Courts*   Appeals from district
courts, with few exceptions, are heard by federal appellate courts, called "circuit
courts." The United States is divided into twelve regional circuits—the first
through eleventh, plus the Court of Appeals for the District of Columbia. (There
is also the "Federal Circuit," which takes appeals from all over the country, but
only on certain issues, like patent cases.)

40   An appeal from a district court must go to the circuit court for that particular
region. For example, Texas is within the Fifth Circuit. California is within the Ninth.
New York is in the Second. Illinois is in the Seventh. The District of Columbia has
its own circuit. If you look in the front of any volume of the "F.2d's" (the Federal
Second) Reporters, you'll see a map of which states are in each circuit. So, if you
lose a case in a federal district court in Texas, you file your appeal with the Fifth

Circuit. If you lose one in a California federal district court, you appeal to the Ninth Circuit.

41   Whoever lost in the district court may appeal. The loser—called in the appellate court the "appellant"—will file an opening brief in the circuit court which explains why the district court's decision was wrong. Typically, the circuit courts limit appellants' briefs to fifty pages. Whoever won below will file an appellee's brief, which is also typically fifty pages. The appellant then usually gets a 25-page reply brief.

42   The appeal will be assigned to a "panel" from among the judges in that particular circuit. A panel usually has three judges. These three judges then read the briefs and sometimes permit a 30-minute (15 minutes per side) oral argument. (Oral argument is becoming rare, which—you guessed it—is [one] reason why legal writing is so important.) Some time after oral argument, the court will issue a written opinion explaining why the district court was right or wrong, and so whether it is affirming or reversing the decision of the district court.

43   Lawsuits may not originally be filed in the appellate courts—each appellate court only *reviews* the decisions of the district courts in its circuit. As Justice Thurgood Marshall was quoted by *The Wall Street Journal,* "such appeals should await the outcome of the trial." It is hard to argue with that.

44   *C. The United States Supreme Court*   If the loser in the court of appeals wants to try, it can ask the United States Supreme Court to review the case. Again, the United States Supreme Court sits alone at the top of the federal judicial pyramid.

45   The principal way by which cases reach the Supreme Court is through the writ of *certiorari.* Whoever lost in the appellate court will write a "petition for a writ of *certiorari,*" which argues why the Court should issue an order (a "writ of *certiorari*") directing the lower court to send up records of the case so that the Supreme Court can consider the issues which it is interested in, to see if the result reached in the case was correct. The loser is called a "petitioner" in the Supreme Court because that's what it's doing; it is petitioning the Court for a writ of *certiorari.* The winner in the circuit court will write a brief opposing *cert* (pronounced like the candy), arguing that either the circuit court decided the issues correctly, or that essentially the issues are just not important enough to warrant the Supreme Court's time, or both. The winner below is called a "respondent" in the Supreme Court because that is what it is doing: it is responding to a petition for a writ.

46   Nine justices (not, mind you, "judges") sit on the United States Supreme Court. Like all federal judges, they are appointed by the President, subject to approval by the Senate, and serve for life unless impeached. One of the nine is appointed Chief Justice, also subject to Senate approval. He (there has never been a female Chief Justice) presides over the Court's sessions and determines which justice will write each opinion.

47   If the Court grants *cert,* then the parties write briefs, much as they did in the circuit court. The Supreme Court then holds an oral argument and will later issue an opinion deciding the case... .

48   The Supreme Court is the ultimate judicial tribunal: if you lose there, it's "game over."

2. The Structures of the State Court Systems

49 The vast majority of cases are handled by state courts. Why? There are far more state courts than federal district courts, there are far more disputes which can be heard only in state court, there are more state laws than federal laws, and there is virtually no federal common law—only federal statutory law. Federal courts are courts of *limited jurisdiction.* Only suits which are expressly recognized by federal law may be filed in federal court. Everything else must go to state court.[5] There is very, very little federal law governing divorce, car wrecks, breach of contract, products liability, and most common disputes. Thus, most cases must go where most of the governing law subsists: in state court.

50   The structure of each state court system varies by state. Each state has between two and four levels of courts. Generally, most states have lower courts of limited jurisdiction. Examples of this kind of court include county courts, family courts, municipal courts, JP (justice of the peace) courts, or small claims courts. The next higher level are the district or superior courts, which also act as appellate courts for cases decided by the courts of limited jurisdiction. Next up are the "true" appellate courts often thought of as intermediate appellate courts. Finally, at the top, sits a court of last resort, usually, but not always, called the state's "supreme court."

51   *A. Courts of Limited Jurisdiction*   At the bottom of each state court "pyramid" are its courts of limited jurisdiction. These can include municipal courts, JP courts, small claim courts, family courts, and the like. These courts have limited jurisdiction. This means that they have jurisdiction to handle cases involving only smaller amounts of money, or only certain kinds of cases (for example, landlord-tenant disputes).

52   Generally, these courts are informal. Parties often file suits without a lawyer; the rules of evidence may not apply; and the judges probably never write opinions that will be published in the reporters. These courts are critically important to solving the problems that confront people every day, but they generally do not add much to the common law, because they do not write opinions that are published in the reporters.

53   *B. District or Superior Courts*   Just above the courts of limited jurisdiction are the district courts. In some states, they are called superior courts. District courts handle the bulk of the state court caseload. They also handle appeals from the courts of limited jurisdiction: the loser in a lawsuit filed in a court of limited jurisdiction can "appeal" up to the district or superior: court, although usually the "appeal" takes the form of a completely new trial—"*de novo*

---

[5]There is something called "diversity jurisdiction," which allows people to file a lawsuit in federal court only because the defendant resides in a different state than the state in which suit is brought. Even in such suits, however, state law is applied to the merits of the dispute.

review"—rather than the review only by written briefs which takes place in the typical appeal.

54   Practice before a state district court is, in broad view, much the same as in a federal district court (discussed above). The procedural rules can be quite different, however, and so the actual daily practice may be very different. For our purposes, however, they are quite similar: the written practice consists of pleadings and motions supported by briefs…

55   *C. Intermediate Appellate Courts*   Intermediate appellate courts exist in many states, and are much like the federal circuit courts. In most states, as a matter of right the loser in a district court can appeal and have a state court of appeals review the district court's decision for error.

56   The briefing practice in state appellate courts is much as it is in the federal circuit courts: main brief, response; reply, followed (perhaps) by oral argument.… .

57   *D. Courts of Last Resort: State Supreme Courts*   At the top of state court systems is a court of ultimate review. In a deliberate scheme to confuse you, New York calls its supreme court the "court of appeals," and Texas has *two* supreme courts—one for criminal matters and the other for civil suits. Most states, thankfully, have only one highest court, and they call it the supreme court.

58   Most state supreme courts act like the United States Supreme Court, taking only those cases in which they are interested and ignoring the others. They will decide whether to take your case based only on the written briefs. This means that only your *writing* can persuade the court to review your case. (Which, you guessed it, is yet another reason writing is so important.)

Review Questions

1. How does Hricik define the law?

2. What is the difference between civil law and common law?

Discussion and Writing Suggestions

1. Does the law as Hricik describes it—a set of rules that create duties—seem different from the way you have previously thought of the law? If so, what were your previous impressions?

2. Based on how Hricik describes the difference between statutory law and case law, what advantages and disadvantages do you see with a legal system based largely on case law, like the one that operates in the United States?

3. If you or someone you know has ever had experience with the legal system—particularly in terms of the way that Hricik describes the process of the typical lawsuit—describe what happened. Based on this experience, what advantages and problems did you find with the system?

How to Present Your Case Systematically and Logically
Veda R. Charrow
Myra K. Erhardt
Robert P. Charrow

The principles of effective argument, as we've discussed them in Part One of this book, apply to law no less than to other disciplines and professional fields. But the special requirements of legal argument call for a more specific set of guidelines than we were able to provide earlier. The following passage, from a widely used textbook, Clear and Effective Legal Writing *by Veda R. Charrow, Myra K. Erhardt, and Robert P. Charrow, will provide some of these guidelines.*

Here, Charrow, Erhardt, and Charrow explain the IRAC (Issue, Rule, Application, Conclusion) approach to organizing legal arguments—one that has been used by generations of law students, but one whose usefulness extends beyond legal writing. Charrow and Erhardt also explain how to construct syllogisms in legal arguments and how to develop the kinds of analogies between similar cases that are basic to legal thinking.

This selection will provide an essential basis for many of the assignments that you will write in the rest of "You, the Jury."

IRAC: Organizing a Complex Legal Document

1   You must always impose order on your writing. Legal documents, in particular, demand a tight, logical structure. In other documents poor organization may interfere with readers' comprehension, but in legal documents poor organization can cause even greater problems. In an adversarial document, for example, your opponents will be looking for any weak spots they can find. A gap in your logic caused by poor organization can give your opponents an opening for attack. In a nonadversarial document, poor organization can make the reader believe that either your knowledge and research are not thorough or that your thinking is not logical... .

2   Thus, the outline for a complex legal document might look like this:

1. Introduction providing a context
2. First claim
   a. What is the *claim* you are making? How are you proposing to resolve the issue or subissue? This can be further subdivided into
      i. A statement of the particular *issue* or subissue you have identified. At this point you may also wish to state how you believe the issue should be resolved.*

---

*This is especially important in persuasive writing, where you want to make a forceful opening statement.

ii. The *rule* of law that is most pertinent to the situation.

iii. Why and how the rule should be *applied* to the facts of your case.

iv. A *conclusion* based upon your analysis and the application of the law to the facts.

(IRAC is the mnemonic for this method of organizing a claim.)

b. What are the *objections* and counterarguments to your claim?

c. What is your *response* to the objections and counterarguments?

d. What is your *conclusion?* This section summarizes your reasoning and restates your claim.

3. Second claim

4. Conclusion

3   This model works well for any level of analysis, from the general analysis of a whole problem down to the analysis of specific subissues. When you have used this model to analyze all of the issues or subissues, you will then be able to come to a conclusion.

1. Identifying and Presenting Issues

4   Your first step in setting up the structure of a complex legal document is to identify the important issues that you will be discussing in your document. Here is an example of a fact situation and the issues that should be analyzed in a brief.

> Jones worked as a salesman for the Southern Corporation. His job required him to provide his own car and deliver perishable supplies to customers on his route. Jones had been told a number of times by his supervisor at Southern that it was extremely important that he stay on a strict time schedule with his deliveries.
>
> On March 10, Jones made a delivery during normal working hours. He returned to the parking lot in which he had left his car and found that Warner's car was blocking his car. After waiting ten minutes for Warner to return, Jones finally decided that he had to leave. Jones tried to move his car, but put a large dent in Warner's bumper and broke one of Warner's headlights in the process. Warner returned just as Jones broke the headlight. Warner demanded payment for the damage to his car and refused to move his car so that Jones could leave. Jones angrily got out of his car and moved towards Warner, yelling that he was already late for his deliveries and that it was Warner's fault. Warner angrily shook his fist at Jones and again demanded payment for the damage to his car. Jones, in anger, hit Warner, knocking him to the ground. Warner had Jones arrested.
>
> After Jones's arrest, Southern Corporation learned from the local police that Jones had been convicted of aggravated assault three years before Southern had hired him. When Southern hired Jones, the corporation did not inquire into his background. Warner is suing Southern for the personal injuries he suffered as a result of Jones's attack.
>
> *Issue 1:* Did the defendant commit an intentional tort [wrongful act] when he knocked the plaintiff to the ground, or was the action privileged?

Issue 2: Is an employer liable for injuries that its employee intentionally inflicted upon the plaintiff while the employee was trying to make deliveries on behalf of the employer?

Issue 3: Can the defendant employer be held liable for negligence in hiring and retaining an employee who has a criminal record for assault if the employer did not investigate the employee's background and does not know of the record?

5   Once you have identified the main issues, you may find that you can deal with them more easily by breaking them down into smaller, more manageable subissues (or sub-subissues). For example, you might see the following subissues under Issue 1.

1. Did the act of the plaintiff in shaking his fist at the defendant place the defendant in imminent threat of physical injury?
   a. If the plaintiff's act placed the defendant in imminent threat of physical injury, did he have a duty to retreat?
   b. If the defendant did not have a duty to retreat, did he use excessive force in repelling the imminent threat?
2. Did the act of the plaintiff in refusing to move his vehicle constitute the tort of false imprisonment?
3. Did the act of the plaintiff in refusing to move his vehicle constitute the tort of trespass to chattel?

2. Presenting the Rule

6   The rule of law that you use in your analysis can come from case law or enacted laws. Once you have established the applicable rule in a particular case, you should present it in a way that will make it easy to apply the law to the facts. For example, if you are discussing a particular tort or crime, or the definition of a particular legal concept, describe it by breaking it up into its elements. Thus, if the issue is whether a defendant has committed a battery, a good way to present the rule would be to take the definition from section 13 of the Restatement (Second) of Torts.

[Section] 13 *Battery: Harmful Contact*

An actor is subject to liability for battery if
a) he *acts intending* to cause harmful or offensive contact with the person of the other or a third person, or an imminent apprehension of such a contact, and
b) a harmful contact with the person of the other directly or indirectly *results* (emphasis added).

7   If you have to synthesize the rule from case law, this will probably take more time and space. This is because you will often need to go through the steps that you took and the sources that you used in your distillation of the rule.

3. Application: Analyzing Facts and Law

8 The next step is to examine the facts and decide whether a rule is satisfied or the elements of an offense or tort are present. You should organize this section so that it follows the order of the elements of the rule. For example, you could discuss the facts in the Jones case by applying them to the elements of battery.

> First, the defendant, Jones, *acted* when he attempted to strike the plaintiff in the parking lot. Second, the defendant *intended* to harm the plaintiff, since he spoke angrily to the plaintiff, shook his fist at the plaintiff, and then struck him. Third, the defendant struck the plaintiff and knocked the plaintiff to the ground. Thus, the defendant's act *resulted in* the harmful contact to the plaintiff.

9   The application section of your document is the most crucial, for it is here that you have to convince your audience that your analysis is sound and that your conclusions follow logically. We have presented only the most basic application of facts to law in the example above... .

4. Anticipating Counterarguments

10 One of the best ways to ensure that you have treated an issue thoroughly is to try to anticipate all possible counterarguments and defenses. Put yourself in your opponent's position: List all of the ways that you can attack or weaken your own argument. Be ruthless. After you compile the list, develop responses or rebuttals for each area of attack.

11   There are a number of counterarguments that the defendant might raise in the battery case. The defendant might attack the way in which you applied the law to the facts; or the defendant might raise the defense that he was using reasonable force to prevent the plaintiff from committing a tort against his property (the plaintiff refused to let the defendant remove his car from the lot) or against his person (the plaintiff prevented the defendant from leaving by holding something of great value to the defendant).

5. Providing a Conclusion

12 The contents of your conclusion will depend upon the length and complexity of the information that you have presented in the other portions of your analysis. For example, if your application section is long and intricate, then you might want to refresh your reader's memory by briefly recounting the steps in your reasoning. If the application section is short, however, you would probably not want to reiterate your reasoning. In either case, you would finish with a statement of your position or your interpretation of the facts and the law. Here is an example of a simple way to conclude the battery issue:

> Because all three elements of battery are present in the defendant's conduct, the defendant is liable for the tort of battery.

6. Organizing a Complex Legal Document: An Example

13 Now that we have presented and explained the different parts of the model on pages 617–18, look at the following fully developed issue analysis. This analysis follows the standard IRAC—issue, rule, application, conclusion—outline.

Issue   The issue presented in this case is whether one spouse can sue the other for injuries caused by the negligence of the other spouse.

Rule   In *Sink v. Sink,* 239 P.2d 933 (1952), this court held that neither spouse may maintain an action in tort for damages against the other. Although a number of states have recently enacted legislation which allows these suits, Kansas has not joined them. This can be seen in the fact that the Kansas legislature has just enacted, in 1981, a law which authorizes any insurer to exclude coverage for any bodily injury to "any insured or any family member of an insured" in its insurance policies. Even though this law does not go into effect until January 1, 1982, it is clear that Kansas's position on interspousal tort immunity has not changed.

Application   In the present case, the plaintiff, who is the defendant's wife, was injured when the car the defendant was driving crashed into a telephone pole. The plaintiff was sitting in the passenger seat at the time of the accident. She sustained a broken leg and cuts and bruises. Although the defendant may have been negligent, the accident obviously involved injuries inflicted by one spouse upon another.

Conclusion   Therefore, this case clearly falls within the mandate of *Sink,* and the plaintiff's case should be dismissed on the basis of Kansas's very viable interspousal immunity.

Counterargument   The plaintiff has claimed that a decision upholding interspousal immunity violates logic and basic principles of justice. She notes that the new law has not yet gone into effect, so that it does not apply to the present case. She also contends that the foremost justification for immunity laws is illogical, since it is based on the premise that personal tort actions between husband and wife would disrupt the peace and harmony of the home. She cites the Restatement of the Law of Torts, which criticizes this justification by stating that it is based upon the faulty assumption that an uncompensated tort makes for peace in the family.

Response   However, it is no more logical to contend that family harmony will be better served if a husband and wife can drag each other into court and meet each other as legal adversaries. In addition, the plaintiff has overlooked a far more persuasive argument for interspousal tort immunity: under Kansas law, any recovery that the plaintiff-wife would obtain if this action were allowed to proceed would inure to the benefit of the defendant-husband. All property acquired by either spouse during the marriage is "marital property" in which each spouse has a common ownership interest. If the injured spouse (plaintiff) should die, the surviving spouse could maintain an action for wrongful death, and could share in any recovery of losses. This result would allow a negligent party

Conclusion   to profit by his own actions. This is a result which would be truly offensive to anyone's sense of justice.

The doctrine of interspousal immunity is as viable today as it was when initially enunciated by this court. It not only fosters family harmony, but also prevents a spouse from profiting from his or her own negligence.

14   For some types of documents, you will want to abbreviate or rearrange the scheme presented above. For example, if you are answering opponent's brief, you could begin by stating the opponent's objections and then follow with your own claims and conclusions. With this order, a separate "response" section may no longer be necessary, since the response may become part of your main argument. For example:

Issue   The issue presented in this case is whether one spouse can sue the other for injuries caused by the negligence of the other spouse.

Subissue   Does Kansas law presently require interspousal tort immunity?

The plaintiff in this case has claimed that a decision upholding interspousal immunity violates basic principles of justice and current Kansas law. She acknowledges that Kansas has enacted a law which authorizes any insurer to exclude coverage for any bodily injury to "any insured or any family member of an insured" in its insurance policies. However, she points out that this law does not establish blanket interspousal tort immunity. Also, because the law has not yet even gone into effect, it does not apply to the present case.

Rule   The plaintiff's reliance on the nature and effective date of the legislation is misplaced. The law to which the plaintiff alludes is one that the Kansas legislature has just enacted, in 1981. Even though this law does not go into effect until January 1, 1982, Kansas' position on interspousal tort immunity was established long ago and has not changed. In *Sink v. Sink*, 239 P.2d 933 (1952), this court held that neither spouse may maintain an action for tort for damages against the other. Although a number of States have recently enacted legislation which explicitly allows these suits, Kansas has not joined them. In fact, the legislation mentioned by the plaintiff makes it clear that Kansas is not attempting to establish a new policy on interspousal immunity, but is merely incorporating its current policy into the laws which govern insurers.

Application   As the plaintiff has pointed out in her brief, she was injured when the car her husband was driving crashed into a telephone pole. Whether or not the defendant was negligent, the accident involved injuries inflicted by one spouse upon another. As such, Kansas' policy on interspousal tort immunity would apply.

Subissue   Is the rationale behind interspousal immunity illogical?

The plaintiff further contends that the foremost justification for immunity laws is illogical, since it is based on the premise that personal tort actions between husband and wife would disrupt family harmony. She cites the Restatement of Torts, which criticizes this justification by stating that it is based upon the faulty assumption that an uncompensated tort makes for peace in the family.

Rule   The plaintiff and the Restatement have overlooked the even greater illogic behind a premise that family harmony can be better served if a husband and wife can drag each other into court and meet as legal adversaries. In addition, the plaintiff has overlooked a far more persuasive argument for interspousal immunity: under Kansas law, any recovery that the plaintiff-wife would obtain if this action were allowed to proceed would inure to the benefit of the defendant husband.

Application   In the present case, the husband and wife could be forced to endure years as legal adversaries, waiting for an interspousal lawsuit to slowly wend its way through a complex legal system. In addition, the defendant could stand to profit by any recovery his wife receives from the couple's insurance.

Conclusion   The doctrine of interspousal immunity is as viable today as it was when initially enunciated by this court. It not only fosters family harmony, but also prevents a spouse from profiting from his or her own negligence.

15   *Some Caveats*   There are several caveats to consider when you use IRAC or any similar outline to analyze the issues in a law school problem. Students sometimes get the impression that they have done a complete, well-rounded analysis of a question once they have taken the obvious issues through the IRAC outline. IRAC can give you a false sense of security if you mistake the thorough analysis of an issue for the thorough analysis of a whole problem or question. Once you have completed analyzing the obvious issues, make sure that you reread the problem to search for subissues or elements of issues that you might have overlooked. These are important and can influence the outcome of your problem.

16   IRAC is merely a framework within which to build your analysis: It should not appear to your readers that you have merely plugged information into a rigid formula. Edit your writing to eliminate the mechanical effects of a series of statements that the issue is *W*, the rule is *X*, the analysis is *Y*, and that, therefore, the conclusion is *Z*... .

Developing a Logical Argument

17 In order to create a logical structure, think about what you are trying to accomplish when you deal with a problem in law. You will often find that you are trying to establish that a specific set of facts fits within a well-settled rule of law. One way to do this logically and systematically is to use the principles of deductive reasoning to set up the skeleton of your legal analysis.

1. Deductive Reasoning in Law

18 You are probably familiar with the basic categorical syllogism. For example:

Major premise: All men are mortal.

Minor premise: Socrates is a man.

Conclusion: Socrates is mortal.

19   Deductive reasoning is the thought process that occurs whenever you set out to show that a minor premise (a specific situation, event, person, or object) fits within the class covered by a major premise (an established rule, principle, or truth) and to prove that, consequently, what applies to the class covered by the major premise must necessarily apply to the specific situation. In short, deductive reasoning allows you to prove that your particular case is covered by an established rule.

20   Deductive reasoning is a cornerstone of legal thought. Lawyers are often called upon to decide how a rule of law applies to a given case. Since the rule is usually stated in general terms and a client's problem is generally very specific, deductive reasoning can be used to bridge the gap between the general and the specific. For example:

Rule of Law (major premise): Courts have held that any agreement made in jest by one party and reasonably understood to be in jest by the other party will not be enforced as a contract.

Facts of our case (minor premise): Robert agreed to paint Lee's entire house, but both Robert and Lee understood that Robert was only joking.

Conclusion: Robert's agreement is not an enforceable contract.

21   These basic steps of deductive reasoning form the skeleton of a legal argument. In fact, the rule, application, conclusion sequence of IRAC forms a simple syllogism: The rule contains the major premise, the application contains the particular facts of the minor premise, and the conclusion sums up the information. [...]

2. Expanding the Syllogism into a Legal Argument

22 The syllogism serves as the skeleton of a legal argument. Once you have created the skeleton, you must flesh it out. For example, once you have the major premise in a particular case, you must present evidence that your specific fact situation does indeed fit within the class covered by the major premise. In the example about painting Lee's house, you would have to show that there was a promise but that both parties knew that it was made in jest, as "jest" has been interpreted by the courts.

23   In the rest of this section, we discuss techniques for expanding the different parts of a syllogism. We present the parts in the order of the standard syllogism, even though you may not always work in this order when you construct your argument.

24   *A. The Major Premise*   In most cases, your major premise will either be a given (you are told what the rule of law is and you must apply it to a set of facts), or you must extract the rule from legal authorities such as constitutions, statutes, regulations, and reported cases. You must then draw the appropriate information from these authorities and present the information so that your rule is well substantiated. In addition, you must define the abstract terms in the rule in order to clarify the rule and make it easier to apply the rule to the facts in your case. […]

25   *B. The Minor Premise*   The most important techniques for expanding your major premise are citing authority and defining terms. The most important technique for expanding your minor premise is analogy, either to the facts of other cases or to the policies underlying other decisions.

26   *Arguing by analogy: similarity of facts.* When you argue by analogy, you reason that if two or more situations are the same in some significant respect, they are likely to be the same in other significant respects as well, so they ought to be classified together. (If you want to *distinguish* your case from others, you show that it is *not* analogous.)

27   You could link the major and the minor premises of the general welfare case by using the following analogy: Funding should be provided for X Auto Company because the case is similar to cases in which the Court has approved Congress's funding in the past. Here is a way you might express this.

28   The facts in the X Auto Company case are very similar to the facts in cases that have already established the scope of "general welfare." In all of these cases, the courts agreed that

1. Private individuals or entities may receive funds from the federal government.
2. Individuals and entities may receive money that they did not personally contribute to the government.
3. Individuals and entities may receive money from the government when it helps them continue to earn money and spend money.

29   *Arguing by analogy: similarity of policy considerations.* Another way to link the major and minor premises is to show that the facts of your case are covered by a particular rule because your case furthers the same social goals as other cases already covered by the rule. For example, in the X Auto Company case, you might argue that your case and the previously decided cases all fulfill the following goals, regardless of the similarities or differences in their facts.

1. They keep individuals from turning to the state for support.
2. They keep the economy balanced and functioning.
3. They show people that the government will intervene if a segment of the population is about to experience an economic crisis.

30   The first step in making a policy argument is to identify what the authors of a rule intended when they created the rule. If you are investigating legislation, try looking at and analyzing legislative history or policy statements in the legislation itself. If you are investigating an opinion, try comparing your case with other cases

that have been decided under the rule and showing that your case will help to further the same goals. You can look at any language in these opinions that sheds light on the objectives of the ruling.

31   Once you have established the purpose of the rule, i.e., what it was intended to accomplish, you can alter your major premise to include this purpose and emphasize the specific facts in your minor premise that suit the major premise. You would then argue that the authors of the rule intended that the rule cover cases like yours and that the principles behind the rule will be dangerously eroded if the court excludes your case.

32   If you were arguing that by analogy to the *Steward Machine* case *X* Auto Company should get federal funds, you might use this analogy on policy considerations:

> The courts have found that federal payments to particular groups or individuals such as the unemployed or the elderly can serve the general welfare because, in the long run, these payments benefit the entire nation. This idea is reflected in the words of Justice Cardozo in *Steward Machine* 301 U.S. 548, 586-587 (1937):
>
> > During the years 1929 to 1936, when the country was passing through a cyclical depression, the number of the unemployed mounted to unprecedented heights... .The fact developed quickly that the states were unable to give the requisite relief. The problem had become national in area and dimensions. There was need of help from the nation if the people were not to starve. It is too late today for the argument to be heard with tolerance that in a crisis so extreme the use of the moneys of the nation to relieve the unemployed and their dependents is a use for any purpose narrower than the promotion of the general welfare.
>
> *X* Auto Company employs hundreds of thousands of employees. In addition, there are thousands of other employees who work in industries that depend on *X* Auto Company. Even though the problems of *X* Auto Company are not on the scale of the problems of the Great Depression, the loss of part of a major U.S. industry would have devastating effects on the U.S. economy as a whole. If federal funds can help *X* Auto Company continue to employ its workers, then thousands of private individuals will continue to earn and spend money. This will help protect the health of the nation's economy.

33   On the other hand, you could counter an argument based on similarity of policy considerations by showing that giving X Auto Company federal funds would widen the scope of the rule beyond the limits intended by those who derived the rule. This widening would have all kinds of adverse effects or troublesome consequences, such as opening the courts to a flood of frivolous litigation.

34   *Setting up an analogy.* To set up an analogy between two cases, using both the facts and the policy issues, begin by making a list of similarities and differences. Here is how you might expand the general welfare example to show that one case that has already been decided involving the old-age benefit provisions of the Social Security Act is or is not analogous to the *X* Auto Company case.

SIMILARITIES	DIFFERENCES
In both situations the recipients may receive money that they only directly paid into the system. For example, Social Security recipients may receive funds in excess of the amount they actually put into the fund. The *X* Auto Company will receive funds that it indirectly paid in the form of taxes, etc.	The recipients of old-age benefits have paid into an insurance fund over the years, while the *X* Auto Company would be receiving money from a nonspecific tax fund that it has not contributed to. Taxes and insurance are not the same thing.
Many individuals who need support will benefit from the federal funds; employees in the case of *X* Auto Company, and older members of the population in the case of old-age benefits.	It is quite a different thing for the federal government to provide funds to a private corporation than to provide them to individuals. The government is set up to benefit members of the general population. It is not the government's purpose to benefit a large private corporation.
The *X* Auto Company funds will help keep the economy healthy because it will keep a major industry alive and will keep *X*'s employees (and employees of other companies that depend on *X*) off of welfare and other forms of state subsidy. Similarly, the old-age benefits of Social Security assure citizens that they will have an opportunity to put money into a fund that they can draw on in their old age, provided they have worked the requisite amount of time to qualify. This keeps older people from having to turn to the state for support.	Giving funds to a private business may actually unbalance the economy, disturbing the free market and fair competition.

35   *C. The Conclusion*   After you have established and developed your major and minor premises, you are ready to reach a conclusion that follows logically from them. You may need to use a cause-and-effect argument to show *how* you came to the conclusion.

36   In law you will often be required to show that there is a cause-and-effect relationship between certain events or actions... .

37   Here is an example of how a cause-and-effect relationship can be established within a deductive argument. First, set up the skeleton of your argument.

General rule (major premise): Under the law of State *X*, the operator of a motor vehicle is liable for his or her wrongful act, neglect, or default if it causes death or injury to another person.

Specific facts (minor premise): The plaintiff was riding in her car on the freeway when the defendant's car hit her from behind. Two days later, the plaintiff suffered severe back pains and headaches.

Conclusion: Therefore, the defendant should be liable for the damages the plaintiff has suffered.

38   If you terminated your argument at this point, it would appear that you had based your conclusion on a faulty premise or assumption: "All pain that occurs within two days of an accident is necessarily caused by the accident." Or your conclusion may appear to result from a *post hoc* fallacy, in which you assert that because event *B* follows event *A* in time, event *A* has therefore caused event *B*. To avoid the appearance that your conclusion does not follow logically from the premises, you must articulate the causal link between events. You could do so by beginning your conclusion with the following information.

There is a good deal of evidence that the plaintiff's injury was caused by the defendant's act of hitting the plaintiff from behind. First of all, the plaintiff's medical records show that the plaintiff did not have a history of back problems or headaches, so there is no possibility that her injuries are part of a recurrent or chronic problem. Also, she has not engaged in any activity or suffered any other injury within the last few years that might have led to back pain or headaches. In addition, Dr. Jones, the plaintiff's physician, has examined the plaintiff and will testify that the pain the plaintiff is experiencing is the kind that the plaintiff would be likely to feel several days after a rear-end collision in an automobile.

39   You would finish your argument by qualifying your conclusion to reflect the evidence you have presented:

Because the evidence from medical records and from an expert demonstrates that, in all probability, the plaintiff's injuries were caused by the defendant's conduct, the defendant is liable for the damage the plaintiff has suffered as a result of that conduct.

40   When you are constructing a cause-and-effect argument, keep the subject matter in mind. If you are working with causation in a complex statistical argument, you must comply with the generally accepted principles of statistical analysis. For example, you may have to adhere to a scientific definition of causation. However, if you are writing about more common types of problems, try to appeal to your readers' sense of how the world works: Present a cause-and-effect relationship that your readers will recognize from their own experience. You can appeal to your readers' common sense and to the "common wisdom

of the community." Remember that judges and other attorneys are part of the community and that they will share this sense of what probably did or did not happen in a given situation.

Discussion and Writing Suggestions

1. In what ways is the IRAC system different from the way or ways you have previously been taught to organize writing? In what ways is it similar?

2. Take an everyday situation involving a conflict between individuals, involving you or someone else you know. Discuss this situation in IRAC format, as if it were a lawsuit and one party was suing the other. Articulate the *issue* at the heart of the conflict, the *"rule"* that you believe applies (even though it is not a legal rule), the *application* of this rule to the situation at hand, your *conclusion*, a counterargument to this conclusion, your response to the counterargument, and your overall conclusion.

3. Select another situation that might provide the basis of a lawsuit, drawing upon either your own experience, the experience of someone you know, or the experience of someone in a work of fiction or film. Develop a syllogism that would apply to this situation, as if you were constructing a legal argument. Formulate the major premise and the minor premise. Develop an argument by analogy, using the double column "Similarities"-"Differences" format indicated by Charrow, Erhardt, and Charrow. Finally, write the complete argument, using IRAC format.

Venezia v. Miller Brewing Company: A Defective Beer Bottle?
Ruthi Erdman

Now that you've read how to discuss a case in IRAC format, you may be interested in having such a discussion available as a model for the kind of writing you're likely to be doing in connection with this chapter. The selection leads off, like most of the rest here, with a statement of the "Facts of the Case," followed by a section of the relevant law. More specifically, you'll consider a case in which a boy's parents sued the Miller Brewing Company when the youngster injured himself after shattering a beer bottle against a telephone pole. The relevant law in this case is the Restatement of Torts, Section 402A: "Special Liability of Seller of Product for Physical Harm to User or Consumer." Should Miller be found liable for the boy's injuries? Does the law on product liability apply in this case? Ruthi Erdman, a writing instructor at Central Washington University, provided the following model paper for her students to use as a guide in responding to other cases in this chapter. We believe that you'll find her discussion helpful.

Patricia VENEZIA, Individually, and as she is next friend of Louis Venezia, a minor, Plaintiffs, Appellants

v.

MILLER BREWING COMPANY et al., Defendants, Appellees
No. 80-1036
United States Court of Appeals, First Circuit
Argued May 8, 1980
Decided July 18, 1980

Facts of the Case*

1   The complaint charged Miller Brewing Company and three manufacturers of glass products with negligence, gross negligence and breach of warranty in connection with the design and manufacture of a glass bottle used as a container for Miller Beer. The complaint alleged that plaintiff, then eight years of age, was playing with friends near his home when he "found a non-returnable Miller High Life clear glass bottle" which had been "discarded by…persons unknown…." During the course of play the "thin walled" bottle, in plaintiff's words, "came in contact with a telephone pole." Plaintiff, in his brief, has clarified this phrase, indicating that he was the party responsible for throwing the bottle against the pole. Following the impact of the glass container with the telephone pole the bottle shattered, and particles of glass entered plaintiff's eye causing severe injury. Plaintiff's basic premise is that Miller and the bottle manufacturers should have been aware of the dangers inherent in their "thin walled" "non-returnable" bottles and should have accordingly designed and marketed a product better able to safely withstand such foreseeable misuse as breakage in the course of improper handling by children.

Statements on the Law[†]

Restatement of Torts, Second

[SECTION] 402A. SPECIAL LIABILITY OF SELLER OF PRODUCT FOR PHYSICAL HARM TO USER OR CONSUMER
   (1) One who sells any product in a defective condition unreasonably dangerous to the user or consumer or to his property is subject to liability for physical harm thereby caused to the ultimate user or consumer, or to his property if
       (a) the seller is engaged in the business of selling such a product, and
       (b) it is expected to and does reach the user or consumer without substantial change in the condition in which it is sold.
   (2) The rule stated in Subsection (1) applies although
       (a) the seller has exercised all possible care in the preparation and sale of his product, and

---

**Venezia v. Miller Brewing Co.* 626 F.2d 188 (1980).

[†]*Restatement of The Law, Second: Torts 2nd.* As Adapted and Promulgated by The American Law Institute at Washington, D.C. May 25, 1963 and May 22, 1964. St. Paul, MN: West Publishing Co., 1965.

(b) the user or consumer has not bought the product from or entered into any contractual relation with the seller....

[Comment]

1   *g. Defective condition.* The rule stated in this Section applies only where the product is, at the time it leaves the seller's hands, in a condition not contemplated by the ultimate consumer, which will be unreasonably dangerous to him. The seller is not liable when he delivers the product in a safe condition, and subsequent mishandling or other causes make it harmful by the time it is consumed. The burden of proof that the product was in a defective condition at the time that it left the hands of the particular seller is upon the injured plaintiff; and unless evidence can be produced which will support the conclusion that it was then defective, the burden is not sustained.

2   Safe condition at the time of delivery by the seller will, however, include proper packaging, necessary sterilization, and other precautions required to permit the product to remain safe for a normal length of time when handled in a normal manner.

3   *h.* A product is not in a defective condition when it is safe for normal handling and consumption. If the injury results from abnormal handling, as where a bottled beverage is knocked against a radiator to remove the cap, or from abnormal preparation for use, as where too much salt is added to food, or from abnormal consumption, as where a child eats too much candy and is made ill, the seller is not liable. Where, however, he has reason to anticipate that danger may result from a particular use, as where a drug is sold which is safe only in limited doses, he may be required to give adequate warning of the danger and a product sold without such warning is in a defective condition... .

4   *n. Contributory negligence.* Since the liability with which this Section deals is not based upon negligence of the seller, but is strict liability, the rule applied to strict liability cases applies. Contributory negligence of the plaintiff is not a defense when such negligence consists merely in a failure to discover the defect in the product, or to guard against the possibility of its existence. On the other hand the form of contributory negligence which consists in voluntarily and unreasonably proceeding to encounter a known danger, and commonly passes under the name of assumption of risk, is a defense under this Section as in other cases of strict liability. If the user or consumer discovers the defect and is aware of the danger, and nevertheless proceeds unreasonably to make use of the product and is injured by it, he is barred from recovery.

Judge's Instructions to the Jury*

FAILURE TO WARN—ESSENTIAL ELEMENTS

1   The essential elements of a claim based upon an alleged defect from failure to warn are:

California Jury Instructions, Civil: Book of Approved Jury Instructions (BAJI). 8th ed. Prepared by The Committee on Standard Jury Instruction Civil, of the Superior Court of Los Angeles County, California. Hon. Stephen M. Lachs, Judge of the Superior Court, Chairman. Compiled and Edited by Paul G. Breckenridge, Jr. St. Paul, MN: West Publishing Co., 1994.

1. The defendant was the manufacturer of a product, namely *beer bottle*;
   (identify the product)
2. The product was defective;
3. The product defect was a cause of injury to the plaintiffs;
4. Plaintiff's injury resulted from a use of the product that was reasonably fore-seeable to the defendant.

2   A product is defective if the use of the product in a manner that is reason-ably foreseeable by the defendant involves a substantial danger that would not be readily recognized by the ordinary user of the product and the manufactur-er knows or should have known of the danger, but fails to give adequate warn-ing of such danger.

IRAC Essay: *Venezia vs. Miller Brewing Company:* A Defective Beer Bottle?

*Facts of the Case**

1   Eight-year-old Louis Venezia was playing outside with some friends near his home when he discovered a new toy: a discarded, empty beer bottle. In the course of the play that followed, Lou threw the bottle against a telephone pole, shattering it. Unfortunately, some particles of the splintered glass flew into Louis's eye, leaving the little boy with severe injuries.

2   Now Louis's mother, Patricia Venezia, is suing the Miller Brewing Company and three glass manufacturers for "negligence, gross negligence and breach of warranty" (*"Venezia"* 630), charging her son's injuries resulted from defects in the design and manufacture of the beer bottle. According to Mrs. Venezia, the company involved in the bottle's manufacture should have realized that by mar-keting a "thin walled" bottle which was "non-returnable" and therefore likely to be discarded, they were creating a hazard (630). The bottle, she claims, was inherently dangerous, as it was not designed to "safely withstand such foresee-able misuse as breakage in the course of improper handling by children" (630).

Issue

3   The issue in this case is whether the defendant, who manufactured a beer bottle that shattered when the plaintiff threw it against a telephone pole, severe-ly injuring his eye from flying glass particles, should be liable for gross negli-gence and for breach of warranty in the design and manufacture of the bottle.

Rule

4   According to the law, anyone who "sells any product in a defective condition unreasonably dangerous to the user or consumer or to his property is subject to liability for physical harm" (Restatement" 630). This rule applies even if "the user or consumer has not bought the product from or entered into any con-tractual relation with the seller" (631), so the fact that Louis Venezia did not

---

*For the purpose of this reading (as opposed to the purpose of a legal writing course) we recommend that the standard IRAC essay be prefaced by a statement of the "Facts of the Case."

actually buy the product is irrelevant. The law also stipulates that the seller is responsible only for "safe condition at the time of delivery" (631). This means that when a product "leaves the seller's hands," it must not, unbeknownst to the consumer, be in a condition "unreasonably dangerous to him" (631). It must be safe for "normal handling and consumption" (631).

Application

5 The Venezias are probably banking on the fact that safe condition at the time of delivery includes "proper packaging" (631). But was the beer sold by Miller "improperly packaged," so as to be "unreasonably dangerous" according to the accepted safety standards of the industry? What constitutes "proper packaging" for beer? True, some manufacturers of beverages such as Squeeze-it and Kool-Aid Splash package their product in soft plastic bottles that will not shatter under any circumstances. But beer is not Kool-Aid. It is intended for an entirely different consumer market consisting solely of adults, since minors cannot legally buy beer. Why should "reasonable consumer expectation" require that the package for an adult beverage be unbreakable? Furthermore, even manufacturers of legal-for-kiddies beverages like Snapple and 7-up are not required to package their drinks in plastic; they use nonreturnable glass bottles that probably would not withstand being hurled against a telephone pole.

6 This brings us to the question of whether Louis Venezia, in throwing the bottle against the pole, contributed to the negligence that resulted in his injury. The law states, quite sensibly, that failure to discover the defect in a product is not negligence on the part of the injured consumer ("Restatement" 631). But if the consumer "voluntarily and unreasonably [proceeds] to encounter a known danger" (631), then he is at fault, even if the product is defective. A user who "discovers the defect and is aware of the danger, and nevertheless proceeds unreasonably to make use of the product and is injured by it…is barred from recovery" (631)—that is, he cannot collect damages from the manufacturer.

7 Is it unreasonable to think that Louis Venezia was aware of the dangerous possibility that the beer bottle might shatter, and proceeded to throw it anyway? It seems unlikely that an eight-year-old child could have been *ignorant* of the shatterable nature of glass. In fact, it seems very likely that Venezia threw the bottle precisely for the thrill of making it shatter, the excitement and power of sending the glass shards flying. Why else do children hurl glass bottles against hard surfaces? Thus, the legal requirement that a product's dangerous condition must be "not…readily recognized by the ordinary user" ("Instructions" 632) is not met here, and Venezia was himself negligent in "encountering a known danger," even if Miller's beer bottle was defective.

8 But it wasn't defective. The final case against the Venezias' suit is that legally, a product is not defective as long as it is "safe for normal handling and consumption" ("Restatement" 631). The manufacturer cannot be held responsible when the consumer subjects the product to misuse:

> The seller is not liable when he delivers the product in a safe condition, and subsequent mishandling or other causes make it harmful…if the injury results from abnormal handling, as where a bottled beverage is knocked against a radi-

ator to remove the cap, or from abnormal consumption, as where a child eats too much candy and is made ill, the seller is not liable. ("Restatement" 631)

Clearly, if knocking a beverage bottle against a radiator to get the cap off is not "normal handling and consumption," then neither is flinging such a bottle against a telephone pole. A bottle cannot be labeled "defective" for breaking under such misuse, even if the breakage results in painful and debilitating injury to a little boy.

Conclusion

9 Of course any decent person will feel sympathy for an eight-year-old boy whose eye has been seriously injured, and of course it is natural for a traumatized, protective mother to look for someone on whom to pin the responsibility. But are the Miller Brewer Company and its glass suppliers really to blame for what happened to Louis Venezia? Is a beer bottle "defective" if it shatters when thrown against a telephone pole? Surely any reasonable court will see that the Miller Company is not liable for negligence or breach of warranty and that to force it to pay damages to the Venezias would be a gross miscarriage of justice.

The Ridiculed Employee:
An Additional Case of Emotional Distress
(Harris v. Jones)

The first selection in this chapter, "The Maiden and the Pot of Gold," presented a case of emotional distress. Now that you have had an opportunity, through the three subsequent selections, to learn more about how the law operates and how legal writing is used to formulate arguments, you are in a position to develop more knowledgeable, systematic responses to another case of emotional distress.

In Harris v. Jones, *a man sues his supervisor for repeatedly ridiculing and mimicking him. Following the facts of the case, as presented in the ruling of the appellate court, we present a number of "Statements on the Law," which help to establish the legal basis of claims for emotional distress. (Refer also to the "Judge's Instructions to the Jury" in the Nickerson case, pages 605–606.)*

William R. HARRIS

v.

H. Robert JONES et al.
Court of Appeals of Maryland
Dec. 9, 1977

Facts of the Case*

1 The plaintiff, William R. Harris, a 26-year-old, 8-year employee of General Motors Corporation (GM), sued GM and one if its supervisory employees, H. Robert

---

*Harris v. Jones. 380 A.2d 611 (1977).

Jones, in the Superior Court of Baltimore City. The declaration alleged that Jones, aware that Harris suffered from a speech impediment which caused him to stutter, and also aware of Harris' sensitivity to this disability, and his insecurity because of it, nevertheless "maliciously and cruelly ridiculed…[him] thus causing tremendous nervousness, increasing the physical defect itself and further injuring the mental attitude fostered by the Plaintiff toward his problem and otherwise intentionally inflicting emotional distress." It was also alleged in the declaration that Jones' actions occurred within the course of his employment with GM and that GM ratified Jones' conduct.

2   The evidence at trial showed that Harris stuttered throughout his entire life. While he had little trouble with one-syllable words, he had great difficulty with longer words or sentences, causing him at times to shake his head up and down when attempting to speak.

3   During part of 1975, Harris worked under Jones' supervision at a GM automobile assembly plant. Over a five-month period, between March and August of 1975, Jones approached Harris over 30 times at work and verbally and physically mimicked his stuttering disability. In addition, two or three times a week during this period, Jones approached Harris and told him, in a "smart manner," not to get nervous. As a result of Jones' conduct, Harris was "shaken up" and felt "like going into a hole and hide."

4   On June 2, 1975, Harris asked Jones for a transfer to another department; Jones refused, called Harris a "troublemaker" and chastised him for repeatedly seeking the assistance of his committeeman, a representative who handles employee grievances. On this occasion, Jones, "Shaking his head up and down" to imitate Harris, mimicked his pronunciation of the word "committeeman" which Harris pronounced "mmitteeman." As a result of this incident, Harris filed an employee grievance against Jones, requesting that GM instruct Jones to properly conduct himself in the future; the grievance was marked as satisfactorily settled after GM so instructed Jones. On another occasion during the five-month period, Harris filed a similar grievance against Jones; it too was marked as satisfactorily settled after GM again instructed Jones to properly conduct himself.

5   Harris had been under the care of a physician for a nervous condition for six years prior to the commencement of Jones' harassment. He admitted that many things made him nervous, including "bosses." Harris testified that Jones' conduct heightened his nervousness and his speech impediment worsened. He saw his physician on one occasion during the five-month period that Jones was mistreating him; the physician prescribed pills for his nerves.

6   Harris admitted that other employees at work mimicked his stuttering. Approximately 3,000 persons were employed on each of two shifts, and Harris acknowledged the presence at the plant of a lot of "tough guys," as well as profanity, name-calling and roughhousing among the employees. He said that a bad day at work caused him to become more nervous than usual. He admitted that he had problems with supervisors other than Jones, that he had been suspended or relieved from work 10 or 12 times, and that after one such dispute, he followed a supervisor home on his motorcycle, for which he was later disciplined.

7   Harris' wife testified that her husband was "in a shell" at the time they were married, approximately seven years prior to the trial. She said that it took her

about a year to get him to associate with family and friends and that while he still had a difficult time talking, he thereafter became "calmer." Mrs. Harris testified that beginning in November of 1974, her husband became ill-tempered at home and said that he had problems at work. She said that he was drinking too much at that time, that on one occasion he threw a meat platter at her, that she was afraid of him, and that they separated for a two-week period in November of 1974. Mrs. Harris indicated that her husband's nervous condition got worse in June of 1975. She said that at a christening party held during that month Harris "got to drinking" and they argued.

8   On this evidence, the case was submitted to the jury after the trial court denied the defendants' motions for directed verdicts; the jury awarded Harris $3,500 compensatory damages and $15,000 punitive damages against both Jones and GM. [The verdict was then appealed by the defendant.]

Statements on the Law*

Restatement of Torts, Second

[Section] 46. OUTRAGEOUS CONDUCT CAUSING SEVERE EMOTIONAL DISTRESS
  (1) One who by extreme and outrageous conduct intentionally or recklessly causes severe emotional distress to another is subject to liability for such emotional distress, and if bodily harm to the other results from it, for such bodily harm.
  (2) Where such conduct is directed at a third person, the actor is subject to liability if he intentionally or recklessly causes severe emotional distress
      (a) to a member of such person's immediate family who is present at the time, whether or not such distress results in bodily harm, or
      (b) to any other person who is present at the time, if such distress results in bodily harm.

[Comment]

1 *d. Extreme and outrageous conduct.*   The cases thus far decided have found liability only where the defendant's conduct has been extreme and outrageous. It has not been enough that the defendant has acted with an intent which is tortious or even criminal, or that he has intended to inflict emotional distress, or even that his conduct has been characterized by "malice," or a degree of aggravation which would entitle the plaintiff to punitive damages for another tort. Liability has been found only where the conduct has been so outrageous in character, and so extreme in degree, as to go beyond all possible bounds of decency, and to be regarded as atrocious, and utterly intolerable in a civilized community. Generally, the case is one in which the recitation of the facts to an average member of the community would arouse his resentment against the actor, and lead him to exclaim, "Outrageous!"

Restatement of The Law, Second: Torts 2nd. As Adapted and Promulgated by The American Law Institute at Washington, D.C. May 25, 1963 and May 22, 1964. St. Paul, MN: West Publishing Co., 1965.

2   The liability clearly does not extend to mere insults, indignities, threats, annoyances, petty oppressions, or other trivialities. The rough edges of our society are still in need of a good deal of filing down, and in the meantime plaintiffs must necessarily be expected and required to be hardened to a certain amount of rough language, and to occasional acts that are definitely inconsiderate and unkind. There is no occasion for the law to intervene in every case where someone's feelings are hurt. There must still be freedom to express an unflattering opinion, and some safety valve must be left through which irascible tempers may blow off relatively harmless steam.

Illustrations [liable]:

3   1. As a practical joke, A falsely tells B that her husband has been badly injured in an accident, and is in the hospital with both legs broken. B suffers severe emotional distress. A is subject to liability to B for her emotional distress. If it causes nervous shock and resulting illness, A is subject to liability to B for her illness.

4   2. A, the president of an association of rubbish collectors, summons B to a meeting of the association, and in the presence of an intimidating group of associates tells B that B has been collecting rubbish in territory which the association regards as exclusively allocated to one of its members. A demands that B pay over the proceeds of his rubbish collection, and tells B that if he does not do so the association will beat him up, destroy his truck, and put him out of business. B is badly frightened, and suffers severe emotional distress. A is subject to liability to B for his emotional distress, and if it results in illness, A is also subject to liability to B for his illness.

5   3. A is invited to a swimming party at an exclusive resort. B gives her a bathing suit which he knows will dissolve in water. It does dissolve while she is swimming, leaving her naked in the presence of men and women whom she has just met. A suffers extreme embarrassment, shame, and humiliation. B is subject to liability to A for her emotional distress....

Illustrations [not liable]:

6   8. A, a creditor, seeking to collect a debt, calls on B and demands payment in a rude and insolent manner. When B says that he cannot pay, A calls B a deadbeat, and says that he will never trust B again. A's conduct, although insulting, is not so extreme or outrageous as to make A liable to B....

7   17. The same facts as Illustration 1 [above], except that B does not believe A's statement, and is only sufficiently disturbed to telephone to the hospital to find out whether it could possibly be true. A is not liable to B.

[Comment on Illustrations]

8   *Severe emotional distress.*   The rule stated in this Section applies only where the emotional distress has in fact resulted, and where it is severe. Emotional distress passes under various names, such as mental suffering, mental anguish, mental or nervous shock, or the like. It includes all highly unpleasant mental reactions, such as fright, horror, grief, shame, humiliation, embarrassment, anger, chagrin, disappointment, worry, and nausea. It is only where it is extreme that the liability arises. Complete emotional tranquility is seldom

attainable in this world, and some degree of transient and trivial emotional distress is a part of the price of living among people. The law intervenes only where the distress inflicted is so severe that no reasonable man could be expected to endure it. The intensity and the duration of the distress are factors to be considered in determining its severity. Severe distress must be proved; but in many cases the extreme and outrageous character of the defendant's conduct is in itself important evidence that the distress has existed. For example, the mere recital of the facts in Illustration 1 above goes far to prove that the claim is not fictitious.

9   The distress must be reasonable and justified under the circumstances, and there is no liability where the plaintiff has suffered exaggerated and unreasonable emotional distress, unless it results from a peculiar susceptibility to such distress of which the actor has knowledge.

10   It is for the court to determine whether on the evidence severe emotional distress can be found; it is for the jury to determine whether, on the evidence, it has in fact existed.

From Harris *ruling:**

11 In his now classic article, *Mental and Emotional Disturbance in the Law of Torts,* 49 Harv.L.Rev. 1033 (1936), Professor Calvert Magruder warned against imposing liability for conduct which is not outrageous and extreme; he observed at 1035 that "Against a large part of the frictions and irritations and clashing of temperaments incident to participation in a community life, a certain toughening of the mental hide is a better protection than the law could ever be," and at 1053, he said:

> "there is danger of getting into the realm of the trivial in this matter of insulting language. No pressing social need requires that every abusive outburst be converted into a tort; upon the contrary, it would be unfortunate if the law closed all the safety valves through which irascible tempers might legally blow off steam."

From Harris *ruling†*

12 "In *Samms [v. Eccles,* 11 Utah 2d 289, 358 P.2d 344 (1961)], the Supreme Court of Utah aptly stated:

> '…[T]he best considered view recognizes an action for severe emotional distress, though not accompanied by bodily impact or physical injury, where the defendant intentionally engaged in some conduct toward the plaintiff, (a) with the purpose of inflicting emotional distress, *or,* (b) where any reasonable person would have known that such would result; and his actions are of such a nature as to be considered outrageous and intolerable in that they offend against the generally accepted standards of decency and morality.'" 210 S.E.2d at 147-148.

---

*[380 A.2d at 615]

†[380 A.2d at 614]

From Harris *ruling:**

13 The "severe emotional distress" required to support a cause of action for intentional infliction of emotional distress was discussed by the Supreme Court of Illinois in *Knierim v. Izzo,* 22 Ill.2d 73, 174 N.E.2d 157 (1961):

> "...not...every emotional upset should constitute the basis of an action. Indiscriminate allowance of actions for mental anguish would encourage neurotic overreactions to trivial hurts, and the law should aim to toughen the pysche of the citizen rather than pamper it. But a line can be drawn between the slight hurts which are the price of a complex society and the severe mental disturbances inflicted by intentional actions wholly lacking in social utility." 174 N.E.2d at 164.

Caselaw: Womack v. Eldridge†

14 We adopt the view that a cause of action will lie for emotional distress, unaccompanied by physical injury, provided four elements are shown: One, the wrongdoer's conduct was intentional or reckless. This element is satisfied where the wrongdoer had the specific purpose of inflicting emotional distress or where he intended his specific conduct and knew or should have known that emotional distress would likely result. Two, the conduct was outrageous and intolerable in that it offends against the generally accepted standards of decency and morality. This requirement is aimed at limiting frivolous suits and avoiding litigation in situations where only bad manners and mere hurt feelings are involved. Three, there was a causal connections between the wrongdoer's conduct and the emotional distress. Four, the emotional distress was severe.

Discussion and Writing Suggestions

1. Assume that you have heard the evidence in *Harris v. Jones,* as summarized in the "Facts of the Case." Assume also, that you have heard the same jury instructions as were given in the Nickerson case (pp. 605–606). Finally, assume that in asking for clarification of "emotional distress," the jury has received additional information in the form of the "Statements on the Law" presented after the "Facts of the Case."

   If you were a member of the jury deliberating on a verdict, how would you vote? Explain your reasoning, specifically referring to the particular facts of the case and to the definitions or explanations of "emotional distress." How do these definitions and explanations either support or fail to support the plaintiff's claim for damages? Emphasize those elements of the case that seemed crucial to you in reaching a determination.

---

*[380 A.2d at 617]

†[210 S.E.2d at 148]

2. Assume that you are an attorney *either* for the plaintiff (Harris) *or* for the defendant (Jones). Assume also, that you have researched the case and discovered a precedent, *Nickerson v. Hodges.* You believe that this precedent can support your position, owing to either its similarities to or differences from the *Harris* case. Write a brief argument to the appellate court in IRAC format explaining how the facts in *Nickerson* are similar to or different from those in *Harris.* (Ask your instructor for the appellate court ruling on *Nickerson*; it is included in the *Instructor's Manual.*) In developing your argument, draw upon relevant statements on the law following the facts of the case. As an IRAC model, see the "beer bottle" essay (pp. 632–34).

3. Have you (or has someone you know) ever suffered emotional distress of the type that would fit the legal definition of this term? If so, lay out the facts of the case in a manner similar to the narratives in this section. Then, using IRAC format, apply the legal standards for a judgment of emotional distress to the event or events you have described.

4. As an alternate assignment to #3 above, select a character in a story, novel, film, or TV show who has suffered emotional distress. Using IRAC format, write a brief either for the plaintiff or the defendant. For example, could Othello charge Iago with intentional infliction of emotional distress? Could "Piggy" in *Lord of the Flies* charge Jack and others?

5. *Group Assignment* : Form a jury, a group consisting of several other members of the class. (It doesn't have to have 12 members.) Choose a foreperson, someone to moderate, though not dominate, the discussion—someone who will keep the deliberations on track and keep the main issues in the forefront. Appoint someone to take notes. You may wish to tape-record the discussion.

   Deliberate on the case before you: study the facts of the case; study the applicable law; apply the law to the facts of the case. Before or while you are developing your own conclusions, take account of other people's arguments. Weigh the merits of these arguments before deciding upon your vote. At the conclusion of discussion, the group will vote on a verdict. (Criminal cases require a unanimous vote; civil cases require a three-quarters majority.) If the jury is badly split, deliberate more in order to reach greater consensus.

   After you arrive at a verdict, work with the foreperson as she or he prepares a report, written in IRAC format, that presents your verdict (as a conclusion), and that explains the issue, the rule, and also summarizes the main points of the discussion in the "counter-argument" and "response" sections.

Assault and Battery on the Gridiron: A Case of Reckless Disregard of Safety
(Hackbart v. Cincinnati Bengals)

Should a professional football player be entitled to collect damages from another player who has injured him in the course of a game? At first, the question seems laughable: after all, if pro football is about anything, it's about organized (sometimes disorganized) violence, and players who aren't willing to run the risk of being injured, it might be argued, have no business playing the game.

Still, there must be some limits to violence, even in football. The game has rules, and one of those rules provides that: "All players are prohibited from striking on the head, face or neck with the heel, back or side of the hand, wrist, forearm, elbow, or clasped hands."* Admittedly, most violations of the rules are penalized by a loss of yardage; but are there particularly extreme cases in which recourse to the law is appropriate?

In June, 1997, millions of people were outraged when Mike Tyson bit off part of Evander Holyfield's ear during a heavyweight title bout in Las Vegas. Tyson was fined $3 million and suspended indefinitely from professional boxing; some commentators noted that Holyfield could have filed a lawsuit against the offender. Even boxing, which is conflict at its most primal, has its rules of fair play, and Tyson clearly and egregiously violated those rules.

The case that follows deals with an incident that occurred during an NFL game played in Denver in September, 1973, between the Denver Broncos and the Cincinnati Bengals. After the initial trial, the case was appealed, first to the United States District Court in Colorado (1977), and then to the U.S. Court of Appeals, Tenth Circuit (1979).

Following the "Facts of the Case," we present "Statements on the Law": section 500 of the Restatement of Torts, 2d., which, the plaintiff argued, applied to the defendant's action.

Dale HACKBART, Plaintiff

v.

CINCINNATI BENGALS, INC. and Charles "Booby" CLARK, Defendants
United States District Court
D. Colorado

Facts of the Case[†]

The Parties

1   The Plaintiff, Dale Hackbart, is a citizen of Colorado who was a 35-year-old contract player for the Denver Broncos Football Club in the National Football League

---

*NFL Rules of Football: Article 1, Item 1, Subsection C.

[†]*Hackbart v. Cincinnati Bengals.* 601 F.2d 516 (1979).

at the time of the incident. He was then 6 feet 3 inches tall and weighed 210 pounds. Mr. Hackbart had 13 years' experience as a professional football player after competing in college and high school football, making a total of 21 years of experience in organized football.

2   The Denver game was the first regular season professional football game for the defendant, Charles Clark, who was then 23 years old with a weight of 240 pounds and a height of 6 feet 1 3/4 inches. Mr. Clark was a contract player for the Cincinnati Bengals Football Club, Inc., defendant herein, which was also a member of the National Football League. Both defendants are citizens of states other than Colorado.

The Incident

3 The incident which gave rise to this lawsuit occurred near the end of the first half of the game at a time when the Denver team was leading by a score of 21 to 3. Dale Hackbart was playing a free safety position on the Broncos' defensive team and Charles Clark was playing fullback on the Bengals' offensive team. The Cincinnati team attempted a forward pass play during which Charles Clark ran into a corner of the north end zone as a prospective receiver. That took him into an area which was the defensive responsibility of Mr. Hackbart. The thrown pass was intercepted near the goal line by a Denver linebacker who then began to run the ball upfield. The interception reversed the offensive and defensive roles of the two teams. As a result of an attempt to block Charles Clark in the end zone, Dale Hackbart fell to the ground. He then turned and, with one knee on the ground and the other leg extended, watched the play continue upfield. Acting out of anger and frustration, but without a specific intent to injury, Charles Clark stepped forward and struck a blow with his right forearm to the back of the kneeling plaintiff's head with sufficient force to cause both players to fall forward to the ground. Both players arose and, without comment, went to their respective teams along the sidelines. They both returned to play during the second half of the game.

4   Because no official observed it, no foul was called on the disputed play and Dale Hackbart made no report of this incident to his coaches or to anyone else during the game. However, the game film showed very clearly what had occurred. Mr. Hackbart experienced pain and soreness to the extent that he was unable to play golf as he had planned on the day after the game, he did not seek any medical attention and, although he continued to feel pain, he played on specialty team assignments for the Denver Broncos in games against the Chicago Bears and the San Francisco Forty-Niners on successive Sundays. The Denver Broncos then released Mr. Hackbart on waivers and he was not claimed by any other team. After losing his employment, Mr. Hackbart sought medical assistance, at which time it was discovered that he had a neck injury. When that information was given to the Denver Broncos Football Club, Mr. Hackbart received his full payment for the 1973 season pursuant to an injury clause in his contract.

The Professional Football Industry

5   The claim of the plaintiff in this case must be considered in the context of football as a commercial enterprise. The National Football League (NFL) is an organization formed for the purpose of promoting and fostering the business of its members, the owners of professional football "clubs" with franchises to operate in designated cities....

6   Football is a recognized game which is widely played as a sport. Commonly teams are organized by high schools and colleges and games are played according to rules provided by associations of such schools.

7   The basic design of the game is the same at the high school, college and professional levels. The differences are largely reflective of the fact that at each level the players have increased physical abilities, improved skills and differing motivations.

8   Football is a contest for territory. The objective of the offensive team is to move the ball through the defending team's area and across the vertical plane of the goal line. The defensive players seek to prevent that movement with their bodies. Each attempted movement involved collisions between the bodies of offensive and defensive players with considerable force and with differing areas of contact. The most obvious characteristic of the game is that all of the players engage in violent physical behavior.

9   The rules of play which govern the methods and style by which the NFL teams compete include limitations on the manner in which players may strike or otherwise physically contact opposing players. During 1973, the rules were enforced by six officials on the playing field. The primary sanction for a violation was territorial with the amounts of yardage lost being dependent upon the particular infraction. Players were also subject to expulsion from the game and to monetary penalties imposed by the league commissioner.

10   The written rules are difficult to understand and, because of the speed and violence of the game, their application is often a matter of subjective evaluation of the circumstances. Officials differ with each other in their rulings. The players are not specifically instructed in the interpretation of the rules, and they acquire their working knowledge of them only from the actual experience of enforcement by the game officials during contests.

11   Many violations of the rules do occur during each game. Ordinarily each team receives several yardage penalties, but many fouls go undetected or undeclared by the officials.

12   Disabling injuries are also common occurrences in each contest. Hospitalization and surgery are frequently required for repairs. Protective clothing is worn by all players, but it is often inadequate to prevent bodily damage. Professional football players are conditioned to "play with pain" and they are expected to perform even though they are hurt. The standard player contract imposes an obligation to play when the club physician determines that an injured player has the requisite physical ability.

13   The violence of professional football is carefully orchestrated. Both offensive and defensive players must be extremely aggressive in their actions and they

must play with a reckless abandonment of self-protective instincts. The coaches make studied and deliberate efforts to build the emotional levels of their players to what some call a "controlled rage."

14   John Ralston, the 1973 Broncos coach, testified that the pre-game psychological preparation should be designed to generate an emotion equivalent to that which would be experienced by a father whose family had been endangered by another driver who had attempted to force the family car off the edge of a mountain road. The precise pitch of motivation for the players at the beginning of the game should be the feeling of that father when, after overtaking and stopping the offending vehicle, he is about to open the door to take revenge upon the person of the other driver.

15   The large and noisy crowds in attendance at the games contribute to the emotional levels of the players. Quick changes in the fortunes of the teams, the shock of violent collisions and the intensity of the competition make behavioral control extremely difficult, and it is not uncommon for players to "flare up" and begin fighting. The record made at this trial indicates that such incidents as that which gave rise to this action are not so unusual as to be unexpected in any NFL game.

16   The end product of all of the organization and effort involved in the professional football industry is an exhibition of highly developed individual skills in coordinated team competition for the benefit of large numbers of paying spectators, together with radio and television audiences. It is appropriate to infer that while some of those persons are attracted by the individual skills and precision performances of the teams, the appeal to others is the spectacle of savagery.

Plaintiff's Theories of Liability

17 This case is controlled by the law of Colorado. While a theory of intentional misconduct is barred by the applicable statute of limitations, the plaintiff contends that Charles Clark's foul was so far outside of the rules of play and accepted practices of professional football that it should be characterized as reckless misconduct within the principles of Section 500 of the *Restatement of Torts, 2d*....

18   Alternatively, the plaintiff claims that his injury was at least the result of a negligent act by the defendant. The difference in these contentions is but a difference in degree. Both theories are dependent upon a definition of a duty to the plaintiff and an objective standard of conduct based upon the hypothetical reasonably prudent person. Thus, the question is what would a reasonably prudent professional football player be expected to do under the circumstances confronting Charles Clark in this incident?

19   Two coaches testified at the trial of this case. Paul Brown had had 40 years of experience at all levels of organized football, with 20 years of coaching professional football. Both Mr. Brown and Mr. Ralston emphasized that the coaching and instructing of professional football players did not include any training with respect to a responsibility or even any regard for the safety of opposing players. They both said that aggressiveness was the primary attribute which they sought in the selection of players. Both emphasized the importance of emotional preparation of the teams. Mr. Brown said that flare-up fighting often occurred, even in practice sessions of his teams.

Statements on the Law*

Restatement of Torts, Second

[SECTION] 500. RECKLESS DISREGARD OF SAFETY DEFINED

The actor's conduct is in reckless disregard of the safety of another if he does an act or intentionally fails to do an act which it is his duty to the other to do, knowing or having reason to know of facts which would lead a reasonable man to realize, not only that his conduct creates an unreasonable risk of physical harm to another, but also that such risk is substantially greater than that which is necessary to make his conduct negligent.

1   *Special Note:* The conduct described in this Section is often called "wanton or wilful misconduct" both in statutes and judicial opinions. On the other hand, this phrase is sometimes used by courts to refer to conduct intended to cause harm to another.

[Comment]

2   *a. Types of reckless conduct.*   Recklessness may consist of either of two different types of conduct. In one the actor knows, or has reason to know [...] of facts which create a high degree of risk of physical harm to another, and deliberately proceeds to act, or to fail to act, in conscious disregard of, or indifference to, that risk. In the other the actor has such knowledge, or reason to know, of the facts, but does not realize or appreciate the high degree of risk involved, although a reasonable man in his position would do so. An objective standard is applied to him, and he is held to the realization of the aggravated risk which a reasonable man in his place would have, although he does not himself have it.

3   For either type of reckless conduct, the actor must know, or have reason to know, the facts which create the risk. For either, the risk must itself be an unreasonable one under the circumstances. There may be exceptional circumstances which make it reasonable to adopt a course of conduct which involves a high degree of risk of serious harm to others. While under ordinary circumstances it would be reckless to drive through heavy traffic at a high rate of speed, it may not even be negligent to do so if the driver is escaping from a bandit or carrying a desperately wounded man to the hospital for immediately necessary treatment, or if his car has been commandeered by the police for the pursuit of a fleeing felon. So too, there may be occasions in which action which would ordinarily involve so high a degree of danger as to be reckless may be better than no action at all, and therefore both reasonable and permissible. Thus one who finds another in a lonely place, and very seriously hurt, may well be justified in giving him such imperfect surgical aid as a layman can be expected to give, although it would be utterly reckless for him to meddle in the matter if professional assistance were available.

Restatement of the Law, Second: Torts 2nd. As Adapted and Promulgated by The American Law Institute at Washington, D.C. May 25, 1963 and May 22, 1964. St. Paul, MN: West Publishing Co., 1965.

4   For either type of conduct, to be reckless it must be unreasonable; but to be reckless, it must be something more than negligent. It must not only be unreasonable, but it must involve a risk of harm to others substantially in excess of that necessary to make the conduct negligent. It must involve an easily perceptible danger of death or substantial physical harm, and the probability that it will so result must be substantially greater than is required for ordinary negligence.

5   *b. Perception of risk.*   Conduct cannot be in reckless disregard of the safety of others unless the act or omission is itself intended, notwithstanding that the actor knows of facts which would lead any reasonable man to realize the extreme risk to which it subjects the safety of others. It is reckless for a driver of an automobile intentionally to cross a through highway in defiance of a stop sign if a stream of vehicles is seen to be closely approaching in both directions, but if his failure to stop is due to the fact that he has permitted his attention to be diverted so that he does not know that he is approaching the crossing, he may be merely negligent and not reckless. So too, if his failure to stop is due to the fact that his brakes fail to act, he may be negligent if the bad condition of the brakes could have been discovered by such an inspection as it is his duty to make, but his conduct is not reckless.

6   *c. Appreciation of extent and gravity of risk.*   In order that the actor's conduct may be reckless, it is not necessary that he himself recognize it as being extremely dangerous. His inability to realize the danger may be due to his own reckless temperament, or to the abnormally favorable results of previous conduct of the same sort. It is enough that he knows or has reason to know of circumstances which would bring home to the realization of the ordinary, reasonable man the highly dangerous character of his conduct…

7   *f. Intentional misconduct and recklessness contrasted.*   Reckless misconduct differs from intentional wrongdoing in a very important particular. While an act to be reckless must be intended by the actor, the actor does not intend to cause the harm which results from it. It is enough that he realizes or, from facts which he knows, should realize that there is a strong probability that harm may result, even though he hopes or even expects that his conduct will prove harmless. However, a strong probability is a different thing from the substantial certainty without which he cannot be said to intend the harm in which his act results.

8   *g. Negligence and recklessness contrasted.*   Reckless misconduct differs from negligence in several important particulars. It differs from that form of negligence which consists in mere inadvertence, incompetence, unskillfulness, or a failure to take precautions to enable the actor adequately to cope with a possible or probable future emergency, in that reckless misconduct requires a conscious choice of a course of action, either with knowledge of the serious danger to others involved in it or with knowledge of facts which would disclose this danger to any reasonable man. It differs not only from the above-mentioned form of negligence, but also from that negligence which consists in intentionally doing an act with knowledge that it contains a risk of harm to others, in that the actor to be reckless must recognize that his conduct involves a risk substantially greater in amount than that which is necessary to make his conduct negligent. The difference between reckless misconduct and conduct involving

only such a quantum of risk as is necessary to make it negligent is a difference in the degree of the risk, but this difference of degree is so marked as to amount substantially to a difference in kind.

Instructions to the Jury*

1 The plaintiff *Dale Hackbart* [also] seeks to recover damages based upon a claim of reckless misconduct by a co-participant in an active sporting event.

2   The essential elements of such a claim are:

1. Plaintiff and Defendant were co-participants in an active sporting event;
2. Defendant'[s] physical conduct caused plaintiff to suffer injury;
3. The defendant intended to injure plaintiff, or was so reckless as to be totally outside the range of the ordinary activity involved in the sport.

3   [A defendant intended to inflict injury if it is established that [he] [she] desired to cause such injury or knew that such an injury was substantially certain to result from [his] [her] conduct.]

4   [A co-participant in an active sport is not subject to liability for an injury resulting from conduct in the course of the sport that is merely accidental, careless, or negligent.]

Discussion and Writing Suggestions

1. If you were a member of the jury deliberating on a verdict, how would you vote? Explain your reasoning, specifically referring to the particular facts of the case and to the definitions or explanations of "reckless disregard of safety" in the *Restatement of Torts*. How do these definitions and explanations either support or fail to support the plaintiff's claim for damages? Emphasize those elements of the case that seemed crucial to you in reaching a determination.

2. Based on the explanations in the *Restatement of Torts,* would you characterize Charles Clark's actions as "negligent" or "reckless"— or neither? Explain.

3. One judge reviewing this case (whose opinion did not necessarily prevail), wrote

   It is wholly incongruous to talk about a professional football player's duty of care for the safety of opposing players when he has been trained and motivated to be heedless of injury to himself. The character of NFL competition negates any notion that the playing conduct can be circumscribed by any standard of reasonableness. [452 F.Supp. at 356]

California Jury Instructions, Civil: Book of Approved Jury Instructions [BAJI]. 8th ed. Prepared by The Committee on Standard Jury Instruction Civil, of the Superior Court of Los Angeles County, California. Hon. Stephen M. Lachs, Judge of the Superior Court, Chairman. Compiled and Edited by Paul G. Breckenridge, Jr. St. Paul, MN: West Publishing Co., 1994.

Another judge reviewing the case (again, whose opinion did not necessarily prevail) wrote:

> … it is highly questionable whether a professional football player consents or submits to injuries caused by conduct not within the rules, and there is no evidence which we have seen which shows this. [602 F.2nd. at 520]

Considering the facts of the case, which of these opinions do you find more persuasive? Explain.

4. One judge reviewing this case noted:

> The NFL rules of play are so…difficult of application because of the speed and violence of the play that the differences between violations which could fairly be called deliberate, reckless or outrageous and those which are "fair play" would be so small and subjective as to be incapable of articulation. The question of causation would be extremely difficult in view of the frequency of forceful collisions. [435 F.Supp. at 358]

Essentially, the judge appears to be saying that given the nature of professional football, there is no way to tell whether a violent act by one player against another is fair or not. Looking at the particular facts of this case, to what extent to you agree?

5. Have you (or has someone you know) ever been a victim of reckless disregard of safety that would fit the legal definition of this term? If so, lay out the facts of the case in a manner similar to the narratives in this section. Then, using IRAC format, apply the legal standards for a judgment of reckless disregard of safety to the event or events you have described.

6. *Group Assignment:* See Discussion and Writing Suggestion #5 in "The Ridiculed Employee" (p. 640) and apply that assignment to this case.

Who Gets the Kids?
Some Cases of Child Custody
(Ashwell v. Ashwell, Wood v. Wood, Fingert v. Fingert, In re B.G., B.A.S. v. G.R.S.)

Custody battles are among the most bitter conflicts fought in the nation's courts—ironic, considering that the adversaries generally began their relationship in an atmosphere of love and trust. In many cases, the divorcing couple is able to resolve the issue of child custody through private negotiation, sometimes with the aid of a mediator. But in cases where they cannot agree on which parent gets which kids, one will generally sue the other, and a judge in a family court must resolve the matter. What usually needs to be decided is which parent gets physical custody—that is, with which parent do the children live most of the time?—as well as what kind of visitation rights are awarded to the other parent, and what kind of child support must be paid by the non-custodial parent. In many cases, a court will rule that a child or children live with one parent part of the week, or the year, and with the other parent, the rest of the time. Such arrangements are only made, of course, if both adversaries are ruled fit parents.

During the first half of the last century, courts almost automatically awarded custody to the mother. This preference arose from the assumption that the mother did not work and was available at home to serve as a full-time caregiver for her children. With more women joining the workforce in the second half of the twentieth century, and with a general movement toward equality of the sexes, awarding custody to the mother no longer became automatic. Judges had to decide whether it would be in the best interest of the child to live with the mother or the father. This "best interest of the child" standard has become the main criterion that determines who gets physical custody.

What factors go in to determining the best interest of the child? The courts look for a stable home environment, where a loving parent takes care of the children's physical and emotional needs: makes sure that they are well fed and housed, sees that they get adequate medical care, ensures that they regularly go to school. The custodial parent has to be financially able to take care of the child (which means, generally, that the parent must be gainfully employed), but otherwise, the relative financial conditions of the two parents is not a factor in awarding custody. The parent with custody must also be considered morally fit by the court; this often precludes the awarding of custody to parents involved in criminal activities, who take illegal drugs, who drink to excess, or who have serious emotional problems. Sexual behavior or promiscuity (or sexual inclination) in itself does not necessarily bar a parent from being awarded custody unless the other parent or the state can show that such behavior has led to the parent neglecting the children's needs. The courts will also consider the age and sex of each child; judges will often award female children to the mother and male children to the father. Finally, courts may also take into account the children's wishes, but those wishes must be based on sound reasons (the child wants to continue going to the same school, for instance, not that the parent doesn't buy the child enough presents).

A significant change in any of the conditions that determined the original settlement (such as a planned out-of-state move by one parent) will often bring the parties back to court, with one arguing that the changed conditions justify a change in custody. And—as is the case in all of the following disputes—a losing party who disagrees with the trial court's judgment may appeal to a higher court for a reversal of the original ruling.

Norma Jeanne ASHWELL, Plaintiff-Appellant

v.

Curtis Lee ASHWELL, Defendant-Respondent
Court of Appeal of California, Third Appellate District
Division 6
August 24, 1955*

1 On August 17, 1953, an interlocutory [temporary] decree of divorce was entered in an action brought by Norma Jeanne Ashwell, appellant herein, against Curtis

---

*Ashwell v. Ashwell. 286 P.2d 983 (1995)

Lee Ashwell, respondent herein. The decree was granted to Norma upon the ground of extreme cruelty and upon default of Curtis. Custody of the four children of the marriage was given to Norma. The oldest of the children was 6 and the youngest less than 2. During the interlocutory period and on January 19, 1954, Curtis filed a notice of motion to modify the interlocutory decree by taking the custody of the children from Norma and awarding that custody to Curtis. The notice of motion stated that the modification sought would be to the effect that Norma was not a fit and proper person to have custody. [...]

2   Norma gave birth to a fifth child on February 14, 1954 (conceived prior to the interlocutory decree). The father of the child was one Barney Cassella. Norma, the five children and Cassella were living in the same house when the motion to modify the decree was heard. Curtis was a master sergeant in the United States Army, stationed in Sacramento [California]. That county had also been the situs of the domicile of the parties when the decree of divorce was granted. Curtis testified he had visited the children about once a week and a number of times had found them in the charge of a 12-year-old girl. He said they were generally raggedly dressed in dirty clothes and appeared to need a bath; that whenever he visited Barney Cassella was always present; that Norma and the children had, after the decree, moved from a residence in Sacramento and were living in West Sacramento, across the river in Yolo County; that on December 23, 1953, at about 10 P.M. he visited there and Cassella answered the door and was improperly dressed (he did not specify in what the impropriety consisted); that Norma then told him she was pregnant, but denied that Cassella was responsible. Curtis stated to the court that if he obtained custody of the children he intended to get a discharge from the Army and take the children back to Virginia to live with his parents who were living on a farm three miles out of Huddleston; that the home was an average home, with access to schools and churches; that his parents were Mormons; that his mother was 45 years of age and his father 54 years old; that he, Curtis, is a mechanic by trade and had been offered a job in Huddleston and expected to support his children from his earnings. He said he had never seen any improprieties between Norma and Cassella.

3   Barney Cassella testified he was a taxi driver employed in Sacramento and since November 1953 had been living in the same house with Norma and the children; that he rented the house; that before that time he rented an apartment from Mrs. Ashwell in Sacramento; that he had had sexual intercourse with her several times, but not since June of 1953; that he was the father of the child she bore February 14, 1954; that when he moved to West Sacramento it was to a house which he rented which had three bedrooms, one of which was occupied by him and his adult nephew, one by Norma with the new baby and the youngest Ashwell child, and the other by the three older children; that he loved Norma and intended to marry her as soon as her divorce became final. Norma testified that Cassella was the father of her last born child; that she and Cassella had had no sexual relations since she became pregnant in June of 1953; that she had not told Curtis at any time that Cassella was not the father of her last born child. In explanation of her conduct she testified that she had been compelled, while living in Sacramento and after her separation from

Curtis, to rent an apartment to Cassella, and that the compulsion was from economic necessity; that she was compelled to leave her Sacramento home because Curtis came there at unreasonable hours and abused and insulted her beyond endurance; that she had moved into a house which Cassella rented because she could not afford a place of her own; that she loved Cassella and intended to marry him as soon as her divorce became final; that she had always properly cared for the children; that she loved them and devoted her full time to their care; that they were healthy and happy. She said: "I am living with Mr. Cassella now because of economic necessity. I receive $100.00 a month from him to apply toward the support of myself and my children. I cannot afford to live separate and apart from him at the present time. If my children were taken back to Virginia, I could not afford to go there to visit, and I would probably never see them again." Two women, neighbors to Norma, testified that Norma was a good mother, cared for her children well and that they appeared to be healthy, happy, normal children; that she was conscientious and never neglected or abused her children in any way.

In re the Marriage of Patricia C. and Frank Howard WOOD, Patricia L. WOOD, Appellant

v.

Frank Howard WOOD, Respondent
Court of Appeals of California, Fifth Appellate District
April 5, 1983*

1 This is an appeal by a mother who has lost physical custody of her two minor children to their father who successfully convinced the trial judge that the mother had engaged in a longstanding effort to interfere with his visitation rights.[...]

Father's Version

2 Father was, at the time of combined hearings, a 30-year-old painting contractor who lived in Bakersfield with his then present wife (a data support operator) and her son by a previous marriage. A school where the minor children of the parties would attend classes was nearby. When the children were with their father they got along well with his new family.

3   Mother moved to Oakland, California, with the children. Thereafter, Father attempted to exercise his visitation rights on alternate weekends, but by the time of the hearing had missed 16 weekends and 6 holidays, allegedly due to actions of Mother. When she moved, Mother refused to give Father her address, telephone number or the name of the school attended by the children. On three occasions, Father notified Mother that he was making the 700-mile round trip from

---

Wood v. Wood. 190 Cal. Rptr. 469 (1983)

Bakersfield to Oakland to exercise his visitation rights, but when he arrived at her house (the location of which he had learned from the children), no one was home. On some occasions when he telephoned the children, Mother refused to let them speak to him. When he wrote to the children, she would not let them reply unless he enclosed a self-addressed, stamped envelope. He asked her to share in the financial burden of transporting the children between Bakersfield and Oakland, but she refused, and when he once attempted to require her to obey the then existing court order by insisting that she pick up the children at his home in Bakersfield, she told him that he would never see the children again.

4   On three occasions when Father was scheduled to drive to Oakland to pick up the children for visitation, he was told by Mother that she had arranged to take them to a baseball game and he would have to delay his visitation. On one occasion he arranged to have a relative pick up the children at her house in Oakland to attend a birthday party in the Bay Area; she refused, stating that he was required to personally exercise his visitation rights. She later agreed to let the relative pick up the children, but when the relative arrived at her home, no one was there. A $5 bill that Father had mailed to the children to buy a present for the party was returned to him, torn in quarters, in one of the self-addressed, stamped envelopes he was forced to provide. Father believed that Mother was attempting to sever his relationship with his children.

5   Father and his present wife reported earnings for tax purposes of $16,201 in 1978, $23,574 in 1979 and $20,988 in 1980. He felt that $75 per month child support per child was adequate and was unable to pay more at that time.

Mother's Version

6   Mother had primary care of the two minor children of the marriage since their birth and custody of them during the five years since the parties separated. Having become a licensed registered nurse since her divorce, she moved to Oakland to work at a hospital there and to be near her relatives. She owned a home, which she and the children shared with Raul Martinez, a student from Argentina who attended a local college and who babysat the children at night while she worked. She had not remarried.

7   Mother testified that she made the children available for Father's visitation on every appropriate weekend, but he frequently did not come to Oakland—he only came once a month. In the past he had become belligerent in dealing with her, used swear words, and harassed her, such as by calling the hospital where she worked. Someone did tear up a $5 bill he had sent to the children and mailed it back to him.

8   Her gross monthly income excluding child support was at the time of the hearing $1,745.12 and her net monthly income, $1,327.60. She could not afford to transport the children from Bakersfield to Oakland, and $75 per month child support per child was inadequate; she requested $150 per child.

Children's "Testimony"

9   Bryan, a first-grader, and David, a fourth-grader, initially expressed a preference to continue living with their mother and visiting their father. There had been

times when their father was supposed to pick them up but their mother would-n't let them go with him. Bryan thought they had moved from Bakersfield so that their father wouldn't make any problems. In response to questions by the court the children indicated that they would be willing to live with their father and have visits with their mother.

10   In the course of argument, Mother's counsel, after learning that the trial court proposed to place the children in the custody of Father, suggested to the court that joint physical custody be ordered. The trial court found both parents fit and ordered joint legal custody but expressed a desire that the maximum relation-ship be maintained by the children with both parents.

11   The court found that for the welfare of the children and to have the maxi-mum beneficial relationship with each parent, greater exposure to the father was desirable, and therefore granted the physical custody of the children to Father, with the visitation rights formerly ordered for him granted to Mother. She was ordered to pick up the children for visitation and Father to pick them up when visitation had concluded. Mother was ordered to pay $75 per child per month child support to Father.

In re the Marriage of Pamela M. and Michael J. FINGERT
Michael J. FINGERT, Respondent

v.

Pamela M. FINGERT, Appellant
California Court of Appeal, Second District
Division 6
July 13, 1990*

1   Pamela Fingert (Pamela) and Michael Fingert (Michael) were married on November 13, 1980, and lived in Ventura County [California]. They separated approximately nine months later when Pamela was pregnant. Michael filed a petition for dissolution of the marriage on December 28, 1981. Their son Joshua was born on February 1, 1982. In January 1983 Pamela and Michael executed a marital settlement agreement in which they agreed to joint legal cus-tody, with actual physical custody to Pamela, and reasonable visitation rights to Michael. The interlocutory decree was entered making orders in accordance with the agreement.

2   During Joshua's first year of life, he and Pamela lived in Ventura. She decid-ed to relocate to Chicago, Illinois, where her family resided. Michael sought and obtained an ex parte restraining order temporarily enjoining Pamela from moving. Pamela changed her plans and relocated to San Diego. The custody order was modified to provide that Pamela was to have physical custody of Joshua except for alternate weekends and certain summer and holiday periods,

---

Fingert v. Fingert. 271 Cal Rptr. 389 (1990).

when the child was to be with Michael. Pamela obtained employment in San Diego in the computer industry and lived there for approximately 18 months. During that period, both Pamela and Michael would drive approximately 100 miles to a half-way point between Ventura and San Diego to exchange Joshua to implement the custody agreement.

3   Pamela accepted a better job which required her to move to San Mateo County. Pamela and Michael, through their attorneys, agreed to an informal modification of the visitation schedule. Michael had Joshua approximately one week per month. Joshua was met by one of his parents at both ends of his flights between the San Francisco and Los Angeles areas.

4   Pamela's father was ailing and wanted to retire from his small publishing business located in Chicago. He asked Pamela to take over the business. Pamela petitioned the court for permission to move to Chicago to take over this business. This request was denied but the court confirmed the informal arrangement agreed upon by the parents by ordering that Michael would have visitation from the second Friday to the third Saturday of each month and during certain summer and holiday periods. Joshua was now in kindergarten, and the arrangement meant he would attend one school for three weeks and another for one week each month.

5   Pamela became concerned about how this arrangement was affecting Joshua and how it would affect him when he started first grade. In April 1988 she filed a motion to modify the custody order to provide for visitation to Michael consistent with Joshua's school schedule. Pamela's suggestion was that Michael have Joshua on weekends, holidays, and during the summer. The parties were ordered to and did meet with a court mediator and a hearing was eventually set for September 12, 1988, by which time Joshua had already begun first grade in San Mateo County.

6   Michael filed a responsive declaration to Pamela's motion in which he suggested that "the optimum living arrangement for my six-year-old boy is for he and his mother to move back into the County of Ventura, allowing Joshua 50 percent time in each home while being a student at only one school." In the alternative, Michael suggested that Joshua live with him for one year and with Pamela the next.

7   In response Pamela argued that requiring Joshua to move to Ventura would not be in his best interests, that he attended the same school in San Mateo County for three years, he was enrolled in his second year in a Sunday school and had participated on the same soccer team for years and has had the same set of playmates ever since he was three years old. She contended that Joshua's "roots" were in San Mateo County.

8   On September 12, 1988, the court heard testimony from Pamela, Michael and Robert L. Beilin, Ph.D., the director and senior mediator of the family relations department on the Ventura County Superior Court.

9   The court mediator testified that he had met with Pamela and Michael, alone and together, and had spent some time with Joshua. He recommended that because of "the significance of the father and son relationship," Michael should be allowed to continue to see Joshua on a regular basis and that "neither a weekend father arrangement, nor paternal visitation during holidays and vacations was the best situation." He felt that "it would be best if Joshua and [Pamela] moved to Ventura in order to make it easier for [Michael] and Joshua to continue to spend time together regularly." He recommended that the court

order Pamela to move back to west Ventura County.

10   Michael testified that he and his son needed to be together because they are father and son and that he and Joshua are very close and their time together is extremely important to them both. Pamela's testimony centered on the ties they had in San Mateo County. She objected to the dislocation in her own life if she and Joshua were ordered to move to Ventura County as recommended by the mediator.

11   The mediator testified that in considering whether Pamela should move instead of Michael, he was "swayed by the fact [Michael] owned a home and 10 year old business in Ventura and offered to help [Pamela] move to Ventura County whereas [Pamela] had only launched [her business] in the San Francisco bay area in the last year, did not have substantial financial ties there, and was not financially in a position where she could meet [Michael's] offer and assist him in relocating."

12   The trial judge stated that he felt there were "...strong equities both ways" and that he considered granting summer custody to Michael and ordering Joshua to continue to spend the school year with Pamela in Northern California. However, the judge explained that he had faith in the court mediator and would follow his recommendations. He ordered that "[t]he minor's residence shall be in Ventura County and shall not be changed from said county without order of this court or written agreement signed by both parties..." and that Michael "financially assist [Pamela] in moving back to West Ventura County at a cost not to exceed $ 1,000.00 in connection with moving expenses."

13   The court acknowledged that its order would "force [Pamela] to Ventura County or else give up custody of her child." He stated it would not make sense to have Michael move because of Michael's "long-standing roots in business in Ventura and his greater ability financially to help [Pamela] relocate."

In re B.G.
Vlasta Z., Plaintiff and Appellant

v.

SAN BERNADINO COUNTY WELFARE DEPARTMENT,
Defendants and Respondents
Supreme Court of California
June 20, 1974*

1 V. G. and B. G. (hereinafter referred to as the children) were born in Czechoslovakia in 1963 and 1964, respectively, the children of the marriage of Bedrich and Vlasta Z. In August 1968, shortly after Soviet troops occupied Czechoslovakia, Bedrich, their father, fled the country with his two children. Vlasta, their mother, did not consent to the children's departure nor did she know about it until she arrived home from work. The father took the children to Munich, West Germany.

2   The father remained in Munich for about six months. During this period he attempted to persuade his wife to join him; she, in turn, sought to convince him

---

In Re B.G. 523 P.2d 244 (1974).

to return to Czechoslovakia with the children.[1] In March 1969, the father's mother and stepfather (hereinafter referred to as grandparents, grandfather, or grandmother), residents of Yucaipa, California, sent the father funds to enable him to come to the United States. The father and children flew to California and entered the United States as political refugees. They went to live with the grandparents; the father found employment and arranged for day care for the children with neighbors, Roy and Madeline Smith. Three weeks after his arrival in California the father collapsed; a medical examination revealed terminal cancer. In June 1969, the father, who was then too weak to write, dictated a "will" to an interpreter in which he stated that the children should remain in the United States.[2] The father died on July 8, 1969.

3   The mother, who was injured in an automobile accident in November 1968, was still recuperating in May 1969, when she first learned that the children's father was seriously ill. The grandparents sent her an airplane ticket but apparently failed to supply the necessary documents to secure a visa.[3]

4   The probation department, informed that the father had died and that the children were staying with the Smiths, who had applied for a foster home license, scheduled a dependency hearing. The department did not orally contact the grandparents, who could not be reached because of their work schedules, but sent them notice of the dependency hearing by mail. It did not notify the mother or any agency, such as the embassy, that might reasonably be expected to forward notice to the mother.[4]

5   On August 29, 1969, the minors appeared in juvenile court in response to petitions filed by the social worker. The petitions stated that: (1) the father had died in California; (2) the "mother's exact whereabouts is unknown; she is presumed living in Czechoslovakia"; and (3) the children are Czechoslovakian nationals. The court found the allegations true, adjudged the minors dependent children of the juvenile court, and placed them in the custody of the welfare department to be maintained in the home of the Smiths as their foster parents.[5]

---

[1]In October 1968, without notice to her husband, Vlasta obtained a Czech divorce decree which awarded her custody of the children. She testified that she undertook these proceedings because she was advised by counsel that a custody decree would facilitate the return of the children to her own country.

[2]This "will" reads as follows: "Request: I, [father], undersigned—born in 1934—hereby request that my children [daughter], age 6—and [son], age 5—should remain in the United States of America. I do not want them to be sent back to Czechoslovakia. My first wish that my mother should have the children. If she is not able to have them or care for them, I would like [the foster parents] to care for them."

[3]The grandparents later sent another airplane ticket accompanied by the required documentation, but the mother denies receiving this second ticket.

[4]The department file includes a dictated notation of July 7, 1969, suggesting that the department was aware of the mother's attempts to secure the return of the children through the auspices of the Red Cross and the Czechoslovakian Embassy; the notation indicates that the department had the mother's address or, at the very least, knew that it could be secured from the grandparents.

[5]After the hearing, the welfare department received a letter from the International Social Service, dated September 8, 1969, acknowledging receipt of the department's letter which had requested help in locating the mother. The service stressed the difficulty of the task but requested more detailed information about the mother's whereabouts. This letter was never answered by the department nor were any further contacts made with the grandparents for over a year.

6 During the next two years the children resided with the foster parents. The matter came before the court for annual review in August 1970, but the mother received no notice of this proceeding; the court confirmed the disposition established by the August 1969 order. During this period the mother and grandmother continued to exchange correspondence, but the mother was never informed that the children were living with foster parents or that they were subject to court supervision. On September 27, 1970, the mother remarried. She continued her efforts to secure help from the Czechoslovakian Red Cross, the Brno Office for the Protection of Children, the Ministry of Foreign Affairs and the Czechoslovakian Embassy in Washington, D.C.

7 In December of 1970, the grandparents visited the welfare department and informed the department that they had received letters from the Czech Embassy indicating that the embassy thought the children were living with the grandparents and had engaged an attorney to institute proceedings to return the children to their mother. In re-examining the file, the social worker discovered an envelope with the mother's address on it, which apparently had been received some time earlier.

8 The matter again came before the court for annual review in August 1971. The court, now aware of the mother's desire to regain custody of her children, continued the case for 30 days. After further continuances, the mother appeared by counsel on November 4, 1971, acknowledged the personal and subject matter jurisdiction of the court, and requested the court to exercise that jurisdiction by transferring custody of the children to her. The court ordered that the children would be continued as dependent children of the court, in the custody of the probation officer, but to be maintained in the home of the mother.

9 The Czech Embassy arranged for the children to fly to Czechoslovakia on November 18, and the parties agreed that a welfare worker, the grandparents, and the foster parents would bring the children to the airport. On November 18, however, the children disappeared. The grandparents told the welfare worker "if you want to know where the kids are, watch T.V." The children and the foster parents appeared on the evening television news; the foster parents announced that they and the minors were going into hiding.

10 The next morning an attorney representing the foster parents filed a petition for writ of prohibition with the Court of Appeal.[6] That court denied the petition on condition that the juvenile court vacate its order of November 4, and reopen the proceedings "for the purpose of conducting the Dispositional Hearing."

11 When that hearing began on February 28, 1972, the foster parents asserted that the juvenile court lacked jurisdiction because of its failure to notify the mother of the August 1969 jurisdictional hearing. The mother's counsel stipulated to the court's jurisdiction over the mother as of the 1969 hearing. The court then denied the foster parents' motion to dismiss. The foster parents petitioned for habeas corpus in the Court of Appeal, again asserting that the juvenile court lacked jurisdiction over the minors, but the Court of Appeal denied the petition.

12 On March 15, 1972, at the end of the dispositional hearing, the juvenile court stated orally its findings and reasoning. The court first noted that everyone

---

[6]On November 23, 1971, the foster parents petitioned for appointment as guardian for the children. The guardianship petition has not been heard because of the pendency of the present proceeding under the Juvenile Court Law.

involved—the mother, the foster parents, and the grandparents—were "fine people," and that the children had received proper and loving care from the grandparents and foster parents.[7] He then expressly found that the mother was a fit parent for the children.[8] The court, however, expressed its concern that the mother had encountered difficulties in relating to both her present and her former husband, that she displayed little warmth toward the children, and that the children had adapted to living in America and largely forgotten the Czech language.[9]

---

[7]The trial judge interviewed the children, who said they preferred to stay with the foster parents. The court observed, however, that the only reasons given by the children for their preference were "childish," and that he gave them no weight in reaching his decision.

[8]"We come to the question of whether [the mother] is a fit or an unfit parent. There has been no evidence presented to this court whatsoever that would indicate that [the mother] is a bad person or an evil person, or that she has ever done anything other than provide adequate food, clothing, shelter, attention for her children while she had them and the child she has now. It is obvious to the court that she is an intelligent woman; she is neat, clean and dresses well. According to the testimony, she has a good job. She owns and maintains an adequate home…Her personal morals appear to be adequate by modern standards…. "

[9]"I can't help but conclude from the testimony that [the mother] has not coped well with the problems of marriage and home and motherhood. I don't know whether this is due to her personal personality or psychological problems, or whether it is due to the culture in which she lives. Maybe, to some extent, it is due to the modern liberation of women movement. She apparently does a good job at her employment, but you can't help but note that both of her marriages were impelled by unwanted pregnancies, that the second child of the first marriage was unwanted.

"I can't help but observe from the testimony, particularly from reading the letters written to her by her first husband, [the father] and saved by her, that there were serious problems between her and [the father]….

"There has been much talk in the evidence about [the mother's] inability to express her warmth, her love for the children.

"… Apparently that has been a problem from the beginning.

"The little evidence we have of her second marriage seems to indicate bad omens for the future.

"I find it difficult to conceive how a woman marrying a younger man and requiring him to sleep in the living room, while she sleeps in the bedroom with the child, can expect a long and happy married life.

"These things, none of them are determinative. They are all just things which are apparently so and which I have to consider….

"I have been extremely empathetic with [the mother], her situation in coming to a strange country, thinking she was just going to come pick up her children and go home apparently very quickly, and finding out that it's going to be a long, drawn-out court battle….

"The evidence makes it quite clear that [the mother] was unable to cope with that situation, and I think just had to hope that upon getting the children back home and learning the language that these things would all work out; but there appeared to be no real effort on her part to start working them out now.

"I have been impressed by all of the evidence that [the mother],…perhaps being a bright woman, being a handsome woman, being a success in her occupation has grown much more accustomed to getting than to giving."

The trial court also relied upon the testimony of Dr. Beukema, a psychiatrist, that the children would suffer emotional damage at being separated from the foster parents and might have difficulty reestablishing a close relationship with their mother.

13   The court concluded that "We have to weigh and balance the good and the bad in both directions and then choose that which, all in all, will be in the best interests of the children.... At any rate, it is the considered decision of the Court and one, I might say, that I arrived only at the tag end of the trial, that the welfare and best interests of the children require that they be continued as dependent children of the Court to be maintained at a home to be selected by the Court; in the meantime to be detained at the home of [the grandparents]." The court rendered no finding whether an award of custody to the mother would be detrimental to the children.[10] After concluding its statement, the court entered a minute order continuing the children in the custody of the probation officer, to be maintained at the grandparents' home pending a probation study. Shortly thereafter, the court returned the children to the foster parents.

14   The mother appeals from the juvenile court's minute order continuing the court's jurisdiction over the children, and denying her legal and physical custody.

In re the Marriage of B.A.S., Petitioner-Appellant [Mother]

v.

G.R.S., Respondent [Father]
Missouri Court of Appeals
St. Louis District
Division Three
Sept. 21, 1976*

1 The parties, married in 1961, have three children, a daughter C, 12, and two sons, B , 11, and E, 8. We find no indication of marital strife prior to 1970 when they purchased a home in St. Peters, Missouri. Personal discord soon surfaced, followed by marriage counseling, reconciliation efforts and finally a March 1973 agreement to separate in June at the end of the school term.

2   Appellant-mother, by prearrangement, moved the children and some furniture to St. Charles. Some quarreling occurred concerning temporary custodial arrangements; but the children, living principally with their mother through the summer of 1973, stayed five nights and two days each week with their father, under a plan designed to accommodate the parents' working hours. After September the children remained in the general custody of their mother, staying Tuesday through Thursday nights with her and three weekends per month with the father until the divorce in May 1975.

---

[10]The juvenile court admitted evidence on political conditions in Czechoslovakia to determine whether the children would encounter any disabilities by reason of their father's defection. The evidence on this point, however, was inconclusive, and the trial judge, in his oral presentation, stated that his decision was not based on political considerations.

*In Re the Marriage of B.A.S. 541 S.W.2d 762 (1976).

3   For eight months following the separation the husband, though requested, provided little or no support for appellant-mother or the children, while with her stating: "He didn't see any reason why he should." In April 1974 he was ordered to pay child support of $60 per week but from time to time arbitrarily deducted amounts from the weekly payments for items such as car insurance premiums for the automobile in appellant-mother's possession and the cost of shoes or similar purchases for the children.

4   In February of 1974 appellant-mother moved to a more suitable apartment less than one-half mile from her place of employment.

5   While at work, appellant-mother could conveniently communicate with the children by phone and sometime before the divorce changed her hours to 6:30 A.M. through 2:30 P.M. permitting her to be with the children on return from school. The respondent-husband points out she could not be with the children at breakfast but the evidence shows breakfast for the children was arranged each morning before she left, the children's clothes laid out, and plans made for the day. Further, as the mother explained, the money she received was insufficient to adequately care for the children and she needed to work. It seems unbecoming to fault appellant-mother for this effort; and if the father feels strongly she should not work, which requires her to be away during the children's breakfast time, this could be readily remedied by increased support payments. As the husband also works, neither can legitimately argue the other's disqualification as custodian because of their respective employment.

6   The living accommodations of each are suitable for the children; and while the jointly-owned home in St. Peters occupied by the husband is more commodious than appellant-mother's apartment, the court has ordered the home "divided equally between the parties," presenting a problem for his custodial claim.

7   Appellant-mother permits the children to have friends in the home for meals and overnight stays. Appellant-mother entered both sons in little league baseball and attended most if not all of their games. She also enrolled the younger son in cub scouts, bought his uniform and furnished the monthly dues.

8   The children keep numerous animals and the only difficulty in this area developed when, without consulting the mother, the father delivered a rabbit that was unsuitable as a pet. A more serious problem occurred when the father, aware of the children's love for their pets, attempted to poison their minds against their mother, saying if the children lived with her they would not be permitted to have animals and she will marry somebody who is "real bad."

9   Witnesses for appellant-mother included the fifth-grade teachers who testified that B was punctual, as clean and neat as other children, participated well in activities, was well-disciplined, courteous, and respectful and although at the beginning was not working up to his grade level, improved after appellant-mother's conference with the teachers. Neither of these teachers had ever seen the child's father.

10 E's third-grade teacher described his manner of dress and personal appearance as much like other children in the class, and though he had been below his grade level in some areas, several months after the conference with his mother E also improved academically. Further, he was not a discipline problem, treated the teachers with respect, and was apparently a very normal child.

11   An employee of the Howard Johnson Restaurant had seen the children on numerous occasions and stated they appeared normal, clean, and neat. Having observed the children with their mother, the witness testified: "She disciplined them but never mistreated" them.

12   The minister of the Calvary Evangelical Methodist Church of St. Charles where appellant-mother had attended for a year confirmed that the children attended Sunday school and church regularly when with the mother and she attended regularly at other times. He also testified the mother and the three children were clean and neat in their appearance. This testimony concerning the children's appearance and conditions in appellant-mother's home were generally corroborated by the father's witness, Mr. Darrill Beebe, a social worker for the St. Charles County Family Services.

13   Though the husband charged the children were dirty and their clothes torn when they came to him on weekends, this evidence came exclusively from him and his mother who admitted attempts to persuade the children to choose her son, the respondent-husband as custodian. Respondent and his mother produced a number of articles of dirty and torn clothing claiming they were those of the children but appellant-mother stated she had not seen most of the items and the clothing she provided the children was usually kept at her home and that provided by the father at his.

14   During the trial, in March 1975, the parties agreed the court should examine the 12-year-old daughter and the 11-year-old son. The 8-year-old child did not appear in the chambers. The testimony of that examination is most revealing and important to our decision.

Trial Court's Interview of the Children

15 The 12-year-old daughter explained she was doing better in school as time went on and described living conditions at the home. She stated a part of her job was to take the clothes to the laundromat, fold them, and bring them home where her mother usually ironed them.

16   She testified her brothers played outside a good deal and would get dirty and this was true whether at her mother's or father's home. The clothes the children wore at the mother's or father's house were the same or similar.

17   She also described matters of grave concern to this court. The father-respondent has repeatedly attempted to poison the minds of the children against the mother. The following responses to the court's nonleading questions tell us much about the parties:

Q. "Has anyone tried to influence you as to whose custody you should be in?"

A. "Yes."

Q. "Who has done that?"

A. "My father."

Q. "What has he done in that respect?"

A. "He tells us that *my mom is no good and if we live with her I won't have any animals and she will marry somebody real bad and they will beat us and everything and stuff like that.*"

Q. "How often does he do this?"

A. "Mostly every weekend when we come out there."

Q. "What are your feelings toward your father and your mother?"

A. "Well, I like them both and everything. It's just *I get sick of hearing my dad talk about my mom, criticizing her and stuff and I don't like it.*"

Q. "Does your mother or anyone in the household other than your mother say anything critical of your father?"

A. "*Never.* Sometimes, you know, say something like tell her that he called her a name or something and she will say, 'I don't want you talking about your father like that.' She won't let me talk about it." (Emphasis ours.)

18   The child stated that she would prefer to stay with her mother and felt that spending three weekends a month with the father was too much as she would prefer to spend more free time with the mother.

19   The court then asked her if she had seen anything improper at the mother's or father's home to which she answered that at the father's home the grandmother "has taken over the place of a mother and I don't think she should," and further that:

"And every time I ask if I can go somewhere I always…my dad always goes, 'Ask your grandmother,' and I don't think it's right because if we have to live with him, all she should be used for is a grandmother not a mother."

20   The court then asked concerning matters she might consider improper in the mother's home and she answered that she gets tired of having chicken all the time stating: "My mom gets chicken all the time and I go over to my dad's house and we have chicken and I'm tired of chicken but I like it still." Pressing this inquiry, the court asked concerning improper associations of either parent with other men or women. The child answered: "My dad never goes out or anything and my mother goes out about once a week and I don't think it's very bad," going on to explain that during the first months of the separation her mother went out only occasionally, returning usually about 11 o'clock and a baby sitter was always employed. The court then asked:

Q. "All right, do you know anything about your mother having…whether she did or did not associate with other men during the time your mother and father were living together. Did you know anything along that line?"

A. "No."

Q. "You did not?"

A. "*My dad tells me that she did but I don't know.* I don't think she did." (Emphasis supplied.)

21   He then directed attention to the matter of morals asking if she had observed anything immoral in the conduct of either the mother or the father to which she answered that her mother and father "don't get along together."

22   The daughter related that on one occasion her father pushed her mother against the bookcase and she started crying and when her mother got up he started pushing her again.

23   On the subject of cleanliness she explained that they had to take baths at her father's house and at her mother's house she took "showers and wash my hair." As far as the children getting dirty and playing she said "we don't have to change clothes unless we go to somebody's house because they are always dirty from playing."

Q. "Is this the same whether you are at your father's or mother's?"

A. "Yes."

24   When asked her personal preference she expressed a desire to live with her mother.

25   The court then examined the 11-year-old son who stated he was making fairly good grades in school, that he was being well-taken care of in both homes, but at his dad's house "we got to get dressed up and everything to go places and stuff and over here we don't just have to get all dressed up and everything." He also stated his father tried to influence him as to which home he should prefer:

Q. "And what has your father done or said to try to influence you?"

A. "He says my mom doesn't take near as much care as my dad and he says he keeps—he watches over us and stuff and my mom doesn't hardly do that."

26   Then he stated that his father does "keep an eye on us more" than his mother does. He said his mother tried to influence him by "getting me stuff and—and taking us some places." [...]

27   Darrill Beebe, who at the court's instance conducted an investigation and home study, testified as to child-parent relationship, living arrangements, financial and general fitness of each parent as custodian. [...] As Mr. Beebe described it, Mr. S was an "over firm person. Very strict. Perhaps more strict than desirable." Appellant aptly stated: "You can't raise children on bitterness and hate." Respondent-father admitted some of these things but stated they were done in a very limited way. Appellant-mother had stated her children's well-being is more important to her than anything else in the world and Beebe's report shows "she feels that they are happier with her since they are close to many friends in the neighborhood and school." In his opinion " [appellant-mother] seems to possess a deep understanding and insight into the respective needs of the children." His comment concerning the father was:

> [He] tends to lack insight into the needs and feelings of his children…He does not appear to have understanding of their individual motivation. [...]

28   His behavior in the past has shown a limited ability to understand the children's respective personalities and motivate them in ways other than harsh discipline. The children have expressed a desire to be with their mother, and the worker feels this is quite significant. Since the children have shown no major disruption in their lives other than poor appearance and some rowdiness due to lack of discipline, it is felt that the present arrangement with their mother should be continued.

[Mr. Beebe's] decision was based "upon observations of her insight into the children's needs and her ability to provide a happy, stable home in which the children appear to be very secure."

29　The father, challenging the mother's suitability, points to the fact she admitted extramarital affairs with seven men during the period 1973 through 1975, though none occurred at the home and the children were unaware of any of the intimacies. The appellant-mother admitted the affairs to Mr. Beebe and again at trial, stating they occurred while the parties were married and at least on two occasions before the separation. During her cross-examination there was some confusion as to statements made in deposition but at trial the witness frankly admitted her intimacies and the record belies respondent's contention these include other men whose names she could not remember.

30　Respondent admitted his daughter preferred to stay with appellant but charges the children were neither clean nor properly clad by her. This contrasted sharply with testimony of independent witnesses, i.e. the teachers, the minister, and the restaurant employee. Though the father and maternal grandmother insist the children bathe more often and are better clothed when with the father, it seems apparent both parties provide adequate clothing, hygienic conditions, and suitable homes.[1] Interestingly, after the separation the mother on three occasions went to the father's home and gave it sorely needed cleanings.

31　The father's conduct was not above reproach as he admitted calling his wife a "whore and a bitch" and in one instance grabbed her and threw her in the bookcase only leaving when she threatened to call the police. These episodes seemed to spring from jealousy or temporary rage, provoked by her dating other men. On the other hand appellant-mother complained that he showed very little affection during the years of their marriage. Appellant-mother admitted her intimacies with other men but believed her dating during the separation of almost two years did not adversely affect the children. She conceded that from time to time her "dates" called to see her at the home and one of them occasionally had meals there. No acts of adultery were committed in the home or in the presence of the children.

Statements on the Law

Uniform Marriage and Divorce Act, §402

The court shall determine custody in accordance with the best interest of the child. The court shall consider all relevant factors including:

(1) The wishes of the child's parent or parents as to his custody;
(2) The wishes of the child as to his custodian;
(3) The interaction and interrelationship of the child with his parent or parents, his siblings, and any other person who may significantly affect the child's best interest;

---

[1]The husband testified the younger son became ill, called him at work, and he took the child to the hospital. Learning this, the mother went to the hospital complaining she should have been notified. It eventuated the child was neither hospitalized nor seriously ill and the occurrence has no strong bearing on the case.

(4) The child's adjustment to his home, school and community; and

(5) The mental and physical health of all individuals involved.

The court shall not consider conduct of a proposed custodian that does not affect his relationship to the child.

California Civil Code §4600 (a)

The Legislature finds and declares that it is the public policy of this state to assure minor children of frequent and continuing contact with both parents after the parents have separated or dissolved their marriage, and to encourage parents to share the rights and responsibilities of child rearing in order to effect this policy. In any proceeding where there is at issue the custody of a minor child, the court may, during the pendency of the proceeding or at any time thereafter, make such order for the custody of the child during minority as may seem necessary or proper. If a child is of sufficient age and capacity to reason so as to form an intelligent preference as to custody, the court shall consider and give due weight to the wishes of the child in making an award of custody or modification thereof. In determining the person or persons to whom custody shall be awarded under paragraph (2) or (3) of subdivision (b), the court shall consider and give due weight under Article 1 (commencing with Section 1500) of Chapter 1 of Part 2 of Division 4 of the Probate Code.

California Family Code §3011 (2001): Factors Considered in Determining Best Interest of Child

1   In making a determination of the best interest of the child in a proceeding described in Section 3021, the court shall, among any other factors it finds relevant, consider all of the following:

(a) The health, safety, and welfare of the child.

(b) Any history of abuse by one parent or any other person seeking custody against any of the following:

(1) Any child to whom he or she is related by blood or affinity or with whom he or she has had a caretaking relationship, no matter how temporary.

(2) The other parent.

(3) A parent, current spouse, or cohabitant, of the parent or person seeking custody, or a person with whom the parent or person seeking custody has a dating or engagement relationship.

2   As a prerequisite to the consideration of allegations of abuse, the court may require substantial independent corroboration, including, but not limited to, written reports by law enforcement agencies, child protective services or other social welfare agencies, courts, medical facilities, or other public agencies or private nonprofit organizations providing services to victims of sexual assault or domestic violence. As used in this subdivision, "abuse against a child" means "child abuse" as defined in Section 11165.6 of the Penal Code and abuse against any of the other persons described in paragraph (2) or (3) means "abuse" as defined in Section 6203 of this code.

(c) The nature and amount of contact with both parents, except as provided in Section 3046.

(d) The habitual or continual illegal use of controlled substances or habitual or continual abuse of alcohol by either parent. Before considering these allegations, the court may first require independent corroboration, including, but not limited to, written reports from law enforcement agencies, courts, probation departments, social welfare agencies, medical facilities, rehabilitation facilities, or other public agencies or nonprofit organizations providing drug and alcohol abuse services. As used in this subdivision, "controlled substances" has the same meaning as defined in the California Uniform Controlled Substances Act, Division 10 (commencing with Section 11000) of the Health and Safety Code.

(e)(1) Where allegations about a parent pursuant to subdivision (b) or (d) have been brought to the attention of the court in the current proceeding, and the court makes an order for sole or joint custody to that parent, the court shall state its reasons in writing or on the record. In these circumstances, the court shall ensure that any order regarding custody or visitation is specific as to time, day, place, and manner of transfer of the child as set forth in subdivision (b) of Section 6323.

(2) The provisions of this subdivision shall not apply if the parties stipulate in writing or on the record regarding custody or visitation.

California Family Code §3020 (2001): Legislative Intent on Child Custody

(a) The Legislature finds and declares that it is the public policy of this state to assure that the health, safety, and welfare of children shall be the court's primary concern in determining the best interest of children when making any orders regarding the physical or legal custody or visitation of children. The Legislature further finds and declares that the perpetration of child abuse or domestic violence in a household where a child resides is detrimental to the child.

(b) The Legislature finds and declares that it is the public policy of this state to assure that children have frequent and continuing contact with both parents after the parents have separated or dissolved their marriage, or ended their relationship, and to encourage parents to share the rights and responsibilities of child rearing in order to effect this policy, except where the contact would not be in the best interest of the child, as provided in Section 3011.

(c) Where the policies set forth in subdivisions (a) and (b) of this section are in conflict, any court's order regarding physical or legal custody or visitation shall be made in a manner that ensures the health, safety, and welfare of the child and the safety of all family members.

California Family Code §3040 (2001): Order of Preference in Granting Custody

(a) Custody should be granted in the following order of preference according to the best interest of the child as provided in Sections 3011 and 3020:

(1) To both parents jointly pursuant to Chapter 4 (commencing with Section 3080) or to either parent. In making an order granting custody to either parent, the court shall consider, among other factors, which parent is more likely to allow the child frequent and continuing contact with the

noncustodial parent, consistent with Section 3011 and 3020, and shall not prefer a parent as custodian because of that parent's sex. The court, in its discretion, may require the parents to submit to the court a plan for the implementation of the custody order.

(2) If to neither parent, to the person or persons in whose home the child has been living in a wholesome and stable environment.

(3) To any other person or persons deemed by the court to be suitable and able to provide adequate and proper care and guidance for the child.

(b) This section establishes neither a preference nor a presumption for or against joint legal custody, joint physical custody, or sole custody, but allows the court and the family the widest discretion to choose a parenting plan that is in the best interest of the child.

California Family Code §3041 (2001): Custody Granted to Non-Parent

Before making an order granting custody to a person or persons other than a parent, without the consent of the parents, the court shall make a finding that granting custody to a parent would be detrimental to the child and that granting custody to the nonparent is required to serve the best interest of the child. Allegations that parental custody would be detrimental to the child, other than a statement of that ultimate fact, shall not appear in the pleadings.

Discussion and Writing Suggestions

1. In *Ashwell v. Ashwell,* should Curtis Lee Ashwell be awarded custody of the four children he had with Norma Jeanne Ashwell? Apply relevant elements of child custody law to this case. To what extent should the following factors be significant in determining who gets custody: (1) Norma's sexual relationship and living arrangements with Cassella before her divorce became final; (2) Curtis' planned move across the country to Virginia; (3) Curtis' Army status; (4) Curtis' testimony about the children being frequently raggedly dressed and dirty when he visited and their being cared for by a 12-year-old babysitter? Take into primary account the best interest of the children.

2. In *Wood v. Wood,* should custody of the children remain, as the trial court judge ruled, with the father? Base your conclusion upon the best interest of the children. Reviewing the three "versions" of the situation—by father, mother, and children—what do you conclude about the actual facts of this case and about which parent was most/least blameworthy in terms of the father's visitations? To what extent should the trial court judge's rulings on custody, child support payments, and visitation arrangements, be upheld; to what extent, reversed? Apply the relevant laws on child custody to the facts of this case.

3. To what extent do you agree with the trial court judge's decision in *Fingert?* Should Pamela be required by the appellate court to either relocate to Ventura or give up custody of Joshua? Discuss the mediator's recommendation (one with which the judge agreed) that the father had a home and an established business in Ventura, whereas the mother "had only launched [her business] in the San Francisco bay area in the last year, did not have substantial ties there, and was not financially in a position where she could meet [Michael's] offer and assist him in relocating." In light of the relevant laws on child custody, consider whether or not the best interests of the child would be served by awarding the father custody.

4. How should the appellate court deal with the custody issue in *B.G.?* Should the children remain in the custody of their foster parents, or their paternal grandparents, or should they be placed in the custody of their natural mother? Among the factors you might consider: (1) the father's dying wishes; (2) the fact that the children were taken by the father without the mother's knowledge and consent; (3) the American grandparents' wishes; (5) the failure of the Welfare Department to contact the mother for a long time; (5) the children's wishes. Consider and discuss also the trial judge's finding that "the mother had encountered difficulties in relating to both her present and her former husband, that she displayed little warmth toward the children, and that the children had adapted to living in America and largely forgotten the Czech language." Apply the relevant laws on child custody to the facts of this case.

5. Applying the relevant laws on child custody to the facts of *B.A.S.,* do you think the interests of the children would best be served if they stayed with the mother or the father? In developing your conclusion, take into account some of the following factors: (1) one parent attempting to prejudice the children's minds against the other parent; (2) each parent's approach to raising his or her children; (3) the mother's extramarital affairs; (4) the expressed wishes of one or more of the children. To what extent does the testimony of the children influence your conclusions? To what extent do you think the court's questions were fair and impartial (that is, not trying to lead the children to respond with particular answers)?

6. If you have had direct experience with or knowledge of the effects of a child custody battle, you may want to comment on the adequacy of the laws governing child custody and of the legal system's ability to deal with custody fights. Given the often intractable conflicts between the parents, in what ways could the law and the court system better deal with child custody issues to minimize the adverse effects on all parties concerned, but particularly on the kids?

"Urban War Zone": A Case of Public Nuisance
(People v. Acuna et al.)

In the summer of 1997, Los Angeles authorities obtained a court injunction against some 300 members of the notorious 18th Street Gang, centered in the largely Latino Pico-Union area of the city. According to authorities, the gang had been involved in murders, robberies, auto theft, drug dealing, and extortion. The injunction prohibited gang members from standing, sitting, walking, or gathering with one another in groups of three or more. It also imposed an 8 P.M.-to-sunrise curfew on gang members under 18 years of age (see pages 672–73).

Anti-gang injunctions are not new. Four years earlier, the city of San Jose in northern California instituted a similar injunction against the VST (Varrio Sureno Treces) gang based in the Rocksprings neighborhood. Violation of the injunction was punishable by six months in jail and a $1,000 fine. In approving the injunction, one justice observed, "Gang members threatened and intimidated residents. For example, a gang member warned a nine-year-old girl who had told police officers where some drugs were hidden that he could cut her tongue out if she ever again talked to the police. In another incident, gang members threatened a Rocksprings resident and vandalized her property after she called the police to report that some gang members urinated in her garage." While applauded by local residents, the injunction was challenged by civil libertarian groups, including the American Civil Liberties Union, which contended, "Simply because these men and women are suspected gang members, they are stripped of a variety of constitutional freedoms, the right to associate, to assemble, and the right to due process. It's guilt by association, without the City showing that the defendants themselves intended to violate the law."

With the ACLU representing the suspected gang members, the case went all the way up to the California Supreme Court. "The People," represented by San Jose City Attorney Joan R. Gallo, argued that the injunction was justified under the provisions of California's public nuisance statute. The defendants argued that the injunction was overly broad, overly vague, and violated their constitutional rights of freedom of association under the First Amendment.

Read the facts of the case, along with the relevant law and the injunction itself. Attempt to determine whether the injunction was justified. Then, formulate a position on some of the underlying issues in this legal conflict—issues concerning the rights of the community on the one hand, and the rights of individuals, on the other.

PEOPLE ex. rel. GALLO, Plaintiff and Respondent

v.

Carlos ACUNA et al., Defendants and Appellants
No. S046980
Supreme Court of California
Jan. 30, 1997

Facts of the Case*

1   At the request of the City Attorney of the City of San Jose (hereafter the City), we granted review to resolve an array of challenges to two provisions of a

---

*"Urban War Zone": A Case of Public Nuisance." *People v. Acuna et al.* 60 Cal. Rptr.2d.

preliminary injunction [see pp. 672–73] entered by the superior court against individual members of an alleged "criminal street gang." The underlying action was instituted under the provisions of sections 731 of the Code of Civil Procedure and 3480 of the Civil Code, the operative core of California's civil "public nuisance" statutes.

2   The 48 declarations submitted by the City in support of its plea for injunctive relief paint a graphic portrait of life in the community of Rocksprings. Rocksprings is an urban war zone. The four-square-block neighborhood, claimed as the turf of a gang variously known as Varrio Sureno Town, Varrio Sureno Treces (VST), or Varrio Sureno Locos (VSL), is an occupied territory. Gang members, all of whom live elsewhere, congregate on lawns, on sidewalks, and in front of apartment complexes at all hours of the day and night. They display a casual contempt for notions of law, order, and decency—openly drinking, smoking dope, sniffing toluene, and even snorting cocaine laid out in neat lines on the hoods of residents' cars. The people who live in Rocksprings are subjected to loud talk, loud music, vulgarity, profanity, brutality, fistfights and the sound of gunfire echoing in the streets. Gang members take over sidewalks, driveways, carports, apartment parking areas, and impede traffic on the public thoroughfares to conduct their drive-up drug bazaar. Murder, attempted murder, drive-by shootings, assault and battery, vandalism, arson, and theft are commonplace. The community has become a staging area for gang-related violence and a dumping ground for the weapons and instrumentalities of crime once the deed is done. Area residents have had their garages used as urinals; their homes commandeered as escape routes; their walls, fences, garage doors, sidewalks, and even their vehicles turned into a sullen canvas of gang graffiti.

3   The people of this community are prisoners in their own homes. Violence and the threat of violence are constant. Residents remain indoors, especially at night. They do not allow their children to play outside. Strangers wearing the wrong color clothing are at risk. Relatives and friends refuse to visit. The laundry rooms, the trash dumpsters, the residents' vehicles, and their parking spaces are used to deal and stash drugs. Verbal harassment, physical intimidation, threats of retaliation, and retaliation are the likely fate of anyone who complains of the gang's illegal activities or tells police where drugs may be hidden.

4   Among other allegations, the City's complaint asserted that the named defendants and others "[f]or more than 12 months precedent to the date of [the] complaint, continuing up to the present time…[have] occupied [and] used the area commonly known as 'Rocksprings'…in such a manner so as to constitute a public nuisance…injurious to the health, indecent or offensive to the senses, [and] an obstruction to the free use of property so as to interfere with the comfortable enjoyment of life or property by those persons living in the…neighborhood."

5   After alleging the usual requisites for equitable relief—the prospect of "great and irreparable injury" and the absence of a "plain, adequate and speedy remedy at law"—the complaint prayed for a broad and comprehensive injunction against defendants' alleged activities in Rocksprings. The superior court granted an ex parte temporary restraining order enjoining all 38 defendants

named in the complaint and issued an order to show cause (OSC) why a preliminary injunction should not be entered.

6   Only five of the named defendants appeared in response to the OSC. Following a hearing, the superior court entered a preliminary injunction against the 33 defendants who had not appeared and continued the matter as to those 5 defendants who opposed entry of a preliminary injunction, leaving the temporary restraining order in force as to them. Eleven of the named defendants (the five who had originally appeared in opposition to the OSC, together with another six of the named defendants) moved to vacate the injunctions. After the matter was briefed and argued, the superior court entered a preliminary injunction. The multi-part decree, consisting of some 24 paragraphs, was the subject of an interlocutory appeal by these 11 defendants.

Statements on the Law

California Penal Code*

1 *[Section] 370. Public Nuisance Defined*   Anything which is injurious to health, or is indecent, or offensive to the senses, or an obstruction to the free use of property, so as to interfere with the comfortable enjoyment of life or property by an entire community or neighborhood, or by any considerable number of persons, or unlawfully obstructs the free passage or use, in the customary manner, of any navigable lake, or river, bay, stream, canal, or basin, or any public park, square, street, or highway, is a public nuisance.

California Civil Code†

2 *[Section] 3479. Nuisance Defined*   Anything which is injurious to health, or is indecent or offensive to the senses, or an obstruction to the free use of property, so as to interfere with the comfortable enjoyment of life or property, or unlawfully obstructs the free passage or use, in the customary manner, of any navigable lake, or river, bay, stream, canal, or basin, or any public park, square, street, or highway, is a nuisance.

3   *[Section] 3480. Public Nuisance*   A public nuisance is one which affects at the same time an entire community or neighborhood, or any considerable number of persons, although the extent of the annoyance or damage inflicted upon individuals may be unequal.

Restatement of Torts, Second‡

[Section] 821b. Public Nuisance

   (1) A public nuisance is an unreasonable interference with a right common to the general public.

Penal Code, Annotated of the State of California, San Francisco: Bancroft-Whitney, 1985.

†*Civil Code, Annotated of the State of California,* San Francisco: Lexis Law Publishing, 1984.

‡*Restatement of The Law, Second: Torts, 2nd.* As Adapted and Promulgated by The American Law Institute at Washington, D.C. May 25, 1963 and May 22, 1964, St. Paul, MN: West Publishing Co., 1965.

(2) Circumstances that may sustain a holding that an interference with a public right is unreasonable include the following:

(a) Whether the conduct involves a significant interference with the public health, the public safety, the public peace, the public comfort or the public convenience, or

(b) whether the conduct is proscribed by a statute, ordinance or administrative regulation, or

(c) whether the conduct is of a continuing nature or has produced a permanent or long-lasting effect, and, as the actor knows or has reason to know, has a significant effect upon the public right.

First Amendment to the U.S. Constitution

1 Congress shall make no law...abridging the freedom of speech, or of the press, or the right of the people peaceably to assemble, and to petition the Government for a redress of grievances.

Text of Preliminary Injunction

The order granting the preliminary injunction enjoins defendants from the following acts:

"(a) Standing, sitting, walking, driving, gathering or appearing anywhere in public view with any other defendant herein, or with any other known 'VST' (Varrio Sureno Town or Varrio Sureno Locos) member;

(b) Drinking alcoholic beverages in public excepting consumption on properly licensed premises or using drugs;

(c) Possessing any weapons including but not limited to knives, dirks, daggers, clubs, nunchukas [*sic;* nunchakus], BB guns, concealed or loaded firearms, and any other illegal weapons as defined in the California Penal Code, and any object capable of inflicting serious bodily injury including but not limited to the following: metal pipes or rods, glass bottles, rocks, bricks, chains, tire irons, screwdrivers, hammers, crowbars, bumper jacks, spikes, razor blades, razors, sling shots, marbles, ball bearings;

(d) Engaging in fighting in the public streets, alleys, and/or public and private property;

(e) Using or possessing marker pens, spray paint cans, nails, razor blades, screwdrivers, or other sharp objects capable of defacing private or public property;

(f) Spray painting or otherwise applying graffiti on any public or private property, including but not limited to the street, alley, residences, block walls, vehicles and/or any other real or personal property;

(g) Trespassing on or encouraging others to trespass on any private property;

(h) Blocking free ingress and egress to the public sidewalks or street, or any driveways leading or appurtenant thereto in 'Rocksprings';

(i) Approaching vehicles, engaging in conversation, or otherwise communicating with the occupants of any vehicle or doing anything to obstruct or delay the free flow of vehicular or pedestrian traffic;

(j) Discharging any firearms;

(k) In any manner confronting, intimidating, annoying, harassing, threatening, challenging, provoking, assaulting and/or battering any residents or patrons, or visitors to 'Rocksprings', or any other persons who are known to have complained about gang activities, including any persons who have provided information in support of this Complaint and requests for Temporary Restraining Order, Preliminary Injunction and Permanent Injunction;

(l) Causing, encouraging, or participating in the use, possession and/or sale of narcotics;

(m) Owning, possessing or driving a vehicle found to have any contraband, narcotics, or illegal or deadly weapons;

(n) Using or possessing pagers or beepers in any public space;

(o) Possessing channel lock pliers, picks, wire cutters, dent pullers, sling shots, marbles, steel shot, spark plugs, rocks, screwdrivers, 'slim jims' and other devices capable of being used to break into locked vehicles;

(p) Demanding entry into another person's residence at any time of the day or night;

(q) Sheltering, concealing or permitting another person to enter into a residence not their own when said person appears to be running, hiding, or otherwise evading a law enforcement officer;

(r) Signaling to or acting as a lookout for other persons to warn of the approach of police officers and soliciting, encouraging, employing or offering payment to others to do the same;

(s) Climbing any tree, wall, or fence, or passing through any wall or fence by using tunnels or other holes in such structures;

(t) Littering in any public place or place open to public view;

(u) Urinating or defecating in any public place or place open to public view;

(v) Using words, phrases, physical gestures, or symbols commonly known as hand signs or engaging in other forms of communication which describe or refer to the gang known as 'VST' or 'VSL' as described in this Complaint or any of the accompanying pleadings or declarations;

(w) Wearing clothing which bears the name or letters of the gang known as 'VST' or 'VSL';

(x) Making, causing, or encouraging others to make loud noise of any kind, including but not limited to yelling and loud music at any time of the day or night."

From *Gallo* Opinion:

1 There are few "forms of action" in the history of Anglo-American law with a pedigree older than suits seeking to restrain nuisances, whether public or private. Actions to abate private nuisances by injunction are the oldest of these apparent twins, which have almost nothing in common except the word "nuisance" itself. Unlike the private nuisance—tied to and designed to vindicate individual ownership interests in *land*—the "common" or *public* nuisance emerged from distinctly different historical origins. The public nuisance doctrine is aimed at the protection and redress of *community* interests and, at least in theory, embodies a kind of collective ideal of civil life which the courts have vindicated by equitable remedies since the beginning of the 16th century.

2   Originally, a public nuisance was an offense against the crown, prosecuted as a crime. The first known statute dealing with public nuisances—enacted in the 12th year of Richard II's reign—had as its subject the pollution of waters and ditches lying near settlements, and provided criminal liability for the offender. The earliest public nuisance statute thus bore a feature that marks the entire field even today: public nuisances are offenses against, or interferences with, the exercise of *rights common to the public.*

3   In this country, as in England, *civil* suits in equity to *enjoin* public nuisances at the instance of public law officers—typically a state's Attorney General—grew increasingly common during the course of the 19th century, a trend that was not without critics.... ["'If a charge be of a criminal nature, or an offense against the public, and does not touch the enjoyment of property, it ought not to be brought within the direct jurisdiction of this court, which was intended to deal only in matters of civil right resting in equity....' *Attorney General v. Insurance Co.,* 2 Johns. Ch. 378..."].

4   With the publication of the Restatement Second of Torts in 1965, the law of public nuisances had crystallized to such an extent that its features could be clearly delineated. Section 821B of Restatement Second of Torts identifies five general categories of "public rights," the unreasonable interference with which may constitute a public nuisance: "the public health, the public safety, the public peace, the public comfort or the public convenience." (Rest.2d Torts, 821B, subd. (2)(a).) A "public right," according to the Restatement Second, "is one common to all members of the general public. It is collective in nature and not like the individual right that everyone has not to be assaulted or defamed or defrauded or negligently injured."

5   In California, the early common law categories of public nuisance, codified in 1872 and still applicable, define anything that is "injurious to health, or is indecent or offensive to the senses, or an obstruction to the free use of property, so as to interfere with the comfortable enjoyment of life or property, or unlawfully obstructs the free passage or use, in the customary manner, of any navigable lake, or river, bay, stream, canal, or basin, or any public park, square, street, or highway," as a nuisance. (Civ. Code, 3479). Civil Code sections 3480 and 3481 divide the class nuisances into public and private. A public nuisance is one which "affects at the same time an entire community or neighborhood, or any considerable number of persons." (Civ. Code, 3480.) Rounding out the taxonomy of the Civil Code, section 3491 provides that "the remedies against a public nuisance are: 1. Indictment or information; 2. A civil action; or, 3. Abatement."

6   Section 370 of the Penal Code mirrors these civil provisions, combining the characteristics of nuisances generally with a distinctly public quality: that a given activity "interfere with the comfortable enjoyment of life or property by an entire *community or neighborhood,* or by any *considerable number* of persons." (Pen. Code, [section 370], italics added.) In *People* ex rel. *Busch v. Projection Room Theater* (1976) 17 Cal.3d 42, 49, 130 Cal.Rptr. 328, 550, P.2d 600, we parsed these code provisions, remarking on "the substantial identity of definitions appearing in Penal Code section 370 and 371, and Civil Code section 3479 and 3480.... After quoting the text of section 370, we observed: "[T]he proscribed

act may be anything which *alternatively* is injurious to health *or* is indecent, *or* offensive to the senses; the *result* of the act must interfere with the comfortable enjoyment of life *or* property; and those affected by the act may be an entire neighborhood or a considerable number of persons, and as amplified by Penal Code section 371 the extent of the annoyance or damage on the affected individuals may be unequal."

Discussion and Writing Suggestions

1. If you were a judge ruling on this anti-gang injunction, would you vote to approve it or to deny it? If you would support some of the 24 provisions, but not others, explain which ones you would support and which you would not. Put another way, which of the provisions do you find reasonable, which unreasonable? Explain.

2. One of the main objections made by defendants was that some provisions of the injunction were overly vague. What examples, if any, of vagueness do you find in the language of the injunction, and what kind of problems might such vagueness pose for its enforcement?

3. The First Amendment to the Constitution states:

   Congress shall make no law respecting an establishment of religion, or prohibiting the free exercise thereof; or abridging the freedom of speech, or of the press; or the right of the people peaceably to assemble, and to petition the Government for a redress of grievances.

   Some have argued that antigang injunctions such as this one violate the First Amendment's guarantee of "the right of the people peaceably to assemble." One judge ruling on this case quoted an opinion by another court, as follows: "The First Amendment generally prevents government from proscribing speech, or even expressive conduct, because of disapproval of the ideas expressed."

   Others have argued that the First Amendment is not absolute: the familiar example is that the right of freedom of speech does not extend to shouting "Fire!" in a crowded theater. In *Madsen v. Women's Health Center* (antiabortion demonstrators versus an abortion clinic), the Supreme Court ruled that "Freedom of association, in the sense protected by the First Amendment, 'does not extend to joining with others for the purpose of depriving third parties of their lawful rights.'"

   To what extent do you believe that the antigang injunction is unconstitutional because it violates the First Amendment?

4. Commenting on this case, Justice Brown wrote:

   From Montesquieu to Locke to Madison [18th-century political philosophers], the description of the pivotal [social] compact remains unchanged: by entering society, individuals give up the unrestrained right to act as they think fit; in return, each has a positive right to society's protection. Montesquieu describes this civil liberty as "that tranquility of spirit which comes from the opinion each one has of his security, and in order for him to have this liberty the government must be such that one citizen cannot fear another citizen."...To hold that the liberty of the peaceful, industrious residents of Rocksprings must be forfeited to preserve the illusion of freedom for those whose ill conduct is deleterious to the community as a whole is to ignore half the political promise of the Constitution and the whole of its sense.... Preserving the peace is the first duty of government, and it is for the protection of the community from the predations of the idle, the contentious, and the brutal that government was invented.

On the other hand, Justice Mosk wrote:

No doubt Montesquieu, Locke, and Madison would turn over in their graves when they learn they are cited in an opinion that does not enhance liberty but deprives a number of simple rights to a group of Latino youths who have not been convicted of a crime. Mindful of the admonition of another great 18th-century political philosopher, Benjamin Franklin, that "[t]hey that can give up essential liberty to obtain a little temporary safety deserve neither liberty nor safety."... [Some of my colleagues] would permit our cities to close off entire neighborhoods to Latino youths who have done nothing more than dress in blue or black clothing or associate with others who do so; they would authorize criminal penalties for ordinary, nondisruptive acts of walking or driving through a residential neighborhood with a relative or friend. In my view, such a blunderbuss approach amounts to bad law and bad policy. Chief Justice [Earl] Warren warned... "Unfortunately, there are some who think that the way to save freedom in this country is to adopt the techniques of tyranny." [Some] here appear to embrace that misguided belief.

Summarize in two or three sentences each the ideas of Justice Brown and Justice Mosk; then explain which position is closer to your own. Draw upon both the "Facts of the Case" and the provisions of the injunction, and provide reasons for disagreeing with the opinions that you do not share.

5. One judge ruling on this injunction pointed out that only 12% of the reports of criminal activity in Rocksprings were believed by the City to be gang-related, with another 2% "possibly gang-related." How does this statistic affect your view of the justification of the San Jose injunction?

6. To what extent do you believe that injunctions such as this one are an effective way of dealing with gangs? If you do not believe they are effective, or justified, what other measures do you believe would be more effective and more justifiable? Put another way, what recourse do residents of neighborhoods affected by gangs have if they wish to live their lives in peace and safety?

7. *Group Assignment:* See Discussion and Writing Suggestion 5 on page 640 and apply that assignment to this case.

The Felled Stop Signs: Some Cases of Homicide
(State of Florida v. Miller, State of Utah v. Hallett)

The following selections deal with two remarkably similar cases, almost 20 years apart. In both cases, the earlier one in Utah, the later one in Florida, teenagers looking for an evening of fun pulled out or pulled down stop signs at intersections. In both cases, their actions resulted in one or more persons killed in automobile crashes. The teens were blameworthy: no one disputed that. But how blameworthy, from a legal standpoint? With what crime should they be charged? To what extent were they directly responsible for the fatalities that occurred? You'll explore these and other issues by reading accounts of the two cases: first, the more recent case, described in an article in the Los Angeles Times (as of publication, no appeals ruling had been issued on this case); second, the "Facts of the Case" section of the earlier case, as described in the ruling of the Utah appellate court. Following these accounts are two statements on the law that will provide guidelines for your deliberations: the first offers excerpts from the "Homicide" section of the Utah Criminal Code, along with definitions of some key terms. The second is a brief distinction (contained in a later legal opinion from an Arizona appellate court) between "negligent homicide" and "manslaughter."

For Fallen Stop Sign, Vandals Face Life
Mike Clary

1   Tampa, Fla.—It was a clear, dark February night when the fates collided in front of Tim's Cafe at a rural intersection where a stop sign lay face-down by the side of the road.

2   One of the vehicles involved was an eight-ton Mack truck loaded with phosphate. The other was a white Camaro carrying three 18-year-old friends on a one-way ride to eternity. Chances are, police said, they never knew what hit them.

3   Tow trucks and sheriff's deputies were still on the scene a few hours later when a fourth young man named Thomas Miller pulled up. He and a friend had just finished working the graveyard shift at a welding shop and were heading to Tim's for breakfast.

4   Miller got out of his car to see the wreckage better and, he recalled later, he stood right next to the fallen stop sign.

5   Now, 16 months after that fatal crash, Miller and two friends stand convicted on three counts of manslaughter, guilty of causing three deaths by pulling that stop sign out of the ground days earlier.

6   Although Miller, 20, and his housemates, Nissa Baillie, 21, and her boyfriend, Christopher Cole, 20, admitted taking about 20 road signs during a late-night

Mike Clary, "For Fallen Stop Sign, Vandals Face Life," *Los Angeles Times,* June 11, 1997.

spree sometime before the fatal crash, they denied tampering with the stop sign in front of Tim's Cafe.

7   But a jury did not believe them.

8   On June 19 Miller, Baillie, and Cole could be sentenced to life in prison in what is believed to be the first case in the United States in which the vandalism of a traffic sign has led to a multiple manslaughter conviction.

9   What has become known as the "stop sign case" has had a wrenching effect on the families of the six young people involved, while sparking a passionate community debate on the nexus of crime and punishment.

10   On one side is Assistant State Atty. Leland Baldwin, who prosecuted the three young people. "I have heard people ask: 'How dare you charge them with manslaughter? This was a prank. It was an unintentional crime,'" she said. "But this was not a prank. These were not young kids. These were young adults. So give me a break."

11   On the other side is Joseph Registrato, chief assistant to the Hillsborough County public defender, which represented Cole and Baillie.

12   "It's one thing to take a car when you're drunk and recklessly kill somebody," Registrato said. "That law is well-understood. But in this case, they may have committed criminal mischief and then later three people died. But others had gone through that intersection and didn't die. So there is a serious question about whether the [fallen] stop sign caused the deaths.

13   "From that they could get life in prison? It's hard to follow the ball here."

Road Sign Theft Called a Commonplace Prank

14 About this there is no debate: The chain of events that led up to that horrific crash in front of Tim's Cafe makes up a cautionary tale of sobering complexity.

15   Joe Episcopo figures at least half the population of America at one time or another has stolen a road sign to hang on a bedroom wall, to win a scavenger hunt or just for kicks.

16   In fact, says Episcopo, a lawyer who represents Miller, road sign theft is so common that, when potential jurors in the case against his client were asked if they had ever taken a sign, half the pool raised a hand and three of those who answered yes ended up being seated on the six-member panel. "Everybody has somebody in their family who takes signs," he said.

17   Indeed, vandalism and theft of road signs is a problem all across the country. After the trial here in the Hillsborough County courthouse was broadcast by Court TV, public officials from as far away as Washington state have been speaking out about the expense and danger resulting from defaced or stolen road signs.

18   In Iowa, a county engineer has announced plans to use the Tampa case as a springboard for a national education campaign on the issue.

19   Dave Krug, Hillsborough County public works department engineer, estimated that 25% of all road signs ever put up in the Tampa area are damaged by vandals, knocked down or stolen. Most road sign vandalism, however, does not result in triple fatalities, attract media attention and provoke heart-wrenching community anguish over wasted lives.

20   Moreover, most sign vandalism does not give rise to the sea of regrets among thousands of people—including at least 11 people who testified in the trial here—who noticed the downed stop sign during the 24 hours preceding the crash and failed to report it.

21   "Well, what did you do?" Baldwin asked of one witness who noticed that the stop sign was down.

22   "We just went back to work, got busy," the witness replied.

Three Target Signs 'for a Rush'

23 Miller, Baillie, and Cole lived together in a rented $300-a-month mobile home on a country road less than three miles from the intersection of Keysville and Lithia-Pinecrest roads in eastern Hillsborough County where the fatal crash occurred just before midnight on Feb. 7, 1996.

24   According to interviews they gave to a local television station and Cole's testimony at trial, the three had been shopping at a nearby Wal-Mart, had drunk a couple of beers and were headed home when one of the three suggested that they take a few railroad signs. Cole told a television reporter that they began taking signs "for a rush."

25   Over a period of a couple of hours and a distance of about five miles, they unbolted and pulled up railroad signs, street name signs, a "Dead End" sign, a "Do Not Enter" sign and—from neighboring Polk County—at least one stop sign, tossing all of them in the back of their pickup truck.

26   Was it fun? Cole was asked. "I suppose so, yeah," he replied. "Yeah, it was fun at the time."

Night of Bowling Ends in Collision

27 Kevin Farr, who worked in his family's data processing business, had been bowling with his father, Les, and his two older brothers on the evening of his death. He rolled a 218 in his final league game and, as he left the bowling alley, he shouted at one of his brothers: "Tell Mom I'll be home between 11 o'clock and 12. I don't want her to worry."

28   From the bowling alley Farr drove to the house of Brian Hernandez, his best and oldest friend, and the pair then picked up Randall White. No one seems to know where they were going.

29   June Farr said that the death of the youngest of her four children has condemned her to live day by day. "And day by day takes on a whole new meaning after something like this," she said. "Sometimes it's more like a few minutes at a time."

30   The case against Miller, Cole and Baillie was circumstantial. There were no fingerprints on the stop sign and no eyewitnesses who put them at the scene. But the fallen stop sign was well within the general area of the thefts to which the three had confessed and prosecutors presented expert testimony that the stop sign appeared to have been pulled from the ground, not run over by a vehicle.

31   The defense also had its own expert witness, a mechanical engineer who testified that the stop sign had been struck by a "lateral force."

Defendants Say They Panicked Next Day

32 Perhaps the most damning evidence against Cole, Miller, and Baillie came from their own statements to police. Ron Bradish, a Sheriff's Department traffic homicide investigator, testified that Cole and Miller admitted that—during their stealing spree—they sometimes would pull signs from the ground and, if a car came by, leave them to pick up later.

33 The day after the fatal crash, the three defendants admitted to police, they panicked. They gathered up most of the stolen signs from inside and outside their mobile home and tossed them off a bridge into nearby Alafia Creek. According to Bradish, Cole said that they got rid of the signs "so no one would think they took the stop sign down at the crash."

34 Held without bail, Cole, Miller, and Baillie are to be sentenced next week after the judge hears from lawyers on both sides, as well as from relatives of the convicted and those who died.

35 While she will not lobby for life sentences, Baldwin says, she will insist on long terms. "I hope this case will be a deterrent, or, at least, somewhat thought-provoking," she said. "Perhaps this is one of the types of cases that have to be tried every generation to remind high school kids and others that vandalism has consequences. And this does have an effect. Just days ago some kids in Leon County [Tallahassee] had a stop sign in a scavenger hunt and the media [publicly] stopped them."

36 Again, Registrato demurs. "This case is useless as a deterrent," he said. "Send these three children to prison for life and the kids in Hillsborough County where it happened won't have a clue about it the next day."

37 Episcopo and Registrato said they have prepared their clients for the worst. Sentencing guidelines call for 28 years to life and Judge Bob Anderson Mitcham has been known to use the suggested maximum as a starting point. Last year he put a man convicted of wounding two Tampa police officers in prison for seven consecutive life terms, ignoring guidelines that called for 14 to 24 years.

38 For June Farr, the sentencing decision seems straightforward. "My child got the maximum penalty and he had no choice in the matter," she said. "They knew exactly what was going to happen. They just didn't know who the victims would be. This was not a prank. Pranks don't kill."

39 To those who would find life in prison too harsh a price to pay for yanking out a stop sign, Farr responds: "They didn't have to go pick out a coffin."

40 Registrato said he would argue that Miller, Cole and Baillie could better atone for their sins and better service society by doing "a couple of years hard time in Florida State Prison and then be required for the next 18 years to go to high schools twice a month and tell about the consequences of criminal mischief."

41 But Miller, Thomas Miller's father, clings to hope that his son will win a retrial and be found not guilty. He acknowledged that his son, who has a juvenile record for theft, has lied to him before. But this time, Miller said, "Tommy says he didn't take that sign and I believe it with all my heart. We know when he's lying."

42 Whatever the outcome, said Miller, 69, a retired postal worker, he knows that the lives of his family, as well as the other five families involved, are forever changed.

43   "I was in court every day," he said, "sitting in the front row on one side, across from the families of the dead boys. We didn't speak but I felt for them.... They lost their children. I understand.

44   "Now they have to understand that I've lost mine. Win or lose, this is a tragedy for both sides."

STATE of Utah, Plaintiff and Respondent

v.

Kelly K. HALLETT and Richard James FELSCH, Defendants and Appellants
No. 15765
Supreme Court of Utah
Oct. 20, 1980

Facts of the Case*

1   On the evening of September 24, 1977, a number of young people gathered at the defendant's home in Kearns. During the evening, some of them engaged in drinking alcoholic beverages. At about 10:30 P.M., they left the home, apparently bent on revelry and mischief. When they got to the intersection of 5215 South and 4620 West, defendant and the codefendant Richard Felsch (not a party to this appeal) bent over a stop sign, which faced northbound traffic on 4620 West, until it was in a position parallel to the ground. The group then proceeded north from the intersection, uprooted another stop sign and placed it in the backyard of a Mr. Arlund Pope, one of the state's witnesses. Traveling further on, defendant and his friends bent a bus stop sign over in a similar manner.

2   The following morning, Sunday, September 25, 1977, at approximately 9:00 A.M., one Krista Limacher was driving east on 5215 South with her husband and children, en route to church. As she reached the intersection of 4620 West, the deceased, Betty Jean Carley, drove to the intersection from the south. The stop sign was not visible, since the defendant had bent it over, and Ms. Carley continued into the intersection. The result was that Mrs. Limacher's vehicle struck the deceased's car broadside causing her massive injuries which resulted in her death in the hospital a few hours later.

Statements on the Law

Utah Criminal Code†

Criminal Homicide

Criminal homicide—elements—designations of offenses
(1)(a) A person commits criminal homicide if he intentionally, knowingly, recklessly, with criminal negligence, or acting with a mental state

---

State of Utah v. Hallett. 619 P.2d 337 (1980).

†*Utah Code Unannotated,* 1996. Vol. 4. Charlottesville, VA: Michie Law Publishers, 1988–96.

otherwise specified in the statute defining the offense, causes the death of another human being, including an unborn child.

Murder

(1) Criminal homicide constitutes murder if the actor:

(a) intentionally or knowingly causes the death of another;

(b) intending to cause serious bodily injury to another commits an act clearly dangerous to human life that causes the death of another;

(c) acting under circumstances evidencing a depraved indifference to human life engages in conduct which creates a grave risk of death to another and thereby causes the death of another;

(d) while in the commission, attempted commission, or immediate flight from the commission or attempted commission of aggravated robbery, robbery, rape, object rape, forcible sodomy, or aggravated sexual assault, aggravated arson, arson, aggravated burglary, burglary, aggravated kidnapping, kidnapping, child kidnapping, rape of a child, object rape of a child, sodomy of a child, forcible sexual abuse, sexual abuse of a child, aggravated sexual abuse of a child, or child abuse…, when the victim is younger than 14 years of age, causes the death of another person…; or

(e) recklessly causes the death of a peace officer while in the commission or attempted commission of:

(i) an assault against a peace officer; or

(ii) interference with a peace officer if the actor uses force against a peace officer.

(2) Murder is a first degree felony.

Manslaughter

(1) Criminal homicide constitutes manslaughter if the actor:

(a) recklessly causes the death of another; or

(b) causes the death of another under the influence of extreme emotional disturbance for which there is a reasonable explanation or excuse; or

(c) causes the death of another under circumstances where the actor reasonably believes the circumstances provide a legal justification or excuse for his conduct although the conduct is not legally justifiable or excusable under the existing circumstances.

(2) Under Subsection (1)(b), emotional disturbance does not include a condition resulting from mental illness.

(3) The reasonableness of an explanation or excuse under Subsection (1)(b), or the reasonable belief of the actor under Subsection (1)(c), shall be determined from the viewpoint of a reasonable person under the then existing circumstances.

(4) Manslaughter is a felony of the second degree.

Negligent homicide

(1) Criminal homicide constitutes negligent homicide if the actor, acting with criminal negligence, causes the death of another.

(2) Negligent homicide is a class A misdemeanor.

Definitions

Requirements of criminal conduct and criminal responsibility
No person is guilty of an offense unless his conduct is prohibited by law and:
  (1) He acts intentionally, knowingly, recklessly, with criminal negligence, or with a mental state otherwise specified in the statute defining the offense, as the definition of the offense requires; or
  (2) His acts constitute an offense involving strict liability.

Definitions of "intentionally, or with intent or willfully"; "knowingly, or with knowledge"; "recklessly, or maliciously"; and "criminal negligence or criminally negligent"

A person engages in conduct:
  (1) Intentionally, or with intent or willfully with respect to the nature of his conduct or to a result of his conduct, when it is his conscious objective or desire to engage in the conduct or cause the result.
  (2) Knowingly, or with knowledge, with respect to his conduct or to circumstances surrounding his conduct when he is aware of the nature of his conduct or the existing circumstances. A person acts knowingly, or with knowledge, with respect to a result of his conduct when he is aware that his conduct is reasonably certain to cause the result.
  (3) Recklessly, or maliciously, with respect to circumstances surrounding his conduct or the result of his conduct when he is aware of but consciously disregards a substantial and unjustifiable risk that the circumstances exist or the result will occur. The risk must be of such a nature and degree that its disregard constitutes a gross deviation from the standard of care that an ordinary person would exercise under all the circumstances as viewed from the actor's standpoint.
  (4) With criminal negligence or is criminally negligent with respect to circumstances surrounding his conduct or the result of his conduct when he ought to be aware of a substantial and unjustifiable risk that the circumstances exist or the result will occur. The risk must be of such a nature and degree that the failure to perceive it constitutes a gross deviation from the standard of care that an ordinary person would exercise in all the circumstances as viewed from the actor's standpoint.

State v. Fisher*

1　*Negligent homicide and manslaughter.* The general rule is that negligent homicide is a lesser included offense of manslaughter. In *State v. Parker,* 128 Ariz. 107, 624 P.2d 304 (App. 1980) [...] the Court of Appeals determined that the only difference between manslaughter and negligent homicide is an accused's

---

State v. Fisher. 686 P.2nd 750 (1984).

mental state at the time of the incident. *See also State v. Montoya*, Ariz. 155, 608 P.2d 92 (App. 1980). Manslaughter is established where a person, aware of a substantial and unjustifiable risk that his or her conduct will cause the death of another, consciously disregards that risk. Negligent homicide is established where a person fails to perceive the substantial and unjustifiable risk that his or her conduct will cause the death of another. The element of the greater not found in the lesser is awareness of the risk.

Discussion and Writing Suggestions

1. You are either (1) a prosecuting attorney or (2) a defense attorney involved with the Miller case. In researching precedents, you find *State of Utah v. Hallett.* For purposes of preparing either your prosecution or your defense, compare and contrast the circumstances of the *Miller* and *Hallett* cases. Consider (a) the activities of the respective defendants prior to the action being prosecuted; (b) their motivations; (c) the relationship between the defendants' actions and the automobile accidents that subsequently occurred; (d) the relative blameworthiness of the defendants; (e) with what crime, if any, the defendants should be charged; (f) any other factors you find relevant. Prepare your findings in the form of a memorandum to the District Attorney (if you are prosecuting) or the partners in your law firm (if you are defending).

2. Read the Utah Criminal Code on homicide, focusing on the distinctions drawn between murder, or manslaughter, or negligent homicide. Should Hallett and Felsch be charged with murder, or manslaughter, or negligent homicide? In a memo to the District Attorney, justify your decision. To help you with your thinking on this subject, review the definitions provided by the Utah Code of various key phrases ("intentionally, or with intent or willfully," "recklessly, or maliciously," etc.) in the Code. Review also the distinction drawn between "negligent homicide" and "manslaughter" in the opinion, *State [of Arizona] v. Fisher* (1984).

3. Hallett argued that the pulling down of a stop sign did not show the required *intent* to constitute negligent homicide. The Utah statute provides that a person is guilty of negligent homicide if he causes the death of another person

> with criminal negligence or is criminally negligent with respect to circumstances surrounding his conduct or the result of his conduct when he ought to be aware of a substantial and unjustifiable risk that the circumstances exist or the result will occur. The risk must be of such a nature and degree that the failure to perceive it constitutes a gross deviation from the standard of care that an ordinary person would exercise in all the circumstances as viewed from the actor's standpoint.

Based on the evidence before you and the inferences you draw from this evidence, do you believe, beyond a reasonable doubt, that the defendant's conduct met the elements of the above statute? Explain, in terms of the defendant's actions, viewed from his standpoint.

4. Hallett argued that the evidence did not support the conclusion that his acts were the *proximate cause* of Ms. Carley's death. To quote from the court's "Opinion," summarizing this argument,

> [Defendant] starts with a uniformly recognized definition: that proximate cause is the cause which through its natural and foreseeable consequence, unbroken by any sufficient intervening cause, produces the injury which would not have occurred but for that cause. His [argument] here is that there was evidence that as the deceased approached from the south, she was exceeding the speed limit of 25 mph; and that this was subsequent intervening and proximate cause of her own death. This is based upon the fact that a motorist, who was also coming from the south, testified that he was going 25 mph and that Ms. Carley passed him some distance to the south as she approached the intersection.

Considering this argument, do you believe that the defendant's action in pulling down the stop sign was the *proximate cause* of the fatal accident? Explain your reasoning.

5. In separate opinions, two judges of the appellate court hearing *Hallett* made the following arguments concerning the defendant's degree of responsibility for the fatality:

Maughan's opinion

> [W]here a party by his wrongful conduct creates a condition of peril, his action can properly be found to be the proximate cause of a resulting injury, even though later events which combined to cause the injury may also be classified as negligent, so long as the later act is something which can reasonably be expected to follow in the natural sequence of events. Moreover, when reasonable minds might differ as to whether it was the creation of the dangerous condition (defendant's conduct) which was the proximate cause, or whether it was some subsequent act (such as Ms. Carley's driving), the question is for the trier of the fact [the jury] to determine.

> Reflecting upon what has been said above, we [believe] that whether the defendant's act of removing the stop sign was done in merely callous and thoughtless disregard of the safety of others, or with malicious intent, the result, which he should have foreseen, was the same: that it created a situation of peril; and that nothing that transpired thereafter should afford him relief from responsibility for the tragic consequences that did occur.

Hall's opinion

> The evidence produced at trial does not discount beyond a reasonable doubt the possibility that the actions of the decedent on the morning of

September 25, 1977, constituted an independent, unforeseeable intervening cause. In this regard, it is to be noted that the evidence produced
at trial clearly established that the accident occurred in broad daylight
and that the stop sign in question had not been removed from the intersection, but merely bent over into a position where it was still marginally visible. Moreover, the word "Stop" was clearly printed in large block
letters on the pavement leading into the intersection. Even if we were to
assume, however, that defendant's action in bending the stop sign over
erased all indication that vehicles proceeding north on 4620 West were
obliged to yield right-of-way, such would render the location of the accident an unmarked intersection. The law requires due care in approaching such intersections, with such reasonable precautions as may be
necessary under the circumstances.

Evidence also appearing in the record indicates that decedent was
moving at an imprudent speed when she entered the intersection.
Although the exact rate of speed is disputed, it is unchallenged that she
had, less than a block behind, passed a truck which, itself, was doing the
legal speed limit. All parties testified that she made no attempt to slow
or brake upon entering the intersection. Under such circumstances, reasonable minds must entertain a reasonable doubt that the defendant's
conduct was the sole efficient legal cause of her death....

I would dismiss the charge of negligent homicide.

Which argument do you find more persuasive? Explain your
reasoning.

6. Try to enter into the minds of the teenagers in the Florida case. One
   of these teens told a TV reporter that they pulled out the traffic signs
   "for a rush." What do you think he meant? Attempt to explain, from
   his point of view (to bewildered adults) why "it was fun at the time"
   to pull out traffic signs. What factors do you think contribute to
   some teenagers finding fun in such antisocial outlets? Suppose, for
   the sake of argument, that the teens were guilty of negligent homicide. Why would they fail to perceive the "substantial and unjustifiable risk that his or her conduct will cause the death of another"?

7. Almost certainly, you have not been involved in activities with such
   horrific consequences as those of the defendants in the Florida and
   Utah cases. Almost certainly, however, all of us have been involved
   in actions, which, under certain circumstances, could have resulted
   in very serious outcomes. And we must be prepared to deal with
   those outcomes. To quote a widespread slogan these days: "Actions
   have consequences." How do we go about determining—and dealing with—our responsibility for the consequences of our actions?
   To what extent are our conscious intentions a factor in our personal
   responsibility? Discuss these issues, drawing upon one or two specific incidents in your own life—or the life someone you know.

8. *Group Assignment:* See Discussion and Writing Suggestion 5 on page
   640 and apply that assignment to one of the cases in this group.

Drag Racing and Death: Some Cases of Manslaughter
(Commonwealth of Pennsylvania v. Levin, Commonwealth of Pennsylvania v. Root, Jacobs v. State of Florida)

Negligence, one of the most common charges in legal cases, is defined (in Black's Law Dictionary) as "the failure to exercise the standard of care that a reasonably prudent person would have exercised in the same situation." Such negligence is a tort (i.e., a private wrong), rather than a crime. But of course, there are degrees of negligence, depending upon the level of recklessness of the individual involved and the seriousness of the consequences. Another kind of legal negligence is "gross negligence": "a conscious, voluntary act or omission in reckless disregard of a legal duty and of the consequences to another party.... " Beyond that lies "criminal negligence," that is, "gross negligence so extreme that it is punishable as a crime...for example, involuntary manslaughter or other negligent homicide.... " As we've seen in the felled stop sign cases, acts that might otherwise be chargeable as lesser offenses (such as vandalism) may be chargeable as manslaughter if they result in the death of a human being.

Of course, a jury may choose not to convict on such a charge, if it concludes that the defendant's actions do not justify a guilty verdict, or if it sees mitigating circumstances. By the same token, appeals court judges may overturn a trial court verdict if they believe that the jury's decision to convict is unsupported by the facts.

The following three cases involve drag racing. In all three cases, the races resulted in one or more fatalities. In all three cases, the defendants were convicted of involuntary manslaughter. In all three cases, the defendants appealed. As in other cases in this chapter, you will read the facts of each case, and you will read jury instructions relevant to the charge. You will also find that in two of the cases, individual judges on the appeal panel disagreed as to whether the conviction should be upheld or reversed. Once again, you are left to make your own judgment, applying the rules to the facts of the cases.

COMMONWEALTH

v.

Ronald LEVIN
Superior Court of Pennsylvania
Nov. 12, 1957

Facts of the Case*

1   Between five and six o'clock in the morning of May 14, 1955, appellant and four other young men were together in a diner at Sixty-third and Lancaster Avenue in the City of Philadelphia. They departed in a car owned and operated by one of them, Robinson. At 5151 Dakota Street appellant transferred to his own car, and drove down Dakota Street. Robinson, with his three passengers, drove down the adjoining street. Both drivers turned right on Fifty-first Street, appellant's car being to the rear. They then turned into Wynnefield Avenue,

---

*Commonwealth of Pennsylvania v. Levin. 135 A.2d 764 (1957).

going west. At Fifty-fourth and Wynnefield Avenue, appellant attempted to pass the Robinson car. Realizing that appellant was trying to pass, Robinson accelerated his speed. The drivers kept going faster, appellant's car being along the side of Robinson car to the left, in such proximity that it could have been touched by the passengers in the Robinson car. When the two cars arrived at Woodbine Avenue, they again bore left. As they approached the 5700 block of Woodbine Avenue, the cars were going approximately 80 miles per hour. One of the passengers, who was seated left rear in the Robinson car, opened his window, and shouted to appellant to get away. Appellant persisted in maintaining his position. The passengers called to their driver, Robinson, to slow down, and he replied: "Well, stop being chicken." The speed finally attained 85 to 95 miles per hour. As the cars reached Fifty-seventh Street appellant turned sharply to the right in front of Robinson, who thereupon lost control of his car, and hit a tree. One of the passengers, Klinghoffer, was thrown to the road and fatally injured.

Statements on the Law*

Instructions to the Jury

Involuntary Manslaughter—Defined

1 Defendant is accused of having committed the crime of involuntary manslaughter in violation of section 192, subdivision (b) of the Penal Code.
2   Every person who unlawfully kills a human being, without malice aforethought and without an intent to kill, is guilty of the crime of involuntary manslaughter in violation of Penal Code section 192, subdivision (b).
3   A killing is unlawful within the meaning of this instruction if it occurred:

  1. During the commission of an unlawful act [not amounting to a felony] which is dangerous to human life under the circumstances of its commission; or
  2. In the commission of an act, ordinarily lawful, which involves a high degree of risk of death or great bodily harm, without due caution and circumspection.

4   The commission of an unlawful act, without due caution and circumspection, would necessarily be an act that was dangerous to human life in its commission.
5   In order to prove this crime, each of the following elements must be proved:
  1. A human being was killed; and
  2. The killing was unlawful.

Due Caution and Circumspection—Defined

6 The term "without due caution and circumspection" refers to [a] negligent act[s] which [is] [are] aggravated, reckless and flagrant and which [is] [are] such a departure from what would be the conduct of an ordinarily prudent, careful person under the same circumstances as to be contrary to a proper regard for [human life] [danger to human life] or to constitute indifference to the consequences of such

---

*California Jury Instructions, Criminal: Book of Approved Jury Instructions [CALJIC] 6th ed. Prepared by The Committee on Standard Jury Instruction Criminal, of the Superior Court of Los Angeles County, California. St. Paul, MN: West Publishing Co., 1996.

act[s]. The facts must be such that the consequences of the negligent act[s] could reasonably have been foreseen. It must also appear that the [death] [danger to human life] was not the result of inattention, mistaken judgment or misadventure, but the natural and probable result of an aggravated, reckless or grossly negligent act.

7   *Opinion in* Levin: In brief, a person is not guilty of involuntary manslaughter unless his unlawful and reckless conduct was the legal cause of the injury and death, and legal cause means conduct which is a substantial factor in bringing about the harm.

8   *Precedent cited in* Levin: In *Stark v. Rowley,* 323 Pa. 522, 187 A. 509, cars A and B were racing side by side. Car A finally dropped back but, in attempting to turn behind car B, skidded across the road and collided with car C. It was held that the driver of car B was jointly responsible with the driver of car A for the resultant injury to the driver of car C, even though there was no contact between car B and car C.

COMMONWEALTH of Pennsylvania

v.

Leroy W. ROOT, Appellant
Supreme Court of Pennsylvania
May 2, 1961

Facts of the Case*

1   The testimony, which is uncontradicted in material part, discloses that, on the night of the fatal accident, the defendant accepted the deceased's challenge to engage in an automobile race; that the racing took place on a rural 3-lane highway; that the night was clear and dry...; that the speed limit on the highway was 50 miles per hour; that, immediately prior to the accident, the two automobiles were being operated at varying speeds of from 70 to 90 miles per hour; that the accident occurred in a no-passing zone on the approach to a bridge where the highway narrowed to two directionally-opposite lanes; that, at the time of the accident, the defendant was in the lead and was proceeding in his right hand lane of travel; that the deceased, in an attempt to pass the defendant's automobile, when a truck was closely approaching from the opposite direction, swerved his car to the left, crossed the highway's white dividing line and drove his automobile on the wrong side of the highway head-on into the oncoming truck with resultant fatal effect to himself.

Statements on the Law

1   *Justice Jones in* Root: This evidence would of course amply support a conviction of the defendant for speeding, reckless driving and, perhaps, other violations of The Vehicle Code of May 1, 1929, P.L. 905, as amended. In fact, it may be noted, in passing, that the Act of January 8, 1960, P.L. (1959) 2118, Sec. 3, 75

Commonwealth of Pennsylvania v. Root. 170 A.2d 310 (1961).

P.S. 1041…makes automobile racing on a highway an independent crime punishable by fine or imprisonment or both up to $500 and three years in jail. As the highway racing in the instant [present] case occurred prior to the enactment of the Act of 1960, that statute is, of course, not presently applicable.

2   In the case now before us, the deceased was aware of the dangerous condition created by the defendant's reckless conduct in driving his automobile at an excessive rate of speed along the highway but, despite such knowledge, he recklessly chose to swerve his car to the left and into the path of an oncoming truck, thereby bringing about the head-on collision which caused his own death.

3   *Justice Bell in* Root: What is involuntary manslaughter? Involuntary manslaughter is a misdemeanor and is very different from murder and from voluntary manslaughter. The prime difference between murder, voluntary manslaughter, and involuntary manslaughter may be thus summarized: Murder is an unlawful killing of another person with malice aforethought, expressed or implied.…

4   Voluntary manslaughter is the intentional killing of another person which is committed under the influence of passion.…

5   Involuntary manslaughter is an unintentional and nonfelonious killing of another person without malice or passion, which results from conduct by defendant which is so unlawful as to be outrageous, provided such conduct is a direct cause of the killing.

6   The unlawful racing by this defendant was not only unlawful, it was outrageous, but it was not a direct cause, i.e., one of the direct causes, of the killing.

7   *Justice Eagen in* Root: The opinion of the learned Chief Justice admits, under the uncontradicted facts, that the defendant, at the time of the fatal accident involved, was engaged in an unlawful and reckless course of conduct. Racing an automobile at 90 miles per hour, trying to prevent another automobile going in the same direction from passing him, in a no-passing zone on a two-lane public highway, is certainly all of that. Admittedly also, there can be more than one direct cause of an unlawful death. To me, this is self-evident. But [say some of my fellow justices,] the defendant's recklessness was not a direct cause of the death. With this, I cannot agree.

8   If the defendant did not engage in the unlawful race and so operate his automobile in such a reckless manner, this accident would never have occurred. He helped create the dangerous event. He was a vital part of it. The victim's acts were a natural reaction to the stimulus of the situation. The race, the attempt to pass the other car and forge ahead, the reckless speed, all of these factors the defendant himself helped create. He was part and parcel of them. That the victim's response was normal under the circumstances, that his reaction should have been expected and was clearly foreseeable, is to me beyond argument. That the defendant's recklessness was a substantial factor is obvious. All of this, in my opinion, makes his unlawful conduct a direct cause of the resulting collision.

9   The act of passing was not an "extraordinarily negligent" act, but rather a "normal response" to the act of "racing." Furthermore, as Hall pulled out to pass, Root "dropped off" his speed to 90 miles an hour. Such a move probably prevented Hall from getting back into the right-hand lane since he was alongside of Root at the time and to brake the car at that speed would have

been fatal to both himself and Root. Moreover, the dangerous condition of which the deceased had to become aware of before the defendant was relieved of his direct causal connection with the ensuing accident, was not the fact that the defendant was driving at an excessive rate of speed along the highway. He knew that when the race began many miles and minutes earlier. *The dangerous condition necessary was an awareness of the oncoming truck and the fact that at the rate of speed Root was traveling he couldn't safely pass him.*

10   *Case-law cited by Justice Eagen in* Root: Wharton, *Criminal Law and Procedure* [section] 68 (1957), speaking of causal connection, says: "A person is only criminally liable for what he has caused, that is, there must be a causal relationship between his act and harm sustained for which he is prosecuted. It is not essential to the existence of a causal relationship that the ultimate harm which has resulted was foreseen or intended by the actor. It is sufficient that the ultimate harm is one which a reasonable man would foresee as being reasonably related to the acts of the defendant." Section 295, in speaking about manslaughter, says: "When homicide is predicated upon the negligence of the defendant, it must be shown that his negligence was the proximate cause or a contributing cause of the victim's death. It must appear that the death was not the result of misadventure, but the natural and probable result of a reckless or culpably negligent act. To render a person criminally liable for negligent homicide, the duty omitted or improperly performed must have been his personal duty, and the negligent act from which death resulted must have been his personal act, and not the act of another. But he is not excused because the negligence of someone else contributed to the result, when his act was the primary or proximate cause and the negligence of the other did not intervene between his act and the result."

M. T. Connell JACOBS, Appellant

v.

STATE of Florida, Appellee
No. G-356
District Court of Appeal of Florida
First District
April 5, 1966

Facts of the Case*

1   The facts are not in dispute. On the critical date appellant, together with several others, engaged in a discussion regarding the relative speed of the automobiles owned by some of them. It was agreed that the Buick owned by Kinchen, one of the participants, was the fastest of the group, but a race would be necessary in order to determine whether the Ford owned by one Carter was faster than the

---

Jacobs v. State of Florida. 184 So.2d 710 (1966).

Chevrolet owned by appellant. The group proceeded to an agreed starting point on State Road 40, a two-lane highway west of Ocala. Appellant's Chevrolet had a broken piston and Carter's Ford had a defective low gear. Because of the condition of Carter's Ford, he was given a head start in the race. Kinchen with the faster car was to go ahead of the other two and judge the winner, but at the last minute changed his mind and started last. Appellant, who left the starting line behind Carter, overtook the latter while traveling at a medium speed of about fifty-five miles an hour. All three vehicles proceeded in a westerly direction along the highway. A witness, Sands, driving along the highway in an easterly direction arrived at the crest of the hill and observed all three vehicles approaching in their correct right lane and traveling at an excessive speed. Sands saw Kinchen's Buick pull out into his left lane in order to pass the middle vehicle, and when he did Sands drove his car off the highway on to the right shoulder of the road. Another witness standing alongside the highway saw appellant's car proceeding westerly at an estimated speed of between fifty and seventy miles an hour. At the same time he observed a vehicle driven by one Buck traveling in an easterly direction at a speed of approximately twenty-five to forty miles an hour. As the Buick vehicle reached the crest of the hill, he met the two vehicles driven by Kinchen and Carter approaching him side by side traveling at an estimated speed of ninety miles and hour. The vehicle driven by Buck proceeding easterly in the south traffic lane met head-on the vehicle driven by Kinchen in a westerly direction which was also in the south traffic lane, resulting in the death of both drivers. At the time of the collision appellant was a quarter of a mile down the road ahead of the vehicles which were following him.

2   Under the foregoing factual situation appellant contends that the State failed to prove by any competent evidence that, as alleged in the information, he operated his vehicle in such a culpably negligent manner as to cause the collision which occurred between the vehicles operated by Kinchen and Buck. Appellant urges that the sole proximate cause of the collision was the culpable negligence of Kinchen over which appellant had no control, and for which he was not responsible. Appellant therefore concludes that the probata fails to conform to the allegata, and the court erred when it refused to direct a verdict in his favor.

Statements on the Law*

[Section] 776.011, Florida Statutes Annotated

1   *Principal in first degree*
2   Whoever commits any criminal offense against the state, whether felony or misdemeanor, or aids, abets, counsels, hires, or otherwise procures such offense to be committed, is a principal in the first degree and may be charged, convicted and punished as such, whether he is or is not actually or constructively present at the commission of such offense.

West's Florida Statutes, Annotated. St. Paul, MN: West Publishing Co., 1992.

3   *Judge Wigginton in* Jacobs: The evidence clearly shows that appellant, together with others, was engaged in what is commonly known as a "drag race" of motor vehicles on a two-lane public highway in Marion County. The race entailed the operation of three motor vehicles traveling in the same direction at excessive and unlawful rates of speed contrary to the laws of this state. While engaged in such unlawful activity one of the three vehicles actively participating in the race was negligently operated in such a manner as to cause the death of the person who drove that vehicle, as well as another innocent party who had no connection with the race. The deaths which proximately resulted from the activities of the three persons engaged in the unlawful activity of drag racing made each of the active participants equally guilty of the criminal act which caused the death of the innocent party. The fact that it was the vehicle driven by the person appointed to judge the outcome of the race which caused the death of the innocent party does not relieve appellant from his responsibility as an active participant in the unlawful event out of which the death arose.

4   In Wharton it is said:

> ...If each of two persons jointly engage in the commission of acts which amount to criminal negligence, and as a result of which a third person is killed, each may be found guilty of manslaughter even though it may be impossible to say whose act actually caused the death.

5   The Supreme Court of Oregon, in the case of *State v. Newberg,* quoted with approval from Clark & Marshall as follows:

> There may be principals in the second degree and accessories before the fact to involuntary manslaughter. Thus, if two men drive separate vehicles at a furious and dangerous speed along the highway, each inciting and abetting the other, and one of them drives over and kills a person, the one thus causing the death is guilty of manslaughter as principal in the first degree, and the other is guilty as principal in the second degree....

6   *Judge Carroll in* Jacobs: I do not see how a reasonable man could lawfully conclude from the evidence adduced at the trial that, beyond a reasonable doubt, the appellant was guilty either of manslaughter or of aiding and abetting the commission of manslaughter. The culpable negligence of Willie Kinchen, as shown by the evidence, was his attempt to pass the two racing cars in the face of oncoming traffic. There is not a scintilla of evidence indicating that the appellant was aware of Kinchen's intention so to pass, and hence I do not think it reasonable to hold that the appellant aided and abetted the said culpable negligence. As I view the evidence, there was no causal relationship between the appellant's conduct in engaging in the drag race and Kinchen's culpable negligence. The only such relationship would have to be the discredited "if it hadn't been for" reasoning (if it hadn't been for the race, the collision would not have occurred), but that reasoning has long been discarded by the courts as insufficient to show proximate cause in civil cases or to show liability in criminal cases.

7   If the appellant is to be held criminally liable for manslaughter because he participated in a race during which an act of manslaughter occurred during the

race, I would think that by the extension of such reasoning the spectators lined up along the road to watch the race might be legally tried and convicted as aiders and abettors to the manslaughter, simply because the collision might not have occurred if they had not congregated and encouraged the racing. By like reasoning, also, I would think that, if the starter in a foot race at a track meet had with culpable negligence loaded his pistol with live cartridges instead of the usual blanks and shot and killed someone in the grandstand, the sprinters might be held criminally liable as aiders and abettors. Such a result, of course, would be absurd. While I recognize that these two extreme illustrations differ from the facts of the case at bar in that the appellant and the other participants may have been violating the law by engaging in a drag race, I do not think that the fact of such violation can fairly be held to overcome the fatal deficiency in the evidence—that there was no proof of a causal connection between the acts of the appellant and the culpable negligence of Willie Kinchen that caused the death in question.

8   I have examined the entire transcript of trial proceedings, and, despite much conflicting and confusing testimony, the following facts appear to me to be established by the testimony concerning the automobile race in question: that the defendant was to race his 1950 Chevrolet against one Charles Carter, driving his Ford, for a quarter-mile distance from Geneva's Restaurant westerly to certain railroad tracks, over a highway (one lane for westbound traffic and one for eastbound); that Willie Kinchen, owner of a 1950 Buick, was to serve as the judge to determine the winner of the race; that Carter was permitted to take off first, because his car had a defective gear; that some seconds later the defendant took off and soon passed Carter's car; that shortly after the defendant had left the starting point, Kinchen jumped into his Buick and soon arrived just behind Carter's car; that in the process of passing Carter's car Kinchen drove his Buick into the eastbound lane and crashed head-on into an oncoming Chevrolet being driven by one Buck who, along with Kinchen, was killed in the collision. There is, in my opinion, not a word of testimony in the transcript from which reasonable men could conclude that the defendant knew that Kinchen was planning to try to pass the racing cars, nor knew that Kinchen had even left the starting point for this or any other purpose, and certainly not a word that the defendant knew or had the slightest notion that Kinchen would be so reckless as to try to pass Carter's car by turning into the east lane in the face of oncoming traffic.

9   In view of this state of the evidence, I do not see how we can hold that the evidence supported the jury's finding that the defendant was guilty of the crime of manslaughter in the killing of Buck, or that he aided and abetted in the commission of that crime.

10   What perturbs me particularly about this case is that I do not think that the above evidence would be sufficient to hold the defendant even civilly responsible for the death of Buck, because, even if the defendant were negligent in engaging in the race, such negligence could not be properly held to have proximately caused Buck's death. As mentioned above, the reasoning is not permissible in civil cases that "if it hadn't been for" a certain act the accident would not or might not have happened and hence the doer of such act is liable for the accident.

Certainly such reasoning, *a fortiori,* should not be used to convict a person of the crime of manslaughter, and yet that's the only kind of reasoning that links up the defendant's conduct to Kinchen's act that resulted in the collision.

Discussion and Writing Suggestions

1. In the Levin case, the defendant argued that he was not guilty of manslaughter because "his car did not come into contact with the victim or some instrumentality which contacted the victim." Do you agree? Explain. If you were on the jury would you vote to convict Levin of involuntary manslaughter, taking into account the jury instructions on the definition of manslaughter and the opinion in the case itself concerning the requirements for a manslaughter conviction?

2. The appeals court panel in Levin offered a precedent for a verdict in this case. Does the precedent, *Stark v. Rowley,* support a manslaughter conviction? What are the essential similarities and differences (if any) between *Stark v. Rowley* and *Commonwealth v. Levin,* as presented here?

3. What are the key similarities and differences between *Levin* and *Root?* Specifically, how comparable are the actions of Levin and Root in directly causing the fatal accidents? How would you judge their relative degrees of responsibility? Should Root be convicted of involuntary manslaughter? Explain, using IRAC format.

4. Justices Jones and Bell in *Root* appear to absolve the defendant of responsibility for involuntary manslaughter (though not of reckless and unlawful driving), maintaining that Root's actions were not a *direct cause* of the fatal accident. Rather, it was the deceased, they maintain, who directly caused his own death when he recklessly pulled out into the path of an oncoming truck. Justice Eagen, however, disagrees with this reasoning, claiming that *Root* was "part and parcel" of the sequence of events that resulted in the fatality. He also cites a well-known criminal law text that supports his idea that a defendant's negligence is not excused simply because someone else's negligence "contributed to the result." With whose arguments do you most agree? Explain.

5. In *Jacobs,* the defendant contended that he was not guilty of involuntary manslaughter because his vehicle was not directly involved in the fatal accident. Do you agree? Explain your verdict, using IRAC format.

6. *Jacobs* is similar to *Root* in that both involve fatal accidents resulting from one car unsuccessfully attempting to overtake another with which it was racing and then crashing directly into a third vehicle.

In both cases, also, the defendant was not directly involved in the crash. To what extent do you see significant differences in the two cases? How do these differences affect your judgment of the two defendants' relative degrees of criminal responsibility?

7. In *Jacobs,* Judge Wigginton appears to take a similar position to Justice Eagen in *Root,* maintaining that a defendant who willingly participates in a drag race cannot escape responsibility for a resulting fatality simply because he was not driving the vehicle directly involved in the crash that killed an "innocent party." Judge Carroll, on the other hand, argues that Jacobs should not be held responsible for Kinchen's recklessness and "culpable negligence." In particular, Judge Carroll relies on the important legal concept of *proximate cause,* defined (in *Black's Law Dictionary*) as "a cause that directly produces an event and without which the event would not have occurred." In Carroll's view, since Jacobs's actions were not the proximate cause of Buck's death, he cannot be held legally responsible for it. Assess Judge Wigginton's and Judge Carroll's positions, referring specifically to *Jacobs,* and, if you choose, also to *Levin* and *Root.*

8. *Group Assignment:* See Discussion and Writing Suggestion 5 on page 640 and apply that assignment to one of the cases in this group.

Legal Glossary

Like every other profession (and perhaps more than most) the law has its own special language—a language often so complicated and obscure that even lawyers have difficulty understanding it. Here is a glossary of legal terms that you will encounter while reading this chapter. The definitions, for the most part, are from The Plain Language Law Dictionary, *edited by Robert E. Rothenberg. In some cases (indicated by "[Black's]" after the definition), they are taken from* Black's Law Dictionary: New Pocket Edition, *edited by Bryan A. Garner. In a very few other cases [indicated in brackets] we have provided definitions that do not appear in the dictionaries. Not included here are terms that are defined in the text itself—for example, when a statute or judicial instruction defines what is meant by "public nuisance" or "defective condition" or explains the meaning of "involuntary manslaughter."*

a fortiori   More effective; with greater reason. (Latin)

abettor   One who promotes or instigates the performance of a criminal act.

affidavit   A written statement of facts, sworn to and signed by a deponent before a notary public or some other authority having the power to witness an oath.

allegata   [Statements that have been declared to be true in a legal proceeding, without yet having been proven.]

alleged   Claimed; charged.

amend   To correct; to change; to alter; so as to correct defects in a document.

appeal   The request for a review by a higher court of a verdict or decision made by a lower court.

appellant   The party who appeals a case from a lower to a higher court.

appellate court   A court with the authority to review the handling and decision of a case tried in a lower court.

appellee   The respondent; the party against whom an appeal is taken.

breach   A violation.

case   A contested issue in a court of law; a controversy presented according to the rules of judicial proceedings.

civil   Of or relating to private rights and remedies that are sought by action or suit, as distinct from criminal proceedings. [Black's]

civil law   Law dealing with civil [private], rather than criminal matters.

codify   A code is a collection of laws; the published statutes governing a certain area, arranged in a systematic manner [thus, to "codify" is to render into law].

common law   1. Law declared by judges in area not controlled by government regulation, ordinances, or statutes. 2. Law originating from usage and custom, rather than from written statutes.

comparative negligence   A term that is used in a suit to recover damages, in which the negligence of the defendant is compared to that of the plaintiff. In other words, if the plaintiff was slightly negligent but the defendant was grossly negligent, the plaintiff may be awarded damages. Or, if the plaintiff was grossly negligent and the defendant only slightly negligent, no award may be granted.

compensatory damages   The precise loss suffered by a plaintiff, as distinguished from punitive damages, which are over and above the actual losses sustained.

continue   To postpone or adjourn a case pending in court to some future date.

contributory negligence   Negligence in which there has been a failure on the part of the plaintiff to exercise ordinary, proper care, thus contributing toward an accident. Such contributory negligence on the part of the plaintiff in a damage suit often constitutes a defense for the defendant.

counsel   A lawyer, an attorney, a counsellor. To counsel means to advise.

court   A place where justice is administered.

criminal law   That branch of the law that deals with crimes and their punishment. In other words, this type of law concerns itself with public wrongs, such as robbery, burglary, forgery, homicide, etc.

culpable   At fault; indifferent to others' rights; blamable; worthy of censure.

decedent   A person who has died.

decision   A judgment or decree issued by a judge or jury; the deciding of a lawsuit; findings of a court.

declaration   [A statement, usually written.]

defendant   A person sued in a civil proceeding or accused in a criminal proceeding. [Black's]

deposition   The written testimony of a witness, given under oath. Such a statement may be presented in a trial, before a trial, at a hearing, or in response to written questions put to a witness. A deposition is also called an affidavit or a statement under oath. *Deponent:* One who gives a deposition.

directed verdict   A situation in which a judge tells the jury what its verdict must be [because the evidence is so compelling that only one decision can reasonably follow] [Black's].

discovery   Compulsory disclosure by a party to an action, at another party's request, of facts or documents relevant to the action; the primary discovery devices are interrogatories, depositions, requests for admissions, and requests for production. [Black's]

diversity jurisdiction   The exercise of federal court authority over cases involving parties from different states and amounts in controversy greater than $50,000. [Black's]

duty   A legal obligation.

enjoin   To forbid; to issue an injunction, thus restraining someone from carrying out a specific act; a court order demanding that someone not do, or do, something.

evidence   Anything that is brought into court in a trial in an attempt to prove or disprove alleged facts. Evidence includes the introduction of exhibits, records, documents, objects, etc., plus the testimony of witnesses, for the purpose of proving one's case. The jury or judge considers the evidence and decides in favor of one party or the other.

ex parte   For the benefit of one party. (Latin) An *ex parte* procedure is one carried out in court for the benefit of one party only, without a challenge from an opposing party.

fact   Something that took place; an act; something actual and real; an incident that occurred; an event.

felony   A major crime, as distinguished from a minor one, or misdemeanor. Felonies include robberies, burglaries, felonious assault, murder, etc.

finding of fact   A conclusion reached by a court after due consideration; a determination of the truth after consideration of statements made by the opposing parties in a suit.

findings   The result of the deliberations of a court or jury; the decisions expressed by a judicial authority after consideration of all the facts.

forms of action   Various kinds of suits brought in the common law.

fungible   A thing that can be replaced readily by another similar thing. For example, a sack of potatoes can easily be replaced by another sack of potatoes.

grand jury   A group of citizens whose duties include inquiring into crimes in their area for the purpose of determining the probability of guilt of a party or parties. Should a grand jury conclude that there is a good probability of guilt, it will recommend an indictment of the suspects.

highest court   A court of last resort; a court whose decision is final and cannot be appealed because there is no higher court to consider the matter.

impanel   To make a list of those selected for jury duty.

indictment   An accusation by a grand jury, made after thorough investigation, that someone should be tried for a crime. When an indictment is handed down, the accused must stand trial for the alleged offense, but the indictment in itself does not necessarily mean that the accused will be found guilty.

injunction   A restraining order issued by a judge that a person or persons can or cannot do a particular thing…. Injunctions may be temporary or permanent.

interlocutory   Temporary; not final or conclusive, as an interlocutory decree of divorce or an interlocutory judgment

interrogatories   A set of written questions presented to a witness in order to obtain his written testimony (deposition) while he is under oath to tell the truth. Interrogatories are part of the right of discovery that a party in a suit has of obtaining facts from his adversary. They often take place prior to the commencement of the trial.

judge   A public official, appointed or elected, authorized to hear and often to decide cases brought before a court of law.

judicial   Anything related to the administration of justice; anything that has to do with a court of justice.

jurisdiction   The power and right to administer justice; the geographic area in which a judge or a court has the right to try and decide a case.

jury   A specified number of men and/or women who are chosen and sworn to look into matters of fact and, therefore, to determine and render a decision upon the evidence presented to them.

justice   The attempt by judicial means to be fair and to give each party his due, under the law.

law   The rules, regulations, ordinances, and statutes, created by the legislative bodies of government, under which people are expected to live.

lawsuit   A dispute between two or more parties brought into court for a solution; a suit; a cause; an action.

liability   Legal responsibility; the obligation to do or not do something; an obligation to pay a debt; the responsibility to behave in a certain manner.

litigation   A lawsuit, a legal action; a suit.

lower court   A trial court, or one from which an appeal may be taken, as distinguished from a court from which no appeal can be taken.

malice   Hatred; ill will; the intentional carrying out of a hurtful act without cause; hostility of one individual toward another.

matter   The subject of a legal dispute or lawsuit; the substance of the issues being litigated; the facts that go into the prosecution or defense of a claim.

negligence   Failure to do what a reasonable, careful, conscientious person is expected to do; doing something that a reasonable, careful, conscientious person would not do. *Contributory negligence:* Negligence in which there has been a failure on the part of the plaintiff to exercise ordinary, proper care, thus contributing toward an accident. *Criminal negligence:* Negligence of such a nature that it is punishable as a crime. *Gross negligence:* Conscious disregard of one's duties, resulting in injury or damage to another. Gross negligence exists when an individual, by exercising ordinary good conduct, could have prevented injury or damage. *Ordinary negligence:* Negligence that could have been avoided if only one had exercised ordinary, reasonable, proper care. Ordinary negligence is not wishful or purposeful, but rather "unthinking." *Willful negligence:* Conscious, knowing neglect of duty, with knowledge that such conduct will result in injury or damage to another.

oath   A pledge to tell the truth; a sworn promise to perform a duty; a calling on God to witness a statement.

obligation   Something a person is bound to do or bound not to do; a moral or legal duty. Penalties may be imposed upon people who fail in their obligations.

ordinance   A local law; a law passed by a legislative body of a city or township or other local government; a statute; a rule.

party   1. A person engaged in a lawsuit, either a plaintiff or a defendant. 2. A person who has taken part in a transaction, such as a party to an agreement or contract.

petitioner   One who presents a petition [a written formal request for a particular thing to be done or a certain act to be carried out] to a court seeking relief in a controversial matter. The person against whom the petition is leveled is called a respondent.

plaintiff   The party who is bringing a lawsuit against a defendant; the person or persons who are suing.

prejudice, with   Indicates a matter has been settled without possibility of appeal.

probata (probatum)   Something proved or conclusively established; proof (Latin). [Black's]

proximate cause   The immediate cause of an injury or accident; the legal cause; the real cause; a direct cause. [A cause that directly produces an event and without which the event would not have occurred. [Black's]]

punitive damages   An award to a plaintiff beyond actual possible loss. Such damages are by way of punishing the defendant for his act.

question of fact   The question of truth, such question to be decided after hearing evidence from both sides in a case. It is the judge's or jury's function to decide questions of fact.

question of law   A matter for the courts to decide, based on interpretation of existing laws pertaining to the matter at hand.

reasonable man   Someone who acts with common sense and has the mental capacity of the average, normal sensible human being, as distinguished from an emotionally unstable, erratic, compulsive individual. In determining whether negligence exists, the court will attempt to decide whether the defendant was a reasonable person.

rebuttal   The presentation of facts to a court demonstrating that testimony given by witnesses is not true.

reckless   Careless; indifferent to the outcome of one's actions; heedless; negligent; acting without due caution.

recovery   The award of money given by a court to the person or persons who win the lawsuit.

redress   The receiving of satisfaction for an injury one has sustained.

requisite   [Required; necessary.]

respondent   A person against whom an appeal is brought.

Restatement of Torts   [A codification of the common law relating to torts (private wrongs) compiled by legal practitioners and scholars; most jurisdictions accept the Restatement as the equivalent of law, even though states have often passed their own laws on matters covered by the Restatements. The first series of Restatements (Restatement First) was begun in 1923; the second (Restatement Second) was begun in 1953. Restatements have been written in many other areas of civil law, such as contracts, property, and trusts.]

restraining order   An order issued by the court without notice to the opposing party, usually granted temporarily to restrain him until the court decides whether an injunction should be ordered. In actuality, a restraining order is a form of an injunction.

reversal   The annulment or voiding of a court's judgment or decision. Such reversal usually results from a higher court overruling a lower court's action or decision.

review   1. To re-examine, consider. 2. The consideration by a higher (appellate) court of a decision made by a lower (inferior) court.

ruling   The outcome of a court's decision either on some point of law or on the case as a whole. [Black's]

statute   A law passed by the legislative branch of a government.

stipulation   An agreement between the opposing parties in a lawsuit in respect to some matter or matters that are connected to the suit. Such stipulations are made in order to avoid delays in the conducting of the trial. Many stipulations consist of the admission of facts to which both parties agree.

strict liability   Liability that does not depend on actual negligence or intent to harm, but is based on the breach of an absolute duty to make something safe.

summary judgment   A means of obtaining the court's decision without resorting to a formal trial by jury. Such judgments are sought when the opposing parties are in agreement on the facts in the dispute but wish to obtain a ruling as to the question of law that is involved.

testimony   Evidence given under oath by a witness, as distinguished from evidence derived from written documents.

tort   A wrong committed by one person against another; a civil, not a criminal wrong; a wrong not arising out of a contract; a violation of a legal duty that one person has toward another. Every tort is composed of a legal obligation, a breach of that obligation, and damage as a result of the breach of the obligation. *Tort-feasor:* a wrongdoer.

tortious   Hurtful; harmful; wrongful; injurious; in the nature of a tort.

vacate   To cancel; to annul; to set aside.

verdict   The finding or decision of a jury, duly sworn and impaneled, after careful consideration, reported to and accepted by the court.

witness   1. An individual who testifies under oath at a trial, a hearing, or before a legislative body. 2. To see or hear something take place. 3. To be present, and often to sign, a legal document, such as a will or deed.

writ   A formal order of a court, ordering someone who is out of court to do something.

RESEARCH ACTIVITIES

LEGAL RESEARCH

Unless the institution you are attending has a law school, it will likely not have the resources you need to do genuine legal research, except at the secondary source level—i.e., general books and periodical articles dealing with legal matters. If you do not have access to a law school library, but are in or near a city that serves as the county seat, you may be able to use the law library at the county courthouse. The public does have access to these libraries, which should contain the basic tools you need to conduct research—legal encyclopedias and dictionaries, legal periodicals and indexes, style manuals, and a set of state, regional, and federal case reporters, and state and federal statutes and codes.

Many college libraries will have a set of Supreme Court decisions (in *United States Reports*), even if they do not have collections of state-level cases in regional or state case reporters, such as the *Pacific Reporter* or the *California Reports.* Supreme Court cases also are available on the web; see below. Thus, you should be able to conduct research on cases, such as *Roe v. Wade,* 410 U.S. 113 (1973), that reached the Supreme Court. (This citation means volume 410 of *United States Reports,* beginning on p. 113. To refer to a statement on a particular page, insert "at" before the page number; thus 410 U.S. at 125).

Legal research has been transformed by the computer revolution, and vast legal databases are now available both online and on CD-ROM, through LEXIS-NEXIS and WESTLAW. If you do not have special access to online sources, however, legal research on the internet is hit or miss. America Online, for example, does have a good site on the law, though it is not comprehensive enough to allow you to conduct systematic research on cases. You will find resources, however, on various federal, state, and local statutes, as well as a number of specialized sites on such issues as constitutional law, and poverty/legal assistance. Some states have placed their statutes online: for example, you may find complete state penal and civil codes on the World Wide Web at

<http://www.findlaw.com/casecode/state/html>.

To find other legal information, try going to the home web page of a law school library and following the links. For example, the Cornell University Law School Library site (with a link to its Legal Information Institute) is at:

<http://www.lawschool.cornell.edu/>.

The Law section of the World Wide Web Virtual Library, maintained by the Indiana University Law School, is at

<http://www.law.indiana.edu/v-lib/>.

The Emory University Law Library Electronic Reference Desk is at

<http://www.law.emory.edu/LAW/refdesk/toc.html>.

The Chicago-Kent College of Law (Illinois Institute of Technology) site is at

<http://www.kentlaw.edu/>.

The Harvard University Law School Library is at

<http://www.law.harvard.edu/Library>.

The University of California at Berkeley's Law School Library is at

<http://boall-363-1.law.berkeley.edu/library/library.html>.

The UCLA Law School's site:

<http://www.law.ucla.edu/Research/>.

Other useful web sites for law:

FindLaw: <http://www.findlaw.com>
Law on the Web (Saint Louis University School of Law):
    <http://lawlib.slu.edu/>.
Georgia State University College of Law:
    <http://gsulaw.gsu.edu/metaindex> (Meta-Index for U.S. Legal
    Research)
Washburn University School of Law: <http://www.washlaw.edu/>
RefLaw, the Virtual Law Library Reference Desk:
    <http://washlaw.edu/washlaw/reflaw/reflaw.html>

Note: The FindLaw site offers a searchable database of all Supreme Court opinions since 1893. Go to: <http://www.findlaw.com/casecode/supreme.html>.

FindLaw also offers access to Federal Circuit Court cases and state codes and cases, though only for recent years. Searchability for these cases varies from state to state.

Federal Circuit Court cases:
    <http://www.findlaw.com/casecode/courts/index.html>
State codes and cases:
    <http://www.findlaw.com/casecode/state.html>

Using an electronic legal database such as LEXIS-NEXIS or WESTLAW is similar to using any other database; you conduct a systematic search, using key terms. If you wanted to conduct research on tobacco cases, and particularly on the issue of the liability of tobacco manufacturers for deaths resulting from their products, your search terms would include the words "tobacco" and "manufacturer" and "death" and "liability" and the appropriate connectors ("and," "or," etc.). Following the search, the WESTLAW system would provide citations to all cases, within the time and regional boundaries you specify, that include these terms. (You can find the same citations, of course, by using printed indexes, such as *West's California Digest*. Such searches will take more time because printed indexes are less flexible than electronic ones that search by combinations of individual terms, and because you have to search the various printed supplements, as well as the basic indexes, to make sure your research is up-to-date.) Be forewarned that you may be charged a fee to use electronic search services.

Although a comprehensive guide to legal research is beyond the scope of this book, the list below includes some of the most useful sources you will need:

LEGAL ENCYCLOPEDIAS

Corpus Juris Secundum (includes case annotations)

American Jurisprudence 2d (includes case annotations)

The Guide to American Law

DICTIONARIES

Words and Phrases (includes definitions and case annotations)

Black's Law Dictionary

Ballentine's Law Dictionary

ANNOTATED DECISIONS INDEXED BY LEGAL TOPIC

ALR (American Law Review) Digest of Decisions and Annotations (extensive annotated cases on selected legal issues)

West's [State] Digest (index to legal issues with case annotations)

PERIODICAL INDEXES

Index to Legal Periodicals and Books

Current Law Index

Current Index to Legal Periodicals (also in microfilm, online, and on CD-ROM)

ELECTRONIC LEGAL PERIODICAL INDEXES

LEXIS-NEXIS (includes *Index to Legal Periodicals and Books* and *Legal Resource Index*)

LegalTrac (CD-ROM) (part of the InfoTrac library)

MODEL CODES AND STATUTES

Restatement of the Law, 2d (covers areas of civil law, such as torts and contracts)

Model Penal Code

FEDERAL CASE REPORTERS (Collections of Case Opinions, in Chronological Order of Decision)

United States Reports (Supreme Court)

Supreme Court Reports, Lawyer's Edition

Federal Supplement (decisions of Federal District Courts)

Federal Reporter (decisions of Federal Circuit courts)

West's Supreme Court Reporter

REGIONAL AND STATE REPORTERS

Pacific Reporter (covers Alaska, Arizona, California, Colorado, Hawaii, Idaho, Kansas, Montana, Nevada, New Mexico, Oklahoma, Oregon, Utah, Washington, Wyoming)

North Eastern Reporter (Illinois, Indiana, Massachusetts, New York, Ohio)

North Western Reporter (Iowa, Michigan, Minnesota, Nebraska, North Dakota, South Dakota, Wisconsin)

Atlantic Reporter (Connecticut, Delaware, Maine, Maryland, New Hampshire, New Jersey, Pennsylvania, Rhode Island, Vermont)

South Western Reporter (Arkansas, Kentucky, Missouri, Tennessee, Texas)

South Eastern Reporter (Georgia, North Carolina, South Carolina, Virginia, West Virginia)

Southern (Alabama, Florida, Louisiana, Mississippi)

(state reporters)

STATUTES, CONSTITUTIONS, CODES

United States Code (U.S.C.)

United States Codes Annotated (U.C.S.A.)

United States Code Service (U.S.C.S.)

(state and local statutes and codes)

COMPUTER-ASSISTED LEGAL RESEARCH

LEXIS-NEXIS

WESTLAW

CITATORS (CITATION GUIDES)

Shepard's Citations (indicates if the case, statute, article, etc., you want to cite as authority has been cited in other cases, statutes, articles, etc. The process of conducting such searches is known as "Shepardizing.")

To give you an idea of how you can find particular cases on particular legal issues, below is from a page of West Publishing Company's *Words and Phrases.* Suppose you want to see how the concept of "malice" has been used in libel cases. The entry on "malice" begins with a series of cross references to related topics, then presents a long series of legal statements on malice that have appeared in legal opinions. Following the "general" category that begins most entries, you can look for the particular area in which you are interested—in this case, libel and slander.

MALICE

See, also,

Civil Action When Malice is not Gist of Action.

Common-Law Malice.

Constructive or Implied Malice.

Deliberate Malice.

Doctrine of Universal Malice.

Fraud or Malice.

Implied Malice.

Inferred Malice.

New York Times Malice.

Presumed Malice.

Secrecy and Malice.

Times Malice.

Willfulness and Malice.

With Malice.

With Malice and Unjustified in Law.

IN GENERAL

In the context of intentional torts, "malice" is defined under Massachusetts law as arising from improper motive or means, including age discrimination. Galdauckas v. Interstate Hotels Corp. No. 16, D.Mass., 901 F.Supp. 454, 465.

"Malice," in context of peer review, means recklessness of consequences and mind regardless of social duty. Cooper v. Delaware Valley Medical Center, 654, A.2d 547, 553, 539, Pa. 620.

"Malice" is wickedness of disposition, hardness of heart, cruelty, recklessness of consequences and mind regardless of social duty. Green v. Pennsylvania Bd. Of Probation and Parole, Pa.Cmwlth. 664 A.2d 677, 679.

"Malice," in defamation cases, means that the defendant knows that the statement is false or that he has reckless disregard for determining whether it is true. Century Management, Inc. v. Spring, Mo. App.W.D., 905 S.W.2d 109,113.

LIBEL AND SLANDER

Evidence supported jury's finding that veterinarian's inquiry of coworker as to whether former employee had drug or alcohol problem were slander per se, and were made out of "malice," rather than in "good faith," and thus were not protected by privilege; imputation of substance abuse reflected on former employee's capacity to perform duties of veterinary assistant, and veterinarian denied asking question when confronted by former employee, but during trial he claimed former employee had become unreliable. Lara v. Thomas, Iowa, 512 N.W.2d 777, 785.

In libel action arising from employer and employee relationship, actual "malice" means publication of statement with knowledge that it is false or with reckless disregard for whether it is false, and falsity coupled with negligence, failure to investigate truth or falsity of statement, and failure to act as reasonably prudent person are insufficient to show malice. Maewal v. Adventist Health Systems/Sunbelt, Inc., Tex.App.-Fort Worth, 868 S.W.2d 886, 893.

"Malice," sufficient to overcome qualified privilege in defamation action, requires showing that defendant acted with knowledge of, or in reckless disregard of, falsity of publicized matter, that is that defendant in fact entertained serious doubts about truth of publication. Mitre v. La Plaza Mall, Tex. App.-Corpus Christi, 857 S.W.2d 752, 754.

"Malice" necessary to overcome qualified privilege in defamation action may be proven by evidence of personal ill feeling, exaggerated language or extent of publication. Strauss v. Thorne, Minn. App., 490 N.W.2d 908, 912.

Essence of "malice" in libel context is not lack of prudence, but actual awareness of probable falsity of published statement. Weinel v. Monkey, 5 Dist., 481 N.E.2d 776, 778, 89 Ill.Dec. 933, 935, 134 Ill.App.3d 1039.

Other West indexes also provide references to relevant articles in legal periodicals. Don't hesitate to ask librarians for assistance in using legal indexes to find cases, articles, and other sources.

Some excellent books for teaching novice legal researchers to find cases, statutes, and articles by topic include:

Cohen, Morris, Robert C. Berring, Kent C. Olson. *How to Find the Law.* 9th ed. St. Paul, MN: Westlaw, 1989. (See also Berring's abridged version of this book, entitled *Finding the Law.*)

Jacobstein, J. Myron, Roy M. Mersky, Donald J. Dunn. *Fundamentals of Legal Research,* 6th ed. Wesbury, NY: Foundation Press, 1994.

CITATIONS FOR CASES COVERED IN THIS CHAPTER

If you would like to follow up on cases covered in this chapter, here are the references. (See Hricik, p. 607, on reading legal citations.)

The Maiden and the Pot of Gold: A Case of Emotional Distress
Nickerson v. Hodges. 84 So. 37 (1920).

*Venezia v. Miller Brewing Co.:*A Case of Products Liability?
Venezia v. Miller Brewing Co. 626 F.2d 188 (1980).

The Ridiculed Employee: Another Case of Emotional Distress
Harris v. Jones. 380 A.2d 611 (1977).

Assault and Battery on the Gridiron: A Case of Reckless Disregard of Safety
Hackbart v. Cincinnati Bengals. 601 F.2d 516 (1979)

Who Gets the Kids? Some Cases of Child Custody
Ashwell v. Ashwell. 286 P.2d 983 (1995).
Wood v. Wood. 190 Cal Rptr. 469 (1983).
Fingert v. Fingert. 271 Cal Rptr. 389 (1990).
In Re B.G. 523 P.2d 244 (1974).
In Re the Marriage of B.A.S. 541 S.W.2d 762 (1976).

"Urban War Zone": A Case of Public Nuisance
People v. Acuna et al. 60 Cal. Rptr.2d 277 (1997).

The Felled Stop Signs: Some Cases of Homicide
State of Florida v. Miller. 2001 Fla App LEXIS 2081 (2001).
State of Utah v. Hallett. 619 P.2d 337 (1980).

Drag Racing and Death: Some Cases of Manslaughter
Commonwealth of Pennsylvania v. Levin. 135 A.2d 764 (1957).
Commonwealth of Pennsylvania v. Root. 170 A.2d 310 (1961).
Jacobs v. State of Florida. 184 So.2d 710 (1966).

RESEARCH TOPICS

1. Select a particular legal issue dealt with in this chapter (for example, emotional distress or drag racing) and research the book and
   periodical indexes to find some interesting recent cases. Use an
   index to legal periodicals if the library has one. Select one of these
   cases and report on its progress. Describe the facts of the case, identify the legal issues involved, describe and analyze the arguments
   on both sides, and discuss the case's outcome.

2. Using some of the Internet legal sites mentioned above, browse the
   Web until you find a topic that interests you (for example, tobacco
   lawsuits). Then, using the hyperlinks, research the topic as fully as
   you are able, online. (Remember to write down, electronically copy,
   or bookmark important URLs, so that you can easily return to
   them.) Write a report *on the progress of your research,* rather than on
   the topic itself. Focus on what you were able to find, using Web
   resources, and what you were unable to find. Explain your frustrations, as well as your high points of discovery. Indicate what other
   information—whether available online or in print—you would
   need to find before being able to complete a report on the topic.

3. Visit the county courthouse (if one is nearby) and sit in for a period
   of time on one or more trials. Report on your observations.
   Describe what you have seen and analyze the various aspects of the
   case or cases: the prosecution and defense lawyers, the defendant,
   the witnesses, the judge, the jury. What conclusions, from this limited observation, can you make about the legal process? What recommendations would you make to better achieve justice—or, at least,
   a higher standard of fairness or efficiency?

4. Research the legal system in a country other than the United States.
   Based upon your own experience or knowledge and upon what
   you have learned in this chapter, how does the process of criminal
   or civil cases in this other country compare to that in the United
   States? Which aspects of the other country's legal system appear
   superior to those of the United States? Which seem inferior? In your
   discussion refer to specific cases tried in the other country's legal
   system. You may choose to focus partially on offenses (such as criticizing the government) that are not crimes in the United States, but
   are in some other countries; however, focus primarily upon the
   ways that the legal system *works.*

5. Many feature films focus on courtroom drama and other legal matters. Examples: *Young Mr. Lincoln* (1939), *Adam's Rib* (1949), *The Caine Mutiny* (1954), *12 Angry Men* (1957), *Witness for the Prosecution* (1957), *Anatomy of a Murder* (1961), *Inherit the Wind* (1960), *Judgment at Nuremberg* (1961), *To Kill a Mockingbird* (1962), *The Paper Chase* (1973), *The Verdict* (1982), *True Believer* (1989), *Class Action* (1991), *A Few Good Men* (1992), *Ghosts of Mississippi* (1996), *A Civil Action* (1998).

View one or more of these films, then report on and draw conclusions from your observations. Using inductive reasoning, *infer* points of law and rules of courtroom procedure from what you see. Point out similarities and differences, where appropriate. For example, *The Caine Mutiny* deals (partially) with a court martial, where the rules of procedure are somewhat different from those in civilian courts. *Judgment at Nuremberg* deals with war crimes tribunals in postwar Germany. *12 Angry Men* deals with jury room deliberations, rather than with the trial itself. *The Paper Chase* deals with a tyrannical law professor attacking the "skullsful of mush" in his students' heads and goading them to "think like a lawyer!"

Good Take, Sweet Prince: *Hamlet* on Film

13

When independent filmmaker Michael Almereyda was planning his high-tech *Hamlet*, featuring a hero who assembles his own video "to catch the conscience of the king," he discovered with some trepidation that the play had already been filmed at least 43 times. Could he contribute any fresh insights, he asked himself, or reveal any previously undiscovered truths about a work that had already attracted some of the most talented artists in theater and film? In the end, he decided to try. And so the tradition continues—several new cinematic *Hamlets* for each generation.

William Shakespeare is, of course, the most celebrated writer in the English language, and *Hamlet*, arguably his most celebrated play. In a recent BBC poll, *Hamlet* was rated the most important work of art in the millennium.* It's understandable, then, that generations of filmmakers have felt challenged to test their creative mettles and distinctive artistic visions on this most archetypal of post-Greek tragedies. Counting Almereyda's version, three major film *Hamlets* have been made in the past decade alone. Several years ago, it seemed that Jane Austen (number 2 on the BBC poll) was the hottest writer in Hollywood, with near-simultaneous major studio productions of several of her novels (not counting clever modernizations like *Clueless*); but there's no question that the bard of Stratford-on-Avon is co-author of more British and American films than any other writer. One film historian reports that Thomas Edison, inventor of the motion picture camera, became the first Shakespearean filmmaker in 1899 when he shot excerpts from a London performance of *King John*.[†] In 1900 (100 years before Almereyda's film) a silent *Hamlet* was filmed in France. The most well-known film *Hamlets* of the 20th century include those directed by Laurence Olivier (1948, starring Olivier); John Gielgud and Bill Colleran (1964, starring Richard Burton); Grigori Kozintsev (1964, starring Innokenti Smoktunovski); Tony Richardson (1969, starring Nicol Williamson); Peter Wood (1970, starring Richard Chamberlain); Franco Zeffirelli (1991, starring Mel Gibson); Kenneth Branagh (1996, starring Branagh); and Almereyda (2000, starring Ethan Hawke).

This chapter will give you an opportunity to view some of the varied artistic visions embodied by four particular *Hamlet* adaptations: those by Olivier, Zeffirelli, Branagh, and Almereyda. Your instructor may arrange for class or individual viewings of one

---

*"The Millenium," [London] Daily Telegraph, 28 Dec. 1999. Online. LEXIS-NEXIS.

[†]Kenneth Rothwell, *A History of Shakespeare on Screen: A Century of Film and Television.* Cambridge: Cambridge UP: 1999: 1.

or more of these films on video or DVD. Or, if these are not available at your institution, you may choose to rent the films you would like to work with. After you have viewed two versions of *Hamlet*—say, those by Zeffirelli and Branagh—you might first ask yourself what overall differences you find in experiencing these two distinctive versions of the same work. Consider first the large questions: because of the differences in direction, actors, acting styles, settings, music, and so on, do the two films appear to represent different interpretations or artistic conceptions of *Hamlet*? Does one version illuminate the play for you more than another? How? Do you like one version more than another? Why? Consider next the smaller, component matters: how does Olivier's reading of the "To be or not to be" speech compare with Gibson's? With Hawke's? How does Branagh's moving camera contribute to the effect and the meaning of the scene in which Hamlet talks to his father's ghost? How does one director's staging of the Hamlet-Laertes swordfight compare and contrast with another's? Who creates the most sympathetic Polonius—and how does our sympathy affect the meaning of the film? We should emphasize that the purpose of looking at one *Hamlet* in light of another or others is not to determine which is the "best" or the "worst," but rather to examine how different and perhaps equally legitimate approaches to a classic play can yield intriguingly varied interpretations, can shed unexpected flashes of illumination upon Shakespeare's characters and their story.

The chapter begins with three preliminary readings designed to prepare you for viewing and better understanding the films. The first reading you should undertake is one that, for lack of space, is not actually included in the chapter but which is nonetheless important, if not essential: the text of William Shakespeare's *Hamlet*. Begin your readings in the chapter with Sylvan Barnet's "Shakespeare"—which provides essential biographical facts about the playwright and a list of his plays and major poems. Next, Edward Hubler, editor of *Hamlet* in the *Complete Signet Classic Shakespeare*, provides a critical commentary, focusing on Hamlet as tragic hero. The first section concludes with Jack Jorgens's "Shakespeare and Nonverbal Expression," which illustrates numerous instances from Shakespearean films in which meaning, emotion, and dramatic power is conveyed to the viewer through such types of nonverbal expression as gesture, camera movement, and sound.

The second and most extensive part of the chapter is divided into four sections, each focused on one of the major films treated. Each section begins with a cinematic outline of the film in question: a list of credits followed by a scene-by-scene summary (keyed to Shakespearean act and scene number and time elapsed) of the action and important camera movements and shots. These cinematic outlines are not intended to serve as a substitute for a viewing of the films, but they should refresh your memory about what you have seen so that you can better provide specific examples in your discussion and writing. Each cinematic outline is followed by a statement (or in the case of Zeffirelli, an interview) by the filmmaker himself, who explains his own approach to *Hamlet* and considers some aspects of the filmmaking process. The statement by the filmmaker in each section is followed by one review of the film, in order to provide you with models for critical analysis. (Of course, you are encouraged to look up additional reviews, as they may help stimulate your thinking—or your indignation.) The Branagh section includes two additional pieces: excerpts from a fascinating diary kept by script consultant Russell Jackson about the rehearsing and filming of Branagh's *Hamlet,* and—to help you understand the difference between a play text and a film script—a side-by-side comparison of two scenes in *Hamlet* as they appear in both Shakespeare's play and in Branagh's screenplay. The chapter concludes with an appendix, "A Glossary of Film Terms," that provides definitions of essential film concepts and thus a vocabulary with which to discuss the cinematic aspects of the various film versions of *Hamlet.*

Shakespeare
Sylvan Barnet

The hero of John Madden's delightful 1998 film Shakespeare in Love *is an interesting fellow, but any resemblance between him and the actual William Shakespeare (1564–1616) is somewhere in-between highly doubtful and nonexistent. As Sylvan Barnet points out in the following piece, we do know quite a bit about Shakespeare, but not nearly enough to support all of the suppositions and speculations that have, over the past four centuries, attached themselves to his life. (One such supposition, held to be quite probable by Shakespeare critic Harold Bloom, is that Shakespeare played the Ghost in the original production of* Hamlet.) *In this introductory selection, Sylvan Barnet sticks to the essential facts about the man generally considered the greatest writer in the English language.*

Sylvan Barnet, formerly a professor of English at Tufts University, is a prolific author and editor of books on a variety of humanities-related subjects, many of which have gone into multiple editions. He is the general editor of The Complete Signet Classic Shakespeare, *the author of* A Short Guide to Shakespeare, *and the editor or co-editor of numerous anthologies of drama and fiction, including* The Genius of the Early English Theater, Tragedy and Comedy: An Anthology of Drama, *and* Types of Drama: Plays and Essays. *Barnet is also the co-editor of several anthologies and textbooks in composition, including* Barnet & Stubbs Practical Guide to Writing, The Little, Brown Handbook, Current Issues and Enduring Questions: Methods and Models of Argument from Plato the Present. *He is also the author of* Zen Ink Paintings; A Dictionary of Literary, Dramatic, and Cinematic Terms; A Short Guide to Writing about Art; *and* A Short Guide to Writing about Literature.

1   Between the record of his baptism in Stratford on 26 April 1564 and the record of his burial in Stratford on 25 April 1616, some forty documents name Shakespeare, and many others name his parents, his children, and his grandchildren. More facts are known about William Shakespeare than about any other playwright of the period except Ben Jonson. The facts should, however, be distinguished from the legends. The latter, inevitably more engaging and better known, tell us that the Stratford boy killed a calf in high style, poached deer and rabbits, and was forced to flee to London, where he held horses outside a playhouse. These traditions are only traditions; they may be true, but no evidence supports them, and it is well to stick to the facts.

2   Mary Arden, the dramatist's mother, was the daughter of a substantial landowner; about 1557 she married John Shakespeare, who was a glove-maker and trader in various farm commodities. In 1557 John Shakespeare was a member of the Council (the governing body of Stratford), in 1558 a constable of the borough, in 1561 one of the two town chamberlains, in 1565 an alderman (entitling him to the appellation "Mr."), in 1568 high bailiff—the town's highest political office, equivalent to mayor. After 1577, for an unknown reason he drops out of local politics. The birthday of William Shakespeare, the eldest son of this locally prominent man, is unrecorded; but the Stratford parish register records that the infant was baptized on 26 April 1564. (It is quite possible that he was born on 23 April, but this date has probably been assigned by tradition because it is the date on which, fifty-two years later, he died.) The attendance records of the Stratford grammar school of the period are not extant, but it is reasonable to assume that the son of a local official attended the school and received substantial training in Latin. The masters of the school from Shakespeare's seventh to fifteenth years held Oxford degrees; the Elizabethan curriculum excluded mathematics and the natural sciences but taught a good deal of Latin rhetoric, logic, and literature. On 27 November 1582 a marriage license was issued to Shakespeare and Anne Hathaway, eight years his senior. The couple had a child in May, 1583. Perhaps the marriage was necessary, but perhaps the couple had earlier engaged in a formal "troth plight," which would render their children legitimate even if no further ceremony were performed. In 1585 Anne Hathaway bore Shakespeare twins.

3   That Shakespeare was born is excellent; that he married and had children is pleasant; but that we know nothing about his departure from Stratford to London, or about the beginning of his theatrical career, is lamentable and must be admitted. We would gladly sacrifice details about his children's baptism for details about his earliest days on the stage. Perhaps the poaching episode is true (but it is first reported almost a century after Shakespeare's death), or perhaps he first left Stratford to be a schoolteacher, as another tradition holds; perhaps he was moved by

> Such wind as scatters young men through the world, To seek their fortunes further than at home Where small experience grows.

4   In 1592, thanks to the cantankerousness of Robert Greene, a rival playwright and a pamphleteer, we have our first reference, a snarling one, to Shakespeare as an actor and playwright. Greene warns those of his own educated friends who wrote for the theater against an actor who has presumed to turn playwright:

> There is an upstart crow, beautified with our feathers, that with his *tiger's heart wrapped in a player's hide* supposes he is as well able to bombast out a blank verse as the best of you, and being an absolute Johannes-factotum is in his own conceit the only Shake-scene in a country.

The reference to the player, as well as the allusion to Aesop's crow (who strutted in borrowed plumage, as an actor struts in fine words not his own), makes it clear that by this date Shakespeare had both acted and written. That Shakespeare is meant is indicated not only by "Shake-scene" but by the parody of a line from one of Shakespeare's plays, *3 Henry VI:* "O, tiger's heart wrapped in a woman's hide." If Shakespeare in 1592 was prominent enough to be attacked by an envious dramatist, he probably had served an apprenticeship in the theater for at least a few years.

5   In any case, by 1592 Shakespeare had acted and written, and there are a number of subsequent references to him as an actor: documents indicate that in 1598 he is a "principal comedian," in 1603 a "principal tragedian," in 1608 he is one of the "men players." The profession of actor was not for a gentleman, and it occasionally drew the scorn of university men who resented writing speeches for persons less educated than themselves, but it was respectable enough: players, if prosperous, were in effect members of the bourgeoisie, and there is nothing to suggest that Stratford considered William Shakespeare less than a solid citizen. When, in 1596, the Shakespeares were granted a coat of arms, the grant was made to Shakespeare's father, but probably William Shakespeare (who the next year bought the second-largest house in town) had arranged the matter on his own behalf. In subsequent transactions he is occasionally styled a gentleman.

6   Although in 1593 and 1594 Shakespeare published two narrative poems dedicated to the Earl of Southampton, *Venus and Adonis* and *The Rape of Lucrece,* and may well have written most or all of his sonnets in the middle nineties, Shakespeare's literary activity seems to have been almost entirely devoted to the theater. (It may be significant that the two narrative poems were written in years when the plague closed the theaters for several months.) In 1594 he was a charter member of a theatrical company called the Chamberlain's Men (which in 1603 changed its name to the King's Men); until he retired to Stratford (about 1611, apparently), he was with this remarkably stable company. From 1599 the company acted primarily at the Globe Theatre, in which Shakespeare held a one-tenth interest. Other Elizabethan dramatists are known to have acted, but no other is known also to have been entitled to a share in the profits of the playhouse.

7   Shakespeare's first eight published plays did not have his name on them, but this is not remarkable; the most popular play of the sixteenth century, Thomas Kyd's *The Spanish Tragedy,* went through many editions without naming Kyd, and Kyd's authorship is known only because a book on the profession of acting happens to quote (and attribute to Kyd) some lines on the interest of Roman emperors in the drama. What is remarkable is that after 1598 Shakespeare's name commonly appears on printed plays—some of which are not his. Another indication of his popularity comes from Francis Meres, author of *Palladis Tamia: Wit's Treasury* (1598): in this anthology of snippets accompanied by an essay on literature, many playwrights are mentioned, but Shakespeare's name occurs more often than any other, and Shakespeare is the only playwright whose plays are listed.

8   From his acting, playwriting, and share in a theater, Shakespeare seems to have made considerable money. He put it to work, making substantial investments in Stratford real estate. When he made his will (less than a month before

he died), he sought to leave his property intact to his descendants. Of small bequests to relatives and to friends (including three actors, Richard Burbage, John Heminges, and Henry Condell), that to his wife of the second-best bed has provoked the most comment; perhaps it was the bed the couple had slept in, the best being reserved for visitors. In any case, had Shakespeare not excepted it, the bed would have gone (with the rest of his household possessions) to his daughter and her husband. On 25 April 1616 he was buried within the chancel of the church at Stratford. An unattractive monument to his memory, placed on a wall near the grave, says he died on 23 April. Over the grave itself are the lines, perhaps by Shakespeare, that (more than his literary fame) have kept his bones undisturbed in the crowded burial ground where old bones were often dislodged to make way for new:

> *Good friend, for Jesus' sake forbear*
> *To dig the dust enclosed here.*
> *Blessed be the man that spares these stones*
> *And cursed be he that moves my bones.*

9   Thirty-seven plays, as well as some nondramatic poems, are held to constitute the Shakespeare canon. The dates of composition of most of the works are highly uncertain, but there is often evidence of a *terminus a quo* (starting point) and/or *terminus ad quem* (terminal point) that provides a framework for intelligent guessing. For example, *Richard II* cannot be earlier than 1595, the publication date of some material to which it is indebted; *The Merchant of Venice* cannot be later than 1598, the year Francis Meres mentioned it. Sometimes arguments for a date hang on an alleged topical allusion, such as the lines about the unseasonable weather in *A Midsummer Night's Dream,* II.i.81–117, but such an allusion (if indeed it is an allusion) can be variously interpreted, and in any case there is always the possibility that a topical allusion was inserted during a revision, years after the composition of a play. Dates are often attributed on the basis of style, and although conjectures about style usually rest on other conjectures, sooner or later one must rely on one's literary sense. There is no real proof, for example, that *Othello* is not as early as *Romeo and Juliet,* but one feels *Othello* is later, and because the first record of its performance is 1604, one is glad enough to set its composition at that date and not push it back into Shakespeare's early years. The following chronology, then, is as much indebted to informed guesswork and sensitivity as it is to fact. The dates, necessarily imprecise, indicate something like a scholarly consensus.

Plays

1588–93	*The Comedy of Errors*
1588–94	*Love's Labor's Lost*
1590–91	*2 Henry VI*
1590–91	*3 Henry VI*
1591–92	*1 Henry VI*
1592–93	*Richard III*
1592–94	*Titus Andronicus*

1593–94	*The Taming of the Shrew*
1593–95	*The Two Gentlemen of Verona*
1594–96	*Romeo and Juliet*
1595	*Richard II*
1594–96	*A Midsummer Night's Dream*
1596–97	*King John*
1596–97	*The Merchant of Venice*
1597	*1 Henry IV*
1597–98	*2 Henry IV*
1598–1600	*Much Ado About Nothing*
1598–99	*Henry V*
1599–1600	*Julius Caesar*
1599–1600	*As You Like It*
1599–1600	*Twelfth Night*
1600–01	*Hamlet*
1597–1601	*The Merry Wives of Windsor*
1601–02	*Troilus and Cressida*
1602–04	*All's Well That Ends Well*
1603–04	*Othello*
1604–05	*Measure for Measure*
1605–06	*King Lear*
1605–06	*Macbeth*
1606–07	*Antony and Cleopatra*
1605–08	*Timon of Athens*
1607–09	*Coriolanus*
1608–09	*Pericles*
1609–10	*Cymbeline*
1610–11	*The Winter's Tale*
1611–12	*The Tempest*
1612–13	*Henry VIII*

Poems

1592	*Venus and Adonis*
1593–94	*The Rape of Lucrece*
1593–1600	*Sonnets*
1600–01	*The Phoenix and the Turtle*

Review Questions

1. On what kinds of evidence does Barnet base the facts he recounts of Shakespeare's life? Why can't we be sure of other alleged facts about Shakespeare?

2. Why do critics conclude that Robert Greene's "upstart crow" verse (cited in paragraph 4) refers to Shakespeare?

3. How do we know that Shakespeare was an actor, as well as a writer?

4. Did Shakespeare make money writing for the theater?

5. How do we know when Shakespeare's plays were written?

Discussion and Writing Suggestions

1. How familiar are you with the life and works of William Shakespeare? Which of his plays and other works (such as sonnets) have you read or seen performed? What is your general impression of Shakespeare at this point?

2. Have you seen any filmed versions of Shakespeare's plays? If so, which ones? What is your impression of these works? Which one(s) did you like best, which one(s) least?

3. Have you ever acted in a Shakespearean play or scene or recited his lines in a dramatic reading, perhaps in an English class? Discuss these experiences.

4. To what extent do you find it difficult to appreciate or enjoy Shakespeare's plays or poems? To what extent do you find his work rewarding?

5. Suppose a biographer several centuries from now was attempting to write your biography. Upon what kinds of available evidence could she or he likely draw? What kind of impression of you might such evidence create? To what extent would such an impression be accurate?

The Tragedy of Hamlet, Prince of Denmark: A Critical Review
Edward Hubler

As the most famous play in the English language, Hamlet *has probably attracted more critical commentary—often contradictory—than any other. The poet and critic Samuel Taylor Coleridge declared that eighteenth century critic Dr. Samuel Johnson "did not understand the character of Hamlet."[1] Another 19th-century critic, William Hazlitt, called Hamlet "the prince of philosophical speculators."[2] Contrarily, a renowned early 20th-century critic, A.C. Bradley asks, "[h]ow can we accept the notion that Hamlet's was a weak and one-sided character?"[3] Harley Granville-Barker calls* Hamlet *"a tragedy of inaction."[4] There are an*

---

[1]*Shakespearean Criticism,* 2nd ed. NY: Dutton, 1811–12.

[2]*The Characters of Shakespeare's Plays,* 2nd ed. London: Taylor and Hessey, 1818.

[3]*Shakespearean Tragedy,* London: Macmillan, 1904.

[4]*Prefaces to Shakespeare,* Princeton: Princeton University Press, 1946.

almost infinite number of ways of approaching the play. The one we have chosen as an introduction for this chapter focuses on the idea of Hamlet *as tragedy and its protagonist as tragic hero. Edward Hubler views* Hamlet *not only in the context of earlier, Greek tragedy, but also in the context of Shakespeare's own development as a tragic playwright—beginning with such early works as* Titus Andronicus, Romeo and Juliet, Richard III, Richard II, *and* Julius Caesar, *and maturing to unparalleled magnificence in the later tragedies,* Hamlet, Othello, King Lear, *and* Macbeth.

Edward Hubler was a professor of English at Princeton University. He is the author of The Sense of Shakespeare's Sonnets *(1952), and the editor of* Shakespeare's Songs and Poems *(1959). The following essay on* Hamlet, *first published in 1963, served as the introduction to the edition of* Hamlet *in* The Complete Signet Classic Shakespeare, *edited by Sylvan Barnet.*

1   Tragedy of the first order is a rare phenomenon. It came into being in Greece in the fifth century B.C., where it flourished for a while, and it did not appear again until some two thousand years later when Shakespeare wrote *Hamlet* in 1600. The second incarnation of the spirit of tragedy differs greatly from the first in form and method. In Shakespeare the comic and the serious are not disassociated. His brightest moments pass quickly into shadow, and laughter often illuminates his darkest scenes. The comic and the tragic stand side by side, giving us a fuller view of the thing observed, neither canceling out the other. A hallmark of Shakespeare's mature work is its simultaneity, the presentation of things and their opposites at the same time. Coleridge called him "myriad-minded." There had been an alternation of the dark and the light in English drama almost from the beginning, but it remained for Shakespeare to make each a part of the other. He was able to do so because he knew that the difference between comedy and tragedy has nothing to do with subject matter. Each is a way of looking at life. Neither gives us a total view of life, nor does Shakespeare in his use of both; but he approaches totality more closely than any other dramatist.

2   In *Hamlet* we laugh at the affected and superficial Osric (this is a lightening before the storm), and we are amused by the garrulous Polonius, whose inadequate worldly wisdom stands in contrast to the deeper truths the play reveals. But the most central use of comedy is Hamlet's mordant wit. His

> Thrift, thrift, Horatio. The funeral baked meats
> Did coldly furnish forth the marriage tables   (I.ii.180–81)

emphasizes his revulsion at his mother's hasty remarriage. His near-hysteria after the Ghost makes its revelation underlines the degree to which the revelation has disturbed him. The audience may laugh at things such as these, but the laughter is not merry. And there will be no laughter at all when, at the close of Hamlet's interview with his mother, he drags the body of Polonius to the exit, remarking, "I'll lug the guts into the neighbor room." Then he pauses at the threshold to say, "Good night, Mother." And he says it with all the tenderness he has, for she has looked into her soul and repented, and in the contest with the king she is now on Hamlet's side. Mother and son are again at one. Bringing this about has been the essential business of the scene, and the dragging of the body (though the body must somehow be removed) is in no way necessary to it. Yet this bit of grotesquerie adds to the multiplicity of the scene's effects without in any way detracting from its deep seriousness.

3   It was Aristotle's belief that a well-constructed plot should be single in issue, and that if any one action were to be displaced or removed, the whole would be disjointed and disturbed. The action of *Hamlet,* however, is far from single in issue, and the play can be judiciously cut for presentation on the stage without serious disturbance of the whole. Shakespeare's plays were so cut in his own theater. The First Folio version of *Hamlet* is based upon the acting version of the play, and it omits some two hundred lines, chiefly reflective passages, which are found in the second quarto. These lines include the soliloquy beginning "How all occasions do inform against me" (IV.iv.32–66). The scene is richer if the soliloquy is included, but its absence does not significantly change the play as a whole. Another passage omitted from the acting version is Hamlet's discourse (I.iv.17–38) on the heavy drinking done in Denmark and the effect of it on the reputation of the Danes. The speech adds little to the action, but in its movement from the particular to the general it helps give the play extension. This is not to suggest that Shakespeare's plays are not unified, but their unity is clearly not Aristotelian.

4   In a tragedy the hero normally comes to the realization of a truth of which he had been hitherto unaware. There is, as Aristotle has it, "a change from ignorance to knowledge"; but in Greek tragedy this may be little more than the clearing up of a mistaken identity. Not so with the tragedies of Shakespeare's maturity. In *Hamlet* and *King Lear,* for instance, there is a transformation in the character of the hero. Toward the close of his play Lear is the opposite of what he had been at the beginning. He has been purged of his arrogance and pride, and the pomp and circumstance of kingship, on which he had placed great store, is to him no more than an interesting spectacle. What matters now is the love of the daughter he had rejected in the first scene. When we first meet Hamlet he is in a state of depression. The world to him is "an unweeded garden" from which he would willingly depart. He has found corruption not only in the state but in existence itself. We soon learn that he had not always been so. Ophelia tells us that he had been the ideal Renaissance prince—a soldier, scholar, courtier, "the glass of fashion and the mold of form." And though we catch glimpses of his former self in his conversations with Horatio, his state of depression continues. By the final scene, however, his composure has returned. He no longer appears in slovenly dress; he apologizes to Laertes, and he treats Claudius with courtesy up to the point at which Gertrude's death discloses the king's treachery and compels him to the act of vengeance.

5   All this is not simply a return to Hamlet's former self. In the course of the action he has grown in stature and wisdom. He is no longer troubled by reasoning doubts, for he knows now that reason is not enough. An overreliance on reason and a belief in untrammeled free will are hallmarks of the Shakespearean villain; the heroes learn better. In the beginning of the final scene Hamlet is still beset from without and within—"thou wouldst not think how ill all's here about my heart; but it is no matter." And it does not matter,

because he has now come to put his trust in providence. Earlier in the scene he had said,

> Our indiscretion sometime serves us well
> When our deep plots do pall, and that should learn us
> There's a divinity that shapes our ends,
> Rough-hew them how we will.   (V.ii.8–11)

This is not, as has been said, "a fatalist's surrender of his personal responsibility." It is the realization that man is not a totally free agent. With this realization Hamlet can face the fencing match and the king's intrigues without concern for self. What matters at the end of an important tragedy is not success or failure, but what a man *is*. Tragedy of the first order moves into the realm of the human spirit, and at the close we contemplate the nature of man. In this respect Shakespeare and the Greeks are the same, but they reach the end by widely divergent paths. We may consider the path which Shakespeare took.

6   Early in his career Shakespeare served an apprenticeship to Christopher Marlowe, but he soon surpassed him, and he took the journey from *Romeo and Juliet* to *Hamlet* on his own. His first so-called tragedy, *Titus Andronicus,* is not a tragedy at all. It is a blood-chilling thriller, and, as a recent production at Stratford-upon-Avon demonstrated, an effective one. The management had to have attendants at the theater to minister to the patrons who fainted as the play's horrors were revealed. A like response to tragedy is impossible. Melodrama such as *Titus* uses horror and grief as entertainment, bringing them as close to the spectator as it can. Tragedy uses them as truth. These, it says, are part of our human heritage, and we must face them. And in the end, partly because they are faced, they lose their terror, and the tragedy passes beyond them. It is not surprising, then, that the greatest tragedies are those involving the greatest horrors, for facing a great horror demands greatness of spirit. This greatness of spirit is what we contemplate at the end of a Shakespearean tragedy. At the close of the tragedy we are not so much concerned with Hamlet or Othello as individuals as with the spirit of man triumphant in defeat.

7   Shakespeare's next attempt at tragedy brings him to the borders of the tragic realm. There is much macabre action and humor in *Richard III,* but the horrors are moral as well as physical, and there is an approach to self-recognition in the remorse Richard feels on waking from his ghost-haunted sleep. This is no longer, or at least not altogether, horror as entertainment. In this play Shakespeare mastered and improved upon Marlowe's techniques. In *Richard II* there is, no doubt, a general indebtedness to Marlowe's *Edward II.* Both kings are weak men who come to a tragic end. Toward the close of Marlowe's play we sympathize with Edward because he is the underdog and because the people who surround him are worse than he, but toward the end of *Richard II* we sympathize with the king because adversity has moved him to a kind of self-realization. There is an approach to the recognition scenes of the later tragedies. Shakespeare has brought his weak and self-willed king to a recognition, if only for a time, of his mortality and the humanity he shares with others. Later, Shakespeare was to do this profoundly with Lear. Here he shows us both power politics at work and

a transformation in Richard, and in his characterization of Richard he shows us how the transfer of power to Bolingbroke was possible without Bolingbroke's being a villain. He eschews comedy and physical action, not, we may be sure, out of any disregard for them, but because other matters came first. At this stage of his career Shakespeare was not able to do at one time all the things that needed to be done. He was later to do so in *Hamlet.* In *Richard II* the primary matters are character and theme. There are impressive tableaux, but there is no action comparable to that of the earlier so-called tragedies.

8   There is more onstage action in *Romeo and Juliet,* and almost all of it is integral to character and theme. The hero and heroine meet, fall in love, mature through adversity, and find that, for them, love is of more worth than life. Nor is their ordeal in vain. They have their love, and their deaths bring peace to Verona. There is laughter in the play, but it is aroused by comic characters. The principals are serious throughout. But the play's laughter and vulgarities are not by any means comic relief. They contribute to a background of lust and hatred against which the story of the young lovers stands in contrast. Besides, Shakespeare's romance is never pure; it is always rooted in reality. It is never in danger of "falling upward, as it were, into vacuity." There is a notable mingling of the comic and the serious in Mercutio's death scene. It has comedy, pathos, and irony, all at once—a promise of things to come. Shakespeare seems never to have viewed things simply, and as soon as he acquired the skill, he made contraries and varying aspects of the same thing stand side by side, nothing canceling anything else out. And so it is here. Mercutio's flippancy in no way reduces the pathos and irony of his death.

9   After *Romeo and Juliet* Shakespeare turned to comedy and the completion of the historical tetralogy he had begun with *Richard II.* The last of this series, *Henry V,* is a fine play of action with England as its subject and England's national hero as its hero, yet it seems to have brought Shakespeare to a dead end. He was at the height of his success and popularity, but he seems not to have been satisfied with the play. He apologizes, and directly too, for the inability of his theater to present the panoply of war. He refers to his stage as "this unworthy scaffold," and to his theater as "this cockpit," "this wooden O," and he begs the audience to imagine what cannot be shown them. Yet in his next serious play he uses the oldest of dramatic conventions—a few soldiers on either side of the stage representing contending armies—without apology. For with this play the essential thing is not the action itself but the idea that it embodies. In *Julius Caesar* the essential thing, the dramatic thing, is the spirit of man, and this can be portrayed without pageantry. What is needed now are words. What matters now is not so much what a man *does* but what he *is.*[1] Brutus is the precursor of tragic heroes to come. As he is brooding on the outcome of the Battle of Philippi, he says,

> O, that a man might know
> The end of this day's business ere it come!
> But it sufficeth that the day will end,
> And then the end is known.   (V.i.122–25)

---

[1] In this paragraph I am indebted to "From *Henry V* to *Hamlet,*" by Harley Granville-Barker, in *Aspects of Shakespeare* (1933).

It might be the voice of Hamlet before the fencing match: "If it be now, 'tis not to come...." In *Richard II* there is no comedy; now, in *Julius Caesar,* there are only a few comic puns early in the play. First things first. But although *Julius Caesar* was Shakespeare's most important achievement to date, it has, perhaps, too great a separation of action and idea. What was needed was a fusion of the two, and this he achieved in *Hamlet.*[2]

10   *Hamlet* has onstage action in God's plenty. A ghost walks the stage; people are killed by stabbing and poisoning; a young woman runs mad, is drowned off-stage, and is buried on stage; two skeletons are dug up and scattered over the stage; armies march, and there is a fencing match that ends in a general slaughter. Yet one scarcely thinks of *Hamlet* as a play of action. There is some comedy, but it is most often used to intensify the serious matters to which it is germane. There are indecencies that were *not* put into the play to please the groundlings. They are the opposite of those employed at the opening of *Romeo and Juliet* to command attention. Hamlet's remarks to Ophelia early in III.ii (the scene of the play-within-the-play) reveal once more his disillusionment with women, and the indecencies of Ophelia's mad songs complete her characterization. Uninhibited in her madness, in a notable anticipation of modern psychology she sings about sex and the father who had dominated her while he lived. To be sure, the play is sometimes diffuse. Everyone is given to generalizing, even the wretched Rosencrantz and Guildenstern. It is, of course, necessary to generalize on the action, and Shakespeare succeeds in doing so; but in the later tragedies he was to do it more compactly. In *Hamlet* Shakespeare was writing tragedy of the first order for the first time, and perhaps he could not be intellectually aware of how to do it until he had once done it, for he had no models to show him the way. (What little he knew of Greek tragedy was through Roman or other adaptations.) In any case, he knew, in 1600, the heights tragedy could achieve, and he was to achieve them again in the next great tragedies—*Othello,*

---

[2]*Hamlet* was first published in 1603. The play is not mentioned in Francis Meres's *Palladis Tamia* (1598), which includes a list of Shakespeare's works. Since Meres mentions so minor a work as *Titus Andronicus,* he would have hardly omitted *Hamlet* had it existed. And it is almost certain that the *Hamlet* played by Shakespeare's company in 1594 and 1596 was not Shakespeare's, for he probably was not yet capable of writing the *Hamlet* we now know; nor is it likely that he revised the story over the better part of a decade, for he worked fast, writing his entire works in the time it took James Joyce to write *Finnegans Wake.* But there is other evidence to narrow the gap between 1598 and 1603—a definite allusion to Shakespeare's *Hamlet* in a note written by Gabriel Harvey in his copy of Speght's edition of Chaucer, published in 1598. Such a note might have been written any time between the publication of the book and Harvey's death in 1631, but in the same note he refers to the Earl of Essex in the present tense. Since Essex was executed on February 25, 1601, it appears that the note was written while Essex was alive and before he made his mad attempt to seize the person of the queen on February 7, 1601. During the fall of 1598 and the following winter, Essex was busy preparing his ill-fated foray into Ireland. He returned in September of 1599. Harvey's reference was therefore presumably made between the autumn of 1599 and early 1601, and it is during that time that *Hamlet* was written. The best date is 1600, which is confirmed by a consideration of Shakespeare's other activities. In 1599 he had rounded out his cycle of history plays with the writing of *Henry V.* He had recently written *The Merry Wives of Windsor* (to please Queen Elizabeth, as tradition has it), and he had completed *Julius Caesar.* He seems to have been looking for new worlds to conquer. He turned to comedy for a while, producing *As You Like It* and *Twelfth Night.* Then came the most important play he had yet written, *Hamlet.*

King Lear, and *Macbeth.* There is a saying that Shakespeare never repeats. In most respects it is not true, but it is true that he never repeated his successes. The four great tragedies are as different from each other as plays of the same genre by the same author could be.

11   In each of the plays the hero is transformed into something he had not been at the beginning of the play. He recognizes that he is other than he was, but in *Hamlet* the recognition scene is not explicit. Hamlet emerges from his state of depression, and if he did not the play would be a study in pathology rather than a tragedy; but we do not see him emerging from it as we see, for instance, the change taking place in Othello's speech beginning with "Behold I have a weapon…" (V.ii.259–82) or in Lear's prayer for the poor:

> Poor naked wretches, wheresoe'er you are,
> That bide the pelting of this pitiless storm,
> How shall your houseless heads and unfed sides,
> Your looped and windowed raggedness, defend you
> From seasons such as these? O, I have ta'en
> Too little care of this.   (III.iv.28–33)

In this speech Lear is the opposite of the arrogant, unfeeling man he had been at the opening of the play, and we are told that he is. Shakespeare liked to be explicit when he could be. At the end of his play, Hamlet, too, is very different from the man who had earlier longed for death, and contemplated suicide. There is no more "fighting" in his soul; like Lear on his way to prison, he is at peace.

12   The movement toward Hamlet's regeneration begins with his reflections on the Player's speech about Hecuba; it advances further in the closet scene, and it reaches its culmination in the gravediggers' scene. Although this scene is crowded with action, it is essentially a meditation on the inevitability of death. It begins lightly enough for such a scene, but it grows steadily more serious, more general, and more personal—more personal to Hamlet, and through its increasing generality more personal to us—until in the end it transcends the macabre. At the opening of the scene it is disclosed that someone presumed a suicide is to be buried. Her name is not mentioned, but we know who she is. After some talk about her right to Christian burial, there is a conundrum: "What is he that builds stronger than either the mason, the shipwright, or the carpenter?" And the answer: "a gravemaker. The houses he makes lasts till doomsday." Hamlet and Horatio enter as the digger breaks into a song about advancing age. In the course of the song he digs up a skull, and Hamlet comments on it: "That skull had a tongue in it, and could sing once. How the knave jowls it to the ground, as if 'twere Cain's jawbone, that did the first murder!" Or it might be "the pate of a politician," or a courtier, or "my Lord Such-a-one…. And now my Lady Worm's, chapless, and knocked about the mazzard with a sexton's spade." While Shakespeare is thus generalizing about the fact of death, another skull is dug up. It turns out to be the skull of Yorick, the king's jester, and the generalization becomes personal: "I knew him, Horatio, a fellow of infinite jest, of most excellent fancy. He hath borne me on his back a thousand times. And now how

abhorred in my imagination it is! My gorge rises at it." Here the scene passes beyond comedy, and Shakespeare tells us so: "Where be your gibes now? Your gambols, your songs?… Now get you to my lady's chamber, and tell her, let her paint an inch thick, to this favor she must come. Make her laugh at that."

13   Hamlet's remarks on the bones are his last comment on the discrepancy between appearance and reality. He is coming to accept reality for what it is. Then as the generalization continues, a funeral procession enters, and Hamlet learns who is to be buried today. He has seen the body of an old friend dug up to make room for the body of the woman he loves. He has looked on death at what is for him its worst. It is after the graveyard scene that the man who had continually brooded on death is able to face it. It seems axiomatic that any horror becomes less horrible once we have looked squarely at it. When we see Hamlet again he can defy augury, for the augurs can foretell only such things as success or failure; but there is nothing, except himself, to prevent a man from facing his own private horror and rising above it. And so it is with Hamlet. When Horatio offers to cancel the fencing match "if your mind dislike anything," he is able to reply, "Not a whit, we defy augury. There is special providence in the fall of a sparrow. If it be now, 'tis not to come; if it be not to come, it will be now; if it be not now, yet it will come. The readiness is all. Since no man of aught he leaves knows, what is't to leave betimes? Let be."

14   "Readiness" here means both submitting to providence and being in a state of preparation. It is not that death does not matter; it matters very much indeed, but readiness matters more. Shakespeare's tragic heroes do not renounce the world. The dying Hamlet is concerned about the welfare of the state and his own worldly reputation. Such values are never denied, but at the end of the tragedies they are no longer primary values. At such moments the central thing is the spirit of man achieving grandeur.

Review Questions

1. How does Shakespearean tragedy, as epitomized in *Hamlet,* differ from classical tragedy, according to Hubler?

2. Hubler points out (paragraph 5) that in moving us "into the realm of the human spirit" and self-knowledge, Greek and Shakespearean tragedy have the same purpose, but they employ different means to achieve this purpose. What does he mean?

3. What is the difference between a "so-called tragedy" like *Titus Andronicus* and a tragedy like *Richard II,* according to Hubler?

4. In what significant way did *Hamlet* represent an advance in dramatic art over Julius Caesar, according to Hubler?

5. What qualities, according to Hubler, link the tragic heroes of Shakespeare's great tragedies—*Hamlet, Othello, King Lear,* and *Macbeth?*

Discussion and Writing Suggestions

1. To what extent are you familiar with Shakespeare's *Hamlet* ? Have you read the play, seen it performed on stage, seen one or more film versions? Explain.

2. Before your reading of Hubler's critical analysis, what was your impression of *Hamlet* and of its protagonist?

3. What makes *Hamlet* a tragedy—other than its sad ending? What, for you, is the significance of the action? What would you say is the central theme of *Hamlet?*

4. If you have read some of the other Shakespearean tragedies that Hubler discusses, to what extent do you agree with his assessment that *Hamlet* represents an advance in the art of tragedy over *Romeo and Juliet* and *Julius Caesar?*

5. If you have read one or more of Shakespeare's later tragedies, to what extent do you agree with Hubler's contention that the protagonists of *Hamlet, Othello, King Lear,* and *Macbeth* are similar (whatever their other differences) primarily in the transformations of character they undergo and in the grandeur they achieve in coming to "accept reality for what it is"?

6. Hubler's yardstick for great tragedy involves the protagonist's achieving a degree of self-knowledge and an acceptance of the world in the process of a significant transformation of character. (Hubler also suggests that in great tragedies, comedy—or at least a comic view of the world—co-exists with tragedy.) To what extent do you find such protagonists in the works of other authors— whether playwrights, novelists, or filmmakers? To what extent do you agree with Hubler's implicit contention that the works featuring such protagonists represent the highest achievement in narrative/dramatic art? Can you cite examples of plays, novels, or films that do not contain such characters but which you nevertheless believe should be ranked highly (if not as highly as *Hamlet*) as art? What, in your view, justifies such high ranking?

Shakespeare and Nonverbal Expression
Jack Jorgens

For some, filmed Shakespeare is inherently debased Shakespeare because film is essentially a visual medium while theater is essentially a verbal medium. A recent critic charged that Kenneth Branagh's Hamlet, *despite retaining all the words of the Shakespeare's text, "actually weakens the script through accompanying visual narratives." The critic objected to Branagh's occasional "pantomimes" in which what the character says is accompanied by a corresponding image: "Presumably, the pantomime is intended to add vitality to the speech, but I would argue that it competes for the audience's attention and thereby diminishes the force of Shakespeare's language."* *

Grigori Kozintsev, director of a celebrated 1964 adaptation of Hamlet, *expresses a different view. A filmed version of Shakespeare, he says,*

> *shifts the stress from the aural to the visual. The problem is not one of finding means to speak the verse in front of the camera, in realistic circumstances ranging from long-shot to close-up. The aural has to be made visual. The poetic texture itself has to be transformed into a visual poetry, into the dynamic organization of film imagery.*†

Paradoxically, writes Jack Jorgens, in Kozintsev's own film version of Hamlet, *the filmmaker "repeatedly demonstrates how a collaborator can be true to the original by altering it."*‡

In the following selection from his book Shakespeare on Film *(1977), Jack Jorgens, professor of literature at The American University in Washington, D.C., illustrates how the visual and aural elements of film enhance the spectator's understanding and appreciation of Shakespeare's plays, not by subverting, but rather by illuminating the meaning of the playwright's words.*

1 There is nothing more *un*-Shakespearean than a film which relies solely on the poetry for its power, unity, and meaning. The words are always important, for on film, as on stage, the actors are like musicians performing a verbal score—badly in the case of [Max] Reinhardt and [William] Dieterle's *Dream,* superbly in the case of [Peter] Hall's. Part of the interpretation will always rely upon the actors' readings—shifts in rhythm and emphasis, pitch and volume—as they mold their parts, build and release tension over the whole arc of the role. A simple pause can force us to anticipate, adjust, reconsider. An unexpected inflection can hint at a flow of emotions and ideas which reveal the meaning of their lines. The very quality of the voice—Marianne Faithfull's worldly, sophisticated Ophelia versus Jean Simmons's timid, innocent one; [Richard] Burton's virile, authoritative Hamlet; Olivier's sighing, melancholy Prince; and [Nicol] Williamson's nasty, snarling nasal one—shapes our response to the character and hence to the play. We can never spend too much time and effort listening to the words—their patterns and meaning.

2   But in films, as in live performances, there is so much more. Plays "mean" in hundreds of nonverbal ways not often stressed in criticism or the classroom. We perceive the words in the context of gestures, costumes, groupings, and movements. The meaning of the action is colored by its setting and the object

---

*Kathleen Lundeen, "Pumping Up the Word with Cinematic Supplements." *Film Criticism* 24.1 (1999): 60.

†*Shakespeare,* 1971. Ed. Clifford Leech and J. M. R. Margeson. Toronto: Toronto UP, 1972. Qtd. in Jorgens: 10.

‡Jorgens, *Shakespeare on Film.* Indiana: Indiana UP, 1977: 13.

involved in it. On the screen, the way lines, shapes, colors, and textures are arranged affects our response, as do music and nonverbal sounds, montage, and the structuring of the action beat by beat, scene by scene. These things communicate "the psychological, physical or sociological realities that lie behind, and not infrequently enrich or deny, the more conscious interchanges of speech."[1] Much of the freedom, the creativity allowed collaborators with an "open" playwright like Shakespeare lies precisely in this fleshing out and orchestration of the nuances of the language and dramatic action.

Gestures

3   Shakespeare thought in terms of eloquent gestures as well as eloquent speeches: Macbeth shattering a festive banquet with shrieks and a drawn sword, Othello putting out the light, Lear kneeling mockingly before Regan for raiment and food and later in earnest before Cordelia for forgiveness, Romeo tossing off the poison as a toast to his love. But a sensitive director will always complement these with other gestures which illuminate a dramatic moment, reveal the meaning of the words, define relationships, or establish a contrast or parallel.[2] Olivier as Richard III locates the point at which his controlled energy becomes uncontrolled when, in an unnecessarily emphatic demonstration of what is to be done to the young Princes in the Tower, he nearly smothers the man who is to do it. In [Tony] Richardson's *Hamlet* a passionate kiss between Laertes and Ophelia shows how the disease of incest has spread outward in the court from the King and Queen. In [David] Bradley's *Julius Caesar* a close-up of flowers being trampled on the marble steps foreshadows the general destruction to follow. Even where Shakespeare has provided the gesture, the actor must articulate it: one Othello stares at the handkerchief in disbelief, another is tortured by its softness and sweet smell, still another tears it in his teeth like a wild animal.

Costume

4   Costume, an extension of the actor's body, is really another form of gesture. It communicates not only sex, age, social class, occupation, nationality, season of the year, and occasion, but subjective qualities—moods, tastes, values. Costumes speak to an audience through line, shape, color, and texture. Often Shakespeare gives some direction—Hamlet's suit of mourning, Osric's foppish hat, Malvolio's yellow stockings—but again much is left to the performing artists. [Orson] Welles makes great comic capital out of the incongruous sight of Falstaff drifting across the battlefield like a huge armored blimp. It is not only his movement but his flowing robes that set Othello apart from the Venetians. Changes in character are often signalled by shifts in dress—Juliet or Ophelia appearing in mourning, Hamlet in a travelling robe, Lear in rags, the young Athenian lovers

---

[1]John Russell Brown. *Shakespeare's Plays in Performance*. Cambridge: Cambridge UP, 1967: 41.

[2]See Arthur Colby Sprague's *Shakespeare and His Actors* (Cambridge, MA: Harvard UP, 1944) and subsequent books for much interesting information on the stage business of Shakespeare's plays, much of which carries over into films.

in the *Dream* in muddy, torn parodies of the civilized, freshly laundered apparel of the opening.

Faces

5   [Ingmar] Bergman once said "our work in films begins with the human face."[3] Despite the complaints of insensitive viewers about the boredom of "talking faces," in many of the best Shakespeare films it is the expressiveness of those faces, controlled from within by the actors and from without by makeup and lighting artists, that generates much of their power: the ferocious mask-face of Washizu in [Akira Kurosawa's] *Throne of Blood,* the obscene grins of Polanski's witches, the immobile brutal faces of Goneril, Regan, and Cornwall in Brook's *Lear.* Recall too the fresh, innocent faces in Zeffirelli's *Romeo and Juliet,* Joe E. Brown's deadpan Flute, Mickey Rooney's Pan-like Puck, Welles's Father Christmas Falstaff, and various incarnations of Gertrude's beauty gone to seed. Quite apart from casting and facial expression, faces are photographed in a great variety of ways: from the front, the rear, or in profile, distorted by reflections and shadows, masked by bars, veils, flames, armor, and "beetle brows." Faces are rouged and powdered, glisten with sweat, are dirty or bloodied. They appear upside down, sway back and forth, are fragmented by the edges of the frame, and all of these things affect the meaning of the dramatic moment.

Groupings

6   Spatial arrangements and relationships, on stage and on film, are metaphoric. To be spatially in between is to be caught in conflict—Gertrude between Claudius and Hamlet, Romeo between Mercutio and Tybalt, Desdemona between Othello and Brabantio. As Othello and Desdemona become estranged in Welles's film, the distances between them become huge. Movements away from one character and toward another often announce a shift in allegiance, as when the lords hastily abandon Hastings when they realize Richard intends to kill him. Rapid regroupings signal confusion, as in the mob in *Julius Caesar* or the lovers in *Dream* who do a kind of dance in which they constantly change partners. Film is capable of capturing larger movements, like the fine assassination scene in Mankiewicz's *Julius Caesar,* where after swimming from blow to blow and wiping the blood from his eyes, Caesar staggers down steps toward Brutus only to receive the fatal thrust. Film far surpasses the stage in portraying the charge and countercharge of battle scenes.

Movements

7   Despite the capacity of theatergoers to "zoom in" on a detail, however, film also has more power to make small movements and relationships huge and important. On film, a glance or the nervous flutter of a fan may be as striking as a forty-foot leap. Motion in films is also complicated by the fact that the camera can move and the focal length of the lens can change, placing the characters,

---

[3]Quoted in Lawson, Film: *The Creative Process,* p. xxii.

setting, objects, and camera in an intricate dance. Distance, perspective, and relationships can change with the fluidity and subtlety of a line of verse. Static theatrical space becomes dynamic. The rhetoric may be very strong, as when the camera races along with charging troops, wanders the halls of Elsinore, or rushes toward Hamlet as he spies the ghost in Kozintsev's film. Or it may be "invisible" as we move with an actor, including or excluding elements of setting, light, or color, shifting tempo to comment quietly on the action.

Settings

8   As in poetry and fiction, rooms, buildings, streets, and landscapes may be saturated with ideas, associations, and emotions in film. Realist or expressionist, settings may reinforce or counterpoint with action, character, themes, and verbal styles. The pastoral scene behind Orsino as he sighs out his melancholy to Viola underscores the distinctly forced, literary quality of his love in Fried's Russian *Twelfth Night.* The innocence of the young children playing outside the cathedral in Castellani's film contrasts with Juliet's new seriousness and maturity as she seeks the Friar.

9   Sometimes the worlds of Shakespeare's plays are single—Denmark in many films is a political, psychological, and philosophical prison, puzzling, unknowable, sinister. Brook's Lear inhabits a world of unrelieved darkness and primitiveness which may conflict with Shakespeare's renaissance language and court but which unquestionably contributes to the intensity of the work.[4] [Renato] Castellani's *Romeo and Juliet* takes place in a beautiful but stifling Verona, emblematic of an old civilization built on rivalry and materialism which imprisons and eventually destroys innocence and love.[5] The exterior of Macbeth's castle in [Orson] Welles's film suggests Faustian aspiration, but inside it is a solipsistic world of dizzying heights, jagged rocks, moonscapes, gnarled dead trees, fog, and Rorschach-test floors from which there is no escape. Sometimes the plays have two worlds and the films elaborate the conflicts between the two: the kingdom of Falstaff versus the kingdom of Henry IV; the daylight world of Theseus and the nocturnal world of Oberon; Venice and Cyprus. In his lush color imitation of Welles's *Othello,* Yutkevitch created a film which, from the splendid shots of the ghost ship under the titles to Othello's death on the ramparts of Cyprus, is saturated with images of the sea, demonstrating that a motif can work as powerfully in setting as it can in poetry.

Props

10 In Shakespeare's plays, props often carry great symbolic weight, but once again it is up to his collaborators to articulate and complement what is indicated explicitly in the text. In Welles's *Macbeth,* the awkward, oversized, horned crown

---

[4]See James Naremore, "The Walking Shadow: Welles' Expressionist *Macbeth," Literature/Film Quarterly* 1 (1973), p. 361.

[5]See Paul A. Jorgensen, "Castellani's *Romeo and Juliet:* Intention and Response," and Roy Walker, "In Fair Verona," both reprinted in Eckert, *Focus on Shakespearean Films.*

blends the Satanic theme with the poetic theme of ill-fitting clothes. In [George] Schaefer's film there are two crowns: a crown of thorns mockingly given Macbeth by the prophetic witches, and the jewelled symbol of the power which Macbeth cannot keep from passing on to Banquo's sons. In Polanski's version, the crown is part of a circular motif which runs through the entire film, from the circle inscribed in the sand by the witches, to the iron collar around Cawdor's neck, to the huge shield at Macbeth's coronation, and the ring to which the baited bear is chained. In [Peter] Brook's *Lear,* the throne is a coffinlike stone enclosure which isolates the King, makes his voice boom out at his subjects, and prefigures death. In Kozintsev's film, it is a huge chair which dwarfs the wispy, white-haired King, who sits on its edge like a child.

11   Occasionally such effects are obtrusive and unsubtle: Duncan riding through a herd of sheep as he goes to be sacrificed at Macbeth's castle, Othello wandering distracted among picturesque classical ruins which are an emblem of his own ruined grandeur. Often, however, they enrich our understanding. In [Franz Peter] Wirth's *Hamlet,* Polonius's monocle reveals both his pretentiousness and his figurative blindness. The flaring flame as Lady Macbeth burns Macbeth's letter reflects her inner fire in Schaefer's film, and the skull-like oil lamp on the table as Antony, Octavius, and Lepidus determine which of their enemies must die underscores the grisly nature of their work in Bradley's *Julius Caesar.*

12   Consider the various uses of the bed in Shakespeare films. In Olivier's *Hamlet* it is a rather abstract symbol, overstuffed, decorated with labial curtains, helping to emphasize the Oedipal nature of Hamlet's conflict. [Tony] Richardson's film shows the bed as a "nasty sty" where overweight Claudius and pallid Gertrude drink blood-red wine and feast with their dogs on greasy chicken and fruit. In films of *Macbeth,* beds connote sterility, brutality, perversion, in *Othello* altars for sacrifice, symbols for love covered with shadows or fragmented by the frame. While in Zeffirelli's *Shrew* the bed is a playful battleground, in *Romeo and Juliet* it is associated with the funeral bier. Not only do words and acts speak in Shakespeare films. *Things* speak.

Composition

13 From one perspective, the camera selects and records things in front of the lens, the most important variables being the apparent distance from the subject (are we involved or detached? do we see individual details or the larger pattern?) and the angle of view. From another perspective, film is a graphic art in which the artist composes images with light and shadow, color and texture, shape and line, within a rectangle. Within shots we "read" a hundred different variables which work on us more or less simultaneously and often carry conflicting messages. Welles makes us *see* the sound of the trumpets in *Othello* by creating a harmony of diagonal lines and bell-shaped mouths. When Richard III's shadow fills the frame or a lens distorts his face as he moves near the camera, we *see* his egotism and warped personality. The formal beauty of the shot in which Washizu kneels beside a rack of arrows before going to kill his lord in *Throne of Blood* suits the cool ironic tone of the film and contrasts vividly with the scene in which he is slain violently with arrows. In *Macbeth,*

Welles uses silhouettes throughout the entire film. Characters and objects are very frequently shown with the source of light behind them, as if they had passed over to a realm beyond light with their dark side forward. A variation of this is seen in the partial lighting of people and things, the constant suggestion that only part of the truth can be seen, only part of the real nature of a person noticed.[6]

Olivier consistently associates Ophelia with light. And as with lighting, colors can clarify conflicts (Capulets against Montagues, English versus French), signal shifts in tone (the draining of color from Zeffirelli's *Romeo and Juliet*), establish an overall atmosphere, or create associations.

Editing and Juxtaposition of Images

14 Composition is a complex tool in film since it also involves creative use of *montage,* the juxtaposition of image with image. If *within* a shot Polanski may contrast the external beauty of Lady Macbeth, her red hair blowing against an intense blue sky, with her voice-over prayer for cruelty enough to kill Duncan, if [Grigori] Kozintsev may set Lear's royal commands ("Know that we…") against a shot of Lear playing with the fool by the fire, if Zeffirelli in *Taming of the Shrew* may place the wedding guests in the top half of the frame and dogs gnawing hungrily on bones in the bottom half, *between* shots the possibilities are infinite. Those who find the written word more expressive and subtle than the visual image might consider the number of meaningful contrasts possible between two shots—contrasts of one color with another, stability with instability, a large pattern with a small detail, one rhythm with another, obscurity with clarity, light with dark, stasis with movement, and a hundred other such juxtapositions. Much of the explosiveness of Shakespeare's verse, Peter Brook has pointed out, results from montage. Words and images constitute many messages, "often crowding, jostling, overlapping one another. The intelligence, the feelings, the memory are all stirred…." Using "free verse on the open stage enabled him to cut the inessential detail and the irrelevant realistic action: in their place he could cram sounds and ideas, thoughts and images which make each instant a stunning mobile."[7]

15 Entrances in Shakespeare often duplicate shock cuts: "Enter Lear, with Cordelia in his arms"; (upon Duncan's expression of amazement at his complete trust of Cawdor) "Enter Macbeth." No wonder then that filmmakers use montage extensively. The filmmaker may seek a comic effect, as when in *As You Like It* Paul Czinner dissolves from the ludicrous, mustachioed, melodramatic villain, Oliver, to the wiggling posterior of a swan; or he may underscore the unity of a mood, as when Welles, in *Chimes at Midnight,* dissolves from rebels hanging motionless from gibbets to the solitary, sick king, and from sleepless Henry, hemmed in by huge stone columns and peering out through barred windows, to his melancholy son Hal before a stagnant, glassy pond. He may estab-

---

[6]Skoller, "Problems of Transformation…," p.419.

[7]Introduction, Peter Weiss, *Marat/Sade* (New York: Pocket Books, 1966), pp. 5–6.

lish a parallel, as when Welles, in *Othello,* dissolves from jealous Bianca, clutching the handkerchief, to Desdemona, worried about its loss; or he may reveal unspoken thoughts, as when in Schaefer's version Macbeth registers the prophetic nature of his act as he hands the scepter and crown to Banquo, who in turn hands them to a young boy.

16   Often scenes are punctuated by associative pairs of shots. Schaefer dissolves in successive shots from Macbeth's brutal kiss of Lady Macbeth to the murderers waiting for Banquo (one of them whittling a stick), linking sex and violence; from dead Banquo's bloody face to the roast pig brought in to the banquet being held in his honor; from Ross's whispers about armies on the way from England (cause) to Lady Macbeth staring out the window at the dawn and Macbeth guzzling wine (effect); from Macbeth resolving to execute each violent thought to the aftermath of such thoughts; and from the burning Scottish village strewn with bodies to England with its sunlight and green trees. But often, in much more subtle ways, such associations and comments are made within scenes as well.

Music

17 From the days of so-called silent films, music has been used to underscore or counterpoint with the tempo and rhythms of physical motion. It has been used to clarify dramatic conflicts, create moods, give a sense of period, provide unity, bridge transitions, punctuate bits of business, and heighten meaning and effect in scores of less easily verbalized ways. Shakespeare himself often used music brilliantly in his plays—Iago's drinking song and Desdemona's willow song, Titania's lullaby, the gravedigger's song—and the filmmaker may simply follow the playwright's directions. Shakespeare has provided another kind of musical accompaniment in his plays however, the music of the words, which has not always received kind treatment in films. Subtle verbal harmonies are often obliterated by the heavy syrup of cliché movie music. Similarly, it sometimes seems that the director is striving with full orchestra to provide the emotional power which his actors cannot. Castellani's *Romeo and Juliet* and [Sergei] Yutkevitch's *Othello* serve quite well to illustrate both faults. They help us understand Brook's decision to strip *King Lear* of musical hyperbole, and help us appreciate critical pronouncements that "additional music has more frequently proved a hindrance than a help in conveying the dramatic poetry."[8]

18   Nevertheless, William Walton's music for *Henry V* is very successful in underscoring the film's great variety of visual styles. Nino Rota's boisterous "Where is the life that late I led?" captures Petruchio's character and the dramatic moment perfectly. And Miklos Rosza's careful development of separate themes for each major character contributes much to Mankiewicz's *Julius Caesar.* There is no hindrance in the obscene rasping pipes which accompany the play within the play done in *commedia* style in Richardson's *Hamlet,* the festive ceremonial music by Walton which dies off in Olivier's *Hamlet* when the observers realize the duel

---

[8]Charles Hurtgen, "The Operatic Character of Background Music in Film Adaptations of Shakespeare," *Shakespeare Quarterly* 20 (1969), p. 53.

is in earnest, and the ironic religious music of Olivier's *Richard III.* Even more powerfully ironic are the angelic chorus which is juxtaposed with the shrieks of wounded horses, clashes of iron, and cries of pain in the battle scene of *Chimes at Midnight,* the sour bag-pipe music signalling the presence of the witches in Polanski's *Macbeth,* and the haunting chants of the chorus and forest spirit in *Throne of Blood.* And in at least two instances this side of opera and ballet— Reinhardt and Dieterle's *Dream* with Mendelssohn's music, and Kozintsev's *Hamlet* with Shostakovich's score—films heavily saturated with music succeed in part because of it.

Nonmusical Sounds

19 Finally, to round out our survey of nonverbal expressive means in realizing Shakespeare on film, let us consider an element used less creatively than almost any other—nonmusical sounds. It has been said that they "have almost no place in the presentation of Shakespeare."[9] Yet Shakespeare's own company used many acoustical "props"—owls, clocks, cannon, tolling bells, battle sounds, crowing cocks, thunder, and so on.[10] Many of the most memorable moments in Shakespeare films are inextricably bound up with such sounds: the crackling of the flames as Lady MacDuff stares in wordless horror at her slaughtered children in Polanski's *Macbeth,* the hollow thud of the gravedigger's hammer as he nails on the lid of Ophelia's coffin in Kozintsev's *Hamlet,* the slam of the massive door which seals in Othello and Desdemona in Welles's film. Welles is often acclaimed for his acoustic artistry because sound in his films is often highly subjective: the dripping noises in the cave in *Macbeth* which suddenly accelerate madly, the soft, slow, irregular ringing of the alarm bell which greets Macbeth's call to arms (Seyton's body is swaying from the bell rope). His *Othello* includes the fine aural collage of celestial chorus, thunder, pounding waves, mandolins, wind, a clanking alarm bell, shouts, barking dogs, and notes from a harpsichord which serve as a transition from Venice to Cyprus, and the blend of laughing soldiers and whores and the cries of gulls as Othello wakes from his fit and stares up at the ramparts.

20   The sheer power of discreetly heightened "natural" sounds often creates meaning as well. There is a grim rightness in sensual Gertrude's horrible, panting death in Richardson's *Hamlet.* The battle which we hear but never see under the fog at the beginning of Polanski's *Macbeth* suggests a brutality and ferocity that literal images seldom achieve. Sounds in Castellani's *Romeo and Juliet* often articulate tomblike spaces eloquently, such as the echoing clank as Romeo smashes a huge iron candlestick on the cathedral altar, or the grinding sound of the tomb lid as Romeo pries it off, suggesting the weight of the forces working to separate the lovers. The birds shriek with laughter as the lovers make fools of themselves in Hall's *Dream.* Whether expressionist, as in the rush of

---

[9]Ibid., p. 57.

[10]See Frances Shirley, *Shakespeare's Use of Off-Stage Sounds* (Lincoln: University of Nebraska Press, 1963), though of course all his nonverbal sounds were not off-stage.

water at the moment of Roderigo's death in Welles's *Othello,* or realist, as in the crunching sound of a knife piercing bone as Macbeth kills Duncan in Polanski's film, nonmusical sounds are often important interpretative tools.

Style

21 To speak with precision and understanding about style in Shakespeare films, we must go far beyond categories which divide films according to their relative distance from the language of poetry and the theatre or which measure in some simpleminded way the relative distance of the film from the original play. We must gauge the truth of the actors' performances and the power of the director's aural and visual images, which often must be thought of as free translations, cinematic equivalents, or re-creations rather than attempts at transparent presentations of Shakespeare's poetic and theatrical images. We should always seek the *why* of filmic techniques, ask how they are integrated into overall patterns which constitute a significant style appropriate both to the spirit of Shakespeare's work and to the collaborative artist's vision. (Clearly the same cinematic style could never suit both *As You Like It* and *Hamlet.*) Shunning pedantic fervor, we should ask how the restructuring from play to film constitutes an interpretative act—inquire in such a manner that we learn about both play and film. (Is it true that all good films stress physical action and plays stress emotional and reflective reaction? Is it more effective on film to show the killing of Duncan, or to leave it to our horrible imaginings?) Style describes many things—acting style, the personal themes and techniques recurring in a particular filmmaker, the genre and period of the play, the proportion and relation of verbal to visual meaning, and much more.

22 In its largest sense, however, style deals with the integration of all expressive effects. Peter Brook praised Kozintsev's *Hamlet* precisely because his "structure is inseparable from his meaning." The film is "a search for over-all meaning as opposed to the many and varied, sometimes dazzling, attempts to capture on the screen the actor-manager's view of the play as imagery, theatricality, passion, color, effects."[11] A unified style need not imply simplistic narrative clarity, reductive concepts, or a single level of dramatic illusion. The strength and truth of the play within the play in Richardson's *Hamlet*—a parodic event in which Claudius becomes a red-nosed clown, Elsinore a flimsy cardboard castle, the cuckolding of King Hamlet a game of sexual leapfrog between the Queen of Hearts and her two royal studs, and the murder as a festive dance around the Maypole turned grotesque as the King is strangled in the brightly colored streamers and the self-crowned murderer leaps into the Queen's arms—its strength and truth is its duplicating in terms of visual style the insane discord in Hamlet's mind. Stylistic truth and unity come from the overall vision of the actors and the film artist. Said Orson Welles,

> With me the visual is a solution to what the poetical and musical form dictates. I don't begin with the visual and then try to find a poetry or music and try to

---

[11] Peter Brook, "Finding Shakespeare on Film," in Eckert, *Focus on Shakespearean Films,* p. 37.

stick it into the picture. The picture has to follow it. And again, people tend to think that my first preoccupation is with the simple plastic effects of the cinema. But to me they all come out of an interior rhythm, which is like the shape of music or the shape of poetry. I don't go around like a collector picking up beautiful images and pasting them together.... I believe in the film as a poetic medium...poetry should make your hair stand up on your skin, should suggest things, evoke more than you see. The danger in the cinema is that you see everything, because it's a camera. So what you have to do is to manage to evoke, to incant, to raise up things which are not really there.[12]

Discussion and Writing Suggestions

1. Jorgens begins his chapter on nonverbal expression by acknowledging the importance of verbal expression, offering several examples from Shakespearean films (versions of *Midsummer Night's Dream* and *Hamlet*). Compare and contrast the verbal delivery of a particular speech from *Hamlet* in two of the Hamlet films treated in this chapter (e.g., the "To be or not to be" speech; Polonius's advice to Laertes; Hamlet's advice to the players). Note how each actor's delivery tends to support a particular interpretation of the character or a particular interpretation of the scene in which the speech occurs. To what extent do the two actors' respective deliveries suggest differing interpretations of the role or the play?

2. Select one of the following nonverbal elements discussed by Jorgens: gestures, costumes, faces. Compare and contrast the use of the element you select in corresponding scenes from two or more of the *Hamlet* films treated in this chapter.

   For example, how do Hamlet's gestures in the play-within-the-play sequence illuminate each filmmaker's treatment of the action at that point? Or, compare and contrast the costumes worn by the ghost or by the fencers in the final scene. Or, compare and contrast the facial reactions of Ophelia in the "nunnery" scene, or of Claudius as he watches the play.

3. Select one of the following nonverbal elements discussed by Jorgens: groupings, movements, settings. Compare and contrast the use of the element you select in corresponding scenes from two or more of the *Hamlet* films treated in this chapter.

   For example, what is the spatial relationship between the players and the audience in the play-within-a-play scene? Where are the spies—Claudius and Polonius—placed relative to Hamlet when he confronts Ophelia in the "nunnery" scene? How does the moving

---

[12]Juan Cobos and Miguel Rubio, "Welles and Falstaff," *Sight and Sound* 35 (Autumn, 1966), p. 160.

camera reinforce the dramatic mood in the final sequences: the duel between Hamlet and Laertes and the speech(es) following the death of Hamlet? What does Elsinore look like, both from the exterior and the interior? How does the architectural design of the castle (or the corporate headquarters, in the case of Almereyda's film) and the Great Hall in which much of the action takes place reinforce the mood of the play (e.g., in the first sequence when Claudius addresses the court, then Laertes, then Hamlet)? Contrast the varying visual impressions of Ophelia's drowning.

4. Select one of the following nonverbal elements discussed by Jorgens: props, composition, montage (juxtaposition of images). Compare and contrast the use of the element you select in corresponding scenes from two or more of the *Hamlet* films treated in this chapter.

   Compare and contrast, for example, the images of Yorick's skull in two or more versions of *Hamlet* or the weapons used by Hamlet and Laertes in their duel. Compare and contrast the images in two or three of the adaptations in which we see Hamlet for the first time. What does the ghost look like when he reveals that he was murdered? How is Hamlet's reaction revealed? How does the camera focus upon Hamlet relative to Claudius when the prince comes upon the king praying after the play sequence? How do the opening and closing shots of each of the films you select reinforce the theme and dominant mood of these films? How do juxtaposed contrasts in color schemes in Almereyda's *Hamlet* indicate dramatic conflicts?

5. Discuss the use of music and nonmusical sounds in one or more of the *Hamlet*s treated in this chapter. Examples: the beating-heart sound of the ghost in Olivier's film; the barking dogs in the scene where Claudius urges Hamlet to cast off mourning in Zeffirelli's film; Patrick Doyle's musical score in Branagh's film, particularly just before the intermission.

6. In the final section of his chapter on nonverbal elements in Shakespearean film, Jorgens considers the various visual and aural elements he has been discussing as components of a unified cinematic style for a particular film. He quotes Orson Welles to the effect that cinematic style must "come out of an interior rhythm, which is like the shape of music or the shape of poetry." Select one of the film *Hamlet*s considered in this chapter. To what degree do you find a coherent, even "poetic" style to convey this particular filmmaker's vision of *Hamlet?* Discuss some of the component elements of this style—e.g., the actors' delivery of particular speeches or lines; the use of gesture, costume, composition, montage, music, and nonmusical sounds to convey the director's sense of the "overall meaning" of *Hamlet.*

[**Note:** To help stimulate your thinking on this and the previous questions, we include here part of Jorgens' own analysis of the visual style of Laurence Olivier's *Hamlet*. Editors.]

Visual Style in Olivier's *Hamlet*

1   Olivier's choice of an abstract setting and unusual shooting style has let him in for some harsh criticism, not merely from critics of the realist school who detest film artifice of all kinds, but from those who address the proper question: "stylization for what?"

> Laurence Olivier tried desperately hard to give *Hamlet* (1948) a worthy visual style, but, as Renoir remarked of its barn-sized sets and deep focus compositions, "you feel dizzy when you look down from a great height? So what? What has that got to do with Shakespeare?" The style *confuses* the issue.[1]

But despite some lapses, Olivier did find a significant style for the play as he viewed it. The heights in the film are not meaningless exercises in vertigo. They are linked to Hamlet's sense of disorientation, to the ghost and to godlike knowledge, and to freedom and aspiration as opposed to the world of compromise, deception, and imprisonment below. The wandering camera not only reinforces Hamlet's disturbed mental state, it links things associatively, as the mind does when moving from thought to thought. Like Hamlet, the camera is on a quest for a meaningful pattern—one which it ultimately finds in the journey at the end of the film.

2   Just as with amusing literalness some critics complained that Olivier's "geography doesn't make sense" when they tried to "sketch a floor plan of the castle,"[2] many assumed that his modulations into a theatrical look and feel were evidence that he had lost control, that his filmic skills were breaking down and that he was falling back on his experience in the theatre. But the theatricality of the various platforms and "scenes" in this composite set (modelled, like the Elizabethan stage, on man's mind as well as on his universe)[3] was deliberate and serves to underscore Shakespeare's use of the "world as stage" metaphor in the play. Hamlet's problem, like the players', involves the paradoxical relationships between word and act, reality and fiction. The play within the play is but one of the many instances in which, knowingly or unknowingly, characters act out scenes for other characters: the ghostly apparition appears to the men on the ramparts; Hamlet observes the court as a hollow pageant, the courtiers applauding Claudius's performances with gloved hands; Polonius is a spectator to Hamlet's scenes with Ophelia and Gertrude (when he attempts to enter the latter, he is stabbed through the curtain—enter Polonius, dead). And Hamlet and

---

[1]Raymond Durgnat, *Films and Feelings* (Cambridge, Mass.: M.I.T. Press, 1971), p. 49.

[2]*Harper's* 197 (Sept., 1948), p. 117.

[3]See Frances Yates, *Theatre of the World* (Chicago: University of Chicago Press, 1969).

Laertes, like the other courtiers, are caught up in a final deadly play, a ritual-ized combat which, like the harmless fiction of "The Murder of Gonzago," sud-denly takes on grisly reality. Words like "show," "act," "seem," "apparition," "shape," "painting" echo throughout *Hamlet*. While the blatant theatricality of Olivier's *Henry V* and *Richard III* reinforces theme only in certain scenes, here it is bound up with the meaning of the whole.

3   A moving camera implies a shifting point of view, and *Hamlet* is above all a play of ambivalent and shifting points of view. We become the ghost drifting down into the castle or sweeping behind a pillar in the closet scene. We become Hamlet instructing the players from off-frame or looking with blurred sight at the waves breaking below. We become Ophelia looking down a long corridor at Hamlet or (her dress of madness touchingly resembling a wedding gown) studying her distracted face reflected in a stream. Olivier's play-within-the-play scene is an epiphany affirming that significance shifts with the per-ceiver; it is a graphic illustration of the subjective nature of reality. As the spectators observe a stylized, mimed murder set to music, the camera slowly travels in a large semicircle behind them, allowing us to see the play from the points of view of Ophelia, the courtiers, Hamlet, Claudius, Gertrude, Polonius, and Horatio. The pantomime becomes in turn a mystery, an exciting fiction, a boring puppet show, an open threat by Hamlet against the king, and a night-marish revelation of a real murder. The moving camera, taken by many as a gimmick to make a stagey work seem filmic, is a symbol of the impossibility of fixity in a world of flux. The characters have no being, but are constantly in process. Hamlet becomes something quite other than the "glass of fashion and the mold of form." Honor-conscious Laertes becomes the willing tool of a cor-rupt king. Sweet Ophelia becomes a tousled whore singing bawdy songs. And guilt eats away at the passion of Gertrude and Claudius until, like Lady Macbeth and Macbeth, they are a torment to each other. No single image, verbal for-mulation, or position of the camera can capture the truth about such persons in process. Says mad Ophelia, "Lord, we know what we are, but know not what we may be."[...]

4   The imagery of Olivier's film, like its conception of Hamlet's world is relatively unsophisticated. Montage between shots is hardly used,[4] save for a few blatant examples such as the dissolve from Gertrude's bed to Claudius swilling wine. Rather, meaning is generated *within* shots: the head of Hamlet's shadow falls upon Yorick's skull (foreshadowing death, and linking him with the role of fool), the ghost seems to rise out of Hamlet's head as it reveals the murder, Claudius and Gertrude slowly ascend stairs to separate rooms while reading Hamlet's let-ters, signalling his success in parting them. Occasionally properties link charac-ters—the wine cup of Laertes as he gives advice to Ophelia, associating him with Claudius, and the Player Queen's blonde wig revealing the link in Hamlet's mind between Gertrude and Ophelia—and changes of costume are used to some

---

[4]Stressed by Donald Skoller, "Problems of Transformation in the Adaptation of Shakespeare's Tragedies from Play-Script to Cinema," Ph.D. dissertation, New York University, 1968, p. 296.

effect. But on the whole, *Hamlet* is a very spare film. There are occasional powerful images—the jagged outline of the steps cutting into Hamlet's figure as he
ascends to his mother's room; Hamlet's torch filling the screen at the climax
of the play scene when Claudius cries "give me light"—but Olivier generally
seeks power through the acting (uniformly competent but nowhere brilliant),
camera movement, set design, and blocking rather than in striking composi-
tions. When the director does consciously compose—as in the tableau of theatrical emblems, the dying king encircled by the spears of his own guards,
Ophelia in the sunlight with pastoral landscapes glimpsed beyond, or floating
down the stream in a Rossetti-like image, the insets of the murder superim-
posed over the ghost's description, or the fight of the two ships over Hamlet's
letter—he is less effective than when the camera floats through the castle,
moves around the characters, or captures them in motion. Save for periodic dissolves into Hamlet's face, iterated images of spying and theatre, thrones, the
bed, recurring crosses (Hamlet's sword, the grave markers, Hamlet's entrance
in the graveyard scene and final leap with arms outstretched), and rounded
shapes associated with Gertrude and Ophelia,[5] recurring visual motifs are few.

5   Though as a visual director Olivier is overfond of tableaux, he often suits physical movements to the rhythms and meanings of the lines in interesting ways.

Laurence Olivier's *Hamlet*

A week before its simultaneous previews in Manhattan and Hollywood, Laurence Olivier's
Hamlet *was the subject of a long cover story in the June 28, 1948 issue of* Time. *"It can be
said of Olivier's version," wrote the anonymous author, "that it contains no single unquestionably great performance, but a complete roll call of fine ones; that it is worked out with
intelligence, sensitivity, thoroughness and beauty, that it has everything which high ambition,
deep sobriety and exquisite skill can give it." After discussing Olivier's particular conception
of the play and the performances of the main actors (with particular attention to the 18-year-
old Jean Simmons, who played Ophelia), the writer concluded: "A man who can do what
Laurence Olivier is doing for Shakespeare—and for those who treasure or will yet learn to
treasure Shakespeare—is certainly among the more valuable men of his time." Olivier's*
Hamlet *went on to win the Academy Award for Best Picture of 1948 (beating out John
Huston's* Treasure of the Sierra Madre, *now generally considered the better film).*

*Such accolades—respectful, if not ecstatic—are indicative less of the film's inherent qualities
(which are considerable) than of Hollywood's long-standing desire to be perceived as "serious" and of its penchant for making and honoring "prestige" films like* Gandhi *(1982),*
Dances With Wolves *(1990), and* The English Patient *(1996). Olivier himself (see next selec-*

---

[5]Noted by Robert Duffy in a paper delivered at the Modern Language Association Seminar,
"Shakespeare on Film" (1974), and to appear in *Literature/Film Quarterly.*

tion) thought that his histrionic style of acting was not well suited to the meditative Hamlet, and in his book On Acting, he gives his performance only qualified praise: "Whatever people may have thought of my Hamlet, I think it was not bad. I know it was not perfection, but it was mine. I did it. It was mine. " (The Motion Picture Academy was more enthusiastic, voting Olivier Best Actor of 1948.) Perhaps what was not so much his was the film's visual style: in another anonymous review entitled "Citizen Dane," appearing in Harper's Magazine, the reviewer pointed out the considerable debt that Hamlet (with its moving camera, its deep focus photography, and its dramatic use of shadows and black and white contrasts) owed to Orson Welles's Citizen Kane, made seven years earlier.

A good deal of the commentary on Olivier's film focuses on the cuts required to get the playing time down to a manageable length of two and a half hours. (Even on stage Hamlet is almost always cut, since the complete play takes more than four hours to perform—the length of Kenneth Branagh's unique uncut version.) Rosencrantz and Guildenstern were entirely cut, as was Fortinbras, who in Shakespeare's play provides a political context for the action. A number of Hamlet's soliloquies are also eliminated, including "O what a rogue and peasant slave am I" (II.ii 560–617) and "How all occasions do inform against me" (IV.iv 32–66). As a result, noted the Time reviewer, Olivier's Hamlet "loses much of the depth and complexity which it might have had." In his essay "Text-Editing Shakespeare" (in Hamlet: The Film and the Play [1948]), Alan Dent, Olivier's collaborator on the screenplay, writes:

> How comes it that I, who dislike Shakespeare being cut, in the theater, by so much as a single obscure line or a single bawdy syllable, can nevertheless hack the masterpieces with utter lack of compunction when it comes to making a film out of any one of the plays. Probably because I possess—and no doubt here I flatter myself—a true conception of the fundamental difference between the two mediums. Also because I possess—and here I do not particularly flatter myself—a strong North-country practicality or common-sense, which makes me aware that the translation from stage or screen cannot be made without loss.

Laurence Olivier (1907–1989) was perhaps the most celebrated stage and screen actor of his generation. Born in Surrey, England, he began acting on stage as a child, performing his first speaking role at age 15 in The Taming of the Shrew. In 1937 he joined the Old Vic theatrical company where he performed the lead in numerous Shakespeare plays—including Hamlet, opposite his wife, Vivian Leigh, in a performance staged at Elsinore Castle in Denmark. During this period, he also became a successful film actor, starring in such Hollywood productions as Wuthering Heights (1939), Rebecca (1939), and Pride and Prejudice (1940).

In 1944 Olivier became co-director (with Ralph Richardson) of the Old Vic and continued to perform Shakespeare, as well as the works of other playwrights from Sophocles to George Bernard Shaw. During this period he not only acted in but also directed several Shakespearean films—not only Hamlet (1948), but also celebrated productions of Henry V (1944) and Richard III (1955). Olivier was knighted in 1947. In 1950 he became director of his own theatrical company, and from 1962-73 he was director of Britain's National Theatre. His other well-known films include The Entertainer (1957), Othello (1965), Sleuth (1972), Marathon Man (1976), and The Boys from Brazil (1978). His television appearances include roles in Long Day's Journey into Night (1973), Love Among the Ruins (1975), Cat on a Hot Tin Roof (1976), Brideshead Revisited (1982), and King Lear (1983). Olivier's autobiography, Confessions of an Actor, was published in 1982; his On Acting appeared in 1986.

The following cinematic outline of Olivier's Hamlet was written by Jack Jorgens and appears in his book Shakespeare on Film (1977).

Cinematic Outline
Jack Jorgens

Hamlet (1948)

Produced and Directed by Laurence Olivier

Laurence Olivier—Hamlet

Basil Sydney—Claudius

Eileen Herlie—Gertrude

Jean Simmons—Ophelia

Felix Aylmer—Polonius

Terence Morgan—Laertes

Norman Wooland—Horatio

Peter Cushing—Osric

Anthony Quayle—Marcellus

Edmond Knight—Barnardo

John Laurie—Francisco

Stanley Holloway—Gravedigger

1. [0:00] Titles over waves pounding rocky shore at the foot of the castle in swirling mist. Boom slowly in toward castle from dizzying height. Olivier (voice-over): "So oft it chances in particular men / That through some vicious mole of nature in them, / By the o'ergrowth of some complexion / Of breaking down the pales and forts of reason, / Or by some habit grown too much: that these men—/ Carrying, I say, the stamp of one defect, / Their virtues else—be they as pure as grace, / Shall in the general censure take corruption /From that particular fault." Boom in on soldiers bearing Hamlet's body. Olivier (voice-over): "This is the tragedy of a man who could not make up his mind." The men on the tower disappear into the mist.

2. (1.1) [2:55] *The Ramparts.* Bernardo climbs spiralling stairs, is challenged by Francisco. Horatio and Marcellus arrive, and they sit to talk of the ghost. Loud heartbeat. They whirl to see crowned, bearded ghost in mist with visor half covering his face. Cock crows, ghost vanishes. Guards search, resolve to tell Hamlet.

3. (1.2) [9:10] *Great Hall.* Camera travels down stairs, past two empty thrones in dark hall, up and rapidly in on Gertrude's bed. Dissolve to Claudius drinking from goblet as courtiers laugh. Claudius addresses courtiers, Laertes, Hamlet. Gertrude tries to rouse Hamlet from his sorrows and melancholy.

Claudius scolds him, announces he is next in succession. All leave but Hamlet, who wanders to empty thrones thinking (voice-over) "Oh that this too too solid flesh...."

4. (1.3) [19:20] *Polonius's Apartment.* Camera glides through archway to Ophelia's reading letter from Hamlet. Laertes advises that "best safety lies in fear," and in turn receives advice from his doddering father as Ophelia fully toys with him. Laertes gone, Polonius reinforces Laertes' advice. Ophelia looks at Hamlet through archway, is called in.

5. (1.2) [24:48] *Great Hall.* Hamlet watches Ophelia go in. The shadows of Horatio and guards appear; they tell him of the ghost. Hamlet walks to empty thrones: "foul deeds will rise...."

6. (1.4) [29:30] *Ramparts.* Hamlet peers over the edge to the sea. Guards pace. Sounds of Claudius's revels below provoke Hamlet to speak against drunkenness. Heartbeat as shot of Hamlet goes in and out of focus. Ghost appears, Hamlet follows to the top of the tower where it tells him of murder, adultery, incest (inset of masked dumb show of poisoning of King Hamlet). Ghost disappears and Hamlet passes out. He wakes, vows revenge, makes others swear secrecy.

7. (2.1) [44:25] *Ophelia's Room.* Ophelia narrates (voice-over) disturbed Hamlet's entrance to her room, peering into her eyes, exit.

8. (2.2) [46:30] *Great Hall.* Polonius interrupts Claudius kissing Gertrude to reveal Hamlet's love for Ophelia. Hamlet above overhears plan to loose Ophelia to him, enters more obviously and mocks senile Polonius, exits. Polonius and King spy as Ophelia prays. Hamlet abuses her, hurls angry threats at arras, pauses to kiss hair of weeping Ophelia, exits. Worried spies come out.

9. (3.1) [1:01:00] *Ramparts.* Camera sweeps up stairs. Orchestral and visual flourishes during "To be or not to be." Exit into fog.

10. (2.2) [1:05:45] *Great Hall.* Hamlet in dark. Polonius announces the actors, reads the genres they have mastered off their playbill. Jovial players enter, Hamlet greets them, sends them with Polonius, asks First Player for "Murder of Gonzago," stares at tableau of instruments, props, costumes, then runs and pirouettes: "The play's the thing."

11. (3.2) [1:08:50] *Great Hall with Stage.* Hamlet instructs chief actor, puts blonde wig on boy, dismisses them and urges Horatio to watch Claudius. Enter courtiers. Hamlet conducts Queen to throne, sits at Ophelia's feet and makes bawdy jokes. Camera wanders behind spectators as the play (all in dumb show) is mimed. Claudius rises, puts his gnarled hands to his eyes, cries "Give me light!" Hamlet thrusts torch near his face, forcing him to flee. Fear and chaos. Wild Hamlet sings standing on throne, tells Horatio ghost was right. Polonius summons Hamlet to Queen. Hamlet alone speaks "Now is the very witching time of night" in dark, prays he will not kill mother, ascends stairs.

12. (3.3) [1:23:20] *King's Chamber.* Polonius announces to King he will spy on Hamlet and Gertrude, exits. Tormented Claudius prays. Hamlet comes upon him, draws his sword, pauses, thinks (voice-over) of doing his enemy good, departs. Claudius finds prayer useless.

13. (3.4) [1:27:35] *Gertrude's Bedchamber.* Polonius urges firmness, hides. Hamlet enters, hurls angry Queen on bed, hears Polonius's cry and thinking it is the King stabs through the arras. He discovers his mistake, pierces his mother's heart with dagger-words, compares portraits of her two husbands, becomes angry and is prevented from violence by presence of ghost (heartbeat, moan). The (to Gertrude) invisible ghost leaves Hamlet to plead once more, kiss and embrace her, and drag Polonius's body away.

14. (4.3) [1:38:05] *Great Hall.* Claudius questions mocking Hamlet about Polonius's body, sends him under guard to England (for execution).

15. (4.5) [1:41:35] *By Stream; Castle Interior.* Ophelia peers at her face in the stream, screams, rushes through her room to the Queen in the Great Hall where she raves. Claudius comes in to hear more ramblings. Horatio follows her off. Gertrude refuses to comfort troubled Claudius. Osric enters with two sailors and Hamlet's letters. King and Queen slowly ascend diverging staircases.

16. (4.6) [1:47:25] *Ophelia's Room.* Horatio watches Ophelia outside, receives Hamlet's letters from sailors. As he reads Hamlet's voice-over description, dissolve to smoke, two ships grappling and parting, Hamlet taken, then back to Horatio reading.

17. (4.5) [1:49:30] *Great Hall.* Ophelia walks through arches to where Laertes, sword drawn, demands to know of his father from the King and Queen. He is shocked as mad Ophelia imagines her father in his empty chair, distributes flowers, kneels at foot of arch, thinks, and exits.

18. (4.7) [1:54:00] *Ophelia's Room; The Stream.* Camera travels into her room. Dissolve to stream. Gertrude's voice-over account as we see Ophelia float by, trailing flowers. The stream with Ophelia gone.

19. (5.1) [1:55:25] *Graveyard.* Gravedigger sings and tosses out skull. With Horatio, Hamlet amused picks up skull, learns it was Yorick's, and philosophizes. A bell rings and they hide as a court funeral procession appears. Grieving Laertes jumps in grave and embraces Ophelia. Hamlet enters, they light. Hamlet declares he loved Ophelia, and exits. All leave but Laertes and Claudius, who leads Laertes out.

20. (4.7) [2:05:30] *Great Hall.* Claudius and Laertes drink and plot against Hamlet, the camera moving up and away three times.

21. (5.2) [2:09:15] *Gallery above Great Hall; Great Hall.* Hamlet praises Horatio's justness and courage. Flighty Osric delivers challenge, falls down stairs. Hamlet speaks of ill about heart. Trumpets and torches as courtiers enter. Hamlet asks Laertes' forgiveness, kisses his mother while Osric gives Laertes an unbated sword. The King promises pearl to Hamlet if victorious. Hamlet wins first pass. Gertrude suspicious of pearl King puts in Hamlet's drink. Hamlet wins second bout. Gertrude seizes cup and drinks despite King's objections. Third bout a draw. Laertes wounds Hamlet from behind. Hamlet attacks, seizes unbated sword, wounds Laertes in the wrist. Queen falls, reveals poison. Hamlet rushes up ramp and orders the doors locked. Laertes reveals he and Hamlet are dead and the King is to blame. Hamlet dives off ramp to Claudius, stabs him repeatedly. Claudius struggles to pick up crown. Soldiers with spears ring him in. He dies by Gertrude. Laertes

dies. Hamlet stands before the throne and all kneel. He sits, asks Horatio to live and tell his story, dies. Horatio orders soldiers to bear Hamlet like a soldier. The camera follows the procession past an archway opening out on the graveyard and showing a firing cannon, past the empty chair with a flower on the arm associated with Hamlet and Polonius, up the stairs past the altar where Claudius prayed, past Gertrude's canopied bed, to the tower where the bearers are silhouetted against the sky. [2:32:40]

Discussion and Writing Suggestions

1. Olivier's opening voice-over—that "This is the tragedy of a man who could not make up his mind," following his reading of lines displayed on screen (Hamlet's words to Horatio and the guards as they await the ghost's appearance on the battlements; I.iv 23–36)—has been the subject of a good deal of criticism. How useful do you think this comment is as an overall interpretation of the play? To what extent do you think that the Shakespearean lines quoted are the key to understanding Hamlet's particular tragedy?

2. How does the ghost's first appearance work cinematically, purely as a horror scene? To what extent does Olivier's use of the moving camera, mist, and music seem "old-fashioned"? How might a more contemporary director handle this scene?

3. After the opening scene on the battlements, the moving camera begins a long, leisurely tour downstairs into various parts of the castle interior. What is the dramatic significance of this transitional sequence? What is the significance of the juxtaposition of shots immediately following this sequence?

4. Cinematically, how is Hamlet first introduced to us? Examine the shot in which we first see him and attempt to deduce Olivier's dramatic intentions at this point.

5. Notice Gertrude's kiss of Hamlet—and Claudius' reaction—after Hamlet agrees not to return to Wittenberg. What is the dramatic significance of this moment for Olivier, the director?

6. Study the staging, the use of cinematography, and the use of sound in the shots portraying Hamlet's first soliloquy ("O, that this too too sullied flesh would melt..."). Discuss Olivier's directorial strategy at this point. To what extent does this sequence help establish Hamlet's character and motivation in the action to follow?

7. Consider the scene where Hamlet is told by Horatio, Marcellus, and Barnardo of ghost's appearances. How does Olivier the actor attempt to deal with the audience's impression that the rational Hamlet may be overly superstitious?

8. What, if anything, does the re-enactment of King Hamlet's murder during the ghost's speech add to the dramatic moment? Why might Olivier have concluded that the ghost's words alone were insufficient, at this point? (Note a similar strategy in the following sequence when Ophelia describes to Polonius how Hamlet came into her room, clutched her in silence, sighed, and then departed.)

9. What is Olivier's purpose in placing the camera where he does when Polonius tells them that he thinks Hamlet is mad? What major visual element does Olivier add toward the end of Polonius' interchange with Claudius and Gertrude, and for what dramatic purpose?

10. What kind of nonverbal means does Olivier use to reveal Hamlet's suspicions that others are spying on his conversation with Ophelia (the "nunnery" scene)?

11. An ascending and descending series of camera shots—from Ophelia lying on the stone steps (end of the "nunnery" scene) to a close-up of the top of Hamlet's head—precedes Hamlet's "To be or not to be speech." Discuss what you think might be Olivier's dramatic rationale for such an unusual visual transition.

12. Discuss the nonverbal means that Olivier uses during the play-within-the-play sequence to reveal the actions and reactions of some of the participants. Focus particularly upon the camera's ever-shifting point of view. If you have seen other screen *Hamlets*, compare Olivier's handling of this scene with that of one or more other filmmakers.

13. During the scene between Hamlet and Gertrude in the latter's bed-chamber, we do not see the ghost, as we did in the earlier scene, though we hear him (and indications of his presence on the sound track) and we see Hamlet's reaction to him. Why do you think Olivier decided to view this part of the scene largely from Gertrude's—and the ghost's—point of view?

14. How does Olivier use nonverbal means to show us the increasing estrangement between Gertrude and Claudius during Ophelia's "mad scene"?

15. Ophelia was thought to have committed suicide. To what extent do the visuals—as well as Gertrude's voice-over—support this conclusion? What do you conclude about Ophelia's death?

16. During the scene when Claudius and Laertes plot the death of Hamlet, Olivier pulls the camera rapidly away from the pair three times. What do you think the director's reason for this repeated camera movement might have been?

17. During the duel scene, how does Olivier make it clear that Gertrude suspects that the wine is poisoned?

18. How does the use of props—goblet, swords, crown—following the swordfight reinforce the story's themes?

19. Discuss the relationship of the traveling shot at the end of the last scene of the film with the traveling shot at the end of the first scene. In what senses do these shots serve as a set of cinematic bookends for the drama?

20. An amusing sequence (8:30–11:00) in John McTiernan's *The Last Action Hero* (1993) parodies Olivier's *Hamlet* by substituting Arnold Schwarzenegger for Olivier against sets resembling those of Olivier's film. Scharzenegger's Hamlet, it goes without saying, is somewhat more decisive—and noisy—than Olivier's. (Hamlet: *[brandishing an Uzi]* Claudius—you killed my fah-ter. *[lights cigar]* Big mistake! *[Blam!]*) View this scene if you are able to rent the film and discuss its comic point. Is it making fun of Olivier or Schwarzenegger? (In an inside joke, the schoolteacher introducing the film to her students is played by Peggy Ashcroft, who was married to Olivier.)

An Essay in *Hamlet*
Laurence Olivier

In his book On Acting *(1986), Laurence Olivier recounts that before he first played the role of Hamlet at the Old Vic, he went to see Ernest Jones, a renowned psychoanalyst and disciple of Sigmund Freud, who was profoundly interested in the play and had written an influential book,* What Happens in Hamlet. *In his book Jones theorized that Hamlet's main problem was that he was suffering from an Oedipus complex. (In Freud's theory, the Oedipus complex—named for the Theban king who unwittingly killed his father and married his mother—is an early stage of male sexual development during which the boy unconsciously wishes to replace his father in his mother's affections—and bed.) For Olivier, Jones' approach to* Hamlet *explained a good deal about the melancholy prince. As he wrote, "Nobody's that fond of his father unless he feels guilty about his mother, however subconscious that guilt may be. Hamlet's worship of his father is manufactured, assumed; he needs it to cover up his subconscious guilt."*

Olivier's fascination with Jones' theory is apparent throughout his version of Hamlet, *in which his mother's bed looms large as a recurring image, and in which it was reputed, many shots were filmed at waist level. Critics have also been fascinated with this particular angle: two articles in a recent issue (April 1997) of Film/Literature* Quarterly *devoted to Shakespeare are entitled "Freud's Footprints in Films of* Hamlet *" and "'In the Rank Sweat of an Enseamed Bed': Sexual Aberration and the Paradigmatic Screen* Hamlets." *Olivier's version is featured heavily in both articles.*

For a brief biography of Laurence Olivier, see the introduction to the immediately preceding "Cinematic Outline." The following selection was first published in The Film Hamlet: A Record of its Production, *edited by Brenda Gross and published in 1948.*

From *The Film* Hamlet: *A Record of Its Production* (1948).

1   When I was making "Henry V" I had thought about a film of "Hamlet," but I had not followed up this idea in any detailed way. When the question of a second Shakespearean film came up, however, "Hamlet" seemed the obvious choice. From my experience on "Henry V," I had learnt that in dealing with "Hamlet," the only real way to solve the problem of adaptation for the screen was to be ruthlessly bold in adapting the original play.

2   I find it very difficult to pin down how and when I first conceived the basic idea for the treatment of the film "Hamlet." Quite suddenly, one day, I visualised the final shot of "Hamlet." And from this glimpse, I saw how the whole conception of the film could be built up.

3   I feel it is misleading to couple Shakespeare's play with the film of "Hamlet," and for this reason. In Shakespeare's play, as in all his plays, there runs a beautifully intricate and complete pattern of character and action. The only satisfactory way of appreciating all that Shakespeare meant by "Hamlet" is to sit down in a theatre and follow a performance of the play in its entirety.

4   The role of Hamlet has always had a great attraction for actors, partly because it is such a long and impressive one, and partly because it is capable of so many and varied interpretations. In the past, actors have played Hamlet according to a number of ideas, and the play has been so cut as to present these different aspects of Hamlet's character.

5   In our editing of the play, so that it would make a film of two and a half hours, instead of a play of four and a half hours, we have worked on the basis of making a new but integral pattern from the original, larger pattern of the play itself. In doing this, we have simplified the story, but inevitably we have lost a good deal.

6   There are so many jewels in "Hamlet" that it is impossible to make cuts in the play without sacrifice. Amongst other characters who play a continuous part in Shakespeare's "Hamlet," we have taken out altogether Rosencrantz and Guildenstern, and also Fortinbras. This is a radical approach to adaptation, and because it is so much more than mere condensation, I feel that the film "Hamlet" should be regarded as an "Essay in Hamlet," and not as a film version of a necessarily abridged classic.

7   From the beginning, we decided that the sets should be planned as abstractions. This linked up with the idea of timelessness which I always associated in my mind with "Hamlet." I saw the costumes as a child might, with the King and Queen looking recognisably regal, rather in a conventional, playing card manner. And the Prince was immemorially clad in the medieval doublet and hose. Ophelia's simplicity was brought out by clothes of almost Victorian innocence.

8   As for the period of the film "Hamlet," it is some time, any time, in the remote past.

9   When we began discussing how to make "Hamlet," it was clear that the methods used for "Henry V" were unsuitable for "Hamlet." In the backgrounds of "Henry V" we had aimed at the effect of missal illustrations. Colour and detail and formally posed figures all combined in making this impression. But in "Hamlet" we wished to achieve the poetic truth ordained by Shakespeare by marrying a sensitive intimacy in the acting to a significant austerity of background.

10   I determined not to let the beautiful medium of black and white be shuffled out of existence by the popular ascendancy of colour on the screen, until
I had explored as thoroughly as possible the beauties and advantages of black
and white, so rarely used for a great subject in recent years. One word, "etch-
ing," has been used, not entirely correctly I think.

11   Colour had been essential for "Henry V." In "Hamlet," I did at one time examine the notion of filming it in subdued colours—blacks, greys and sepias. But on
further consideration, I felt that the final effect would not really have justified the
extra problems which use of the technicolor camera always involves. When we
came back to our decision to use black and white, it had the added immediate advantage, that it could be combined with deep focus photography, whereas we could not have done this had we used colour.

12   Apart from the obvious advantage, for a film in verse, that deep focus photography enabled us to shoot unusually long scenes, it had the extra merit of
lending itself to shots of extreme beauty. I have in mind in particular one shot
nicknamed, "The longest distance love-scene on record."

13   In this scene, Hamlet is sitting in a chair, and through a long series of arches,
he sees Ophelia coming towards him. Unknown to Hamlet, she has been
warned by her brother, and particularly by her father, to avoid the Prince, and
this time, Polonius is hiding behind a pillar. He is invisible to Hamlet, but Ophelia
can see him, and when he beckons her away, she turns aside. But to Hamlet,
and to the audience who see her from behind Hamlet's shoulders, it looks as
though Ophelia has avoided him of her own free will. With the use of deep
focus photography, every line of her figure is beautifully distinct as she walks
slowly down the long corridors.

14   In some cases, an actor is over 150 feet away from the camera, yet with
deep focus he is seen by the audience with perfect clearness.

15   We have purposely planned the film with spacious, empty sets. No piece of
furniture appears on the screen unless it plays a necessary part in the film,
either when it is first seen, or later on in the story. In this way, each piece,
whether table, chair or bed, becomes an object of increased significance, and
makes its own tiny contribution to the general pattern of the film.

16   In film work, my preference is for the job of director. I would have liked to
have found an actor of sufficient standing to carry the role on whom I could
have impressed my interpretation of the character of Hamlet without the actor
resenting it. For myself, I feel that my style of acting is more suited to stronger
character roles, such as Hotspur and Henry V, rather than to the lyrical, poetical role of Hamlet.

17   In the end, I thought it simpler to play Hamlet myself, but one reason why I
dyed my hair was so as to avoid the possibility of Hamlet later being identified
with me. I wanted audiences seeing the film to say, not, "There is Laurence
Olivier dressed like Hamlet," but "That is Hamlet."

18   In the production of the film, I would first of all rehearse the actors in the
appropriate scenes. If Hamlet were included, then I used an "understudy" for
grouping and so on. Then I would rehearse myself, and with Reginald Beck and
Anthony Bushell standing by, with advice and suggestions, the scenes would
be shot.

19   When work on the floor was finished, the film moved to another stage, in the cutting rooms, where Reginald Beck, that erstwhile best of all cutters, and I, still supervised it. It is a mistake to think that a film is virtually finished when the actors go home. A great deal of rarely publicised work goes on, concerned with editing the film, adding sound and visual effects, fitting in the music to the appropriate sequences, and generally arriving at the final copy of the film.

20   In our script of "Hamlet," I believe—and I hope—that we have made the story easy to follow for people who are deterred by Shakespeare himself. The actual story of Hamlet is both fascinating and alive. It cuts cleanly away from the older-fashioned concept of heroism and villainy, where characters are irrevocably black or white.

21   "Hamlet," the greatest of all plays, which has kept commentators enthralled for four centuries, was the first to be created by an author with the courage to give his audience a hero with none of the usual excursions of heroism. Perhaps he was the first pacifist, perhaps Dr. Jones is sound in his diagnosis of the Oedipus complex, perhaps there is justification in the many other complexes that have been foisted on to him—perhaps he just thought too much, that is, if a man can think too much…. I prefer to think of him as a nearly great man—damned by lack of resolution, as all but one in a hundred are.

Discussion and Writing Suggestions

1. Why does Oliver call his film "An Essay in Hamlet"? To what extent do you agree with his contention that "The only satisfactory way of appreciating all that Shakespeare meant by *Hamlet* is to sit down in a theatre and follow a performance of the play in its entirety"? At what point do cuts in this or any other play prevent the audience from appreciating "all that [the playwright] meant"?

   In considering your response, you might want to recall whether you have seen, perhaps on a DVD, any of the "deleted scenes" that have been filmed for an important movie and then cut. (For example, the DVDs for Steven Spielberg's *Close Encounters of the Third Kind* (1977) and Stephen Soderbergh's *Erin Brockovich* (2000) include a number of deleted scenes. Francis Ford Coppola's *Apolocalypse Now Redux* (2001) restores several scenes cut from the original 1979 film.) To what extent do cuts detract from the writer's meaning? To what extent are the playwright's (or screenwriter's) words sacrosanct?

2. Olivier discusses why he thought that color, so necessary to his earlier Shakespearean adaptation, *Henry V,* would not work in *Hamlet,* and why the latter film had to be shot in black and white. To what extent do you agree with his reasoning? Considering that some later *Hamlet*s were, in fact, shot in color, did Olivier make the right decision?

3. In paragraph 12, Olivier discusses one particular shot, which he calls "The longest distance love-scene on record." (The shot—just before the interchange in which Hamlet tells Ophelia to "Get thee to a nunnery," comes from Act III, Scene 1.) Compare and contrast this shot with corresponding shots in other film *Hamlet* s and explain how different directorial choices about how to shoot this sequence create different effects—and perhaps different meanings.

4. Olivier explains that he finally decided to take on the role of Hamlet himself, though he would have preferred to find another capable actor who would be comfortable with the director's interpretation of the character. What do you think of Oliver's performance (and his appearance; note his rationale for dying his hair)? Consider his use of voice and gesture, his facial expressions, his use of pauses, his movements. If you have seen other film versions of *Hamlet,* compare Olivier's performance of the role to that of other actors—perhaps Mel Gibson, Kenneth Branagh, Ethan Hawke.

Review of Olivier's *Hamlet*
Margaret Marshall

When Olivier's Hamlet *was released, the director was in a sense competing against himself: four years earlier, he had directed and starred in a film version of* Henry V *that had earned universal acclaim. (In fact, for 45 years no other director attempted to film* Henry V, *fearing that Olivier had created the definitive cinematic production—until in 1989 the young Kenneth Branagh realized a very different vision of the play, one that was held the equal of Olivier's in imagination and dramatic power.)*

Oliver's Hamlet *was also generally received with high approbation, though some critics were ambivalent about this austere, black-and-white rendition. Reviewers praised the acting, the brooding set of Elsinore (which, some pointed out, made no architectural sense, however dramatically powerful), the fluid and expressive camera movements, and even the extensive cuts that both focused and simplified the action of the play. Olivier's interpretation of* Hamlet, *however—particularly, his Freudian perspective, necessitating an unusually youthful Gertrude (Eileen Herlie, who played Hamlet's mother, was 13 years younger than Olivier)—was sometimes met with raised critical eyebrows.* The following review, by arts critic Margaret Marshall, appeared in the October 23, 1948 issue of* The Nation, *shortly after the film's release.*

1   Watching this motion-picture version, one realizes first of all that Elsinore, both in sound and significance, has always been, for the reader or the spectator, no more—and no less—than a dark, rich, but unfigured setting which heightens the

---

*Sixteen years later Herlie would once again play Gertrude, in a 1964 film version of *Hamlet,* directed by Bill Colleran and John Gielgud, and starring Richard Burton as the prince.

values of the play itself as the black rim of a volcano intensifies the brilliance and heat of the fires burning within. Mr. Olivier has made Elsinore a concrete castle in an actual landscape; and these tangible battlements and steps of stone, this actual wind and sea, dreamlike though they are, inevitably dissipate some of the intensity and continuity of the blaze of passions and of language that is "Hamlet." As a result the play becomes, if I may throw in more images, a sequence rather than a spiral, a stream rather than a maelstrom.

2   I am not at all sure that such plays as "Hamlet" or "Macbeth" or "Lear" can be translated into films of comparable power, but if it is possible then it could be done only by a director who was himself enough of a genius and enough of a revolutionary to disregard all the conventions either of filmmaking or of producing Shakespeare.

3   Mr. Olivier is not that director—as a matter of fact he falls, here, between the two sets of conventions—but I wish to add quickly that his "Hamlet" is nevertheless very much worth seeing and hearing. It is a serious and sincere and beautifully mounted production of a great play; and there are elements in it which might well be incorporated in that perfect film I have posited.

4   I am thinking particularly of Ophelia as she is created by Jean Simmons, under the direction, of course, of Mr. Olivier. I say created advisedly, for both in the play as written and as I have seen it produced—though I have not seen all even of the more recent productions—Ophelia has always seemed to me a two-dimensional lay figure who might have been taken over from allegory. Neither she nor her young love, her madness, and her death seemed real, or central to the story of Prince Hamlet. In this production Ophelia becomes a person in her own right; her suffering is not merely represented by gestures and costume but directly communicated. The performance is in itself very moving. And this realization of Ophelia has effects on the play as a whole. For one thing, it points up the conflict of forces in the character of Hamlet by dramatizing the suffering it inflicts upon another and innocent human being. Again, since Ophelia is a character and not a lay figure, the role of Hamlet's mother is inevitably a little reduced. There are two women in the play, not one. And this effect is emphasized, whether by design or not, by the casting of Hamlet's mother not as the ripe matron of middle age, greedy for life and fearful of old age, but as a rather young woman whose relationship with her son is more than ever ambiguous.

5   Miss Simmons's and Mr. Olivier's interpretation of Ophelia may be "wrong," but it is an exciting and fresh interpretation and it does no violence to the text.

6   Olivier's Hamlet struck me as competent and faithful and a little shallow. He does not plumb the depths either of weakness or of strength in Hamlet's character. As the film opens we are told that "Hamlet" is "the story of a man who could not make up his mind," and at times this rather banal and quite inadequate description appears to have been Olivier's directive for his performance. I liked the device of presenting some of the soliloquies as thought—we hear the voice but the lips are still—though at times one has the impression merely of a close-up too long drawn out.

7   Of the rest of the cast, Polonius and Osric are very good; Horatio and Laertes are adequate; the King is inadequate but not disturbingly so. The gravedigger—there is only one—is funny, but his broad cockney sounds somewhat out of

place in Elsinore. The cuts and telescopings, it seemed to me, have been done with care.

Discussion and Writing Suggestions

1. Marshall begins her review by arguing that the "concrete castle in an actual landscape" of Elsinore portrayed in Olivier's film detracts from the power of the passions and the language of the play. To what extent do you agree with this view?

2. Marshall singles out for praise the performance of Jean Simmons as Ophelia, who "points up the conflict of forces in the character of Hamlet by dramatizing the suffering it inflicts upon another and innocent human being." But then in paragraph 5, she suggests that Simmons's "interpretation of Ophelia may be 'wrong.'" What is your own impression of Simmons's performance and Olivier's dramatic interpretation of the character that this performance implies? If you have seen other Ophelias—for example, Helena Bonham Carter in Zeffirelli's film or Kate Winslet in Branagh's, explain which you prefer and why.

3. Marshall is lukewarm about Olivier's performance as Hamlet. She particularly objects to the voice-over at the beginning of the film announcing that "This is the story of a man who could not make up his mind," complaining that "this rather banal and quite inadequate description appears to have been Olivier's directive for his performance." To what extent do you agree with this assessment? Does this announcement help focus the meaning of the play or does it oversimplify it? If the latter, what alternate description might you provide?

Franco Zeffirelli's *Hamlet*

It's one thing for a Hamlet *film to feature an established Shakespearean stage actor like John Gielgud, Laurence Olivier, Nicol Williamson, or Richard Burton. But when Franco Zeffirelli selected Hollywood action hero Mel Gibson (star of the slam-bam* Mad Max *and* Lethal Weapon *movies) to play the melancholy Dane, eyebrows were raised. Richard Corliss summed up the initial critical smirks in the opening of his* Time *magazine review:*

> *A Hollywood story conference. Suit gets up and says, "I've got a great idea for a Mel Gibson movie. He's this prince among men, strong and sensitive, whose father dies suspiciously, like in* Star Wars. *Next thing, the woman he loves is cozying up to a guy Mel thinks is the murderer, like in* Ghost. *Plus he and his girl friend*

argue all the time, like in Pretty Woman. *It's driving him crazy! Then the girl drowns and he gets blamed for it, like in, I dunno,* A Place in the Sun. *So the girl's broth-er picks a fight with Mel like in the* Rocky *movies. [...] Rants a lot, roughs up his co-stars, kills people. We even have one of those 'make my day' lines for Mel. He gets hold of his rival and mutters, 'O.K., tough guy, ya wanna be...or ya wanna not be?' It's a sure $100 million domestic. Whaddaya say?"**

More dryly, Stanley Kauffmann begins his New Republic *review by remarking, "Mel Gibson's greatest advantage in* Hamlet *is that no one expected much of him."[†] But Zeffirelli surprised the doubters. While few would rank this particular* Hamlet *(1991) with the greatest Shakespearean films, Mel Gibson's robust and often moving performance surprised critics and audiences alike. (Even the hard-to-please Kauffmann conceded, in his next sentence, "Thus the little that he accomplishes is mildly impressive.")*

Zeffirelli's film looks very different from Olivier's. Besides being in color, both the interior and exterior settings of the later film seem more primitive and earthy than those in Olivier's film. Zeffirelli skips the opening scene on the castle battlements (where the sentries discuss the appearance of the ghost) and sets the first interchange between Claudius and Hamlet in the confined crypt where the old king has been laid to rest, rather than in the spacious great hall in Olivier's (and later in Branagh's) film. The costumes seem heavier, as do the weapons. (In the duel scene, Hamlet and Laertes fight with broadswords, rather than with the traditional rapiers.) And what Olivier only suggested about Hamlet's sexual feelings for his mother Zeffirelli makes considerably more explicit.

Franco Zeffirelli (b. 1923) had extensive theatrical experience—and two other Shakespearean films to his credit—before embarking on Hamlet. *Born in Italy, he studied architecture at the University of Florence. In the late 1940s he worked as a scenic designer for Luchino Visconti's operatic productions, and when Visconti began making films, Zeffirelli served as assistant director. In the 1950s he began directing his own productions, including operas (some star-ring Maria Callas) and Shakespearean plays. (In the 1970s and 1980s he would direct pro-ductions at the Metropolitan Opera in New York.) In the late 1960s Zeffirelli became a film director and won acclaim for productions of* The Taming of the Shrew *(1967), starring Richard Burton and Elizabeth Taylor, and* Romeo and Juliet *(1968), starring the then-unknown actors Leonard Whiting and Olivia Hussey. His other films include* Brother Son and Sister Moon *(1972),* The Champ *(1979),* Endless Love *(1981),* La Traviata *(1983),* Otello *(1986) (based on Verdi's opera, rather than Shakespeare's play),* Jane Eyre *(1996),* Tea with Mussolini *(1999),* Callas Forever *(2001), and a TV movie,* Jesus of Nazareth *(1977) (with Laurence Olivier).* Zeffirelli: An Autobiography *was published in 1986.*

Cinematic Outline
Editors

Hamlet (1991)

Adapted and Directed by Franco Zeffirelli

Mel Gibson—Hamlet

Alan Bates—Claudius

"Wanna Be...or Wanna Not Be? Time, 7 Jan. 1991: 73.

[†]The New Republic, *28 Feb. 1991: 24.*

Glenn Close—Gertrude

Helena Bonham Carter—Ophelia

Nathaniel Parker—Laertes

Stephen Dillane—Horatio

Ian Holm—Polonius

Paul Scofield—Ghost

Michael Maloney—Rosencrantz

Sean Murray—Guildenstern

Trevor Peacock—The Gravedigger

John McEnery—Osric

1. [00:00] *Titles over castle on promontory into sea.* Successively closer shots of castle as titles proceed. Tilt down from top of castle, revealing a row of mounted, armored soldiers with lances raised. Pan left, revealing more soldiers. Close-ups of individual soldiers and groups of soldiers.
2. (1.2) [2:13] *Interior of crypt.* Legend—"Royal Castle of Elsinore: Denmark." Pan left, revealing King Hamlet lying in open coffin. Gertrude approaches coffin, overcome by emotion, and is comforted by Polonius, as Claudius observes. A hand gathers dirt from container, throws it on king's body; pan along arm to reveal Hamlet as Claudius speaks. Mourners place lid on coffin; Claudius places sword on lid. Gertrude throws herself on coffin, sobs, observed silently by Claudius and Hamlet. Hamlet walks out of dark crypt, begins to climb stairs leading out.
3. (1.2) [4:55] *Exterior of Castle. Great Hall.* Claudius (voice over at first): "Though yet of Hamlet's, our dear brother's death, the memory be green…" Pan left as nobles whisper to one another as Claudius speaks.
4. (1.2) [6:02] *King's Chamber.* Laertes asks Claudius to allow him to return to France.
5. (1.2) [6:49] *Exterior of Castle. King's Chamber.* Gertrude runs happily to Claudius; they kiss, then go inside to find Hamlet sitting in darkened room. Claudius urges Hamlet to leave off mourning. Claudius exits; Gertrude tries to console Hamlet, who agrees to stay at Elsinore. High angle shot of Gertrude running happily toward her ladies-in-waiting. Cut to Hamlet, alone: "Oh that this too too solid flesh would melt…" Through the window, he sees Gertrude happily embracing Claudius; the two ride off.
6. (1.3) [12:17] *Exterior, Shoreline. Polonius' Chamber. Exterior of Castle.* Laertes bids Ophelia farewell, advises her to be wary of Hamlet. Polonius says goodbye to Laertes, advises him how to behave while abroad, as Hamlet observes from rampart. Polonius reinforces Laertes's advice to Ophelia.
7. (1.2) [16:45] *The Ramparts. A Balcony, inside.* Hamlet greets Horatio, Marcellus, and Francisco. They tell him they have seen the ghost of Hamlet's father.
8. (1.4) [21:00] *Great Hall. The Ramparts.* Camera pans across revelers at banquet, dogs eating scraps off the floor. Hamlet complains to Horatio of the drunken scene. Hamlet reflects: "So oft it chances in particular men…"

Moving camera reveals ghost (not armored). Ghost beckons and Hamlet follows, resisting efforts of the others to stop him.

9. (1.5) [26:40] *Ramparts.* Ghost tells Hamlet about his murder at Claudius' hands. Ghost leaves; Hamlet vows revenge. Banquet scene, from Hamlet's point of view, with Claudius and Gertrude embracing. Horatio, Marcellus, Francisco reappear. On top of battlements, Hamlet's swears them to secrecy about ghost.

10. (2.1) [36:00] *Exterior: Castle. Ophelia's room.* As Polonius observes, Hamlet silently enters Ophelia's room, grasps her hand, stares at her wildly, sighs, and leaves.

11. (2.1) [37:45] *Great Hall.* Polonius reports to Claudius and Gertrude that Hamlet is mad, reads them his cryptic note to Ophelia. He suggests they spy on Hamlet the next time the prince encounters Ophelia. Hamlet appears on balcony, reading a book. Polonius engages him in conversation, standing on ladder to get closer to Hamlet, who, mocking the old man, knocks back the ladder, causing Polonius to fall.

12. (3.1) [44:35] *Great Hall.* Gertrude tells Ophelia she hopes her beauty and virtues will cure Hamlet's madness. Polonius tells Ophelia to walk, as he and the King and Queen withdraw, Hamlet enters; Ophelia attempts to return his gifts. Hamlet notices shadow of one of the spies. He berates Ophelia with being two-faced, and leaves in a rage. Claudius tells Polonius he intends to send Hamlet to England (Hamlet overhears this).

13. (3.1) [49:15] *Crypt.* Hamlet soliloquizes, over the body of his father: "To be or not to be…"

14. (2.2) [53:10] *Exterior: Castle. Hut.* Camera dollies toward rider on horseback. Cut to grazing horse as Hamlet lies on rocks. Other riders—Rosecrantz and Guildenstern—approach. After greeting them, though with some suspicion, he and they ride to country inn, where, over food, his friends confess they were sent for by Claudius. Hamlet tells them of his melancholy. Players ride up in wagon, are greeted by Hamlet. The company rides to castle, where they are welcomed by all. Hamlet tells Polonius to look after players; sees Rosencrantz and Guildenstern report to king. Alone, Hamlet reproaches himself for not taking action against Claudius. Noticing players, he gets the idea to trap Claudius with a play: "The play's the thing/Wherein I'll catch the conscience of the King."

15. (3.2) [1:03:15] *Great Hall.* Hamlet looks over preparing players with satisfaction, asks Horatio to observe Claudius during play. Polonius introduces players to audience. Hamlet asks Polonius about his previous acting experience, then refuses a seat by Gertrude to sit with Ophelia. He is merry with Ophelia but advises her to "Get thee to a nunnery." Player King and Queen swear eternal love to one another. Hamlet tells Claudius the play is called "The Mousetrap." In dumb show, the players re-enact the murder of King Hamlet at Claudius' hands. Claudius drops his goblet, puts hand to ear; others, including Hamlet and player-murderer, observe his reaction. Claudius, dazed, becomes aware of others' staring at him, attempts to laugh it off, shouts, "Give me some light!" and staggers off. To Gertrude's shock, a jubilant Hamlet embraces and dances with players. He exults with Horatio,

then kisses Ophelia goodbye. Rosencrantz and Guildenstern tell Hamlet that Gertrude wants to see him. Hamlet goes off: "'Tis now the very witching time of night…"

16. (3.3) [1:15:38] *King's Chamber.* Hamlet comes upon distraught, praying Claudius, prepares to kill him at last, then decides to wait until later, when king is less prepared to go to heaven.

17. (3.4) [1:17:00] *Queen's Bedchamber.* Polonius hides as Hamlet enters. He berates Gertrude, advances upon her with a sword; when she screams, Polonius makes a movement behind the arras. Hamlet plunges his sword into the arras, pulls it back to reveal the dead Polonius. Hamlet compares for Gertrude the pictures (one in locket around her neck) of her two husbands. As he becomes increasingly enraged—to the point of lying on top of her and simulating sexual movements—Gertrude stops his words with a kiss. Ghost, unseen to Gertrude, reappears to Hamlet. Ghost reminds Hamlet of his "almost blunted purpose," tells Hamlet to comfort Gertrude. Hamlet speaks more gently to Gertrude, asks her not to go to Claudius' bed tonight. Shamed, she agrees. Hamlet drags away Polonius's body.

18. (4.1) [1:26:25] *Queen's Bedchamber. Great Hall.* Gertrude tells Claudius that Hamlet has killed Polonius.

19. (4.3) [1:27:20] *Stairwell. Great Hall.* Claudius questions Hamlet (wearing Polonius's cap) about Polonius' whereabouts. Hamlet reveals where the body lies. Claudius tells Hamlet he is being sent to England. After Hamlet leaves, the king tells Rosencrantz and Guildenstern to accompany Hamlet (they are carrying, unbeknownst to them, warrants for his execution).

20. (3.4) [1:30:10] *Great Hall. Courtyard.* Hamlet tells Gertrude he is aware of the letters carried by Rosencrantz and Guildenstern, and he intends to deal with them as they deserve. He rides away. She watches him from bottom of castle steps.

21. (4.5) [1:31:15] *Ocean. The Ramparts. Great Hall. Courtyard.* Shot of Hamlet's ship sailing on sea. Long shot of castle in rain. Ophelia, mad, emerges from behind rampart, climbs to top battlement, approaches soldier, fingers his face and tunic, while reciting mad phrases. She is led away by another soldier as Gertrude watches from steps. Claudius enters; Ophelia raves to members of court, exits. Claudius tells Horatio to follow Ophelia and watch her closely. In courtyard, Horatio picks up Ophelia and carries her away.

22. [1:37:30] *Ship on ocean. Below deck. England.* Hamlet retrieves Claudius' letters from pouch while Rosencrantz and Guildenstern sleep. Voice-over of Claudius giving death warrant. Hamlet substitutes his own letters in their place. In England the two are dragged to the block; the executioner's ax falls.

23. (5.4) [1:38:50] *Elsinore Battlements. Great Hall.* Pull back from battlements to reveal Laertes riding toward castle. Laertes threatens Claudius, runs into castle, is restrained by soldiers. Claudius speaks soothingly to Laertes, who hears sounds of Ophelia's voice from great hall, beyond. Laertes runs in to find Ophelia, mad, sitting on throne. Ophelia distributes flowers to all. Shocked reaction to her state.

24. (4.6) [1:42:30] *Woods. Stream. Great Hall.* In gully, outside castle wall, Ophelia wanders, through trees, to brook. Gertrude describes her death (at

first, in voice over) to Claudius and Laertes. Overhead shot of stream. Camera tilts up to reveal ocean behind hills.

25. (5.1) [1:44:20] *Graveyard.* Dissolve to Hamlet and Horatio, riding on horse-back. Camera pans from them, across graveyard, to gravedigger, singing song and digging grave. Hamlet questions gravedigger, reflects on skull of Yorick. Funeral procession. Hidden, Hamlet and Horatio observe mourners. Hamlet appears as Laertes says goodbye to Ophelia. Laertes confronts Hamlet, puts hands around his throat; the two are pulled apart. Hamlet declares his love for Ophelia and exits; Gertrude bids Horatio keep watch over Hamlet.

26. (4.7) [1:51:30]. *Corridor and Great Hall.* Claudius and Laertes plot to kill Hamlet, will make his death look like an accident.

27. (5.2) [1:53:28] *Gallery above Great Hall. Great Hall.* Osric tells Hamlet of Claudius' wagering on Hamlet's swordsman skills in a match with Laertes. Hamlet accepts. Horatio is worried, but Hamlet is determined. Claudius and Laertes plot about poisoned sword. Hamlet looks out window, sees sea beating against rocks; shot of setting sun: "The readiness is all." Osric welcomes Hamlet to Great Hall. Laertes sheathes unbated sword (not a rapier). Trumpets. Claudius, Gertrude and retinue enter. Hamlet asks Laertes' pardon. Claudius pours wine. Trumpets again; match begins. Hamlet gets first hit. Claudius drops pearl in poisoned wine. For comic effect, Hamlet pretends to be overcome by weight of sword, winks at Gertrude. After next bout, Hamlet prances merrily, to general laughter, then launches fake sneeze at Osric. Hamlet gets next hit. Gertrude picks up and drinks poisoned wine. Reaction from Claudius. Laertes selects poisoned sword. During next bout, Gertrude begins to feel effects of wine. She looks toward half-empty goblet, realizes that she has drunk poison, looks past goblet to Claudius, who stares back in fear. Third bout ends in draw; as Hamlet turns his back, Laertes cuts his arm with poisoned sword. Surprised, then enraged, Hamlet leaps at Laertes, knocks sword out of his hand, picks up Laertes' sword. The two fight; Hamlet jabs Laertes with poisoned sword. Consternation as Gertrude falls. Queen dies. Hamlet orders doors locked; Laertes reveals plot to Hamlet, blames Claudius, dies. Hamlet pursues fleeing Claudius, stabs him with sword, then forces him to drink the rest of the poisoned wine. Claudius dies. Hamlet kisses dead Gertrude's hand. Hamlet falls, asks Horatio to tell his story and "absent thee from felicity awhile." Hamlet dies. From above, camera pulls back to reveal courtiers circled around Hamlet and Horatio. End titles roll.

Discussion and Writing Suggestions

1. How does Gibson's interpretation of Hamlet seem different from Olivier's? Consider the physical appearance of the two actors, their costumes, the way they deliver their lines, their gestures and movements, the way they act and react, the way they interact with

others. Are the overall conceptions of character, despite surface differences, essentially similar or essentially different? Explain.

2. After an establishing shot of Elsinore castle, Zeffirelli's *Hamlet* begins with the camera traveling past rows of armed soldiers and mourners before moving inside the crypt where the dead king lies in his coffin. We next see Gertrude weeping over the body of her husband. Contrast this opening to the one in Olivier's *Hamlet*, which begins (like Shakespeare's play) on the castle battlements and which is followed by Gertrude's and Claudius' wedding celebration. How do the two films' openings signal different dramatic approaches to the tragedy to follow?

3. Contrast our first view of Hamlet in Zeffirelli's film—a hand casting dirt on his father's body—with our first view of the prince in Olivier's film. How do these contrasting introductory views suggest different dramatic approaches to Hamlet by the two directors?

4. Zeffirelli breaks Shakespeare's (and Olivier's) wedding celebration scene (I:ii) into four separate scenes (counting a brief, wordless exterior scene between Gertrude and Claudius). What do you suppose his strategy for doing this might have been?

5. Compare the visuals in Hamlet's "O that this too too sullied flesh would melt" in Zeffirelli's film with those in Olivier's. How do the two filmmakers attempt to make different dramatic points in this scene?

6. Note Zeffirelli's staging of the scene where Polonius gives advice to Laertes—particularly the setting, the interchanges between Ophelia and Laertes. Contrast this to the staging of the corresponding scene in Olivier's film. What differences do you find? Do you find any significance in these differences?

7. Consider the differences between Zeffirelli's staging of the scene where the ghost tells Hamlet of his murder at Claudius' hands with Olivier's staging of the same scene. Note, for example, what the ghost looks and sounds like, as well as Hamlet's reactions to what he hears, as well as the atmospherics created by each director. To what extent do the two scenes create different effects upon the viewer?

8. During the scene where Hamlet berates Ophelia after she returns his gifts, the camera circles Ophelia, mimicking Hamlet's movements around her. What dramatic purpose is served by such movements?

9. In Olivier's film, Hamlet speaks his "To be or not to be" speech at the very top of the castle; in Zeffirelli's, at the very bottom, in the crypt. To what degree do the different settings affect the dramatic impact of the speech?

10. The scenes where Hamlet meets Rosencrantz and Guildenstern, and then rides to a wooden enclosure to eat with them and meet the players, look something like a classic American western. Why do you suppose Zeffirelli chose to stage the scenes in this manner? How do they further his distinctive approach to *Hamlet?*

11. Contrast the scene in Zeffirelli's film where Hamlet conceives the idea of using the players to "catch the conscience of the king" to the corresponding scene in Olivier's film. How do the differing treatments by the two filmmakers emphasize correspondingly different facets of Hamlet's character?

12. Zeffirelli moves Hamlet's lines urging Ophelia to "get thee to a nunnery" forward to the play-within-the-play scene. What dramatic purpose is served by this transplantation? How does Gibson's delivery of the lines differ from Olivier's?

13. Compare and contrast the staging of the play-within-the-play sequence in Olivier's and Zeffirelli's films. Focus both upon the dramatic elements (Zeffirelli's including more of Shakespeare's dialogue) and the cinematic ones (including reaction shots of various characters in the scene.)

14. Compare Zeffirelli's treatment of Ophelia's madness with Olivier's. How is Helena Bonham Carter's approach different from Jean Simmons'? How do the two films produce contrasting dramatic effects in these scenes? If you have seen Branagh's version, bring Kate Winslett's Ophelia into the discussion. (In the latter case, note the medical "treatment" of Ophelia's madness.)

15. In Zeffirelli's film, the scene where Laertes witnesses his sister's madness is shot primarily in close-ups. In Olivier's film, the scene is shot primarily in long and medium shots. To what extent do the different viewpoints produce different dramatic effects?

16. Compare and contrast Zeffirelli's and Olivier's handling of the scene in which Osric informs Hamlet and Horatio of Claudius' wager.

17. During the duel, Gibson's Hamlet sometimes appears to be putting on his "antic disposition." Why do you suppose Zeffirelli might have chosen to have Gibson play the scene in this way? What dramatic purpose might it serve?

18. Unlike Eileen Herlie's Gertrude (in Olivier's film), who appears to be aware that the wine has been poisoned before she drinks it, Glenn Close's Gertrude (in Zeffirelli's) does not realize this until after she has drunk the wine and begun to feel its effects. Which interpretation do you believe is more dramatically persuasive, and why?

19. Compare and contrast the closing shots of Zeffirelli's and Olivier's films. To what extent do you think Zeffirelli made a sound dramatic choice in not showing Hamlet's body being borne away by soldiers?

Breaking the Classical Barrier (Interview with John Tibbetts)
Franco Zeffirelli

It is difficult to approach a celebrated work like Hamlet *without preconceptions—preconceptions often based on previous experiences with the play. Critic Roger Ebert summed up the feeling of many critics when approaching an overly familiar work:*

> *I had a professor in college who knew everything there was to know about* Romeo and Juliet. *Maybe he knew too much. One day in class he said he would give anything to be able to read it again for the first time. I feel the same way about* Hamlet. *I know the play so well by now, I have seen it in so many different styles and periods and modes of dress, that it's like listening to a singer doing an old standard. You known the lyrics, so the only possible surprises come from style and phrasing.*

In the following selection, Franco Zeffirelli explains how he attempted to surprise and delight audiences with the distinctive "style and phrasing" he brought to his vision of Hamlet. *Ebert was surprised to find the style of Zeffirelli's* Hamlet *refreshingly "upbeat." He concludes, "We never feel, as we do sometimes with other productions, that events happen arbitrarily. Zeffirelli's great contribution to 'popularizing' the play has been to make it clear to the audience why events are unfolding as they are."**

This interview first appeared in Film/Literature Quarterly, *April 1994. Tibbetts, an editor of this journal, has also edited, co-edited, or authored several books on film, including* Introduction to the Photoplay: 1929, A Contemporary Account of the Transition to Sound in Film *(1977),* The American Theatrical Film: Stages in Development *(1985),* Dvořák in America, 1892–1895 *(1993),* The Encyclopedia of Novels into Film *(1998), and* The Cinema of Tony Richardson: Essays and Interviews *(1999).*

1 As Franco Zeffirelli recalls in his autobiography, he was born a *bastardino*, or "little bastard," near Florence in 1923. Unable to take the name of his biological father, Corsi, he was a *nescio nomen*, or "no name." Later he took the name "Zeffirelli," which was adapted from a reference in an aria in Mozart's *Cosi fan tutte* to the *Zeffiretti*, or "little breezes." He studied architecture as a student and later fought in the Resistance in the hills around Florence during World War II. He claims that his ambitions to work in stage and cinema were confirmed by

---

*Review of *Hamlet. Chicago Sun-Times,* 18 Jan 1991. Online. 16 June 2002. <http://suntimes.com/ebert/every_reviews/1991/01/630427.html>.

a screening of Olivier's *Henry V* and by a subsequent association in the 1940s and early 1950s with mentor Luchino Visconti. He became a successful opera director, guiding the careers of such luminaries as Maria Callas and Joan Sutherland. But his theatrical films, including the Shakespearean cycle—*The Taming of the Shrew* (1967), *Romeo and Juliet* (1968), *Othello* (1987), and *Hamlet* (1990)—have established his reputation for general audiences.

2   Zeffirelli has been frequently criticized for a style he describes as "lavish in scale and unashamedly theatrical." Yet, undeniably, his pictures (which also include *Brother Sun, Sister Moon,* 1972, *Jesus of Nazareth,* 1975, and *Endless Love,* 1984) have appealed to a mass audience with their blend of flamboyant imagery and spectacle with scrupulous care and craftsmanship. Arguably, more viewers have encountered grand opera and Shakespeare through his films than through the work of any other contemporary artist. He is the complete film-maker who oversees every aspect of the design, story, and production. It was Laurence Olivier, who, during the filming of *Jesus of Nazareth,* said of Zeffirelli: "No matter what we do, in the end Franco has the scissors!"

3   I met Franco Zeffirelli in December 1991 on the occasion of a series of press interviews he granted during the première of *Hamlet.*

John C. Tibbetts
University of Kansas

4   QUESTION: *Is Shakespeare a "hard sell" these days?*
ZEFFIRELLI: Impossible! We tried to interest studios here, but they weren't interested at all. We had to go the independent route. I don't know why they were nervous; we had had great success with *The Taming of the Shrew* and *Romeo and Juliet.* I remember more than ten years ago when the people at Paramount told me that Shakespeare never worked in the movies. Now you are young and you may not know that when I had done *Romeo and Juliet* a few years before, it had resurrected Paramount from the ashes! No matter, they just decided that Shakespeare doesn't work. You go to them with figures and a track record, but they don't listen. The way we did *Hamlet,* finally, was to go with three different companies, including Nelson, Carolco, and Sovereign Pictures. Barry Spikings, with Nelson, is English and I've known him for years. He's been a great fan and friend of mine. When we got Mel Gibson and Glenn Close, he was the one who finally said, "Come on, let's do it!"

5   QUESTION: *How important was getting the Gibson name?*
ZEFFIRELLI: It was vital. But it was a two-edged thing. On the one hand, for anything with Gibson you can find financing; on the other hand, you get people who doubt, who say, "Gibson, Gibson as Hamlet...?" For Gibson it was extreme-ly risky. He was very brave. He put his career on the line. Imagine if we did not succeed, he might be the joke of the industry. He has a new audience now. His fans go, too. But I tell you, it took great nerves from Mel.

6   QUESTION: *Was it also a risk when you did* Taming of the Shrew *with Burton and Taylor?*
ZEFFIRELLI: They were at the peak of their careers. Richard Burton was the most famous Shakespearean actor of his time. Elizabeth Taylor was the great-

est beauty of the day. It was extremely easy. It was supported by him, personally, and by Columbia. The big problem was later with *Romeo.* Despite the success of *Taming of the Shrew,* when I immediately suggested a little, lean *Romeo,* instead of a big fat budget thing—just a crust of bread—everybody said, "No way." I wanted to prove that Shakespeare can work without the big names.

7   QUESTION: *How difficult was it to bring* Hamlet *in at just over two hours?*
ZEFFIRELLI: The kind of story we wanted to do automatically meant some areas of the original play became unnecessary. They fell away by themselves, like dried branches. I never cut down so little from the first assembly to the final version than I did here. At first it was two hours and forty minutes. We cut down only half an hour. Unheard of. My first cut of *Romeo and Juliet* was five hours twenty. And we came down to a little over two hours. I'd love to go back to my original!

8   QUESTION: *Describe your first meeting with Gibson.*
ZEFFIRELLI: I come from the city of Machiavelli. I know one thing: In the heart of every actor, no matter how big or famous, there is this thorn, this stinging thing, that they wish to do Shakespeare. I talked with Dustin Hoffman before and I told him I was going to do *Hamlet.* He asked me, with whom? I told him, Mel Gibson. Dustin just almost fainted. He told me, "My dream has always been to play Hamlet!" Everybody wants to do Hamlet. So you can be sure that you hit a note there, you ring an alarm, a bell, in the ears of every actor. He will not say no. With Mel we had a brunch, which turned into a lunch, and then into a tea and dinner. We separated and he was convinced.

9   QUESTION: *Did anything about Gibson come as a surprise to you?*
ZEFFIRELLI: I was already informed that he had done some Shakespeare when he was young. I also was madly in love with his voice. It was something I liked, perhaps because of my operatic training, whatever. And his voice is a magnificent, bronzed, rich voice. There was something in him that made me very, very excited about the possibility. It was mainly that he could be a 16th-century character. He looks like a young Michelangelo now, with his hair and beard. The classical structure. And the humor. He's capable of a very nasty humor! That's one of my main regrets in the adaptation—that we did not trust ourselves enough to put in more humor. Because Shakespeare knew perfectly well what he was doing. He injected a sudden humor. Perhaps people are uneasy about *Hamlet* now, though—they don't know if they should laugh or not.

10 QUESTION: *Generally speaking, what are the challenges in bringing* Shakespeare *to a modern audience?*
ZEFFIRELLI: I think it's making the language acceptable, that you can understand it, that it's almost colloquial. You look at Shakespeare's earlier plays, like *Romeo and Juliet,* and a much more baroque language, a more flourishing language than, say, *Antony and Cleopatra* or *King Lear.* I think our actors have done this miracle. They have to speak a language that is beautiful, yes, but more "primitive" and spare, in a way. Look at the scenes with Paul Scofield. You're not aware of a "classical barrier" between you and him. He speaks in a way that you understand every single word. And Mel, for all his realism, he makes "To be or not to be" not a poetical aria, but a real suffering and a real problem that you understand. People who are not familiar at all with the speeches tell me that for

the first time they understand it. In trying to make it clear to himself, Mel helps others to understand it better. That was for me the main problem. The story is already so magnificent!

11 QUESTION: *Is reaching a mass audience your biggest priority?*

ZEFFIRELLI: You know, I think culture—especially opera and Shakespeare—must be available to as many people as possible. It irritates me that some people want art to be as "difficult" as possible, an elitest kind of thing. I want to give these things back to the people. All my training has been a preparation for the one medium that can do that, the motion picture.

12 QUESTION: *Let's get back to* Hamlet. *Have you ever staged it before?*

ZEFFIRELLI: I did it on stage in Italy with a superb cast and brought it to the Festival des Nations in Paris. Later we toured it to Russia and Eastern Europe. That was in 1964. Always I wanted to bring it to the cinema. Either the actor wasn't ready or I was not, or the money was not.... Every project has its own season.

13 QUESTION: *In* Hamlet *you achieve a distinctive kind of "look" with cinematographer David Watkin. Tell me about your work with him.*

ZEFFIRELLI: I like always to work with him. We did *Jesus of Nazareth* together. I had lost my cameraman, Armando Nannuzzi, who had become a director himself. David knows how to recreate the look of the "Old Masters." He can make a "still life" out of each set. I enjoy how we worked out a special kind of light for the duelling scene in *Hamlet.* We shot in that huge area with light coming in from openings in the walls. Then we took huge white sheets and placed them from one end of the hall to the other to bounce the light, to reflect it back into the scene. Even the white shirt of Hamlet became a kind of reflector and you can see the light on Laertes's face brighten when he gets closer. An extraordinary effect. All of this is possible too with special lenses and the film stock. And we kept the colors to a more black-and-white look, yes?

14 QUESTION: *Quite a difference from the charge that you usually work in highly saturated, vivid colors!*

ZEFFIRELLI: Color is devastating here, but in this way: I keyed the whole movie to mostly grays and ash colors, a "medieval-primitive" look, the look of a society that is brutal and made of stone. Whenever a few rich colors *do* come out, the effect is even more vivid. In that sense, this is one of the most colorful films I've ever done—but only because the few rich colors stand out so much from the grays. That way, you become inebriated by those colors.

15 QUESTION: *Hamlet himself continues to fascinate us, doesn't he?*

ZEFFIRELLI: Hamlet really was a window opened onto the future. He invented the "modern man." You'd like to meet him personally, if you could, today, because he'd be so exciting and interesting.

16 QUESTION: *Some film critics complain that Gibson's character is too old compared to the relative youth of Glenn Close's Gertrude.*

ZEFFIRELLI: They don't know what they're talking about! They absolutely don't know what they're talking about! Hamlet here is 33, or 34, which at that time was a mature adult. His mother is still young enough to be exuberant sexually, a wildcat who wants to have sex with her new husband at every minute, behind every pillar. She's so hungry for sex. She must be around 45. And that fits very well. She could have had Hamlet at a very young age, you see, even as early as 13—which was common to that time because women were married as soon as they were capable of having children. It works perfectly for us.

17 QUESTION: *In your autobiography you say that from childhood the world of theater has always represented something larger than life. Can you recall an example of that?*

ZEFFIRELLI: We've been talking about the Middle Ages, yes? Well, I grew up in the Tuscan countryside, which has always had for me a taste of the real Italy of the Middle Ages. I spent summers watching the traveling troupes of performers who would come and perform. They kept lamps on the floor in front of them which would throw diabolical shadows on the walls behind them— something I often do in my movies. They told stories and acted them out with shouts and blows and gestures. I have always felt these players were the true descendants of the world of Boccaccio, and I've always believed more in their fantasies than in anything else.

Discussion and Writing Suggestions

1. In the introduction to the interview Tibbetts notes that Zeffirelli's style has been characterized (by the director himself) as "lavish in scale and unashamedly theatrical." Tibbetts also mentions the "flamboyant imagery and spectacle" that characterize some of Zeffirelli's other films—some of this spectacle deriving no doubt from his experience directing grand opera. To what extent do you find evidence of these lavish, theatrical spectacles in *Hamlet?* Cite scenes that exhibit these qualities and explain whether or not you think they effectively bring out the meaning of the play—or a particular approach to the play.

2. In the interview, Zeffirelli first focuses on Mel Gibson, praising the actor for bringing a new dimension to the role (as well as for being instrumental in obtaining financing for the film) and for making Shakespeare's language more accessible than it has been in some other productions. To what extent do you agree that Gibson is convincing as Hamlet and that his performance helps us to understand the meaning of the play? Cite particular scenes or speeches, perhaps comparing Gibson's delivery to Olivier's.

3. Zeffirelli discusses the use of color in his *Hamlet,* noting how he "keyed the whole movie to mostly grays and ash colors," with occasional dramatic emphasis by more vivid colors. Cite illustrations of the effective use of color in the film. For example, how does the color scheme of the opening scene in the crypt help set the mood of the play? At what points do the colors become richer and how are such vivid colors used dramatically to further the meaning of the play?

4. Toward the end of the interview, Zeffirelli discusses the age relationship between Hamlet and Gertrude, as portrayed by Gibson
   and Glenn Close. To what extent do you think the relative age of
   the actors helps further Zeffirelli's interpretation of the relationship
   between son and mother? If you have seen Olivier's *Hamlet,* how
   do the relative ages of Hamlet and Gertrude (Olivier was 17 years
   older than Eileen Herlie, who played the queen) affect the dramatic
   meaning of their relationship?

Review of Zeffirelli's *Hamlet:* Monarch Notes
David Denby

Zeffirelli's Shakespearean adaptations are audience friendly (both Taming of the Shrew
(1967) and Romeo and Juliet *(1968) were commercial successes), but have not always
met with critical esteem. John Simon summarized Zeffirelli's style as "fancy production values
and disrespect for the work of art."* Of* Romeo and Juliet, *Pauline Kael wrote, "Franco Zeffirelli
goes in for strenuous knockabout stuff—for brawling, cavorting young men and for revels
and roistering that have an awful way of suggesting the supers at the opera trying to keep
the stage 'active.'"† Although, on balance, most critics found Zeffirelli's* Hamlet *praiseworthy,
the kind of reservations expressed in the following review by David Denby were not atypical.
Denby, currently a film critic for* The New Yorker, *wrote this review when he was film critic
of* New York *magazine. It appeared in the January 21, 1991 issue. Denby is the editor of
Francois Truffaut's film script* The 400 Blows *(1969), co-edited (with Jay Cocks) a collection of film reviews,* Film 73/74 *(1974), and authored* Great Books: My Adventures with
Homer, Rousseau, Woolf, and other Indestructible Writers of the Western World *(1996), an
account of his experience re-taking, in middle age, a Great Books course he originally took
as an undergraduate at Columbia University.*

1   Mel Gibson, star of Franco Zeffirelli's *Hamlet,* is ravaged by sadness and batted
    about by his feelings. He is certainly not a Hamlet "sicklied o'er with the pale cast
    of thought," not a contemplative and intellectual man, a puzzle to himself, a bru-
    tally candid young ironist who enjoys imposture and wit and taunting paradoxes—
    some of the elements that might be found, by a different actor, in this most
    protean of roles. This Hamlet is fidgety (Gibson wags his head back and forth as
    he talks), balled up much of the time though capable of sudden bursts of loose-
    limbed energy. Goosey rather than graceful, he seems less a prince and heir to
    the throne—"the glass of fashion and the mould of form"—than a rumpled and
    sleepless graduate student strung out on too much coffee.
2   Bangs and a scraggly beard obscure the handsome outlines of Gibson's fore-
    head and chin. By fuzzing his looks in this way, he escapes, I suppose, the

---

*"The Taming of the Shrew" in *Movies into Film: Film Criticism 1967–1970.* New York: Delta, 1971: 28.

†"Romeo and Juliet" in *5001 Nights at the Movies.* New York: Holt, 1985: 500.

charge of being a mere movie-star Hamlet. But his movieness still shows, not so much in his appearance as in his voice, which is growly and unstable, cracking too easily. Gibson, an excellent screen actor, did some work onstage before going into movies, but his voice lacks music, a singing line. *Hamlet,* after all, is not *Julius Caesar* or *Macbeth;* there's no way of bulling through the verse, some of the most beautiful and delicate Shakespeare ever wrote. Gibson's matter-of-factness is not just a technical limitation but a spiritual one. He reads the speeches very simply, with great intensity; he is always intelligible and sometimes moving, but nothing in the performance soars, and his temperamental range is much too narrow.

3   He's a likably unassuming actor, eager to please, and certainly preferable to Nicol Williamson, whose nasty, spasmodic, "modern" Hamlet in Tony Richardson's 1969 film was a near-travesty. For the record, however, Gibson can't compare with Laurence Olivier, whose 1948 production, despite its oddities and aesthetic missteps and a few boring passages, still sets the cinematic standard for the play. Olivier's Hamlet was a much more *formidable* man, intellectually volatile, arrogant, even a bit wicked in his enjoyment of baiting other people. Yet Olivier could be very still and quiet, even tentative, as if he were exploring the familiar words for the first time and was astonished by their meanings. Olivier drew us inside; the soliloquies were spoken as interior monologues—as Hamlet's thoughts. But then—then!—Olivier would shift gears, lift his arms, shout and prance, and in all of Heaven and Earth there was nothing so exciting. Gibson's Hamlet doesn't rouse us that way, and he never stands outside himself as Olivier did, viewing himself as an actor; he doesn't have the mental agility for that. His Hamlet is a sincere fellow in terrible misery, whereas Olivier's was a neurotic genius who transcended dread in moments of ecstatic clarity.

4   Zeffirelli, working with screenwriter Christopher De Vore, has dropped quite a lot of the play (as did Olivier) in order to make a film of manageable length. The beginning of "O what a rogue and peasant slave am I" is gone. So is "How all occasions do inform against me" and Hamlet's instructions to the players. Of the play within the play, only the dumb show and a few lines remain, which renders Gertrude's "The lady doth protest too much" almost meaningless. Fortinbras, the stalwart soldier who restores order to the collapsing kingdom of Denmark, is gone, though Rosencrantz and Guildenstern, Hamlet's wormy "friends," are still there. The tendency of these cuts and many others is to take the play out of the realm of politics and philosophy, to reduce it to its origins as a family saga and revenge tragedy, and then to simplify even that. The physical action has been expanded, but the play's amazing reach is gone—its sense of man as godlike but corruptible, a paragon who decays—the range that makes it the universal drama of Western literature.

5   Clipped and corseted, this *Hamlet* doesn't breathe. The big moments follow hard upon one another, making the play seem more like a collection of set pieces and famous quotes than ever. And yet, given the limits Zeffirelli has established for himself, he has done surprisingly well. I've never been a fan of his work in opera or film; this movie, however, is much more forceful than his earlier, buffoonish attempts at Shakespeare: the teenage, pop-romance *Romeo and Juliet* and the roaring, tedious *Taming of the Shrew.*

6   The production is businesslike and dramatic rather than (as before with Zeffirelli) decorative and hollowly flamboyant. The exteriors were shot at a variety of castles in England and Scotland, the shots combined so as to make the setting seem like a single building, and the realistic approach is remarkably handsome—gray stone, parapets, arches, lots of raw sunlight, and an alternation of open and semi-enclosed spaces, perfect for intrigue and spying. Spatially, the play makes more sense than usual. The Ghost, in the bitterly eloquent person of Paul Scofield, is not a hollow-voiced spook but a tormented man unable to lie in peace. As Ophelia, Helena Bonham-Carter, who has grown up a great deal, is a shrewd, intense girl who cracks, not the usual melodious ninny pushed this way and that.

7   But sometimes realism as a production strategy leads Zeffirelli into absurdities. *Hamlet* is set in the Middle Ages, but Shakespeare, building an exciting climax, has Hamlet and Laertes duel with light-weight rapiers from his own period. Zeffirelli mistakenly corrects the anachronism, which causes the actors, now struggling with rather heavy medieval broadswords, to fall all over the set. The duel is supposed to begin as an elegant and playful exhibition, something like a tennis match, which then degenerates into mayhem, but staged this way, it's a lurching mess from the start.

8   A middling-good film, then, which does no terrible harm to Shakespeare. Alan Bates, merry and insinuating, is the most convincingly intelligent and threatening Claudius I've seen. Ian Holm, as Polonius, is more a busy ferret, full of stupid plots, than a pompous windbag. For all his foolishness, he's a threat, too. Glenn Close, with long gold braids, is very grand as Gertrude; she seems to have wandered in from a heroic production out of an earlier age. Poor queen and mother! Olivier emphasized the Oedipal passion between Hamlet and Gertrude; Zeffirelli attempts to outdo him by having Hamlet pin Gertrude to her bed and, panting, actually move his body up and down on her. I guess Zeffirelli couldn't resist one moment in truly terrible taste.

Discussion and Writing Suggestions

1. Denby first assesses Gibson's overall interpretation of Hamlet. In the way he moves and talks, the author remarks, Gibson "seems less a prince and heir to the throne [...] than a rumpled and sleepless graduate student strung out on too much coffee." To what extent do you agree with this assessment? Does Gibson's manner as Hamlet enhance or detract from his performance as Hamlet?

2. In considering Gibson's delivery of Shakespeare's words, Denby finds the actor wanting, arguing that "his voice lacks music," and that while aspects of his performance deserve praise, "nothing [...] soars, and his temperamental range is much too narrow." Do you agree with this judgment? Find examples from the film that either support or rebut Denby's assessment. If possible, compare Gibson's delivery of particular lines or speeches with Olivier's.

3. Denby compares Gibson's Hamlet unfavorably to Olivier's. He argues that Olivier had greater dramatic range in the part and greater "mental agility" than Gibson. To what extent do you agree that Olivier is a superior Hamlet to Gibson? Cite examples of particular speeches or sequences that effectively compare and contrast the two actor's performances.

4. The duel at the end of the Zeffirelli's film, Denby argues, is a "lurching mess." Compare and contrast the duel as staged in Olivier's film with the duel in Zeffirelli's. Which staging do you prefer and why? Which do you think comes closest to the spirit of Shakespeare's intent at this point in the play?

5. In the conclusion of his review, Denby asserts that the bedroom scene between Hamlet and Gertrude was "in truly terrible taste." Your thoughts?

Kenneth Branagh's *Hamlet*

Kenneth Branagh burst into public prominence as a film director and Shakespearean actor in 1989, at the age of 29, with the release of Henry V. *For almost half a century no other director had had the temerity to film* Henry V *and risk comparison with Laurence Olivier's triumphantly theatrical and heroic 1944 film. Critics were quick to make the comparison and almost unanimously declared that Branagh had met the challenge. As* Washington Post *reviewer Hal Hinson wrote:*

> *Forty-five years ago, Laurence Olivier directed and starred in his own brilliant history-making production of* Henry V *and, in doing so, announced his arrival as a thunderclap talent on both sides of the camera. Branagh with his* Henry *has accomplished a similar feat, and while his work doesn't supplant Olivier's, it is worthy of a place beside it. He has made a* Henry V *for his time, and a masterful one. The king is dead, long live the king.**

Olivier's wartime film, with its patriotic tone and exciting battle sequences, was widely viewed as a stirring contribution to the nation's morale and fighting spirit in its life-and-death struggle against the Nazis (in a manner similar to Sergei Eisenstein's 1938 battle epic Alexander Nevsky, *set in medieval Russia, but intended partly as a warning to Hitler's armies, within striking distance of the border). Branagh's film—post-Vietnam—retains Shakespeare's patriotic spirit, but unlike Olivier's, focuses heavily on the miseries of war. As Hinson notes, "if there is glory in the heavy clanging of metal against metal and metal against flesh as the rains fall and the mud sucks at the soldiers' boots, it is a grim devastating glory—a glory weighted with sorrow."*

**Washington Post,* 15 Dec. 1989. Online. 23 Aug. 2001. <http://washingtonpost.com/wp-srv/style/longterm/movies/henryvhinson.htm>

Branagh followed up his success in Henry V *with another widely acclaimed Shakespearean adaptation,* Much Ado About Nothing *(1993), once again co-starring with his wife, Emma Thompson.* Hamlet, *which has long held a fascination for Branagh (see his "Making* Hamlet," *following), was released in 1996. Branagh's film is unique among* Hamlets *in incorporating the full text of Shakespeare's play (as a result, running over four hours.) Fortinbras, Rosencrantz, and Guildenstern, severely or entirely cut in Olivier's and Zeffirelli's films, were restored, giving Branagh's film a political and social dimension absent from the earlier versions. In another bold directorial stroke, Branagh moved the medieval story of Hamlet into the mid-nineteenth century, setting the action not in a brooding castle, but in massive Blenheim Palace, ancestral home of the dukes of Marlborough (the current duke had a small role as an officer in Fortinbras' army). A vast interior set, representing the great hall in which much of the action takes place, featured mirrored walls, spacious balconies, and a striking black and white checkered floor. With his reputation as an adapter of Shakespeare, Branagh also was able to attract a gallery of international stars, including Julie Christie, Gerard Depardieu, John Gielgud, Charlton Heston, Kate Winslet, Robin Williams, Jack Lemmon, and Billy Crystal. Perhaps most important, for the role of Claudius, Branagh secured Derek Jacobi, the actor who had first inspired him with his love of Shakespeare through his own theatrical performance as Hamlet and who had some years later directed his protégé in the role.*

Now, indeed, Branagh appeared to be inviting comparisons to Olivier. As with Henry V, *the critical applause was almost unanimous. Despite some isolated carps (John Simon of the* National Review *complained, "Much as I have searched back issues of the Wittenberg University catalogue, I cannot find courses in circus skills such as knife throwing."*), critics hailed the new* Hamlet, *declaring it not only a worthy successor to Olivier's film, but also the definitive film version of Shakespeare's most celebrated play. As the hard-to-please Stanley Kauffmann noted in* The New Republic, *"Kenneth Branagh wins two victories in* Hamlet. *He has made a vital, exciting film; and he has triumphed over the obstacles he put in his own way."[†] Richard Corliss of* Time *magazine declared, "Next to this, all other movie versions, from Laurence Olivier's to Mel Gibson's, seem like samplings—a Reduced Shakespeare Company run-through of* Hamlet's *greatest hits."[‡]*

Born in Belfast, Northern Ireland, in 1960, Branagh moved to London at age 9, where he acted in school plays, and in 1981 graduated from the Royal Academy of Dramatic Art. He made his professional debut six weeks later, and in 1984 became the youngest actor in the history of the Royal Shakespeare Company to play the lead in Henry V. *In 1987 Branagh co-founded the Renaissance Theatre Company, for which he wrote, produced, and directed.*

Branagh has appeared in film or TV productions of the works of other major playwrights, including Henrik Ibsen's Ghosts *(1986), Eugene O'Neill's* Strange Interlude *(1987), Christopher Fry's* The Lady's Not for Burning *(1987), and John Osborne's* Look Back in Anger *(1989). Other films directed by Branagh include* Dead Again *(1991),* Peter's Friends *(1992), Mary Shelley's* Frankenstein *(1994),* In the Bleak Midwinter *(1995), and another Shakespearean adaptation (staged as a 1930s style musical),* Love's Labour's Lost *(2000). Branagh has also appeared in films directed by others, including* Othello *(1995) and* Celebrity *(1998).*

---

*National Review, 10 Feb. 1997: 57.

[†]The New Republic, 27 Jan. 1996: 26.

[‡]Time, 10 Jan. 1997: 72

Hamlet (1996)

Adapted and Directed by Kenneth Branagh

Kenneth Branagh—Hamlet

Derek Jacobi—Claudius

Julie Christie—Gertrude

Kate Winslet—Ophelia

Michael Maloney—Laertes

Richard Briers—Polonius

Nicholas Farrell—Horatio

Timothy Spall—Rosencrantz

Reece Dinsdale—Guildenstern

Rufus Sewall—Fortinbras

Jack Lemmon—Marcellus

Brian Blessed—Ghost

Charlton Heston—Player King

Rosemary Harris—Player Queen

Billy Crystal—First Gravedigger

Robin Williams—Osric

Gerard Depardieu—Reynaldo

Jon Gielgud—Priam

Judi Dench—Hecuba

Richard Attenborough—English Ambassador

John Mills—Old Norway

The following outline of Kenneth Branagh's Hamlet *was prepared by the editors of this book.*

1. (1.1) [00:00] *Exterior, Palace at night.* Initial titles on black background; "HAMLET" appears as name carved on base of (unseen) statue. Camera travels left from base to reveal palace in background. Clock chimes the hour. Camera tracks apprehensive Francisco as he patrols and surveys the snowy landscape. Camera travels back past palace, revealing, foreground, the head of the statue of King Hamlet. Francisco appears to see or hear something, braces; camera travels down body of statue, whose hand seems suddenly to unsheathe its sword. Barnardo, yelling, "Who's there?" brings Francisco down to the ground. The two recognize one another; they rise in front of the massive gates of the palace. Horatio and Marcellus appear, bid farewell to departing Francisco. Barnardo and Marcellus tell Horatio of the ghost. Ghost appears: to dramatic music, camera dollies toward armed, silhouetted figure against mist. Overhead shot of three men rapidly retreating inside gate, toward palace; they hide behind pillar, lances oustretched. Ghost disappears.

Marcellus asks Horatio what the ghost might portend; shots of preparations for war. Horatio tells of conflict between King Hamlet and old Fortinbras of Norway. Inserts of young Fortinbras preparing to revenge the death of his father by King Hamlet and the forfeiture of Norway's lands to Denmark. Ghost appears again, this time with face illuminated. Horatio asks ghost to speak; ghost withdraws. Dawn. The three resolve to tell Hamlet what they have seen.

2. (2.2) [10:10] *Great Hall.* Fanfare. Camera travels past assemblage as Claudius and Gertrude make their entrance, past rows of assembled courtiers, toward camera. Claudius addresses court about his marriage. He rips up Fortinbras's message insisting on return of forfeited lands. Insert of Fortinbras, in front of map of Denmark, preparing for war. Claudius dispatches Cornelius and Voltemand to take a message to "old Norway," uncle of Fortinbras. He grants Laertes' request to be allowed to return to France. Camera travels past applauding courtiers to reveal motionless Hamlet, dressed in black, hands clasped in front of him. Claudius and Gertrude attempt to rouse the brooding Hamlet from his melancholy. Hamlet agrees not to return to Wittenberg; Claudius is gratified. Hamlet, back to camera, stands under falling confetti, as Claudius and Gertrude exit. The Great Hall empty, Hamlet soliloquizes: "O that this too too sullied flesh would melt..." Horatio, Marcellus, and Barnardo enter; Hamlet greets them enthusiastically. They withdraw to an anteroom, where Horatio tells the prince of the ghost. Hamlet says he will join them on the watch tonight. After he ushers them out, he walks past rows of books ("My father's spirit? In arms? All is not well"), pulls one out and leafs through it, stopping at a page illustrating "Demons."

3. (1.3) [27:30] *Palace exterior. Polonius' Chamber.* Camera tracks Laertes and Ophelia, walking arm in arm, on wintry ground in front of palace, as Laertes bids his sister farewell, and advises her to be wary of Hamlet. They are observed by Hamlet, as he meets with fencers. Polonius enters, greets Laertes. Inside, he advises Laertes how to behave while abroad. Upon Laertes' exit, Polonius reinforces Laertes's advice to Ophelia. Inserts of Hamlet and Ophelia making love. Polonius forbids Ophelia from seeing Hamlet again.

4. (1.4) [35:10] *Corridor. Exterior. Woods.* As Hamlet, Horatio, and Marcellus prepare to wait for ghost, inserts (to Hamlet's voice over) of Claudius in drunken revelry, then taking Gertrude to bed as courtiers close door behind the couple. Hamlet complains to Horatio of the debauches. He reflects: "So oft it chances in particular men..." Ghost appears, outstretching arm. Shots of the three from ghost's point of view. Ghost beckons again, and Hamlet follows, resisting efforts of the others to stop him. Hamlet runs through woods, following ghost; earth spouts fire, sulphur; trees fall. Inserts of ghost and embalmed King Hamlet, on coffin.

5. (1.5) [39:15] *Woods.* Ghost, at first unseen (camera travels across trees, in mist), tells Hamlet, "Mark me!" Hand clutches Hamlet's throat; dolly in rapidly toward ghost, face illuminated, then Hamlet. Sulphur erupts from ground. Ghost (extreme close-up of mouth) tells Hamlet about his murder at Claudius' hands. Blood pours out of ear three times. Flashback inserts of

Claudius, Gertrude, Hamlet, and King Hamlet in palace, Claudius embracing Gertrude, unlacing her bodice. Dumb show of the murder of King Hamlet by Claudius. Ghost takes his leave, disappears; Hamlet vows revenge. Horatio, Marcellus, Francisco reappear. Hamlet swears them to secrecy about ghost, who speaks from earth to insist on their silence. Lightning, sulphur eruptions, earthquakes. Horatio, Marcellus, and Francisco swear on Hamlet's sword. Earth closes up again.

6. (2.1) [51:25] *Exterior of Palace. Polonius's Chamber.* Polonius (with prostitute in room) dispatches Reynaldo to Paris to give Laertes money and notes and to make indirect inquiries about his behavior. Reynaldo exits; Ophelia enters frantically and tells Polonius of a visit by Hamlet, who grabs her wrist, stares at her intently, sighs piteously, unhands her, and leaves, backing out. Sympathetic Polonius resolves to tell king.

7. (2.2) [58:25] *Exterior, Palace. Claudius's and Gertrude's Bedroom. Great Hall. Exterior of Palace. Great Hall.* Claudius welcomes Rosencrantz and Guildenstern. Camera, at first quickly, then more slowly, circles around them, then pans, tracking Claudius, to reveal servants making up the king and queen's bed, on which Claudius sits down. Gertrude enters, also welcomes the pair, hoping that they can improve Hamlet's mood. Camera tracks company as they leave bedroom, move down hallway. Polinius enters, tells Claudius that ambassadors to Norway have returned. Camera tracks Claudius and Polonius from rear as they move into Great Hall, where fencers are practicing. The two stop momentarily, as camera half circles around them, Polonius telling Claudius he has discovered the cause of Hamlet's madness, but advising the king first to hear the ambassadors. Claudius and Gertrude move toward their thrones, the camera reverse tracking them from front. Fencers exit.

Ambassadors, Voltemand and Cornelius report (inserts of the following actions) that Fortinbras has been rebuked by his uncle, old Norway, for preparing to make war on Denmark. Fortinbras has agreed to desist from aggressive designs and to use his troops to make war on Poland, passing peacefully through Denmark on the way. Ambassadors exit. Polonius tells Claudius and Gertrude that Hamlet is mad. He brings in Ophelia, who distractedly reads note Hamlet has just sent her. Polonius continues reading; flashback inserts of half-dressed Hamlet telling words of his note to happy Ophelia. They kiss. Return to Polonius, telling king and queen that he forbade Ophelia from seeing Hamlet, and attributing Hamlet's melancholy to this fact. He suggests that he and the royal pair spy on Hamlet the next time he encounters Ophelia. They agree.

Hamlet appears on the balcony, reading a book. Claudius and Gertrude withdraw; Polonius approaches Hamlet to find him wearing a skull mask. Polonius follows Hamlet as they walk on balcony, berates him as dishonest. Polonius follows Hamlet outside palace, takes his leave. Rosencrantz and Guildenstern enter on miniature train. They banter awhile; then, as they walk on the snowy plain, Hamlet tells them that Denmark is a prison. They walk into the courtyard; Hamlet, suspicious, forces them to admit that they were sent for by the king and queen. Hamlet tells them of his melancholy as they walk up the steps. Rosencrantz and Guildenstern tell Hamlet of the players; he responds enthusiastically. They go inside to the balcony overlooking the Great Hall.

Polonius enters and tells Hamlet of players' visit. Hamlet descends the stairs into Great Hall to greet the players. Camera circles them twice. Hamlet recites a speech ("The rugged Pyrrhus…") he once heard the chief player perform. Chief player recites speech about Priam and Pyrrhus and the burning of Ilium (action dramatized in dumb show as player recites). Hamlet asks chief player if the company can perform "The Murder of Gonzago" and if he can insert a short speech he will write. Hamlet takes leave of Rosencrantz and Guildenstern and Horatio. Hamlet goes to adjacent library, berates himself for not taking decisive action against Claudius ("O, what a rogue and peasant slave am I…"), resolves to catch the guilty Claudius by means of the play. He fells model king standing on rampart of model castle.

8. (3.1)[1:30:35] *Corridor. Great Hall.* Claudius and Gertrude question Rosencrantz and Guildenstern about Hamlet. Camera circles as Claudius tells Gertrude that he and Polonius will spy on Hamlet as he meets Ophelia. Camera stops its motion to fix on Claudius as Polonius makes a remark ("'Tis too much proved, that with devotion's visage/And pious action we do sugar o'er/The devil himself") that cuts him to the quick. Claudius and Polonius withdraw behind a mirrored door. Camera tracks Hamlet from behind as he enters, looking around warily. Staring at the mirrored door (camera focusing on his reflection), he soliloquizes: "To be or not to be…" Claudius flinches as Hamlet takes out his "bare bodkin." Ophelia enters. They kiss. She offers to return his gifts; he denies giving her any. Suspicious, he questions her honesty, denies ever having loved her, tells her to "Get thee to a nunnery." As Ophelia starts at a noise, Hamlet realizes that they are being observed. He drags her down the hall, opening several of the mirrored doors, looking for the spies. Shot from behind mirrored door, Ophelia's face pressed by Hamlet against it; Claudius, alarmed, slams door on other side; he and Polonius flee. Hamlet opens door, rushes into room, puts his ear against a picture on wall, listening for evidence of the spies' flight. Hearing nothing, he exits. Ophelia laments Hamlet's condition. Claudius and Polonius enter. King, not convinced that Hamlet is mad, decides to send Hamlet to England. Polonius offers to spy on a conversation between Gertrude and Hamlet.

9. (3.2) [1:44:30] *Palace exterior. Balcony of Great Hall. Anteroom. Great Hall.* Horatio reads newspaper article: "NORWEIGIAN ARMIES ADVANCE: PRINCE FORTINBRAS IN COMMAND." Close-up insert of Fortinbras. Camera tracks Hamlet, as he walks on balcony, giving advice to the players. Hamlet leaves players, asks Horatio to observe Claudius as the play progresses. Close-up of Claudius and Gertrude kissing; they pull apart and camera tilts down to reveal stage in Great Hall, audience applauding. Hamlet questions Polonius about his previous acting experience. Hamlet sits by Ophelia, loudly banters with her. Play begins: dumb show, then player king and queen declare their love to one another; player king sleeps, is poisoned in the ear by usurper. Reactions by Claudius, Gertrude, Polonius, Rosencrantz and Guildenstern, and other members of audience. Hamlet interrupts performance to explain

its significance to Claudius and members of the audience. Player murderer pours poison in ear of player king; insert of death of King Hamlet; camera dollies in to close-up of Claudius, who rises and exits, followed by retinue. Hamlet exults to Horatio. Rosencrantz and Guildenstern enter to tell Hamlet of Claudius's rage, and that Gertrude has sent for him. Polonius enters, urges Hamlet to see Gertrude. Hamlet agrees; all but Hamlet exit.

10. (3.3) [2:04:05] *Claudius's Chamber. Gertrude's Chamber.* Claudius reiterates to Rosencrantz and Guildenstern, his determination to send Hamlet to England. They exit; Polonius enters and tells Claudius he will spy on the conversation between Gertrude and Hamlet. Hamlet, against open window in his chamber: "'Tis now the very witching time of night..." Hamlet's voice over toward end of his speech, as we see distraught Claudius, in his chamber: "O, my offense is rank, it smells to heaven..." Hamlet comes upon Claudius praying, prepares to kill him; but reconsiders (inserts of King Hamlet dying, earth opening, closing, Claudius hiding behind door), determines to wait until Claudius is less prepared to go to heaven. In Gertrude's chamber, Polonius hides behind arras. Hamlet enters, berates Gertrude. He grabs hold of the locket around Gertrude's neck; she cries out, Polonius calls for help, Hamlet stabs him from behind the arras. Polonius dies. Hamlet continues berating his mother. Hamlet forces Gertrude to compare the two pictures of his father and uncle. At the height of his rage, Gertrude implores him to speak no more "daggers." Ghost appears (unseen to Gertrude), tells Hamlet not to forget his purpose, urges him to soothe Gertrude. He speaks more gently to her, urges her not to go to Claudius's bed tonight. Hamlet reminds her that he must go to England but will deal with the treacherous Rosencrantz and Guildenstern; he drags Polonius's body out, leaving a distraught Gertrude.

11. (4.1) [2:24:30] *Hallway. Gertrude's Chamber.* Gertrude tells Claudius of Hamlet's killing Polonius. Claudius runs toward pool of blood where Polonius lay. He instructs Rosencrantz and Guildenstern to find Hamlet and determine where he has put Polonius's body. Camera rapidly pulls away from Claudius and Gertrude comforting one another.

12. (4.2) [2:27:25] *Ophelia's Chamber. Hamlet's Chamber.* Soldiers, bayonets drawn, burst in upon sleeping Ophelia, looking for Hamlet. Rosencrantz and Guildenstern come into Hamlet's chamber asking him what he has done with the body. Camera reverse tracks as Hamlet leads the two, and soldiers, through various rooms, including Great Hall. Ophelia enters; Hamlet runs away, as others pursue. He slams door behind him. A rifle is leveled at his head.

13. (4.3) [2:29] *Claudius's Chamber.* Claudius muses that he must deal carefully with Hamlet, who is beloved by the people. Rosencrantz and Guildenstern enter, followed by soldiers, dragging in Hamlet (and restraining Horatio). Hamlet refuses at first to say where he has put Polonius, is slapped by Claudius, finally tells where the body is. Claudius tells Hamlet he must go to England immediately; Hamlet is dragged out by soldiers. Claudius tells Rosencrantz and Guildenstern to follow him; they exit and Claudius reveals his plan to have Hamlet killed upon his arrival in England. Body of Polonius is borne by soldiers as Ophelia screams.

14. (4.4) [2:32:35] *A Plain in Denmark.* Ophelia's screams persist in voice-over; long shots of misty plain. Fortinbras, mounted with other soldiers, asks Norweigian captain to request safe passage through Denmark from Claudius, as the army proceeds to make war on Poland. Fortinbras' soldiers march. In another part of the plain, Hamlet, accompanied by Rosencrantz and Guildenstern, asks the Norweigian captain about the troops of Fortinbras and their purpose in Denmark. Hamlet, in soliloquy: "How all occasions to inform against me/And spur my dull revenge..." Camera, at first slowly, then more rapidly, pulls away from Hamlet, revealing icy landscape; music's volume rises to climax as Hamlet berates himself for his continuing inaction (he has good reason to act, while Fortinbras's determined troops have none). As shot concludes, he appears a speck on the barren landscape. INTERMISSION. [End tape 1 [2:38:00]]

15. (4.5) [Tape 2: 0:00] *Great Hall.* Claudius voice-over ("When sorrows come, they come not in single spies, /But in battalions...") to montage of shots, some of which we have recently seen: exterior of palace, Hamlet stabbing Polonius, Hamlet being dragged off, Ophelia distraught, courtiers whispering, Laertes, Claudius pacing and fretting. Ophelia, shot from above, slams herself into the walls of a closet, Gertrude, from above, with Horatio and a serving woman, listening to her. They discuss her condition. Ophelia, in strait jacket, enters, distracted, Gertrude trying to soothe her. Claudius enters. Ophelia continues to rave, in verses. She makes sexual motions; insert of Hamlet and Ophelia in bed. Ophelia exits, pursued by Claudius, who sends Horatio after her. Shots of many running feet. A messenger tells Claudius that Laertes has returned; the mob demanding that he be made king. Laertes enters, at the head of the "rabble," demanding, "Where is this king?" In terror, Claudius and Gertrude retreat to their thrones, then stand their ground; soldiers force out mob. Laertes runs at Claudius with his sword, is restrained by Gertrude. Gradually, Claudius soothes Laertes, declaring that he is guiltless of Polonius's death. Camera tracks Ophelia, distracted, in nightdress, as she runs into Great Hall, toward, and then away from amazed Laertes. Ophelia and Laertes reflected in door mirrors as he speaks gently to her. She gives imaginary herbs and flowers to Laertes, sings, then exits. Claudius assures the stricken Laertes that he will labor with him to "let the great axe fall" on the true perpetrator of the "offenses" against his father and sister.

16. (4.6) [14:35] *Exterior, Palace. Corridor. Courtyard.* A gentleman tells Horatio that seafaring men have letters for him. Horatio opens peephole to door in corridor, revealing mad Ophelia being hosed down in cell. Horatio turns away. Left alone, Ophelia takes key out of her mouth. In courtyard, Horatio meets seafarers, who give him Hamlet's letter. Horatio reads letter about his ship being chased by pirates; he boarded their ship and became friends with them; Hamlet asks Horatio to deliver letters to Claudius and then to join him as soon as possible.

17. (4.7) [16:25] *Polonius' Chamber.* Claudius explains to Laertes why he has not yet taken stronger action against Hamlet. King agrees to help Laertes in his revenge. Messenger brings Claudius Hamlet's letters. Hamlet writes

that he is back in Denmark and will see Claudius tomorrow. Claudius plots with Laertes to kill Hamlet in a way that will lay no blame on them: Hamlet will be challenged to a fencing match and Laertes will kill him with a poisoned sword. If that fails, Claudius will prepare a poisoned goblet of wine. Gertrude enters with news of Ophelia's drowning in a stream. Camera dollies in on Gertrude as she describes the scene. Grief-striken Laertes exits; Claudius asks Gertrude to come with him to help calm Laertes; she remains where she is. Insert of drowned Ophelia below the water.

18. (5.1) [29:05] *Exterior, Palace. Graveyard.* Gravediggers debate whether a suicide deserves a Christian burial. After some riddling, second gravedigger exits; Hamlet and Horatio enter. Hamlet comments on gravedigger's merry mood and the former identities of the skulls gravedigger unearths from the grave and lines up in neat row—a politician, a courtier, a lawyer. Gravedigger is questioned by Hamlet, pulls out skull of Yorick. Hamlet reminisces about Yorick. Skull of Yorick morphs into face of Yorick in dumb show amusing the court. Hamlet reflects on the transitoriness of life and of the eventual passage of all power and beauty to death. Upon a noise in the distance, Hamlet and Horatio conceal themselves. Gravedigger prepares grave. Claudius, Gertrude, Laertes, and retinue enter, bearing Ophelia's coffin, which they lower over grave. Laertes objects to brief ceremony; priest replies that suicides are not entitled to more. Hamlet realizes that it is Ophelia who is to be buried. As dirt is thrown on coffin, frantic Laertes jumps into grave, opens coffin to reveal Ophelia, rages at her death. Hamlet reveals himself; Laertes grabs him around the throat, is pulled off by soldiers. Restrained by another soldier and Horatio, Hamlet declares that he loved Ophelia as much as "forty thousand brothers," then speaks more gently to Horatio and exits. Claudius sends Horatio after Hamlet, urges Laertes to bide his time, keeping in mind the plot that they have hatched to kill Hamlet.

19. (5.2) [45:55] *Exterior of Palace from behind gates, bright daylight. Balcony of Great Hall. Hamlet's Chamber. Great Hall.* Guard patrols in front of gates. Hamlet tells Horatio how, on the ship, the day before the seafight with the pirates, he found the warrant for his execution carried by Rosencrantz and Guildenstern, then substituted his own forged warrant for the execution of the bearers. Hamlet has no regrets about Rosencrantz and Guildenstern, but is sorry about how he behaved to Laertes, resolving to improve matters between them. Osric enters, to Hamlet's amusement, with news of Claudius's wager on Hamlet's fencing skills against Laertes. Hamlet accepts the wager; Osric exits. Insert of apprehensive guard patrolling in front of gates. A lord enters to tell Hamlet the king and queen await him. Horatio is worried about the upcoming match; Hamlet is confident, though melancholy ("…if it be not now, yet it will come. The readiness is all"). They embrace.

   In the Great Hall (a red carpet down the center), the company waits. Hamlet and Horatio, Laertes and his second, enter from opposite ends of the carpet, meet at the center. Claudius and Gertrude approach the center at a right angle. Claudius joins Hamlet's and Laertes's hands. Hamlet asks Laertes's pardon; voice-over continues, as we see montage of guard patrolling outside palace, frozen landscape, close-up of Fortinbras turning his head forward, Fortinbras' troops on the march; close-up of amazed guard in front of palace seeing troops; a hand grabs guard's mouth from behind; Fortinbras's troops, in formation, march, away from camera, toward palace; Hamlet's speech to Laertes continues. With icy reserve, Laertes accepts Hamlet's offer of love and clasps his hand. Courtiers applaud. Hamlet and Laertes take off their robes and prepare for the match. Claudius orders wine set on the table, promises a pearl to the winner. Claudius drinks to Hamlet. Hamlet and Laertes fence; Hamlet wins first bout ("A hit, a very palpable hit"). Claudius and Gertrude rejoice; Claudius drinks wine, drops a pearl in goblet, offers Hamlet the goblet; Hamlet says he will drink after the bout. In courtyard, Fortinbras' soldiers attack defenders, prepare to scale walls of palace. Second bout between Hamlet and Laertes; much thrusting and parrying, ending with another "touch" by Hamlet. Joyful Gertrude takes goblet to Hamlet, gives him handkerchief, then drinks from the goblet, to Claudius' shouted "Gertrude [a pause, while he recollects himself, then a quiet, imploring] do not drink!" She drinks. Laertes's second bates his sword with the poison. Dejected Claudius sits on throne. Gertrude, losing her balance, sits next to him.

Inside the palace, a guard opens a second-story window to see Fortinbras' advancing troops; he sounds the alarm, but the enemy is already inside and pushes him aside; through the open window, we see columns of troops advancing toward palace. In the Great Hall, Hamlet banters with Laertes, who rushes toward him and cuts him on the shoulder. An unbelieving, then enraged Hamlet pursues Laertes across the hall. In the confusion with Laertes and Hamlet fall, and Hamlet picks up Laertes's poisoned sword. Panic among the audience as Hamlet and Laertes go up the stairs to the balcony to continue the fight. Hamlet wounds Laertes. Laertes lunges at Hamlet, who dodges; Laertes falls over balcony to floor below, to general consternation. Gertrude realizes that she has been poisoned by the wine. Hamlet orders the doors locked. Laertes tells Hamlet that he is dying; the sword has been poisoned, blames the king. Hamlet hurls the envenomed sword over the balcony, into the back of the fleeing Claudius. With another sword, Hamlet cuts the rope holding the chandelier, which falls toward and against Claudius's throne. Using the rope, Hamlet lowers himself to the floor of the Great Hall, runs to throne, forces poisoned wine down Claudius's throat. Laertes asks Hamlet to exchange forgivenesses. Outside, Fortinbras rides through rows of his victorious soldiers. Hamlet asks Horatio to tell his story and "absent thee from felicity awhile," also says Fortinbras "has my dying voice" [approval as next king]. Guns sound from outside. Hamlet dies.

Fortinbras' soldiers crash through balcony windows, bayonets drawn; other soldiers run across Great Hall; yet others crash through windows on opposite balcony. Soldiers point their guns from balcony toward floor of Great Hall. Reverse track of Fortinbras entering Great Hall. English ambassador enters with news that Rosencrantz and Guildenstern are dead. Horatio asks that Fortinbras order the bodies removed in proper state, promises to tell the story of how these deaths came about. Fortinbras sits on throne; the crown is placed on his head. He orders four captains to bear Hamlet out and the soldiers to shoot in tribute. Overhead shot of Hamlet's body, arms outstretched, borne out between rows of soldiers. Dissolve to Hamlet (another overhead shot), in royal outfit, grasping sword, lying in coffin, against snowy ground; camera pulls back to reveal numerous mourners, with palace in the background; chorus on soundtrack swells. Long shot of palace, soldiers in mid-ground, a single soldier in foreground ascending ladder set against base of statue of King Hamlet. Rope is tied around neck of statue; sledge hammer pounds head; various parts of statue are smashed. Statue's head, in close-up, comes falling down—as it does, concealing "HAMLET" carved on base. End titles.

Discussion and Writing Suggestions

1. Branagh's *Hamlet* presents the full text of Shakespeare's play. The implications of this decision begin to emerge in the first scene, as Horatio explains to the sentries the recent history of young Fortinbras's preparations against Denmark. To what extent do such restored speeches—absent from Olivier's, Zeffirelli's, and other film versions—make Branagh's film more stagy, less cinematic? How does the filmmaker attempt to deal with this issue? To what extent do you think his efforts are successful?

2. Toward the end of the first scene, Horatio notes, "But look, the morn in russet mantle clad/Walks o'er the dew of yon high eastward hill." Discuss the effectiveness of the visual that accompanies these lines.

3. Compare and contrast our first sight of Hamlet in Branagh's film with corresponding shots in Olivier's and Zeffirelli's. Discuss, for example, how the two main antagonists, Hamlet and Claudius, are placed in relation to the setting and to others in the scene.

4. During his first soliloquy ("O, that this too too sullied flesh would melt") Branagh chooses not to follow Olivier's lead in having the words spoken in voice-over, as if he were thinking them. Rather, he speaks the lines aloud, as would a stage actor. Comment upon this strategy and its effectiveness.

5. Discuss the dramatic use of nonverbal elements in the scene where Horatio, Marcellus, and Barnardo tell Hamlet of the ghost's appearance.

6. Contrast the staging of the scene where Polonius offers advice to Laertes with the corresponding scenes in Olivier and Zeffirelli. To what extent does the staging and cinematography of each scene influence our view of the characters of Polonius, Laertes, and Ophelia?

7. Polonius's admonitions to Ophelia about Hamlet are intercut with scenes of the pair making love. To what extent do you believe that this directorial decision supports Shakespeare's intent about the sexual nature of their relationship? To what extent are the intercuts dramatically necessary?

8. Comment on the staging of the scene where Hamlet talks to the ghost—set not on the castle battlements (as in the play and the other two films), but in the frozen woods. Note, for example, how Branagh uses camera movement, intercutting (in particular, of shots depicting the recent past in the palace), extreme close-ups, music, sound, and visual effects.

9. During the scene when Polonius asks Reynaldo to investigate Laertes, we see a prostitute on Polonius's bed. To what extent do you think that such dramatic license is justified, in terms of what we know about Polonius?

10. Unlike Olivier and Zeffirelli, Branagh does not attempt to dramatize the story that Ophelia tells her father about Hamlet's recent strange behavior (his coming to her room, clutching her in silence, sighing, and then withdrawing). To what extent do you think Branagh was justified in choosing to rely entirely on Ophelia's words?

11. In the scene where Polonius informs the king and queen that Hamlet is mad, Branagh changes Shakespeare's text by having Polonius call in Ophelia to read portions of Hamlet's letter to her. (Note that in Olivier's and Zeffirelli's films, Ophelia is not present during this scene, and Polonius both reads the letter and comments upon it.) Ophelia runs from the room after reading the letter. When Polonius continues reading, we see a shot of Hamlet and Ophelia after their lovemaking, with Hamlet saying to Ophelia the words in his letter. What dramatic effect does Branagh achieve by bringing in Ophelia, at this point, both in the present and in flashback?

12. Contrast Branagh's version of the scenes showing the arrival of Rosencrantz and Guildenstern with the corresponding scenes in Zeffirelli's film. How do the very different settings of the two films, as well as the different acting styles of Branagh and Gibson, affect the mood and dramatic significance of each sequence?

13. As Claudius discusses Hamlet with Rosencrantz and Guildenstern, and he and Polonius prepare to spy on Hamlet's encounter with Ophelia, the camera makes several circles around the company. What dramatic purpose do you think is served by such restless, ever-changing shifts in point of view?

14. Compare and contrast Branagh's treatment of Hamlet's "To be or not to be" speech with Olivier's and Zeffirelli's. How does the set-

ting of each scene, as well as the actor's delivery, affect the dramatic meaning of the speech?

15. Branagh's full-text version of *Hamlet* naturally includes all of the dialogue between the players in the play-within-the-play sequence. (Olivier's version includes only the dumb show prologue; Zeffirelli's includes a highly truncated version of the dialogue.) Discuss the benefits and possible drawbacks of presenting this scene in its entirety. In your response, consider the nonverbal elements of Branagh's scene.

16. In playing the scene with Rosencrantz and Guildenstern after Claudius's abrupt departure from "The Mousetrap," Gibson and Branagh approach Hamlet at this point from somewhat different angles. Notice how the two actors in their respective films move, deliver their lines, and interact with other characters in the scene. From what you can determine, how do Branagh and Zeffirelli differently interpret Hamlet's state of mind at this time?

17. Notice that Claudius's reaction upon discovering that Hamlet has killed Polonius—Act IV, scene 1 in Shakespeare's play—is recorded by Branagh in a single, unusually long (almost 3 minutes) traveling shot. What dramatic purpose do you think is served by the way that this scene has been filmed?

18. Discuss the effectiveness—or ineffectiveness—of the scene immediately preceding the Intermission, when Hamlet, alone on the icy plain, delivers the speech, "How all occasions do inform against me…" Note the role of the setting, the pictorial composition, the camera, and Patrick Doyle's music during this shot.

19. Though Branagh has been extraordinarily faithful to Shakespeare's text, he has made some changes for cinematic purposes. For example, the film resumes after the Intermission (Act IV, scene 5) with a voice-over by Claudius extracted from a speech to Gertrude later in the scene, a speech illustrated with visual quotations from earlier in the film, as well as new scenes—for example, of Ophelia confined to a padded cell. Lines by an anonymous "Gentleman" in Shakespeare, who informs Gertrude of Ophelia's condition, have been assigned to Horatio and a nurse. Discuss the effectiveness of this particular sequence that opens the second part of the film.

20. Unlike Olivier and Zeffirelli, Branagh chooses not to illustrate Gertrude's report of Ophelia's death with shots of Ophelia in the stream. (We do see a brief shot of Ophelia under the water, but not until after the scene concludes.) Do you think that Branagh should have illustrated this reported event (as he did other reported events, such as the poisoning of Hamlet's father or even, in the next scene, Yorick alive and jesting) or that he was right to keep the visual focus on Gertrude and Laertes in this scene?

21. In one of Branagh's most daring innovations for a *Hamlet* film, the final scene is intercut (beginning with Hamlet's asking for Laertes's forgiveness before the duel begins) with shots of Fortinbras' invading army marching towards and eventually forcing its way into the great hall of Elsinore. Discuss the ways that this ending affects the meaning of *Hamlet,* particularly in comparison to the film versions by Olivier and Zeffirelli.

22. Comment on the final sequence in Branagh's *Hamlet,* with Hamlet's body being borne away (as in Olivier's film) and subsequently lying in state, followed by the pulling down and smashing of the statue of Hamlet's father. What effect does this conclusion have upon the meaning of the play, as Branagh appears to conceive it?

Making *Hamlet*
Kenneth Branagh

In a series of interviews connected with the premiere of Hamlet *Branagh talked about the making of the film, why he was attracted to the project in the first place, and what he hoped to accomplish. Responding to PBS interviewer Charlie Rose about why he loved great plays, he said, "you know, as [theater critic] Kenneth Tynan once said, the experience of watching a great play means that we sometimes understand a little more about why we're alive. Well, when I left [a performance of* Hamlet *starring Derek Jacobi] I don't know if I understood that, but I did feel alive. I felt better. I [...] went away with a feeling of excitement that stayed with me for days."* In another interview, Branagh explained the bracing effect of re-interpreting Shakespeare:*

> *For many people there continues to be the sense that this writer and his work, which has this Masterpiece status, is something to fear and dread, something that will somehow expose their lack of learning or intelligence. My experience has been that when people have had a good experience with Shakespeare, it's beyond perhaps just the snob factor, and feeling rather clever, it's something that can open up a certain part of themselves which, from that point, starts to be much less intimidated by great works of literature.†*

In the following selection, which serves as the Introduction to Branagh's edition of the Hamlet *screenplay (1996), Branagh further discusses his long-standing passion for Shakespeare's great tragedy and why he burned to make his own film version.*

A brief biography of Kenneth Branagh may be found in the headnote to the previous selection.

1   As I write this, I am one month away from completing a project which has consumed me, to varying degrees, for the last twenty years.

---

*Interview, *The Charlie Rose Show,* 23 Dec. 1996.

†Gary Crowdus, "Sharing an Enthusiasm for Shakespeare: An Interview with Kenneth Branagh. *Cineaste* 24.1 (1998): 35.

2   I first encountered *Hamlet* when Richard Chamberlain, T.V.'s Doctor Kildare, played the title role on British television. I was eleven years old and from a background (Irish, Protestant, working-class) which had given me little preparation for watching Shakespeare. I was sufficiently distracted on that Sunday evening to leave my overdue homework uncompleted. I felt very uneasy when the Ghost of Hamlet's father appeared. There were no great special effects to heighten the audience's fear, but the atmosphere of the scene was unsettling. I was dragged away from the screen shortly afterwards to a tardy bedtime. It continued to affect me as I tried, unsuccessfully, to sleep. I wasn't sure that I had liked what I saw (the play I mean, not the performances) but it certainly stayed with me. Enough for me to resort to Shakespeare as an excuse when I was carpeted the following morning for my poor homework.

3   Over the following few years, *Hamlet* took on different shapes. One was a picture of Laurence Olivier on the cover of an old L.P. record, lying (unused) in a corner of the English Department Stock Room. Later still, the record itself was played in class, the master's sepulchral reading of 'To Be Or Not To Be' set against Walton's eerie score. I knew nothing of 'fardels' or 'bodkins', but I knew that here was 'something'. By the age of fifteen, though, Shakespeare had still taken no special hold of my imagination. I was interested in soccer and girls. Shakespeare was for swots.

4   Surprisingly, however, what did grab my attention at this time was a television serialization of Robert Graves's *I, Claudius* [about the first four Roman emperors]. I was particularly impressed by the actor playing the title role. His name was Derek Jacobi, and I noticed, with some excitement, a small ad in the entertainment section of our local newspaper announcing that Derek Jacobi "of T.V.'s *I, Claudius* fame" was to appear in *Hamlet* at the New Theatre, Oxford.

5   I rang to book my ticket. A new adventure for me. My theatre-going had been limited to a couple of organized school trips prior to this. But I wanted to see this man in the flesh. I still hadn't read the play, so for all I knew, I might be treated to some of the stuttering which had impressed me so much in his television performance. I travelled to Oxford, some half an hour away by train, my first real independent outing as an adolescent. The pavement outside the theatre was thronged with ticket holders, and I discovered it was the very first performance of this production by the Prospect Theatre Company. Excitement was in the air, and from my first glimpse of the poster, with a haunted Jacobi staring into some bleak beyond, I was aglow with anticipation.

6   Much later I read a remark by the distinguished critic Kenneth Tynan, who said "the difference between a good play and a great play is that after the experience of a great play we understand a little more about why we are alive." My theatre-going experience at that point gave me little scope for comparison but I was convinced as I left the theatre that evening that I had experienced—not just watched, but truly experienced—something unique. The story was gripping, and I wanted at every moment to know "what happened next." Much of the language I did not understand and yet the actors' commitment to each line convinced me that I knew what they were feeling. As Ophelia lost her reason, I was moved to tears. I was passionate in my longing for Claudius to receive his come-uppance, and the sword fight at the end was as thrilling as any football match.

7   But as I travelled home that summer evening twenty years ago my overwhelming feeling was of having connected with an extraordinary energy. In the play itself and chiefly in the character of Hamlet I experienced the insistent hum of life itself. He was passionate, humorous, cruel, intelligent, courageous and cowardly, but unmistakably and gloriously brimming over with life. In this production and in Jacobi's performance I had been taken on an emotional roller-coaster. It made me reflect on my relationships with my parents, the prospects of my adolescent love affair. It set my heart and my head racing. I felt I had encountered a genuine force of nature, and on that journey home and for sometime afterwards, its memory made me glad to be alive. But then I was fifteen.

8   Nevertheless, the damage was done. I began to read the play, to read more of Shakespeare. I resolved to become an actor. Tempting though it is to re-write one's personal history with the benefit of hindsight, I believe that much of what has followed in my life was affected by that experience.

9   My training at the Royal Academy of Dramatic Art was the next point at which I could pursue this passionate interest. At twenty, having 'collected' as an audience member the performances of a dozen other Hamlets (including the films by Olivier and Kozintsev), I gave my first performance of the role. Regarding its success, I would borrow Richard Briers' self-assessment of his own RADA Prince—"I may not have been the best Hamlet but I was the quickest." But the experience taught me much about the practical demands of the role: massive physical exertion culminating in a complicated fight that an exhausted actor at the end of the play would happily do without. I felt the thrill of playing the role, but at the end of the run I knew little more about the Prince of Denmark than I had five years earlier.

10   There was a stronger sense of this four years later in 1984, when I played Laertes in a production for the Royal Shakespeare Company. It was invaluable to watch the central character (played by Roger Rees) from a different vantage point. I was able to observe much more clearly what is said about him by others, and worry less about the Prince's own words. Here too was a chance to view the whole play, but from within. I was made aware of the double family tragedy. All of the Polonius clan and all of the royal family—dead, at the finale. And in Fortinbras's accession to the throne there is the sense of a national tragedy—the end of an era. The weight of sadness is felt across the whole play, not confined to one man.

11   Derek Jacobi stepped back into my "Hamlet" life once more, when in 1988 he directed me in the role for The Renaissance Theatre Company. As a director of the company I had originally asked him to produce *Richard II* with another actor, but he suggested *Hamlet* and asked me to play the title role. My actor's vanity got the better of me and I said yes.

12   Even so, I was unready. I produced a hectic Hamlet, high on energy but low on subtlety and crucially lacking depth. I was aware that something Jacobi himself had brought effortlessly and effectively to the role was life experience. He had the confidence as an actor to do less. A longer exposure to the 'whips and scorns of time' in his own life gave him an easy weight which underlined the depths of Hamlet's thinking and gave a necessary counterpoint to the frenzied and frantic elements of Hamlet's personality.

13   The chief lesson of the production was that I should do it again and that the time must be right. It had to be when I still fulfilled the age requirements for the Prince but when I had the courage to bring a slightly older and more complex self to the role. When I had the confidence to let the acting energy take care of itself and, as Hamlet, to live more completely in the moment. As the years went by, I was never less than fascinated by other actors' Hamlets. The play still held its attraction for me, but it remained artistically as unfinished business.

14   On radio in 1992 I had my first taste of the full text, and a splendid opportunity to explore the play's language with a focus and significance that was uniquely offered by the medium, in which the spoken word dominates. With the full text, the gravitational weight of the play seemed to increase. While arguments will always rage about exactly what constitutes a "full text" I had no doubt that this version offered rich opportunities for the actors, particularly in the supporting roles. I felt I understood much more about Polonius with the inclusion of the often cut scene with his 'agent' Reynaldo. The complexity of Claudius's manipulations in the full version of the scene where he plots with Laertes, helped to flesh out a richer portrait than the conventional stage villain. And there were, to my taste, fascinating excursions on the state of the Elizabethan theatre, and jaundiced summations of the legal profession and of court life. On top of the domestic tragedy which engulfs a royal family the play seemed an all-embracing survey of life. It was harsh, vigorous and contemporary in feel.

15   I resolved that were I to attempt the role again, it should be using this full text.

16   The opportunity arose when Adrian Noble invited me to play the title role in a new Royal Shakespeare Company production which opened in 1992. He concurred with me that we should use what some critics have referred to as the "eternity" version. Now, at thirty-three, the part seemed at last to be "playing me." There were no surprises in the obstacle course of great set pieces, and I felt as if I had been in training for this attempt. The performance matured as it had not before, and continued to surprise me, not least by the way in which the full text offered a much more comfortable playing experience for the actor. It was more imaginatively paced. One could take advantage of the "breaths" that Shakespeare had given the actor. Paradoxically it was much less physically exhausting to play, and the cumulative weight of the longer evening made for an immensely powerful finale.

17   By this time I had had two experiences of filming Shakespeare and my film-maker's instincts made me long—even as I explored it within a fine production like Adrian's—to take the play into the cinema in its fullest form. I longed to allow audiences to join Fortinbras on the plain in Norway, to be transported, as Hamlet is in his mind's eye, back to Troy and see Priam and Hecuba. I felt that all my experience with the play and with Shakespeare was leading me in one direction.

18   My attempts to finance a film version had been in motion since the opening of *Henry V,* but the perpetual reluctance of film companies to finance Shakespeare had frustrated each attempt.

19   In 1995 Castle Rock Entertainment finally agreed to follow this dream, by financing a full-length version which would perhaps be followed by an abridged version at a more traditional length. The pages that follow, record the attempt.

20   The screenplay is what one might call the "verbal storyboard." An inflexion of

a subjective view of the play which has developed over the years. Its intention was to be both personal, with enormous attention paid to the intimate relations between the characters, and at the same time epic, with a sense of the country at large and of a dynasty in decay.

21   The style is a development of my other Shakespeare film work. Among its principles are a commitment to international casting; a speaking style that is as realistic as a proper adherence to the structure of the language will allow; a period setting that attempts to set the story in a historical context that is resonant for a modern audience but allows a heightened language to sit comfortably. Above all, we have asked for a full emotional commitment to the characters, springing from belief that they can be understood in direct, accessible relation to modern life.

22   As I mentioned before, at the time of writing, the film is yet to be completed. The sound and music mix are in their final stages. So I for one am unsure of the results. I've brought as much intelligence as I can to its execution but in the end mine is not an intellectual approach, but an intuitive one. For better or worse, I am still connected to the feeling that had overwhelmed me all those years ago, when first I saw the play live. For audiences familiar or unfamiliar with the story, that's what I'd like to pass on.

23   That I should have pursued the play's mysteries so assiduously over twenty years continues to puzzle me. But, it's what I do, and this is what I've done. As the great soccer manager Bill Shankly once said, describing the importance of football, "It's not a matter of life and death. It's much more important than that." Certainly for me, an ongoing relationship to this kind of poetry and this kind of mind is a necessary part of an attempt to be civilized. I am profoundly grateful for the opportunity to explore it.

24   The hold it has over me will not lessen its grip. Michael Maloney, who plays Laertes in the film, told me recently of an impending production in which he will play the Prince. I found myself as excited as ever to discuss interpretation, casting, language—everything. For I believe I've come happily to realize that of course I cannot explain *Hamlet*, or even perhaps my own interpretation of *Hamlet*.

25   This film is simply the passionate expression of a dream. A dream that has preoccupied me for so many years. I cannot really explain that either. The reasons are in the film. The reasons are the film.

26   Goethe said, "A genuine work of art, no less than a work of nature, will always remain infinite to our reason: it can be contemplated and felt, it affects us, but it cannot be fully comprehended, even less than it is possible to express its essence and its merits in words."

27   After twenty years, I'm happy to say, I think I know what he means.

Discussion and Writing Suggestions

1. Branagh stresses that from the beginning of his experience with *Hamlet* to the present, he has lacked a complete understanding of the work, though it has exerted an increasingly powerful hold over his imagination and his creative efforts. What is it about *Hamlet* that appears to so

strongly fascinate him? What do you think he means when he says (in paragraph 25), "The reasons are in the film. The reasons are the film"?

2. In paragraph 10 Branagh explains that when he played Laertes in *Hamlet* some years after playing the lead, he was able to consider the action of the play from a different vantage point and had "a chance to view the whole play, but from within." To what extent might such an experience have implications for any of us—not necessarily as actors, but rather as members of the audience, who generally focus on the action from the limited point of view of the protagonist?

   For example, when we view a film, we generally identify with the hero and hope the hero prevails over his or her antagonist—either a villain or an unsympathetic character. But would playing the role of the antagonist—or trying to see the action from the antagonist's point of view—help us to better understand, if not actively sympathize, with that character? Think of examples of dramas in which you may have too hastily judged one or more characters. Perhaps you thought too harshly of the antagonist or too sympathetically of the protagonist or, more broadly, did not see "the whole play… from within."

3. Branagh spends some time explaining his rationale for making an uncut (four hour) *Hamlet.* To what extent do you think he was justified in this decision? If you have seen the Olivier and/or Zeffirelli *Hamlet*s, does the action of Branagh's version seem clearer? Do the characters in his film appear more fully developed and motivated? Does the social and political context provided by the full text enhance your experience of the play? Or does the four-hour length blur the dramatic focus—and make the film seem interminable?

4. Branagh closes with a quotation by the poet and dramatist Johann Wolfgang von Goethe (1749–1832). What do you think Goethe means by this quotation? Can you think of a particular "genuine work of art" that exemplifies his idea? Does it make the idea clearer or more confusing to make an analogy between a work of art and "a work of nature"?

Review of Branagh's *Hamlet*
Roger Ebert

As indicated earlier, Branagh's Hamlet *drew widespread critical raves. The following review by Roger Ebert, probably the best-known film critic in America, is representative. Ebert, who began his career as a sportswriter, currently appears on the weekly TV film review show "Ebert & Roeper at the Movies." For 23 years before Richard Roeper became his co-host (after the death of Gene Siskel), Ebert was half of the "Siskel and Ebert" show. In 1975 he was awarded the Pulitzer Prize for the nationally syndicated film criticism column he has written since 1967 for the* Chicago Sun-Times. *Since 1970 he has conducted lectures on film at the University of Chicago Fine Arts Program and is an adjunct professor of cinema and media studies at the University of Illinois at Urbana-Champaign. Ebert serves as a jury member for the Sundance, Montreal, Chicago, Hawaii, and Venice Film Festivals. He is the author of 15 books, including the annual editions of* Roger Ebert's Movie Year Book; Roger Ebert's Movie Home Companion *(1985);* Two Weeks in the Midday Sun: A Cannes Notebook *(1987);* Roger Ebert's Book of Film *(1997);* I Hated, Hated, HATED This Movie *(2000); and* Ebert's Bigger Little Movie Glossary: A Greatly Expanded and Much Improved Compendium of Movie Clichés, Stereotypes, Obligatory Scenes, Hackneyed Formulas, Shopworn Conventions, and Outdated Archetypes *(1999).*

This review originally appeared in the Chicago Sun-Times *in January 1997 and is available on Ebert's Web site, <http://suntimes.com/ebert/index.html>.*

1 There is early in Kenneth Branagh's "Hamlet" a wedding celebration, the Danish court rejoicing at the union of Claudius and Gertrude. The camera watches, and then pans to the right, to reveal the solitary figure of Hamlet, clad in black. It always creates a little shock in the movies when the foreground is unexpectedly occupied. We realize the subject of the scene is not the wedding, but Hamlet's experience of it. And we enjoy Branagh's visual showmanship: In all of his films, he reveals his joy in theatrical gestures.

2 His "Hamlet" is long but not slow, deep but not difficult, and it vibrates with the relief of actors who have great things to say, and the right ways to say them. And in the 70-mm. version, it has a visual clarity that is breathtaking. It is the first uncut film version of Shakespeare's most challenging tragedy, the first 70-mm. film since "Far and Away" in 1992, and at 238 minutes the second-longest major Hollywood production (one minute shorter than "Cleopatra"). Branagh's Hamlet lacks the narcissistic intensity of Laurence Olivier's (in the 1948 Academy Award winner), but the film as a whole is better, placing Hamlet in the larger context of royal politics, and making him less a subject for pity.

3 The story provides a melodramatic stage for inner agonies. Hamlet (Branagh), the prince of Denmark, mourns the untimely death of his father. His mother, Gertrude, rushes with unseemly speed into marriage with Claudius, her husband's brother. Something is rotten in the state of Denmark. And then the ghost of Hamlet's father appears and says he was poisoned by Claudius

4 What must Hamlet do? He desires the death of Claudius but lacks the impulse to act out. He despises himself for his passivity. In tormenting himself he drives his mother to despair, kills Polonius by accident, speeds the kingdom toward chaos and his love, Ophelia, toward madness.

5 What is intriguing about "Hamlet" is the ambiguity of everyone's motives. Tom Stoppard's "Rosenkrantz and Guildenstern Are Dead" famously filtered all the action through the eyes of Hamlet's treacherous school friends. But how does it all look to Gertrude? To Claudius? To the heartbroken Ophelia? The great benefit of this full-length version is that these other characters become more understandable.

6 The role of Claudius (Derek Jacobi) is especially enriched: In shorter versions, he is the scowling usurper who functions only as villain. Here, with lines and scenes restored, he seems more balanced and powerful. He might have made

a plausible king of Denmark, had things turned out differently. Yes, he killed his brother, but regicide was not unknown in medieval times, and perhaps the old king was ripe for replacement; this production shows Gertrude (Julie Christie) as lustfully in love with Claudius. By restoring the original scope of Claudius' role, Branagh emphasizes court and political intrigue instead of enclosing the material in a Freudian hothouse.

7   The movie's very sets emphasize the role of the throne as the center of the kingdom. Branagh uses costumes to suggest the 19th century, and shoots his exteriors at Blenheim Castle, seat of the duke of Marlborough and Winston Churchill's childhood home. The interior sets, designed by Tim Harvey and Desmond Crowe, feature a throne room surrounded by mirrored walls, overlooked by a gallery and divided by an elevated walkway. The set puts much of the action onstage (members of the court are constantly observing) and allows for intrigue (some of the mirrors are two-way, and lead to concealed chambers and corridors).

8   In this very public arena Hamlet agonizes, and is observed. Branagh uses rapid cuts to show others reacting to his words and meanings. And he finds new ways to stage familiar scenes, renewing the material. Hamlet's most famous soliloquy ("To be or not to be…") is delivered into a mirror, so that his own indecision is thrust back at him. When he torments Ophelia, a most private moment, we spy on them from the other side of a two-way mirror; he crushes her cheek against the glass and her frightened breath clouds it. When he comes upon Claudius at his prayers, and can kill him, many productions imagine Hamlet lurking behind a pillar in a chapel. Branagh is more intimate, showing a dagger blade insinuating itself through the mesh of a confessional.

9   One of the surprises of this uncut "Hamlet" is the crucial role of the play within the play. Many productions reduce the visiting troupe of actors to walk-ons; they provide a hook for Hamlet's advice to the players, and merely suggest the performance that Hamlet hopes will startle Claudius into betraying himself. Here, with Charlton Heston magnificently assured as the Player King, we listen to the actual lines of his play (which shorter versions often relegate to dumb-show at the back of the stage). We see how ingeniously and cleverly they tweak the conscience of the king, and we see Claudius' pained reactions. The episode becomes a turning point; Claudius realizes that Hamlet is on to him.

10   As for Hamlet, Branagh (like Mel Gibson in the 1991 film) has no interest in playing him as an apologetic mope. Branagh is an actor of exuberant physical gifts and energy (when the time comes, his King Lear will bound about the heath). Consider the scene beginning "Oh, what a rogue and peasant knave am I…," in which Hamlet bitterly regrets his inaction. The lines are delivered not in bewilderment but in mounting anger, and it is to Branagh's credit that he pulls out all the stops; a quieter Hamlet would make a tamer "Hamlet."

11   Kate Winslet is touchingly vulnerable as Ophelia, red-nosed and snuffling, her world crumbling about her. Richard Briers makes Polonius not so much a foolish old man as an adviser out of his depth. Of the familiar faces, the surprise is Heston: How many great performances have we lost while he visited the Planet of the Apes? Billy Crystal is a surprise, but effective, as the gravedigger. But Robin Williams, Jack Lemmon, and Gerard Depardieu are distractions, their performances not overcoming our shocks of recognition.

12   At the end of this "Hamlet," I felt at last as if I was getting a handle on the play (I never expect to fully understand it). It has been a long journey. I read it in high school, underlining the famous lines. I saw the Richard Burton film version, and later Olivier's. I studied it in graduate school. I have seen it onstage in England and the United States (most memorably in Aidan Quinn's punk version, when he scrawled graffiti on the wall: "2B=?"). Franco Zeffirelli's version with Gibson came in 1991. I learned from them all.

13   One of the tasks of a lifetime is to become familiar with the great plays of Shakespeare. "Hamlet" is the most opaque. Branagh's version moved me, entertained me and made me feel for the first time at home in that doomed royal court. I may not be able to explain Hamlet, but at last I have a better idea than Rosencrantz and Guildenstern.

Discussion and Writing Suggestions

1. Ebert begins his review by pointing out a noteworthy shot in which Hamlet unexpectedly comes into the foreground during the wedding celebration for Claudius and Gertrude. As Ebert says, "We realize the subject of the scene is not the wedding, but Hamlet's experience of it." Find other examples in Branagh's *Hamlet* of imaginative uses of the camera to help create dramatic meaning. How does our *viewpoint*, established by either a still or a moving camera, contribute to the effect of the scene?

2. In paragraphs 5 and 6, Ebert discusses the "ambiguity of everyone's motives," mentioning Gertrude and Ophelia, but focusing particularly upon Claudius, who "might have made a plausible king of Denmark, had things turned out differently." Compare Ebert's handling of this topic with Branagh's own, in paragraph 10 of "Making *Hamlet*."

3. In paragraphs 7 and 8, Ebert considers the distinctive way in which Branagh shoots familiar scenes—the "To be or not to be" soliloquy, the "Get thee to a nunnery" scene between Hamlet and Ophelia, the scene where Hamlet comes upon the praying Claudius. Note what Ebert says about how the way that one of these scenes is shot helps create a particular dramatic meaning, and then compare Branagh's approach to this scene with either Olivier's or Zeffirelli's. What differences do you find? How do these differences create a different kind of dramatic effect?

4. Ebert notes that Branagh's *Hamlet* is unique in presenting all of the players' dialogue in the play-within-the-play scene. In other versions, the scene is presented merely as "dumb show." Compare and contrast Branagh's play scene with those in Olivier's and Zeffirelli's films and explain to what extent you agree with Ebert about the value of presenting the players' dialogue. Won't audiences get the dramatic point if the players merely pantomime their actions—particularly since Shakespeare himself provided for a pantomime *before* the dialogue? Is dialogue redundant at this point? Or is it dramatically necessary?

5. Compare and contrast Ebert's comments about being able "to explain *Hamlet*" with similar comments made by Branagh during the course of "Making *Hamlet.*" Why should people who are so thoroughly familiar with this play be not fully confident that they can "explain" it? In what sense do Branagh and Ebert appear to be using the word "explain"?

Rehearsing and Filming *Hamlet:* A Film Diary
Russell Jackson

During the rehearsals and filming of Hamlet, *Russell Jackson, Associate Director of the Shakespeare Institute, and Branagh's long-time script consultant, kept a diary, one that provides a fascinating record of how a large scale film project like this is produced. Jackson focuses primarily on the actors as they proceed from their preliminary readings and conceptions of their characters to the nuts-and-bolts problems they face as they interact not only with other actors, but also with complex sets, props, cameras, lights, sound equipment, and snow-making and earthquake-making machines. Especially interesting is Jackson's record of how the actors struggle to flesh out both their own and Branagh's interpretations of their roles. Just how should Hamlet—and Ophelia—play their "mad" scenes? How should Branagh speak Hamlet's most famous soliloquy—"To be or not to be?"—without sounding trite? How can he address his speech to a mirror without the lights and cameras reflecting in the image? How can Hamlet send a chandelier flying down onto Claudius's throne without killing Derek Jacobi? (Interestingly, Olivier was worried about a similar problem and spends some time in his autobiography discussing the logistics of this scene.**)*

In one of his interviews Branagh describes the crucial role of Russell Jackson to the production:

> *Russell is someone with a very rich understanding of the textual history of Shakespeare's plays and an immense knowledge of Shakespearean performance, so he's a useful bridge between academia and his own knowledge of the ways in which, somehow, the play simply works, or how this difficult bit that the actor is having trouble understanding, and that no amount of textual analysis will clarify, works. So Russell is a reference point for actors in rehearsal who, for instance, may have an issue with having to perform a much shorter version of a speech or a piece of prose. Often they'll go to him and talk about the whole speech and sometimes, as a result of that, I will be led to understand that I perhaps cut too deeply or that I need to restore a line or two that continues an idea inside the language that I had under-estimated in terms of its importance for the actor.*†

These excerpts from Jackson's diary originally appeared in Branagh's edition of the Hamlet *screenplay.*

---

*Laurence Olivier, *Confessions of an Actor: An Autobiography.* New York: Simon and Schuster, 1982: 152–54.

†Gary Crowdus, "Sharing an Enthusiasm for Shakespeare: An Interview with Kenneth Branagh. *Cineaste* 24.1 (1998): 35.

What follows is taken from a diary of the rehearsals and shooting of [Branagh's] *Hamlet.* In selecting from the three and a half months of work, I've tried to convey film-making's combination of the serious and the trivial, the glamorous and the mundane. […]

Every morning the crew assembles its trolley-loads of equipment, and the Director, the Director of Photography and their entourages arrange the set-ups for the first shots of the day. The actors rehearse the scene, and the stand-ins take their places so it can be lit. When each shot has been done, we move to another set-up. The actors either return to their dressing-rooms while this is being done, or stay on set to read, chat or do the crossword—though they need to keep their sense of the scene and the character, and may not want simply to pass the time of day. To make their job harder, scenes are often shot out of sequence. Sometimes even the shots that make up a scene are filmed out of order, and not always on consecutive days. At the end of every working day, when we hear the magic word 'wrap' and have tomorrow's call-sheet we can pack up and go home. (Though usually there are rushes to be viewed, and some people still have a lot of note-making and checking to do.)

I ought to explain briefly the function of a few members of the unit. The Script Supervisor keeps watch over dialogue or moves, logs photographic data for each take the director decides to have printed, maintains and is responsible (amongst other things) for the "Bible" of the film, the marked continuity script. If we wanted to know what we were doing next (and in some cases what we had just done) Annie Wotton, our Script Supervisor, was the fount of all knowledge. The First Assistant Director (Simon Mosley) is responsible to the Director for the organisation of the set, and the Director of Photography (Alex Thomson) supervises the work of the camera team and the lighting. The props department has 'stand-bys' to place props on the set, go round with blowtorches lighting candles, and so forth. Costume and make-up have their own personnel on the set, so that the day's call-sheet might list half a dozen actors and still require catering for more than a hundred people. Two trolley-loads of electrical equipment are always in attendance, for sound and video, the latter providing video relay and a recording of each shot as the camera sees it.

So where do I fit into this labour-intensive artistic industry? Hugh Cruttwell and I have worked with Kenneth Branagh for some years on various projects, including his Shakespeare films. Hugh has a watching brief on Ken's own performance and is also part of the support system for the actors in general. I'm there to help with textual matters, which range from queries about specific words and lines to broader questions of interpretation affecting speeches or scenes. These can't (or shouldn't) be divorced from matters that are, strictly speaking, Hugh's department: we work together, as extra eyes and ears for the director. Most of the time during shooting, our place is by the video monitors, and what follows is largely *Hamlet* seen from that point of view—or, in the usual abbreviation, p.o.v.

Wednesday 3 January

Rehearsals Begin

First morning in Shepperton. This may be one of the major British studios but it's not, on first sight, impressive. Located in a semi-suburban hinterland southwest of London, it seems at first like an industrial estate, a jumble of sheds, hangars, workshops, and what look like builders' yards, with a mansion trapped in the middle of it all like a genteel hostage from Edwardian England. Small electric trucks (some with '101 Dalmatians' blazoned on their cab) ferry lamps, equipment, food around between the offices, stages and workshops. The canine spectacular is well on in shooting: graceful white dogs with black spots are much in evidence. One low white building, painted with Dalmatian-style spots, is the home of the puppies ('Caution—Puppies at play') and inmates in various sizes bounce or amble about in their runs. One is being trained to trot alongside a bicycle, another to follow a row of silver-paper covered boxes and then pounce on it at command.

We're in the elegant board-room of the old house, round a long green-baize covered table. First session is with Derek Jacobi (Claudius) and Julie Christie (Gertrude), plus Ken, Orlando Seale (his "acting double"), Annie Wotton (Script Supervisor), Simon Mosley (First A.D.), Hugh Cruttwell.

Ken distributes phials of a herbal "Rescue Remedy" (only half a joke, admitting nervous apprehension). Everyone has read the screenplay, and the actors have already had some discussion of their roles with Ken, but these days of rehearsal before we begin shooting will give everyone time for reappraisal, adjustments and (most important) finding out how the story will be told by *this* company of actors, in *these* circumstances. We won't start with a read-through: better to edge towards the play. We discuss royal families (including the current one), privacy, politics, and draw towards a reading of the scenes when Claudius and Gertrude are together. There's talk about the issue of complicity between them (not at all, so far as murder is concerned) and the "essential" Claudius, which she took (and part of him still takes) as loving, kind, a "good" man. Derek goes along with this, though he and Hugh Cruttwell remind us of Hamlet's very different point of view. Gertrude and Claudius feel responsible for Hamlet but Claudius has another agenda she knows nothing about—concerning the potential threat posed by her son.

After lunch the Polonius family join us, with Horatio. By now we feel able to discuss frankly and simply (and off the record) our own experiences of family, bereavement, grief. (This is not just to canvass ideas about the emotions of the play to draw on them in performance: it also establishes common ground among us.) Then we try to imagine an "ideal" family, successful and well-balanced according to current middle-class notions, professional but not competitive, materially well-off but not showy—which (we agree) turns out quite repulsive. Then on to the Polonius family.

Polonius (Richard Briers) was promoted by new king. Laertes (Michael Maloney) is in Paris getting the gentlemanly accomplishments (N.B. not at Wittenberg). Ophelia (Kate Winslett) and Hamlet have been having an affair (yes, they have been to bed together, because we want this relationship to be as serious as possible) since the death of Hamlet senior. (Effect of a surge of feeling in time of bereavement and crisis?) Then we visit the set, particularly the State Room, which fills the whole of Stage A. Actors seem to be getting the Elsinore air in their nostrils. Slowly, alone, Julie walks along one mirrored wall. Ken announces that in a fortnight's time he hopes to have a "performance" of the whole play, if possible without scripts and certainly without set or costumes.

Thursday 4 January (morning)

Ken gives us all copies of a questionnaire, a magazine-style personality quiz ("Which of your characteristics do you most/least admire?", "If you were to die and come back in another form, what would you like to be?" and so on). The actors fill this in as their characters, the rest of us as ourselves, and Tim Spall and Reece Dinsdale (Rosencrantz and Guildenstern) arrive half-way through as though coming late to a party—which may be exactly the position their characters are in when they get to Elsinore. Then we have to exchange the forms, and guess who wrote which. Some surprises among the 'characters' (Horatio wants to translate Virgil's *Aeneid* into Danish) but mainly a consolidation of the ideas we have been pushing round so far, a good way of taking stock of the court.

Later more on the Polonius family. Believable intensity in the Polonius/Ophelia talk about Hamlet: not simple oppression from him and rebellion from her, but she can't tell him what's been going on. After much talk, paraphrasing lines, trying moves, Ken runs the scene with them just sitting on chairs side by side: stronger, more frustrated, with a greater sense of her being cornered. Kate Winslett plays Ophelia as vulnerable but not cowed, Dickie Briers is getting more than anger in Polonius—some loving apprehension. We try having her present when Polonius tells the king and queen he has found the cause of Hamlet's madness, and to take this further by making her read out Hamlet's love-letter—usually read by Polonius. We decide this is (a) too cruel an ordeal for her to be put through by our Polonius (b) too extreme so early in the story—so we will split the difference and have her read some of it only.

Thursday 4–Monday 8 January

We work through scenes, trying various approaches, finding snags, problems, opportunities. Ophelia's motivations in returning Hamlet's love-tokens are considered: she is going further than Polonius suggested in any instructions we have heard, and whatever her father and the king expect from this confrontation, she has her own agenda (perhaps to find out why Hamlet is behaving this way to her, to put him on the spot?). The kinder and more circumspect Polonius seems, the harder it will be for her to betray him—hence her lying to Hamlet ('Where's your father?—At home, my lord'). In "To be or not to be" Ken wants to show Hamlet alone with his mirror image(s) in the vast space of the mirrored hall. He has to be careful not to give the soliloquy an energy or momentum that it does not need—those qualities are coming soon enough in what follows when he encounters Ophelia. Ken steers Derek towards seeming even more vulnerable as Claudius, "quietly anxious" about Hamlet after "nunnery" scene, rarely openly angry, even when Rosencrantz and Guildenstern have screwed up. So, when he does flare up, becomes desperate, it will be more shocking.

[…]

Wednesday 10 January

Rehearsal on set with Robin Williams (Osric), Nick Farrell (Horatio) and Ken, to set up Osric scene in Hamlet's study. This is our first exposure to a fully-dressed set, stuffed with the impedimenta of Hamlet's artistic and literary enthusiasms. For the first time there are discussions of camera set-ups, lighting, etc. Now we are no longer in the technical-free environment of the board-room. We discuss dividing up the scene, but agree that it needs to take place in this private room, except for the very opening (which we do on the hall balcony). Robin is inventive, full of comic "turns" and voices but not aggressive or showy (at lunch he gives us, among other things, 'Gandhi, the musical'). He is careful to see Osric as a person—a landowning upstart, but with his own sense of place and purpose. Details: he looks round the room nervously (but only a brief glance) while waiting for Hamlet to answer him.

While we're rehearsing, a striking figure appears, ushered in by a bearded stranger: a woman in an extravagant art deco outfit, all angles and black-and-white lines from head to toe. At first I assume this is one of the ultimate fashion victims of the movie business on a day out—then realize it's Glenn Close in full fig as Cruella de Vil.

Thursday 11 January

Shoot the scene. Osric at first confident, not very flamboyant or aggressive, but as the scene progresses he is less easily conciliatory with Hamlet, a bit surer of his own fashionable rightness, even when taunted about the fancy words he uses. (But it's still an ordeal: eyes show he's had enough, and he manages to collide with a chair when he bows.) Robin has found the physicality: the painfully restrict-ing boots, tight new uniform, make him stiff and awkward, undermine the high status he has awarded himself. Pround at first of having been told to go to see Hamlet, by the end he is glad to get out. Lack of space in study means that we sit in our overcoats in the dimly-lit, cold State Hall, watching monitors, and thread our way through cables and lights to get into the set. Catering is in a tent against the outside of the stage, and feels like a garden-party gone wrong, with hot-air blowers fighting a rear-guard action against icy wind under canvas walls. Later (as a bonus and while we're in the study) we shoot Hamlet's scene with Horatio just before the fencing match—"providence in the fall of a sparrow." Somehow it does-n't work: Ken a bit too lyrical, not stern enough, too sorry for that sparrow? We'll come back to this in a couple of months' time, but it was worth having a go now.

Monday 15—Wednesday 17 January

More rehearsal, some on the set. Among other things, a session with Derek and Julie and their attendants to get a sense of how this court works. Discretion, status, and the significance of living close to royals are discussed. We also work on Ophelia's "mad" scenes. In the first she will be frightening, not all "pretty," and almost beyond communication as Gertrude and Claudius try to get through to her. In the second (with Laertes) she is stiller, less confrontational. She is being treat-ed with a mixture of shock treatment (using water) and fairly brutal confinement, partly in accordance with some nineteenth-century notions of how to deal with the insane, but also because she is a political threat that has to be contained.

Then, on Wednesday, the promised run-through takes place, with no costumes and a few props. A private "studio" version. The acting area is a large square in the middle of the State Hall's tiled floor, marked off with candlesticks on stands, and the working lights are lowered so that we see it virtually by candlelight. The whole play is acted in sequence, with a five-minute break in the middle. Those not "on" watch from the sides, along with heads of technical departments. When he's not on, Ken wanders round watching action from various angles—which somehow seems to embody both his two roles as actor and director, and Hamlet's own dual role as well (plotter/victim).

Some revelations: Claudius's "goodness" is paying off, and the solution to the Hamlet problem seems to be displays of more love, apparently sincere and caring, until Hamlet has taken matters well beyond the bounds of acceptable (or excusable) behaviour by killing Polonius. Gertrude is well-defined, Horatio clear and passionate, Hamlet still a bit too sane in "Fishmonger" scene with Polonius, the Ophelia/Laertes relationship not right (too playful?). This is an invaluable opportunity for us all to get a sense of the whole play, to see where there are strengths and weaknesses—and in a technology-free environment.

Tuesday 23 January

After four days off, back to rehearse the Players' scenes. Charlton Heston (Player King) is sitting at the end of the board-room, drinking coffee, when we arrive. He moves straight in on verbal queries about his speeches, which he has gone through with a fine-toothed comb: Ken and Rosemary Harris (Player Queen) arrive and we read through, then move into next room to get it on its feet. Heston becomes more relaxed, begins to see acting opportunities rather than possible problems. Quest for a quasi-Chekhovian feeling (intimacy, sadness) in the speeches between the "play" king and queen, rather than starting out from a notion of their being in a quainter, more "old-fashioned" style than the rest of Shakespeare's play (the verse will do that anyway). At lunch Heston and Harris are expansive, anecdotal, at home. Afterwards, on to the first meeting with the Players and the 'Pyrrhus' and 'Hecuba' speech. The size of the performance will come from Heston's natural command and physique: we work now on expressive detail. Players' background discussed: they used to run a theatre, but times are bad, and they have been forced to take to the road. Still an impressive bunch—though a command performance is just what they need right now. Actor-managerish names provided for them (Horatio and Ermingard Hamilton and two further generations of their family). We imagine that the actor who plays the poisoner fancies himself as an innovator and may have an eye on the Hamilton troupe for himself.

Wednesday 24 January

Last full day of rehearsals: work on the play scene and Hamlet's meeting with the Players, who begin to seem a sort of ideal, alternative family. (The only one we see that is not dysfunctional?) The dumb-show is choreographed, then run again and again to make it faster, snappier. The State Hall is now practically ready, and without realizing it we have slipped onto the "real" set. At the end of the afternoon, everyone is called onto the State Hall set—all the crew, carpenters, painters, workshop staff, most of the principal actors, about two hundred of us. The play-scene bleachers are filled to overflowing. Ken makes a short speech. Some of us have worked with him since he started in the theatre, many (including several crew) have worked on his other films. This is the fulfillment of an ambition since 1972 when he was at school. We need to keep a high level of efficiency, attention, commitment. Then we have drinks, to "wet the baby's head": tomorrow the long haul starts.

Thursday 25 January

First Day of Principal Photography

We start with the long tracking shot of Hamlet talking to the Players, "Speak the speech, I pray you…" with background activity (chandelier raised, attendants passing). A complex speech with a lot of detail in action around it. When Hamlet reaches group of Players in the corner, Heston remarks on the effect of his being with these people (warm colours in costume, family group), in contrast with starchy, well-drilled formality of our military court.

Friday 26 January

Snow outside, and icy wind. Inside the sound stage, flaring gas jets, high bleachers with ranks of courtiers in shades of red and gold. Bits of scene including dumb show. Shots from balcony down to stage. How we do this determines shots for succeeding days. Ken doesn't at first find the sense of "antic" in his teasing Polonius before the play—it seems as though it's a sideshow they have both anticipated. Then it gets edgier, less amiable. Later Hamlet is angrier, cruder with Claudius, too. The Players now look picturesque and vaguely 'medieval' in costumes they must have carted lovingly across Europe.

[…]

Thursday 1 February

Players greeted, in long travelling shot in our hall of mirrors, so that the few acting problems pale beside the logistical ones. Heston on epic form in "Hecuba" speech, with a touch of Moses in a low angle shot where he is holding out his arms, but quiet—resonant, expressive voice and face made for the camera. (Like Depardieu, one of the great screen faces.) Chats about films and Shakespeare, including Olivier's abortive plans to do *Macbeth*, which he discussed with Heston several times.

(Question: how do you address a screen legend? Answer from camera crew, a mixture of deference and familiarity: "A bit to the left please, Chuck, sir.")

Friday 2 February

First big court scene. King and queen approach the dais down the corridor, then seen from corridor p.o.v., swishing towards thrones with their attendants, in eerie silence (music on sound track will make a great difference here). Later we turn round to film their departure, with multiple cameras and a snowstorm of confetti that we hope not to have to repeat.

This is a day dominated by logistics and problem of getting maximum effect from crowd. The sense of a public occasion with the extras in serried ranks produces different performances: Derek gives Claudius's speech with a brio (and he does the whole lot) that will be qualified in the close-ups. Finale is confetti snowstorm, with Hamlet alone on the dais, but the most striking sight of the day is after the lights have been switched off. Alone, holding a plastic bag with her belongings in one hand, and clutching her script and the train of her wedding dress with the other, Julie stands pensively among heaps of confetti in the dim and empty hall. (Unfortunately, no photographer is at hand.)

[…]

Tuesday 6 February

Over to another, smaller sound stage for the first day in the woods. (Hamlet's first scene with the Ghost, and its aftermath.) Powdery snow outside (Dalmatians identifiable against it by their spots) and snowy powder (finely shredded paper) inside. At first it seems like Siberia, but with the doors closed and the lights it's soon like the Mediterranean, especially for actors in layers of heavy uniform. The woodland almost fills the stage, and is built over a cellar full of hydraulics. In the working lights it resembles a display in a garden centre, with trees and branches bedded in with loam and held up with wires and iron stakes. Smoke and the wonderful cold morning light arranged by Alex Thomson (Director of Photography) change it into a mysterious, haunted woodland. First contact with special effects: bursts of flame and shaking forest and floor. In the middle of all this, there's acting to be done. Hamlet has to seem in a state of high anticipation and apprehension. The mad or "antic" behaviour has to come later when he warns that he may have to behave oddly, but now he mustn't seem too sober for a man fired by the need for revenge, awed by the Ghost's commands, horrified by the news of the murder. (Before each take, as the camera starts running, we hear Jack Lemmon murmur "magic time" to himself.)

[…]

Tuesday 13 February

Blemheim Palace, First Day of Location Shooting

Cold wet morning in the grounds of Blenheim Palace. Our first set-up is outside the side gate of the extraordinary piece of English early eighteenth-century baroque that was the (enormously expensive) reward of a grateful nation for the military prowess of the first Duke of Marlborough. We will be spending a fortnight encamped in the grounds from early morning to late at night like a small army, with a base camp of trailers and tents and fleets of minibuses and off-road vehicles to ferry personnel and equipment about. Now a bitter wind cuts across the lake, blowing our snow around. This is mostly detergent foam sprayed by teams of men and women in oilskins who stand in rows supporting lengths of hose across their shoulders, linked to tanks and compressors on lorries: a cross between some arcane rural ritual and an airport firecrew.

The first shot has Rosencrantz and Guildenstern arriving by miniature train, which has been dressed up as a vintage steam locomotive. (Smoke charges like fireworks in chimney.) Polonius meets them first: "You go to seek the lord Hamlet, there he is." Radio microphone signal is faint. (Sound department, over headphones: "Polonius isn't behaving very well. I'll probably have to change his aerial.") Then Hamlet, doublet all unbrac'd, greets them. Chat turns serious when prisons are mentioned: smiles freeze in apprehension (as well as literally) and R. and G. are already out of their depth, their skin-deep jauntiness wearing thin. Ken needs to sustain Hamlet's mood from a scene we haven't shot yet ("Fishmonger") which precedes this immediately in the script. Hamlet is bitter, evasive, now backfooting them, now attacking, now genial—their job isn't going to be easy.

Set-up for these first lines of long conversation seems interminable, compounded by the need to get snow just right. The "green-room," a mobile home parked nearby, is a refuge, but heated like a sauna, and every burst of shooting is heralded by an invasion from make-up and wardrobe, so that it soon becomes as crowded as the Marx Brothers' stateroom in *A Night at the Opera*. As everyone is wearing the most layers of clothing possible, space gets even tighter. Catering now includes soup and bread at one o'clock, and evening hot snack: cold weather rations.

Blenheim in different lights: orangey glow to stone, responding to shifting sun, a formidable Winter Palace. Courtyard is covered in our snow, this time paper rather than foam. The great open space is bounded by the wings of the building, and guarded by a splendid wrought-iron gate to which our Art Department has added "Danish" crests and flanking rows of "iron" railings. There are also two very convincing sentry-boxes. (Blenheim, of course, was not built as a fortress, but we need to suggest that Claudius has taken some measures to defend his palace.) Rushes are shown in the Palace restaurant, and we sit snugly at tables watching the screen and eating lunch out of styrofoam trays. On the screen are events from another, warmer, indoor world. In the afternoon we set up for night's shooting at Palace gates, with sentry in snow. We finally reach the first line of the play. Snow on snow now, with close-up detail in salt and finely powdered paper which are dusted onto railings with a hand brush.

[...]

Thursday 22 February

The Norwegians invade. (Call-sheet includes "His Grace the Duke of Marlborough" as an officer.) The army charges across courtyard with fixed bayonets—only some of them rubber, and not the ones in front. We stand our ground in the portico, with Duchess of M. and her dog on the steps to repulse the invasion. Will the dog go for them? (No, it obviously thinks the whole business is further proof of human folly.) Then the cavalry make a statelier progress. Troops line up for tracking shots and close-up on Rufus (Fortinbras) and his Captain (Jeffrey Kissoon) and officers (including Duke of M.), as they ride up to take possession. Rufus looks as though he really wants it, but knows it's easily won. Intense eyes, darkly handsome, calmly self-assertive. (Ken: "No glam spared on this film.")

[...]

Saturday 24 February

Last day at Blenheim. Out in the driving rain and down to the bridge over the lake, for Fortinbras' men to demolish statue, bits of which (in ready-broken version) lie in a corner like fragments of a giant chocolate Santa Claus. As weather worsens, and our *ersatz* snow is threatened, this gets more urgent. We get a take in before a furious downpour. Tourists with umbrellas appear by the gate, all decanted from one bus, and brave the drizzle to snapshoot each other by the sentry boxes (which we have added, along with the railings). Our people up there shoo them away. Grim entrenched atmosphere down by the statue, constant discussion of weather reports (which are phoned in from the Meteorological Office). Most of what can be done with dialogue on location has been achieved, but we need shots like this for sense of place and scale. I go back to our hotel in Woodstock for lunch. Meet Nick Farrell and we spend half an hour at an antiques fair in the town hall. Odd moment of remembering we're just camped out on the edge of a busy little town where normal Saturday afternoon life goes on.

"Angels and ministers" at sunset, dealt with quickly and efficiently. Then other angles and close-ups, and close in on Ken for "By heaven I'll make a ghost of him that lets me." Ken thinks of saying "stops" for "lets," anxious not to be misunderstood at this moment. Worrying, because it's a famous line and it seems a shame to compromise like this. After he's watched first take on the monitor I hear myself almost yelling, "No, 'lets' is fine—it'll be clear enough what you mean!" Then odd silence and general laughter. "Well, I think I know what you feel about that one." (We go for "lets.") Wrap at about nine, back to hotel. Ken awards himself steak and chips with ketchup, breaking strict training regime, to celebrate end of location shoot.

[...]

Friday 1 March

More graveyard. Important to remember in the middle of all this where we have got to emotionally. So, when Hamlet says "This is Laertes, a very noble youth" he isn't telling Horatio something he may not know: Hamlet thinks aloud, begins to take in the situation—and has deduced who is in the coffin. (Which raises question as to why Horatio didn't tell him before now that Ophelia was dead—to which there is no good answer.) Julie's Gertrude is tragically adrift in her grief, which makes it doubly odd immediately before the takes, when the First Assistant calls for "Checks, please" and make-up, hair, costume and props departments gather round her and adjust tiny details of her appearance (such as flicking the feather on her hat). Kate arrives in late afternoon, made up and costumed for coffin, but with her own big black boots on. Gets in so we can check lights. (Ken: "The boots will be on either side of your head, Kate"). A runner from the production office comes with a telephone message from L.A. for Kate, but we don't know where she is, so messenger departs—then we remember she's in the grave.

[...]

Wednesday 6 March

"Fishmonger" scene, with Hamlet teasing Polonius: potentially most difficult in play for Hamlet? Easy to be amusing, but Ken is urged by Hugh to go for the bitterness: convincing imitation of "madness," thoughts of Ophelia ("Have you a daughter?"), lingering impression of encounter with Ghost. The last of these is harder to perceive directly. First shot in chapel gallery, with skull mask. Then two shots, one on either side of hall balcony. In the second, Ken plays "madder," positively playful, vicious in listing details of old man's appearance.

Thursday 7 March

Edging towards "To be…." First a long, complex circling shot to take us from R. and G. being quizzed on their success in sounding out Hamlet ("And can you by no drift of conference…?") to Ophelia being placed with a prayer book for Hamlet to "affront" her. Acting and text all fairly secure, but reflection-dodging taxes the concentration. This takes its toll on lines and moves. Ken sits at the monitor, hunched forward on his chair willing them on with impatient involuntary gestures, like a punter at a racecourse—helpless, unable to influence his horse. Two acceptable takes, one very good.

For a time it seems as though we will never reach "the" soliloquy, then suddenly we set up for it, with track to accompany Hamlet to mirror: the isolation we discussed in rehearsals, and (so far as possible) the sense of an infinite regression of mirror reflections. The first take is simple, but not shaped by sense of argument. This should seem the "Wittenberg" mode of his mind, intellectually trained, reflective. Later takes are clearer in argument, more specific and vivid in details of the "whips and scorns" a man must endure, getting a sense of wonder in the thought of the "undiscovered country" after death. We sit by monitor in one of the side "rooms" behind the doors, oddly quiet between takes. The unit (professional, pragmatic, not consciously inclined to any sentimental "reverence" for the work in hand) seems to be affected by the aura of this speech—or perhaps simply by its power? Covers, like large quilts, are piled on the camera to damp down the sound of its motor: operator and focus-puller huddle under them.

Friday 8 March

Ken and Kate come in early to rehearse "nunnery" scene with Hugh, then the camera and lighting teams are shown in and the crew set-up for the first section, up to his realizing she has betrayed him. There's a momentary pause after "Well, well, well," then they giggle together, then kiss, then she offers the "remembrances" (love-letters) and he flares up. How does she get to that point? Why does she return them? In rehearsal we reminded ourselves that she's not been *told* to do this by her father, so "which I have longed long to redeliver" is spoken from her heart—or at least is what she is trying to convince herself of. What she has wanted for a long time is an explanation. But for a moment we see what the reconstruction of their love could be like. Then it gets worse, she can't go back now, she falters when he asks 'Where's your father?' Kate is stronger, tougher on the successive takes, but this is the moment of no return. At the end of the scene, Hamlet flings her down in doorway. Kate, in heap against the door frame, speaks "O what a noble mind is here o'erthrown" in one shot, as camera moves in on her. (Between takes she darts into the side-room of the hall where we lurk with the monitors: "Chaps, did you see my eyes? Did I have them open against the door?" "Should I take "O heavenly powers restore him" in to myself a bit?")

[…]

Wednesday 13 March

Rehearsal at 10.00 for first sections of scene between Gertrude and Hamlet and the death of Polonius. Blood is a practical problem once he has been stabbed: we mustn't get any on the bedspread or her dress (no repeats available). At first Dickie is a little too brusque with queen—he marches in, tells her very sharply what to do. A brief bow is then added as he opens the doors, but Ken wants to keep it brisk, with sense that everything is falling apart, less time for politeness. We end the day with Hamlet heaving Gertrude onto the bed ("leave wringing of your hands"), which Julie does with a precisely placed flying lunge. ("Where do you want me?")

Friday 15 March

Gertrude and Hamlet sit together on sofa. A few minor adjustments, but plays well from first take. Tenderer now than in rehearsal, and in fact the only time when mother and son are seen together like this. Lull in the storm—then they look across to where Polonius lies in a pool of blood. The main acting decision is how to treat the section near the end, beginning at "Not this by no means…," where Hamlet is sarcastically describing what he doesn't want her to do. In rehearsal we considered the possibility of this being despair and contempt, with Hamlet unable to trust her ("Oh, I know you'll give in and tell him") but we didn't follow that line, and now as we work on the scene it is clear that version couldn't be motivated by the way Julie asks "What shall I do?," and that Hamlet is in fact getting carried away with disgust for Claudius ("the bloat king") as he imagines what would happen if she gave his game away. As so often, Hamlet seems to relish in vivid detail any picture he conjures up for himself.

The final shots are of Polonius's body, looking towards the forlorn pair on the sofa, pool of blood in foreground. Job demarcation: blood on floor is props department, blood on clothes is costumes, blood on Dickie is make-up. Rules relaxed to let make-up pour the blood on costume and face. We soon get through all the "blood donor" jokes.

This is the last of the series of "big" emotional scenes between Hamlet and Gertrude or Ophelia. When we wrap, Ken is relieved, but will only allow himself big sigh of relief when rushes are O.K. (In the end they weren't—some shots had to be redone because of a processing fault.)

Saturday 16 March

Long single shot to go down corridor as Claudius dashes to find out what is happening, then into his room with Gertrude, out into corridor again, into bedroom, back out to send off Rosencrantz and Guildenstern and then embracing Gertrude tightly as camera tracks back leaving them lonely and fearful. Decision that Claudius will be impatient with her for a moment as she tries to excuse Hamlet, then more comforting and finally himself insecure. When he goes into her room, should Claudius kneel by pool of blood? Doesn't it take a beat too long? Derek: "No, I can do it all, kneel, look at pictures, move—just watch me!" While we rehearse shot in king's apartment, Tim and Reece do a soft-shoe shuffle routine in the doorway behind Derek's back. Julie, puzzled, asks Ken "Will you be in this scene?"—"No, I'll be over there" (behind camera)—"Oh, I'd forgotten, you're the director too."

All this takes three hours to light, but single shot here repays time in number of pages covered and impetus it gives to action. Court in crisis, and R. and G. have become even more haplessly embroiled: sent off to find a royal psychopath at large and armed. Another shot takes an hour to set up, but covers a long sequence from Claudius bursting into room ("It likes us not…") and sending R. and G. off to England with Hamlet, then the soliloquy that makes clear to the audience his anxiety to kill his nephew. R. and G. propitiate him. Tim is anxious about his elaborate speech ("massy wheel" etc.)—but his anxiety feeds that of the character, wonderful moment of comedy as R. digs himself further into the mire and G. watches coolly. Relaxed atmosphere by end of day: a big sequence dealt with.

[…]

Wednesday 20 March

Ophelia's first mad scene, shot on two cameras, one wide, one medium. At first little sign of the Ophelia we used to know, then, as she begins to recall Polonius, it changes, and the fullest effect is there in later shots, close-ups, with the hyperventilating, sobbing mania—she dips down below the camera's frame as though going *down* for air ("O.K. I'll go again" a few deep breaths, then up into view and sobbing.) In the middle of all this Kate can change a word or a line-reading. (Ken: "It's almost unbelievably painful. Once more with a higher eye-line.")

Most important change is in her first entrance, which now begins as a run at full tilt into the hall, then is slowed down, and as a consequence twice as affecting—she seems to be looking for someone when she asks "Where is the beauteous majesty of Denmark?" (Julie's hair and the high-ruffed collar on her dress make her look like Sarah Bernhardt: Derek points out that he has to make do with one haircut and three uniforms while she gets a different outfit in every scene.)

Kate, in her "madhouse" combination of straitjacket and shift, jokes about having found her outfit for the Oscar ceremony (Vivienne Westwood?). Sitting on floor, during a respite, she waves, does "potty" acting (lolling head, hands waving): thumbs-up cheerfully exchanged. Not a chatting day, though—everyone reading between shots, like a library or a doctor's waiting room.

[…]

Saturday 30 March

Yet more fight. At one point Hamlet and Laertes approach one another solemnly, like prize-fighters, down the long red carpet in front of the entire court, reach the middle—and crack up laughing. So 130 people "corpse," all at once.

Desperate hacking and slashing upstairs. We never see the totality that will be there when the bits are joined together—indeed, there was never a "complete" sword fight, but we now have enough components to show it twice over.

Julie's death—trying out each movement, turn of head at end, smile. Derek, reacting to fight, must remember to notice queen crumpling. Weary extras round staircase, more like a Victorian painting than ever—except for one lady prostrate at back with her legs only in view, which makes it more like the aftermath of an orgy. Another has taken her shoes off and used her fan to cool her feet. Rather than be slaughtered *en masse,* our Danish aristocrats flee—which shows how rotten the state is and also saves massively on stage-management and cleaning bills. Only a loyal band remains—determined by who can work on Monday. For one long shot we do the departure of the rest, which Simon orchestrates from the balcony with his loud-hailer: "Pandemonium!!!" (lasts 30 seconds, then) "Shut the doors as you go!" (for continuity).

Monday 1 April

A strangely desultory day, with Ken a bit withdrawn, anxious to get this done. Death of queen in detail, reactions—Derek has to get fear, desperation in "she swoons to see them bleed" and also (tellingly) the fact that this is his last attempt to lie. Then we start on his death (which will involve several shots of varying degrees of complexity for swinging chandelier, sword flying at him, etc.).

Tuesday 2 April

Fortinbras's army arrives in the hall. Scaffolding towers and crash mats behind the set walls (for stunt men to swing through windows). Practice for troops crossing, closing doors, pointing guns downstairs, while the stuntmen will hurtle in above. Cameras shooting from several angles. Then Fortinbras stalks down the corridor. We probably have two goes at the invasion. Conferences with various departments: stunts, art dept. camera, effects. Decision needed on how many repeats of the "sugar" glass window-panes we have. The stuff crumbles to powder underfoot, makes splinters that look nasty, litters floors on upper level, and the windows take a while to set back. Starting with a big shot helps the day. Ken: "I'm making six films at once. This is *Diehard.*" Later shoot chandelier pinning Derek down in the throne: in fact it really does so, not stopping as soon as expected, giving a better shot than we could have asked for—luckily without really damaging Derek.

Wednesday 3 April

Derek's last day: Claudius plotting with Laertes. When we set up for Gertrude's entrance (with news of Ophelia's suicide) the positions of the table and sofa are "cheated" to accommodate camera angles. Michael now sits on a box at the table, like a small boy allowed to sit with the grown-ups: Ken asks if camera crew would like to cheat anything else. "We could put Julie on castors." Meanwhile on the headphones we can hear her behind the door getting ready, summoning up distress.

The speech to be as little of an elocution piece as possible—numbed, shocked detachment, as camera moves in on her relentlessly. Then close-ups on Claudius. Laertes, grief-stricken, leaves quietly, not in a rush. Claudius is concerned merely to get him back on course for the sake of his plot—which Gertrude of course does not know about. He seems to blame her for upsetting Laertes. ("How much I had to do to calm his rage…") When Claudius leaves, she does not follow. She shows no sign of affection for him from now on.

A drama and a ceremony today. The first is a fire on set. As first scene is being set up, we hear shouts of "fire," and see smoke and a red glow above ceiling of corridor. A drape has blown against one of the lamps and in these dry, dusty conditions, has taken fire. Stage cleared, blaze contained and doused by studio fire crew, then Surrey brigade arrive and Tim Harvey (Production Designer) persuades them not to hose down the whole set. Disaster has been averted, little time lost.

The ceremony: Derek completes his work on the film and there's the usual applause, especially strong in his case. Then he springs a surprise. He holds up a small red-bound copy of the play, that successive actors have passed on to each other with the condition that the recipient should give it in turn to the finest Hamlet of the next generation. It has come from Forbes Robertson, a great Hamlet at the turn of the century, to Derek, via Henry Ainley, Michael Redgrave, Peter O'Toole and others—now he gives it to Ken.

[…]

Wednesday 10 April

Laertes dies, followed by Hamlet. Hamlet's emotions? They include urgent need for Horatio to tell the story. Physical details a problem: Ken anxious to avoid being cradled by Horatio as in a *pietà,* or spending a lot of time on the floor. Problems carrying him out: getting the bearers to walk in step and not sway too much. (Unfortunately Fortinbras specifies *four* captains as bearers so we can't sneak in a couple more.) Should doors be shut, or Hamlet carried to end of corridor in shot? (Both tried.) Here for a session of publicity photos, Kate passes through from time to time in a bewildering selection of Ophelia's costumes, like a rapid re-run of the play.

[…]

Saturday 13 April

Final day. The news on the lens problems is better, and we won't need to save the State Hall set or even perhaps do any reshooting with Derek and Michael. (In the end, none was needed.) So this really is the final day of the complete unit.

Reshooting Hamlet and Gertrude on the couch. Her reactions made more specific by Julie. Dickie Briers in and bloodied for the last time. Gore spread again by the gallon, perhaps a bit thicker than last time, and Alfie (props) on his knees with a paintbrush, as Ken and Julie chat on a sofa in the background—so on the video monitor this looks even more like a do-it-yourself programme ("Be sure to use firm, even brushstrokes…").

Final shots of the film are in State Hall. First a "cover" for Hamlet's turn to see Ophelia after "To be or not to be…" During line-up for this an A.D. has been lashed to a post with a fireman's hat on his head and a banana in his flies—which is revealed to Ken in the rehearsal as he turns to where Kate should be. ("But soft you now—the fair Ophelia??") Then the last shot of all: he comes down the rope and grabs the poisoned drink from table. Ken is left dangling for a few seconds, then "action"—he lands, gets the goblet, runs off out of shot—a couple of takes and suddenly that's it. "Check that please." "Gate good." Final wrap of film. Last farewell applause of the film. Short speech by First Assistant, then everyone is invited to a drink in Ken's dressing-room. Hamlet, coming off set: "Well, we have a go, don't we?"

Discussion and Writing Suggestions

1. In the January 4 entry, Jackson notes how Richard Briers (Polonius) and Kate Winslet (Ophelia) tried different readings of the scene in which Polonius tells the king and queen about Hamlet's letter (II.ii.85–128). View this scene in the film and judge whether Branagh's decision to "split the difference" was a dramatically effective one. If possible, compare this scene in Branagh's film with the corresponding scenes in Olivier's and Zeffirelli's.

2. Notice that the first scene filmed (January 25) is that of Hamlet addressing the players (III.ii). Why do you suppose that movie scenes are not shot in the same order as will appear in the finished film? (Note also the acting problems that this practice sometimes creates: in the February 13 entry, Jackson remarks that when first meeting Rosencrantz and Guildenstern, "Ken needs to sustain Hamlet's mood from a scene we haven't shot yet ("Fishmonger") which precedes this immediately in the script.") What factors are most likely to determine the order of shooting?

3. Select one of the scenes Jackson discusses: e.g., the invasion of the Norwegians shot on February 22 or Hamlet's determination to follow the ghost, shot two days later. View this scene and then "reverse-engineer" it from the point of view of direction, lighting, camera movement, and so on. What kind of cinematic decisions must Branagh and his crew have made to achieve the effects that appear on screen and on the sound track? For example, what might have been the effect if the camera had been located in another position—perhaps from above? If the action had been viewed through a sequence of stationary shots, rather than through a single travelling shot? If an actor had moved in a different way than she or he actually did? If the lights had been harsher—or softer? If there had been no music—or a different style of music?

4. On March 8, Branagh filmed the "nunnery" scene (III.i.90–191) between himself and Kate Winslet (Ophelia). Jackson recalls how the actors tried to determine just why Ophelia feels it necessary to return Hamlet's letters and how Ophelia's line readings are meant to reflect the feelings she has both for Hamlet and for her father. View this scene in Branagh's film and also the corresponding scene in either Olivier's or Zeffirelli's film, and discuss any differences of interpretation you detect.

5. Here's your chance to play director. Study a particular scene in Shakespeare's *Hamlet*. Decide how the scene should be staged and acted if you were filming it. Convert the scene, as written by Shakespeare, into screenplay format. In stage directions indicate the kinds of emotion the actors should bring to their lines, their facial expressions, gestures, and movements. Although cinematic ele-

ments are generally not included in a screenplay (that would constitute an unwarranted incursion by the screenwriter into the province of the director and the cinematographer), you may also wish to add directorial notes about shots, camera movements, and camera angles. In a separate paragraph or two, discuss your interpretation of the scene, as it informs your screenplay.

[**Note:** To get an idea of how Shakespeare's words might be converted to a screenplay, see the following side-by-side comparison of the sequence described by Jackson in his entry for March 16 (IV.i and ii). Editors.]

Act IV

Scene I. The castle.

Enter King and Queen, with Rosencrantz and Guildenstern.

KING   There's matter in these sighs. These profound heaves
    You must translate; 'tis fit we understand them.
      Where is your son?
QUEEN   Bestow this place on us a little while.

[*Exeunt Rosencrantz and Guildenstern.*]

       Ah, mine own lord, what have I seen tonight!   5

KING   What, Gertrude? How does Hamlet?

QUEEN   Mad as the sea and wind when both contend
    Which is the mightier. In his lawless fit,
    Behind the arras hearing something stir,
    Whips out his rapier, cries, "A rat, a rat!"   10
    And in this brainish apprehension[1] kills
    The unseen good old man.

KING   O heavy deed!
    It had been so with us, had we been there.

    His liberty is full of threats to all,
    To you yourself, to us, to every one.   15

    Alas, how shall this bloody deed be answered?
    It will be laid to us, whose providence[2]
    Should have kept short, restrained, and out of haunt[3]
    This mad young man. But so much was our love

---

[1]*brainish apprehension* mad imagination

[2]*providence* foresight

[3]*out of haunt* away from association with others

Interior/Corridor Night

To see Claudius, Rosencrantz and Guildenstern plus Guards, striding along the corridor as Gertrude comes out of her apartment.
Claudius goes straight to his wife.
CLAUDIUS   There's matter in these sighs, these profound heaves,
> You must translate. 'Tis fit we understand them.
> Where is your son?
GERTRUDE (to Rosencrantz and Guildenstern)
> Bestow this place on us a little while.
Rosencrantz and Guildenstern and the Attendants move away and Claudius and Gertrude move into the King's apartments.

Interior/King's Apartments Night

We follow them as Claudius and Gertrude face each other.
GERTRUDE (shaking)   Ah, mine own lord, what have I seen tonight!
He touches her, holds her. But she does not respond.
CLAUDIUS (gently but firmly)   What, Gertrude? How does Hamlet?
She talks as if her mind were somewhere else. Which it probably is.
GERTRUDE   Mad as the sea and wind when both contend
> Which is the mightier. In his lawless fit,
> Behind the arras hearing something stir,
> Whips out his rapier, cries 'A rat, a rat!',
> And in this brainish apprehension kills
> The unseen good old man.
Gertrude moves away.
CLAUDIUS (appalled)   O heavy deed!
> It had been so with us had we been there.
Claudius moves back into Gertrude's apartment to the pool of blood on the floor and searches behind the arras.
CLAUDIUS (continuing)   His liberty is full of threats to all—
> To you yourself, to us, to everyone.
Angry now. Paranoid. He kneels down by the blood.
CLAUDIUS (continuing)   Alas, how shall this bloody deed be answered?
> It will be laid to us, whose providence
> Should have kept short, restrained, and out of haunt
> This mad young man.
Rationalizing at a thousand miles an hour.
CLAUDIUS (continuing)   But so much was our love,

We would not understand what was most fit,   20
But, like the owner of a foul disease,
To keep it from divulging, let it feed
Even on the pith of life. Where is he gone?

QUEEN   To draw apart the body he hath killed;
O'er whom his very madness, like some ore   25
Among a mineral[4] of metals base,
Shows itself pure. 'A weeps for what is done.

KING   O Gertrude, come away!
The sun no sooner shall the mountains touch
But we will ship him hence, and this vile deed   30
We must with all our majesty and skill
Both countenance and excuse. Ho, Guildenstern!
Enter Rosencrantz and Guildenstern.

Friends both, go join you with some further aid:
Hamlet in madness hath Polonius slain,

And from his mother's closet hath he dragged him.   35
Go seek him out; speak fair, and bring the body
Into the chapel. I pray you haste in this.
[*Exeunt Rosencrantz and Guildenstern.*]

Come, Gertrude, we'll call up our wisest friends
And let them know both what we mean to do
And what's untimely done…[5]   40
Whose whisper o'er the world's diameter,
As level as the cannon to his blank[6]
Transports his poisoned shot, may miss our name
And hit the woundless[7] air. O, come away!

My soul is full of discord and dismay.   *Exeunt.*   45

---

[4]*Among a mineral* vein of gold in a mine

[5]*done* … (Something has dropped out of the text here.)

[6]*blank* white target

[7]*woundless* invulnerable

We would not understand what was most fit,
But, like the owner of a foul disease,
To keep it from divulging, let it feed
Even on the pith of life.

He snaps at Gertrude as she enters her apartments.

CLAUDIUS (continuing)   Where is he gone?

She pulls herself out of her reverie to make some desperate attempt at a defence of the son she cannot but love.

GERTRUDE   To draw apart the body he hath killed,
O'er whom—his very madness, like some ore
Amongst a mineral of metals base,
Shows itself pure—a weeps for what is done.

He will have none of this. It's action stations. National crisis. The heir to the throne has killed the Prime Minister.

CLAUDIUS   O Gertrude, come away!
The sun no sooner shall the mountains touch
But we will ship him hence; and this vile deed
We must with all our majesty and skill
Both countenance and excuse.

He moves out into the corridor where Rosencrantz and Guildenstern stand, aghast.

CLAUDIUS (continuing)   Ho, Guildenstern!
Friends both, go join you with some further aid.
Hamlet in madness hath Polonius slain,

This is all much more than they can deal with.

CLAUDIUS (continuing)   And from his mother's closet hath he dragged him.
Go seek him out, speak fair, and bring the body
Into the chapel. I pray you haste in this.

Rosencrantz and Guildenstern go.

He tries to be gentle again with her as she joins him.

CLAUDIUS (continuing)   Come, Gertrude, we'll call up our wisest friends
And let them know both what we mean to do
And what's untimely done. So envious slander,
Whose whisper o'er the world's diameter,
As level as the cannon to his blank,
Transports his poisoned shot, may miss our name
And hit the woundless air. O, come away!

He pulls her to him, comforting each other.

CLAUDIUS (continuing)   My soul is full of discord and dismay.

Cut to:

[Scene II. The castle.]

Enter Hamlet.
HAMLET Safely stowed.
GENTLEMEN (*Within*) Hamlet! Lord Hamlet!
HAMLET But soft, what noise? Who calls on Hamlet?

O, here they come.
Enter Rosencrantz and Guildenstern.

ROSENCRANTZ What have you done, my lord, with the
  dead body?   5
HAMLET Compounded it with dust, whereto 'tis kin.

ROSENCRANTZ Tell us where 'tis, that we may take it thence
  And bear it to the chapel.

HAMLET Do not believe it.
ROSENCRANTZ Believe what?   10
HAMLET That I can keep your counsel and not mine
  own. Besides, to be demanded of[8] a sponge, what
  replication[9] should be made by the son of a king?

ROSENCRANTZ Take you me for a sponge, my lord?

HAMLET Ay, sir, that soaks up the King's countenance,[10]   15
  his rewards, his authorities. But such officers do the
  King best service in the end. He keeps them, like an
  ape, in the corner of his jaw, first mouthed, to be

---

[8]*demanded of* questioned by

[9]*replication* reply

[10]*countenance* favor

Interior/Palace Rooms—Montage Night

Soldiers on red alert.
Alarms go off.
The hunt for Hamlet is on!
Cut to:

Interior/Palace Night

Guards break into Ophelia's room. She is terrified. Her bed is searched, with
her still in it!
Cut to:

Interior/Chapel Stairs Night

Hamlet finishes disposing of Polonius's body.
HAMLET   Safely stowed.
ROSENCRANTZ AND GUILDENSTERN (O/S)   Hamlet, Lord Hamlet!
HAMLET   But soft. What noise? Who calls on Hamlet?
He rushes through and into the adjoining Ante-Room.

Interior/Ante-Room Night

HAMLET   O, here they come.
Where he is joined by a panting Rosencrantz and Guildenstern. What a
surprise.
ROSENCRANTZ   What have you done, my lord, with the dead body?
They circle each other in the large room. Wary of a quick move.
HAMLET (cheerful)   Compounded it with dust, whereto 'tis kin.
Courtiers and Soldiers arrive throughout the scene, cornering the Prince.
Hamlet leads them around the Hall, through the remains of the theatre.
ROSENCRANTZ   Tell us where 'tis, that we may take it thence
        And bear it to the chapel.
Hamlet fixes him with a particularly contemptuous glare.
HAMLET   Do not believe it.
ROSENCRANTZ   Believe what?
HAMLET   That I can keep your counsel and not mine own. Besides, to be
        demanded of a sponge—what replication should be made by the son
        of a king?
Rosencrantz can barely tolerate this so-called 'wit'.
ROSENCRANTZ   Take you me for a sponge, my lord?
He talks as if filling him in on a particularly useful piece of information.
Meantime the room starting to fill up with other guards, and their dogs.
HAMLET   Ay, sir, that soaks up the King's countenance,
        his rewards, his authorities. But such officers do the
        King best service in the end. He keeps them, like an
        Ape an apple in the corner of his jaw, first mouthed to be

last swallowed. When he needs what you have
gleaned, it is but squeezing you and, sponge, you   20
shall be dry again.

ROSENCRANTZ   I understand you not, my lord.
HAMLET   I am glad of it: a knavish speech sleeps in a foolish ear.

ROSENCRANTZ   My lord, you must tell us where the   25
    body is and go with us to the King.
HAMLET   The body is with the King, but the King is not
    with the body. The King is a thing—

GUILDENSTERN   A thing, my lord?
HAMLET   Of nothing. Bring me to him. Hide fox, and   30
    all after.   *Exeunt.*

last swallowed. When he needs what you have
gleaned, it is but squeezing you, and, sponge, you
shall be dry again.

With this Hamlet grabs Rosencrantz around the neck, taking him hostage
against the growing Crowd.

ROSENCRANTZ   I understand you not, my lord.

HAMLET   I am glad of it. A knavish speech sleeps in a foolish ear.

They start to move in on him.

ROSENCRANTZ   My lord, you must tell us where the body is, and go with us to
the King.

HAMLET   The body is with the King, but the King is not with the body.
The King is a thing—

Hamlet throws Rosencrantz back to the Crowd.

GUILDENSTERN   A thing, my lord?

HAMLET   Of nothing. Bring me to him.

He appears to go with them willingly. They go towards the stairs as Ophelia
runs down

OPHELIA   My lord!

HAMLET   Hide fox and all after.

Hamlet escapes, Rosencrantz and Guildenstern and the soldiers begin the
chase.

Cut to:

Interior/Lower Hall Rooms Night

Chaos. Close shots of the dogs, the troops, Rosencrantz and Guildenstern.
Hamlet runs through room after room, hidden door after hidden door, we track
beside them. Surely he, who knows this spy-infested rabbit warren, can escape?

But no, as he closes the door in his apartment, apparently safe...a gun
barrel trains itself on his head.

Michael Almereyda's *Hamlet*

The camera tracks the scruffy young man as he cruises the aisles of a Blockbuster video store. "To be or not to be…," we hear in voice-over. This is the startling vision of Michael Almereyda's modern dress Hamlet *(2000). The innovation is not so much that the story of Hamlet has been set in contemporary times. Such adaptations as* The Rest is Silence *(1960), set in post-war Germany, and* Strange Brew *(1983), a comedy set in Canada, took the same route. But unlike other filmmakers who merely appropriated Shakespeare's story, Almereyda retained Shakespeare's language. (Not very much of it, to be sure; this* Hamlet *is cut even more drastically than Olivier's.) It is the tension between the language and the settings that accounts for so much of the eerie power of Almereyda's film. "Watching the movie requires a certain suspension of disbelief," conceded the director in an interview. "People don't really talk like that. But the language has a tone and its own life and its own logic. I hope you get acclimated and you're in it, so that you can just forgive words you don't understand or even words that don't seem quite right, because of the general sense and the force of it."**

Michael Almereyda is the archetypal "indie" (independent) filmmaker, one who produces or finances his own pictures on a proverbial shoestring without the benefits—or drawbacks—of major studio backing. Born in 1960 in Overland Park, Kansas, Almereyda earned enough money from rewriting other people's scripts to make his first film, a 26-minute short called "A Hero in Our Time," and starring Dennis Hopper. His first feature, Twister *(1988) (not the 1996 tornado movie) left him somewhat disillusioned with studio filmmaking (the project was controlled by Vestron Pictures); and his next film,* Another Girl, Another Planet *(1994), was financed with $10,000 from his own pocket, and shot with a Fisher Price toy camera.* Nadja *(1995), about a vampire in Manhattan (and this time shot with a plastic toy video-camera), became a cult hit. In 1998 he made* Trance*, a horror film about an "Irish druid witch mummy" who pursues an alcoholic woman's soul.*

After briefly reviewing Almereyda's career, interviewer Jeffrey Anderson prepared to discuss the director's current project: "Oh yeah, and your [new] movie is based on arguably the single greatest piece of literature yet produced by human hands."[†] The skepticism about the fit between director and subject may have been justified, but Almereyda surprised everyone by producing one of the most imaginative and compelling films of the year. Some critics, indeed, hated the film for what they considered its desecration of Shakespeare, but most were intrigued and impressed by Almereyda's unique take on the play. The director and his actors had produced a compelling re-interpretation of Hamlet *for a new, "information age" generation accustomed to interacting with the world through fax machines, video monitors, and laptops. This* Hamlet *is not one that is likely to supplant Olivier's or Branagh's versions. But it is one that is worth watching and talking about.*

Cinematic Outline
Editors

Hamlet (2000)

Adapted and Directed by Michael Almereyda

Ethan Hawke—Hamlet

---

*Qtd. in Jeffrey M. Anderson, "Interview with Ethan Hawke and Michael Almereyda," *Combustible Celluloid.* 4 May 2000. Online. 23 Aug. 2001. <http://www.combustiblecelluloid.com/hawke.shtml>

[†]Crowdus.

Kyle MacLachlan—Claudius

Diane Venora—Gertrude

Liev Schreiber—Laertes

Julia Stiles—Ophelia

Bill Murray—Polonius

Karl Geary—Horatio

Sam Shepard—The Ghost

1. [0:00] Open on a view of NYC towers through the back window of a limousine. Legend reads: "New York City, 2000/The King and C.E.O of Denmark Corporation is Dead/The King's widow has hastily remarried his younger brother/The King's son, Hamlet, returns from school, suspecting foul play…"

2. (2.2) [0:52] Times Square: Hamlet walks across the street to his room at Hotel Elsinore. In his room, recorded on his personal video player, we see grainy B&W images of Hamlet himself, speaking: "I have of late…lost all my mirth.…/What a piece of work is a man.…" (from 2.2) His phone rings. On the screen, images of animal skeletons, the Gulf War, and a B-2 bomber taking off. "And yet to me what is this quintessence of dust?"

3. [2:35] Title screen: "Hamlet" (blood-red background)

4. (1.2) [2:40] Panning shot of a hotel press conference: Hamlet is carrying a small video camera and monitor as he circles the room. Claudius announces his marriage to Gertrude, and the defeat of the takeover attempt by Fortinbras (tearing in half, to loud applause, a *USA Today* paper with "Fortinbras Makes Bid on Denmark Corporation" headline). In the foyer afterward, Claudius grants Laertes permission to return to France.

5. (1.2) [5:34] Walking down Manhattan's Park Avenue, Claudius and Gertrude implore Hamlet to "cast thy nightly color off," and "go not to Wittenberg."

6. (1.2) [7:43] [Brief wide shot of Ophelia, seated in front of a large fountain.] In his room, Hamlet, seated before an armada of computer-video equipment: "O that this too too [sullied/solid] flesh would melt…" He is watching old video footage of his father and mother together ("she would hang on him/As if increase of appetite had grown/By what it fed on.…") Close-up of Ophelia on the screen as he ends the soliloquy: "But break, my heart, for I must hold my tongue." [Cut to Ophelia before the fountain again, balancing on the edge of the pool.] Enter Horatio, Marcella (a woman), and Barnardo. Horatio relates his encounter with the apparition of Hamlet the King. (The first encounter with the ghost from 1.1 is told here through a flashback; the ghost had been sighted on the video surveillance monitors in the basement of the elevator lobby.) Scene ends with Hamlet alone in close-up; voice-over: "Foul deeds will rise…."

7. (1.3) [14:26] Laertes and Ophelia in their father's apartment: "Fear it, Ophelia." Polonius enters, delivers the "to thine own self be true" speech, while Ophelia, from an overhead stair landing, takes photographs of her father and Laertes. Laertes departs for France.

8. [19:35] Gertrude and Claudius ride at night through midtown in the back seat of a limo. (He is reading *USA Today*, which reads "Denmark Thwarts

Fortinbras." Hamlet sits opposite, sulking. They exit the limo and walk through a cordon of media.) [No dialogue.]

9. (1.4; 1.5) [20:27] While Horatio and Bernardo watch the video monitors downstairs, the apparition comes to Hamlet on the balcony of his apartment at the Elsinore. The apparition embraces Hamlet, urges him to "Remember me," and disappears. We hear the squeal of a modem and watch the Denmark Corporation logo appear on the screen as Hamlet says "The time is out of joint. O cursed spite / That ever I was born to set it right." Horatio and Marcella catch a glimpse of the apparition on the balcony—"There are more things in heaven and earth, Horatio, than are dreamt of in your philosophy"—and again it is gone.

10. (1.3) [27:25] Polonius advises Ophelia in their apartment: "Do not believe his vows." As Polonius says this, he reaches down to tie Ophelia's shoe lace.

11. [29:40] Wide shot of birds scattering over a church at sunset. A Buddhist monk speaks on the video screen "You need other people in order to be; you need other beings in order to be." Hamlet is looking at the image of Ophelia on his hand-held video monitor.

12. [30:50] Hamlet sits in a diner, writing in his notebooks, to Ophelia. He walks to her Lower East Side apartment, where she is working in her darkroom, developing photos. Hamlet embraces her, and gives her the poem he has been working on. Polonius comes up the stairs carrying a balloon bouquet; Hamlet kisses Ophelia and leaves, brushing past Polonius and dropping the poem, which Polonius quickly picks up and reads. High shot of Hamlet walking past the Key Food grocery on the street below. [no dialogue]

13. (3.1) [33:11] Hamlet is watching himself "live" on his video-monitor, while he holds a gun to his head and contemplates suicide. He rewinds and watches the tape of himself again.

14. (2.2) [33:45] Wide-angle shot of a high-rise against the blue sky. Shift to interior of the office building high above the East River. We see segments of this scene through a security-camera monitor. Polonius speaks directly to the camera: "Still harping on my daughter...He is far gone." Hamlet walks into Claudius' office, brandishing a pistol, but the office is empty.

15. (2.2) [35:45] On the deck of an indoor swimming pool, surrounded by the Manhattan skyline bathed in morning sunlight, Polonius tells Gertrude and Claudius "Your noble son is mad." While Polonius reads Hamlet's poem, Ophelia, seen from below the water's surface, imagines herself plunging into the pool.

16. (3.1) [40:04] Sepia-tone shot of old NY buildings at dusk. Inside a Blockbuster Video outlet, Hamlet wanders the aisles, while the "To Be or Not To Be" soliloquy is spoken in voice-over, then shifts to "live" speech. (Scenes from "Crow II: City of Angels" are playing on the in-store monitors.)

17. (2.2) [42:34] In a dark nightclub, Hamlet greets Rosencrantz and Guildenstern. The dialogue takes place in tableaux shots, illuminated by green and blue disco lighting, while young dancers rave in the background.

18. (3.1) [44:42] In Claudius and Gertrude's bedroom. High-angle shot from above. Over the speaker-phone, Rosencrantz and Guildenstern report on

the state of Hamlet, while Gertrude and Claudius drink champagne and cavort on the bed.

19. (2.2) [45:31] Hamlet's room at the Elsinore, dimly lit by the glare of a television screen. Hamlet watches James Dean ("this player here") on the television: "What would he do / Had he the motive and the cue for passion / That I have?" The scene shifts to Hamlet's computer video-editing desk, where we see Hamlet's film-in-progress, *The Mouse Trap,* as he edits it, on one monitor screen, Laurence Olivier as Hamlet, holding the skull of Poor Yorick, in another. "The play's the thing / Wherein I'll catch the conscience of the King." Fade to black.

20. (3.1) [47:07]—Open on a close-up of an invitation to the opening of Hamlet's "film/video," *The Mouse Trap.* In Claudius' office, Polonius is fitting Ophelia with a microphone so that Gertrude, Claudius, and Polonius can eavesdrop on her meeting with Hamlet. Cut to image of an outdoor fountain as Ophelia wipes away her tears. Ophelia, first seen through the security peep-hole, arrives at Hamlet's apartment at the Elsinore, to return his "remembrances." Cut to an airplane high above as Hamlet says "I loved you not." Hamlet flies into a rage when he discovers the wire. Tracking shot of Ophelia on her bicycle. In her apartment, Ophelia burns photos of Hamlet while we hear his voice on her answering machine ("I give thee this plague for thy dowry.... Get thee to a nunnery..."). Close-up on a burning photo in the sink, while Hamlet screams on the answering machine: "I say we shall have no more marriage." Scene ends on a close shot of Hamlet, checking out a foot-high stack of videos from Blockbuster. Fade to black.

21. (3.2) [52:28] The screening room, where Hamlet's film will be shown. Hamlet instructs Horatio to watch the King. *The Mouse Trap* is shown in the screening room. Intercut reaction shots of Claudius and Gertrude, visibly disturbed by the film. (The film is a silent montage of images and clips, depicting, roughly, the events of the murder of Hamlet the Elder as recounted by his ghost.) Claudius and Gertrude run from the screening room as the film ends; Hamlet follows, tucking a pistol into his belt as he goes. On the street below, Hamlet tries to hail a taxi while we hear in voice-over "For some must watch, while some must sleep; / Thus runs the world away." Rosencrantz and Guildenstern surprise Hamlet, jumping into the cab on either side of him. Shift to Hamlet alone on the street outside Denmark Corporation headquarters. Hamlet disguises himself as Claudius's limo driver.

22. (3.3) [59:12] Claudius, on his way out through the lobby of Denmark Corp, boards the limo. He speaks with Rosencrantz and Guildenstern, via the limo's mobile phone, to set the trap for Hamlet in England. Hamlet leaves the speaker on and overhears their conversation from the driver's seat. Close-up of Claudius's hand ("What if this cursed hand..."). Wide shot of the limo in Times Square, as Hamlet turns to aim the gun at Claudius. He lowers the pistol and abandons the car in front of a theater. Close shot of Claudius alone on the street, stock-ticker scrolling behind him.

23. (3.4) [1:01:56] Polonius visits Gertrude in her apartment. Hamlet knocks, and Polonius hides in the closet, behind its mirrored doors. Hamlet and Gertrude struggle; we see them reflected in the mirror. Hamlet fires a shot

through the mirrored door, killing Polonius. As Hamlet screams at his mother in her bedroom, the ghost appears sitting opposite in a chair (Gertrude cannot see the apparition). In the basement, Hamlet drags the corpse of Polonius to its hiding place. He calls his mother from a pay-phone to conclude the dialogue ("One word more, good lady.") He drags the corpse around a corner, trailing blood along the floor.

24. (4.2; 4.3) [1:09:32] Close-up of Hamlet's eye. Long shot reveals he is sitting in a laundromat, watching clothes spin in a dryer. Rosencrantz and Guildenstern interrogate Hamlet. Claudius arrives, with two bodyguards, at the laundry, and continues to ask Hamlet to reveal the location of Polonius's body. Claudius and his men beat Hamlet until he reveals the location, then they banish him to England "with fiery quickness." At JFK airport, Hamlet arrives in the limo, escorted by Gertrude (drinking, walking unsteadily, wearing sunglasses), Claudius, and his men, who put him on the plane to England.

25. (4.4) [1:14:15] Close up of a stack of postcards in Hamlet's hands as he sits on the plane. He looks back to see Rosencrantz and Guildenstern a few rows behind him. Hamlet delivers the "How all occasions do inform against me" soliloquy as he wanders the aisles of the 747, looking for a vacant lavatory. Shot of a small child on its mother's lap. Hamlet addresses himself in the bathroom mirror: "from this time forth / My thoughts be bloody or be nothing worth!"

26. (4.5) [1:17:22] Wide shot of the spiral central walkway at the Guggenheim Museum, where Ophelia walks along the railing. Cut between wide shots of Ophelia and close-ups of Gertrude, drinking champagne and mingling. Voice over is Gertrude: "To my sick soul, as sin's true nature is...." Ophelia joins Gertrude on the walkway, as Claudius rushes to their side. Ophelia is escorted, kicking and screaming, from the gallery, by Claudius' guard. Long shot from across the gallery of Laertes' confrontation with Claudius. They retreat into a glassed-in ante-room. Ophelia enters from the other end of the room, tossing Polaroid snapshots to the floor like flower-petals ("There's rosemary...and there is pansies..."). Laertes embraces her.

27. (4.5; 4.7) [1:22:04] In their bedroom, Claudius and Gertrude, framed by the mirrored closet doors, examining the bullet hole in the door. Laertes arrives at the door. Claudius and Laertes talk in the sitting room ("put me in your heart for friend..."), accompanied by a bodyguard. Claudius hands Laertes a gun (presumably Hamlet's) in a plastic bag. We see a neon Paine Webber sign across the street, behind Laertes. While they talk, a fax machine in the room rings, receives a fax. Claudius reads the fax from Hamlet, announcing his pending return the next day. Close-up of Laertes's hands, where he holds a hair-pin belonging to his sister. As Claudius and Laertes plan to poison Hamlet during a duel with Laertes, Gertrude enters with news of Ophelia's death. Cut to a high overhead shot of Ophelia's body, floating in a semi-circular fountain pool. Close in on a police officer dragging her from the fountain. In the water floats the box in which she held all her remembrances of Hamlet, now floating loose in the water. Fade to black.

28. (5.1) [1:27:56] Hamlet emerges through automatic doors at JFK airport, and is greeted by Horatio. They ride off on a motorcycle as airplanes pass

overhead on approach. Tracking and trailing shots of Horatio and Hamlet as they ride the motorcycle along the expressway toward Manhattan. As a group of children run along a hill through a cemetery, they pull into the cemetery on the bike. Quick shot of a grave-digger, singing while he digs. They come over a hill and arrive at Ophelia's funeral. Close-up on Hamlet and Horatio as they witness Laertes's grief. Laertes jumps into the grave and tries to open her casket. Hamlet approaches and addresses Laertes, offers his hand to hoist him from the grave. They fight among the headstones.

29. (5.2) [1:31:35] Trailing shot of Hamlet and Horatio riding the motorcycle with the Manhattan skyline at dusk in the background. Close up of Hamlet, wearing a red motorcycle helmet. Brief shot of the ghost watching over Marcella as she sleeps. Hamlet narrates to Horatio his escape from England. Flashback to the airplane, where Hamlet discovers the orders for his death on Rosencrantz's laptop (while Rosencrantz and Guildenstern are asleep). Hamlet and Horatio talk in the kitchen. A fax is received, announcing the wager from the King. Hamlet glimpses his father's ghost over Horatio's shoulder.

30. (5.2) [1:35:55] Close-up of Claudius's hand pouring white powder into a wine glass. Cut to Hamlet at his desk, taking photos down from the wall; he pauses to look upon two snapshots of Ophelia. Horatio smiles. Hamlet turns out the light and leaves the room. Wide shot of Manhattan skyline. On the rooftop, Laertes and Hamlet don their fencing gear. As they choose their weapons, the camera pans across the gathered audience on the rooftop. Claudius smokes a cigarette while the two men fence. Gertrude, apparently knowingly, drinks the (poisoned) wine intended for Hamlet. She hugs him, wiping his brow with her napkin. Laertes lunges at Hamlet, holding a pistol in place of his foil. As they struggle, two shots are fired, wounding both of them. Close-up of Gertrude's horrified reaction. As Bernardo and Horatio look on, Laertes tells Hamlet "the king's to blame." Horatio helps Hamlet to his feet. Hamlet fires three shots at Claudius, who slumps to the ground, leaving a trail of blood along the rooftop railing. Intercut extreme close-ups of Hamlet's eye with grainy black and white video images of Ophelia, Gertrude, Hamlet's father. The last image is Hamlet kissing Ophelia, as Hamlet speaks his last: "—the rest is silence." Close-up of Horatio's face as he watches Hamlet die. Wide shot of a high-altitude jet contrail overhead, behind the silhouette of a public statue ("... flights of angels sing thee to thy rest!") Fade to black.

31. (5.2; 3.2) [1:44:32] On a television screen, anchor Robert MacNeil recites the closing lines. Behind him, a graphic announces "Fortinbras: Denmark's New King." As the credits roll, we see his final script scrolling across the screen of a teleprompter. His final lines are a conflation of lines spoken by Fortinbras and the First Ambassador in 5.2 with lines spoken by the Player King in the play-within-the-play in 3.2: "This quarry cries on havoc. O proud death, / What feast is toward in thine eternal cell, / That thou so many princes at a shot / So bloodily hast struck? // The sight is dismal. // Our wills and fates do so contrary run / That our devices still are overthrown; / Our thoughts are ours, their ends none of our own." 5.2.366–69; 3.2.209–11.

Discussion and Writing Suggestions

1. This version of Hamlet immediately announces its contemporary, urban setting ("New York, 2000"). How does the filmmaker use setting, imagery, and music to establish a tone for the film? How does the contemporary setting and costuming create an effect different from the "historical" versions of the film?

2. For some people, the contemporary settings, costumes, and technology featured in Almereyda's *Hamlet* are simply incompatible with both the language and the essential situations of Shakespeare's play, and therefore they cannot accept the basic premise of the film. Discuss your thoughts about this potential problem. To what extent is the very idea of a contemporary *Hamlet* untenable?

3. Almereyda's film, like Olivier's, begins with a quotation from later in the play; in this case, we see Hamlet on a video monitor reciting some lines ("I have of late, but wherefore I know not, lost all my mirth …")(II.ii.303ff.) that later in the play he speaks to Rosencrantz and Guildenstern, in explaining why he has been acting so strangely. The video takes of Hamlet are followed by some newsreel images of explosions and other shots of real or potential violence. Discuss the significance of this opening for Almereyda's approach to *Hamlet*.

4. One of the first scenes introduces a theme that runs throughout the film: technology. How is Hamlet's use of video technology used in the film to expand our understanding of Hamlet's character and motivations?

5. During the scene where Gertrude and Claudius implore Hamlet to "cast thy nighted color off," the characters, walking up Park Avenue, are shot in a reverse tracking movement, from a low angle that emphasizes the tall Manhattan office buildings in the background. What do you think Almereyda's strategy might have been in filming the scene this way?

6. We see several images of Ophelia before she actually speaks on screen. What kinds of images is she associated with? How is imagery used to add depth and foreshadowing to her character?

7. Several scenes in this film seem disconnected from the main plot. For example, in one scene, we see a shot of birds scattering over a cathedral, followed by a few moments of a Buddhist monk on videotape. What effect and message do you think these shots are meant to convey? Why do you think the filmmaker has inserted them?

8. Voice-over is frequently used in this film as a way to present soliloquy. Choose one such scene and discuss the effect of using voice-over as opposed to traditional dramatic presentation.

9. The first encounter with the ghost of Hamlet's father is told through a flashback (scene 6). How is that flashback presented? Do Horatio and Barnardo doubt what they have seen? How do they understand and respond to the apparition?

10. Examining the non-verbal elements (gesture, movement, facial expression) in the scene where Polonius gives advice to Laertes (as well as such verbal elements as intonation and manner of delivery), what can you infer about the relationship between father and son? To what extent do you sense a different relationship between Bill Murray's Polonius and Liev Schreiber's Laertes from those between corresponding characters in the films by Branagh, Zeffirelli, and Olivier? Alternately, examining the previous scene, you may want to focus on the relationship between Schreiber's Laertes and Julia Stiles' Ophelia, as opposed to their cinematic forbears.

11. Describe the visual presentation of the meeting between Hamlet and his father's ghost. How is the scene presented? How does Hamlet react to his father's appearance?

12. Both Hamlet and Ophelia are visual artists in this version: Hamlet is a video/filmmaker, and Ophelia is a photographer. What themes do they explore in their art? How does their use of visual media work in the film to present and explore their characters?

13. During the (swimming pool) scene where Polonius tells Claudius and Gertrude that he thinks Hamlet is mad, Almereyda places much of the dramatic focus on Ophelia. Branagh does this also in his film, though to a lesser degree. How and why do you think the filmmaker creates such an emphasis? Contrast Olivier's or Zeffirelli's treatment of the same scene. Note that in Shakespeare's play, Ophelia does not appear in this scene.

14. How does this film present the relationship between Gertrude and Claudius? Is it a political relationship? Sexual? Romantic? What filmic techniques does Almereyda use to offer glimpses into the nature and function of their relationship?

15. Are we to believe that Gertrude is complicit in the death of the elder Hamlet in this film? How much does she know about the events that have transpired? What clues do we have as to the depth of her awareness and complicity? How does Almereyda's presentation of Gertrude compare to other film versions?

16. In perhaps his most daring—and notorious—staging sequence in *Hamlet,* Almereyda sets the "To be or not to be" scene in a Blockbuster store, with Hamlet cruising the aisles to the soliloquy voice-over. What do you think is Almereyda's strategy here? Notice which section he is cruising in and what is showing on the store monitors at the time. Recall, too, that earlier in the film we

saw a video image of Hamlet, a gun to his head, attempting this same speech.

17. Contrast Ethan Hawke's manner in the "Get thee to a nunnery" sequence—at least until he discovers the microphone she is wearing—with those of earlier Hamlets in the same scene. To what extent is this a different man, with a different agenda than the Hamlet of Gibson or Branagh?

18. What kind of images do we see in Hamlet's video "The Mousetrap"? To what extent do you think that this sequence of images serves as a contemporary equivalent of the dumb show and the dialogue between the player king and queen in Shakespeare's play and earlier film versions?

19. Discuss the dramatic effectiveness of the scene where Hamlet, masquerading as Claudius's chauffeur, prepares to kill him as he confesses. Why does this Hamlet pull back without firing his gun?

20. Contrast Ophelia's mad scenes (in the Guggenheim Museum) with corresponding scenes in one or more earlier Hamlets. Setting apart, how do the interactions among the various characters show a different set of personal dynamics than those in Olivier's, Zeffirelli's, or Branagh's *Hamlet* at this point in the story? Is this an Ophelia we have not seen before?

21. Discuss the images that appear on screen from the time Hamlet speaks his dying words to the first section of the end credits. How do these images relate to Almereyda's distinctive approach to *Hamlet?*

22. In a review of Almereyda's *Hamlet* for *Cineaste* (25.4, 2000: 37–40), Martha P. Nochimson argues that it is difficult for a modern *Hamlet* to be dramatically convincing, given that the characters in Shakespeare's play behaved according to "Shakespearean coils of political hierarchy, authority, and the implacable Great Chain of Being"—social influences that no longer exist to anywhere near the same degree in contemporary America. As an example, she cites the case of Polonius:

   > Polonius is personally a fool in the original play, but his connection to the monarchy as a loyal retainer invests him with the consequence of his place in the scheme of things. He has been stripped to less than zero in the corporate setting, as has any sense of authority he might have. This Polonius is a cipher. As a result, the famous advice scene in which the old boy tells Laertes as he departs for Paris, "This above all, to thine own self is true," is almost unplayable. Polonius is a suit, with not even the buttress of convention to support his empty clichés.

   To what extent do you think that Nochimson has a valid point? Does the fact that today's social and cultural order is radically different from that which existed in Shakespeare's time mean that not only the language, but also the action of the play is archaic and unconvincing?

The Rotten State of Denmark Corp.
Michael Almereyda

In one of his interviews, Almereyda, describing the shooting of the swordfight between Hamlet and Laertes, gives some insight into the life of an independent filmmaker:

> We got on the roof and it started raining and it was cold and all the actors and extras were cold. Our fencing equipment suppliers took their equipment in a fit of pique at 2 in the morning and left us dangling. It was overwhelming. I don't think that's the best part of the film, but I have a great editor and she worked with it. All the actors worked very hard. It was just the one scene we were really disappointed by. We really wanted it to be great.*

This incident may help explain Almereyda's approach to the conclusion of the swordfight. His "unbated and envenomed" sword repossessed, Laertes pulls an "Indiana Jones": he shoots Hamlet with a gun.

In the following selection Almereyda explains why he was attracted to the idea of making yet another film version of Hamlet *and his rationale for making the first high-tech adaptation of Shakespeare's tragedy. This piece first appeared as a column in the London* Sunday Telegraph *on December 17, 2000.*

1   "If I feel physically as if the top of my head were taken off," Emily Dickinson once said, "I know that is poetry."

2   I'll get back to this in a minute.

3   We were in the lobby of a bank in midtown New York at 3 A.M., filming that scene—you know the one—in which the ghost of Hamlet's father (Sam Shepard) appears on a surveillance monitor, prompting Hamlet's spooked pals to dash to the elevator to check it out. After the second take, one of the producers turned to me and said, "This reminds me of Scooby-Doo." I didn't feel insulted. It wasn't the first or last time I had to face the implicit question: What are we doing here? Why Hamlet—again—here and now?

4   The answer leads back to Emily Dickinson by way of Orson Welles, who conjured up a version of Macbeth in 1948, shooting for 21 days on an RKO sound stage cluttered with fantastic, soggy-looking papier-mache sets. Welles described his film as "a rough charcoal sketch" of the play, and this remark, alongside the finished picture, provoked in me a sharp suspicion that you don't need lavish production values to make a Shakespeare movie that's accessible and alive. Shakespeare's language, after all, is lavish enough. The meaning and emotion are all embedded there, line for line, word for word.

5   In the last 400 years, who more than Shakespeare has been so directly responsible for transmitting the particular electrical charge that Emily Dickinson described—the recognition of sudden and contrary meanings colliding in your brain, a certain top-of-your-head-being-taken-off feeling? Dickinson herself felt

*Jeffrey M. Anderson. "Interview with Ethan Hawke and Michael Almereyda." *Combustible Celluloid.* 4 May 2000. 23 Aug. 2001. <http://www.combustible.celluloid.com/inthawke.shtml>.

the ceiling lift when reading Shakespeare. After first taking in a volume of his plays, she was prompted to ask: "Why is any other book needed?"

6   At any rate, I was visited by an elemental desire to film Shakespeare. It was, as Emily would have it, practically a physical impulse—like wanting to go swimming in the ocean, or running out into a storm at night. Then again, maybe it wasn't so purely hedonistic. I had some hope that my reflexes as a film-maker would be tested, battered and bettered. That I'd be swept along into deeper Shakespearean currents.

7   I was hovering over various possibilities and I was resisting *Hamlet*. It seemed too familiar, too obvious, and it's been filmed at least 43 times. Better to leave it to high-school productions, spoofs and skits and The Lion King. As T.S. Eliot noted years back, *Hamlet* is like the Mona Lisa, something so over-exposed you can hardly bear to look at it.

8   But masterpieces are definably masterpieces because they have ways of manifesting themselves in our everyday lives. The play, and the character, seemed to be chasing me around New York. I passed high-school kids quoting Hamlet on the street. I was informed of the existence of a Hamlet porno film ("To f— or not to f—"). And I found myself thinking back to my first impressions of the play, remembering its adolescence-primed meaning for me—the parallels between the melancholy Dane and my many doomed and damaged heroes and imaginary friends: James Agee, Holden Caulfield, James Dean, Egon Schiele.

9   I was struck by the fact that no film of *Hamlet* features a truly young man. The most definitive, conspicuous modern incarnations—Olivier, Richard Burton, Kevin Kline, Mel Gibson—were all at least 40 when they tackled the part (Kenneth Branagh, at 35, seemed hardly any younger). Why not entrust the role to an actor in his twenties? The character takes on a different cast when seen more clearly as an abandoned son, a defiant brat, a poet, a perpetual student—a radiantly promising young man who doesn't quite know who he is (the play's famously simple first line is, "Who's there?")

10   Given the story's familiarity, it seemed altogether natural to locate a new *Hamlet* in the immediate present, to translate the Danish kingdom into a multimedia corporation, and to watch the story unfold in penthouse hotel rooms, sky-level office corridors, a coffee shop, an aeroplane, the Guggenheim Museum. The chief thing was to balance respect for the play with respect for contemporary reality—to see how thoroughly Shakespeare can speak to the present moment, how they can speak to each other.

11   When I showed Ethan Hawke a six-page treatment and explained my intention—to shoot fast and cheap in New York, to film in super-16mm, to make everything as urgent and intimate as possible, keeping all spoken dialogue as written by Shakespeare but set within and energised by a contemporary context—Ethan got it immediately. He trusted me and was ready, with a breathtaking absence of Hamlet-like equivocation, to leap in.

12   Ethan's contributions were essential. He made a case for Hamlet as someone whose hesitation to kill Claudius is justified, contrary to the questionable imperatives of revenge or a bloodthirsty audience. Hamlet doesn't need to kill Claudius, Ethan insisted, once he's made the man face his own guilt: "There's

nothing in the body of Shakespeare's work that suggests he thinks murder is a good thing." The level of vulnerability Ethan brought to the role, the quality of imploding self-doubt, is tempered by this conclusion, as is our entire treatment of the story.

13   Meanwhile I was watching every version of *Hamlet* available. And, of course, I never stopped reading the play, which carries the best advice for any director: "Suit the action to the word, the word to the action." This is so smart and simple it's almost stupefying.

14   The screenplay came together quickly and even easily—a process of channelling and distillation. From what I can tell, global corporate power is as smoothly treacherous and absolute as anything going in a well-oiled feudal kingdom, and the notion of an omnipresent Denmark Corp provided an easy vehicle for Claudius' smiling villainy. And it's more meaningful to explore how Shakespeare's massive interlocking themes—innocence and corruption, identity and fate, love and death, the division between thought and action—might be heightened, even clarified, when colliding with the spectacle of contemporary media-saturated technology.

15   Shakespeare, after all, has Hamlet caught in the wheels of his own hyperactive mind, enthralled by "words, words, words." The film admits that images currently keep pace with words, or outstrip them, creating a kind of overwhelming alternate reality. So nearly every scene in the script features a photograph, a TV monitor, an electronic recording device of some kind. The play-within-the-play becomes Hamlet's home-made video projection. Polonius (Bill Murray) eavesdrops on his daughter (Julia Stiles) by wiring a microphone to her shirt. (This was Ethan's inspiration, courtesy of Linda Tripp.)

16   Of course, the film contains some dazzling contradictions. Not least the fact that this *Hamlet*, skidding into being on a perilously low budget, happens to feature a notably high-profile cast—prominent actors all working for basic rates of pay—is further testament to Shakespeare's supernatural status as the great leveller, unifier of mighty opposites.

17   In most cases, the actors were my first choices for the roles. Sam Shepard confided that he'd never worked so hard on a part, never felt so challenged. Bill Murray disingenuously volunteered that nobody had ever asked him to play Shakespeare before. It also emerged that Murray, in the course of an action-packed career, had never taken on a film in which he was obliged to die, whereas Ethan Hawke had always resisted roles requiring his character to kill someone. And here we all were—all the actors in the film—coerced by Shakespeare into doing miraculous work.

18   It's a truism that every movie is made three times: in the writing, in the shooting and in the editing, each process generating new contingencies and surprises. And so, many of our best and worst ideas fell by the wayside—sacrificed for the sake of clarity and momentum and to dodge mistakes, making this latest *Hamlet* the most condensed straight film adaptation in English. Entire scenes were dropped, Shakespeare's text was further trimmed and the result is, inevitably, an attempt at *Hamlet*—not so much a sketch but a collage, a patchwork of intuitions, images and ideas. "Who's there?"—the famous stark first line was finally cut, with great reluctance. But we never stopped asking

ourselves the question. Shakespeare's most inexhaustible play keeps throwing back infinite answers.

Discussion and Writing Suggestions

1. In the first part of his article, Almereyda makes several references to the American poet Emily Dickinson. Why does he feel that Dickinson's comments help explain why he wanted to make yet another film version of *Hamlet?* Does your experience of Almereyda's *Hamlet* help reinforce Dickinson's ideas? Explain.

2. Almereyda argues that one significant shortcoming of most other recent film versions of *Hamlet* is that they feature actors who are too old for the part of Hamlet. (The prince, after all, is still going to college.) Consider the age factor both in Almereyda's film and in the previous versions covered in this chapter. In view of the subject matter of the play, to what extent is Ethan Hawke (30) a better fit for the role of Hamlet than Laurence Olivier (41 when he made the film), Mel Gibson (35), or Kenneth Branagh (35)?

3. Almereyda focuses on Hawke's interpretation of why Hamlet refuses for so long to kill Claudius. "The level of vulnerability Ethan brought to the role," notes Almereyda, "the quality of imploding self-doubt, is tempered by this conclusion [that he 'doesn't need to kill Claudius,' that Shakespeare does not endorse murder, even for revenge], as is our entire treatment of the story." After viewing Hawke's performance, to what extent do you agree that his self-doubting and vulnerable manner (as opposed, for example, to Gibson's and Branagh's more assertive styles) make good dramatic sense?

4. In paragraphs 13 and 14 Almereyda explains why "nearly every scene in the script features a photograph, a TV monitor, an electronic recording device of some kind." What was your own reaction to this information-age *Hamlet?* To what extent did you experience a disconnect between the modern technology, the action of the drama, and Shakespeare's language? To what extent did the technology reinforce the action and the language?

5. In the final section of his article Almereyda expresses regret that so much had to be cut from the film. Like Olivier, who called his work an "essay" in *Hamlet,* Almereyda writes of his film as an "attempt...a collage, a patchwork of intuitions, images and ideas." To what extent do you feel that the film suffered from not including such well-known scenes as the opening "Who's there?" sequence or the gravedigger scene? To what extent does the action seem choppy or unmotivated as a result of such cuts?

Review of Almereyda's *Hamlet:*
The Prince Is Dead, Long Live the Prince
Alexandra Marshall

Predictably, for such a radical re-conception of a famous work, the reviews of Almereyda's Hamlet *were more sharply polarized than those of Olivier's, Zeffirelli's, and Branagh's versions. Traditionalists deplored the contemporary updating of Shakespeare's play. John Simon wrote, "In the mesmerizingly real-seeming medium of cinema [...], ten sore thumbs would stick out less than Shakespeare's language surrounded by laptops and limousines, skyscrapers and neon lights."* Stanley Kauffmann dismissed the film for relying on "gimmicks" and charged that Almereyda was uninterested in the play's"beauty."† But other critics were enthralled. David Denby wrote, "Almereyda has produced a ripely melancholy version of the play, and many of the translations into contemporaneity strike me as oddly right..."‡ Elvis Mitchell declared, "Mr. Almereyda has created a new standard for adaptations of Shakespeare, starting with an understanding of the emotional pull of the material that corresponds with its new period and setting."§*

The following review by Alexandra Marshall first appeared in the June 19, 2000, issue of The American Prospect. *Marshall is the author of five novels, including* The Brass Bed *(1986),* Something Borrowed *(1997), and* The Court of Common Pleas *(2001).*

1   The fast-paced disjointedness of Almereyda's film makes this Hamlet acutely expressive of our own exploding culture.

2   On multiple video monitors at his Manhattan apartment in the Hotel Elsinore, the modern Hamlet (Ethan Hawke) mesmerizes himself with his own distressed image. At Blockbuster Video, he rents action films by the dozen, all the better to create his frightening movie-within-a-movie that is his version of the play wherein he'll "catch the conscience of the king." His girlfriend Ophelia (Julia Stiles) has her own darkroom and carries around a bunch of Polaroid proofs that will scatter around her like fallen leaves as she herself disintegrates. Typical of their generation, Hamlet and Ophelia try to escape into the technologies of image making, but because this *Hamlet* is none other than Shakespeare's tragedy, their essential identities, and thus their fates, are as bound—and sealed—as ever.

3   With any contemporized rendering of Shakespeare, there are always those who feel the plays can't be authentic if the stagecraft isn't as "Shakespearean" as the language. But we are reminded in the 1947 revised edition of The Yale Shakespeare that "the outline of the story of Hamlet, as we are familiar with it, is first found in the Historica Danica of Saxo Grammaticus, a Danish chronicler who lived at the end of the twelfth century." When Shakespeare's play was performed by his company, it was by definition a *Hamlet* in modern dress.

---

*"A Will, But No Way," *The Nation,* 19 June 2000: 59.

†"The Muses in Manhattan," *The New Republic,* 5 June 2000: 26.

‡"Flesh and Blood," *The New Yorker,* 15 May 2000: 105.

§"Hamlet: A Simpler Melancholy in a Different Denmark," *The New York Times,* 12 May 2000. 16 June 2001. <http://www.nytimes.com/library/film/051200hamlet-film-review.html>.

tlesis

4   The Hamlet boldly imagined for our time by the film maker Michael Almereyda—who tells a preview audience that he made the movie "in a hurry, for very little money"—is a rich achievement. Hamlet and Ophelia are the casualties not only of character but of an all-too-familiar corporate power-lust. As the Denmark Corporation's CEO/king, Hamlet's uncle Claudius (Kyle MacLachlan) is frighteningly without conscience. He has married Hamlet's adulterous mother, "our sometime sister, now our queen" Gertrude (Diane Venora), whose own innocence and guilt converge before our eyes as she reluctantly comes to her own palpable realization of all that has gone wrong. Despite the intrinsic familiarity of the play's story line, this movie version has a momentum of its own—enhanced by its frantic and fractured vision of life in the big city—so that even though we know at the beginning that by the end they will all be dead, Almereyda generates genuine emotional suspense as well as an active curiosity about how the film will deliver the known tragic outcome. Every line spoken by the actors was written by William Shakespeare, but the busy background noise and fast-paced disjointedness of Almereyda's film version make this Hamlet acutely expressive of our own exploding culture. While the young Hamlet broods, what Claudius calls "the hectic in my blood" seems to circulate throughout.

5   The characters in this Hamlet are conveyed—with the multiplicity of perspective that also marks our era—as an ensemble of complex personalities with layered and sometimes discomforting histories together. Here the actors display a depth of thought about the characters they play that is not often visible when *Hamlet* reaches the screen. Almereyda's achievement is that his actors project—and in close-up!—the fundamental interior transformations that drive the action. And in a play so famously ambiguous, this clarity, while unavoidably provisional, is nevertheless welcome.

6   For example, a decision has been made here about Gertrude's intentions as she takes up the poisoned cup and drinks from it, a decision for which Almereyda credits a director's notation from a stage production in the 1970s (in the margin of the script was written, "Gertrude knows"). Others may be more comfortable with a less deliberate interpretation, but I think that this "knowing" on Gertrude's part—knowing that her new husband intends to kill her son—provides a tragic gravity that is missing when her death by poisoning is played as entirely accidental. Diane Venora brings a veteran's power to the role of Gertrude, which she again performed this past winter in an acclaimed stage production at the Public Theater in New York City, with Hamlet played by the gifted Liev Schreiber, who plays Ophelia's brother Laertes in this film version. In other words, there is a real theatrical authority invested here, and this strength seems by extension to empower those other actors—Bill Murray as Polonius, Sam Shepard as the ghost of Hamlet's father, and Ethan Hawke, for that matter who might not at first come to mind as right for their roles, but who become so.

7   Stunning without question is Julia Stiles, who embodies Ophelia with an authenticity equal to Diane Venora's Gertrude. In this film, we truly experience Ophelia's madness as the high-cost consequence of her insight. In contrast to the usual, more illusive representations of a solitary Ophelia, here we have a complex character whose decline is tangibly a response to Hamlet's own dete-

rioration. And this Gertrude and Ophelia, so accessible in their internal development, make us aware of how much of the story we have missed in less "modernized" Hamlets with their unexplored women.

8   According to Julia Stiles in a brief telephone interview, her own sense of the character was arrived at once she understood Ophelia as a young woman "who was trying to please everybody, even though Hamlet and her father send contradictory messages." The popular book *Reviving Ophelia,* says Stiles, helped her see the tragic impact upon the self-image of young women who are "suffocated by their environment and this need to please." Most useful—because, as she says, "Shakespeare never writes stage direction"—were the "visuals" that Almereyda wrote into the script, which conveyed, without words, the intensity of feeling between Ophelia and the other characters. Stiles says she admired Almereyda's various concrete choices in the making of this film, and at the same time, what she rediscovered about Shakespeare was the wide-open range of possibility of interpretation.

9   One such possibility is presented in the persuasive invention of *Gertrude and Claudius,* the new novel by John Updike, which tells Updike's version of the story-before-the-story told in Shakespeare's play. In the novel, we are invited to imagine a Claudius who is driven primarily by his desire for Gertrude, which prompts a different interpretation of his ambitions for the throne of her husband the king, his brother. Necessarily too, then, does Updike's Gertrude gain in both dimension and sympathy. The reader experiences her, in the novel's three parts, as the daughter of a king and the wife of two subsequent kings. And as the mother of a presumptive fourth, the future King Hamlet, Gertrude is thus given the means to instruct Ophelia—with the generosity of feeling that in Shakespeare resides only between the lines—about the nature of female compliance. "Men are beautiful enemies we are set down among," Gertrude tells Ophelia in Updike's novel. "If we have been compliant with one man, they reason, we may be also with another. The wish to be agreeable we take in with our mother's milk, alas."

10   In his own vivid telling, Updike, too, brings the story forward in time, beginning his novel in the late twelfth century and moving the story (by changing the names) into Shakespeare's time and (by exploring the point of view of Claudius as a stepfather) to the verge of our own. The characters are so actual—even with their ancient names and antique speech—that, like Almereyda's Hamlet, Updike's novel enlarges the conversation about the nature of love and power, of loyalty and betrayal. And, as in any telling of this mythic story, its success has less to do with where in time or place it is set than with how psychologically complete and emotionally true is our experience of it.

11   Other screen Hamlets over the years have taken other approaches. Helpful for its literal representation of the whole text of *Hamlet*, word for word, is the epic-length Kenneth Branagh film (1996), which includes all the scenes usually left, for the sake of pacing, on the cutting room floor. In this production, Kate Winslet is uneven as Ophelia, whom she represents as a Botticelli Venus, and Julie Christie's Gertrude is never the dramatic equal of either her husband (Derek Jacobi's Claudius) or her son (Kenneth Branagh's own Hamlet). And yet this complete version has the real advantage of displaying both of these women

as the characters Shakespeare wrote and therefore as more complex than, when edited, they are often rendered.

12   Laurence Olivier's 1948 film, for instance—in which, like Branagh, he both stars and directs—is so melodramatic to a modern sensibility that it is almost comic, an effect reinforced by the physical resemblance between the young Olivier and Steve Martin. But it suffers even more from the fact that Ophelia and the queen are played with blank faces that seem rarely to crack into meaningful expression, and like Branagh, Olivier essentially stages the play as a one-man show.

13   If the Olivier version seems too stylized, the Franco Zeffirelli film version (1990), by contrast, is too casual. As Hamlet, Mel Gibson offers too little evidence of the internal struggle that is at the heart of the play, which has the awful effect of disembodying the great soliloquies. The characterization is undermined by a cuteness on the part of Gibson—as when Hamlet winks at his mother in a comic sword scene which, in turn, makes all the more difficult the other adjoining roles, especially that of Gertrude (Glenn Close) and Ophelia, who is bravely played by a girlish Helena Bonham Carter.

14   With the illumination that Almereyda and Updike have brought to the story, the lack of compelling women in other versions now seems an overwhelming gap. To know the play is to want to know it better, and yet, the one certainty in any discussion of *Hamlet* is that there's no such thing as a final word.

15   "Absent thee from felicity awhile, And in this harsh world draw thy breath in pain, To tell my story." This is Hamlet's last charge to his friend Horatio. It is a pleasure to find the challenge taken up once again, and met.

Discussion and Writing Suggestions

1. In paragraph 4, Marshall alludes to a paradox—that even though we know how events will turn out in the end, an imaginative reworking of a familiar work can still hold us in "emotional suspense" and "active curiosity." To what extent do you think that this is true of Almereyda's film? To what extent is it true, as a general rule? Consider other adaptations that have been made of familiar works—everything from *Jane Eyre* to *Great Expectations.* What elements of the film—other than the outcome of the plot—keep us in suspense?

2. "Almereyda's achievement," writes Marshall, "is that his actors project—and in close-up!—the fundamental interior transformations that drive the action." Marshall cites, as one example, Gertrude's displaying knowledge that the cup of wine has been poisoned. To what extent do you agree with Marshall's comment? Cite other examples of particular moments in the film that exemplify Marshall's conclusion.

3. Marshall singles out Liev Schreiber (Laertes), Diane Venora (Gertrude), and Julia Stiles (Ophelia) for praise. Even those critics

who disliked Almereyda's film acknowledged the skill of these particular actors. Reviewers were more divided on others in the cast,
including Ethan Hawke and Bill Murray (Polonius). In your opinion, who were the strongest actors? The weakest? Explain.

4. Marshall quotes Julia Stiles (Ophelia) concerning "the tragic
   impact upon the self-image of young women who are 'suffocated
   by their environment and the need to please.'" To what extent
   does such an interpretation help you to understand Ophelia's
   motivation and her ultimate fate? Does such an interpretation
   ring as true in the 20th century (the setting of this *Hamlet*) as it
   did in the 17th?

5. Marshall thinks that Ophelia and Gertrude, as portrayed in
   Branagh's film by Kate Winslet and Julie Christie, are not as dramatically "compelling" (particularly in their relationship with men)
   as the two women in Almereyda's. And the women in Olivier's
   film, she claims, are even weaker than those in Branagh's. To what
   extent do you agree with this assessment? Cite particular scenes in
   the films that support your conclusion.

6. Marshall objects to the "cuteness" underlying Mel Gibson's characterization of Hamlet, as well as the overly "casual" approach of
   Zeffirelli's film. To what extent do you agree with this assessment?

Film Glossary
David Bordwell
Kristin Thompson

The following glossary defines some of the key terms you will find useful in discussing film. Written by David Bordwell and Kristen Thompson, both of the University of Wisconsin, it is excerpted from their film text Film Art: An Introduction *(4th ed.).*

We have rearranged the terms into the following categories: CINEMATOGRAPHY, which includes the **photographic** *aspects of the shot (film stock, exposure, color of black and white, filters, focal length, special effects, etc.), the* **framing** *of the shot (angle, height, distance of framing, various types of camera movement, zooms), and the* **duration** *of the shot; MISE-EN-SCENE (literally, staging an action), which includes* **setting, lighting, costume,** *and the* **behavior of the characters/actors;** *EDITING (the joining of shot to shot, with various types of relationships possible:* **graphic, rhythmic, spatial, temporal);** *SOUND; and NARRATIVE aspects.*

CINEMATOGRAPHY

cinematography   A general term for all the manipulations of the film strip by the camera in the shooting phase and by the laboratory in the developing phase.

angle of framing   The position of the frame in relation to the subject it shows: above it, looking down (a high angle); horizontal, on the same level (a straight-on angle); looking up (a low angle). Also called "camera angle."

crane shot   A shot with a change in framing accomplished by having the camera above the ground and moving through the air in any direction.

dolly   A camera support with wheels, used in making *tracking shots.*

establishing shot   A shot, usually involving a distant framing, that shows the spatial relations among the important figures, objects, and setting in a scene.

extreme close-up   A framing in which the scale of the object shown is very large; most commonly, a small object or a part of the body.

extreme long shot   A framing in which the scale of the object shown is very small; a building, landscape, or crowd of people would fill the screen.

following shot   A shot with framing that shifts to keep a moving figure on-screen.

framing   The use of the edges of the film frame to select and to compose what will be visible onscreen.

front projection   Composite process whereby footage meant to appear as the background of a shot is projected from the front onto a screen: figures in the foreground are filmed in front of the screen as well. This is the opposite of *rear projection.*

long shot   A framing in which the scale of the object shown is small; a standing human figure would appear nearly the height of the screen.

long take   A shot that continues for an unusually lengthy time before the transition to the next shot.

matte shot   A type of process shot in which different areas of the image (usually actors and setting) are photographed separately and combined in laboratory work.

mixing   Combining two or more sound tracks by recording them onto a single one.

mobile frame   The effect on the screen of the moving camera, a *zoom lens,* or certain *special effects;* the framing shifts in relation to the scene being photographed. See also *crane shot, pan, tilt, tracking shot.*

normal lens   A lens that shows objects without severely exaggerating or reducing the depth of the scene's planes. In 35-mm filming, a normal lens is 35 to 50 mm. See also *telephoto lens, wide-angle lens.*

pan   A camera movement with the camera body turning to the right or left on a stationary tripod. On the screen, it produces a mobile framing which scans the space horizontally.

point-of-view shot   (POV shot) A shot taken with the camera placed approximately where the character's eyes would be, showing what the character would see; usually cut in before or after a shot of the character looking.

process shot   Any shot involving rephotography to combine two or more images into one, or to create a special effect; also called "composite shot." See also *matte shot, rear projection, special effects.*

racking focus   Shifting the area of sharp focus from one plane to another during a shot; the effect on the screen is called "rack focus."

rear projection   A technique for combining a foreground action with a background action filmed earlier. The foreground is filmed in a studio, against a screen; the background imagery is projected from behind the screen. The opposite of *front projection.*

reestablishing shot   A return to a view of an entire space after a series of closer shots following the *establishing shot.*

reframing   Short panning or tilting movements to adjust for the figures' movements, keeping them onscreen or centered.

shot   1. In shooting, one uninterrupted run of the camera to expose a series of frames. Also called a *take.* 2. In the finished film, one uninterrupted image with a single static or mobile framing.

shot/reverse shot   Two or more shots edited together that alternate characters, typically in a conversation situation. In *continuity editing,* characters in one framing usually look left, in the other framing, right. Over-the-shoulder framings are common in shot/reverse-shot editing.

special effects   A general term for various photographic manipulations that create fictitious spatial relations in the shot, such as *superimposition, matte shots,* and *rear projection.*

superimposition   The exposure of more than one image on the same film strip.

take   In filmmaking, the shot produced by one uninterrupted run of the camera. One shot in the final film may be chosen from among several takes of the same action.

telephoto lens   A lens of long focal length that affects a scene's perspective by enlarging distant planes and making them seem close to the foreground planes. In 35-mm filming, a lens of 75-mm length or more. See also *normal lens, wide-angle lens.*

tilt   A camera movement with the camera body swiveling upward or downward on a stationary support. It produces a mobile framing that scans the space vertically.

tracking shot   A mobile framing that travels through space forward, backward, or laterally. See also *crane shot, pan,* and *tilt.*

wide-angle lens   A lens of short focal length that affects a scene's perspective by distorting straight lines near the edges of the frame and by exaggerating the distance between foreground and background planes. In 35-mm filming, a wide-angle lens is 30 mm or less. See also *normal lens, telephoto lens.*

zoom lens   A lens with a focal length that can be changed during a shot. A shift toward the *telephoto* range enlarges the image and flattens its planes together, giving an impression of moving into the scene's space, while a shift toward the *wide-angle* range does the opposite.

MISE-EN-SCENE

mise-en-scene   All the elements placed in front of the camera to be photographed: the settings and props, lighting, costumes and make-up, and figure behavior.

high-key lighting   Illumination that creates comparatively little contrast between the light and dark areas of the shot. Shadows are fairly transparent and brightened by fill light.

key light   In the three-point lighting system, the brightest illumination coming into the scene.

low-key lighting   Illumination that creates strong contrast between light and dark areas of the shot, with deep shadows and little fill light.

three-point lighting   A common arrangement using three directions of light on a scene: from behind the subjects (backlighting), from one bright source (key light), and from a less bright source balancing the key light (fill light).

screen direction   The right-left relationships in a scene, set up in an establishing shot and determined by the position of characters and objects in the frame; by the directions of movement; and by the characters' eyelines. *Continuity editing* will attempt to keep screen direction consistent between shots.

EDITING

editing   1. In filmmaking, the task of selecting and joining camera takes. 2. In the finished film, the set of techniques that governs the relations among shots.

axis of action   In the *continuity editing* system, the imaginary line that passes from side to side through the main actors, defining the spatial relations of all the elements of the scene as being to the right or left. The camera is not supposed to cross the axis at a cut and thus reverse those spatial relations. Also called the "180° line."

continuity editing   A system of cutting to maintain continuous and clear narrative action. Continuity editing relies upon matching screen direction, position, and temporal relations from shot to shot.

crosscutting   Editing that alternates shots of two or more lines of action occurring in different places, usually simultaneously.

cut   1. In filmmaking, the joining of two strips of film together with a splice. 2. In the finished film, an instantaneous change from one framing to another. See also *jump cut.*

cut-in   An instantaneous shift from a distant framing to a closer view of some portion of the same space.

dialogue overlap   In editing a scene, arranging the cut so that a bit of dialogue or noise coming from shot A is heard under a shot of character B or of another element in the scene.

dissolve   A transition between two shots during which the first image gradually disappears while the second image gradually appears; for a moment the two images blend in *superimposition.*

eyeline match   A cut obeying the *axis of action* principle, in which the first shot shows a person looking off in one direction and the second shows a nearby space containing what he or she sees. If the person looks left, the following shot should imply that the looker is offscreen right.

fade   1. *Fade-in:* A dark screen that gradually brightens as a shot appears. 2. *Fade-out:* A shot gradually darkens as the screen goes black. Occasionally fade-outs brighten to pure white or to a color.

graphic match   Two successive shots joined so as to create a strong similarity of compositional elements (e.g., color, shape).

jump cut   An elliptical cut that appears to be an interruption of a single shot. Either the figures seem to change instantly against a constant background, or the background changes instantly while the figures remain constant.

match on action   A continuity cut that places two different framings of the same action together at the same moment in the gesture, making it seem to continue uninterrupted.

montage   1. A synonym for *editing.* 2. An approach to editing developed by the Soviet filmmakers of the 1920s; it emphasizes dynamic, often discontinuous, relationships between shots and the juxtaposition of images to create ideas not present in either one by itself.

montage sequence   A segment of a film that summarizes a topic or compresses a passage of time into brief symbolic or typical images. Frequently dissolves, fades, superimpositions, and wipes are used to link the images in a montage sequence.

SOUND

diegetic sound   Any voice, musical passage, or sound effect presented as originating from a source within the film's world. See also *nondiegetic sound.*

nondiegetic sound   Sound, such as mood music or a narrator's commentary, represented as coming from a source outside the space of the narrative.

offscreen sound   Simultaneous sound from a source assumed to be in the space of the scene but in an area outside what is visible onscreen.

sound bridge   1. At the beginning of one scene, the sound from the previous scene carries over briefly before the sound from the new scene begins. 2. At the end of one scene, the sound from the next scene is heard, leading into that scene.

synchronous sound   Sound that is matched temporally with the movements occurring in the images, as when dialogue corresponds to lip movements.

NARRATIVE

ellipsis   In a narrative film, the shortening of *plot* duration achieved by omitting intervals of *story* duration.

motif   An element in a film that is repeated in a significant way.

narrative form   A type of filmic organization in which the parts relate to each other through a series of causally related events taking place in a specific time and space.

plot   In a narrative film, all the events that are directly presented to us, including their causal relations, chronological order, duration, frequency, and spatial locations. Opposed to *story*, which is the viewer's imaginary construction of all the events in the narrative.

scene   A segment in a narrative film that takes place in one time and space or that uses crosscutting to show two or more simultaneous actions.

sequence   Term commonly used for a moderately large segment of a film, involving one complete stretch of action. In a narrative film, often equivalent to a *scene.*

story   In a narrative film, all the events that we see and hear, plus all those that we infer or assume to have occurred, arranged in their presumed causal relations, chronological order, duration, frequency, and spatial locations. Opposed to *plot,* which is the film's actual presentation of certain events in the narrative.

SYNTHESIS ACTIVITIES

1. Compare and contrast the opening sequences (or some other sequence of your choice, such as the play-within-a-play scene, the death of Polonius scene, or the gravedigger scene) in two or more film versions of *Hamlet*. How does the way each filmmaker chooses to open his film—or to treat your selected scene—reveal his distinctive approach to the play? What themes are emphasized by the choice of dialogue, camera movement, lighting, editing, sound? In your discussion focus on particular details that appear to you to be representative of the filmmaker's "take" on *Hamlet*.

2. Compare and contrast Olivier's, Zeffirelli's, Branagh's, and Almereyda's approach to *Hamlet*, based largely on the personal statements each makes about his film. In making your comparisons you might want to consider some of the following points: How do the filmmakers' various motivations in making their own film versions of *Hamlet* compare? What was each striving primarily to accomplish? How well did each feel he had accomplished his main goal? Consider what each says about the play's theme, character,

conflict, the match of cinematic style to dramatic theme, acting, music, and other dramatic and cinematic elements. Finally, which statements do you feel were the most successful (interesting, informative), which the least successful in communicating the directors' visions? Explain.

3. Branagh's *Hamlet*—running four hours—is the only uncut adaptation of the play. To what extent do you think that Branagh was right in choosing to use the complete text? How would you assess Branagh's choice in light of what Olivier and Almereyda say about the necessities of cutting Shakespeare's play?

4. Select at least two characters in *Hamlet* and compare and contrast the performances of the actors who play those characters in at least two film adaptations of the play. Take into account that different cinematic styles and different thematic emphases may require different styles of acting and different types of actors. That said, which filmic portrayals of Hamlet, Claudius, Ophelia, Gertrude, Polonius, Laertes, etc., seem most satisfactory to you? Which seem least satisfactory? Explain.

5. Drawing upon Jorgens's essay as a model, write a paper on nonverbal expression in *Hamlet*. Re-viewing the films (or refreshing your memory by means of the cinematic outlines), show how the filmmakers' use of (select from among the following) gesture, costume, faces, grouping, movements, settings, props, composition, juxtaposition of shots or images, and musical and nonmusical sounds in one or more of the films creates dramatic meaning, apart from the words actually spoken by the actors.

6. One of the main ways to differentiate stage and screen Hamlets is to categorize them as tending to be passive, vacillating, and weak, on the one hand, or tending to be active, decisive, and strong, on the other. Olivier's and Hawke's Hamlets appear to fall into the first category, Gibson's and Branagh's into the second. Consider one screen Hamlet of each type, note particular moments in the films that appear to support your interpretation (and perhaps other moments that appear to refute it) and write a report on your findings. Draw upon the critical outlines and relevant criticism (as well as close observation of the films, themselves) to support your argument.

7. Michael Almereyda is only the most recent director of *Hamlet* to explicitly raise the issue of whether Hamlet and his story have any relevance for the 21st century. Taken at the most literal level, of course, the issue of what a son should do about an uncle who pours poison in his brother's ear and thereby becomes king in his place is of limited relevance to most people sipping a Starbucks mochaccino while reading *USA Today*. On a less literal level, one can argue that human nature changes little from one historical era to another. The kinds of things people think and do in response to the actions of others; their frustrations, anxieties, and rages; and their loves and

their hatreds are not bounded by local time or space. Find examples in at least two of the films treated in this chapter which support the conclusion that *Hamlet* remains a work that illuminates the human condition—regardless of the era in which it is staged.

8. One of the issues that every director of *Hamlet* must contend with is how to portray the relationship between Hamlet and Gertrude—particularly in the crucial scene (III.iv) where Hamlet rebukes his mother in her bedroom after the play-within-the-play. To what degree should the director fill the scene with sexual tension? As indicated in the introduction to "An Essay in *Hamlet*," Olivier adopted a Freudian approach, in which Hamlet's Oedipus complex becomes the chief motivating force in his disgust with Gertrude.

   Other filmmakers have also gone the Freudian route, not always to critical approval. In his *New Republic* review of Zeffirelli's film, Stanley Kauffmann notes, "when Hamlet is berating his mother, he lies on top of her on the bed, mimicking sex and finishing with a hot kiss. Freud has often been enlisted in this scene but never less subtly. What must her late husband's ghost, who has been invisibly watching, think of these goings-on?"*

   Drawing upon at least two film versions of Hamlet, explore this question of how different filmmakers' interpretations of the Hamlet–Gertrude relationship are revealed in their films, both through acting and other cinematic means. You may find it useful to look up some critical commentary upon this topic. The April 1997 issue of *Film/Literature Quarterly*, for example, features two articles on the subject: "Freud's Footprints in Films of *Hamlet* " by Philip Weller and "'In the Rank Sweat of an Enseamed Bed': Sexual Aberration and the Paradigmatic Screen *Hamlet*s" by James R. Simmons, Jr.

9. Based on your reading of Shakespeare's play and on your viewing of at least two film versions of *Hamlet*, discuss the problems involved in adapting the play from stage to screen. Discuss also, how some solutions that filmmakers have devised in response to these problems appear to be more successful than other solutions. Consider, for example: (1) how to deal with soliloquies and other 16th–17th century stage conventions; (2) how to use physical space; (3) how to find non-verbal equivalents for Shakespeare's language—more specifically, how to use the special visual and aural qualities of cinema to translate the essence of *Hamlet* from stage to screen; (4) how to deal in film with events that are only recounted by characters in the play; (5) how to direct actors for the camera, as opposed to for the stage; (6) how to deal with the audience's not understanding substantial parts of Shakespeare's language?

---

*Review of *Hamlet*, *The New Republic*, 23 Feb. 1991: 25.

10. Write an introductory chapter for a film textbook explaining such basic film concepts as camera movement, camera angle and position (relative to the subject), mise-en-scene (framing the action), editing, lighting, setting, color, music, nonmusical sounds, acting, costume, props, and special effects, using examples from various film *Hamlet*s to illustrate these concepts. For example, what can we learn about effective use of camera angle and movement from watching two or three of the sequences showing Hamlet's body being borne away? How do different camera strategies create different effects? Could a reasonably talented person who had seen no other films than Branagh's and Almereyda's *Hamlet*s make a reasonably effective film on another subject by carefully studying these filmmaker's cinematic techniques?

RESEARCH ACTIVITIES

1. Select the film version of *Hamlet* that most interests you and write a report on its critical reception. Locate reviews, both in print and online sources. (Take care to check the credentials of the reviewers: For what publications do they write? What else have they published?) Organize your report by topic (e.g., the director's overall vision of the play, the film's dramatic or visual qualities, the adequacy of the acting) rather than by source (individual reviewer).

   For critical commentary and reviews of individual films, see film review listings (alphabetically listed under "Moving Pictures" or "Motion Pictures") in the *Reader's Guide to Periodical Literature*, print or online versions. See also *Film Index International on CD-ROM* (covers films from 1930 to the present), *Film Review Annual* (collections of film reviews, 1981 to the present), *The New York Times Film Reviews* (1913 to the present), *International Index to Film Periodicals* (1972 to the present), *Film Literature Index* (1973 to the present), *Variety Film Reviews*, *Magill's Cinema Annual* (1982 to the present).

   Two especially useful Web sources on film are The Internet Movie Database (IMDb) <us.imdb.com/> and The Movie Review Query Engine (MRQE) <http://www.mrqe.com/>.

2. In her review of Almereyda's *Hamlet*, Alexander Marshall compares the director's reconception of the characters and action of Hamlet to the reconceptions presented in John Updike's 2001 novel *Gertrude and Claudius*. Read this novel and then compare and contrast its treatment of Gertrude and Claudius with the treatment of these characters in one or two of the film versions treated in this chapter.

3. Select a literary work that has been adapted into film at least twice—perhaps another play by Shakespeare (e.g., *Romeo and Juliet*)

or a work by a novelist (e.g., Charles Dickens, Charlotte Brontë, Jane Austen, George Orwell, Ernest Hemingway, William Golding). You may wish to consult John Tibbetts's *The Encyclopedia of Novels into Film* (1998). View the films based on this work and look up reviews and other background information. (See information on locating reviews in Research Activity 1, above.) Which of the adaptations did reviewers generally find more successful? Why? Did the reviewers discuss some dramatic or novelistic elements that resisted adaptation to film? Were reviewers unhappy with omissions made by the filmmaker from the original work? Did reviewers feel that the filmmaker and the actors had sufficient comprehension of the original work?

4. What kinds of critical commentary have been made about Shakespeare's *Hamlet* during the past ten or fifteen years, and how does that commentary differ in critical focus and method from commentary written earlier in the century? You can find earlier commentary in editions of *Hamlet* that include critical excerpts, such as *The Signet Classic Shakespeare.* You might also check anthologies of Shakespeare criticism, such as *Twentieth Century Interpretations of* Hamlet: *A Collection of Critical Essays,* edited by David Bevington (Prentice Hall, 1968). For more recent commentary, check the *PMLA Bibliography,* either print or online versions, as well as *Hamlet* commentary in books by Shakespearean scholars such as Harold Bloom's *Shakespeare: The Invention of the Human* (Riverhead, 1998) and contemporary collections of *Hamlet* criticism such as Richard Corum's *Understanding* Hamlet *: A Student Casebook to Issues, Sources, and Historical Documents* (Greenwood, 1998).

5. Select a film that has been adapted from a work of fiction and research the problems involved in transferring this particular work from the page to the screen. One of the best-known accounts of such an adaptation is Lillian Ross's *Picture* (1952), which gives a detailed account of the making of John Huston's adaptation of Stephen Crane's Civil War novel *The Red Badge of Courage.* Use both print sources and online/CD-ROM databases to discover other accounts of the process of making a film based on a literary work. There are innumerable sources on the making of *Gone With the Wind* and *The Wizard of Oz*—though much of this material is Hollywood press agentry or gossip journalism. [In some cases, "The Making of…" videos may be useful; see Eleanor Coppola's documentary, *Hearts of Darkness: A Filmmaker's Apocalypse* (1991), on the making of her husband's (Francis Ford Coppola's) *Apocalypse Now.*] Don't neglect contemporary accounts in newspapers and magazines, particularly the trade papers (if you have access to them), such as *Variety* and *The Hollywood Reporter.*

6. Locate the script for a film based on a short story or a novel. (If your college or university has a film studies department, that department

or the college library may have a collection of film scripts. You might also call nearby college and university libraries, some of which may hold special film collections.) Read the story or novel, and then read the script. Finally, watch the film adaptation. Write a three-way comparison-contrast in which you examine differences and similarities in plot, characters, and tone among the three. Check the online catalog at your library for available film scripts. Locate the novel, play, or story; locate the film on video or DVD. When you have all three elements available, begin your work.

7. Research the role of the screenwriter in the production of films (which, for this assignment, need not be adaptations). When in the process of a film's creation does the screenwriter become involved? To what extent does the screenwriter stay involved through film production? What differences do screenwriters find between writing original scripts and writing adaptations? In the hierarchy of people involved in the creation of a film—producer, director, cinematographer, actors—what is the screenwriter's relative value? There are many ways of calculating value, the most important one for Hollywood being money. What are screenwriters paid, relative to other talent?

8. Investigate and explain the process by which a work of fiction or drama becomes a candidate for adaptation and then an actual film. You will need to investigate the "movie-making machinery" of Hollywood and of independent studios to learn how literary properties are sold. What is the role of the original writer of the literary work in the sale of his or her work for possible adaptation? What is the role of the literary agent? The producer? Do directors acquire the rights to literary works? What is an "option"? What percentage of literary works put under agreement eventually become films?

Credits

CHAPTER 1

Page 7: "The Future of Love: Kiss Romance Goodbye, It's Time for the Real Thing" by Barbara Graham, *UTNE Reader,* November/December, 1996. Reprinted by permission of the author.

Page 22: "Why I Will Never Have A Girlfriend" by Tristan Miller. Reprinted from http://www.nothingisreal.com/. Reprinted by permission of the author.

CHAPTER 2

Page 54: "A Message to President Clinton and the 105th Congress: A Simple One-Step Plan to Solve the Education Crisis." J. Morton Davis. *The New York Times* Jan. 18, 1998, *Week in Review,* p. 18. Reprinted by permission of J. Morton Davis, Chairman, D.H. Blair Investment Banking Corp.

CHAPTER 3

Page 89: From: Mark Naison, "Scenario for Scandal." *Commonweal,* 109 (16), Sept. 24, 1982. Reprinted by permission.

CHAPTER 4

Page 102: Sanjiv N. Singh, "Cyberspace: A New Frontier for Fighting Words," *Rutgers Computer and Technology Law Journal* 25.2 (1999): 283.

Page 103: Rob Kling, "Social Relationships in Electronic Forums: Hangouts, Salons, Workplaces and Communities," *CMC Magazine* 22 July 1996, 4 Feb. 2000 <http://www.december.com/cmc/mag/1996/jul/kling.html>.

Page 103: Sonia Maasik and Jack Solomon, eds., *Signs of Life in the USA* (Boston: Bedford Books, 1997) 701.

Page 104: Deborah Branscum, "Life at High-Tech U," *Newsweek* 27 Oct. 1997: 78–80.

Page 104: Brittney G. Chenault, "Developing Personal and Emotional Relationships Via Computer-Mediated Communication," *CMC Magazine* May 1998, 20 March 2000. <http://www.december.com/cmc/mag/1998/may/chenault.html>.

Page 105: John Suler, "Cyberspace Romances: Interview with Jean-François Perreault of *Branchez-vous,*" *The Psychology of Cyberspace,* 11 Dec. 1996, 7 April 2000 <http://www.rider.edu/users/suler/psycyber/psycyber.html>.

Page 106: Jennifer Wolcott, "Click Here for Romance," *The Christian Science Monitor* 13 Jan. 1999, 23 Feb. 2000 <http://www.csmonitor.com/durable/1991/01/13/fp11s1-csm.shtml>.

Page 106: Bonnie R. Morris, "You've Got Romance! Seeking Love Online: Net-Based Services Change the Landscape, If Not the Odds, of Finding the Perfect Mate," *New York Times on the Web* 26 Aug. 1999, 23 Feb. 2000 <http://www.nytimes.com/library/tech/yr/mo/circuits/index.html>.

CHAPTER 5

Page 132: "Ban the Bargains" by Bob Ortega as appeared in *The Wall Street Journal,* October 11, 1994. Copyright © 1994. Permission conveyed through the Copyright Clearance Center, Inc.

Page 134: "Eight Ways to Stop the Store" by Al Norman, reprinted by permission from the March 28, 1994 issue of *The Nation.*

Page 136: Sarah Anderson, "Wal-Mart's War on Main Street." *The Progressive* Nov. 1994: 19–21. Reprinted by permission from *The Progressive,* 409 E. Main Street, Madison, WI 53703.

CHAPTER 7

CHAPTER 8

Page 329: Review of Stanley Milgram's Experiment on Obedience as appeared in *American Psychologist,* 1964. Copyright © 1964 by the American Psychological Association. Reprinted (or adapted) with permission of The American Psychological Association and Diana Baumrind.

Page 336: From *Obedience* by Ian Parker as first appeared in *Granta* 71: Shrinks. Reprinted by permission of PFD on behalf of Ian Parker.

Page 347: "The Mind Is a Formidable Jailer" [The Stanford Prison Experiment] by Philip K. Zimbardo, *The New York Times Magazine,* April 8, 1973. Copyright © 1973 The New York Times Co. Reprinted by permission of The New York Times.

Page 360: Excerpt from *On Disobedience and Other Essays* by Erich Fromm. Copyright © 1981 by the Estate of Erich Fromm. Reprinted by permission of HarperCollins Publishers, Inc.

Page 365: "The Organization Kid" by David Brooks as appeared in *The Atlantic Monthly,* April 2001. Reprinted by permission of the author.

CHAPTER 9

Pages 384, 386: From "Ethics and Business" in *The New World of Business: Ethics and Free Enterprise in the Global 1990s* by Robert C. Solomon. Copyright © 1994 by Rowman & Littlefield Publishers, Inc. Reprinted by permission of Littlefield Adams Quality.

Pages 385, 394: From *Ethics and the Conduct of Business* by John R. Boatright, copyright © 2000 by Prentice-Hall, Inc. Reprinted by permission of Pearson Education, Inc., Upper Saddle River.

Page 386: "Double Expense Account" from *American Business Values,* Third Edition, by Gerald F. Cavanagh, copyright © 1990 by Prentice-Hall, Inc. Adapted by permission of Pearson Education, Inc., Upper Saddle River, NJ.

Page 390: "The Case of the Collapsed Mine" from *Business Ethics,* 5/e by Richard T. DeGeorge, copyright © Reprinted by permission of Pearson Education, Inc., Upper Saddle River, NJ.

Page 394: "Ethics in Business" from *American Business Values,* Third Edition, by Gerald F. Cavanagh, copyright © 1990 by Prentice-Hall, Inc. Adapted by permission of Pearson Education, Inc., Upper Saddle River, NJ.

Page 409: "Peter Green's First Day" by Laura L. Nash. Reprinted by permission of the Harvard Business School of Publishing.

Page 412: "Love and Business" from *Business Ethics: A Philosophical Reader* by White, Thomas, copyright © 1993 by Thomas I. White. Reprinted by permission of Pearson Education, Inc., Upper Saddle River, NJ.

Page 415: "The Serpent Was There" by Margot Langstaff and Joseph Badaracco, Jr. Reprinted by permission of the author.

Page 420: "Is this the Right Time to Come Out?" by Alistair D. Williamson from *Ethical Issues in Business: A Philosophical Approach,* Sixth Edition, edited by Thomas Donaldson and Patricia H. Werhand. Copyright © 1993 by the Harvard Business School Publishing Corporation; all rights reserved.

Page 423: "Why Should My Conscience Bother Me?" by Kermit Vandivier, from *In the Name of Profit* by Robert Heilbroner, copyright © 1972 by Doubleday. Used by permission of Doubleday, a division of Random House, Inc.

CHAPTER 10

Page 440: Flegal KM, Carroll MD, Kuczmarski RJ, Johnson CL. Overweight and obesity in the United States: prevalence and trends, 1960–1994. *Int J Obesity,* 1998;22:39–47.

Page 448: Figure 4 BMI Tables from *Eat, Drink and Be Healthy* by Walter C. Willett, D.C., as adapted from *Nutrition and Your Health: Dietary Guidelines for Americans* (1995). Copyright © 2001 Harvard

University, President and Fellows of Harvard College. Reprinted with the permission of Simon & Schuster.

Page 451: "Gaining on Fat" by W. Wayt Gibbs, *Scientific American,* August 1996. Copyright © 1996 by Scientific American, Inc. All rights reserved.

Page 461: "Too Much of a Good Thing" by Greg Crister, *The Los Angeles Times,* July 22, 2001. Copyright © 2001, Los Angeles Times Syndicate. Reprinted by permission.

Page 464: NAAFA (National Association to Advance Fat Acceptance) Policy: Dieting and the Diet Industry as found on www.naafa.org. Reprinted by permission of the NAAFA.

Page 469: "Fat and Happy: In Defense of Fat Acceptance" by Mary Ray Worley as found on www.naafa.org. Reprinted by permission of the NAAFA.

Page 474: "Too 'Close to the Bone'": The Historical Context for Women's Obsession with Slenderness by Roberta P. Seid from *Feminist Perspectives on Eating Disorders,* edited by Patricia Fallon, Melanie A. Katzman, and Susan C. Wooley (pp. 3–16). Copyright © 1994 The Guilford Press. Reprinted by permission of The Guilford Press.

Page 487: "Fat and Happy?" from *Never Satisfied: A Cultural History of Diets, Fantasies and Fat* by Hillel Schwartz. Copyright © 1986 by Hillel Schwartz. Reprinted with the permission of The Free Press, a Division of Simon & Schuster, Inc.

Page 495: "Food Product Design," from *Fast Food Nation* by Eric Schlosser. Copyright © 2001 by Eric Schlosser. Reprinted by permission of Houghton Mifflin Company. All rights reserved.

Page 503: "The Man Who Couldn't Stop Eating" by Atul Gawande from *Complications* by Atul Gawande, copyright © 2002 by Atul Gawande. Reprinted by permission of Henry Holt and Company, LLC.

CHAPTER 11

Page 523: From *Universality of the Folktale* by Stith Thompson, copyright © 1951 by Henry Holt and Co., Reprinted by permission of Henry Holt and Company, LLC.

Page 527: "Cinderella" from *Fairy Tales* by Charles Perrault, translated by Geoffrey Brereton (Penguin Books, 1957). Translation copyright Geoffrey Brereton, 1957.

Page 531: From *Grimm's Tales for Young and Old* by Jakob & Wilhelm Grimm, translated by Ralph Manheim, copyright © 1977 by Ralph Manheim. Used by permission of Doubleday, a division of Random House, Inc.

Page 536: Excerpt from "When the Clock Strikes" from *Red as Blood* by Tanith Lee. Copyright © 1983 by Tanith Lee. Reprinted by permission of DAW Books, Inc.

Page 548: Tuan Ch'êng-Shih, "The Chinese Cinderella Story" by Translated by Arthur Waley. *Folklore,* 58, March 1947, pp. 226–238. Reprinted by permission of the Folklore Society.

Page 549: Excerpt from "Cinderella in Africa" by William Bascom from *Cinderella: A Folklore Casebook.* Edited by Alan Dundes. Reprinted by permission of Garland Publishing, Inc.

Page 553: "The Algonquin Cinderella" from *World Tales: The Extraordinary Coincidence of Stories Told in All Times, in All Places* by Indries Shah. Copyright © 1979 by Technographia, S.A. and Harcourt Brace & Company. Reprinted by permission of Harcourt, Inc.

Page 555: Textual excerpts from *Walt Disney's* CINDERELLA as adapted by Campbell Grant. © Disney Enterprises, Inc.

Page 557: "Cinderella" from *Transformations* by Anne Sexton. Copyright © 1971 by Anne Sexton. Reprinted by permission of Houghton Mifflin Company. All rights reserved.

Page 560: *Gudgekin the Thistle Girl and Other Tales.* New York: Knopf, 1976. Copyright held by John Gardner (deceased).

Page 567: "Cinderella" from *The Uses of Enchantment* by Bruno Bettelheim, copyright © 1975, 1976 by Bruno Bettelheim. Used by permission of Alfred A. Knopf, a division of Random House, Inc.

Page 575: "'Cinderella' and the Loss of Father-Love" from *The Stepmother in Fairy Tales: Bereavement and the Feminine Shadow* by Jacqueline M. Schectman. Copyright © 1993 by Jacqueline M. Schectman. Reprinted by permission of Jacqueline M. Schectman.

Page 590: "Cinderella's Stepsisters" by Toni Morrison. Copyright © 1979 by Toni Morrison. First appeared in *Ms. Magazine.* Reprinted by permission of International Creative Management.

CHAPTER 12

Page 601: *Nickerson v. Hodges.* 84 So. 37 (1920). Used by permission.

Page 605: *California Jury Instructions, Civil: Book of Approved Jury Instructions (BAJI).* 8th ed. Prepared by The Committee on Standard Jury Instruction Civil, of the Superior Court of Los Angeles County, California. Hon. Stephen M. Lachs, Judge of the Superior Court, Chairman. Compiled and Edited by Paul G. Breckenridge, Jr. St. Paul, MN: West Publishing Co., 1994.

Page 607: David Hricik, "The American Legal System." *Law School Basics, A Preview of Law School and Legal Reasoning.* Copyright " 1996, 1997 by David Hricik. Published by Nova Press.

Page 617: Veda Charrow, et al., "How to Present Your Case Systematically and Logically." *Clear and Effective Legal Writing, 2e.* Boston: Little, Brown 1995. Used by Permission of the Publisher.

Page 629: "*Venezia v. Miller Co:* A Defective Beer Bottle?" Essay by Ruthi Erdman. Used by permission.

Page 630: *Venezia v. Miller Brewing Co.* 626 F.2d 188 (1980). Used by permission.

Page 630: *Restatement of The Law, Second: Torts 2nd.* As Adapted and Promulgated by The American Law Institute at Washington, D.C. May 25, 1963 and May 22, 1964. St. Paul, MN: West Publishing Co., 1965.

Page 634: *Harris v. Jones.* 380 A.2d 611 (1977). Used by permission.

Page 641: *Hackbart v. Cincinnati Bengals.* 601 F.2d 516 (1979). Used by permission.

Page 669: *People v. Acuna et al.* 60 Cal. Rptr. 2d 277 (1997). Used by permission.

Page 677: "For Fallen Stop Sign, Vandals Face Life" by Mike Clary, *The Los Angeles Times,* June 11, 1997. Copyright © 1997, Los Angeles Times. Reprinted by permission.

Page 681: *State of Utah v. Hallett.* 619 P.2d 337 (1980). Used by permission.

Page 681: The code sections reprinted or quoted verbatim in the following pages are taken from the Utah Code Annotated, Copyright © 1996 by Lexis® Law Publishing, a brand of Matthew Bender & Co., Inc. and are reprinted with permission. All rights reserved.

Page 688: *California Jury Instructions, Criminal: Book of Approved Jury Instructions [CALJIC]* 6th ed. Prepared by The Committee on Standard Jury Instruction Criminal, of the Superior Court of Los Angeles County, California. St. Paul, MN: West Publishing Co., 1996.

CHAPTER 13

Page 713: From the Introduction: "The Tragedy of Hamlet Prince of Denmark," by Sylvan Barnet, edited by Edward Hubler, in *The Complete Signet Classic Shakespeare.* Copyright © 1972 Harcourt Brace & Company. Reprinted by permission.

Index of Authors and Titles